"To Woody,
of the Caldwell an[illegible]
boys and the First Tennessee

ALSO FOR GLORY MUSTER

I salute you for
keeping the memory alive

Don [illegible]
12-23-08

Also for Glory Muster

The Story of the Pettigrew Trimble Charge at Gettysburg

Don Ernsberger

ISBN: Hardcover 978-1-4363-7439-2
Softcover 978-1-4363-7438-5

This book was printed in the United States of America.

To order additional copies of this book, contact:
Xlibris Corporation
1-888-795-4274
www.Xlibris.com
Orders@Xlibris.com
53945

Contents

Preface 9

Chapter One — The Road to Gettysburg 13
Chapter Two — The First Day 25
Chapter Three — The Morning of Glory 43
Chapter Four — The Bombardment 88
Chapter Five — The Advance 95
Chapter Six — Emmitsburg Road 120
Chapter Seven — "Also for Glory" 138
Chapter Eight — The Aftermath 174
Chapter Nine — Return to Virginia 188

Bibliography — Books and Articles 213
Archive Collections 219
Photo Credits 645

The Army of Northern Virginia
Pettigrew—Trimble Command
July 3, 1863

Third Corps—Lieutenant General A.P. Hill

Heth's Division—*commanded by General James J Pettigrew*

Archer's Brigade—commanded by Colonel Birkett Fry (13th Al)

5th Alabama Battalion
13th Alabama
1st Tennessee
7th Tennessee
14th Tennessee

Pettigrew' Brigade—commanded by Colonel James Marshall (47th NC)

11th North Carolina
26th North Carolina
47th North Carolina
52nd North Carolina

Davis's Brigade—commanded by Brigadier General Joseph R. Davis

2nd Mississippi
11th Mississippi
42nd Mississippi
55th North Carolina

Pender's Division—*commanded by Major General Isaac Trimble*

Scales's Brigade—commanded by Colonel William Lee Lowrence

13th North Carolina
16th North Carolina
22nd North Carolina
34th North Carolina
38th North Carolina

Lane's Brigade—commanded by Brigadier General James H. Lane

7th North Carolina
18th North Carolina
28th North Carolina
33rd North Carolina
37th North Carolina

Preface

July the third 1863 it seems, will forever be associated with an event known by almost everyone as "Pickett's Charge" . . . the day more than 12,000 officers and men in Robert E. Lee's Army of Northern Virginia charged forward at the Union defenses at Gettysburg.

Almost since that day onward, the label given to that assault has focused on the commander of less than half of the troops who made the attack—Major General George Pickett. Pickett whose Division constituted only three of the nine brigades in the afternoon assault has become the namesake of the entire effort. Scores of books written since the Civil War ended have labeled the assault "Pickett's Charge" and have focused almost all of their coverage and analysis on the three brigades of Virginians under Pickett. One classic work "Pickett's Charge in History and memory" by Carol Reardon was even written to study the reasons why the assault became known as "Pickett's Charge" over time.

As a student of Civil War battles, I too had focused most of my attention over the years on the role of George Pickett's regiments that day. My own writing focused on the 69th Pennsylvania "Irish Volunteers" from Philadelphia who faced Pickett's men at the wall in 1863. As my Civil War library grew, it became clear to me that books that were designed to describe that "Grand Assault" on July 3 were uniformly constructed with eighty to ninety percent of their coverage on the details of the Pickett division. Only the barest minimum of attention was given in most of these works to the actions of the troops from Tennessee, Alabama, North Carolina and Mississippi who constituted the entire left wing of the attack that day under Generals Pettigrew and Trimble. There had been some writing done on individual Confederate officers who were in the other half of that assault with the divisions of Heth and Pender but very few. Several excellent studies appeared over the years in the pages of Gettysburg Magazine. Michael W. Taylor, a lawyer and Civil War scholar in North Carolina did several articles on the role of North Carolina troops that day. Books appeared on various North Carolina and Mississippi regiments which included a chapter on Gettysburg. In general however, there was a need for a book to be written which focused exclusively on the "other half" of the Confederate assault that day in July 1863. This would be my task.

There were reasons why so much of the historical writing about the Confederate assault of July third focused on the regiments from Pickett's Division. It had nothing to do with any bias that historians had either for Virginia or against North Carolina. It started shortly after the battle during the Civil War due to the predominance of Richmond Virginia newspaper coverage of the Gettysburg campaign in general and the July third attack in particular. However, the real reason had more to do with the availability of primary resources for the historians who have written on the "Charge". The fundamental reality of the Confederate assault is that the men of Pickett's Division (15 regiments) were fresh arrivals on the battlefield and all compiled service data and documentation regarding their Gettysburg role focused on their role on one day July Third. The twenty seven regiments under the command of Generals Pettigrew and Trimble that day had almost all fought in battle on the first of July, many with terrible losses in men and leadership. In fact only 6 regiments of this group were fresh troops.

Researchers who investigate the individual soldiers who fought at Gettysburg with the regiments under Pettigrew and Trimble are struck at once with a classic research problem. Many of the individual compiled service files for men killed, wounded or captured typically read as follows "Private James Hamby 23 years old enlisted Caldwell County 4/30/61 killed Gettysburg July 1-3." OR "Sergeant Leonidas Pearsall 20 year old enlisted Duplin County 10/1/61 wounded and captured Gettysburg July 1-5". In essence the official records often did not make clear to the researcher the day on which the death or wound or capture occurred. Because of this, the creation of an accurate rooster of companies and regiments has always been difficult. Thus, statistical data that provides empirical support for analysis was lacking.

My decision to undertake the three year research project which would result in this book would require me to begin with the standard reference sources such as found in the National Archives in Washington DC or in works such as *North Carolina Troops, 1861-1865: A Roster*. Next, I would review a number of detailed regimental works such as *Covered with Glory* by Rod Gragg and *"Duty, Honor, Valor: The Story of the Eleventh Mississippi Infantry Regiment,"* by Steven H. Stubbs and *"The Thirty-Seventh North Carolina Troops. Tar Heels in the Army of Northern Virginia,"* by Michael C. Hardy.

Finally an extensive search of the internet would yield a collection of excellent regimental and company studies and letters from veterans.

Eventually in order to examine pension files and archive collections I would have travel to Jackson Mississippi, Raleigh North Carolina and Nashville, Tennessee. In these places the pension papers and archives would yield answers for the focus I would need. Slowly but surely the factual information came together to identify the dates and the names and locations. The rough information from primary resources could then be refined and quantified.

Needless to say I borrowed generously from some of the finest general works on the July 3rd action from authors such as Jeffry Wert, Stephen Sears, Michael Priest, Richard Rollins, and Earl Hess.

I am indebted to a number of individuals who personally assisted me with my research. Tamra Stephens has spent years studying the 13th Alabama infantry and provided me with accurate data on their ranks at Gettysburg. Michael W Taylor from North Carolina provided several excellent articles and advice in phone conversation. Early in my research, Timothy Mulligan in Maryland provided me with valuable data and charts concerning the 1st Tennessee Infantry. Frequently over the years John Heiser of the Gettysburg National Military Park library made available to me the valuable resources found in their regimental files and book collections.

Finally I acknowledge the help provided by over 50 descendants of the men who fought with Pettigrew and Trimble who I was able to locate by internet and to gain insights on personal lives, adventures and military records.

Those familiar with the literature on the Confederate assault July 3, 1863 will of course recognize the structural similarity of this work to the classic of Pickett's Charge literature . . . Kathy Harrison's & John Busey's 1986 work.

First Lieutenant John Thomas James with Company D of the 11th Virginia who fought to the south of Pettigrew and Trimble in the July 3rd assault summed up the entire charge this way, "We gained *nothing but glory* and lost our bravest men". Those from North Carolina and Tennessee and Mississippi and Alabama that day echoed his thoughts knowing that they too had fought *also for glory*.

CHAPTER ONE

The Road to Gettysburg

There was a time when bridges spanned the Potomac River at Shepherds Town Virginia, but the war years had seen them burnt and destroyed. The logical crossing point therefore would be the old fording spot known by the locals as Pack Horse Ford. It had been used for as long as white men had lived in the area as a ford for wagons and before them as a crossing point for the Indian tribes. It was located less than two miles downstream where the approaches on both sides were far less steep than the high banks near the town. The water there was slower moving and less deep. The site was remembered by some of the men in A.P. Hills Corps as the scene of the Battle of Shepherds Town back in September 19-20 1862 during the retreat from Sharpsburg. For a few regiments in A.P. Hill's old "Light Division" now with Pender it was a memorable sight. For Private George Frazier in Company E of the 7th Tennessee it was memorable sight indeed. He had fought in those very fields in the distance and had an artillery shell fragment cut his rifle into two pieces injuring his shoulder. After eight weeks in the hospital he would return to duty. After Gettysburg, he would later be captured at The Wilderness. **(George Frazier, Compiled Service Records, National Archives)**

Early in the morning of Thursday June 25, 1863 the marching regiments from North Carolina and Tennessee and Mississippi and Alabama would enter the town from the south on the Berryville Road. They would enter the town of whitewashed wooden board houses and brick buildings that sat overlooking the Potomac River on a steep bluff.

Shepherds Town, even then, claimed to be oldest town in the region. In 1734, Thomas Shepherd was granted 222 acres on the south side of the "Potomack" river. From that tract, he selected fifty acres and laid out a town. Naming the place Mecklenburg. the town was officially chartered in 1762 by the Virginia General Assembly. Thomas Shepherd was the sole trustee. He owned the town and had the responsibility to conduct its government. In 1798 it was renamed Shepherds Town. The ford had been a familiar crossing spot for families settling the Shenandoah Valley in the early 1700s. The interconnections between families in Virginia's Shenandoah Valley and the rich farmland of Pennsylvania's Cumberland valley were strong and many a young Virginian had distant cousins living in the areas of Carlisle and Chambersburg and Gettysburg. More than twenty natural springs feed the small creek that enters the south end of town. The creek never runs dry; it meanders through backyards, under houses, across alleys and beneath streets. This setting was conducive to millers, tanners, potters, smiths and other artisans. As a result, by 1800 Shepherds Town boasted 1,000 inhabitants.

The area had seen troops cross before . . . troops marching off to battle. In 1775, General George Washington issued a call for "Virginia Volunteer Riflemen." Captain Hugh Stephenson filled the ranks of his company in Shepherds Town. His troops departed from there on July 16, 1775. Their march to Massachusetts crossed the river here and then covered 600 miles in 24 days. Now in 1863 troops would be crossing the Potomac and heading to battle in the same direction.

As civilization spread a covered wooden bridge had been built on large stone pillars in the 1840's with a wagon roadway on top. A roadway leads to Sharpsburg, Maryland. Because of the high cliffs on both sides where the town stood, the bridge stood high in the air. But at the start of the war the bridge was destroyed and now there was only the ford.

This crossing would find men crossing the river who thought of themselves as part of Pender's Division or Heth's Division but who would soon return to the Potomac River known as Pettigrew's and Trimble's. At the spot where they crossed there was an old burned cement mill, Boteler's Cement Mill, which had been destroyed at the Battle of Shepards Town September 18-20 1862. Some of these men had fought here in the post Sharpsburg battle. Men in Archer and Scale's regiments remembered well the short but fierce fight they had had here back on September 20, 1862. Archer's brigade had lost 55 men killed and wounded and Scales (then commanded by Pender) lost 63. The 22nd North Carolina alone in the middle of the fighting had lost 12. The men in Company K of the 22nd NC remembered how their newly elected Captain Charles Burgin had been wounded in the fight and later died. The men of the 38th North Carolina remembered how their Lieutenant Colonel Robert Armfield had been hit in the hand by a bullet while waving his sword in the middle of their charge. They had elected him Lieutenant Colonel and he was disabled in the battle resigning shortly thereafter. Also with the 38th were eight members of the Lackey family, cousins and brothers ranging in age from 21 to 30 in Company G. They had all enlisted in Alexander County, NC on November 2, 1861. They had all also remembered how they almost lost their brother William when he was wounded at this very spot back in September 1862—near the very place they were about to ford. All the family had survived unharmed since that day . . . . Gettysburg would end that record. First Sergeant John Crawford in Company I of the 34th remembered how he had been badly wounded in that attack down the hill and would spend months recovering in a hospital. The Steadman brothers in Company I of the 34th knew well this place. John had been badly wounded here by the river and had been cared for by his brother James.

Both would be wounded before seeing this river again. So too would Private Jonathan Miller in Company A who had been shot in the thigh here last September. The soldiers of Company C of the 34th NC remembered sadly how their newly appointed Second Lieutenant Robert Dickerson was mortally wounded at this very place. Two men in the 16th North Carolina had been wounded at the Shepardstown battle in 1862 but would survive this invasion. Musician Joseph Johnson (Co. K) had been wounded in the neck and Private Israel Higgins (Co. G) had been wounded as well. Indeed this crossing was a place of memories for many.

The men of the 38th NC with Scales remembered that the fighting at Shepards Town had cost them their Lt. Col. Robert Franklin Armfield's career as a Confederate officer came to an end when he resigned his commission on January 14, 1863 due to disability from wounds received at the battle of Sheperdstown on September 20, 1862. Returning to the Old North State, Armfield became North Carolina's state attorney in 1863.

Footnote—The Battle of Shepherdstown had occurred when Lee was retreating from the battle of Sharpsburg in September 1862. To protect his retreat, Lee had Pendleton, his chief of artillery place several batteries of guns on the cliffs guarding the Potomac River ford along with several regiments of infantry. An artillery dual across the river resulted in the Confederates running low on ammunition and in a Union raiding party of about 500 men crossing the river and driving back the rebel cannons and infantry. In the retreat 5 cannons were lost and Pendleton panicked and communicated with Lee that his reserve artillery had been seized. Lee immediately ordered several Brigades of A.P. Hill "Light infantry" to push back the Union troops. Pender's Brigade, Archer's Brigade and Gregg's South Carolinians were rushed back to the river. Three Union brigades crossed the river on the morning of September 20th and were hit head on by the attacking Confederates. The rebel troops were on the high ground and could fire down into the Union forces. Union commanders pulled back their forces to the other side of the river but the 118th Pennsylvania ignored orders and made a stand on the Virginia side. They were overwhelmed by the attacking Confederates from North Carolina, Tennessee and Alabama.

As he crossed at Shepherds Town General James Lane must also have remembered this spot and a scene that he would recall well past the end of the war . . . . "Here the regiment was compelled to lay all day on the Virginia shore, and the enemy, from the opposite side of the river, fired artillery at every individual soldier who dared expose himself. When Colonel Lane, then in command of the brigade, General Branch having been killed at Sharpsburg, called to a litter to know who had been wounded and received the reply: "Lieutenant Long, of your regiment," he approached and expressed the hope that the lieutenant was not seriously hurt. The latter replied: "I have been shot in the back; the ball has gone through me and I am mortally wounded." Taking his colonel's hand, he put it inside of his shirt on the slug which was under the skin of his breast, and added:

"I am a young man. I entered the army because I thought it right, and I have tried to discharge all my duties." Then that young hero, with his colonel's hand still on that fatal slug, asked in a most touching tone: "Though I have been shot in the back, will you not bear record, when I am dead, that I was always a brave soldier under you?" **(History of the 28th North Carolina, From the Charlotte, N. C Observer Feb 17, 1895. General James H. Lane.)**

It was 150 yards across to Maryland . . . huge boulders in the water here and there . . . small muddy spots where the water was deep. By 6:00 AM that morning Thursday June 25th they were in the cold water . . . . crossing. Many of the soldiers stripped naked, hold their weapons and clothing and leathers high over their head and cross the Potomac. Some would fall over hidden stones at the river bottom and end up with everything soaked. Most would wade across and redress in Maryland. Regiment by regiment they crossed.—the men of Pettigrew's North Carolina Brigade; the men with Archer from Tennessee and Alabama; with Davis from Mississippi and all those North Carolinians with Lane and Scales. Heth's Division of Hills Corp numbering 7,458. Pettigrew's Brigade numbered 2,581. The 26th North Carolina numbered more than 800.

Veterans of the 52nd NC remembered years later that Sergeant Matthew Goodson in Company A loudly and cynically announced as they crossed the river that he felt that few of the men in his regiment would return to Virginia **(Janie Wagoner, "*Story of Cabarus Confederate Soldiers Retold*", The Concord Daily Tribune, January 18, 1934, p 6)** The 36 year old merchant would die July 3.

One of the most common memories that soldiers with Pettigrew and Trimble had years later of the march to Pennsylvania was the role of band music in the adventure. On the morning before the crossing of the Potomac The 26th NC band was awake at 4:30 AM playing tunes such as "The Girl I Left Behind Me" as the men assembled into marching formation. And again once across the river, the band of the 26th North Carolina and the band of the 11th NC were ordered by General Pettigrew to play music as the entire Division crossed. Popular tunes such as "Maryland my Maryland", "Listen to the Mockingbird" and "Wait for the Wagon" echoed down the valley. **(Lineback Journal June 24-28, 1863, Julius Lineback Papers, SHC)** One soldier in the 26th NC Company G, Private Thomas Perrett would long remember the joyful feelings stirred by the music and by the soldiers joining in singing. **("A Trip That Didn't Pay", Thomas Perrett Papers, NCDAH)**

"June 25th—Leaving Bivouac at an early hour, we moved forward about a mile, which brought us to the ford across the Potomac about one mile below the little village of Shepherdstown. Here a scene of some grandure, of no little novelty, presented itself. Not a pontoon bridge was to be seen. The river, however, was fortunately low, reaching, near the farther bank a depth of about three feet. The channel, some hundred yards in width, seemed one living mass of horsemen, footmen, wagons, artillery and every other accompaniment of a grand army, struggling forward amid shouts and yells of every conceivable character. The men had, for the most part, donned a costume which reached a very near approximation to that of the "Highland Laddie".

The current was quite strong and the rocks at the bottom, provokingly sharp. Occasionally this combination of obstacles would get the mastery of some unfortunate being, who, loosing his footing, became a thorough a Baptist as accidental immersion could possibly make him, only to have added to his misfortune, the provoking influences of the unrelenting peals of laughter and a variety of derisory epithets of his more fortunate companions. We made but a temporary halt for preparation, when, entering the stream, we crossed over, as those preceding us had done I for the first time "waded the Potomac". There were many here with us, however, who had, more than once, performed this task. Moving out a few hundred yards from the river, we were halted, to await the coming up of the remainder of the Brigade which delayed us but a comparatively short time." **(Far from Home—The Diary of Lt. William Peel, p 34-35)**

The Commissary Sergeant of the 5th Alabama battalion, William Fulton would remember the crossing this way "As Commissary Sergeant for the Fifth Alabama Battalion of Infantry I had a horse to ride and this was one pleasant feature of this march. Where I got my horse, bridle and saddle I have entirely forgotten, it is a little singular that I should forget this, when I have a clear recollection of other things of not such importance to me at least I know I was mounted all right, and was elated over my good fortune, and this is all I now recall. When and where we crossed the Potomac I can't remember. However, I distinctly remember the boys wading across up to their waist in places, and my riding across on my horse, and when we reached the other side the jokes and jibes flew thick and fast as the wet garments clung to them and the water in their shoes made a sloshing noise as they hurried along to close up ranks. **(William Frierson Fulton, Family Record and War Reminiscences, 1919)**

Once across the regiments would again assemble in brigades and begin the march north to Sharpsburg, some 6 miles distant. Here they would travel through the town, see the pot marks of shell damage in the stone houses from the battle the year before and move past the Dunkard Church and the battlefield. Just as troops from North Carolina had remembered their 1862 experiences at Shepards Town as they crossed the Potomac, many Confederates who had fought at Sharpsburg thought back to that battle. One soldier with Company A of the 2nd Mississippi, Sergeant George Turner Bynum recalled well his earlier visit as he wrote in his dairy . . . "June 25. Crossed the Potomac by wading and passed through the battle field of Sharpsburg, which was fought September 17, 1862. Much sign of the conflict is visible. The low mounds which cover the bones of those who fell, the furrowed ground, and scarred trees—all speak more plainly than words of that terrible conflict. I saw the ground over which we charged on that memorable occasion and the very spot where I was wounded. Sad, sad thoughts are recalled by again reviewing the old battleground." **(G.W. Bynum Diary Extracts. Quoted in *Confederate Veteran*, XXXIII (1925): pp. 9-10.)**

Then came a 5 hour march to Hagerstown where they would rest for the night in fields at the southern edge of the town near Funkstown which had been known as Jerusalem Town until recently and was known for its old flour Mill.

In the days before reaching this point a number of officers and men had fallen ill or were exhausted from the march to the point that they were left behind. Confederate hospital operations had been established at Fredericksburg and at Front Royal and Winchester for these men. A careful examination of the June 30th muster rolls of several regiments show a number officers and men listed as sick and some of these contain side notes such as "left behind at Fredericksburg" or "left behind at Front Royal". Some of these men would play a role in the weeks to come. Captain John Powell Co H ; Lieutenants Joseph Patterson (Co K) and William West (Co A) all were 42nd MS officers left behind sick but who would be brought forward later to Falling Waters, Maryland.

That Thursday evening, Colonel John Fite commanding the 7th Tennessee Infantry got permission from his Brigade commander James Archer to go into town that night "to buy a new hat". Instead of a buying a hat Fite visited the local saloon and when he left he bumped into Archer in the town square. The two men then went out again to again to a local home where they spent some time with some young ladies and some champagne.

Fite and Archer got separated and the Colonel ended up sleeping that night in the back of an ammunition wagon. He had been unable to ride his horse back to camp. **(Memoirs of Col. John Fite, Tennessee State Library, p 83)**

The next morning in a light rain, Friday June 26th, the Confederate forces marched through the streets of Hagerstown and had the chance to observe the reactions of the town folk there. The 26th North Carolina and 11th North Carolina bands led the march playing lively tunes. Behind them with Pender the 33rd NC and 22nd NC bands kept up the pace. The marching plan was to have all of A.P. Hills Divisions take the roads that skirted the mountains to the east thus enabling Longstreet's entire Corps to use the major pike that ran north along the railroad tracks from Hagerstown to Carlisle. This would result in the brigades of Pender and Heth traveling in a less direct, often twisting, route north through small towns and villages that had rarely seen any small movements of armed men let alone the passage of a giant army. The 7th Tennessee, Colonel Fite's regiment, had not gotten on the road until later in the morning because their Colonel was still hung over from the hat-hunting trip the night before. When the regiment finally caught up to the rest of the Brigade, a confrontation occurred between Archer and Fite over the late departure of the 7th. As both men were still feeling the effects of their drinking others around them thought that Fite might soon be under arrest. However Archer settled the debate by telling Fite to join him for another drink. Within 8 days they would both be under arrest as prisoners of the Yankee army. **(Memoirs of Col. John Fite, Tennessee State Library, p 83)**

The men with Archer and Pettigrew and Davis left the edges of Hagerstown and moved on to the Leitersburg Pike. Winding its way up to Marsh Mill and the small village of Leitersburg. From there it would be about 6 miles to the Pennsylvania State line still marked by the Mason-Dixon markers. The road here was known both as Hagerstown Road and old Leitersburg Pike and ended at Waynesboro Pennsylvania. It would be a full day of marching to Rocky Forge, just south of Waynesboro where they would make camp and spend Friday night.

One soldier from the 38th (Co. H) North Carolina who deserted on the way to Gettysburg was Private Julian Fletcher Hamilton a 20 year old who had enlisted in Randolph County on March 5, 1863. The notation on his prisoner card states "When he was just 18 his family 'really pushed him' into the Confederate army. One day he decided he couldn't stand it any longer, so he left. As he waded across a creek he was captured by the Yankees . . . After the war ended he was ashamed to come home and so worked and made his living mostly in the vineyards of a Catholic priest in Ohio" (**North Carolina Divisions of Archives and History, Private Collection 1215)**

"Marched at 9 AM toward Waynesboro, Pa. Made 12 miles and stopped to bivouac 2 miles from Waynesboro. Rain all day. Country fine, houses & barns good. The crops look well. The people refuse to sell anything to the soldiers but give them milk, bread, butter. They show little fear of being damaged by our troops. The country is very hilly, the roads all turnpikes. **(Civil War Diary of Augustus L.P. Vairin 2nd Mississippi Infantry CSA (Co B)**

The regiments which had organized bands among the brigades of Heth and Pender were the 26th North Carolina; the 11th North Carolina in Pettigrew's Brigade and the 55th North Carolina with Davis plus the 33rd with Lane and the 16th with Scales. Except for Archer's brigade, each of the brigades in both Heth's and Pender's Division was staffed with a small group of excellent musicians to provide a marching pace for the invasion.

The Third Corp under Hill was busy, as were all of Lee's legions, in gathering supplies to be shipped back to Virginia. One of the major reasons for this invasion was to resupply Lee's army through the Fall by shipping livestock, flour, grain, and goods back to Virginia. "We are taking everything we need", wrote Junius Lineback, a musician with Pettigrew's Brigade, "horses, cattle, sheep, flour, groceries and goods of all kinds. We gathered up thousands of beeves. enough to feed our army until cold weather" **(Junius Lineback Journal, June 26, 1863, Junius Lineback papers SHC)** To achieve this goal men were detailed from the ranks of all of Heth's and Pender's Divisions for the purpose of locating, "requisitioning" "and purchasing (with Confederate dollars) every wagon and carriage found in the path of the invading army. Following this came the task of loading all of the supplies and sending them south to Hagerstown and then to Shepardstown or Williamsport.

In his address at Gettysburg in 1903, Colonel John Lane who had been the Lieutenant Colonel of the 26th North Carolina during the Gettysburg campaign, told a story about a group of soldiers who had marched north to Pennsylvania in a far less joyful mood then their comrades. These were the men who had been caught as deserters and had been sentenced to be shot. They were kept under guard at the rear of each regimental formation, marching along knowing that they were to be executed. Lane told of riding back with them and asking them if they would fight for the Confederacy when the battle began, as it surely would. Lane knew many of them personally and knew that most had deserted because they missed their families back home and did not relish invading the North. Most of these men would pledge their loyalty and be back in the ranks before Gettysburg. **(Address at Gettysburg by Colonel John R. Lane, Raleigh News and Observer, July 6, 1903)**

Friday night June 26th was spent in fields south of Waynesboro along both banks of the Marsh creek. Marsh creek winds for miles and miles and eventually feeds the waters of the Antietam creek before flowing into the Potomac River. The following morning the men from Tennessee and Alabama were in the lead as Archer's Brigade followed by Heth and Pettigrew and Davis marched through the town of Waynesboro before the sun had even risen. Mixed into their marching ranks were the 4 artillery batteries of Garnett. As the sun rose in the east Pender's division with Perrin and Lane and Scales and Thomas headed north through Waynesboro along with the 4 batteries of Poague. AP Hills old Light Division set the pace for the journey North. The next eight hours would take them on the Mont Alto road from Waynesboro through the small villages of Quincy, Fox Hill and the small hamlet of Mont Alto, nestled in the hills. Here, in 1859, John Brown had assembled his "liberation army" in a small Episcopal church before heading to Harper's Ferry. And here, after the failed Harper's ferry raid, one of his men Captain John Cooper had been arrested then returned to be hung with Brown. The road was now close to the mountains and it curved back west and then downhill toward The Chambersburg Pike where the rest of Lee's Army would be approaching. After eight hours of marching with no foraging, the men of AP Hill's Corps approached the town of Fayetteville, Pennsylvania along the Conocheague Run. "27 Saturday 5 AM marched 7 miles to Fayetteville 5 miles and 1 mile to the bivouac making a total of 16 miles today. The people refuse Confederate money. Camp is in the mountains on the road to Baltimore. The people seem quite friendly & come to see us." **(Civil War Diary of Augustus L.P. Vairin 2nd Mississippi Infantry CSA (Co B)**

Fayetteville was directly on the Chambersburg Pike which was the major east—west roadway connecting the area first to Gettysburg then York then Lancaster. Camp was established 3 miles south of the town and the regiments of Lane and Scales and Pettigrew and Davis would stay here for two days, resting from then long walk from Virginia. The only notable event recorded during this two day rest period involved a group of Mississippi soldiers from Davis's brigade who wandered into the town of Fayetteville and had to be gathered up by several companies of the 26th North Carolina on provost duty. This period of rest gave many men an opportunity to write letters home. For many, it would be the final communication between son and mother and husband and wife. The themes in these letters are several; optimism about the coming success of the Confederate invasion; astonishment at the rich bounty of the farmlands they had found in Pennsylvania and finally the usual exchange of news about anecdotal adventures mixed with a longing for home and family.

Private Vairin in Company B of the 2nd Mississippi had a chance to make a longer than usual entry into his diary during this rest period. "28 Sunday, cloudy & warm. Remained in camp all day. Our commissaries and quartermasters are gathering horses, beef cattle from the people in great numbers. Some of our men forage after chickens, eggs, butter, vegetables, apple butter, honey etc." **(Civil War Diary of Augustus L.P. Vairin 2nd Mississippi Infantry CSA (Co B)**

Commissary Sergeant William Fulton with the 5th Alabama Battalion was a farm boy and wrote home about his observations of the Pennsylvania farmland. "Through Pennsylvania we were struck with the similarity of the farms and the farm houses, all made after the same pattern. We were struck, too, with the good barns, sometimes better than the dwellings of the owners, and a big bell on top of each barn. The clover and wheat fields looked very enticing to us who were from the cotton fields of Alabama. The horses in the clover fields were great, big footed, clumsy, awkward things, so different from our Alabama horses and although theirs were a great deal heavier and more suited for draught purposes we greatly preferred ours which were more active and could endure more service without jading. Gen. Lee issued a very stringent order against straggling and depredating. Rights of private property were to be strictly respected and there was to be no meddling with that which belonged to private citizens, under penalty of severe punishment. Soldiers seemed to consider chickens and fruits of all kinds to be exempt from this general order, judging from the way they acted with regard to these.

A soldier ran a chicken under a large stack of wheat straw, and going under after it discovered horses and wagons and other things hid away under these straw stacks to protect them from 'The rebels'. This was reported to the proper authorities and a search instituted which revealed many things of importance to the commissary and quartermaster's stores" **(William Frierson Fulton, Family Record and War Reminiscences, 1919)** Lee's orders had indeed been clear and they were posted with all commands and all regiments . . . .

Chambersburg, June 27th, 1863

"The commanding general has observed with marked satisfaction the conduct of the troops on the march, and confidently anticipates results commensurate with the high spirit they have manifested. No troops could have displayed greater fortitude, or better performed the arduous duties of the past ten days. Their conduct in other respects has, with few exceptions, been in keeping with their character as soldiers, and entitles them to approbation and praise. There have, however, been instances of forgetfulness on the part of some, that they have in keeping the yet unsullied reputation of the army, and that the duties exacted of us by civilization and Christianity, are not less obligatory in the country of the enemy than in our own. The commanding general considers that no greater disgrace could befall the army, and through it our whole people, than the perpetration of the barbarous outrages upon the innocent and defenseless, and the wanton destruction of private property that have marked the course of the enemy in our own country. Such proceedings not only disgrace the perpetrators and all connected with them, but are subversive of the discipline and efficiency of the army, and destructive of the ends of our present movements.

"It must be remembered that we make war only upon armed men, and that we cannot take vengeance for the wrongs our people have suffered, without lowering ourselves in the eyes of all whose abhorrence has been excited by the atrocities of our enemy, and offending against Him to whom vengeance belongeth, and without whose favor and support, our efforts must all prove in vain.

"The commanding general, therefore, earnestly exhorts the troops to abstain with most scrupulous care from unnecessary or wanton injury to private property; and he enjoins upon all officers to arrest and bring to summary punishment all who shall, in any way, offend against the orders of this subject.

R. E. Lee, General."

Regarding the conditions of the land and farms they encountered in Pennsylvania, Lieutenant Julius Joyner Company F 47th NC wrote home to his mother "This has been called a land of milk and honey and is indeed such compared with our desolated country pillaged and burned by the plundering Yankees . . . . What has become of Hooker, I do not know, but one thing is certain, he does not interrupt us and if he does he will be severely chastised." **(Julius Joyner letter to Mother June 29, 1863, NCU archives)**

Private Samuel Hankins (Co E, 2nd Mississippi) remembered years later the Pennsylvania farmland. "That night we camped in Pennsylvania just over the line. As we marched along the next day we found most of the homes abandoned, the owners having fled to the mountains. Some in their haste to depart had not even shut their doors, leaving everything exposed. Nothing was molested by our men. I did not see the smoke going up from a single dwelling or any other building fired by our men while in the enemy's country. The citizens expected it by way of retaliation. Our army took only food for man and beast and exchanged old army mules for their large, overgrown horses. This was a mistake, as one mule is worth a dozen horses for military service." **(Samuel W Hankins, "Simple Story of a Soldier", Confederate Veteran September 1912-May 1913)**

On Sunday night a concert was given by the North Carolina bands from the 26th, 11th, 33rd and 22nd regiments and the men settled to sleep. By 3:00AM Monday June 29 marching orders arrived and the men were awoke, camp was broke and then the order was recalled. Time for breakfast and then by 11:00am the compan the Brigades were formed. With Archer's Tennessee and Alabam army marched east down Chambersburg Pike toward the hills. Be and his Mississippians.

Except for the 42nd Mississippi which was detached that morning to scout for enemy cavalry near Fairfield, which they fought and chased off. Behind Davis was Pettigrew with the men from North Carolina. Artillery batteries were shuffled between the brigades. Pender's brigades of Lane and Scales were far in the rear.

The advanced guard reached the burnt ruins of the Caledonia Iron Furnace, torched with a vengeance by Early days before. Caledonia forge was owned by abolitionist and Northern firebrand Thaddeus Stevens. By noon they were through the pass and that night Monday June 29th they made camp in fields near Cashtown, Pennsylvania. The Brigade wagons were moved forward to Cashtown itself and guarded.

The next morning orders arrived from General Heth that General Pettigrew was to take three regiments east along the pike into Gettysburg for a reconnaissance-in-force. The orders were given to pile up all knapsacks and place all men who were too ill to march on guard duty. But before the expedition could begin the Regimental muster had to be taken and this June 30th muster would become the basis for future historians understanding of what men were about to go down in history. The 26th, 47th and 11th North Carolina along with a collection of empty wagons for gathering supplies plus Maurin's Donaldsville Artillery (4 guns) were ready to move. The 52nd NC was left behind in part because some of its companies had been involved in extra duties. One company for example, Company B, had been sent to Fairfield and engaged in skirmish wit the 8th Illinois Cavalry **(Clark, North Carolina regiments, pp 40-41)** One man who was there wrote ". . . . halting on the 29th at Cashtown, a village at the foot of the mountains on the Baltimore and Chambersburg pike, and distant about six miles northwest from Gettysburg. Here we rested until the morning of 1 July. On the evening of the 29th Company B, Fifty-second Regiment, under command of First Lieutenant W.E. Kyle, was detailed to picket the Emmitsburg road at a village called Millertown, about five miles to the right of the camp, and during the night had a skirmish with a picket post held by the enemy's cavalry. During the night of the 30th the company was withdrawn and reported at camp. **(Manarin, L.H.,** *North Carolina Troops, 1861-'65*, **Raleigh, 1966.)**

It was a rainy morning and the roads would be muddy and the stream swollen. The first site would be the famous Cashtown Inn alongside the road as it moved downward toward the valley floor. As General Pettigrew passed the picket line of the 55th Virginia (Brockenbrough's Brigade) he invited their Colonel, William Christian, to join the march. And since they were about to be relieved of picket duty the 55th joined in. Now heading east for seven miles these four regiments with wagons and artillery slowly moved down the pike four abreast with a skirmish line out in front of the lead regiment. Soon they reached a slight rise known as Herr's Ridge where another tavern and Inn was located. From this vantage point the tops of the churches in Gettysburg could be seen. Pettigrew

…under orders to not engage any troops he may meet. At Herr Ridge he sent out a …l regiment skirmish line. Probably the 47th North Carolina. Off in the distance it was clear that Union Cavalry was posted along the opposite ridge beside a farm and barn. Pettigrew's orders were clear, so he pulled back his skirmish line and ordered the entire expedition to turn around and head back to Cashtown. Protected by the 47th, the group retraced their 7 mile steps. Arriving back in Cashtown Pettigrew reported to Heth and reported his findings. Heth was not quick to accept that Union Cavalry had arrived in the town but after discussion he accepted Pettigrew's view.

The men of Tennessee and Alabama and Mississippi and North Carolina camped that night in fields about three miles east of Cashtown . . . a place called New Salem. The orders were given that in the morning Heth's entire Division was moving East. The night brought several short showers of rain and a last night's sleep for many. "On the night of June 30 we bivouacked on the summit of a high mountain, during which a heavy rain fell, drenching us." **(Samuel W Hankins, "Simple Story of a Soldier", Confederate Veteran September 1912-May 1913)**

Chapter Two

The First Day

Heth's Division

"Archer's brigade left camp at the lead of Heth's Division on July 1, starting at 5 A.M. The brigade took the front of A.P. Hill's Corps, with General Davis' Mississippi brigade following, The Fifth Alabama Battalion was at the very front of Archer's Brigade. This Battalion and fifty men drawn from the Thirteenth Alabama Regiment were deployed to the right of the road leading to Gettysburg as skirmishers to drive in the Federal outposts. They encountered the cavalry about five miles out from Gettysburg and began to push them back. After driving them four miles, the skirmish line halted west of Willoughby Run, a small stream, when Archer's Brigade advanced over and beyond the skirmish line and soon engaged the enemy's main line of battle." **(William Frierson Fulton, Family Record and War Reminiscences, 1919)** At the same time Davis' Brigade was doing the same thing on the north side of Chambersburg Pike with skirmishers drawn from each of the three regiments he had on the field.

The Advance of Davis and Archer

On the morning of July 1, 1863 the Davis's Brigade was the second brigade in line behind Archer's Brigade and as they approached Gettysburg were put into battle line on the north side of Chambersburg Road. The 11th Mississippi was kept to the rear to guard the wagon trains while the brigade was placed in order from south to north. The Forty-second Mississippi, Col H. R. Miller commanding, on the right; Fifty-fifth North Carolina (with 655 officers and men), Col. J. K. Connally commanding, on the left, and Second Mississippi, Col. J. M. Stone commanding, in the center—skirmishers thrown forward, and the brigade moved forward to the attack. Lieutenant Colonel David W. Humphreys of the 2nd Mississippi was also detached with a large detail to help guard wagons and would not be in the fight.

Calhoun Rifles Private Samuel Hankins in the 2nd Mississippi remembered the beginning of the battle. "The following morning we marched down from the mountain to the pike that led to Gettysburg and then on in that direction. Between nine and ten o'clock on July 1 we halted at the foot of a hill and fronted, when our Colonel (John M. Stone) came down the line, stopping in front of each company and giving instructions. On reaching ours he remarked: 'Men, clean out your guns, load and be ready. We are going to have it.' Our first Lieutenant Whitley, had been under arrest a few days for disobeying some petty order and had kept along with the company at will. To him the Colonel remarked, 'Lieutenant Whitley, you can take command'. 'Thank You Colonel' said Whitley, obeying. We then marched to the top of the hill." **(Samuel W Hankins, "Simple Story of a Soldier", Confederate Veteran September 1912-May 1913)**

Between the brigade and the town, and very near it, was a commanding hill in wood, the intervening space being enclosed fields of grass and grain, and was very broken. On Davis's right was the turnpike and a railroad, with deep cuts and heavy embankments, diverging from the turnpike as it approached the town. On the high hill, the Union forces had artillery, with infantry supports. The line of skirmishers advanced, and the brigade moved forward about 1 mile, driving in the enemy's skirmishers, and came within range of his line of battle, which was drawn up on a high hill in a field a short distance in front of a railroad cut. "In the meantime we had thrown out a skirmish line, J.B. Gambrell, now a noted Baptist divine in Texas, was then a gallant young lieutenant and a member of our regiment, and no braver man ever lived. He was given command of our skirmishers, who soon became engaged all along the line, while the artillery duel began. We moved forward while our line of skirmishers kept pressing back that of the enemy" **(Samuel W Hankins, "Simple Story of a Soldier", Confederate Veteran September 1912-May 1913)**

After a short contest, the order was given to charge, and promptly obeyed. The Union forces made a stubborn resistance, and stood until Davis's men were within a few yards, and then gave way, and fled in much confusion, but rallied near the railroad, where they again made a stand, and, after desperate fighting, with heavy loss on both sides, Union troops fled in great disorder toward the town, leaving Davis's brigade in possession of his commanding position and batteries.

1st Sgt August Varin recalled the opening of the day this way in his diary . . . .

1st July Wednesday, clear, The regt. returned from picket at 7 AM & stopped a short time to rest at Cashtown & get the rations cooked by those we left in camp. About 9 AM marched toward Gettysburg. We had no idea of a battle yet until we crossed a small bridge. We were halted, taken through the manual of arms by Col. Stone, arms inspected & ordered to load at will. As we approached the town we went through a wheatfield on the right of the road to support a battery, soon after moved to the left of the pike. Sent out a skirmish line & moved forward, going over many plank fences—hard work for me, who was gaulded badly by the march. About 1/2 mile from the town we met the enemy, the 16th New York being the first we met. We were in a clover field on high ground, they in a corn field 100 yards off in the hollow. We soon annihilated them, so one of their sergeants afterward told me, for we drove the remnant of them back. They fought well & fell mostly on the line they occupied. Passing their lines we pushed on & saw a brass battery[171] advance to open fire on us but before they could unlimber we killed or wounded every man and horse but one, who galloped off. **(Vairin Diary, July 1, 1863)**

After a short interval, Union forces again returned in greater numbers including a Union artillery battery and the fight was renewed. Being opposed by greatly superior numbers, Davis's regiments gave way under the first shock of his attack, many officers and men having been killed or wounded, and all much exhausted by the excessive heat; but the line was promptly formed, and carried to its former position, and, while there engaged, a heavy force was observed moving rapidly toward their right, and soon after opened a heavy fire on their right flank and rear. This movement forward by Pennsylvania and New York troops convinced Davis to retire to regroup.

Davis gave the order to retire, which resulted in leaving a large number of officers and men in the railroad cut, who were captured. Large numbers of officers and men from the 2nd Mississippi and the 42nd Mississippi were lost here and most did not return to ranks even after the later Union retreat through town. Most of the 2nd Mississippi were caught in the Railroad Cut as were companies B and G of the 42nd. A man who was there with the 2nd Mississippi recalled "Our men thought the railroad cut would prove a good breast work but it was too deep and in changing front the men were all tangled up and confused" **(Vairin Diary, July 1, 1863)** 1st Sgt Augustus Vairin in Company B was a 43 Tippah, Mississippi watchmaker who would survive the first but be wounded and captured on the third. Vairin was one of the few to escape the Railroad Cut. Varin recorded the entire morning events in his diary "While preparing to go after the guns we saw a Yankey division which had captured Pettigrew's brigade on our right advancing. An old railroad cut on our right our men thought would prove a good breastwork but it was too deep & in changing front the men were tangled up & confused. Here we lost a number of men. I did not go into the cut, seeing its danger, & I cautioned all I could to get out by the right flank. Some did, but those on the left were surrounded by Major Blair. Those of us who got out of the difficulty fell back. Others of our troops came up in time & we gained that day's battle, but the regt. was reduced fearfully." **(Vairin Diary, July 1, 1863)** In Varin's company of 66 men that day 53 were killed, wounded or captured, Major Blair who surrendered his sword and many of his men in the trap wrote later.

In the midst of this combat a fight broke out over possession of the flag of the 2nd Mississippi. Color Bearer Private William Murphy a 22 year old Tishomingo farmer would be captured with the flag after a fight which he described after the war. "My color guards were all killed and wounded in less than five minutes, and also my colors were shot more than one dozen times, and the flag staff was hit and splintered two or three times. Just about that time a squad of soldiers made a rush for my colors and our men did their duty. They were all killed or wounded, but they still rushed for the colors with one of the most deadly struggles that was ever witnessed during any battle in the war. They still kept rushing for my flag and there were over a dozen shot down like sheep in their mad rush for the colors. The first soldier was shot down just as he made for the flag, and he was shot by one of our soldiers. Just to my right and at the same time a lieutenant made a desperate struggle for the flag and was shot through the right shoulder. Over a dozen men fell killed or wounded, and then a large man made a rush for me and the flag. As I tore the flag from the staff he took hold of me and the color. The firing was still going on, and was kept up for several minutes after the flag was taken from me . . . (Murphy letter to Dearborn, June 29, 1900.)

Major John Blair himself later wrote "By the time we reached a deep cut in the railroad—for the want of officers and other causes—all the men were jumbled together without regard to regiment or company" **(John Blair to Henry Lyman letter, June 9, 1888, *Historical sketch of the 147th New York Volunteers*, New York Monuments Commission 1900)** Captain Wollard of Company B 42nd Mississippi lost almost his entire company in about five minutes. "The Brigade of the enemy in our front had but to come up & take us in, which they did after killing a number of men all around me, several of my own company. I tried to make my way out and escape but the press was very great and just as I was trying to squeeze through a big Wisconsin man thrust his bayonet at me and said, 'give me that sword & stop your men from shooting here or we will kill the last damned one of you.'"**(Wollard Diary July 1, 1863)** Wollard's company went in with 61 men and lost 40 of them. By the time the company made it back to Virginia only 5 remained.

One of the men wounded in the Railroad cut was Private Samuel Hankins in Company E of the 2nd Mississippi, "I was wounded in the Railroad Cut. A minie ball struck me on my instep and broke the bones of my foot, lodging against the heel leader. I am thankful it was not in the heel. The wound was most painful" **(Samuel W Hankins, "Simple Story of a Soldier", Confederate Veteran September 1912-May 1913)** Hankins company Entered the battle with forty six men. By the night of the third only two remained unhurt or uncaptured, Privates Rufus Jones and Berry Scott.

The perspective of the 55th North Carolina which was on the left flank of the Davis Brigade focuses on their role as rear guard in the retreat through the railroad cut . . ." "The Fifty-fifth Regiment was on the left of the brigade, and owing to the character of the ground was the first one to come into view of the enemy, and received the first fire in the battle. It was a volley fired by the Fifty-sixth Pennsylvania Regiment, commanded by Colonel Hoffman, of Cutler's Brigade. Two men in the color guard of the regiment were wounded by this volley. The regiment immediately returned the fire and inflicted considerable loss upon the Fifty-sixth Pennsylvania Regiment. The Eleventh Mississippi Regiment was on detail duty that morning, so only three regiments of our brigade, the Second and Forty-second Mississippi Regiments, and the Fifty-fifth North Carolina, were present. The regiments in our front were the Seventy-sixth New York, the Fifty-sixth Pennsylvania and the One Hundred and Forty-seventh New York of Cutler's Brigade. After the enemy's position became known by their first fire, our brigade charged them in magnificent style. The left of our regiment extended considerably beyond the right of the enemy's line—and at the proper time our left was wheeled to the right. The enemy fled from the field with great loss. From the beginning of this engagement it was hot work. While the regiment was advancing, Colonel Connally seized the battle flag and waving it aloft rushed out several paces in front of the regiment. This drew upon him and the color guard the fire of the enemy and he fell badly wounded in the arm and hip. His arm was afterwards amputated. Major Belo, who was near him at the time, rushed up and asked him if he was badly wounded. Colonel Connally replied: "Yes, but do not pay any attention to me; take the colors and keep ahead of the Mississippians." After the defeat of the forces in front of us, the brigade swung around by the right wheel and formed on the railroad cut. About one-half of the Fifty-fifth Regiment being on the left extended beyond the cut on the embankment. In front of us there were then the Ninety-fifth and Eighty-fourth New York (known as the Fourteenth Brooklyn) Regiments, who had been supporting Hall's battery, and were the other two regiments of Cutler's Brigade, and the Sixth Wisconsin, of the Iron Brigade, which had been held in reserve, when the other regiments of that brigade were put in to meet Archer's advance. Just then the order was received to retire through the road-cut, and that the Fifty-fifth North Carolina cover the retreat of the brigade. The Federal Regiments in front of us threw themselves into line of battle by a well executed movement notwithstanding the heavy fire we were pouring into them, and as soon as their line of battle was formed, seeing a disposition on our part to retire, charged. They were held in check, as well as could be done, by the Fifty-fifth Regiment covering the retreat of the brigade; a part of the regiment was in the road-cut and at a great disadvantage. One of the Federal officers on the embankment, seeing Major Belo in the cut, threw his sword at him, saying: "Kill that officer, and that will end it." The sword missed Major Belo, but struck the man behind him. Major Belo directed one of the men to shoot the officer and this was done. This somewhat checked their charge, and we fell back to another position. The loss of the regiment was very great in killed and wounded, and a large number were captured in the road-cut. **(Cooke, Fifty-Fifth Regiment)**

This action occurred around 1 p.m. The Mississippi troops that remained were pulled back to the west to regroup. About 3 p.m. a division of Lieutenant-General Ewell's corps came up on Davis's left, moving in line perpendicular and the brigade was again moved forward, and, after considerable fighting, reached the suburbs of the town, into which the enemy had been driven. The men, being much exhausted by the heat and severity of the engagement, were rested, and about sunset were ordered to bivouac about 1 mile to the rear.

One final incident had occurred with the 2nd Mississippi troops during this movement of Ewell's Corps (Daniel's Division). Sometime after 3:00PM before the Scale' assault on Seminary Ridge. The flag company of the 149th Pennsylvania was moved forward from their regimental line to draw Confederate artillery fire away from the flank of the Union line. Colonel Stone noticed the flag and called for volunteers to rush and take it.

3rd Lieutenant Altas K. Roberts of Company H and four men of his company volunteered to lead a party to capture the enemy colors. As 21 year old Roberts' squad rushed forward and surprised the Pennsylvanians located near a fence, a hand-to-hand struggle ensued. Lieutenant Roberts, reached the fence first, but to the surprise of the squad, the hidden color guard rose up and killed the former Chesterville, Mississippi farmboy.

In the confusion that followed, the gun of one of Lieutenant Roberts' men, Private Henry McPherson, failed to fire three of the Union color guard were running away with the 149th flag and one of his comrades as prisoner. McPherson recapped his gun and fired at the color bearer hitting him in the leg. He then rushed forward, seized the colors from the wounded man and, braving a hail of bullets from the Union line, brought in the flag. **(J. H. Strain. "Heroic Henry McPherson," Confederate Veteran, XXXI (1923): p. 205) (Compiled service records Henry McPherson Co H 2nd Mississippi, National Archives)**

The 55th North Carolina also returned to the fighting later that afternoon . . ." From that time until 3 o'clock in the afternoon we were not engaged. About that time Early came in with fresh troops from the left. We formed in line with them on their right and were hotly engaged in the battles of that afternoon, driving the enemy before us and capturing a number of prisoners. At sundown we were in the edge of Gettysburg, and the regiment was placed behind the railroad embankment just in front of the Seminary. In the afternoon Lieutenant Colonel Smith, while the regiment was waiting in reserve, walked towards the right to reconnoiter and was mortally wounded and died that night. Major Belo was also severely wounded in the leg just as the battle closed that evening. Davis' Brigade, during the night, was moved from its position on the railroad cut near the Seminary to a piece of woods across Willoughby Run, west of the mineral springs, and there rested." **(Cooke, Fifty-Fifth Regiment)**

In the July 1 engagement the losses in men and officers were very heavy; of 9 field officers present, but 2 escaped unhurt. Colonel Stone, of the Second Mississippi, and Colonel Connally, of the Fifty-fifth North Carolina, were both wounded while leading their men in the first charge. Stone was able to serve in command while wounded. Lieutenant Colonel. M. T. Smith, of the Fifty-fifth North Carolina, was mortally wounded. Major Belo, of the same regiment, was severely wounded and later died. Lieutenant-Colonel Moseley and Major Feeney, of the Forty-second Mississippi, were both severely wounded. A large number of the company officers were killed or wounded.

Meanwhile Archer's Brigade had been heavily involved to the south of the Chambersburg Road. At 5:00 AM on July 1, 1863 the division of Henry Heth moved eastward along the Chambersburg Road toward Gettysburg. Archer's Brigade was in the lead with the 13th Alabama in the front. Union cavalry skirmishers fired on the advancing rebel column as they neared Marsh creek but withdrew as the 5th Alabama Battalion and several 13th Alabama companies were deployed as skirmishers. The 13th Alabama contingent was commanded by Lieutenant William Crawford with some of his company C and all of companies B and G.

Private William Bird and his friend Samuel Biekly (Co C 13th AL) had risen early on the morning of July 1 and set out on their own expedition . . ." carrying with us four or five canteens apiece and haversacks, we succeeded in getting our canteens filled with cherry wine, and in passing through a fine cherry orchard, we both were up a cherry tree, eating the finest cherries I ever saw. When we heard the long roll beating to fall in to go into the Gettysburg fight, we hastened down from the tree, picked up our canteens of wine and made for Regiment, but when we arrived at the camping ground our Regiment and Brigade were gone. But we found our guns and knapsacks and put off in search or our Regiment, and in a short distance overtook our Company and distributed our wine among them . . ." **(Bird, William, *Stories of the Civil War, Company C, 13th Regiment of Alabama Volunteers,* Columbiana, AL: Advocate Press, circa 1900.)** (Author note: Interestingly, the muster report for Private Samuel Biekly (Buckley) reads "absent sick" on both July 1 & July 3. It is not known if this report is inaccurate or whether the effect of the cherry wine was at fault.)

Private Elijah Boland in Co. F of the 13th Alabama remembered reaching "a small village of a few brick houses "just before the firing began. In her writings on the 13th Alabama, historian Tamara Stephens relates an interesting story about the advance of the Archer Brigade toward Herr Ridge . . . . "As members of the 5th Alabama Battalion momentarily sought shelter behind a small house, a snarling dog 'raised an objection' to their presence. Soon the dog's owner appeared and asked what was happening. Upon being told that a battle was at hand, the surprised man asked, 'By whom'? The soldiers responded, 'by General Lee and the Yankees.' The framer said, ' Tell Lee to hold on just a little until I get my cow out of the pasture,' and then ran off to preserve his livestock.

Passing through a wheat field, part of the 13th Alabama soon upon an obstacle in their path—a house occupied by 'an old lady and a large yellow dog,' probably the same dog the 5th Alabama Battalion had just encountered. As they maneuvered around the house, the dog bit several of the men. They shot the dog which "'of course layed him out", according to Pvt. Bird. The old lady 'got stirred up' because not only was her dog dead, but also that some of the men had 'knocked down her ash-hopper.' Bird thought this 'gave her room to believe the Rebels were terrible fellows,' and noted she' did not fail to tell us so.' Leaving the angry old lady behind hurling insults at them, Archer's men pushed the Union skirmishers off Herr Ridge and then halted at the woods. From this vantage point they could see the Federal position at McPherson Ridge." **(Tamara Stephens manuscript; Letters of Commissary Sgt. William Fulton & Private William H. Bird (Co C)**

Archer's Brigade was deployed to the south side of the Chambersburg Road and was arranged North to south 7th Tennessee, 14th Tennessee, 1st Tennessee and to the far right the 13th Alabama. The 5th Alabama Battalion was out in front as skirmishers. The Brigade moved forward toward Willoughby Run and the Herbst woods. The left regiments, 7th & 14th Tennessee, soon came under fire while the two right regiments moved ahead, reached the creek and crossed. Soon the Union counterattack started as the Iron Brigade went into action. The 4 regiments of the Iron Brigade (2nd & 7th Wisconsin; 24th Michigan and 19th Indiana—north to south) moved forward. Because the Iron brigade was larger than Archer's brigade the 19th Indiana and parts of the 24th Michigan on the Union left moved around the Flank of the 13th Alabama and crossed the creek to their south. Soon the 13th Alabama and then the 1st Tennessee were rolled up and in retreat. Then, Archer's entire Brigade was headed back to Herr's Ridge with Brigadier General James Archer and a cluster of men around him taken as a prisoner. Captain Turney of Company K of the 1st Tennessee described the action this way . . . "The sharpshooters, under command of Major Buchanan, of the First Tennessee, encountered the Federal advance some three miles southwest of Gettysburg. The enemy fell back slowly, resisting our approach, until General Archer ordered a halt when we were within about one mile of the town. General Heth soon arrived, and ordered Archer forward, as he said, to ascertain the "strength and line of battle of the enemy." Archer suggested that his brigade was light to risk so far in advance of support. Upon being ordered forward a second time, he advanced about two hundred yards, when we met with stubborn resistance, having encountered the enemy's line of battle. For thirty minutes the firing was severe, and the smoke of battle hovered near the ground, shutting out from view the movements of the Federal forces. When the enemy's fire ceased, I dropped on my knees, and, looking beneath the hanging smoke, saw the feet and legs of the enemy moving to our left. This I communicated to General Archer, who doubted its possibility, saying: "I guess not, Captain, since Gen. Joe Davis is to occupy that timber to our left." By the time I reached my line a brigade of the enemy under General Reynolds was upon our left, capturing General Archer, with quite a percentage of his brigade, including a portion of the left of the First Tennessee. During the excitement attending the capture of General Archer, I succeeded in escaping with the major part of my company, falling back some two hundred yards to the skirt of timber." **(Captain J.B. Turney, "The First Tennessee at Gettysburg", Confederate Veteran, VII (1900), pp 528-529)**"

Well, we soon formed the line again and we had to pass down a long slant, and that was the prettiest line of battle I think I ever saw. Our regiment was on the right of the Brigade and I believe our Brigade was on the right of the Division. So we went down the sloe to a ravine, but before we reached it, Capt. B.A. Brown was detailed off with fifteen or twenty men to watch a flank movement and try to prevent it. So on we went down the hill with Lieut. H.W. Pond I command of the remainder of the company. We finally arrived at the ravine, crossed the clearest stream; pebbles on the bottom nearly knee deep. Rose a rugged step bluff, and entered a wheat field about a half mile west of Gettysburg. When we got up on the hill we seen a line of skirmishers some one hundred yards in front: the field officers were cheering their men and urging them forward. Lieut H.W. Pond is one of those long keen good-ones; he was there urging on his company; when all of a sudden a heavy line of battle rose out of the wheat and poured a volley into our ranks, it wavered and they charged us, and we fell back to the ravine again, and before we could possibly rally, it seemed to me there were 20,000 Yanks down in among us hollowing surrender. I had discharged my gun at them just before they got us, and of course I had to surrender. There were two officers and a private or two ran up to Lieut. Pond, saying surrender! surrender and the Lieutenant looked at me and said: Bird, what in the hell shall I do? I remarked, I don't see what you can do, but surrender, and he threw down his sword." **(Bird, William, *Stories of the Civil War, Company C, 13th Regiment of Alabama Volunteers*, Columbiana, AL: Advocate Press, circa 1900.)**author note : B.A. Brown was actually a Lieutenant of Company C which was commanded by Captain Walter Taylor (also captured July 1)

The action on the first day would greatly weaken the five regiments. The First Tennessee lost 4 killed 27 wounded and 57 captured for a total of 88 (300 Officers and men remaining). The 13th Alabama lost 7 killed 28 wounded and 117 taken prisoner. (162 officers & men left) The 7th Tennessee 1 Killed 9 wounded 29 taken prisoner. (219 left) The 14th Tennessee lost none killed 4 wounded 47 prisoner (230 remaining) and the 5th Alabama lost 10 wounded leaving 121 remaining for July 3.

The Advance of Pettigrew's Brigade

Marshall's brigade at Gettysburg was originally Pettigrew's brigade under Major General Henry Heth. Brigadier General James Pettigrew had been severely wounded at Seven Pines during the Peninsular campaign and during his recovery period held no Brigade position. After his recovery four North Carolina regiments were placed under his command in the summer of 1863 for the Pennsylvania invasion. (11th NC, 26th NC, 47th NC and 52nd NC)

Early on the morning of July 1, Pettigrew's brigade moved down the pike toward Gettysburg. When within about 2½ miles of the town, they deployed to the left of the pike, but soon crossed over to the right, other regiments of the division having been engaged for some time. They took up position in rear of the batteries after moving to the right. After remaining in this position about half an hour, exposed to a random fire from the enemy's guns, losing probably a dozen men killed and wounded, Pettigrew received orders to advance, moved forward about half a mile, and halted in a skirt of woods.

The following is the position of the regiments in the brigade: On the right (south), the Fifty-second North Carolina, next the Forty-seventh North Carolina, then the Eleventh North Carolina, and on the far left (north) the Twenty-sixth. In front was a wheat-field about a fourth of a mile wide; then came a stream, with thick underbrush and briars skirting the banks. Beyond this was again an open field, with the exception of a wooded hill directly in front of the Twenty-sixth Regiment, about covering its front. During this lull Heth reformed his lines and placed his two damaged brigades (Archer & Davis) to the flanks. Meanwhile Rode's division arrived on oak Hill and attacked from the north. Colonel John Brockenbrough's Virginian regiments prepared to forward to combat the "bucktails" near the Chambersburg Pike while Pettigrew would fight the "black hats".

Skirmishers being thrown out, the brigade remained in line of battle until 2 p.m., when orders to advance were received. While they waited the right companies were under fire from a group of Union sharpshooters on top of the barn that was over by the Fairfield road. 23 year Lieutenant John Lowe in Company G crawled out to a fence line that ran toward the barn and in a few shots "took them out". At about 2:30PM The brigade moved forward in beautiful style, at quick time, just with the brigade on their left, commanded by Colonel Brockenbrough. When nearing the branch referred to, the Union forces poured a galling fire into the left of the brigade from the opposite bank, where they had massed in heavy force while Pettigrew's regiments were in line of battle in the woods. The Forty-seventh and Fifty-second, although exposed to a hot fire from artillery and infantry, lost but few in comparison with the Eleventh and Twenty-sixth. On went the command across the branch and up the opposite slope, driving the enemy at the point of the bayonet back upon their second line. This second line was encountered by the Twenty-sixth, which took severe losses including its "boy" Colonel Henry Burgwyn killed and its Lieutenant Colonel John Lane wounded in the neck and mouth. while the other regiments were exposed to a heavy shelling. Colonel Marshall commanding the 52nd NC was concerned about Union cavalry to his south and at one point formed his men into defense squares. Next he swung his men across the Fairfield Road and shifted east. The Union single line in the field was engaged principally with the fight against the Eleventh and Forty-seventh NC. The 47th was met "by a furious storm of shells and canister and further on by the more destructive rifles of the *two* army corps confronting us . . . . After a desperate struggle this (line) yielded and the second line was met and quickly broken to pieces" **(John Thorp, Memories of Gettysburg, GNMP)** These Union regiments did not observe the Fifty-second, which flanked their left, until they discovered themselves by a raking and destructive fire into their ranks, by which they were broken. On this second line, the fighting was terrible—Pettigrew's men advancing, the Union stubbornly resisting, until the two lines were pouring volleys into each other at a distance not greater than 20 paces. With the 11th North Carolina 3rd Lieutenant William B Taylor (Co A) described the scene to his parents in a letter home after the battle. "drove them like sheep . . . it was an awful cost but we paid it to them twofold. The Iron Brigade Yankeys tried to stand but it was know use. Stood within 20 yards of each other for 15 minutes but they had to give way. Major Ross was killed. Our company and part of company F and D and I went ahead of the balance of the brigade and Ross was with our company He was shot with grape in the right side, and it went nearly through him, it was about the size of an egg. He lived for four hours and we buried him. I got a piece of plank, put his name on it with his rank for a head board." **(Lieutenant William Taylor, letter home, Histories of the North Carolina Regiments 5:640)** At last the Union forces retreated. They again made a stand in the woods, and the third time they were driven from their position, losing a stand of colors, which was taken by the Twenty-sixth North Carolina. The fierceness of the line to line volleys was remembered by 26th North Carolina Sergeant J.T. Hood in Company F . . . "Volleys of deafly missiles were sent into our ranks which mowed us down like wheat before the sickle" **(Hood, J.T.C. "The 26th Regiment at Gettysburg." Lenoir**

News Topic. April 8, 1896) Another soldier in the 26th NC Corporal James Dorsett (Co E), who was wounded described the action this way. "The bullets were flying around me like hailstones in a storm. Lot's of men near me were falling to the ground, throwing up their arms and clawing the earth. The whole field was covered with gray suits soaked in blood." **(Dorsett, Wilber, "Fourteenth Color-Bearer, p 5)**

While the Twenty-sixth was still engaged, the rest of the line, having cleared the field and being exposed to a heavy fire from the enemy's batteries, were ordered to fall back, which they did in perfect order. The Twenty-sixth, not receiving the order, were now engaged in collecting ammunition from the enemy's dead, being entirely out themselves. Just as they were ready to advance again, General Pender's division passed over them. They followed on, and after a lengthy wait assisted in driving the enemy from the heights on the edge of the town. Then the entire Brigade halted. That night the brigade bivouacked in the woods they had occupied previous to making the charge.

In the midst of this action Major General Harry Heth was hit by a bullet in the head. His life was saved because, a couple of days earlier, he had gotten a new felt hat in Cashtown which was too large and so his quartermaster, had folded up a dozen or so sheets of paper and stuffed them inside the hat, creating a snug fit. Heth survived the bullet because of the cushioning the wrapped paper provided but was knocked unconscious for the remainder of the day. "I am confidently of the belief that my life was saved by this paper in my hat," Heth commented later. Heth's part in the battle of Gettysburg was over as Brigadier James Pettigrew took his place in command of the division

The Twenty-sixth lost more than half its men killed and wounded, among them Col. H. K. Burgwyn, Jr., killed, Lieut. Col. J. R. Lane seriously wounded, both with the colors, with many other most valuable officers. The 26th had gone into battle with 843 officers and men and had only 212 left unhurt. Col. C. Leventhorpe of the Eleventh, and Major E. A. J Ross were lost—the former wounded severely, the latter killed—with many officers and men. The losses by the 52nd and the 47th were less severe. That evening Colonel Marshall of the 52nd NC was given command of the brigade as General Pettigrew was promoted to replace the wounded General Heth. Pettigrew as the new brigade commander ordered all detailed men back into the ranks for coming battle and on the next day moved forward to support the abortive attack by Brigadier General Wright's attack but the brigade arrived too late to take part in that action. That evening they returned to the protected hollow behind seminary ridge.

Pender's "Light" Division

Pender's division, camped on the northern side of the Chambersburg Pike in the Cashtown Gap, got on the Pike at 8 o'clock in the morning on July 1 and marched toward Gettysburg in the rear of Heth's division. Perrin's brigade was in the lead, followed by Scales, Lane and Thomas. At 9:30, as Perrin reached Marsh Creek, Pender heard the boom and crackle of Maj. Gen. Henry Heth's Division's fight just ahead, and stopped to form a line of battle, with the Pike in the center, about 2 miles to the east of McPherson's Ridge, where the battle was being fought. The subsequent slow advance through the fields on the hot morning fatigued the men and, in the absence of orders, kept Pender's brigades from joining the desperate fighting between Heth's men and the Union First Corps. Pender's brigades finally reached Herr Ridge a little before noon, just as Heth's men were being repulsed in their front. Instead of rushing into action, Pender halted on the ridge. This was a distinct difference in General Pender's usual aggressive style. Pender then took some time to redeploy on Herr Ridge, and there his brigades rested until around 2:30 that afternoon, when Heth's division renewed its attack in Pender's front. Although Pender was ordered to support Heth, Heth declined any assistance in the afternoon attack, so Pender merely advanced slowly at first, keeping within supporting distance of Heth's line. Heth, in fact, got far more fight than he expected from the Union First Corps defenders on McPherson's Ridge, and could have used the help of Pender's men, but he received a disabling wound at the height of the attack and had not request timely assistance. Corps commander Hill was evidently too sick to order Pender's men forward, and Pender himself did not consult with anyone or push forward on his own initiative when he saw the trouble Heth's men had gotten into.

Doubleday was therefore able after Pettigrew's successful assault, to withdraw his command into a consolidated position on Seminary Ridge where the men threw down fence rails for a barricade and waited as the Confederates formed on McPherson's Ridge for a final assault. But driving Doubleday's command from Seminary Ridge proved more deadly than Hill and his division officers had planned.

In the first arrangement of the troops of Pender's light division, Lane's brigade was on the extreme left, and Scale's brigade on his immediate right, with Scale's left resting upon the turnpike leading from Cashtown to Gettysburg. McGowan's (South Carolina) brigade was on Scale's right. Thomas Georgia Brigade was on detached duty guarding the wagon trains and protecting the Confederate artillery batteries. A few minutes after the line of battle was thus formed, the brigade received orders to advance. After marching about a quarter of a mile without any casualty, the brigade was halted, and put in rear of the artillery belonging to A. P. Hill's corps. Here General Lane's brigade was changed to the extreme right of the division, leaving Scale's brigade on the extreme left, without any change of position. For the remainder of the action Lane would be tied up, under orders from Pender, keeping track of Union cavalry forces to the south.

The Action of Lane's Brigade

Lane's Brigade was largely untested on the first day of battle. On the morning of July 1, Lane's Brigade moved through Cashtown, in the direction of Gettysburg, and formed line of battle in rear of the left of Heth's division, about 3 miles from the latter place, to the left of the turnpike, in the following order: Seventh, Thirty-seventh, Twenty-eighth,

Eighteenth, and Thirty-third North Carolina Regiments, the right of the Seventh resting on the road. After marching nearly a mile in line of battle, we were ordered to the right of the road, and formed on the extreme right of the light division. The brigade had suffered heavy casualties at Chancellorsville and many officers and men were still recovering in hospitals in Virginia. Most would return to the brigade in September and October after the Gettysburg campaign. The Seventh Regiment was deployed as a strong line of skirmishers some distance to the right and at right angles to the line of battle, to protect the brigade's flank, which was exposed to the enemy's cavalry. Pettigrew's and Archer's brigades were in the first line, immediately in their front. The brigade was soon ordered forward again after taking this position, the Seventh Regiment being instructed to move as skirmishers by the left flank. In advancing, Lane gained ground to the right, and, on emerging from the woods in which Pettigrew's brigade had been formed. Soon the brigade line had passed Archer's right flank and the brigade's front was open to Union attack.

The brigade moved forward about a mile, and as the Seventh Regiment had been detained a short time, Colonel Barbour commander of the 37th North Carolina threw out 40 men, under Captain Hudson (Company G), to keep back some of the enemy's cavalry, which had dismounted and were annoying us with an enfilade fire. Co G moved across this open field at quick time until a body of the enemy's cavalry and a few infantry opened upon them from the woods, when the men gave a yell, and rushed forward at a double-quick, the whole of the enemy's force beating a hasty retreat to Cemetery Hill.

Lane's right now extended into the woods above referred to, and his left was a short distance from the Fairfield road. On passing beyond the stone fence and into the peach orchard near McMillan's house, Lane was ordered by General Pender not to advance farther unless there was another general forward movement. As he could see nothing at that time to indicate such a movement, and as one of the enemy's batteries on Cemetery Hill was doing some damage, Lane ordered the brigade back a few yards, so the left flank might take shelter behind the stone fence. Lane's brigade remained in this position that night; and next day, before the heavy artillery firing commenced, the Thirty-third and Eighteenth Regiments was moved to the left of Lieutenant-Colonel Garnett's battalion of artillery, so they might be better sheltered and be out of the enemy's line of fire.

The Attack by Scales' & Perrin's Brigades

As Lane was engaging light Union cavalry action, Scale's brigade was again ordered to advance, which it did in good order, and under a severe artillery fire from the enemy in the front—twelve guns of Stevens and Stewart's batteries. While advancing, a regiment or two of Union troops about half a mile in the front, marching in line of battle on the north side of the road parallel to the turnpike, and directly toward the road appeared. They very soon engaged a regiment of Confederate troops men (part of General Davis' brigade who had survived the Railroad cut trap), who were advancing on the opposite side of the road. A heavy fight ensued, in which Davis's brigade, overpowered by numbers, started giving way. Seeing this, Scales brigade quickened their step, and pressed on with a shout to their assistance. The enemy, with their flank thus exposed to Scale's charge, immediately gave way, and fled in great confusion to the rear.

Scales brigade pressed on until coming up with the line in their own front, which was at a halt and lying down. This would have been the rear of Brockenbrough's Brigade which had been regrouping west of McPherson's ridge. Scales received orders to halt, and to wait for the line in front line to advance. For the purpose of keeping in the proper supporting distance, Scale's again ordered an advance, but, after marching one-fourth of a mile or more, again came upon the front line of Confederate forces (Pettigrew's Brigade), halted and lying down. The officers on this part of the line informed Scale's that they were without ammunition and would not advance further. At this point Pender, who was usually an aggressive commander failed to order an attack on the Union forces then establishing a defensive line on the ridge where the Lutheran Seminary was located. Pender also did not bring up artillery to support the upcoming attack.

It was not until about 4:00 P.M. that Pender got the order from Hill to launch his attack on the Union line, now withdrawn to Seminary Ridge, the last line of defense in front of Gettysburg.

The tactical situation for Scale's at this point was that Union artillery had been moved to the north side of Chambersburg Road up on a slope. Artillery which would be able to fire into his left flank as he advanced. In addition, the hesitation of General Pender had enabled the Union to build breastworks and artillery emplacements connecting the Seminary buildings forming a wall of cannons and infantry rifles across the ridge. Scales alignment was from north to south the 38th NC (*229 men*), which would attack just south of the road directly at the newly placed guns; the 13th NC (*232 men*), 34th NC (*329 men*), 22nd NC (*321 men*) and the 16th NC (*321 men*). It should be noted that the Union guns placed on the slope between the Chambersburg road and the railroad line were pointed into the valley so the 38th North Carolina would not be charging directly into their canister fire. The converging fire of the Union guns would strike most effectively the middle regiments of Scales attack.

When Pender finally ordered the attack, after receiving orders from Hill, Scale's five regiments passed over the remains of Heth's forces, went up the ascent, crossed the ridge, and commenced the descent into the swale just opposite the theological seminary. Pender had plunged ahead with only two of his four brigades, with Scales on the left with his left touching the Chambersburg Pike and Perrin on the right. Here, the brigade encountered a most terrific fire of grape and shell on their flank, and grape and musketry in their front, but the brigade pressed on at a double-quick until it reached the bottom, a distance of about 75 yards from the ridge they had just crossed, and about the same distance from the college, in their front. Here, General Scale's received a wound from a piece of shell, and was disabled. Scales himself wrote this account of the effect of the federal artillery in his official report "Every discharge made sad havoc in our line, but we still pressed on at a double-quick until we reached the bottom . . . here I received a painful wound from a piece of shell, and was disabled. Our line had been broken up, and now only a squad here and there marked the place where regiments had rested. Every field officer of the brigade except one was disabled during the attack, and the brigade lost nine officers killed, forty five wounded and one missing. The ranks were thinned by the loss of thirty nine men killed, three hundred and thirty six wounded, and one hundred and fifteen missing."

The Scales attack began to stall at this point and only 15 to 20 minutes later when Perrin's men were able to break through the Union left did Scale's move forward (Now under the command of Lowrence from the 34th NC) Scale's losses were tremendous. His losses in officers were severe. By the time Pender's attackers reached the ravine 200 yards in front of Union line, Scales' brigade had been obliterated by a storm of canister fire from the blue gunners in their front, and Perrin's brigade continued the charge alone.

The initial Confederate attack in the valley had met a storm of concentrated artillery and musketry fire that nearly destroyed General Alfred Scales' North Carolina brigade and severely crippled part of a South Carolina brigade commanded by Colonel Abner Perrin. Outnumbered, low on ammunition and with his rear threatened, there was nothing more Union commander Doubleday could achieve by holding Seminary Ridge. There was no alternative but to retreat through Gettysburg to Cemetery Hill. Just as the orders to withdraw were given to the Union regiments, The South Carolinians were ordered to attacked again. Despite a severe cross fire and heavy casualties suffered during their first charge, Colonel Perrin's South Carolinians exploited a narrow gap in the Union line and raced onto Seminary Ridge just as the Union officers ordered their men to pull out. After about a half hour of bloody fighting, Pender's men had finally forced the Yankees off the ridge. Perrin ordered two of his regiments to pursue the retreating Federals and the incensed South Carolinians raced after the refuges in blue, taking prisoners and shooting down those who refused to surrender. What began as an orderly retreat soon turned into a confused race through Gettysburg as soldiers trotted through unfamiliar streets and alleys while other lost souls ploughed into the crowd from intersecting streets. Adding to the chaos was the lack of orders to direct the refugees to Cemetery Hill, the Union rallying point. Lost soldiers ran from one street to another to find themselves confronted by armed Confederates. Others took refuge in cellars and buildings, only to be rooted out and taken prisoner. Disorganized after their victory and having suffered huge losses, some men from Scale's pursued the retreating Union forces into Gettysburg before halting for the day. Pender brought up Thomas's Brigade that evening and posted the full division on Seminary Ridge facing east with its left on the Fairfield Road.

Day Two

For most of the regiments in Heth and Pender's Division the Second Day of the battle of Gettysburg was a day of rest and recovery. For many regiments the losses of July 1 had crippled them as fighting units. Officers had been particularly targeted it seemed in the ranks of Scales brigade and Davis's brigade.

General Pettigrew (now in command for Heth), sensing the need for combating the depression that the huge number of casualties had brought his regiments looked up into the cloudy sky and saw that the light drizzle in the morning would further expand the gloom and decided to use some psychology. He immediately ordered the members of the 26th NC and the 11th NC bands to report to his headquarters. In addition, the order went out that all cooks and detailed soldiers were to report to their regiments and prepare for combat duty. Pettigrew ordered that roll calls were to be taken and burial details assigned. Members of the band feared that they to would be given rifles for combat duty. When they arrived at Pettigrew's headquarters they were told that they should be prepared to play music the entire day to keep up the spirit of the troops. The 26th and the 11th combined bands. **(Julius Lieback Papers, SHC)** One would assume the 55th NCV musicians were added. By mid morning the concert began and tunes such as "Old North State" and "Dixie" and "Bonnie Blue Flag" could be heard across the battlefield. Even Polkas were played. The English visitor Lieutenant Colonel Freemantle recalled "When the cannonade was at it height, a Confederate band . . . began to play polkas and waltzes, which sounded very curious, accompanied by the hissing and bursting of the shells **(Freemantle Diary, p 208)**

1st Sgt Augustus Varin had a brush with death himself on Day two. "*2nd July Thursday*, We were moved about 1 mile to the right of yesterday's battle & rested all day, gathering arms & c. From our bivouac we could see the battlefield of this day. I was struck on the head by a glancing ball which addled me for the rest of the day so I did no more that day. Col. Stone was hurt & disabled by a piece of shell." **(Varin Diary, July 2)**

Some of Pender's regiments did not have it so easy. Several of the regiments were given skirmish duty on the second day. In the 33rd North Carolina companies E and F under Lieutenants Caldwell and Gibbs were out most of the day. "On the second day our line of battle was not engaged but there was a very strong picket fighting in front of us and as it was the turn of his company to go out on skirmish he (John Caldwell) was skirmishing all day and was not relived until about sundown. He took his skirmishers out in gallant style and during the day lost two of his company killed and several wounded. I* was sent out to him by General Lane with an order during the day and our conversation took place in an open field under a heavy fire from the enemy's sharpshooters and of course was brief. This was the last conversation I had with him because I was sent off with a detachment that night and did not return until just as our line commenced advancing the next day. John Happoldt (3rd Lt Co D) says he and Johnny had a long conversation the day before the charge and that he told him he never expected to see his relations again . . . ." **(Willoughby F. Avery Co C to Cousin Mary Caldwell, Tod Caldwell Papers #128, Southern Historical Collection)**

Several companies of the 28th North Carolina with Lane also had skirmish duty on the second day. Captain Edward Lovell the 21 yr old commander of Company A was wounded in the right arm while out on the front line.

For many men the second day was a day to tend to their wounds and to bury the dead. Many men would be focused on caring for their friends and comrades. Private Samuel Hankins in Company E of the 2nd Mississippi had been wounded in the ankle and told years later of how close he had come to death"

(Samuel W Hankins, "Simple Story of a Soldier", Confederate Veteran September 1912-May 1913)

While leading his troop deployment on the 2nd day of fighting, Major General Dorsey Pender was wounded in the fleshy part of the thigh by a shell fragment. Although a small entrance wound, the shrapnel severed a major artillery and brought forth much blood. Reluctantly Pender had to go to the rear and would play no further part in the battle. Deemed too valuable to be left behind to be captured, Pender wound be carried back across the Potomac in a wagon. Despite the difficult ride and an infection setting in it was thought that he would recover, however, as his condition seemed to be improving. Later at Staunton, Virginia he began heavy bleeding and his surgeon felt the artery impossible to repair and the leg was amputated. Pender died within a few hours after the operation on July 18, 1863.

On the evening of July 1 First Lieutenant William Peel of Company C 11th Mississippi walked over a section of the battlefield . . . "Implements of war were scattered in every direction, where here and there lay horses in every conceivable degree of mutilation. Our wounded had all been taken to the Hospitals, & some of the Yankees had been taken from the field, while those who were still there had been collected into a grove of forest tress. There are perhaps few stages of suffering of which the imagination can conceive, that were not there represented. I saw one poor fellow, lying stretched on his back. He must have been lying down when he was struck, for a minnie ball had struck him near the top of his head & and appeared to go directly in. There was quite a quantity—a handful it seemed to me of his brains that had issued forth from the wound & was lying on the ground. The man appeared perfectly unconscious, but was breathing freely, then after 2,4 hours from the time he was shot." **(Peel Diary—July 2, 1863)**

Finally, two important developments occurred on the Second Day at Gettysburg. Because of the wounding of Major General Heth and Major General Pender there would be a need to find leadership for their divisions. The oft criticized decision by Lt. General A.P. Hill to use these regiments in the Third Day assault would require new leadership. Brigadier General James Pettigrew would be advanced from the command of his Brigade to take the place of Heth. Major General—at large Isaac Ridgeway Trimble would be shifted from Ewell's command to replace the dying Pender.

Both men had been recommended for promotion. Trimble in fact had the blessing of Stonewall Jackson himself who wrote "I respectfully recommend that Brig. Gen. I.R. Trimble be appointed a Maj. Gen. It is proper, in this connection, to state that I do not regard him as a good disciplinarian, but his success in battle has induced me to recommend his promotion. I will mention but one instance, though several might be named, in which he rendered distinguished service. After a day's march of over 30 miles he ordered his command . . . to charge the enemy's position at Manassas Junction. This charge resulted in the capture of a number of prisoners and 8 pieces of Artillery. I regard that day's achievement as the most brilliant that has come under my observation during the present war."

Pettigrew had earned the respect of his fellow Brigadiers and was well known as a scholar and a military commander. But the reality of the day was this—Now. not only would crippled regiments be selected to assault the Union line on the third of July, but they would be under commanders who had little knowledge of their Divisions or experience in handling such large numbers of men.

"The four Wilkins brothers of Company E (11th Mississippi) shared a small fire and meager rations that night. Private Henry Wilkins while sharpening his "D Guard" fighting knife, asked, 'Boy's, do you remember all that fuss and fanfare when we mustered in at Crawfordsville?' Charlie Wilkins replied: 'Yeah I thought we were off on a lark . . . Things ain't so grand now are they? We're all sick and starving and them Yankees just keep on a'coming, no matter how many of 'um we shoot" **(Steven H. Stubbs; *Duty * Honor * Valor:*, p 417)**

Chapter Three

The Morning of Glory

The sun rose in the sky over the Union defenses at around 5:00 in the morning. The men along the Confederate battle line squinted to see what awaited them eastward across the valley. Breakfast would be followed by Morning Muster call as the men of North Carolina, Mississippi, Tennessee and Alabama began what would be for many their last day of life.

The regiments had spent the evening before in the valley behind Seminary ridge. They would be moving up closer to the front mid morning once the day's scenario was established.

To boost the number of fighting men for the assault, men who had been detached to duties such as cooking and pioneer corps and hospital detail were recalled to duty. "The cooks were given muskets etc. in fact everything was done to get as many fighting men in ranks as possible." **(Thomas Cureton to John R Lane, June 22, 1890, OR Supplement 5:427)**

Archer's Brigade
Commanded by Colonel Fry (13th Alabama)
1st Tennessee

The 1st Tennessee regiment was organized April 21, 1861 in Winchester, Tennessee under the leadership of Peter Turney. Companies came from Franklin, Lincoln, Coffee and Grundy Counties. On May 17 the regiment moved to Richmond Va. where they were drilled by students from VMI. They were originally known as the First Confederate Infantry. Attached to Bee's Brigade—Johnson's Division they fought at First Manassas. When three Tennessee Regiments were sent west, the regiment acquired the name First Tennessee Infantry. They fought with Hatton's Brigade at the Peninsula, and Archer's

Brigade at Cedar Run, 2nd Manassas, Fredericksburg (where Colonel Turney was wounded) and Chancellorsville. The regiment was led north to Gettysburg by Lt. Colonel Newton George with strength of 389 officers and men plus 8 staff.

In the fighting on July 1st had cost the 1st Tennessee a number of captured soldiers due to their position on the left of the line which had been turned. They suffered 4 killed, 27 wounded and 57 taken prisoner. Their Adjutant, William Watson, was one of the captured.

8:00 A.M. Report

Company A was commanded by 1st Lieutenant Jesse Gunn a 20 year old Coffee County farmer. The Pelham Guards" had two 2nd Lieutenants and would field 36 men on July 3. They had lost nine two days before including two Sergeants and a Corporal.

"The Tullahoma Guards" Company B had ten casualties on July 1st including their 2nd Lieutenant William Muses who was wounded and captured. This day they would be commanded Captain William Daniel a 21 year old Chattanooga farmer who had been wounded in the face at Sharpsburg. They would have 26 officers and men available for duty.

Company C, commanded by Captain Aaron Alexander who had been wounded at Second Manassas. The "Mountain Boys" had lost 8 on July 1 including three Corporals and would have 29 available.

34 year old Captain John Bevall would lead the "Ridgedale Hornets" (Co D).
His first Lieutenant William Farris had been wounded along with 12 others leaving 26 officers and men.

Mr. John T Taylor of Lynchburg, Tennessee had personally financed Company E at the beginning of the war and the "Lynchburg Rangers" was now led by Captain Thomas Mann. Mann had been wounded at Second Manassas. Today he would lead 26 men forward assisted by 1st Lt Anderson Eaton who also had been wounded at second Manassas. Ten had been lost on July 1.

Captain James Thompson, of Company F had been captured along Willoughby Run. And his 2nd Lieutenant William Nuckles killed. "The Salem Invincibles" had lost 11 that day and would fight with 29 officers and men this day under the command of 1st Lieutenant Thomas Foster 30 years old from Winchester, Tn.

"The Fayetteville Guards" commanded by 1st Lieutenant James Manley would go in action with 38 men on July 3. Company G's Captain Davis Clark had been wounded in the left ankle on July 1 as one of four losses.

A 27 year old Sheldon Creek farmer, Captain Thomas Arnold would lead 34 fighters into the battle today. "The Sheldon Creek Boys" (Co H) had lost a dozen casualties two days before.

Company I would be commanded by Captain Henry Hawkins from Cowen County. They had only taken three losses July 1 and would have their full complement of officers to lead the "Cowen Guards" this day

Finally Company K, the "Boons Hill Minutemen" was led Captain Jacob Turney a 32 year old Boons Hill Lincoln County farmer. Turney had been wounded at Gaines Mill, Fredericksburg & Chancellorsville. He had lost seven in the first day's fight and would advance with two officers and twenty one men today.

13th Alabama

Organized in Montgomery Alabama the regiment, under Col Birkett Fry, was sent to Richmond and placed into Colquitt's Brigade. They fought at Seven Pines with 7 killed and 45 wounded. At Antietam they were both in the cornfield action and at Sunken Road. Their losses at Fredericksburg were light but at Chancellorsville they lost half of their 450 men in the fighting. After Chancellorsville, they were transferred to the Archer Brigade and continued to be commanded by Col Fry. A total of 311 officers and men marched north with the 13th Alabama to Gettysburg.

In the fighting on July 1st the 13th Alabama was on the left flank of the Archer advance and was flanked and overrun. As a result they had severe losses of 119 captured plus 7 killed and 28 wounded. They would have only157 officers and men available on July 3. Regimental Commander Fry, who was nicknamed by his men "old Nicaragua", was promoted to Brigade commander after the capture of Brigadier General James Archer on the first.

8:00 A.M. Report

Company A which had been severely damaged on the first day fight would be led by Sergeant Nathaniel Brantley a 17 year old former student from Rehobeth Tennessee.

"The Camden Rifles" would have only 5 other men in the attack. 17 men had been lost on July 1 including both Lieutenants. One Private. William Hayes had been wounded slightly in the neck and face yet went into action July 3.

The "Southern Stars" Company B was commanded by 1st Lieutenant Hardy Gibson after the wounding of Captain Charles E Chambers two days before. Chambers had been the only casualty and the company would have 24 men in action today.

Company C like Company B did not have many losses on July (only 4). The 26 men from Talladega County would be led by Captain Walter Taylor and three Lieutenants.

Captain Algernon Sidney Reaves was a 22 yr old clerk from Randolph Co. He was wounded along with two of his three Lieutenants on July 1 as he led Company D. Losses that day totaled 21. Twenty six year old 2nd Lt Thomas Strong would take command of the 14 remaining men. Private Ansel Brown had been slightly wounded in the right arm on 7/1 but reported for duty

The "Randolph Raiders", Company E had only eight men available for duty. 1st Lt John Dixon Robinson, a 29 year old Eastville farmer, would lead them. Twenty had been lost on the first day.

Twenty five casualties had been the loss of Company F from Elmore County. 25 year old teacher 1st Lt James Simpson would command the remaining twelve soldiers.

Company G had lost only two men on July first. They would advance this day with twenty four men commanded by Captain Robert Cook, 23 year old Greenville former college student and his two Lieutenants. The "Yancy Guards" had been on the left flank of the regiment two days before.

Company H was known as the "Coosa Mountaineers" and had twenty casualties including their Captain Stephen R. Allison who was captured. The remaining 17 men would be led by 21 year old Lieutenant George Callaway. One soldier who was long gone was Private Eugene Bently. Bently would be taken prisoner after the battle in Greencastle, Pa and on the back of his prisoner card would be noted these words "was going to school in Alabama living with uncle when forced to join army deserted before crossing mountains found Union lines". His card reads "Captured 7/7/63 Greenwood (sic Greencastle) Pa" **(Eugene Bentley, compiled service record, National Archives, Washington DC)**

The "Invincibles", Company I, had lost their 1st Lt. Lawson D. Ford captured on July 1 along with 24 others. Today they would be commanded by 2nd Lt. William Ellis a 22 year old Roanoke farmer. They would number 14 in the advanced.

All three of the Green brothers in Company I had been captured on July 1. One by one they had all joined the 13th Alabama starting with William in July 1861 and then Nathaniel in February 1862 followed by Jasper in March 1862.

"Tom Watts Rebel men", Co K, had been hard hit at Chancellorsville. They entered Gettysburg with only 19 men and one officer, 3rd Lt. William H. Burgess, who was captured with 12 others on the first day. The remaining six men were led by 29 year old mechanic Sergeant Jefferson Savage.

7th Tennessee

The regiment was organized in Sumner County east of Nashville in October 1861 under Colonel Robert Hatton and trained in Big Spring, Va. After participating in the West Virginia campaign, the unit joined Hatton's brigade at the Peninsula and fought under Brigadier James Archer at Cedar Run, 2nd Manassas and Fredericksburg. At Second Manassas S.G. Shepard was commander. At Fredericksburg they were involved in a counter attack where they lost 38 men killed and wounded. At Chancellorsville they helped to take and hold Hazel Grove and captured the Chancellor house. Placed in A.P. Hill's III Corps, Heth's Division, Archer's Brigade, under Col. John Fite they marched north to Gettysburg with 314 officers and men plus 11 staff.

In the fighting on July 1st the 7th had lost 1 killed 9 wounded and 29 taken prisoner. This would leave 219 available for the assault.

8:00 A.M. Report

Company A was commanded by 1st Lt George Cowen after the loss July 1 of Captain John Dowell who was wounded and captured. These men from Alexandria, and DeKalb County had four other casualties that day and would take 23 into combat today.

The men from Smith County in Company B were commanded by Captain John Allen. They were a large company and had lost only five on the first day and would have 47 men available for duty on the third.

Sumner County, Tennessee was represented by brevet Captain John Fry and company C with 32 officers and men. Only five had been lost on the first day including their original Captain John Elliot who was captured.

Company D, commanded by Captain Marcus Welsh was known as the "*Harris Rifles*". On July 1 2nd Lt John Carter and four others were captured. Twenty Six officers and men were ready to advance.

Commanded by Captain Robert Miller, who had been wounded at Sharpsburg, "The Sumner County Rifles" had lost only two men in the fighting July 1. Thirty Two men and 3 officers reported for duty on the morning of July 3.

Company F was led by Captain Asaph Hill who enlisted in Nashville as Sergeant Major of the regiment. Hill had been wounded three times already in the war at Gaines Mill, Antietam and Berryville. *"The Statesville Tigers"* from Wilson County had no losses on the first day's battle and would number only 16 this day, having lost many at Chancellorsville.

Sam Shepard's old company, the Hurricane Rifles" from Wilson County was commanded by Captain William Graves. Company G had lost five on the first day including two lieutenants and would have twenty four reporting for duty this morning.

"The Grays" from Wilson County had lost two Sergeants and a private on the first day. Company H was commanded by Captain William Tate and had eighteen men available for duty.

Company I would be commanded by Captain James Oren Bass age twenty five.
"The Silver Spring Guards" from Wilson County had twenty nine available men on July 3 having lost only three prior.

Two Sergeants and two privates had been the loss by Company K on the opening day of the Gettysburg battle. "The Blues" from Wilson county would be commanded by Captain Archibald Norris and three Lieutenants with 23 enlisted men.

14th Tennessee

The regiment was organized Camp Dungan in Montgomery County Tennessee and then sent to Virginia under Colonel Forbes. It served with Jackson in the valley campaign and then marched to Richmond for the peninsular fighting. When three Tennessee regiments were sent back west the 14th was placed into the "Tennessee Brigade" of Brigadier General Hatton and later James Archer. The regiment fought at Sharpsburg, 2nd Manassas, Fredericksburg and Chancellorsville. At Chancellorsville it helped seize and hold Hazel Grove. The regiment marched north under the command of Lt. Colonel James Lockert with a strength of 209 officers and men plus 9 staff. Colonel McComb was absent with wounds from Chancellorsville and Major Milton Morris was on furlough during Gettysburg campaign. In the fighting on July 1st The 14th Tennessee lost none killed, 4 wounded and 44 prisoners. One of the wounded was Sergeant Major Robert Moore. This would give them strength of 158 remaining on the third.

With the loss of all of their officers at Chancellorsville Company A was commanded by Sergeant Junius Kimble at Gettysburg. Captain William Thompson's death and severe losses in the company resulted in only 26 men arriving in Gettysburg and four of these were lost July 1. The Clarksville, Montgomery County, Tennessee company would go into battle led by one Sergeant and two corporals.

Company B's Captain Howell Avrit was on furlough and was captured in Tennessee.

The Montgomery County company would be led by 1st Lt. William Shelby who had enlisted in Clarksville. Nineteen men and three officers would make the advance on July 3rd after losing 5 the first day in battle.

"The Pepper Guards." From Robertson County had 22 men available on July 3 commanded by Captain James Dale from Springfield, TN. Company C Losses on July 1 had been two captured and one wounded.

Stewart County had supplied the men for Company D. Captain Hegler had been wounded at Chancellorsville and was in hospital during the entire campaign. The company entered Gettysburg with 21 officers and men under Company Commander 1st Lieutenant brevet Captain John Settle, the only officer remaining after the capture of 2nd Lt William Hagler on Day One. The three losses on the opening day brought he number of fighting men to 18 for the third.

Company E from Stewart County was under the command of 1st Lt Benjamin Elvis Outlaw. Outlaw commanded a large company of 43 when he entered Gettysburg and lost only three captured and one sick by the third of July. One of his wounded was 1st Lt. John Largent who had been wounded at Fredericksburg

Company F had been disbanded on May 23, 1863 before the Gettysburg campaign due to severe losses from Chancellorsville. 32 men transferred to Co E although many were hospitalized during June-July.

Captain Harry Bullock from Montgomery County commanded Company G. A Sergeant and eight Privates had been lost July 1 and the company would have twenty two report for duty July Third.

July One had seen twelve men in Company H captured including Captain William Moore and 3rd Lt John Moore. 1st Lt. Charles Mitchell from Clarksville was the ranking officer remaining to command the remaining men of the Company who numbered twenty eight.

Company I had major losses in the Chancellorsville fighting including their captain William Winfield who was wounded. 2nd Lt Thomas Gilbert arrived in Gettysburg with only 13 men and lost three on the first day. The company of eleven would advance on the third.

Captain Thaddeus Bowling who enlisted Clarksville had been wounded at Chancellorsville but recovered for the Gettysburg campaign. The Montgomery County men in Company K had four casualties on the first and would fight with twenty under Bowling on this day.

Company L also from Montgomery County, Tennessee commanded by 1st Lt. Alexander Collins had lost five of its twenty two members on the first, including its Captain Thomas Herndon. The remainder would fight on the third.

5th Alabama Battalion

Organized in Montgomery Alabama the regiment was shipped east to Manassas, Va. and put into Richard Ewell's Brigade. They were stationed in a Confederate artillery fort during the Battle of First Manassas. General Robert Rode's became brigade commander and the 6 company regiment was grouped with 6th & 12th Alabama and 12th Mississippi. At the battle of 7 Pines they lost 27 killed and 128 wounded out of 660 in action. At Gaines Mill and Malvern Hill another 15 killed and 58 wounded (including Major Van De Graf). Sharpsburg cost then 11 killed and 39 wounded. The 5th Battalion (now 4 companies were heavily involved at 2nd Manassas The regiment was in reserve at Fredericksburg but took severe losses as part of Jackson's flank attack at Chancellorsville losing 24 killed 133 wounded and 121 taken prisoner . . . Under Major Van de Graf the four company battalion was reduced to three added to Archer's brigade and marched to Gettysburg with 132 officers and men plus 6 staff.

Commanding the three companies of the 5th Alabama Battalion was Major A. Sebastian Van de Graff, aged 31 who had attended both Yale and the University of Richmond. He was a Sumter County Lawyer before the war. His career started as Captain of Company A of the 5th Alabama Battalion and he had been severely wounded at Gaines Mill. He was in fact reported as killed on the Brigade report. He had been wounded again at Fredericksburg in the middle of the fighting there. The Battalion originally had six companies but was reduced by fighting at Gaines Mill, and Fredericksburg to four. In May of 1863 Company D was eliminated with the men integrated into the remaining three companies.

In the fighting on July 1st ten men in the 5th Alabama Battalion were wounded. This left one hundred twenty two soldiers available for the July 3 fight.

8:00 A.M. Report

On the morning of July 3 the total strength of the battalion was 122 officers and men. Major Van de Graff and Sergeant Major Baker Roberts made up the field officers.

Staff officers included Assistant Surgeon William Pearson, Assistant Surgeon A.D. Hamilton, Hospital Steward John Turk, Assistant Quarter Master Richard McCormack and Commissary Sergeant William Fulton.

Company A "The North Sumter Rifles" was led by Captain Wade Ritter with two Lieutenants Bowling Branch and Charles Dennison plus 42 men. There losses on July 1 had only been three men wounded. Lieutenant Charles Dennison was an interesting story. He had been born in New York City and had lived in Chicago before moving south to Alabama.

Company B "The Calhoun Sharpshooters" was led by Captain A.N. Porter as they entered Gettysburg with First Lieutenant John Robinson by his side. 48 men remained on duty after the loss of four wounded on July first including both Captain Porter and 2nd Lieutenant James Wilson.

Company C "The White Plains Rangers" was led by 1st Lieutenant William Clay because of Captain James Reese' absence with sickness. His 2nd Lieutenant was Walter Bray. With them would be 27 men after the loss of three wounded on July 1.

Pettigrew's Brigade
Commanded by Colonel John Marshall
52nd North Carolina

Organized June 1862 under Colonel Marshall and Lieutenant Colonel Marcus Parks, the regiment was send to Petersburg, Va. and to Drury's Bluffs near Richmond for defense operations. In August they returned to North Carolina to fight at the battle of Goldsboro and in the New Bern campaign. In April 1863 they returned to the Richmond, Va. defense lines and then were assigned on June 1 to Major General Henry Heth's Divisions A.P. Hill's Corps. Five regiments from North Carolina were combined under the leadership of Brigadier General James Pettigrew—The 11th, 26th, 44th, 47th, and 52nd. From there they joined Lee's Army as it marched north to Gettysburg with 553 men commanded by Colonel James Keith Marshall and Lt. Colonel Marcus Parks.

In the fighting on July 1st forty eight men were lost either killed, wounded or captured.

8:00 A.M. Report

Company A, The Cabarrus Riflemen" was commanded by Captain John Alexander a 35 year old tailor. By his side was 1st Lt James M. Cook who had previously been a Sergeant in the 20th NC. A total of fifty three men remained on July from the estimated fifty six who came to Gettysburg.

"The Randolph Guards" were Company B of the 52nd. They were commanded by Captain Jesse Kyle a Randolph Co farmer and by 1st Lt. William with forty two soldiers. Their losses on July 1 had been four men.

Company C known as the "Orapeake Guards" was led by Captain George Gilliam, a 29 yr old Gates County. Merchant assisted by 19 year old 1st Lt John Warren. The company had lost five men on July 1 and would go into action with twenty eight.

Commanded by Captain Leonidas Gibson Company D had lost six in the first days fighting and would be at strength of fifty two. 1st Lt Isaac was the "McCulloch's Avengers" second in command.

33 year old Captain Benjamin Little and 1st Lt Milton Austin a 36 yr old Richmond County merchant were in charge of Company E—"The Richmond Regulators". Their strength on the morning of July 3 was 4 officers and forty three men. They had lost seven two days before.

The forty five men of the "The Wilkes Grays" Co F were led by two men who had been merchants before the war, Captain Nathaniel Foster 32 yr old Wilkes Co. and 1st Lt William Carmichael 20 yr old Wilkes Co. Losses on July 1 had been nine.

Company G, the "Dry Pond Dixies" was led by Captain James Kincaid, with 63 men reporting for duty. His 1st lieutenant was James Wells a Lincoln Co. farmer. Company G had lost three men two days before.

The Spring Hill Guards was being led this day by Captain Eric Erson who had transferred from 1st North Carolina regiment. The company had lost three on July 1 and would go into battle with four officers and forty eight men. Their 1st Lieutenant was Lawson Dellinger.

Captain John McCain of the Stanley Rebels had been killed on July 1 among five casualties. Company I would be led this day by 1st Lt James Hearne a 28 year old Stanly Co. merchant with fifty one men under his command.

The "Fighting Boys" was an appropriate name for the officers and men of Company K. Their 23 year old former student Captain Aurelius Blackburn had been killed on July 1 and command fell to 22 year old former student 1st Lt Junius Goslen. Goslen would be assisted by a former teacher 28 year old 2nd Lt Romulus Cox. A total of three men had fallen in battle on day One and fifty nine remained.

47th North Carolina

Organized in March 1862 near Raleigh under Colonel Sion Rogers the 47th regiment was in action in eastern North Carolina under Colonel Rogers who became Attorney general of the state and Lt. Col George Faribault took command. In July 1862 they were rushed to the Richmond defenses and then assigned provost guard duty in Petersburg. In early 1863 five regiments from North Carolina were combined under the leadership of Brigadier General James Pettigrew—The 11th, 26th, 44th, 47th, and 52nd and sent first to North Carolina to operate with the Army of D.H. Hill and then in May to Richmond. From there they joined Lee's Army as it marched north to Gettysburg with 567 officers and men under the command of Colonel George Faribault.

In the fighting on July 1st the 47th was involved with combat with 567 men and sustained some 117 casualties.

8:00 A.M. Report

Company A was commanded by Captain John Thorpe. Thorpe later wrote that he had "82 trigger pullers on 7/1". His 1st Lt. George Westray had been wounded in the arm & groin in the first days fighting. The "Chicora Guards" had lost thirteen on July 1 and would serve as the skirmish line for the regiment on July 3 with 73 men.

Franklin County, North Carolina was the home of Company B commanded by 30 year old Captain Joseph "Honest Joe" Harris. His First Lieutenant was 1st Lt. Sherwood Evans age 35. A total of 58 men were ready for action on July 3 with July 1 losses being ten.

With the loss of Captain Campbell Iredell a 26 year old druggist from Wake Co K who had his "arm shot off" on July 1, First Lieutenant George Whiting a 21 yr old druggist and 2nd Lt Nathaniel Brown a 22 year old watchmaker took control of Company C. With losses of eight on July 1, 39 men were prepared to fight July 3.

The "Castalia Invincibles" had a 39 year old Captain George Lewis as commander. Company D had lost nine men on the first day of the battle and with the assistance of 30 year old 1st Lieutenant Richard Drake, Lewis would lead 43 men forward on the third.

Company E was led by Captain John Norwood a 31 yr old teacher from Wake Co. He had brought seventy one men to Gettysburg and had losses of eleven on July 1. His 1st Lieutenant 30 yr old former merchant Ray would aid him in leading fifty eight men into battle.

A physician before the war, Captain William Lankford age 29, would lead the "Sons of Liberty" into battle. Company F had lost nine on the opening day and would take thirty three in on the third. Julius Joyner was their First Lieutenant under Lankford's command.

Commanded by Captain Joseph Davis a 34 year old lawyer, Company G was enlisted in Franklin and Granville Counties in March of 1862. Another physician 1st Lt. Pleasant Peace age 46 was with Davis in the fight. Peace had been a poet before the war as well as a doctor. With losses of nineteen on July 1 the company of 63 men was down to forty four for today's assault.

The commander of the "North Carolina Tigers"—Company H was Captain Sidney Mitchell his 1st Lieutenant Thomas Lasater And he brought fifty four men to Gettysburg, loosing ten in the first day battle.

Company I was led this day by Captain John Brown and 1st Lt. William Harrison. The men from Northern Wake County had entered Gettysburg with 74 and had losses on July 1 of eleven.

Finally Company K's loss of their Captain Robert Faucette who was wounded in the thigh on 7/1 would place command in the hands of 19 year old 1st Lt. James Watson and 2nd Lt. Thomas Taylor a 28 year. The "Alamance Minute men" had forty four men prepared for battle having lost 17 on July 1.

26th North Carolina

The regiment was organized in the summer of 1861 under the command of Colonel Zebulon Vance. They saw action near New Bern and were sent to Va. to participate in the Peninsular campaign including the attack on Malvern Hill. The 26th was sent south to North Carolina to deal with Union advances along the coast where Colonel Vance left to be elected Governor of North Carolina and was replaced by Lt. Colonel Burgwyn. In early 1863 five regiments from North Carolina were combined under the leadership of Brigadier general James Pettigrew—The 11th, 26th, 44th, 47th, and 52nd and sent first to North Carolina to operate with the Army of D.H. Hill and then in May to Richmond. From there they joined Lee's Army as it marched north to Gettysburg with 843 officers and men under the command of Colonel Henry King Burgwyn.

In the fighting on July 1 The 26th was decimated losing 543 of its officers and men.

8:00 A.M. Report

In command of the 26th North Carolina as they moved into position on July 3 was Major John Jones. This would be the first time he commanded the regiment in battle. With Colonel Burgwyn dead and buried and Lieutenant Colonel Lane mortally wounded "Knock" Jones would take his men forward, a regiment severely reduced from the first day's action. In a letter to his father after the battle he wrote that as he watched his men take position he wondered to himself whether they had been too badly mauled on July 1 to be effective in battle and would he be able to inspire them to action. **(John Jones letter to his father 17 July 1863)** Jones counted 230 men in line, down from the more than 800 man regiment that had gone into action on the 1st of July. But Lieutenant Underwood had no such second thoughts, later recalling that "To the great surprise of everyone, the brigade seems as ready for the fray on the morning of the third day as it had been on the morning of the first." **(Underwood, "Twenty-Sixth Regiment: 361")**

Company E was down to 12 Company A to 14 Company K had 37 and company F which had one man left on the evening of July 1 now had grown to 6. Company H went in with a dozen. **(Major John Jones letter of July 30, 1863 from Culpepper, Va.)**

Company A continued to be commanded by Captain Samuel Wagg with only 14 enlisted men left. Wagg was one of only three Captains still in command. "The Jeff Davis Mountaineers" had lost 78 soldiers in the first day fight. 1st Lt. Ambrose B Duvall and 2nd Lt Jacob Houck had both been wounded and 3rd Lt Levi Gentry would be the only other officer reporting.

The death of Captain William Wilson age 22 had placed Thomas Cureton in command and he was brevetted Captain of Company B, "The Waxsaw Jackson Guards". After the loss of 76 the first day Private William Estridge was elected as 3rd Lieutenant to work by Cureton's side with the remaining thirteen soldiers in the company.

1st Lieutenant William Porter took the place of Captain Isaac Jarratt who had been wounded in the face and hand in Company C. The "Wilkes Volunteers" would go into battle with forty three men after losing fifty two in battle on the First.

Company D had twenty five men left after the July 1 battle. Three of their four officers including Captain James Adams had been wounded. Command fell to 28 year old 1st Lt. Gaston Broughton. The "Wake Guards" had mustered 83 men two days before but lost 58 in battle.

Company E, "The Independent Guards" was still commanded by Captain Stephen Brewer age 27, another one of three surviving Captains. Only 12 men remained from the total of eighty two who arrived in Gettysburg. Their loss of seventy on July 1 would make the company into a tiny squad. They had flanked the colors.

Company F had but one man unwounded on July 1, Sergeant Robert Hudspeth. He had been able to gather up 6 men from detached duties and now commanded a company of seven. The "Hilbriten Guards" flanked the colors July 1 and had been destroyed.

20 year old Captain Henry Clay Albright was the other surviving company commander on July 1. His "Chatham Boys" company of 89 officers and men had lost fifty six in the whirlwind fight on July 1. At one point in that battle his company had held the regimental flag. Expert marksman 1st Lt. John Lowe was second in command.

Captain James McIver was the 29 year old commander of "The Moore Independents" Company H in 1863 but he was on a furlough during the Gettysburg campaign and his 1st and 2nd Lieutenants had both been wounded July 1. 1st Lt. Murdoch McLeod was wounded in the shoulder & breast and 2nd Lt. George Wilcox had been wounded in the left foot & side "while carrying flag". Command fell to 22 year old 3rd Lt. John McGilvary Moore who received a flesh wound on July 1 but would lead on 7/3. But Moore would only lead 12 men into battle. Seventy nine had been lost on July 1.

"The Caldwell Guards had lost Captain Nero Bradford, their 37 year with bullet in his left lung. Company I would have 1st Lt. Milton Blair as commander. The "Guards had arrived in Pennsylvania with 87 officers and men and lost 56 on July 1.

Thirty Seven men remained in Company K after the first days fighting of the 103 who came to Gettysburg. With Captain J.C. McLaughlin wounded in the left hand and 1st Lt. Thomas

Lilly wounded in the hip, 2nd Lieutenant Jesse Henry was in command. 1st Sergeant John Briley assisted Henry with the leadership duties. The loss of 66 on day One was severe but one of the lightest loss rates of all the companies of a decimated regiment.

One of the immediate problems in setting the company lines in each regiment was the selection of the new Color guard. In the 26th North Carolina Sergeant William Smith from Company K would carry the colors. Private Daniel Thomas (Company E) and Private Thomas Cozart (Company F) would be at his side. Major Jones continued to set the company positions ignoring the fact that some companies such as F & H were down to less than a dozen men. Company E was down to eleven men under Captain Stephen Brewer, while Company D was one of the largest with 25.

11th North Carolina

The regiment was organized in May 1862 when the 1st North Carolina "Bethel Regiment" reorganized for three year service. The "Bethel regiment" had fought in the early battles of the Peninsular campaign. The reorganized regiment was kept in North Carolina for the defense of Wilmington and saw action in fighting there. In early 1863 five regiments from North Carolina were combined under the leadership of Brigadier General James Pettigrew—The 11th, 26th, 44th, 47th, and 52nd and sent first to North Carolina to operate with the Army of D.H. Hill and then in May to Richmond. From there they joined Lee's Army as it marched north to Gettysburg with 645 men and 45 officers under the command of Colonel Collett Leventhorpe.

In the fighting on July 1st the eleventh lost 288 men including their Colonel wounded in the left arm and hip and Major Ross killed. With Lieutenant Colonel William Martin sick back in Fredericksburg regimental command would shift to senior Captain William Grier of company H.

8:00 A.M. Report

Company A, "The Charlotte Grays, was led by Captain William Hand with the assistance of 1st Lt. Charles Alexander. There were 86 officers and men who entered the battle July 1 or as one officer stated "82 trigger pullers". Losses that day reduced strength to 30 men and four officers.

Captain Mark Armfield and 1st Lt Thomas Parks commanded the men from Burke County in Company B. They had lost thirty men on July 1 and went into battle of July 3 with 3 officers and forty eight men.

The soldiers of Bertie County, North Carolina in Company C were commanded by Captain Francis Bird. 1st Lt Thomas Cooper was killed on July 1 and his duties were performed by 2nd Lt Edward Outlaw. The strength of the unit was sixty four on July 3 after losing twenty four men July 1

Burke County had provided the soldiers for Company D of the 11th NC. They had come to Gettysburg with 68 men commanded by Captain Calvin Brown. In the fighting on July 1 1st Lt W.J. Kincaid had been severely wounded and his place taken by 18 year old 2nd Lt. Louis Elias. Other losses on the first day were twenty seven men.

Captain William Kerr led Company E on both days at Gettysburg. His 1st Lieutenant 33 yr old John Clanton had been wounded and captured July 1 along with thirty one other men from the company. Company E strength on July 3 was twenty nine.

Captain Edward Small and 1st Lt. Stephen Roberts led Company F during the Gettysburg battles. Their 2nd and 3rd Lieutenants, Rea and Hoskins, were both wounded on July 1. The company arrived with sixty one officers and men and lost nineteen the first day.

Company G of the 47th had damaged severely by the fighting on July 1

Captain John Freeland had survived the fighting but lost all three of his Lieutenants killed 1st Lt. John McDade; 2nd Lt. Nathaniel Tenney; 3rd Lt. James Williams. First Sergeant Jones Watson would assist with leadership for the thirty eight men who remained on July 3.

Day one had taken out both junior officers in Company H commanded by Captain William Grier. 1st Lt. James Lowrie had been killed and 2nd Lt. John Knox wounded. Along with them were seven other casualties. With all of the Field officers out of action Captain Grier took charge of the regiment and his company of 35 men would be commanded by Sergeant Stephen Blankenship a 28 yr old.

Lincoln County's Company I officers were very fortunate on July 1 with all officers and Non Comms surviving unscratched. Company commander Captain Albert Haynes 1st Lt. David Coon would lead the fifty six men of the company July 3 with far different results.

Finally Company K was commanded by Captain James Young and 1st Lt. John A. Burgin. Seventy four Bumcombe County soldiers arrived with Company K on July 1. Twenty seven were lost in battle that day.

Davis's Brigade
Commanded by Colonel Joseph Davis
55th North Carolina

Organized in the spring of 1862 they were formed near Raleigh from companies from all over the state of North Carolina. They were first active in the Suffolk, Va. Campaign while stationed with the North Carolina department. Colonel John Connally commanded the regiment. They later were formed with the 2nd, 11th and 42nd Mississippi regiments into Davis's brigade in June 1863. They marched north to Gettysburg with 640 officers and men plus 9 staff under the command of Colonel John Kerr Connally.

"Our regiment had suffered so greatly on the first that in this charge it was commanded by Captain Gilreath (Co B) and some of the companies were commanded by non-commissioned officers. But the men came up bravely to the measure of their duty . . ."

(Cooke, "*Fifty-Fifth Regiment*", p. 299) Their Colonel John Kerr Connally killed, Lt. Colonel Maurice Smith mortally wounded and Major Alfred Belo severely wounded in the leg, command would fall to Captain George Gilreath of Company B.

In the fighting on July 1st the 55th North Carolina had severe losses in their fight along the Chambersburg Road. Their estimated losses were 298 in killed, wounded and captured. The number of men remaining to fight on July 3 was 390.

8:00 A.M. Report

Company A was commanded by Captain Albert Upchurch a 27 year old Wilson Co. merchant. The company lost 36 men on July 1 but no officers. 1st Lt Benjamin Briggs assisted Upchurch with the attack July 3. Strength that day was four officers and forty men

Company B with 31 year old Captain George Gilreath commanding the regiment after the loss of all three field officers, Captain John Peden was promoted to Captain on the morning of July 3. He would be assisted by 22 year old 2nd Lt Hiram Greer. The Wilkes County company lost twenty men on July 1 from a total of fifty one.

The "Cleveland Grays" had lost their Captain Edward Dixon wounded on July 1. The company would be commanded by 2nd Lt. Philip Elam, a 30 yr old Minster because the 1st Lt. George Bethel was captured in the first day's fight. Company C had a strength of eighty one on July 1 and had lost 40 that day.

With the loss of 33 year old Captain Silas Randall on 7/1 with a face wound, 1st Lt. William Townes was the only remaining officer in Company D. Losses on the first day included the Captain as well as 27 year old brother 2nd Lt James Randall with facial wounds and 3rd Lt Joseph Cabaniss. The Cleveland farmers lost 27 other men that day and would have fifty one remaining.

Two Sergeants and 25 men were lost from Company E on the first days fight. The company of Pitt County would be led by 24 year old Captain Howell Whitehead on the third. Thirty six men and officers remained to assault to Union lines.

Captain Peter M Mull was still absent wounded from head and lung injuries suffered in North Carolina fighting. Command of Company F had passed to 1st Lt. Joseph Hoyle a 25 year old teacher from Cleveland Co. The "South Mountain Rangers" had lost about half their men (33) in the fighting on the first day but none of their officers.

Company G was commanded by 1st Lt. Narcus Stevens, after the loss of Captain Walter Whitted with wounds to his face and right leg. "The North Carolina rebels" had lost heavily in the July 1 fighting including the Captain wounded and 2nd Lt. Mordecal Lee killed plus forty one others. The company was down to 15 men and two officers for the assault today.

"The Archer Boys"—Company H were commanded by Captain Edward Fletcher Satterfield. Their losses on July 1 had been 22 out of 57 including two officers 1st Lt. Nicholas Lillington wounded in the thigh and 2nd Lt Benjamin Blount captured

July First had cost Company I about half of their men. This would include their Captain Wilson Williams captured and former teacher 3rd Lieutenant Burton Winston wounded in the side and captured. The remaining thirty two men in the "Franklin Farmers" would be commanded by 1st Lt. Charles Cooke a 19 year old Franklin County student

Lastly, Company K had fairly low losses in the first day's fighting (3 killed, 5 wounded, 7 wounded and captured and one captured unwounded). Two of these men were the 1st and 3rd Lieutenants, Stovall and Rooster. The men from Grenville County would be one of the strongest companies on 7/3 with 66 officers and men commanded by Captain Robert Thomas

2ND Mississippi

Organized in the 4 counties of North eastern Mississippi in May 1861 with William Clark Faulkner as Colonel the regiment was shipped to Harper's Ferry, Va. and placed under the command of Brigadier General Bernard Bee along with the 11th Mississippi and the 1st Tennessee and 4th Alabama.

They participated in the 1st Manassas battle where Brigadier General Bee was killed and after Col. Faulkner left the service the new Colonel was John Stone. Next they were sent to Yorktown on the Peninsula and then to the valley with Stonewall Jackson. After arriving with Jackson's Division they turned around and marched back to the peninsula with Writing's Brigade participating in Gaines Mill and Malvern Hill. At Antietam the brigade was led by Law's under Hood. In spring 1863 they were shifted to Davis's Mississippi Brigade (2nd, 11th, 42nd Mississippi and the 55th North Carolina). The regiment marched north with officers and 492 men plus 12 staff under the command of Colonel John M Stone.

The men of the 2nd Mississippi came from small towns in the Northeast corner of the state. The regiment was largely recruited in the Spring of 1861. About 70%

identified themselves as farmer or planters. The rest of the occupations ranged from clerks to students, teachers to carpenters. The average age of the unit was 23-24 years old. However, the average age of the last company to be recruited in the spring of 1862(Company L) was almost 28 years old. This reflected the fact that the Confederate government had begun a draft and available manpower to be recruited was already reduced by the Spring of 1862. **(Stanley F Horn, The Army of Tennessee, Norman, OK p. XI)**

In the fighting on July 1st the 2nd Mississippi had been devastated. The fight on the first day in the fields and at the Railroad cut had cost the 2nd Mississippi as many as 400 of its 492 men. The report on captured Confederates from the action at the Railroad Cut alone claimed 7 officers and 225 men captured from the three Davis regiments, mostly from the 2nd Mississippi. Their losses in the fighting before the Railroad disaster were also heavy.

8:00 A.M. Report

On the morning of July 3 the 2nd Mississippi numbered about as few as 90 enlisted men and 28 officers ready for duty. They would be commanded by Lieutenant Colonel David W Humphries who had missed the action of July 1 while on duty guarding wagons. The regiments had lost many of its most experiences officers in addition to its Colonel John Stone wounded and Major John Blair captured in the Railroad Cut.

Company A commanded by 22 year old Captain Andrew Walker had lost two of its officers on July 1. 1st Lt George Ralston and 3rd Lt. James McKay had both been wounded. The "Tishomingo Rifleman" had lost 47 and would fight on July 3 with eight men and two officers.

Company B was commanded by Captain John Buchanan a 43 year old Tippah blacksmith. The "O'Conner Rifles" had lost 1st Lt. John Lauderdale killed in the first days fight. 2nd Lt William Moody a 26 yr old druggist and Lt Hugh "Luke" Byrn a 23 year old Tippah clerk would remain with fifteen enlisted men of the original 66 who came to Gettysburg. Many of the enlisted men had surrendered at the Railroad Cut.

The "Town Creek Rifleman" Company C had been fortunate in the first days fighting all four of its officers had returned from the RR Cut unwounded. The company would be commanded by Captain John Storey a 26 yr old Itawamba clerk leading thirty four men on July 3.

The officers of Company D the "Joe Mathews Rifles" had also been fortunate, only losing fourteen men in the first day's fight. Nineteen would be led into battle July 3 by Captain Robert Brandon 24 yr old Tippah Co. farmer and both Lieutenants.

Company E had almost been wiped out at the Railroad Cut losing both of its senior Lieutenants. It would be commanded July 3 by 3rd Lt Benjamin Richardson a 28 year old Guntown farmer. Only 10 men of the original 56 remained to fight with the "Calhoun Rifles".

The "Magnolia Rifles" was Company F commanded by 31 year old lawyer Captain Henry Powers. All three Lieutenants had survived unhurt from the Day One fight. Thirty nine men would follow their 4 officers forward today. Twenty had been lost on July 1.

Commanded by 1st Lt. John W. Dillard, a 25 year old Pontotoc County businessman, Company G would number eleven. The loss of Captain Thomas Crawford a 29 yr old clerk who had fought on the first but had taken sick put Dillard in command with the help of 2nd Lt. James Combs. "The Pontotoc Minutemen" had lost twenty three July One.

Also hard hit at the Railroad Cut were the "Coonwah Rifles". Company H would be commanded by 1st Lt David Marlin a 28 year old Chesterville teacher after the wounding of Captain William Cunningham in his right arm and left hip 7/1. 3rd Lt Altas Roberts 21 yr old Chesterville farmer had been killed in the fight over the colors of the 149th Pa two days before. Thirty men remained on July 3 after losses of thirty six.

Captain Richard Leavell a 24 year old Pontotoc Co teacher had led the "Cherry Creek Rifles" and had been captured at the Railroad Cut, along with 2nd Lt John Stevens and many others. The remaining twenty three men of Company I would now be led by 1st Lt Artaxeres Sory

All of the officers in Company K, "The Iuka Rifles" survived unharmed on July First even though the losses at the Railroad Cut had been heavy (31). Commanded by Captain Henry Terry, who had been wounded at 2nd Manassas, the company would field thirty seven men on July 3.

42nd Mississippi

Organized May 1862 in North Central Mississippi under the command of Colonel Hugh Miller the regiment was sent to the Richmond Defenses and served there from July 1862 to June 1863. In June 1863 they were made part of the Davis brigade (2nd, 11th, 42nd Mississippi and the 55th North Carolina). They marched north to Gettysburg with 803 soldiers and officers.

There was a feeling in the 42nd Mississippi that their Brigade commander Joseph R. Davis was not fit for the command of the brigade. Sergeant Major George Miller had written home to his mother on June 5, 1863 that "Genl Davis is in Miss. On furlough and Stone 'the mighty' is in command. Davis is looked for I believe, but if he doesn't stay with the brigade any more than heretofore, he had better stay away altogether, as he was absent about every other week." Miller also wrote of Davis's work ethic, "has no sort of fancy for anything requiring exertion of any sort—is always running off somewhere and absent, and yet is silly enough to think that he ought to hold some important command" **(George Miller to Mother, letter owned by Mr. Bob F. Thompson)**

In the fighting on July 1st many men from the 42nd had been trapped in the Railroad Cut as they pulled back from the Union counterattack by Cutler's Brigade. Because the 42nd was on the left of the Confederate line many got through the cut or avoided it by running behind it. Companies B and G appear to have had the most captured there. Of the over 596 officers and men in a regiment which had never been in combat before the 42nd would lose 270 of its men on the first.

8:00 A.M. Report

With Lt. Colonel and Major William Feeney both wounded and out of action. Colonel Miller would lead the remainder of the regiment into battle.

One incident was later told about Colonel Hugh R. Miller's talk with the troops as they lined up that morning and one soldiers reaction. "After forming his line Col. Hugh Miller walked own the line, and stated that if there was a man there who could not stand the smell of gunpowder he had better step out, for we were going into a fight. To my astonishment one poor fellow went to him and said, 'Colonel, I just can not go into a fight today, for if I do I will get wounded or killed'. The Colonel, with an oath, ordered him back into line." **(Andrew Park, *"Some of My Recollections of the Battle of Gettysburg"*, Arkansas History Commission)**

That morning Reverend Witherspoon of the 42nd Mississippi staff made a decision, he would not stay behind in the coming battle and would take up a rifle to fight. He would move forward with his regiment that day **(Witherspoon Diaries, University of Mississippi Archives)**

Company A was missing both Lieutenants on the morning of July 3. 1st Lt Thomas Pleasants had been left sick in Fredericksburg sick on the march north and 2nd Lt William Bamburg had been wounded on the first along with thirty two other members of the "Carroll County Fencibles" Captain Andrew Nelson would command the remaining thirty one men of the company.

The "Senatobia Invincible" was almost wiped out in the fighting at the Railroad Cut on July 1 losing 43 men killed, wounded or captured including their Captain Leander Woollard a 28 year old lawyer captured as well as 36 year old druggist 2nd Lt John Godfrey. Command of the remaining nineteen men would far to 3rd Lieutenant Benjamin Wham

Company C, "Nelm's Avengers" was commanded by 1st Lieutenant James Nail a 28 year old mechanic. Captain Wiley Smith a 25 year old physician was absent \from the campaign. The company had thirty seven present July 3 having lost 22 on the first.

The first day's fighting cost twenty five men to Company D including Captain Robert Locke who was wounded in the breast. 2nd Lieutenant George Houze was killed in the action. Command of the thirty men remaining fell to 35 year old 1st Lt Matthew Jones. The company nicknamed "Captain Locke's Company" had arrived at Gettysburg with fifty five.

All of the officers in Company E commanded by Captain Henry Davenport made it safely through the first days fighting. The "Davenport Rifles" had only ten casualties on the first day at Gettysburg and would have thirty six men ready for Action July 3.

Company F was involved in heavy fighting July 1 losing Captain Thomas Clark aged 41 and both of his sons Albert & Jonathan all killed. 29 others would fall as well mostly killed and wounded. The companies nickname was "Captain Clark's Company" and 24 year old 1st Lt James Seals of Oxford, Mississippi would take command of the remaining thirty one soldiers. The company had been severely handled in the fighting prior to the Railroad Cut action.

Author personal conversations with the great grandson of Captain Clark suggest that the second son Jonathan may have survived July 1 and been killed July 3 . . . "I also have circumstantial evidence—very good though. A person walking around the battlefield found a carved headboard in a weed patch with the inscription Capt. Clark and son (not sons) and another Capt buried in the same grave. This headboard hung on a wall in the Civil War Museum in Richmond until it was moved to Chicago where we think it still resides in a lot of artifacts that have been boxed for years. We think Jonathan, with help, buried his father and brother and carved the small headboard after fighting the first. None of this can be documented but has been handed down to family and friends by word of mouth. All my old time kin are long gone so I can't even verify this. According to a source where the headboard was found it was not in the park area, instead its on Marsh Creek which was in the battlefield zone." **(Charlie Clark, Bruce, Mississippi)**

One company that suffered many men captured and wounded in the Railroad cut (43) was Company G commanded by Captain James Gaston who was killed. 33 year old 1st Lt Thomas Smith would take command of the "Gaston Rifles" and the thirty three remaining men of the seventy seven who arrived in Gettysburg.

Captain John Powell age 36 had been a sheriff in Grenada, Mississippi before the war. He took sick on the march north and command of company H went to 24 year old 1st Lt Frank Ingram from Grenada. Company H nicknamed "Captain Powell's Company" would have to wait 2 weeks to see their old commander having lost 22 men on July 1. They would march into battle with forty seven soldiers July 3.

The normal commander of Company I was Captain Jefferson Meek who was an amazing 53 years old and not surprising was on furlough during the Gettysburg campaign. His place was taken by 1st Lt Robert Buchanan age 24. The "Mississippi Reds" had lost the other two lieutenants on July 1. 2nd Lt William Waldron was wounded and died the next day. 3rd Lt. William Harmon was mortally wounded. Harmon family tradition suggests that Lt. Harmon had been wounded in the leg and was transported South dying either on July 14th or July 20th. Twenty other men were casualties that day leaving thirty five to serve July 3.

Lastly Company K was commanded July 3 by Captain Goldsboro Mears age 31. Left behind sick in Virginia was 32 year old 1st Lt Joseph Patterson. Patterson would return to his regiment at Williamsport and be wounded in the arm at Falling Waters on July 14. The "Pontotoc Minutemen" had suffered badly at Chancellorsville and fielded only forty three on July 1 losing twenty that day.

11th Mississippi

Organized at Corinth Mississippi in May 1861 under the command of Lt. Colonel Liddell the regiment was shipped to Harper's ferry, VA and placed under the command of Brigadier General Bernard Bee along with the 2nd Mississippi and the 1st Tennessee and 4th Alabama.

Two companies of the Eleventh participated in the 1st Manassas battle where Brigadier General Bee was killed. The remainder under Colonel W.H. Moore arrived after the battle. Next they were sent to Yorktown on the Peninsula and then to the valley with Stonewall Jackson. After arriving with Jackson's Division they turned around and marched back to the peninsula with Whiting's Brigade participating in Gaines Mill and Malvern Hill battles. At Antietam, the brigade was led by Laws under Hood. In spring 1863 they were shifted to Davis's Mississippi Brigade (2nd, 11th, 42nd Mississippi and the 55th North Carolina). The regiment marched north under the command of Colonel Francis Marion Green with 432 soldiers and officers

The rest of the Davis brigade was excited as their fourth regiment, the 11th Mississippi finally arrived on the field from Cashtown. They had been sorely missed while on wagon guarding duty. The Eleventh was a tough fighting unit respected by the entire brigade. Colonel Francis Green and his full field officer staff had led them into line boosting the morale of the battered other three regiments. The 11th was respected as a special unit. "Perhaps no regiment entered the service with a larger number of professional men in its ranks. Physicians were especially represented, both officers and privates." **(Rietti, *Military Annals of Mississippi*, p 147)** The Eleventh had seen tough duty in other battles and now weighted in with about 49 officers and 386 men. Said one historian of the 11th "The Eleventh was made up in large measure from the choicest spirits in the state—intelligent, honorable and brace, and was a tried and trained body that had won fame upon many bloody fields before Gettysburg" **(McFarland, "The Eleventh Mississippi Regiment at Gettysburg, p 563)**

In the fighting on July 1st the Eleventh had been on duty guarding wagons and suffered no casualties. One of the hardest fighting regiments in the division, the Eleventh would be at full strength but full strength was only 43 officers and 389 men due to their heavy losses in almost every battle since the war began.

8:00 A.M. Report

An early account of the role played by North Carolina troops on the third day at Gettysburg talks about the unique condition of the 11th Mississippi. “When on the afternoon of the third day of July 1863 Pettigrew, Trimble and Pickett’s divisions marched into that ever-to-be remember slaughter pen, there was one regiment in the first named division, the 11th Mississippi, which entered the assault fresh, carrying in 325 officers and men. After losing 202 killed and wounded, it with the brigade left the field in disorder” **(W.R. Bond, *Pickett or Pettigrew: an historical essay*, W.L.L. Hall Publisher, Scotland Neck, NC 1888, p 41)**

Company A of the 11th was the famous “University Grays”, so named because of the large number of students from University of Mississippi who had joined the company ranks at the beginning of the war. The original number of soldiers in the company was 70 of which 33 were students. By Gettysburg the numbers had been reduced to about 39 officers and men. It should be noted that there were University of Mississippi students and graduates in several other companies of the 11th NC such as Company H. The company was officially commanded by Captain Simon Marsh who enlisted in Oxford, Mississippi and was promoted to Captain in September 1862 but he had resigned sick in June so command was in the hands of First Lieutenant John Moore

“Coahoma Invincibles” Company B commanded by 21 year old Captain William David Nunn from Friars Point, Mississippi and First Lieutenant L. M. Suddoth had 38 men on duty with them on the morning of July 3.

Captain George W. Shannon who later became Major and Lieutenant Colonel led Company C assisted by First Lieutenant William H. Peel. “The Prairie Rifles” reported with 4 officers and 24 men.

Company D was commanded by Captain John R. Prince 26 yr old from Philadelphia, Mississippi. First Lieutenant Isaac M. Kelly and fifty one men were by his side with the “Neshoba Rifles”.

The “Prairie Guards” were under the leadership of Captain Henry P. Halbert and First Lieutenant William Henry Belton. Company E would bring 4 officers and 35 men to battle.

Company F was known as the "Noxubee Rifles" and was commanded by Captain Thomas J. Stokes a 25 year old planter from Macon. His First Lieutenant Charles O. Brooks had been wounded at Sharpsburg. Together they would command forty one men in the coming battle.

The young men of Lafayette County had organized a militia company before the Civil War started in Oxford, Mississippi and named the company after the popular Congressman L.Q.C Lamar. Their motto was "Semper Paratus" (Always Ready). They often served as a skirmishing Company. They were commanded at Gettysburg by Captain William G. Nelms age 27 who had been wounded at Sharpsburg. Assisting Nelms with the 29 men and three other officers of the "LaMar Rifles" Company G was First Lieutenant Henry G. Fernandez who enlisted in Oxford.

Company H was known as the "Chickasaw Guards" consisting of 43 officers and men commanded by Captain Jamison H. Moore and First Lieutenant Thomas W. Hill—enlisted Houston. Company H was the color company in the battle to come.

"The Van Dorn Reserves"—Company I had as their commander for most of the war Captain Stephen Cocke Moore he was sick during the Gettysburg Campaign but fought and would later resign in February 1864. 1st Lieutenant William Word would assist with his Second Lieutenant William H. Clopton plus 2 officers and 41 men.

Thirty Eight men reported for duty July 1 in Company K commanded by Captain George Bird who replaced Captain James Standley on June 28th. Standley—age 22—from Carrolton had been wounded at Seven Pines and after a length recovery had resigned. First Lieutenant John T. Stanford—who had recently been promoted in June would assist Bird with the leadership of the "Carroll Rifles"

Lane's Brigade
Commander by General James Lane

In the fighting on July 1st Lane's Brigade was ordered to provide flank protection for the Pender assault in light of Union cavalry activity to the south of the field. All five regiments were stationed along the Fairfield Road with a skirmish line from the 37th North Carolina. Colonel Barbour commander of the 37th North Carolina threw out 40 men, under Captain Hudson (Company G). The only casualties for the day were a few men wounded in the skirmish line. One report lists four and one lists seven.

33rd North Carolina

The 33rd Regiment NC Infantry was organized in Raleigh in September 1861 under the leadership of Princeton graduate Colonel Lawrence Branch. The regiment served at the fighting around New Bern and then transferred to Virginia where Branch was selected to head the brigade. The regiment lost 75 men in the fighting on the Peninsula; 8 at 2nd Manassas and Brigadier General Branch was killed at Sharpsburg. It lost 41 at Fredericksburg and was heavily involved at Chancellorsville and lost 42% of its 480 men there. (202 k/w/c) The strength of the regiment on the march to Gettysburg was 368 officers and men under the command of Colonel Clark Moulton Avery. Like many of the officers and men of the 33rd NC, Colonel C.M. Avery had been wounded at Chancellorsville and had recovered just in time to make the journey North.

The strength of the 33rd was greatly reduced by the numbers killed, wounded and captured at Chancellorsville and many of the wounded would not return until September.

8:00 A.M. Report

Company A was commanded by Captain Henry Baker 24 years old from Halifax in Iredell Co. His First Lieutenant was James Summers a 34 year old mechanic who had been captured at Chancellorsville. Company A had forty one reporting for duty July 3.

1st Lt Ebenezer Price commanding Company B had been wounded at Cedar Mountain before taking the place of wounded Captain Thomas Gatlin who was hit in the right elbow at Chancellorsville. "Clark's Guard" numbered forty six officers and men on July 3 with 2nd Lt Peyton Anthony who had been wounded at Chancellorsville assisting 1st Lt. Price.

The "Cabarrus Hornets" were led by Captain David Corzine who had been wounded at Chancellorsville assisted by 1st Lt. Willoughby Avery. Company C numbered fifty two men on July 3.

Company D had been in turmoil for many months prior to Gettysburg. Their Captain Oliver Tyrel Parks had been relieved of command in January for "conduct unbecoming an officer" and for "leaving his company in the face of the enemy". His replacement was 1st Lieutenant James Hunt. However sometime before the Gettysburg campaign Parks was reinstated by the War Department and Hunt demoted back to 1st Lt. The "Wilkes Regulators" would number thirty three able bodied men for the attack.

Forty three year old Captain William Parker from Edgecombe Co. had been wounded in the head at 2nd Manassas but returned to command Company E in the Gettysburg campaign. His 1st Lt Lewis Babb had been wounded in the face at Chancellorsville and second in command fell to 2nd Lt. John "Jimmy" Caldwell, the 18 year old son of the future Governor of North Carolina. Forty officers and men were ready for duty with these men from Gates County on July 3.

In Company F forty four officers and men reported for duty under the command of Captain James Weston who had been captured at New Bern, NC. the year before. The leadership of the "Dixie Invincibles" was aided by 1st LT James Gibbs who had been captured at Fredericksburg

Company G was known as the "Cumberland Rangers" and was headed by Captain William Callais. Callais had been wounded at Chancellorsville but recovered in time to join the regiment heading north. He would be assisted in leading the thirty one men of Company G by 1st Lieutenant Joseph Mills.

Hyde County provide the men for Company H under the command of Captain Riddick Gatling and 1st Lt George Sanderlin. The strength of the company on the morning of July 3 was twenty eight.

Company I "The Confederate Stars" had been led by 21 year old 2nd Lt. Lafayette Goslin ever since 1st Lt. John Anderson was wounded in the knee at Chancellorsville. Former Captain George Stowe had his thumb shot off and was captured at Fredericksburg. 3rd Lt. Isaac Farrow would assist the leading the fifty one men of the company on July 1.

Lastly Company K was led by Captain Henry Granger a 23 year old from Greene Co. Company K had been in turmoil for some time since 1st Lt William Taylor had tried to resign several time then deserted. Then newly Brevetted 1st Lt James Walton was wounded in the shoulder at Chancellorsville and 2nd Lt Spier Whitaker became regimental Adjutant. This placed 1st Sgt James Dockery a 19 year old second in command of the thirty three men who fought on July 3.

18th North Carolina

The 18th North Carolina regiment was founded in August 1861 at Camp Wyatt near Wilmington NC. Colonel was T.J. Purdie. They saw service in North Carolina until the summer of 1862 when they were shipped to the Peninsula campaign. There they were attached to the brigade of Brigadier Lawrence Branch. Branch was killed at Sharpsburg and replaced by Col. James Lane. The 18th was not involved in the fighting at Sharpsburg but at Chancellorsville they lost both their commander Colonel T.J. Purdie killed and their flag captured by the 7th NJ. Their new commander would be Colonel John Decatur Barry who would lead the 346 officers and men to Gettysburg.

8:00 A.M. Report

Company A "The German Volunteers" was the name of Company A of the 18th North Carolina infantry regiment. The name came from the fact that the first recruits to the regiment were recent German immigrants in New Hanover County. Ironically, almost all of the original recruits were discharged in April 1862 for being non citizens. Captain Benjamin Rinaldi was appointed 5/27/62 and was wounded at Second Manassas. He returned in time to lead the company to Gettysburg. He would be aided by 2nd Lt David Bullard 25 years old in leading thirty men.

Captain Marcus Buie would command the "Bladen Light Infantry"—Company B on July 3. The 25 yr old had been appointed just after the Chancellorsville battle and would be assisted by 1st LT Thomas Wiggins 23 years old from Bladen County. The company would have three officers and thirty seven men ready for combat.

Company C was led by Captain Van Richardson. Forty seven men would fight with the "Columbus Guards No 3" in the assault on Cemetery Ridge. Eighteen year old 1st Lt Owen Smith would assist in leading.

The original company commander still led the "The Robeson Rifle Guard" at Gettysburg. Captain Alexander Moore 21 years old and 2nd Lt. Alfred Rowland 19 years old would command the thirty eight men who reported for duty. 1st Lieutenant Neil Townsend had been wounded at Chancellorsville.

Company E "The Moore's Creek Rifle Guards" was led by captain John Moore at 3 years old. 1st Lt. George Washington Corbett who had been wounded at Malvern Hill assisted the leadership of the forty eight men who were prepared for battle.

"The Scotch Boys" under Captain Alfred Moffit numbered forty five on July 3. The 24 yr old merchant had enlisted in Randolph County and was aided with Company F by 1st Lt. Archibald McGregor age 24. Two men from Company F had been wounded by fire from Union cavalry on July 1. Privates Henry Thrower and James Waters.

Company G was known as the "Wilmington Light Infantry". Captain John Poisson a 31 year old former clerk from New Hanover County had been wounded at Fredericksburg. 23 year old 1st Lt. William Dixon helped lead the thirty seven men who reported for duty.

Captain Francis Wooten led the "Columbus Vigilants" helped by 1st Lt. Archibald McCollum a 26 year old carpenter. Company H would have forty officers and men in action this day.

Company I was commanded by Captain Thomas Lewis who had been wounded in the hip and 2nd Manassas and again wounded at Chancellorsville. The "Wilmington Rifle Guards" had lost both Lieutenants wounded (Joseph Bridger & George Huggins) in May and neither had returned. Forty men arrived with Company I on July 1.

Lastly, The "Bladen Guards" were Company K of the 18th North Carolina. Commanded by 1st Lt. Alfred Tolar who had been promoted to brevet Captain after the promotion of Captain Thomas Wooten to Major and then wounded at Chancellorsville. The twenty one year old Bladen County farmer was assisted in leading the forty one men of Company K by 2nd Lt Evander Robison age 25.

28th North Carolina

The 28th North Carolina was organized in August 1861 and placed into the "Cape Fear" District under Commander Colonel James Lane. They were later shifted to Va. for the Peninsula campaign and would be placed in Branch's Brigade. Branch would be killed at Sharpsburg and Colonel Lane of the 28th would replace him as Brigade commander. The new Colonel of the regiment would be Samuel Lowe. At Fredericksburg the regiment was in action losing 16 killed and 49 wounded. They would be in combat at Chancellorsville losing 12 officers and 77 men as casualties. Under the command of Colonel S.D. Lowe they marched north to Gettysburg with 346 officers and men.

8:00 A.M. Report

Company A was led by Captain Edward Lovell age 21 with 1st Lt. Elijah Thompson age 28 who had been wounded at Second Manassas. The "Surrey Regulators" would field thirty nine officers and men on July 3

At age 31 Captain Thomas Smith from Gaston County, NC was in command of Company B. At his side was 22 year old 1st Lt. Robert Rhyne who had been wounded at Chancellorsville but returned. "The Gaston Invincibles" would number thirty eight in the assault.

The "South Fork Farmers" were Company C of the 28th North Carolina. Captain James Linebarger age 25 was their commander. Linebarger had been wounded twice before at Fredericksburg and at Chancellorsville. He would command forty five men on July 3 assisted by 1st Lt. Marcus Throneburg who had been captured at Hanover Courthouse.

Company D had as its commander Captain John Randall. The Stanley Yankee Hunters would field thirty one officers and men July 1 with Edmund Moose at 38 years old as 1st Lieutenant.

Captain Niven Clark a 28 year old officer from Montgomery County, NC had been wounded at Glendale and was in command of Company E. 1st Lt. James Ewing was second in command and had been wounded in the leg at Fredericksburg. The "Montgomery Grays" would put thirty men into the field this day.

"The Yadkin Boys" had been racked with political infighting before the Gettysburg campaign. In 1862 there had been a bitter election for Company Commander between the incumbent John Kinyoun and a challenger Thomas Apperson. The rift within the company had never healed. With Apperson as commander and his brother, Peter, as First

Sergeant company F numbered thirty one men and had as its first Lt. John Truelove 31 years old from Yadkin County.

Company G was commanded by Captain Elijah Morrow who also had been wounded at Chancellorsville but returned. He was assisted by 1st Lt. George McCauley age 31 yr. "The Guards of Independence" would put thirty eight fighting men into action July 3

The "Cleveland Regulators" was company H of the 28th North Carolina. Their Captain was 43 year old Gold Holland and their 1st Lieutenant was Milton Lowe. A total of thirty officers and men would march with them on July 3

The 28 year old commander of Company I was Captain Simon Bohannon of Yadkin Co, NC. "The Yadkin Stars" fielded thirty six men on July 3 with 1st Lt. Jordan Snow as second in command.

Finally Company K—"The Stanley Guards". Their Captain John Moody was sick in Virginia and 1st Lt. James Crowell who had been wounded at 2nd Manassas was in command assisted by 2nd Lt. Adam Stone. Company K would field thirty nine officers and men.

37th North Carolina

The regiment was organized at Camp Fisher, NC in November 1861. The fighting around New Bern saw the regiment in its first combat in heavy fighting. After transfer to Virginia as part of Branch's Brigade the regiment was in heavy combat at Hanover Courthouse taking considerable causalities.

Colonel Lee was regimental commander until he was killed at Frazier's farm. At Sharpsburg, where Brigadier General Branch was killed, the regiment had light losses (only 4 wounded) while protected with a stone wall. General 3Lane took command of the brigade and again at Chancellorsville the regiment was in heavy fighting with 34 killed and 193 wounded. Colonel Barbour commanded the regiment during this time but now due to his injuries Lt. Colonel William Morris was in command with 379 officers and men. The 37th was a tough fighting regiment which an examination of the past wounds of its officers will show.

8:00 A.M. Report

Company A was commanded by Captain William Alexander. The "Ashe Beauregard Rifles" had their 1st Lieutenant 18 year old Thomas Norwood with a total strength of twenty two men.

Captain Andrew Critcher of Company was still absent from his Chancellorsville wound and command was in the hands of 1st Lt. Joseph Todd who had been wounded in the arm at Fredericksburg. The “Watauga Marksmen” numbered twenty nine officers and men and had as their 2nd Lieutenant Nathaniel Horton.

The “Mecklenburg Wide Awakes”, Company C, was led by Captain Lawson Potts who had been twice wounded. First in the thigh and 2nd Manassas and first in the hip at Ox Hill. The company had forty five men prepared for battle on July 3 with 1st Lt. John Brown on duty.

Company D’s Captain Jackson Bost was a 30 year old medical doctor from Union County. Bost had been captured at Hanover Courthouse in 1862 and also at Chancellorsville. He had been paroled in time to return to his unit, The “North Carolina Defenders” The 1st and 2 Lt both had been wounded at Chancellorsville as well and 3rd Lt Wesley Battle would help Bost lead the fifty men who reported for duty on July 3.

Captain William Nicholson age 25 had previously been Adjutant of the regiment. The “Watauga Minute Men” would field forty four officers and men on July 3 with 1st Lt Johiel Eggers who had been captured at Hanover Courthouse in June 1862.

The “Western Carolina Stars” had as a commander Captain John Petty who had recovered from his Chancellorsville wounds. The 1st Lt of Company F Felix Tankersley was still absent wounded at Chancellorsville and so 23 year old 2nd Lt. John Forrester wounded in the knee at Ox Hill and Captured at Fredericksburg would assist leading forty men into battle.

The skirmish line on July 1 had been Company G—“The Alexander Soldiers”. Captain Daniel Hudson age 26 from Alexander County had led his line out to meet the Union cavalry scouting out the flank of Pender’s Division. His thirty six men had suffered a few wounded. His 1st Lt. was James Pool a 22 year old who had been twice wounded first at Cedar Mountain and then at Second Manassas.

Company H’s Captain Henry Fite was still absent wounded after Chancellorsville as was the 1st Lieutenant. 2nd Lt. George McKee 20 years old was in command of the “Gaston Blues”. McKee had been awarded the “Badge of Distinction” at Chancellorsville and would command thirty nine men with the help of his 1st Sergeant John Ormand.

“The Mecklenburg Rifles”—Company I were led by 1st Lieutenant William Ellis due to Captain William Stitt still being absent wounded in the thigh at Chancellorsville. 2nd Lt. Adam Yandle had recovered from the wounded arm he suffered at Chancellorsville and would help lead the forty men in Company I.

Lastly Company K’s Captain William Fetter had thirty seven officers and men on July 3rd. The 23 year old Captain of the “Alleghany Tigers had been wounded in the thigh at

2nd Manassas and would be court—martial after the Gettysburg campaign. 1st Lt. Thomas Armstrong would later take his place but would assist him at Gettysburg.

7th North Carolina

The 7th North Carolina Regiment was formed in August 1861 at Camp Mason and trained in Bern, NC. They saw service in North Carolina until the summer of 1862 when they were shipped to the Peninsula battlefields. The regiment was there involved in the fighting at Hanover Courthouse. They were part of General Lawrence Branches Brigade (AP Hill's Light Infantry) and when he was killed at Sharpsburg, Colonel James Lane of the 28th North Carolina then took command of the Brigade. Colonel Campbell took command but was killed. The regiment lost heavily at Chancellorsville. In the march to Gettysburg under Major John McLeod Turner 291 officers and men participated.

8:00 A.M. Report

Company A from Iredell and Alleghany Counties was under the command of Captain John Knox a 23 year old student who had been wounded at Fredericksburg. His 1st Lt. Pinkney Carlton was wounded at Chancellorsville but recovered in time to join the campaign to Pennsylvania. Company A had thirty six officers and men prepared for battle July 3. The company had lost one of the few casualties from July 1 when Private Noah Baker was wounded on the skirmish line.

Captain James Harris was 23 years old in command of the Cabarrus County volunteers. The strength of the company on July 3 was thirty. 21 year old William Harris from Cabarrus Co. was his 1st Lieutenant.

The men from New Hanover County in Company C had lost their Captain James McKeithan wounded at 2nd Manassas and were led at Gettysburg by 1st Lt. Walter MacRae. With thirty officers and men present and accounted for they would advance at Cemetery Ridge.

Company D was led by Captain Timothy Cahill. The 1st Lieutenant of the Mecklenburg County *"auslanders" was* 1st Lt Thomas Mulloy a 22 year old clerk from Charleston, SC. Their strength after severe losses at Chancellorsville would be three officers and eighteen men.

1st Lt Joshua Vick was a 20 year old enlisted Nash farmer before the war. He took command when former Captain Hamilton Graham resigned in the summer. Company E would go into action with twenty six officers and men.

Company F's Captain Thomas Williamson was wounded in the arm at Chancellorsville and still had not returned to command. 1st Lieutenant Daniel Kinney, age 26, who had been promoted to Sergeant back in November 1862 for "gallant conduct" in battle would lead the thirty three men from Rowen County.

Captain Andrew Hill would command the "Wake Rangers" with a strength of 3 officers and thirty six men. 1st Lt Simpson Weatherspoon who had been wounded at Second Manassas would assist in leading Company G.

Company H was commanded by 22 year old Captain James Harris. The strength of the company on July 3 was thirty two officers and men with John Alexander as 1st Lieutenant.

With Captain James McCauley wounded at Chancellorsville and still absent in the hospital, Brevet 2nd Lt. DeWitt Smith a 35 year old teacher from enlisted Iredell Co led Company I into battle twenty eight men strong.

Lastly Company K was led a group of officers who had seen battle before. Captain Nathan Pool age 32 had been wounded at Fredericksburg. 1st Lt. Robert Teague had been wounded at Gaines Mill and 2nd Lt Arthur Walker had been wounded at W Malvern Hill plus was awarded the "Badge of Distinction" for bravery at Chancellorsville. The Alexander County, North Carolina men numbered thirty five on July 3.

Scales Brigade
Commanded by Colonel Lowrance (34th NC)
38th North Carolina

Organized on January 17, 1862 at Camp Mangum (near Raleigh) for twelve months service, two days later the regiment was transferred to Confederate service. On February 10th, 1862 they were ordered to Richmond Virginia and to Weldon to guard some railroad lines. The following April the regiment was reorganized to serve three years (or for the duration of the war) in Joseph R Anderson's brigade. Colonel William Hoke was the original commander. The regiment fought from Gaines Mill to Chancellorsville as part of Pender's Brigade. With Pender's promotion to Division commander Colonel Alfred Scales of the 34th NC became Brigadier. Under the command of Colonel Hoke the regiment marched north to Gettysburg with 216 officers and men.

In the fighting on July 1st The 38th was closest to the Chambersburg road and least subject to the Union artillery fire. However all of its Field officers were out of action wounded by the end of the fighting. Colonel William Hoke who had been wounded before at Mechanicsville was hit in the leg and Lieutenant Colonel Ashford who had been hit in the leg at 2nd Manassas was wounded again. The 38th reported losses of 65 killed and wounded. With the loss of so many officers many men would be missing in action "unaccounted for" during the next few days.

8:00 AM Report

The losses from July 1 had seriously crippled the leadership of 38th North Carolina. The field officers were all down wounded and command was in the hands of Captain Thornburg of Company H. The total number of men available for the July 3 assault was about 150.

Company A lost three men in the fighting July 12. The "Spartan Band" was led both days by 1st Lt. Alsa Brown a 20 year old from Duplin County who had been awarded the "Badge of Distinction" for bravery at Chancellorsville. Captain Nichols Armstrong was still recuperating from his wound at Harper's Ferry back in September 1862. Company A would advance on July 3 with 10 officers and men.

The "Men of Yadkin" was a small company which had been hurt badly at Chancellorsville. The Company was commanded by 28 year old Capt. Augustin Blackburn who had brought his slave (Alfred "teen") north with him. Losses on July 1 had been 6. Blackburn's 1st Lt. was Samuel Wilder a 33 year old cabinetmaker. Strength on the morning of July 3 for Company B was 10.

Company C was led by Captain John Wilson age 33 who would later become Major. The company had been hard hit at Chancellorsville and came to Gettysburg with only twenty one men plus four officers. Captain Wilson was the only officer to not be killed or wounded July 1. The "Sampson Farmers" would lose twelve that day including 1st Lt. Rufus Allen wounded and later died; 2nd Lt. Hosea wounded on the scalp and 3rd Lt. George Daughtry killed. The company would be down to seven men by the morning of July 3.

With Captain Henry Darden wounded in the right shoulder on July One command of Company D—"The Sampson Plowboys" was in the hands of 24 year old 1st Lt. John Robinson. In addition to Captain Darden and also 3rd Lt. William Faison wounded in the right leg, nine others fell in the attack on the Seminary buildings. Company D would advance into battle July 3 with four men.

Captain Duncan McRae of Company E who was "known for his bravery" had been killed at Chancellorsville with many of his men placing the leadership of "The Richmond Boys" with 1st Lt. Olfred Dockery. Losses July 1 were light (5 wounded) and Dockery plus Second Lieutenant William Covington led seven men on the third.

Company F would be led by 3rd Lt. Hiram Davis a 31 year old mechanic after the loss of 2nd Lieutenant Alonzo Deal July 1 with a wound in the side. Deal had been wounded before at Mechanicsville. The original Captain Daniel Roseman had resigned because of wounds suffered. The "Catawba Wildcats" had suffered a total of 15 casualties on the first day leaving eight.

The "Rocky Face Rangers" was led both days by Capt. George Flowers 21 years old from Alexander County and. 1st Lt. Richard Sharp who had been awarded for gallantry at 2nd Manassas. Captain flowers had been Wounded in the scalp at Mechanicsville in 1862 and would later become Regimental Major. Losses for Company would be fifteen on July 1 leaving seven men prepared for duty.

After day One, 26 year old Captain William Thornburg who had been wounded slightly took command of the 38th Regiment as senior Captain. Thornburg had been wounded before in the fighting near Richmond Virginia in the summer of 1862. The "Uwhallie Boys" suffered heavy losses on July1 totaling 14. 1st Lt. Isaac Kearns would command the company of eleven officers and men in Thornburg's absence.

Company I was known as the "Cleveland Marksmen" and had suffered light losses of nine on July One. Captain David Magness was in command with 1st Lt. William Blanton who had been previously a Private in the 56th NC. Total strength July 3 14.

Company K's Captain Daniel Monroe commanded "The Carolina Boys", a regiment strong with Scotch—Irish. His 1st Lt. John Ray who had been wounded in the mouth at Mechanicsville had been wounded in the right ankle on July 1 (one of ten casualties). His place was taken by 2nd Lt. Hugh McDonald. Total reporting on July 3 was nine.

13th North Carolina

The 13th regiment was organized in May of 1861 in Garysburg, North Carolina under the command of Colonel Pender and joined the Confederate Army as part of Colston's brigade. During the Peninsular Campaign the losses were 29 killed and 80 wounded. At Sharpsburg they lost 49-killed and 149 wounded. With Colonel Pender promoted to Brigadier, Alfred Scales took command of the regiment. Suffering 37 killed and wounded at Fredericksburg, the regiment was part of Jackson's flank attack at Chancellorsville where they lost 216 Killed/ wounded and captured. Here Colonel Scales was wounded in the thigh but recovered for the Gettysburg campaign as a Brigadier were the regiment entered the battle with 232 officers and men under the leadership of Colonel Joseph Hyman. In the fighting on July 1 Scales was wounded again by a shell fragment as he charged across the field towards the Lutheran Seminary Buildings.

In the fighting on July 1st most of the leaders of the 13th North Carolina were put out of action. Losses that day were 133 men killed, or wounded. The Thirteenth would have about 45 officers and men available July 3. With the loss of so many officers many men would be missing in action "unaccounted for" during the next few days.

8:00 A.M. report . . .

With the wounding of both Colonel Joseph Hyman and Major Eilah Withers on July 1, command of the 13th NC fell to Captain Ludolphus Henderson (Co A). The 13th North Carolina had numbered only 180 men and 30 officers of the first day at Gettysburg and had lost almost 150 on the assault on the Seminary. The return of a detail of men numbering 15 who had been left behind at Greencastle, Pa boosted the strength of the regiment on the morning of July 3 to 45 soldiers commanded by Captain Ludolphus Henderson (Co A) a 27 year old dentist who enlisted in Caswell County 4/29/61. Henderson would be wounded this day on the advance and again later at Cold Harbor. Four Captains and ten Lieutenants remained to provide leadership. **(Nathan Smith, letter to the Raleigh Observer, November 30, 1877)** This is conformed by the memory of 27 year old Lieutenant James Bason who was wounded on the first day "My recollection is that by the third day there were no more than forty or fifty men left for duty" **(James Bason letter to the editor September 28, 1877 from Reidsville, NC)**

Commanding Company A was Captain Ludolphus Henderson a 27 year old dentist from Caswell County and 1st Lt. James Williamson a 20 yr old. The "Yanceyville Grays" had lost eight men on July 1 including 1st Lt. James Williamson who had been wounded before at Chancellorsville now wounded in the thigh and 1st Sgt John Jones. On the morning of July 3 twelve men reported for duty.

Capt. William Robinson was a 27 year old doctor from Mecklenburg who had been wounded at Sharpsburg. He served as second senior captain of the regiment. The "Raneleburg Riflemen" Co B lost 14 men on July 1 and had ten remaining for action July 3.

Company C was commanded by Sgt William Farley because all officers had been killed or wounded on the first day. Captain William Rainey was wounded and would be too weak to move July 5th (he would die 7/9/63); 1st Lt. William Brandon was wounded and also be captured July 5th (and die July ninth). The "Milton Blues" had lost thirteen men July 1 and would be left with ten.

The "Leasburg Grays" or Company D was led on the third by Captain Thomas Stephens a 24 year old teacher from Caswell County. 1st Lt. William Woods a 22 year old student had survived to help lead the eleven remaining men from the company. Fifteen men were lost on July 1.

Company E's 2nd Lt. William Andrews led the men on July 3. The "Alamance Regulators" had taken heavy casualties at Chancellorsville and arrived in Gettysburg with only twenty seven men. Of these fifteen were lost on the first day including their Captain Thomas Martin a 22 year old former student wounded in the left hip as well as the 1st Lieutenant and three Sergeants. Martin would recover and later become Major of the regiment.

Corp. Matthew Ijams would lead Company F on July 3 after the loss of all officers. The 21 yr old would command only eleven men. All the rest of the twenty nine who came to Gettysburg were casualties. The "Davey Grays" had lost Captain Franklin Williams a 25 year old teacher who had been wounded before at Fredericksburg and was now hit in the left leg as well as 2nd Lt. Nimrod Sain a 34 year old carpenter who was also wounded.

Company G would find Sgt. Richard Stallings a 27 yr old clerk as its commander on July 3. Acting commander 2nd Lt. Rufus Atkinson a 23 year old teacher had been wounded on July 1. The company's Captain John Fuqua had been wounded at Chancellorsville and its 1st Lt Charles Civallier had been wounded at Boonsboro and was absent wounded. The "Edgecombe Rifles" lost thirteen men on July 1 and had fifteen remaining.

The "Rockingham Guards"—Company H was commanded by Captain Thomas Lawson with the help of 2nd Lt Nathaniel Smith after 1st Lt James Smith a 25 year old medical student had been wounded in the ankle on 7/1. Nine men were lost with Smith leaving eleven remaining.

Company I was led by 1st Lt. William Winchester a 23 year old clerk from Rockingham County. Winchester had been wounded at Chancellorsville as had his Captain Robert Ward but Winchester had returned to the company. 3rd Lieutenant Roland Williams assisted leading the seven remaining men from the "Rockingham Rangers" after losses of ten on July 1.

Company K was led on July 3 by Captain Hugh Guerrant Rockingham Co. The "Dixie Boys" would have eleven men available for the assault. Lost on the first day were sixteen men plus 1st Lt. William Nunally a 28 year old merchant killed and 3rd Lt. William Totten wounded in the leg requiring amputation.

34th North Carolina

The regiment was organized the winter of 1861 at High Point and Raleigh. After spending some time in North Carolina, the regiment was transferred to the Army of Northern Virginia. They participated in the Peninsular campaign and suffered heavy losses at Gaines' Mill and later at Chantilly. The regiment was attached to "Stonewall" Jackson for the Second Manassas campaign. After helping to capture Harper's Ferry in September 1862, the Thirty-fourth was placed in charge of the pontoon bridge and was entrusted with the counting and discharging of the prisoners, after conducting them to the Maryland side of the river. On 20 September the regiment assisted in driving back the Federal force which followed General Lee into Virginia, killing many of them at Shepherdstown, while attempting to recross the river on a dam. After Fredericksburg and Chancellorsville the regiment came under the leadership of Colonel William Lowrance and Lt. Col George Gordon a former British Army officer. 300 men and 37 officers went north to Gettysburg.

In the fighting on July 1st about 60 officers and men were killed or wounded. With the loss of so many officers many men would be missing in action "unaccounted for" during the next few days

8:00 A.M. Report . . .

With the promotion of Colonel William Lowrence into the command position after the wounding of Brigadier General Scales, command of the 34th was given to Lieutenant Colonel George Gordon, a former British military officer.

Captain Hiram Abernathy was the only remaining officer in Company A after July. Abernathy had formerly been Lieutenant Colonel of the 34th North Carolina and was appointed in June as Senior Captain. The "Laurel Springs Guard" had lost both of their lieutenants on July 1. 1st Lt. Bartlett Martin was wounded in the shoulder and 2nd Lt. George Woody wounded in the head. Eleven men remained with the "Laurel Spring Guard to fight on July 3.

Company B was led by Captain Joseph Byers a 31 year old from Cleveland County. The "Sandy Run Yellow Jackets" 1st Lieutenant was David Harrill age 25 who had been captured at Chancellorsville. Company B lost four men on July 1 and went into battle with eleven officers and men.

On the evening of July 1 Company C, "The Rutherford Rebels" had been given a new commander. Their Captain Francis Twitty was promoted to Major and First Lieutenant John Young was promoted to Captain. Former Major George Clark had been killed in the attack on the Seminary Buildings. On that day Company C itself lost four casualties. 2nd Lt. Lorenzo Wilkie would assist Young in leading the remaining eighteen men into battle.

The "Oakland Guards" was the nickname of Company D led by Capt. Carmi McNeely. Both of his Lieutenants had survived the first day fight unharmed while the company lost three. Returned to the company was Corporal Theodore Kisler who had been wounded at 2nd Manassas and was honored for "skill, good bearing and gallant conduct as a soldier". The strength of Company D on the Third Day was ten officers and men.

Both lieutenants had also survived in Company E under the command of Capt. Micajah Davis a 25 year old farmer from Lincoln Co. The "Shady Grove Rangers" lost eight men on July 1 and went into battle on July 3 with 3 officers and twenty men.

In Company F Captain David Hoyle who was a 33 year old millwright from Cleveland County headed the "The Floyd Rifles". Losses on July 1 had been ten including 1st Lt. Jacob Hogue who was wounded. The 38 yr old would return on July 3 to fight again with fourteen others from his company.

July 1 was a day of major loss for the "Mecklenburg Boys of Company G. Captain George Norment their 29 year commander who had been wounded at Gaines Mill was wounded in the left hip. 1st Lt. Alexander Cathy was wounded in the leg requiring amputation. 3rd Lt. John Abernathy age 21 was killed. Total losses July 1 were eight. Only 2nd Lt. James Todd age 24 remanded as an officer to lead the remaining fourteen Company G soldiers on the third day at Gettysburg.

"The Rough and Readys" (Co H) had light losses on the first day at Gettysburg (only four lost) and their commander Captain John Roberts and 1st Lt. Joseph Camp would go into battle on the third with almost a full force of twenty three.

Company I on the other hand was severely damaged by action at the Seminary July 1 losing twelve men including three of the four officers. Captain James Wood was wounded in the head & right arm. 1st Lt. Henry Jenkins was wounded as well and 22 year old 3rd Lieutenant George Huntley was killed. Command of the company fell to surviving 2nd Lt. Thomas Phillips age 19 who had been wounded himself in the right thigh at 2nd Manassas. He would lead "The Rutherford Band" of 9 men on the final day of battle.

Company K The Montgomery Boys was commanded by 1st Lt. Thomas Haltom at the age of 43 one of the oldest officers in the regiment. A former merchant he became commander when Captain George Clark was promoted to Major in June (only to be killed July 1) The "Montgomery Boys" would lose a 2nd Lieutenant and a 1st Sergeant plus seven others on July 1 and be left with 16 men on July 3.

22nd North Carolina

Formerly the 12th Volunteers, completed its organization near Raleigh, North Carolina, in July, 1861 under Colonel James Pettigrew. The unit was ordered to Virginia and assigned to the Aquia District in the Department of Northern Virginia. The regiment was composed originally of twelve companies, but two of them, "C" and "D," were very soon transferred to other commands, and the lettering, A, B, E, F, G, H, I, K, L, and M, for the ten companies was retained. Later the regiment was brigaded under Generals Pettigrew, Pender, and Scales. It fought with the army from Seven Pines to Chancellorsville. In April, 1862, this regiment contained 752 men, reported 161 casualties during the Seven days' Battles', had 6 killed and 57 wounded at Second Manassas and 1 killed and 44 wounded at Fredericksburg. It lost 30 killed and 139 wounded at Chancellorsville and its Colonel C Cole was killed. 321 officers and men marched into Gettysburg under the command of Lt. Colonel William Mitchell.

In the fighting on July 1st the 22nd was heavily hit by Union artillery protecting the seminary buildings attacked by Pender's assault. Losses for the day were estimated to be 83 in killed and wounded. This would leave about 137 men and officers for the assault July 3.

With the loss of so many officers many men would be missing in action "unaccounted for" during the next few days.

8:00 A.M. Report . . .

The "Caldwell Rough & Ready Boys" in Company A were led by Captain William Clark who had been wounded at Malvern Hill and again wounded in the hand at Fredericksburg. Losses on July were eight including 1st Lt. Joseph Clark 26 years old wounded in the right arm. Eighteen men remained for the July 3 assault.

Company B was led by Captain. Joseph Conley. The "McDowell Rifles" had lost six men on July 1. With 1st Lt James Higgins dismissed 20 year old 2nd Lt. George Gardin who had been captured at Seven Pines assisted the Captain in leading the ten men who remained.

"The Guilford Men" were Company E of the 22nd North Carolina. Capt. Martin Wolfe 33 years old from Guilford County was their commander. The officers of the company were seasoned veterans. Wolfe had been wounded in the leg at 2nd Manassas. 1st Lt. Robert Cole was wounded at Chancellorsville and 2nd Lt. Andrew Busick was wounded at Sharpsburg. Losses on day One were eleven leaving fourteen men ready for action July 3.

Company F was known as the "Alleghany True Blues". 2nd Lt. Shadrach Caudilla 20 year old from Alleghany County was in command because former Captain William Mitchell had been promoted to Lt. Col on May 3 and 1st Lt. David Edwards has resigned disabled after a hip wound at Fredericksburg. Five lost on July 1 left eight ready for action on the Third Day at Gettysburg.

The officers of Company G had seen their share of battle wounds. Capt. George Graves had been wounded at Sharpsburg leading the "Caswell Rifles". 1st Lt. Peter Smith a 24 year old had also been wounded at Sharpsburg and on July 1 in the left hand along with seven others killed or wounded. 2nd Lt Martin Cobb had been wounded in the left thigh and right eye at Chancellorsville. Eleven men remained after the Seminary Building attack.

Company H "The Stokes Boys" with seventeen men was commanded this day by 2nd Lt. John Martin who had been Court-martialed back in April 1863 but had his sentence of dismissal remitted by the Secretary of War. Martin moved into command when Former Captain William Loving resigned April 22,63 and 1st Lt Christopher Smith resigned wounded. Company H had lost sixteen on July 1

Severe losses occurred in Company I on July 1 leaving 24 year old student 3rd Lt. Burwell Birkhead in command of the "Davis Guards". Capt. Gaston Lamb was wounded in both thighs on 7/1. 1st Lieutenant John Palmer and 2nd Lt. Isaiah Robbins were both killed. Both men had been wounded at Chancellorsville but returned for the Pennsylvania campaign. The year 1863 had not been a good one for the officers of Co I 22nd NC. They would attack with fifteen men having lost nine of the first day.

The "McDowell Boys" were led on July 3 by 22 year old 2nd Lt. John Burgin. The company K Captain William Goodling had been wounded in the left arm in the first days fight (total loss—eleven men) and 1st Lieutenant Joseph Burgin had been captured at Chancellorsville and dropped as officer after his parole. The strength of the company on July 3 would be twelve.

Company L had lost 2nd Lt. Oliver Pike with wounds of the hand and leg on July 1 along with seven other casualties. Captain Clarkson Horney 20 year old Randolph County farmer would command "The Uwharrie Grays". 1st Lt. Yancey Johnson 22 years old would help led the remaining twelve into battle.

Lastly, "The Randolph Hornets" Company M was commanded by Captain Columbus Silver who had been wounded both at Glendale and Chancellorsville. Losses on July 1 were eight out of twenty seven officers and men present on July 1. 1st Lt. James Robbins who was also wounded at Chancellorsville would be second in command.

16th North Carolina

Organized for 12 month service June 1861 in Burke County Western North Carolina. Trained in Raleigh as the "Burke Tigers" Glendale losses were 33-killed 199 wounded; Fredericksburg losses 6—killed 48 wounded Chancellorsville losses 105 KWC. The regiments Field officers were mostly killed and wounded by June 1863 and the 321 officers and men went to Gettysburg under the command of Calvin McLoud who was Captain of Company H.

In the fighting on July 1st The 16th was in the middle of the attack on the Seminary buildings held by Union infantry and artillery. The regiment would suffer considerable casualties. Their losses on July 1 numbered about 63 officers and men. With the loss of so many officers many men would be missing in action "unaccounted for" during the next few days.

8 A.M. Report . . .

With no Field Officers remaining, command of the 16th North Carolina had fallen to the Captain of Company H, Captain Calvin McCloud. Colonel John McElroy and Lieutenant Colonel William Stowe had both been badly wounded at Chancellorsville. Contemporary accounts record that about 80 men of the regiment were battle ready on July 3. The nine member band would stay behind to care for wounded.

Captain Solomon Carter had been badly wounded at Chancellorsville and was still absent during the Gettysburg campaign. Company B was commanded by First Lieutenant Ira Profit age 29 and 2nd Lt John Rhea who would later be arrested after the battle and court-martialed. Sixteen Madison County men would be available for duty on July 3rd after a loss of seven in the fighting on Seminary Ridge July 1.

Yancy County was the home of Company C commanded by Captain Nelson Wilson age 26 and 27 year old 1st Lt William Jasper. Jasper had been wounded at Seven Pines and had been captured at Fredericksburg. The "Black Mountain Boys" lost six men on July 1 and would go into combat with fourteen on July 3.

Company D was commanded by Capt Adolphus McKinney. 1st Lt King was 20 years old from Rutherford County like most of the Company. 3rd Lt Thorn age 25 was wounded on July 1 and died 7/30/63. Company D had five casualties that day and would be a strength of fourteen for July 3.

Capt Cloud a 22 year old from Burke Co. later became Colonel but on July 3rd commanded the "Burke Tigers" Company E with the assistance of 1st Lt Kaylor a 28 yr old. The Tigers had lost five men on July 1 and fielded fifteen on July 3.

Six men were lost in Company F from Buncombe County North Carolina on July 1. The company was commanded by 1st Lt. Milton Blackwell. After the resignation of Captain Alexander Jones and the loss of 2nd Lt William Boyd who was sick during this period, 3rd Lt. Dowe Alexander assisted. Alexander had been wounded in the shoulder at 2nd Manassas. Fourteen men remained to attack on July 3. One man from Company F who did not charge forward that day seems to have been Private Mias Wilson. The 20 year old soldier appears to have deserted his unit sometime after The July 1 fighting and showed up at the farm of Mr. Joseph Bayly outside Gettysburg and asked to be hidden until after the battle. Wilson would never leave Gettysburg. Long after the battle, he worked on the Bayly farm and then turned to farming himself. He died in Gettysburg March 19, 1921 an accepted member of the community. It is unclear if he ever returned to North Carolina to explain his "disappearance" at the Battle of Gettysburg. **(Account of Mrs. Joseph (Harriet) Bayly file V8-5 GNMP library)**

Rutherford County had produced Company G commanded by 1st Lt John McEntire who took leadership after the wounding of Captain Lawson Erwin at Fredericksburg. His second in command, 2nd Lieutenant George Mills was wounded by a shell on 7/1. His 3rd Lt John Ford age 30 was killed. Ford had been Color Sergeant at Fredericksburg where he was wounded. Mills and Ford were one of thirteen casualties on day one leaving nineteen men in line on July 3.

With Captain Calvin McLoud leading the regiment, Company H had lost seven men on the July 1 attack on the seminary buildings. 1st Lieutenant C.L. Robinson had been killed at Chancellorsville and assisting Captain McLoud was 2nd Lt Lee Allman. The Macon county men would number fourteen on the morning of July 3.

Company I Captain John Lane had been wounded at Fredericksburg and 2nd Lieutenant Thomas Brittain had been wounded in the arm at Chancellorsville. This left 1st Lieutenant John Mills to command Company I. In the first day's fighting Mills was wounded in the right leg and Sergeant Alfred Gash would lead the company on the third. Henderson County soldiers lost eight men on July 1 and have twelve available for July 3.

Nine men had been lost in Company K on July 1 with 28 year old Captain John Camp in command. Twenty four officers and men were in action on the third. One Polk County man who had been wounded slightly by a shell fragment during the artillery action on the second, Private John Williams appeared in line that morning ready to go.

The behavior of the 16th North Carolina this day would lead to some perplexing yet unanswered questions.

"On the morning of the 3rd, Lane's and Scales North Carolina brigades were sent, under the command of Major-General Trimble, to the right to reinforce Longstreet. After getting in our position our new commander rode down the line and halted at different regiments and made us little speeches—saying he was a stranger to us and had been sent to command us in the absence of our wounded general, and would led us upon Cemetery Hill at 3 o'clock **(Octavious A Wiggins, Clark's Regiments, Vol. II p. 661)** Wiggins also remembered Trimble stating that "no guns should be fired until the enemy line was broken and that I should advance with them to the farthest point"

As the men of Pettigrew's (now Marshall's) Brigade moved into line they were clearly aware that two other brigades were in position to support them if needed, "Billy' Mahone's Virginians and General Carnot Posey's Mississippians. Surely these 10 regiments would spring into action if the Union line was broken.

To the rear of Davis' brigade Dr H.H. Hubbard of the 2nd Mississippi set up his hospital operation and dressing station in a swale about a mile from town. With him would be other senior surgeons Robert Taggart of the 42nd and Dr. Benjamin Green of the 55th When the cannonade would begin they would expect a slow stream of stretcher bearers bringing victims of shell fragments and tree limb injuries. It had been the duty of the assistant surgeons from each regiment that morning to set up field stations. Assistant Surgeon Dr. James Wilson wrote about the morning preparation. "Early in the morning I was ordered to my command. I had been constantly engaged during the previous day and half the night attending the wounded of the first day's battle, then I slept three hours, hastily ate my breakfast and hurried to the battlefield. I found Holt and Shields waiting for me and together started out to find a suitable location. **(Wilson, The Confederate**

Soldier, p. 120) (author note: Assistant Surgeon Joseph Holt of the 2nd Mississippi had been a pre-war surgeon; Asst. Surgeon William Shields with the 11th Mississippi had enlisted Harpers Ferry, Virginia in June of 1861) Other assistant surgeons would include Assistant Surgeon Legrand James Wilson, a 27 year old who had enlisted in Grenada, Mississippi on May 5, 1862 and the 55th's assistant Surgeon W.T. Parker.

In the lull that followed the movement of the regiments to their forward battle positions, a number of men were able to survey the fields of the coming engagement. From Company B of the 26th North Carolina Thomas Cureton, now Captain following the death of Captain William Wilson, moved slightly forward of the regiment to observe the features of Cemetery Ridge across the valley. With him was Captain Samuel Wagg of company B of the 26th. They viewed the valley and saw that the Union forces lined the distant horizon. Captain Cureton had been slightly wounded by a bullet on July 1, a graze on his left shoulder but would be ready for action this day. **(T.L. Cureton to "Dear Sir", 15 June 1890 & 22 June 1890, John Lane Papers, SHC)**

From the 14th Tennessee Captain June Kimble would also venture out in front of the regimental line to view the fields that must be crossed. He later recalled "I sought to locate the point on Cemetery Ridge about which our Brigade and our regiment would strike the enemy provided our advance be made in a straight line. Realizing what was before me and the brave boys with me. I asked aloud the question 'June Kimble, are you going to do your duty today?—I'll do it so help me God." When Kimble returned from his scouting mission Private P.S. Waters (14th TN Co A) asked him how things looked and Kimble replied "Boys, if we have to go it will be hot for us . . ."

From the 11th Mississippi Third Lieutenant Pleasant Goolsby of Company E scouted out the terrain that his regiment would soon cross. Goolsby reported that the men were to charge over a mile across an open field and then attack the "blue-bellies" who are entrenched behind a stone wall recalled Private Tom Wilkins years later. **((Steven H. Stubbs; *Duty * Honor * Valor:*, p 420)**

What all these men would see was a wide valley of small rolling slopes covered in fields of clover, wheat and grass. Off in the distance stood two small white buildings to the north and a series of stone walls and fences marking the location of federal infantry and artillery. Most noteworthy was the clump of small trees at the center and the fact that the farmland in front sank as it approached the Emmitsburg road and then rose up toward the crest.

An unidentified soldier with the 26th N.C. would later write his thoughts as he sat waiting for the opening of the action, "On the morning of the Third, we were aroused to a sense of our situation, and no man who viewed that ground but felt that when the charge was made that all thought would be, blood must flow and gallant spirits must take their final flight." **(Rollins Pickett's Charge: Eyewitness Accounts: 54; Underwood, "Twenty-Sixth Regiment: 277")**

By twelve O'clock the brigade and regimental commanders were briefed on their assignments. The brigades of Brockenbrough and Davis would head for those two small whitewashed buildings while the brigades of Marshall and Fry would charge the center to the left of the copse of trees and the forward wall before it. To their right the Virginians of Pickett would take that forward wall as the forward regiments of Marshall and Fry fired into the flanks of the Union infantry at that forward wall . . . . breaking them and crushing their position.

As the lull continued men of the Tennessee and Alabama regiments with Fry held a worship service and sang some hymns and the men of the 26th could hear their prayers and songs in the distance. Captain Cureton recalled years later. **(T.L. Cureton to "Dear Sir", 15 June 1890 & 22 June 1890, John Lane Papers, SHC)** One man among them, the color bearer of the 13th Alabama carefully attached a sharp lance head to the regiments flagstaff for the coming fight. **(I.T Miller, Confederate Veteran, 2 (1895) p 281)**

E.M Hays (22nd N.C. Co M) with Scales recalled the period before the bombardment "There was kicking in my command about the balance of the Pender Division getting out of the attack" . . . "The Tar Heels of both Brigades, small in number as they were, had the determination to try" **(E.M Hayes to John Bachelder October 15, 1890, Vol. 3 pp. 1776-1777)**

Lieutenant William Peel of the 11th Mississippi would later write poetically of the look on the men's faces as they pondered their future. "the ashen hue that lingered upon every check, showed the accuracy with which the magnitude of the task before us was estimated, while the firm grasp that fixed itself upon every musket & the look of steady determination that lurked in every eye, bespoke an unflinching resolution to 'do or die'" **("Diary of William Peel", Mississippi State Archives)**

Years later, one of these surgeons Dr. James Wilson would recall the conditions of the field station he would use for the upcoming battle . . . . "We had three walls of stone between ourselves and the battlefield, which would protect us against bullets, grape and canister, and here we prepared for the coming storm and caring for our wounded, which consisted chiefly in extracting bullets, ligating bleeding vessels, checking hemorrhages in different ways, splinting broken limbs so that the poor sufferers could be sent in ambulances to the real hospital for appropriate treatment. This hospital was usually two or three miles in the rear of the battlefield. To apply the term hospital to this field station was really a misnomer. But here the Assistant Surgeon got in his ministrations of mercy to the wounded. Often we had the pleasure of saving life by the ligation of an artery or application of a tourniquet. Here often had the sad pleasure of writing down the last messages of love and affection to the dear ones at home, whispering words of consolation and hope into the ears of the dying." **(Wilson, The Confederate Soldier, p. 120)**

THE CONFEDERATE ADVANCE

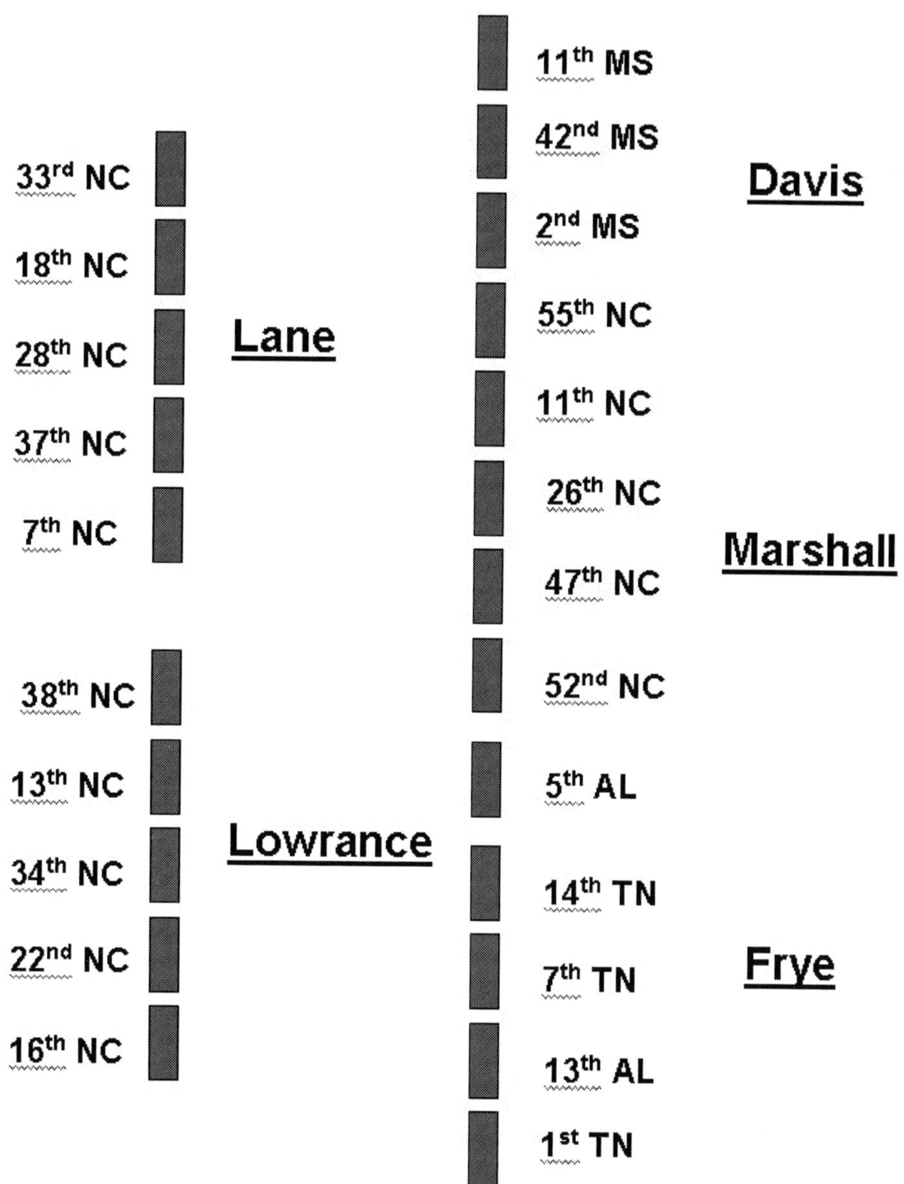

Chapter Four

The Bombardment

Captain Benjamin Little commanding the extreme right company of the 52nd North Carolina was in a position that morning to observe a council of Confederate leadership . . .

"Generals Lee, Longstreet, Hill and a number of general officers met in a shady bottom near a little branch. Lee sat on a stump, was reading a paper of some kind a long time before the action . . . . **(Andrew Cross. The War, Battle of Gettysburg and the Christian Commission. 1865, pp 26-27)**

About 1 o'clock PM, the report of a cannon to the far right was heard and was quickly answered by another far away to the left; these were the signal guns which announced the opening of one of the severest artillery duals the world has ever known. The earth fairly shook for two hours. then the firing ceased almost as suddenly as it had commenced and the infantry moved forward. **(Octavious A Wiggins, Clark's Regiments, Vol. II p. 661)**

On the right flank of Pettigrew's line Colonel Burkett Fry, who was hit by a fragment in his right shoulder called the cannonade "that deadly storm of hissing and exploding shells" **(B.D Fry, Pettigrew's Charge at Gettysburg, SHSP, (VII p 92))**

Two men in Fry's original regiment (13TH AL) who were hit by incoming artillery were 1st Lieutenant James Simpson Company F and First Lieutenant Hardy Gibson a 25 year old Cusseta farmer. In a letter to his mother July 8 after the battle, Simpson explains the event . . . "We only had one officer killed in our Regt, Lt. Gibson, a particular friend of mine. I was laying with my arm on him when he was killed by a shell passing right through his head and body, a fragment of the same shell struck me on the temple inflicting a sore little wound but I am on duty again." **(Simpson to Mother letter, July 8, 1863, Allen-Simpson Papers #29, Southern Historical Collection)** Interestingly, Lieutenant Simpson explains his own wounding slightly different in the letter he sent his wife on July 16th . . . "I received my wound just as the line started to advance and it stunned me so that I was compelled to go to the rear." **(Simpson to wife letter, July 16, 1863, Allen-Simpson Papers #29, Southern Historical Collection)**

Corporal James Bradley in Company B the 7th Tennessee saw a solid shot land within inches of his head as he hugged the ground **(F.S. Harris, *From Gettysburg*, The Lebanon Democrat August 10, 1899)**

Sergeant June Kimble 14th Tennessee Company A remembered the concussions ". . . loose grass, leaves and twigs arose from six to eight inches above the ground, hovered and quivered as birds about to drop." **(June Kimble, *Tennesseans at Gettysburg—The Retreat*, CV (XVII :460)**

Assistant Surgeon L.J Wilson in the 42nd Mississippi wrote that "The air seemed to be in a state of vibration and produced a very strange feeling in one's head" **(LeGrand J. Wilson, The Confederate Soldier (Memphis: Memphis State University Press, 1973, p 120)**

The surgeon of the 2nd Mississippi H.H. Hubbard remembered that the bombardment sounded like "the crash of Krakatoa and Pele in violent eruption"

Lieutenant William Peel in Company C of the 11th Mississippi saw a shell penetrate the body of 2nd Lieutenant Daniel Featherstone (Company F) and explode. While Private Andrew Baker from a different perspective saw Featherstone's skull split open from the blast.**(Michael Priest, *Into the Fight*, p 71)**

Peel described the scene this way . . . "In the hottest of the cannonading I heard a shell strike in the right of the reg't & turning over, as I lay on my back. I looked just in time to witness the most appalling scene that perhaps ever greeted the human eye. Lt. Daniel Featherstone from Noxubee County, was the unfortunate victim. He was a large man—would have weighted perhaps two hundred pounds. He was lying on his face, when the shell struck the ground near his head & ricochet, entered his breast, exploded about the same time & knocking him at least ten feet high & not less than twenty feet from where he was lying." **(Peel Diary, July 3, 1863)**

Baker described years later the same scene . . . . "I was a member of the University Grays, with position next on the right of the Noxubee Rifles, and remember one Featherstone in the Noxubee Rifles. While we were lying down on Seminary Ridge at Gettysburg, just behind our batteries, during the most unprecedented cannonade every witnessed on earth, and just before we went into the charge on Cemetery Heights, Featherstone was struck by a cannonball and thrown several feet in the air, his head being split wide open." **(Love, *Mississippi at Gettysburg*, p 44-45)**

Quite possibly the same blast wounded nearby Private Thomas J. Boatner in "The "Chicksaw Guards"—Company H of the 11th. Boatner was wounded by a shell fragment in the hip as he waited out the cannonade. **(Thomas Boatner, Compiled service records, National Archives)**

As the temperature continued to rise details were sent back to the rear to bring water forward to the troops. 17 year old Private W.W. Scales in Company E of the 11th Mississippi was assigned to one detail, but afraid he might miss the assault, asked for a substitute. Several men quickly volunteered to take his place and soon water was available during the bombardment. **(Love, *Mississippi at Gettysburg*, P. 43)** (Author note: The two volunteers were Privates Charles Cooper and William Broadfoot . . . neither would return in time for the assault)

Private Andrew Park (Co I 42nd Mississippi) wrote of the bombardment "We were lying down in an open field with nothing to protect us except a small ditch; and the sun was coming down on us pretty hot. Two Brigades were in this ditch and behind us was General Lee's artillery of about three hundred and sixty pieces. All of these guns of both armies were firing at the same time and it seemed as if every shell came out way. Of course we got as close to the ground as possible. I do not think that mortal men ever heard such an artillery duel as we did at that time. "**(Andrew Parks, Some of my Recollections of the Battle of Gettysburg, Arkansas Historical Society)**

At the right of Davis's line was the 55th North Carolina. Captain Howell Whitehead in Company E wrote in his diary, "we had a great many men killed. I saw one shell explode and kill five horses and two men in 20 yards of me. I also saw a shell strike a man who was lying flat on the ground. It seemed to raise him 10 to 12 feet in the air and literally shake him into mince meat . . ." (Whitehead Diary, July 3, 1863) Brigade Commander Davis wrote in his report that "Flying iron, tree limbs and splinters filled the woods . . . killing two men and wounded twenty-one during the next two hours." **(OR Series I, XXVII, Part II, p 650)**

The fury of the bombardment was not only on the infantry. Confederate artillerymen had to both fire their guns and withstand un protected, the Union artillery response. One graphic recollection was penned by Private Felix Gallaway with Captain Hugh Ross and the Georgia artillery in the McMillian Orchard. Gallaway wrote of his surprise of seeing the entire Union artillery line silent while his guns fired round after round but knew that soon shot and shell would be returned. And returned it was as leaves and tree branches scattered all around his men once Union counter fire began. His gun section fared well as Union guns never really got their exact range. **(Felix Richard Gallaway, Gettysburg—The battle and the Retreat, Confederate Veteran XXI:338)**

The Confederate Artillery

In front of the brigades of Pettigrew were the batteries of Confederate guns. To the far right in front of the 1st Tennessee and 13th Alabama was the Charlotte Artillery commanded by Captain Joseph Graham. This battery consisted of 2 Napoleon smoothbores and two 12lb Howitzers. manned by men from North Carolina. In front of the left wing of Archer were the guns of Captain James Wyatt in the Ablemare Virginia Artillery. This battery was composed of one 10lb Parrott rifle and two three inch rifled cannon. Next, to the north, were the two Companies (A & C) of the Sumter Battalion led by Captains Hugh Ross and John Wingfield. With a total of seven guns, they fired from a position at the point where Pettigrew's old Brigade, now commanded by Col. John Marshall, touched Archer's brigade. Behind them lay the 52nd North Carolina and 47th North Carolina. The Sumter Battalion, from Georgia, had a variety of cannons including two 20 lb Parrotts, a 12lb howitzer, a 3" Parrott Navy rifle and two 3" rifled cannon. Next in line northward was the Fredericksburg Battery commanded by Captain E. Marye with 2 Napoleon smoothbores and 2-10lb Parrott rifles. Directly behind them was the left wing of Marshall's brigade (the 26th NC & 11th NC). Next came the batteries in front of Davis's Mississippi Brigade (plus of course the 55th North Carolina). The Crenshaw Battery (Virginia) under Captain E.B. Brunson and the Pee Dee artillery from South Carolina commanded by Lieutenant William Zimmerman occupied this space. Brunson had 2 Napoleon's and 2 12lb Howitzers while Zimmerman had four 3' rifled cannon. The Pee Dee artillery (sometime called McIntosh's artillery) had been among the guns that had opened up the first day's battle providing cover for Heth's opening attack. Finally in front of Davis's flank stood 4 Napoleon's with the Purcell Artillery led by Virginian Joseph McGraw. The Purcell Artillery was also known by many as the Pegram Battery after the man who gave it fame at Fredericksburg. These 30 cannons in front of Pettigrew and Trimble would draw intense Union counter battery action.

In the Union lines the effect of the Confederate guns was being felt. A number of Union guns were disabled and the infantry was impacted . . . . "Up and down the Union line the infantrymen endured the maelstrom,helpless to respond to the ceaseless bombardment. For the troops of Alexander Hays' division in Ziegler's Grove, severed limbs from the oak and hickory trees added to the danger. It was "perfectly awful, murderous" according to a 108 NY man. One Federal soldier noted that the birds in the grove began to fly wildly in the air, "all out of their wits with fright." Numbers of men in the New York regiment "were so shook up" they began to waver. Lt. David Shields of Hays' staff rode to them, shouting encouragement and telling them to stay at their posts. Some of them broke for the rear. "It was an appalling sight," complained Shields. Officers in the 108th drew swords, threatening to use them on any man who left the ranks. Brigade commander Colonel Thomas Smyth went to the regiment to restore order and was stuck in the face with a piece of shell." **(Wert, Jeffry D. *Gettysburg Day Three*, p 169)**

Up front with Marshall's brigade Captain Thomas Cureton (now promoted and in command of Company B 26th NC)) remembered that the sound was like an earthquake as incoming and outgoing fire shook the ground. **(T.J. Cureton to "Dear Sir," June 22, 1890, John Lane Papers, SHC)** Another soldier from North Carolina remembered the sound to be like a massive passing thunder storm "The lumbering of the thunder overhead was but as the wail of an infant to the roar of a lion in comparison with the deafening roar that shook the ground" **(Gibbon, Personal Recollections of the Civil War: p 146)** from near the same location another soldier Joseph Wheeler in Co. D of the 26th NC recalled that the sky "was clouded with smoke, and the air filled with shrieking shot and shell . . . until it seemed as through hell itself had broken loose." **(Joseph Wheeler, Reminiscences of Gettysburg, p 213)**

One of the most famous stories about the intensity of the bombardment centers around Private Jeremiah Gage of Company A of the 11th Mississippi who was hit with a shell fragment which torn his left arm and his abdomen. Being told that he was fatally wounded he wrote a final letter to his mother . . . .

> Gettysburg Penn.
> July 3rd.
>
> My dear Mother
>
> This is the last you may ever hear from me. I have time to tell you that I died like a man. Bear my loss best you can. remember that I am true to my country and my greatest regret at dying is she is not free and that you and sisters are robbed of my worth what ever that may be. I hope this will reach you and you must not regret that my body can not be obtained. It is a mere matter of form anyhow. This is for sisters too as I can not write more. Send my dying release to Miss Mary . . . you know who.
>
> J.S. Gage
> Co. A. 11th Miss.

Later as he neared death, Gage said: "Boys, come near me, its growing dark. I can't see you. Come round me and take my hand."

His last words were; "I want you to bury me . . . . I want to be buried like my comrades. deep, boys, deep, so the beast won't get me."

Dr John Holt who treated Gage reported "I turned to him and he pointed to his left arm. I quickly exposed it and found that a cannon ball had nearly torn it away between the elbow and the shoulder. I made some encouraging remark—when he smiled and said : Why, Doctor that is nothing; here is where I am really hurt, and he laid back his blanket and exposed the lower abdomen torn from left to right by a cannon shot, largely carrying away the bladder, much intestine, and a third of the right half of the pelvis; but in both wounds so grinding and twisting the tissues that there was no hemorrhage." **(Dr. John Holt, quoted in Maud Morrow Brown, The University Grays: Company A, Eleventh Mississippi Regiment; Army of Northern Virginia, 1861-1865 (Richmond, Virginia Garrey and Massie (1940)**

An eye witness to the fatal wounding of Jeremiah Gage was Private H.Q. Bridges who had caught up with the 11th at Harper's Ferry and joined there in May of 1862. He was wounded in the fighting later that day but had been near Gage when the shell exploded.

In 1913 he would write a letter to Gage's married sister in New Orleans . . .

Mrs. V.G. Armistead
2616 Royal St
New Orleans, La

Sixth District Court
717 E 15th Street
Kansas City, Mo 7/26/1913

". . . . We were in the battle the first day until dark; the second we were not in action, but in the afternoon of the third day we were in a strip of woods hard by Emmitsburg Road about one mile south of the town. I was within a few feet of him when he was struck . . . . My remembrance at this long distance is that Jere was sitting in a posture while most of us, except of course the officers, were lying down. Presently a 24 lb shell exploded immediately in front of us and Jere called out that he was hit, one fragment of the shell almost tearing away his left arm from the socket, and another fragment hitting him in the abdomen. Jim Dailey, also one of our mess, being litter bearer that day at once gathered him up and bore him away to the field hospital about 200 yards to the south of us."

H.Q Bridges
(Author note :Hugh Quinn Bridges Co. A)

(Author note: Jim Dailey's brother Frank would be killed in the fighting July 3)

Another Mississippi soldier who survived the bombardment 29 year old Private John B Crawford Company D—Capt. Locke's Company raised in Marshall County, wrote his wife afterward that "If the crash of worlds and all things combustible had been coming in collision with each other, it could not have surpassed it seemingly. To me it was like the magazine of Vengeance blown up." **(John B Crawford to wife July 8, 1863 Crawford Civil War Letters MDAH)** "The ground fairly shook beneath the feet of the assembled armies from the terrible concussion." **(Brown, University Grays: p 37)**

For the regiments of Trimble the bombardment seemed less intense as they were far behind the Confederate artillery beyond the woods in the fields. Colonel Avery commanding the

33rd North Carolina wrote "On the 3rd day we occupied the 2nd line in an open field under the heaviest artillery bombardment I have ever heard or seen. The heat was so intense that I went to the front of my regiment under a solitary tree. Having noticed that Johnny (2nd Lt John Caldwell Co E) and John Happoldt (3rd Lieutenant Co D) seemed shaken by the heat, I made them come forward and lie down by me for an hour." **(Letter from Colonel C.M. Avery to Tod and Mrs. Caldwell, July 18, 1863, Southern Historical Collection #128)**

Captain William L Thornburg (Co H 38th NC) would soon be hit on the advance and lose an eye but he remembered the cannonade that preceded his wounding "On the third day after being exposed for several hours to the enemy's shells while supporting our own batteries . . . . A perfect shower of shot and shells" **(William Thornburg letter to Raleigh Observer, September 25, 1877, from Company Shops, NC)**

Some Union shells did hit the area occupied by Trimble's men. Private Aurelius Dula a 20 year old soldier in the 22nd NC who had been wounded at Gaines Mill was hit by pieces of exploding shell during the bombardment which wounded his right foot, right leg & left arm. **(Aulelius Dula letter to mother, July 22, 1863, UNC Archives)**

Yet in the middle of this hell some men could focus on distractions. One story told by many men was of a fox that had run straight into the ranks of the 7th North Carolina at the height of the cannonade. "On the 3rd July 1863 at Gettysburg when the fearful cannonade was at its height on our right, a fox alarmed for its safety came at full speed from the direction of the enemy's lines and in it's attempt to pass our lines it was surrounded by laughing and yelling officers and men and Major Tuner of the 7th dispatched it with his sword. This incident shows the makeup of the North Carolina Confederate soldiers, and that no danger, however great, deterred him from the enjoyment of a little sport" **(Captain James Harris, Clark's Regiments, 7th North Carolina)**

Visitors today on the fields of Gettysburg still see such foxes running through the fields and it seems that on that day in July of 1863 several foxes met their death. Private Wilbur von Swarigen in Company K of the 28th North Carolina at the age of 80 years recalled another such incident. "Reynard was stoned to death. This old red fox was "rousted" from his lair and ran from pillar to post. Wherever he ran the "rebel yell" was raised until a well directed rock killed him" **(Van Swaringen Reminiscences, GNMP library collection)**

CHAPTER FIVE

The Advance

Suddenly the Artillery bombardment ceased and Sergeant June Kimble 14th Tennessee Company A recalled taking a deep breath as he thought about what would happen next as his comrades would soon march out upon that field. (**(June Kimble, *Tennesseans at Gettysburg—The Retreat*, CV (XVII :460)**

It was a grand sight as far as the eye could see to the right and to the left two lines of Confederate soldiers with waving banners pressing on into the very jaws of death . . . **(Octavious A Wiggins, Clark's Regiments, Vol. II p. 661)**

General Pettigrew never received a direct order to advance but saw Picket's Regiments forming up and then gave the command to his Brigades. The word was passed down to regimental commanders and soon the men from Mississippi and Tennessee and Alabama were on their feet and forming up as well. Here and there a few men had been overcome by the heat but one officer 32 year old 3rd Lieutenant William B Taylor (Co A) in the 11th North Carolina saw men "fainting all along the line before starting on the charge" **(William B. Taylor to mother July 29, 1863 in Mast, Six Lieutenants p 13)**

With his Brigade Colonel Fry recalled that he had lost a number of enlisted men and officers during the cannonade and was happy that at last his men could move forward instead of being trapped in an artillery barrage. "After lying inactive under that deadly storm of hissing and exploding shells, it seemed a relief to go forward to the desperate assault." **(B.D. Fry, Pettigrew's Charge at Gettysburg, SHSP (VII:92)** Fry was a veteran who had faced artillery before at Sharpsburg and at Seven Pines in addition to his early career in the Mexican War.

One of Fry's officers in the 7th Tennessee, Captain Tate of Company H was immobilized by a Union shell explosion early in the advance . . . "At Gettysburg Capt. Tate was so stunned by the first cannon-shot from the enemy that his comrades left him for dead, but he rallied and rejoined his command later that day." **(Confederate Veteran, 1898, p 275)**

The geography of the fields to be crossed by the Brigades of Pettigrew and Trimble varied widely and the result was several different patterns emerged. On the right of Pettigrew, Fry's men had been located in a hollow area, "a finger of trees and brush" one man called it. Thus somewhat protected they had experienced less direct cannon fire during the bombardment. As they assembled, these men from Tennessee and Alabama could not see their target and in fact had first to march up an elevation as they began for the first 300 yards. Only when they reached a point eighty percent away from the Union lines could they view the panorama of the battlefield. This also provided early protection from direct view by even the sharpest Union artillery telescope.

The opposite geographic scenario was true of the Brigade of Davis to the other end. Davis's regiments looked out over the entire battlefield as they assembled and had to march downhill for the first 200 yards until they approached the back fields of the Bliss farm. This helps explain why the reports concerning Davis suggest that his regiments, which started late" rushed ahead to not only catch up but pass Marshall's brigade. The downhill path aided their speed.

Finally, in the center Marshall faced the most even and level ground. It is far more level a path from the starting point of the Marshall advance through the Bliss Farm and over Stevens Run. The visitor to the battlefield today can both view and walk these three very different paths.

The major feature which dominated the landscape of the Pettigrew-Trimble assault was the large Bliss House and barn that sat astride the attack route. The Bliss barn was a huge construction consisting of two stories. The building was over 70 feet long and 35 feet wide. It had the traditional overhang construction with a dirt ramp leading to the second story. The lower level was built of stone and had windows and barn doors which could be used by sharpshooters. The second story was built of brick and had another set of windows and doors as well. It is estimated that 100 men could occupy the barn effectively. The large house which sat 30 yards to the Northwest was also large and two stories. It had three separate front doors facing south. It is estimated that in the two days of fighting around the Bliss House and Barn over 800 casualties were suffered by both sides. Between the morning of July 2 and the burning of the barn and house by soldiers from the 14th Connecticut late in the morning of July 3 possession of the property had changed hands 11 times. By the opening of the bombardment the house and barn had both been burnt to the ground but the smoldering ruins clearly marked the middle of the Pettigrew-Trimble terrain.

At one point in the early advance General Pettigrew rode out to the front of his old brigade now commanded by Colonel Marshall stating "Now Colonel for the honor of the good old North State. Forward" **(Underwood; 26th Regiment p 365)**

Captain Louis Young riding along side General Pettigrew as his aide wrote later that the day seemed "beautifully clear. before us lay bright fields and a fair landscape, embracing hill and dale and mountain . . . and beyond, fully three-fourths of a mile away, loomed Cemetery Ridge it's heights capped with cannon. **(Young, *Pickett's Brigade at Gettysburg*, p 127)**

While Marshall and Fry's regiments moved forward it was clear that Davis and Brockenbrough had yet to leave the protection of the trees. Pettigrew's chief of staff Louis G. Young was sent to retrieve Davis but ran into Davis's regiments emerging from the woods as he approached. Young was told to forget the role and value of Brockenbrough who in Pettigrew's opinion could play no effective role in the fight due to poor leadership and demoralization. **(Young; Battle of Gettysburg, p 5)**

After clearing the woods, Sergeant Kimble, Co A 14th Tennessee, rushed forward of the battle line and reviewed the regiment. "Turning his back upon the Federals, he faced the line and studied it from right to left. The magnificent spectacle of the regiment emerging into open ground with the breathtaking precision of the Prussian Guards left an indelible impression upon him which he could never find the words to adequately describe." (dramatically painted by Michael Priest, *Into the Fight*, p 87). At the same moment on the opposite end of the Pettigrew Line with the 11th Mississippi troops Lieutenant William Peel in Company C scanned the faces of his men and was struck by the gray faces sensing that each knew the seriousness of the task ahead **(Diary of Lieutenant William Peel," Mississippi State Archives)**

The seasoned reader of literature on Gettysburg and in particular on the July 3 assault must by now have thought, "When will the author discuss whether Pettigrew had created a single or a double line advance for his regiments from Fry down through Davis? To the less veteran student an explanation is in order. For years, the debate has raged between historians regarding the issue of whether General James Pettigrew created for this particular assault a rather unique formation of two separate lines or was his advance in the typical regimental pattern of 10 companies abreast. Many have suggested and provided powerful evidence that for this assault Pettigrew ordered each of the brigades and therefore regiments to place half their companies in a line supported some 10 yards back by the other half of the companies. This would result in strength in depth for each brigade. To the Union observer this would create the image of a skirmish line followed by a first and second Pettigrew line followed by a third Trimble line. This is exactly the image many in blue reported. However, equally determined critics suggest that no evidence of any command by Pettigrew to create such a pattern exists; that such a pattern would be so unusual in battle that some mention would have been made in official reports of it's unique nature. Both sides provide excellent evidence for the debate. This author himself has gone back and forth on both sides of the issue. After examining the literature and the evidence for over three years in preparation for this writing of this book, I find no compelling case for the two line theory and consider it a product of the poor visibility of the observers in the Union lines.

For the reader to gain perspective of the line of march, a walking tour of the fields at Gettysburg is recommended. The downward sloping field of clover and weeds runs 1,500 yards then bottoms out as it reaches the Bliss House and barn with surrounding orchards and small shade trees. By the time of the July 3 advance the Bliss house and barn had been burnt to the ground and what remained were collapsed chimneys and smoldering ruins. Through these ruins and scattered barn yard debris they would travel a short distance on the Bliss farm slope. Another 200 yards of slightly downward sloping would bring the advancing forces to the ruined fence line that marked the location of Stevens Run, a shallow ditch filled on rainy days with running water but this day in July 1863 only traces of mud remained. As the rebels crossed Stevens Run they entered fields of ripened grain which would run all the way 800 yards to the Emmitsburg Road ahead.

As the regiments passed by the artillery batteries and headed out into the open fields at least one artilleryman with the Charlotte Artillery Private Joseph Graham recalled that the infantry advanced steadily "but I fear with too feeble determination" hearing one soldier state "That is worse than Malvern Hill" "I don't hardly think that position can be carried" **(Max R. Williams "Awful Affair" p 48)**

Yet the sight of the six brigades of Pettigrew and Trimble marching forth in three (or was it two?) massive lines across the fields proved breathtaking to both Yankee and Confederate. One group of Confederate observers on Seminary Ridge viewed the advance and observed that the splendid lines of Pettigrew and Trimble seemed cover twice the distance as Picket's These officers shouted "Here they come! There they are! Hurrah! Thinking one later noted that it must be Hill's Whole Corps on the advance **(Shallow, Southern Bivouac, February 1886. Hoke p 396)** A Yankee officer would write "The whole line of battle looked like a stream or river of silver moving towards us" **(Harwell, Two Views of Gettysburg: p 189)** In the 12th New Jersey Private William Haines called the advance "the grandest sight . . . their lines looked to be as straight as a line could be, their bayonets glistening in the sun from right to left, as far as the eye could reach . . ." **(Haines, History of Company F of the 12th NJ Volunteers, p 42)**

Another rather unusual view came from Private Asa S. Hardman who was a Union prisoner from the 3rd Indiana Cavalry being held in the attic of a house on Seminary Ridge directly next to the Confederate lines "Suddenly, the rebel batteries also became silent and while I watched, *three long lines* of rebel infantry sprang out in front of their guns, and pausing a moment as if to take long breath, seemingly pitched forward like a resistless wave that threatened to destroy everything in its path. I never saw such a sight before and I never want to see it again. It was grand beyond my power to describe. I saw them pause an instant, and then shot forward, with their lines as true as if on dress parade with their muskets at 'right shoulder shift' their elbows touching the left. As our artillery, which had suddenly found voice, ploughed great gaps in their lines, they would close up and still move forward with an impulse that seemed irresistible" **(Asa Sleath Hardman, "As a Union Prisoner at the Battle of Gettysburg", Civil War Times Illustrated, I, No 4 (July,1962, P 49)**

2nd Lieutenant S.A. Ashe with Marshall's brigade looked at the soldiers and battle flags and remembered "their bright guns gleaming in the noonday sun and their innumerable battle flags flying in the breeze, making as fine a pageant as was ever seen on any field of battle." **(Captain S.A. Ashe "The Pickett-Pettigrew Charge" p.141)**

Captain John H Thorp of Company A with the 47th North Carolina later wrote about the effect of an exploding shell on the company next to his. "We were met by a furious storm of shells and canister and further on by the more destructive rifles of the two army corps confronting us. One shell struck the right company, killing three men, and exploding in the line of file closers, by the concussion, felled to the earth every one of them. The other companies were faring no better. Still our line, without a murmur, advanced, delivering its steady fire amid the rebel yells . . ." ***("The 47th NC at Gettysburg",* by Captain John H Thorp, Rocky Mount, NC, and 9 April, 1901)**

Private Albert Caison Co I of the 26th North Carolina knew what was coming "He looked at the federal artillery waiting ahead, and concluded that an untold number of men now marching alongside him would soon be cut down like harvested grain. Even after calculating the odds, however, he remained confident that the Yankees would soon be routed." **(Gragg, Covered with Glory, p 185; Caison, "Southern Soldiers": p160)**

Yet Lieutenant William Peel Co C 11th MS) wrote in his diary in a Union prison camp before dying there that the scene of beauty quickly changed to carnage "Far over the field to the front, at the distance of perhaps a little less than a mile & near the top of the ascent, there lay a long dark line, parallel with our advancing front, which a stranger would probably not have understood, but which we recognized as a stone fence—something very common in this section of country. Nor were we blind to another important fact: that behind this fence, on the more elevated knolls, was ranged the enemy's scowling artillery.

The peaceful contemplation of the scene however was destined to be short lived. Our debut into the field was greeted with abroad-side from the long line of artillery that sent a storm of screaming howling shells, across the field that burst & tore the timber behind us in a frightful manner. Volley after volley resounded as broadsides were forth, until they subsided into one unbroken roar, louder than the thunder-peals of Heaven. Shells screaming and bursting around us scattered their fragments & projectiles in every direction." **(Diary of Lieutenant William Peel," Mississippi State Archives)**

The late start of Davis and even later start of the Brockenbrough regiments would result in poor coordination of the four front brigades for the remainder of the assault. It appears that Davis's command would be acting almost independent for the remainder of the charge from the beginning until they would dash separately upon the Union works around the Bryan barn and the wall to the west of the Barn. One man who had decided to join the advance was Reverend Thomas Witherspoon Chaplin of the 42nd Mississippi who reportedly "took a gun and went into battle" **(Thomas Dwight Witherspoon Papers, University of Mississippi Collection)**

The two brigades under Trimble's command—Lawrence and Lane seemed to start advancing exactly as planned. Trimble later noted "there was no hesitation in my command at the start" **(Letter from General Trimble, Raleigh Observer November 30, 1877, pp 33-34)**

"In a few minutes after the start, we were obliqued rapidly to the left to take the place of Brockenbrough's Brigade, which had broken. **(Octavious A Wiggins, Clark's Regiments, Vol. II p. 661)**

Colonel Burkett Fry wrote that the Union artillery started ripping huge holes in his and Marshall's brigades but that the troops kept closing ranks and kept going as if on parade. Private James Bishop with the White Plains Rangers (Co C 5th AL battalion) was wounded in the back by a shell fragment before he reached the road. Private Thom Denson with Company F of the 1st Tennessee was reported to have been killed on the advance as well. In the 7th Tennessee Co G was the flag company. Commanded by Captain William Graves who was wounded most of the 24 man company would remain at the road and loose only 2 killed and 4 wounded. Two would be captured at the road.

Watching from Cemetery Ridge Captain Winfield Scott in the 126th NY recalled that he was "so absorbed with the beauty and grandeur of the scene that I became oblivious to the shells that were bursting around us." **(Scott, Pickett's Charge as seen from the front lines: *Gettysburg Magazine*, pp10-11)**

Across the fields the Confederate troops could see what waited for them. One Private in the charge remembered "We could see the mouths of the gaping cannon waiting for us to get in range to pour bushels of grape and canister into our ranks . . ." **(Martin Hazlewood, *Gettysburg Charge* 1896)** Private Benjamin Thomas in Co E of the 52nd NC was hit in the back with a shell fragment halfway across the field.

Union artillery rained in on the front three brigades of Fry, Marshall and Davis while Lawrence and Lane some 150 yards to their rear seems to have escaped heavy incoming artillery rounds at least until they reached the shallow stream of Steven's Run in front of the Bliss House. Major J. McLeod Turner of the 7th North Carolina recalled after the war "the line of battle was as good as I ever saw; our loss up to within a few yards of the road had been very slight." **(Michael Taylor, "North Carolina at The Pickett-Pettigrew-Trimble Charge at Gettysburg"** ***The Gettysburg Magazine*****, no 8 (January 1993)**

General Trimble summarized the position of his line in a letter in 1877. "When the charge commenced, about 3:00 o'clock I followed Pettigrew's (Heth) division about 140 yards in rear, a sufficient distance to prevent the adverse fire raking both ranks as we marched down the slope. Not with standing the losses as we advanced, the men marching with the deliberation and accuracy of men on drill. I observed the same in Pettigrew's line. When the later was within 150 yards of the Emmitsburg Road, they seemed to sink into the earth under the tempest of fire poured into them." **(I.R. Trimble letter to the Raleigh Observer, November 30, 1877)**

Yet the men of Scales and Lane's Brigades saw what was coming as they crossed what Colonel William Lowrance later called in his OR report "a wide, hot and already crimson plain" **(OR 27, 2 p 659)** Lourance goes on to state "We advanced upon the enemy's line, which was in full view, at a distance of one mile. Now their whole line of artillery was playing upon us, which was on an eminence on our front, strongly fortified and supported by infantry. While we were thus advancing, many fell, I saw but few in that most hazardous hour who even tried to shirk duty. All went forward with a cool steady step, but ere we had advanced over third-thirds of the way, troops from the front came tearing through our ranks, which caused many of our men to break . . . **(Civil War Record of Lt. William Jasper Edney of Jack's Creek, Yancey County)**

General Lane wrote in 1877 his summary of the role of Union artillery on his men, "As soon, however as Pettigrew's and Trimble's divisions fairly appeared in the open ground at the top of Seminary Ridge, furious discharges of artillery were poured on them from the line in their front and from their left flank by artillery which overlapped them near Gettysburg. To the artillery was soon added small arms in a ceaseless storm as they marched down the smooth, even slope." **(Letter from General Lane to Raleigh Observer from Va. Ag'l and Mech'l College Blacksburg, Va., September 7, 1877)**

When artillery finally found the range of Trimble's two brigades Lieutenant Colonel William Asbury Speer of the 28th North Carolina was knocked down by a shell explosion that killed two and wounded three around him. **(Speer,** ***Voices from Cemetery Hill*****, p.107)**

In Company I of the 28th NC, the old company of Lt. Col William A. Speer, 5 men were taken out by one exploding shell. "Jones Holcomb, Jonas MaCokey were killed dead. A shell exploded in the line as we were charging, killing them both dead, wounding 3 others and knocking me down." **(Speer to Father & Mother July 10, 1863 from Hagerstown, Md, in Speer, Voices from Cemetery Hill, pp 105-107)**

Private James South in Company A of the 34th North Carolina with Scales was knock senseless with a shell concussion while advancing **(James South, Compiled Military Records, National Archives)**

One veteran with the rear Trimble line, Acting Adjutant of the 38th North Carolina Lieutenant Henry Moore stated, "We reached another fence, which was on the side of the road. Here we halted and endeavored to reform our line with the men who had become mixed up from different commands." The adjutant of the 38th NC wrote to a newspaper after the war "No one who was not in it can imagine the terrible fire of the batteries on the right and those Parrots on Round Top. And the batteries in front were very busy" . . . . "Our men falling in every direction" **(letter from Henry Moore, *Raleigh Observer*, November 29, 1877)**

However the Union artillery was still doing its harshest damage on the front line advance. From south to north along the line. Lt. James M Simpson of the 13th Alabama was hit by a shell fragment early in the movement and went to the rear. He wrote his wife later "I think I was providentially saved by the wound for had (I gone) across the field there would have been little probability of my escape." **(James Simpson to wife July 16, 1863, Allen Simpson papers UNC)** In the cluster of men around Flag bearer Private Wiley Woods Company F of the 1st Tennessee were two brothers, Stant and Thomas Denson. Stant would fall on the way to Emmitsburg Pike while his brother would promise Woods that he would take the flag if Woods would fall. **(Wiley Woods, *The First Tennessee Flag at Gettysburg*, CV Battles William Perkins Library Duke University**)

In the same location, Lieutenant John Moore Co. B in the 7th Tennessee would write that the sound was "a deepening roar that no exaggeration of language can heighten" **(Moore; *Battle of Gettysburg,* p 250)**

In his colorful narrative after the war senior Captain J.B. Turney Co. K with the 1st Tennessee recalled that . . . for three miles from right to left we charged in an unbroken line, across the fields; through the ravines over fences—on we went, bent on victory or death. The lead rained; gallant Colonel George, of the First Tennessee fell wounded; thirty steps farther and Colonel Fry was checked by an enemy bullet—wounded in the leg. He called to me and asked for Colonel George, and, when informed of his wound, said to me 'Captain, take command of the regiment. Proceed with the charge, but don't stop to fire a gun.' **(Captain J.B. Turney, "The First Tennessee at Gettysburg", Confederate Veteran, VII (1900), pp 535-537)**

In Company C of the 47th North Carolina, 1st Lieutenant George Whiting a 21 year old druggist from Wake Co wrote that there was "decimation of our ranks" from the artillery fire. His Captain Campbell Iredell had his "arm shot off" and died during the advance and Whiting took command. Captain Iredell was also a druggist by trade and the two had enlisted together February 27, 1862 into Company C in Wake County. **(George M. Whiting to editor, March 18, 1867, Paris Papers; Compiled Service records, National Archives)** In the same company, Corporal R.B. Beddington (Company C) a 26 year old carpenter was severely wounded by a shell during the advance and later died. The second Lieutenant Nathaniel Brown was shocked by a shell but only had a fragment graze on his middle finger of his right hand.

34 year old lawyer, Captain Joseph J. Davis (Co G 47th NC) reported "My company was next to the extreme left of the regiment and when not far from the enemy's works, say not more than 100 yards a Sergeant of an adjoining company (Serg. Gilliam, I think, of Alamance) called my attention to the fact that the troops the left of us were giving way and stated that all his officers had been shot down and asked what to do? I looked and saw that at some distance to the left of us, the troops had given up but our supports were then advancing in admirable style and I think that not more than 100 and fifty yards to our rear. I called the Sergeant's attention to this and said: "our supports are coming and we an whip them yet" Colonel Graves, who was to the right of me had kept the regiment well in hand and was urging the men on and we advanced 50 or 60 yards further and to within 30 or 40 yards of the enemy's works (nothing but the road intervening) when I discovered the day was lost. The supports had not come up and as far as I could see, on either side of me, our troops had given way." Davis would be captured and held until the end of the war. (Author note: Sgt. Jesse Gilliam was killed minutes later. The 28 year old Co. K soldier with the "Alamance Minutemen" had two brothers wounded on July 1) **Hon. Joseph Davis September 20, 1877 to the Raleigh Observer, from Louis, NC)**

(Author note Davis, who became a Judge after the war, mentions that Sgt Gilliam told him that that all his officers (Co K) had been "shot down". This would have included 1st 19 year old Lt. James Watson wounded in the right check of his face on the advance and 2nd Lt. Thomas Taylor 28 years old appointed 3/13/62 and 3rd Lt. Felix Poteat 26 years old enlisted Camp Campbell 7/25/62.

One of the first to fall in the 11th North Carolina with Marshall was Private N. O. Harris a 24 yr. old from Mechlenburg in Company A. He would be hit by a fragment from a bursting shell in his right shoulder and return to a medical station. The 30 men in his company would advance that day under the command of brothers Captain William Hand and 2nd Lieutenant Robert Hand. Captain Hand would be captured at the road and his brother Robert would be hit in the back while retreating (only to be captured in a hospital wagon in Greencastle, Pa days later). The surviving officer 22 year old 3rd Lieutenant William Taylor would report that only 8 men made it back to the lines from his company.

The flag bearer of the 47th North Carolina, Private Robert Weeden, a 21 year old from Alamance County in flag Company K was wounded in the thigh by a shell as he crossed the fields. He was taken back to Seminary ridge and taken south where he died on July 23rd. In his regiment Captain John Brown, age 34, and Lieutenant John Jones, age 22, in

Company I were also wounded in the advance. Both Wake County officers would survive and Brown would be wounded again both at Bristoe Station and Ream's Station.

General Pettigrew himself behind Marshall's brigade was wounded soon in the advance as shell fragments broke some bones in his left hand.

The flag bearer of the 1st Tennessee Wiley Woods (Co F) saw several comrades go down wounded around him by artillery fragments before he crossed the Emmitsburg road. **(Wiley Woods, The First Tennessee Flag at Gettysburg, *Confederate Veteran Papers*)**

To the left in Davis's brigade A single shell explosion over the 11th Mississippi took out five soldiers in the company of William Peel soon after passing through the artillery batteries. **(William Love, *Mississippi at Gettysburg*, p 44)** Peel described the shells which "burst and tore the timber behind us in a frightful manner" **(Peel Diary, p 29)**

One Mississippi officer wrote later that the fragments of shell resulted in "decimation of our ranks" **(George Whiting—Editor, March 17, 1867, Paris Papers UNC)** Still, many of the Union shots flew overhead striking the tree line where the Mississippi troops had been before the advance. Lieutenant William Peel observed with relief.

To counter their slow start, Davis's regiments moved forward at a double pace resulting in a bunching of the line. The result: better targets for artillery bursts. Yet Davis himself recalled later that the men "displayed great coolness" "never for a moment did they cower" remembered one proud soldier from Mississippi **(Love, *"Mississippi at Gettysburg", p* 43)**

Yet Davis would suffer terrible casualties from the Union artillery before he reached the road. "The 11th Mississippi would lose 312 of its 592 men in Pickett's Charge, and easily a third to a half that number fell before Yankee Artillery." **(Stephen Sears, *Gettysburg*, p 425)** Brigade Commander Davis reported that "Not a gun was fired at us until we reach ed a strong post and rail fence about three-quarters of a mile from the enemy's position when we were met by a heavy fire of grape, canister and shell, which told sadly upon our ranks" . . . . The enemy fire commanded our front and our left with fatal effect." **(Davis OR Report Series I, XXVII, Part II, p.651)** The worst hit, of course, was the 11th Mississippi which had not been in the action on July 1. When Brockenbrough's regiments left the field the 11th Mississippi was open to flanking fire from both artillery and infantry. One man from the 11th 29 year old Private W.P. Heflin (Company D "The Neshoba Rifles") wrote after the war that "our line was so cut down and demoralized by the enemy's batteries before we got in gunshot distance that we could not carry the works. Heflin remained at the road wounded and would be captured. **(Heflin, *Blind Man*, 24-25)**

One of the first flag bearers to fall in the advance was Ensign and Color Sergeant William "Billy" O'Brien with the 11th Mississippi. A shell exploded directly in front of him killing him instantly. The flag he carried was blown into the air and retrieved by Private Joseph Smith of Company. Smith soon was hit by a bullet in the mouth. **(Compiled Service files)**

One shell exploded in the midst of Company E "The Prairie Guards" taking out 5 men. "The Prairie Guards" in the next 30 minutes would lose it's Captain, three lieutenants and 4 of 5 Sergeants, mostly all killed . . . . "Immediately past the fence, a large shell exploded above Company E (11th Mississippi) killing five members of that company. The concussion rendered Private Tom Wilkins unconscious, and when he cam too, he found himself in smoke and a hail of fire. Wilkins recalled 'I ran forward in a daze and up ahead I saw a few of my friends. When I caught up, I looked for my three brothers. I finally found Charlie'. Charlie sobbed as he told his brother the dreadful news, 'That shell killed both Davy and Henry'. The concussion had also blown away Tom Wilkin's Enfield rifle, but he quickly found another and charged on amid the 'maelstrom of chucks of shot and shell' screaming 'You blue-bellied bastards'" **(Steven H. Stubbs; *Duty * Honor * Valor*, p 425)**

Years after the Battle of Gettysburg former Lieutenant Colonel of the 42nd Mississippi Dr. Hillary Moseley wrote a moving account of the advance into battle, about being under fire and the numbness and detached quality he felt during the Gettysburg assault. His stream of consciousness writing captures best captures the bombardment of sensations experienced by the thousands of soldiers who advanced through the fields under fire.

"With the heavy, pealing notes of the artillery and the occasional sharp crack of the rifles, preceding all battles, begins the untold misery and suffering incidental to war. The wailing mean of the dying, the piercing shriek of the wounded are only silenced and hushed by the avalanche of passions wrought upon one in the excitement of great battle. The artillery's roar, the rattling volleys of small arms are unheard and unnoted in the excitement of the moment. Man seems to be wrought up to a point of mental intoxication and, for a time, seems to be totally oblivious of all else, but the work of death before him. To me it seems, for the moment, a frenzied dream, in which demoniac thoughts (if thoughts at all) pervade my whole nature. Comrades fall unheeded by my side. The groan or prayer of anguish may be heard, but leaves no impression upon the brain. I remember having seen the wounded and the dead, but it was only a vision, I received at the moment.

One impression—a soldier shot down just before me—the ball passing through and flitting by with that peculiar zip. As I was stepping past him, another ball crashed into his thigh, and though dying, he uttered a confusion, my whole life seemed to consist of moving my men forward. Interestingly the boys began to move on like disconcerted animals and they stood motionless. I exerted myself until I was completely exhausted. I remember sitting down for a moment to rest and recover breath but it was only for a moment. Seeing confusion more manifest, I gathered the men by their arms and gave them a good shake, and set them to firing on general stimulation until the whole line was pouring into the enemy a most deadly fire: Seeing a few men dodge off under cover, I rousted them back into line and the word was, again passed to charge, then exultant, on we moved . . ." **(Dr Hillary Moseley, "Journal of Dr. Hillary Moseley, Batesville, Mississippi)**

Historians such as Earl Hess and Stephen Sears estimate that perhaps only 50 men from the 11th Mississippi got past the road and most of those headed for the Bryan Barn.

It seems that some men of the 42nd Mississippi got mixed in with them and perhaps even drifted to their left ((**Andrew J Baker, Tribute to Capt. Magruder and Wife, Confederate Veteran Vol. 6, No. 11 (November 1898), p 507) (Col. Hugh Reid Miller, 42nd Mississippi Volunteers, and the Pickett-Pettigrew-Trimble Assault Gettysburg Magazine Issue Thirty Five January 2007)**

Adjutant S.A. Ashe of Pender's Division was impressed as "They moved in quick time and with admirable precision as if on some gala day parade. It was glorious spectacle, evoking admiration from foe and friend alike" **(Captain S.A. Ashe "The Pickett-Pettigrew Charge" p.141)**

Several Union skirmishers remained at the Bliss Barn, which by now had been burnt to the ground. One of these seems to have wounded Lt. James Newsom (Company H) of the 47th North Carolina in the shoulder. Newsome ran to his Captain and volunteered to take command of the company but needless to say was told to return to his position. In the same regiment, Company I commander Captain John Brown was put on his back by a shell burst but urged his men forward by waving his sword. **(Rogers, *Additional Sketch,* p 105)**

The first serious threat to the left of Pettigrew's line came as the skirmishers of the Davis Brigade passed the point where the 8th Ohio was located to their left (at a point directly west of the Trostle house along Emmitsburg Pike. Lt. Colonel Franklin Sawyer of the 8th Ohio recalled that "it looked as if their line of march would sweep our position, but as they advanced their direction lay considerably to our left, but soon a strong line with flags directed it's march immediately upon us **(Franklin Sawyer,** A Military History of the Eighth Regiment Ohio Infantry, **(Cleveland) 1881 p 130)** Private Thomas Potter of the 8th Ohio recounted in an 1882 newspaper story that "The left of their line came opposite Company H's position on the skirmish line, it was a magnificent sight, their well-dressed lines and colors flying" **T.S. Potter, "The Battle of Gettysburg", *National Tribune*, August 5, 1882 GNMP Library file)**

After crossing Stevens run and a fence line, which had largely been torn down during the see-saw fighting around the Bliss House and Barn, the advancing rebels would have to march through a field of ripened wheat.

Once again geographic features need to understood to see the impact of the land itself on the attack. Once across Stevens Run, the land pattern of the field changes. The Northern (or left side) of the fields rise slightly to form what is almost a knoll toward the road and toward town. This rise caused the left of Davis to be more visible that the right of Davis. The 11th Mississippi therefore emerged up this slight slope to occupy a "horizon line". The fire from both the cannons on Cemetery hill and the rifles of the 8th Ohio, which were still far off but approaching cut deep into these men of the 11th Mississippi. Conversely the swale resultant from this rise to the left gave some protection to the right regiments of Davis and enabled them to be less visible. Perhaps the shift of some companies of the 42nd Mississippi to their left was influenced by these factors. Once again the visitor to Gettysburg today can experience these geographic distinctions by walking from the Bliss farm site toward the Emmitsburg road aiming at the Bryan Barn and noting the distinctions between the rise to the left and the flat ground to the right.

This rise in elevation is where massive numbers of 11th Mississippi soldiers were killed and wounded. Here fell Colonel Green and Major Reuben Reynolds

The impact of the fence lines must also be considered. Much of the fence line was perhaps down at this point but fence lines running both east-west and north-south were never conveniently ordered to slice between regiments but rather often caused companies in each regiment to be separated from their normal neighbor companies.

At this point men may have started dropping off from the attack, Michael Priest in his book *Into the Fight,* calls their actions at this point a "stampede" . . . . "rout" . . . "streamed from the ranks in squads". But an examination of his evidence shows that his citations are based upon Priest's reinterpretation of the very words of the men who are cited. For example when Lt. Colonel Turner of the 7th North Carolina claims he saw men of Brockenbrough's Virginia brigade retreating, Priest says that Turner was mistaken and that the men were really from North Carolina. Or when he cites Pickett ordering two aides to "stem the Carolinian rout" by riding back to Longstreet he provides no evidence that their mission had anything to do with retreating North Carolinians. Finally, when he quotes Lieutenant William Peel tell his men "Steady Boys, slow Don't break yourself by running" Priest makes it seem as if Peel was talking to men who were heading back to the Confederate lines instead of actually moving too quickly forward. When Priest states that General Trimble saw "a great many of the 11th North Carolina and 26th North Carolina on the left of Marshall's line remain behind", he provide no citation or quote at all and explains that his math calculations of Marshall Regimental loses prove that Trimble would have seen such a sight. Still there were men who took advantage of the ruins of the burned Bliss barn and House and the Stevens creek bed to take cover and drop from the charge.

A reading of James Longstreet's letters of 1884, 1887 and 1896 show a very different analysis of the strength of the left flank of the Pettigrew Trimble advance. Longstreet seems to suggest that he had concerns at first regarding the weakness of Pettigrew's (read Davis's) and Trimble's (read Lane's) left flank but that after sending messengers to address the problem that the assault continued without serious injury from the left flank. This, of course stands in total opposition to those historians who see the 11th and 42nd Mississippi and the 33rd North Carolina has ravaged by Union attack and collapsing with the result being a collapse of Davis's brigade and Lane's entire left. Longstreet writes in 1896 "Colonel Latrobe was sent to General Trimble to have his men fill the line of the broken brigades, and bravely they repaired the damage . . . Trimble mended the battle of the left in handsome style . . ." **(James Longstreet, *From Manassas to Appomattox* (Philadelphia: J.B. Lippincott & Co. 1896 pp 393-394)** Longstreet's regard for the men of North Carolina that day was recorded in an article he wrote in 1887 "There is no doubt that the North Carolinians did as well as any soldiers could have done under the circumstances . . . They certainly made sufficient sacrifice, and that was all we had left to do that day." **(James Longstreet, *"Lee's Invasion of Pennsylvania"*, Century Magazine Vol. 23 (1887), pp 622-636) Finally Longstreet** Finally, Longstreet in 1884 wrote a letter to Emerson Bicknell who was in a Union regiment on Pettigrew's Left flank on July 3 stating "At it's (the Union attack on Pettigrew's left flank) first appearance I sent orders for a counter-move. I think the order was sent by Col. Osmon Latrobe, now of Baltimore . . . At the first appearance of the troops of this move, I recognized it as one that would break up my assault: But I looked the movements of the 3rd Corps—A.P. Hills as certain to break the intended flank move." **(James Longstreet to Emerson L. Bicknell. January 4, 1884)**

All of the regiments under Pettigrew's Command were under strict orders to hold their fire until they reached the Emmitsburg Road fences. With one exception mentioned by Trimble years later (Some of Marshall's men) the rebel troops waited as ordered. **(Trimble to W.H. Swallow February 8, 1886, *Bachelder Papers* Vol. 2, 1199)**

The Union commanders had placed a strong skirmish line out in front of their defensive positions and as a result skirmish fire against the advancing rebel lines was unusually strong. The rebel skirmish line consisted of one company per regiment. The result was that considerable fighting took place early in the advance between these relatively heavy skirmish units. Some of the Union skirmishers extended halfway between the pike and the bliss farm. As the Confederate skirmish lines neared Emmitsburg Pike the Union lines were called in and blue uniforms rushed back to the stone wall positions. The accounts of this withdrawal vary widely from a story of an orderly retreat punctuated by occasional volleys of fire to one account where one federal observer recalled that the skirmishers ran "like so may frightened sheep" Some of the skirmishers had been wounded in the fighting and remained behind to be captured or were helped back by comrades. Others mixed in with whatever regiment they happened to find as they climbed back over the wall **(Christopher Mead letter to wife, July 6, 1863, Brake Collection, USAMHI; Whellock Veazey to G. Benedict, July 11, 1864, Veazey Papers; Testimony of George Hanson, 72nd Pa VS Gettysburg Monument Commission, pp 51-53)** One Confederate observer, Major Joseph Englehart praised the determination of the Union skirmish line in front of his men, and was led to believe that there was a full Union defense line located at the Emmitsburg Road. A line which, of course did not exist but which may well be the source of all of the Confederate accounts about "breaking the enemy works" **(Report of Major Joseph H Englehard, November 4, 1863, OR, 1,27, pp 659-660)**

As the troops from Tennessee approached the Emmitsburg Pike fences 2nd Lieutenant John Moore recalled that the explosion of artillery and the resultant smoke and flame was like a fog-like "darkened magnificence" Also with Tennessee was Sergeant Junius Kimble (Co A 14th TN) who remembered the ease at which the first several fences were crossed. "Soon shot & shell were plowing through the Confederate ranks; but on, steadily on the line moved with never a waver or break save as gaps were rent by solid shot or exploding shell. The first fence was soon reached and quickly toppled over by hand and upon the points of bayonets. No check but on we moved. The second fence shared the fate of the first, and without a halt the column went forward as if to victory. The third obstacle appeared, a strong well-built post or slab fence, too strong to be quickly torn away. Realizing this, over the fence the Confederates sprang, thus pausing for a moment in some confusion; but reforming quickly the line, still unbroken but terribly punished, rushed forward undismayed. Moore also noticed that the artillery fire coming from the right (Little Round Top) was as severe as the fire from ahead. **(June Kimble, "Tennesseeans at Gettysburg—The Retreat" Confederate Veteran CV, XVIII (1910), pp460-461) (Moore, *Battle of Gettysburg,* p 251)**

Moore's observation about the effect of artillery fire from Little Roundtop (Rittenhouse) and from McGilvery's batteries is also mentioned by Louise G Young who noticed that troops with Marshall were shifting to the left and bunching as enfilade fire came in from the south (which of course created even better targets.)

Private Drury Wall (Co D 52nd NC) was a 21 year old Stokes Co farmer who was hit in the leg with a shell fragment as he advanced along side his brother John. He was able to return to his lines where his leg was amputated. He would be captured on July 5th at the Confederate hospital. His 20 year old brother would survive the battle and be captured on July 14th at Falling Waters Maryland. Neither brother would survive the war.

In the 47th NC Corporal R.B. Bedington (Co C from Wake County) fell to shellfire before reaching the road as did Private Daniel Bates Company D in the 11th MS from Philadelphia, Ms. who was wounded by a shell fragment in the head. Another soldier to be felled by shell fire was Private William Nunnery a 32 yr old in Company H of the 26th North Carolina who was wounded in the leg.

Somewhere just past Stevens Run Colonel Marshall was knocked from his horse by the concussion of an exploding shell. He remounted and continued forward behind his brigade line. At about the same time as Marshall was knocked from his horse several men recalled that the entire Pettigrew line paused briefly to realign just as it passed the Bliss Farm and approached the Stevens Run. Captain Albert Haynes in Company I of the 11th North Carolina believed that the reason for the brief halt was that Marshall's regiments had gotten slightly ahead of the rest of the division causing the need for realignment. He argued after the war that there had been two such halts (one just before the Stevens Run and another between Stevens Run and the Emmitsburg Pike). **(A.S. Haynes to editors, October 8, 1877, Grimes Papers SHC-UNC)**

Somewhere on the advance, perhaps just before the Emmitsburg Road Private Eligah Messer Co F with the 2nd Mississippi was hit in the chest. He would be helped back to the rebel lines and almost die of gangrene while being transported back to Virginia where he recovered.

Just as Colonel James Marshall's men reached the first fence at Emmitsburg Pike the Colonel shouted to his aide Captain Stockton Heth "We do not know which of us will be the next to fall". Moments later he was hit in the head with two bullets. In front of him at about the same moment Sergeant William Smith carrying the flag of the 26th North Carolina was hit with shrapnel and went down.

A witness to Marshall's death was 19 year old Lieutenant John Warren of company C "The Orapeake Guards" (52nd NC). In a letter to Marshall parents from a cousin the details of his death were given . . . .

Ordnance Office
Lynchburg, VA
6th October 1863

My dear uncle-

It becomes my painful duty to inform you, and my dear Aunt, that I have received information through a letter to Mrs. Dr. Warren, from a friend in Baltimore, that according to Lieut. Warren's statement, Jimmy was killed *instantly* on the 3rd day's fight at Gettysburg. Warren says that he was killed near him and that he was shot in the forehead and expired immediately. I fear there can be no mistake about it, as Warren lay wounded on the field for *three days* and makes the statement without *any qualification* . . . . Capt. Stockton Heth (son of Jacob Heth) saw Jimmy a few moments before he heard that he was killed, and had a few moments conversation with him, in the midst of the lead and iron hail, and that Jimmy remarked to him in words to this effect "we do not know which of us will be the next to fall" and dashed on with his command with that cool courage for which he was so remarkable; and in a few moments was killed dead on the field. **(F. Lewis Marshall letter (VMI Archives Manuscript #0165)**

Lieutenant Warren himself was wounded in the lung, wrist and thigh and captured shortly thereafter as was his Captain George Gilliam a 29 year old merchant from Gates' County who was hit in the thigh.

The one or two brief pauses by the entire Pettigrew line had two effects. First it allowed the Trimble line to close the gap behind and also shift regiments to help on the left flank. Second, it created an image in the eyes of those far away that the Pettigrew line was wavering in their advance rather than just realigning. What had been created both Davis's late start and by Marshall's brief pauses was an uneven jerky advance.

One more geographic note must be made. If one walks today along the path of Pettigrew's and Trimble's advance, one is struck by the fact that the white washed Bryan Barn and House loom directly at the center of the line advance. The common idea that the Bryan farm stood off past the far edge of the action is troublesome as one can see both by they geography and by the accounts of some of Davis's men coming at the Bryan Barn from the north as the road was crossed and violence escalated.

As the first Pettigrew Confederates reached the Emmitsburg Road, had time been frozen, they could have seen the vast force in blue that waited for their arrival. Some 5,000 Union troops, from Pennsylvania to their right to Ohio on their left. Troops bolstered by no fewer than 8 still functioning artillery pieces still in action to their front with more than 30 pieces behind those on higher ground. In this frozen moment they would have seen that the solid stone wall that protected the Union infantry line was not a straight wall running along the hill's crest at the all but rather a wall that rested down the crest to their right but which made a sharp eastward turn running up toward the crest some 75 yards before turning at a right angle to move along the crest northward. This feature would mean that the regiments on Pettigrew's and Scales right flank would reach a stone wall sooner than the remainder of the Brigades (as would all of Pickett's Virginians) The other feature that was striking is that at the Northern end of the Union line there stood a whitewashed house and barn along the stone wall and a small fence and path running from the barn down to several small structures and the Emmitsburg Pike. Because the crest of Cemetery Ridge converged with the Emmitsburg Road the rear stone wall converged as well and in point of fact the Northern End of the stone wall was but half the distance of the imposing stone angle where the wall made its eastward turn. The implication of this twist in topography is that the center of Pettigrew's Brigade would have farther to charge before reaching the Union troops at the stone wall than would either flank. To further confuse the eye, a light fence line overgrown with brush and a few small trees ran northward about 50 yards from the forward stone wall angle. This had the effect of obscuring from view the fact that the center of the position about to be attacked was hollowed out as discussed above. The final note of topography is often ignored by historians but is quickly realized when walking the battlefield even today. A perpendicular ridge runs from the forward stone wall angle down toward the pike and with a rise of some 15-20 feet this ridge makes it impossible for troops marching eastward on opposite sides of this ridge to see each other. Even today a person standing half way up the hill in front of the 69th Pa monument can not see a person standing halfway up the hill in front of the rear stone wall. In fact, a person standing half way up the hill in front of the 69th Pa monument is unable to see the light fence with overgrown brush at all.

THE FEDERAL DEFENSE

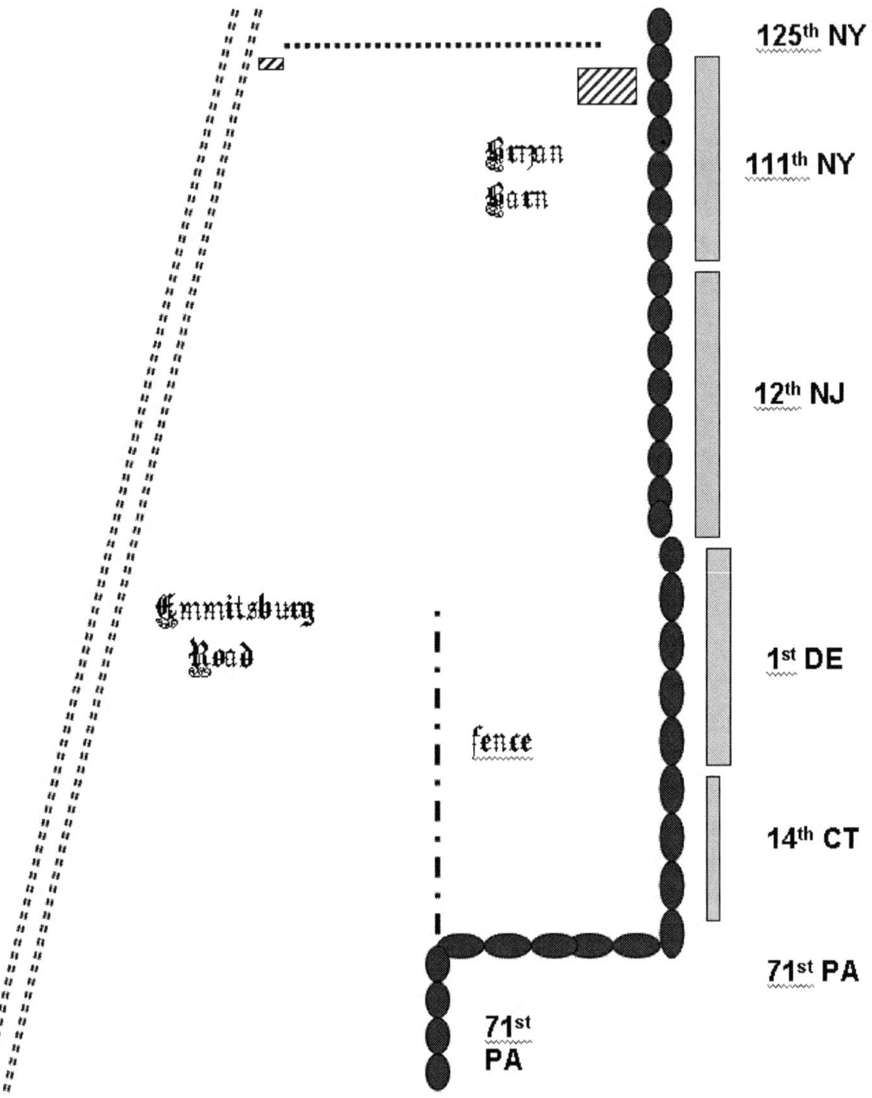

Who were the Union troops behind these impressive defenses? To the far right of Pettigrew's, and in Pettigrew's rear, Scale's brigade were the Irishmen of the 69th Pennsylvania. Unseen by Pettigrew's men, they would occupy the forward wall from the point where Cushing's remaining two guns were still in service off to the south. They would be the anchor as Pickett's regiments swarmed around their flanks. The first visible soldiers in blue to the right would be the men of four companies of the 71st Pa, without their flags, as these remained with their other 6 companies up at the crest. Company K at the stone angle with companies G, H, & C to the south. Some 125 men, assigned to protect Cushing northern flank would occupy the high point of the perpendicular ridge and thus were in the unique position of being able to view both Pickett's and Pettigrew forward advance. But their unique position would be a dangerous one since they were only 4 of 10 companies in strength and since Pettigrew's right flank would reach them far before his center got close to the rear wall.

The next Union soldiers along the defense line would be situated far to the rear (some 75 yards) where the wall again turned and ran 260 yards northward. Here stood Colonel Thomas Smythe's Second Brigades of General Alexander Haye's Third Division. The wall at the point was and is the highest and most impressive of all the stone walls. Even today only a rare tourist can climb it's heights. Arnold's battery of six guns had stood at the point where the stone wall turned again north but had been effectively knocked out of action during the bombardment. Perhaps one gun remained serviceable. The 14th Connecticut with their officers and men had moved into position where Arnold's guns had operated and waited in two ranks for the attack.

The men from Connecticut were among the few who were armed with Sharp breech loading rifles which gave them extra firepower. At least several of their companies had such guns. They were veterans of some of the bloodiest fighting at Antietam, Fredericksburg and Chancellorsville. There appears to be no reserve behind the Connecticut men. The Chaplin of the 14th wrote that his men "had no supporting troops behind it's single thin line" and others recalled how thin the Connecticut line appeared during the fight. **(Stevens, *Fourteenth Connecticut Regiment*, p 23 ; Morton, *Sparks from the Camp Fire*, National Tribune 1899, p 33)**

Next in line were the officers and men of the 1st Delaware Infantry. These men from Delaware had been lead through most of the war by their current Brigade Commander Thomas Smyth but now in the past 24 hours they had seen their Lieutenant Colonel Edward Harris arrested; his successor Captain Thomas Hizatr wounded and were commanded this morning by Lieutenant John F Dent.

Next to the men from Delaware was the 12th New Jersey, well known for the "buck & ball" muskets which were deadly in close combat. Some 400 in number commanded by Major John Hill. Hill, who had provided heroic leadership at Chancellorsville was new to command but had overseen action of several 12th regiment companies the day before in raids on the Bliss Farm out to the front of the defensive lines (and now filled with advancing rebel regiments). Beside and behind the right flank of the 12th New Jersey was the 111th New York overlapping the whitewashed Bryan Barn. Unseen to any mortal man advancing toward this line was a second line of armed men composed of two regiments from New York State, the 125th and the 39th New York. The 39th New York appears to have been shifted northward as the action began instead of moving forward to reinforce the left of the 12th New Jersey and right of the 1st Delaware. The 39th's seizure of the flags of the 11th and 42nd Mississippi flags demonstrates this fact.

But the Union defense did not end at the Bryan Barn. Stretching northward along a much shorter stone wall were the New York regiments, the 108th NY and the 126th NY stationed there to protect the right flank of the Union defense. Telescopes told the Union commanders that the northern edge of the Confederate attack would more than overlap the Bryan barn and these 2 New York regiments plus the reserve in the rear were give the task of making sure the Confederate left did not sweep over Zeigler's Grove. The right companies of the 126th New York practically reached the Emmitsburg Pike here closing to the ridgeline. The old Trostle House stood to their right and marked the end of their line.

The remaining Union force to the farthest north position was the 8th Ohio. Several companies of the regiment were spread out as skirmishers off in the fields and the main force took cover behind an embankment along the pike where the roadway sank into the slight hillside. It was here and not at the position currently marked by the 8th Ohio monument that these men had settled in during the bombardment. The fact that the 8th Ohio was much farther up the pike toward the town of Gettysburg alters the usual interpretation of what happened on the northern end of the assault field. Historically most writers presented a battleground where the Bryan barn was the most northern extent of Confederate assault, but recent scholarship suggests that with the 8th Ohio and consequently the 126th New York both farther north that some rebel infantry action occurred to the north of the Bryan barn. (see footnote)

Note—The actual starting position of the 8th Ohio main body of troops was a dirt embankment alongside the Emmitsburg just to the town side of the old Trostle house. The Trostle house stood during the battle on the east side of the Emmitsburg Road approximately where the driveway to the Visitor center now enters Steinwehr Ave. The actual dirt embankment is long gone but would have been directly in front of the McDonald's today. It is clear that the forward motion of the Ohio in bringing up additional men to their skirmish line did not take them at first toward the Davis advance but rather toward the short-lived advance of Brockenbrough's Brigade. To the east of the 8th Ohio grouping were elements of the 108th New York, 126th NY and 125th New York, all still well north of the Bryan barn and in fact well north of the Visitors Center driveway today. Colonel Sawyer of the 8th Ohio reported that after the breakup of Brockenbrough's Brigade his regiment moved south carefully firing into the ranks of Confederates still advancing on the assault. He and others reported coming to a position where the men were able to rest their rifles on a fence rail and aim more steadily at the gray ranks. This rail fence was located in 1863 along a line that today would divide the Battle Theatre building from the Kentucky Fried Chicken Restaurant. (My thanks to Guide Karlton Smith for his excellent analysis of these positions and to Keith Snipes for his excellent article in Gettysburg Magazine Issue #35 *"The Improper Placement of the 8th Ohio Monument; A Study of Words and Maps")*

Trimble Advance
Lane 7—37—28—18—33

Commanding the left wing regiment of Lane's Brigade, the 33rd NC was Colonel Clark Avery who recalled the opening of the advance. "At a given signal we moved forward in the charge. After passing a wood we had to charge ¾ of a mile in open field in full view of the enemy on an eminence. The first line soon gave way & we had the full benefit of artillery and musketry. Steadily we moved forward. First the right of the Division gave way the right of the Brigade at this juncture I saw that my regiment and another only remained in line (author note: the 33rd & 18th). **(Letter from C.M. Avery to Tod and Mrs. Caldwell, July 18, 1863, Southern Historical Collection #128)**

One man from the 33rd who was wounded during the advance was Private Mathias O'Neal in company F who was wounded when "a bomb shell exploded near his face otherwise shocking and injuring him" **(Mathias O'Neal, Compiled Service records, National Archives)**

One of the first casualties in the advance from the 28th North Carolina was Sergeant Jesse Woodson Cockerham. He was a file closer in the advance and was killed instantly by shell fragments. His brother, William, who was a private in his company (Co A) saw Jesse fall. Family tradition states that William placed a handkerchief over his dead brother's face before rushing to rejoin the advancing company. Sergeant Cockerham was 30 years old and had been captured earlier in the war at Hanover Courthouse. His brother William had been wounded at Chancellorsville and would later be captured at the Wilderness.

Another tragic incident in the advance would occur as Private Alan Carpenter, a 21 year old soldier in Company D would be marching with his 19 year old brother Churchill when an explosion would kill the younger brother. Alan moved forward toward the Emmitsburg Road to continue the fight. A short time later as the 28th retreated back across the field, the field was so thickly covered with dead and wounded that many soldiers could not prevent themselves from stepping on bodies of the fallen. At one point, Allen stepped on a dead body and looked down in horror to see that it was his dead brother Churchill. **(interview with Mrs. Rose Almond, great granddaughter of Allen Carpenter)**

Another early casualty from the 28th North Carolina was Private William Martin in Company C. Martin had gained fame earlier in the war as an expert marksman. He would be commentated by General James Lane himself for his outstanding shooting skills at

Fredericksburg. The "South Fork Farmer" had "coolly sat on the track and called to his comrades to watch the Yankee colors, then fired and down they went. This was done repeatedly. Captain Lovell, of Company A . . . stood on the track all the time waving his hat and cheering his men; and strange to say, neither he nor Martin was struck." James Lane, "Twenty-Eighth Regiment", in Clark, Histories of the North Carolina Regiments, 2: pp 475-476) Captain Lovell was wounded in the right arm in the July 2 fighting.

Ironically Martin was never himself hit by rifle fire but rather wounded twice by artillery shell fragments. First at Glendale, where he was hit by a shell fired by a Union gunboat in the James River and then while advancing across the fields this day during the Trimble advance, wounded by fragments in the left arm and shoulder. He would be hit again by artillery at Petersburg where he would be wounded in the head, pelvis and right leg. He would live to surrender at Appomattox.

The Colonel of the 28th Colonel S.D. Lowe was taken out of action during the advance. "My rank was Colonel commanding the 28th NC Regiment—325 men. We advanced about a mile starting just in the rear of Pettigrew's (Marshall's left, which brigade closing and dressing to the right, we to the left, in less than half the distance uncovered us and left us front line. Over 300 yards from the enemy's works I received a severe wound from a Minie ball and was carried to the rear." **(Colonel S.D. Lowe to Raleigh Observer October 17, 1877 from Iron Station, NC)**

As the 28th North Carolina advanced a father and his two sons would be in line and all would survive the fight. Private John Draughan in Company A was a 52 year old blacksmith from Surray County, NC His two sons Isaac (age 22) and William (age 26) would march beside him and retreat with him. The senior member of the family would be killed in May 1864 in the Wilderness. The two sons would survive the war.

There were 10 members of the Bolch extended family who served in the 28th North Carolina during the war. By Gettysburg some were already dead. Private Logan Bolch in Company C of the 28th had two brothers Anthony and Emanuel killed at Chancellorsville. Cousins Aaron and Abel marched forward with him on July 3. Logan was hit someplace shortly before reaching the Emmitsburg Pike by a bullet that hit him in the upper right arm below the shoulder. He was able to return to his lines where he was placed in a Confederate hospital but not evacuated. His cousin Aaron would also be wounded and captured that day. **(Affidavit of Elijah Killian, Pension file of Mrs. Joann Adfam Bolch, North Carolina pension applications files)**

The key feature of the Trimble advance was the split in Lane's Brigade into two separate thrusts. Major J. McLeod Turner in command of the 7th North Carolina explained "I looked ahead and saw Pettigrew advancing in good order. The left three regiments (of Lane's Brigade) then oblique left and the right two regiments obliqued right . . . . Leaving a gap in our lines. Our losses were slight as we approached the road. **(J. McLeod Turner**

letter to Raleigh Observer, October 10, 1877, Raleigh NC) This placed three Lane regiments the 33rd, 18th and 28th on the left supporting Davis while the 37th and 7th ended up supporting the Scales attack . . . . or backing up Pettigrew.

One of the best explanations of this split came years later in a letter written by Lt. Colonel William Morris who was commanding the 37th NC that day. "Heavily engaged with the enemy our Brigade was ordered to double quick and we soon became part of the first line forming on Pettigrew's left, the 7th on the right of our Brigade on Pettigrew's left. About this time I heard the command by General Lane to left wheel but before I could repeat the Command Tremble being in the vacancy between the 7th & 37th ordered a bayonet charge which resulted in separating Lane's Brigade. While the 7th and all on the right of Colors of the 37th obeyed Tremble, the remainder changed direction to the left. (Author note: Companies K, A & G)

Just at this point about midway from the skit of woods & the enemy's works there was considerable elevation both on our right and left so that we could not see what was going on any great distance right or left. The right of my regiment being on low ground was not so much exposed to the flanking fire consequently we obeyed Trimble's command & charged with the 7th to within a short distance of the turnpike road & found the enemy posted both in the road and behind the stone fence some 40 paces distance on the crest of the hill . . ." **(Letter from Lt. Col William Morris to Colonel W. Saunders, October 1, 1877, Dallas NC, GMNP Library Collection)**

During this split of the Lane Brigade a shell exploded in the ranks of 28th North Carolina. Private Sidney Choplin was one of four brothers who joined the 28th North Carolina Company F "The Yadkin Boys" in June 18, 1861. One by one the siblings were killed or severely wounded. Brothers Joseph (killed—Gaines Mill), Robert (mortally wounded—Gaines Mill, Wesley (wounded-Ox Hill). During the charge by Lane's Brigade Sidney died as well. Before the war he had served as a deputy sheriff.

The officers of the 7th were surprising candid in their writings after the war with regard to the action taken by their regiment. Major Turner in command wrote "As we reached the road I saw the enemy leave their works and retreat over a hill. I called out to my men and the whole line rushed forward. But before we could reach the works their reinforcements arrived back at the works. When we reached the road we had to tear down fences. We tore down the first but the second would not fall. I climbed over the fence and advanced about ten yards with some of my men and was shot down. The men who climbed over returned to the road and lay down. **(J.McLeod Turner letter to Raleigh Observer, October 10, 187, Raleigh, NC)** The officers of companies H, A & F were equally candid—

20 year old Nash County 1st Lieutenant Joshua Vick (Company E 7th NC) had been shot in the left knee as he approached the Emmitsburg Pike and was taken off the field by some of

his men. At the time he noted that the regiment was still in good order **(Joshua Vick letter to Raleigh Observer, September 26, 1877, Selma NC),** while Private Wilbur Swaringer 28th NC Co K, after the war told of passing a soldier from the 55th North Carolina who had been hit by a shell during the advance holding his bowels in his hands.

Trimble Advance
Scales 16-22-34-13-38

Some 160 yards behind, of course were those regiments of Trimble . . . .

The advance of the 100 men left in the 38th North Carolina was described by 3rd Lieutenant Henry Moore "As we emerged from the woods we were nearly three fourths of a mile from the federal lines. We could see about a mile of enemy's works. We suffered very little from the enemy fire until about half way across the field. We climbed a diagonal fence running across the field and climbed it. We were now greeted by heavy doses of canister. Our men were falling in every direction but we managed to struggle on.

About 200 yards from the enemy we reached another fence which confused us considerably. The fire from enemy artillery and infantry were terrible and we were reduced to a mere skirmish line" **(Letter from Henry Moore November 6, 1877, Warsaw NC, UNC Archives Collection)**

Many in the Trimble line could not see what was happening to those with Pettigrew who preceded them. Moore with the 38th NC recalled. "We had not been in the enemy's line for more than five or ten minutes before a courier came galloping down from the enemy's left and spoke to an officer and said "General, we are all right" . . . I know nothing of the number of men in Pettigrew's brigade, or their position that day. If they in our front they certainly lost many men, as the field was dotted with the dead and wounded." **("H. C Moore to the Editor, *Raleigh Observer*, November 6, 1877)**

The command of the 38th North Carolina regiment had fallen to Captain Thornburg of Company H but his wounding during the advanced resulted in some confusion in the lines. The 38th had to cross a wooden fence prior to the Emmitsburg Road fences about 150 yards out. "I was in command of the 38th NC on the 2nd and 3rd day at Gettysburg. We advanced about a half a mile when I was shot down (lost right eye) . . . It was about an hour before I was gotten entirely out of danger" **(Letter from Captain William Thornburg to Raleigh Observer, September 25, 1877, from Company Shops, NC)**

As the regiments of Scales (Lowrence) moved forward Lieutenant R.L. Moir (Company H 13th NC) was wounded by a shell fragment and fell. The 2nd Lieutenant would find his way back to his lines and later become a Captain. He had been wounded in Chancellorsville only 2 months before. About the same time the acting commander of the 13th was also hit. Captain Ludolphus Henderson, senior Captain from Company A would fall and his place taken by Company B's Captain William B Robinson. Robinson was a 27 year old doctor who had been wounded at Sharpsburg and would later be wounded at Spotsylvania.

19 year old Lieutenant T.D. Lattimore with Company F of the 34th NC (Scales) recalled "We marched into the assault with magnificent appearance, but were repulsed and driven back in disorder." **(Letter to the editor Charlotte Democrat 1877)**

One of the men in Lattimore's regiment who marched with him until knocked senseless by a shell concussion was 28 year old Private James South from Ashe County. South, in company A, had been wounded before at 2nd Manassas and would later be promoted to Corporal.

Color Bearer Lawrence Birkhead who had just turned 21 was carrying the flag of the 22nd North Carolina in the fields before the fenced road and was wounded by shell fire. His brother Francis, age 23, was also hit. Both would recover and his brother Francis would later become First Sergeant.

In the 16th North Carolina, Private Aaron Wall a 24 year old in Company D was thrown to the ground with the percussion of an exploding shell. He would be gathered up later and returned to his lines with "shell shock". **(Compiled service files, 16th NC, National Archives)**

CHAPTER SIX

Emmitsburg Road

First to reach the road were the Alabama and Tennessee men under Fry. One man Lieutenant John Moore Company B in the 7th Tennessee remembered it well "The time it took to climb to the top of the fence seemed to me an age of suspense. It was not a leaping over; it was rather an insensible tumbling to the ground in the nervous hope of escaping the thickening missiles that buried themselves in falling victims, in the ground and in the fence, against which they rattled with the distinctness of large rain drops patterning on a roof." **(Moore; *Battle of Gettysburg,* p 250)**

1st Lt James Simpson, a 25 year old Tallassee teacher was wounded at the beginning of the advance and his 2nd Lieutenant Robert Ashurt reached the road commanding the 11 men who remained with Company F. Four more of these men from Elmore County would fall this day. Lt. Simpson wrote his mother a few days after the battle. "It was the strongest position I have ever seen and I wondered at our Genl making any attempt to storm them. I saw that they could not be taken before the charge" **(James M Simpson to mother, July 8, 1863, Allen and Simpson Family papers, UNC)**

Corporal George Powell in Company C of the 14th Tennessee carried the flag up to the first fence at the road when he was shot down. The flag was then taken over the fence by Private Thomas Davidson who made it to the second fence and was wounded. He handed the flag next to Sergeant Robert Mockbee saying "Bob, take the flag, I am shot." The flag then crossed the second fence. (**C.Wallace Cross, Ordeal by Fire: A History of the Fourteenth Tennessee Volunteer Infantry regiment, CSA (Clarksville, TN, 1990)**

At the same time and place the flag of the 1st Tennessee was held by Color Bearer Wiley Woods with Private John McLeer by his side. **(Wiley Woods, The First Tennessee Flag at Gettysburg, CV Battles William Perkins Library Duke University**) **(Shepard Report OR, II, 647)**

Moore also wrote elsewhere, "We reached the first slab or plank fence and the men clambered over with the speed of a stampeded retreat". **(Ibid)**

Moore also recalled that as he reached the first fence he glanced backward and watched as two riders rode along the rear of his line. One was covered with blood and both rode back toward the Bliss Barn. Suddenly Moore saw one rider went down with his horse in a twisted pile and the other disappeared from view. **(Moore; *Battle of Gettysburg,* p 249)**

Major General Trimble wrote in his memoirs after the war "While at the fence, the exposure was dreadful. The incessant discharge of canister, shell and musketry was more than any troops could endure." **(Isaac Trimble, Clark, Histories from North Carolina, p. 564)**

It seems that the first wave to cross the first fence waited for a few seconds hugging the ground until their officers inspired them, to cross the second fence and advance. Very few who did so would return. Major William Williamson, who had been wounded in the arm at Gaines Mill remained at the road and would be captured.

Private John Dornan in Company A of the 5th Alabama Battalion took bullets in his right leg and his right side as he climbed the fence. **(John Dornan, Compiled Service File, National Archives)**

One of the first to cross the second fence must surely have been Private Kimble of the 14th Tennessee who wrote later that as he crossed the final fence he looked up and down the fence line and was "an eyewitness of the most vivid and stupendous battle scene doubtless that ever fell to mortal man "**(June Kimble, "Tennesseeans at Gettysburg—The Retreat" Confederate Veteran CV, XVIII (1910), 461)**

One of the men from Tennessee who did hold and wave the flag from the roadbed was Private Mockbee of the 14th Co B who recalled "The waving battle flags seemed to be the special mark as soon as we came in range of the small arms" **(Cooke, "Gallant Tennesseans in Gettysburg Charge", *Richmond Times Dispatch,* April 3, 1910)**

Captain Jacob Turney who had taken command of the 1st Tennessee had fallen behind his company and rushed to the pike as many of his men were already crossing. "By the time I reached my line it was to the first plank fence that enclosed the Emmitsburg. How like hail upon a roof sounded the patter of the enemy's bullets upon that fence. Onward swept the columns, thinned now and weakened, the dead behind, the foe in front, and no thought of quarter. The second fence was reached, and scaled now no impediment save the deadly fire of ten thousand rifles that barred our head—long charge. It was one hundred and fifty yards now of open field. Who would reach the goal? **(Captain J.B. Turney, "The First Tennessee at Gettysburg", Confederate Veteran, VII (1900), pp 535-537)**

Some must have thought that the task was impossible but Captain Benjamin Little (Company E 52nd North Carolina, who lost his arm in the attack) recalled "The only 'giving away' I could see on the part of Pettigrew's Brigade was the 'giving away' by falling to the earth killed or wounded" **(Michael W. Taylor, North Carolina in the Pickett-Pettigrew-Trimble Charge at Gettysburg, p. 84)**

Captain Little in Company E had taken a bullet in his left arm as he climbed the plank fence and was helped back to the ground by one of his men Private W.F. Sandford. They both would be captured. Later Sanford would be paroled and become the regimental chaplain.

Adjutant John H. Robinson of the 52nd summed up the action years later tells how his regiment "moved gallantly and steadily forward under the covering fire of our guns until it reached a point beyond which it was unsafe to fire over our heads. Steadily the advance was made, and as steadily and coolly met with a murderous fire from the enemy's cannon, charged with grape, shrapnel and canister. Still the line advanced, and at every step our comrades fell on every side killed or wounded. Still we advanced under the incessant discharge of the cannon, assisted by the infantry's rifles, and had almost attained success, when by the overpowering force and almost impregnable position of the enemy, our lines were forced back, and then the slaughter was terrific." **(Clark, Histories of the North Carolina Regiments, III, p 238)**

Many men of the 47th and 26th North Carolina recall that as they reached the Emmitsburg Road two events occurred just prior to the mounting or knocking down of the post & rail fence of the West side of the road. First the Confederate artillery suddenly stopped firing, fearing that past the pike rebel shells would find rebel targets. The end of Confederate cannon fire brought a momentary lull and quiet to the scene and then many recalled a volley from the 26th North Carolina just as they reached the western fence. Perhaps men had been firing prior but this relative silence created a condition where this volley was heard by all . . . . of course within seconds the massive Union volley of canister and bullets from the heights ahead would blurr and overwhelm all other sounds. Finally as they neared the Emmitsburg Road, Pettigrew's troops opened fire with a powerful volley. It was 'a terrible crash", according to a Yankee officer on the ridge ahead. They fired while they were advancing—, and they were well within range to do serious damage to the enemy. The Federal infantry were still crouched behind the stone wall, however, and the volley had minimum impact" **(Rod Gragg, Covered with Glory, p 191)**

Apparently Company G of the 47th North Carolina largely stayed at the road instead of advancing. Their casualty figures show a large number of men captured on July 3 and another large number later captured at Falling Waters Maryland. Captain Davis made it clear that the company never went past the roadbed. **(Honorable Joseph J Davis letter of September 20, 1877 to Raleigh Observer)** With his company at the left end of the

47th, it is probable that they could see around the northern end of the front wooden fence and realize what lay ahead at the rear stone wall.

First Lieutenant Julius Sidney Joyner age 23 with Company F, who had written his mother about the "land of milk and honey" was hit in the hand with a Yankee bullet as he rallied his men in the roadbed. In company A of the 47th there were 4 members of the Batchelor family and four members of the Bissett family in line that day. All eight survived the assault without injury . . . . A rare story indeed on July 3, 1863.

Captain John Thorp with Company A remembered clearly the difference between the fight on July 1st and the situation his men faced on July 3rd at the road. "On the 1st as it double quicked on Reynolds, it (The 47th) had an equal chance with the enemy and had hurled 30,000 bullets in their faces. On the 3rd they had attempted to march 1,000 yards in quick time through a raking fire of cannon and minies, with virtually no chance to use their minies—soldier's main weapon."**(John H Thorpe, *Memories of Gettysburg letter*, GNMP library)**

In Company I of the 11th NC 2nd Lt. Lemuel Hoyle was wounded but able to return to his lines. In a letter to his mother, the Lincoln County officer said that "the fighting was perfectly fearful, and the slaughter tremendous Our men fought with the accustomed valor and determination of Southern soldiers but in vain." **(Lemuel J Hoyle letter to mother July 12, 1863 Hoyle Papers, UNC)**

With Colonel James Marshall killed command of the entire Brigade now fell on the shoulders of Major John Jones who earlier had wondered if he could inspire his own men of the 26th North Carolina. As Jones took command, the flag of the 12th New Jersey suddenly was unfurled and was caught by the breeze. At the same time, the division flag—a huge blue cloverleaf on a field of white was raised to the same breeze. **(OR I, 27 pp 158-159)**

In the 26th North Carolina color-bearer Thomas Cozart (Co I) was hit and the regimental flag was grabbed by others. Sergeant Jake Rush in the same Caldwell Guards company was hit by four bullets at the same moment just as he was about to touch the first rail and fell bleeding in the wheat. He would lay there for two days unable to move but would captured recover and be able to fight again at Ream's Station and surrender at Appomattox. His tale of capture would be one of horror. Sergeant Bush had been hit by two bullets in the right thigh, one in his left arm and another through his right side and lung. As he lay bleeding, after the general retreat, he was almost hit again by a Yankee firing at a wounded Confederate officer (probably 1st Lt. Gaston Broughton Co D) who was crawling back toward safety. The officer turned around and crawled toward the Union lines for help. Rush rolled down a short slope and came to rest next to a dead soldier who had a half full canteen. **(Bush Remembrances, NCDAH, pp3-4)**

First Sergeant Alexander Dunlap in Co H (26th NC) The Moore Independents" was hit in the leg and fell in the roadbed. He heard Sergeant Rush calling out for water.

Second Lieutenant James Greer, of the Caldwell Guards Co I, also fell wounded as he crossed the first fence. Greer **(Regimental History James T Adams papers, NCDAH)**

Artillery shell and canister filled the air while volley after volley of Union infantry rifles poured thousands of projectiles at the fence lines along the road. "One board of the slab fence at the point crossed (first by Marshall and then) by Brigadier General Alfred Scales brigade measuring 14 inches by 16 feet was perforated by 836 musket balls." **(Gregory Coco, On the Bloodstained field" (Gettysburg, Pa Thomas Publications1987) p 32**

From the Union vantage point it looked like slaughter, Chaplain Henry Stevens of the 14th Connecticut wrote many years later "Our men were ordered to withhold their fire until the Confederates were Across the Emmitsburg road. As soon as the Confederates began to climb the hither fence the men opened fire upon them." **(Henry Stevens letter June 10, 1905 NCDAH)**

The tension of the drama was captured in the memory of a Union officer "The click of the locks as each man raised the hammer to feel with his fingers that the cap was on the nipple; the sharp jar as a musket touched the stone upon the wall when thrusting in aiming over it, and the clicking of the iron axles as the guns were rolled up by hand a little further to the front, were all the sounds that could be heard." **(Harwell, Two Views of Gettysburg: pp. 189-190)**

For the men of Marshall and Fry's brigades who crossed the first fence constructed of post and rail and then looked up behind the second fence composed of post and slab, the scene was one of terror. Yet another fence stood half way between the road and the Union infantry behind their stone wall two Hundred Yards away. Yet another fence to cross before getting in close to the enemy. Chaplin Henry Stevens recounted that the men saw the crossing of the Emmitsburg Roadbed as "a dreadfully bloody one" **(Reverend Henry S Stevens June 10, 1905, Stevens Papers NCDAH)**

Major John Jones remembered it this way. "As we got within two hundred yards of the enemy we commenced firing and the storm of lead was beyond description. As we advanced we received a fire from our left as our brigade to the left had given way and the enemy flanked us. I had only about 60 men left at this pint and that small number was diminishing every moment." **(John Jones letter July 30, 1863 from Culpepper, Va.)**

Another man who made it to the road and was able to later escape was First Sergeant William Snelling in Company D of the 26th. He recalled many men wounded in the roadbed that were unable to retreat. **(Snelling letter September 25, to Raleigh Observer, from Raleigh, NC, UNC Archives)** Snellings' superior, 2nd Lieutenant George Wilcox wrote

"WE crossed the road and went to the enemies' works. MY company went with about 25 men. We were captured after being hit at the enemy works about 10-15 minutes. The 47th regiment was on our right as we went in." **(Gaston Broughton letter from Raleigh NC October 15, to Raleigh Observer, UNC archives)**

2nd Lt. George Wilson had been wounded on July 1 carrying the flag. He talked to the men who did attack on July 3 And recalled these details . . . "The 26th had no more than 150 men by the third day" . . . His company went in with 10-12 men commanded by a Sergeant. They lost about half killed and wounded. He remembered the fate of the men of the flag Color Guard; Sgt Smith (Co K) was killed . . . . Private Cozart (Co F was killed . . .

Captain Brewer (Co E) was wounded. Private Thomas (Co E) was wounded . . . Sergeant Brooks (Co E) was captured. **(George Wilcox Letter to Raleigh Observer, from Creraw S.C. October 1877)**

After the battle in a letter home, Captain William Kerr of the 11th North Carolina reported home about the fate of a number of men from his local section of Mecklenberg County. Most of these men were either in Company E with Kerr or with his good friend Lieutenant W.B. Taylor in Company A. Company A under Captain William Hand (who was captured) began the fight on July 1 with 91 men but had only 30 go forward in the attack July 3. Eight would make it back to their lines. Sergeant Major I.G. McCorkle who was with Company A but had been promoted to Sergeant Major was wounded at the road. Kerr's friend Taylor was unhurt but would be later wounded both at The Wilderness and at Petersburg. The First and Second Sergeants, 22 year old Richard Alexander and J.N. Ernheardt were both wounded (in the left shoulder and right side respectively). Finally he reported that his 2nd Lt. Robert Hand was wounded in the back during the retreat (author note Hand would be captured in the wagon train at Greencastle, Pa on July 5th) **(William Kerr to Mother, August 14, 1863, UNC Archives)** Kerr's company had been heavily hit on July 1 and had very few casualties on July 3.

"The storm of lead which met us was beyond description. Grape and canister intermingled with minies and buckshot. The smoke was so dense I could hardly see my own men." **(Captain Albert Haynes Co I, 11th North Carolina, Hewett OR Supplement)**

In Company I of the 11th North Carolina five members of the Hafner family, brothers and cousins, came to Gettysburg. On July 1, John Hafner was killed in the fighting. This day Adolphus was killed. The remaining three would suffer arm wounds in the fighting but survive. George, Hosea and Jacob all would be hit during the assault on the Union Wall. Jacob's arm would be amputated and he would be captured. George and Hosea would be transported back to Virginia and safety.

"In obedience to orders the line moved gallantly and steadily forward under fire of our guns until it reached a point beyond which it was unsafe to fire over our heads. Steadily the advance was made, and as steadily and coolly met with a murderous fire from the enemy's cannon, charged with grape, shrapnel and canister. Still the line advanced, and at every step our comrades fell on every side, killed or wounded. Still we advanced under the incessant discharge of the cannon, assisted by the infantry's rifles, and had almost attained success, when by the overpowering force and almost impregnable position of the enemy, our lines were forced back, and then the slaughter was terrific . . . . Lieutenant-Colonel Parks was shot through both thighs, and fell into the hands of the enemy, and our brave and dashing Major Richardson sealed, with his life, his devotion to the cause he loved so well, and for the advancement of whose success he had striven so zealously. He was instantly killed by a rifle ball while leading the left wing of his regiment. Of the line officers, but few escaped wounds or capture . . . . We fell back to the point from which the attack was made, rallying all whom it was possible to reach, and reforming our shattered lines." **(Adjt John H. Robinson in Manarin, L.H., *North Carolina Troops, 1861-'65*, Raleigh, 1966.)**

For Davis no such fence existed and because the road moved closer to the Union line as it approached Gettysburg the distance to be covered was less and less filled with obstacles.

The 55th North Carolina was the right regiment of General Davis's other wise solid Mississippi brigade. Stripped of shelter from the 300 foot long rail fence that ran north from the outer angle, the 55th was in clear sight of the 12th New Jersey 69 caliber "buck and ball" weapons. Captain Howell Whitehead was wounded in both the head and hand in the roadbed and would be captured July 5th in Greencastle Pa by Federal cavalry while riding in a hospital wagon. Many in the 55th stayed at the road rather than attack up the slope . . . but not all some would die almost to the stone wall.

Here also fell the watchmaker Private Augustus Vairin in the 2nd Mississippi (Co B), badly wounded and then captured near the roadbed. He later claimed that every one of the men with him was either killed wounded or captured except one. **(Civil War Diary of Augustus L.P. Vairin, 2nd Mississippi Infantry CSA)** Nearby in Company B of the same regiment fell Private David Hill a 35 yr old Tippah surveyor who was hit in the right leg and captured. Hill had been a successful civil engineer and educator before the war and enlisted at the outbreak. He would recover in a Baltimore hospital and be exchanged to fight again and be captured again at Hatcher's Run

Somewhere near the road Private Levi Rhodes in Company I of the 42nd Mississippi was wounded in the left thigh and went down. The Sardis Mississippi soldier would be captured after the fighting died down and after the war would move to Texas. **(Correspondence with J.R. Rhodes great great grandson)**

But the twin fences of the Pike would provide the men of Davis's brigade with enough problems. As the 11th Mississippi took the pike, men of Company D started to climb the second fence to attack. First Lieutenant John Moore of Company A rushed up to tell the men to wait until the entire Regimental line was formed before advancing. Sergeant Andrew Jackson Baker of Moore's own company, The University Grays, shouted at him "John's for heaven's sake, give the command to charge" Moore hesitated and Baker screened ":Charge" himself and was hit as he spoke. Those in the roadbed took a final pause awaiting the order to advance the regiment. **(Andrew J Baker, "Tribute to Captain Magruder and his Wife", CV (VI:507)** There seems to be some confusion About Baker's rank during this battle. Some historians have called him a Lieutenant and he appears on the muster rolls as a private. There is some evidence that after July 1 he was brevetted at a Sergeant. The records of the regiment show that Baker and a small squad surrendered in the road as the battle ended.

At the same time Company C of the 11th seems to have held at the road, surrendering a dozen men there at the end of the fight. Their Captain, George Shannon, had been wounded in the advance and the officers remaining ended up surrendering in the road bed. This included Lieutenants William Peel and George Lusher Also surrendering at the road was 25 year old Sergeant John Morris was with them with a leg wound.

It is not entirely clear how many men from Company E made it to the Emmitsburg Road. Many fell in the fields approaching the dual fences. Many others reached the road and stayed. When the battle was over Company E was destroyed as a fighting unit and would later be merged with Company H. While "the Prairie Rifles" Company C gained fame for rushing toward the Bryan Barn, The Lownes County "Prairie Guards" Company E lost heavy in the advance and fought it out in the roadbed. When it was over their Captain Henry Halbert was mortally wounded. All three Lieutenants were killed or wounded. All four Sergeants were killed or wounded and one of the two Corporals were dead. Only 20 year old Corporal John T Morgan of Crawfordsville made it back of the 39 who charged that day.

Yet further obstacles besides a new fence were there as Private Andrew Parks Co I in the 42nd Mississippi would recall. "The Yankees were stationed behind a rock wall or fence; and we had to charge through an open field and up a hill which was covered with reed clover and running briars, which made it more difficult for us to get along." **(Andrew Parks, Some of my Recollections of the Battle of Gettysburg, Arkansas Historical Society)**

One of the men who fought bravely that day was Private Thomas Martin in Company D of the 42nd Mississippi. He was later awarded the Roll of Honor for his conduct. Later he was severely wounded at Wilderness and after the war went on to become a Deputy US Marshall. In 1893 he would be shot to death on his front porch by moonshiners he had been investigating. (Personal communication with descendants) Another 42nd Mississippi Roll of Honor recipient was Private J.P. Ticer in Company I who was cited by his officers for bravery in the fight. He would be later captured at Falling Waters. Finally, another soldier, who had displayed courage in the fight on the first day and was cited for the Roll of Honor, was Private Henry Storey (Co C) who would be killed in the attack along with his brother, the Captain of the company.

Private Richard Bridges (Co A 11th Mississippi) later wrote his parents that he was hit in the leg with a shell fragment entering his leg just below the knee penetrating about an inch but not breaking the bone as he crossed the road. Bridges was able to climb back over the west fence and return to his lines. In his letter, he told about witnessing the wounding of his cousin Hugh Bridges during the advance . . ." Hugh once wrote home and told a gay joke on me about throwing down my gun and cartridges and skedaddling when wounded . . . Now Hugh went ahead until he was shot and then he dropped everything and did some of the best running you ever read about **(Private Richard Bridges to Parents, July 12, 1863)**

The last words heard by a number of men in Company K from their Captain George Bird Jr. were "Rally Boys and go over that fence." He died moments later from multiple bullet wounds. Command fell to First Lieutenant John Stanford who was soon hit in the right shoulder but was able to return to his lines. **(Bird / Stanford; Compiled Service Files)**

It is difficult to know exactly how many of the men of Fry's and Marshall's and Davis brigades crossed both fences and charged up that hill. One Confederate observer Randolph Shotwell in Pickett's Division wrote later that 1,000 to 1,200 of Fry's and Marshall's brigades made it past the road. But Shotwell was with the 8th Virginia and it is doubtful if he ever had an accurate glimpse down Emmitsburg Road from his position. **(Shotwell, Virginia and North Carolina at the Battle of Gettysburg p 94)**

Colonel John Fite of the **7th** Tennessee believed that no more than half of his regiment made it across the first fence and that no more than 50 made it across the second fence. "What wasn't shot down, fell down" Lieutenant John Moore Co B 7th Tennessee wrote "Our line was greatly weakened by a great part of the charging column, I mean the front line, remaining in the Emmitsburg Road. I think not more than two thirds crossed it. I know that when I reached the top of the second fence there seems to remain a line of battle in the road." Moore believed after the war that the cause of the repulse was the fences and the inviting roadbed. There seems to be no way to motivate so many men to leave the protection of the roadbed. **(Letter of John Moore Bo B 7th Tn.).** At the wall Private Christopher Mead in the 12th New Jersey, armed with "buck & ball" muskets, observed "We opened up on them and they fell like grain before the reaper." **(Christopher Mead to wife letter July 6, 1863 GNMP park file—12th NJ)**

General Trimble now saw that his 10 regiments must be rushed forward to mingle with and then to pass by the remnants of the Pettigrew line. Trimble would later describe the event. "We passed over the remnant of their line and immediately after some one close by my left sang out 'three cheers for the Old North State', when both brigades sent up a hearty shout, on which I said to my aide, 'Charlie, I believe these fine fellows are going into the enemy's line" **(Clark, Histories from North Carolina, p. 564)** Charlie Grogan, Trimble's aide was captured as was Trimble himself, wounded in the leg, along with other members of his staff such as Lieutenant Samuel Boyer Davis, at the road. Trimble was placed beneath an elm tree.

As stated above, General Lane's report creates the impression that the left shift of his brigade happened after the crossing of the Emmitsburg Road which conflicts with most other accounts. Lane wrote in his August 13, 1863 report "As soon as Pettigrew's Brigade gave back, Lowrance's brigade and my own, without ever being halted took position of the troops on the left who were still contesting the ground with the enemy. My command never moved forward more handsomely. The men reserved their fire in accordance with orders until within good range of the enemy and then opened with telling effect, repeatedly driving the cannoners from their pieces, completely silencing the guns in our immediate front and breaking the line of infantry which was formed on the crest of the hill. We advanced to within a few yards of the stone wall, exposed all the while to a heavy raking artillery fire to the right. My left was here very exposed, and a column of the enemy's infantry was thrown forward in that direction, which infiltrated my whole line. This forced me to withdraw my brigade, the troops on the right having already done so." **(Report of Brigadier James Lane, August 13, 1863, OR 1,27, 666-667)** If we couple the references to "raking artillery fire to the right" and "column of enemy's infantry" to the left with the fact that no mention is made of a road or pike fences, it is clear that the scene described occurred about 100 yards to the west of the fence and that Lane's sense of breaking both artillery and infantry at the far stone wall is inaccurate. Once again in 1877 Lane writes "when the right of my command was within a short distance of the stone fence used by the enemy as a breastwork, one of General Longstreet's staff officers came dashing through a hot fire with orders from Longstreet to move by brigade rapidly to the left as the enemy had thrown out a flanking force in that direction—this force was already pouring a destructive fire into us. As soon as I could dismount from my wounded and plunging horse, I ordered Colonel Avery in command of my left regiment to move to meet the force above refereed to, when he quickly replied, "My God General, do you intend rushing your men into such a place unsupported, when the troops on the right are falling back?' Seeing it was useless to sacrifice my brave men, I ordered my brigade back . . . ." **(James Lane letter to Raleigh Observer, September 7, 1877).** Once again the sequences agree but the entire action was occurring 100 feet to the west of the Emmitsburg Road and the Stone Walls were far distant. Important to note is that Lane appears unaware that many of his men had by this time crossed the road and were acting independent of his command and orders. Most likely the 33rd and 18th NC were still within his command range. Trimble's account of the same movement is far less dramatic. "I took in two North Carolina brigades . . . we marched ¾ of a mile under terrible fire past the first line and reached appoint some 200 yards from the breastworks—here the men broke down from exhaustion & the fatal fire & went no further but walked sullenly back to their entrenchments" **("Civil War Diary of I.R. Trimble," Maryland Historical Magazine, XVII (1922), 1-2)** Again this viewpoint is from the rear of the Division line.

Lane's Left 33rd—18th—28th

One soldier from Lane's 33rd North Carolina regiment who got past the fences (just barely) was Major Joseph Saunders. His regiment was the left flank regiment of Lane's Brigade and had taken severe flanking fire from Ohio troops on their way to the wall. Saunders survived the war and captivity at Johnson's island Ohio and talked of his final conscious moments after crossing the second fence. He claimed to have seen a Yankee color bearer to his left take to his heels followed by most of his Yankee regiment. This must have occurred at the point where the Long Lane meets Emmitsburg Pike. Saunders, realizing that a gap had appeared, ordered what was left of the 33rd North Carolina to move forward (toward the Bryan farm lane). This was the last detail he remembered of the fight as he was hit by a bullet that dropped him to the ground and shattered his mouth and teeth. **(Clark, Histories from North Carolina. p 566 (Conversations with Joseph Saunders)** His brother William (with the 46th North Carolina) heard about the wounding second hand and telegrammed the family "was shot, a bullet having entered his cheek and passed out the back of his head—he was alive when last seen . . ." **(Saunders Papers, SHC)** A version of the wounding also appeared in an unidentified newspaper clipping found at the Southern Historical Society library stating "He was wounded several times and during the Battle of Gettysburg was shot through the head and mouth, leaving about two-thirds of his teeth in Pennsylvania. His death was considered certain and he was reported among those killed."

Companies C & D of the 33rd crossed the fences ahead of the rest of the regiment and 2nd Lieutenant Finley Jones age 28 who had been wounded at Chancellorsville was wounded again and this time captured. (Finley Jones, Compiled Service Record, National Archives)

Private Richard Reeves would be unwounded during the attack and was captured with men from his company "The Moore's Creek Rifle Guards Co E 18th North Carolina in the road bed as the battle ended. He would be later wounded at the Wilderness. **(Richard Reeves, Compiled service file, National Archives)**

Chaplin Francis Kennedy of the 28th NC reported later that Private Wilbur Swaringen in Company K had been seen shot in the lower neck and shoulder (and later captured) while crossing the fence with Captain Moody. Wilbur's 19 year old brother Henry was killed in the road by his side. Swaringen later told of being hit "where the shoulder and the neck unite" and falling on the west side of the fence. As he lay bleeding his regiment had to fire both forward and to the left as bullets poured down the pike from Union forces moving in. "I was in the second line of battle crossing a plank fence when my rifle fell on one side and I fell on the other, about 75 or 80 yards from the enemy, who were behind a stone wall on Cemetery Ridge. Our troops went only a short distance after I was wounded when they fell back, many killed and disabled. The roar of battle slackened somewhat and I felt the blood trickling down my breast. **(Van Swaringen Reminiscences, GNMP library collection)**

Another soldier in the 28th, in Company E, was 25 year old Private Nathaniel Cook from Montgomery County, NC. Cook, whose brother, Lewis, had been shot down wounded beside him at Chancellorsville was shot in he left arm sometime while advancing on the Yankee lines. Nathaniel had been wounded before in the fighting around Richmond and his brother Lewis would recover and be wounded again at the Wilderness. Nathaniel would not be able to make it back to his lines. He would be captured, have his arm amputated and die at a Gettysburg hospital September 1.

The Linebarger family provided leadership to Company C "The South Fork Farmers".

The captain of the 28th NC company at Gettysburg was James Linebarger who had been wounded both at Fredericksburg and at Chancellorsville in the midst of the fighting. The senior Sergeant was Levi Linebarger who would become 1st Sergeant after the battle. Privates Avery and Jacob would advance with Trimble's Division. After the battle, two younger members would join the company and survive the war. As the company approached the fences Captain Linebarger would be wounded in the groin (but make it back to his lines) and Private Jacob would be mortally wounded dying two days later.

Lane's Right 37th—7th

Lt. Colonel William Morris commanding the 37th NC years later discussed the actions of his regiment "At any rate we obeyed Trembles command & charged the enemy out of the road & from behind the stone fence. We went within a few paces of the stone fence. Now being on high ground we could see a considerable distance on our right. I discovered at once that the extreme right had given way. (Author note: As one crosses the Emmitsburg Road at this point one is on higher ground and can see the positions far down the pike to the South. However, once crossing the road the elevation drops again and the rightmost positions are blinded from view) but seeing mcn immediately on our right (7th NC and Scales regiments) some in the road and some between the road and the stone fence. I still felt no fears as to the final result, but soon my attention was called to the left by a volley from the enemy. I made inquiry for the General Tremble immediately was informed that he was severely wounded and carried to the rear. I then changed front to the left & became engaged with the flanking party and in this engagement we suffered severely. Lieutenants Batte *(3rd Lt Wesley Battle Co D W—left arm (amp.) died 8/22,)*

Horton *(2nd Lt. Nathaniel Horton Co B W-left shoulder)*, Peel *(1st Lt. James Pool 22 yr old W Cedar Mtn. W 2nd Manassas WC 7/3)* & Norwood *(1st Lt Thomas Norwood Co A 18 years old W-breast 7/3 & Captured)* was wounded. Captain Alexander and myself was all the officers that were not wounded." **(Letter from Lt. Col William Morris to Colonel W. Saunders, October 1, 1877, Dallas NC, GMNP Library Collection)**

Morris might have also mentioned 3rd Lieutenant Iowa Michigan Royster who was also wounded with the group. Royster who was new with the regiment, having been transferred from the cavalry, was hit in the right upper leg while in the road bed. Somehow he managed to pass the road and "while singing Dixie" and ""waving his sword" was hit again by canister or a shell fragment in the chest and lungs. Nearby in Company E Lieutenant Octavius Wiggins watched him go down "I can see him now in his new uniform with flashing sword, he cheered his men on apparently totally oblivious of the fact that a shrapnel bullet had already passed through his right leg . . ." **(Octavius A Wiggins, Thirty Seven Regiment, Clark's Regiments, Vol. II p. 224)**

By the time the Brigades of Lane (especially the right regiments) and Lowrence had reached the twin fences of the Emmitsburg Pike many rails were down. Some had been torn down by Pettigrew's men and others collapsed under grape and canister shot. The 37th North Carolina regiment "sprang over the fence followed by the whole command" according to Lieutenant Thomas Norwood of Company A. Norwood continued to tell how he and Lieutenant Iowa Michigan Royster (from Company G) pushed on past the first fence when Royster was wounded in the thigh. **(Michael Taylor "North Carolina in the Pickett-Pettigrew-Trimble Charge at Gettysburg *Magazine* No 8 (January 1993: 77)** In the same regiment 3rd Lieutenant Wesley Battle Co D "North Carolina Defenders NC "North Carolina Defenders" was wounded in the left arm while in the road and later captured and cared for by a Union soldier Kenneth Hickey of the 12th Massachusetts Co E until he died. For those in Scales Brigade who remembered the final breakthrough on July 1 back at the Seminary a very different Union line existed . . . . "The Yankees were harder to push back" than two days before later wrote E.M Hays in Scales Brigade **(E.M Hayes to John Bachelder October 15, 1890, Vol. 3 pp.1776-1777)** Another man to fall in the 37th as he approached the fence was Private Joseph Benjamin Burleyson a 22 yr old who had enlisted in Mecklenburg County. He had cousins in the 28th North Carolina who reported his wounding and capture home after the battle. Burelyson had been wounded in the hand at Fredericksburg.

Second Lieutent Octavius Wiggins of Company E 37th NC claimed that his men crossed the Emmitsburg Pike fences "Over the Emmitsburg road we went and rushed for the stone wall, the line all the while seems to be melting away. **(Octavius A Wiggins, Thirty Seven Regiment, Clark's Regiments, Vol. II p. 661)**

Private John Austin was a 24 year old soldier from Union county who had been wounded at Glendale and had won the Badge of Distinction for bravery at Chancellorsville. He appears to have taken a place at the fence in the Emmitsburg Road and fired away at Yankee troops until the remains of his company (Co D 37th NC) surrendered.

Another soldier decorated for bravery at Chancellorsville who was wounded and captured at the road was from one of the hardest hit companies of the 7th. 2nd Lt Arthur Walker (Co K) had been wounded at Malvern Hill and had been awarded the "Badge of Distinction" for his actions at Chancellorsville. Walker was hit by bullets in the gut & the breast yet managed to make it back to his lines.

As the troops of the 7th North Carolina approached the road Major Turner had the wisdom to tell his men to "rush against and push down": the western fence along the pike. This they did with the inertia of a solid line of advancing soldiers at the quick step. Turner reports that the first fence did go down but that the slowdown which occurred in the road bed took away all the forward motion of the regiment and the second fence was impossible to destroy. Thus climbing over was the only option. By this point all of the 7th color guard was killed or wounded on the field.

Turner having been wounded (in the abdomen) just after crossing the road later wrote "I crawled to the road and turned command over to Captain James Harris. He and some others offered to carry me back. At that point the enemy was advancing on our right. Harris and others did escape. I was captured. Parts of our line did advance to the wall but most stayed and fired from the road. **(J. McLeod Turner letter October 10, to Raleigh Observer, Raleigh NC)** The bullet that hit Turner would enter from the front and then strike his spinal column paralyzing him

The surviving officers of the 7th NC were very candid after the war in discussing the reluctance of their companies in climbing over two sets of fences and charging up a hill through a whirlwind of shell and canister and bullets. The right companies F, A, & H all appeared to settle into the roadbed and fire away at the Yankee positions uphill ahead.

Second Lieutenant Daniel Kinney of wing Company F wrote in 1877 "We went to the turnpike road. No orders were given to retreat. I was captured and most of my men . . . The Yankees fell in on our right and rear. The balance of the regiment escaped up the turnpike to the left . . . most of Company F were was wounded and captured. I think there were only three men of Company F that were captured that were not wounded" **(Daniel Kinney letter to Raleigh Observer, October 23, 1877, Clemmonsville, NC)** Company A (next to Company F) saw a few men advance but most stayed at the road as well. 1st Lieutenant Pickney Carlton in the same year wrote "We advanced to about 40 yards of the works. No member of my company reached the worksl. The command to fall back was given to an aide to General Trimble. In my company we had 8 killed, 12 wounded and 2 captured. In the regiment 86 killed 256 wounded and 28 captured. We started out on the 3rd with about 400 men and came out with 40. When we feel back all the fighting on the right had ended" **(Pickney Carlton letter to Raleigh Observer September 26th, 1877, Statesville, NC)**

After the wounding of Major Turner command was taken by Captain James Harris Company H. He recalled remaining in the road until the fighting was drawing down. "We reached a road enclosed on both sides by a plank fence about 30 yards from the enemy works and did not go farther without support. In a few moments after reaching the road we saw that Picket's forces were falling back. I took command After Major Turner was wounded and we stayed there until the Yankees on our right came down to the road and threatened our right. The Yankees in front of us never crossed their works to advance on us. We had at least 50-60% of our officers and men killed or wounded." Lieutenant Thomas Mulloy also mentions the loss of the regimental flag and of all of the color bearers. To his left Companies D and G both lost their Captains (Cahill & Hill) but perhaps the actions of the 37th NC prompted some crossing of the fences by these left companies. One indication of this is found in Lieutenant Thomas Mulloy (Co D) account when he wrote that "There was a road running parallel to the enemies' works and about 80 yards in front with high post and rail fence on the side of the road next to the enemy. We reached this fence as an organized body and about half of the men and most of the officers crossed the fence and some of them reached the works. A few but not over a dozen of my company reached the enemy works some of whom were lost there. Among the wounded were the commanding office of the regiment, who was wounded and captured, the Captain of my own company (Captain Timothy Cahill—wounded in the right leg and later captured July 5) and two or three other officers slightly" (Author note: One of these wounded officers was Philadelphia born 2nd Lieutenant Pasqual Agostini a 24 yr old Italian merchant who had moved south before the war and was wounded in the arm and foot) **(Thomas Mulloy letter to Raleigh Observer, September 29, 1877, Charleston SC)** In Company F of the 7th NC Private Richard Franklin Fleming was a 21 year old who was wounded in the roadbed and then captured. Fleming would recover and be wounded again at Wilderness and then be promoted to Corporal.

Scales Left Regiments 38—13—22

One gets the impression that there must have either been a gap between the 7th NC Regiment of Lane and the 38th Regiment of Scales OR that the 38th had moved ahead faster than the 7th on Lane's right wing. The hesitance of the right companies of the 7th NC to move beyond the Emmitsburg Road and the lack of any mention of Scales regiments to their right suggest this.

According to 2nd Lieutenant Henry Moore the 38th North Carolina hit the fence line at an angle and the effect "deranged our line very much". The regiment was faced with two problems at this point. First was the flow of soldiers from Pettigrew's line (52nd & 47th NC) who had enough of the fight and were retreating back across the road And second the need to order the line and climb over the second fence. Not many men in the 38th achieved this difficult task. "Our men kept up a weak fire through the plank fence" is how Moore remembered it.

Consequently the 38th (Scales left Regiment) 2nd Lieutenant Henry Moore and 1st Lieutenant A.J. Brown seem to among those who lasted the longest in the roadbed and who after their capture had a perspective of the fields to their front. "About 150 yards from the enemy a part of our line struck another fence which confused us considerably. The fire from the enemy's artillery and infantry was now terrible and we were reduced to a mere skirmish line. We reached another fence which was on the side of the road. Here we halted and endeavored to reform our line with the men who had become mixed up from different commands. I spoke to Captain A.S Cloud who was that day in command of the 16th North Carolina regiment and asked him what we should do. He replied "We will hold on here until we get help". I looked back and saw some troops apparently moving in our direction but they were some distance in the rear. They finally disappeared and I suppose they were ordered back" Moore along with Lieutenant A.J. Brown surrendered. Brown, 1st Lieutenant in Company A had been awarded the "Badge of Distinction" for bravery at Chancellorsville and the 20 year old Duplin County officer would survive the battle. Moore, himself, learned after the war that after the retreat only about 40 men remained from the 38th North Carolina commanded by a first lieutenant **(H.C Moore to the Editor, *Raleigh Observer*, November 6, 1877)** The commanding 1st Lieutenant was 1st Lt. John Robinson 24 yr old from Sampson Co. 10/22/61 (later promoted to Captain)

One of the few officers from the Brigade leadership to make it to the road and escape was Acting Brigade Adjutant general D.M. McIntire who was able to leave the pike and run back to the west. **(H.C Moore to the Editor, *Raleigh Observer*, November 6, 1877)**

Captain Rowland W. Williams with Company I 13 NC made it to the road with his company and recalled "Lowrance's Brigade fired from the road for a bout ten minutes before falling back." Williams's cousin in the same company (The Rockingham Rangers), 1st Lieutenant W.H. Winchester had his right foot shot off except the heel string, which he cut off with a knife before being captured. Winchester had also been wounded at Chancellorsville. **(memoirs of Rowland Williams, letter to Clark's regiments)**

Another 13th North Carolina officer who made it to the road was Lieutenant Henry Walker in company B, whose brother Levi had been wounded on the first day and lost his left leg to amputation. Henry would survive the battle only to be wounded on the skirmish line two weeks later and have his left leg amputated as well)

In Company H of the 13th NC, 3rd Lieutenant Nathan Smith, who would later become temporary adjutant, also made it to the road and wrote in his report "Our part of the line advanced splendidly and the enemy was driven from the works in front of our troops. In action, we lost 23 men killed and wounded with some others captured in the works. We were the last or among the last to reach the rear." **(Nathan Smith letter to the editor, 1877; Clark's Regiments Vol. 1, pp 698-69)** One half of the survivors, including Smith, would be captured later at Falling Waters. Smith and his brother, Lieutenant James Smith, had both been students before the war. James had been wounded in the ankle on July 1.

Finally from the 13th NC is the report of Major Elijah Withers who was wounded on the first. "I was wounded on the first and was replaced by Captain L.B. Henderson of company A. He was wounded about 30 feet from the enemy works. When he was shot he noticed that the troops on the right had already given way and that the fire was worse from the left and the right than from his front. When he was wounded the troops were entering the first line of breastworks having driven out the federals. A federal officer was trying to rally his men and shot with his pistol Private Tollie (note: actually by now Corporal Trollinger (Company K) a 22 year old former clerk from Rockingham NC. The popular "Tollie" had been wounded in the thigh at Chancellorsville and rose from Private to Corporal to Sergeant Major of the regiment) The Yankees fled to their second line and then we were hit from the right and left. 'Tollie' was carried to the rear and survived . . . . Captain H.L. Guerrant of Company K also informs me that his men entered the enemy works and stayed until driven out by attacks from the right and left." (Major Elijah Withers report, Clark's regiments Vol. 1)

The reader needs to take into account in these recollections a striking distinction in the use of the terms "wall" and "works" in almost all of these memories. The existence of a final wooden fence line which runs 300 feet to the North from the Stone Wall angle clearly provided a very different perspective of the Union defense for men of Scales Brigade as well as the right two regiments of Lane (7th NC & 37th NC). It is in the memories of these soldiers that we most frequently see references to "enemy works" while the perspective of those to their left (Lane's 28th NC, 18th NC and 33rd NC) as well as Davis's Brigade and Marshall's left regiments (11th & 26th NC) almost always speaks of stone walls. Success in taking the "enemies' works" seems to have meant successful advance to the forward wooden fence. This writer has come to the conclusion that the middle regiments of the Trimble line were most often content to settle into the roadbed, while the flanks of both Lane and Lowrence tended to move ahead past the pike fences.

Scales Right Regiments 22nd NC 16th NC

Some men from the 16th and 22nd North Carolina on Scales right flank followed their flag across the road. Some would make it to the wooden fence halfway to the stone wall but others such as Private John Brown in Co B and 2nd *Lieutenant* William Byrd in Company C of the 16th went part way and then turned around to return to the wall. One officer with the 53rd Virginia, Major John C Timberlake later recalled seeing these men slow down and then reverse direction claims to have shouted to them "For God's sake, come on" **(Supplement to the OR, V Part 1, p 336)**

However it is not clear exactly where Timberlake was himself when he shouted this plea since many from the 53rd Virginia themselves never made it past the roadway. The behavior of the 16th North Carolina is perplexing to historians. The evidence suggests that some of the regimental companies made it as far as the road and beyond and yet other companies seem to have fallen back well short of the goal. The company commanders of companies F, I and K all were relieved on command or court-martialed shortly after the battle and the casualty figures for these three companies reveal minor losses for July 3rd.

FOOTNOTE In companies F, I and K of the 16th North Carolina we note a number of disciplinary actions taken after the Battle of Gettysburg. Company F was led that day by 25 year old 1st Lt. Milton Blackwell. He had been appointed in March 1862 and was Court-martialed In September 1863 and reduced to a Private. Sergeant Alfred Gash, age 20, commanded company I on July 3 after the wounding of the last remaining officer on July 1. He would be reduced in rank to a Private a month after Gettysburg. Finally Captain John Camp 28 yr old leader of Company from Polk county was court-martialed and dismissed shortly after he battle. So that the record is clear, a number of commanding officers did a fine job on the third. Captain Cloud in company E was later was promoted to Lieutenant Colonel of the regiment and several Company commanders (Lt. Ira Profitt—Co A, Captain Adolphus McKinney—Co D and 1st Lt John McEntire—Co G were captured in the fighting and spent time in prisons)

Chapter Seven

"Also for Glory"

The mad dash on the right side of the Pettigrew line had seen a group of men from Tennessee and Alabama rush forward toward the stone angle of the forward wall. Colonel Shepard reports that at this point "The line both right and left, a far as I could observe, seemed to melt away until there was but little left" **(Shepard report OR II, 647)** The flag of the 14th Tennessee in the middle of Fry's brigade was in the hands of Private Thomas Davidson as the second fence was crossed. But he went down with a bullet wound shouting "Bob, take the flag. I am shot" **(C.Wallace Cross, Jr. Ordeal by Fire: *A History of the Fourteenth Tennessee Volunteer Infantry Regiment CSA* (Clarksville, TN p 72)**

The Yankee perspective of the move past the pike fences was recorded in his report by General Alexander Hayes who reported that he had his men run through a manual of arms as the rebels maneuvered the roadway and then "four lines rose from behind our stone wall and before the smoke of our first volley had cleared away, the enemy in dismay and consternation, were seeking safety in flight." **(Hayes Report, July 8, 1863.OR.I, p 455)**

Fry's Right Flank 13th Alabama & 1st Tennessee

But the infantrymen who were firing the shots told it somewhat differently. "When the charging columns reached the road our infantry opened with all the vigor that they could use, adding still further to the enemy's confusion, and by the time the second fence and the one nearest to us was crossed, about one hundred and fifty yards away, there was no semblance of formation remaining, only a great mass of desperate men pushing on, the color-bearers keeping well to the front." **(Fleming, ed., Hays, p 458")** The massive blasts at the crossing of the second pike fence followed by a second barrage at the nearest fence each reduced the Tennessee and Alabama numbers (plus men from the 52nd and 47th North Carolina of Marshall's right. The 26th and the 11th NC of course never faced the inner fence nor had the protection it must have provided. Still some men from Archer's brigade did ran that gauntlet and survive because some made it to the outer stone angle and joined with Virginians from the 56th and 28th Virginia under Garnett.

Just who were these men? Some like Springfield's Private George Powell of Company C 14th Tennessee died at the wall from the bullets coming at them from three directions. Powell was a Color Corporal. Another who died there was Private John McClure 35 year old Salem farmer who had enlisted April of 1861.

Several lived to tell the tale including Sergeant Junius Kimble from the 14th Tn. (Co A); Sergeant Robert Mockbee from Company B; Captain John Turney (K) and Private Wiley Woods (I) of the 1st Tn; and Captain Archibald Norris Co (Co K 7th Tn). The tale they weave tells us of Sergeant Mockbee handing the 14th Tennessee flag to Private Columbus Horn (Company G) the Mockbee taking it up again until it was snatched up again by Corporal George Powell (Co. C). The last memory was of "Boney" Smith who was quite possibly a black servant taking it to the fence where he was killed and it was captured **(C.Wallace Cross, Jr. Ordeal by Fire: *A History of the Fourteenth Tennessee Volunteer Infantry Regiment CSA* (Clarksville, TN p 72)** The tale of Boney Smith is an interesting one. Even his race seems to be a matter of debate. The rosters of the 14th Tennessee do not carry his name yet he is mentioned by a number of survivors as having carried the flag near the end and being killed. He is always referred to as being a tall lankey man. One Connecticut Soldier Sergeant Ben Hirst of the 14th Connecticut wrote after war about a tall Confederate at the distant fence placing the flag of the 14th Tennessee against the fence rail and standing up tall "looking us calmly in the face" and then being shot down by several bullets. He said nothing about the race of the man.(Bee, *Boys from Rockville*, p 450)

The 14th Tennessee Commander Lt. Colonel James Lockert had enlisted in Clarksville back in June of 1861. He had been wounded during the rush up the hill by bullets in both thighs and laid on the ground wounded and bleeding until the fighting ended and he was captured.

There were also those who fought at the stone wall and were able to retreat back across the fields to avoid capture. The commander of the "Mountain Boys" Company C 1st Tennessee Captain Aaron Alexander was a 25 year old Winchester farmer who enlisted April 21, 1861. He had been wounded at 2nd Manassas would be later wounded again at the Wilderness, but this day at Gettysburg he would go as far as any man and return unhurt. His good friend, and fellow Captain, Thomas Arnold with the "Shelton Creek Boys" Company H would not dare the running retreat and would be taken prisoner. As would Company I's Captain Henry Hawkins.

Colonel Fry, the 42 year old Tallassee Lawyer, was hit in the leg, sword in hand, on the slope halfway up from the pike. The Colonel was with his men of the 13th Alabama and shouted "Go on, It will not last five minutes longer" **(Fry, *Pettigrew's Charge at Gettysburg*, p**

93) Nearby Major A.S. Van de Graff Commanding the 5th Alabama had fallen down just past the roadway' second fence and had been able to crawl back to the roadbed. He told his wife a few days later that by this time he was "overheated and broken down" **(Van de Graf to wife letter, GNMP library)**

One of the most interesting accounts of what happened inside the outer stone angle was told by Captain John Turney (Co K 1st Tennessee) who as senior Captain would have taken command with the wounding of both Colonel Frye and Colonel George. Turney tells of the charge up the hill and provides insight into the events that followed the climbing of the stone wall which once protected Company K of the 71st Pa. "In wonderful order, at double quick time, we continued the charge: and not until we were within about fifteen steps of the stone wall did I give the command to fire. The volley confused the enemy. I then ordered a charge with bayonets, and on moved our gallant boys. Another instant we were engaged in a desperate hand-to-hand conflict for the possession of the fragile wall of masonry that held out as the sole barrier between the combatants. Each man seemed to pick his foe and it fell my lot to struggle with a stalwart Federal officer, who made a vicious thrust at my breast. I parried it just in time. Thus, for a few moments the contest settled as a death struggle, and one triumphant shout was given as the federals in our immediate front and our right yielded and fled in confusion to a point just back of the crest of the hill, abandoning their artillery.**(Captain J.B. Turney, "The First Tennessee at Gettysburg", Confederate Veteran, VII (1900), pp 535-537)** (Authors note: From my previous research on this action, the group of Northern soldiers that Turney fought was Company K of the 71st Pa. Four companies of the 71st remained at the front wall when the rest of the regiment was withdrawn back to the crest. The 71st companies remaining were Companies K, G, H, and C from north to south along that segment of the wall. The testimony of Sergeant Major William Stocker of the 71st make clear the viewpoint of the same action from the Union perspective "I saw them come to the road and just as they got to the road the gun was fired and after they passed the fence they came on with a great rush. I saw one or two of our men start for the rear and I must say that, at the time I thought it rather cowardly . . . The men who were with me stood and fought, and the enemy came in great numbers, and, as I remember, there was a great boulder which formed a sort of stepping stone and made it easy to get over the wall, and they appeared to mass at this a place, I suppose on account of it being easier to get over, and came over the wall in overwhelming numbers. They came with such force that they seemed to rebound and go back, like a wave receding from the shore, and as they went back they took us with them. (Author note" The large boulder mentioned by Stockton is still at the same location today and his description of the rebels surging and receding matches Turney's account of a crossing followed by a quick retreat and entrenchment.—The officer with the sword mentioned by Turney was probably 2nd Lieutenant William McDaid, then commanding Company K—since McDaid, who escaped to the rear, would have been the only Union soldier with a sword at that location) "When we got to the other side of the wall, they ordered us to the rear, but I told the men to stay where they were. Then, a non-commissioned officer was ordered to take us back but he didn't do it . . . We laid there along that boulder and the rebels knelt along the wall as far as I could see to our left; kneeling down, firing over the wall . . . We were right in among them, there was one on each side of me . . . . I heard the water rattling in his canteen ad asked him to give me a drink but he would not do it . . . . While we were lying there, the five of us agreed among ourselves to escape if we got the opportunity. I was to give the word, which would be the signal, and we would jump altogether to get over the wall, it being impossible to have done so singly. Previous to that a number of balls were striking the wall all around our heads while we were on the opposite side of it; the balls came from the rear and we supposed it was some of our troops. I raised my head to see where they came from and over to the extreme left I saw some of our troops, on their left, and I then found that our men had gotten to their rear and on their flank, and then I gave the order to jump and we all jumped over the all and ran in a body and we were met in the rush by our regiment and another and we immediately commenced taking the rebels prisoners." **(Testimony of William Stocker,** ***72nd Pa vs. the Gettysburg Monument Commission*****, DATE, pp 242-244)** Stocker's story is confirmed by the account of Private Wiley Woods, who would be captured at this wall. Some of the Yankees "hollowed out we surrender and no officer said anything. I said crawl over to our side & you shanty be hurt." These Union men became the prisoners Stockton testified about. **(Wiley Woods, The 1st Tennessee Flag at Gettysburg, Confederate Veterans Papers, SCL-DU**

Thus, the retreat witnessed by Captain Turney was the rapid withdrawal by these four companies of the 71st. That still left companies I, A & F of the 69th Pennsylvania to Turney's right. The fight of the four companies of the 71st were not made without cost. Just in Company K facing Turney, in addition to the four men mentioned by Adjutant Stocker who were temporarily captured. Five men were killed and five wounded in the fighting **(Ernsberger,** ***At The Wall*****, pp. 604-607)**

(Killed—Sgt Thomas Cosgrove, Corporals John Duggan & James Haggerty and Privates Levi Dellinger & Reuben Miller) (Wounded—Sgt Andrew Monaghan, Corporals Peter Quinn & Henry Ottinger and Privates George Fitzgibbons & John Maroney)

Turney continues his recollection by discussing the situation at the stone after the retreat of the 71st companies. "I now mounted the rock wall and found everything successful to my right, while the center and left of Archer's Brigade had failed (author note—Turney would come under fire later after making this statement from other Alabama and Tennessee survivors. Turney's leftward (northward) view at this point, would have been of a long stretch of fence line running north from the Stone Wall angle, behind which many men of the remainder of Archer's brigade had taken cover. "I decided to throw a column beyond the works and enfilade the lines to my left, and succeeded in taking with me my own company (Co K) and parts of others.

The volleys we fired were effective, and created confusion enabling Capt J.H. Moore, and possibly others of the Seventh Tennessee and Captain J.H. Taylor, of the thirteenth

Alabama to lead their companies over the works. (Note—The "works" mentioned by Turney are of course the stones along the forward fence line not the main Union Wall)l. A few of the Fifth Alabama also crossed. (Author note—The Turney version of this action became a topic of hot debate after publication, however, most of the details of the story are consistent with records concerning soldiers from various Archer regiments who ended up either killed, wounded or captured at the stone wall angle. In addition, Turney's recollection is consistent with the recollections of both Adjutant Stockton of the 71st and various men of the 56th Virginia. Given the choice of either standing at the fence line running south under murderous fire or shifting to the right where temporary success seemed to be occurring, it is not unbelievable that many made the later choice.

Turney further wrote "By this time, at a distance of only about thirty yards, and behind the crest of the hill, I noted the reforming of the Federal lines. This necessitated a withdrawal to a position behind the stone wall, and there we joined the balance of the First Tennessee. After a desperate, but unsuccessful, effort to dislodge us the enemy again retired over the crest of the hill. I then made a second effort to cross the works and enfilade but by this time our lines . . . were being beaten back by a most destructive fire; and as our opposition melted in their front, the enemy turned a deadly fire upon the unprotected squad of First Tennesseans, who, together with a few of Garnett's Virginians (56th Va.) had the second time crossed the works. The artillery as well as the musketry belched forth destruction to our little band, and we were forced to drop back behind the wall." **(Captain J.B. Turney, "The First Tennessee at Gettysburg", Confederate Veteran, VII (1900), pp 535-537)**

It must be remembered that the 13th Alabama right next to the 1st Tennessee went into the fight on the third with about 158 officers and men. They had been the hardest hit in Archer's Brigade in the fighting against the Iron Brigade in the McPherson woods. Their loses this day would be 6 killed, 24 wounded who returned, 12 wounded and captured and 41 captured unwounded. Especially hard hit would be Companies B, D and G. The commanding officer of Company B "The Southern Stars" 1st Lieutenant Hardy Gibson would be killed as he led most of his men past the pike and up to the outer stone wall. There 60% of his 24 total were lost. Six were wounded and seven were captured unwounded in company B. Captain Walter Taylor (Co D) would lose half his men fighting to the outer wall: 4 killed, 4 wounded, 8 captured. Captain Robert Cook's men in the "Yancy Guards" (Co G) would suffer 6 wounded and 8 captured. The casualty figures for the 13th Alabama give a clue to which companies probably remained at the road as well. Company commander 26 year old 2nd Lieutenant Thomas Strong would be part of the 70% loss suffered by Company D of the 13th Alabama that day with 10 out of 14 men captured but only one of these wounded. Companies A, F, H and I all had lower loss levels. **(Tamra Stephens, *History of the 13th Alabama manuscript*)**

There were other men from Tennessee who wrote of this fight at the stone wall after the war. Sergeant Junius Kimble of the 14th Tennessee (Co A) "Still, after practical annihilation, the remnant of these glorious Confederates keep going forward, until they silenced the guns and stood in the works of the enemy. Those enemy who remained in the works were prostrated at our feet, practically prisoners, with arms upon the ground, not firing a shot. For five, perhaps ten, minutes we held our ground and looked back for a prayed for support. It came not, and we knew that their battle of Gettysburg was ended. Many of this brave remnant choose surrender rather than run the gauntlet of the enemy's fire. Among others, I refused to yield and made a break for my liberty in the face of their guns." **(June Kimble, "Tennesseeans at Gettysburg—The Retreat" Confederate Veteran CV, XVIII (1910), pp460-461)** There were at least three men from Company H at the stone wall with Turney, Privates Arnold, Hawkins and Alexander and at least three men from Company F as well, Lieutenant Foster and Privates Wiley Woods and Sergeant Eli Cox (all would be captured there) 2nd Lt John Moore (Co B 7th Tn) claimed in his pension to have been with these men at the wall and escaped. Captain Walter Taylor (Co C with the 13th Alabama) was captured and claims to have been at the stone wall as well **(Tennessee Confederate Service Pension files)**

The regimental commander of the 14th was Lt. Colonel James Lockhart. He was wounded in both thighs as they rushed forward toward the fence from Emmitsburg Road. Sergeant June Kimble then commanding Company A had this to saw about Lockhart . . . "His fearless leadership had long since won the admiration and confidence of his regiment, and superiors in rank. Because he was ever in the thickest of the fight, and never got a scratch, he was daubed "Old Ironclad." They declared that the enemy couldn't hit him with a bullet, much less kill him. This good fortune, luck or providence, whatever the reader may call it, at last forsook him in that mortal struggle at the foot of Cemetery Ridge at Gettysburg, on July 3d and last day. In that world famous, Pickett's Charge, Lt. Col. Lockhart commanded his regiment, the 14th Tenn. and as always leading some ten or twelve paces in advance e of his line, and some fifty or less yards from the enemies works, this gallant soldier fell, pierced by a bullet, with both thighs broken. It was at first supposed, a mortal wound, but with the surgeon's skill aided by the patient's indomitable will power and an unimpaired constitution, carried him safely over but ended his service as an active soldier" **(June Kimble statement, The First State Bank of Eastland, Gettysburg National Military Park Library, 14th Tennessee file)**

The confusion of this outer stone angle is difficult to accurately determine but the combined accounts of both Archer and Garnett survivors seems to tell the following tale. The four companies of the 71st Pa which were left forward by their commander to cover the wall between Cushing remaining guns and the outer angle broke to the rear after taking a volley from both the 56th and 28th Virginia as well as men firing obliquely from the 1st Tennessee and the 13th Alabama. These four companies of the 71st lost about 12 men killed or severely wounded and about another dozen captured as Virginians, Tennesseans and Alabamans volleyed and leapt the stone wall. Once over these men found themselves staring into the guns of the 72nd Pa at the top of the crest. However, since the 72nd was just completing a shift to the north and preparing to volley, most of the rebels were able to jump back across the stonewall and take cover. The subsequent 72nd volley did some damage including probably killing General Garnett on horseback some 20 feet behind the stonewall. However, now the 72nd Pa was on the horizon line of the crest and the Confederates had the wall as protection. In the moments that followed, volleys from the Archer and Garnett men killed and wounded over 50 men of the 72nd and all the time more men from the 14th Tennessee and the 28th Virginia were drawn to the firefight. The 72nd, raked with volley, pulled back beyond the crest to regroup and just at the same moment Armistead's Brigade arrived, their commander sensing a general Union withdrawal ordered what would be the second (even larger) crossing of the stonewall. **(Ernsberger, Paddy Owen's Regular's, Vol. II, pp 603-607)** The flag of the 14th Tennessee would not make the sideways shift to the stonewall but would be found some 20yards to the left along the fence. **(J.B. Smith, The Charge of Pickett, Pettigrew and Trimble", Battles and Leaders, Vol. III, p. 354)**

Captain Turney's final account recalls the end of the struggle at the stone wall. He discusses seeing General Armistead cross the wall and being wounded. "Seeing the impossibility of effective work from behind the wall and the shattered condition of our lines, I hastily called the captains of my regiment for conference. Captains Thompson (Author note—here Captains Turney's memory is faulty as Captain James Thompson Co. F had been captured on July 1), Hawkins (Henry Hawkins Co. I—captured), Arnold (Thomas Arnold Co H—captured), and Alexander (Aaron Alexander Co. C—escaped) responded. While we were conferring, a courier arrived and, calling for the officer in charge, told me General Lee's orders were to hold my position, as Ewell had broken the lines on the extreme left. These orders settled the question and brought us face to face with the critical elements of that decisive battle. To the left of the First Tennessee our lines had completely given way, thus enabling the enemy to concentrate its fire—not only from our center but from our left—directly upon my command . . . . Some of the Virginians to our right had already yielded. For Ten minutes (sic) still we remained the target . . . . Retreat across the open was now impossible, and a white flag was reluctantly hoisted by a Virginia regiment to my right (56th Va.) and thus it was that those of the First Tennessee who survived the struggle and had not escaped yielded themselves as prisoners . . . except a flesh wound in my neck and a number of bullet holes in my clothes, I was unharmed" **(Captain J.B. Turney, "The First Tennessee at Gettysburg", Confederate Veteran, VII (1900), pp 535-537)**

The thick smoke made it impossible for Union troops at the wall to see clearly and inevitably contradictory stories emerge about what they saw. One clear example is two stories that seem to have factual basis told by two different men from the 14th Connecticut. Clearly they each had looked to their left and saw through the smoke images Rebel soldiers who had climbed up on the stone wall at the forward angle. One reported that a "daring and audacious Confederate jumped on a cannon that had been left about 30 feet in front of the wall, then waved his hat for the men to come with him, he was riddled with bullets". Factually this seems to blend together the location of Cushing's #1 gun with the action of Tennessee troops crossing the wall and being fired upon by then72nd Pa. (Charles Page, History of the Fourteenth Regiment, Connecticut Volunteer Infantry, pp 142-156) Another Connecticut man looked in the same direction at the same time and through the smoke saw the soldier waving a flag and being knocked over by a gunner with a sponge or a rammer. **(Diary of Captain George Bowen, The Valley Forge Journal, Vol. II, No 1 June 1884, 135)** This is similar to the recollection of Sergeant Major Stockton of the 71st Pa who told of a gunner knocking down a rebel with his plunger **(Testimony of William Stockton, 72nd Pa VS Gettysburg Memorial Commission)**

By the time the fighting at this stone wall was over at least 4 companies of the First Tennessee would have been devastated in this fighting. Captain Turney's own company K had three wounded and six captured. Company I under Captain Thomas Hawkins would also lose three wounded but 9 captured. Company H would have one killed 9 wounded and 15 captured. In this company the three Cashion brothers, Andrew, Gabriel and William would all be wounded or captured.

Fry's Left Flank 5th Alabama & 7th Tennessee

Meanwhile further to the left along the inner fence line the 5th Alabama and 7th Tennessee and part of the 14th, divorced from the firefight with the 72nd Pa and the forward stone wall exchanged fire with the men of Hay's regiments (mostly the 14th Connecticut) behind the farther and thicker rear stonewall. "The color bearer of the 5th Alabama Battalion carried its flag near the stonewall before he was shot down "not more than ten rods distant" **(Charles Page, *History of the 14th Regiment, Connecticut Volunteer Infantry* (Meridian, Connecticut, 1906, pp142-156).**

Commissary Sergeant William Fulton, Fifth Alabama, who did not make the charge, talked to the returning and surviving members of his regiment. His memory of the role of the 13th years later told of ". . . the line is never broken and their pace is not slackened until they reach the enemy's lines and here amid smoke and carnage the deadly work gocs on until our en are forced by the overwhelming odds to fall back. The color bearer of the Fifth Alabama is shot down, the flag falls to the ground. Private Bullock of Co, "C" raises it again. He is shot. Then Private Manning of Company "B" lifts it again as it floats out on the breeze Manning is killed. Then Private Gilbert of Co "a" seizes it and succeeds in bearing it to the rear where we were forced to retreat. This was a bloody charge. Many poor fellows were left stretched upon the field, dead or severely wounded." **(William Frierson Fulton, Family Record and War Reminiscences, 1919)**

At the fence, Captain John Allen leading Company B of the 7th was hit and assumed dead by his men . . . "Capt. Allen was conspicuously brave. He was wounded in nearly every engagement. He particularly distinguished himself in the desperate charge at Gettysburg. On the third day, and was there so severely wounded that he was left for dead on the field. His strong vitality pulled him through, however, and after a long time in prison he secured an exchange, returned to command of his company before Petersburg . . ." (Confederate Veteran, Nov 1901, p 495)

Another Captain in the 7th Asoph Hill (Company F) died at the fence. "He walked all the way to Gettysburg at the head of his company. When that fatal day and the world's greatest charge was ordered, Capt Hill stepped to the front smiling, as was his custom on such occasions. He carried his company to the 'stone wall' so well known in that battle. Capt. Alexander (note: Corporal Benjamin Alexander at the time), who was perhaps the last man who ever spoke to him, told me afterwards that Capt. Hill stood waving his sword to his men, urging them forward in the face of one hundred pieces of artillery in front . . . Capt Alexander thinks death was instantaneous: **(Confederate Veteran, 1901, p 160)**

The First Sergeant of Company B 5th Alabama Battalion, David Turner took a bullet in the right shoulder and would be captured at the fence line. Private Robert Womach (Co H 7th Tennessee) took a bullet in his right arm at the fence but would make it back to his own lines. His arm would be amputated later.

The rush from the Pike to that fence line had been costly, One of the few who lived, June Kimble wrote later of the loss. Private Theodore Hartman (Co A 14th Tennessee) grabbed Kimble's shoulder as they rushed up the slope. Private William McCulloch was at Kimble's other side shouting "I am with you" before a bullet hit him in the head. **(Kimble, W. H. McCulloch," MC)** The flag of the 7th Tennessee would finally be saved when Captain Archibald Norris (Co K) from Nashville, tore it from its staff and tucked it under his coat (A.S. Van de Graff letter to wife, July 8, 1863)

From the Union view it seemed that this forward fence line marked the boundary of how far the rebels could advance. "none could get over a low rail fence a short distance in front of the stone wall without our permission" wrote Sergeant Hirst in the 14th CT **(Robert Bee, *The Boys from Rockville*, p 150)** It must be remembered that while today this restored fence line still stands to mark the spot, the many larger rocks appeared to be piled up along some segments back in 1863. It is clear that the men from Delaware and Connecticut saw this fence and rock formation as significant. One man wrote about thoughts before the cannonade began "some of the boys were about to tear down a fence that ran partway across the field in our front, but some of the Division or Brigade staff stopped them saying that the fence might be of more use in another direction" **(Report of the Joint Committee, p 12)** It must be remembered that two of the companies in the 14th were equipped with Sharps breech loading rifles. These two companies which had been out on skirmish duty were placed at the far right of the Connecticut line and poured forth a wall of fire into particular rebel companies opposite them.

Another reference to this front fence and piles of rock is found in Colonel Samuel Shepard of the 7th Tennessee's account of the movement forward of his men. "The men advanced directly upon the enemy's work, the first line of which was composed of rough stones. The enemy abandoned this, but just in the rear was massed a heavy force." One might assume that Shepard observed forward Union skirmishers rushing back through this fence line and rocks and perhaps turning to fire as they did. **(OR, vol. 27, pt 2, p 247)**

Two men from the 7th Tennessee who were hit who were hit on the slope were Colonel Fite himself and 1st Lieutenant F.A. Timberlake from Nashville in Company B. Near them Lt. Colonel Newton George a farmer from George's Store of the 1st Tennessee had been struck down as well. All three were captured at the end of the fighting. George was trying to crawl back toward the road when a Union soldier would run up to him and tell him to hand over his sword. The Lt. Colonel said he would prefer to give it to an officer but after the bluecoat threatened to run him through with a bayonet, the sword was surrendered.

Company I of the 7th Tennessee had stayed together in a bunch. Several of the men made it all the way to the fence. Corporal James Bass later recalled that Corporal Brad Anderson (age 22) and Private Charlie Lane were both wounded near him at the fence along with Private Jim Walpole. Anderson's brother, Oren helped care for him in that spot until rounded up by Union soldiers. They would all become prisoners in Fort Delaware . . . However 2nd Sergeant John Jennings and Corporal John Sullivan fought at the fence line but were able to escape. Jennings was wounded and was helped off by comrades. Sullivan was also wounded and ended up too badly hurt being captured in the Confederate hospital July 5. Like Albert Wilkerson they had returned with wounds. **(James Bass, Tennessee Pension Report collection)** Bass recalled that only Private John Eatherly from his group was killed fighting there. His brother Martin had been killed earlier during the advance. Private John McCall probably stopped at the road. He later wrote in his pension report that of the 47 men in his company B who started the attack, 40 were killed, wounded or captured. He claimed that fully half stopped at the road. **(John McCall, Tennessee Pension Report Collection)**

This occupation of the outer stone wall became a rallying cry for the post war North Carolinians who resented the focus of historians who dubbed the assault "Pickett's Charge" and painted a portrait of Pettigrew and Trimble as being merely supporting players. One of the first pamphlets published with this contrary view was entitled *Pickett Or Pettigrew* by Captain W.R. Bond. In it he states, "Archer's, Scales' and Pettigrew's own brigade went as far and stayed as long or longer than Pickett . . . . The left of Garnett's and Armistead, all of Archer's and Scales (but that all means very little, neither of them at the start being larger than a full regiment) plus a few of the 37th took possession of the works, which the enemy had abandoned on their approach" **(W.R. Bond, Pickett or Pettigrew: an historical essay, W.L.L. Hall Publisher, Scotland Neck, NC 1888, p 41)**

An officer back at the road watching this action unfold was Captain James Harris Co B of the 7th North Carolina. Looking forward and to his right through the smoke of battle Harris saw "... the remnants of Pettigrew's commands immediately in Lane's front, that escaped destruction from the tempest of iron and lead hurled at them closed to the right, and a glance in that direction revealed the fact that our troops on the right were in possession of the 'projecting angle' of the Federal line but unfortunately they were too weak and too much disorganized to long maintain the position, or advance with any hope of success. **(James Harris, *Historical Sketches* (Moorestown, N.C. 1893)**

Louis Young who was Pettigrew's aide-de-camp wrote a year after the battle of the condition of what remained of Marshall and Archer's brigades by the time the stone wall originally held by the 71st Pa was taken. "The right of the line formed by Archer's and Pettigrew's (Marshall's) brigades rested on the works (author—actually half on the "works"—fence line and half on the "works"—stone wall), while the left was further removed, say forty to sixty yards. Subjected to a fire even more fatal than that which had driven back the Brigades to our left, and the men listening in vain for the cheering commands of officers, who had fallen, our Brigade gave way likewise, and simultaneously with it, the whole line. The supports under Gen. Trimble did not advance as far as we had." **(Louis S. Young to Major William J. Baker, February 10, 1864. Francis Winston Papers, North Carolina State Archives and History.)**

Marshall Right Flank 52nd NC & 47th NC

The right flank position of the 52nd North Carolina required these men to first reach the final fence and then pausing there to volley then charge forward the remaining 50 feet. This task proved almost impossible and only three officers names are mentioned of men who attempted in that task; Captain Benjamin Little (Co E); Major Q.A. Richardson and Lieutenant Col Marcus Parks (who would be wounded in the thigh). In the case of Captain Little, he remained conscious after being hit in the left arm with a bullet and listened to the fury around him. He recalled seeing the bodies of his dead and wounded comrades and hearing the roar of gunfire. He would be captured and have his left arm amputated. **(Caison, Southern Soldiers in Northern Prisons, p 366)** Captain Little, a 33 year old farmer commanded the "Richmond Regulators" wrote to his wife "The ground between the enemy's works and where I lay was thickly strewn with killed and wounded" Captain N.C. Hughes on Marshall's staff took a mortal wound as he charged up the slope and Major John Richardson bled to death after being hit with multiple bullets near the stone wall. **(Benjamin Little letter to wife, July 20, 1863, Little Papers, UNC)**

Later in 1877, Little wrote "I was shot down when within 50 yards of the enemy's works . . . as to 'coming to the rear', very few ever got to the rear at all, all the badly wounded being taken prisoners, a few only getting back and they as best they could when al was over . . . Officers and men were about that time mowed down so rapidly and the fighting so hot, that orders could not be heard if given" **(Letter from Benjamin Little to Raleigh Observer, September 20, 1877 from Little's Mills, Richmond County, NC)**

The Major of the 52nd John Richardson was commanding the left wing of the regiment and was killed "instantly by a rifle ball while leading the left wing of the regiment". The Lieutenant Colonel who took command when Marshall was promoted, Lt. Colonel Marcus Parks had been already wounded in both thighs at the road and would be captured. Company I of the 52nd had severe losses and probably had many men who made it to the front fence. "The Stanley Rebels" suffered at least 45 casualties having lost their 31 year old Captain John McCain killed on July 1 27 year old Lieutenant Willis Randal was wounded in the left hand and 1st Sergeant 25 year old Buckner Crowell was wounded in the right thigh and captured. The killed and mortally wounded losses were very high suggesting that this company moved ahead of many. Company C in the 52nd was also devastated losing every officer and Non-Comm except one with losses of enlisted men of about 50%. These losses in the "Orapeake Guards" were heaviest in the captured category with eighteen. Company A lost all of it's officers and it's first Sergeant plus a large number of wounded. A Total of 24 Captains and Lieutenants fell as many of the regiment crossed the fields, the road and reached the front fence. Finally, there are about 25 men with Captain James Kincaid who were killed, wounded or captured with their commander at the road or on the slope. Their Captain being mortally wounded and captured.

Facing the final fence were the remaining men of the 47th North Carolina. At least one unnamed Private was recorded to have been wounded for a second time as he reached the wooden rails. The remaining color-bearer fell just a few feet in front. **(J. Rogers Brown, "Additional Sketch Forty-Seventh Regiment ", Clark's *Histories*, III, p 108)** The names mentioned from the 47th in this area include Captain Joseph Davis (Co. G); Sergeant Jesse Gilram (Co. K) and Lieutenant Colonel John Graves. One account in the Grime's Paper's at University of North Carolina claims that 150 of the men with the 11th North Carolina made it to within 50 yards of the Stone Wall position. "I was in about fifty yards (I think nearer) of the wall when I was shot down, so says Lieut. Ramsour who saw me fall and he went forward with about 150 men left in our regiment to a fence at or near the wall. He says that he dressed our lines under that galling fire and then retreated". **(Captain Albert Haynes Co I, 11th NC letter to Raleigh Observer, October 8, 1877,)** Captain Haynes from Lincoln County was wounded twice during the attack and was able to make his way back after dark found medical care by 11:00 PM only to be captured in the Confederate Hospital on July 5th. Haynes would suffer wounds in his right fibula and shoulder. He later recalled "we were all cut down—no one but wounded left in my company, save two" (Sergeant Walter Ramsuer & Private Robert Glenn). His 1st Lt. David Coon had been wounded in the right foot in both eyes during the advance. His 2nd & 3rd Lieutenant were both wounded as well **(Chapman, More Terrible than Victory, p 113)** Company E of the 47th would have terrible losses with four out five men killed and wounded during the charge.

The men of the 1st Delaware facing this charge would never forget the impact of their volleys. "We were cautioned to hold our fire until the rebels began to climb the fence along the Emmitsburg Road. When this obstacle was reached their ranks were thrown into some confusion, when, at the word 'fire' shouted by General Hayes, commanding the Division, such an appalling sheet of flame burst forth from our line that the rebel ranks melted away like wax, and none of them reached a point in our front nearer than fifty yards." Remembered Private William Seville**(Seville, *History of the First Regiment Delaware Volunteers*, p 81)**

In Company C of the 47th 1st Lieutenant Nathaniel Brown would survive but would report 3rd Lieutenant Norfleet and Corporal Gaston Utley killed beside him and Lieutenant Whiting wounded in the head and left behind to be captured. Sergeant L.M. Green was shot in the face to be captured as well. Sergeant Lt. Colonel John Graves had led a small group of men forward halfway to the stone wall where they took cover in a shallow ravine. With bullets and canister hurling over their heads and at times into their mass, these men fired occasionally toward the wall but all ended up being captured. Graves would be wounded and Major Archibald Crudup would be wounded in the breast, neck, and left arm. **(Louis Young to W.J. Baker, February 10, 1864 Richmond Daily Enquirer)** Lieutenant Norfleet, by the way was incorrectly reported as dead, but was in fact wounded in the groin (in hand to hand combat) and was captured. He later was promoted to 2nd Lieutenant. Lieutenant Brown would write home that among his enlisted men Privates Nicholas Gill, Joseph Woodward and John Johnson were killed in the close up fighting and Private John Done was shot in the lungs and captured. (Privates George Partin and J.W. Pilkeron were captured after the fighting died down.) **(Louis Young to W.J. Baker, February 10, 1864 Richmond Daily Enquirer)**

Downhill closer to the road elements of Companies G & K had occupied a similar gully and under the command of Captain Joseph Davis, commander of Company G, also fired toward the wall. Sergeant Jesse Gilliam (Co K) had two brothers Abner and John who had been wounded on the first of July. Gilliam shouted to Captain Davis that all the other officers were down and that the regiments to their left were weakened. Davis shouted back "Our supports are coming and we can whip them yet". Soon however, a retreat was ordered. In the fighting, Sergeant Gilliam was killed and Captain Davis would be taken captive. **(Joseph Davis to editors, September 20, 1877, Grimes papers SHC-UNC)** Davis's company G would suffer severe losses. Davis's account is puzzling since in it Sergeant Gilliam announces that all his company officers were down yet the records only show that 1st Lieutenant James Watson had been hit. The 3rd Lieutenant Felix Poteat may have been acting as Adjutant that day but the whereabouts of 2nd Lt. Thomas Taylor at this point is unknown. Finally, Company I of the 47th regiment, which had lost their two top commanders during the advance would suffer the most of any company with 57 men killed and Wounded.

Marshall Left Flank 26th NC & 11th NC

In the centre with Marshall we find two regiments (26th NC & 11NC) directly facing the huge stone wall behind which hundreds of Hay's men are waiting, while the right two regiments faced the final wooden fence line which perhaps provided light cover from the eyes and guns of the 14th Connecticut and 1st Delaware.

Next to the left in regimental order, the 26th North Carolina moved forward facing the "buck & ball" of the 12th New Jersey & the rifles of the125th NY. Free from the obstacle of the final wooden fence the remnants of the regiment charged forward. "We crossed the road and went to the enemy's works where we continued fighting until most of the regiment I was captured. The 47th regiment was on our right as we went into the fight . . . We were captured after being at the enemy's works some ten or fifteen minutes, the enemy closing in on us from our rear" remembered Captain Gaston Broughton of company D. Broughton would be hit in the foot while advancing up the hill.

"In my company there were 5 killed, 6 wounded and from 5-6 missing. We were in with only about 25 men." **(Gaston Broughton to Raleigh Observer, October 15, 1877)**

A cluster of men either almost reached the wall or actually died at the rocks including Sergeant William Smith (Co K) ; Private Thomas Cozart (Co. F) ; Captain Steven W. Brewer (Co E but now in command), Private Daniel Thomas (E) and Sergeant James Brooks (Co E.). Captain Cureton (Co B was wounded in the shoulder but kept moving forward. The flag passed hands several times but was captured at the wall by the 12th New Jersey. At one point Captain Brewer was seen holding it aloft until he fell. First Sergeant William Snelling (Co D) was said to have made it close to the wall as survive as well. While Private Albert Caison (Co I) later wrote about crossing the road and running up the hill until hit in the hip and the hand and captured. **(G.C Underwood, The History of the Twentieth-Sixth Regiment of the North Carolina Troops (Goldsboro, N.C.: Hall 1901, pp 365-366)** Captain Cureton in the 26th NC summarized this final thrust best . . . the regiment was "reduced to a skirmish line by the constant falling of the men at every step, but still they kept closing to the colors." The flag had gone forward and men gave their lives to follow it. **(Thomas Cureton to Lane, June 22, 1890, Lane Papers SHC-UNC)** A testimony to the handful of men who made it up the slope is the recollection of Lieutenant Charles Troutman of the 12th New Jersey who testified about rebels close enough to the wall to be hit by rocks thrown by his men who had run out of ammunition or did not have time to reload their buck and ball muskets. Another New Jersey Lieutenant William Potter wrote about a single rebel soldier who broke out from the small pack of gray and ran ahead to be killed about twenty feet out from the wall. **(Toombs, New Jersey Troops, p 300)**

Another soldier with the New Jersey 12th recalled the same young rebel who had charged ahead. Shields recalled that after the battle many of his comrades walked out to examine the body with a bullet through his brain. The young rebel who was still alive for some time was unconscious but alive "as could be seen by the blubbers on his lips" **(Shields letter to Grimes Collection UNC)**

Sergeant Robert Hudspeth of the 26th's decimated Company F was one of only six men to survive the first days fighting in good enough shape to make the charge this day. Hudspeth made it just past the fence and half way to the stone wall but then turned around and retreated. As he crossed the fields a shall explosion knocked him to the ground. He would survive and fight in battles through 1864 only to die of sickness in a Confederate hospital before the war ended.

Shortly behind them many had fallen on the way up the slope. Captain Wagg took several pieces of grapeshot through his body and died instantly. Lieutenant Emerson from company E fell wounded but managed to crawl back to the roadbed and later escape. His company commander captain Brewer had held the flag on the way up the slope but was cut down. The flag was then grabbed by Private Daniel Boone Thomas (Co E) the last remaining member of the color guard. **(Emerson, Lieutenant J.R Emerson, Co E 26th Regiment N.C.Troops**) The final two men to make it close to the wall on the flank of the 26th seems to have been 22 year First Sergeant William Snelling (Co D Wake County Guards) (and 22 year old Private Thomas Cozart (Co F Hilbriten Guards) who would both be seen by Lt. William Potter of the 12th New Jersey "These two men like spray driven from a wave, marked the farthest limit of the enemy's advance in our front." (Toombs, New Jersey troops) both would die in the gunfire. Meanwhile at the middle of the 26th line the attack was stalling and all eyes were on two men from the flag Company E advancing, one holding the regimental flag. Private Daniel Thomas, wounded, held the tattered pieces of the 26th NC flag and beside him was 1st Sergeant James Brooks. Both had served with the "Independent Guards" Co E since the beginning of the war and were old friends from Cartersville, NC. At 22 they had enlisted together on May 28, 1861 along with Daniel's two older brothers John and Nathaniel. Now, they were advancing to their death toward the stone wall. They looked to their left and saw the flag of the 47th North Carolina go to the ground within ten feet of the stone wall. Then, the men of the 12th New Jersey suddenly stopped firing and in admiration of these two brave men perhaps all guns were silent. Suddenly a soldier behind the wall yelled "Come over on this side of the Lord" and suddenly hands reached out a pulled the two young men over the stones to safety. The torn and bloodstained flag was captured. Both would be imprisoned along with Daniel's brother Nathaniel and all would fight in later battles. **(Rose, Colours of the Gray, p 38; Underwood, "Twenty-Sixth Regiment, 366-374)**

"The brigade dashed on, and many had reached the wall, when we received a deadly volley from the left. The whole line on the left had given way, and we were being rapidly flanked. With our thinned ranks and in such a position, it would have been folly to stand, and against such odds. We therefore fell back to our original position in rear of the batteries.

After this day's fight, but one field officer was left in the brigade. Regiments that went in with colonels came out commanded by lieutenants.—**After battle report of Major John T. Jones, Twenty-sixth North Carolina Infantry, commanding Pettigrew's brigade (on the Gettysburg campaign, July 3, 1863)**

Finally, the regiment at the Northern end of the Marshall line the 11th North Carolina had lost all eight of the color bearers by the time the regiment reached the road the flag may not have passed the road. (note-the flag was finally rescued by Captain Francis Bird of the 11th North Carolina (Co C.) who was able to take it all the way back to Seminary Ridge and safety after the wooden staff was twice hit by bullets). **(Edward R Outlaw, Clark Histories I pp.589-590)** Lieutenant Colonel William J. Martin of the 11th recalled years later the horror he witnessed. "a slaughter pen" was the vision he saw when remembering the blood and the loss of men all around him. **(Martin, Eleventh North Carolina Regiment, SHSP 23)** Captain Albert Hayes and Lieutenant Oliver Ramseur (both from Company I) were said to have gone farthest of the 11th NC soldiers. Both would be wounded, Hayes crawling back to safety and Ramseur captured. Meanwhile some wounded Confederates were beginning to crawl forward unarmed toward the stone wall itself for protection from the cannon fire and bullets. One Private William Mull in Company B had a brother, Ezra, and a cousin, John in the 55th NC. William made it to the fence. His brother was in the regiment directly to his left. William survived as did his brother and cousin. Another soldier who made it to the fence was Private William Madison Suggs in Company G of the 11th NC. He got to the fence, fired some rounds at the enemy and then retreated back to the road. There, exhausted, he was captured and taken away. **(Nancy Crabtree, North Carolina State Archives, Civil War widow pension application files)**

Davis Brigade Right Flank 55th NC & 2nd MS

Davis's brigade on the far left would have far fewer men reach the final enemy positions. Facing the 39th NY, 108th New York and 111th New York plus flanking fire from the 126th NY only a few men would reached the Bryan Barn or circle the barn from the North, hidden by the heavy smoke. But yet, some brave soldiers from each of the Davis regiments were either found killed or wounded then captured all along the wall. The thick smoke from the belching cannons and rifles created a fog through which rebels could advance unseen and Yankees often would be firing blindly forward. Only this can explain how some Confederates would be found later dead and wounded so close to what had to be a living hell storm.

There is some evidence to believe that Davis's survivors actually may have reached the fences of the Emmitsburg Road ahead of the Pettigrew men. Several observers noted that the Davis regiments "pushed forward in advance of the general line with too much impetuosity and was driven back" **(James H. Lane to editors, September 7, 1877,**

Grimes Papers, SHC-UNC) This would make sense since Marshal's line may have halted once or twice to realign. One of the frequent criticisms of Davis as a commander is that he often failed to keep his brigade front in order and often failed to prevent uneven advances.

The right regiment of Davis's brigade was the 55th North Carolina and three men who did both cross the road fences and rush up the hill were Captain Edward Fletcher Satterfield (Co. H), 2nd Lt. D.T. Falls (Co C) and Sergeant J. Augustus Whitley (Co E) Satterfield died and Falls and Wiley were wounded and taken prisoner. Both men would later document the position where Satterfield was killed for Colonel Bachelder **(Five Points in the Record of North Carolina, North Carolina Literary and Historical Society-1904 p 36)** Edward Satterfield had enlisted in the "Archer Boys" at the beginning of the war. Thomas Falls was a 23 year old clerk in the "Cleveland Grays" from Cleveland County described by his comrades as "boyish-looking" and J. Augustus Whitley was a 21 year old Pitts County farmer.

Satterfield's death was reported to his family by several comrades. Private J.D Williams reported that several men of the company saw Satterfield hit with a shell as he advanced up the slope. The regiment's assistant quartermaster Captain William Webb wrote the family, "Several; of his men told me that in charging the heights he was in advance of his company, that they saw him when struck by a shell, and that his body was torn almost into fragments." **(Satterfield and Merritt Papers SHC, Wilson Library, UNC)** In 1895 Lieutenant Falls and Sergeant Whitley returned to Gettysburg and took part in driving wooden stakes into the spot where they had charged and where Captain Satterfield had been killed. "Lieutenant Falls and Sergt. Whitley showed me over the ground over which they had charged and the point they reached, which point as noted on our maps and in our journal is twenty steps south of the (Brien) Barn and just nine yards west of the stone wall which Pettigrew and Trimble tried to storm. Whilst we were driving stakes to mark to exact spots reached by them and also where Captain Satterfield, of Person County, has fallen near them, several officers and men of the Thirty-ninth New York Regiment of Willard's brigade. came up to the stone wall near us and said that while, of course, they could not identify the men, they could swear that a thin line of rebels did reach the very spot where we were driving those stakes . . . **(Major W.M. Robbins "Longstreet's Assault at Gettysburg: 3 July 1863" in Clark, Histories of the Several Regiments and Battalions, Vol. 5, pp 110-112**

The role of the 55th NC on July 3 was years later summarized by then 1st Lieutenant Charles Cooke (Co I) who added fuel to the debate about the North Carolina role In the July 3 charge (The farthest to the front" debate) "Our regiment had suffered so greatly on the 1st that in this charge it was commanded by Captain Gilreath, and some of the companies were commanded by non-commissioned officers. But the men came up bravely to the measure of their duty, and the regiment went as far as any other on that fatal charge, and we have good proof of the claim that a portion of the regiment led by Captain Satterfield, who was killed at this time, reached a point near the Bennet barn, which was 'more advanced than that attained by any other of the assaulting columns.' Lieutenant T.D. Falls, of Company C, residing at Fallstown, Cleveland County, and Sergeant Augustus Whitley, of Company E, residing at Everitt's, in Martin County, who were with Captain Satterfield, have recently visited the battlefield, and have made affidavit as to the point reached by them. This evidence has been corroborated from other sources and the place has been marked by the United States commission, and the map herewith copied from the United States official survey of this historic field will show the position attained by these men of the Fifty-fifth Regiment, in relation to other known objects on the battlefield such as the Benner barn and the Bronze Book which marks the high-water mark of the struggle for Southern independence. The measurements for the map were made by the late Colonel Batchelder, of the United States Commission, and by Colonel E.W. Cope, United States engineer, for the field. This map shows that those killed 'farthest to the front' belonged to the Fifty-fifth North Carolina Regiment. **(Cooke, Fifty-Fifth Regiment)**

The 2nd Mississippi's Lieutenant Colonel David Humphries had been killed in the advance. One soldier remembered that "No one seemed to be in command" another later wrote "lines became so shortened and thin as they neared the wall as to be nearly or wholly indiscernible and indistinguishable in the smoke, even nearby, and much more at a distance." **(Winschel, Heavy was their loss" Gettysburg Magazine, #3 July 1990, pp82-83).** The 2nd Mississippi had lost their battle flag in the railroad Cut on July 1 and this day Luke Byrn (Co B) would carry the new one into battle. In some accounts Byrn is labeled as a Sergeant in this battle yet the official compiled records show that the 23 year old from Tippah was promoted to 2nd Lieutenant after doing recruiting duty back in Mississippi in the summer of 1862. He not only saved the flag but made it back to his own lines with a wound. He would be captured in a wagon in Greencastle, Pa July 5th.

He would be sent to Johnson Island, Ohio. There he became sick, was paroled and returned home. (Author note: Other accounts argue that a Sergeant Christopher Columbus Davis in Co D carried the flag and hid it under his body after being wounded) Others who leaped the fences and charged up the hill only to be cut down included Captain Robert Brandon, age 24, in Company D who would be wounded and captured. The leader of the "Joe Matthews Rifles" would die in a Chester, Pa hospital on July 15. In Company H Lieutenant David Marlin was killed. The 28 year old member of the "Coonewah Rifles" had been a teacher before the war. William Moody, age 21, who was a Lieutenant in Company A (the "Tishomingo Rifleman") would be wounded and captured and die the same day in Yankee hands. Lieutenant Benjamin Richardson in Co E was killed as well. The 28 year old Guntown, Mississippi farmer made it halfway to the stonewall. **(Rowland, *Military History of Mississippi*, pp 4-42)**

Davis Brigade Left Flank 42nd MS. & 11th MS.

To the left was the 42nd Mississippi and the 11th. The 42nd had been damaged in the fighting on the 1st of July7 and was down to about 250 effectives but the 11th was a fresh regiment having not seen duty on the opening day.

The mad dash by the 42nd Mississippi was witnessed by Private Andrew Parks in Company I who recalled "Our colors were shot down three times before reaching the wall. Parks is credited by some historians as being a Sergeant in the battle but the compiled service records clearly show that the 30 year old Grenada, Mississippi was a private. Shortly after the battle he contracted typhoid fever and there is no evidence he ever rose to Sergeant. Lieut. Davenport of Company K of the 42nd regiment (actually Captain Henry Davenport Company E) seized the colors and planted then on top of the wall but was immediately shot down by the enemy." **(Andrew Parks, Some of my Recollections of the Battle of Gettysburg, Arkansas Historical Society)**

Yet their commander Colonel Stone was far to the left of this position by this moment.

Most of the 42nd Mississippi struck the Union line south of the Bryan barn. Yet the Colonel of the 42nd seems to have fallen north of the barn. Several witnesses cite Colonel Hugh Reid Miller falling mortally wounded at the small stone wall which runs from the Bryan barn to the Emmitsburg Pike (in those days connecting the small wooden shack at the end of the Bryan Lane. "On the third day of July, the third day of the battle of Gettysburg, in the desperate charge upon the enemy's works, he was mortally wounded through the left (lung), he lay in a few feet of a little white frame house on the Emmitsburg pike road some twenty five yards from their line of stone fences, together with Captain Magruder, the A.A. Gen'l of our brigade, who died and was buried a few feet of where he lay . . ." **(September 2, 1863 letter of Robert A Miller)**

An excellent presentation of evidence regarding this action is given by Dr. Robert Himmer in his article "Col. Hugh Reid Miller, 42nd Mississippi Volunteers, and the Pickett-Pettigrew Trimble Assault" in Gettysburg magazine Issue Number Thirty-Five. Himmer writes "It may seem odd, then, that the colonel of the 42nd fell north of the Brian Barn. It is possible that he had become disoriented and separated from his command, or that he had elected to lead men of his command and the adjacent 11th Mississippi (which was without field officers by this time) in an effort to take Woodruff's murderous guns. But the fact that he fell close by the brigade adjutant, Captain Magruder, who one might normally expect to find near the brigade commander, suggests another explanation. Was Colonel Miller leading the brigade?" **("Col. Hugh Reid Miller, 42nd Mississippi Volunteers, and the Pickett-Pettigrew Trimble Assault",** ***Gettysburg Magazine*****, 35, p 60)**

Statements by Lt. John Egan commanding the leftmost section of Woodruff's Union artillery suggest that a rebel attack on his left flank was unfolding at this very time. If well may be that the Confederates were attempting to flank the Union forces and ran directly into the right guns of Woodruff's battery on the north side of the Bryan Barn.

Egan wrote later "Woodruff came to me and said he feared the enemy was coming up a little lane on my left, and I must at once move and fire down it." **(John Eagan, The Bachelder Papers, Vol. 3 p 1794)** A soldier with the infantry besides Woodruff's guns recalled "Their determination was evident in their frequent attempts to advance against Woodruff's battery" **(Pierce, History of the First Regiment of Artillery, p 170)**

The inscription on the monument of the 125th NY speaks of the Confederate line extending and overlapping the Union position. The burial records also support the fierce fighting that occurred in the Bryan lane. About 200 Confederate bodies were buried on the west side of the Emmitsburg Pike and some 106 were buried on the east side of the pike around the Brian tenant shack.

A memoir of Private Andrew Baker Company A of the 11th Mississippi locates the position of Captain Magruder's fall as being "a little house . . . . just against which the end of a stone fence rested on either side behind which a small group of Confederates had taken cover" Baker relates the fall of Magruder who had urged the men forward and "leaped the stone fence on the western side of the house and was shot down at once, either as he was going over the fence or was just getting over it." **(Andrew J Baker, Tribute to Capt. Magruder and Wife, Confederate Veteran Vol. 6, No. 11 (November 1898), p 507)** Baker himself is also described as falling "within ten feet of the stone wall and twenty feet to the left of the barn." Baker has enlisted in the regiment at Manassas, Va. back after the 1861 battle and would end up a prisoner at Gettysburg. **(Love, "Mississippi at Gettysburg", p 46))**

The "small group of Confederates" that Baker saw included Lieutenant William Peal of Company C "The Prairie Rifles" who wrote in his diary this description "Four brave men had already fallen under the colors of our Regt & now the fifth bore them aloft & rushed boldly forward to embrace if need be the fate of the other four. Color Corporal 36 year old William "Billy" O'Brien (Company H) had held the flag but fell advancing on the hill. The flag staff was now cut in two midway the flag, but without one moment's pause, the never-flinching little Irishman (George Kidd Co C who had been wounded at Seven Pines and would be wounded again and captured in this fight) grabbed it, a flag now dangling in graceless confusion, from one corner still pushed fearlessly, upon the stone fence. Thirteen of our Regt had concentrated upon the colors, as if to constitute its guard. We were some yards in advance of the line, & now found ourselves within about thirty yards of the stone fence. Immediately before us was small framed house—about twenty feet square—the farther end of which joined the fence. Springing forward we secured its shelter, gaining at the same time, a position, within twenty five feet of the Yankees behind the fence. The boys betook themselves to the work before them in good earnest.

A number of shots were fired, which must have proven very fatal, as the distance was so small. Thinking the line rather a long time coming up, I looked to the rear. The state of my feelings may be imagined, but not described, upon seeing the line broken & flying in full disorder . . ." **(Diary of Lieutenant William Peel," Mississippi State Archives.)**

Other men who were reported to have carried the flag of the 11th Mississippi were James M. Griffin and William Marion both from Company H. There is an account from the Union side of this exchange. Lieutent George Bowen of the 12th NJ had just fired his rifle and saw a Confederate behind the Bryan lean forward and point his rifle at him. Just then one of his fellow officers fired and hit the rebel in the forehead killing him . . . one of the thirteen with Peel was dead. Among these thirteen were, in addition to Private George Kidd and Lieutenant Peel, were Lieutenant Robert A. McDowell with the Chicksaw Guards Co H and Sergeant Samuel Caruthers (Co H). Robert's brother Frank was wounded but made it back to hisown lines. Possibly also Private Andrew J. Baker joined them and called for a charge. Killed at the barn beside him was Sergeant Eli Peel, William's brother and Private William Marion in Company H. Captain George Bird of Co K who had been carrying the torn flag and shattered staff was probably there as well and killed. Bird had been the sheriff of Carrolton County before the war and his heroic action in this fight resulted in him being promoted posthumously to Captain shortly afterward according to one account but his service record shows him promoted to Captain on the march to Gettysburg. Private William Smith in the "Chicksaw Guards" Company H was wounded in the mouth. Finally, one story has Private Joseph Marable placing the tattered flag on the stone wall and being clubbed in the head by a Yankee rifle butt. Research into this incident provides more confusion than clarity. There were three brothers in the 11th Mississippi in this attack. Joseph Marable was a 23 yr old who had been wounded at Seven Pines . It is likely that he was the individual in this account. His brother William, however, was a Private and was killed in the fighting on July 3. Perhaps this 24 year old was the holder of the flag. On the other hand the third brother John, who had been wounded at Malvern Hill was also there and was wounded and captured in the same area. Two other men wrote after the war about being at or near the Bryan Barn in the fight, Private Rhesa Hawkins (Co K) and Private Archibald Turner (Co K).

29 year old Wiley Heflin in the "Nesoba Rifles" Company D of the 11th Ms recalled that by this time "our line was so cut down and demoralized by the enemy's batteries before we got in gun shot distance that we could not carry the works" He would be wounded in the foot and ankle and captured at the road. **(Heflin, *Blind Man on the Warpath*, pp.24-25)**

With the 11th's color company H (The Chickasaw Guards) 2nd Lt Baxter McFarland witnessed the rush to the wall "Lines became so shortened and thin as they neared the wall as to be nearly or wholly indiscernible and indistinguishable in the smoke, even when nearby and much more so at a distance." The 24 yr old McFarland had been wounded at

Gaines Mill in 1862. **(McFarland, *"The Eleventh Mississippi Regiment At Gettysburg"*, Mississippi Historical Society V II, p 565)**

McFarland survived the war and later became a Judge. He had been a law student at the University of Mississippi before the war. He described the final rush this way in a speech he often gave after the war . . . . "then charging with a yell, the few undaunted survivors impetuously rushed through the 'hell of fire' of arms to and near the wall continuing the battle there at close quarters for a short time" **(McFarland, *"The Eleventh Mississippi Regiment At Gettysburg"*, Mississippi Historical Society V II, p 551)**

Company H was to the right of the 11th Mississippi regimental line and here Sergeant Warren D. Reid, a 22 year old student, rushed forward only to be wounded and captured on the slope. Reid would be wounded again at Cold Harbor. Only three of the 27 men in his company came back unscathed with 15 killed and 9 wounded and or captured.

With the University Grays, First Lieutenant John V. Moore was wounded and captured some 20 feet north of the Bryan barn where he drifted with Colonel Miller of the 42nd Mississippi and some of his own men. Perhaps these were the three men who were credited with making it close to the stone wall but not connected to Peel's approach to the Bryan Barn.

Letters home after the battle told of three other men from the company charging the wall. Private Andrew Jackson Baker (later Lieutenant) was reported to have made it within 10 feet of the wall and escaped. Privates W.F. DeGaffenreid and Thomas McKie were reported to have been killed as they rushed forward but DeGaffenreid's compiled service records shows him as wounded and captured. He was later wounded again at Weldon Railroad. Thomas McKie's cousin Joseph was wounded and captured that day. The total losses from Company A "The University Grays" was reported to be 14 killed and 17 wounded/ captured in the fray.

Written on the back of a daguerreotype of Private Thomas McKie now in the possession of his sister's great granddaughter are these words written by his sister during the war "was with Gen. Pickett at that charge, charged the bloody angle and was fatally wounded in the charge there, died in enemy hands on the 4th, body never recovered. His cousin Joe McKie was wounded in the same battle was taken prisoner at the time." **(Maud Morrow Brown, The University Grays: Company A, Eleventh Mississippi Regiment; Army of Northern Virginia, 1861-1865 (Richmond, Virginia Garrey and Massie (1940)**

Sergeant James D. Love had enlisted in Crawfordsville early in the war and was wounded in the left leg and then captured. He said later of the fighting between the Emmitsburg Road and the Union lines "It had become a soldiers battle, in which the Southerners watchword, 'The grave of a hero or victory' was being gloriously exemplified." **(Love, *"Mississippi at Gettysburg"* p 44)** Sergeant Love fought with The "Prairie Guards—Company E 11th Mississippi.

In trying to understand the advance of the 11th Mississippi and the death of Colonel Miller in his flank attack one needs to examine exactly where the famed eighth Ohio was located on the flank of Davis. Conflicting evidence exists as to the position of the Eight Ohio during the very time that Colonel Miller and his small group were attempting to flank the Union forces by moving north of the Bryan barn. It is clear that the Eighth Ohio and parts of the 125th New York had moved southward and were pouring fire into the 11th Mississippi. What is not clear, however is where this forward movement began or how this action is consistent with small elements of the 42nd Mississippi and 11th Mississippi sliding northward to end up attacking the Bryan Barn from the left. If the Eighth Ohio started where traditionally they are credited (and where their monument today stands) it is hard to accept any forward motion by ether the small group of 40 of 50 11th Mississippi attackers or the equally small number of men from the 42nd Mississippi who seemed to be able skirt the wooden building along the Emmitsburg Pike at the end of the Bryan Lane and then to move through the fields rightward to the Bryan Barn. Recent research and authorship by Keith Snipes in "The Improper Placement of the 8th Ohio Monument; A Study in Words and Maps" suggests that the Eighth Ohio's original position was back at a road bed in front of the Trostle house along the west side of Emmitsburg Pike and that their movement southward took longer than previously asserted thus allowing the left flank of the 11th Mississippi to move to the road and elements of rebels (along with Colonel Miller) to cross the road and move northward toward the 125th New York that was swinging down from the hill. Evidence from a number of men from the Eight Ohio suggests that most of that regiment began their movement toward the Davis flank as far as 300 yards away and that that motion took as long as five minutes. (Today of course this original position is covered with small shops and sidewalk but the position shows clearly in the 1877 Tipton & Myers photograph of the areas) **(Keith Snipes, "The Improper Placement of the 8th Ohio Monument; A Study in Words and Maps", Gettysburg Magazine No. 35, pp 69-93)**

By the time this small group from the 11th Mississippi made to the field approaching the Bryan Barn, almost all of their officers were down or had fallen behind. It must be remembered that this regiment was taking the blunt of the flanking fire from the North as the 8th Ohio and the 125th New York edged closer moving down the pike and surrounding fields from the Trostle home. The Colonel Francis Marion Green had not made it to the Emmitsburg Road. Nor it seems had the new Lieutenant Colonel Alexander H. Franklin. Nor it seems did Major William Benjamin Lowry who had been wounded at Seven Pines.

Only the new acting adjutant A.A. William T. Magruder made it across. Magruder had replaced Adjutant Thomas C. Holliday when he was promoted to Brigade Staff.

Losses of officers in the 11th Mississippi were particularly severe in this attack. Before even reaching the road Captains Raines (A) Holbert (E) and Jamison Moore (H) had been killed and their fellow Captains Shannon (C) and Nelms (G) wounded. At least 10 Lieutenants were down before reaching the pike as well. Captain Nunn of company B was killed and on his body lying in the roadbed was found the watch of Assistant Adjutant Magruder.

Many of the remaining men in the 11th were killed or wounded advancing up the hill or took cover in the roadbed from the fire now coming from both front and left. Captain Thomas Stokes was apparently one man from Company F of the 11th Mississippi who moved up the hill. The 25 year old planter from Noxubee County was severely wounded and would be captured. His First Lieutenant Charles Brooks had been wounded at Sharpsburg and would be captured here at Gettysburg.

Company I of the 42nd Mississippi had already lost 23 men on July 1 and the only men not killed or wounded on July 3 according to one survivor were the three shortest men in the unit . . . . "Reached Gettysburg 1st day of July and entered the fight with 52 men in the company. Fifteen men were shot on the famous railroad cut. Fought all that day and came out with the loss of 23 men. Did nothing on the second day. Fought the third day and came out with three men in the company who were not shot; these were the smallest men in the company—Don Still, Green Cain, Tince Harmon. I had my left hand wounded." **(Diary of James Alfred "Bud" Conner, Co I 42nd MS)**

The rifle fire at the point was not all one way. The murderous volleys of the Union troops from New York and New Jersey and Delaware and Connecticut behind that stone wall were answered by fire from Confederates who had taken cover at the road and by random shots by the small clusters who advanced up the hill. The color bearer of the First Delaware was hit and the 111th New York had four color bearers shot as was their Colonel Clinton MacDougall in the left arm. Colonel Eliakim Sherrill Brigade commander was shot in the abdomen while on his horse. Brigade commander Thomas Smyth was cut by shell fragments during the fight. Artillery Commander Woodruff was mortally wounded as well.

The left side of the Pettigrew-Trimble line was recorded later by one Union officer with the 126th New York to have made three distinct attacks upon the position of Hayes. These attacks were said to have been "separate" and "distinct" and desperate". **(Winfield Scott, "Pickett's Charge As Seen from the Front Line" MOLLUS California war papers no 1)** This would imply that three waves of rebel troops advanced beyond the fences: first portions of Davis and Marshall, then the regiments of Lane and then a final tragic combination of men who had taken cover in the roadway.

One medical officer with the Union army watched the attack as it died out "The rebel officers after making forlorn and desperate attempts to rally their men found all their efforts in vain, for the men opposed them stood immovable & resolute as the ground on which they fought. The line began to break into hopeless & despairing squads of men, many of whom ran in and surrendered. **(Diary of Francis Moses Wafer, Queen's University Library, Kingston, Ontario, Canada)**

Earl Hess in his classic work "Pickett's Charge The Last Attack at Gettysburg" summarizes the situation of Pettigrew's Division attack this way. "It is possible that only 250 of Fry's men,

700 of Marshall's command, 50 of Davis's brigade and certainly none of Brockenbrough's Virginians crossed Emmitsburg Road." This author feels that the number for Davis's is too low given the numbers of dead Confederates buried near the Bryan Shack site and the evidence of fighting along a wider range than most historians have acknowledged.

THE TRIMBLE LINE
Lane's Left Flank 33rd NC & 18th NC

As combat played itself out along the front line of Pettigrew, the regiments of Trimble were about to close in across the road and up the hill but in fact only a few small groups of men from a few regiments made that effort. "Then the rebel yell sounded over the roar of battle—it was Lane's brigade clambering over the Emmitsburg Road fences. Composing the left wing of Trimble's division, Lane's brigade had been rushed forward by Trimble even before he received Pettigrew's summons from Captain Young . . . General Lane and his North Carolina regiments had rushed in behind Davis's troops, reaching the Emmitsburg Road moments behind them. Lane's men managed to push down at least one section of the first fence, but they found the second one too sturdy and had to climb it . . . They spilled over the fences, merged with the stubborn survivors of Davis's brigade and surged up the slope together toward the stone wall—waved on by the fallen wounded of Davis's brigade." **(Rod Gragg, Covered with Glory, p 194-195) (Letters from Captain P.C. Carlton & Lt. Colonel W.G Morris)**

As mentioned earlier a few men with Major Joseph Saunders, who had been promoted after Chancellorsville, managed to get beyond the road but were shot down by the intense fire from their left. Saunders himself would be wounded in the mouth and captured. It would seem that the arrival of the Eight Ohio did more close range rifle fire damage to the 33rd and 18th North Carolina then it did to the 11th Mississippi which suffered more from artillery fire.

Major Saunders account suggests that what remained of the 33rd had crossed the road and had started to wheel to the left. This would require him as the Left guide to push the regiment back to the right. That would explain Colonel Avery on the right of the line being closer to the stone wall at this point. "I went to about 60 yards of the stone wall where I was wounded in the mouth and captured. I distinctly remember just before I was shot seeing the flag bearer of the enemy get up and run followed by his regiment so that nothing kept our regiment from going right into the enemy works. I was shot by the enemy flanking us on the left. I was at the time acting as left guide for Col. Avery directing the line of march more to the right, as to strike the enemy works in a straight line. Our lines caught up to Pettigrew and merged to become one line . . . . There can be no mistake about this. If you will write to Col. W.G. Morris (37th NC who was in the attack and captured, I think he can give you a more accurate account. Colonel Morris was as cool a man under fire as I ever saw, very deliberate and mythological in his movements." **(Letter of September 22, 1877 to the Raleigh Observer, from Avon Farm, NC, UNC Archive Collection)**

This account, if accurate, would explain the 33rd slanting to the left and facing New York troops who may just have pulled back and reformed to await the advance of the 33rd & 18th NC and what remained of the 11th & 42nd Mississippi under Colonel Miller.

When Morris wrote his account he makes it clear the two step process that occurred. First at the road and then at what he calls the "stone fence". What is problematic here is that the 33rd North Carolina clearly did not face the wooden fence (with all of the stones along its base). This fence would have been far to the south near where Scale's advanced. Thus the only "stone fence" Morris could have faced is the fence line (and stone base) that ran from the Bryan barn toward the Emmitsburg Road, suggesting that his men were moving diagonal into a pocket. "Pettigrew (Marshall's) and Archer's (Fry's) men reached the enemy's works a little in advance of us and succeeded in driving the enemy from his works (note: the road fences) in their front, but were exposed to a flanking fire from both right and left. They laid down, some in the road, some on the crest of the hill near the stone fence and beckoned to us to come on. Gen. Trimble then ordered us to charge the enemy's works in our front. This order was promptly obeyed . . . . we drove the enemy in front of us from his position in the road, then from behind the stone fence and held this position at least half an hour (???) Right here between the road and the stone fence (the enemy having disappeared from our front) we became engaged with a flanking party on our left and was soon surrounded and captured. Six officers on the right of my regiment were wounded in the enemy's works and captured. Among the number was the lamented Lieut. Battle (3rd Lt. Co D "The North Carolina Defenders"37th NC), whose wound proved fatal. Lieutenant Horton (2nd Lt, Co B "The Watauga Marksmen) 37th NC) was shot through the left lung" **(Lt. Col W.G. Morris Letter to Raleigh Observer, October 1, 1877 from Dallas, N.C.)** (author note: It is interesting that Morris mentions men from the 37th NC which was to his far right as being the one's who were "in" the enemy works.

This further suggests that the left regiments of Lane's brigade were fighting on a diagonal by this point).

The Colonel of the 33rd, Clark Moulton Avery wrote a letter to the parents of 2nd Lieutenant John "Jimmy" Caldwell (Co E) on the 18th of July explaining the death of their son during the peak of the fighting. The letter best describes the height of the action by the 33rd after their remnants crossed the road.

> "My Dear Sir,
>
> I delayed until this time in writing you with the fine hope that I could write you certainly with regard to the fate of your gallant son in the late fight at Gettysburg.
>
> My regiment was engaged in the fight on the 1st July and although greatly exposed suffered very little on the 2nd. We were under shelling all day. On the 3rd we were ordered forward to storm the heights.

We advanced to within forty yards of the enemy's works and it was there that my little friend fell. I saw him but a few moments before we were ordered to fall back discharging his whole duty. You can not imagine my feelings after reforming my regt. To find him absent and after being told that he was seen to fall forward on his face .... He was in command of his company but by this he was not more exposed that he otherwise would have been. The other Lieutenant of his company (3rd Lieutenant John Cowper) fell about the same time and I suppose to have been killed. (Author note: Actually Cowper was wounded in the left lung and captured but never recovered—died 10/14/63 in a Confederate hospital in South Carolina).

A wounded Lt who was near Jimmy (but was able to walk off the field) thinks he was shot in the breast .... (probably was Lieutenant James Gibbs Co F)

Very truly yours
C.M. Avery"

(Letter from C.M. Avery to Tod and Mrs. Caldwell, July 18, 1863, Southern Historical Collection #128) (Author Note: Tod Caldwell later became the Governor of North Carolina)

**** THE CONTROVERSEY**

Subsequent letters from Colonel Avery to the Caldwell family on July 28th give us more information about the fighting but also generate a controversy about he death of John "Jimmy" Caldwell. It seems that a letter had been send to the Caldwell family stating that John "Jimmy" was seen advancing "in front" of his company when shot. The source of this information appears to be two men who in fact were wounded on the 1st of July.

Colonel Avery denies this stating "The story of Good (that he was killed far in front of his company is positively untrue. The proper place for a line officer is in the rear of his command and he is not permitted to go to the front unless his company falters." **(Letter from C.M. Avery to Tod and Mrs. Caldwell, July 28, 1863, Southern Historical Collection #128)**

1st Lieutenant Willoughby Avery Co C (who was the nephew of Colonel Avery and the cousin of John) wrote a letter to his cousin Mary a few weeks after the battle about the death of her brother and about some men in the 11th North Carolina who claimed to have seen him.

"No one in the 11th Regt could have seen him for they (11th regt) was in the first line of battle that advanced and they had fallen back sometime before our line reached the point where he fell. Johnny was not acting rashly when he was shot, he was not our in front of his company but was at his proper place in the line. He had been in command of his company ever since he joined us. Two Lts of his company had been killed at

Chancellorsville and the other wounded. The Capt. was away sick. Lt. Cowper, who was appointed when Johnny was, also fell and was left upon the field. I have made every endeavor to find out all I could about where and how he fell. His company was on the left of the regiment and mine and Lt. Happodts (3rd Lt Co D) on the right so neither of us saw him when he fell and with the exception of one or two of his men Lt. Anthony who was the only person to see him fall and Anthony who was himself severely wounded but managed to get off the field says he saw Johnny when he was hit and that he threw his hands up to his head and fell forward on his face. This was the last that was seen of him by any member of the regiment. Our Major and six other company officers were shot down near this same spot and left on the field." **(Willoughby F. Avery Co C to Cousin Mary Caldwell, Tod Caldwell Papers #128, Southern Historical Collection)**

(Author note: 2nd Lt Peyton Anthony was new to the regiment being transferred 4/23/63 He was wounded at Chancellorsville and wounded again this day in the ankle

Another soldier from the 33rd NC who appears to have made it close to the Union lines was 28 year old Private Edward Shore in Company I. Shore was captured at Fredericksburg and again captured in the Pettigrew—Trimble charge. He wrote his wife after being imprisoned at Fort Delaware and then paroled sick to City Point, Va.

"Dear wife I seat myself this evening to write you a few lines to let you know how I am getting along . . . . I was taken prisoner at Gettysburg on the third day of July . . . I want to know whether you have herd whether Frank Kiger got killed or not. I herd he got killed at Gettysburg. (author note: Corporal Frank Kiger (Co I) was killed during the attack) We had to charge a battery, we charged right up to it. They cut our men down as fast as our men came up. I could have walked a good ways on dead men close to the battery. Our regiment was cut up powerfully. Our Brigade suffered mightly bad . . ." **(Edward Shore letter, Augustine Shore letters, Woodruff Library—Emory University Folder 1, Box2)**

(author note: Augustine Shore was Edward's brother in the same company. He was captured along with Edward at Fredericksburg but not at Gettysburg. Edward was later wounded in the right arm at Spotsylvania and had an amputation. Both survived the war)

(Corporal Frank Kiger was one of a group of brothers in Company I who were killed and wounded and captured at Gettysburg)

22 year old First Sergeant Augustus Floyd Co D "The Robeson Rifle Guard" 18th NC was hit past the road by a bullet in the thigh and remained there until finding an opportunity to run back to safety. His autobiography makes it clear that the 18th NC had been able to follow in the path of the 11th & 42nd Mississippi and move past the Emmitsburg Pike and advance toward the Bryan Barn. "I know Lane's Brigade went nearer than the line in front of us for I saw them fall back about 100 yards from the enemy, and we went up within about 20 yards. Some came back, and some stayed there dead or as prisoners. I was wounded, near the enemy works, in the thigh. I stepped behind an old blacksmith

shop (the Bryan front buildings on the Pike) about 150 yards from the enemy's works to examine my wound for I had to cross that same old open field to get back to our artillery I soon concluded that my wound was only a flesh wound and started again for the rear in double quick time." **(Augustus Evander Floyd, Autobiography, Fairmount, NC)**

Lane's Right Flank 28th NC—37th NC—7th NC

The flag of the 28th North Carolina was captured on the East side of the Emmitsburg Pike after the battle so it is safe to say that the color guard of this regiment crossed the two fences. But it is unlikely that many of the men followed. Most recall lying down in the road bed seeking shelter and firing at Yankee figures far in the distance.

Up front however the perspective was different as some clusters of Trimble's men made it up the hill, mostly to die but some to retell the tale. As the action at the front continued closely behind the Pettigrew Line came these men of Lane and Lowrence. By this time the 8th Ohio had reached the fence where they stopped and fired into the Confederate left. The 33rd and 18th North Carolina had been pretty much spent by the time they reached the road dealing with the left flank threat but their effort made it possible for the 28th, 37th and 7th to largely reach the two fences of the pike intact. But the fences they found there were even stronger and more formidable than southward along the pike. Many men found it impossible to clear this final obstacle and although they did not face the secondary fence because it ended to their south, these men were much closer to the Union guns and rifles because of the angle of the road as it entered Gettysburg town.

Lieutenant Royster (Co E 38th NC), already wounded in the thigh rushed forward waving his sword and singing Dixie was struck again in the chest and lungs and went down for a final time. His fellow officer in Company E recalled the scene in 1901 "I can see him now in his new uniform with flashing sword, he cheered his men on apparently totally oblivious of the fact that a shrapnel bullet had already pierced his right leg." **(Octavius Wiggins "Thirty-Seventh Regiment in Walter W Clark, ed Histories of the Several Regiments and Battalions from North Carolina in the Great War, 1861-1865 Vol. 2, p 224)**

In the middle of the action at this point was Lieutenant Thomas Norwood of Company A 37th NC. Norwood wrote "Several officers, myself among the number, sprang over the fence followed by the whole command as far as I know. The cannoners then left their guns (???). I rushed forward thinking the day was ours, and when within twenty yards of the enemy's works (Author: here we can assume Stone Wall) was called by Lieut Mickle (2nd Lt. Co K "The Alleghany Tigers" 37th NC) who told me that our line had fallen back. Just then he and I and Lieut. Royster (the only other man that I remember seeing so near the works) were shot down. I do not know by whose command the retreat took place. Mickle and Royster were killed. I was dragged over the breastworks by the Federal Sergeant where I found several prisoners from different commands, but do not know when or how they got there, as I soon fainted." **(Letter from Lt. Thos. Norwood to Raleigh Observer, October 6, 1877 from Fayetteville, Tenn)**

"Norwood wrote home after the battle of Mickle's death 'He and I were shot at the same moment; he uttered one shriek and afterwards was motionless and quiet, so there was no doubt that he was killed.'"

1st Lieutenant Pickney Carlton with the 7th North Carolina Company to the right of Norwood summarized the attack this way . . . "W advanced to about 40 yards of the works. No member of my company reached the wall. The command to fall back was given by an aide to General Trimble. In my company we had 8 killed, 12 wounded and 2 captured. Our regiment started out with 400 and came out with 40. **(Pickney Carlton letter to Raleigh Observer, September 26, 1877 from Statesville, NC, UNC Archive collection)**

Scales Left Flank 34th NC—13th NC—38th NC

The five regiments with Scales (Lowrance) also reached the Emmitsburg Pike and crossed but by this time most men who had made it that far took cover in the road bed with scant protection from the plank fence line. Here they were bombarded both with cannon and with rifle fire from above. In fact, later, when one of the Tennessee soldiers Lieutenant John Moore (Co B 7th Tennessee retreated back down the slope he encountered a mass of men in what he called the "horrid confusion in the lane" with frightened soldiers mixed in with bodies and wounded comrades. He saw that the road had not been safety for the many dead scattered in the roadbed among "splintered and riddled" fence rail and that "the very grass was scorched and withered by the heat" of exploding shells. **(Moore, Battle of Gettysburg, p 251)**

It seems that one soldier from the 34th was able to find cover after crossing the road. Corp. Malachi Hovis was a 20 year old soldier from Lincoln County (Company E 34th NC). He was able to find a gully in the field about 100 yards from the stone all and there he fired at the Yankees in blue. "In the open field I got down in a gully beside a wounded Yankee I took for dead. I load and took ten good shots at the Yankees who were but one hundred yards away. When I had loaded and raised up for the eleventh shot the Yanks were gone. When I announced this to some of the other boys, the dead Yankee raised up and said 'You've got me this time' I said 'I thought you were dead" . . . . but the Yankees were not gone and Hovis ended up taking his prisoner back to the Confederate lines where he found his wounded 1st Lieutenant 23 year old James Tiddy. Tiddy had been wounded in the foot. "I found Jim Tiddy with his foot shot off and made the Yankee and Private Levi Wacaster of our company carry Tiddy back to the liter bearers" **(Memoirs of Reverend John Malachi Hovis)** 1st Lieutenant Tiddy would lose the foot and be captured July 5th.

On the other hand in the same regiment and same company (Co E) Private Benjamin F Carpenter made it clear in 1877 that "We charged and went into the works. Some of the men were on the works with the colors of the 16th North Carolina when Picket's men ran (what did not surrender) This allowed the enemy to flank us and we had to cut our way back" **(Benjamin Carpenter letter to Raleigh Observer, November 12, 1877)** Carpenter, who later became a judge after the war, asserts that some of the men in his regiment (the 34th NC) at the far *left* of Scales line somehow got mixed up with the men of the 16th NC at the far *right*)

Two officers from the 13th North Carolina who survived the fight were 3rd Lieutenant Nathaniel Smith (Co H) and Captain Hugh L. Guerrant of Company K. Smith wrote in 1877 "On the third day we were recruited up to 45 men and this number we carried into the fight. Our part of the line advanced splendidly and the enemy were driven from the works in our front. In the action we lost 23 men killed and wounded and some few were captured in or about the works" **(Nathaniel Smith letter to Raleigh Observer, November 30, 1877)** Captain Guerrant insisted that men of Scales brigade "entered the Yankee works and stayed there until driven out by the enemy advancing on their position". This view was shared by Major Elijah Withers who was wounded on July 1 and not in the action but who talked with survivors. **(Letter from Colonel Elijah B Withers to Raleigh Observer, October 8, 1877, from Danville, Va.)** (Author note:

Smith whose brother 1st Lt James was wounded in the ankle on July 1 would be captured at Falling Waters Maryland two weeks later. He would remain in prison until the end of the war. With the Captain and both senior Lieutenants down, Nathaniel would command the company at the road.

A Lieutenant with the Rockingham Rangers Co I 13th NC, William Winchester had been badly wounded in the right foot in the roadbed, the bullet completely severing his foot except the heel tendon. He tried to crawl back to Seminary Ridge and even asked a retreating soldier to take his knife and amputate the foot. He would be captured and die. **(North Carolina troops 5:366)**

3rd Lt. Henry Moore, a 27 yr old from Duplin Co made it to the wall with what was left of his company "The Spartan band" (Co A 38th NC). After reaching the pike and it's fences Moore remembered that confusion set in and while a number men climbed the fences and continued forward, they soon turned around and returned. Most men remained with Moore and fired at the Yankees through the fence rails. **(Henry Moore letter November 6, 1877, Grimes Papers SHC-UNC)**

The 38th NC advanced to within a few feet of the wooden fence line but near the end of the fight a group of Union soldiers rushed out from a ditch and captured about 30 of the men of the 38th. In Company A every man was shot down except 3rd Lieutenant Henry.C. Moore and 1st Lieutenant Alsa.J. Brown both of whom were captured. Corporal Lewis Thomas of Company A was killed firing over the rails. Only 40 men from the regiment would return to their own lines. **(Compiled service files, 38th North Carolina Infantry Regiment,**

National Archives) (Lt. Colonel George Flower, Clark's regiments Vol. II pp 692-693) (Henry Moore letter to Raleigh Observer, November 6, 1877, from Warsaw NC)

Captain George Flowers would write a report about the wounding of 29 year old 1st Lt. Isaac Kearns who was hit in the left ankle and would die of blood poisoning on July 24. Kearns had been at the fence line and tried to escape but was shot as he moved down the slope toward the road. **(Letter from Lt. Colonel John Ashford September 18, 1877 from Clinton, NC)** Ashford had been wounded on the 1st and was not in the action on the 3rd but talked with the survivors "The 38th was involved in the charge of the 3rd. We lost two officers beyond the works who were captured Captain Alsa Brown (Co A) and Lieutenant Kearns (Co H). Captain Brown (actually 39 year old 1st Sgt Hampton Brown) and Lieutenant McIntyre were engaged but returned to their lines. The 38th lost about 30 prisoners beyond the works, besides quite a number killed." **(Letter from John Ashford to Raleigh Observer, September 18, 1877, from Clinton, NC)**

Lieutenant McIntyre who doubled as Adjutant of the 38th himself wrote of his role in 1877. "A large portion of my own command reached the enemy works . . . I lost a large portion of officers and men killed and captured inside the enemy's works. I suppose we held the works some fifteen minutes or more. I recollect very distinctly seeing two of the officers of my own regiment surrender to the enemy inside their works and they are now both living and perhaps could give you some information; they are Capt. A.J. Brown, White Hall, Wayne County and Lieut H.C. Moore, Faison's Duplin County, both gallant officers. **(Letter from Adjutant-General D.M. McIntyre to Raleigh Observer, October 1, 1877 from Mount Olive, NC)** (Author note the two prisoners mentioned were from Company A, 1st Lt. Alsa Brown a 20 year old from Duplin Country who had earned the "Badge of Distinction" at Chancellorsville and 3rd Lt. Henry o a 27 year old also from Duplin County. Brown would be exchanged March 1864 and be promoted to Captain, Moore would remain a prisoners until after the war. First Sergeant David Thompson would become commander of the company for the remainder of the fight.

Henry Moore who was that day 3rd Lieutenant of Company A of the 38th North Carolina wrote about the end of the fight." By now we were mixed up with other units. I talked with Captain Cloud who was that day in command of the 16th NC *(author note : actually Captain Calvin McCloud 23 year old of Company H16th NC—commanding)* Our men kept up a weak fire from the road fence. The enemy fire then slackened and we limbed the fence and attempted to advance. They rushed out to meet us and our left collapsed and we surrendered. Some of our captured men attempted to escape and were shot down" **(Letter of Henry Moore November 6, 1877 from Warsaw, NC, NCU archives)**

Division commander Trimble's task was to keep funneling troops across the road and up the hill, but soon it was clear that the attack was a failure and Trimble ordered withdrawal. Just on the western side of the fences of Emmitsburg Pike Major General Isaac Trimble was hit by bullet, "I was shot through the left leg on horseback near the close of the fight my fine mare after taking me off the field died of the same shot—Poor Jinny, noble horse, I grieve to part thus." **(Isaac Trimble, "Civil War Diary of I.R. Trimble," Maryland Historical Magazine, XVII (1922), 1-2)**

Scales Right Flank 22nd NC—16th NC

The 22nd NC seems to have mostly stayed at the fence line, however some men in two companies after the war claimed to have climbed the wall and moved through the ranks of the 7th Tennessee and 5th Alabama Battalion and engaged Union forces at the wall. Opposite these men was the 1st Delaware. In the dense smoke a group of men of the First Delaware charged down the slope. The records show that Color Sergeant John Dunn participated in the charge, although no witness claims that he took the regimental flag with him. Lieutenant William Smith, at the time commanding the regiment, went as well with these group of men and was reported to have been killed running down toward the fence. Command then passed to Lieutenant Dent. **(Seville, History of the First regiment, p 83) (William P Seville to John T Dent, OR 27)** What makes this tale even more interesting is that stories among survivors of the 38th North Carolina tell of actually capturing Union men who rushed down the slope only to be taken prisoners by the still active rebels. Glenn Tucker in his early work Gettysburg states "Lowrance's 38th North Carolina reversed the normal process by capturing 30 Federal prisoners besides the works and shooting many. **(Glenn Tucker, *Gettysburg*, 1958)** Tucker's unfootnoted assertion remains speculation since searches of the Union roosters of the 12th NJ, 14th Ct and 1st Delaware fail to produce such a number of MIA or POW names.

For every man from Trimble's Division who crossed that road another made a choice to retreat back toward the safety of the Seminary ridge. "That fire was too much and we 'Turkeyed' in fine style admitted one North Carolina soldier after the war. Trimble in his OR report made it clear that he did not attempt to turn around those who passed by him in flight by this point in the battle. **(Trimble, North Carolinians At Gettysburg, p 58)**

Yet even as their Division commander saw a need to order withdrawal, scores of men such as those of the 22nd and 16th were already too far in advance and too heated by combat and pressed forward to carry the banners of the Trimble regiments beyond the roadbed. Most would not return. At the far right of the Scales line was the 16th North Carolina. Evidence suggests that many of these soldiers had been able to move forward in a cluster. The reason was the dense smoke and the fact that they were hidden both by the scrubbed fence line running north of the forward stone angle and by the intense therefore distracting combat at the wall by Tennessee & Alabama & Virginia troops. Today a monument to the 26th North Carolina stands to the mark the spot where historians years ago incorrectly thought the North Carolina came closest to the Federal Wall. The monument was placed there in spite of the fact that overwhelming evidence suggested that the 26th actually had faced the 12th New Jersey much farther North along the slope. In addition, almost all first hand reports and placed the 26th further north. The source of the confusion was always an account of the action of the last remaining gun of Arnold's battery (gun number four) which was not withdrawn from position and was left loaded with canister. As the battle seemed to be winding down a cluster of rebels appeared through the fog headed for the stone wall. Later reports from some of the remaining cannoners stated that "the gap made in that North Carolina regiment was simply terrible". One man said that he saw the flag of the 26th North Carolina at the front. However, the flag of the North Carolina had already been seized from the hands of Private Thomas by men of the 12th New Jersey. All the evidence regarding regimental position indicates that the flag was in fact that of the 16th North Carolina . . . . a "26" and a "16" being confused in the smoke and fury. Author Rod Gragg tells the tale in his classic work on the 26th North Carolina "Up on the slope to his right, Yankee gun crews on Cemetery Ridge were hurriedly pulling the serviceable guns of Arnold's Battery out of line to save them from capture. One of the Rhode Island gunners, however was determined to take a final shot. Gun number—four was charged with a lethal double load of canister and its gunner, Private William C. Barker stood with lanyard in hand waiting to fire. The gun covered the slope in front of Hay's left wing—the section defended by the men of Connecticut, Delaware and New Jersey. For some reason as the thin gray line surged before the muzzle of the gun, Private Barker hesitated. In his line of fire were North Carolina troops—one Yankee artilleryman would claim they were from the 26th—and at such close range the double load of canister could not miss. Still the gunner hesitated. 'Barker', shouted his Sergeant, 'why the devil don't you fire that gun! Pull, Pull'. Finally the gunner jerked the lanyard, and in a blast of fire and smoke, bucketfuls of lead balls tore into the gray line. 'The number four obeyed orders,' a Federal artilleryman would recall, 'and the gap made in that North Carolina regiment was simply terrible.'" **(Rod Gragg, Covered with Glory, p 199)**

With remnants of Scales Brigade 3rd Lieutenant H.C. Moore (Co A 38th NC) told how the fighting ended. "Our men kept up a weak fire through the plank fence. The enemy's fire slackened and we climbed the fence and attempted to advance. They rushed out from their works to meet us and we were fired upon by a flanking party to our left who close din upon us and compelled us to surrender." (**"H.C Moore to the Editor, *Raleigh Observer*, November 6, 1877)**

Some of the men in the 16th North Carolina had managed to work their way up to the outer angle wall and would join up with the remnants of the Tennessee and Alabama troops that had chased the 71st Pa away from that position earlier. Other men from the 16th and perhaps the 22nd North Carolina managed to mix in with elements of Fry's brigade along the fence line extending north from the outer angle wall. Both groups would surrender to Union forces as the attack stalled and ended. **(Mills, History of the 16th North Carolina, p 38)** Some men had been able to move back in the dense smoke that covered the field. In fact the smoke was remembered as so dense that the wounded Colonel Fry remembered that Union troops kept firing for several minutes after rebels either escaped or raised white flags or pieces of paper in surrender. **(Fry, Pettigrew's Charge at Gettysburg, P 93)**

First Lieutenant William Jasper Edney of Company C 16th NC stated that the left side of Scales Brigade touched the enemy works (the outer stone wall and the forward fence) ". . . with the remaining few we went forward until the right of the brigade touched the enemy's breastworks . . . . The natural inquiry was 'what shall we do?' and none to answer the men answered for themselves, and, without orders, the brigade retreated, leaving many men on the field unable to get off . . ." **(Civil War Record of Lt. William Jasper Edney of Jack's Creek, Yancey County)**

As the assault began to falter General Lane was thrown from his horse. Captain John Thorp of Company A 47th North Carolina had been a part of the skirmishers for Pettigrew's advance and had taken up a position at the western fence firing at the Yankees at the wall. Company A "The Chicora Guards" out of Nash County NC had moved forward and battled the Union skirmish line. At this point Captain Thorp was separated from his regiment and probably from his company as well. He saw Lane to the west of the road and fences on horseback "in the attitude of urging his men forward with his hand; a moment later a large spurt of blood leaped from the horse as he rode up, and the rider and horse went down in the smoke and uproar." Lane recovered and continued in command **(Thorp, Forty-Seventh Regiment, p 81)**

Near the end Lt. Gulian Weir's Battery C of the 5th US Artillery wheeled into position where Arnold's guns had been and began firing into what he called later "a dense body of the enemy", although several members of the 14th Connecticut were killed and wounded by his first discharges.

Colonel Lowrence reported in his post battle report that his regiments had been "reduced to mere squads" Small groups of men would soon be retreating "leaving many of the field unable to get off, and some, I fear, unwilling to undertake the hazardous retreat" **(Lowrence letter to Joseph Engelhard, August 12, 1863)**

A few of the Tennessee soldiers who had take cover debated whether to surrender or run for safety. One group with Lieutenant Ferguson Harris of the 7th Tennessee commanding Company H, debated the issue. One man, Private Thomas Holloway shouted "let's never surrender" and was hit in the head by a bullet as he spoke. Another rebel soldier was hit in the back as he ran not twenty yards from the road. Another ("Black" Dunn—Sergeant Blackman Dunn Company E) shouting "They've got to get more blood out of men before I surrender" However Dunn did try to make a run for it and was shot down about twenty steps down the hill. Another soldier Private John Hale lay on the ground beside Holloway and lived through the firestorm to be captured without a wound.**(F.S Harris Letter, Lebanon Democrat, August 10, 1899)** Harris himself would return to his own lines using two rifles as crutches. He would become deathly sick the next day.

One of the few Tennessee soldiers to make it all the way to the stone wall and then all the way back to the starting point was Sergeant June Kimble (Co A 14th Tennessee) who had enlisted with his entire Company at Camp Dungan early in the war. He ran down the slope to the road and there stopped, picked up a rifle and started firing at Union soldiers still at the distant wall. He told the tale of firing repeated shots at a red shirted Union artilleryman and missing each time. A young soldier beside him was also firing and suddenly jumped up to retreat and was hit in the head by a bullet, dropping beside Kimble. Kimble laid down his rifle and ran for the fields. He could hear the bullets land all around him and fearing that he would be hit in the back turned around and walked backward to Seminary Ridge. **(June Kimble: An Incident at Gettysburg, Tennessee Regiments Collection Museum of the Confederacy)**

The bullets continued to fly in both directions. Among the 14th Connecticut one Corporal, William Goodell shouted out to his men "I would rather be killed than beaten today". He died from a rebel marksman a few moments later. The 14th Connecticut continued firing at the rebels hidden behind the fence line and the rocks along the fence until white cloths and outstretched hands were seen. The firing stopped and weary men in gray rose up and moved forward to surrender. (Bee, *The Boys from Rockville*, p. 144)

1st Lt John Hicks age 32 had been born in Tennessee but lived in Mississippi when the war started. He had been wounded at Sharpsburg. He survived the forward attack and was leading his company back in retreat when a Yankee bullet hit him in the back. He would report that his cousin 21 year old Corporal Joseph Jasper Cox had been killed in the advance and would, after recovery fill out the paperwork needed to settle Cox's account.

Chapter Eight

The Aftermath

The retreat back across the fields was nearly as dangerous as the attack across them had been. An enthusiastic Yankee enemy fired cannon and rifle at men as they moved back toward Seminary Ridge. At least one third of the distance back could be reached by rifle fire and as troops in blue rushed forward toward the Emmitsburg Pike captured prisoners by the hundreds they also leaned their rifles against the still standing study plank fences and fired into the backs of retreating Confederates.

Lieutenant Frederick Colson with the artillery recalled that . . . "The whole field was dotted with our soldiers, singley and in small groups, coming back from the charge, many wounded, and the enemy were firing at them as you would a herd of game." **(Frederick Colson memoir, 14, Campbell-Colson Papers, UNC-SHC)**

22 year old Captain Henry Clay Albright of Company G in the 26th NC, who was later wounded at Ream's Station made it back to his lines but always felt that the rifle fire was more dangerous on the retreat than it had been on the attack. **(Henry C Albright Papers, GHM)**

Sergeant June Kimble from the 14th Tennessee remembered clearly how he got away. "For about one hundred yards, I broke the lightning speed record." (Kimble, *Tennesseans at Gettysburg*, p 451)

Each soldier had to make a choice. Private Wilbur von Swirigen in Company K of the 28th North Carolina recalled his decision. "I saw plainly that it meant death to retreat across the open field a half a mile or more. The enemy was barely shooting over my head at our retreating men. The dead and wounded were many on both sides. Just under the crest of the hill scores of dead and crippled fine artillery horses lay writing in death—From Lee's battery of nearly one hundred guns just one hour previously." **(Van Swaringen Reminiscences, GNMP library collection)**

General James Pettigrew was wounded in the hand and calmly walked back towards his lines. His aide Louis Young walked with him for a while but then Lt Thomas Cureton of the 26th caught up with him and offered assistance. Pettigrew offered Cureton his unwounded arm and the two continued walking back to their lines. **(T.J. Cureton to Dear Sir, June 22, 1890. Lane Papers, SHC)**

General Isaac Trimble who by this point was wounded with a bullet in the leg had made the decision for his men. When his aide Charles Grogan told him that the men of his Brigades were starting to far back and asked if he should try to urge them to return to the fight, Trimble responded "Charlie, the best thing for these brave men to do is to get out of this"

One of the Trimble men who did make it back was 1st Sergeant Augustus Floyd Company D of the 18th NC. Floyd made it back to his lines after starting behind the small wooden blacksmith shack along the Emmitsburg Pike. He described his return years later in his autobiography. "I got back and fell into a hole dug out near our artillery, rested a few minutes and came out past our men rallying and being rallied. I went to a Field Hospital about two miles from the battlefield. The doctor progged my wound for a ball and found that my pants had not been penetrated, but driven with the ball to the bone, which made a large hole. I think it was a grapeshot from a cannon that probably struck some other object before striking me."**(Augustus Evander Floyd, Autobiography, Fairmount, NC)**

Union cannon fire fell into the midst of rebel troops already returned to the start point of the attack. It is worth repeating the story told by 3rd Lieutenant Fergus Harris of 7th Tennessee Co H in Captain William Tate's command of the aftermath of the assault and of the carnage evidence by the returning wounded soldiers. In 1899, some 37 years after the battle an aged Captain Fergus (he always used his rank at the end of the war) returned to visit Gettysburg. He walked the battlefield and dictated a story to the local newspaper. It is a story that bears repeating.

"A beautiful carriage drive winds its serpentine way along the crest of Cemetery Ridge, up and over little Round Top, around and own to Devil's Den. Immense boulders lie above ground all over these two mountains and on the top of one of these a beautiful life-like statue to General Warren who discovered the Round Top and was first to seize it twelve hours after General Lee had ordered General Longstreet to occupy it. We drove away south and west and back again to Sprangle's woods, where we lay during the artillery duel preceding this charge. You will remember Alexander's artillery was just in our front, and we lay behind a slight crest of the hill where I saw a tremendous shot, almost spent, fall within a few inches of Jim Bradley's head. You will remember that when we arose and formed a line we advanced into an open field slightly depressed, in front of Spangle woods. Marching a short distance to the front, we formed in line, beside and touching Garnett's brigade, with Armistead just in the rear. While standing there I could not realize that thirty-seven years had passed and became almost oblivious to my surroundings. I imagined again I could see that great line sway back and forth—my mind as in a dream. I saw myself coming out again, using two guns as a pair of crutches, until rescued by Old Artillery (John Lanier Co F). I imagined I could see General Lee again as he rode back and forth on his old white horse begging the men to rally. I thought I could see Bill Young (3rd Sergeant Co I) being ordered by Gen. Lee to take command of General Heth's division, and ordering men to stop, which, when they would not do it, he knocked them down with the butt of his gun. There stood before my eyes again the picture of Gen. lee asking Bill Yong if any of his officers had come out, who, pointing just on the brow of the hill, said, 'There comes Col. Shepard now,' I imagined I could see Gen. Lee ride up to Col. Shepard and say, 'Colonel, tell your men it is my fault: take command of these men, form them, and drive those people (pointing to the Yankees) back if they over here.' I thought I saw again the grandest compliment I ever knew paid to a man in my life when Gen. Lee turned around, patting Bill Young on the shoulder, saying, 'My brave boy, if I had an army like you this would not have happened.' I imagined that I could again see Jack Moore (2nd Lt. Company B) as he dragged himself up the rise and said to Col. Shepard,:'Colonel, if them damned fellows hadn't broken on the right we could have held that ridge.' I imagined again that I could see the old 7th Tenn. Formed with only thirteen men left in line . . . I thought of Jim Martin (1st Lt. Co D) as I saw him coming back with his arm all torn and bleeding. A grim smile passed over my face as I thought of Dick Palmer (Private Co D), who only received a pair of shoes that morning, after marching all the way to Gettysburg bare-footed. Under the rules observed, had he not received the shoes he would not have had to go into the battle, but Rufe McClain (Acting Brigade Quarter Master) gave him a pair that morning. I thought of John Harlin (Co H), Ben Ferrell (Co D), Dick Palmer (Co D), Byrd Willmouth (2nd Lt Co A), Old Artillery (John Lanier (Co. F) and various others whose names I cannot now remember, as they came up the hill amid a perfect hurricane of shot and shell, each bearing a wounded man.

A singular coincidence happened to me there. I remember as I was being brought out by Old Artillery, to have seen the "Black Ram" (Sergeant James Grissom Co G) assisting Captain Bob Miller (Co E), who was seriously wounded in the foot. The shells were so thick that we were paying not so much attention as we did at first, but one big fellow came screaming along and it seemed as if it would hit us in spite of all we could do. "Black Ram" dropped captain Miller and jumped about ten feet to his let close to the stump of a large tree, which seemed only recently to have been cut. Just as he stooped the shell struck him on the shoulder and seems to have exploded at the same time. It literally tore him into a thousand pieces and dug a great hole into the ground. I was not making any notes in my memorandum book that day, but I noticed distinctly the spot and easily located it today. The great stump is only a small piece of rotten wood there now, but enough to designate it. This field is now in corn, and while I was relating this circumstance to the commissioners, a man who was ploughing the corn was standing there listening, and he said 'I will get you a piece of the shell that killed the Black Ram'. He drove his long keen bull tongue into the ground deeper than it has ever been ploughed before, and then in the exact spot brought o the surface a piece of shell which I am certain is the piece that killed the 'Black Ram'. I have brought the relic home with me and now have it. Capt. Jim Martin (then 1st

Lt. James Martin Co D) says 'Black Ram's' name was Grissom and he belonged to Col. Shepard's old company (Co G), that his people yet live in Wilson County. If they will take this relic and take care of it as a memento of one of the finest of America's soldiers, and of the battlefield of Gettysburg, I will give it to them. The old fences yet stand on each side of the Emmitsburg road, and so full of bullet marks that it is impossible to put your finger on it without striking one." **(F.S Harris Letter, Lebanon Democrat, August 10, 1899)**

Another memory of General Lee's interaction with the retreating troops was recorded in his reminiscence by Commissary Sergeant William Fulton "As our command rallied and formed in the rear Gen. Lee rode by and asked 'What troops are these?' When informed that it was Archer's Brigade he ordered them to support a battery that had just opened near by on the enemy's line. His parting words were "Remember that adversity puts men to the test; in prosperity all are true" Through our lines had been repulsed with fearful shock, yet they were soon readjusted and an advance by the enemy would have met a hot reception. It seems there was little danger of their attempting it as they had enough." **(William Frierson Fulton, Family Record and War Reminiscences, 1919)**

One Confederate engineer, Lt. William Gordon, was impressed by the way the survivors of the attack maintained order as they returned to the protection of Seminary Ridge. I was . . . "particularly impressed by the appearance the men made in coming back, so slowly and so deliberately that at first I thought they were wounded men or prisoners." **(Gordon Memoirs p 140)** One the other hand men recalled years later the panic and confusion of the retreat which "commenced a rout that soon increased to a stampede and almost demoralization of all the survivors of this noted charge without distinction of regiments or commands" **(H.T. Owen, *Pickett at Gettysburg*)**

2nd Lieutenant Octavius Wiggins with the 37th NC (Co E) insisted that the retreat was orderly. "When the order came to retire, those who were spared did so in perfect order—never anything like a panic, as some people think—and halted at the position from which they had started." **(Octavious A Wiggins, Clark's Regiments, Vol. II p. 661)**

Private Andrew Parks had been wounded in the knee but made it back somehow to his own lines. "The few of us that were left got back to where we started from. Some companies had not more than five men left. Nine others and myself were all that were left out of fifty five that we went in with. Two Lieutenants and nearly all of the missing in my company were killed. About ten were taken prisoners." Parks was with Company I of the 42nd Mississippi **(Andrew Parks, Some of my Recollections of the Battle of Gettysburg, Arkansas Historical Society)**

The lone North Carolina regiment in Davis's brigade, the 55th NC, was devastated. It's lost in officers was extreme. All four of the Field officers had been killed or wounded in the fighting on July 1st. Colonel John Kerr had been wounded in the left arm and right hip; Lieutenant Colonel Maurice Smith had been killed by a fragment in his side; Major Alfred Belo had been wounded by a shell on the night of the 1st and Adjutant Henry Jordan had been captured. This left 31 year old senior Captain Gilreath (Co B) to command the entire regiment in the attack. He was killed. Command of the 55th North Carolina after the battle passed to 25 year old First Lieutenant Marcus Stevens in Company G. The North Carolinians had lost 9 of it's 10 Captains and 19 of it's 30 lieutenants.

Lieutenants Moore and Brown from the 38th North Carolina were taken to the original position of Arnold's Union battery after their capture and they were is position to look out over the field they had crossed during the attack. "We were then at an abandoned battery a few feet in front of their infantry lines. I now perceived that they had been protected by a cut in the rear which seemed do run parallel to the road which we had crossed . . . some of our men attempted to escape but were shot down. We had heard no order to retreat, and I don't think any such order was given. After our party was captured there was a lull in the firing along the whole line; a shell would be thrown occasionally.

1st Sergeant Augustus Varin, in the 2nd Mississippi, who had been in the midst of the hardest fighting, summed up his experiences rather calmly his in diary entry for the day, "*3 July Friday*, clear. About 7 AM the remnant of our regt.—60 guns strong—marched to the battlefield & after the cannon ceased firing we joined in making the last grand charge which was so disastrous to our army. We were on the right of Genl. Heath's command & were in the thickest of the fight, where we lost all our men but one, either killed, wounded or captured. I was badly wounded & in time was sent to David Island hospital near New York where I remained till November & returned to Richmond for exchange. (Varin's company B had 66 men when they arrived at Gettysburg. They would lose 48 on the first day and 13 more on July 3. One man was wounded and three more captured on the retreat back to Virginia) **(Varin Diary July 3, 1863)**

One memory that Private Tom Wilkins (Co E 11th Mississippi) had of his arrival back at the McMillan Woods with his broken right leg reminds us of the context of the war in which he was engaged . . . "All of the little black servants owned by the University Greys were standing in a row wringing their hats in their hands, with tears streaming down their dusty cheeks. Each boy cried out his master's name, but no master answered. The University Greys had ceased to exist. They were all gone—gone to glory up Cemetery Ridge." **(Stubbs, Duty, Honor, Valor, p 431)**

An officer with the 80th New York, Major Walter Van Rensselaer wrote in his diary about rounding up of Confederate prisoners . . ." When near a sash of timber, I discovered a rebel flag behind a fence in the hands of an officer—I demanded its surrender—he replied "not by a damned sight" and fired at me with his revolver wounding me in the small of the back. I lunged at him with my saber when he fired again, the ball striking my saber scabbard—five or six of my boys came to the rescue and he surrendered, followed by his whole regiment—they came over the fence like a flock of sheep. **(Diary of Walter A. Van Rensselaer, Gettysburg National Military Park)**

One of the many mortally wounded officers in Pettigrew's line was Captain James Kincaid Company G 52nd North Carolina. He was brought in by the 14th Connecticut and talked with Corporal Alexander McNeil who wrote in a letter the next month "I had a long conversation with a Captain of the 52nd North Carolina. He was severely wounded and we carried him into our lines & laid him down. I gave him coffee to drink twice, while waiting for a stretcher to carry him to the hospital. He was sensible intelligent man." **(Alexander McNeill letter August 16, 1863 US Army Military History Institute, Carlisle, Pa)**

In the roadbed, Captain James Harris, 23 year old commander of Company B 7th Tennessee, knew that the attack had failed and understood the choices available. The Cabarus County officer recalled "To remain and be captured, or run the gauntlet of the enemy's batteries and escape, was our only alternative and the latter, (The bravest act of the day), was resorted to every man going to the rear as fast as his well neigh exhausted nature would, spurred onward by dangers which the heroic courage of the day failed to surmount." **(James Harris, *Historical Sketches*, pp 35-36)**

Private Wilbur von Swarigen in Company K of the 28th was now a prisoner being taken back to the rear. He observed the horror around him "I will never forget a young Mississippi man of the Fifty-Fifth regiment crying and looking for a doctor, holding his bowels in his hands, torn by a piece of shell. I directed him to a federal surgeon not far away. **(Van Swaringen Reminiscences, GNMP library collection)**

Such comradeship was frequently found after the battle ended. Private William Madison Suggs in Company G of the 11th NC was a prisoner after the battle. Years later he wrote an affidavit for the widow of a soldier he had helped on the battlefield. "I was returning to the ground which we passed near the stonewall, he called to me, I looked and saw Wm. E Crabtree of Chapel Hill lying on the ground. He was known to me and I asked him where he was wounded. he pulled up his shirt showed me a wound in the point of the belly that must have gone through his bowels. On retreat I was taken prisoner and was taken under guard. He asked me to help him to the rear. He put his arms around my neck and I carried him twenty yards when he asked me to put him down. I did so and he—back upon the ground and I am satisfied died there and the being prisoner I was ordered on and was not allowed to remain with him." **(Nancy Crabtree, North Carolina State Archives, Civil War widow pension application files)** Suggs was paroled and later would rise to both Corporal and Sergeant of his company.

Amidst all the carnage a scene occurred which brought cheers and exultation to the Union troops of Hayes Division yet at the same time shame and bitterness to the battered warriors of the south who could look up from the ground and see the sight. General Alexander

Hayes ordered his staff to find him several Confederate battle flags and on horseback leaped the stone wall and was handed a captured rebel banner. He placed the flag on the ground and holding the pole in his hand dragged the flag of one rebel regiment along in the dirt and blood and filth of battle riding first southward toward the connecting wall and then turning around rode north to the Bryan barn. His two staffers did likewise and then threw the remnants of these banners into the pile of dead and wounded rebels.

Private Heflin was unable to retreat due to bullets in his foot and ankle. He had pleaded for help from other retreated soldiers in the roadway but was abandoned. After being taken prisoner a Yankee soldier helped him to the Bryan shack (located at the point where the Bryan lane hit Emmitsburg Road). A Confederate shell sailed through the building without exploding and Heflin was led hobbling back toward Taneytown road. **(Heflin, *Blind Man on the Warpath*, pp.24-25)**

Later that afternoon a chaplain from a Maine regiment was walking over the battlefield when he heard "a feeble voice calling 'Doctor come here' It was Lieutenant Royster (Co G 37th NC) calling out. The chaplain found Royster 'fearfully wounded through the lungs, one thigh shattered and other wounds' The chaplain told Royster that he was no doctor, but a minister. Royster's reply was 'you are the doctor I need, none other will do my any good now" **(Michael Hardy The Gettysburg Experiences of Lt. Iowa Michigan Royster, 37th North Carolina Volunteer Infantry Regiment)**

The 14th Tennessee had left Clarksville, Tennessee with more than 960 men in 1861 and had marched into Adams County Pa with 365. After the first of July it numbered 60 soldiers and by nightfall on the 3rd of July all but three had fallen . . . .

"Thus the band that once was the pride of Clarksville has fallen . . . . A glom rests over the city, the hopes and affections of the people were wrapped in the regiment . . . Ah! what a terrible responsibility rests upon those who inaugurated this terrible war." **(Civil War in Song and Story, P 220)**

In front of the 12th New Jersey lay the men of the 26th North Carolina, "Dead and dying everywhere, the ground almost covered with them; their wounded and prisoners coming I into our ranks by the hundreds; some crawling on their hands and knees, others using two muskets as crutches." **(Foster, New Jersey and the Rebellion, p. 305)**

Private Albert Caisson (Co I 26th NC) tried to leave the field as the fire slackened but was quickly surrounded by Yankees who demanded he surrender. One of the few from the 26th to return was Lieutenant Hudspeth who was running back toward his lines when an artillery shell exploded and knocked him to the ground but he jumped up and ran all the way back to his lines. He had been the sole unwounded man in Company F on the first of July and he would survive this day as well without a wound.

Commissary Sergeant William Fulton, back at the Confederate lines, wrote that the remainder of troops from the five regiments of Archer's brigade were ordered to guard a near by artillery battery "General Lee rode by and asked 'what troops are these?' His parting words were "Remember that diversity puts men to the test; in prosperity all are true." Though our lines had been repulsed with fearful shock, yet they were soon readjusted and an advance by the enemy would have met a hot reception" **(Family Record and War Reminiscences by William Fulton Jr., Livingston, Alabama 1919)**

Lieutenant Peel taken prisoner with what remained of the Confederates who had reached Bryan's barn described the aftermath. ". . . in a moment more a white flag floated from behind the corner, around which the moment before, our accurately aimed muskets had belched their deadly contents into the ranks of the enemy. An old Seg't (Probably Sergeant Thomas Greer Co A 111th New York) came out & took charge of us, and ordered us through the gate that was open on the left of the barn. As passed through, all unarmed of course, a Yankee soldier brought down his musket & with its muzzle right at the breast of one of our party, was on the point of firing. I cringed for the safety of my brave comrade, and shuttered at the thought of seeing him thus butchered, but just at this crucial juncture, our Serg't sprang forward, knocked up the musket & with a word of reproach, asked the soldier if he did not see that these men had surrendered. In passing the line, we were surrounded by a crowd of soldiers . . . . We were hurried on under a strong guard. Our retreating line had, in the mean time, repassed our line of artillery, which immediately resumed it's fire. Shells came screaming through the air & began to burst around us. They flew thicker & faster as the greater number of pieces opened, and I saw several vary narrow escapes . . . For half a mile we were thus exposed to the fire of our own guns. Hobbling along as best we were able—most of us wounded—hurried at every step by our impatient guard, we at length reached the Baltimore pike, where we found the second line of battle."**(Diary of Lieutenant William Peel," Mississippi State Archives)**

Sergeant George Bowen with the 12th New Jersey reminds us of the horror of that attack with his description of a dying young Confederate in front of the stone wall, "partially paralyzed by two bullets in his head, but stubbornly using his working hand to pull clumps of grass—which he tried fruitlessly to stuff in his head wounds." **(Rod Gragg, Covered with Glory, p 205)**

One Union soldier with the first Delaware regiment Private John Dunn who had faced the 47th North Carolina never forgot the scene in front of his position "I never saw dead and wounded men lay so thick. From a space about seventy-five feet back to the opposite side of the pike you could walk over the dead bodies of men." **(John Dunn testimony, *Report of Joint Committee*, p 15)**

A number of Confederate prisoners still were spunky after their capture. One Union soldier recalled a Confederate looking around while being taken over the wall and seeing so few Yankee soldiers, "Where are your men, I mean those you had here when you gave us such volleys as we advanced" When told that this was the entire Union force the rebel exclaimed "My God, we could have gone through you as it was if we's known how few your were." **(Samuel McIntyre letter to Clinton MacDougal, June 27, 1880)**

Lieutenant Colonel Dawes, years later, told a story about riding horseback to headquarters carrying the flag of the 2nd Mississippi which had been taken on July 1st in the Railroad cut. As he passed by a wounded soldier from Mississippi, the soldier cried out 'You have our colors, let me se them' . . . Dawes wrote 'The poor fellow was quite affected to see his colors, and I did all I could to comfort him" **(Dawes," *Service with the Sixth Wisconsin Volunteers*" p. 368)** (author note—There is a strong chance that the rebel soldier was 2nd Lt "Luke" Byrn of the 2nd Mississippi who had been in the color company. The 23 year old Tippah clerk had been with the O'Conner rifles since June 1861 and was wounded and captured July 3 near that location. Other historians suggest that the man may have been Sergeant William Davis who also had carried the flag during the attack. One soldier who was captured two days before and spent prison time with Davis, Private D.J. Hill, suggested that Davis was the man. **(Hill to Dawes, Sept. 12, 1893, Rufus Dawes Letters, McCain Library and Archives, University of Southern Mississippi)**

In front of the wall lay hundreds of dead and dying men, "I counted 16 dead bodies on one rod square, and the dead in every direction lay upon the field in heaps and scattered as far as the eye could reach, wrote one man in the 125th New York **(Longacre, To Gettysburg and Beyond, p 137)**

The rounding up of prisoners; the taking of battle flags and the search to find the fate of comrades left lasting images in the minds of those who were there. Lieutenant Gaston Broughton of Company D, 26th North Carolina recalled that he looked around him as he lay on the field with a wounded foot and saw that but eight of his 25 men who made the charge remained alive unwounded. Colonel Birkett Fry's wounded thigh resulted in his being captured and seeing all around him dead of his command. As Fry told it he was surrounded by dead and dying comrades and unable to crawl back to his own lines, "I was of course left a prisoner" **(Fry, Pettigrew's Charge at Gettysburg" SHSP, Vol. 7, pp 91-92)**

In front of the Bryan barn lay hundreds of Confederate dead and dying. ". . . the Confederate dead could be seen lying in heaps. Hundreds of the charging line prostrated themselves on their backs in the Emmitsburg road and waved their hats and handkerchiefs in token of surrender. Some of the bravest rushed close to the main Union line and fell a few yards away." **(Erza Simons, A Regimental History: The One Hundred and Twenty-Fifth New York State Volunteers, pp 136-138)**

The 11th Mississippi which had born the brunt of Union flank attacks had gone into the battle with 393 officers and men would see 110 of them killed, 193 wounded and

37 captured unhurt. That left only 53 men remaining for duty. The small number of unwounded captured is in sharp contrast to the numbers taken unwounded from the regiments who had access to the protection of the sunken roadbed between the fences.

Once it was clear that the assault had failed, Confederate artillery opened up on the Union position once again. Assistant Surgeon Francis Wafer with the 108th New York, who was charged with going to the aid of wounded from both armies, was puzzled by this bombardment. "The enemy commanders . . . now reopened their artillery indiscriminately upon friend and foe. Whether this was done in a clumsy attempt to cover the retreat or punish their men who had surrendered remains to be explained. The later suspicion has been aroused by some of the prisoners stating that they were threatened to be fired upon by artillery if they broke. But this course probably prevented our line making any counter charge and permitting more of their men to escape from the field." **(Diary of Francis Moses Wafer, Queen's University Library, Kingston, Ontario, Canada)**

Much as been written about the "capture" of Confederate flags during the cleanup fighting and in general these capture records do give us indications of where Union and Confederate regiments squared off in general. The end of the battle saw a mad rush forward of Union soldiers anxious to take prisoners and grab fallen flags. The Yankee regiment directly opposite each Confederate regiment of course had the best chance to seize flag and sword and captive. The men of the 14th Connecticut were able to take both flags and officers from the 1st & 14th Tennessee as well as the 7th and 5 Alabama. Likewise the 12th New Jersey had a premium on the banners of the 26th and 47th North Carolina. The taking of the flag of the 14th Tennessee by the Sergeant Major of the 14th Connecticut is an exciting tale. Out pacing two fellow soldiers (one of whom was shot dead) William Hincks dashed down from the stone wall to seize the banner leaning up against the wooden fence, swinging his sword at nearby Confederates, and then ran back to the cheers of his "nutmeg state" comrades. Hincks later recalled that at that point he was more concerned with the fire of his Union comrades than he was of Confederate bullets.

Captain Benjamin F Little (Co E 52nd NC) who had a severe arm wound was taken back to the Union lines. He later wrote his wife "All the badly wounded were taken prisoner when I was captured. I was led to the enemy rear and saw men killed and wounded immediately at the enemy works. My company was reduced to a squad" Little would lose his arm and be imprisoned until March 6, 1864. Promoted to Lt. Colonel he would be unable to serve because of his wound. **(Benjamin Little letter to wife, July 20, 1863, Little Papers, UNC)**

Little later recalled in 1877 "I lay where I fell until the fight was over, perfectly conscious and no retreating men ever passed my line of vision and I was so situated that I had a good view . . . When I was taken prisoner and borne to the enemy's rear, I passed over their works, and found some of my men killed and wounded immediately at their works.

Of my company, three commissioned officers went into the fight—all were wounded, and my company was reduced to a mere squad" (The other two wounded officers were 1st Lt Milton Austin a 36 year old Richmond County merchant who was wounded in the right foot and 2nd Lt Martin McDonald a 23 year old Richmond County farmer wounded and captured) **(Benjamin Little letter to Raleigh Observer, September 20, 1877)**

Captain George Bowen of the 12th New Jersey described what it was like to go out in the fields in front of the Union defenses after dark. "As soon as it was dark I with many others went out over the field, had my canteen filled with water before starting, giving a drink to such of the wounded that I found, soon it was empty, it was a long way to go for more, so filled my canteen from a ditch beside the Emmitsburg road. This road was filled with their dead, the ditch was piled up with them. I did not think about the water being bloody, it was dark so could not see, knew it was muddy, but that kind of water I had frequently had to drink. I gave some of this to a wounded man, he said 'can't you get me some cool clear water that is not so full of blood that I can not drink it. This is the first time we have had the privilege of going over a battlefield immediately after a fight, one time is enough, the sight and sound were terrible, no one can give an idea of what it is like, the pain and misery of those poor fellows whom we shot down a few hours ago—it is heart breaking sight" **(Bowen, "The Diary of Captain George D. Bowen, p 134)**

Captain James Kincaid of the 52nd NC (Co G) had been wounded in the thighs and lay helpless on the slope near the forward fence. He was carried to the Union lines where a Corporal O'Neil of the 14th Connecticut had a conversation with him as he lay waiting for to be taken to an aide station. "I had a long conversation with a Captain of the 52nd North Carolina regiment, He was severely wounded and we carried him into our lines and laid him down. I gave him coffee to drink twice, while waiting for a stretcher to carry him to hospital. He was a sensible intelligent man. He told me the South had been rough and harsh with North Carolina troops all through, since the War commenced. He told me that it was because the State of North Carolina did not secede quite soon enough to suit some of the other slave states. He told me too that the State of South Carolina ought to be sunk. That, he said, was where the trouble started." **(letter from Alexander McNeil, August 16, 1863, USMHI, Carlisle, Pa collection)**

Sergeant William Jenkins of the 7th North Carolina (co G) had several serious wounds and lay dying under a grove of trees behind the front wall of Hayes Division. Union officer Abner Small offered the dying soldier a drink of water and wrote of the incident "My duties permitting, I went among the wounded in a grove on the left of our position, where lay many hurt survivors of the Rebel attacking force; men of Pickett's Division and Heth's and Pender's. I proffered what assistance I could. I remember stopping beside one poor fellow who was shot through the body, His wants were few. 'Only a drink of water; I'm cold; so cold. Won't you cover me up? His mind wandered, and he murmured something about his mother. Then he had a clear sense of his condition, would I write to his home, and say how he loved them, and how he died 'Tell the about it won't you' Father's name is Robert Jenkins. My name is Will. I thought I heard him say he belonged to the 7th North Carolina and came from Chatham County. His words faltered into silence. I covered his face." **(GNMP Library, 7th NC File)** Jenkins would be buried in the Orchard of the Frey Farm, where many men of the 69th Pa "Irish Volunteers" were laid to rest.

Captain John Thorpe Company A of the 47th North Carolina recalled the scene at the end of the fight "The skeleton of its former self it (the regiment) returned to the place whence it began its charge and began business without a field officer, and during the balance of the day and the succeeding night welcomed the return of several our members who, unscathed or wounded in various degrees, crawled from the field of carnage, for the space between the armies continued neutral ground being covered by the wounded of both." **(John Thorpe, *Memories of Gettysburg, GNMP*)**

In the darkness of the night of July 3, 1863 Private William "Bill" Cook slowly crept back on to the field of battle searching for the body of his brother Columbus Cook (both in Company D of the 11th Mississippi). He found his brothers body in the fields west of the Emmitsburg road and knowing that he could not carry him back to Confederate lines buried him in a shallow grave. The Cook brothers (6 in number) all fought at Gettysburg in Company D. Brothers Jacob and John were both wounded and captured on July 3. Oldest brother Thomas would be captured at Falling Waters. **(Clark, NC Regiments / Compiled Service files, National Archives)**

One of the most detailed reports of the 47th North Carolina came in a letter written home by 1st Lieutenant Nathaniel Brown of Company C. On July 10 at Hagerstown Maryland he had a chance to write a detailed report of the actions of his company which became, no doubt, the basis for information in the surrounding Wake County towns. A watchmaker before the war, Brown, age 26 had been in the middle of the action but suffered only a graze on the middle finger of his left hand.

> Camp of the 47th Regt N.C.T.
> Hagerstown, Md July 10, 1863
>
> MY DEAR FATHER AND MOTHER—Thank God I am once more permitted to write you, and let you know that I have been spared through the hard fought battles of the 1st and 3rd of July at Gettysburg, Pa. I came out unhurt, with the exception of a slight graze on the middle finger of my right hand. I was shocked by a shell also. Wee have to mourn the loss of many thousands of our poor soldiers who fought their last fight. In our company Color Sergeant E.C.N. Green and Private Hansel Poole were killed instantly on the 1st of July. Capt. Iredel's arm was shot off, and he has since died. Several of the men were wounded but not seriously.

On July 3rd, Lt. Norfleet was wounded severely if not mortally and Corporal Gaston Utley killed. Lt. Whiting, L.M. Green and Corpl. R.B. Beddington were wounded and left on the field. Lt. W was shot in the head Corpl. B struck by a shell and whether killed not known. Privates John Done, Nicholas Gill, John Johnson, Geo. Partino, J.W. Pilkerton and Joe Woodward are missing. Lt. Col Graves, Major Crudup and Adjutant Powell were seen to fall and have not been heard from. Jim Andrews was wounded and left on the field. (author note—Sergeant Jim Andrews was a neighbor back home who served in Company H "The North Carolina Tigers" and died on the field that day)

The officers missing from the regiment are Lts. Evans (B) Whiting (C), Drake (D), Joyner (F), Newsom (H), Watson (K) Captain Davis, Lt. Col Graves, Major Crudup, and Adjutant Powell. (note—author added company designations)

The following are the officers wounded and taken off the field. Col G.H. Fairbault, slightly in right arm, Lts. Westray Bunn(A), Perry (B), Norfleet (C), Ray (E), Robinson (E), Gill (F), Tunstall (G),

Williamson (G), Womble (H), Jones Rogers (I) and Captain Faucette (K). Lt Rogers (I) is slightly wounded in the leg and is with his company.

Sergts Syme and Hall and Geo Moore and Ed Williams (all in Co C) are safe as are Deems Smith and Bragg (author note—The two drummers of Co. C). Rufus Ruth of the 14th regt had his arm amputated at the shoulder. Billy Hayes is safe.

Gen. Pettigrew was wounded in the left arm and had his horse shot under him.

N.L.B

(Letter to Mother and Father from 1st Lt Nathaniel Lane Brown Co C 47th NC, GNMP Library collection)

Captain Benjamin Little would become a source of information on his regiments loses in the weeks following the battle as he wrote frequent letters to his wife and was able to report on wounded members of the 55th North Carolina. In a series of eight letters over the next two months news of both death and recovery was sent south.

The very next day after the assault Captain John J Young, the assistant quartermaster of the 26th North Carolina wrote a letter to Governor Zebulon Vance (also former commander of the Regiment) to tell him of the sever losses of his old command.

"Near Gettysburg, PA., July 4, 1863.

My Dear Governor:

I will trespass a few minutes upon your indulgence to communicate the sad fate that has befallen the old Twenty-sixth. The heaviest conflict of the war has taken place in this vicinity. It commenced July 1, and raged furiously until late last night. Heth's division, of A. P. Hill's corps, opened the ball, and Pettigrew's brigade was the advance. We went in with over 800 men in the regiment. There came out but 216, all told, unhurt. Yesterday they were again engaged, and now have only about 80 men for duty. To give you an idea of the frightful loss in officers: Heth being wounded, Pettigrew commands the division and Major J. Jones our brigade. Eleven men were shot down the first day with our colors; yesterday they were lost. Poor Colonel Burgwyn, jr., was shot through both lungs, and died shortly afterward. His loss is great, for he had but few equals of his age. Captain McCreery, of General Pettigrew's staff, was shot through the heart and instantly killed' with them Lieutenant-Colonel Lane through the neck, jaw, and mouth, I fear mortally; Adjutant James B. Jordan in the hip, severely; Captain J. T. Adams, shoulder, seriously; Stokes McRae's thigh broken; Captain William Wilson was killed; Lieutenants John W. Richardson and J. B. Holloway have died of their wounds. It is thought Lieutenant M. McLeod and Captain N. G. Bradford will die. Nearly all the rest of the officers were slightly wounded. I. A. Jarratt I had forgotten to mention-in the face and hand. Yesterday, Captain S. P. Wagg was shot through by grape and instantly killed; Lieutenant G. Broughton in the head, and instantly killed, Alexander Saunders was wounded and J. R. Emerson left on the field for dead. Captain H. C. Albright is the only captain left in the regiment unhurt, and commands the regiment. Lieutenants J. A. Lowe, M. B. Blair, T. J. Cureton, and C. M. Sudderth are all of the subalterns. Colonel Faribault, of the Forty-seventh, is severely wounded. Lieutenant-Colonel J. A. Graves and Major A. D. Crudup supposed killed. Colonel Marshall and Major J. Q. Richardson, of the Fifty-second, supposed to be killed. Lieutenant-Colonel Parks dangerously wounded; Colonel Leventhorpe badly wounded; Major Ross killed. Our whole division numbers but only 1,500 or 1,600 effective men, as officially reported, but, of course, a good many will still come in. The division at the beginning numbered about 8,000 effective men. I hear our army is generally badly cut up. We will fall back about 5 miles, to draw the enemy, if possible, from his impregnable position. It was a second Fredericksburg affair, only the wrong way. We had to charge over a mile a stone wall in an elevated position. I learn the loss of the enemy is terrible. We have taken 10,000 or 15,000 prisoners in all. Yesterday, in falling back, we had to leave the wounded; hence the uncertainty of a good many being killed late yesterday evening. I must close.

Yours truly,

J. J. Young, Captain, and Assistant Quartermaster.

(Young to Vance letter July 4, 1863, *The War of the Rebellion: A Compilation of the Official Records of the Union and Confederate Armies*)

Chapter Nine

Return to Virginia

The plans for Lee's Retreat back to Virginia were formulated in the darkness of July 3 and organized all day the fourth. The role of the regiments that constituted the Pettigrew—Trimble assault would be central to the effort. There would be two separate paths back to Williamsport where the Potomac would be crossed. All of those in Heth's and Pender's Divisions wounded too badly to fight would be placed in an Ambulance Train that would travel westward through Cashtown Gap and then turn south before Chambersburg through New Franklin and then from there to Greencastle and then on to Williamsport. This path would be filled with ambulances, wagons, confiscated buggies and carts and would stretch eventually some seventeen miles in length. To protect these battered men from Pettigrew's and Trimble's regiments, cavalry units under the command of General Imboden would be interspersed along with artillery batteries throughout the seventeen mile train as well as in the lead and the rear.

Meanwhile the fighting forces of Heth and Pender would be marched down the Fairfield road as part of the active regiments closer to the mountains and to the Union army. This train would go through Fairfield and the Monterey Pass then to Waynesboro Hagerstown and Williamsport. Both groups would be subject to the possibility of attacks by Union cavalry forces that were both to their east and in some cases to their west.

The positions of the regiments which had assaulted the Union lines on July 3rd were as follows: The Third Corps wounded with Imboden were first in line on the road to Cashtown: Pender's Division (right behind the Third Corps Quartermaster train) followed by Heth and then by Anderson. Thus wounded troops with Scales and Lane would arrive first in Williamsport.

On the other route A.P. Hill's Corps infantry would also be first to retreat. The able bodied soldiers from Third Corps who traveled by the Fairfield route would follow the Army's Reserve trains and Ewell's Three Division Trains and be arranged as follows : Anderson, Pender and then Heth. Only after Hill had cleared the Monterey Pass and established defensive position would Longstreet and finally Ewell pass through.

Before these two retreating armies could begin the trek, logistics concerning artillery and cavalry support as well as vehicles for the march had to be placed in order. In addition, the decision would be made concerning which soldiers were physically able to travel and which need be left behind. Everywhere and every day for the next week would be the rain . . . . heavy downpours or scattered showers turning all roads and fields into mud quagmires.

Private Thomas Bailey was a member of the Pioneer Corps for Heth's Division and had been detailed from Company E of the 47th North Carolina. Bailey kept a diary during the entire Gettysburg Campaign and his entries provide us with a unique viewpoint concerning the retreat of Heth's Division. On July 4th in preparation for the retreat Bailey's pioneers repaired a railway bridge across a small stream which would be used for wagons. **(Mary Lewis, The Life and Times of Thomas Bailey, Gettysburg National Military Park Archives, 47th NC folder)**

The field hospitals of Pender's and Heth's Division were located alongside the Chambersburg road at the farms of the Lahr and Heintzelman families. The wounded of both divisions were to be found in farmhouses and barns all along the Chambersburg Pike and Marsh Creek valley. Part of the process on the morning of July 4th was to determine who would stay and who would go. "The surgeons continued the work incessantly, until the morning of the 4th, without having finished the work before them. Orders had been received the night previous to have the wounded made speedily ready to send them forward to Winchester. Every mind is now absorbed in getting them off. Those able to walk were immediately started and wagons and ambulances filled. We left any fellows too badly wounded to risk their uncertain transportation. Captain Cooper furnished the major and me a spring wagon and a large blind horse We were soon comfortably fixed and on the way with an immense wagon train some ten miles long. **(Dr Hillary Moseley, "Journal of DR. Hillary Moseley, Batesville, Mississippi)**

As the Confederate army prepared to withdraw back to Virginia decisions needed to be made regarding which medical staff would remain with the wounded non-movable soldiers. In the 42nd Mississippi Thomas Dwight Witherspoon, the Reverend who had taken up a rifle and went into the July 3 charge, would remain with about 300-400 severely wounded from Davis's brigade. Witherspoon would care for these troops, be captured and then would be given permission to take the body of Colonel Hugh Miller back south. Witherspoon's regiment suffered 43 killed or mortally wounded on the 3rd; 73 captured (most of who were wounded) and 43 wounded and returned to Confederate lines.

Assistant Surgeon LaGrand James Wilson was not anxious to remain in Pennsylvania. The 29 year old Grenada native was first ordered to stay with the severely wounded but told his commander Dr. H.H. Hubbard "Doctor, I will obey orders but if you have any duty more dangerous or more arduous, let me have it. I don't want to fall into the hands of the enemy, although I know they will treat me right'. I am real cranky on this subject please give me something else.' Dr Hubbard replied 'I have a train of wounded to start for Williamsburg. Can you be ready in half and hour? . . . . Wilson was on that train. **(Wilson, The Confederate Soldier, p.125)**

One soldier who was picked to remain was Private John Kennedy Minyard of Company A 42nd Mississippi who had been wounded in the side on July 1. He recalled in his 1916 pension papers years later having been wounded by a shell fragment in the side and of losing an eye as well. **(Indigent pension of John Minyard, Mississippi State Records)**

For many the choice was easy. A careful examination of the list of men who volunteered to stay behind with the wounded reveals a large number of men whose brothers had been wounded in the fighting on July 1. In many cases the siblings had already spent considerable time caring for their wounded brothers and the choice to stay behind was clear. An examination of the muster rolls shows many instances of this pattern.

Of an estimated 1,300 sick and wounded from Pender's Division at the Heintzelman and Samuel Lohr farms about 700 would be left behind. The Lohr farm was located about ¼ mile north of the Marsh Creek. Most of the houses and barns along the Marsh creek and Willoughby's Run were filled with battered men. From Heth's Division an equal number were told to remain to be cared for by Confederate surgeons, volunteers and the arriving Union army. This would bring the total number of wounded and sick men in these two divisions to be transported to Williamsport at about 1,400, almost 1000 of whom would be veterans of the fated July 3 assault.

Some men were given a choice . . . "Dr Cheek came to me and told me that the army was falling back and asked if I wanted to go back in a wagon or stay and be taken prisoner. I preferred to go back in a wagon, so I was put in one with Capt. Lamb, Capt. Conley, Lieutenant Pike and Sergt. Cunningham all of my regiment and we made out way to Williamsport without anything to eat or drink. We traveled all night and all day and in the evening reached the Potomac River. It was raining and by this time the river was full and we could only get over the ferry. Our wagon train was there, a great many wounded who could walk, artillery and a great number of stragglers. Late in the evening, a force of Federal Cavalry appeared and we all expected to be captured, but one officer in command gathered up all armed teamsters, stragglers, and everyone who could shoulder a gun and made a display of force and fired some volleys into them and they left but during the excitement I crawled out of the wagon and on to the ferry boat and crossed to the Virginia shore." **(Memoirs of Private A.J. Dula Co A 22nd NC)**

On the very next day after the Pettigrew—Trimble Assault General Robert E lee did something that rarely occurred in the war. He personally wrote a short note to the commanding general of the Union army on a personal matter. He wrote to General George Meade inquiring about the condition of Colonel Hugh Miller of the 42nd Mississippi who had been wounded and taken prisoner the day before . . . .

> Gen. Robert E Lee to Commanding General, Army of the Potomac, July 4, 1863
>
> To the Commanding Officer, Army of the Potomac
> General:
>
> The son of Col. Hugh Miller, 42nd Regiment Mississippi Volunteers, who was wounded and take prisoner in the engagement of yesterday, is very anxious to learn of his father's condition. Any information you may be able to furnish concerning the fate of Col. Miller will be thankfully received.
>
> I am General Respectf'y
> Your obt. Svt.
> R.E,. Lee
> General

Among the first to be loaded on the wagons would be the wounded commanding officers of the two Divisions which had been Heth's and Pender's. Lieutenant Colonel Lane of the 26th NC, Colonel Stone of the 2nd Mississippi and Major Belo of the 55th NC were placed in ambulances. Two of General Archer's wounded staff, Captains G.A. Williams and Robert Harris Archer as well as Captain Hughes of Pettigrew's staff rode in another. Colonel Leventhorpe of the 11 NC and his wounded adjutant Henderson Lucas rode along together. Other ambulances carried officers such as Lieutenant Robert Hand of Company A 11th NC wounded in the back; 2nd Lieutenant James Randall Co D 55NC wounded in the face and Captain Howell Whitehead Co. E 55th NC wound in the head and hand. Private Joseph King Co I of the 11th Mississippi had been wounded in the groin. Private John Shitle of the 55th NC rode in a wagon with a side wound. All around the wagons and ambulance assembled the "walking wounded" with head and arm wounds but able to walk besides the vehicles.

Two Generals in Hills Corps who were badly wounded would be taken in the front of the Pender train on orders of General Imboden: William Dorsey Pender and Alfred Scales. "As an advance guard I had placed the 18th Virginia Cavalry, Colonel George W. Imboden in front with a section of McClanahan's battery. Next to them, by request, was placed an ambulance carrying, stretched side by side, two of North Carolina's most distinguished soldiers, Generals Pender and Scales, both badly wounded, but resolved to bear the tortures of the journey rather than become prisoners. I shared a little bread and meat with them at noon, and they waited patiently for hours for the head of the column to move. The trip cost poor Pender his life. General Scales appeared to be worse hurt, but stopped at Winchester, recovered, and fought through the war. **(John Imboden, *The Confederate Retreat from Gettysburg*, Battles and Leaders of the Civil War, Vol. 3, pp 420-429)**

Pender's train of wounded was moved forward to west of Cashtown on the afternoon of July 4th along with its cavalry and artillery protectors. Heth's soldiers would remain in their hospitals until after midnight and then be loaded into the wagons and ambulances. Pender started west at 4:00PM and by dark was climbing over Cashtown pass. By 3:00 AM the men from Mississippi, North Carolina Tennessee and Alabama who had been torn apart fighting with Davis, Marshall and Fry were underway. About the same time the front of Pender's train arrived in New Franklin and by 4:00AM were in Greencastle. A Union cavalry night attack by Captain Ulrich Dahlgren with 100 Union troopers on the Quartermaster section of Pender's column slowed things down but was beaten off. The front of Heth's column reached New Franklin by noon and by 4:00 were passing through Greencastle. Most of the men who survived the trip with the wounded train remembered hellish scenes of screaming wounded men, some begging to die, others leaving the wagons to crawl off by the roadside or to nearby farms. All along the way hundreds were dying and being buried in shallow graves beside the road. Mile by mile the wounded train continued south on the 60 mile trip to the Potomac.

Lt. Colonel Hillary Moseley of the 42nd Mississippi was with the wounded in the train "We had not proceeded far before one of those mountain torrents poured down upon us with its avalanche of waters saturating everything about us. We had oil clothes to protect us, but it was all unavailing. Soon we were moving quite a brisk rate for such an immense cavalcade. We traveled all night and nobly did our horse sustain his look for strength and endurance. The major slept all the way. With the pain in my foot and the uneasiness and fear of an attack on our train, I slept none . . . . A large portion of our road was a good turnpike. On this we got along admirable, but after dark we diverged to the left by way of Greencastle, over a bad road. To the badly wounded, it was a night of terror. Their piercing shrieks could be heard far away. "**(Dr Hillary Mosely, "Journal of Dr. Hillary Mosely", Batesville, Mississippi)**

Traveling along with Heth's wounded were the 26th and 11th North Carolina regimental bands that had played such an important part of the march north. Now in retreat they played no stirring march tunes but marched along through the mud with everyone else.

Julius Lineback would write about "a motley procession of wagons, ambulances, wounded men on foot, straggling soldiers and band boys, splashing along in the mud, weary, sad and discouraged." Lineback himself with several of his fellow band members got lost in the dark and sat under a tree until morning in the pouring rain. **(Lineback Papers Vol. II, UNC)**

General Imboden had remained behind at Cashtown and then would ride ahead all night to the head of the marching column. In that ride he would experience the full range of experiences that the battered men of Pettigrew's and Trimble's regiments would endure . . .

"After dark I set out from Cashtown to gain the head of the column during the night. My orders had been peremptory that there should be no halt for any cause whatever. If an accident should happen to any vehicle, it was immediately to be put out of the road and abandoned. The column moved rapidly, considering the rough roads and the darkness, and from almost every wagon for many miles issued heart rending wails of agony. For four hours I hurried forward on my way to the front, and in all that time I was never out of hearing of the groans and cries of the wounded and dying. Scarcely one in a hundred had received adequate surgical aid, owing to the demands on the hard working surgeons from still worse eases that had to be left behind. Many of the wounded in the wagons had been without food for thirty-six hours. Their torn and bloody clothing, matted and hardened, was rasping the tender, inflamed, and still oozing wounds. Very few of the wagons had even a layer of straw in them, and all were without springs. The road was rough and rocky from the heavy washings of the preceding day. The jolting was enough to have killed strong men, if long exposed to it. From nearly every wagon as the teams trotted on, urged by whip and shout, came such cries and shrieks as these: "Oh God! Why can't I die? My God! Will no one have mercy and kill me Stop! Oh! For God's sake, stop just for one minute; take me out and leave me to die on the roadside." I am dying! I am dying! My *poor wife,* my dear children, what will become of you?

Some were simply moaning; some were praying and others uttering the most fearful oaths and execrations that despair and agony could wring from them; while a majority, with a stoicism sustained by sublime devotion to the cause they fought for; endured without complaint unspeakable tortures, and even spoke with cheer and confront to their unhappy comrades of less will or more acute nerves. Occasionally a wagon would be passed from which only low, deep moans could be heard.

No help could be rendered to any of the sufferers. No heed could be given to any of their appeals. Mercy and duty to the many forbade the loss of a moment in the vain effort then and there to comply with the prayers of the few. On! On! We must move on. The storm continued, and the darkness was appalling. There was no time even to fill a canteen with water for a dying man; for, except the drivers and the guards, all were wounded and utterly helpless in that vast procession of misery. During this one night I realized inure of the horrors of war than I had in all the two preceding years." **(John Imboden, *The Confederate Retreat from Gettysburg*, Battles and Leaders of the Civil War, Vol. 3, pp 420-429)**

Some men went through the hell of the experience and were left by the roadside. Others climbed out of the wagons and sought help from farm families. Private Charles Nuttal Co G 47th North Carolina had been wounded in the leg July 1 and wrote about his experiences . . . "I was put in an ambulance and after traveling twenty miles the ambulance broke down and I was left on the road. There I laid by myself for two days and nights without food or water. From there I was taken to a private house of Mr. Samuel

B Millers and was taken prisoner after staying there three weeks. I was carried to a hospital at Chambersburg Pa." **(Charles Nuttel letter, Gettysburg National Military Park Archives, 47th NC folder)**

Back at Gettysburg men are still dying and clinging to life

By the evening of the 5th Gregg's Union Cavalry had rounded up and seized all the hospitals filled with Confederate wounded too badly damaged to have been loaded on wagons. Most of these badly wounded would be left in the Confederate hospitals but some would be transported to Union hospital care.

Lieutenant James Seals of company F 42nd Mississippi had been hit by five bullets during the July 3 charge and had been carried back to a Union hospital there he had an arm amputated and was close to death. Emily Sonder a volunteer nurse from Philadelphia wrote about caring for Seals "I wrote letter yesterday for Lt. Seal of the 42nd Mississippi, a very interesting young man . . . . We had scarcely entered the field of labor when someone came and begged my to see a young Mississippi Lieutenant . . . Lying on the ground in front of one of the larger hospital tents, was a young man whose face as I looked at him, seemed that of one of my own kindred, the same blue eyes, brown hair and light complexion. With sorrow, I spoke of his coming North on the wrong side . . . In reply to my offer of service, he said I could do nothing for him. He was groaning in spirit, and suffering greatly, having been wounded in five places, and also suffered amputation . . . Yesterday I wrote his farewell message to his wife, which he was scarcely able to utter, even in faint whisper." **(Emily Sounder letter to Sister-in-law July 20, 1863)**

Private Logan Bolch from Company C of the 28th NC had originally enlisted as a nurse in the regiment but his wife wrote years later "he could not endure that and he was put into the regulars service". One of the men he served with during his nursing duties was a Private Elijah Killian, a blacksmith before the war. Bolch had been wounded in the upper right arm during the fighting and having made it back to his lines was placed in the care of his old comrade Elijah Killian. On July 5th Bolch was not selected to make the journey back to Virginia in the wagon train of wounded and he and Killian were taken prisoner.

Killian wrote years later, ". . . said Logan Bolch was wounded in the Battle of Gettysburg, Pa and was sent to field hospital where he, the said E. Killian, was detailed for a nurse from his Co. and he further states that said Bolch was wounded in the right arm below the shoulder and that he held said Bolch while the doctor amputated his arm and that he remained in the field hospital 2 weeks and then was moved to the Hospital in Baltimore where he died from the effects of the wound." **(Affidavit of Elijah Killian, Pension file of Mrs. Joann Adam Bolch, North Carolina pension applications files)** Logan oldest son Nathaniel reportedly joined the Confederate army after hearing of his father's death.

The Senior Brigade Surgeon of Davis's Brigade stayed behind with about 400 of the brigade wounded. Dr. Benjamin J Ward had graduated from University of Louisiana (now Tulane) and had attended Atlanta Medical College. When the war started he joined Company K of the 11th Mississippi as a Private but soon his talents were recognized and he became the brigade Chief Surgeon. He was headquartered in a field hospital along side Willoughby Run. In his personal papers he tells the tragic story of the task he faced in caring for hundreds of men who were wounded and soaked by the rainfall . . . . "We were confronted with a sad spectacle. The poor fellows were wet and chilled, their wounds were soaked with dry water, and none of them had a change of clothes. Nearby were a farmhouse and a very large brick barn which was filled with straw. I walked up to the house and was met by a typical Pennsylvania farmer. I saw the hard lines in his face and realized the rigor of the judgment spot before which I stood. How I did wish for the eloquence of Paul that I might have made the old Hessian Felix tremble. I did my best. I wanted straw worse than the Israelites did at the brickyards of Egypt, but could not get it without money. I told him I had not a dollar of funds that could be current in his country, and reminded him that on the battlefields of Virginia many Federal wounded had fallen into my hands, and that I always attended to them the same and attentions given to my own wounded; but he was not in the 'reciprocity' business. I then inquired how much he would charge for straw enough to make beds for a certain number of wounded, as I wanted it only for the worst and most helpless cases. He replied that I might have the straw for five dollars.

I walked back with a heavy heart, and feel yet the anguish that seized me when I looked on the pale and pinched features of those intrepid and bleeding boys a thousand miles from home dying upon the bare, wet, inhospitable soil of a heartless enemy without even an old Confederate blanket between them and a dying couch. I told them I had not a dollar with which to purchase straw to make them a bed.

Beverly Daniel Young (Co I, 11th Mississippi) was sitting down by a tree waiting for his clothes to dry on him. He put his hand in his pocket, took out a five-dollar gold piece, the last he had and that he had saved thru many months of hunger and want for such an emergency as had now overtaken him, and said 'Here Doctor, take this and pay old Shylock for his straw!' I replied that he was going to a Yankee prison, that he was badly wounded and would sorely need that money, and that I did not fell that it was right to take it. He said 'Yes, take it and provide for those boys; they are worse off than I am'. I went back, dropped the coin in the old man's hand, and his eyes glittered like a basilisks's as he clutched it. (Author note: The basiliska is a mythical Greek snake which kills by its stare) I think his greed was the more gratified because it was blood money. We all went to work, packing the straw in our arms, stripping the wet clothes from the boys, and covering them naked in the straw while we hug their soiled, bloody garments out to dry.

(Author note: Doctor Ward remained with his men and was then sent to Fort McHenry for five months before being returned to Richmond. Private "Bev" Young was sent to David's Island hospital in New York where he died of his wounds August 29, 1863) **(Benjamin Ward Family Papers, University of Mississippi Archives)**

The able bodied troops from Mississippi, North Carolina and Tennessee and Alabama that could still fight continued their 50 mile trek over Monterey Pass and through the towns of Waynesboro . . . . Their first goal was the town of Hagerstown Maryland.

Even as Lee's Army moved South, the search for the dead of Gettysburg by relatives began. Not only did the parents and wives and siblings of Union dead travel to Gettysburg but as the word spread through the South so to did the reactions. One striking advertisement appeared by the end of July in Gettysburg newspaper—LOST a large size double case watch and link chain belonging to Captain W.T. Magruder, C.S.A. who was killed at Gettysburg; and thought to have been placed in the possession of Captain W.D. NAY, (note—actually Nunn) Co B 11th Mississippi Regt, who died July 13th at 1st Army Corp, 2nd Division Hospital, and who it is supposed, gave it to someone previous to his death for safe keeping. The full value of the watch will be given for its return and the information gratefully received. Apply to: Mary C Magruder, 64 Courtland Street, Baltimore.

Meanwhile back with the wounded train, the men from Pettigrew and Trimble's regiments had made it over the mountains and through New Franklin. First Pender's division and then Heth's approached Greencastle.

Cunningham Crossroads Attack

"10 o'clock Sunday the 5th found us, safe at Greencastle, 14 miles distant from Williamsport. We were, near this point attacked by a small body of cavalry, taking possession of a section of artillery and about 40 wagons. Our cavalry soon assembled and retook all that we had lost except for our artillery horse. Wee were soon again all right and on our way, through still dogged by watchful enemy. We arrived at Williamsport early in the evening. **(Dr Hillary Moseley, "Journal of DR. Hillary Moseley, Batesville, Mississippi)**

Dr Mosely, indeed, underestimated the attack by this "small body of cavalry" in part because his section of the wounded train had passed the point of attack. This attack at an intersection known as Cunningham Crossroads, would be the single biggest Union cavalry threat to the wounded and sick men in the trains of Heth's division and would result in the largest capture of Confederate soldiers who had been casualties of the Gettysburg fighting on the retreat to Williamsport.

The attack at Cunningham's Crossroads was the work of Captain Abram Jones of the First New York Cavalry who was in command of a special raiding unit composed of about 130 troopers from his command and about 80 troopers from the Twelfth Pennsylvania Cavalry. Jone's plan was to launch a surprise attack on the wounded train at a point where the road from Mercersburg, Pennsylvania intersects with the north-south Cumberland Valley Turnpike. He hoped that a surprise attack on the artillery-cavalry segment of the train would confuse the Confederates long enough for his men to grab several hundred wagons and force them to detour to Mercersburg, Pennsylvania. Hiding behind a ridge, Jones waited and at dusk struck the column in the middle of the Heth ambulance section.

The Confederates were at first routed and more than 100 wagons seized. Confederate cavalry regrouped and counter attacked, recapturing some wagons. Jones and his detail rushed west with their captives. With no time to waste, the ambulance trains and their protectors ignored the fleeing Jones and hurried south towards Williamsport.

The Cunningham Crossroads attack would capture some major remaining leaders of the regiments from Mississippi, Tennessee, Alabama and North Carolina who had been at the front of the July 3 attack. Colonel Leventhorpe of the 11th North Carolina was the highest ranking officer taken. Key officers from the 55 North Carolina and the 2nd Mississippi were taken as well. General Archer's staffers Archer and Williams were seized.

From the 11th NC Lieutenant Robert Hand Co A who had been wounded in the back as well as Captain Howell Whitehead of Co E from the 55th NC. 27 year old 2nd Lt James Randall from Co D 55th North Carolina with his face bandaged was also seized in his ambulance. Officers captured from the 2nd Mississippi included Quartermaster Majijak Suratt; Captain John Buchanan Co B; and Chaplin M.W. Frierson. The chaplains brother Sergeant William Frierson was also taken. Several wounded men from the 55th NC were being carried in one wagon which was captured . . . 2nd Lieutenant James Randall (Co D) and privates John Shitle and John Dudley. Two surviving but badly wounded officers from the 13th Alabama, Captain Charles Cambers and 1st Lieutenant Mark Kemp with a fractured hip were taken.

Among the "walking wounded" were a large number of men from the 1st Tennessee including both 2nd Lieutenants from Company A George Parks (Co A) and Joshua Warren plus Corporal Wootson Northcutt. The records show at least eight others from the 1st Tennessee gathered up by Yankee horseman. On particularly tragic case was that of Private William Cashion (Co G) who had been wounded both on July 1 and 3. A total of 308 wounded men plus at least the same number of drivers and guards were taken prisoner and herded to Mercersburg, Pa. 100 Wagons and 300 horses were also captured.

One officer who did escape what would have been certain capture was Lieutenant Colonel James Lane of the 26th North Carolina. Wounded July 1 in the throat and mouth he was sick and unable to eat any solid food. As the attack began, Lane climbed out of his ambulance grabbed his horse which was tied to the back of the ambulance and rode off to escape. Lane would survive and make it back to the service.

Somewhere near Cunningham's Crossroad another adventure was unfolding. Private William Lea (Co A 11th Mississippi) who had been wounded on July 3 was able to secure a horse on the wounded train retreat. He moved ahead of the wagon train and found refuge from Union cavalry at the home of a farmer. After evading capture he was able to ride into Williamport. **(William Lea compiled service file notes)**

Into Williamsport

Finally by 6:00 PM the first of Pender's division in the wounded train arrived at Williamsport. Even as the attack at Cunningham Crossroads was underway, wagons at the front of the column were rolling into Williamsport. Those attacked but not taken by Captain Jone's attack would roll into town around 8:00 PM By this time there had already been a pile up wagons from the Reserve Trains and from the leading wagons of the Quarter Master train.

Imboden had worked a miracle. He had taken over 6,000 wounded and sick over a 60 mile journey attacked by various sized Union cavalry units and delivered most of them to Williamsport. Now his task was to ferry them across the Potomac while holding off Union cavalry units that were growing stronger and stronger.

General Robert E Lee himself wrote a commendation to General John Daniel Imboden on the work he had achieved. ""In passing through the mountains in advance of the column, the great length of the trains exposed them to attack by the enemy's cavalry, which captured a number of wagons and ambulances, but they succeeded in reaching Williamsport without serious loss. They were attacked at that place on the 6th by the enemy's cavalry, which was gallantly repulsed by General Imboden." **(OR Vol. 27, part 2, p. 309)**

Others wrote about what awaited the wagon train of wounded once they arrived. "On arrival at Williamsburg [Williamsport], on the river, I found the whole wagon train of General Lee's army held by high water. A portion of the Federal cavalry made a demonstration with some artillery and shelled the train. Colonel [J. M.] Stone of the Second Mississippi, Major [R. O.] Reynolds of the Eleventh, and myself, went around and got all the able-bodied men to take places in the trenches in front of us. Besides these, numbers of teamsters and detailed men, soldiers retiring for sick leave, furlough, etc., were drawn up, and checked the Federals and saved the wagon train." **(Memoirs of Major Belo, 55th North Carolina)**

Hagerstown, Maryland

With the Potomac River at full flood, it was clear that the able bodied elements of the Army of North Virginia were going to have to set up defensive positions stretching from Hagerstown to the Potomac river south of Falling Waters. The battle ready troops of A.P. Hills Corps crossed over the mountains and wound their way down the muddy roads through Waynesboro and into Hagerstown. The engineers of Lee's army were already surveying and building defensive positions along a series of ridges to protect the convoys of wounded now in Williamsport crossing the river slowly on a few ferries that had been assembled. With the river at full flood and with several days needed to ferry the ambulances and wagons filled with mangled and battered wounded soldiers, The Army of Northern

Virginia would have to make a defensive stand. The troops who had marched and fought under Davis and Pettigrew and Archer and Scales and Lane would now take up trench positions in the middle of the new Confederate defense line. What was left of the 26th North Carolina and the 1st Tennessee and the 42nd Mississippi and the rest of Pettigrew's units took up a position near a brick school house just east of the road leading from Hagerstown to Downsville and along the Marsh Creek. To their immediate north towards Hagerstown were what remained of the soldiers of the 33rd North Carolina and the 7th and the 16th and the rest of Scales and Lane's brigades along the ridge running south west of Hagerstown. Today little remains of that mammoth defensive line. A railroad line runs parallel to Marsh creek running along what was in July 1863 a massive defense line. In July 1863 from the 8th to the 13th this defensive position was all that stood between Robert E. Lee's Army of Northern Virginia and disaster. The men who manned it were a skeleton of the force that had marched into Pennsylvania. The 42nd Mississippi was under the command of Captain Andrew Nelson of Company A; the 55th North Carolina was led by Lieutenant M.C. Stevens of Company G and the entire brigade once known as "Pettigrew's" was under the leadership of wounded Major John Jones of the 26th who had been wounded on both days.

Pioneer Thomas Bailey's entries in his diary paint a picture of the logistics necessary to give Robert E Lee's army a chance to survive. Bailey marched with his regiment through Fairfield toward Hagerstown . . . .

. . . . The retreat was continued during the whole of the night in a southern direction along a sloppy road, as sloppy as I ever saw, by Fairfield in the neighborhood of which the troops rested a while on Sabbath morning of the 5th of July, After noon, the retreat was resumed across the mountain to Frogtown where we again rested on the afternoon of the 6th (July 1863), then marched by Waynesburg and Lightersburg; 7th (July 1863 Passed Hagerstown about which our forces halted for several days . . . . **(Mary Lewis, The Life and Times of Thomas Bailey, Gettysburg National Military Park Archives, 47th NC folder)**

While at Hagerstown July 8th, Major Van de Graff of the 5th Alabama Battalion had an opportunity to write his wife and tell her of the battle. He described the actions of July 1 & 3 and listed some of the men from his old company who were lost. He told her of his present condition. "The next evening we fell back and have retreated to this place. WE sent our wounded back, but they were all nearly captured by the enemy. Our entire loss must be heavy. Two wagons from each regiment was sent back loaded with wounded, and that was attacked and captured by the Calvary of Enemy. We lost nearly four hundred wagons. I think we will recross the River as soon as it becomes fordable. We have not heard a word from home. Our army was buoyant and full of life and the repulse wholly unexpected by officers and men. My health has not been good and I am worn out with exposure and hardships of the last week. I have not been able to change my clothing for ten days, and don't know where we will meet the wagon train again. I will write to you every opportunity I meet with, but have little hope of hearing from you." **(Van de Graff letter, GNMP Park Library)**

While the third Army Corps took position, a pitched battle occurred in the streets of Hagerstown between advancing Union cavalry and the rear guard of Lee's army.

While entrenched at Hagerstown, Lieutenant Henry Jackson Walker, whose brother Levi Jasper had lost a leg on July 1 lost his leg on the picket line. Their friend William J Thompson, who had started as a musician and then was shifted to the infantry, wrote home to his Mother and Sister about the incident. "It was here that Jackson Walker got his leg broke. He was out on Skirmish one of the Yankee Skirmishers shot him. Jasper was left at the hospitals in Pennsylvania and fell into the hands of the Yankees" **(William J. Thompson letter July 20, 1863, New York Historical Society)** (The story of the Walker brothers is an interesting one. Both brothers lost their left legs below the knee during the Gettysburg campaign. Jasper would be captured and paroled by October. Jackson would be captured but not paroled until May of 1864. After the war Levi became engaged to marry and on the day of the wedding he slipped and broke his cork leg replacement. His brother Henry promptly offered the loan of his left artificial leg for the ceremony.

In the midst of this deadly serious business an incident occurred that spread humor throughout the Confederate camps. On July 10th, Thomas Norwood, an officer from the 37th North Carolina captured in the thick of the July 3 fighting, walked into rebel lines having escaped from a Gettysburg hospital . . . "while the regiment was at Hagerstown, Lt. Norwood came marching into camp disguised in the most ridiculous looking and fitting countyman's suit of clothes imaginable, having secured it at Gettysburg in one of the houses around the hospital, and although suffering greatly from his wound, he managed by his wit and cunning to march through the Federal lines and into ours; he was sent to the headquarters of General lee and took a cup of coffee with that distinguished personage." **(*North Carolina Troops, 1861-1865: A Roster.* 37th North Carolina, Thomas Norwood entry)**

Lt. Colonel William A Speer of the 28th NC wrote home shortly after the battle and Discussed the losses that had occurred in his old company I during the July 3 attack. ". . . Jones Holcomb, Jonas MaCokey were killed dead. A shell exploded in the line as we were charging, killing them both dead, wounding 3 others and knocking me down." Sgt. Cast and Buchanan supposed killed. Sgt. Hendricks wounded through the legs and in the hands of the enemy. John G. Holcomb—thigh and hand, left at our hospital and in the Yankee hands. J.G. Danner mortal, since dead. E.H. Reece severe and left D.C. Hall. _____ is across the lines. J.G Reynolds is in the Yankee lines wounded. Sgt S. Bohanon slight. H.H. Snow sever. M. Carter severe. N.C. Dozier slight. Berry Harding struck 3 times slightly. C.V. Hutchens, S.N. Johnson both slight. All these are inside our own lines. Capt.

Apperson took in 24 men and only came out with 4 unhurt. Col. Lowe out. Marler in the Yankee hands. Captain Lovell's company—every man in it was struck. Lowell wounded sever—T.T. Thompson wound very severely." **(Speer to Father & Mother July 10, 1863 from Hagerstown, Md, in Speer, Voices from Cemetery Hill, pp 105-107)**

Colonel Hugh Miller of the 42nd Mississippi had been wounded and captured On July 3. The regimental chaplain Thomas Wright Witherspoon and the Colonel's son Ordinance Sergeant Edwin Miller had stayed behind to find the Colonel. Meanwhile the other son George Miller—Sergeant Major of the regiment who was wounded in the thigh on July 1 had been taken on the wounded train to Williamsport and had been transported by the ferry back to Virginia. Here on July 11th he wrote to his mother about the ordeal. Miller feared that his mother had been moving around Virginia and had not heard of her husbands capture and possible death.

"Mrs Russell's Winchester, Va
July 11, 1863

My Poor Mother,

As far as my maimed fingers will admit I will try and write you of the fate of al of us.

I sent you a dispatch as soon as they brought me here telling you of my terrible fear of my poor father's loss and of my being wounded slightly in the hand and severely through the thigh and of my being here. I am afraid you may not yet receive the dispatch nor the letter written by Captain Jones to Andrew Clark in case you had left Uncle Eppa's and followed us. Oh God grant that you have not gone to Culpepper and missed us, for then I may not see you for weeks. Capt. Jones I told to write to Andrew Clarke all that we knew of my poor fathers fate, and he was requested to write to you immediately if you had gone from Cumberland. All we know of poor father is that he was left supposed to be mortally wounded on the field between the enemy's lines and ours, that he said to one of our officers on leaving him, "I am wounded, and I fear mortally." More than this I could not hear from anyone, but I fear that the worst is too-too terribly true. Our poor Eddy staid with Mr. Witherspoon to try to find him and either bring him back or at least inert him decently. They were left to stay with the wounded, left in the enemies hands, and intended asking permission of the enemy to search for him. They sent me off with the wounded and I have not heard anything since from them, Ma. Good save my poor brother at least . . . .

Your affect son
George Miller

Lee's plan was to buy time while the Potomac River returned to its normal levels and while a floating pontoon bridge was being built at Falling Waters. During this pause one small ferry at Williamsport would continue taking ambulances and wagons filled with wounded men across the Virginia and return with ammunition and supplies for Lee's army. A second ferry would be built and added in a few days. The pause would last from July 7th to July 13th. Returning with the empty ferryboats would be reinforcements to strengthen the army. Two regiments, the 58th Va. and 54th North Carolina were brought across to Williamsport. In addition, men who had taken sick on the trip North back in June were gathered from the hospitals at Front Royal and Shepherdstown and sent to Maryland as reinforcements. A careful examination of the lists of men left behind sick in Virginia show a number who appear to have returned to their regiments and took part in the rear guard action.

An example of this return is the case of 1st Lieutenant Thomas Pleasants in Company A of the 42nd Mississippi. Pleasants had been left behind sick in Port Royal Virginia during the march north and his records shows that he was not present at the fighting in Gettysburg on July 1-3. However he was wounded in the arm during the fighting at Falling Waters of July 14th. A close examination of his company shows another 5 soldiers who also returned with him to Falling Waters. Five Privates from Company C are also listed as sick and hospitalized on the march north yet returned to their regiment by the time it reached Hagerstown. One Private, James Johnson, was wounded in the rear guard action and two brothers Donald Jones and John Jones were captured. Private James Rowell in company E was in fact killed in the Falling Waters fighting yet was sick under care in Winchester during the Gettysburg action. Company G had 5 soldiers in this pattern of whom 4 were captured in Falling Waters after crossing the Potomac. One of these was Sergeant Joshua Benela who was wounded and captured. The service record of Captain John Powell of Company H 42nd Mississippi states that he was "left behind sick in Front Royal and pressed into service to return to Falling Waters". His Sergeant Eli Spears was hospitalized with him and returned to be captured there. A careful examination of the medical records of the 42nd Mississippi show at least 23 such cases.

The job of building a new pontoon bridge fell to the pioneer Corps. Once again Private Thomas Bailey provides a look at the logistics . . . .

. . . . The Pioneer Corps were sent forward to Williams Port to build pontoon boats . . .

10th (July 1863) several other corps were also engaged on this work, had to toat plank half a mile on our shoulders;

11th (July 1863) warm threatening weather, river falling fast;

12th (July 1863) finished boats, carpenters took them down to Falling Waters. The pick and shovel hands marched down the canal, made a dirt bank across it and dug down the bank of the Potomac River;

13th (July 1863) finished bridge by 10 o'clock sufficiently for two wagons to cross and by 2 o'clock thirty or forty had crossed. **(Mary Lewis, The Life and Times of Thomas Bailey, Gettysburg Military Park Museum archives, 47th NC folder)**

The retreat from Gettysburg required a reorganization of almost all of the regiments who had attacked with Pettigrew and Trimble. Adjutant John H. Robinson of the 52nd North Carolina detailed the reorganization and the retreat . . . . In consequence of the death of our field officers on the 3d, Captain B.F. Little, of Company F, was commissioned Lieutenant-Colonel, and Captain Eric Erson, of Company H, was commissioned Major, the officers of Companies E and H were each promoted one grade, as were also the officers of Companies I and K, in consequence of the death of Captains McCain and Blackburn. On account of the bad roads and caution observed on retiring, we did not reach Hagerstown, Md., until the 10th. Finding the waters of the Potomac so much swollen from recent heavy rains as to make fording impracticable, and General Lee's pontoon bridge partially destroyed, we halted at this place. On the morning of the 11th our regiment went into line of battle about three miles from the town, expecting General Meade would attack us as soon as he had come up. We held this line until the night of the 13th, wit occasional skirmishing between the picket lines. During this halt the pontoon bridge had been repaired so as to be available, and was thrown across the Potomac at Falling Waters. The rain had been falling nearly every day since we began to fall back from Gettysburg, and consequently the roads were in a horrible condition. During the 13th wagon trains were put in motion to cross the river, and at night the troops from our portion of the line were withdrawn and marched for the pontoon bridge, but the roads were so cut up by the heavy wagon trains and the artillery as to make them almost impassable, and our march was necessarily slow." **(Adjt John H Robinson in Manarin, L.H., *North Carolina Troops, 1861-'65*, Raleigh, 1966.)**

The flow of the wounded from Heth's and Pender's Divisions continued while the pontoon bridge was being built. As they arrived at Williamsport, those who were able to continue were ferried across the Potomac. Those who were too sick or injured were hospitalized in the warehouses and Lutheran Church property in Williamsport. Meanwhile the destruction of the original pontoon bridge by Yankee raiders left a massive pile up and backlog of wounded and the entire fighting force of the Army of North Virginia stuck in Maryland.

Nearly three hundred men, too badly wounded to continue would be cared for at Williamsport and at Hagerstown. Dr J.M. Gaines of Hagerstown, who was a surgeon with the 18th Virginia was ordered by General Lee to led this operation. He remained with the wounded from July 13th to August 12 when the last surviving soldier was sent north to Chester Pa. He then went with them to Point Lookout and to Fort Delaware. In his report to The Governor of Virginia he lists the names of all those who were under his care. Included on this list are 41 men who had fought with the regiments of the Pettigrew-Trimble Charge. **(Gaines, Sick and Wounded Report pp 1-20)**

"I started on a wagon with other wounded men the next morning for Winchester, Va. We were detailed at Williamsport as the Potomac River had risen so much we had to cross on floats. While waiting to be carried over, some Yankee cavalry tried to capture our wagons but were driven back and we crossed over on the evening of the 4th and 5th of July and went to Winchester.**(Augustus Evander Floyd, *Autobiography*, Fairmount, NC)**

Once across the Potomac the wounded were taken to Winchester, Va. The most severe were taken directly to Richmond for care and others were placed in homes in the Winchester area. For many wounded soldiers instructions were given to seek aid as best they could. One such case was the story of Private James Alfred "Bud" Conner (Vo I 42nd MS) who had been wounded in the hand on July 1 and was with the wounded train which went to Williamsport to cross with the ferry . . . . "To Bunker Hill, WV July 6, Winchester, Va. July 7th. Before we got to Winchester, we were in a very long hard rain, food was scare and we were very hungry. Bought a few pies wrapped in heavy brown paper for 25 cents each. Upon arriving in Winchester, we went to a vacant hotel, the Union, built afire and cooked some corn bread and boiled some beef. At Winchester we were examined by the board surgeon to see who was wounded enough to go to Richmond for treatment. I had to go. I got so I couldn't hardly walk. I had a terrible time for a few days, suffering intensely all the time with a swollen hard and arm, nothing hardly to eat and in lots of misery. I saw a house a few yards down from the road—went to the door. Gave a very poorly dressed lady 25 cents for a piece of bread that had failed to rise. At the next house I asked for something to eat and received a pitcher of milk and some butter. When they saw my bread they gave me some much better. That night I stayed in a barn with several other soldiers. I heard them talk about the place where they got supper across the road. The next morning I was so sore I could not walk. The soldiers left me at my request—they were too weak to help me. In sort time I heard someone in the lot and called. A young lady came to the door. She went back to the house and got the rest of the family to come see me. The man said he would carry me to Harrisonburg, Va. after I had been fed. He gave me bread and butter. I rode his horse bareback. There had the middle finger of my left hand dressed. Without delay I started looking for someone to take me to Staunton, Va. While sitting on the hotel steps, I asked a boy to see if he could find a way for me to get to Staunton. In the meantime, an old lady came to see what was wrong with me—she got me a hoe handle to walk with. I told her I wanted somebody to take me to Staunton. She said she knew a man who would let me ride in his wagon to Staunton the next morning. The next morning I got into the wagon after paying the owner $5 for the rip. I gave all the change I had left to the old lady. I got to Staunton on July 12th. Got on the afternoon train and went to Richmond. To Richmond on July 13th. Stayed there all night—into the hospital the next day. July 14th, admitted to MS soldier's hospital where they removed my middle finger 14 days after being wounded and treated the infection until the last of September, when I was dismissed." **(Diary of James Alfred "Bud" Conner, Co I 42nd MS) . . .** (Author note—Private Conner returned to his regiment) . . . . While Private Conner was seeking medical care in Richmond, the story of Lee's Retreat continued in Maryland.

As the wounded reached Richmond they began to write home about their wounds. Some letters were pessimistic about the chances for the Confederacy but others showed resolve to fight on . . . . "Well . . . The Gibraltar of the South has fallen and my home is entirely surrounded by the enemy, and one who will rejoice to destroy everything I have. Yet, they can not conquer me. When everything is gone, I will take the Indians motive and fight them for revenge with a more deadly hate. When the Indian sees his hut burned, his squaw murdered and his happy hunting ground laid waste, then he is not subdued but steals his heart and sharpens his tomahawk for revenge. Thus . . . the people of the South fight on and fight forever if necessary **(Private Richard Bridges (Co A 11th Mississippi) letter to parents from Richmond hospital July 12, 1863)**

As Confederate units successfully crossed the Potomac River and reached Winchester, Virginia, many men wrote letters home. Many were not certain that the mail they had sent home from Maryland or Pennsylvania ever reached their destination . . . . One such case was Sergeant Joseph Drury Joyner who served as Ordinance Sergeant for the 7th North Carolina who had written his mother from Hagerstown Maryland a week before.

Wincester, Va
July 15th, 1863

Dear Mother

I wrote you a letter from Hagerstown Md on the 9th and sent it to Wincester to be mailed by a wounded soldier but fearing he neglected to do so, as soldiers are not very reliable, I will write again. You have no doubt have heard the particulars of the battle of Gettysburg more fully than I could give them, Therefore I will only such information as will interest you. I saw Uncle James at Hagerstown after the battle. He had seen Bro Algeron. Both had participated in the battle but escaped unhurt. Bro Sidney is missing suppose to be taken prisoner with several others of the company. John & Sidney Ellis came through safely. Thomas Speed was mortally wounded. Captain Williams company went into action with 46 men and came out with only three a great many being taken prisoners. Capt Williams is a prisoner. We left the army in Md day before yesterday. There is only one ordinance wagon left with each brigade. I understand Longstreet's troops have recrossed the river. The Yankee army is in Leesburg. Write soon as I have not have a letter since May. I would write more if I have time.

Your Affectionate Son
J.D. Joyner

(Sergeant Joseph Joyner to Mother, July 15, 1863, Gettysburg Park Library V7-NC-7)

By 11:00 PM on the night of July 11th the 800 foot long pontoon bridge was complete and the Army of Northern Virginia had a means of escape. The plan was to continue the use of the small ferries to take the last of the wounded across the Potomac and at the same time to pull the three Corps of the Army of Northern Virginia out of their defensive lines and across the river. While the ferry operation could continue all day on the 12th, the darkness of the night of July 13th would have to arrive before Lee's three Army Corps could evacuate. The job of "rear guard" was given to the regiments that had fought the "Pettigrew—Trimble Charge". The men of Heth's and Pender's old Corps would be last to leave the trenches and last to cross the river. Ewell's Corps would ford the Potomac (now down in level at several places) upstream from Williamsport. Longstreet's Corps would cross the new floating bridge and then be followed by Anderson's Division of Hill's Corps. Only then would the remaining men from Heth and Pender's Divisions be able to leave.

The Pettigrew Story / Falling Waters

In the middle of the night on July 13th Heth's old division moved away from their fortifications and marched toward Falling Waters Maryland where the waters of the Potomac had reseeded enough to use the floating bridge built to the Virginia shoreline. It took twelve hours of hiking that night to go the seven miles because the mud was thick and it was raining. Confederate engineers had prepared a defensive line about a mile from the river including artillery berms but no artillery was left behind. Heth's men arrived at the defense line as the sun came up and collapsed exhausted. Feeling that there was a cavalry screen out in front the exhausted men stopped in a field about a mile and a half from the river to rest and prepare for orderly evacuation. The men soon fell asleep feeling safe.

Lieutenant William Fulton, the 22 year old Commissary Sergeant with the 5th Alabama Battalion recalled later in his memoirs his arrival at the new rear guard defensive positions "tired, foot sore, wet, hungry and literally frazzled out, our division lay down in the old field in the edge of which was an apple orchard" **(Fulton, *War Remembrances*, p 81)**

Around 11:00 in the morning a small troop of Union cavalry came through the woods and, assuming the scattered rebels to be a small group of deserters. The 50 horsemen in blue charged up the road and through the fields. Pickets shouted a warning and some men prepared to fire. However the order to fire was countered by Heth, who thought the horseman were Confederates. Most of the men did not have loaded weapons. Quickly the 50 troopers were in the midst of the Tennessee and North Carolina soldiers. What followed was hand to hand combat as rebels clubbed Yankees from their horses and Yankees pierced rebels with their swords.

In the midst of this short struggle, General James Pettigrew took aim with his revolver at one unhorsed trooper and the gun misfired. The cavalryman fired at Pettigrew hitting him in the stomach. Pettigrew would die from the wound. This group of Union riders were mostly killed or captured in the fray after this surprise attack General Heth gathered his men even tighter and waited to cross the pontoon bridge. Just as they began to cross a larger force of Union cavalry swooped own in the loading area and captured almost 500 Confederates including 90 from the 11th North Carolina, 54 from the 47th NC, 71 from the 52 NC and 55 men from the 26th North Carolina in Jones' Brigade (Major Jones having succeeded Colonel Marshall). Fry's Brigade lost 15 with the First Tennessee, 7 taken from the 7th Tennessee.

Private John McCall in the 7th Tennessee wrote years later about the surprise attack by the Yankee cavalry at Falling Waters. He remembered seeing Confederate troops swinging their rifles like clubs and knocking Yankee cavalry off their horses. He observed Captain Norris from Company K kill three Yankees and Lieutenant William Baber kill two. In the midst of the fighting McCall and a comrade ran to a fence and were pursued by a Yankee cavalryman. His comrade saw a loaded rifle, grabbed it and shot the Yankee from his horse. **(John McCall, "Seventh Tennessee, Battle of Falling Waters, p 406)** 23 year old Private Nevel B. Staten in the 26th NC (Co.B) killed the Yankee who shot Pettigrew by dropping a large rock on his chest.

In the midst of the fighting against these Michigan cavalrymen, 1st Lt.+ James Simpson was almost captured and ended up losing his sword . . . "they charged right into us cutting and thrusting with their sabers, and firing on us with pistols calling out 'Surrender, you damn Rebels" our men not having time to load, pitched in with their guns and knocked a good many of them off their horses and soon got them scattered and gained time to load and fire. One of them seemed to have a particular spite on me, and selected me for his victim, tried to ride me down, and finding I could avoid him he drew his pistol and I unfortunately fell into a ditch, and when I rose and turned he had his pistol cocked, and presented right in my face calling out "G-d D-n your, surrender or I will blow your brains out. I told him all right, I did not care to be shot and he, thinking he had a prize started off with me to the Yankee lines. I went a short distance with him and he happened to discover that I has a sword, and presenting his pistol again made me give it up, I only went a little way with him before we came to a fence and I jumped over that and made my heels do good service until I was safe in our lines again. I was then safe with the loss of my sword which I regretted very much, for it has been my close companion through a good many battles, but I had only one alternative, to give it up or be shot and did not hesitate as to my decision between the two." **(Letter to Wife July 16th, 1863, Allen-Simpson Papers, SHC #929.)**

Not everyone escaped—Among the men who had not been at Gettysburg were a small group from Company G "The Lamar Rifles" 11th Mississippi. They had been rushed across the Potomac River, rejoined their regiments and formed the rear guard. One man, Private John Brown wrote about the attack of Kilpatrick's cavalry near the river and of the death of one comrade who had not gone to Gettysburg but would die in the final day of the campaign. "While engaged in the battle of falling Waters I discovered a Federal in the panel of a fence, some thirty yards to my left. What attracted my attention was his moving his gun, to get, as I though, Comrade Harley, who was just to my right, on a line, in order that he might get both of us with the same shot. The Federal shot missed me but got Harley. (author note: 2nd Sergeant Joshua Harley Co G) I did not look to see the results of the shot but took aim at my antagonist, then I looked to see the result and found comrade Harley, as I thought, mortally wounded. To my astonishment I found that Harley and I were fighting Kilpatrick's Cavalry. Our command was running for dear life in the direction of the Potomac River where we had a pontoon bridge. As soon as I discovered the situation I beat a hasty retreat in the direction my command had gone. I had not gone far until looking back, I saw one of Kilpatrick's men pursuing me at full speed. While I continued to run, I reloaded my gun, and by this time my pursuer had gained considerably on me; and I, continuing to run if possible faster, wheeled and fired on him. Not looking back to see what the result was, I continued to run. I had gone but a short distance when he was so close on me that his steed jarred the earth under me; then I heard him draw his saber. By this time I was nearly exhausted, and I began zigzagging in order to prevent my pursuer from cutting me down. I succeeded in reaching a small tree, which stood in my line of retreat; and just as I ran under the tree, my pursuer came down at me with his saber; but fortunately he struck a limb of the tree. I immediately threw up my hands, saying that I surrendered." **(LaMar, pp 66-69)** (author note: Private Brown hit his first Yankee target between the eyes but ended up a prisoner of war. Sergeant Harley survived and recovered as a prisoner)

Colonel McComb, who was not present at Falling Waters, in his after battle report evaluated the Confederate resistance this way . . . "such close quarters that it was almost impossible to miss. The officers for once had a good opportunity to use their side arms with telling effect. It was aid that Capt. Norris of the 7th Tenn. Regt brought down three with his Colt Navy at short range. At any rate of the more than two hundred Michigan Cavalry who composed this squadron which proved to be the advance guard of Kilpatrick's Corps, only a few were left to tell the tale. But the canteens of most of those left on the field told the tell as to why they were so desperately brave and foolhearty. **(McComb Memoirs, The Museum of the Confederacy Collection, Richmnd, Va, P 47)**

The losses in the brief fight at Falling Waters were from Archer's Brigade one killed and 2 wounded. Davis's Brigade suffered several killed and about 15 wounded and some prisoners. 27 skirmishers out on the line from Lane's brigade were captured. Captain Thomas Cureton was claimed by many to be the last man to cross over the floating bridge with the 26th North Carolina. **(Our Living and Our Dead, September 1874, pp 29-32) (Confederate veteran 6 (1898) p 406)**

Private Andrew Parks of the 42nd Mississippi (Company I) who had been wounded in the knee during the July 3 charge remembered that at Falling Waters "My regiment only had

145 engaged and we lost forty five men in this engagement" **(Andrew Park, *"Some of My Recollections of the Battle of Gettysburg"*, Arkansas History Commission)**

Two brothers in the 33rd North Carolina company F had survived the fight in Gettysburg and were part of the group waiting to cross the Potomac River. Private Augustus Shore a 22 year old veteran would be wounded in the fight with the Union cavalry and captured. His younger brother Naaman was able to escape but deserted in November only to return shortly thereafter.

3rd Lieutenant Nathan Smith Co H 13th NC had fought without injury on both the 1st and the 3rd of July. However he would be part of the 11 men who were captured at Falling Waters. This would cut the strength of the survivors of the 13th North Carolina from 22 to 11 commanded by Captain Robinson of Company B **(Nathan Smith report, Clark's regiments, Vol. 1, pp 698-699)** The report of the wounded Colonel J.H. Hyman on October 23, 1863 stated that the regiment lost 149 men from July 1-3 at Gettysburg with another 20 lost July 14th. The clerk for company C tallied 5 killed, 6 wounded and 1 missing from the 16 who started the campaign. **(Colonel J.H. Hyman, Roll of Honor Report, October 28, 1863)**

In the 2nd Mississippi four men were decorated and entered on the Roll of Honor for courage during the rear guard fight at Falling Waters. Corporals Stephen Braddock from Co B and G.M. Easterwood from Company G as well as Privates Miller (E) and Nunnelee (H) all resisted the Union attacks and were praised by their officers. 23 year old Braddock would be killed later that year at Bristoe Station.

General Heth wrote later that his plan for the withdrawal was based on leapfrogging his troops. He placed Lane's Brigade as a heavy line of skirmishers about 500 yards to the rear of his own men and then passed his men through the Lane ranks to form again a strong skirmish line for Lane to pas through. Heth later wrote of his problems . . . "it was not surprising that in attempting to reach the road, over ravines impassible at many points, and through a thick growth and woods, and over a country which both men and officers were unacquainted, that many of them were lost and fell into the hands of the enemy, who pushed vigorously forward on seeing that I was retiring. **(Heth, Henry "Report of General Heth of the Affair at Falling Waters", pp 198-199)**

To help with the retreat some units were called back from the riverbank to hold back Union cavalry attacks . . . . "The exposure to rain, to which we had been subjected for so many days, had left the rifles of our men in such bad condition that but few would fire at first, and to this fact is attributes the losses we sustained—had the guns of our men exploded when first tried, not a man of the attacking party would have been left to tell the tale, and valuable lives would have been saved. This engagement caused a general advance on the part of the enemy, and that portion of General A.P. Hill's Corps not yet over the river was hurried to the support of Pettigrew. We formed line of battle to meet the advance, though all of our artillery having passed the river, we had none in line; but skirmishing with the enemy and fighting and falling back, we held them in check until the whole army had crossed, with all of the wagons and artillery, save two pieces, the horses drawing which had become so exhausted as to be unable to move them, and before fresh horses could be procured the rear of the army had passed them. The whole army thus crossed the river successfully in the face of a large body of the enemy. The loss in our regiment (52nd NC), however, was considerable, its commanding officer, Captain Nathaniel A. Foster, being among the number captured. **(Adjt John H. Robinson, Manarin, L.H., *North Carolina Troops, 1861-'65*, Raleigh, 1966.**

An entry in his journal of July 26 told of the news received by the 42nd' Mississippi's Lt Colonel Hillary Mosely about his regiments losses back at the Williamsport fighting. "Just heard from the 42nd at the battle of Williamsport, and again we lose heavily, 7 killed, 10 wounded and 27 missing or prisoner. Among the dead is said to be the brave and noble-hearted Price of Co. A. Poor Frank, how deeply I lament your early fate. Like my own noble boy, pure, gentle and unobtrusive: but on the battlefield, the bravest of the brave. Leading where only daring spirits dare to go and continue to go forward when other men might quail. May the clods of Maryland rest gently on Frank Price's unmarked resting place" **(Dr Hillary Moseley, "Journal of DR. Hillary Moseley, Batesville, Mississippi)** (note Sergeant Frank Price age 20 had enlisted as a Private in Grenada Mississippi into Company A "The Carroll Fencibles" and had fought in almost every battle of the war.)

Finally all of the men from Tennessee, North Carolina, Mississippi and Alabama were across the river or were prisoners in Union hands. One again many different versions would appear concerning which regiment was actually the last to cross.

General Lane wrote a brief history of his old regiment, the 28th NC, and told of their role in the retreat back to Virginia "On the 12th (of July) it formed line of battle near Hagerstown, Maryland, threw up breast-works and skirmished with the enemy until the night of the 13th. The retreat from Hagerstown through mud and rain was worse than that from Gettysburg, which was "awful." Some fell by the wayside from exhaustion, and the whole command was fast asleep as soon as halted for a rest about a mile from the pontoon bridge at "Falling Waters." On the morning of the 14th, Lane's brigade alone covered the crossing at "Falling' Waters," and Captain Crowell, of the Twenty-eighth commanded its skirmishers. After all the other troops were safely over the Potomac, the whole brigade retired in splendid order and the enemy opened with its artillery just as the bridge swung loose from the Virginia shore." ***(History of the 28th North Carolina, Charlotte, N. C Observer Feb 17, 1895. Written by General James H. Lane.)*** *(author note: James Crowell was still a lieutenant in Company K at this point)*

In contrast to the story as told by General Lane, the regiments of Scales claimed to be the last to leave Maryland. They were cut off from the crossing and the confusion that marked the end of the Confederate Invasion of 1863 were recorded by him in his official report "When the army began crossing the Potomac near Falling Waters, Maryland, which, along with the rest of Pender's division, had been consolidated into division of General Heth, became part of the rear guard . . . *[We} arrived there [Falling Waters] at 10 o'clock on the morning of the 14th; and, while resting for a few hours ere we crossed, . . . were attacked by a squad of cavalry, which caused some detention. Then, all being quiet, I moved off, as directed, toward the river, but ere I had gone more than 300 yards, I was ordered by General Heth to take the brigade back to the support of those who were acting as rear guard . . . . [T]he men were quite exhausted from pressure of heat, want of sleep, want of food, and the fatigue of marching; and at this very moment I found the troops on our right giving way . . . . Then I was ordered to join on their right, and, while making a move to do this effect, ere we had come to the top of the hill on which they were, I rode forward, and saw the whole line in full retreat some 200 or 300 yards to my rear; the enemy was pursuing, and directly between me and the bridge. The move, I understand since, was made by order, but I received no such orders, in consequence of which I was cut off. But I filed directly to the rear, and struck the river some three-quarters of a mile above the bridge, and so cut off many of our men who were unwilling to try to pass, and captured many more who failed from mere exhaustion; so in this unfortunate circumstance we lost nearly 200 men.* **(Official Records, Series I, Vol. XXVII, pt 2, p. 672)**

The 13th Alabama had come to Gettysburg with 311 officers and men. On July 1 they lost 154 and on July 3rd they went into battle with 157 men plus 5 field officers. By the end of that day they had lost another 83. They would lose 7 more captured on the way back to Virginia. 72 men would remain.

Many in the rear guard of Heth's Division were forced by the appearance of both federal cavalry and infantry to run for the pontoon bridge with "every man for himself" . . . "Only a few minutes elapsed before the large fields to our right and front was covered with Kilpatrick's cavalry and they were already closing in on the right of our line where they captured some of Heth's division. When the orders were given for each man to make his way to the river as best they could and then a wild race commenced to reach the pontoon bridge. Most of Archers brigade made their way threw a body of woods threw which ran a small stream and by following the general direction of this branch we soon reached to toe path of the Chesapeake and Ohio canal which runs alongside of the river. We were none too soon in reaching this point for when we looked up the toe path the head of a column of federal infantry were in sight marching in column of fours and one important fellow some hundreds yards in advance orders a squad of us to surrender. We called him to us as if hesitating and when he came up not withstanding his assurance that "the war as over" we took him in tow on the towpath and made double quick time for the bridge a short distance below. We could hear the resounding foot beats of our comrades as they hurried over and our own movements were quick as well. When coming in sight of the bridge, we beheld the men with uplifted axes ready to cut the ropes and let it swing around to the south side of the river. More then one pleading voice was heard to call out "don't cut that rope, there is lots of our men over here yet". The towpath prisoner was carried to General Lee and he was informed of the approach of the enemy on the tow path when he ordered a battery to throw a few shells across the river which checked there advance on the bridge, and in a short time the ropes was cut and it swung around leaving quite a number of our men to fall into the hands of the enemy." **(McComb Memoirs, The Museum of the Confederacy Collection, Richmond, Va, pp 47-49)**

One Private with the 11th Mississippi walked off the pontoon bridge and passed by the Regimental band assembled on the Virginia shore. Gabe Smither (Co G) shouted to the band leader "Stewart, by blood, play Dixie" and soon the tune was being played and the "Rebel Yell" was sounded on the Virginia shoreline. **(Love, *Mississippi at Gettysburg*, IX, p. 50-51)**

As the final Confederate troops reached the Potomac and rushed across the river, many looked back and felt the pain of all they had endured. One soldier who was the sole survivor of his company, Corporal John T Morgan of Company I, 11th Mississippi, summed up the emotion he felt when many years later near the end of his life, he wrote "All my company officers were swept to death or wounded, and when I marched out towards the Potomac the lone man of my company I wept that I was not slain with the rest of my dear comrades whom I loved like brothers and would have died for any of them. This day and this awful battle I can never forget, and those dear boys, many of whom lie somewhere in unknown graves. Through thirty-five years have swept away, the memory of that awful day hangs on my memory as bright as if it was only yesterday. In after campaigns I have sought death that I might be with my comrades, but not a shot nor a shell ever came to relieve me, and I am here yet to ponder over the past and fight all those Virginia battles over again, and weep for those dear comrades that are gone; and how I went through the whole war and never missed a battle and never received a wound is something mysterious to me. It might have been on account of the prayers of my mother, I don't know, for I was her baby boy." **(John T. Morgan letter, Mitchell Memorial Library, Mississippi State University)**

Bibliography

Books and Articles

A Bandsman's Letters to Home from the War." Moravian Music Journal. 36 (Spring 1991).

"Albert Stacey Caison". *Confederate Veteran* 29 (March 1921).

Archer, John M. "Remembering the 14th Connecticut Volunteers", *Gettysburg Magazine*, no.9, July 1993.

Ashe, S.A. "The Charge at Gettysburg", North Carolina Booklet, vol 1, no. 11 (March 10, 1902)

Bee, Robert L. *The Boys from Rockville: Civil War Narratives of Sgt. Benjamin Hirst, Company D, 14th Connecticut Volunteers*, Knoxville, University of Tennessee Press, 1998.

Bird, William, *Stories of the Civil War, Company C, 13th Regiment of Alabama Volunteers,* Columbiana, AL: Advocate Press, circa 1900.

Brown, Kent Masterson. *Retreat from Gettysburg*, Chapel Hill: University of North Carolina Press, 2005

Brown, Maud Morrow. *The University Greys; Company A Eleventh Mississippi Regiment Army of Northern Virginia 1861-1865*, Richmond, Va Garrett and Massie, 1940.

Burgwyn, William "Unparalleled Loss of Company F" Southern Historical Society Papers 28 (1900).

Bush, Jacob A. "From 1861 to 1865 as I Remember." Lenoir (N.C.)Topic March 25, 1922

Busey, John W, and David G. Martin, *Regimental Strengths at Gettysburg*, Baltimore: Gateway Press, 1982

"Celebration of the Great Charge at Gettysburg", *Raleigh News and Observer*. July 7, 1903.

Christ, Elwood W. *"Over a Wide, Hot . . . . Crimson Plain": The Struggle for the Bliss Farm at Gettysburg July 2nd and 3rd, 1863*, Baltimore: Butternut and Blue, 1993.

Clark, Walter. History of the Several Regiments and Battalions from North Carolina in the Great War 1861-65. Five vols. Reprint. Wendell, N.C.: Broadfoot's Bookmart, 1982

Cockrell, Thomas D., and Michael B. Ballard, eds. *A Mississippi Rebel in the Army of Northern Virginia: The Civil War Memoirs of Private David Holt*, Baton Rouge and London, Louisiana State University Press, 1995.

Coddington, Edwin B. *The Gettysburg Campaign: A Study in Command*. New York: Charles Scriber's Sons, 1968

Cooke, Charles M. "Fifty-Fifth Regiment", in *Histories of the Several Regiments and Battalions of North Carolina,* Ed. Clark, III

Cross, Wallace. *"An Ordeal by Fire": A History of the 14th Tennessee Infantry Regiment"*. Clarksville-Montgomery County Historical Society, 1988.

Dorsett, Wilber, "Fourteenth Color-Bearer", Carolina Magazine, 1932

Ellis, Billy, *Tithes of Blood: A Confederate Soldiers Story*, Southern Heritage Press 1998

Ernsberger, Donald. *Paddy Owen's Regular's*, Random House Press, Xlibris Press, Philadelphia, Pa 2003

Fleming, George Thornton, ed. *Life and Letters of Alexander Hays*. Pittsburg, Pa.: Gilbert Adfams Hays, 1919

Friscoe, Thomas Conner, *The Compiled Diary and notes of Private John Alfred Conner Co I 42nd Mississippi*, Possession of great great grandson

Freeman, Douglas Southall, *Lee's Lieutenants: A Study in Command*. Three vols., New York: Charles Scriber's Sons, 1942-44.

Fry, Burkett D. "Pettigrew's Charge at Gettysburg." *Southern Historical Society Papers* 7 (1879)

Gaines, Dr. J.M. *Sick and Wounded Confederate Soldiers at Hagerstown and Williamsport: A Report to the Governor*, published in Southern Historical Society Papers, Vol. XXVII, Richmond Jan-Dec 1899

Gragg, Rod. *Covered with Glory, The 26th North Carolina Infantry at the Battle of Gettysburg*. New York: Harper Collins Publishers, 2000.

Haines, William P. *History of the Men of Co. F with Description of the Marches and Battles of the 12th New Jersey Vols.*, Camden, N.J.: C.S. Magrath, 1897.

Hardy, Michael. "The Gettysburg Experiences of Lt. Iowa Michigan Royster, 37th North Carolina Volunteers Infantry Regiment, *Gettysburg Magazine*, no. 29, 2003

Haxlewood, Martin W. "Gettysburg Charge." *Richmond Dispatch*, January 26, 1896.

Hess, Earl J. *Pickett's Charge—The Last Attack at Gettysburg*. Chapel Hill: University of North Carolina Press, 2001.

Heth, Henry. "Report of General Heth of The Affair at Falling Waters," Southern Historical Society Papers, Vol. VII, (Jan-Dec 1879)

Himmer, Robert. "Col. Hugh Reid Miller, 42nd Mississippi Volunteers, and the Pickett-Pettigrew-Trimble Assault, *Gettysburg Magazine*, no. 35, 2006

Hood, J.T.C. "*The 26th Regiment at Gettysburg*." Lenoir News Topic. April 8, 1896

Johnson, Robert Underwood, and Clarence Buel, eds, *Battles and Leaders of the Civil War*. Four vols. Reprint. New York and London: Thomas Yoseloff, 1956.

Krick, Robert K. *Lee's Colonels: A Biographical Register of the Field Officers of the Army of Northern Virginia*, Dayton, Ohio: Morningside Bookshop, 1979.

———— *Staff Officers In Gray*: Chapel Hill, NC: University of North Carolina Press, 2003

LaMar Rifles Survivors Association, *"History of the Lamar Rifles"*, 1901, Bonnie Blue Press reprint.

Lane, John R. "Address at Gettysburg". *Raleigh News and Observer*, July 6 1903

Leinbach, Julius, *Regiment Band of the 26th North Carolina*. Edited by Donald M McCorkle. Winston-Salem, N.C. Moravian Music Foundation Publications, 1958.

Lindsley, John Berrien, ed. *The Military Annals of Tennessee*. First Series. Nashville: J.M. Lindsley & Co., 1886.

Long, Roger. "Major Joseph H. Saunders, 33rd North Carolina, C.S.A., *Gettysburg Magazine,* No 10, January 1994.

Love, D.C. *The Prarie Guards*. Columbus, Miss: n.p. 1890

Love, William. "Mississippi at Gettysburg" Publications of the Mississippi Historical Society IX (1906)

Mast, Greg *State Troops and Volunteers: A Photographic Record of North Carolina's Civil War Soldiers.* Volume I. Raleigh: North Carolina Department of Cultural Resources, 1995.

Manarin, L.H., *North Carolina Troops, 1861-'65*, Raleigh, 1966.

Moon, W. H. "Beginning of the Battle of Gettysburg," *Confederate Veteran 33* (1925)

Morgan, John T. letter 1898, Special Collections, Mitchell Memorial Library, Mississippi State University

Peel, William: Diary, Special Collections, Mitchell Memorial Library, Mississippi State University

Priest, John Michael, *Into the Fight: Pickett's Charge at Gettysburg*, Shippensburg, Pa: White Mane Books, 1998.

Rearson, Carol. *Pickett's Charge in History and Memory*, Chapel Hill and London: University of North Carolina Press, 1997.

Rollins, Richard. "The Damned Red Flags of Rebellion": The Confederate Battle Flag at Gettysburg. Redondo Beach, C.: Rank and File Publications, 1997.

________ ed., *Pickett's Charge: Eyewitness Accounts*. Redondo Beach, Ca. Rank and File Publications, 1994

Rowland, Dunbar. *Military History of Mississippi 1803-1898*. Reprint, Spartanburg, S.C.: Reprint Company, 1978.

Satterfield, John R. "Farthest at Gettysburg: The Story of a Confederate Captain", *Gettysburg Magazine*. No. 26, July 2002.

Sears, Stephen W. *Gettysburg*, Boston, New York: Houghton Miffl in, 2003

Seville, William P. *History of the First Regiment, Delaware Volunteers, from the Commencement of the "Three Months" Service to the Final Muster-Out at the Close of the Rebellion*. Reprint. Baltimore: Gateway Press, 1986.

Shultz, David, and Richard Rollins, "Measuring Pickett's Charge." *Gettysburg Magazine* no. 17, July 1997.

Snipes, Keith. "The Improper Placement of the 8th Ohio Monument: A Study of Words and Maps", *Gettysburg Magazine*, no. 35, 2006.

Southern Historical Society Papers. Fifty-two vols. Reprint. Millwood, N.Y.: Kraus Reprint Co., 1977.

Speer, Allen Paul, *Voices from Cemetery Hill*, Over Mountain Press, 1997

Stewart, George R. *Picket's Charge: A Microhistory of the Final Attack at Gettysburg, July 3, 1863*, Boston: Houghton Miffl in, 1959.

Stubbs, Steven H. *Duty, Honor, Valor: The Story of the 11th Mississippi Infantry Regiment*, Quail Ridge Press, 2000

Taylor, Michael W. "Col. James Keith Marshall: One of Three Brigade Commanders Killed in the Pickett-Pettigrew-Trimble Charge, *Gettysburg Magazine*, no. 15, July 1996.

________. "North Carolina in the Pickett-Pettigrew-Trimble Charge at Gettysburg", Gettysburg Magazine, no. 8, January 1993

________. "The Unmerited Censure of Two Maryland Staff offi cers, Maj. Osmun Latrobe and First Lt. W. Stuart Symington." *Gettysburg Magazine*, no 13, July 1995

"The Battle of Shepherdstown" Antietam National Battlefield: National Park Service, n.d.

The Survivors Association of the LaMar Rifles, *History of the LaMar Rifles*. Topeka: Bonnie Blue Press, 1901

Trimble, Isaac R. "North Carolinians at Gettysburg." Our Living and Our Dead, vol. 4 (March-August, 1876).

Trinque, Brace A. "Arnold's Battery and the 26th North Carolina." Gettysburg Magazine, no. 12, January 1995.

________. Confederate Battle Flags in the July 3rd Charge," Gettysburg Magazine, no. 21, July 1999.

Tucker, Glenn, *High Tide at Gettysburg*, New York,: Bobbs—Merill, 1958

Turney, J.B. "The First Tennessee at Gettysburg." *Confederate Veteran 3* (April 1885)

Tuttle C.A. "F" and "I" of the 26th Regiment from 1861 to 1865" *Lenoir News Topic.* May 11, 1922.

U.S. War Department. The War of Rebellion: A Compilation of the Official Records of the Union and Confederate Armies. One hundred and twenty eight vols. Washington D.C. Government Printing Offi ce, 1880-1901.

Ward, Benjamin F. and family papers, University of Mississippi Archive Collection

Wert, Jeffry D. *Gettysburg Day Three*, U.S.A. New York: Simon & Shuster, 2001

Wilds, Ellen Sheffield, *Far from Home—The Diary of Lt. William Peel 1863-1865,* Carrolton, MS, Pioneer Publishing (2005)

Wilson, Clyde N. *The Most Promising Young Man of the South: James Johnston Pettigrew and His Men At Gettysburg*. Abilene, Texas: McWhiney Foundation Press, 1998.

Wilson, LeGrand James.The Confederate Soldier. Edited by James W. Silver, Memphis, Tn: Memphis State University Press, 1973

Winchel, Terrace J. "Heavy Was Their Loss: Joe Davis' Brigade at Gettysburg, Part I & II." Gettysburg Magazine, no. 3, July 1990.

Young, Louise G. *"Pettigrew's Brigade at Gettysburg."* Our Living and Our Dead, vol.1. no 6 (February 1875)

Archive Collections

Gettysburg National Military Park. Administrative Archives. Gettysburg, Pennsylvania
    Regimental Files
    Reunion Files
    Monument Files

Letter Collection, *Raleigh Observer*, November 29, 1877

Library of Congress, Manuscript Division, Washington D.C.

Mississippi Department of Archives and History, Jackson, Mississippi
    Applications for Pensions
    Letter Collection
    William Peel Diary
    A.L.P. Vairin Diary

Museum of the Confederacy, Eleanor Brockenbrough Library Collections

National Archives, Washington D.C.
    Compiled Service Records
    Regimental muster files
    Pension Files

North Carolina Department of Archives and History, Raleigh North Carolina
    Confederate Pension Applications
    Regimental Muster Rolls
    Letter Collections

Tennessee State Library and Archives
Results of Survey of Tennessee Veterans
Applications for Pensions files
Letter Collection

The Bachelder Papers: *Gettysburg in their Own Words*. Vol 1 & 2. Edited by David Ladd and Audrey Ladd. Dayton Ohio: Morningside House, Inc. 1994

U.S. Army Military History Institute, Carlisle, Pennsylvania
Letter Collections

DOUBLE LINE ASSERTIONS

Captain Samuel Armstrong 125th NY (commanding Skirmishers from Sherrill brigade) "the second line did not support the first efficiently"
"*the third line* did not get at all into the thick of the fight"

Sgt Issac Barnes Co E 125th NY "As far as you could see they were advancing in *three lines of battle*, the first and second were marching in solid column, third in battalions and divisions in order, if necessary, to fill up in strength broken and weak places . . . when the first column had advanced within 10 or 12 rods of us, it was not—they were dead men. The second column pressed on, but shared the same fate, or nearly so. And our shots were reaching the third, and had thinned their ranks badly, when they turned and fled." **(Sgt. Issac Barnes to Oliver Waite August 2, 1863)**

Captain Stratton 12th New Jersey (at the wall)
"The first line had been annihilated, the second was retreating, all broken and battered, one half left behind; *the third* falling back in good order"
(Stratton, "The Gettysburg Campaign", p. 43)

Captain George Bowen 12th New Jersey "Looking up we saw them . . . coming in *three lines of battle* . . . bayonets fixed their lines dressed as if on parade." **(Bowen, The Diary of Captain George D Bowen, p 133)**

Asa S Hardman (3rd Indiana Cavalry—prisoner in attic of house on Seminary Ridge) "Suddenly, the rebel batteries also became silent and while I watched, *three long lines* of rebel infantry sprang out in front of their guns, and pausing a moment as if to take long breath, seemingly pitched forward like a resistless wave that threatened to destroy everything in its path. I never saw such a sight before and I never want to see it again. It was grand beyond my power to describe. I saw them pause an instant, and then shot forward, with their lines as true as if on dress parade with their muskets at 'right shoulder shift' their elbows touching the left. As our artillery, which had suddenly found voice, ploughed great gaps in their lines, they would close up and still move forward with an impulse that seemed irresistible" **(Asa Sleath Hardman, "As a Union Prisoner at the Battle of Gettysburg", Civil War Times Illustrated, I, No 4 (July, 1962, P 49)**

Also for Glory Muster

The Rosters of the Pettigrew-Trimble Assault

Lt. General A.P. Hill
Commander Third Corps
Army of Northern Virginia

Major General Harry Heth
Commander Second Division
Third Corps
Army of North Virginia

Colonel R. H. Chilton
Adjutant and Inspector General
Army of Northern Virginia.

Captain W.N. Starke
Asst. Adjutant. Gen., Third Corps,
Army of Northern Virginia

Brigadier General James Archer
Commander Third Brigade
Second Division—Third Corps
Army of Northern Virginia

Colonel Burkett Fry
Senior Colonel Third Brigade
Second Division—Third Corps
Army of Northern Virginia

Capt. William Brown
Assistant Adjutant and Inspector General.

Brigadier General James Pettigrew
Commander First Brigade
Second Division—Third Corps
Army of Northern Virginia

Colonel James Marshall
Senior Colonel First Brigade
Second Division—Third Corps
Army of Northern Virginia

Brigadier General Joseph Davis
Commander Fourth Brigade
Second Division—Third Corps
Army of Northern Virginia

Third Army Corps

Army of Northern Virginia
Commanded 7/1—7/3 Lieutenant General Ambrose Powell Hill

Assistant Adjutant General Captain William Norborne Starke—27 years old—UVA
Assistant Adjutant & Inspector General Robert J. Wingate—33 year old—Frankford, Ky—West Point
Aide-de-Camp—Lieutenant Francis Travis Hill—23 years old—Culpeper, Va—VMI Harvard Law
Aide-de-Camp—Lieutenant Murray Taylor—19 years old—Falmouth, Va—VMI
Chief of Artillery—Colonel Reuben L. Walker—
Engineering Officer—Major Conway R. Howard—31 years old—Richmond, Va—Washington, Coll.
Ordinance Officer—Major Phillip Beverley Stanard—28 years old—Spotsylvania, Pa—BMI
Signal Officer—Captain Richard H.T. Adams—23 years old—Lynchburg, Va—Merchant
Quarter Master—Major James Gavin Field—37 years old—Culpeper, Va—Lawyer
Assistant Quarter Master—Captain Henry S. Field—35 years old—Colpeper, Va—Farmer
Commissary of Substance—Major Edward Baptist Hill—42 years old—Culpeper, Va—Hotel Keeper

Second Division Third Corps

Army of Northern Virginia
Commanded 7/1 Major General Henry Heth
Commanded 7/3 Brigadier General James Pettigrew

Assistant Adjutant General—Major Randolph Harrison Finney—28 years old—Powhatan, Va

Assistant Adjutant & Inspector General—Captain Henry Heth Harrison—43 years old—Fluvanna, Va—USN

A.A.A.G. Lieutenant Benjamin Franklin Steward (later K Spotsylvania)—27 years old—Westmoreland, Va.

Aide-de-Camp—Captain Stockton Heth 24 yr old brother of Henry Heth—24 years old—Richmond, Va—VMI

Aide-de-Camp—Captain Louis Young—31 years old

Aide-de-Camp Lieutenant Miles Cary Selden—39 years old—Merchant

Engineering Officer—Lieutenant William O. Slade

Ordinance Officer—Captain James Williamson Archer—33 years old—Clerk

Signal Officer—Lieutenant Edmund Burke—Alabama—US Cavalry

Quarter Master—Major Henry Clay Deshields—31 years old—Northumberland, Va—UVA

Assistant Quarter Master—Major Alexander W. Vick—28 years old—Lawyer

Commissary of Substance—Major Phillip Contee Hungerford—34 years old—Montros, Va—Farmer

Major (Dr.) H. H. Hubbard, Chief Surgeon—Captain W. H. Atwold, Assistant Chief Surgeon

Division Wagon Master—Captain John Cage

Scouts—PrivateWilliam L. Nooner 23 yr old enlisted 5/10/61 W Sharpsburg **W 7/1**
Private Albert Richey 27 yr old painter enlisted 1861

Third Brigade Second Division Third Corps

Army of Northern Virginia
Commanded July 1 Brigadier General James Archer
Commanded July 3 Colonel Burkett Fry

Assistant Adjutant General—Captain Robert Harris Archer—43 years old—Maryland—US Army—**W 7/1 C 7/5 Greencastle, Pa**

Acting Inspector General & Aide-de-Camp—George Archer Williams—36 years old—Balt. Md. **W-twice 7/1 C 7/5 Greencastle, Pa**

Aide-de-Camp—Lieutenant Oliver H. Thomas—San Francisco Lawyer

Ordinance Officer—Lieutenant George Lemmon—27 years old—Baltimore, Md—Merchant **C 7/5 Cashtown**

Quarter Master—Captain Rufus Peter McClain—25 years old—Lebanon, Tn

Commissary of Substance—Major Dick R. Hankins—32 years old—Wilson, Tn—Book Dealer

Courier Private Thomas Barnes (14th TN) enlisted Camp Duncan 5/14/61 (later C-Wilderness)

Brigade Commissary Corp Gad Castlemann (7th Tn Co C) W-Gaines Mill

FIRST TENNESSEE REGIMENT

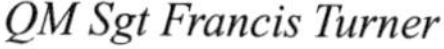

QM Sgt Francis Turner

Private Isaac Caldwell Co C

Field & Staff

Colonel Peter Turney original Colonel 36 yr old enlisted Winchester, TN 4/29/61 W-face & neck Fredericksburg Absent W

Lt Col Newton George 23 year old Georges Store farmer enlisted 4/27/1861 **C 7/3**

Major Felix Buchanan 26 year old enlisted Fayetteville, TN 4/25/61 **C 7/3** (later W Thigh Weldon RR)

Adjutant. William Watson 26 yr old enlisted Wincheser,Tn 4/29/61 **C 7/1** died in prison 2/8/64

Sergeant Major Thomas Turner 24 yr old Salem farmer enlisted 4/29/1861

Surgeon Dr. Pearson Monroe Jordan **C 7/5** with wounded

Assistant Surgeon Steven Dance 27 year old Lynchburg resident enlisted 4/29/1861

Assistant Surgeon John Blake (C Antietam—detailed as nurse) **C 7/5** with wounded Ft. Delaware

Hospital Steward William Miles 26 year old Fayetteville farmer enlisted 4/29/1861

Medical Sgt James Milliken 26 year old Boons Hill Lincoln County farmer enlisted 4/29/1861

Quarter Master William Brannan 32 year old Winchester farmer enlisted 4/29/1861 (later C Sailor's Creek)

QM Sergeant Francis Turner 39 yr old enlisted Franklin Co. 4/29/61

Commissary Sergeant Howard Newman 24 yr old enlisted Winchester, TN 4/29/61

Company A "*Pelham Guards*"

1st Lt Jesse Gunn 20 year old Coffee County farmer enlisted 4/29/1861 **W 7/3 C 7/5** (W Gaines Mill)

2nd Lt George W. Parks 33 yr old enlisted Pelham, Tn W-left arm & leg **C 7/3** Greencastle, Pa

2nd Lt Joshua Warren 35 year old Grundy Co farmer sick at Gettysburg **W 7/3 C 7/5 Greencastle, Pa—Chester Hosp**

1st Sgt Nathaniel Elliot 20 year old Murfeesboro merchant (later W-abdomen Wilderness)

Sgt Madison Parks 24 year old Hillsboro farmer enlisted 4/29/1861 W Gaines Mill

Sgt Henry Phillips 24 year old Hillsboro farmer enlisted 4/29/1861 (later W Mine Run)

Cpl. George Campbell 24 year old Pelham farmer enlisted 4/29,1861 **W/C 7/3**

Cpl. Wootsen Northcutt L. enlisted 8/26/1861 **W 7/3 C 7/5 Greencastle** (later killed Wilderness)

Cpl. William Pattie 24 year old Pelham farmer enlisted 4/29/1861 **C 7/14 Falling Waters** W 2nd Manassas

2nd Cpl. Alexander Sanders age 22 Grundy Co. farmer enlisted 4/29/1861 (later W Selma. Al)

3rd Cpl. A.J. Taylor enlisted 7/26/1861 C 7/14/63 at Falling Waters, Md Pt Lookout to Elmira—died

Private Augustus Austell 21 year old enlisted 4/29/1861 (later W-foot Weldon RR—Sgt)

Private Joel Barnes (later C 11/9/63Culpepper, Va)

Private Lewis Cash 24 year old Coffee county farmer enlisted 4/29/1861 **C 7/3**

Private Henry Farris 21 year old Hillsboro farmer enlisted 4/29/1861 (later K Spotsylvania)

Private John Hamilton Gunn 20 year old Hillsboro farmer enlisted 9/21/1861 (later Sharpshooter C Hatchers Run)

Private John Hayes conscript (later C 11/63 Culpepper, Va)

Private Thomas Howell 19 yr old clerk from Baltimore, Md **C 7/24** (in hiding)

Private Benjamin Layne 31 year old Hillsboro farmer enlisted 4/29/1861 (later teamster)

Private Milton Sanders 25 year old Pelham farmer enlisted 4/29/1861 **W 7/3** W Chancellorsville

Private George Lovelace 20 year old Pelham farmer enlisted 4/29/1861 (later deserted 2/27/64)

Private Robert Miller 30 year old Hillsboro farmer enlisted 4/29/1861 **W-arm/C 7/3**

Private James McClure enlisted 8/26/1861 (later litter bearer)

Private Benjamin Parks 27 year old Pelham farmer enlisted 4/29/1861 **W 7/3 C 7/5 Greencastle**

Private W.R. Pattie 24 yr old enlisted Pelham, Tn 4/24/61 W-2nd Manassas **C 7/14 Falling Waters, Md**

Private John Patton 25 year old Grundy County farmer enlisted 4/29/1861—lost musket (later C Mine Run)

Private Andrew Jackson Phipps 22 year old Pelham farmer enlisted 4/29/1861 **C 7/3 at wall**

Private David Phipps 26 year old Pelham farmer enlisted 4/29/1861

Private Joshua Roberts 22 year old Altamont farmer enlisted 4/29/1861 **W 7/3** (later deserted 7/26/63)

Private John Rose 21 year old Hockersville farmer enlisted 4/29/1861 (later deserted 3/1/64)

Private George Sherrill Coffee Co. farmer enlisted 3/18/1863 **C 7/3**

Private William Tate 26 year old Pelham farmer enlisted 4/29/1861

Private Robert Taylor 24 year old Hillsboro farmer enlisted 4/29/1861 W-chest 2nd Manassas (later Sgt)

Private Charles Townsend21 year old Tullahoma farmer enlisted 4/29/1861 (later C North Anna)

Private George Walls 29 year old Hillsboro farmer enlisted 4/29/1861 **deserted 7/23/63**

Private John Wilkinson 22 year old Pelhal farmer enlisted 4/29/1861

Teamster Roberts Hollins (Brigade level) enlisted 8/27/1861

Teamster John Warren Grundy Co farmer enlisted 6/5/1861 (later W Wilderness)

July 1 Casualties

Sgt Jesse Cornelison 24 yr old enlisted Hillsboro, TN 5/8/61 C **7/1**

Corp John Goodman 24 yr old enlisted Pelham, TN 4/29/61 C **7/1**

Corp Andrew Jackson Phipps enlisted Yorktown 4/29/61 C **7/1**

Private Issac Cornelison enlisted Winchester 4/29/61 K **7/1**

Private George Cunningham enlisted camp Fsher 9/21/62 C **7/1**

Private Islam Dunn enlisted Yorktown 4/29/61 WC **7/1**

Private Raleigh Harris 27 yr old enlisted Hillsboro W-Chancellorsville C **7/1**

Private J.V. "Issac" Howard C **7/1**

Private Harvey Lambert enlisted Camp Fisher 9/21/61 C/ **7/1**

Company B "*Tullahoma Guards*"

Captain William Daniel 21 year old Chattanooga farmer W-face Sharpsburg

1st Lt Jesse Gunn 24 yr old enlisted Hillsboro, Tn 4/29/61 **W 7/3 C 7/5**

2nd Lt James Hubbard 25 yr old enlisted Tullahoma, Tn 4/29/61 W-left shoulder Sharpsburg

1st Sgt Noah Spears 24 year old Winchester farmer enlisted 4/29/1861 **W-back / C 7/3** W Fredericksburg & Chancellorsville

Sgt Milton Byrom 27 year old Winchester farmer enlisted 4/29/1861 W-elbow Fredericksburg **C 7/14 Falling Waters**

Sgt Leonard Kennedy 24 year old Winchester farmer enlisted 4/29/1861 W Fredericksburg

Cpl. Benjamin Anderson age 22 Franklin Co farmer enlisted 4/29/1861 (later W Wilderness)

Cpl. Abraham Evans 21 year old Winchester farmer enlisted 4/29/1861

Private T.H. Allen enlisted 4/1/63 **C 7/3** (later deserted 6/64)

Private Thomas Ayers 27 year old Winchester farmer enlisted 4/29/1861

Private James Bell 24 year old Winchester farmer enlisted 4/29/1861

Private William Blanton 27 year old Winchester farmer enlisted 4/29/1861

Private Joshua Brown 20 year old Lynchburg farmer enlisted 4/29/1861

Private Henry Bunn 26 year old Winchester farmer enlisted 4/29/1861

Private John Erskine 31 year old Williamson Cy farmer enlisted 4/29/1861 W 2nd Manassas (later W Wilderness)

Private Jeptha Fletcheer 23 year old Winchester farmer W-foot Fredericksburg (later deserted 8/25/64)

Private Henry Fowler 32 year old Winchester farmer enlisted 4/29/1861 **W 7/3 C 7/5 Greencastle** (later C Wilderness)

Private Jason Green 28 year old Bedford Cty farmer enlisted 4/29/1861

Private Lewis Holder 23 year old Winchester farmer enlisted 4/29/1861 W 2nd Manassas **C 7/14 Falling Waters, Md**

Private James Hubbard 25 year old Winchester farmer enlisted 4/29/1861

Private Johnson Jordan 23 year old Rutherford Cty farmer (later W Mine Run / W Wilderness)

Private Samuel McCutheon 30 year old Coffee Co farmer enlisted 4/29/1861 **C 7/3**

Private Josiah Marshall 23 year old Fayetteville farmer enlisted 4/29/1861 **C 7/3**

Private Thomas Reese 21 year old Winchester farmer enlisted 4/29/1861

Private Finas Simpson **C 7/3** Ft Delaware—died

Private E. Smith **C 8/11/63** (deserter) Orleans, Md—old Capitol Prison

July 1 Casualties

2nd Lt William Muses 25 yr old enlisted Winchester 4/29/61 **WC 7/1**

Sgt James Smith 22 yr old enlisted Winchester 4/29/61 **C 7/1**

Sgt Robert Newman 22 yr old enlisted Winchester 4/29/61 W-Chancellorsville **C 7/1**

Cpl William Campbell 23 yr old enlisted Winchester 4/29/61 **C 7/1**

Pvt. William Allen 18 yr old enlisted Tullahoma, Tn 4/29/61 W-Sharpsburg **C 7/1**

Pvt John Carroll enlisted Yorktown 4/29/61 W 2nd Manassas C **7/1**

Pvt. Francis Morgan 25 yr old enlisted Winchester 4/29/61 C **7/1**

Pvt. Richard Putnam 23 yr old enlisted Winchester 4/29/61 C **7/1**

Pvt. James Pylant 20 yr old enlisted Winchester 4/29/61 C **7/1**

Pvt. A. Winchester C **7/1** died in prison 10/5/63

Company C "*Mountain Boys*"

Captain Aaron Alexander 25 year old Winchester farmer enlisted 4/29/1861 W 2nd Manassas (later W Wilderness)

1st Lt Samuel Estill 27 year old Franklin County farmer enlisted 4/29/1861 (later C Wilderness)

2nd Lt Alfred Johnson 42 year old Winchester carriage maker (later commanded Co F)

1st Sgt Stanton Denson 28 year old Winchester farmer enlisted 4/29/1861 W-shoulder 2nd Manassas

Sgt Benjamin Jones 25 year old Winchester farmer enlisted 4/29/1861 (later C Wilderness)

Cpl. Thomas Foster 27 year old Winchester farmer enlisted 4/29/1861 **C 7/3**

Cpl. Andrew Caldwell 31 year old Winchester farmer enlisted 4/29/1861 W 2nd Manassas

Cpl John Kinningham 31 year old Winchester farmer enlisted 4/29/1861 (later nurse)

Cpl. George T. Parks 24 year old Winchester farmer enlisted 4/29/1861 **C 7/3**-Ft Delaware—died (buried Finns Pt)

Cpl Benjamin Price 27 year old Winchester farmer enlisted 4/29/1861

Private Willis Brannan 30 year old Winchester farmer enlisted 4/29/1861 **C 7/3**

Private Marshall Bradbury 27 year old Winchester farmer enlisted 4/29/1861

Private Henry Brannan 22 year old Franklin County farmer enlisted 4/29/1861

Private William H. Brannan 31 year old Winchester farmer enlisted 4/29/1861

Private John Brazelton 23 year old Winchester farmer enlisted 4/29/1861 (later W-head Mine Run)

Private Charles Coleman 30 year old Winchester farmer enlisted 4/29/1861 (later Blacksmith)

Private James Estill Franklin County farmer enlisted 2/27/1863 **W 7/3** (later W-knee ream's Station)

Private Hopkins Farris 25 year old Winchester farmer enlisted 4/27/1861 **C 7/3**

Private John Fitzhugh 25 year old Davidson farmer enlisted 4/29/1861 (later Sgt Maj)

Private William Garner 26 year old Franklin County farmer enlisted 4/29/1861 **W-lung 7/3** (later W-Hatchers Run)

Private Thaddeus Green 23 year old Franklin County farmer enlisted 4/29/1861

Private Robert Hodges 27 year old Winchester farmer enlisted 4/29/1861 **W/C 7/3** died

Private George Hexter 22 year old Georges Store farmer enlisted 4/29/1861 (detailed as nurse)

Private George W. Parks enlisted Winchester, Tn 11/8/62 **W 7/3 C 7/5 Greencastle** (later W-ankle Wilderness)

Private Milbern Ratliff Fayetteville farmer enlisted 11/62 (later W Weldon RR)

Private Robert Reeves 25 year old Winchester farmer enlisted 4/29/1861 (later deserted 10/64)

Private Curtis Rich 30 year old Nashville farmer enlisted 4/29/1861 **C 7/3** Ft Delaware

Private David Slatter enlisted 11/8/1862 W-Chancellorsville **W 7/3**
Private Henry Statem 21 year old Winchester farmer enlisted 4/29/1861
Private Dr Hopkins Lacey 25 year old Winchester farmer enlisted 4/29/1861 W 2nd Manassas

Teamster James Sharp 27 year old Franklin County farmer enlisted 4/29/1861

July 1 Casualties

Cpl. Richard Gillespie 24 yr old enlisted Winchester 4/29/61 **C 7/1**
Cpt Henry Robertson enlisted Winchester 4/29/61 **W-left forearm C 7/1** (later K Wilderness)
Pvt. Harrison Bradbury 27 yr old enlisted Winchester 4/29/61 **C 7/1**
Private Issac Caldwell 24 yr old enlisted Winchester 4/29/61 Sharpshooter **W 7/1 C 7/5 Greencastle, Pa** (later Corp)
Pvt Thomas Denson 24 yr old enlisted Winchester 4/29/61 **W-left forearm 7/1**
Pvt. James Martin 28 yr old enlisted Franklin Co. 4/24/61 **C 7/1**
Pvt. Andrew Sims 31 yr old enlisted Winchester 4/29/61 **C 7/1**

Company D "*Ridgedale Hornets*"

Captain John Bevell 34 year old Franklin County farmer enlisted 4/29/ 1861 **W 7/3** (later C Petersburg)
2nd Lt John Tribble 21 year old Winchester farmer enlisted 4/29/ 1861
Sgt Milton Byron 27 year old Winchester farmer enlisted 4/29/ 1861 W-elbow Fredericksburg **C 7/14 Falling Waters**
Cpl. Henry Bolen 20 year old Tullahoma farmer enlisted 4/29/ 1861—leg Fredericksburg **C 7/14 Falling Waters**
Cpl. William Lewis 25 year old Ridgeville farmer enlisted 4/29/ 1861 W Fredericksburg **W-leg C 7/14 Falling Waters**
Cpl. William Majors enlisted 10/10/1861 in Franklin County—detailed to care for wounded **C 7/5**
Private James Allen 27 year old Harrogate farmer enlisted 4/29/1861 **W-leg C 7/3**-Ft Delaware
Private Thomas Anderson 26 year old Ridgeville farmer enlisted 4/29/ 1861
Private Rody Anthony 22 year old Bedford County farmer enlisted 4/29/ 1861 W-Chancellorsville **W-thigh C 7/3**
Private Little Brown 21year old Franklin County farmer enlisted 4/29/ 1861 **C 7/14 Falling Waters**
Private Milton Byrom 27 year old Winchester farmer enlisted 4/29/1861 **C Falling Waters 7/15**

Private Elijah Chambers 24 year old Ridgeville farmer enlisted 4/29/ 1861 W 2nd Manassas (later W Wilderness)

Private James Cook enlisted 9/16/1861 deserted 7/22 Front Royal, Va

Private Joshua Dean enlisted 4/27/1862 W Fredericksburg

Private T. Ellis **C 7/3**-Ft Delaware (died of smallpox) buried Finn Pt. NJ

Private Benjamin Erwin Gilmer Co WVa farmer C Fredericksburg

Private John Fanning 33 year old Franklin County farmer enlisted 4/29/ 1861 W 2nd Manassas **W 7/3 C 7/5 Greencastle, Pa**

Private William Hendrix 28 year old Ridgeville farmer enlisted 4/29/ 1861 W 2nd Manassas W/C Sharpsburg deserted 7/22

Private William Lewis **W Falling Waters 7/14 C 7/15 Martinsburg WV**

Private William Mires 25 year old Ridgeville farmer enlisted 4/29/ 1861 W Gaines Mill **deserted 7/63**

Private Allen Pollock 23 year old Ridgeville farmer enlisted 4/29/ 1861 W-thigh Fredericksburg **K 7/3**

Private John Rogers 23 year old Winchester farmer enlisted 4/29/ 1861

Private George Sanders 25 year old Franklin County farmer enlisted 4/29/ 1861 W Bristoe W Spotsylvania

Private John Thomas deserted Flint Hill, Va 7/24/63

Private Wiley Tribble enlisted at Ridgeville 10/10/1861 (later Sgt / 1st Sgt)

Private George Weaver 26 year old Franklin County farmer enlisted 4/29/ 1861 deserted 7/24 Flynt Hill, Va

Nurse James Byrom 25 year old Winchester farmer enlisted 4/29/ 1861 W Fredericksburg (lost hand) **C 7/15 Williamsport**

Teamster John Beaver 26 year old Ridgeville farmer enlisted 4/29/ 1861

Teamster John Cobble 24 year old Ridgeville farmer enlisted 4/29/ 1861

Teamster Issac Mitchell 25 yr old enlisted Winchester 4/29/61 **W-leg 7/5 amp.**

July 1 Casualties

1st Lt William Farris 29 yr old enlisted Ridgeville 5/8/61 **W 7/1 C 7/5 Greencastle, Pa**

Sgt Robert Anthony 25 yr old enlisted Ridgeville 4/29/61 **W 7/1 C 7/5 Greencastle, Pa**

Sgt Larkum Rogers 18 yr old enlisted Winchester 4/29/61 W-Sharpsburg **W 7/1 C 7/5 Greencastle, Pa**

Cpl. Joseph Bolin 23 yr old enlisted Ridgeville 4/29/61 C 7/1

Cpl. Robert Majors 25 yr old enlisted Ridgeville 4/29/61 W-Sharpsburg **C 7/1**

Pvt. James Adams 24 yr old enlisted Ridgeville 4/29/61 **C 7/1**

Pvt. James Freeman 27 yr old enlisted Ridgeville 4/29/61 **C 7/1**

Pvt. Jacob Mitchell 23 yr old enlisted Winchester 4/29/61 **WC 7/1 died 7/3 buried Hollywood cem**

Pvt. George Ready 20 yr old enlisted Winchester **C 7/1**
Priv. Thomas Rogers 26 yr old enlisted Ridgeville 4/29/61 reduced from Sgt. **C 7/1**
Pvt. J.A. Simms 23 yr old enlisted Ridgeville 4/29/61 **C 7/1**
Pvt. Joseph Timmes 26 yr old enlisted Winchester 4/29/61 W-hip Fredericksburg **C 7/1**

June 30, 1863 desertions
Private Benjamin Hutton deserted Cashtown, Pa
Private William Hines (on the road)

Company E "*Lynchburg Rangers*"

(formed March 1861 / Financed by Mr. John T Taylor—many men transferred to Forest Escort Company—TN)

Captain Thomas Mann Lynchburg farmer enlisted 4/29/1861 W 2nd Manassas (later K Wilderness)
1st Lt Anderson Eaton 25 year old Lynchburg farmer enlisted 4/29/1861 W 2nd Manassas (later W Wilderness)
Sgt Martin Hawkins 23 year old Lynchburg farmer enlisted 4/29/1861 **W 7/3** (later W Spotsylvania)
Sgt Kindred Bobo 23 year old Lynchburg farmer enlisted 4/29/1861 (later deserted 4/23/64)
Sgt William Cowen 22 yr old enlisted Lynchburg, Tn 4/29/61 **W 7/3** later C Petersburg)
Sgt. Rufus Crawford 22 year old Lincoln County farmer enlisted 4/29/1861 **W 7/3**
Sgt Thomas Parks 23 year old Lincoln County farmer enlisted 4/29/1861
Cpl. A.A. Colwell 22 year old Lincoln County farmer enlisted 4/29/1861 **W 7/3**
Cpl. William Hutchinson 24 year old Lynchburg farmer enlisted 4/29/1861 W Harper's Ferry **W 7/3** (later W Hatcher's Run)
Cpl. Milton Parks 20 year old Lincoln County farmer enlisted 4/29/1861 **W 7/3 C 7/5**
Cpl. Felix W. Motlow 22 year old Lynchburg farmer enlisted 4/29/1861
Cpl. Alexander Womack 30 year old Lynchburg farmer enlisted 4/29/1861 **W 7/3**
Private Alexander Bailey 21 year old Lynchburg farmer enlisted 4/29/1861 W Fredericksburg W Chancellorsville **deserted 8/12**
Private Felix Bedford 20 year old Lynchburg farmer enlisted 4/29/1861 W Gaines Mill (later W Petersburg)
Private Benjamin Berry 21 year old Lincoln County farmer enlisted 4/29/1861 W/C 2nd Manassas detailed as nurse **C 7/5**
Private Thomas Eaton 23 year old Lynchburg farmer enlisted 4/29/1861
Private Franklin Edens enlisted 11/10/1862 from Lynchburg
Private E.M. Ewing C Sharpsburg
Private John Felps 21 yr old enlisted Lynchburg, Tn 4/29/61 W-Sharpsburg **W 7/3**

Private James Johnson conscript from Rockingham, Va

Private John McCullough 20 year old Lincoln County farmer enlisted 4/29/1861 (later K Petersburg)

Private Zadock Motlow 31 year old Lynchburg farmer enlisted 4/29/1861 (later Wagon Master)

Private Benton Norton 24 year old Bedford County farmer enlisted 4/29/1861 W-leg 2nd Manassas **W 7/3 C 7/5**

Private James Rives 20 year old Lynchburg student enlisted 4/29/1861 **deserted 8/12/63**

Private James Robinson 23 year old Lynchburg farmer enlisted 4/29/1861 (later teamster)

Private John Strawn 23 year old Lincoln County farmer enlisted 4/29/1861 **W-arm 7/3** (later W Wilderness)

Private William Shaw 24 year old Lynchburg farmer enlisted 4/29/1861

Ambulance Driver William banks enlisted 4/27/1862

Medical Staff Private Stephen Dance

Nurse Private Benjamin Berry C 7/5 at hospital—Ft Delaware

Teamster Thomas Chapman 26 year old Lincoln County farmer enlisted 4/29/1861

Teamster James Kirkland 24 year old Lynchburg farmer enlisted 4/29/1861 (later deserted 3/64)

Teamster D. Motlow—detailed as forage master

Teamster Pvt. Felix Motlow 25 yr old enlisted Lycoming 4/29/61 **C 7/5 with train**

July 1 Casualties

Sgt. Thomas Spencer 23 yr old enlisted Lycoming 4/29/61 **W-abdomen C 7/1**

Cpl. David Robertson 25 yr old enlisted Lynchburg 4/29/61 W-Sharpsburg **W 7/1 C 7/5 Greencastle, Pa**

Pvt. Thomas Allison 23 yr old enlisted Sheldon Creek 4/27/61 **C 7/1**

Pvt. Owen Bailey **W 7/1 C 7/5 Greencastle, Pa**

Pvt. Josiah Brandon enlisted Lynchburg 4/29/61 W-grapeshot Fredericksburg **C 7/1**

Pvt. John E. Cates 25 yr old enlisted Lynchburg 4/29/61 **W 7/1 C Greencastle, Pa** (Died 9/21 Phila hospital buried PNC)

Pvt. Maze Enochs 30 yr old enlisted Lynchburg **W-face-& thigh C 7/1**

Pvt Claiborne Felps 25 yr old enlisted Lycoming 4/29/61 **C 7/1**

Pvt. James Mitchell enlisted Lycoming 4/29/61 **C 7/1**

Company F "*Salem Invincibles*"

1st Lt Thomas Foster 30 year old Winchester farmer enlisted 4/29/1861 as Lt.(resigned) reenlisted 11/8/1862 **C 7/3**

Sgt John Counts 23 year old Salem farmer enlisted 4/29/1861 Drum Major

Sgt John Cox 24 year old Winchester farmer enlisted 4/29/1861 **C 7/3**
Sgt John Hall 23 year old Winchester farmer enlisted 4/29/1861 **K 7/3**
Sgt John King 24 year old Winchester farmer enlisted 4/29/1861 (later died 11/9/64 disease)
Sgt Matthew Mann Winchester farmer enlisted 4/29/1861 W-neck 2nd Manasssas **W 7/3 C 7/6** Greencastle died Ft Delaware
Cpl. James Rowell 26 year old Salem farmer enlisted 4/29/1861 W-leg Chancelorsville **C 7/3**
Cpl.George Williams 32 year old Salem farmer enlisted 4/29/1861 **C 7/3**
Private George Bowling 24 year old Salem farmer enlisted 4/29/1861 **K 7/14 Falling Waters**
Private James Brazelton 22 year old Franklin County farmer enlisted 4/29/1861 deserted 7/24 Flynt Hill, Va
Private James Crawley 23 year old Salem farmer enlisted 4/29/1861 . . . . Pioneer Corps
Private Thomas Denson Salem farmer **K 7/3** (during advance)
Private Thomas Farris 22 year old Winchester farmer enlisted 4/29/1861
Private William Farris enlisted 11/2/1862 at Winchester
Private O.B. Gilmer C Sharpsburg 9/19/62 returned to unit
Private Richard Green reenlisted 11/1/62 at Winchester **W 7/3 C 7/5**
Private Richard Hill Hunts Station farmer enlisted 9/20/1861
Private Nathaniel Lisco detailed to Division Wagon Train **C 7/5**
Private James Martin 28 year old Salem farmer enlisted 4/29/1861 **C 7/3**
Private James Mason Enlisted 4/27/1861 in Salem W-knee Chancellorsville **MIA 7/3** returned
Private Richard Mason reenlisted 4/29/1862 Yorktown, Va W Seven Pines **K 7/3**
Private William Mason 27 year old Salem farmer enlisted 4/29/1861 W-knee Chancellorsville (deserted Flynt Hill, Va 7/24/63)
Private John McClure 35 year old Salem farmer enlisted 4/29/1861 **K 7/3**
Private Thomas Oliver 24 year old Winchester farmer enlisted 4/29/1861
Private Avery Reeves 24 year old Salem farmer enlisted 4/29/1861 C Sharpsburg W Fredericksburg (deserted 7/24 Flynt Hill, Va)
Private George Simmons 37 year old Salem farmer enlisted 4/29/1861 C Chancellorsville **W 7/3** (deserted Flynt Hill, Va 7/24)
Private Samuel Smith 22 year old Salem farmer enlisted 4/29/1861 (later Sgt W-leg Petersburg)
Private William Williams Winchester farmer enlisted 2/26/1863 (deserted Flynt Hill, Va 7/24/63)
Private Henry Wilson enlisted 9/25/1861 at Salem **C 7/3**-Ft Delaware died (buried Finn's Pt NJ)
Private Wiley Woods 32 year old Salem farmer enlisted 4/29/1861 **Flag Bearer C 7/3**
Musician Minor Little enlisted 3/1863 detailed as kettle drummer

July 1 Casualties

Capt James Thompson 30 yr old enlisted Winchester 4/29/61 W-Cedar Run **C 7/1**
2nd Lt William Nuckles 31 yr old enlisted Franklin Co. 5/8/61 **K 7/1**
Cpl. James Baxter 34 yr old enlisted Winchester 4/29/61 **C 7/1**
Pvt. William Arnett enlisted Winchester 4/29/61 **C 7/1**
Pvt. Martin Brazelton 24 yr old enlisted Winchester 11/12/62 **K 7/1**
Pvt. Frederick Lee 22 yr old enlisted Winchester 4/29/61 **WC 7/1**
Pvt. Solomon Mitchell 28 yr old enlisted Salem, TN 4/24/61 W-2nd Manassas **C 7/1**
Pvt. Thomas Rosborough 31 yr old enlisted Salem, TN 4/24/61 **C 7/1**
Pvt. Richard Shepard enlisted Winchester 11/12/62 **WC 7/1**
Pvt. Jones Turner 20 yr old enlisted Winchester 4/29/61 C 7/1
Pvt. Newton Williams enlisted Winchester 11/10/62 **W-arm 7/1 C 7/5 Greencastle, Pa**

Company G "*Fayetteville Guards*"

1st Lt James Manley 28 year old Fayetteville farmer enlisted 4/29/1861 **W-arm & thigh / C 7/3** died Camp Letterman 8/6

2nd Lt Richard Routt 28 year old Fayetteville farmer enlisted 4/29/1861 C Seven Pines W Chancellorsville

3rd Lt James Grant 26 year old Lincon County farmer enlisted 4/29/1861 **C 7/3**-Pt Lookout

1st Sgt John Thore 32 year old Fayetteville farmer enlisted 4/29/1861

Sgt J.H. Shreve served entire war with regiment

Sgt John Cathey 23 year old Fayetteville farmer enlisted 4/1861 **W 7/3**

Sgt William Moore 28 year old Fayetteville farmer enlisted 4/29/1861 (later QM clerk)

Sgt Francis Weaver 26 year old Fayetteville farmer enlisted 4/29/1861 (later 1st Lt)

Corp. William Cashion 22 yr old enlisted 9/61W Seven Pines & Gaines Mill **W 7/1 & W left leg 7/3 (amp) C 7/5 Greencastle**

Cpl. N.P. Mynatt C Sharpsburg returned to unit before 7/1/63

Private Thomas Ables 19 year old Fayetteville farmer enlisted 4/29/1861

Private John Alexander 23 year old Fayetteville farmer enlisted 4/29/1861 (later ambulance driver)

Private John Alford 32 year old Fayetteville farmer enlisted 4/29/1861 (later ambulance driver)

Private John Blake 31 year old Lincoln County farmer enlisted 4/29/1861 **W 7/3 C 7/5**—Ft Delaware

Private George Bulock 27 year old Fayetteville farmer enlisted 4/29/1861

Private Archibald Cashion Lincoln County farmer enlisted 4/27/1861 (later W Bristoe—W Wilderness)

Private Alexander Clark 23 year old Fayetteville farmer enlisted 4/29/1861 **W 7/3**

Private James Cowen 35 year old Franklin County farmer enlisted 4/29/1861 (later C Wilderness)
Private Ezekiel Crawford enlisted 12/12/62 from Lincoln County (later C Wilderness)
Private John Eastland 21 year old Lincoln County farmer enlisted 4/29/1861 W Sharpsburg (deserted 7/25/63)
Private Andrew Edmundson enlisted 10/27/1861 (later C Hatcher's Run)
Private Colville Edmundson 20 year old Fayetteville farmer enlisted 4/29/1861 **W/C 7/3** Ft Delaware (escaped)
Private C.W. Emerson enlisted 4/10/62 Corith Ms (later C Wilderness)
Private Nathan Estell 25 year old Winchester farmer enlisted 4/29/1861 (later W Petersburg)
Private Wilson Fox 22 year old Fayetteville farmer enlisted 4/29/1861 (deserted 7/23/63)
Private Leroy Ham Lawrence County, Tn conscript (deserted 11/27/63)
Private Philip Koonce 26 year old Fayetteville farmer enlisted 4/29/1861 (later Sgt—died 12/63)
Private William McClellan enlisted 10/27/1861 at camp Fisher W-hip Cedar Run, Va (later W Petersburg)
Private John McCollum East Tenn conscript (deserted 11/27/63)
Private John McKinney 23 year old Fayetteville farmer enlisted 4/29/1861 **C 7/3**
Private John Millard 25 year old Fayetteville farmer enlisted 4/29/1861 W Gaines Mill W Fredericksburg **W 7/3**
Private Thomas O'Bryan 25 year old Fayetteville farmer enlisted 4/29/1861 W Gaines Mill W 2nd Manassas
Private Benjamin Smith 22 year old Fayetteville farmer enlisted 4/29/1861 W 2nd Manassas **W 7/3 C 7/5**
Private Thomas Smith 22 year old Fayetteville farmer enlisted 4/29/1861 **W-arm&head 7/3**
Private George Stewart substitute reported 1/63 **K 7/3**
Private George Stonebreaker Fayetteville farmer enlisted 4/29/1861 W 2nd Manassas **C 7/3** (later W Petersburg)
Private Nathan Whitaker 26 year old Fayetteville farmer enlisted 4/29/1861 (later teamster)

Teamster James Hampton
Teamster Cpl. Alfred Kelso 24 year old Fayetteville farmer enlisted 4/29/1861 (later Brigade teamster)
Teamster William Whittington (later W Wilderness)
Ambulance Driver Private John Alexander
Ambulance Driver Private John Alford

July 1 Casualties

Captain Davis Clark 28 yr old enlisted Fayetteville 4/29/61 **W-left ankle 7/1**
Pvt. James Beavert 23 yr old enlisted Fayetteville 4/29/61 W-ankle Chancellorsville **W 7/1**
Pvt. Milton Diemer 21 yr old enlisted Fayetteville 4/29 /61 **C 7/1**
Pvt. Gabe Moore enlisted Fayetteville 11/10/62 **W-left buttock C 7/1** (later C Wilderness)

Company H *"Shelton Creek Boys"*

Captain Thomas Arnold 27 year old Sheldon Creek farmer enlisted 4/29/1861 **C 7/3**

1st Lt George Pickett enlisted Fayetteville 9/25/1861 **W 7/3 C 7/5**

2nd Lt Thomas George Georges Store farmer enlisted 10/4/1861 W 2nd Manassas **W 7/3** (later Captain / C Sailors Creek)

Sgt William A. Cashion 23 year old Georges Store farmer enlisted 4/27/1861 W Sharpsburg W Fredericksburg **C 7/3**

Sgt. James Hunt 22 year old Georges Store farmer enlisted 4/27/1861 **W 7/3 C 7/5** Greencastle, Pa

Sgt Edward Myrich enlisted Flyntville Tn 9/25/1861 **K 7/3**

Sgt John Simmons 23 year old Georges Store farmer enlisted 4/29/1861 W-leg 2nd Manassas **WC 7/3**

Sgt Young Stiles 22 year old Georges Store farmer enlisted 4/29/1861 **W 7/3 C 7/5**

Sgt. Willis White 30 year old Georges Store farmer enlisted 4/27/1861 W 2nd Manassas **W-thigh/C 7/3**

1st Cpl John Baxter 18 year old Knox County farmer enlisted 4/29/1861

Corp. William Faulkner 26 year old Georges Store farmer enlisted 4/27/1861 **C 7/5** *sick during attack*

Cpl. Thomas Harper 23 year old Lincoln County farmer enlisted 4/27/1861 **W 7/3 C 7/5** Greencastle, Pa

Cpl. George McGehee 23 year old Georges Store farmer enlisted 4/27/1861 (deserted 3/14/64) returned

Cpl. Benjamin Shelton 22 year old Georges Store farmer enlisted 4/29/1861

Private John Baxter 2 year old George Store farmer enlisted 4/29/1861 (later Corporal)

Private Thomas Boggs Franklin County farmer enlisted 4/29/1861 **C 7/3** Ft Delaware

Private James Bray enlisted Camp Fisher, va 10/5/1861 W Fredericksburg **W 7/3**

Private Andrew Casion 24 year old Sheltons Creek farmer enlisted 4/29/1861 **W 7/3**

Private Gabriel Cashion 19 enlisted George Store 11/1/62 **W 7/3 C 7/5** Greencastle—Ft Delaware

Private Young Cashion Enlisted 10/4/1861 at Georges Store

Private William T Christian enlisted Sheltons Creek **K 7/3**

Private Hance Hunter 30 year old Georges Store farmer enlisted 4/27/1861 **C 7/3**

Private George Ingland 27 year old Georges Store farmer enlisted 4/27/1861 W 2nd Manassas **C 7/3**-Ft Delaware

Private Josiah Land 25 year old Georges Store farmer enlisted 4/29/1861 **C 7/3**

Private Michael Luttrell 29 year old Georges Store farmer enlisted 4/27/1861 W Shepardstown **W 7/3** (later Ambulance Driver)

Private Robert McGehee enlisted 11/2/62 Lincoln County **W 7/3**

Private Milbern Ratcliff enlisted 11/62 Fayettville (later W Weldon RR)

Private Samuel Ratliff 20 year old Georges Store farmer enlisted 4/29/1861 (later K Mine Run)

Private Peter Shelton 23 year old Georges Store farmer enlisted 4/29/1861 **W 7/3 C 7/5**
Private George Simmons 37 year old Salem farmer enlisted 4/29/1861 C Chancellorsville **W 7/3** (later deserted 7/24/63)
Private Jared Simmons enlisted 11/1/62 George Store **K 7/3**
Private Pleasant Snoddy 23 year old Georges Store farmer enlisted 4/29/1861 W-face 2nd Manassas **C 7/3**
Private John Taylor enlisted 3/16/63 at Fayetteville **C 7/3**-Ft Delaware—died (buried Finn Point, NJ)
Private James Tripp 26 year old Georges Store farmer enlisted 4/29/1861
Private Samuel Walker 23 year old Georges Store farmer enlisted 4/29/1861 **C 7/3**-Ft Delaware
Private Alexander Womach 24 yr old George's Store enlisted 4/29/61 **W 7/3**

Drummer John Faulkner 22 year old student enlisted at Georges Store 4/29/1861
Teamster William Jolly 27 year old Georges Store farmer enlisted 4/29/1861

July 1 Casualties

Cpl. Richard Womach 22 yr old enlisted George's Store W Sharpsburg **W 7/1** (later Sgt)
Cpl. Joseph Allison 22 yr old enlisted Sheldon Creek 4/29/61 **C 7/1**
Cpl. William Faukner 24 yr old enlisted George's Store 4/29/61 **W 7/1 C 7/5 Greencastle, Pa**
Pvt. Francis Alexander enlisted Fayetteville, TN 6/10/63 **C 7/1**
Pvt Ambrose Bennett 20 yr old enlisted Sheldon Creek 4/29/61 W-hip 2nd Manassas / W leg Fredericksburg **C 7/1**
Pvt George Counts 22 yr old enlisted Lincoln Co, TN 5/8/61 **C 7/1**
Pvt Meredith Land enisted camp Fisher 4/29/61 **C 7/1**
Pvt Michael Luttrell 29 yr old enlisted Sheldon Creek 4/29/61 **W 7/1** (later amp driver)
Pvt Martin Shackleford 24 yr old enlisted Sheldon Creek 4/29/61 **C 7/1**
Pvt Henry Shelton enlisted George's Store 11/1/62 **W 7/1**
Pvt. William Carroll Stewart 24 yr old enlisted Sheldon Creek 4/29/61 **WC 7/1**
Pvt Asa Street 20 yr old enlisted Sheldon Creek 4/29/61 **C 7/1** (later K Wilderness)

Company I "*Cowen Guards*"

Captain Henry Hawkins 28 year old Cowen farmer enlisted 4/29/1861 **C 7/3**-Ft Delaware
1st Lt. George Bowers 24 year old Winchester farmer enlisted 4/29/1861 W-leg Fredericksburg **C 7/3** (later C Weldon RR)
2nd Lt William Cowan 23 year old Winchester farmer enlisted 4/29/1861 W 2nd Manassas W Chancellorsville
3rd Lt Willis Brannan transferred from Co C

1st Sgt Charles Hoffman 40 yr old enlisted Cowen, Tn 4/20/61

Sgt Issac Miller 23 year old Winchester farmer enlisted 4/29/1861 **C 7/3**

Sgt Levy Elliot enlisted 3/12/63 Winchester, TN (later C Wilderness)

Sgt Squire Hawkins 32 year old Winchester farmer enlisted 4/29/1861

Sgt. Joseph Lenehan 21 year old Winchester farmer enlisted 4/29/1861 **WC 7/3** Chester Hospital

Cpl. Francis Bowers 23 year old Winchester farmer enlisted 4/29/1861 WE 2nd Manassas **C 7/3** Ft Delaware

Cpl Thomas Hawkins 22 year old Winchester farmer enlisted 4/29/1861 **C 7/3** Ft Delaware

Cpl James Hill 23 year old Winchester farmer enlisted 4/29/1861 W Fredericksburg (later K Wilderness)

Cpl Farley Wade 21 year old Franklin County farmer enlisted 4/29/1861

Private David Anderson enlisted in Franklin County 9/8/1861 W Chancellorsville **W 7/3 C 7/5** Greencastle, Pa

Private J.H. Bowers Enlisted 11/1/62 Winchester (later C Wilderness)

Private John Bowers enlisted 11/1/62 W-leg Fredericksburg (served until 10/63)

Private Issac Clifton 28 year old Marion laborer enlisted 4/29/1861 W Chancellorsville W Bristoe Station

Private C.P. Cochran enlisted 3/11/63 at Winchester

Private Maxwell Hines 20 year old Winchester farmer enlisted 4/29/1861 **W-thigh C 7/3** Chester Hospital

Private James Holland 24 year old Winchester farmer enlisted 4/29/1861 **C 7/3** Ft Delaware—died

Private John Kelly 29 year old Winchester farmer born in Switerland enlisted 4/29/1861 **W 7/3** died Richmond hospital

Private Daniel Lenehan age 24 enlisted in Cowen, Tn 8/1/1861 **C 7/13** Falling Waters

Private Matthew Nichols 22 year old Winchester farmer enlisted 4/29/1861 W Gaines Mills (deserted 11/27/63)

Private William Rogers 21 year old Franklin County farmer enlisted 4/29/1861 (deserted 10/15/64

Private Issac Stewart enlisted 10/7/1861 from Franklin County W Fredericksburg **C 7/13** Falling Waters, Md

Private E.F. Stowe C Sharpsburg returned to regiment

Private James Young enlisted 11/1/62 at Winchester **C 7/3** Ft Delaware

Nurse Private Issac Stewart W Fredericksburg C Falling Waters 7/14 (with wounded)

Teamster William Brazelton (later W Petersburg)

July 1 Casualties

Cpl. Joseph Hawkins 28 yr old enlisted Winchester 4/29/61 **C 7/1**

Private Richard Green enlisted Winchester 4/29/61 **W 7/1 C 7/5 Greencastle, Pa**

Pvt Andrew Ross 23 yr old enlisted Cowen, TN 4/29/61 w-right side Chancellorsville **C 7/1**

Pvt George Young enlisted Winchester 4/29/61 **C 7/1**

Company K "*Boon's Hill Minutemen*"

Captain Jacob Turney 32 year old Boons Hill Lincoln County farmer enlisted 4/29/1861 W Gaines Mill/Fredericksburg & Chancellorsville **C 7/3**

1st Lt James Holland Boons Hill Lincoln County farmer enlisted 4/29/1861 (medal for gallantry at Gaines Mill)

2nd Lt John Farrar 24 year old Lincoln County farmer enlisted 4/29/1861 (later K Wilderness)

Sgt John Harden 21 year old Lincoln County farmer enlisted 4/29/1861 **C 7/3**

Sgt George Sawyers 24 year old Boons Hill Lincoln County farmer enlisted 4/29/1861

Cpl. Felix Boyle 37 year old Boons Hill, Lincoln County farmer enlisted 4/29/1861

Cpl. Michael Denham 24 year old Lincoln County farmer enlisted 4/29/1861 W Seven Pines

Cpl John Sanders 24 year old Boons Hill Lincoln County farmer enlisted 4/29/1861 W Fredericksburg

Cpl Hugh Zimmerman 24 year old Lincoln County farmer enlisted 4/29/1861 (later C Wilderness)

Private William Douthit 24 year old Lincoln County farmer enlisted 4/29/1861 (later teamster)

Private James Farrar enlisted 11/10/62 Boons Hill, Tn **C 7/14 Falling Waters**

Private Manoah Hampton 22 year old Lincoln County farmer enlisted 4/29/1861 W Fredericksburg **C 7/14 Falling Waters**

Private Pleasant Hampton 23 year old Lincoln County farmer enlisted 4/29/1861 W Fredericksburg **C 7/3** Ft Delaware—died

Private John Massey 22 year old Boons Hill Lincoln County farmer enlisted 4/29/1861 W Gaines Mill

Private Joseph McKinney 32 year old Boon's Hill Lincoln County farmer enlisted 4/29/1861 **W-finger 7/3**

Pvt. William Oldham enlisted Lincoln County **C 7/3** later W Wilderness / W Petersburg

Private Marion Sharp 23 year old Lincoln County farmer enlisted 4/29/1861 **K 7/3**

Private Thomas Stewart 23 year old Lincoln County farmer enlisted 4/29/1861 **C 7/3** Ft Delaware—escaped

Private Albert Turney 20 year old Boons Hill Lincoln County farmer enlisted 4/29/1861 W Chancellorsville **WC 7/3**

Private James Turney 26 year old Boons Hill Lincoln County farmer enlisted 4/29/1861 W 2nd Manassas (deserted 12/63)

Private Andrew West 24 year old Lincoln County farmer enlisted 4/29/1861

Private James Woodward 25 year old Boons Hill Lincoln County farmer enlisted 4/29/1861 (blacksmith)

Private Samuel Wright 26 year old Boons Hill Lincoln County farmer enlisted 4/29/1861 **W-head C 7/3**

Private Thomas Wright 23 year old Boons Hill Lincoln County farmer enlisted 4/29/1861 **C 7/14 Falling Waters**

Teamster George Barnes 32 year old Lincoln County farmer enlisted 4/29/1861

Teamster George Brames enlisted 4/27/62 at Yorktown, Va

Teamster Levi Carpenter 26 year old Boons Hill, Lincoln County farmer enlisted 4/29/1861

July 1 Casualties

Cpl. Cornelius Hedgepath 25 yr old enlisted Lincoln Co. 4/29/61 **W 7/1 C 7/5 Greencastle, Pa**

Pvt Napolean Abbott 25 yr old enlisted Boones Mill Lincoln Co. 5/8/61 **C 7/1**

Pvt. Robert Davis 27 yr old enlisted Lincoln Co. 5/8/61 **W 7/1** (later Sgt)

Pvt Marcus Emmons 25 yr old enlisted Lincoln Co. 4/29/61 **WC 7/1**

Pvt. George Garrett 25 yr old enlisted Lincoln Co 4/29/61 **WC 7/1**

Pvt James Massey 21 yr old enlisted Lincoln Co 4/29/61 **C 7/1**

Pvt Cyrus Moores 20 yr old enlisted Boones Mill, Lincoln Co. 4/29/61 W Chancellorsville **C 7/1**

THIRTEENTH ALABAMA REGIMENT

Corp. James Averitt Co A

Private Evan Ballard Co G

Field & Staff

Colonel Birkett D Fry age 42 Cotton Manufacturer enlisted July 19, 1861 W-Seven Pines, Sharpsburg, Chancellorsville. **W-leg C 7/3**

Lt. Colonel James Aiken 31 yr old from S.C. Captain Co D W Chancellorsville Absent W

Major John Smith enlisted Roanoke Co. AL Appt 4/30/63 Killed Chancellorsville

Sergeant Major Burette O. Holman age 28 Camden lawyer enlisted 4/1/63 **C 7/1**

Adjutant Louis Broughton age 26 Student from Greenville enlisted July 19, 1861

Surgeon Henry Clarkson age 30 Columbia SC Physician enlisted March 10, 1862

Assistant Surgeon Abner Arnold age 26 Physician from Washington La. enlist April 9, 1863

Company A *"Camden Rifles"*

Sgt Nathaniel Brantley 17 year old student from Rehobeth

Corp. William L. Hayes 7/18/61 Bridgeport, Al W-Seven Pines **W-slightly in face, neck 7/1 fought on 7/3 C**

Private Virgil Carstarphen 25 year old farmer from Camden

Private Issac Handly 20 year old student from Camden

Private Harrison Martin 26 year old farmer from Camden **C 7/3**

Private John Morgan 22 year old farmer from Pine Hill

July 1 Casualties

1st Lt. Calvin C. Sellers 25 yr old lawyer enlisted 7/6/ 61 Bridgeport, Al **C 7/1**
2nd Lt. Joseph L. Moore 26 yr old enlisted 7/6/ 61 Bridgeport, Al **C 7/1**
Sergeant Aubudon Gullett enlisted 7/19/61 Bridgeport, Al; **C 7/1**
Sergeant Jackson Welch 29 yr old mechanic enlisted 7/6/ 61 Bridgeport, Al **C 7/1**
Corp. James B. Averitt enlisted 7/19/61 Montgomery, Al **C 7/1**
Corp. Duncan McCaskill 26 yr old enlisted 7/6/ 61 Bridgeport, Al **C 7/1**
Private Homer Adams enlisted 3/23/63 Nottingham, Al **C 7/1 (died 12/23/63)**
Private Edward J. Bailey 36 yr old mechanic enlisted 7/6/61 Bridgeford, Al **C 7/1**
Private George DeMoth enlisted 7/25/61 Bridgeport, Al **C 7/1**
Private B. O. Holman enlisted 7/25/61 Bridgeport, Al **C 7/1**
Private Henry Kirkwood 32 yr old 31 yr oldenlisted 7/25/61 Bridgeport, Al **C 7/1**
Private Hiram A. McClure 34 yr old enlisted Bridgeport, Al **C 7/1**
Private Robert P. Nevill 28 yr old dentist enlisted 7/6/61 **C 7/1**
Private John W. Reeves 28 yr old enlisted 7/6/ 61 Bridgeport, Al **C 7/1**
Private Thomas J. Sadler 25 yr old enlisted 7/6/ 61 Bridgeport, Al **C 7/1**
Private Jesse B. Skinner 23 yr old enlisted 7/6/ 61 Bridgeport, Al **C 7/1**
Private Jeremiah Tucker 23 yr old enlisted 7/6/61 Camden, Al **C 7/1**
Private Thomas C. Williams 21 yr old student enlisted 7/6/ 61 Bridgeport, Al **C 7/1**

Company B *"Southern Stars"*

1st Lt Hardy Gibson 25 year old Cusseta farmer enlisted 7/17/1861 **K 7/3 during bombardment**
2nd Lt Charles Dean 24 year old LaFayette farmer enlisted 7/19/1861 **W 7/3**
Sgt William Wright 22 year old Montgomery farmer enlisted 7/19/1861 **C 7/3**
Corp William Barron 20 year old Tuskegee farmer enlisted 7/19/1861
Corp John Brunson 27 year old Tuskegee farmer enlisted 7/19/1861 **C 7/3**
Corp James Freeman 19 year old Ufaupee farmer enlisted 7/19/1861
Private Stephen Bailey 21 year old Tuskegee farmer enlisted 7/19/1861 **W/C 7/3**
Private James Barron 20 year old Tuskegee farmer enlisted 5/30/1863
Private Thomas Bazemore 20 year old Rockford farmer enlisted 7/19/1861
Private Henry Cannon 25 year old Dadeville farmer enlisted 3/23/1863 **C 7/3**
Private James Dozier 24 year old LaFayette farmer enlisted 7/19/1861 **W 7/3**
Private Jefferson Gleaton 29 year old Tallassee farmer enlisted 7/19/1861
Private John Hand 24 year old Salem farmer enlisted 3/13/1863 **C 7/3**
Private Phillip Henly 28 year old Columbus, GA mechanic enlisted 4/30/1863
Private David Honeycutt 28 year old Dadeville farmer enlisted 7/19/1861 **W/C 7/3**
Private John Kelley 34 year old Montgomery farmer enlisted 7/19/1861
Private William LaFour 38 year old Tuskegee painter enlisted 7/19/1861 **C 7/3**

Private John McKay 25 year old Tuskegee mechanic enlisted 7/19/1861
Private John McLaughlin 34 year old Montgomery farmer enlisted 3/18/1863 **C 7/3**
Private George Mitchell 20 year old Montgomery painter enlisted 7/19/1861
Private James Stallings 20 year old Ufaupee farmer enlisted 7/19/1861 **SW/ C 7/3**
Private Jefferson Stallings 32 year old Ufaupee farmer enlisted 7/19/1861 **W 7/3**
Private William Teal 26 year old Montgomery bookkeeper enlisted 7/19/1861 **C 7/3**
Private Andrew Williams 28 year old Montgomery mechanic enlisted 7//19/1861

July 1 Casualties

Captain Charles E Chambers 29 yr old mechanic enlisted 7/19/61 Montgomery **W-thigh, hand & head C 7/5 Greencastle, Pa c***aptured with letters home from several men*

Company C "*Talladega County*"

Captain Walter Taylor 27 year old Wetumpka merchant enlisted 7/15/1861 **C 7/3**
Lt. Henry Pond 29 year old Rockford farmer enlisted 7/15/61 **C 7/3**
Lt. William Crawford 20 year old Rockford farmer enlisted 7/19/1861
Lt. Bailey A. Bowen 27 year Wetumpka mechanic enlisted 7/15/1861
Sgt Hastings Todd 33 year old Burkeville farmer enlisted 7/19/1861
Corp William Lawson 18 year old Burkeville farmer enlisted 7/19/1861
Corp John Speer 23 year old Burkeville farmer enlisted 7/15/1861 **K 7/3**
Private Dixon Adcock 20 year old Wetumpka farmer enlisted 7/19/1861 **K 7/3**
Private Samuel W Biekly (Buckley) 20 yr old enlisted Wetumpka 7/18/61 listed as "absent sick" for 7/1 & 7/3 ???
Private Nicholas Carnochan 21 year old Wetumpka sadler enlisted 4/27/1861
Private Marion Dunlap 22 year old Nixburg farmer enlisted 7/19/1861
Private William Ellis 22 year old Nixburg farmer enlisted 9/17/61
Private George Freeman 19 year old Nixburg farmer enlisted 3/23/1862 **K 7/3**
Private Absalom Harwell 20 year Wetumpka farmer enlisted 7/19/1861 **W/C 7/3**
Private William Harwell 22 year old Wetumpka farmer enlisted 7/19/1861
Private Lloyd Hastie 35 year old Nixburg teacher enlisted 7/19/1861 **W 7/3**
Private Benjamin Johnson 22 year old Fishpond farmer enlisted 3/23/1862 **SW 7/3**
Private John Johnson 21 year old Tallahassee farmer enlisted 7/19/1861
Private William Martin 32 year old Wetumpka farmer enlisted 7/19/1861 **C 7/3**
Private George Mason 25 year old Tallahassee farmer enlisted 7/19/1861
Private Robert Mason 22 year old Tallahassee farmer enlisted 7/19/1861
Private John Maston 22 tear old Wetumpka farmer enlisted 9/15/1861 **C 7/3**
Private Alexander McAllister 22 year old Wetumpka farmer enlisted 7/19/1861 **C 7/3**
Private Riley Owens 19 year old Wetumpka farmer enlisted 7/19/1861
Private Thomas Owens 22 year old Wetumpka farmer enlisted 7/19/1861

Private John Richards 22 year old Nixburg farmer enlisted 7/19/1861 **C 7/3**
Private Theodore Rouse 22 year old Nixburg farmer enlisted 7/19/1861 **C 7/3**
Private William Thompson 24 year old Burkeville farmer enlisted 7/19/1861 **C 7/3**
Private Jacob Vann 24 year old Crops Plain farmer enlisted 7/19/1861
Private George Willbanks 21 year old Equality farmer enlisted 7/19/1861 **C 7/3**
Private Alexander Wright 19 year old Wetumpka farmer enlisted 7/19/1861 **W 7/3**

July 1 Casualties

Corp. Ebenezer P. Ferguson enlisted 7/19/61 Montgomery, Al **W-slightly in hand 7/1**
Private David Bailey enlisted 7/19/61 Montgomery, Al C-Sharpsburg **C 7/1**
Private William H. Bird enlisted 7/19/61 Montgomery. Al **C 7/1**
Private James R. Rodgers 18 yr old enlisted 7/19/61 **C 7/1**

Company D "*Montgomery & DeKalb County*"

2nd Lt Thomas Strong 26 year old Oakfusie farmer enlisted 7/19/1861 **C 7/3**
Private William Armstrong 23 year old Arbacoochee farmer enlisted 6/12/1861
Private James Avery 21 year old Wedowee farmer enlisted 7/19/1861 **C 7/3**
Private Ansel W. Brown 23 yr old enlisted 9/9/61 Randolph Co. Al **W-right arm 7/1 fought on 7/3 C**
Private Jeremiah Dingler 25 year old Fox Creek farmer enlisted 7/19/1861
Private James Goddard 26 year old Arbacoochee minor enlisted 7/19/1861
Private William Hilton 29 year old Wesobulga farmer enlisted 7/19/1861
Private Benjamin Hood 21 year old Fox Creek farmer enlisted 7/19/1861 **C 7/3**
Private John Hood 23 year old Fox Creek farmer enlisted 7/19/1861 **C 7/3**
Private James Howell 23 year old Delta farmer enlisted 7/19/1861 **SW 7/3**
Private William Keith 20 year old Arbacoochee farmer enlisted 9/6/1861 **C 7/3**
Private John Keller 22 year old Arbacoochee farmer enlisted 3/13/1862 **C 7/3**
Private Andrew Ray 23 year old Arbacoochee farmer enlisted 7/19/1861 **C 7/3**
Private Eralbun Reaves 23 year old Wedowee farmer enlisted 7/19/1861 **C 7/3 0-1-0-9**

July 1 Casualties

Captain Algernon Sidney Reaves 22 yr old clerk enlisted Randolph Co. **W 7/1**
1st Lt. Mark W. Kemp 24 yr old physician enlisted as Asst. Surgeon 7/19/61 promoted **W-hip 7/1 C 7/5 Greencastle**
2nd Lt. Elridge W. Reeves 24 yr old enlisted 7/19/61 Montgomery Al. **C 7/1**
Sergeant John Howell 28 yr old enlisted 7/19/61 Randolph Co. **C 7/1**
Sgt. Virgil Hunter—enlisted 7/6/61 Randolph Co Al. **W-slightly in side C 7/1 (later C Spotsylvania)**

Corp. Seaborn H. Dunken 24 yr old enlisted 7/6/61 Randolph Co. **W-head 7/1 C 7/5 (later C Spotsylvania)**
Corp. John N. Moore 25 yr old enlisted 7/19/61 Montgomery Al. **C 7/1**
Private James H. Able 31 yr old transferred from 44 Alabama 5/63 **C 7/1**
Private Henry Bellah 25 yr old enlisted 7/6/61 Randolph Co. Al **W-left lung C 7/1**
Private James V. Harlan 25 enlisted 7/6/61 Randolph Co. Al **C 7/1**
Private Joel Thomas Hatton 23 yr old enlisted 7/6/61 Randolph Co. Al **C 7/1**
Private Thomas N. Howle 35 yr old enlisted 7/6/61 Randolph Co. Al **C 7/1**
Private Samuel P. Kennedy enlisted 7/14/61 Montgomery, Al **C 7/1**
Private Charles Mann 21 yr old enlisted 7/19/61 Montgomery Al. **C 7/1**
Private Joseph Mauk 26 yr old enlisted 7/19/61 Montgomery Al. **C 7/1**
Private Thomas F. McCullough 28 yr old blacksmith enlisted 2/23/63 Randolph Co. **C 7/1**
Private Benjamin J. Shelton 30 yr old enlisted 7/19/61 Montgomery Co. Al. **C 7/1**
Private David C. Stephens 23 yr old enlisted 7/19/61 Montgomery Co. Al. **C 7/1**
Private Matthew Waldrop 24 yr old enlisted 7/19/61 Montgomery Co. Al. **C 7/1**
Private Sebron M. Waldrop 24 yr old enlisted 7/19/61 Montgomery Co. Al. **C 7/1**
Private William York—49 yr old enlisted 9/9/61 Randolph Co. **W-thigh 7/1 C 7/5 Greencastle**

Company E "*Randolph Raiders*"

1st Lt John Dixon Robinson 29 year old Eastville farmer enlisted 7/12/1861 **W/7/3 C 7/5 Greencastle**
2nd Lt Titus McSwain 24 year old Gold Ridge farmer enlisted 7/12/1861 **C 7/3**
Sgt Marcus Herring 21 year old Gold Ridge farmer enlisted 9/16/1861
Private William Brown 34 year old Arbacoochee farmer enlisted 3/1/1863 **W-leg Falling Waters 7/14 C 9/21/63**
Private John Edwards 24 year old Lost Creek farmer enlisted 7/12/1861 **K 7/3**
Private William Eubanks 28 year old Fox Creek farmer enlisted 9/6/1861
Private John Shaffiett 21 year old Eastville farmer enlisted 7/12/1861 **SW 7/3**
Private Ambrose Hanson 29 year old Bowden GA farmer enlisted 7/12/1861 **1-1-1-1**

July 1 Casualties

Sergeant James S. L. Kerr 30 yr old enlisted 7/26/61 Montgomery, Al **C 7/1**
Sergeant William P. Rainey 21 yr old enlisted 7/12/61 Randolph Co. **W 7/1**
Corp. James Mitchell 34 yr old enlisted 7/12/61Randolph Co. **C 7/1**
Private Joseph Alewine 30 yr old enlisted 7/26/61 Montgomery, Al **C 7/1**
Private Wiley J. Bean 40 yr old enlisted 9/3/61 Eastville, Al **C 7/1 died 1/13/64**
Private Benjamin A. Burdett 30 yr old enlisted 7/26/61 Randolph Co. Sgt 1862 demoted **C 7/1**
Private William Burtt 40 yr old enlisted 2/19/63 Randolph Co. **C 7/1**

Private William B. Cagle 35 yr old enlisted 3/8/62 Eastville, Al **W-upper hip 7/1** (Later K Bristoe Station)
Private William Kelley 22 yr old enlisted 7/26/61 Randolph Co **MW 7/1 died 7/25/63**
Private Robert J. Kennedy 31 yr old enlisted 7/26/61 Randolph Co. Al W-Seven Pines **C 7/1**
Private Thomas J. Lovvorn 20 yr old enlisted 7/12/61 Randolph Co. **K 7/1**
Private William F. Lovvorn 24 yr old enlisted 4/12/62 Randolph Co. **C 7/1**
Private Isaac Mitchell 22 yr old 7/12/61 Randolph Co. **C 7/1**
Private John Mitchell 21 yr old enlisted 7/12/61 Randolph Co. **C 7/1**
Private James D. Rodgers 21 yr old enlisted 9/1/61 Randolph Co. **K 7/1**
Private Samuel M. Thompson 18 yr old enlisted 3/6/61 Randolph Co. **W-left shoulder 7/1**
Private William D. White 17 yr old enlisted 2/19/63 Randolph Co. **C 7/1**
Private Thomas J. Wiggins 23 yr old enlisted 2/19/63 Randolph Co. **C 7/1**
Private William Wilson 26 yr old enlisted 3/3/62 Randolph Co **C 7/1**
Private Ezekiel Yancy 19 enlisted 9/1/61 Randolph Co. **C 7/1**

Company F *"Elmore County"*

1st Lt James Simpson 25 year old Tallassee teacher enlisted 7/19/1861 **W head 7/3 at start of advance** almost C 7/14
2nd Lt Robert Ashurst 24 year old Tallassee farmer enlisted 2/26/1862
Sgt Thomas Thompson 29 year old Tallassee farmer enlisted 9/3/1862
Sgt William Castleberry 20 year old Central Institute farmer enlisted 7/19/1861
Private Richard Baker 20 year old Loachopoka farmer enlisted 7/19/1861
Private Jarmony Ballard 26 year old Tallassee farmer enlisted 8/30/1862
Private William Betts 27 year old Equality farmer enlisted 7/19/1861
Private Henry Cooper 20 year old Wetumpka farmer enlisted 7/19/1861 **slight W 7/3**
Private Edward Terrell Griffin 20 year old Tallassee farmer enlisted 9/30/1862 **SW-left arm 7/3 amp. C 7/5**
Private George McKissack 20 year old Tallassee farmer enlisted 7/19/1861
Private Walter Meeks 18 year old Tallassee laborer enlisted 7/19/1861
Private William Owens 29 year old Tallassee farmer enlisted 10/25/1861 **W 7/3**
Private Stephens Price Notasulga farmer enlisted 7/19/1861

July 1 Casualties

Sergeant William G. Baird 22 yr old enlisted 7/19/61 Montgomery, Al **C 7/1**
Sergeant Simeon Wilkie 34 yr old peddler enlisted 7/19/61 Montgomery, Al **C 7/1**
Corp. Francis M. Pope 23 yr old enlisted 7/19/61 Montgomery Co. **C 7/1**
Corp. Jacob L. Williams 44 yr old enlisted 7/19/61 Montgomery, Al **W-knees 7/1**
Private John Baggett 33 enlisted 3/20/62 Nohope Co. Al **C 7/1**
Private Elijah T. Boland 16 enlisted 2/7/62 Montgomery, Al **C 7/1**

Private Hiram H. Britt 22 enlisted 7/19/61 Montgomery, Al C South Mtn 9/14/62 **W-slightly 7/1 C 7/14**
Private James U. Carter 20 enlisted 7/19/61 Montgomery, Al **C 7/1**
Private Benjamin L. Estes 23 enlisted 7/19/61 Montgomery, Al **C 7/1**
Private Hezekiah H. Estes 48 yr old enlisted 6/28/62 Richmond, Va **C 7/1**
Private John F. Fox 22 yr old enlisted 7/19/61 Montgomery, Al **C 7/1 died smallpox 11/19/63**
Private Francis Fuller 20 enlisted 7/19/61 Montgomery, Al C-Sharpsburg **W-leg slightly 7/1**
Private Thomas Galloway 20 enlisted 3/20/62 Monroe Co, Al **C 7/1**
Private Campbell Gems 20 yr old enlisted 7/19/61 Montgomery, Al **C 7/1**
Private John W. Gilbert 18 yr old enlisted 1/5/63 Montgomery, Al **K 7/1**
Private John Hanby 30 yr old enlisted 7/19/61 Montgomery, Al **W-hand slightly 7/1**
Private Elijah C. Hancock 22 yr old enlisted 7/19/61 Montgomery, Al W-Seven Days **C 7/1**
Private John W. Hendricks 20 yr old enlisted 7/19/61 Montgomery, Al **C 7/1**
Private Isaac W. Kennedy 19 yr old enlisted 9/3/62 Montgomery, Al **W lungs 7/1 left at Falling Waters 7/14 died**
Private W.F. Ransom 20 7/19/61 18 yr old enlisted 3/18/63 Montgomery **C 7/1**
Private Joseph Vinyard 20 yr old enlisted 7/21/61 Montgomery Al. **C 7/1**
Private Samuel Walts 26 yr old enlisted 7/19/61, Montgomery Al. **W-hip slightly 7/1**
Private Sylvanius Wilkie 34 yr old peddler enlisted 7/19/61 Montgomery Al. **C 7/1**
Private Wiley H. Wood 22 yr old enlisted 7/21/61 Montgomery **C 7/1**

Deserted
Private James M. Hammock 20 yr old enlisted 7/19/61 Montgomery, Al **deserted 7/1 AM C 7/14 (Old Capitol Prison)**

Company G *"Yancy Guards"*

Captain Robert Cook 23 year old Greenville student enlisted 7/19/1861 **K 7/14**
1st Lt Richard Cook 24 year old Greenville farmer enlisted 7/19/1861
2nd Lt William Glasgow 29 year old Greenville farmer enlisted 7/19/1861 **C 7/3**
Sgt. Henry Roach 25 year old Greenville farmer enlisted 7/19/1861 **W 7/3**
Sgt. David Staggers 25 year old Greenville farmer enlisted 7/19/1861
Cpl. James Cook 19 year old Greenville farmer enlisted 7/19/1861 **C 7/3**
Cpl. Alvin Owen 21 year old Millville farmer enlisted 7/19/1861
Private Evan Ballard 23 year old Greenville farmer enlisted 7/19/1861 **W 7/3**
Private Shadrick Carter 28 year old Raneville farmer enlisted 12/27/1861
Private John Edson 25 year old Greenville farmer enlisted 7/19/1861 **C 7/3**
Private John Halman 18 year old Greenville farmer enlisted 7/19/1861 **SW 7/3**

Private Benjamin Hastings 22 year old Greenville farmer enlisted 7/19/1861
Private William Jackson 21 year old Millville farmer enlisted 7/19/1861 **C 7/3**
Private John Johnson 30 year old Oaky Streak farmer enlisted 7/19/1861
Private Anson Kent 25 tear old Millville farmer enlisted 7/19/1861 **C 7/3**
Private John Lasiter 27 year old Greenville farmer enlisted 7/19/1861 **C 7/3**
Private Nathaniel Long 28 year old Raneville farmer enlisted 7/19/1861
Private William Phillips 26 year old Leon farmer enlisted 7/19/1861 **C 7/3**
Private Jacob W. Pickett 30 year old Greenville farmer enlisted 7/19/1861 **SW / C 7/3 died 7/28/63**
Private William Pitts 26 year old Oaky Streak farmer enlisted 7/19/1861
Private Henry Ridgeway 23 year old Millville farmer enlisted 7/19/1861 **W/C 7/3**
Private Capen Smith 34 year old Greenville farmer enlisted 7/19/1861 **W 7/3**
Private William Terrell 45 year old Millville farmer enlisted 7/19/1861
Private David Trotman 28 year old Raneville farmer enlisted 7/19/1861
Private Thomas Wright 23 year old Milleville` farmer enlisted 7/19/1861 **C 7/3**

July 1 Casualties

Private James C. Harrison 32 yr old enlisted 7/19/61 Montgomery Al **C 7/1**
Private Robert A. Redman 42 yr old enlisted 7/19/61 Montgomery Al **C 7/1**

Company H "*Coosa Mountaineers*"

1st Lt George Callaway 21 year old Weogulfka farmer enlisted 6/17/1861
Sgt Issac Adams 29 year old Rockford mechanic enlisted 3/27/1862
Sgt Moses Adams 22 year old Rockford farmer enlisted 3/2/1862
Cpl Jacob Flournoy 22 year old Travellers Rest farmer enlisted 7/2/1861
Private John Bradley 20 year old Weogulfka farmer enlisted 3/26/1862
Private Milton Bullard 33 year old Sylcauga grocer enlisted 7/2/1861
Private William Connoway 23 year old Travellers Rest farmer enlisted 7/2/1861
Private Francis Conoway 25 year old Travellers Rest farmer enlisted 8/22/1862
Private Thomas Foster 34 year old Rockford farmer enlisted 3/25/1862
Private Mathew Glenn 22 year old Travellers Rest farmer enlisted 7/2/1861
Private Joseph Herren 27 year old Rockford farmer enlisted 3/8/1862
Private William Hoard 22 year old Indian Springs farmer enlisted 3/7/1862
Private William Holmes 22 year old Yeogulfka farmer enlisted 7/2/1861 **C 7/3**
Private Earle Jones 26 year old Yeogulfka farmer enlisted 7/2/1861 **C 7/3**
Private Constantine McDonald 20 year old Rockford farmer enlisted 3/8/1862
Private Raleigh Phillips 22 year old Rockford farmer enlisted 3/2/1862
Private Winburn Terrell 20 year old Rockford farmer enlisted 7/2/1861 **W 7/3**
Private Richard Wood 20 year old Rockford farmer enlisted 7/2/1861

Casualties 7/1

Captain Stephen R. Allison enlisted 7/2/61 Coosa Co. Al **C 7/1**
Sergeant Henry C. Teel 25 yr old enlisted 7/2/61 Coosa, Al **C 7/1**
Corp. William H. Blankenship 23 yr old enlisted 6/29/61 Coosa Co. Al. **W-slightly in head 7/1**
Corp. John B. Brown 35 yr old enlisted 6/29/61 Coosa Co. Al. **C 7/1**
Corp. George S. Gulledge 21 yr old enlisted 7/2/61 Coosa Co. Al. **C 7/1**
Private James A. Allison 23 yr old clerk enlisted 7/8/61 Griffin, Al **W-slightly 7/1 (later C Spotsylvania)**
Private Major Hezekiah Allen enlisted 6/29/61 Coosa Co. Al. **W-slight 7/1 C 7/5 (Chester Hospital)**
Private Young Brown 23 yr old enlisted 6/29/61 Coosa Co. Al. **C 7/1**
Private John S. Dennis 21 yr old enlisted 6/29/61 Coosa Co. Al. C-Sharpsburg **C 7/1**
Private Samuel Deupriest 25 yr old enlisted 6/29/61 Coosa Co. Al. **C 7/1**
Private Henry J. Gilder 26 yr old dentist enlisted 5/12/62 Coosa Co. Al. **C 7/1**
Private George A. Harmon 24 yr old enlisted 7/22/61 Coosa Co. Al. W Sharpsburg **C 7/1**
Private William P. Holmes 32 yr old mechanic enlisted 3/5/62 Coosa Co. C 7/1
Private Nais Kilpatrick 26 yr old enlisted 7/2/61 Coosa, Al **C 7/1**
Private Albert A. Parrish 26 yr old enlisted 7/2/61 Coosa, Al **C 7/1**
Private George W. Sconyers 22 yr old enlisted 3/8/61 Coosa, Al **C 7/1**
Private Harrison Sconyers 22 yr old enlisted 3/21/62 Coosa, Al **C 7/1**
Private Andrew J. Stubbs 25 yr old enlisted 7/2/61 Coosa, Al **C 7/1**
Private Thaddeus W. Wright 32 yr old enlisted 7/2/61 Coosa, Al **C 7/1**

Deserted
Private Eugene Bentley 16 yr old enlisted 2/1/62 Coosa Co. Al. **deserted 6/30 C 7/5 (Greenwood, pa-sic)**
Union records state "left army before it crossed the Mountains captured 7/5" "was going to school in Alabama. Living with uncle when forced to join army"

Company I *"Invincibles"*

2nd Lt. William Ellis 22 year old Roanoke farmer enlisted 7/19/1861 **slightly W 7/3**
Sgt. Thomas Phillips 35 year old Roanoke farmer enlisted 9/23/ 1861
Sergeant William B. Stephens 19 yr old enlisted 7/19/61 Roanoke, Al **K 7/3**
Cpl. David Howe 23 year old Roanoke mechanic enlisted 7/19/1861
Private Elias East 23 year old Roanoke farmer enlisted 7/19/1861 **C 7/3**
Private Thomas East 21 year old Roanoke farmer enlisted 7/19/1861
Private Benjamin Estes 20 year old Roanoke farmer enlisted 9/17/1862

Private Chesley Ford 22 year old Roanoke mechanic enlisted 2/15/1862
Private Francis Garrison 27 year old Roanoke farmer enlisted 10/17/1862
Private James Garrison 24 year old Roanoke farmer enlisted 10/17/1862
Private James Grant 24 year old Roanoke farmer enlisted 7/19/1861 **SW 7/3**
Private Daniel Johnston 23 year old Roanoke farmer enlisted 7/19/1861 **MWC 7/3 died 9/12/63**
Private W.B. Johnston 21 year old Roanoke farmer enlisted 2/22/1862
Private Thomas Knowles 21 year old Roanoke farmer enlisted 4/22/1862 **W 7/3**
Private James Philips 17 year old Roanoke farmer enlisted 9/22/1862

Casualties 7/1

1st Lt. Lawson D. Ford 23 yr old mechanic enlisted 7/19/61 Randolph Co. Al. **C 7/1**
Sergeant Nathaniel G. Johnston 22 yr old enlisted 7/19/61 Randolph Co. **W-severely in left arm C 7/1**
Sergeant Joseph McClendon 23 yr old enlisted 7/19/61 Randolph Co. **C 7/1**
Sergeant Harrington Wood 35 yr old enlisted 7/19/61 Randolph Co. **C 7/1**
Corporal John B. Carlisle 21 yr old enlisted 7/19/61 Montgomery, Al **C 7/1**
Corporal John Reynolds 29 yr old enlisted 7/19/61 Randolph Co. **C 7/1**
Private Judson B. Andrews 22 yr old enlisted 3/4/62 Roanoke, Al. **C 7/1**
Private William W. Andrews 30 yr old enlisted 7/19/61 Montgomery, Al **W-severely in thigh 7/1** (later C Spotsylvania)
Private James M. Clark 23 yr old enlisted 7/26/61 Randolph Co. Al. **C 7/1 died**
Private Green A. Gann 29 yr old enlisted 7/19/61 Roanoke, Al. **C 7/1**
Private Jasper M. Green 28 yr old enlisted 3/5/62 Roanoke, Al. **C 7/1**
Private Nathaniel B. Green 31 yr old enlisted 2/28/62 Roanoke, Al. **C 7/1**
Private William J. Green 34 yr old enlisted 7/19/61 Roanoke, Al. **C 7/1—died**
Private Isaac C. Hendon 27 yr old enlisted 7/19/61 Roanoke, Al. **C 7/1**
Private Wiley B. Henton 34 yr old mechanic enlisted 10/24/62 Randoplh Co. Al. **W-severely in arm 7/1**
Private Nathan L. Hutchens 34 yr old enlisted 7/19/61 Randolph Co. **W-severely in hip 7/1**
Private William B. Johnston 22 yr old enlisted 7/19/61 Roanoke, Al. **C 7/1**
Private John L. Lemmonds 29 yr old enlisted 7/19/61 Roanoke, Al. **C 7/1**
Private Lewis M. Long 28 yr old enlisted 9/25/61 Roanoke, Al. **C 7/1**
Private Jackson W. Mickle 22 yr old enlisted 7/19/61 Randolph Co. **C 7/1**
Private William H. Moon 20 yr old enlisted 7/19/61 Randolph Co. **C 7/1**
Private James B. Phillips 18 yr old enlisted 7/19/61 Randolph Co. **C 7/1**
Private Joseph G. Posey 20 yr old enlisted 7/19/61 Randolph Co. **C 7/1**
Private George Ramsey 22 yr old enlisted 7/19/61 Randolph Co. **C 7/1**
Private John T. Speights 21 yr old enlisted 7/19/61 Randolph Co. **C 7/1**

Company K "*Tom Watts Rebel Men*"

Sgt Jefferson Savage 29 year old Cusseta mechanic enlisted 7/26/1861
Sgt Jesse Savage 20 year old Cusseta farmer enlisted 7/26/1861
Private Otis Owen 20 year old Corn House farmer enlisted 7/26/1861
Private Loftin Reaves 25 year old Corn House farmer enlisted 7/26/1861
Private Thompson Reaves 25 year old Corn House farmer enlisted 7/26/1861
Private John Sharp 20 year old Corn House farmer enlister 10/27/1862 **C 7/3**
Private Joseph Whitaker 21 year old Wedowee farmer enlisted 9/1/1861 **C 7/3**

July 1 Casualties

3rd Lt. William H. Burgess 23 yr old clerk enlisted 5/10/62 Randolph Co. **W C 7/1**
Sergeant Joseph S. Savage 29 yr old carpenter enlisted 7/26/61 **W 7/1**
Private Samuel P. Blackman 23 yr old shoemaker enlisted Randolph Co 7/26/61 **C 7/1** died Typhoid Fever 9/10/63
Private John H. Boyd 26 yr old enlisted 9/10/61 Yorktown, Va **C 7/1**
Private William R. Bryan 22 yr old shoemaker enlisted 7/12/61 Montgomery, Al W-Sharpsburg **C 7/1**
Private E. B. Camp 22 yr old enlisted Randolph Co. Al 8/13/62 **C 7/1**
Private James R. Cline 19 yr old enlisted Randolph Co. Al. 7/26/61 W-Sharpsburg **C 7/1**
Private Felix C. Cunningham 37 yr oldenlisted Randolph Co. Al. 7/26/61 **C 7/1**
Private Burton Hardeman 26 enlisted Randolph Co. Al. 7/26/61 **W-wounded throat & neck 7/1 died 7/20/63**
Private Benjamin F. Parish 25 yr old enlisted 7/26/61 Randolph Co. **C 7/1**
Private Martin V. Parish 22 yr old enlisted 7/26/61 Randolph Co. **C 7/1**
Private James W Ward enlisted 7/26/61 Randolph Co. **C 7/1**
Private M. B. Wiggins 32 yr old enlisted 7/31/61 Randolph Co. **W-slightly 7/1**

FOURTEENTH TENNESSEE REGIMENT

Field & Staff

Colonel McComb 32 yr old Clarksville, TN absent with wounds from Chancellorsville (W Sharpsburg)
Lieutenant Colonel James Lockert 35 yr old. enlisted Clarksville 5/17/61 "Old Ironclad" **W-thighs C 7/3**
Major Milton Morrisenlisted Ft Donelson 5/18/61 on furlough from 2nd Manassas head wounds during Gettysburg campaign

Adjutant William Munford 26 yr old enlisted Clarksville 5/17/61 (later C Wilderness)
Sergeant Major Robert Moore 25 yr old enlisted Clarksville 5/17/61 **W-abdomen 7/1**

Surgeon A.J. Ernoy 23 yr old doctor commissioned 11/62 **C 7/5 with wounded**
Assistant Surgeon Thomas Norfleet enlisted Clarksville 5/17/61 appt 1/14/63 C 7/5 with wounded
Hospital Steward John Gholson 23 yr old enlisted Clarksville appt 3/63 **C 7/5 with wounded**
Hospital Steward A. Prichett enlisted Springfield 5/16/61
Quartermaster Sgt John Barnes Clarksville 5/17/61
Ordinance Dept Henry Garrigus enlisted camp Duncan 5/14/61 W-hand Cedar Run
Ordinance Sergeant James Jenkins Clarksville 5/17/61
Commissary Duty Robert Goosetree (Co A) 26 yr old brickmaker enlisted Camp Duncan 5/14/61
Chief Musician & Regt Bugler Harry Clark 35 yr old enlisted Bristol, TN 7/28/61 (Later C-HR)

209-47 = 162 7/4 (60 men)
Captain Bruce.L. Phillips in command after 7/3 (old Co F Commander)

Company A *"Clarksville, Montgomery County"*

Captain William Thompson (Killed at Chancellorsville)
Sgt Junius Kimble 23 yr old enlisted Camp Duncan 5/14/61
Sgt William Green enlisted Springfield . . . courier for Heth
Cpl. Charles Donoho enlisted Camp Duncan 5/14/61
Cpl. James Kennedy enlisted Camp Duncan 5/14/61 **C 7/3**
Private Jesse Allensworth enlisted Camp Duncan 5/14/61 (courier for Gen Hill)
Private A. Anderson enlisted Camp Duncan 5/14/61 . . . detailed as QM
Private Richard Armistead enlisted Camp Duncan 5/14/61
Private Thomas Barnes enlisted Camp Duncan 5/14/61 (courier for Gen. Archer)
Private Samuel Cryer enlisted Camp Duncan 5/14/61
Private Benjamin Davidson enlisted Camp Duncan 5/14/61 (Ambulance Driver)
Private David Dorris enlisted Camp Duncan 5/14/61 **WC 7/3**
Private Robert Evans enlisted Camp Duncan 5/14/61
Private Theodore Hartman enlisted Camp Duncan 5/14/61 **C 7/3**
Private Christopher Kelly enlisted Camp Duncan 5/14/61
Private William Lester enlisted Camp Duncan 5/14/61 **C 10/8/63**
Private George Lynes enlisted Camp Duncan 5/14/61
Private Cornelius Mehigan enlisted Camp Duncan 5/14/61 **W 7/3**
Private William Nichols enlisted Camp Duncan 5/14/61 **C 7/3**

Private Robert Perryman enlisted Camp Duncan 5/14/61
Private George Rasor enlisted Clarksville TN 5/27/61 **C 7/14**
Private Robert Shackleford enlisted Clarksville TN 5/27/61 **C 7/3 died**
Private Davis Sullivan enlisted Camp Duncan 5/14/61
Private P.S. Waters enlisted canp Duncan **K 7/3**

Teamster Wade Glenn enlisted Camp Duncan 5/14/61

July 1 Casualties

Private Henry Armistead enlisted Big Springs TN 9/1/61 **C 7/1**
Private Francis Barnes enlisted Camp Duncan 5/14/61 **C 7/1**
Private George Grimes enlisted Camp Duncan 5/14/61 **C 7/1**
Private Ben Haskins enlisted Clarksville TN 5/27/61 **C 7/1**

Company B *"Palmyra, Montgomery County"*

Captain Howell Avrit was on furlough but was captured in TN
1st Lt. William Shelby enlisted Clarksville TN 5/27/61 **C 7/14**
2nd Lt William Hicks enlisted Clarksville TN 5/27/61 **WC 7/3 died 8/10 Chester hospital buried PNC**
3 rd Lt Patrick Bateman Ft Donelson 5/18/61 **W 7/3 C 7/5 Greencastle**
Sgt John Fletcher enlisted Clarksville TN 5/27/61 **W right arm 7/3 C 7/3**
Sgt James Hicks enlisted Clarksville TN 5/27/61
Sgt Robert Mockbee enlisted Clarksville TN 5/27/61
Cpl. John Buchanan enlisted Clarksville TN 5/27/61
Cpl. Richard Steele enlisted Camp Duncan 5/14/61
Private John Davis enlisted Clarksville TN 5/27/61
Private William Davis enlisted Clarksville TN 5/27/61
Private Thomas Dunbar Big Springs, Va 8/61 **C 7/3**
Private John Hamlett enlisted Clarksville TN 5/27/61 **C 7/3**
Private Samuel McFalle enlisted Camp Duncan 5/14/61
Private Charles McGan enlisted Clarksville TN 5/27/61 **C 7/3**
Private James Nesbitt enlisted Camp Duncan 5/14/61
Private James Quinn enlisted Clarksville TN 5/27/61
Private William Riley enlisted Camp Duncan 5/14/61
Private Edward Steele enlisted Camp Duncan 5/14/61
Private David Suss enlisted Clarksville TN 5/27/61 **C 7/14 Falling Waters**
Private Sylvanus Trotter enlisted Clarksville TN 5/27/61
Private Cincinatus Wall enlisted Camp Duncan 5/14/61

July 1 Casualties

Cpl. Hamlin Childs enlisted Clarksville TN 5/27/61 **C 7/1**
Private William Broom enlisted Clarksville TN 5/27/61 **C 7/1**
Private John Dicks enlisted Clarksville TN 5/27/61 **C 7 /1**
Private James Myers enlisted Camp Duncan 5/14/61 **C 7/1**
Private Richard Stewart enlisted Clarksville TN 5/27/61 **W 7/1 C 7/5**

Company C "*The Pepper Guards.*" Robertson Co.

Captain James Dale 27 yr old enlisted Springfield, TN 5/16/61 W 2nd Manassas
3rd Lt James Howard enlisted Springfield, TN 5/16/61
1st Sgt Thomas Cornell enlisted Springfield, TN 5/16/61—sick after 7/3
Sgt Cullen Blackburn enlisted Springfield, TN 5/16/61 (later QM)
Sgt Mathew Powell enlisted Springfield, TN 5/16/61
Cpl. Gustavis Brewer enlisted Springfield, TN 5/16/61 **W 7/3**
Cpl. Thomas Simmons enlisted Springfield, TN **W 7/3 died 7/27**
Private George Braden enlisted Springfield, TN 5/16/61 **C 7/14 Falling Waters**
Private Robert Burns enlisted Springfield, TN 5/16/61 **C 7/14 Falling Waters**
Private Charles Cannon enlisted Springfield, TN 5/16/61 **C 7/3**
Private Andrew Coate enlisted Springfield, TN 5/16/61 **WC 7/3**
Private J.H. Chris **WC 7/3 died 7/10**
Private A.W. Christ **W hand C 7/3**
Private Willis Farmer enlisted Shelbyville,TN 5/14/63 **C 7/3**
Private James Fisher enlisted Springfield, TN 5/16/61 **WC 7/3 died**
Private Lewis Glascow enlisted Springfield, TN 5/16/61 **WC 7/3**
Private Edward Kirk enlisted Springfield, TN 5/16/61
Private Benjamin Madole enlisted camp Duncan 5/14/61 **C 7/3**
Private William McDonald enlisted Springfield, TN 5/16/61 **C 7/14 Falling Waters**
Private Robert Murphy enlisted Springfield, TN 5/16/61
Private George Powell enlisted Springfield, TN 5/16/61 **K 7/3**
Private Nicholas Rose enlisted Springfield, TN 5/16/61 **W 7/1 fought & C 7/3**

Teamster James Mitchell enlisted Springfield, TN 5/16/61

July 1 Casualties

Private James Hedley enlisted Springfield, TN 5/16/61 **C 7/1**
Private John Jones enlisted Springfield, TN 5/16/61 **C 7/1**
Private Archer Samuel enlisted Springfield, TN **W arm 7/1**

Company D "*Stewart County*"

Captain Hegler was wounded at Chancellorsville and was in hospital

1st Lt./ Captain John Settle 22 yr old W 2nd Manassas enlisted Fort Donelson **K 7/3**
Sgt Hubbard Carrsey enlisted Dover 5/18/61
Sgt James Moore enlisted Dover 5/18/61 **C 7/3**
Sgt James Noble enlisted Dover 5/18/61
Sgt William Thompson enlisted Dover 5/18/61 **C 7/3**
Cpl. Fountain Lewis enlisted Dover 5/18/61
Cpl. George Sinclair enlisted Dover 5/18/61
Private Jethro Bass enlisted Dover TN 5/18/61 **C 7/14 Falling Waters**
Private John Buckner enlisted Nashville,TN 5/20/61 **C 7/3**
Private James Burns enlisted Dover TN 5/18/61 **C 7/3**
Private James Edwards enlisted Clarksville TN 5/27/61
Private William Hart enlisted Dover 5/18/61 **C 7/3**
Private John Hogan enlisted Dover 5/18/61
Private John Locke enlisted Dover 5/18/61
Private Joshua Pugh Ft Donelson 5/18/61 **C 7/3**
Private Albert Roberts enlisted Nashville 5/20/61
Private Andrew Taylor enlisted Dover 5/18/61
Private Charles Wafford enlisted Dover, Tn 5/18/61 **K 7/3**
Teamster William Hankins Dover, TN 5/18/61
Teamster Elijah Puckett Dover 5/18/61

July 1 Casualties

2nd Lt William Hagler enlisted Dover 5/18/61 **C 7/1**
Private Robert McKinney enlisted Dover 5/18/61 **C 7/1**
Private Edward Moore enlisted Dover 5/18/61 **C 7/1**

Company E "*Stewart County*"

Captain Benjamin Outlaw yr old enlisted Dover, Tn 5/18/61 (later K Petersburg)
2nd Lt Cornelius Crockerall enlisted Camp Duncan **C 7/3**
Sgt John Brigham enlisted Ft Donelson 5/18/61
Sgt William Randle enlisted Ft. Donelson 5/18/61 **C 7/3**
Sgt Samuel Scarborough enlisted Ft. Donelson 5/18/61
Sgt John Wall enlisted Nashville TN **C 7/3**
Cpl. William Bryant enlisted Ft Donelson 5/18/61 **WC 7/3**
Cpl. Abitul Morris enlisted Camp Dungan
Private George Barnes enlisted Ft Donelson 5/18/61 (detailed as Pioneer)

Private Willie Barnes enlisted Ft Donelson 5/18/61
Private William Barnes enlisted Ft Donelson 5/18/61
Private Elliot Bigham enlisted Ft Donelson 5/18/61
Private James Brack enlisted Ft Donelson 5/18/61
Private Thomas Champion enlisted Ft Donelson 5/18/61 **W 7/3** (later pioneer)
Private Colman Clark enlisted Ft Donelson 5/18/61
Private William Clark enlisted Ft Donelson 5/18/61
Private Alan Dunn enlisted Ft Donelson 5/18/61
Private Newton Hamilton enlisted Ft. Donelson 5/18/61 **K 7/3**
Private David Johnson enlisted Ft. Donelson 5/18/61
Private Thomas Kernall enlisted Ft. Donelson 5/18/61 **WC 7/3**
Private Robert King enlisted Ft. Donelson 5/18/61 . . . later sick
Private Thomas Marberry enlisted Ft. Donelson 5/18/61 **C 7/14**
Private Henry McAskell enlisted Ft. Donelson 5/18/61
Private John McAskell enlisted Ft. Donelson 5/18/61
Private William McAskell enlisted Ft. Donelson 5/18/61 **K 7/14/63**
Private John Murphy enlisted Ft. Donelson 5/18/61
Private Dudley Parker enlisted Ft. Donelson 5/18/61 **WC 7/3**
Private Pleasant Parrott enlisted Ft. Donelson 5/18/61
Private James Ray enlisted Ft. Donelson 5/18/61 **C 7/14**
Private George Robertson enlisted Ft. Donelson 5/18/61 **C 7/3**
Private Joseph Shemwell enlisted Ft Donelson 5/18/61 **C 7/3**
Private Thomas Sikes enlisted Ft Donelson 5/18/61 **C 7/3**
Private Joel Smith enlisted Ft Donelson 5/18/61 **C 7/3**
Private John Smith enlisted Ft Donelson 5/18/61
Private Thomas Smith enlisted Ft Donelson 5/18/61
Private William Smith enlisted Ft Donelson 5/18/61 **C 7/3**
Private Milton Spurgin enlisted Ft Donelson 5/18/61
Private William Thompson enlisted Ft Donelson 5/18/61
Private William Vickers enlisted Ft Donelson 5/18/61

Teamster Thomas Fielder enlisted Ft Donelson 5/18/61
Teamster Henry Brake enlisted Ft Donelson 5/18/61 **deserted 8/30/63**

July 1 Casualties

1st Lt. John Largent enlisted Ft. Donelson 5/18/61 W-Fredericksburg **W 7/1 C 7/5 Greencastle, Pa**
Private Augustus Boyd enlisted Ft Donelson 5/18/61 **C 7/1**
Private George Marberry enlisted Ft. Donelson 5/18/61 **sick 7/1 & 7/3**
Private David Parker enlisted Ft. Donelson 5/18/61 **C 7/1**

Company E 14th Tennessee
Captain Benjamin Outlaw Commanding

Company G *"Montgomery County"*

Captain Harry Bullock 27 yr old enlisted Camp Duncan 5/14/61 MW 4/2/65 left shoulder
Sgt Bailey Bowers enlisted Camp-Duncan 5/14/61) (W Chancellorsville)
Sgt James Brantley enlisted camp Duncan 5/14/61
Sgt George Halyard enlisted camp Duncan 5/14/61
Sgt William Randall enlisted Ft Donelson 5/18/61 **C 7/3**
Cpl. William Brantley enlisted camp Duncan 5/14/61
Cpl. William Hogan enlisted camp Duncan 5/14/61
Private Andrew Cherry enlisted camp Duncan 5/14/61
Private John Choate enlisted camp Duncan 5/14/61 **WC 7/3**
Private Columbus Horn enlisted camp Duncan 5/14/61 **W 7/3**
Private Cornelius Horn enlisted camp Duncan 5/14/61
Private Frank Lisonby enlisted Camp Duncan 5/14/61
Private Cordle Norfleet enlisted Camp Duncan 5/14/61 **W 7/14**
Private George Norfleet enlisted Ednay, Va 9/30/61
Private Dudley Parker enlisted Ft. Donelson 5/18/61 **WC 7/3**
Private Pleasant Parrott enlisted Ft. Donelson 5/18/61

Private James Ray enlisted Ft. Donelson 5/18/61 **C 7/14**
Private George Robertson enlisted Ft. Donelson 5/18/61 **C 7/3**
Private William Shepard enlisted camp Duncan 5/14/61 **C 7/3**
Private John Shoat enlisted camp Duncan 5/14/61 **C 7/3**
Private James Smith enlisted camp Duncan 5/14/61
Private Richard Smith enlisted camp Duncan 5/14/61
Pioneer Davis Vickers enlisted Nashville detached as Pioneer 6/63

July 1 Casualties

Sgt Thomas Davidson enlisted camp Duncan 5/14/61 **C 7/1**
Private James Acree enlisted camp Duncan 5/14/61 **C 7/1**
Private Lee Dota enlisted camp Duncan 5/14/61 **C 7/1**
Private Lark Leick enlisted camp Duncan 5/14/61 **C 7/1**
Private Andrew McNeil enlisted Clarksville **C 7/1**
Private Gustauus Norfleet enlisted Camp Duncan 5/14/61 **C 7/1**
Private H.A. Norfleet enlisted Clarksville **C 7/1**
Private William Page enlisted Camp Duncan 5/14/61 **C 7/1**
Private David Parker enlisted Ft. Donelson 5/18/61 **C 7/1**

Company H *"Clarksville, Montgomery County"*

1st Lt. Charles Mitchell enlisted Clarksville 5/23/61
2nd Lt Irwin Beaumont enlisted Clarksville 5/23/61
1s Sgt George Rice enlisted Clarksville 5/23/61
Sgt John Hurst enlisted Clarksville 5/23/61 **C 7/14 Falling Waters, MD**
Private Eugene Anderson enlisted Clarksville 5/23/61
Private Benjamin Ballentine enlisted Clarksville 5/23/61
Private Rolfe Carden enlisted Clarksville 5/23/61 **C 7/3**
Private Michael Caton enlisted Martinsburg 10/62
Private Joseph Chilton enlisted Clarksville 5/23/61
Private Benjamin Coleman enlisted Clarksville 5/23/61 **C 7/14 Falling Waters, MD**
Private James Fields enlisted Camp Duncan C 7/14 **Falling Waters, MD**
Private B.F. Froman enlisted Clarksville 5/23/61
Private Andrew Howell enlisted Clarksville 5/23/61 **WC 7/3**
Private Henry Jackson enlisted Clarksville 5/23/61
Private Benjamin Johnson enlisted Clarksville 5/23/61
Private James Johnson enlisted Clarksville 5/23/61
Private William McCullock enlisted Clarksville 5/23/61 **K 7/3**
Private George Moody enlisted Clarksville 5/23/61
Private Dan Neblett enlisted Clarksville 5/23/61 **W 7/3 C 7/5**

Private J.J. Nicholson enlisted Martinsburg, Va **K 7/3**
Private Robert Pritchett enlisted Clarksville 5/23/61 (lost musket)
Private William Riter enlisted Clarksville 5/23/61
Private Sim Rogers enlisted Clarksville 5/23/61
Private George Spencer enlisted Clarksville 5/23/61
Private John Thomas enlisted Clarksville 5/23/61

Teamster Robert Chiles enlisted Clarksville 5/23/61 **C 7/5**
Ambulance Driver Drew Smith enlisted Clarksville 5/23/61
Cpl. James Braden enlisted Clarksville 5/23/61 ***(Commissary Dept—not in fight)***
Private James Jones enlisted Clarksville 5/23/61 (courier for Hill)
Private Napoleon Leaville enlisted Clarksville 5/23/61 (courier for Hill)
Private Robert McCullock enlisted Clarksville 5/23/61 (clerk for Archer)
Private Thomas McManus enlisted Clarksville 5/23/61 detached butcher

July 1 Casualties

Captain William Moore 25 yr old W 2nd Manassas enlisted Clarksville 5/23/61 **C 7/1**
3rd Lt John Moore 26 yr old enlisted Clarksville 5/23/61 **C 7/1**
Sgt James Ligon enlisted Clarksville 5/23/61 **C 7/1**
Cpl. Daniel Jackson enlisted Clarksville 5/23/61 **C 7/1**
Private Edward Bringhurst enlisted Clarksville 5/23/61 C-Fredericksburg **C 7/1**
Private Thomas Kirby enlisted Clarksville 5/23/61 **C 7/1**
Private James Madison enlisted Clarksville 5/23/61 **C 7/1**
Private Warren Madison enlisted Clarksville 5/23/61 **C 7/1**
Private William Neblett enlisted Clarksville 5/23/61 **C 7/1**
Private James Solomon enlisted Clarksville 5/23/61 **C 7/1**
Private John Spencer enlisted Clarksville 5/23/61 **C 7/1**
Private E.A. Tarrvater enlisted Clarksville 5/23/61 **C 7/1**

Company I *"Robertson County"*

2nd Lt Thomas Gilbert enlisted Springfield TN 5/25/61
3rd Lt William Durrett enlisted Springfield TN 5/25/61
Sgt Horation Petty enlisted Springfield TN 5/25/61 (C-Fred)
Sgt Richard Porter enlisted Springfield TN 5/25/61
Cpl. Robert Baldwin enlisted Springfield TN 5/25/61 **C 7/3**
Cpl. John Hall enlisted Springfield TN 5/25/61 **C 7/3**
Private Thomas Baldwin enlisted Springfield TN 5/25/61 **W 7/3**
Private Galien Benson enlisted Springfield TN 5/25/61 (later C Wilderness)

Private James Dorris enlisted Springfield TN 5/25/61
Private Gilbert Flood enlisted Springfield TN 5/25/61
Private Dan Rogers enlisted Clarksville 5/27/61 **C 7/3**

Teamster William Summerville enlisted Haynesville, TN
Teamster John Maudy enlisted Springfield TN 5/25/61

July 1 Casualties

Private Daniel Durrette enlisted Springfield TN 5/25/61 **C 7/1**
Private Patrick Krisle enlisted Springfield TN 5/25/61 **WC 7/1**
Private James Kiger enlisted Springfield TN 5/25/61 **C 7/1**

Company K *"Montgomery County"*

Captain Thadeus Bowling enlisted Clarksville TN 5/27/61 (W-Chanc)
1st Lt. John Jenkins enlisted Clarksville TN 5/27/61
2nd Lt William Glifton enlisted Clarksville TN 5/27/61
Sgt Hugh Dickson enlisted Clarksville TN 5/27/61 **C 7/3**
Sgt James Bobbitt enlisted Clarksville TN 5/27/61 later sick
Sgt John Randell enlisted Clarksville TN 5/27/61
Cpl. David Herring enlisted Clarksville TN 5/27/61
Private David Blanton enlisted Clarksville TN 5/27/61
Private William Collier enlisted Clarksville TN 5/27/61 **W right thigh C 7/3**
Private William Comperry enlisted Clarksville TN 5/27/61
Private James Crotzer enlisted Clarksville TN 5/27/61 **WC 7/3**
Private William Davis enlisted Clarksville TN 5/27/61
Private Robert Hitt enlisted Clarksville TN 5/27/61
Private John Howard enlisted Nashville TN
Private John Jett enlisted Clarksville TN 5/27/61 (later K Petersburg)
Private Thomas C Jett enlisted Clarsvill;e, TN 5/27/61
Private Drew Marshall enlisted Clarksville TN 5/27/61
Private D. Pierce enlisted Clarksville TN 5/27/61 **K 7/3**
Private Peter Rudolph enlisted Clarksville TN 5/27/61 **WC 7/3**
Private Samuel Small enlisted Clarksville TN 5/27/61
Private George Smith enlisted Clarksville TN 5/27/61

Teamster Matthew Smith enlisted Clarksville TN 5/27/61
Teamster James Smith enlisted Clarksville TN 5/27/61

July 1 Casualties

Private James James enlisted Clarksville TN 5/27/61 **C 7/1**
Private William Moses **C 7/1**
Private John Rogers enlisted Clarksville TN 5/27/61 **C 7/1**
Private Mark Swift enlisted Clarksville TN 5/27/61 **C 7/1**

Company L *"Montgomery County"*

1st Lt. Alexander Collins enlisted Clarksville TN 5/27/61 **W 7/3**
Sgt J.K. Chester enlisted Clarksville TN 5/27/61
Sgt Mack Smith enlisted Camp Duncan 5/14/61 **WC 7/3**
Sgt Harrison Trice enlisted Camp Duncan 5/14/61 **WC 7/14 Falling Waters**
Sgt Henry Trice enlisted Camp Duncan 5/14/61
Cpl. Ephraim Manson enlisted Clarksville TN 5/27/61 **C 7/3**
Cpl. Samuel Taylor enlisted Camp Duncan 5/14/61 **W 7/3**
Private James Butler enlisted Clarksville TN 5/27/61
Private John Dycus enlisted Clarksville TN 5/27/61
Private R.F. Grafton enlisted Clarksville TN 5/27/61 **C 7/14 Falling Waters**
Private Junius Ingram enlisted Clarksville TN 5/27/61
Private Nathan McCormack enlisted Camp Duncan 5/14/61
Private Steve Rives enlisted Camp Duncan 5/14/61 **C 7/3**
Private James Trammill enlisted Fort Donelson
Teamster John Robertson enlisted Clarksville TN 5/27/61
Teamster John Maudy enlisted Clarksville TN 5/27/61

July 1 Casualties

Captain Thomas Herndon enlisted Clarksville TN 5/27/61 **C 7/1**
Cpl. Edward Hewell enlisted Clarksville TN 5/27/61 **C 7/1**
Private James Burnine enlisted Camp Duncan 5/14/61 **C 7/1**
Private John Chester enlisted Clarksville TN 5/27/61 **C 7/1**
Private James Cox enlisted Clarksville TN 5/27/61 **C 7/1**
Private George Riggins enlisted Camp Duncan 5/14/61 **C 7/1**
Private Adam Stark enlisted Clarksville TN 5/27/61 **fought 7/1 nurse 7/3**

SEVENTH TENNESSEE REGIMENT

Lt. Colonel Sam Shepard

Lt. Furgus Harris Co H

Field & Staff "Hurricane Rifles"

Colonel John Amenas Fite 31 yr old enlisted Dekalb Co. grad Cumberland University 1855 Captain Co B promoted Col 4/8/63 wounded three times: Mechanicsville, Cedar Mountain, and Chancellorsville. **WC 7/1**

Lieutenant Colonel Samuel G. Shepard 33 yr old Wilson County framer Captain Company G appt Major 7/9/62

Appt Lt. Col. In command 7/3 reached wall and ran back

Major William Williamson 35 yr old enlisted Greenville Captain Co H W-arm Gaines Mill **W-right arm C 7/3**

Adjutant George Howard enlisted Camp Trousdale 5/30/61 W-scalp—Gaines Mill)(Commanded Regt at Sharpsburg) **C 7/3**

Sergeant Major Samuel Jennings—

Assistant Surgeon James Fite enlisted Nashville 5/20/61

Hospital Steward James Webb

Ordinance Sgt Alexander Piper

Ordinance Guard George Kittrell enlisted Yorktown 4/26/62

Quartermaster Sergeant Rufus McClain (Acting Brigade QM)

Quartermaster Sergeant Holliday Stratton enlisted Yorktown 4/26/62

Commissary Sergeant Walter Atwell enlisted Yorktown 4/26/62

Commissary Sergeant Robert Floyd

Wagon Master D.J. Vaugh (Co I) enlisted Yorktown 4/26/62
Forage Master Jesse Gillespie enlisted Yorktown 4/26/62
Butcher Elmore Roney detailed Commissary Dept 11/20/62
Regimental Sutler James Bradley

Company A *"Alexandria, DeKalb County"*

1st Lt George Cowen enlisted Yorktown 4/26/62 **K 7/3**
2nd Lt Burgess Wilmath enlisted Yorktown 4/26/62
1st Sgt James Winfrey enlisted Yorktown 4/26/62 **K 7/3**
Sgt. John Cheek enlisted Yorktown 4/26/62
Sgt. George Reasonover
Sgt. John Williams enlisted Yorktown 4/26/62 **K 7/3**
Cpl. William Griffin enlisted Yorktown 4/26/62
Private James Abner enlisted Nashville 5/20/61
Private John Close enlisted Yorktown 4/26/62
Private James Donnell enlisted Yorktown 4/26/62 **C 7/3**
Private Alphonse Emerique enlisted Yorktown 4/26/62
Private Francis Foutch enlisted Yorktown 4/26/62 **C 7/3**
Private Levi Foutch
Private James Harris enlisted Yorktown 4/26/62 (later became Chaplin)
Private William Hullet enlisted Yorktown 4/26/62 (later deserted 8/27/63)
Private John Johnson enlisted Yorktown 4/26/62
Private George Lamberson enlisted Yorktown 4/26/62 **C 7/3**
Private John Luck enlisted Yorktown 4/26/62
Private Theodore Moores enlisted Yorktown 4/26/62
Private George Murray
Private John Nix enlisted Yorktown 4/26/62 **C 7/3**
Private William Willaby enlisted Yorktown 4/26/62 **C 7/14** (later died in prison)
Private Wesley Yeargin

July 1 Casualties

Captain John Dowell enlisted Yorktown, Va 4/26/62 **W/C 7/1**
Cpl. Thomas Goodner enlisted Yorktown, Va 4/26/62 **C 7/1**
Private Joab Baileff enlisted Yorktown, Va 4/26/62 **WC 7/1 died 7/7**
Private William Lamberson enlisted Yorktown, Va 4/26/62 **C 7/1**
Private Thomas Sneed enlisted Yorktown, Va 4/26/62 **C 7/1**

Company B *"Smith County"*

Captain John Allen enlisted Nashville 5/20/61 wounded several times **WC 7/3**
1st Lt. Francis Timberlake enlisted Nashville 5/20/61 **WC 7/3**
2nd Lt John Moore enlisted Nashville 5/20/61
2nd Lt John Lapsley (later W Cold Harbor)
Sgt Anthony Apple enlisted Nashville 5/20/61 **C 7/3**
Sgt Charles McClaine enlisted Yorktown 4/26/62 **C 7/3**
Sgt Leonidas Thompson enlisted Nashville 5/20/61 **C 7/14**
Cpl. James Bradley enlisted camp Trousdale
Private Francis Bass enlisted Yorktown 4/26/62
Private Henry Beasley **K 7/3**
Private David Black Camp Trousdale 6/2/61
Private Andrew Blair enlisted Carthage 11/8/62
Private John Bolton enlisted Nashville **C 7/3**
Private William Bolton enlisted Carthage 11/8/62 (later deserted 7/20/63)
Private Andrew Bradley Camp Trousdale 6/2/61 **C 7/3**
Private William Bradley Camp Trousdale **WC 7/3**
Private William Conditt enlisted Nashville 5/20/61
Private Henry Dawson enlisted Nashville 5/20/61
Private Isaac Dawson enlisted Nashville 5/20/61 (later deserted 7/20/63)
Private Samuel Derrickson enlisted Nashville 5/20/61 **C 7/14**
Private Samuel Duke enlisted Nashville 5/20/61 (later deserted 9/18/63)
Private James Hale Camp Trousdale 7/15/61 **C 7/3**
Private John Hale Camp Trousdale 7/15/61
Private John Hall enlisted Nashville 5/20/61 **C 7/3**
Private Branch High enlisted Nashville 5/20/61 **C 7/14**
Private Thomas Hubbard Camp Trousdale **WC 7/3**
Private George Huhes enlisted Nashville 5/20/61
Private William Jarred enlisted Nashville 5/20/61
Private John Johnson enlisted McMannville 4/4/63
Private Richard Johnson Camp T **C 7/14**
Private Samuel King enlisted Nashville 5/20/61 **WC 7/3**
Private John McCall enlisted Nashville 5/20/61 reached wall—ran back (in fight at Falling Waters)
Private William McGee **WC 7/3**
Private George McKenny enlisted Nashville 5/20/61
Private Henry Mitchell enlisted Nashville 5/20/61
Private James Paty enlisted Nashville 5/20/61 **K 7/3**

Private Benjamin Perry
Private Ira Royster enlisted Nashville 5/20/61 **C 7/14**
Private James Sexton enlisted Nashville 5/20/61 (later Deserted 8/4/63)
Private German Shoemaker enlisted Nashville 5/20/61
Private Eleazer Smith enlisted Nashville 5/20/61 (later deserted 8/4/63)
Private Benjamin Thackston enlisted Nashville 5/20/61 **W 7/3**
Private Robert Thompson enlisted Nashville 5/20/61 **C 7/14**
Private Fountain Timberlake enlisted Nashville 5/20/61 **C 7/3**
Private Nathaniel Trimble enlisted Nashville 5/20/61 **C 7/3**
Private Albert Womac enlisted Nashville 5/20/61
Drummer Francis McReeves enlisted Nashville 5/20/61

July 1 Casualties

Private Joseph Hopkins enlisted Carthage 11/8/62 **C 7/1**
Private James Horn enlisted Nashville 5/20/61 **C 7/1**
Private David Lynch enlisted Nashville 5/20/61 **W 7/1 C 7/4**
Private John Patterson enlisted Nashville 5/20/61 **C 7/1**
Private Henry Rison enlisted Nashville **WC 7/1** (died Chester Hospital)

Company C *"Gallatin, Sumner County"*

1st Lt John Fry enlisted Gallatin TN 5/25/61 W-Seven Pines W-Chancellorsville (resigned 9/11/63)
2nd Lt William Baber enlisted Yorktown 4/26/62 (later W-Cold Harbor)
2nd Lt Elijah Boddie enlisted Yorktown 4/26/62 (later C Wilderness)
1st Sgt Oliver Foster enlisted Yorktown 4/26/62 (later Capt C Wilderness)
Sgt James Douglas enlisted Yorktown 4/26/62 (later deserted)
Sgt Balie Jackson enlisted Yorktown 4/26/62 W-Seven Pines **C 7/3** Fort Delaware
Sgt Richard Rutledge enlisted Gallatin 4/24/62 (had Bright's disease dismissed 12/64)
Sgt Thomas Woodall enlisted Yorktown 4/26/62
Sgt Jefferson Lower enlisted Yorktown, Va 4/26/62 **C 7/15 (in hiding)**
Cpl. Julius C. Edwards enlisted Yorktown 4/26/62
Cpl. David Jenett enlisted Yorktown 4/26/62 (later K Mine Run)
Cpl. Thomas Reed enlisted Yorktown 4/26/62 Hospitalized 8/1/62
Cpl. Charles Shaub enlisted Yorktown 4/26/62 **C 7/16**
Private Daniel Branhan enlisted Yorktown 4/26/62 deserted 7/9
Private Thomas Brasmahan enlisted Yorktown 4/26/62 **C 7/3 (at fence) escaped C 7/6**
Private James K.P. Buck enlisted Yorktown, Va 4/26/62 W-leg Seven Pines **C 7/3**
Private Alfred Brown enlisted Yorktown 4/26/62 W-arm Seven Pines absent 8/25/63

Private James Buck enlisted Yorktown 4/26/62 **WC 7/3**
Private Stephen Cantrell enlisted Yorktown 4/26/62
Private Curran J. Clendenning enlisted Yorktown 4/26/62 W-left hip and temple Seven Pines **C 7/3**
Private William Elliot enlisted Yorktown 4/26/62 W-head Seven Pines **W-neck C 7/3**
Private Samuel F. Forbis enlisted Yorktown 4/26/62 W-arm Seven Pines
W-heel 2nd Manassas (later W-head Wilderness)
Private William Kirkpatrick enlisted Yorktown 4/26/62
Private Thomas Lownsbrough enlisted Yorktown 4/26/62
Private Jefferson H. Lowery Hospital Nurse / Baggage Guard deserted 7/11/63
Private Benjamin Rutherford teacher enlisted Yorktown 4/26/62 W-Seven Pines **C 7/3** Fort Delaware—escaped
Private Reuben Searcy enlisted Yorktown 4/26/62
Private Charles J. Shaub enlisted Yorktown 4/26/62 **C 7/16** Falling Waters
Private James Turnage enlisted Yorktown 4/26/62
Private Charles Watkins enlisted Yorktown 4/26/62 W Seven Pines **C 7/3**
Private Henry White a weaver who enlisted 7/15/61 in Gallatin TN deserted 7/11/63 **C** Hagerstown
Private Charles Winham enlisted Yorktown 4/26/62 (later W Mine Run)
Teamster William Taylor enlisted Yorktown 4/26/62 detailed 2/9/62

July 1 Casualties 5

Captain John Elliot enlisted Yorktown 4/26/62 **WC 7/1**
Private Calvin Buck enlisted Yorktown 4/26/62 C 7/1 Fort Delaware—escaped
Sgt Nathan L. Guthrie enlisted Yorktown 4/26/62 W-Gaines Mill **C 7/1**
Private James Clendenning enlisted Yorktown 4/26/62 C 7/1
Private Rufus Hester enlisted Yorktown 4/26/62 **C 7/1** Fort Delaware—died

Company D *"The Harris Rifles"* Wilson County

Captain Marcus Welsh enlisted Nashville (later C Hatchers Run)
1st Lt. James Martin enlisted Yorktown 4/26/62
2nd Lt Andrew Miller
Sgt Robert Irby enlisted Yorktown 4/26/62
Sgt. Romanoff Little enlisted Yorktown 4/26/62 deserted 12/24/763
Sgt William Ralston enlisted Yorktown 4/26/62 **W 7/3 C 7/5**
Sgt John Webster **C 7/3**
Cpl. John Donnell enlisted Yorktown 4/26/62 **C 7/14**
Cpl. Barthomew Stevens enlisted Yorktown 4/26/62
Private John Canary enlisted Richmond 6/11/62 **W 7/3 C 7/5**

Private Ben Carson enlisted Yorktown 4/26/62
Private Samuel Evitts enlisted Yorktown 4/26/62
Private William Evitts enlisted Yorktown 4/26/62
Private Benjamin Ferrill enlisted Yorktown 4/26/62
Private Thomas Hatcher enlisted Nashville 1861 **C 7/3**
Private John Hawkins enlisted Yorktown 4/26/62
Private William Hawkins enlisted Yorktown 4/26/62
Private James Hearn enlisted Yorktown 4/26/62 **C 7/3**
Private Thomas Johnson enlisted Yorktown 4/26/62 **C 7/3**
Private Thomas H. Johnson enlisted Yorktown 4/26/62 (transferred to Teamsters)
Private William Lamkin enlisted Yorktown 4/26/62
Private William McLenden enlisted Yorktown 4/26/62
Private Richard Palmer enlisted Yorktown 4/26/62
Private Luther Ralston enlisted Yorktown 4/26/62
Private James Watkins enlisted Yorktown 4/26/62
Private Andrew Whitehead enlisted Nashville 5/20/61 **C 7/3**
Teamster Solomon Williams

July 1 Casualties

2nd Lt John Carter enlisted Nashville 5/20/61 **C 7/1**
1st Sgt Hart Harris enlisted Nashville 5/20/61 **W 7/1**
Cpl. James Freeman enlisted Nashville 5/20/61 **C 7/1**
Private Richard Hearn enlisted Nashville 5/20/61 **C 7/1**
Private Robert "Rice" Hughes enlisted Yorktown 4/26/62 **W 7/1 C 7/5**

Company E *"Gallatin, Sumner County"*

Captain Robert Miller W-Sharpsburg **W head & leg 7/3**
1st Lt Alexander Hogan enlisted Yorktown 4/26/62 **C 7/14 Falling Waters**
2nd Lt William McCall enlisted Yorktown 4/26/62 "Gallantry-Sharpsburg" **C 7/3**
Sgt Jesse Cage enlisted Yorktown 4/26/62 (later W Petersburg)
Sgt Blackman Dunn enlisted Yorktown 4/26/62 **C 7/3 escaped**
Sgt James Garrett enlisted Yorktown 4/26/62 **W-groin & right knee 7/3**
Sgt John Puckett enlisted Yorktown 4/26/62 W Groveton **WC 7/3**
Cpl. William Clendening enlisted Yorktown 4/26/62 W 2nd Manassas
Cpl. William Garrett enlisted Yorktown 4/26/62 **C 7/3**
Corporal Marcus Hurst enlisted Yorktown 4/26/62 **WC 7/3 died 7/23**
Corp Henry Williams enlisted Yorktown 4/26/62 (later W-Wilderness)
Private Elisha Blackburn enlisted Yorktown 4/26/62 W Chancellorsville (later W Bristoe)
Private Milton Brown enlisted Munnville TN 3/63 **W 7/3**

Private William Cole enlisted Yorktown 4/26/62
Private Daniel Elam enlisted Yorktown 4/26/62
Private John Eidson enlisted Yorktown 4/26/62 **C 7/3**
Private Francis Frazier enlisted Yorktown 4/26/62 W-left knee **C 7/3** died 7/11
Private George Frazier W Shepardstown (later W Wilderness)
Private George Freeman enlisted Yorktown 4/26/62
Private Henry Graves enlisted Yorktown 4/26/62 (later Sgt)
Private James Gray enlisted Yorktown 4/26/62 W-breast Sharpsburg **W 7/3 C 7/5**
Private John Idson enlisted Yorktown 4/26/62 **C 7/3**
Private W.G. Keeoph enlisted Yorktown 4/26/62 **C 7/3**
Private Hugh Kirkpatrick enlisted Yorktown 4/26/62 **C 7/14**
Private William A. Kirkpatrick enlisted Yorktown 4/26/62 W-Seven Pines **C 7/3**
Private H.A. Kirkpatrick enlisted Yorktown 4/26/62 **C 7/14/ Falling Waters**
Private William Lewis enlisted Yorktown 4/26/62 **C 7/14**
Private Joseph Love enlisted Yorktown 4/26/62 **WC 7/3 died**
Private William Matherly enlisted Yorktown 4/26/62 **C 7/3**
Private James Montgome enlisted Yorktown 4/26/62
Private Francis Williams enlisted Yorktown 4/26/62
Private James Williams enlisted Yorktown 4/26/62 (later K Weldon RR)
Private Joseph Williams **C 7/3**
Private Charles Wilson enlisted Yorktown 4/26/62 **C 7/3**
Teamster John Cage Wagon Master (later Captain Quartermaster)
Teamster Jesse Gillespie detailed as Forage Master 3/3/63
Teamster George Hamilton enlisted Yorktown 4/26/62 **C 7/7/63 (on retreat)**
Teamster Faustulus Hughes enlisted Yorktown 4/26/62 W Groveton detailed 6/17/63

July 1 Casualties

Private William Keopf enlisted Yorktown 4/26/62 **C 7/1**
Private William Matterly enlisted Yorktown 4/26/62 **C 7/1**

Company F *"The Statesville Tigers"* Wilson County

Captain Asaph Hill enlisted Nashville 5/20/61 as Sgt Major
W Gaines Mill, Antietam, Berryville **K 7/3—grapeshot breast died 7/8**
1st Lt John Sloan enlisted Yorktown 4/26/62
2nd Lt Thomas Jennings **WC 7/3**
Sgt John Jennings enlisted Yorktown 4/26/62 W-Sharpsburg **C 7/3**
Sgt John Lanier enlisted Yorktown 4/26/62
Cpl. John Keaton enlisted Yorktown 4/26/62 **C 7/3**
Cpl. Abner Watt

Private Richard Coley enlisted Yorktown 4/26/62
Private James Craft enlisted McMunwell 3/63
Private George Dunn
Private Gideon Jennings **C 7/3**
Prtivate Archibald Johnson enlisted Yorktown 4/26/62 **C 7/3**
Private William Ragain enlisted McMinnville, TN 3/12/63 **C 7/3**
Private Thomas Sullivan enlisted Yorktown 4/26/62
Private Jeremiah Turner enlisted Yorktown 4/26/62
Private Robert Whitlock enlisted Yorktown 4/26/62

July 1 Casualties

None

Company G "*Hurricane Rifles*" Wilson County

Captain William Graves enlisted Yorktown 4/26/62 **W 7/3**
1st Lt Newton Jennings *W-right shoulder Fredericksburg (on furlough)*
1st Sgt William Baird enlisted Yorktown 4/26/62 **K 7/3**
Sgt George Huddleson enlisted Yorktown 4/26/62
Sgt Thomas Jackson enlisted Yorktown 4/26/62
Sgt Richard Vaugh enlisted Yorktown 4/26/62 **W 7/3 C 7/5**
Cpl. Ben Curray enlisted Yorktown 4/26/62
Cpl. Richard Queensbury enlisted Yorktown 4/26/62
Cpl. Thomas Sullivan enlisted Yorktown 4/26/62
Private Hartwell Birdshaw enlisted Yorktown 4/26/62 **WC 7/3** died 7/15
Private John Curray enlisted Yorktown 4/26/62
Private Andrew Foster **W 7/3 C 7/6**
Private James Grissom enlisted Yorktown 4/26/62 **K 7/3 after retreat by artillery**
Private William Harrison enlisted Yorktown 4/26/62
Private John Hawks enlisted Yorktown 4/26/62
Private Edward Hide enlisted Yorktown 4/26/62 deserted 7/16/63
Private Medicus King enlisted Yorktown 4/26/62
Private Peter Lannon
Private John Nelson enlisted Yorktown 4/26/62
Private James Olliver enlisted Yorktown 4/26/62
Private William Olliver enlisted Yorktown 4/26/62
Private Luke Roberson enlisted Yorktown 4/26/62
Private John Roberts enlisted Yorktown 4/26/62 **K 7/3**
Private George Sims enlisted Yorktown 4/26/62

July 1 Casualties

2nd Lt William Robbins enlisted Yorktown 4/26/62 C 7/1
3rd Lt John Ingram enlisted Yorktown 4/26/62 **W 7/1 C 7/4**
Private William Allen enlisted Nashville 5/21/61 C 7/1
Private William H Harrison enlisted Yorktown 4/26/62 **K 7/1**
Private John Kennedy enlisted Nashville 6/1/61 **C 7/1**

Company H *"The Grays"* Wilson County

Captain William Tate enlisted Yorktown 4/26/62 **shocked during bombardment / recovered by evening**
3rd Lt. Fergusen Harris enlisted Yorktown 4/26/62 (made it to the road) **W-head & foot 7/3** sick 7/4/63
Sgt John Hamilton enlisted Yorktown 4/26/62 **C 7/3**
Sgt John Williamson enlisted Yorktown 4/26/62
Cpl. Ben Alexander enlisted Nashville 5/20/61 **C 7/3 (later Captain)**
Private Winfield Eatherly recruited at Shiloh, TN 4/26/62
Private David Hamilton enlisted Yorktown 4/26/62
Private Joseph Hamlton enlisted Nashville 5/20/61
Private John Harlin enlisted Yorktown 4/26/62
Private Thomas Holloway **K 7/3**
Private Thomas King enlisted Yorktown 4/26/62
Private Robert Lindsay enlisted Yorktown 4/26/62
Private Wilburn Morris QM Department (handicapped)
Private John Ruitland enlisted Yorktown 4/26/62 **C 7/3**
Private Rolando Swain
Private William Wade enlisted Yorktown 4/26/62 **C 7/3**
Private John Williams enlisted Yorktown 4/26/62 **C 7/5**
Private Robert Womack enlisted Yorktown 4/26/62 **W right arm 7/3**
Private Roger Word enlisted Yorktown 4/26/62
Pioneer James Hibbs

Clerk for major Vick William Wharton
Drummer recruited at Camp Gregg 6/63
Teamster Samuel Alexander enlisted Nashville 5/20/61

July 1 Casualties

Sgt John Miller enlisted Yorktown 4/26/62 **C 7/1**
Sgt Lewis Westbrook enlisted Yorktown 4/26/62 **C 7/1**
Private William Hewgley enlisted Yorktown 4/26/62 **C 7/1**

Company I *"The Silver Spring Guards"* Wilson County

Captain James Oren Bass (25) enlisted Yorktown 4/26/62
2nd Lt Thomas Clemens (22)
1st Sgt Jesse Jennings (24)
2nd Sgt John Jennings (21) **W 7/3** carried off
3rd Sgt William Young (22) enlisted Yorktown 4/26/62
4th Sgt John Clemens (24) (later W Petersburg)
1st Cpl. Peter Bashaw (27) enlisted Yorktown 4/26/62 **W 7/3 C 7/5**
4th Cpl. Brad Anderson (22) enlisted Nashville 5/20/61 **WC 7/3** near stone wall
Private Clint Anderson (27)
Private. Orrin Anderson (27) enlisted Nashville 5/20/61 **WC 7/3** near stone wall
Private Frank Bass (28)
Private James Criswell (20) enlisted Yorktown 4/26/62
Private Robert Criswell Y enlisted Yorktown 4/26/62
Private Turner Criswell (29)
Private John Eatherly (19) enlisted Yorktown 4/26/62 **K 7/3** near stone wall
Private Martin Eatherly (23) enlisted Yorktown 4/26/62 **K 7/3**
Private Issac Griffin enlisted Yorktown 4/26/62
Private George Guire enlisted Yorktown 4/26/62
Private William (Pos) Gwynn (27) enlisted Yorktown 4/26/62 deserted 9/15/63
Private Joseph Hamblin enlisted Yorktown 4/26/62
Private George Hellums enlisted Yorktown 4/26/62
Private Clem Jennings (24) enlisted Yorktown 4/26/62
Private James Jetton enlisted Yorktown 4/26/62
Private William Johnson 23 yr old enlisted Yorktown 4/26/62 **K 7/3**
Private Charles Lane enlisted Yorktown 4/26/62 **WC 7/3** near stone wall
Private William Orgain sick 8/4/63
Private William Parker enlisted Yorktown 4/26/62 sick 8/1/63
Private Sion Peak (27) enlisted Nashville 5/20/61
Private Ben Sullivan enlisted Yorktown 4/26/62
Private John B Vivrett enlisted Yorktown 4/26/62
Private Rufus Vivrett enlisted Yorktown 4/26/62
Private Albert Wilkinson **W 7/3**
Private James Walpole **WC 7/3** near the wall

Musician Enos Jennings

July 1 Casualties

Private John Robinson enlisted Yorktown 4/26/62 **C 7/1**
Private Eli Smith enlisted Yorktown 4/26/62 **WC 7/3**
Private John Sullivan enlisted Yorktown 4/26/62 **W 7/1**

Company K *"The Blues"* Wilson County

Captain Archibald Norris enlisted Nashville 5/20/61
1st Lt Martin Beard enlisted Nashville 5/20/61 **C 7/3**
2nd Lt David Phillips **C 7/3**
3rd Lieutenant Mitchell Anderson enlisted Nashville 5/20/61 **K 7/3**
Sgt William Cato enlisted Yorktown 4/26/62
Cpl. William Lane enlisted Yorktown 4/26/62
Private Robert Anderson enlisted Nashville 5/20/61 **C 7/3**
Private Ales Benson enlisted Yorktown 4/26/62
Private Charles Brandon enlisted Yorktown 4/26/62 **C 7/3**
Private William Clemens enlisted Yorktown 4/26/62
Private John Drake enlisted Yorktown 4/26/62 **C 7/14**
Private William Griffin enlisted Yorktown 4/26/62
Private William Johnson enlisted Yorktown 4/26/62 **C 7/3**
Private John Lane enlisted Yorktown 4/26/62 **W 7/3 C 7/5**
Private John R Lane
Private James martin enlisted Yorktown 4/26/62
Private James H Marbrey enlisted Nashville 1861 **K 7/3**
Private James Moxley **W 7/3** died 7/16
Private John Nettle enlisted Yorktown 4/26/62
Private Joseph Palston
Private John Powell
Private Daniel Riggan enlisted Yorktown 4/26/62
Private James Seat enlisted Yorktown 4/26/62 **W 7/3 C 7/5**
Private James Smert sick 8/63
Private William Sneed enlisted Yorktown 4/26/62
Private James Tarpley enlisted Yorktown 4/26/62 (later C Wilderness)
Private Thomas Tinsbloom enlisted Yorktown 4/26/62 (later C Wilderness)

Drummer Chris Raney
Pioneer John Reed enlisted Nashville 5/20/61

July 1 Casualties

Sgt Henry William enlisted Yorktown 4/26/62 **C 7/1**
Sgt James Woodland enlisted Yorktown 4/26/62 **C 7/1**
Private Henry Forbis enlisted Yorktown 4/26/62 **C 7/1**
Private Thomas Johnson enlisted Yorktown 4/26/62 **C 7/1**

Captain John Allen (Co B), General William McComb & Captain Furgus Harris (Co H)

FIFTH ALABAMA BATTALION

Field & Staff

Major A.S. Van de Graaff—31 yr old enlisted Sumter Co, AL 5/26/61 w Gaines Mill / Fredericksburg **C 7/3** (Captain of Co A at start of war)

Sergeant Major Baker Roberts enlisted Sumter, AL 5/26/61 appointed 4/12/62

Assistant Surgeon William Pearson enlisted 3/13/62 Sumter, AL as Private appointed 1/63

Assistant Surgeon Issac Pearson 24 yr old enlisted as Private Sumter, AL promoted 3/5/62

Assistant Surgeon A.D. Hamilton enlisted Orange Court House, Va appointed 6/16/62

Hospital Steward John Turk enlisted Calhoun, AL 3/4/61

Assistant Quarter Master Richard McCormack enlisted Sumter Co AL 5/25/61 w-2nd Manassas

Commissary Sergeant William Frierson Fulton (memoirs) 22 yr old enlisted Sumter Co AL (later Lt)

Company A *"The North Sumter Rifles"*

Recruited in Sumter County Alabama in the Spring of 1861. Trained for two months then sent to Richmond, Va. Present at the first battle of Manassas as artillery unit.

Captain Wade Ritter enlisted 5/26/61 Sumter, Al 3rd LT to Capt 9/4/62 (later commanded battalion)

1st LT Bowling Branch enlisted Sumter, Al 5/26/62 Corp to 2nd Lt to 1st LT

2nd LT Charles Dennison born NYC moved to Chicago then Alabama enlisted **W/C 7/3 (deserted)**

Sgt Thomas Ormond enlisted 5/26/61 Sumter, Al

Sgt. Thomas White enlisted 7/10/61 Manassas, Va C Chancellorsville **W-thigh C 7/3** (later 1st Sgt)

Corp Taylor Bradshaw enlisted Sumter Co, Al 5/21/61

Corp James Long enlisted Gainesville, AL (later Sgt)

Private Joseph Barnes enlisted Manassas, Va 7/28/61 w 2nd Manassas

Private Milledge Braley enlisted Sumter Co, Al 5/26/61

Private George Boyd enlisted Gainesville, Al 5/26/61

Private James Bradshaw enlisted Gainesville, Al 5/21/61

Private Albert Brunson enlisted Mobile, Al 5/25/61 **W/C 7/3**

Private William Cashman enlisted Mobiloe, Al 5/25/61

Private Leonidas Clary enlisted Mobile, AL 8/20/61 **W 7/3**

Private Patrick Caffney enlisted Mobile, Al 6/26/61 **C 7/3**

Private Peter Clark enlisted Sumter Co, Al 8/20/61
Private Francis Crooks enlisted Gainsville, Al 8/20/61
Private George Denton enlisted Sumter C, Al
Private Issac Denton enlisted Sumter, Al 5/26/61 acting Sgt Major 1/63
Private John Dornan enlisted Mobile AL 6/25/61 **W right leg / side C 7/3**
Private William Frost enlisted Sumter Co, Al 5/25/61
Private William Fulton enlisted Sumter Co, Al 5/26/61 (later Lieutenant)
Private John Freeman enlisted Mobile Al 5/25/61 W Gaines Mill
Private Thomas Gilbert enlisted Sumter Co Al W Gaines Mill (carried flag back to road)
Private John Holloway enlisted Sumter Co, AL 6/23/61 W Gaines Mill
Private John Hadley enlisted Sumter Co, AL 6/12/61 W Cedar Mtn (later courier)
Private Oscar Hadley enlisted Gainsville, Al 3/13/62 (later Ord Sgt)
Private Peter Hart enlisted Mobile, Al 5/25/61 **W 7/3**
Private Jesse Hutchins enlisted Livingston, Al 4/5/61
Private William Ivy enlisted Sumter Co 5/26/61 (lost bayonet in charge)
Private Lucian Jones enlisted Gainsvuille 3/13/62 **C 7/3**
Private W. Bolivar Jones enlisted Gainsville, Al
Private Noah Little enlisted Sumter Co, Al 5/26/61
Corp James Long enlisted Sumter Co, Al 5/26/61 (later Sgt)
Private William Long enlisted Sumter Co, Al 5/26/61 **W 7/3**
Private John Moore enlisted Sumter Co, Al 5/16/61 (later Cm Sgt)
Private Samuel Moore enlisted Mobile, AL 5/26/61
Private Barney McDevitt enlisted Mobile, AL 5/26/61
Private Charles Myers enlisted Mobile, AL 3/1/61 (lost bayonet)
Private Robert Markham enlisted Mobile, AL 3/10/61
Private John Ormond enlisted Sumter Co, AL 5/26/61 (later Corp)
Private Willis Peel enlisted 5/26/61 Sumter. Al (sometimes teamster) **C 7/3**
Private Thomas Robertson enlisted 5/26/61 Sumter, Al **C 7/3**
Private James Tureman enlisted Sumter Co, AL 5/26/61 **W-shoulder 7/3 C 7/5**
Private Alexander Watt enlisted 5/26/61 Sumter, Al
Sgt (Wagon Master) Young Harris enlisted Gainesville, Al 8/26/62
Teamster Chares Dunning enlisted Gainesville, Al 3/26/61
Teamster Benjamin Little wagon master
Private Thomas Long enlisted Gainesville, AL 5/26/61 detached as courier for General Archer

July 1 Casualties

Private Thomas Barnes enlisted 5/26/61 Sumter, Al W-Peninsula **W 7/1 leg C 7/5**
Private Wesley Cole enlisted Sumter Co, AL 8/20/61 **W 7/1**
Private Columbus Worley enlisted 3/14/61 Gainesville, Al **SW-leg (amp) 7/1 C 7/5**

Company B *"Calhoun Sharpshooters"*

Recruited in Jacksonville, Alabama in August 1861. Trained and then traveled to Virginia to join Battalion.

1st Lieutenant John Robertson enlisted 8/19/61 Calhoun, Al **W 7/3 C 7/5 (died 7/9/63)**
1st Sgt David Turner enlisted Calhoun. AL 8/19/61 **W-shoulder/C 7/3**
Sgt John Dinnan enisted Calhoun, Al **K 7/3**
Sgt James Crow enlisted Calhoun, Al 8/19/61 **W 7/3**
Sgt John Denman enlisted Calhoun, Al 8/19/61 **K 7/3**
Sgt Wilburn Denman enlisted Calhoun, Al 8/18/61 **W 7/3**
Corp George Matthews enlisted Calhoun, AL 8/10/61 **C 7/3**
Corp. David Pollard enlisted 3/31/61 Calhoun, Al **W foot 7/3**
Private William Anderson enlisted Calhoun, Al 8/18/61
Private Asbury Beal enlisted Calhoun, Al 8/19/61
Private Martin Beal enlisted Calhoun, Al 8/19/61
Private James Bishop 38 yr old enlisted Calhoun, Al W-Cedar Mtn. **W-back C 7/3**
Private Jackson Bonds 19 yr old enlisted Calhoun, Al 3/4/62 W-hand Fredericksburg
Private John Black enlisted Calhoun, Al 3/4/62 **K 7/3**
Private Augustus Bryant enlisted Calhoun, Al 8/19/61 (later Corp—Sgt)
Private John Bullock enlisted Calhoun, Al 8/19/61 **W-right hip 7/3 C 7/5**
Private Patrick Bond enlisted Calhoun, Al 8/26/61 **WC 7/3**
Private Wyatt Chadwick enlisted Calhoun, Al 3/13/62
Private Jackson Chandler 26 yr old enlisted Calhoun, Al 3/13/62 **WC 7/3**
Private Reuben Craft enlisted Calhoun, Al 8/19/61 W-Mechanicville
Private John Dial enlisted Calhoun, Al 8/19/61
Private Phillip Humphries enlisted Calhoun, Al 8/10/61
Private William Hollingsworth enlisted Calhoun, Al 8/26/61
Private William Hill enlisted Calhoun, Al 8/19/61
Private Edward Henson 25 yr old enlisted 3/13/62
Private Charles Hudgins enlisted Mobile, Al 3/10/62
Private William Goins 19 yr old enlisted Calhoun, Al 3/2/62
Private Thomas Johnson enlisted Calhoun, Al 8/19/61
Private Thomas Kirkpatrick enlisted Calhoun, AL (later Corp)
Private Thompson Lambert enlisted Calhoun, AL 6/19/61 **C 7/3 died**
Private Alexander Logan 27 yr old enlisted Oxford, AL 3/19/62
Private John Martin enlisted Calhoun, AL 8/10/61 (later Sgt)
Private Thomas Martin enlisted Calhoun,AL 8/19/61 **W 7/3 C 7/5**
Private Benjamin Manning enlisted 3/31/61 Oxford, Al (held flag—killed) **K 7/3**
Private George Manning enlisted 3/31/61 Oxford, Al
Private Pleatus McCaghren 20 yr old enlisted Oxford, MS 3/18/62
Private William McCaghren enlisted Oxford, Oxford, MS 8/26/61
Private John McCollum enlisted Calhoun, AL 8/26/61

Private Benjamin Mount enlisted Calhoun. AL 8/19/61 (later detached amb corps)

Private Richard Mount enlisted Calhoun, AL 8/19/61 C-Sharpsburg (later detached amb corps)

Private Thomas Owens enlisted 8/19/61

Private James Porter enlisted 4/26/61 Montgomery, Al **SW-fractured left radius 7/3**

Private William Ripley enlisted 3/3/62 Calhoun, Al **left sick as nurse c 7/5**

Private Augustis Spraggins enlisted Calhoun, AL 2/6/63 W/C 7/3

Private Francis Vincent enlisted Calhoun, AL 8/19/61 W 2nd Manassas

Private James White enlisted 8/19/61 Calhoun, Al C 9/7/62

Private Daniel Wilson enlisted 8/10/61 Calhoun, Al W-Fredericksburg **C 7/5 stayed with wounded brother 2nd LT**

Private Francis Witt enlisted 8/19/61 Calhoun. Al later detached Ambulance Corps

Blacksmith Thomas Dickson enlisted Calhoun, Al 8/10/61

Wagon Master Elihu Griffin enlisted Calhoun, Al 8/19/61 **WC 7/3**

Teamster Gabriel Griffin 21 yr old enlisted Calhoun, Al 3/12/62 **C 7/5**

Drummer Thomas Sullivan enlisted Calhoun, AL 2/18/63

July 1 Casualties

Captain A.N Porter enlisted 8/19/61 Calhoun, Al W-Fredericksburg **W 7/1**

2nd LT James Wilson enlisted 8/19/61 Calhoun, Al **W 7/1**

Private Duncan Bartlett enlisted Mobile, Al; 5/28/61 **W 7/1**

Private John Borlash enlisted 8/19/61 Calhoun, Al medal of honor Chancellorsville **W 7/1**

Company C *"The White Plains Rangers"*

Recruited in Calhoun County, Alabama. Shipped to Richmond and joined battalion at Dumfries, Va.

Captain James Reese enlisted 9/3/61 White Plains, Al—sick during campaign

1st Lt William Clay enlisted White Plains 3/20/62

2nd Lt Walter Bray enlisted Calhoun, Al 9/2/61

Sgt John Clay enlisted Calhoun, Al 9/3/61 (appt Sgt. 7/1/63)

Sgt Abraham Green enlisted Calhoun, Al 9/3/61 (appt 7/1/63)

Sgt George Williams enlisted 9/3/61 Calhoun **K 7/3**

Sgt William Cambron enlisted Calhoun Co 9/3/61

Corp. William Glenn enlisted White Plains 9/3/61

Corp. Thomas Morgan enlisted 3/6/61 White Plains, Al **C 7/3**

Corp David Smith enlisted Calhoun, AL 9/3/61

Private James Alred enlisted White Plains

Private Wade Andrews enlisted 9/3/61 White Plains, Al (ambulance driver—called up) **C 7/3**

Private James Bishop enlisted Calhoun Co, Al W-shell fragment in back 7/3

Private John Bullock enlisted 8/10/61 Calhoun Co. Al (takes flag—shot) **WC 7/3**
Private Bannister Burns enlisted 9/3/61 Calhoun Co. Al. (later Teamster)
Private B.J. Chandler enlisted Calhoun Co 9/3/61
Private Harrison Gibson enlisted Calhoun 9/3/61
Private John Grubbs enlisted White Plains (later Ambulance Driver)
Private W.R. Hilburn enlisted White Plains 3/8/62 **WC 7/3**
Private Charles Isham enlisted Calhoun, AL 9/3/61 **C 7/3**
Private Alexander Jones enlisted White Plains. AL 9/13/61 **W 7/3**
Private William Morgan enlisted 3/6/62 White Plains, Al **C 7/3**
Private David Mount enlisted 3/6/62 White Plains, Al **C 7/3**
Private Robert Murray enlisted 9/3/61 Calhoun Co. Al **WC 7/3**
Private Francis Newton enlisted 9/3/61 White Plains, Al **C 7/3**
Private Jasper Steadman enlisted Calhoun, AL 9/3/61
Private Newton Steadman enlisted Calhoun, AL 9/3/61
Private William Smith enlisted 9/3/61 White Plains, Al
Private Joseph Thomas enlisted 9/3/61 White Plains, Al **C 7/3**
Private C.H. York enlisted 9/3/61 White Plains, Al **W 7/3**

Ambulance Driver Private Henry Hilburn enlisted White Plains, Al 9/3/61
Teamster Wesley Burns enlisted White Plains 9/3/61
Teamster Levi Vice (Reserve Ordinance Train) enlisted Calhoun, AL 9/3/61

July 1 Casualties

Private W.G. Canibrow enlisted 9/3/61 White Plains, Al **W 7/1**
Private D.J. McClellan 3/20/62 White Plains, Al **W 7/1 (later Corp)**
Private Robert Yarbourgh enlisted 9/3/61 Calhoun, Al **W 7/1**

Post War Reunion of Fifth Alabama Battalion

First Brigade Second Division Third Corps

Army of Northern Virginia
Commanded July 1 Brigadier General James Pettigrew
Commanded July 3 Colonel James Marshall

Assistant Adjutant General—Captain Nicholas Collins Hughes 23 years old UNC **W hip & spine 7/1 died 7/15**

Assistant Inspector General—Captain W.W. McCreery 26 year old West Point graduate **K 7/1 "bullet through the heart"**

Buried Oakwood Cemetery Raleigh NC

Aide-de-Camp—Lieutenant Louis G. Young 30 years old Grahamville, SC **W-three times 7/1-7/3**

Volunteer Aide-de-Camp—Lieutenant William Blount Shepard 19 years old Elizabeth City NC

Ordinance Officer—Lieutenant Walter Henderson Robertson 22years old Amelia, Va—UVA **W-left leg 7/1**

Quarter Master—Major George Pumpelly Collins 27 years old—NYC

Commissary of Substance—Major William J. Baker 47 year old Gates Co, NC St. Mary's College—banker

Courier Private George Freeman (7th Tennessee Co E)

FIFTY SECOND NORTH CAROLINA REGIMENT

Private Drury Wall Co D

Lt. Romulus Cox Co K

Field & Staff

Colonel James Keith Marshall (commanding Brigade) 24 yr old VMI graduate, teacher enlisted Edenton NC. Captain Co. M 1st NC appointed Colonel 52nd NC 4/23/62 **K 7/3**

Lieutenant Colonel Marcus Parks Captain Co. F appointed major 4/18/62 appointed Lt. Col 4/25/62 **W-both thighs C 7/3**

Major John Richardson 27 yr old appointed Major 4/29/62 "Killed instantly by rifle ball while leading left wing **K 7/3**

Adjutant John H. Robinson 26 yr old Raleigh merchant 2nd Lt. Co B appointed Adjutant 3/16/63

Sergt Major Robert G Baines Sgt Co.K promoted 9/62 **W knee& hand C 7/3 died 7/13**

Aide de camp Captain N.C. Hugh

Surgeon James Foulkes Captain Co B appointed 9/26/62

Assistant Surgeon William H Lilly 30 yr old physician enlisted Montgomery Co. appointed 9/26/62

Chaplin James Cline Methodist Episcopalian appointed 7/11/62 resigned 8/24/63

Assistant Quartermaster John Gatling 2nd Lt. Co C appointed 12/2/62

(later Brigade Asst. QM)

Commissary Sergeant Henry Clay Turner Sgt. Co I appointed 5/1/62

Ordinance Sergeant Thomas Richardson enlisted Camp Johnson 7/5/62 as private Co C appointed 9/62

Company A *"Cabarrus Riflemen"*

Captain John Alexander 35 yr old Cabarrus Co. tailor **W-right arm 7/3**
1st Lt James M. Cook previously Sgt in 20th NC **K 7/3**
2nd Lt Alexander Hurley 36 yr old Cabarrus Co sheriff enlisted 3/21/62 **W-head 7/3**
3rd Lt Joseph Hill 29 yr old Cabarrus Co carpenter enlisted 3/21/62
1st Sgt Matthew Goodson 36 yr old Cabarrus Co merchant enlisted 3/21/62 **K-lungs 7/3**
Sgt John Fetzer 20 yr old Cabarrus Co teacher enlisted 3/21/62
Sgt Alfred Smith 33 yr old Cabarrus Co farmer enlisted 3/21/62 **WC 7/3**
Sgt Charles Walter 24 yr old Cabarrus Co farmer enlisted 3/21/62 (later W CH)
Cpl.George Blume 24 yr old Cabarrus Co farmer enlisted 3/24/62 **WC 7/3**
Cpl. John Brown 21 yr old Cabarrus Co farmer enlisted 3/21/62 (later C-Wilderness)
Cpl. John Cline 27 yr old Cabarrus Co farmer enlisted 3/21/62 (later C Bristoe)
Cpl. George Misenheimer 20 yr old Cabarrus Co farmer enlisted 3/21/62 W-both legs **C 7/3**
Cpl Thomas Van Pelt 30 yr old Cabarrus Co farmer enlisted 3/21/62 (later Sgt)
Private Benton Barnhardt 21 yr old Cabarrus Co farmer enlisted 3/21/62 (later C Bristoe)
Private Tobias Barnhardt 31 yr old Cabarrus Co farmer enlisted 3/21/62 **WC 7/3**
Private Allison Blackwelder 36 yr old Cabarrus Co farmer enlisted 3/26/62 **WC 7/3**
Private Charles 32 yr old Cabarrus Co farmer enlisted 3/26/62 **W-leg C 7/3 died**
Private Columbus Blackwelder 20 yr old Cabarrus Co. farmer enlisted 3/21/62 (C Bristoe)
Private Ransome Blackwelder 25 yr old Cabarrus Co. stable worker enlisted 3/21/62
Private Joseph Blume 24 yr old Cabarrus Co wagonmaker enlisted 9/1/62 **W left arm C 7/3**
Private William Blume 22 yr old Cabarrus Co wagonmaker enlisted 3/21/62 **WC 7/3**
Private William H Blume 24 yr old Cabarrus Co farmer enlisted 3/21/62 **WC 7/3**
Private James Brown 36 yr old Cabarrus Co farmer enlisted 4/8/62 **WC 7/3**
Private Richard Cooke 19 yr old Cabarrus Co farmer enlisted 3/21/62 (later Corp)
Private Jeremiah Cress 26 yr old Cabarrus Co laborer enlisted 3/21/62 (later W Bristoe)
Private William Dry 24 yr old Cabarrus Co laborer enlisted 3/21/62 (later C Bristoe)
Private Daniel Eddleman 22 yr old Cabarrus Co laborer enlisted 3/21/62 **W 7/3**
Private William Eudy 36 yr old Cabarrus Co farmer enlisted 3/21/62 **C 7/3**
Private Andrew Eury 30 yr old Cabarrus Co farmer enlisted 3/21/62 **W 7/3**
Private Adam Fink 29 yr old Cabarrus Co farmhand enlisted 3/21/62 **C 7/3**
Private Henry Goodnight 44 yr old Cabarrus Co farmer enlisted 3/21/62 (later C Bristoe)
Private Caleb Hagler 23 yr old Cabarrus Co farmer enlisted 3/21/62 **K 7/3**
Private John Hamilton 21 yr old Cabarrus Co farmer enlisted 3/21/62 **C 7/3**
Private Henry Isenhour 22 yr old Cabarrus Co farmer enlisted 3/21/62
Private Robert W Johnston 21 yr old Cabarrus Co farmer enlisted 3/21/62 **WC 7/3**
Private Robert W Johnson Sr 36 yr old Cabarrus Co farmer enlisted 4/12/62
Private Addison Joyner 40 yr old Cabarrus Co farmer enlisted 3/21/62 **C 7/14**
Private Daniel Lipe 20 yr old Cabarrus Co farmer enlisted 3/21/62 (C-Bristoe)
Private Thomas Ludwig 21 yr old Cabarrus Co farmer enlisted 3/21/62 (C-Bristoe)

Private Joseph M. Miller 34 yr old Cabarrus Co farmer enlisted 3/21/62 **WC 7/3 died 2nd Corps hospital 7/21**

Private James Misenheimer 30 yr old Cabarrus Co farmer enlisted 9/1/62 **K 7/3**

Private John Morrison 22yr old Cabarrus Co farmhand enlisted 9/1/62 (Later C Wild)

Private Gibson Nesbitt 18 yr old Cabarrus Co farmer enlisted 3/21/62 (later W Jones farm)

Private John Page 21 yr old Cabarrus Co farmer enlisted 3/21/62 **K 7/3**

Private John Poteat 36 yr old Cabarrus Co farmer enlisted 3/21/62

Private Thomas Poleat 24 yr old Cabarrus Co farmer enlisted 3/21/62 **W right thigh C 7/3**

Private Henry Powles 25 yr old Cabarrus Co farmer enlisted 3/21/62 **W 7/3 C 7/5**

Private George Rice 18 yr old Cabarrus Co farmer enlisted 3/21/62

Private William Rice 20 yr old Cabarrus Co farmer enlisted 3/21/62 **WC 7/3 died 8/20**

Private Rufus Safrit 21 yr old Cabarrus Co farmer enlisted 3/21/62 (later Corp)

Private Mathias Smith 28 yr old Cabarrus Co farmer enlisted 3/21/62 **C 7/3** died Pt Lookout

Private Jackson Stancil 31 yr old Cabarrus Co farmer enlisted 3/21/62 **W-right elbow C 7/3**

Private Martine Starnes 24 yr old Cabarrus Co farmer enlisted 3/21/62 **W right shoulder 7/3**

Private Greensbury Suther 22 yr old Cabarrus Co farmer enlisted 3/21/62

Private John Suther 33 yr old Cabarrus Co farmer enlisted 3/21/62 (later W Spots)

Private Richard Suther 22 yr old Cabarrus Co farmer enlisted 3/21/62

Private James Wallace 26 yr old Cabarrus Co farmer enlisted 3/21/62 **W 7/3**

Private John Wallace 24 yr old Cabarrus Co farmer enlisted 3/21/62

Private Martin Walter 19 yr old Cabarrus Co farmer enlisted 3/21/62 **W forearm 7/3**

Teamster Adam Barnhardt 22 yr old Cabarrus Co farmer enlisted 3/21/62

Ambulance Driver Willliam DeMarcus 50 yr old Cabarrus Co farmer enlisted 3/21/62

July 1 Casualties

Sgt Thomas Fleming 34 yr old Cabarrus Co farmer enlisted 5/14/62 **W 7/1**

Private Junius Beaty 21 yr old Cabarrus Co manufacturer enlisted 3/21/62 **W 7/1**

Private William Joyner 20 yr old Cabarrus Co blacksmith enlisted 3/21/62 **W 7/1**

Private James Keziah enlisted 3/21/62 **W 7/1 C 7/14**

Company B *"Randolph Guards"*

Captain Jesse Kyle Randolph Co farmer enlisted 3/15/62 (later C North Anna)

1st Lt. William Kyle Randolph C farmer enlisted 3/15/62 **W-head 7/3**

2nd Lt. James Huske Randoplh Co farmer enlisted 10/28/62 **W 7/3**

1st Sgt Alson Rush 22 yr old Randolph Co farmer enlisted 3/12/62

Sgt Alexander Hall 28 yr old Randolph Co carpenter enlisted 3/7/62 **W-leg 7/3**

Sgt Thomas W Ledwell 23 yr old Randolph Co farmer enlisted 3/7/62 **WC 7/3**

Cpl. Lovelace Hall 20 yr old Randolph Co farmer enlisted 3/8/62 (later C Bristoe)
Cpl. Franklin Luther 23 yr old Randolph Co farmer enlisted 3/12/62 **W-right leg C 7/3**
Private Henry Auman 26 yr old Randolph Co farmer enlisted 3/6/62
Private Milton Bell 24 yr old Randolph Co farmer enlisted 3/12/62 **C 7/5**
Private Kerney Bolen 32 yr old Randolph Co farmer enlisted 3/7/62 **WC 7/3**
Private Stanton Brunell enlisted April 1863 **W-knee C 7/3**
Private Jacob Callicott 21 yr old Randolph Co farmer enlisted 3/6/62 **WC 7/3**
Private J.F. Cashatt 26 yr old Randolph Co farmer enlisted 11/7/62 **W7/3 C 7/14**
Private John Dunning 27 yr old Randolph Co farmer enlisted 3/7/62 **C 7/14**
Private Zebulon Foard 25 yr old Mecklenburg Co farmer enlisted 3/7/62 (later C-Wild)
Private Andrew Goins 28 yr old Randolph Co farmer enlisted 3/7/62 (later Corp)
Private Thomas Grissom 27 yr old Randolph Co farmer enlisted 3/12/62 (later W Bristoe)
Private William Hoover 28 yr old Randolph Co farmer enlisted 3/7/62 **W 7/3**
Private Absalom Jerrald 53 yr old Randolph Co farmer enlisted 3/12/62
Private William Jerrald 26 yr old Randolph Co farmer enlisted 3/21/62 **C 7/14**
Private Issac Kearns 35 yr old Randolph Co farmer enlisted 3/7/62 **WC 7/14**
Private Thomas Kearns 22 yr old Randolph Co farmer enlisted 5/13/62 (later C Bristoe)
Private James Kernegay 25 yr old Duplin Co farmer enlisted 10/1/62 **WC 7/14**
Private James King 32 yr old Randolph Co farmer enlisted 3/6/62 **C 7/4**
Private Jason Ledwell 21 yr old Randolph Co farmer enlisted 3/7/62 **W 7/14**
Private Thomas Ledwell 55 yr old Randolph Co farmer enlisted 3/7/62 **C 7/14**
Private John Lewallen 32 yr old Randolph Co farmer enlisted 3/7/62
Private John Medley 43 yr old Randolph Co farmer enlisted 3/10/62 **W-head 7/3**
Private James Messick 27 yr old Yadnik Co farmer enlisted 3/7/62 **WC 7/3**
Private P.G. Murray 29 yr old Guilford Co farmer enlisted 3/6/62 **W-right leg C 7/3**
Private Morris Nelson 22 yr old Randolph Co farmer enlisted 3/24/62 **WC 7/3**
Private William Pearce 29 yr old Randolph Co farmer enlisted 3/6/62 **C 7/9**
Private James Presnell 35 yr old Randolph Co farmer enlisted 3/24/62 **K 7/3**
Private Stanton Presnell 23 yr old Randolph Co farmer enlisted 3/12/62 **W-knee & hand C 7/3**
Private Jesse Reaves 21 yr old Duplin Co farmer enlisted 10/1/62 **W 7/3 C 7/4**
Private Archibald Rush 46 yr old Randolph Co farmer enlisted 3/6/62 **C 7/7**
Private William Scott 30 yr old Randolph Co farmer enlisted 3/6/62 **WC 7/3**
Private Wiley Shaw 20 yr old Randolph Co farmer enlisted 4/8/62
Private Leroy Smith 21 yr old Mecklenburg Co farmer enlisted 10/1/62 **W 7/3**
Private Andrew Strider 23 yr old Randolph Co farmer enlisted 3/6/62 (later W-Bristoe)
Private John Trotter 20 yr old Randolph Co farmer enlisted 3/6/62 (later Corp)
Private Joseph Vanderford 26 yr old Randolph Co farmer enlisted 3/6/62
Private William Vanderford 23 yr old Randolph Co farmer enlisted 3/6/62
Private Nathan Walker 27 yr old Randolph Co farmer enlisted 3/12/62 (C-Bristoe)
Private Spain Williams 31 yr old Randolph Co farmer enlisted 3/6/62 **W 7/3**
Private Samuel Williams 26 yr old Randolph Co farmer enlisted 11/11/62 (later C Wilderness)

July 1 Casualties

Private William Hammond 32 yr old Randolph Co farmer enlisted 3/12/62 **W 7/1 C 7/5**
Private William Lamb 23 yr old Duplin Co farmer enlisted 3/7/62 **W 7/1**
Private Joel Strider 29 yr old Randolph Co farmer enlisted 3/6/62 **W 7/1 C 7/14**
Private Josiah Surrat 18 yr old Randolph Co farmer enlisted 3/25/62 **W 7/1**
Private Andrew Yates 27 yr old Wake Co. carpenter enlisted 3/6/62 **W 7/1 C 7/5**

Company C *"Orapeake Guards"*

Captain George Gilliam 29 yr old Gates Co. merchant enlisted 4/27/62 **W-thigh C 7/3**
1st Lt John Warren 19 yr old Chowan Co 4/24/62 **W-lung,wrist,thigh C 7/3**
2nd Lt David Parker 21 yr old Gates Co. farmer enlisted 4/24/62 **C 7/14**
Sgt Caleb Hayes 31 yr old Gates Co farmer enlisted 2/27/62 **W-right thigh C 7/3**
Sgt David Savage Gates Co farmer enlisted 2/27/62 **K 7/3**
Sgt William Speight 33 yr old Gates Co farmer enlisted 2/27/62
Sgt Anderson Ward Chowan Co. farmer enlisted 3/19/62 **C 7/3**
Cpl. Calvin Blanchard Gates Co farmer enlisted 2/27/62 **W-hip C 7/3**
Cpl. Thomas Mathias 28 yr old Gates Co farmer enlisted 2/27/62 **C 7/3**
Private Elijah Baker 34 yr old Gates Co enlisted 2/27/62 **C 7/3**
Private Eldridge Blanchard Gates Co farmer enlisted 5/10/62 **C7/3**
Private Moses Byrd 33 yr old Gates Co. farmer enlisted 2/27/62 **C 7/3**
Private Lewis Carter 28 yr old Gates Co farmer enlisted 2/27/62 **W-shoulder C 7/3 died**
Private James Ellis 20 yr old Gates Co farmer enlisted 2/27/62
Private Elmore Eure 22 yr old Gates Co farmer enlisted 2/27/62 (father was Corp)
Private James R. Eure 24 yr old Gates Co farmer enlisted 2/27/62 **W-head 7/3 (died 9/20 Chester hospital buried PNC)**
Private Preston Eure 23 yr old Gates Co farmer enlisted 2/27/62
Private James Floyd 24 yr old Gates Co farmer enlisted 2/27/62
Private George Harrell 21 yr old Gates Co farmer enlisted 2/27/62
Private William Harrell 20 yr old Gates Co farmer enlisted 2/27/62 **C 7/3**
Private Jacob Hofler 21 yr old Gates Co farmer enlisted 2/27/62 **C 7/3**
Private Jesse Hyatt 32 yr old Gates Co farmer enlisted 2/27/62 **C 7/3**
Private Joshua Jones 21 yr old Chowan Co farmer enlisted 2/27/62 **C 7/3**
Private Richard Lassiter 21 yr old Gates Co farmer enlisted 2/27/62 **C 7/3**
Private Isaac lee 21 yr old Gates Co farmer enlisted 2/27/62 **C 7/3**
Private Allen Perry 20 yr old Gates Co farmer enlisted 2/27/62 (later W-CH)
Private John Rawles 20 yr old Gates Co farmer enlisted 2/27/62 **W-hip 7/3**
Private Simon Riddick 20 yr old Gates Co farmer enlisted 2/27/62 (later W-Bristoe)
Private William Sprull Gates Co farmer enlisted 5/10/62 **C 7/3**
Private Bryant Umphlet 34 yr old Gates Co farmer enlisted 2/27/62 (Later C-Bristoe)

Private William Walker enlisted Wayne Co. 2/28/63 **W right leg 7/3**

Teamster Benjamin Owens 30 yr old Gates Co farmer enlisted 2/27/62
Teamster Robert Redd Gates Co farmer enlisted 2/27/62

July 1 Casualties

Cpl. Daniel Eure 42 yr old Gates Co farmer enlisted 2/27/62 **C 7/1**
Cpl. Daniel Trotman 31 yr old Chowen Co farmer enlisted 2/27/62 **W 7/1**
Private Oliver Butler 28 yr old Chowen Co. farmer enlisted 3/1/62 **W 7/1 C 7/14**
Private Josiah Ellis 23 yr old Gates Co farmer enlisted 2/27/62 **W-foot C 7/1**
Private Allen Lassiter 24 y old Gates Co farmer enlisted 2/27/62 **W-head 7/2 skirmisher**
Private Augustus Ward Chowen Co farmer enlisted 3/17/62 **W 7/1**

Company D *"McCulloch's Avengers"*

Captain Leonidas Gibson 34 yr old Stokes Co farmer enlisted 3/19/62 **W-head&leg 7/3**
1st Lt Isaac Nelson 25 yr old Stokes Co farmer enlisted 3/19/62 **C 7/3**
2nd Lt John Fowler 39 yr old Stokes Co farmer enlisted 3/19/62
3rd Lt Samuel Rierson 21 yr old Stokes Co farmer enlisted 3/19/62 (later C-Bristoe)
1st Sgt Aderson Myers 32 yr old Stokes Co farmer enlisted 3/19/62 **W left arm&hip 7/3**
Sgt Phillip James 24 yr old Stokes Co farmer enlisted 3/19/62 **W-arm 7/3**
Sgt Samuel Krause 25 yr old Stokes Co mechanic enlisted 3/19/62 **C 7/3**
Sgt Dewitt Tuttle 20 yr old Stokes Co farmer enlisted 3/19/62 (later K Ream's Station)
Cpl. John Tuttle 22 yr old Stokes Co farmer enlisted 3/19/62 (later Sgt)
Cpl. Charles Williams 20 yr old Stokes Co farmer enlisted 3/19/62
Private Eli Barker 21 yr old Stokes Co farmer enlisted 10/1/62 **C 7/3**
Private David Bowman 21 yr old Stokes Co farmer enlisted 2/20/63 **W-right leg 7/3 C 7/4**
Private Joseph Bowman 29 yr old Stokes Co farmer enlisted 3/19/62 **C 7/3**
Private David Bowman 21 yr old Stokes Co farmer enlisted 2/20/62 **W-right leg 7/3**
Private Joseph Bowman 29 yr old Stokes Co farmer enlisted 3/19/62 **C 7/3**
Private James Branson 20yr old Stokes Co farmer enlisted 3/19/62 **W-leg 7/1 C 7/4**
Private Allen Brewer 19 yr old Stokes Co farmer enlisted 3/19/62 (later W Bristoe)
Private William Brown 42 yr old Stokes Co farmer enlisted 3/19/62 **W-right thighC 7/3**
Private Claiborn Cape 50 yr old Stokes Co farmer enlisted 3/13/62 **C 7/3**
Private J.W. Carmichael 36 yr old Stokes Co farmer enlisted 10/21/62 later C Wilderness
Private Benjamin Cofer 19 yr old Stokes Co farmer enlisted 3/19/62 W-right arm **C 7/3**
Private Isaac Davis enlisted at Camp French Va 10/21/62 **K 7/3**
Private Robert Davis 21 old Stokes Co farmer enlisted 3/19/62 **K 7/3**
Private Adam Denny 36 yr old Stokes Co mechanic enlisted 3/19/62

Private James Fulton 31 yr old Stokes Co farmer enlisted 5/1/62 **W-breast 7/3**
Private Reuben George 43 yr old Stokes Co farmer enlisted 5/12/62 **C 7/3**
Private Lee Gibson 20 yr old Stokes Co farmer enlisted 3/19/62 **C 7/3**
Private William Hopkins 27 yr old Stokes Co farmer enlisted 3/19/62 W-left ankle **C 7/3**
Private George Jackson 19 yr old Stokes Co farmer enlisted 3/19/62
Private Alexander Jester 22 yr old enlisted Camp French 10/21/63 **WC 7/3**
Private Isaac Landers 28 yr old Stokes Co farmer enlisted 3/19/62 **W-right hand & leg C7/3**
Private John Landers 35 yr old Stokes Co farmer enlisted 3/19/62 (later Corp)
Private Zachariah Landers 25 yr old Stokes Co farmer enlisted 3/13/62 later C-Wild
Private William Ligon 20 yr old Stokes Co farmer enlisted 3/19/62 **K 7/3**
Private Matthew Marshall 23 yr old Stokes Co farmer enlisted 3/19/62
Private Richard Marshall 39 yr old Stokes Co farmer enlisted 3/13/62 (later W-Bristoe)
Private John Starns 40 yr old Stokes Co farmer enlisted 10/21/62 (later C Bristoe)
Private Gideon Tuttle 25 yr old Stokes Co farmer enlisted 3/19/62 **WC 7/14**
Private Jefferson Tuttle 23 yr old Stokes Co farmer enlisted 3/19/62 **W-right arm C 7/3**
Private Drury Wall 21 yr old Stokes Co farmer enlisted 3/19/62 **W-leg 7/3 C 7/5**
Private John Wall 20 yr old Stokes Co farmer enlisted 3/19/62 **C 7/14**
Private David Westmoreland 22 yr old Stokes Co farmer enlisted 3/19/62 **C 7/3**
Private Edward Young 30 yr old Stokes Co farmer enlisted 3/19/62 **C 7/14**
Private Edward H Young 41 yr old Stokes Co farmer enlisted 3/19/62 **C 7/3**
Private Robert Young 40 yr old Stokes Co farmer enlisted 3/19/62 **C 7/3**
Private Benjamin Zeigler 24 yr old Stokes Co farmer enlisted 3/19/62 **C 7/3**
Private Samuel Ziegler 22 yr old Stokes Co farmer enlisted 3/19/62 **W-head 7/3** (later K-Spots)

July 1 Casualties

Cpl. John Allen 26 yr old Stokes Co farmer enlisted 3/19/62 **W 7/1**
Cpl. John White 28 yr old Stokes Co farmer enlisted 3/19/62 **W 7/1**
Private James Banson 20 yr old Stokes Co farmer enlisted 2/20/63 **W-leg 7/1**
Private Robert Golding 24 yr old Stokes Co farmer enlisted 3/19/62 **W 7/1 C 7/14**
Private John Hancock enlisted Camp French 10/21/62 **K 7/1**
Private James Leaman 37 yr old Yadkin Co farmer enlisted 10/21/62 **K 7/1**
Private William Simmons 20 yr old Stokes Co farmer enlisted 3/19/62 **W 7/1**

Company E *"The Richmond Regulators"*

Captain Benjamin Little 33 yr old Richmond Co. farmer enlisted 3/8/61 **W-left arm C 7/3 at road** (Later Lt. Col)
1st Lt Milton Austin 36 yr old Richmond Co merchant enlisted 3/8/61W **W right foot 7/3**

2nd Lt Martin McDonald 23 yr old Richmond Co farmer enlisted 3/8/61W **WC 7/3**
3rd Lt. Thomas Baldwin 31 yr old Richmond Co farmer enlisted 3/8/62
1st Sgt William Brookshire 33 yr old Richmond Co farmer enlisted 4/4/62 (later Comm Sgt)
1st Sgt John Ewing 25 yr old Richmond Co farmer enlisted 3/8/62 **W-knee C 7/3**
Sgt Isaac Gately 30 yr old Richmond Co farmer enlisted 3/8/62 (later W Jone's Farm)
Sgt Robert Gibson 27 yr old Richmond Co farmer enlisted 4/14/62 W 7/1 **C 7/5**
Cpl. Benjamin Covington 24 yr old Richmond Co farmer enlisted 4/4/62 **WC 7/14**
Cpl. Joseph Covington 19 yr old Richmond Co farmer enlisted 3/8/62 (later W Bristoe)
Cpl. William Kennedy 22 yr old Richmond Co farmer enlisted 3/8/62
Cpl. William Roper 18 yr old Richmond Co farmer enlisted 3/19/62 **C 7/3**
Cpl. John Wade 34 yr old Richmond Co farmer enlisted 3/8/62 **C 7/3**
Private Daniel Baldwin 30 yr old Richmond Co farmer enlisted 3/8/62 **C 7/5**
Private Madison Baldwin 33 yr old Richmond Co farmer enlisted 3/8/62 **C 7/5**
Private William Barmer 19 yr old Richmond Co field hand enlisted 3/8/62 **C 7/14**
Private Martin Chappell 34 yr old Richmond Co farmer enlisted 3/10/62 **W right thigh C 7/3**
Private Rolin Chappell transferred from 44th NC **W 7/3 C 7/6 (died Phila hospital buried PNC)**
Private John Covington 18 yr old Richmond Co farmer enlisted 3/10/62 **C 7/14**
Private Thomas Covington 23 yr old Richmond Co farmer enlisted 3/8/62 **W 7/3**
Private Thomas T Covington 20 yr old Richmond Co farmer enlisted 2/16/63
Private William Covington 55 yr old Richmond Co farmer enlisted 3/19/63 **C 7/3**
Private Anderson Driggers 33 yr old Richmond Co farmer enlisted 3/8/62 **C 7/3**
Private John Galloway 25 yr old Richmond Co farmer enlisted 4/28/62 (later C Wild)
Private George Green 35 yr old Richmond Co farmer enlisted 4/3/62 (later C Bristoe)
Private George Harvell 52 yr old Richmond Co farmer enlisted 4/2/62 **WC 7/3**
Private John Hasty 24 yr old Richmond Co farmer enlisted 3/8/62 **C 7/3**
Private W. Frank Landford WC 7/3
Private Starling McDonald 21 yr old Richmond Co farmer enlisted 4/5/62 **W-left shoulder C 7/3**
Private John McDuffie 28 yr old Richmond Co farmer enlisted 4/10 /62 **C 7/14**
Private Murdock McDuffie 37 yr old Richmond Co farmer enlisted 2/16/62 (later C Bristoe)
Private Lauchlin McKay 52 yr old Richmond Co farmer enlisted 4/4/62 **K 7/3**
Private Benjamin McLendon transferred from 38th NC 4/22/63
Private John McNair 25 yr old Richmond Co farmer enlisted 3/8/62 (later W Wild)
Private William McNair 31 yr old Richmond Co farmer enlisted 3/8/62
Private James Maner 36 yr old Richmond Co farmer enlisted 3/8/62 **K 7/3**
Private John Mason 20 yr old Richmond Co farmer enlisted 3/8/62 (later K Jone's Farm)
Private Daniel Meacham 34 yr old Richmond Co farmer enlisted 4/16/62 (later C Bristoe)
Private Robert Meacham transferred from 38th NC 2/10/63 **C 7/14**
Private William Moore Richmond Co farmer enlisted 4/16/63 **C 7/3**

Private John Morgan 32 yr old Richmond Co farmer enlisted 3/8/62 **C 7/14**
Private John Nichols 31 yr old Richmond Co farmer enlisted 3/8/62 **C 7/3**
Private William Patterson 24 yr old Richmond Co farmer enlisted 3/8/62 **W-right leg 7/3**
Private Charles Robinson Richmond Co farmer enlisted 4/4/62 **K 7/3**
Private Dennis Sanford 19 yr old Richmond Co farmer enlisted 4/15/63 (later C Bristoe)
Private William Frank Sanford 23 yr old Richmond Co farmer enlisted 4/10/62 **C 7/3** (helped Capt. Little)
Private Daniel Sedberry 40 yr old Richmond Co mechanic enlisted 3/8/62 (later C Bristoe)
Private Willis Shankle 39 yr old Richmond Co farmer enlisted 3/19/62 **W-thigh 7/3**
Private Calvin Shepard 21 yr old Richmond Co farmer enlisted 4/13/62 **C 7/14**
Private Eli Shepard 19 yr old Richmond Co farmer enlisted 3/25/62 **C 7/14**
Private Martin Shepard 23 yr old Richmond Co farmer enlisted 3/10/62
Private Jonathan Strickland 22 yr old Richmond Co farmer enlisted 3/8/62 **C 7/3**
Private George Swink 22 yr old Richmond Co farmer enlisted 11/8/62 **W-right foot C 7/3**
Private Benjamin Thomas 35 yr old Richmond Co farmer enlisted 4/4/62 **W-back (shell) 7/3**
Private James Thomas 20 yr old Richmond Co farmer enlisted 4/15/63
Private Robert Thomas 31 yr old Richmond Co farmer enlisted 5/3/62 **K 7/3**
Private William Thrower 23 yr old Richmond Co farmer enlisted 5/5/62 **K 7/3**
Private Atlas Webb 32 yr old Richmond Co farmer enlisted 3/19/62 **C 7/14**
Private John Webb 23 yr old Richmond Co farmer enlisted 3/17/62 **C 7/3**
Private Robert Webb 26 yr old Richmond Co farmer enlisted 4/10/62 **C 7/3**
Private William Webb 20 yr old Richmond Co farmer enlisted 3/10/62 (later Sgt)
Private Thomas Woodward 24 yr old Richmond Co farmer enlisted 10/12/62 **WC 7/3**

Blacksmith Private Enos Smith old Lenoir Co blacksmith enlisted 3/8/62
Teamster Edward Hicks 20 yr old Richmond Co farmer enlisted 3/8/62
Teamster Lauchlin McKinnon 23 yr old Richmond Co farmer enlisted 3/13/62

July 1 Casualties

Sgt Thomas Capel 27 yr old Richmond Co farmer enlisted 5/2/62 **W 7/1**
Sgt Samuel Crouch 35 yr old Richmond Co farmer enlisted 3/8/62 **W 7/1 C 7/5**
Cpl. Daniel Gay 22 yr old Richmond Co farmer enlisted 3/19/62 **W 7/1**
Private Elijah Gibson 30 yr old Richmond Co farmer enlisted 3/17/62 (deserted 7/21)
Private Brinkley Hinson 21 yr old Richmond Co farmer enlisted 4/12/62 **W 7/1 C 7/5**
Private John Paul 49 yr old Richmond Co farmer enlisted 3/8/62 **C 7/14**
Private George Thompson 20 yr old Richmond Co farmer enlisted 4/4/62 **W 7/1** (later K Petersburg)
Private Steven Thompson 18 yr old Richmond Co farmer enlisted 4/4/62 **W 7/1**

Company F *"The Wilkes Grays"*

Captain Nathaniel Foster 32 yr old Wilkes Co. merchant enlisted 3/14/62 **C 7/14 while in command of regiment**

1st Lt William Carmichael 20 yr old Wilkes Co. merchant enlisted 3/14/62

2nd Lt Jacob Parleir 25 yr old Wilkes Co. farmer enlisted 3/14/62

3rd Lt Joseph Hall 20 yr old Wilkes Co. merchant enlisted 3/14/62 (later W Jones Farm)

1st Sgt Elijah Vannoy 19 yr old Wilkes Co. farmer enlisted 4/5/62 **K 7/3**

Sgt John Foster 19 yr old Wilkes Co. farmer enlisted 3/14/62 (later W Bristoe)

Sgt William A Foster 24 yr old Wilkes Co. farmer enlisted 3/14/62 **WC 7/3**

Sgt William A. Hall 21 yr old Wilkes Co. farmer enlisted 4/5/62 **WC 7/3**

Cpl. John Emerson 19 yr old Wilkes Co. farmer enlisted 4/5/62 **W 7/3**

Cpl. James Mock 27 yr old Wilkes Co. farmer enlisted 3/14/62 **C 7/3**

Cpl. Henry Sebastian 24 yr old Wilkes Co. farmer enlisted 4/5/62 W-head &Thigh **C 7/3**

Private Abram Absher 34 yr old Wilkes Co. farmer enlisted 9/22/62 **W 7/3**

Private Adam Absher 34 yr old Wilkes Co. farmer enlisted 9/22/62 (later W Glove tavern)

Private Alfred Absher 33 yr old Wilkes Co. farmer enlisted 9/22/62

Private Benjamin Absher 29 yr old Wilkes Co. farmer enlisted 9/22/62 **C 7/14**

Private Tobias Absher 23 yr old Wilkes Co. farmer enlisted 9/22/62 (later W North Anna)

Private Ausburn Anderson 34 yr old Wilkes Co. farmer enlisted 9/22/62 **WC 7/3**

Private Larkin Bishop 22 yr old Wilkes Co. farmer enlisted 3/14/62 **C 7/14**

Private Elam Bowles 20 yr old Wilkes Co. farmer enlisted 9/22/62 (later W Bristoe)

Private Simpson Bowles 25 yr old Wilkes Co. farmer enlisted 4/5/62 **W 7/3** (later C Bristoe)

Private Johnson Broyhill 19 yr old Wilkes Co. farmer enlisted 4/5/62

Private Anderson Cain 24 yr old Wilkes Co. farmer enlisted 3/14/62 (later Cpl.)

Private Thomas Carlton 22 yr old Wilkes Co. farmer enlisted 3/14/62

Private Abner Caudill 19 yr old Wilkes Co. farmer enlisted 3/14/62 **C 7/14**

Private Marion Chapel 24 yr old Wilkes Co. farmer enlisted 3/14/62

Private Solomon Chapel 20 yr old Wilkes Co. farmer enlisted 4/5/62 **W-right side C 7/3**

Private James Church 27 yr old Wilkes Co. farmer enlisted 3/14/62 **C 7/14**

Private John Church 22 yr old Wilkes Co. farmer enlisted 3/14/62

Private William Church 18 yr old Wilkes Co. farmer enlisted 3/14/62 W-right thigh **C 7/3**

Private Joseph Cockerham 36 yr old Wilkes Co. farmer enlisted 3/14/62 (later C Bristoe)

Private Columbus Dowel 22 yr old Wilkes Co. farmer enlisted 3/14/62

Private John S. Foster transferred from 54th NC 10/62 (later W Bristoe Station)

Private William Glass 27 yr old Wilkes Co. farmer enlisted 9/22/62 (deserted 8/22/63)

Private Daniel Hall 25 yr old Wilkes Co. farmer enlisted 9/22/62 **C 7/6**

Private Nathaniel Hall 19 yr old Wilkes Co. farmer enlisted 4/5/62 (deserted 8/63)

Private William H. Hall 20 yr old Wilkes Co. farmer enlisted 4/5/62 (later C Bristoe)

Private John Hamby 23 yr old Wilkes Co. farmer enlisted 3/14/62 (later C Wild)

Private John Handy 25 yr old Wilkes Co. farmer enlisted 9/22/62 **C 7/3**

Private Marcus Handy 21 yr old Wilkes Co. farmer enlisted 9/22/62 **WC 7/3**

Private Wyatt Harris 23 yr old Wilkes Co. farmer enlisted 3/14/62 **W-leg C 7/3**
Private Jabez Hendren 20 yr old Wilkes Co. farmer enlisted 4/5/62 **K 7/3**
Private John Higgins 16 yr old Wilkes Co. farmer enlisted 4/5/62
Private John Hix 35 yr old Wilkes Co. farmer enlisted 4/5/62 **C 7/14**
Private William Hutchison 20 yr old Wilkes Co. farmer enlisted 9/22/62 **K 7/3**
Private John Kilby 20 yr old Wilkes Co. farmer enlisted 4/5/62 WC 7/3
Private Joseph Lundy 19 yr old Wilkes Co. farmer enlisted 3/14/62 (later C Bristoe)
Private Zebedee Lundy 22 yr old Wilkes Co. carpenter enlisted 3/14/62 **W 7/3** (later C Bristoe)
Private John Marlee 33 yr old Wilkes Co. farmer enlisted 3/14/62
Private Harvey Marlow 35 yr old Wilkes Co. farmer enlisted 3/14/62 **C 7/14**
Private John Owens 27 yr old Wilkes Co. farmer enlisted 4/5/62 (deserted 7/25/63-returned)
Private Martin Parks 20 yr old Wilkes Co. farmer enlisted 3/14/62 (later K CH)
Private Smith Price 27 yr old Wilkes Co. farmer enlisted 3/14/62 (later W Bristoe/C Wild))
Private Finley Queen 24 yr old Wilkes Co. farmer enlisted 4/5/62
Private William Queen 20 yr old Wilkes Co. farmer enlisted 4/5/62 **C 7/14**
Private Andrew Reavis 23 yr old Wilkes Co. mechanic enlisted 3/14/62
Private John St Clair 20 yr old Wilkes Co resident enlisted 9/22/62
Private Martin Sebastain 21 yr old Wilkes Co resident enlisted 9/22/62 **W-right leg C 7/3**
Private Jesse Sumerlin 36 yr old Wilkes Co. farmer enlisted 4/5/62 (nurse) **C 7/5**
Private Aaron Tucker 24 yr old Wilkes Co. farmer enlisted 4/5/62 (later W Reams's)
Private Abram Voncannon 27 old Wilkes Co. mechanic enlisted 3/14/62 **C 7/14**
Private William Waggoner 20 yr old Wake Co farmer enlisted 6/3/62
Private James Warren 19 yr old Wilkes Co. farmer enlisted 4/5/62 **W-shoulder & thigh 7/3**
Private John Watts 21 old Wilkes Co. farmer enlisted 3/14/62 **W-right shoulder 7/3**
Private Franklin Williams 23 old Wilkes Co. farmer enlisted 4/5/62 **WC 7/3**
Private John Williams 20 old Wilkes Co. farmer enlisted 4/5/62 **K 7/3**
Private Joseph Woods 37 yr old Wilkes Co farmer enlisted 3/14/62 **C 7/14**

Musician John Pierce enlisted Franklin Co 11/15/62
Chief Musician Robert Warren 19 old Wilkes Co. farmer enlisted 3/14/62

July 1 Casualties

Private Horton Bishop 20 yr old Wilkes Co. farmer enlisted 3/14/62 **W 7/1**
Private David Bullis 22yr old Wilkes Co. farmer enlisted 3/14/62 **WC 7/1**
Private John Evans 26 yr old Wilkes Co. farmer enlisted 3/14/62 **W 7/1**
Private Nathan Hall 19 yr old Wilkes Co. farmer enlisted 3/14/62 **W-left leg 7/1 C 7/5**
Private Jesse Havener 20 yr old Wilkes Co. farmer enlisted 3/14/62 **WC 7/1**
Private James Johnson 31 yr old Wilkes Co. farmer enlisted 3/14/62 **W-left leg 7/1 C 7/5**

Private William Smithy 29 yr old Wilkes Co resident enlisted 9/22/62 **W-left leg 7/1**
Private James Watts 21 yr old Wilkes Co. farmer enlisted 3/14/62 **W-left elbow 7/1**

Blacksmith Isham Burchett 33 yr old Wilkes Co. farmer enlisted 3/14/62 **(W 7/2 bombardment)**

Company G *"The Dry Pond Dixies"*

Captain James Kincaid 25 yr old Lincoln Co. farmer enlisted 3/25/62 **W-left thigh C 7/3 died 8/27**
1st Lt. James Wells Lincoln Co. farmer enlisted 3/23/62 (later C-Wild)
2nd Lt. John Gatens Lincoln Co. farmer enlisted 4/26/62 (later W Bristoe)
3rd Lt. Henry Wells 26 yr old Lincoln Co. farmer enlisted 3/22/62 **W 7/3**
1st Sgt William Thompson 33 yr old Lincoln Co. farmer enlisted 3/23/62 **WC 7/3 died**
Sgt Leroy Dellinger 26 yr old Lincoln Co. farmer enlisted 3/23/62 **W 7/3**
Sgt John Little 27 yr old Lincoln Co. farmer enlisted 3/22/62 **C 7/3**
Sgt Levi Shelton 33 yr old Lincoln Co. farmer enlisted 3/22/62 **C 7/14**
Sgt Thomas Thompson 29 yr old Lincoln Co. farmer enlisted 3/22/62 **W left thigh 7/3**
Cpl. James Norwood 46 yr old Lincoln Co. farmer enlisted 3/25/62 **W 7/3** (later C Bristoe)
Cpl. Joseph Robinson 23 yr old Lincoln Co. farmer enlisted 3/23/62 **W-left arm-right shoulder-left thigh 7/3 died 9/9**
Cpl. Robert Sifford 25 yr old Lincoln Co. resident enlisted 4/10/62 **W-right leg C 7/3**
Cpl. William Smith 31 yr old Lincoln Co. farmer enlisted 3/22/62
Private David Abernathy 25 yr old Catawba Co. farmer enlisted 3/21/62 **K 7/3**
Private Milton Abernathy 28 yr old Lincoln Co. farmer enlisted 3/23/62 **W 7/3**
Private Henry Brotherton 21 yr old Lincoln Co. farmer enlisted 3/23/62 **W 7/3**
Private James Caldwell 20 yr old Lincoln Co. farmer enlisted 3/23/62 **WC 7/3**
Private J.P. Cranford 32 yr old Randolph Co. resident enlisted 11/3/62 **WC 7/3**
Private Henry Davis 26 yr old Randolph Co. resident enlisted 11/3/62 (later C Wilderness)
Private Lorenzo Dellinger 20 yr old Lincoln Co. farmer enlisted 9/22/62
Private Jacob Edwards 20 yr old Lincoln Co. farmer enlisted 3/23/62 **C 7/3**
Private William Edwards 19 yr old Lincoln Co. farmer enlisted 3/23/62 (later Cpl / W CH)
Private Harrison Gant 23 yr old Lincoln Co. farmer enlisted 3/20/62
Private Jefferson Gant 40 yr old Lincoln Co. farmer enlisted 3/12/62 **C 7/3**
Private Joe Goodson 22 yr old Lincoln Co. farmer enlisted 3/23/62
Private John F. Goodson 25 yr old Lincoln Co. farmer enlisted 3/20/62 **C 7/3**
Private John W Goodson 19 yr old Lincoln Co. farmer enlisted 3/20/62 (later W Bristoe)
Private Reuben Goodson 22 yr old Lincoln Co. farmer enlisted 3/20/62
Private Thomas Hagar 26 yr old Lincoln Co. farmer enlisted 3/9/62 (later W Jone's Farm)
Private Adam Hager 27 yr old Lincoln Co. farmer enlisted 3/17/62 **C 7/3**

Private Monroe Hager 28 yr old Lincoln Co. farmer enlisted 9/22/62 **C 7/14**

Private James Hager 24 yr old Lincoln Co. farmer enlisted 3/17/62

Private John Hager 27 yr old Lincoln Co. farmer enlisted 3/9/62

Private Robert Hager 20 yr old Lincoln Co. farmer enlisted 3/17/62 (later C Wild)

Private Jacob Hinshaw 29 yr old Randolph Co. Quaker drafted 11/3/62 **C 7/5 as nurse**

Private Thomas Hinshaw 32 yr old Randolph Co. Quaker drafted 11/3/62 **C 7/5 as nurse**

Private Joseph Howard 23 yr old Lincoln Co. farmer enlisted 3/19/62 **K 7/3**

Private McDonald Hunt 28 yr old Lincoln Co. farmer enlisted 6/30/62 (later K Globe Tavern)

Private Sidney Kidds 28 yr old Lincoln Co. farmer enlisted 9/22/62 **C 7/14**

Private Archibald Lucky 39 yr old Lincoln Co. farmer **C 7/14**

Private David Lucky 35 yr old Lincoln Co. farmer enlisted 3/23/62 (later C Wild)

Private John Lucky 27 yr old Lincoln Co. farmer enlisted 3/23/62 **C 7/14**

Private James Munday 18 yr old Lincoln Co. student enlisted 3/23/62

Private Jeremiah Munday 20 yr old Lincoln Co. farmer enlisted 3/23/62 (later W Bristoe)

Private William Munday 22 yr old Lincoln Co. farmer enlisted 3/23/62 **C 7/3**

Private Albert Nixon 26 yr old Lincoln Co. farmer enlisted 3/21/62 **C 7/14**

Private Archibald Nixon 40 yr old Lincoln Co. farmer enlisted 3/25/62 **W-thigh C 7/3 (amp) died 7/19**

Private Franklin Nixon 37 yr old Lincoln Co. farmer enlisted 3/12/62 **C 7/3**

Private George Nixon 35 yr old Lincoln Co. farmer enlisted 3/25/62 **W-head 7/3 died 7/20**

Private John Nixon 35 yr old Lincoln Co. farmer enlisted 3/25/62 **W-left shoulder 7/3**

Private William Potts 19 yr old Lincoln Co. farmer enlisted 6/30/62 (later C Bristoe)

Private James Reagan 19 yr old Lincoln Co. farmer enlisted 3/1/63

Private Michael Redding 27 yr old Randolph Co. farmer enlisted 11/3/62 **deserted 7/5**

Private James Reed 20 yr old Iredell Co. farmer enlisted 3/22/62 **W-right arm 7/3**

Private Thomas Reed 29 yr old Lincoln Co. farmer enlisted 3/22/62 **W-thigh & hand C 7/3**

Private John C.Robinson 25 yr old Lincoln Co. farmer enlisted 3/22/62 **C 7/3**

Private John H Robinson 25 yr old Lincoln Co. farmer enlisted 3/23/62 (later Cpl)

Private Thomas Robinson 21 yr old Lincoln Co. farmer enlisted 3/23/62 **C 7/12**

Private Henry Russell 26 yr old Lincoln Co. farmer enlisted 11/2/62 **C 7/3**

Private John Sexton 27 yr old Randolph Co. farmer enlisted 11/3/62 (deserted 7/7/63)

Private James Sherrill 19 yr old Lincoln Co. farmer enlisted 3/25/62

Private William Sherrill 18 yr old Lincoln Co. farmer enlisted 3/1/63

Private John Sifford 38 yr old Lincoln Co. farmer enlisted 3/23/62 **C 7/14**

Private William Sifford 35 yr old Lincoln Co. farmer enlisted 3/10/63 **W-left leg C 7/3**

Private Daniel Thompson 19 yr old Lincoln Co. farmer enlisted 3/22/62 **W-groin & right thigh C 7/3**

Private John Thompson 20 yr old Lincoln Co. farmer enlisted 3/22/62 **C 7/3**

Private John Tucker 28 yr old Lincoln Co. farmer enlisted 4/28/62 **C 7/12 Hagerstown**

Private James Wilkerson 22 yr old Lincoln Co. farmer enlisted 3/22/62 **C 7/3**

Ambulance Driver Solomon Young 28 yr old Lincoln Co. farmer enlisted 9/22/62
Teamster James Cashion 28 yr old Lincoln Co. farmer enlisted 4/25/62
Private Cyrus Barker 31 yr old Randolph Co. Quaker farmer enlisted 11/3/62 (Nurse) **C 7/5**
Private Nathan Barker 22 yr old Randolph Co. Quaker farmer enlisted 11/3/62 (Nurse **C 7/5**

July 1 Casualties

Private P.C. Cranford 31 yr old Randolph Co. resident enlisted 11/3/62 **(deserted 7/2)**
Private William Howard 31 yr old Lincoln Co. farmer enlisted 2/22/62 **W-thigh 7/1 C 7/4**
Private Sidney Nixon 36 yr old Lincoln Co. farmer enlisted 3/17/62 **W 7/1 C 7/14**
Private Thomas Norwood 29 yr old Lincoln Co. farmer enlisted 3/22/62 **W 7/1 C 7/14**
Private William Prim 23 yr old Lincoln Co. farmer enlisted 3/17/62 **W-right ankle 7/1**

Company H *"Spring Hill Guards"*

Captain Eric Erson Lincolnton merchant; born in Sweden; transferred from, 1st NC **W-right hand 7/3** (later Lt. Col)
1st Lt Lawson Dellinger Lincoln Co farmer transferred 3/25/62 **WC 7/3**
2nd Lt. William Arent 23 yr old Lincoln Co.farmer promoted 3/25/62 **W-right leg 7/3 C 7/5 died**
3rd Lt. Peter Beal 27 yr old Lincoln Co. farmer enlisted 3/25/62 (later C Wild)
1st Sgt William Rutledge 24 yr old Lincoln Co. farmer enlisted 4/24/62 (W-Wild)
Sgt Samuel Randleman 22 yr old Lincoln Co. farmer enlisted 3/25/62 (later Lt.)
Sgt Marcus Loftin 31 yr old Lincoln Co. farmer enlisted 3/25/62 **C 7/14**
Sgt John McCall 29 yr old Lincoln Co. farmer enlisted 3/25/62 **C 7/3**
Cpl. John Dellinger Lincoln Co. farmer enlisted 3/25/62 (later Sgt)
Cpl. John Goodson 25 yr old Lincoln Co. farmer enlisted 3/25/62 (later Sgt)
Cpl. Rufus Helderman Lincoln Co. farmer enlisted 4/28/62 **K 7/3**
Cpl. Richard McCorkle 39 yr old Lincoln Co. farmer enlisted 3/25/62 **W-left arm 7/3**
Private William Abernathy 29 yr old Lincoln Co. farmer enlisted 11/11/62 (later K CH)
Private David Anderson 24 yr old Lincoln Co. farmer enlisted 11/11/62
Private Albert Bynum 24 yr old Lincoln Co. farmer enlisted 7/25/62 (deserted 7/25/63)
Private James Franklin Bynum 22 yr old Lincoln Co. farmer enlisted 7/8/62 **W 7/3**
Private William Bynum 19 yr old Lincoln Co. farmer enlisted 3/25/62 **C 7/3**
Private Marcus Caldwell 27 yr old Lincoln Co. farmer enlisted 3/25/62 **W-right hand C7/3**
Private William Carpenter 19 yr old Lincoln Co. farmer enlisted 3/25/62 **W 7/3 died**
Private Ephraim Chesser 29 yr old Lincoln Co. farmer enlisted 3/25/62 (deserted 7/25/63)
Private Albert Dellinger 19 yr old Lincoln Co. farmer enlisted 3/25/62
Private Isaac Dellinger 29 yr old Lincoln Co. farmer enlisted 7/6/62 (nurse C 7/5)

Private Monroe Dellinger 25 yr old Lincoln Co. farmer enlisted 7/6/62 **C 7/14**
Private Noah Dellinger 19 yr old Lincoln Co. farmer enlisted 3/25/62 (later W Bristoe)
Private Admiral Earney 24 yr old Lincoln Co. farmer enlisted 4/19/62 (later W Bristoe)
Private Lafayette Earney Lincoln Co. farmer enlisted 3/25/62 **C 7/14**
Private David Eddleman 31 yr old Lincoln Co. farmer enlisted 3/25/62 **C 7/3**
Private David Fisher 35 yr old Lincoln Co. farmer enlisted 1/30/63 **C 7/14**
Private James Fisher 19 yr old Lincoln Co. farmer enlisted 3/25/62 (deserted 7/25/63)
Private Sidney Forney 19 yr old Lincoln Co. farmer enlisted 3/25/62 (later Cpl.)
Private John Friday 19 yr old Lincoln Co. farmer enlisted 3/25/62 (later W Petersburg)
Private Abner Goodson 27 yr old Lincoln Co. farmer enlisted 7/6/62 **W-left leg C 7/3**
Private George Goodson 32 yr old Lincoln Co. farmer enlisted 7/6/62 (later Sgt)
Private Rufus Goodson 26 yr old Lincoln Co. farmer enlisted 7/6/62
Private William Hawkins 23 yr old Lincoln Co. farmer enlisted 7/6/62 **WC 7/3**
Private George Helderman 29 yr old Lincoln Co laborer enlisted 7/6/62 (later C Bristoe)
Private John Honeycut 23 yr old Lincoln Co. farmer enlisted 7/6/62 (later K Bristoe)
Private Christopher Hope 32 Lincoln Co. brick mason enlisted 7/6/62 **W-right leg C 7/3**
Private Moses Hovis 20 yr old Lincoln Co. farmer enlisted 3/25/62 **WC 7/3**
Private Westley Hovis 31 yr old Lincoln Co. farmer enlisted 7/6/62 **W-thumb 7/3**
Private Cephas Keener 32 yr old Lincoln Co. farmer enlisted 3/10/62
Private David Keener 22 yr old Lincoln Co. farmer enlisted 3/25/62 (later W Bristoe)
Private David A Keener 26 yr old Lincoln Co. farmer enlisted 7/6/62 (later W-N.Anna)
Private John Lawing 21 yr old Lincoln Co. farmer enlisted 3/25/62 **W 7/3**
Private William Lawing 26 yr old Lincoln Co. farmer enlisted 10/24/62 **W-left leg C 7/3**
Private Andrew Moore 21 yr old Lincoln Co. farmer enlisted 3/25/62 (later Cpl.)
Private Clabern Nance 24 yr old Gaston Co. farmer enlisted 3/25/62 **C 7/14**
Private Lawson Nance 22 yr old Gaston Co. laborer enlisted 3/25/62 (deserted 7/25/63)
Private Hosea Parker 26 yr old Lincoln Co. laborer enlisted 7/6/62
Private John Parker 24 yr old Lincoln Co. farmer enlisted 3/25/62 **W-left chest 7/3** (later W—leg Jones Farm (amp)
Private Franklin Perkins 24 yr old Lincoln Co. farmer enlisted 10/24/62 (later W-Petersburg)
Private James Queen 33 yr old Lincoln Co. farmer enlisted 3/25/62 (later W-Wild)
Private Joseph Richardson 27 yr old Lincoln Co. farmer enlisted 11/11/62 **C 7/14**
Private James Saunders 19 yr old Lincoln Co. farmer enlisted 3/25/62 **W-thigh 7/3 died**
Private Thomas Saunders 21 yr old Lincoln Co. farmer enlisted 3/25/62 **W-thigh 7/3**
Private Thomas Stewart 20 yr old Lincoln Co. farmer enlisted 3/25/62 **K 7/3**
Private Lafayette Stroup 21 yr old Lincoln Co. farmer enlisted 7/6/62 **C 7/3**
Private Robert Stroup 21 yr old Lincoln Co. farmer enlisted 3/25/62 **C 7/14**
Private Wesley Stroup 28 yr old Lincoln Co. farmer enlisted 3/25/62 **W-right foot 7/3**
Private David Summerow 20 yr old Lincoln Co. farmer enlisted 2/10/63 **C 7/3**
Private Henry Summerow 24 yr old Lincoln Co. farmer enlisted 4/29/62 **W-leg 7/3** (later Cpl.)

Private David Summey 18 yr old Lincoln Co. farmer enlisted 3/25/62 **W jaw-right leg 7/3**
Private Sidney Thompson 26 yr old Lincoln Co. farmer enlisted 3/25/62 **C 7/3**
Private John Weathers 27 yr old Lincoln Co. farmer enlisted 4/27/62 **W-left arm C 7/3**
Private Oliver Weathers 25 yr old Lincoln Co. farmer enlisted 3/25/62

Teamster John Haynes Lincoln Co. farmer enlisted 7/6/62
Teamster William Hope 40 yr old Lincoln Co. farmer enlisted 3/25/62
Orderly William Friday 20 yr old Lincoln Co. farmer enlisted 3/25/62—Brigade

July 1 Casualties 4

Private James Bynum 23 yr old Lincoln Co. farmer enlisted 3/25/62 **W 7/1 C 7/5**
Private George Gibson 49 yr old Lincoln Co. farmer enlisted 3/25/62 **C 7/14**
Private James McCaul 20 yr old Lincoln Co. farmer enlisted 3/11/62 **W 7/1**
Private Isaac Williams 25 yr old Lincoln Co. farmer enlisted 3/25/62 **W 7/1**

Company I *"The Stanly Rebels"*

1st Lt James Hearne 28 yr old Stanly Co. merchant enlisted 3/29/62 (took command)
2nd Lt Samuel Lilly 28 yr old Stanly Co. farmer enlisted 3/29/62 (later W-CH)
3rd Lt Willis Randall 27 yr old Stanly Co. farmer enlisted 3/29/62 **W-left hand C 7/3**
1st Sgt Buckner Crowell 25 yr old Stanly Co. farmer enlisted 3/25/62 **W-right thigh C 7/3**
Sgt James Forrest 26 yr old Stanly Co. farmer enlisted 3/25/62
Sgt Reuben Harris 36 yr old Stanly Co. farmer enlisted 3/25/62 **WC 7/3**
Sgt Manlove Kimray 31 yr old Stanly Co. farmer enlisted 3/25/62 **C 7/14**
Sgt William Smith 22 yr old Stanly Co. farmer enlisted 3/25/62 (later K Bristoe)
Cpl. Daniel Lowder 29 yr old Stanly Co. farmer enlisted 3/25/62 **C 7/14**
Cpl. William Mason 26 yr old Stanly Co. farmer enlisted 3/25/62 **K 7/3**
Private A.S. Allen 29 yr old Stanly Co. farmer enlisted 9/8/62 (later C Bristoe)
Private Nathan Almond 25 yr old Stanly Co. farmer enlisted 3/25/62 (later C Bristoe)
Private John Austin 25 yr old Stanly Co. farmer enlisted 3/25/62 **W-left hand C 7/3**
Private Henry Barringer 21 yr old Stanly Co. farmer enlisted 3/25/62 **K 7/3**
Private Jackson Bird 32 yr old Stanly Co. carpenter enlisted 3/25/62 **W-right shoulder C 7/3**
Private Edmond Blalock 27 yr old Stanly Co. farmer enlisted 3/25/62
Private John Callaway 26 yr old Stanly Co. farmer enlisted 3/25/62 **C 7/14**
Private T.K. Colson 19 yr old Stanly Co. farmer enlisted 3/1/62 **W-left foot C 7/3**
Private Julius Creps 19 yr old Stanly Co. farmer enlisted 3/25/62 **C 7/3**
Private George Crowell 34 yr old Stanly Co. farmer enlisted 3/25/62 **W 7/3**
Private Edmund DeBerry 21 yr old Stanly Co. farmer enlisted 3/25/62 **WC 7/3**
Private Boggan Dees 37 yr old Stanly Co. farmer enlisted 9/25/62 (deserted 8/5/63)

Private Christopher Dry 32 yr old Stanly Co. farmer enlisted 3/25/62 **K 7/3**
Private George Dry 26 yr old Stanly Co. farmer enlisted 3/25/62 **C 7/3**
Private William Farmer 29 yr old Stanly Co. farmer enlisted 3/25/62
Private Eben Fry 39 yr old Stanly Co. farmer enlisted 3/25/62 **W-shoulder C 7/3**
Private John Fry 36 yr old Stanly Co. farmer enlisted 3/25/62
Private Joseph Haskell 23 yr old Stanly Co. farmer enlisted 4/28/62 (later 1st Sgt)
Private Alfred Hatley 28 yr old Stanly Co. farmer enlisted 3/25/62 **W-leg C 7/3 died**
Private Doctor Hinson 18 yr old Stanly Co. farmer enlisted 3/25/62 **C 7/14**
Private Julius Howell 29 yr old Stanly Co. farmer enlisted 4/28/62 **C 7/14**
Private Lewis Hudson 36 yr old Stanly Co. farmer enlisted 3/25/62 (later C Bristoe)
Private Isaac Ivy 27 yr old Stanly Co. farmer enlisted 3/25/62 **C 7/3**
Private Julius Kendall 34 yr old Stanly Co. farmer enlisted 3/1/62 **K 7/3**
Private George Kirk 32 yr old Stanly Co. farmer enlisted 3/25/62 **C 7/14**
Private Parham Kirk 33 yr old Stanly Co. farmer enlisted 4/28/62 **K 7/3**
Private J.T. Lanier 19 yr old Stanly Co. farmer enlisted 9/25/62 **K 7/3**
Private Robert Lilly 23 yr old Stanly Co. farmer enlisted 3/25/62
Private Enoch Littleton 24 yr old Stanly Co. farmer enlisted 3/25/62 **C 7/3**
Private George Lowder 20 yr old Stanly Co. farmer enlisted 3/25/62 **W-right hand 7/3**
Private William Lowder 32 yr old Stanly Co. farmer enlisted 5/14/62 **WC 7/3**
Private John McInnis 17 yr old Stanly Co. farmer enlisted 3/25/62 **W 7/3** (later Sgt)
Private Hammett Maners 19 yr old Stanly Co. farmer enlisted 3/25/62 **C 7/14**
Private James Marbry 27 yr old Stanly Co. farmer enlisted 3/25/62 **W 7/3**
Private Ezekiel Martin enlisted Spring 1863 **K 7/3**
Private James Mason 21 yr old Stanly Co. farmer enlisted 3/25/62 (later C Wilderness)
Private Atlas Melton Stanly Co farmer enlisted 3/1/63 **C 7/14**
Private Joseph Melton 51 yr old Stanly Co. farmer enlisted 3/25/62 **W-left side 7/3**
Private Martin Morgan 30 yr old Stanly Co. farmer enlisted 5/1/62 **C 7/3**
Private Robert Morris 32 yr old Stanly Co. carpenter enlisted 4/26/62 **WC 7/3**
Private Ezekiel Morton 34 yr old Stanly Co. farmer enlisted 3/25/62 **K 7/3**
Private Henry Pence 49 yr old Stanly Co. farmer substituted 3/6/62 **C 7/3**
Private Noah Pence 28 yr old Stanly Co. farmer enlisted 4/25/62 **W-left arm C 7/3**
Private James Perry 22 yr old Stanly Co. farmer enlisted 3/25/62 **K 7/3**
Private John C. Pickler 22 yr old Stanly Co. farmer enlisted 3/25/62 **WC 7/3 died**
Private John Pickler 29 yr old Stanly Co. farmer enlisted 3/25/62 **C 7/14**
Private James Poplin 28 yr old Stanly Co. farmer enlisted 3/25/62 **W-right thigh C 7/3**
Private William Randle 34 yr old Stanly Co. farmer enlisted 7/1/62
Private Jacob Sell 18 yr old Stanly Co. farmer substitute 3/25/62 **K 7/3**
Private John Sell 37 yr old Stanly Co. farmer enlisted 3/25/62 **K 7/3**
Private Solomon Sell 57 yr old Stanly Co. farmer enlisted 5/17/62 **W-hip C 7/3**
Private James Shankle enlisted Stanly Co. 3/1/63 **WC 7/3 died 7/6**
Private Noah Shaver 33 yr old Stanly Co. farmer enlisted 3/25/62 **K 7/3**
Private D.A. Sides 35 yr old Stanly Co. farmer enlisted 3/25/62 **C 7/3**

Private Eli Smith 29 yr old Stanly Co. farmer enlisted 3/25/62 **WC 7/3**
Private Green Smith 28 yr old Stanly Co. farmer enlisted 3/25/62 (later Cpl)
Private Reuben Smith 18 yr old Stanly Co. farmer enlisted 3/25/62 **W-right thigh 7/3 C 7/5**
Private Eli Swaringen 24 yr old Stanly Co. farmer enlisted 3/25/62 (later Sgt)
Private Risden Thompson 19 yr old Stanly Co. farmer enlisted 3/25/62 **W-left thigh C 7/3 died**
Private John Tolbert 34 yr old Stanly Co. farmer enlisted 4/26 /62 (deserted 8/5/63)
Private William Upchurch 37 yr old Stanly Co. farmer enlisted 3/25/62 **WC 7/3**
Private John Waller 29 yr old Stanly Co. farmer enlisted 4/28/62 **W-thigh C 7/3 died**

Teamster Merritt Blalock 21 yr old Stanley Co. farmer enlisted 3/25/62 (later W-Spots)
Teamster Daniel Moyer 44 yr old Stanly Co. farmer substituted 3/25/62 (later K Globe Tavern)

July 1 Casualties

Captain John McCain 31 yr old Stanly Co. farmer enlisted 3/29/62 **K 7/1**
Private J.M. Avett 27 yr old Stanly Co. farmer enlisted 9/25/62 **W 7/1**
Private John Laney 21 yr old Lincoln Co. farmer enlisted 7/6/62 **W 7/1**
Private John Rogers 29 yr old Stanly Co. farmer enlisted 12/4/62 **K 7/1**
Private Jacob Shankle 35 yr old Stanly Co. farmer enlisted 3/25/62 **W 7/1**
Private John Shankle 49 yr old Stanly Co. farmer enlisted 3/25/62 **C 7/14**

Company K *"The Fighting Boys"*

1st Lt Junius Goslen 22 yr old Forsyth Co.student enlisted 4/3/62 (in command 7/3)
2nd Lt Romulus Cox 28 yr old Forsyth Co. teacher enlisted 4/3/62 (later W Globe Tavern)
3rd Lt. Virgil Walker 23 yr old Forsyth Co. teacher enlisted 4/3/62 (later C Burgess Mill)
1st Sgt William Wallace 22 yr old Wae Co. farmer enlisted 3/22/62 (later W Jone's farm)
Sgt Gideon Clayton 26 yr old Forsyth Co. farmer enlisted 3/22/62 **WC 7/3**
Sgt Francis Hardgrove 20 yr old Forsyth farmer enlisted 3/22/62 (later W Bristoe)
Sgt Thomas Pratt 22 yr old Forsyth farmer enlisted 3/22/62 **K 7/3**
Cpl. Thomas Davis 20 yr old Forsyth Co. farmer enlisted 3/22/62 **C 7/3**
Cpl. Lauriston Elliot 21 yr old Forsyth farmer enlisted 3/26/62 **W-right forearm C 7/3**
Cpl. James Ingram 27 yr old Forsyth farmer enlisted 3/22/62 **C 7/14**
Cpl. William Pratt 22 yr old Forsyth farmer enlisted 3/22/62 **C 7/3**
Private Henry Bowen 31 yr old Forsyth farmer enlisted 3/22/62 **W-thigh & ankle C 7/3**
Private Micajah Brown 21 yr old Wilkes Co. farmer enlisted 10/30/62
Private William Browning 17 yr old Forsyth farmer enlisted 3/22/62 **C 7/14**
Private Alexander Carmichael 21 yr old Forsyth Co. farmer enlisted 3/22/62

Private John Carmichael 23 yr old Forsyth farmer Co. enlisted 3/22/62 (later detailed as baker)
Private Thomas Carmichael 19 yr old Forsyth farmer enlisted 3/22/62 **WC 7/3**
Private Nathan Craft 27 yr old Forsyth carpenter enlisted 3/22/62 (later C Bristoe)
Private Yancey Crews 18 yr old Forsyth farmer substituted 5/5/62 **C 7/5 as nurse**
Private Hamilton Davis 31 yr old Forsyth blacksmith enlisted 3/22/62 **W-ankle C 7/3 died**
Private George Dull 24 yr old Forsyth farmer enlisted 3/13/62 **W-left leg C 7/3**
Private Henderson Dull 26 yr old Forsyth farmer enlisted 3/13/62 **WC 7/3**
Private Leroy Elliot 19 yr old Forsyth farmer enlisted 7/10/62 **W-arm C 7/3**
Private James Glasscock 27 yr old Forsyth Co. farmer enlisted 3/18/62 **C 7/14**
Private Silas Hampton 31 yr old Forsyth farmer enlisted 10/30/62 **W-leg 7/3 C 7/14**
Private Lewis Hardgrove 23 yr old Forsyth farmer enlisted 3/18/62 **C 7/3**
Private Thomas Hardgrove 22 yr old Forsyth farmer enlisted 3/22/62 **C 7/14**
Private Moses Hauser 35 yr old Forsyth farmer enlisted 3/18/62 **W-hand & thigh 7/3**
Private Edward Hine 30 yr old Forsyth Co. farmer enlisted 3/18/62 **C 7/3**
Private Theodore Hine 33 yr old Forsyth farmer enlisted 2/10/62 **C 7/3**
Private William Holdeer19 yr old Forsyth farmer enlisted 3/18/62
Private Thomas Jennings 31 yr old Forsyth farmer enlisted 4/30/62 (later C Burgess Mill)
Private Jesse Johnson 23 yr old Forsyth farmer enlisted 3/18/62 **W-thigh C 7/3**
Private John Johnson 20 yr old Forsyth farmer enlisted 3/22/62 W-Goldboro
Private William Johnson 26 yr old Forsyth farmer enlisted 3/22/62 **W-thigh C 7/3**
Private John Jones 19 yr old Forsyth farmer enlisted 3/18/62 **W 7/3 C 7/14**
Private Adam Kiger 23 yr old Forsyth farmer enlisted 3/18/62
Private Solomon Livengood 37 yr old Forsyth farmer enlisted 2/10/63 **C 7/3**
Private John McKnight 23 yr old Forsyth Co. farmer enlisted 3/22/62 **W-leg C 7/3**
Private John McMillan 37 yr old Forsyth farmer enlisted 3/18/62
Private James Martin 22 yr old Forsyth farmer enlisted 3/14/62 **C 7/14**
Private John Martin 20 yr old Forsyth farmer enlisted 3/14/62 (later W Bristoe)
Private Alexander Merritt 22 yr old Forsyth farmer enlisted 10/8/62 **C 7/3**
Private Thomas Mickey 32 yr old Forsyth farmer enlisted 3/18/62 **W-foot C 7/3**
Private Henry Moore 20 yr old Davidson Co. farmer enlisted 10/8/62 **C 7/3**
Private Robert Moser 22 yr old Forsyth Co. farmer enlisted 3/22/62 (later C Spots)
Private Marvill **Padgett** 26 yr old Rowen Co. farmer enlisted 10/8/62 **C 7/3**
Private Thomas Parham 29 yr old Forsyth Co. farmer enlisted 3/18/62 **W-right arm C 7/3**
Private Jacob Pegram 20 yr old Forsyth Co. farmer enlisted 3/18/62
Private Joseph Pegram 24 yr old Forsyth Co. farmer enlisted 10/8/62 **W-hand C 7/3**
Private Jacob Petree 37 yr old Forsyth Co. farmer enlisted 3/22/62 **C 7/3**
Private James Powers 23 yr old Forsyth Co. farmer enlisted 3/18/62 **K 7/3**
Private Francis Pratt 29 yr old Forsyth Co. farmer enlisted 5/10 62 **C 7/14**
Private Richard Ransom substitute Forsyth farmer enlisted 3/22/62 (later W Bristoe)
Private William Reedy 24 yr old Forsyth farmer enlisted 10/10/62 (later W Petersburg)
Private Edmund Sams 27 yr old Forsyth farmer enlisted 3/22/62 **C 7/3**

Private John Sapp 19 yr old Forsyth farmer enlisted 3/18/62 (later C Bristoe)
Private Michael Sapp 22 yr old Forsyth farmer enlisted 3/22/62 (later C Bristoe)
Private John Shouse 34 yr old Forsyth farmer enlisted 2/10/63 **C 7/3**
Private James Snipes 32 yr old Forsyth farmer enlisted 3/22/62
Private John Snipes 23 yr old Forsyth farmer enlisted 5/10/62
Private Wiley Snipes 21 yr old Forsyth farmer enlisted 5/10/62 **C 7/3**
Private John Starbuck 20 yr old Forsyth farmer enlisted 2/10/62 **W-left thigh C 7/3**
Private Amos Transou 19 yr old Forsyth farmer enlisted 2/10/62 **W-head 7/3** (later Sgt)
Private Alfred Walker 19 yr old Forsyth farmer enlisted 5/16/62 (later C Spots)
Private David Westmoreland 22 yr old Forsyth farmer enlisted 3/22/62 **K 7/3**
Private Oliver Westmoreland 19 yr old Forsyth farmer enlisted 3/22/62 **C 7/14**
Private George Yeates 23 yr old Forsyth farmer enlisted 3/22/62 **C 7/3**

July 1 Casualties

Captain Aurelius Blackburn 23 yr old Forsyth Co. student enlisted 4/3/62 **K 7/1**
Sgt William Dawson 28 yr old Forsyth Co. farmer enlisted 3/22/62 **K 7/1**
Private William Cordell 56 yr old Forsyth Co. farmer enlisted 3/26/62 **C 7/14**
Private John Pendry 31 yr old Forsyth Co. laborer enlisted 3/22/62 **W-breast (shell) 7/1 C 7/5**
Private Bennett Sprinkle 39 yr old Forsyth farmer enlisted 2/10/62 **C 7/14**

FORTY SEVENTH NORTH CAROLINA REGIMENT

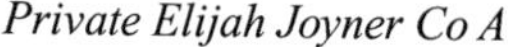

Private Elijah Joyner Co A

Private James Yates Co H

Field & Staff

Colonel George Faribault 33 yr old Captain Co E 14th NC appointed Lt Col 4/9/62 promoted 1/5/63 **W-right shoulder & foot 7/3**

Lieutenant Colonel John Graves 40 yr old Captain Co A 13th NC appointed Major 4/8/62 promoted 4/5/63 **WC 7/3**

Major Archibald Crudup 47 yr old Captain Co B appointed Major 1/5/63 **W-breast, neck, left arm C 7/3**

Adjutant Thomas Powell 25 yr old enlisted Wake Co. appointed 7/31/62 **W-right eye 7/3 C 7/4**

Sergeant Major Pascahll Page 27 yr old enlisted Wake Co. 10/20/62 promoted 4/14/62

Quartermaster Samuel Bridgers 22 yr old clerk enlisted 2/22/62 to Co G appointed 3/1/63

Quartermaster Clerk Frank Timberlake 23 yr old teacher enlisted Franklin Co. 2/20/62 detailed 11/62

Assistant Quartermaster James Thomas appointed 7/8/62 (later QM Brigade)

Quartermaster Carpenter Edward Gillespie 38 yr old enlisted Alamance Co. 4/23/62

Assistant Commissary of Subsistence Benjamin Justice appointed 7/21/62

Commissary Sergeant Rufus Temple 35 yr old enlisted Wake Co 5/5/62 promoted 8/62

Surgeon Franklin White 28 yr old physician appointed 3/1/63 **C Williamsport 7/5**

Assistant Surgeon 31 yr old physician enlisted Franklin Co 8/9/62

Hospital Steward 25 yr old school teacher enlisted Franklin Co. 3/28/62 Appointed 5/3/63
Hospital Steward Jonathan Stone transferred 4/62 reported to duty 2/63
Ordinance Sergeant George Hines 26 yr old merchant enlisted 3/1/63 detailed 3/63
Brigade Courier Benjamin Matthews enlisted Camp Mangum 5/16/62 **W-left arm C 7/3**
Brigade Courier Frederic Backus 19 yr old enlisted Granville Co. 3/3/62

Company A *"Chicora Guards"*

Captain John Thorpe enlisted 3/1/62 (wrote article) "82 trigger pullers 7/1" plus officers (4)
2nd Lt Sidney Bridgers 23 yr old enlisted Franklin Co. 2/18/62 (later W-right side Bristoe Station)
3rd Lt Benjamin Bunn enlisted 9/24/62 **W 7/3**
1st Sgt Joseph Partin 20 yr old enlisted Halifax Co 2/9/62 **C 7/3**
Sgt Charles Braswell 23 yr old enlisted Nash Co 1/23/62 (later C Bristoe Station)
Sgt James Deans 23 yr old enlisted Nash Co 2/29/62
Sgt. William Stott 25 yr old enlisted Nash Co 3/3/62
Color Cpl. William Chambee 22 yr old enlisted Nash Co 3/26/62 **W 7/3** (later W Bristoe Station)
Corp. Irvin Eatman 19 yr old enlisted Nash Co 3/10/62 (later C Bristoe Station)
Private Edmond Abernathy 21 yr old enlisted Camp Vance 10/18/62 (later WC Burgess Mill)
Private Abijah Baines 35 yr old enlisted Nash Co 2/4/62 **C 7/3**
Private Edmond Bass 24 yr old enlisted Nash Co 2/24/62 (later C Burgess Mill)
Private William Bass 49 yr old enlisted Nash Co 2/24/62 **C 7/14**
Private Jordan Batchelor 36 yr old enlisted Nash Co 5/3/62 C 7/14
Private Richard Batchelor 23 yr old enlisted Nash Co 1/1/63 (later C Bristoe Station)
Private Wright Bachelor 34 yr old enlisted Nash Co 2/4/62 (later C Bristoe Station)
Private Jackson Bissett 28 yr old enlisted Nash Co 4/19/62 ***C 7/14***
Private Joseph Bissett 19 yr old enlisted Nash Co 2/5/62 (later W Burgess Mill)
Private Josiah Bissett 28 yr old enlisted Nash Co 4/4/62 (later W Burgess Mill))
Private Manoah Bissett 17 yr old enlisted Nash Co 5/3/62 (later W Bristoe, Spotsylvania, Cold Harbor)
Private William Boone 27 yr old enlisted Nash Co 3/3/62 **C 7/14**
Private Lovett Boykin 18 yr old enlisted Nash Co 3/7/62 **W-breast 7/3** (later C Bristoe Station)
Private Lemuel Braswell 20 yr old enlisted Nash Co 2/24/62 **C 7/14**
Private Patrick Henry Braswell 19 yr old enlisted Nash Co 10/1/62 (later W Bristoe Station)
Private Augustus Chambee 21 yr old enlisted Nash Co 1/29/62 (later Corp)
Private Jonathan Cockrell 19 yr old enlisted Nash Co 2/24/62 **WC 7/3 died teamster called up**

Private Nicholas Collins 20 yr old enlisted Nash Co 2/24/62 (later detailed as Baker)
Private Neverson Cone 19 yr old enlisted Nash Co 2/24/62 **W-leg C 7/3 died**
Private John Daly 19 yr old enlisted Lenoir Co 5/14/62 **C 7/3**
Private Jesse Davis 36 yr old enlisted Nash Co 2/22/62 (later C Bristoe Station)
Private Ransom Dodd 19 yr old enlisted Nash Co 3/1/63 **W 7/3** later Corporal
Private William Dozier 20 yr old enlisted Nash Co 2/4/62
Private Edward Finch 25 yr old enlisted Nash Co 3/7/62
Private William Finch 32 yr old enlisted Nash Co 4/19/62 (later detailed as cook)
Private Vine Glover 19 yr old enlisted Nash Co 3/10/62 (later C Bristoe Station)
Private Isham Hagwood 31 yr old enlisted Nash Co 4/19/62 (later C Bristoe Station)
Private Andrew Henderson 29 yr old enlisted Nash Co 4/23/62 **W 7/3** (later C Burgess Mill)
Private Bartley Jones 18 yr old enlisted Nash Co 3/7/62 (later C Bristoe Station)
Private Eli Joyner 23 yr old enlisted Nash Co 2/24/62 **W-side 7/3—died 7/6**
Private John Joyner 19 yr old enlisted Nash Co 2/24/62
Private Kinchen Joyner 19 yr old enlisted Nash Co 4/30/62 **W-hips 7/3** (later W Bristoe Station)
Private William Joyner 22 yr old enlisted Nash Co 2/24/62 **C 7/14**
Private Stephen Lamm 27 yr old enlisted Nash Co 2/14/62 ***W-wrist** 7/3 (later detailed QM dept)*
Private Thomas Lamm 38 yr old enlisted Nash Co 4/10/62 ***C 7/14***
Private William Lamm 31 yr old enlisted Nash Co 2/24/62 ***W-both thighs C 7/3***
Private Gilbert Lewis 22 yr old enlisted Nash Co 5/15/62 **K 7/3**
Private Joseph Manning 19 yr old enlisted Wilson Co 5/15/62 (later C Bristoe Station)
Private Caswell Matthews 34 yr old enlisted Nash Co 2/24/62 **C 7/14**
Private John Morgan 20 yr old enlisted Nash Co 5/9/62 (later W-left foot Petersburg)
Private Kerney Morgan 25 yr old enlisted Nash Co 2/23/62 (W-right leg Ream's Station)
Private William Morgan 18 yr old enlisted Nash Co 3/7/62 (later C Bristoe Station)
Private John Morris 36 yr old enlisted Nash Co 3/1/63 **C 7/14**
Private William D. Murray 25 yr old mechanic enlisted Nash Co 2/24/62 **C 7/14**
Private William G. Murray 23 yr old enlisted Nash Co 2/23/62 (later W Bristoe Station)
Private James O'Neal 25 yr old enlisted Nash Co 4/25/62 **C 7/3**
Private Elijah Patterson 26 yr old mechanic enlisted Nash Co 2/12/62 (later C Bristoe Station)
Private Sidney Patterson 44 yr old enlisted Nash Co 2/12/62 (later C Bristoe Station)
Private James Perry 20 yr old enlisted Nash Co 2/24/62 ***W-thigh C 7/3***
Private John Perry 48 yr old enlisted 1/23/62 (deserted 7/27/63—returned) FATHER
Private James Puckett 19 yr old enlisted Nash Co 1/28/62 **W-leg 7/14**
Private William Riley 43 yr old enlisted Nash Co 5/15/62 **W-both thighs 7/3**
Private Samuel Sellers 21 yr old enlisted "Sunny South" 2/8/62 **W-abdomen C 7/3**
Private Bryant P Strickland 26 yr old enlisted Nash Co 5/12/62 C 7/3
Private James Strickland 20 yr old enlisted Nash Co 1/23/62
Private Lemon Strickland 19 yr old enlisted Nash Co 2/18/62

Private Marcus Strickland 21 yr old enlisted Nash Co 1/28/62 **K 7/3**
Private William Strickland 31 yr old enlisted Wilson Co 3/10/62 (later C North Anna River)
Private William Taylor 34 yr old enlisted Nash Co 2/24/62 (later C Bristoe Station)
Private Wren Tinsdale 28 yr old enlisted Nash Co 5/20/63 **W-right leg C 7/3**
Private William Tolbert 27 yr old enlisted Battleboro, NC 2/2/62
Private John Turner 18 yr old enlisted Nash Co 2/24/62 (later C Bristoe Station)
Private Willis Warren 20 yr old enlisted Nash Co 5/15/62 (later Corp & Sgt W Ream's Station)
Private Jeremiah Westray 24 yr old enlisted Nash Co 3/13/62 (later W Wilderness)

Teamster Joel Wells 24 yr old enlisted Nash Co 2/14/62 **C 7/14**
Teamster Benjamin Whitley 26 yr old enlisted Camp Mangum 5/10/62
Teamster William Whitley 33 yr old enlisted Nash Co 2/23/62 (later provost guard)

July 1 Casualties

1st Lt. George Westray enlisted 4/11/62 **W-arm & groin 7/1** (later W Bristoe Station K Cold Harbor)
Sgt John Barnhill 24 yr old enlisted Nash Co 2/8/62 **W 7/1** (later W Bristoe Station)
Sgt William Cone 27 yr old enlisted Nash Co 2/23/62 **W-shoulder & head 7/1** (later W Wilderness)
Sgt. Zachariah Westray 21 yr old enlisted Nash Co 1/29/62 **W 7/1**
Cpl. Seymour Warren 22 yr old enlisted Nash Co 3/5/62 **W 7/1-C 7/5** (later W-left leg Cold Harbor)
Private Williamson Abernathy 29 yr old enlisted Nash Co 1/29/62 **K 7/1**
Private James Bunn 44 yr old enlisted Nash Co 2/23/62 **W 7/1 C 7/5**
Private Richard Dozier 44 yr old enlisted Nash Co 2/11/62 **K 7/1**
Private William Edwards 22 yr old enlisted Nash Co 2/11/62 **W-hand 7/1** (W Bristoe Station)
Private Martin Green 28 yr old enlisted Nash Co 5/2/62 **W-right hand 7/1**
Private Abijab Griffin 37 yr old enlisted Nash Co 10/10/62 **W 7/1** (later W Bristoe Station)
Private Gilliam Lewis 20 yr old enlisted Nash Co 5/15/62 **W 7/1**
Private Emerson Puckett 32 yr old enlisted Nash Co 2/12/62 **K 7/1**

Company B *"Franklin County"*

Captain Joseph "Honest Joe" Harris 30 yr old enlisted 2/24/62 **WC 7/3**
1st Lt. Sherwood Evans 35 yr old enlisted 2/24/62 **W-shoulder & left hand C 7/3** (two middle fingers amp)
2nd Lt Hugh Perry 22 yr old enlisted 3/15/62 **W-left leg 7/3**
3rd Lt William Chamblee On Furlough

1st Sgt Wiley Clifton 22 yr old enlisted Franklin Co 5/28/62 (demoted 9/1/63)
1st Sgt William Phillips 33 yr old enlisted Franklin Co 5/15/62
Sgt John Pearce 24 yr old enlisted Franklin Co 2/28/62 **W-head 7/3**
Corp. Peyton Massey enlisted Franklin Co 5/2/62 **C 7/3**
Corp. Western Perry 20 yr old enlisted Nash Co 1/23/62
Private Grandberry Allen 23 yr old enlisted Franklin County 3/15/62 (later Corp & Sgt)
Private Leven Allen 37 yr old enlisted Franklin Co 2/28/62 **W 7/3**
Private Matthew Arnold 25 yr old enlisted Franklin Co 2/28/62 (later K Ream's Station)
Private James Baker 26 yr old enlisted Franklin Co 5/2/62 **WC 7/3**
Private Willis Bolton 22 yr old enlisted Franklin Co 5/13/62 (died of disease 1/12/64)
Private Berry Bryant 18 yr old enlisted Nash Co 3/5/63 (later C Burgess Mill, Va)
Private Archibald Bunn 32 yr old enlisted Wake Co 3/5/62 left sick **C 7/5**
Private Ellis Bunn 36 yr old enlisted Wake Co 2/22/62 (later W Bristoe Station)
Private George Bunn 19 yr old enlisted Franklin Co 3/3/62
Private James Bunn 19 yr old enlisted Franklin Co 3/6/62 ***W-left thigh C 7/3***
Private Marion Bunn 18 yr old enlisted Franklin Co 4/29/62 **W-cheek 7/3 C 7/5**
Private George Carter 29 yr old enlisted Franklin Co 4/9/63 (later W Ream's Station)
Private John Cheves 35 yr old enlisted Franklin Co 5/15/62 (later Corp & Sgt)
Private Thomas Cheves 22 yr old enlisted Franklin Co 2/26/62 **K 7/3**
Private William Cone 25 yr old enlisted Franklin Co 2/26/62 **W-left foot 7/3 C 7/5**
Private James Cook 31 yr old enlisted Franklin Co 2/26/62 **W-left arm 7/3 C 7/5**
Private Thomas Cook 19 yr old enlisted Franklin Co 2/26/62 (later C Spotsylvania)
Private Lemuel Cooley 15 yr old enlisted Franklin Co. 3/11/62 **WC 7/3 (died 7/14/63)**
Private Curby Denton 25 yr old enlisted Franklin Co. 2/22/62 (later K—"by a tree" 8/64)
Private Fenner Denton 17 yr old enlisted Franklin Co 2/26/62
Private Joseph Dixon 20 yr old enlisted Franklin Co 5/26/62
Private Henry Etherridge 21 yr old enlisted Franklin Co 5/26/62 (later W Bristoe Station)
Private Wiley Ferrell 19 yr old enlisted Wake Co 5/16/62
Private Henry Gay enlisted Franklin Co 6/4/63 **C 7/14**
Private Josiah Green 22 yr old enlisted Franklin Co 2/28/62 **W-neck 7/3**
Private Marcilers Harris 19 yr old enlisted 10/13/63 (later Sgt)
Private Hardy Hicks 27 yr old enlisted Franklin Co 5/26/62
Private William Hicks 39 yr old enlisted Franklin Co 3/5/62
Private Alexander Hopkins 18 yr old enlisted Franklin Co 2/26/62 **W 7/3**
Private John Jeffreys 33 yr old enlisted Franklin Co 2/27/62 (later Corp)
Private Dennis Johnson 19 yr old enlisted Franklin Co 4/21/62 **W 7/3 C 7/5**
Private Seth Jones 18 yr old enlisted Franklin Co 3/11/62 (later W-finger Ream's Station)
Private Lemon Joyner 35 yr old enlisted Franklin Co.
Private Bryant Martin 28 yr old enlisted Franklin Co 2/28/62
Private Archibald Medlin 46 yr old enlisted as substitute Wake Co. 4/11/63 **C 7/14**
Private Hartley Medlin 47 yr old enlisted Franklin Co 2/22/62 **C 7/14**
Private Hartley Medlin 47 yr old enlisted Franklin Co 2/22/62 **C 7/5 as nurse**

Private James Medlin 21 yr old enlisted Franklin Co 2/22/62 **W-hand 7/3**
Private John Medlin 27 yr old enlisted Franklin Co 2/26/62 (later K Spotsylvania)
Private James Moss 21 yr old enlisted Franklin Co 2/22/62 **W-hand 7/3**
Private Marion Moye 17 yr old enlisted Franklin Co 3/6/62 **K 7/3**
Private William Moye 33 yr old enlisted Franklin Co 5/15/62 (later W-hand Wilderness / W-shell Cold Harbor
Private James D Pearce 19 yr old enlisted Franklin Co 2/16/62 (later W-right hand & shoulder Cold Harbor)
Private Lee Pearce 21 yr old enlisted Franklin Co 2/27/62
Private Barham Perry 22 yr old enlisted Franklin Co 2/28/62 (later Corp W Hatcher's Run))
Private James Perry 40 yr old enlisted Franklin Co 4/11/63 (later W Petersburg)
Private Kerney Perry 25 yr old enlisted Franklin Co 5/16/62 (later Corp W Hatcher's Run)
Private Lindsay Perry enlisted Nash Co. 5/4/62 C 7/5 Fayette, Pa (later K Burgess Mill)
Private Wesley Perry 34 yr old enlisted Franklin Co 5/17/62 (later K Ream's Station)
Private Calvin Pippin 33 yr old enlisted Franklin Co 5/15/62
Private Wesley Pippin 26 yr old enlisted Franklin Co 5/15/62
Private William Privett 19 yr old enlisted Franklin Co 2/26/62
Private Jimesson Pucket 30 yr old enlisted Franklin Co 3/15/62 **K 7/3**
Private Richardson Rice 32 yr old enlisted Franklin Co 4/28/62 **C sick 7/5**
Private John Riley 17 yr old enlisted Franklin Co 3/5/62 C 7/14 (joined US Service)
Private Reuben Rogers 46 yr old enlisted Franklin Co 2/22/62 **left sick and captured 7/5**
Private Lee Tant 43 yr old enlisted Franklin Co 2/27/62 **W-both legs 7/3** (later W Wilderness)
Private Thomas Tant 37 yr old enlisted Franklin Co 3/6/62 (died disease 12/7/63)
Private William Tucker 23 yr old enlisted Franklin Co 4/21/62
Private Burkley Upchurch 32 yr old enlisted Franklin Co 2/27/62
Private John Upchurch 23 yr old enlisted Franklin Co 5/2/62 (later C Burgess Mill)
Private William Wiggs 23 yr old enlisted Franklin Co 3/5/62 (later Corp & Sgt W Burgess Mil)
Private Starling Wood 48 yr old enlisted Franklin Co 2/27/62 **C 7/5 as nurse**
Private Washington Wood 18 yr old enlisted Franklin Co 2/27/62

July 1 Casualties

Sgt Augustus Bryant 26 yr old enlisted Nash Co 3/4/62 **W-left leg 7/1 C 7/5 (amp)**
Private Abijab Carter 35 yr old enlisted Franklin Co 5/15/62 **W-arm 7/1**
Private William Gay 34 yr old enlisted Franklin Co 5/13/62 **W-legs 7/1 C 7/4** (died 7/4)
Private Abihu Johnson 20 yr old enlisted Franklin Co 2/22/62 **W-thigh 7/1 C 7/5 attending wounded**
Private William Meacom 18 yr old enlisted Franklin Co 4/21/62 **W-left thigh & chest 7/2**
Private James Pearce 18 yr old enlisted Franklin Co 2/22/62 **W-arm 7/1**
Private Chesley Perry 27 yr old enlisted Franklin Co 3/26/62 **K 7/1**

Private Gideon Phillips 19 yr old enlisted Franklin Co 2/26/62 **W-right foot 7/1**
Private Richmond Phillips 21 yr old enlisted Franklin Co 2/27/62 **W-foot 7/1 C 7/5**
Private Joseph Stallings 31 yr old enlisted Franklin Co 5/1/62 **W-thigh 7/1 C 7/5**

Company C *"Wake County"*

1st Lt. George Whiting 21 yr old druggist enlisted Wake Co 2/27/62 **W-head C 7/3 (later Capt)**
2nd Lt Nathaniel Brown 22 yr old watchmaker enlisted Wake Co 2/22/62 (later 1st Lt) **(Finger wound 7/3)**
3rd Lt Marmaduke Norfleet elected 11/1/62 **W-groin "hand to hand combat" C 7/3 (later 2nd Lt)**
1st Sgt L.M. Green 19 yr old enlisted Wake Co. 2/11/62 **W-face C 7/3**
Sgt Thomas Bunch 26 yr old enlisted Wake Co. 2/25/62 (later C Bristoe Station)
Sgt William Hall enlisted 2/21/62 (later hospital guard C Burgess Mill)
Sgt John transferred 2/21/62 (AWOL 11/63—returned C Burgess Mill)
Sgt. Edward Williams 20 yr old enlisted Wake Co. 11/9/62 (later C Bristoe Station)
Cpl. Jacob Adams 27 yr old lawyer enlisted Wake Co 2/17/62 (later C Bristoe Station)
Cpl. Robert Beddington 26 yr old carpenter enlisted Wake Co. 3/11/62 **K 7/3 (shell in advance)**
Cpl. Henry House 26 yr old enlisted 2/3/62 (later W-left leg Bristoe Station)
Cpl. Rufus Sanders 19 yr old enlisted Wake Co. 2/3/62 **W-arm 7/3**
Cpl. Gaston Utley 47 yr old enlisted Wake Co. 2/23/62 **WC 7/3 died**
Private M. Bishop 23 yr old enlisted Wake Co. 2/27/62 **C 7/14**
Private H.H. Bunch 24 yr old enlisted Wake Co. 2/25/62 (deserted 8/23/63—returned)
Private Julius Bunch 19 yr old enlisted Wake Co. 2/25/62 **W-right leg 7/3 C 7/5**
Private Samuel Carr 26 yr old carpenter enlisted Wake Co. 3/1/62 **C 7/3** (later joined US Service)
Private Isiah Cates 38 yr old enlisted Wake Co. 10/22/62 **W-head 7/3**
Private Atlas Denton 32 yr old enlisted Wake Co. 1/18/62 Color bearer
Private Haywood Dixon 26 yr old enlisted Wake Co. 2/24/62 (later C Bristoe Station)
Private John Done 21 yr old enlisted Wake Co. 3/1/62 **W-lungs C 7/3** (died 11/22)
Private John Edmonds 19 yr old laborer enlisted Wake Co. 1/21/62
Private J.T. Ferrell 24 yr old enlisted Wake Co. 2/18/62
Private Thomas Ferrell 23 yr old enlisted Wake Co. 2/15/62 **C 7/14**
Private H.H. Forrest enlisted Camp Mangum 5/15/62 (later W Bristoe Station)
Private Rufus Fowler 24 yr old enlisted 1/25/62 (later W left leg Bristoe Station)
Private Nicholas Gill 19 yr old clerk enlisted Wake Co 3/3/62 **K 7/3**
Private John Glover 34 yr old enlisted Wake Co. 1/17/62 (later W-right leg & left arm Bristoe Station)
Private James Goodwin 19 yr old enlisted Wake Co. 2/4/62

Private Joseph Haley 35 yr old enlisted Wake Co. 3/3/62 **C 7/14**
Private James House 23 yr old enlisted Wake Co. 2/13/62 **WC 7/3**
Private John Johnson 18 yr old enlisted Wake Co. 2/18/62 **K 7/3**
Private James Jones 19 yr old enlisted Wake Co. 3/1/62
Private William Justice 19 yr old enlisted Wake Co. 2/1/63 (Later W-arm Petersburg)
Private William Keith 28 yr old carpenter enlisted Wake Co. 1/18/62 (deserted 8/63—returned)
Private James Lowe 23 yr old enlisted Halifax Co 2/19/62 **C 7/5**
Private Etheldred Matthews transferred 10/62 (later C Burgess Mill)
Private Ransom Matthews 21 yr old enlisted Wake Co. 3/1/62 (later C Burgess Mill)
Private A.H. Maynard 32 yr old enlisted Wake Co. 2/10/62 **C 7/14**
Private William Maynard 35 yr old enlisted Wake Co. 2/10/62 **C 7/14**
Private Drewry Mewborn 22 yr old enlisted Lenoir Co 10/21/62 (later C Bristoe Station)
Private George Moore 21 yr old enlisted Wake Co. 2/21/62 **C 7/14**
Private James O'Daniel 25 yr old enlisted Wake Co. 10/20/62 **C 7/14**
Private W. O'Daniel 23 yr old enlisted Wake Co. 10/20/62 (deserted 8/26/63—arrested)
Private George Partine enlisted camp Mangum 5/10/62 **C 7/3**
Private John Partin transferred 9/18/62 (deserted 8/26/63—returned)
Private John Pilkinton 27 yr old enlisted Franklin Co 1/18/62 **C 7/3**
Private William Pollard 22 yr old enlisted Wake Co. 3/1/62 (deserted 8/26/63—returned)
Private James Pool 24 yr old enlisted Wake Co. 3/4/62 (deserted 8/26/63—returned)
Private Ransom Pool 31 yr old enlisted Wake Co. 1/18/62 (later detached as shoemaker)
Private Weston Rogers 22 yr old enlisted Wake Co. 2/17/62 (deserted 8/26/63—returned W-Wilderness)
Private William Sanders 19 yr old enlisted Camp magnum 3/3/62 **C 7/14**
Private James Stephens 29 yr old enlisted Guilford Co 10/22/62 (later Corp & Sgt)
Private Bartlett Underwood 40 yr old enlisted Wake Co. 2/27/62 **W-knee 7/3** (deserted 8/26/63—returned W-Bristoe Station)
Private Alfred Webster 18 yr old enlisted Wake Co. 2/5/62 (later W Wilderness)
Private Christopher Woodward 32 yr old enlisted Wake Co. 1/18/62
Private Joseph Woodward 26 yr old enlisted Wake Co. 1/18/62 **K 7/3**
Private William Wright 19 yr old tobacconist enlisted Wake Co. 3/10/62

Teamster Hilliard Rogers 19 yr old enlisted Wake Co. 2/12/62
Drummer William Smith transferred 7/1/62
Musician W.P. Bragg 18 yr old printer enlisted Wake Co. 3/24/62

7/1 Casualties

Captain Campbell Iredell 26 yr old druggist enlisted Wake Co 2/27/62 **K "arm shot off" 7/1**
Sgt E.C.N. Green 22 yr old enlisted Wake Co. 2/10/62 **K 7/1**

Private John Bishop carpenter enlisted wake Co 7/2/62 **W 7/1 C 7/4** (later C Burgess Mill)
Private N.N. Bunch 22 yr old enlisted Wake Co. 7/7/62 **W-thigh 7/1**
Private Preston Kelly 46 yr old shoemaker enlisted Wake Co. 1/18/62 **W-face, hand & breast 7/1**
Private Hansel Pool 26 yr old enlisted Wake Co 1/18/62 **K 7/1**
Private James Royster transferred 4/30/63 W-left thigh & knee **7/1 C 7/14**
Private William Stephens 20 yr old enlisted Wake Co. 3/1/62 **W-wrist 7/1 C 7/14**

Company D *"Castalia Invincibles"*

Captain George Lewis 39 yr old enlisted Nash Co 2/27/62 (later W-left thigh Bristoe Station)
1st Lt. Richard Drake 30 yr old enlisted Nash Co 2/24/62 **WC 7/3**
2nd Lt William Blount 2nd Lt transferred 12/2/62 (later W-right arm Bristoe Station)
3rdLt John Winbourne 30 yr old enlisted Nash Co 3/3/62 (later 1st Lt)
1st Sgt Nathaniel Caudell 33 yr old enlisted Nash Co 2/23/62
Sgt Rufus Daniel 31 yr old enlisted Wilson Co 5/14/62 **C 7/14**
Sgt William Drake 24 yr old enlisted Nash Co 2/22/62 **W 7/3 C 7/5**
Sgt Dempsey Eure 25 yr old enlisted Nash Co 3/3/62 (later W-wrist Jones farm)
Cpl. Allison High 26 yr old enlisted Wilson Co. 5/14/62 (later Sgt)
Corp. Edwin Powell 25 yr old enlisted Nash Co 2/21/62 (later Sgt)
Cpl. Rufus Pullen 37 yr old enlisted Nash Co. 2/21/62 **W-hip 7/3 C 7/5**
Private Gideon Bass 18 yr old enlisted Nash Co 2/24/62
Private Rufus Bell 28 yr old enlisted Nash Co 3/6/62 **C 7/3**
Private Joel Bottoms 19 yr old enlisted Wilson Co 10/18/62 **W 7/3 C 7/5**
Private John Brown 19 yr old enlisted Nash Co 2/24/62
Private Dorsey Deans 24 yr old enlisted Nash Co 10/18/62 (later C Bristoe Station)
Private Augustus Delbridge 26 yr old enlisted Nash Co 2/22/62 **W-head 7/3** (later C Bristoe Station)
Private Barnsey Driver 29 yr old enlisted Wayne Co 3/1/63 **W 7/3 C 7/5 died**
Private Calvin Driver 26 yr old enlisted Nash Co 2/24/62 **C 7/5**
Private Zackariah Driver 31 yr old enlisted Duplin Co 2/10/63 **C 7/14**
Private William Griffin 29 yr old enlisted Griffin Co 4/27/62 (later C Hatcher's Run)
Private Robert Harper 24 yr old enlisted Nash Co 2/24/62 (deserted 8/23/63—returned C Bristoe Station)
Private Amacy Hicks 36 yr old enlisted Nash Co 3/14/62 **W-neck C 7/14**
Private Henderson High 22 yr old enlisted Wilson Co 5/14/62 (deserted 7/28/63—returned)
Private Huel Hinton 19yr old enlisted Johnston Co 18/10/62
Private Alsie Hopkins 22 yr old enlisted Nash Co 2/24/62 **W-arm 7/3** (laterW-Wilderness)
Private Emerson Johnson 24 yr old enlisted Nash Co 3/3/62 **MW-bowels C 7/3**

Private Bryant Jordan 35 yr old enlisted Nash Co 2/24/62
Private Cornelius Joyner 34 yr old enlisted Nash Co 2/24/62 **W-right knee 7/3**
Private Henry Joyner 36 yr old enlisted Nash Co 7/2/62
Private Berry Lee 35 yr old enlisted Nash Co 4/22/62 **W-knee C 7/3** (died 8/4)
Private William J Lee 19 yr old enlisted Wayne Co 3/18/62 (later hospital nurse)
Private Caswell Lewis 26 yr old enlisted Wilson Co 5/14/62
Private Josiah Lewis 36 yr old enlisted Nash Co 10/18/62 **C 7/5**
Private O.K. Massey 35 yr old enlisted Nash Co 4/27/62 (later Corp K Cold Harbor)
Private Goodman Massingale 28 yr old enlisted Nash Co 3/18/62 (later FW Bristoe Station)
Private William May 17 yr old enlisted Nash Co 2/24/62 (later W Bristoe Station)
Private Robert Melton 20 yr old enlisted Nash Co 2/22/62 **WC 7/3 died 7/25**
Private Benjamin Murray 19 yr old enlisted Nash Co 3/1/63 (deserted 8/23/63 returned)
Private Joseph Peacock 19 yr old enlisted Nash Co 7/1/63 on march **C 7/14** (later Corp)
Private Amos Pearson 19 yr old enlisted Nash Co 2/24/62 3/1/63
Private Needham Price 31 yr old enlisted Johnston Co 10/18/62 (deserted 1/20/64)
Private Granbury Proctor 31 yr old enlisted Nash Co. 2/24/62 (later C Burgess Mill)
Private Emelius Pullen 42 yr old enlisted Nash Co. 2/24/62 **left sick C 7/5**
Private Ruffin Ricks 26 yr old enlisted Nash Co. 10/18/62 **WC 7/3**
Private Spencer Ricks 34 yr old enlisted Nash Co. 3/1/63 **W-thigh 7/3** (later C Bristoe Station)
Private Benjamin Roe 32 yr old enlisted Nash Co. 2/24/62 (later C Burgess Mill)
Private John Rose 26 yr old enlisted Nash Co. 3/18/62 **C 7/14**
Private Granberry Rowe 27 yr old enlisted Nash Co. 3/3/63
Private George Smith 25 yr old enlisted Nash Co. 3/18/62
Private Sidney Smith 31 yr old enlisted Nash Co. 3/18/62 (later nurse)
Private Kennel Tant 33 yr old enlisted Nash Co. 2/24/62
Private James Turner 38 yr old enlisted Wilson Co. 4/27/62 (died of disease 4/64)
Private Ashley Ward 19 yr old enlisted 7/1/63
Private John West 19 yr old enlisted Nash Co. 6/13/63 (later w-left arm C Bristoe Station)
Private George Wilder 17 yr old enlisted Wayne Co. 3/18/62 **W 7/3 C 7/5**
Private Willie Williams 35 yr old enlisted Nash Co. 2/27/62 **W C 7/14**
Private William Winborne transferred from Co A 9/1/62
Private Alexander Winstead 35 yr old enlisted Nash Co. 2/27/62 (later Corp W-Bristoe Station)
Private Burton Winstead 33 yr old enlisted Nash Co. 4/27/62 **C 7/14** (later K Burgess Mill)
Private John Winstead 31 yr old enlisted Nash Co. 4/27/62

July 1 Casualties

Private Elijah Coggin 48 yr old enlisted Nash Co 2/24/62 **W 7/1 C 7/5**
Private Joseph Deans 21 yr old enlisted Nash Co 10/18/62 **W 7/1 C 7/5**
Private John Floyd 23 yr old enlisted Davidson Co 3/26/62 **W 7/2** (later C North Anna River)

Private Joseph Higgins 38 yr old enlisted Nash Co 3/8/62 **W-knee and left leg 7/1 C 7/5**
Private Manly High 33 yr old enlisted Wilson Co 5/14/62 **W-leg 7/1**
Private Larkin Hyatt 19 yr old miller enlisted Camp Mangum **W-left hand 7/1 C 7/5**
Private William Norwood 24 yr old enlisted Camp Magnum 3/5/62 **K 7/1**
Private Benjamin Stone 33 yr old enlisted Camop Mangum 5/2/62 **Stunned by shell 7/1 C 7/5**
Private Rufus Stone 22 yr old enlisted Nash Co. 2/24/62 **W-right hip 7/1 C 7/5**

Company E *"Wake County"*

Captain John Norwood 31 yr old teacher enlisted Wake Co. (later C Burgess Mill)
1st Lt. Erastus Ray 30 yr old merchant enlisted Wake 2/27/62 **W-leg 7/3**
2nd Lt Leonidas Robertson 32 yr old enlisted Wake 2/27/62 **W-ankle 7/3**
3rd Lt William Dunn 27 yr old merchant enlisted Wake 5/12/62 (later C Burgess Mill)
1st Sgt William Hunter 19 yr old enlisted Wake Co 2/18/62 **W-thigh 7/3**
Sgt. William Hill 21 yr old enlisted Wake Co 1/20/62
Sgt James Norwood 26 yr old enlisted Wake Co 3/4/62
Sgt Joseph Norwood 25 yr old enlisted Wake Co 1/20/62
Sgt. Robert Thompson 19 yr old enlisted Chatham Co 2/8/62 (commanded Co at Appomattox)
Corp Charles Clark 29 yr old enlisted Wake Co 2/3/62 **C 7/5**
Corp. Dawson Johnson 23 yr old wheelwright enlisted Wake Co 2/28/62 **C 7/14**
Corp. Priestly Mangum 32 yr old enlisted Laws Store 1/21/62 **C 7/3**
Private James Adkins 28 yr old enlisted Wake Co 2/28/62 W-thigh **C 7/3**
Private Nathaniel Belvin 40 yr old enlisted Wake Co 2/27/62 (later C Ream's Station)
Private Samuel Bridgers 25 yr old enlisted Wake Co 3/4/62 **C 7/3**
Private Andrew Brogdon 33 yr old enlisted Camp Mangum 3/7/62 **C 7/3**
Private William Cooper 26 yr old enlisted 1/25/62 **W-thigh 7/3**
Private Bryant Creech 44 yr old enlisted Wake Co 2/21/62
Private James Cross 29 yr old enlisted Wake Co 3/21/62
Private Washington Cross 41 yr old enlisted Wake Co 1/25/62
Private William Dancy 41 yr old tailor enlisted Camp Mangum 2/27/62 (later W Bristoe Station)
Private John Davis 25 yr old enlisted Wake Co 1/21/62 **K 7/3**
Private James Dew 34 yr old enlisted Laws Store 1/21/62 **W-foot 7/3** (later W-hand Jone's Farm)
Private Wyatt Dew 29 yr old enlisted Wake Co 3/8/62 **C 7/3**
Private John Glenn enlisted Wake Co. 4/1/63 (later C Burgess Mill)
Private William Gooch 47 yr old enlisted as substitute 3/21/63 **C 7/3**
Private James Gower 34 yr old enlisted Wake Co 3/3/62 **C 7/3**
Private Tiller Grady 31 yr old enlisted Wake Co 3/15/62 **C 7/3**

Private Almi Harrison 40 yr old enlisted Wake Co 1/20/62 **C 7/3**

Private John Honeycutt 18 yr old substitute enlisted Camp Mangum 5/12/62 **W-left leg 7/3**

Private William Honeycutt 19 yr old enlisted Wake Co. 1/25/62 (later Corp)

Private Barney Jones 27 yr old enlisted Wake Co 3/5/62

Private Battle Jones 25 yr old enlisted Wake Co 5/3/62 (later C Bristoe Station)

Private William Lamb 31 yr old enlisted Wake Co 2/17/62 **WC 7/3** (later joined US Service)

Private Jeptha Lassiter 24 yr old enlisted Wake Co 5/13/62

Private Norfleet Lassiter 30 yr old blacksmith enlisted Chatham Co 3/8/62 (later C Bristoe Station)

Private Dorris Mangum 19 yr old enlisted Wake Co 3/4/62 (later W Ream's Station)

Private Jason Mangum enlisted Wake Co. 7/15/62 **K 7/3**

Private W.B. Marcom 37 yr old enlisted Wake Co 2/24/62 **K 7/3**

Private Hubbard Maynard 24 yr old enlisted Halifax Co.

Private Josiah Maynard 37 yr old enlisted Halifax 3/7/62 (later W-hand Wilderness)

Private Sidney Maynard 26 yr old enlisted Wake Co 3/8/62 **K 7/3**

Private William Medlin 27 yr old enlisted Wake Co 3/3/62 **W-thigh C 7/3 (died)**

Private Gaston Mooneyham 24 yr old enlisted Wake Co 1/18/62 **W-wrist 7/3** (later W-shoulder Wilderness)

Private James Nipper 29 yr old enlisted Wake Co 1/25/62 deserted-captured-"whipped" (later C Bristoe Station)

Private John Page 23 yr old enlisted Wake Co 3/3/62 **C 7/3**

Private Marion Powers 26 yr old enlisted Wake Co 1/27/62

Private James Pugh 23 yr old enlisted Wake Co 2/27/62 **C 7/3**

Private James Richardson 28 yr old enlisted Wake Co 1/18/62

Private William Richardson 36 yr old enlisted Wake Co 1/18/62 **W-right arm 7/3**

Private Leonidas Roles 25 yr old clerk enlisted Wake Co 2/24/62

Private Chesley Searles enlisted 2/12/62 (later C Bristoe Station)

Private Henry Smith 17 yr old enlisted Wake Co 3/12/62

Private James Sykes 19 yr old substitute enlisted Wake Co 1/20/62 (later W-arm Wilderness)

Private W.S. Taylor 28 yr old enlisted Wake Co 5/11/62

Private Joseph Terry 25 yr old enlisted Wake Co 1/20/62 (later W—Stomach Wilderness)

Private William Terry 35 yr old enlisted Wake Co 1/20/62

Private Alsey Watkins 35 yr old substitute enlisted Wake Co 3/4/62 **K 7/3**

Private John Watkins 24 yr old enlisted Wake Co 2/24/62 **W-neck C 7/3**

Musician William McDowell 45 yr old substitute enlisted Wake Co 1/21/62 (later W Burgess Mill)

Drummer Silas Boykin 35 yr old carpenter enlisted Wake Co 1/20/62

Teamster Benjamin Taylor 30 yr old enlisted Wake Co 2/21/62 (later K Bristoe Station)

Pioneer Private Thomas Bailey 41 yr old enlisted 2/19/62 (later W Cold Harbor C Hatcher's Run))

July 1 Casualties

Corp. Richardson Honeycutt 19 yr old teacher enlisted Chatham Co. 2/8/62 **W-breast 7/1**

Private John Carpenter 16 yr old enlisted Wake Co 2/27/62 **W-right arm 7/1 C 7/5**

Private Dionysius Jackson enlisted wake Co. 5/5/63 **W 7/2**

Private John McDade 40 yr old enlisted Wake Co 2/27/63 **W-hip & left arm 7/1**

Private Thomas Medlin 21 yr old enlisted Wake Co 1/20/62 **K 7/1**

Private W.A. Medlin 17 yr old enlisted Wake Co 11/25/62 **K 7/1**

Private Calvin Rabon 23 yr old substitute enlisted Wake Co 1/27/62 **K 7/1**

Private Benjamin Smith enlisted Wake Co 2/12/63 **W-breast 7/1**

Private James Snead enlisted 10/21/62 **K 7/1**

Private Jubal Upchurch enlisted wake Co 2/12/63 **W-hip 7/1 (died)**

Private William Wilson 24 yr old enlisted 3/7/62 **K 7/1**

Company F *"Sons of Liberty"*

Captain William Lankford 29 yr old physician enlisted Franklin Co 2/22/62 (later Major)

1st Lt. Julius Joyner 23 yr old enlisted Franklin Co. 3/11/62 **W-hand C 7/3**

2nd Lt Sylvanus Gill 22 yr old teacher enlisted Franklin Co 3/11/62 **W-head & right hand 7/3**

3rd Lt Hugh Crichton 21 yr old clerk enlisted Franklin Co.2/14/62 (later W-head Spotsylvania)

1st Sgt Albert Dement 29 yr old mechanic enlisted Franklin Co. 2/1/62 **WC 7/3 died 7/23**

Sgt. Henry Coggin 20 yr old clerk enlisted Franklin Co. 2/13/62 **C 7/3**

Sgt. Sidney Ellis 20 yr old clerk enlisted Franklin Co. 2/21/62 (later 1st Sgt 3rd Lt C Burgess Mill)

Sgt. Thomas Hoswell 21 yr old enlisted Franklin Co. 3/8/62 **W-hand 7/3**

Cpl. William Benningfield 34 yr old clerk enlisted Franklin Co. 3/4/62 (later Sgt)

Cpl. Zachariah Gill 22 yr old enlisted Franklin Co. 5/23/62 (later Sgt)

Cpl. Leonidas Spencer 20 yr old enlisted Franklin Co 3/4/62 **W 7/3** (later Sgt)

Private James Alford 23 yr old enlisted Franklin Co. 2/14/62 (later Sgt C Burgess Mill)

Private Francis Alley 51 yr old substitute enlisted Franklin Co 4/10/62 (died at home on furlough 1864)

Private John Benningfield 31 yr old enlisted Franklin Co 3/8/62 **W 7/3**

Private E.W. Berkheard enlisted Wake Co 10/10/62 **C 7/14**

Private James Bragg 19 yr old enlisted Granville Co. **K 7/3**

Private John Carter 19 yr old enlisted Franklin Co. 2/21/62

Private William Coghill 28 yr old enlisted Franklin Co. 8/21/62 (later C Bristoe Station)

Private Norfleet Dent 33 yr old teacher enlisted Franklin Co. 2/23/62 (later W Wilderness)

Private James Dickerson 37 yr old enlisted Franklin Co. 2/28/62 **W 7/3** (later C Bristoe Station)

Private William Dickerson 51 yr old enlisted Wake Co. 4/27/62 **WC 7/3** (died 10/14)

Private Willis Dickerson 19 yr old enlisted Granville Co. 2/22/62

Private Jesse Duke 20 yr old enlisted Franklin Co. 4/62 **W-breast C 7/3**

Private Charles Edwards 26 yr old enlisted Franklin Co **K 7/3**

Private William Edwards 21 yr old enlisted Franklin Co. 3/1/62 **W 7/14 died**

Private John Ellis 19 yr old enlisted Franklin Co **W 7/3**

Private Marcus Evans 21 yr old enlisted Granville, Co. 2/18/62 (W-right thigh Ream's Station)

Private Jesse Fulghum 20 yr old enlisted Franklin Co. 2/14/62 **W-thigh 7/3**

Private Daniel Fuller 23 yr old enlisted Franklin Co. 3/4/62

Private Joseph Harris 19 yr old enlisted Franklin Co. 2/22/62 **C 7/14**

Private Hudson Harris 51 yr old substitute enlisted Franklin Co. 5/1/63 ***C 7/3***

Private Wyatt Harris 24 yr old enlisted Franklin Co. 3/4/62 ***W-neck C 7/3***

Private William Hill 19 yr old enlisted Franklin Co. 3/4/62 **W 7/3**

Private Alexander Holmes 26 yr old enlisted Franklin Co. 2/1/62 ***W 7/3 C 7/5***

Private Rufus Holmes 26 yr old enlisted Franklin Co. 3/8/62 ***K 7/3***

Private J.W. Katner 19 yr old enlisted Rowan Co. **K 7/3**

Private Alexander Mitchell 19 yr old enlisted Franklin Co. 3/1/62 ***C 7/3***

Private John Mitchell 19 yr old enlisted framklin Co. 2/14/62 ***W 7/3*** *(later Corp)*

Private William Pearce 19 yr old enlisted Franklin Co 3/10/62 (later Corp)

Private Willis Pearce 33 yr old enlisted Franklin Co 2/28/62 **C 7/3**

Private Thomas Pruitt 22 yr old enlisted Franklin Co 2/62 **K 7/3**

Private John Sandeford transferred 4/10/62 **W-right hip C 7/3**

Private Julian Timberlake 18 yr old enlisted Franklin Co 3/1/62 (later WC Bristoe Station)

Private Gaston Wiggins 26 yr old enlisted Franklin Co 2/18/62 (later W Bristoe Station)

Private Alonzo Williams 29 yr old enlisted Franklin Co 5/62 **W-side 7/3** (later C Bristoe Station)

Private Joseph Winston 18 yr old substitute enlisted Franklin Co 5/4/62

July 1 Casualties

Sgt. Atlas Mitchell 26 yr old enlisted Franklin Co 4/19/62 **W-groin 7/1** (later W-right hand Spotsylvania)

Private Isaiah Alley 20 yr old mechanic enlisted Franklin Co 2/11/62 **W-left shoulder & left leg 7/1 died 7/5**

Private Charles Clifton 17 yr old enlisted Franklin Co. 3/10/62 **"arm shot off" 7/1**

Private Cornelius Freeman 20 yr old enlisted Franklin Co. 2/10/62 **W 7/1** (later W Bristoe Station—Sgt)

Private David Fuller 31 yr old enlisted Franklin Co. 5/8/62 **W 7/1**

Private Thomas Fuller 22 yr old enlisted Franklin Co. 2/10/62 **W-hand 7/1** (later W Bristoe Station)

Private Ennels Lamb 41 yr old enlisted Wake Co. 10/10/62 **W 7/1**

Private Pugh Tharington 22 yr old enlisted Franklin Co 2/18/62 **W-arm 7/1**

Private Richard Warmouth 35 yr old enlisted Franklin Co 2/19/62 **W-shoulder 7/1**

Company G *"Franklin & Granville Co."*

Captain Joseph Davis 34 yr old lawyer enlisted in Franklin Co 3/5/62 **C 7/3**

1st Lt. Pleasant Peace 46 yr old physician & poet enlisted Granville Co 2/24/62 (later W-left shoulder Cold Harbor)

2nd Lt. George Tunstall 24 yr old clerk enlisted Franklin Co 2/15/62 **W-left thigh 7/3** (later W-face & left thigh)

3rd Lt. George Williamson 30 yr old carpenter enlisted Granville, Co 2/22/62 W-right side face 7/3

1st Sgt. Joseph Moss 34 yr old enlisted Granville Co. 2/22/62 **WC 7/3**

Sgt. George Horner 27 yr old teacher enlisted Granville Co 2/22/62 C 7/3

Sgt. Charles Reid 17 yr old student enlisted Franklin Co 2/15/62

Sgt. Lysander Turner 27 yr old school teacher enlisted Granville Co. 2/22/62 **W-left thigh C 7/3**

Cpl. Thomas Jackson 20 yr old enlisted Franklin Co 5/28/62 (later K Petersburg)

Corp Marcellus Joyner 19 yr old student enlisted Franklin Co 2/25/62 (later courier)

Cpl. Alexander Smith 28 yr old trader enlisted Granville Co. 2/22/62

Cpl. William Watkins 21 yr old tobacconist enlisted Granville Co.

Private Benjamin Ball 28 20 yr old enlisted Franklin Co 2/22/62 (later Ambulance driver)

Private Jasper Barham 46 yr old enlisted Wake Co. 5/4/63 **C 7/3**

Private William Batchelor 39 yr old enlisted 2/11/63 **C 7/3**

Private Henry Benton 18 yr old enlisted Franklin Co 4/18/63 **C 7/3** (later joined US Service)

Private James Blackley enlisted 3/10/63 (later hospitalized with disease)

Private Rufin Blackley 21 yr old enlisted Camp Holmes 7/22/62

Private P.S. Bobbitt 20 yr old enlisted Franklin Co 5/6/62 **W-bladder C 7/3** (died 8/20)

Private Jordan Bowden 26 yr old enlisted Franklin Co 4/22/62 (later W Spotsylvania)

Private Rufus Bowden 20 yr old enlisted Franklin Co 4/22/62 (later C Burges Mill)

Private Edwin Brumet 26 yr old carpenter enlisted Granville Co. 2/22/62 (later K Wilderness)

Private James Carlile 18 yr old trader enlisted Franklin Co. 2/25/62

Private John Carlile 18 yr old enlisted Franklin Co. 5/15/62—TWINS

Private Thomas Carr 26 yr old enlisted Granville Co 2/25/62 **K 7/3**

Private Thomas Carroll 26 yr old mechanic enlisted Franklin Co. (later W-face & hand Petersburg)

Private Thomas Debnam 18 yr old enlisted Franklin Co 3/27/62 (later died sickness)
Private Levi Dickerson 36 yr old enlisted Granville 2/26/62 **C 7/3**
Private Anderson Duke 24 yr old tobacconist enlisted Granville Co.
Private Madison Edwards 25 yr old enlisted Franklin Co 5/6/62
Private Everett Fowler 21 yr old enlisted Franklin Co 2/22/62 **K 7/3**
Private Henry Fuller 32 yr old enlisted Granville Co. 5/4/62 (later K Cold Harbor)
Private Jonathan Fuller 27 yr old enlisted Granville Co. 5/6/62 (later deserted)
Private George Harper 22 yr old enlisted Franklin Co 2/10/63 (later C Bristoe Station)
Private James Harper 34 yr old enlisted Franklin Co 2/2/62 (later pioneer)
Private Leonard Harris 24 yr old enlisted Camp Holmes 7/22/62 **C 7/14**
Private Benjamin Hawkins 22 yr old student enlisted 3/1/62
Private George Hicks 39 yr old enlisted Franklin Co 3/3/62 **C 7/3** (later c Burgess Mill)
Private Leonidas Hicks 36 yr old enlisted Granville Co 2/3/63 **C 7/14**
Private William Holmes 23 yr old enlisted Granville Co. 2/22/62
Private Joseph Horner 19 yr old enlisted Camp Holmes 5/1/63 **C 7/14**
Private Rufus Horner 23 yr old enlisted Granville Co 5/6/62 (later Sgt W-left thigh Ream's Station)
Private A.A. Hunt 29 yr old enlisted Franklin Co 4/22/62 **W-left leg C 7/3** (amp)
Private William Jones 22 yr old enlisted Franklin Co 2/20/62 (later C Bristoe Station)
Private John Joyner 21 yr old enlisted Franklin Co 2/18/62 (later teamster)
Private Sidney Joyner 19 yr old enlisted Franklin Co 5/1/62 (later W Spotsylvania)
Private Norfleet Layton 38 yr old enlisted Franklin Co 3/10/63 **C 7/5**
Private H.G. Leonard 27 yr old enlisted Camp Holmes 10/8/62 (later W Petersburg)
Private Iverson Longmire 33 yr old Granville Co 2/22/62
Private A.A. McBurth 54 yr old enlisted Franklin Co 2/23/63 **C 7/3**
Private Robert Massey 29 yr old enlisted Franklin Co 2/18/62 (later K-Ream's Station)
Private A.T. May 19 yr old enlisted Franklin Co 2/23/62
Private Henry Medlin 17 yr old enlisted as substitute 4/18/62 **C 7/3 sick 7/5**
Private William Morris 18 yr old enlisted Granville Co 2/22/62 (later Corp K 4/64)
Private Lewis Moss 20 yr old enlisted Granville Co
Private John Nutall 23 yr old enlisted Granville Co 2/23/62
Private Thomas O'Mara 20 yr old enlisted Granville Co. **W-head & left leg C 7/3**
*Private A. Overton 23 yr old enlisted Granville Co. 5/6/62 **C 7/3***
Private George Overton 19 yr old enlisted Granville Co 2/22/62
Private James Parrish 31 yr old cabinetmaker enlisted Granville Co. 2/22/63 (later Pioneer)
Private A.D. Patterson 23 yr old enlisted Camp Holmes 9/27/62
*Private James Patterson 26 yr old enlisted Franklin Co 2/11/63 **C 7/14** (later W-leg Petersburg)*
Private Richard Pearson enlisted Franklin Co 3/10/63 **K 7/3**
Private Howell Perry transferred 3/10/62
Private W. H Perry 37 yr old enlisted Franklin Co 2/10/63
Private Hay Pleasants 19 yr old enlisted Wake Co. 4/18/62 **W-scalp 7/3**

Private James Sledge 19 yr old enlisted Franklin Co 2/11/62
Private William Smith 20 yr old enlisted Granville Co **K 7/3**
Private William Spain 24 yr old enlisted Franklin Co 2/24/62 **W-face C 7/3**
Private William Stone 39 yr old enlisted Franklin Co 3/10/63 **C 7/3**
Private R. Strickland 36 yr old enlisted Nash Co 2/23/63 (later C Burgess Mill)
Private W.H. Tharington 19 yr old enlisted Franklin Co 5/5/62 **K 7/3**
Private James Uzzell 17 yr old student enlisted Franklin Co. 3/29/62 (later Corp & Sgt C Burgess Mill)
Private Benjamin Weaver 23 yr old enlisted Granville Co. 2/22/62 **C 7/3**
Private Gaston Wilder 30 yr old enlisted Wake Co. 4/4/62 (later W-ankle Petersburg)
Private Irvin Wilder 31 yr old enlisted franklin Co 2/25/62 ***W-jaw 7/3***
Private James Wyche 19 yr old enlisted Granville Co. **W-arm C 7/3** (died 8/12)
Private Walter Young 18 yr old mechanic enlisted Franklin Co. 2/15/62

Teamster Benjamin Thomas 36 yr old carpenter enlisted 3/3/62 assigned as ambulance driver 1/63

July 1 Casualties

Sgt. Elijah Jackson 21 yr old enlisted Franklin Co 5/5/62 **W-Abdomen 7/1**
Corp. William Burge 17 yr old student enlisted Franklin Co 3/10/62 **W-thigh & foot 7/1**
Private Benjamin Ayscue 20 yr old enlisted Franklin Co 2/20/62 **W-both arms 7/1**
Private William Bowden 37 yr old enlisted Franklin Co 3/10/63 ***K 7/1***
Private John Bradford 16 yr old enlisted Granville Co. **W-left shoulder 7/1** (later C Burgess Mill)
Private Stephen Dement 20 yr old enlisted Granville Co 2/22/62 **W-scalp 7/1**
Private Washington Dorsey 22 yr old enlisted Granville Co. 3/1/62 **W-wrist 7/1** (in 3rd attack)
Private Albert Green 19 yr old enlisted Franklin Co 5/5/62 **W-thigh 7/1** (later W-Wilderness)
Private Lemuel Hayes transferred 1/1/63 **W-left thigh 7/1** (later K Petersburg)
Private Wiley Hubbard 52 yr old harness maker enlisted Franklin Co as substitute 3/12/62 **W-arm C 7/1**
Private Wiley Jones 19 yr old enlisted Franklin Co 2/25/62 **W-leg 7/1** (later W Petersburg)
Private Calvin Long enlisted Franklin Co 3/10/63 **W-left leg & thigh 7/1** (died 8/29)
Private Joseph May 23 yr old enlisted Franklin Co 5/1/62 **W-shell 7/1** (later CS Navy)
Private Samuel Nance 27 yr old enlisted 5/6/62 **W-side 7/1 C 7/14**
Private Charles Nutall 22 yr old enlisted Granville Co 2/22/62 **W-leg 7/1 C 7/6 Chambersburg, Pa**
Private Josiah Phelps 21 yr old enlisted Franklin Co 3/3/62 **W-left thigh 7/1** (later W Burgess Mill)
Private Thomas Pulley 24 yr old tobacconist enlisted Granville Co 2/22/62 **W-thigh 7/1**
Private James Thomason 21 yr old enlisted Granville Co. 2/22/63 **W-neck 7/1**

Private Leander Tunstall 19 yr old enlisted Camp French 9/30/62 **W-shoulder 7/1** (later C Hatcher's Run)
Private S.D. Weaver 27 yr old enlisted Granville Co. 2/16/62 **K-breast and stomach 7/1**

Company H *"North Carolina Tigers"*

Captain Sidney Mitchell 31 yr old elected 3/17/62 from Wake Co. (later C Hatcher's Run)
1st Lt. Thomas Lasater transferred 6/19/62
2nd Lt James Newsom elected 7/19/62 **W-head, shoulder & thigh on advance C 7/3**
3rd Lt. John Womble 22 yr old clerk enlisted Wake Co. 3/24/62 **W-right leg 7/3**
1st Sgt James Andrews 19 yr old clerk enlisted Wake Co. 3/17/62 **K 7/3**
Cpl. Henry Johnson 19 yr old enlisted Wake Co 3/7/62 **W 7/3 (later Sgt)**
Cpl. Joseph Page 22 yr old enlisted Wake Co 6/6/62 **W-arm & head 7/3** (later Sgt)
Cpl. Amos Royster 21 yr old enlisted Wake Co 3/7/62
Cpl. Joseph Upchurch 22 yr old enlisted Wake Co. **C 7/3**
Private Rufin Barbee 36 yr old enlisted Cahtham Co. 3/16/62 (later W Wilderness C Burgess Mill)
Private Ansil Beckworth 25 yr old enlisted Wake Co. 3/7/62 (later c Burgess Mill)
Private Alfred Bryles 24 yr old enlisted 10/27/62 **C 7/5**
Private William Carpenter 24 yr old enlisted Wake Co. 7/18/62 (later C Burgess Mill)
Private F.M.Certain 21 yr old enlisted Wake Co 3/7/62 **K 7/3**
Private Wright Certain 39 yr old enlisted Wake Co. 2/11/63 (later W-right thigh Cold Harbor)
Private Wiley Chamblee 51 yr old enlisted Wake Co. 3/7/62 **WC 7/3**
Private Matthew Crocker 24 yr old enlisted Wake Co 3/7/62 **C 7/3**
Private William Crocker 26 yr old enlisted Wake Co 6/29/62 (later W-right leg & left thigh Bristoe Station)
Private Eli Damper 22 yr old enlisted Wake Co 3/7/62 (later C Burgess Mill)
Private Charles F. Debnam enlisted Wake Co. 2/7/63 (Cousins)
Private Charles R Debnam 19 yr old enlisted Wake Co. 2/7/62 (later Corp)
Private James Edwards 18 yr old enlisted wake Co. 3/7/62
Private Wiley Faggett 51 yr old enlisted Wake Co. 3/17/62 **W-right thigh C 7/3**
Private William Ford 33 yr old enlisted Wake Co. 3/7/62
Private Thomas Franklin 27 yr old enlisted Wake Co. 3/7/62 **C 7/14**
Private E.G. Hales 28 yr old enlisted Wake Co. 10/17/62
Private William Henry 52 yr old enlisted Wake Co 3/7/62 **C 7/14**
Private Paschal Herdon 35 yr old enlisted Orange Co. 10/20/62 (later C Burgess Mill)
Private William Horton 23 yr old enlisted Wake Co 5/16/62
Private John Johnson 26 yr old enlisted Wake Co 3/7/62 ***W-leg C 7/3 (died 7/30)***
Private Sylvester Johnson 21 yr old enlisted Wake Co 10/17/62 (later W-thigh Burgess Mill)
Private Anderson King 22 yr old enlisted Wake Co 4/25/62 (later Corp K Hather's Run)

Private Eli King 23 yr old enlisted Wake Co 4/13/62 ***C 7/3***
Private Leroy King 19 yr old enlisted Wake Co 4/25/62 ***W-right ankle C 7/3*** *(later C Burgess Mill)*
Private Henry Knight 19 yr old enlisted Wake Co 5/16/63 **W 7/3 C 7/5**
Private Seth Lee 19 yr old enlisted Wake Co 3/24/62 **WC 7/3**
Private Jasper Lowe 26 yr old enlisted Wake Co 4/22/62 **C 7/5**
Private Benjamin Lynch 19 yr old enlisted Wake Co 3/11/62 (transferred 8/63)
Private George Lynn 24 yr old enlisted Wake Co 3/7/62 **C 7/14**
Private Charles McGee 24 yr old enlisted Wake Co 4/23/62 (later C Burgess Mill)
Private Joseph McGee 19 yr old enlisted Wake Co 10/21/62 (later W Globe Tavern)
Private John Moring 22 yr old enlisted 6/30/62 (deserted 8/63)
Private Peyton Moring 19 yr old enlisted Wake Co. 4/23/62 (later W-right side chest Petersburg)
Private Henry Page 19 yr old enlisted Wake Co 3/7/62 **W-hand 7/3**
Private Wiley Paggett 51 yr old enlisted Wake Co 3/16/62 **K 7/3**
Private James Partin 20 yr old enlisted Wake Co 3/7/62
Private Henry Rollins 37 yr old enlisted Wake Co 3/5/62
Private Amos Royster 21 yr old enlisted Wake Co 3/7/62 (later W Cold harbor)
Private Steven Scroble 34 yr old enlisted Wake Co. 3/11/62 (later W Bristoe Station)
Private Willie Shamley enlisted Wake Co. **C 7/3**
Private Alfonsa Shuford 26 yr old enlisted Rowan Co. 10/17/62 (later died of disease 11/63)
Private William Sorrel 19 yr old enlisted Pitt Co. 3/23/62 **C 7/14** (later joined US service)
Private Ometa Tetterton 31 yr old enlisted 11/18/62 (later C 9/63)
Private Parker Upchurch 35 yr old enlisted Wake Co. 3/11/62
Private Thomas Upchurch 19 yr old enlisted Camp Vance 10/16/62 **W-right thigh 7/3**
Private Hilliard Yates 39 yr old enlisted Wake Co 3/11/62
Private **James Yates** 19 yr old enlisted Chatham Co. 3/16/62

July 1 Casualties

Sgt William Ivey 36 yr old substitute enlisted Wake Co 3/7/62 **W-hand 7/1**
Sgt Joseph Mills 21 yr old enlisted Wake Co 4/28/62 **W 7/1**
Private Joseph Hancock 19 yr old enlisted Randolph Co. 10/25/62 **W-foot 7/1**
Private Troy Jinks 24 yr old enlisted Wake Co 3/7/62 **K 7/1**
Private James Joyner 51 yr old mechanic enlisted Wake Co 3/7/62 **K 7/1**
Private Lucius McNeill 21 yr old enlisted Wake Co 3/5/62 **deserted 7/1**
Private Jefferson Mills 19 yr old enlisted Wake Co 3/27/62 **W 7/1**
Private Hilliard Mills 19 yr old enlisted Wake Co 4/22/62 ***W-both arms 7/2*** *(later W Wilderness)*
Private Hilliard Olive 19 yr old enlisted Wake Co 4/25/62 **W-shoulder & face C 7/1**
Private James Sears 18 yr old substitute enlisted Wake Co 3/7/62 **W-both shoulders 7/1**

Company I *"North Wake County"*

Captain John Brown 34 yr old enlisted Wake Co. 3/13/62 **W 7/3 shell** (later W Bristoe Station & Ream's Station—died)

1st Lt. William Harrison 22 yr old enlisted Wake Co. 3/13/62 (later W Jerusalem Plank Rd)

2nd Lt. John Jones 22 yr old enlisted Wake Co. 3/13/62 **W-right leg 7/3** (later 1st Lt.)

3rd Lt. Julius Rogers 18 yr old student enlisted Wake Co. 5/8/62 **slight W-leg 7/3** (later W Cold Harbor)

1st Sgt Alexander Harris 20 yr old enlisted Wake Co. 3/13/62 **W-leg 7/3** (later 3rd Lt)

Sgt Dempsey Blake 33 yr old enlisted *Wake Co. 3/11/62 (later 1st Sgt)*

Sgt James Driver 29 yr old enlisted Wake Co. 5/9/62 **W-foot C 7/3** (later hospital nurse)

Sgt Samuel Earp 26 yr old enlisted Wake Co. 2/21/62 (later W Bristoe Station)

Sgt. J.A. Hicks 26 yr old enlisted Wake Co. 3/4/62 **W 7/3 died 7/13**

Cpl. Isiah Blake 27 yr old enlisted *Wake Co. 5/2/62* ***W-left foot C 7/3***

Cpl. William Shephard 25 yr old enlisted Wayne Co. 2/22/62 **C 7/3**

Private Josiah Atkinson 31 yr old enlisted Wake Co. 5/10/62 (later W Bristoe Station)

Private Henry Babb 26 yr old enlisted Wake Co. 5/10/62

Private James Blake 22 yr old enlisted *Wake Co. 5/4/62* ***Missing 7/3*** *(later C Burgess Mill)*

Private Josiah Boyette 22 yr old enlisted Wake Co. 5/12/62 **C 7/3**

Private Calvin Broughton 33 yr old enlisted Wake Co. 5/10/62 **C 7/6**

Private George Broughton 23 yr old enlisted Wake Co. 5/12/62 **C 7/14**

Private Paschall Brown 28 yr old enlisted Wake Co. 3/3/62 (later W North Anna)

Private William Brown 29 yr old enlisted Wake Co. 3/4/62 **W-shoulder C 7/3** (later W Ream's Station)

Private A.M. Bryan 31 yr old enlisted Wake Co. 5/9/62 (later Corp)

Private William Bryan 23 yr old enlisted Wake Co. 5/9/62 **C 7/14** (later C Burgess Mill)

Private John Carpenter 20 yr old enlisted Wake Co. 5/9/62 **C 7/3**

Private William Carpenter 23 yr old enlisted Wake Co. 5/9/62 (later W Ream's Station)

Private Calvin Cope 19 yr old enlisted Wake Co. 10/4/62 **W-left thigh 7/3** (later W-Petersburg)

Private George Crabtree 49 yr old substitute enlisted Wake Co. 4/11/62 **W 7/3**

Private John Crabtree 23 yr old enlisted Wake Co. 2/24/62 W-2nd Manassas (later C Burgess Mill)

Private Thomas Daniel 53 yr old substitute enlisted Wake Co. 5/8/62 **C 7/5**

Private William Daniel 46 enlisted **C 7/3** (later joined US Service)

Private Calvin Evans 25 yr old enlisted Wake Co. 5/6/62 (later W left leg (amp) Bristoe Station—died)

Private James Evans 29 yr old enlisted Wake Co. 5/6/62 (died pneumonia 2/64)

Private George Neel 19 yr old enlisted Mecklenburg Co. 2/1/63 **W-left arm 7/1 C 7/5**

Private William Evans 23 yr old enlisted Wake Co. 5/6/62 (later W Bristol Station)

Private John Ferrell 42 yr old enlisted Wake Co. 5/12/62 (later W lung & thigh Bristoe Station—died)

Private Abner Fletcher 19 yr old enlisted Wake Co. 3/3/62 ***C 7/3***

Private William Fletcher 24 yr old enlisted Wake Co. 5/8/62 ***C 7/3***

Private William Fowler 18 yr old enlisted Wake Co. 5/6/62 deserted-returned

Private Augustus George 21 yr old enlisted Wake Co. 5/13/62 (died disease 11/63)

Private McRae George 19 yr old enlisted Wake Co. 5/12/62 ***W-arm & bowels 7/3 Died 7/5***

Private William George 19 yr old enlisted Wake Co. 2/24/62 (later C Bristoe Station)

Private Joseph Gooch 24 yr old enlisted Wake Co. 3/3/62 (later K Bristoe Station)

Private George Gullie 24 yr old sawyer enlisted Wake Co. 3/5/62 **WC 7/14**

Private William Hales 29 yr old enlisted Wake Co. 5/14/62 **W 7/3**

Private John Harp 20 yr old substitute enlisted Wake Co. 10/11/62

Private Jesse Harris 27 yr old enlisted Wake Co. 2/21/62 **WC 7/3**

Private George Hayes 27 yr old enlisted Camp Mangum 5/1/62

Private Green Hill 31 yr old shoemaker enlisted 5/2/62 **C 7/3** (later joined US Service)

Private Alonzo Hilton 22 yr old enlisted Granville, Co. 2/24/62 (later hospital nurse)

Private James Hopson 27 yr old enlisted Wake Co. 5/8/62 (later W Bristoe Station)

Private Joseph Hopson 19 yr old enlisted Wake Co. 5/6/62 **C 7/3**

Private Alexander Jones 37 yr old enlisted Wayne Co. 5/7/63 (later C Bristoe Station)

Private James Lee 22 yr old enlisted Wake Co. 2/19/62 **WC 7/3**

Private Asbury Marshall 27 yr old enlisted 5/8/62 **C 7/3**

Private Francis Medlin 36 yr old enlisted 2/24/62

Private James Medlin 25 yr old enlisted Camp Mangum 5/16/62 W-back shoulder ***C 7/3***

Private Samuel Medlin 62 yr old enlisted Camp Mangum 5/9/62 (later discharged for age) FATHER

Private Sidney 22 yr old enlisted Camp Mangum 5/16/62 (later W-hand Wilderness)

Private B.A. Mimms 27 yr old enlisted Wake Co. 5/9/62 **C 7/3**

Private William Morris 29 yr old enlisted Wake Co. 5/2/62 **W-eye & left hip 7/3** (later Sgt. & C Burgess Mill)

Private Wiley O'Neal 20 yr old enlisted Wake Co. 2/19/62 **C 7/3**

Private William Patterson 51 yr old enlisted Martin Co. **C 7/5**

Private John Pollard 27 yr old enlisted Wake Co. 5/9/62 (later W-left thigh Bristoe Station)

Private Wright Rigsby 19 yr old enlisted Wayne Co. 5/8/62 **W-foot 7/3**

Private Hiram Rochelle 41 yr old enlisted Wayne Co. 3/1/62 (later W Wilderness)

Private George Rochelle 43 yr old enlisted Wayne Co. 3/1/62 ***W-shoulder C 7/3***

Private Thomas Ross 39 yr old enlisted Wayne Co. 3/7/62 **K 7/3**

Private Pleasant Scoggins 46 yr old enlisted Wayne Co. 4/3/62 (later W Petersburg) FATHER

Private Rappso Scoggins 18 yr old enlisted Wayne Co. 3/6/62 (later discharged sick)

Private Reuben Scott 21 yr old enlisted Wake Co. 3/3/62 **C 7/5 sick**

Private John Smith 19 yr old enlisted Wake Co. 5/9/62 **K 7/3**

Private William Smith 29 yr old carpenter enlisted Orange Co. 3/12/62
Private John Watts 19 yr old enlisted Wayne Co. 3/7/62 (later C Burgess Mill)
Private William Watts 22 yr old enlisted Wake Co. 3/12/62 (later W Ream's Station)
Private James Wood 23 yr old enlisted Camp Mangum 5/12/62 ***W-thigh C 7/3*** *(later Sgt)*
Private John Wood 25 yr old enlisted Camp Mangum 5/12/62 (later C Bristoe Station)

Teamster Samuel Edgerton 29 yr old enlisted Wake Co. 3/13/62 (later C Burgess Mill)
Private William Massey 42 yr old enlisted Granville Co. 2/24/62 (detailed as cook)

July 1 Casualties

Sgt Woodley Bevers 22 yr old enlisted Wake Co. 3/7/62 **W-arm C 7/1** (later Sgt)
Private Wiley Allmond 23 yr old enlisted Wake Co. 5/6/62 **W-thigh 7/1** (later C Bristoe Station)
Private William Anderson 23 yr old enlisted Granville Co. 3/4/62 **W 7/1**
Private G.A. Boyette 51 yr old enlisted Wake Co. 5/12/62 **W-hand 7/1**
Private Benjamin Broughton 29 yr old enlisted Wake Co. 5/12/62 **W-"Arm shot off" 7/1**
Private John Fowler 39 yr old enlisted Wake Co. 3/6/62 **W 7/1**
Private Robert Hall 23 yr old enlisted Wake Co. 2/24/62 **K 7/1**
Private Joseph Scott 19 yr old enlisted Wake Co. 3/8/62 **W 7/1**
Private Hollum Sturdivant 20 yr old enlisted Wake Co. 5/9/62 **W 7/1** (later Corp)
Private Frank Williams 23 yr old enlisted Wake Co. 3/9/62 **W-chest C 7/1**
Private Sanders Wood 26 yr old enlisted Wake Co. 3/9/62 ***W-back 7/1***

Company K *"Alamance Minutemen"*

1st Lt. James Watson 19 yr old appointed 3/13/62 **W-left cheek C 7/3**
2nd Lt. Thomas Taylor 28 yr old appointed 3/13/62 (later C Burgess Mill)
3rd Lt. Felix Poteat 26 yr old enlisted Camp Campbell 7/25/62 (later Adjt W—right arm Ream's Station)
1st Sgt Jesse Gilliam 28 yr old enlisted Alamance Co. 4/19/62 ***K 7/3***—2 brothers
Sgt. James Foster 31 yr old enlisted Alamance Co. 4/24/62
Sgt. Albert Love 35 yr old blacksmith enlisted Alamance Co. 2/28/62 **C 7/3**
Sgt. James Ross 22 yr old enlisted Alamance Co. 2/28/62 (later 1st Sgt)
Corp. James Garrison 19 yr old enlisted Alamance Co. 2/27/62 ***K 7/3*** *(near wall)*
Corp James Mc Garrsion 19 yr old enlisted Alamance Co. 4/26/62 (later W Bristoe Station)
Cpl. William Love 24 yr old enlisted Alamance Co. 7/7/62 (later W-thigh Ream's Station)
Cpl. David Rose 19 yr old enlisted Alamance Co. 2/27/62 (died disease 6/64)
Cpl. Jacon Waggoner 19 yr old enlisted Alamance Co. 2/28/62 (later Sgt W Cold Harbor)
Private James Apple 24 yr old enlisted Alamance Co. 4/21/62 (later C Burgess Mill)
Private Patterson Apple 28 yr old enlisted Alamance Co. 4/21/62 (later C Burgess Mill)

Private Zachariah Apple 25 yr old enlisted Alamance Co. 2/28/62 (later C Burgess Mill)
PrivateWilliam Baldwin 33 yr old enlisted Alamance Co. 4/18/62 **C 7/3**
Private George Barker 37 yr old enlisted Alamance Co. 2/19/62 **K 7/3**
Private John Boon 20 yr old enlisted Alamance Co. 7/14/62 (later Teamster Wheelwright/Carpenter)
Private Philemon Boon 17 yr old enlisted Alamance Co. 2/27/62 (later W-lost thumb Cold Harbor)
Private William Boon 29 yr old enlisted Alamance Co. 5/12/63
Private James Brannock 25 yr old enlisted camp French 11/1/62
Private Sanford Busick 32 yr old enlisted Alamance Co. 4/21/62 (deserted 8/25/63)
Private M.D. Byrum 18 yr old enlisted Alamance Co. 4/22/62 (W-left ankle Ream's Station)
Private Anderson Clapp33 yr old enlisted Alamance Co. 2/28/62 (later CS Navy)
Private Henry Danielly 31 yr old enlisted Alamance Co. 4/18/62 **W-shoulder 7/3** (died 8/5)
Private William Edwards 25 yr old enlisted Alamance Co. 4/19/62
Private William Foster 20 yr old enlisted Alamance Co. 4/21/62 (later C Burgess Mill)
Private Jacob Foust 23 yr old enlisted Alamance Co. 2/27/62 (later W-leg & hip Bristoe Station)
Private Willis Harder 24 yr old enlisted Alamance Co. 2/28/62
Private John Herron 19 yr old enlisted Alamance Co. 2/27/62 (later W-hand Bristoe Station)
Private James Hornbuckle 19 yr old enlisted Alamance Co. 4/21/62 **W 7/3**
Private Milton Huffines 21 yr old enlisted Alamance Co. 3/5/62 (later C Burgess Mill)
Private Asa Iseley 39 yr old enlisted Alamance Co. 2/28/62
Private Christian Iseley 22 yr old enlisted Alamance Co. 5/16/62 (later W Wilderness)
Private William Iseley 19 yr old enlisted Alamance Co. 4/26/62 ***W-both legs 7/3*** *(died 8/28)*
Private Samuel Linens 18 yr old enlisted Alamance Co. 3/25/62 (later W-leg Cold Harbor)
Private William Linens 24 yr old enlisted Alamance Co. 2/27/62 (later W Wilderness)
Private Taylor Linnen 17 yr old enlisted Camp Mangum. 4/2/62 (later K Wilderness)
Private Daniel Lowe 19 yr old enlisted Alamance Co. 2/28/62 (later W left arm Cold Harbor)
Private George Loy 38 yr old shoemaker enlisted Alamance Co. 5/63 (discharged illness)
Private Joseph Loy 20 yr old enlisted Alamance Co. 3/14/62 (later C Burgess Mill)
Private James McCauley 18 yr old enlisted Alamance Co. 2/19/62 **C 7/3**
Private John Matkins 28 yr old enlisted Alamance Co. 4/21/62 (later W Wilderness)
Private William Nease 20 yr old enlisted Alamance Co. 2/28/62 **WC 7/3**
Private Robert Pyles 27 yr old enlisted Alamance Co. 4/21/62 (hospitalized 8/25/63 scurvy)
Private David Ross 19 yr old enlisted Alamance Co. 3/7/63 ***W-head C 7/3***
Private Edward Ross 20 yr old enlisted Alamance Co. 4/21/62 ***WC 7/3 (brother SGT)***
Private Alpheus Sharp 19 yr old enlisted Alamance Co. 2/27/62 ***W-hand 7/3*** *(later W-thigh Petersburg*

Private Michael Sharp 20 yr old enlisted Alamance Co. 2/27/62 ***C 7/3***

Private Henry Simpson 24 yr old enlisted Dunn's Hill 10/1/62 (later detached to Engineers Corps)

Private Jefferson Simpson 23 yr old enlisted Alamance Co. 4/19/62 **C 7/3**

Private Lemuel Simpson 36 yr old enlisted Alamance Co. 2/28/63 (later W-left buttock Wilderness)

Private Luke Simpson 22 yr old enlisted Alamance Co. 2/28/62

Private Morgan Simpson 31 yr old enlisted Alamance Co. 2/27/62 (later W Wilderness—died)

Private Daniel Smith 21 yr old enlisted Alamance Co. 10/1/62

Private William Smith 24 yr old enlisted Alamance Co. 4/21/62 **C 7/14**

Private Julius Summers 18 yr old enlisted Alamance Co. 3/5/62 (later Corp)

Private George Sutton 28 yr old enlisted Alamance Co. 4/28/62 (deserted 8/24/63—returned C Burgess Mill)

Private Lindsay Sutton 23 yr old enlisted Alamance Co. 3/14/62 (deserted 8/24/63—returned K Cold Harbor)

Private John Swain 20 yr old enlisted Alamance Co. 2/23/63 **W-thigh 7/3** (later W-left leg Cold Harbor)

Private Samuel Swing 18 yr old enlisted Alamance Co. 3/5/62 (deserted 7/22/63—returned W Cold Harbor)

Private John Tarpley 21 yr old enlisted Alamance Co. 4/26/62 (later Sgt W Burgess Mill)

Private Charles Thomson 19 yr old enlisted Alamance Co. 2/278/62 (deserted 7/22/63—returned W-Jones farm)

Private Andrew Tickle 22 yr old enlisted Alamance Co. 4/30/62 ***W-back & breast C 7/3 died***

Private Calvin Tickle 19 yr old enlisted Alamance Co. 3/13/63 (later W-right shoulder Cold Harbor)

Private Charles Tickle 22 yr old enlisted Alamance Co. 2/28/62 (later W-right leg Hatcher's Run)

Private George Tickle 19 yr old enlisted camp Mangum 4/30/62 ***K 7/3***

Private Julius Tickle 21 yr old enlisted Alamance Co. 4/30/62 ***W-arm, leg and eye 7/3*** *(later K Wilderness)*

Private Levi Tickle 24 enlisted wake Co. 9/14/62 **W 7/3**

Private Henry Waggoner 29 yr old enlisted Camp Mangum 3/13/62 (later W Cold Harbor C Burgess Mill)

Private John Waggoner 26 yr old enlisted Alamance Co. 2/28/62

Private David Webb 30 yr old enlisted Alamance Co. 2/28/62 (deserted 8/24/63—returned C Bristoe Station)

Private Robert Weeden 21 yr old enlisted Alamance Co. 4/19/62 **W-thigh 7/3 color bearer** died 7/23/63

Blacksmith Teamster Austin Willis 36 yr old mechanic enlisted Alamance Co. 2/27/62
Teamster Corporal Patterson Boon 22 yr old enlisted Alamance Co. 3/14/62 Wheelwright / Carpenter
Teamster Daniel May 27 yr old enlisted Alamance Co. 2/28/62 (later K Wilderness)

July 1 Casualties

Captain Robert Faucette 26 yr old appointed 3/13/62 **W-thigh 7/1** (later W Bristoe Station)
Private Thomas Brannock 28 yr old enlisted Alamance Co. 3/17/62 **K 7/1**
Private Anthony Foster 18 yr old enlisted Alamance Co. 4/21/62 **W 7/1**
Private George Garrison 20 yr old enlisted Alamance Co. 2/27/62 ***K 7/1***
Private Henry Geringer 24 yr old enlisted Alamance Co. 4?30/63 **W-thigh C 7/1**
Private Abner Gilliam 23 yr old enlisted Alamance Co. 4/21/62 **W-right shoulder C 7/1**
Private John Gilliam 22 yr old enlisted Alamance Co. 4/21/62 **W-thigh C 7/1**
Private Madison Loy 23 yr old enlisted Camp Mangum 5/10/62 ***W-left arm C 7/1 (amp)***
Private James Kernodle 20 yr old enlisted Alamance Co. 11/1/62 **W-arm 7/1**
Private William Kernodle 21 yr old enlisted Alamance Co. 3/26/62 **W 7/1** (later Corp)
Private William Matkins 29 yr old enlisted Alamance Co. 4/28/62 **W-head, shoulder & arm 7/1**
Private Silas Matkins 22 yr old enlisted Alamance Co. 3/11/62 **W 7/1**
Private Lewis Patten 19 yr old enlisted Alamance Co. 3/17/62 **K 7/1**
Private John Summers 23 yr old enlisted Alamance Co. 2/28/62 **K 7/1**
Private Absalom Tickle 30 yr old enlisted Alamance Co. 4/21/62 ***W-head, Shoulder & arm C 7/1 died***
Private Simeon Tickle 44 yr old enlisted Alamance Co. 4/28/62 ***W-head & thigh 7/1*** *(later W-knee Hatcher's Run)*
Private Thomas Underwood 24 yr old enlisted Alamance Co. 3/11/62 **K 7/1**

TWENTY SIXTH NORTH CAROLINA REGIMENT

Colonel Henry Burgwyn *Lt. Colonel John Lane* *Major John Jones*

Field & Staff

Colonel **Henry King Burgwyn** enlisted 19 yr old VMI graduate promoted Col 8/19/62 at age 22 **K-lungs 7/1**

Lieutenant Colonel **John Randolph Lane** 28 yr old Chatham appointed 8/19/62 **W-jaw, mouth, neck 7/1** (later W Wilderness / Ream's Station)

Major **John T. "Knock" Jones** 22 yr old enlisted Caldwell Co. appointed 9/27/62 **W 7/1 W 7/3** (in command) (later K Wilderness)

Adjutant James Jordan enlisted Holy Sprimg NC 5/29/61 appointed 8/27/61 **W-hip 7/3 C 7/5**

Sergeant Major Montford "Stokes" McRae promoted 3/1/63 **W-left thigh C 7/1**

Quartermaster Joseph J. Young appointed 3/1/62 (later Brigade QM)

Assistant Commissary Phineas Horton 36 yr oldappointed 10/4/61

Surgeon Lewellyn Warren appointed 8/28/62 **C Williamsport 7/5/63**

Assistant Surgeon William Gaither appointed 11/16/61 (later Surgeon)

Assistant Surgeon John Barry appointed 4/1/63

Hospital Steward Benjamin Hinds promoted 5/1/63

Hospital Stewart **Bryant Dunlap** Physician (Pa Medical College) . . . (treated Lt Colonel John Lane wounds)

Chaplin Styring Moore appointed 9/15/62

Commissary Sergeant Jesse Ferguson appointed 3/1/62

Ordinance Sergeant E.H. Hornaday enlisted Camp Burgwyn 10/10/61 detailed 4/26/62

Regimental Band

Chief Musician Samuel Mickey 24 yr old enlisted Camp French 11/1/62
Musician Daniel Crouse enlisted Craven Co. 3/9/62 (later C Amelia CH)
Musician Alex Gibson enlisted Craven Co. 3/9/62 (later C Amelia CH)
Musician Thomas Hackney 20 yr old enlisted "Cartersville" 5/28/61 promoted 6/63
Musician Julius Lineback enlisted Camp French 11/1/62 kept diary (later C Amelia CH)
Musician Alexander Meining 39 year old enlisted Craven Co. 3/9/62
Musician L.L. Mickey enlisted Camp French 11/1/62
Musician James Peterson 35 year old enlisted Petersburg 8/15/62
Musician William Reich enlisted Petersburg 7/7/62
Musician Henry Sidall 17 yr old enlisted Petersburg 11/1/62 (later C Amelia CH)
Musician Julius Transon enlisted Lenoir Co. 5/28/62
Drum Major Joseph Hackney 21 yr old enlisted "Cartersville" 5/28/61 promoted 6/63 **W 7/1 C 7/5**

Company A *"Jeff Davis Mountaineers"* 92

Captain **Samuel Wagg** 23 yr old enlisted Ashe Co. 7/1/61 **K 7/3 (shot through with grape)**
3rd Lt. Levi Gentry enlisted Ashe Co. 3/27/62 **C 7/14** (later 2nd Lt)
1st Sgt James Duvall (later 3rd Lt. W Bristoe Station W Glove Tavern—died
Corp. Troy Sheets 21 yr old enlisted Ashe Co 5/17/61 (later C Bristoe Station)
Private James P Ashley 25 yr old enlisted Ashe Co. 3/27/62 (later Sgt)
Private Joseph Ashley 24 yr old enlisted Ashe Co. 5/17/61 **C 7/3**
Private Edward Barker 21 yr old enlisted Ashe Co. 3/27/62 **W-face & left thigh 7/3 died 8/13/63**
Private Flemin Doughton 37 yr old enlisted Ashe Co 5/17/61 C New Bern NC **C 7/14**
Private John Estridge 36 yr old carpenter enlisted Ashe Co 3/27/62 **C 7/3**
Private Hugh Farington Ashe co farmer enlisted Camp French 10/9/62 **C 7/3**
Private George Fisher 23 yr old enlisted Ashe Co 5/17/61 **C 7/3**
Private Joseph Gentry 25 yr old enlisted Ashe Co 5/17/61 C New Bern, NC ***W 7/3 C 7/5***
Private John Houck 18 yr old enlisted Ashe Co 3/27/62 ***W-leg 7/3***
Private Issac Landreth 25 yr old enlisted Ashe Co 5/17/61 **C 7/3**
Private Jonathan Miller 36 yr old enlisted Camp French 10/9/62 ***K 7/3***
Private Josh Pendergrass 31 yr ld enlisted Ashe Co 3/27/62 **W-left hip C 7/3**
Private William Pennington 22 yr old enlisted Ashe Co 3/27/62 **W-left leg 7/3 C 7/5**
Private Riley Perkins 26 yr old enlisted Ashe Co 3/27/62 **K 7/3**
Private William Reaves 22 yr old enlisted Ashe Co 5/17/61 **K 7/3**
Private Solomon Roten 31 yr old enlisted Ashe Co 10/9/62 **K 7/3**
Private Meredith Stamper 21 yr old enlisted Ashe Co 5/17/61 (later transferred CS Navy)
Private John Vanover 20 yr old enlisted Ashe Co 5/17/61 **C 7/3**

Private Alfred Wagg 18 yr old enlisted Ashe Co 3/27/62 (later Corp / Sgt)
Private Eli Young 28 yr old enlisted Ashe Co 5/17/61 **C 7/3**

Teamster James Duvall 24 yr old enlisted Ashe Co 3/27/62

7/1 Casualties

1st Lt. Ambrose Duvall 29 yr old enlisted Ashe Co. 5/17/61 **W-left hand 7/1**
2nd Lt. Jacob Houck 26 yr old enlisted Ashe Co. 5/17/61 ***W 7/1*** (later 1st Lt W Bristoe Station)
Sgt Isaac Carter 24 yr old enlisted Ashe Co. 5/17/61 **W-left leg 7/1 C 7/5**
Sgt James Lane 23 yr old enlisted Ashe Co 5/17/61 **W 7/1**
Sgt. Lewis Jones 26 yr old enlisted Ashe Co 5/17/61 **W 7/1 C 7/5** "on his return from Gettysburg"
Corp. Joseph Doughton 22 yr old enlisted Ashe Co 5/17/ 61 W 7/1 **C 7/14**
Corp. Elijah Smith 21 yr old enlisted Ashe Co 5/17/61 **W 7/1** (later 1st Sgt)
Corp. Samuel Wayman enlisted Ashe Co 5/17/61 **W-left shoulder-right knee 7/1**
Private Tivis Ashley transferred 5/1/62 **W 7/1 C 7/5**
Private James Baker 22 yr old enlisted Ashe Co. 5/17/61 ***K 7/1***
Private Jacob Baker 32 yr old enlisted Ashe Co. 7/28/61 ***W-left foot 7/1 (died 7/16)***
Private Ambrose Baker 17 yr old enlisted Ashe Co. 5/10/62 (deserted 7/20/63)
Private Joseph Baldwin 34 enlisted at Camp French 10/9/62 **W-left thigh 7/1 C 7/5**
Private Hugh Ballou 31 yr old enlisted Ashe Co. 3/27/62 **K 7/1**
Private Lee Ballou 18 yr old enlisted Ashe Co. 3/1/63 **W-left arm 7/1**
Private Jesse Bare 18 yr old enlisted Ashe Co. 5/15/63 **W-left hip 7/1** (C Bristoe Station)
Private Lee Bare 21 yr old enlisted Ashe Co. 5/17/61 **K 7/1**
Private Ambrose Barker 35 yr old enlisted Ashe Co. 3/27/62 **W-right shoulder 7/1** (later W Cold Harbor)
Private John Billings 20 yr old enlisted Ashe Co. 5/17/61 (later K Wildernesss)
Private Michael Black 31 yr old enlisted Ashe Co. 10/9/62 **W 7/1 C 7/5**
Private Albert Blevins 20 yr old enlisted Ashe Co. 3/27/62 ***W-left leg 7/1***
Private Bartlett Blevins 19 yr old enlisted Ashe Co. 3/27/62 ***W 7/1*** *(later C Bristoe Station)*
Private Felix Blevins 19 yr old enlisted Ashe Co. 5/17/61 ***W-right foot 7/1 C 7/5***
Private Horton Blevins 24 yr old enlisted Ashe Co. 5/17/61 C New Bern, NC ***W-forehead 7/1*** *(later Corp)*
Private Levi Blevins 28 yr old enlisted Camp French 3/15/63
Private Stephen Blevins 28 yr old enlisted Ashe Co. 10/9/62 ***K 7/1***
Private William Blevins 19 yr old enlisted Camp French 10/9/62 (later W Bristoe Station)
Private Thomas Burgess 27 yr old enlisted Ashe Co. 5/17/61 **W 7/1 C 7/5**
Private Christian Burkett 23 yr old enlisted Ashe Co. 5/17/61 **C 7/14**
Private Hiram Calaway 19 yr old enlisted Ashe Co. 3/27/62 **W-right shoulder 7/1**
Private H.H. Campbell 19 yr old enlisted Ashe Co. 3/27/62 **W 7/1 C 7/5**

Private Arms Clark 30 yr old enlisted Ashe Co 3/1/63 **W 7/1 C 7/5**

Private William Davis 21 yr old enlisted Ashe Co. 5/17/61 **W-leg 7/1 C 7/5**

Private Walter Denney 31 yr old enlisted Ashe Co. 10/9/62 **W-right leg 7/1 C 7/5**

Private Uriah Denny 37 yr old enlisted Ashe Co. 5/17/61 **W-right leg C 7/1**

Private Maston Duvall 22 yr old enlisted Ashe Co 3/27/62 **W 7/1 C 7/5**

Private Calloway Farmer 24 yr old enlisted Ashe Co 3/27/62 (later K Bristoe Station)

Private Noah Farmer 20 yr old enlisted Ashe Co **W 7/1** 3/27/62

Private John Fields 22 yr old enlisted Ashe Co 5/17/61 W 7/1 **C 7/14**

Private Lowry Grimsley 20 yr old enlisted Ashe Co 5/17/61 **W 7/1 (later W Cold Harbor)**

Private Nicholas Gentry 32 yr old enlisted Ashe Co 5/17/61 C New Bern (later K Bristoe Station)

Private George Harless 21 yr old enlisted Ashe Co 5/17/61 (later W Bristoe Station)

Private John Hash 20 yr old enlisted Ashe Co 5/17/61 C New Bern, NC (later W Bristoe Station)

Private James Hash 21 yr old enlisted Ashe Co 5/17/61 C New Bern, NC **W-left arm 7/1**

Private Andrew Hawthorne 19 yr old enlisted Ashe Co 3/27/62 ***W 7/1*** *(later C Spotsylvania)*

Private Washington Houck 18 yr old enlisted 3/27/62 ***W-arm 7/1 C 7/5***

Private Henry Hughs enlisted Ashe Co 3/27/62 **WC 7/1**

Private Marshall Hurley 18 yr old enlisted 3/15/63 **K 7/1**

Private William Hurley 23 yr old enlisted Ashe Co 5/17/61 C New Bern, NC (Later W-right arm Wilderness)

Private Nauman Loggins 23 yr old enlisted Ashe Co 5/17/61 **W-right leg C 7/1**

Private William McMillan 33 yr old enlisted Ashe Co 5/17/61 (deserted 7/31/63)

Private Isham Miller 21 yr old enlisted Camp French 10/9/62 (later C Wilderness)

Private G.R. Mink 23 yr old enlisted Ashe Co 10/9/62 (deserted 8/1/63—returned 3/64)

Private Freeland Mitchell 25 yr old enlisted Ashe Co. 3/1/63 **W 7/1**

Private George Nye 35 yr old enlisted Ashe Co 5/17/61 **W 7/1**

Private Granville Osborn 22 yr old enlisted Ashe Co 5/17/61 **W-left arm 7/1**

Private Zachariah Osborn 21 yr old enlisted Ashe Co 5/17/61 C New Bern, NC

Private Nathan Phipps 24 yr old enlisted Ashe Co 5/17/61 WC New Bern NC **W 7/1 died 8/1/63**

Private J. Plummer 27 yr old enlisted Ashe Co 5/17/61 **W-right leg C 7/1**

Private Mitchell Plumber 24 yr old enlisted Ashe Co 5/17/61 **W 7/1**

Private William Porter 19 yr old enlisted Ashe Co 3/1/63 (later C Bristoe Station)

Private Calvin Reedy 25 yr old enlisted Ashe Co 3/27/62 **W 7/1** (later ambulance driver)

Private Jackson Reid 19 yr old enlisted Ashe Co 5/17/61 C New Bern, NC (deserted 8/1/63)

Private Andrew Reeves 24 yr old enlisted Ashe Co 5/17/61 **W-right arm 7/1 C 7/4**

Private James Roberson 23 yr old enlisted Ashe Co 5/17/61 (later W Bristoe Station K Wilderness)

Private Ashley Roten 26 yr old enlisted Ashe Co 5/17/61 (deserted 8/1/63)

Private Alexander Sanders 17 yr old enlisted Ashe Co 4/20/62 **W 7/1 C 7/14 Williamsport**

Private Abraham Sheets 33 yr old enlisted Ashe Co 10/9/62 **W 7/1 (later C Spotsylvania)**
Private Ira Stamper 20 yr old enlisted Ashe Co 5/17/61 C New Bern, NC ***W 7/1***
Pri*vate John Stamper 20 yr old enlisted Ashe Co 5/17/61* ***color-bearer W-right shoulder 7/1***
Private Louis Stedham 20 yr old enlisted Ashe Co 5/17/61 **W 7/1** (later C Weldon RR)
Private Callaway Taylor 20 yr old enlisted Ashe Co 5/17/61 **K 7/1**
Private Cleveland Taylor 21 yr old enlisted Camp French 10/9/62 **W-right leg 7/1**
Private William Taylor 24 yr old enlisted Ashe Co 7/28/61 **W-jaw 7/1** (later Corp)
Private T.M. Testament 19 yr old enlisted Ashe Co 3/27/62 **K 7/1**
Private William Tredway 21 yr old enlisted Ashe Co 5/17/61 C New Bern **W-right leg 7/1** (later Sgt)
Private James Turner 31 yr old enlisted Ashe Co 3/27/62 **W 7/1 C 7/5** (later Corp)
Private Lafayette Yates 23 yr old enlisted Ashe Co 5/17/61 (later W Bristoe Station C Spotsylvania)

Musician Harrison Miller 21 yr old enlisted Ashe Co 5/17/61 **W 7/1 C 7/5**

Company B *"Waxhaw Jackson Guards"*

Brevet Captain Thomas J. Cureton 25 yr old enlisted Union Co 6/5/61 *promoted 7/2/63* **W-shoulder 7/3** (later W Spots)
3rd Lt. William Estridge 25 yr old enlisted Union Co. **Private to 3rd Lt 7/2** (later W Bristoe Station)
Sgt. Leroy Hilton 21 yr old enlisted Union Co 6/5/61 (later W Wilderness)
Sgt. George Richards 28 yr old miner enlisted Union Co. 6/5/61 **C 7/5** (joined US Service)
Private Green Austin enlisted Union C 8/1/61 **W-right leg 7/3 C 7/5**
Private John Dulin enlisted Camp Mangum 9/21/62 **W 7/3 C 7/5**
Private Henry Fesperman 23 yr old enlisted Union Co 6/5/61 **W-left leg 7/3 (later W Jaw Wilderness)**
Private Benjamin Hamby enlisted camp Mangum 9/21/62 **W 7/3**
Private John Huffstickler 19 yr old enlisted Union Co 6/5/61 **W-hip 7/3**
Private William Inman 31 yr old enlisted Union Co 6/5/61 **C 7/3**
Private Eli Laney 23 yr old enlisted Union Co 6/5/61 ***K 7/3***
Private William Laney 22 yr old enlisted Union Co 6/5/61 **WC 7/3 (died 7/10)**
Private Isaac Mattox 25 yr old school teacher enlisted Monroe, NC 6/5/62
Private Amos Pigg enlisted Union Co 8/17/61 **K 7/3**
Private Nevel Staten 23 yr old enlisted Union Co. 6/5/61 (later Corp K Wilderness) *(helped move Colonewl Burgwyn's body and killed Yankee killer of Pettigrew with a rock)*
Private Thomas Whitaker 30 yr old enlisted Union Co. 6/5/61 **W 7/3 C 7/20** Martinsburg, Va

Musician Bazel Johnson 24 yr old enlisted Union Co 6/5/61

July 1 Casualties

Captain William Wilson 22 yr old enlisted Union Co appointed 1/9/63 **K 7/1 "while gallantly leading his men up the hill through McPherson's woods"**

1st Lt. Edward Brietz elected 3rd Lt 1/5/63 appointed 1st Lt 7/2 **W 7/1 C 7/5**

2nd Lt. John William Richardson 28 yr old enlisted Union Co 6/5/61 **K 7/1 buried Oakwood Cemetery Raleigh**

1st Sgt Samuel Walkup 24 yr old enlisted Union Co. 6/5/61 ***W-left leg & thigh 7/1***

Sgt. Ellis Chaney enlisted Union Co. 8/17/61 W-face & right shoulder **7/1 C 7/6**

Sgt. Hampton Thomas 24 **W-right leg 7/1 C 7/5**

Sgt. Andrew Wyatt enlisted Camp Mangum 9/21/62 deserted 12/62 arrested sentenced to death / pardoned **K 7/1**

Corp. David Huffstickley 24 yr old enlisted Union Co 6/5/61 **W 7/1 C 7/14**

Corp. Marshall Mullis 23 yr old enlisted Union Co. 6/5/61 (W Bristoe Station)

Corp. James Rogers 29 yr old enlisted Union Co. 6/5/61 (later W-lungs Bristoe Station)

Corp. Robert Rogers 22 yr old enlisted Camp Wilkes 10/17/61 **WC 7/1**

Corp. Leroy Seacrest enlisted Union Co 8/1/61 **W-right leg 7/1 C 7/5**

Private William Austin 23 yr old enlisted Union Co 6/5/61 **W 7/1**

Private Albert Broom 19 yr old enlisted Union Co 6/5/61 **W 7/1 C 7/5**

Private Thomas Broom 19 yr old enlisted Union Co 6/5/61 (later W-arm Wilderness K-Globe Tavern)

Private James Burke enlisted Camp Mangum 9/28/62 (W Bristoe Station)

Private Calvin Church enlisted Camp Mangum 9/21/62 **W 7/1 C 7/5** (later C Hatchers Run)

Private H.M. Church enlisted Camp Mangum 9/21/62 **W 7/1 C 7/5**

Private Joel Church enlisted Camp Mangum 9/21/62 **C 7/14**

Private William Clayton enlisted Camp Mangum 9/21/62 (later K Cold Harbor)

Private James Cook 28 yr old enlisted Union Co 6/5/61 **W-leg C 7/1 died 7/23**

Private Moses Costly 19 yr old enlisted Union Co 6/5/61 (later W-Cold harbor died)

Private Alfred Eason enlisted Unuion Co 8/17/61 **W 7/1 C 7/5** (later Corp)

Private Doctor Estep enlisted Camp Mangum 9/21/62 **C 7/14** (later joined US service)

Private Hardy Estep enlisted Camp Mangum **K 7/1**

Private James Fincher 23 yr old enlisted Union Co 6/5/61 **WC 7/1 died 7/10**

Private William Fox enlisted Camp Mangum 9/21/62 **C 7/14**

Private William Friezeland enlisted Union Co. 3/28/63 **W 7/1 C 7/5**

Private George Glenn enlisted Union Co 3/29/63 (later W Wilderness)

Private Robert Glenn enlisted Union Co 1/29/63 **W-arm 7/1 C 7/5**

Private William Glenn enlisted Union Co 6/5/61 (later died 3/6/64)

Private John Griffin 30 yr old enlisted Union Co 6/5/61 **K 7/1**

Private Sheldon Hays 25 yr old enlisted Union Co 6/5/61 **W 7/1** (died 7/19 Chester hospital buried PNC)

Private Charles Helms enlisted Union Co 6/5/61 W Malvern Hill **W 7/1 C 7/5**

Private Franklin L. Honeycutt enlisted Union Co 8/1/61 **K-head 7/1 "carrying colors"**

Private Wilburn HoneycutT enlisted Camp Burgwyn 9/8/61
Private Burrel Knight 23 yr old enlisted Union Co 6/5/61 **W 7/1 C 7/5**
Private Jehu Laney 22 yr old enlisted Union Co 6/5/61 C 7/5
Private Samuel Laney 19 yr old enlisted Union Co 6/5/61 C 7/14
Private Samuel Laney 19 yr old enlisted Union Co. 6/5/61 **C 7/14** (later W-leg Ream's Station)
Private William Laney 22 yr old enlisted Union Co. 6/5/61 WC 7/1
Private John McCain 23 yr old enlisted Union Co. 6/5/61 **W-both arms 7/1** (later W Wilderness)
Private John McCorkle enlisted Union County 8/1/61 **W 7/1 C 7/5**
Private Columbus McManus 20 yr old enlisted Union Co. 6/5/61 **W-neck 7/1 C 7/5**
Private George McManus 23 yr old enlisted Union Co. 6/5/61 **W-foot 7/1 C 7/5**
Private Henry McManus 22 yr old enlisted Union Co. 6/5/61 **W 7/1**
Private Milus McRory enlisted Union Co. 8/17/61 (later W Bristoe Station)
Private John McWhorter 20 yr old enlisted Union Co. 6/5/61 **K 7/1**
Private James Nichols enlisted Wilkes Co 9/21/62 **W-head 7/1**
Private Alexander Osborne 23 yr old enlisted Union Co. 6/5/61 W Malvern Hill **W 7/1 C 7/5**
Private Milton Osborne 19 yr old enlisted Union Co. 6/5/61 **C 7/14**
Private William Pardue 26 yr old enlisted Union Co. 6/5/61 **C 7/14**
Private Benjamin Phillips 20 yr old enlisted Union Co. 6/5/61 **C 7/3** (joined US Service)
Private William Phillips 25 yr old enlisted Union Co. 6/5/61 **W 7/1 C 7/5**
Private Darlin Pressler enlisted Union Co 2/14/63 (later C Bristoe Station)
Private John Ray enlisted Wilkes Co 9/21/62 **C 7/14**
Private Thomas Richards 31 yr old miner enlisted Camp Vance 12/4/61 **C 7/5**
Private Brinkly Richardson 28 yr old enlisted Union Co. 6/5/61 (later Sgt)
Private James Richardson enlisted Camp Mangum 12/29/62 **C-7/3**
Private Sampson Richardson enlisted Wake Co8/17/61 **W-right arm 7/1 C 7/5**
Private Sylvanus Richardson 20 yr old enlisted Union Co. 6/5/61 **C 7/1-7/5**
Private James Robinson 23 yr old enlisted Union Co. 6/5/61 **C 7/5** (joined US service—deserted-rejoined Rgt Sgt)
Private Robert Robinson 24 yr old enlisted Union Co. 6/5/61 (later C Bristoe Station joined US service)
Private Anderson Rogers 23 yr old enlisted Union Co. 6/5/61 **W-thigh 7/1**
Private Robert Rogers 22 yr old enlisted Camp Wilkes 10/17/61 **WC 7/3** died 8/21
Private John Rollins 22 yr old enlisted Union Co. 6/5/61 **W-left arm 7/1** "carrying colors" (later W Wilderness)
Private John Simpson 22 yr old enlisted Union Co. 6/5/61 (later W face & chest Wilderness)
Private M.L. Starnes enlisted Union Co 2/14/63 **W 7/1 C 7/5**
Private Thomas Starnes 23 yr old enlisted Union Co. 6/5/61 **WC 7/1 died 7/21**
Private Marcus Sykes 23 yr old mechanic enlisted Union Co. 6/5/61 **W 7/1 C 7/14** (later joined US service)

Private Demsey Tucker enlisted Iredell Co 9/28/62 (later K Bristoe Station)
Private Henry Walkup 19 yr old enlisted Union Co. 6/5/61 ***W-right arm C 7/1 (amp)***
Private Israel Walkup enlisted Union Co. 12/29/62 ***W-left arm 7/1 C 7/5***
Private B.R. White enlisted Union Co 12/29/62 **C 7/5**
Private Theophilus Woody enlisted Camp Mangum 9/21/62 (AWOL 9/63)
Private Washington Wyan enlisted Camp Mangum 9/28/62
Private Adam Wyatt enlisted Camp Mangum 9/21/62 **K 7/1**

Company C *"Wilkes Volunteers"*

1st Lt. William Porter 26 yr old enlisted Wilkes Co 6/12/61 **C 7/3**
2nd Lt. John Harris 24 yr old enlisted Wilkes Co 6/12/61 (later C Bristoe Station)
3rd Lt. Rufus Horton 28 yr old enlisted Camp French 12/12/61 **W 7/3**
1st Sgt Jesse Triplett 29 yr old enlisted Wilkes Co 6/12/61 ***K 7/3***
Sgt. William Curtis 24 yr old enlisted Wilkes Co 6/12/61 W Malvern Hill (detailed brigade Ord Sgt)
Sgt. David Hall 25 yr old enlisted Wilkes Co 6/12/61 **W 7/3 C 7/14**
Sgt. Samuel Pryor 30 yr old enlisted Wilkes Co 6/12/61 **C 7/14** (later 1st Sgt)
Corp. Benjamin Welch 26 yr old enlisted Wilkes Co 6/12/61 (later C Bristoe Station)
Corp. George Welch 24 yr old enlisted Wilkes Co 6/12/61 (later K Hatchers Run)
Private Wesley Bullis 28 yr old enlisted Wilkes Co 3/20/63
Private Wesley Combes 21 yr old enlisted Wilkes Co 6/12/61 **C 7/5**
Private Elisha Cox 37 yr old enlisted Pitt Co 5/20/63 **W 7/3 C 7/5**
Private David Dancy 24 yr old enlisted Wilkes Co 6/12/61
Private A.M. Davis 32 yr old enlisted Camp Holmes 9/21/62 **W 7/3**
Private John Dixon 25 yr old enlisted Camp Holmes 10/17/62 **W 7/3** (later C Spotsylvania)
Private William Edmisten 25 yr old enlisted Wilkes Co 6/12/61 (later C Bristoe Station)
Private James Eller 25 yr old enlisted Wilkes Co 6/12/61 **C 7/5**
Private Leander Eller transferred to company 1/63 **C 7/3**
Private Pinkney Foster 22 yr old enlisted Wilkes Co 6/12/61 **W-left leg C 7/3**
Private Charles Gilbert 24 yr old enlisted Wilkes Co 11/15/61 (later K Bristoe Station "carrying colors")
Private Henry Hall 21 yr old enlisted Wilkes Co 6/12/61 (deserted 8/29/64)
Private Pinkney Hall 21 yr old enlisted Wilkes Co 6/12/61 (later W-hand Cold Harbor)
Private Samuel Hall 23 yr old enlisted Wilkes Co 6/12/61 **W-right thigh C 7/3**
Private Josiah Millsaps 27 yr old enlisted Wilkes Co 6/12/61 **C 7/14** (later Corp)
Private Madison Minton 30 yr old enlisted Wilkes Co 6/12/61
Private William F. Parsons transferred 1/63 **WC 7/3** (later C Hatcher's Run)
Private William N Parsons 28 yr old enlisted Pitt Co. 3/20/63 (AWOL 8/63-returned W-Wilderness)

Private William Rhodes 23 yr old enlisted Camp Holmes **C 7/14**
Private Calvin Simmons 22 yr old enlisted Wilkes Co 6/12/61 (later C Wilderness)
Private Jesse Souther 23 yr old enlisted Camp Holmes ***W 7/3*** *(later K Glove Tavern)*
Private Joshua Souther 24 yr old enlisted Wilkes Co 6/12/61 W Malvern Hill ***W-left Shoulder 7/3***
Private James Welch 23 yr old enlisted Camp Holmes 10/17/62 **C 7/14**
Private Alfred Yates 18 yr old enlisted Wilkes Co 6/12/61 (later C Spotsylvania—joined US service)
Private Jesse Yates 21 yr old enlisted Wilkes Co 6/12/61 (deserted 9/9/63)

July 1 Casualties

Captain Issac Jarratt 23 yr old enlisted Carteret Co 10/8/61 appointed 10/28/62 **W-face & hand 7/1** (later W left lung Spotsylvania)
Sgt. Franklin Chappel 22 yr old enlisted Wilkes Co 6/12/61 **W-right thigh 7/1**
Corp. Benjamin Bullis 34 yr old enlisted Wilkes Co 6/12/61 **W 7/1 C 7/5**
Corp. John Reeves 22 yr old enlisted Wilkes Co 6/12/61 **W 7/1** (AWOL 8/63 returned)
Private Franklin Adams 24 yr old enlisted Camp Holmes 12/11/62 **W-left thigh 7/1** (later C Burgess Mill)
Private James Adams 28 yr old enlisted Camp Holmes 9/21/62 (later W Wilderness)
Private Monroe Alley 30 yr old enlisted Camp Holmes 12/11/62 **W 7/1** (later W Wilderness)
Private Benjamin Auton 24 yr old enlisted Camp Holmes 12/11/62 **W 7/1**
Private James Ball 21 yr old enlisted Wilkes Co 6/12/62 **W 7/1**
Private Harrison Barlow 25 yr old enlisted Camp Holmes 12/11/62 **W-right ankle 7/1** (later K Cold Harbor)
Private John Bell 22 yr old enlisted Wilkes Co 6/12/61 **W-left thigh 7/1 C 7/5**
Private Malin Brown 23 yr old enlisted Wilkes Co 6/12/61 **W-side 7/1**
Private John Bullis enlisted Camp Holmes 9/21/61 (later C Bristoe Station)
Private Simeon Bullis 27 yr old enlisted Wilkes Co 6/12/61 **W 7/1 C 7/5**
Private A. Bumgarner 30 yr old enlited Wilkes Co 3/20/63 **K 7/1**
Private John Cranfield 23 yr old enlisted Wilkes Co 6/12/61 **K 7/1**
Private James Curtis 23 yr old enlisted Wilkes Co 6/12/61 **K 7/1**
Private James Dudley 30 yr old enlisted Wilkes Co 6/12/61 **W 7/1**
Private James Edmisten 38 yr old enlisted Wilkes Co 6/12/61 **W 7/1** (later W Bristoe Station died 10/31)
Private Abraham Edmonson transferred from Co A 4/12/62 **W 7/1** (later C Bristoe Station)
Private John Foster 35 yr old enlisted Wilkes Co 6/12/61 **W 7/1** (later W Cold Harbor)
Private Triplett Hamby 31 yr old enlisted Wilkes Co 6/12/61 **W 7/1**
Private Esley Higgins 25 yr old enlisted Wilkes Co 6/12/61 (later Sgt & 1st Sgt K Ream's Station)
Private John Hinson 37 yr old enlisted Wilkes Co 6/12/61 (deserted 9/8/63—returned)

Private William Holder 23 yr old enlisted Wilkes Co 6/12/61 **W 7/1**
Private James Johnson 21 yr old enlisted Wilkes Co 6/12/61 **W 7/1** (later W-right arm Wilderness)
Private Eli Joins 37 yr old enlisted Wilkes Co 6/12/61 **SW 7/1**
Private Franklin Keeton 22 yr old enlisted Camp Holmes 10/17/62 **K 7/1**
Private G.E. Kemp 27 yr old enlisted Camp Holmes 12/11/62 **K 7/1**
Private B.F. Lewis 31 yr old enlisted Camp Holmes 9/21/62 **K 7/1**
Private James Lewis 29 yr old enlisted Camp Holmes 9/21/62 **W 7/1** (later C Bristoe Station)
Private Joseph Lewis 20 yr old enlisted Wilkes Co 6/12/61 (later WC Bristoe Station)
Private Joshua Lewis 22 yr old enlisted Wilkes Co 6/12/61 (later K Bristoe Station)
Private Franklin McDaniel 21 yr old enlisted Wilkes Co 6/12/61 **W-left leg 7/1**
Private James Melton 25 yr old enlisted Wilkes Co 6/12/61 **W-left shoulder 7/1** "with the colors"
Private Thomas Minton 21 yr old enlisted Wilkes Co 6/12/61 **W-left arm 7/1 C 7/5** (K Burgess Mill-carrying colors)
Private Andrew Moss 30 yr old enlisted camp Holmes 12/1/62 **W 7/1 C 7/5** (later C Wilderness)
Private Benjamin Nance 22 yr old enlisted Wilkes Co 6/12/61 W-right thigh Malvern Hill **C 7/14**
Private James Nance 20 yr old enlisted Wilkes Co 6/12/61 **C 7/14**
Private William Nance 25 yr old enlisted Wilkes Co 6/12/61 **W 7/1** (later Corp)
Private Anderson Nichols 23 yr old enlisted Wilkes Co 6/12/61 **K 7/1**
Private Anderson Nicholson 21 yr old enlisted Wilkes Co 6/12/61 **K 7/1**
Private Alfred Parsons 23 yr old enlisted Wilkes Co 6/12/61 **W 7/1**
Private Payton Parsons 23 yr old enlisted Wilkes Co 6/12/61 **W 7/1**
Private Caleb Rupard 33 yr old enlisted Camp Holmes 12/11/62 **W 7/1**
Private Thomas Simmons 24 yr old enlisted Wilkes Co 6/12/61 **K 7/1**
Private Asa Triplett 25 yr old enlisted Camp Holmes 9/21/62 **W-back 7/1** (later Corp & Sgt)
Private Elbert Triplett 21 yr old enlisted Camp Holmes (C Wilderness)
Private J.W. Triplett 22 yr old enlisted Camp Holmes 9/21/62 (later W-knee Bristoe Station)
Private Hilary Tripett 27 yr old enlisted Camp Holmes 9/21/62 **W 7/1**
Private Thomas Watts 18 yr old enlisted Camp Holmes 9/21/62 **W-neck 7/1**
Private William Welch 24 yr old enlisted Wilkes Co 6/12/61 **W 7/1** (later Sgt)

Company D *"Wake Guards"*

1st Lt. Gaston Broughton 28 yr old enlisted Wake Co 5/29/61 **W-foot C 7/3**
Sgt. William Utley 19 yr old enlisted Wake Co 6/10/61 5/29/61 ***W-right arm C 7/3*** *(later 1st Sgt)*

Corp. Henry Booker enlisted Wake Co 5/29/61 **W 7/3** (later Sgt W-face Wilderness)
Corp. Wiley Burt 21 yr old enlisted Wake Co 5/29/61 (later Sgt 1st Sgt)
Private Sidney Austin 18 yr old enlisted Wake Co 5/8/63 **W-right hip 7/3**
Private Wesley Baker 22 yr old enlisted Wake Co 6/10/61 **W 7/3 C 7/5**
Private N.F. Bryan 25 yr old enlisted Wake Co 5/29/61 C New Bern, NC **K 7/3**
Private William Burt 23 yr old enlisted Wake Co 5/29/61 W New Bern, NC **C 7/3** (later W Shoulder Cold Harbor)
Private John Chamblee 28 yr old enlisted Camp Holmes 10/1/62 **C 7/3**
Private Hawkins Gilbert 23 yr old enlisted Wake Co 5/29/61 C New Bern, NC **K 7/3**
Private Theophilus Holleman 20 yr old enlisted Wake Co 5/29/61 **C 7/3**
Private F.M. Langston 23 yr old enlisted Camp Magruder 5/9/62 **K 7/3**
Private J.P. Langston 18 yr old enlisted 3/18/63 **C 7/14**
Private W.W. Langston 26 yr old enlisted Wake Co 5/29/61 C New Bern, NC **C 7/14**
Private Nathan Nordan 24 yr old enlisted Wake Co 6/10/61 **W-head & left leg 7/3**
Private Solomon Pearson 19 yr old enlisted Wake Co 6/10/61 **C 7/3**
Private James Wallace 26 yr old enlisted camp Holmes 1/20/63 **C 7/14**
Private Joseph Wheeler 30 yr old enlisted Wake Co 5/19/62 (letter)
Private Joseph White Union Co farmer **C 7/14** (later joined US Service)
Private Abner Williams 27 yr old enlisted Camp Holmes 9/22/62 **C 7/14**
Private Aquilla Williams 24 yr old enlisted Camp Holmes 9/22/62 **C 7/14**
Private Marshall Williams 25 yr old enlisted Camp Holmes **C 7/3**
Private Jesse Wyatt 23 yr old enlisted Camp Holmes 9/22/62 **C 7/3**
Private John Wyatt 25 yr old enlisted Camp Holmes 9/22/62 **W-head 7/3 C 7/14**
Private Simeon Young 23 yr old enlisted Wake Co 6/10/61 C New Bern, NC **C 7/3**

Teamster N.G. Godwin 23 yr old enlisted Wake Co 6/10/61

July 1 Casualties—

Captain **James Theophilus Adams** 23 yr old enlisted Wake Co 5/29/61 W-hip Malvern Hill **W-left shoulder 7/1** (later Lt. Col)
2nd Lt. James Jones 23 yr old enlisted Wake Co 5/29/61 **W-right thigh 7/1** (later W Spotsylvania)
3rd Lt Marion Woodall enlisted Wake Co 8/19/61 4/21/62 **W-knee C 7/1**
1st Sgt William Utley 22 yr old enlisted Wake Co 6/10/61 **W 7/1**
Sgt. William C. Booker 24 yr old enlisted Wake Co 5/29/61 C New Bern, NC **W-left leg 7/1**
Sgt. William H. Booth 30 yr old enlisted Wake Co 6/10/61 **W 7/1** died 8/20/63
Sgt. Britton Utley 21 yr old enlisted Wake Co 5/29/61 **W 7/1**
Corp. Thomas Hunter 31 yr old enlisted Wake Co 5/29/61 C New Bern NC **WC 7/1** died
Private Samuel Atkins 30 yr old enlisted Wake Co 8/19/61 **W 7/1 C 7/5**
Private Simeon Austin 22 yr old enlisted Wake Co 5/29/61 C Hanover CH **W 7/1** (later Corp C Burgess Mill)

Private Alexander Baker 20 yr old enlisted Wake Co 6/10/61 **W 7/1**

Private Jackson Baker 23 yr old enlisted Wake Co 8/19/61

Private Joseph Baker 23 yr old enlisted Wake Co 6/10/61 **W-hand 7/1 C 7/5**

Private William E. Booker 21 yr old enlisted Wake Co 6/10/61 **W left ankle 7/1**

Private Joseph Burt 26 yr old enlisted Wake Co 8/19/61 **K 7/1**

Private Jesse Burt 24 yr old enlisted Wake Co 6/10/61 (twins) **W 7/1** (later W Bristoe Station)

Private Robert Burt 24 yr old enlisted Wake Co 5/29/61 (twins) C New Bern, NC (later Corp)

Private J.H. Bynum enlisted 6/20/62 **K 7/1**

Private John Camp 27 yr old enlisted Camp Holmes 6/10/61 **W-left thigh 7/1 C 7/5**

Private William Champion 24 yr old enlisted Wake Co 5/29/61 C New Bern, NC **W 7/1** (later K Bristoe Station)

Private Dallas Crawford 21 yr old enlisted Wake Co 8/19/61 C New Bern, NC **W 7/1** (later W Bristoe Station)

Private Thomas Cordle 20 yr old enlisted Wake Co 6/10/61 **W 7/1 C 7/5** (later C Burgess Mill)

Private Joseph Dancy 20 yr old enlisted Wake Co 9/22/62 **W-right thigh 7/1**

Private Andrew Ford enlisted Camp Holmes 10/1/62

Private Stephen Fuquay 22 yr old student enlisted Wake Co 6/10/61 **W-arm 7/1**

Private James Gilmore 18 yr old enlisted Camp Holmes 1/20/63 **W 7/1** (later W Bristoe Station)

Private S.W. Godwin 26 yr old enlisted Camp Magruder 5/9/62 **W 7/1**

Private Paschal Gower 25 yr old enlisted Wake Co 6/10/61 musician at start of war-demoted

Private Willis Hamilton 36 yr old enlisted Wake Co 5/29/61 **W 7/1**

Private Wesley Hamilton 20 yr old enlisted Wake Co 5/29/61 **W 7/1** (later C Burgess Mill)

Private J.P. Honeycutt 24 yr old enlisted Wake Co 5/29/61 **W 7/1** (later C Bristoe Station)

Private Reuben Hunter 22 yr old enlisted Wake Co 5/29/61 **W 7/1** (later K Wilderness)

Private Alexander Jones 28 yr old enlisted Camp Holmes 1/20/63 **W 7/1** (later WC Bristoe Station)

Private John Jones 18 yr old enlisted Wake Co 6/8/63 **W 7/1** (later W-left knee Bristoe Station)

Private David Jenkins 29 yr old enlisted Camp Holmes 10/162 **W 7/1**

Private Sidney Jones 22 yr old enlisted Wake Co 8/31/61 C New Bern, NC **W-left shoulder 7/1 C 7/5**

Private Walter Jones 20 yr old enlisted Wake Co 5/29/61 **W 7/1 C 7/5**

Private George Washington Kelly 30 yr old enlisted Wake Co 6/10/61 **color bearer W-ankle & arm by shell fragment 7/1 C 7/5**

Private H.W. Langston 22 yr old enlisted Wake Co 5/29/61 **W 7/1** (later K Wilderness)

Private William McDonald 23 yr old enlisted Camp Holmes 10/1/62 **W 7/1 C 7/5**

Private L.D. Mangum transferred 12/1/62 **W 7/1 C sick 7/5**

Private Quinton Maynard 19 yr old enlisted Wake Co 6/10/61 **W 7/1**

Private George Morris 19 yr old enlisted Camp Holmes 1/20/63 **W 7/1** (later C Bristoe Station)

Private John Nordan 26 yr old enlisted Wake Co 6/10/61 **W 7/1** (later W-right arm C Bristoe Station)

Private William Norris 21 yr old enlisted Bogue Island, NC 9/10/61 C New Bern, NC **W 7/1** (later Corp)

Private Thomas Oliver 21 yr old enlisted Camp Holmes 9/22/62 **K 7/1**

Private Martin Overby 30 yr old enlisted Wake Co 6/10/61 **W 7/1 C 7/5** (later joined US Service)

Private George Partin 23 yr old enlisted wake Co 5/29/61 **W-arm 7/1 (amp)**

Private Henderson Ray 20 yr old enlisted Wake Co 8/19/61 **W 7/1** (later C Bristoe Station)

Private William Rogers transferred 10/24/62 **W 7/1** (later W Bristoe Station)

Private William Smith 22 yr old enlisted Wake Co 6/10/61 C New Bern, NC **W 7/1** (later K Bristoe Station)

Private James Stephens 24 yr old enlisted Wake Co 5/29/61 C New Bern, NC (later C Bristoe Station)

Private Eli Tredway 22 yr old enlisted Camp Holmes 9/22/62 **W 7/1** (later W Bristoe Station)

Private Rufus Trenshaw 25 enlisted Camp Holmes 9/22/62 **W-head 7/1 C 7/5** (later W-right leg Wilderness)

Private John Wingler 30 yr old enlisted 9/22/62 (later K Bristoe Station)

Private Reinhardt Wingler 23 yr old enlisted Camp Holmes 9/22/62 **K 7/1**

Private Cornelius Wood 22 yr old enlisted Wake Co 5/29/61 C New Bern, NC **W 7/1 C 7/5**

Company E *"Independent Guards"*

Captain **Stephen Brewer** 27 yr old enlisted Cartersville, NC 5/28/61 **W 7/3 "while carrying flag" C 7/5 Greencastle** (later Sheriff)

1st Lt. John R. Emerson 24 yr old enlisted Cartersville, NC 5/28/61 **W 7/3 C 7/5 died NY hospital**

2nd Lt. William Lambert 30 yr old enlisted Cartersville, NC 7/1/61 **survivor** (later C Burgess Mill)

1st Sgt James Brooks 22 yr old enlisted 5/28/61 **reached wall C 7/3** (later W Petersburg) later teacher

Private William M. Cheek 30 yr old enlisted Cartersville 5/28/61 slightly **W 7/1** returned **W 7/3** (later C Petersburg)

Private Jesse Petty 22 yr old enlisted Cartersville, NC 5/28/61 **W-left hip & left thigh 7/3**

Private John Phillips 20 yr old enlisted Cartersville, NC 5/28/61 W Malvern Hill **W-neck & left hand 7/3 C 7/5**

Private John Smith 28 yr old enlisted Cartersville, NC 10/26/61 **C 7/14**

Private James Tally 21 yr old enlisted Cartersville, NC 5/28/61 **WC 7/3** died 7/8

Private Robert Tally 28 yr old enlisted Cartersville, NC 5/28/61 **survivor** (later W left leg C Bristoe Station)

Private Daniel Boone Thomas 22 yr old enlisted Cartersville, NC 5/28/61 ***reached wall WC 7/3***

Private Nathaniel Thomas 27 yr old enlisted Cartersville, NC 5/28/61 ***C 7/3***

Private Levi Welch 25 yr old enlisted Cartersville, NC 6/1/61 **W-left arm 7/3**

Musician (Drummer) Thomas Hackney 20 yr old enlisted Cartersville, NC 5/28/61

July 1 Casualties

3rd Lt. Orren Hanner 20 yr old enlisted Cartersville, NC 5/28/61 W Malvern Hill **W 7/1 C 7/5 Greencastle**

Sgt. James Ellis 25 yr old enlisted Cartersville 5/28/61 **W 7/1 C 7/5**

Sgt. Jefferson Mansfield 25 yr old enlisted Cartersville, NC 5/28/62 Color Sergeant 7/1 **W-right foot 7/1 C 7/5**

Sgt. William Merritt 26 yr old enlisted Cartersville, NC 5/28/61 **W-thigh 7/1 C 7/5**

Sgt. Neal Kidd 24 yr old enlisted Cartersville 5/28/61 (later C Bristoe Station)

Corp. George Fitts 23 29 yr old enlisted Cartersville, NC 5/28/61 (later Sgt)

Corp. James Dorsett 19 yr old enlisted Cartersville 7/5/61 **W-chest & left shoulder 7/1 C 5**

Corp. William Edwards 21 year old enlisted Cartersville 5/28/61 **W 7/1** (later C Burgess Mill)

Corp. James Martindale 24 yr old enlisted Cartersville, NC 5/28/61 **W-chest 7/1** (later W Bristoe Station)

Corp. John Phillips 30 yr old enlisted Cartersville, NC 5/28/61 **K 7/1**

Private Brant Adcock 36 yr old enlisted Cartersville 3/8/62 (later W Bristoe Station)

Private John Adcock transferred 4/62 **W 7/1**

Private John Beal 20 yr old enlisted Cartersville 6/1/61 (later W Bristoe Station C Spotsylvania)

Private Joseph Andrew 24 yr old enlisted Cartersville 3/8/62 **W-left foot 7/1**

Private Benjamin Beal 24 yr old enlisted Cartersville 6/1/61 **K 7/1**

Private William Borroughs 21 yr old enlisted Cartersville 8/20/61 **W 7/1** (later C Burgess Mill)

Private Elijah Brewer 37 yr old enlisted Chatham Co. 3/1/63 (later W Bristoe Station)

Private Eli Brewer 22 yr old enlisted Chatham Co. 5/15/62 (later W Cold Harbor)

Private Gerry Brewer 23 yr old enlisted Chatham Co. 3/1/63 (later Corp)

Private Nathan Brewer 19 yr old enlisted Chatham Co. 3/8/62 **W 7/1**

Private Josiah Brooks 23 yr old enlisted 5/28/61 (discharged 9/63)

Private John Brooks 20 yr old enlisted Cartersville **K 7/1**

Private Thomas Burke transferred 4/5/63 **W 7/1**

Private Daniel Carter 24 yr old enlisted Cartersville 5/28/61 **W 7/1** died 7/20 Winchester, Va

Private John Carter transferred 6/19/62 **W-right eye 7/1**

Private William Caviness 22 yr old enlisted Chatham Co.5/8/61 **W 7/1 C 7/5**
Private John Cheek 25 yr old enlisted Cartersville **W-knee 7/1 C 7/5 died**
Private Middleton Cheek transferred 1/63 **W 7/1 C 7/5**
Private Robert Cheek 23 enlisted Cartersville 5/28/61 **W 7/1 C 7/5**
Private Joseph Claridy 18 yr old enlisted Chatham Co 3/1/63 **W 7/1** (later W-finger Wilderness)
Private John Crutchfield enlisted 7/19/62 (later transferred to 41st NC)
Private William Crutchfield 29 yr old enlisted Cartersville, NC 5/28/61 **C 7/4** South Mtn, Md
Private S.J. Dorsett transferred 4/62 **W 7/1 C 7/5**
Private John Dowd 20 yr old enlisted Cartersville 5/18/61 **W 7/1**
Private David Foster 29 yr old enlisted Cartersville, NC 5/28/61 **K 7/1**
Private Issac Edwards 18 yr old enlisted Chatham Co 1/1/63 **W 7/1 C 7/4**
Private William P. Elington 25 yr old enlisted Camp Wilkes 11/4/61 **WC 7/1** died 7/21 (moved Col Burgwyn's body)
Private Joseph Ellis 19 yr old enlisted Chatham Co. 5/28/61 (later K Ream's Station)
Private Laban Ellis 28 29 yr old enlisted Chatham Co. 5/28/61 **W 7/1 C 7/5**
Private Green Fields 24 yr old enlisted Cartersville, NC 5/28/61 **W-right knee 7/1**
Private James Fields 24 yr old enlisted Cartersville, NC 5/28/61 **W-left arm "shot off" 7/1**
Private Manly Forrester 18 enlisted Chatham Co 3/8/62 **W-left leg 7/1 C 7/5**
Private Nathaniel Foster 20 yr old enlisted Cartersville, NC 5/28/61 **W 7/1 C 7/5**
Private William Gee transferred 6/19/62 **W 7/1** (later W-knee Bristoe Station)
Private Joseph Harper 29 yr old enlisted Chatham 5/28/61 **K 7/1**
Private William Harper 35 yr old enlisted Cartersville, NC 5/28/61 **W-left leg 7/1**
Private John Hart 20 yr old enlisted Cartersville, NC 5/28/61 **K 7/1**
Private Alfred Howard 19 yr old enlisted Chatham Co. 9/22/62 **K 7/1**
Private Richard Jenkins 24 yr old enlisted Cartersville, NC 6/5/61 (later W Bristoe Station)
Private John Jones 20 enlisted Chatham 9/22/62 (later C Bristoe Station)
Private John Jones 21 yr old enlisted 5/19/61 (later W-back Bristoe Station)
Private James Johnson 29 yr old enlisted Chatham Co. 5/15/62 **W 7/1** (later W Bristoe Station)
Private Willis Jones 28 yr old enlisted Cartersville 5/28/61 **W 7/1**
Private John Lambert 21 yr old enlisted Cartersville, NC 5/28/61 **W-left foot 7/1** C Wilderness
Private James **McDaniel** 29 yr old enlisted Cartersville, NC 5/28/61 **W 7/1 C 7/5 died**
Private Edwin McManus 25 yr old enlisted 8/23/61 **W 7/1** (later 3rd Lt)
Private James McMath 21 yr old enlisted Cartersville, NC 5/28/61 W Malvern Hill **W 7/1**
Private John Mobley 21 yr old enlisted Cartersville, NC 5/28/61 **K 7/1**
Private Charles Moody 28 enlisted Chatham Co 9/5/62 **W-left shoulder & both legs 7/1**
Private James Moody 24 yr old enlisted Cartersville, NC 5/28/61 (later W Bristoe Station)
Private Irvin Nall 26 yr od enlisted Chatham Co 9/22/62 (later W-left leg Cold Harbor)
Private Martin Nall 22 yr old enlisted Cartersville, NC 5/28/61 **W-left ankle 7/1 C 7/5**

Private Thomas Needham 22 yr old enlisted Randolph Co 6/22/61 (later C Bristoe Station)
Private William Needham 28 yr old enlisted Cartersville, NC 5/28/61 **W 7/1**
Private John Norwood 22 yr old enlisted Cartersville, NC 6/3/61 **W-back 7/1 C 7/4**
Private Everet Page 25 yr old enlisted 5/28/61 **W 7/1 died**
Private Henry Perry 23 yr old enlisted Cartersville, NC 7/1/61 **K 7/1**
Private George Phillips 24 yr old enlisted Cartersville, NC 5/28/61 W-left hip Rawls Mill, Va (later W—left leg Bristoe Station)
Private Richard Phillips 28 yr old enlisted Cartersville, NC 5/28/61 **W 7/1** (later C Bristoe Station)
Private Thomas Phillips 21 yr old enlisted Cartersville, NC 5/28/61 **K 7/1**
Private John Powers 26 yr old enlisted Chatham Co. **W-left foot 7/1 C 7/5**
Private Henry Rogers 25 yr old enlisted Cartersville, NC 7/5/61 W Malvern Hill **K 7/1**
Private John Russell 27 yr old enlisted Cartersville, NC 5/28/61 **K 7/1**
Private Allen Shields 27 yr old enlisted Cartersville, NC 5/15/61 **W-right leg C 7/1** (amp died Chester Pa 7/30)
Private Green Smith 27 yr old enlisted Cartersville, NC 5/15/61 W Malvern Hill **K 7/1**
Private Levi Smith 21 yr old enlisted Cartersville, NC 5/28/61 W-right hand New Bern NC
Private Thomas Smith 29 yr old enlisted Cartersville, NC 5/15/62
Private Atlas Stanley transferred 5/15/62 **W 7/1** (later C Spotsylvania)
Private Noah Smith 23 yr old enlisted Cartersville, NC 5/28/61 **W-right shoulder 7/1 C 7/5**
Private Robert Smith 21 yr old enlisted Cartersville, NC 5/28/61 **W-neck & shoulder 7/1**
Private Wiley Smith 25 yr old enlisted Cartersville, NC 5/15/62 **K 7/1**
Private Lewis Teague 38 yr old enlisted Cartersville, NC 5/28/61 **W 7/1** (later Sgt)
Private John Thomas 25 yr old enlisted Cartersville, NC 5/28/61 (later C Bristoe Station)
Private Hezekiah Vestal 22 yr old enlisted Cartersville, NC 5/28/61 (later C Burgess Mill)
Private Oren Vestal 23 yr old enlisted Cartersville, NC 5/28/61 (later W-arm Bristoe Station)
Private Adolphus Welch 20 yr old enlisted Chatham Co 5/15/62 W-leg New Bern, NC (later C Bristoe Station)
Private Abram Vestal 39 yr old enlisted Chatham Co 3/1/63 **W 7/1**
Private James Ward 30 yr old enlisted Cartersville, NC 5/28/61 **K 7/1**
Private Stephen Ward 25 yr old enlisted Cartersville, NC 6/1/61 **W-right hip 7/1**
Private Henry Welch 28 yr old enlisted Cartersville, NC 5/28/61 **W 7/1** (later W Bristoe Station)
Private Robert Welch 28 yr old enlisted Cartersville, NC 5/28/61 **WC 7/1**
Private William Welch 23 yr old enlisted Cartersville, NC 5/28/61 W-Malvern Hill **W 7/1 C 7/5**
Private Issac Wilkie 20 yr old enlisted Chatham Co 3/1/63 **W 7/1 C 7/4**

Drum Major Joseph Hackney 21 yr old enlisted Cartersville, NC 5/28/61 **W 7/1 C 7/5**

Company F *"Hilbriten Guards"*

Sgt. / Lieutenant Robert Hudspeth 26 yr old enlisted Caldwell Co 7/15/61 promoted to Lieutenant 7/2
W-knocked down and stunned by shell" 7/1 fought again W 7/3
Sgt. John Tuttle 19 yr old enlisted Caldwell Co 7/15/61 (later K Bristoe Station) *"survivor"*
Private George W. Coffey 22 yr old enlisted Caldwell Co.3/20/61 (later C Bristoe Co.)
Private Jesse Patterson Coffey 19 yr old enlisted Caldwell Co 7/15/61 (deserted 7/15/63 Winchester, Va)
Private Thomas Cozart 22 yr old enlisted Caldwell Co 7/15/61 carried flag after Sgt Smith **K 7/3**
Private Abraham Hutson 20 yr old enlisted Wake Co 10/19/62 **C 7/5**
Private John Kincaid 21 yr old enlisted Caldwell Co 3/20/62 **W-shoulder 7/3 C 7/5**
Private William Payne transferred 1/1/63 **W-"in body" 7/3 C 7/14**
Private John Sudderth transferred 1/15/63 W-right thigh **C 7/3** (later Corp)

7/1 Casualties

Captain Romulus Tuttle 20 yr old enlisted Caldwell Co. 7/15/61 promoted 10/16/62 **W-right leg 7/1** (later W-breast Wilderness)
1st Lt. Charles Sudderth 28 yr old enlisted Caldwell Co. 3/20/62 promoted 10/16/62 **W-right hand 7/1**
2nd Lt. Abner Hayes 23 yr old enlisted Caldwell Co. 7/15/61 promoted 10/16/62 **W 7/1** (W-breast Bristoe Station / K Cold Harbor)
3rd Lt. John B. Holloway 29 yr old enlisted Caldwell Co **K 7/1**
1st Sgt Caleb Estes 23 yr old enlisted Caldwell Co 7/15/61 **W 7/1 C 7/14** (later C Burgess Mill)
Sgt. Henry Coffey 20 yr old enlisted Caldwell Co 7/15/61 **W-wrist 7/1 C 7/5**
Sgt. J.T. Hood 26 yr old enlisted Caldwell Co 7/15/61 **W-left foot & thigh 7/1 C 7/5**
Color Corp. John Bowman 36 yr old enlisted Caldwell Co. **W-both legs 7/1**
Corp **Andrew Courtney** 26 yr old enlisted Caldwell Co 7/7/62 **W-left leg 7/1 amp C 7/5**
Corp. John Nelson 23 yr old enlisted Camp Wilkes 11/6/61 W-right hip Rawl's Mill (later C Bristoe Station)
Corp. Simeon Phlyaw 23 yr old enlisted Caldwell Co 7/15/61 fired first shot 7/1 **W-thigh 7/1 C 7/5**
Private Hezekiah Annas 34 yr old enlisted Wake Co. 1/7/63 **W-thigh 7/1 C 7/5** (later W-Wilderness)
Private George Arney 36 yr old enlisted Caldwell Co. 1/7/63 **W-right leg 7/1 C 7/5**
Private Sidney A. Badger 22 yr old enlisted Camp Wilkes **W-right leg 7/1** (amp) C 7/14 Williamsport
Private Joseph Baldwin 18 yr old enlisted Caldwell Co 2/20/63 **W-thigh 7/1 C 7/4**
Private Zeror Beach 26 yr old enlisted Caldwell Co 7/15/61 **W 7/1 C 7/5**

Private William Bean 18 yr old enlisted Caldwell Co 3/20/62 **W-foot 7/1** (later W Bristoe Station)

Private William Bradford 18 yr old enlisted Caldwell Co. 1/7/63 **W-arm 7/1** (later W Wilderness C Hatcher's Run)

Private Nathan Bradshaw 20 yr old enlisted Caldwell Co 7/15/61 C New Bern, NC **W-knee 7/1**

Private R.W. Braswell 33 yr old enlisted Caldwell Co. **W-breast 7/1**

Private Robert Braswell 28 yr old enlisted Petersburg 10/15/62 **K-head 7/1**

Private Jiles Calloway 34 yr old enlisted Caldwell Co. 3/20/62 **C 7/14** (later C Hatcher's Run)

Private Robert Caswell 35 yr old enlisted Caldwell Co 1/5/63 **K-head 7/1**

Private Redman Church 30 yr old enlisted Caldwell Co. 3/20/62 **W-foot 7/1**

Private Joseph Clark 18 yr old enlisted Caldwell Co. 3/20/62 **W-arm 7/1** (later C Spotsylvania)

Private William Clarke 38 yr old enlisted Wake Co. 1/5/63 W-foot, leg & shoulder **7/1/63**

Private Mortimore Clonts 22 yr old enlisted Caldwell Co. 7/15/61 **W-hip 7/1** (died 11/8/63)

Private Asbury Coffey 29 yr old enlisted Caldwell Co 3/20/62 **W-"fingers shot off" 7/1**

Private Cleveland Coffey 26 yr old enlisted Caldwell Co. 3/20/62 **W 7/1 died 7/3**

Private J.G. Coffey 24 yr old enlisted Caldwell Co 7/15/61 **W-left arm 7/1 C 7/4** (amp) died 8/23

Private J.H. Coffey 23 yr old enlisted Camp Burgwyn 10/1/61 **K-breast 7/1**

Private Thomas Coffey 28 yr old enlisted Caldwell Co 3/20/62 **W-breast C 7/1** (died 8/12/63)

Private William Coffey 19 yr old enlisted Caldwell Co 3/20/62 **W-thigh 7/1**

Private Henry Courtney 20 yr old enlisted Caldwell Co 7/15/61 **W-right thigh 7/1 C 7/5**

Private Solomon Crisp 29 yr old enlisted Caldwell Co 3/20/62 **W-left thigh 7/1 C 7/4**

Private H.C. Crump 18 yr old enlisted Caldwell Co 3/20/62 **W-arm 7/1**

Private Thomas Crump 21 yr old enlisted Caldwell Co 3/20/62 **W 7/1** Died 7/8/63

Private Nathaniel Culbreath 26 yr old enlisted Caldwell Co 3/20/62 **W-side 7/1** (later K Wilderness)

Private Joshua Curtis 23 yr old enlisted Caldwell Co 7/15/61 **W 7/1 C 7/15** Williamsport, Md (joined US Service)

Private Thomas Curtis 23 yr old enlisted Wake Co 10/10/62 **W-thigh 7/1 C 7/4**

Private William Curtis transferred 11/62 **W-arm 7/1 C 7/5** (amp)

Private James Deal 30 yr old enlisted Wake Co. 1/5/63 **K 7/1**

Private Rufus Erwin 35 yr old enlisted Wake Co. 1/5/63 **W-shoulder 7/1** (died 7/15/63)

Private William Fleming 35 yr old enlisted Wake Co. 1/7/63 **K 7/1**

Private James Gilbert 26 yr old enlisted Caldwell Co 3/20/62 **W 7/1** (later W Wilderness)

Private Jackson Gragg 23 yr old enlisted Caldwell Co 3/20/62 **K 7/1**

Private Henry Hayes 20 yr old enlisted Caldwell Co 3/20/62 **W-shoulder 7/1 C 7/5**

Private George Holloway 24 yr old enlisted Caldwell Co 7/15/61 W Malvern Hill **W-right leg 7/1** (later Sgt)
Private J.M. Holloway 23 yr old enlisted Caldwell Co 7/15/61 **W-breast 7/1/63 C 7/14** (died 10/18/63)
Private George Washington Hood 22 yr old enlisted Caldwell Co 7/15/61 W Malvern Hill **W-hip 7/1** (later W-thigh Bristoe Station)
Private Paul Howell 26 yr old enlisted Caldwell Co 7/15/61 **W-thigh 7/1 C 7/4** (later C Spotsylvania)
Private A.M. Hudspeth 24 yr old enlisted Caldwell Co 7/15/61 **W-face 7/1** (later K Bristoe Station)
Private George Huspeth 21 yr old enlisted Caldwell Co 7/17/62 **W-leg 7/1 C 7/4**
Private Ambrose Hudson 18 yr old enlisted Wake Co. 10/19/62 **W-shell 7/1 C 7/14**
Private William Kirby 23 yr old enlisted Caldwell Co 7/15/61 **W-shoulder 7/1** (later Corp C Bristoe Station)
Private Philip Largent 29 yr old enlisted Caldwell Co 3/20/62 **W-thigh 7/1** (later C Bristoe Station)
Private John Lewis 24 yr old enlisted Caldwell Co 7/15/61 **K 7/1**
Private William Lewis 18 yr old enlisted Caldwell Co 3/20/62 **C 7/3**
Private J.B. Littlejohn 22 yr old enlisted Caldwell Co 7/15/61 **W 7/1** Died 7/3/63
Private Elcanna Mathis 34 yr old enlisted Caldwell Co 2/4/63 **W-arm 7/1**
Private **James D. "Jimmy" Moore** 17 yr old enlisted Caldwell Co 7/15/61 **W-neck & left thigh 7/1**
Private George Morgan 26 yr old enlisted Caldwell Co 7/15/61 **W-arm 7/1** (died 7/31/63)
Private Noah Page 35 yr old enlisted Wake Co. 1/5/63 **W-thigh 7/1 C 7/5**
Private Alison Perkins 21 yr old enlisted Caldwell Co 7/15/61 **W-side 7/1** (later W Bristoe Station)
Private Joseph Phillips enlisted 3/20/62 ***K 7/1***
Private W.E. Phillips enlisted 3/20/61 W Malvern Hill ***K 7/1*** *. . . . Twin brothers*
Private Gideon Philyaw 23 yr old enlisted Caldwell Co 7/15/61 **W-hip 7/1**
Private George Porch 24 yr old enlisted Caldwell Co 7/15/61 **W-thigh 7/1**
Private John Porch 19 yr old enlisted Caldwell Co. **W-back 7/1** (later C Hatcher Run)
Private Pinkney Powell 19 yr old enlisted 2/20/63 **W-head 7/1** (later C Bristoe Station)
Private Malcolm Rader 19 yr old enlisted Caldwell Co. 3/20/62 **W-shoulder 7/1 C 7/5**
Private Wade Rich 23 yr old enlisted Caldwell Co. 8/9/61 **W-arm 7/1**
Private William Rich 19 yr old enlisted Caldwell Co 7/15/61 **W-head 7/1** (later W Bristoe Station)
Private Joseph "Jo" Setser 20 yr old enlisted Camp Holmes 10/9/62 **W-leg 7/1 amp C 7/4** (died 7/17/63)
Private Thomas Setser 23 yr old enlisted Camp Carolina 8/9/61 **W-right thigh 7/1** (later Sgt—W Spotsyvania)
Private W. "Eli" Setser 19 yr old enlisted Caldwell Co 7/15/61 **W-thigh 7/1 C 7/4** (died 7/4/63)

Private Joseph Shork 32 yr old enlisted Wake Co. 1/5/63 **K 7/1**

Private Hosea Stallings 20 yr old enlisted Camp Carolina 8/9/61 **W-shoulder 7/1 C 7/4** (died 8/26/63)

Private William Stallings 18 yr old enlisted 3/1/63 **W-left leg 7/1** (died later disease)

Private Toliver Sudderth transferred 1/15/63 **W-finger 7/1** (later W right leg Bristoe Station)

Private John Taylor 20 yr old enlisted Caldwell Co 7/15/61 **K 7/1**

Private Benjamin Taylor 23 yr old enlisted wake Co 8/9/61 **W-left heel 7/1** (later C Spotsylvania)

Private Larkin Thomas 23 yr old enlisted Caldwell Co 3/20/62 **color bearer W-left arm 7/1**

Private Smith Thomas 22 yr old enlisted Camp Wilkes 12/2/61 **W-arm 7/1 as color bearer C 7/14**

Private James Thompson 19 yr old enlisted Caldwell Co 3/20/62 **W-shoulder 7/1** (later C Bristoe Station)

Private W.M. Thompson 18 yr old enlisted Caldwell Co 3/20/62 **K 7/1**

Private M.L. Townsell 22 yr old enlisted Caldwell Co 3/20/62 ***K 7/1 twins***

Private William P Townsell 22 yr old enlisted 7/15/61 Caldwell County (deserted 11/1/63)

Private Columbus Tuttle 18 yr old enlisted Camp Vance 12/17/61 **W-right arm 7/1** (later W-left arm Bristoe Station)

Private John Underdown 18 yr old enlisted Caldwell Co. 3/20/62 **W-breast 7/1**

Private Richard Upchurch 33 yr old enlisted Caldwell Co 7/15/61 C New Bern, NC **W-hand 7/1**

Private William Upchurch 25 yr old enlisted Caldwell Co 3/20/62 **W 7/1** (later C Bristoe Station)

Private Joseph Winkler 46 yr old enlisted Caldwell Co 3/20/62 **W-back 7/1**

Private Israel Zimmerman 35 yr old enlisted Wake Co 1/5/63 **W-knee 7/1 C 7/14 Hagerstown Died 7/24**

Musician George Sherrill 26 yr old enlisted Caldwell Co 7/15/61

Deserters

Private Larkin Coffey 24 yr old enlisted Caldwell Co 3/20/62 deserted in Maryland

Company G *"Chatham Boys"*

Captain Henry Clay Albright 20 yr old enlisted 7/10/61 promoted 10/12/62 (later K Squirrel Level Petersburg) commanded the regiment 7/4

1st Lt. John A. Lowe 23 yr old enlisted Chatham 6/10/61 promoted 10/12/62 "excellent shot" (later W left lung Bristoe Station)

2nd Lt. Austin Johnson 25 yr old 6/10/61 promoted 10/12/62 (later W left armpit Bristoe Station)

1st Sgt. Samuel Teague 24 yr old 6/10/61 promoted 10/62 (later 3rd Lt)

Sgt. Franklin Matthews 24 yr old enlisted Chatham Co 6/10/61 W Malvern Hill (later reduced to Private)

Corp. Horace Siler 19 yr old enlisted Chatham Co 3/6/62 **W 7/3**

Corp. Jesse Smith 27 yr old enlisted Chatham Co 6/10/61 (later Sgt C Wilderness)

Private Eli Branson 19 yr old enlisted Chatham Co 6/10/61 (later C Bristoe Station)

Private William Branson 24 yr old enlisted Chatham Co 6/10/61 (later Corp)

Private Henry Brown enlisted Wake Co 11/17/62 C Bristoe Station

Private John Brown 20 yr old enlisted 6/10/61 (later Corp)

Private Murphy Edwards 23 yr old enlisted 9/10/61 C 7/14 (later Corp C Burgess Mill)

Private Wiley Edwards 28 yr old enlisted Chatham Co 6/10/61 **C 7/14** (later C Burgess Mill)

Private William Foushee 20 yr old enlisted Wake Co 9/10/62 (later W-Wilderness AWOL 10/64)

Private Joseph Gilbert 21 yr old enlisted Camp Vance 11/29/61 (sick detached 12/63 to 1/65)

Private Thomas Hinshaw 27 yr old enlisted Chatham Co 6/10/61 C New Bern, NC (died 2/2/64 disease)

Private Loammi Johnson 20 yr old enlisted Petersburg, Va 11/17/62 (later C Bristoe Station)

Private Wiley Prentiss Kirkman 22 yr old enlisted Chatham Co 6/10/61 C New Bern, NC ***C 7/5***

Private Abraham Lane 22 yr old enlisted Chatham Co 6/10/61 brother of Lt Col Lane (later QM Sgt)

Private Alson McCay 19 yr old enlisted Chatham Co 3/6/62 (later K Bristoe Station)

Private David McPherson 20 yr old enlisted Chatham Co 6/10/61 C New Bern NC (later C Bristoe Station)

Private Issac McPherson 29 yr old enlisted Chatham Co 6/10/61 (later C Bristoe Station)

Private John Marley 19 yr old enlisted Chatham Co 3/6/62 **C 7/5** (detailed as nurse for wounded)

Private Riley Neese 26 enlisted 3/6/62 **K 7/3**

Private William Overman 47 yr old enlisted Chatham Co 6/10/61 **C 8/15/63**

Private William Patterson 27 yr old enlisted Chatham Co 6/10/61 (reduced from Sgt to Private 11/62)

Private Thomas Perrett 19 yr old enlisted Chatham Co 6/10/61 "excellent shot" **W 7/1—two wounds** (later Corp/Sgt W Spotsylvania)

Private James Purvis 30 yr old enlisted Graham's Station 6/10/61 (later C Wilderness)

Private John Roberts transferred 9/10/62 **C 7/14** (later joined US Service)

Private Jasper Rogers 24 yr old enlisted Chatham Co 6/10/61 **C 7/14**

Private Merritt Rosson 29 yr old enlisted Chatham Co 6/10/61 (later C Bristoe Station)

Private James Sheridan 28 yr old enlisted 3/6/62 (later K Bristoe Station)

Private James Siler 21 yr old enlisted Chatham Co 6/10/61 C New Bern, NC (later W Spotsylvania)

Private William Siler enlisted 8/13/62 **C 7/3**
Private Marion Smith 20 yr old 9/10/62 (later W Wilderness)
Private Solomon Smith 20 yr old enlisted Chatham Co 6/10/61 **K 7/3**
Private William Snotherly 22 yr old substitute enlisted Chatham Co 3/6/62 **W 7/3**
Private Jarratt Tilman 22 yr old enlisted Wake Co. **W 7/1**
Private Henry T. Vestal 24 yr old enlisted Chatham Co 3/6/62 **C 7/14** Williamsport Hospital
Private Alfred Way 26 yr old enlisted Chatham Co 6/10/61 **C 7/3** (later joined US Service)

Musician John Record 23 yr old enlisted Chatham Co 6/10/61 (later Corp C Bristoe Station)
Teamster Alexander Lineberry 21 yr old enlisted Chatham Co 3/6/62 (later W Globe tavern—teamster)

July 1 Casualties

3rd Lt. William Lane 32 yr old enlisted Wake Co 9/1/61 promoted 10/12/62 **W-right foot 7/1**
Sgt David Edwards 23 yr old enlisted Chatham Co 6/10/61 **K 7/1**
Sgt. Hiram Johnson 30 yr old enlisted Chatham Co 6/10/61 W Malvern Hill Color Guard **W 7/1** (later 1st Sgt)
Sgt. William Preston Kirkman 25 yr old teacher enlisted Chatham Co 6/10/61 ***W 7/1*** *(died 7/2)*
Corp. William Carter 22 yr old enlisted 6/10/61 W Malvern Hill **W-left shoulder 7/1** (later Sgt)
Corp. John Moran 27 yr old enlisted Chatham Co 6/10/61 **W-head 7/1 C 7/5** (died 8/22/63)
Private John Adcock 22 yr old enlisted 7/10/61 **W-arm 7/1 C 7/5**
Private Issac Allred 22 yr old enlisted Chatham Co ***W 7/1 C 7/5*** *(later hospital nurse)*
Private William Allred 37 yr old enlisted Chatham 2/1/63 ***K 7/1***
Private Rufus Barnes enlisted 9/10/62 **W 7/1** (died 8/9/63)
Private Colin Bowdoin 25 yr ld enlisted Chatham Co **K 7/1**
Private Jasper Bray 19 yr old substitute enlisted Chatham Co 3/6/62 (later Musician)
Private William Bray 22 yr old enlisted 6/10/61 **C 7/14**
Private Irvin Bridges 28 yr old enlisted 3/6/62 **W 7/1** (later W Spotsylvania)
Private Marshall Brown 26 yr old enlisted Chatham Co. 3/6/62 **K 7/1**
Private Henry Buchanan enlisted 9/10/62 **K 7/1**
Private Andrew Burke 31 yr old 3/6/62 **W 7/1 C 7/5**
Private Samuel Carter 19 yr old enlisted Chatham Co. **3/9/63 W-left leg 7/1 C 7/5**
Private John Edwards 19 yr old substitute enlisted 3/6/62 **W-trunk & left arm 7/1 C 7/5**
Private John Fogleman 23 yr old enlisted Chatham Co 3/6/62 ***W-left hand 7/1*** *(later C Bristoe Station)*
Private Young Fogelman 20 yr old Chatham Co. enlisted 6/10/61 ***W 7/1 C 7/5***
Private Thomas Gardner 31 yr old enlisted Wake Co 9/10/62 **W 7/1** (later C Burgess Mill)
Private Henry Garrett 19 yr old enlisted 12/1/62 ***K 7/1***
Private William Garrett 20 yr old enlisted Chatham Co 6/10/61 ***K 7/1***

Private John Halstead 20 yr old enlisted Chatham Co 6/10/61 **W-right leg 7/1** (died at home 7/13)

Private Quimby Hicks 20 yr old enlisted Chatham Co 6/10/61 **W 7/1 C 7/5**

Private Henry Johnson 22 yr old enlisted Chatham Co 6/10/61 **W-thigh 7/1** (later Corp)

Private Thomas Johnson 19 yr old enlisted Chatham Co 3/6/62 **WC 7/1**

Private William Johnson 22 yr old enlisted Petersburg, Va 9/10/62 **W-left arm 7/1 C 7/5**

Private Willis Johnson 19 yr old substitute enlisted Chatham Co 3/6/62 **W-finger 7/1**

Private James Jones 24 yr old enlisted Wake Co. 9/10/62 **W-head 7/1 C 7/5**

Private John Jones 24 yr old enlisted Wake Co. 9/10/62 **W 7/1** (later C Bristoe Station)

Private Isaac Jordan 37 yr old enlisted Chatham Co 2/6/63 **W 7/1 C 7/5**

Private Richard Jordan 19 yr old substitute enlisted Chatham Co 3/6/62 **W 7/1**

Private William Jordan 23 yr old enlisted Chatham Co 6/10/61 **W 7/1** (later Corp C Burgess Mill)

Private George E. Badger Kirkman 19 yr old enlisted Petersburg, Va 9/10/62 ***K 7/1***

Private Henry Clay Bascom Kirkman 20 yr old student enlisted Chatham Co 6/10/61 ***W-foot C 7/1*** *died 9/1/63*

Private William Lineberry 28 yr old enlisted Chatham Co. 3/6/62 W Malvern Hill **W 7/1** (later C Bristoe Station)

Private John R Marley 20 yr old enlisted Chatham Co 6/10/61 **K 7/1 carrying colors**

Private Larkin Moon 18 yr old enlisted 3/6/62 **W 7/1** (later W Spotsylvania)

Private George Moran 28 yr old enlisted Petersburg, Va 8/12/62 **W 7/1 C 7/5**

Private Samuel Moran 23 yr old enlisted Chatham Co 6/10/61 **W-right leg 7/1 C 7/5** (amp)

Private Duncan Murchison 23 yr old enlisted Chatham Co 6/10/61 **W-left thigh 7/1 C 7/5**

Private William Murchison 28 yr old enlisted Chatham Co 6/10/61 **W-right leg 7/1 C 7/5** (later Sgt)

Private John Nelson 24 yr old enlisted Chatham Co 6/10/61 **W 7/1 C 7/5**

Private Washington Nelson 20 yr old enlisted Chatham Co 6/10/61 C Harrison Landing **W 7/1 C 7/5**

Private George Norwood 18 yr old enlisted Wake Co 9/10/62 **W 7/1 C 7/4** (later C Burgess Mill)

Private Nathaniel Norwood 21 yr old enlisted 3/6/62 **K 7/1**

Private Gilliam Norwood transferred 8/8/62 **W 7/1 C 7/5** (later C Wilderness)

Private Elias Parish 22 yr old enlisted Chatham Co 6/10/61 **W 7/1 C 7/5**

Private Isaac Patterson 30 yr old enlisted 9/10/62 **W-abdomen & right arm 7/1 C 7/5**

Private John Pike 29 yr old enlisted Chatham Co 6/10/61 **W-leg 7/1 (amp) C 7/5 died**

Private William Rains 23 yr old enlisted Chatham Co 6/10/61 **W 7/1 C 7/5** (later joined US Service)

Private David Record 31 yr old enlisted Chatham Co 6/10/61 **W-left arm 7/1** (later killed Petersburg)

Private Thomas Record 29 yr old enlisted Chatham Co 6/10/61 **W 7/1** (later Sgt)

Private William Reeves 20 yr old enlisted Chatham Co 6/10/61 W Malvern Hill **W-head 7/1 died**

Private Samuel Rightsel 19 yr old enlisted 9/10/62 **W-left shoulder 7/1** (later C Wilderness)

Private James Rosson 18 yr old enlisted 1/1/63 **W 7/1**

Private John Siler 18 yr old enlisted 9/8/62 **W 7/1**

Private William Terry 33 yr old enlisted Petresburg, Va 8/12/62 **W-left leg 7/1 C 7/4**

Private George Vinson 24 yr old enlisted Chatham Co 6/10/61 **W-left arm 7/1** (amp)

Private John Vinson 27 yr old enlisted Chatham Co 3/6/62 W Malvern Hill deserted / pardoned **W 7/1** "carrying colors"

Private Anderson Way 23 yr old enlisted Chatham Co 3/6/62 **K 7/1**

Private Lewis Wicker 35 yr old enlisted Chatham Co 6/10/61 **K 7/1**

Company H *"Moore Independents"*

Captain James McIver 29 yr old enlisted Moore Co. 6/3/61 promoted 6/16/62 on furlough (later resigned 7/26/64)

3rd Lt. John McGilvary 22 yr old enlisted Moore Co. 6/3/61 W-leg **7/1 flesh wound fought on 7/3**

1st Sgt Alexander Dunlap 23 yr old enlisted Moore Co. 6/6/61 in command of company 7/3 ***W-leg 7/3 C 7/5***

Sgt. Lauchlin Currie 23 yr old enlisted Moore Co. 6/3/61 **W 7/3** (later K Wildernesss)

Sgt. Neil McIntosh 22 yr old enlisted Moore Co. 6/6/61 (later C Spotsylvania) . . . brother killed 7/1

Corp. Daniel McDonald 20 yr old enlisted Moore Co. 6/3/61 (later Sgt) (THREE BROTHERS)

Corp. Neil McDonald 20 yr old enlisted Moore Co. 6/6/61 (later K Bristoe Station)

Corp Charles Shaw Richmond Co. school teacher enlisted Moore Co 3/62 **W-chest 7/3** (later W Bristoe Station)

Private Neill Currie 37 yr old enlisted Moore Co. 6/3/61 ***K 7/3***

Private William Nunnery 32 yr old enlisted Moore Co. 6/3/61 **W-shell wound leg 7/3** (later C Bristoe Station)

Private Jordan Tyson enlisted Camp French 10/5/62 ***W 7/3***

Private John Warick 24 yr old enlisted Moore Co. 6/6/61 **C 7/3**

Private Andrew Williams enlisted Moore Co 3/13/62 W 2nd Manassas **W-chest 7/3**

July 1 Casualties

1st Lt. Murdoch McLeod 30 yr old enlisted Moore Co. 6/3/61 **W-shoulder & breast 7/1** (later C Wilderness)

2nd Lt. George Wilcox 27 yr old enlisted Moore Co. 6/3/61 **W-left foot & side "while carrying flag" 7/1 C 7/4 escaped**

Sgt. James Gilliam enlisted Moore Co. 6/3/61 **W 7/1 C 7/4** (later 1st Sgt)

Sgt. Auley McAuley 23 yr old enlisted Moore Co. 6/3/61 **K 7/1**
Sgt. James McLeod enlisted Moore Co. 6/3/61 **K 7/1**
Sgt. Charles Roberts 23 yr old enlisted Moore Co. 6/3/61 **W 7/1** (later K Wilderness)
Corp. Zacharias Hogan 27 yr old enlisted Moore Co. 6/25/61 **W-right thigh 7/1 C 7/4**
Corp. John McKinnon 27 yr old enlisted Moore Co. 6/6/61 **K 7/1**
Corp. William McNeill 33 yr old enlisted Moore Co. 6/6/61 (later K Bristoe Station)
Corp. Samuel Short 20 yr old enlisted Moore Co. 6/6/61 **K 7/1**
Private Daniel Bailey enlisted camp Holmes 11/2/62 **W 7/1** (later W-right arm Wilderness)
Private William Blue enlisted Moore Co. 5/15/62 **W 7/1** (later W Wilderness)
Private Bradley Brady 33 yr old enlisted Moore Co. 6/3/61 **W 7/1 C 7/4**
Private Malcolm Brewer 22 yr old enlisted Moore Co. 6/3/61 **W 7/1**
Private William Brewer enlisted Moore Co 3/13/62 **K 7/1**
Private Jesse Brown enlisted Moore Co 3/11/62 **K 7/1**
Private Page Brown enlisted camp Holmes 11/8/62 (later W Bristoe Station)
Private James Buchan enlisted Moore Co. 6/3/61 (Later Corp)
Private Artemus Caddell enlisted Moore Co. 6/3/61 (later W Bristoe Station)
Private James Caddell enlisted Moore Co. 6/6/61 (later died disease)
Private Archibald Clark enlisted Camp Holmes 1/20/63 **K 7/1**
Private Lochlin Currie 24 yr old enlisted Moore Co. 6/3/61 (later 1864 transferred to local defense forces)
Private Levi Davis enlisted Camp Holmes 10/11/62 **W-thigh 7/1**
Private Noah Deaton 24 yr old enlisted Moore Co. 6/6/61 (later C Bristoe Station)
Private William Dowd 22 yr old enlisted Moore Co. 6/6/61 **W-left leg & foot 7/1**
Private Absalom Fry 29yr old enlisted Moore Co. 6/3/61 **W 7/1 C 7/4**
Private George Fry 22 yr old enlisted Moore Co. 6/3/61 **W-breast 7/1 C 7/5** (later C Hatcher's Run)
Private Joseph Fry enlisted Moore Co 3/15/62 (later K Bristoe Station)
Private Nathan Fry 28 yr old enlisted Moore Co. 6/6/61 (later C Bristoe Station)
Private David Graham 27 yr old enlisted Moore Co. 6/3/61 **W 7/1** (later C Bristoe Station)
Private William Graham enlisted Moore Co. 6/661 **W 7/1**
Private Christopher Harrison 27 yr old enlisted Moore Co. 7/1/61 **W 7/1 C 7/5** (later C Hatcher's Run)
Private Thomas Hogan enlisted Camp French 10/5/62 **W 7/1** (later C Burgess Mill)
Private Benjamin Hollingsworth 23 yr old enlisted Moore Co. 6/8/61 (later WC Bristoe Station)
Private Nelson Hunsacker enlisted camp Holmes 10/11/62 (later W-breast Bristoe Station)
Private Samuel Johnson enlisted Moore Co. 3/15/62 **W-right arm & right side 7/1**
Private Thomas Johnson 21 yr old enlisted Moore Co. 6/6/61 **K 7/1**
Private John Jordan enlisted as substitute Moore Co. 8/10/62 (later W Wilderness)
Private John Keith enlisted Moore Co. 6/6/61 **W 7/1** (later Corp)
Private John Kerr **C 7/14**
Private Joel Lawhon 22 yr old enlisted Moore Co. 6/3/61 (later W Wilderness)

Private Archibald McCallum enlisted Camp Holmes 1/12/63 **W-left thigh 7/1**
Private Daniel McCaskill 24 yr old enlisted Moore Co. 6/3/61 **W-right hip 7/1 C 7/5** died 11/17 Baltimore buried Loudon Park Cem
Private William McDonald 22 yr old enlisted Moore Co. 6/3/61 (later W Bristoe Station)
Private Samuel McIntosh 23 yr old enlisted Moore Co. 6/6/61 **K 7/1**
Private Colin McKinnon transferred 5/12/62 **K 7/1**
Private William McKinnon 27 yr old enlisted Moore Co. 6/6/61 **W 7/1 C 7/5**
Private Duncan McLeod 20 yr old enlisted Moore Co. 6/18/61 **W 7/1** (later Corp)
Private Aaron Malone 33 yr old enlisted Moore Co. 6/3/61 W Malvern Hill **W 7/1 C 7/5** W-left hand-Petersburg C Hatcher's Run)
Private Daniel Malone enlisted Moore Co. 6/3/61 **K 7/1**
Private William Malone 28 yr old enlisted Moore Co. 6/6/61 (later W Bristoe Station)
Private Jonas Maness 20 yr old enlisted Moore Co. 6/3/61 **W 7/1 C 7/5**
Private John Martin 28 yr old enlisted Moore Co. 6/3/61 **WC 7/1**
Private John Medlin enlisted Morre Co. 6/6/61 **W-groin & right hip 7/1 C 7/4**
Private Bryant Moore 21 yr old enlisted Moore Co. 6/3/61 **C 7/14**
Private William Moore 23 yr old enlisted Moore Co. 6/3/61 (later C Bristoe Station)
Private Ashly Muse enlisted Moore Co. 3/13/63 **K 7/1**
Private John Parsons 20 yr old enlisted Moore Co. 6/3/61 **W 7/1**
Private Benjamin Perry enlisted at Camp Holmes 10/11/62 **C 7/1-7/5** (W Wildernesss)
Private William M Persons enlisted Moore Co 2/10/63 **W 7/1 C Winchester 8/2/63 died 8/3 buried Stonewall Cem, Winchester**
Private Eli Seawell enlisted Moore Co. 3/14/62 (later W Wilderness)
Private Jesse Seawall 20 yr old enlisted Moore Co. 6/3/61 **W 7/1**
Private Joseph Seawall enlisted Camp Holmes 11/8/62 **W 7/1**
Private Thomas Shaw 33 yr old enlisted Moore Co. 6/3/61 (later died disease 10/64)
Private Washington Shaw enlisted Moore Co 3/12/62 (later Corp)
Private Andrew Stutts enlisted Camp Holmes 10/11/62 **W 7/1** (later W-mouth Bristoe Station)
Private Lindsay Stutts enlisted Moore Co 5/10/62 **W-leg 7/1 C 7/5**
Private Eli Teague enlisted Moore Co. 3/10/62 (later C Bristoe Station)
Private Dawson Tyson enlisted Moore Co. 3/10/62 (hospitalized from mule kick 7/17/63)
Private Henry Tyson enlisted Moore Co. 3/1/62 W 7/1
Private James Tyson enlisted Camp French 10/5/62 (later W-thigh Bristoe Station)
Private William Vuncannon 25 yr old enlisted Moore Co. 6/6/61 **W 7/1** (later C Bristoe Station)
Private John Warner enlisted Moore Co 3/12/62 **W 7/1** (later Sgt)
Private A.S. Warren enlisted Moore Co. 3/12/62 (later K Bristoe Station)
Private Harmon Wilcox enlisted Moore Co. 2/10/63 **K 7/1**
Private Robert Wilcox 23 yr old enlisted Moore Co. 6/3/61 **W-left thigh 7/1** (later Sgt)
Private Andrew P Williams enlisted Moore Co. 3/13/62 **W-both thighs 7/1**

Private Henry Williams enlisted Camp Holmes 10/11/62 (later W left thigh Bristoe Station)
Private John Williams enlisted Camp Holmes 10/11/62 (later W-right shoulder Wilderness)
Private Alexander Williamson enlisted Moore Co 3/11/62 **W 7/1** (later W-arm C Bristoe)
Private J.Kelly Williamson 24 yr old enlisted Moore Co. 6/3/61 **W-left thigh 7/1**
Private Henry Yow enlisted Camp Holmes 10/11/62 W-**left arm 7/1 C 7/4**

Musician Joseph Hill 29 yr old enlisted Camp French 11/1/62
Musician Neill Smith enlisted Camp Burgwyn 10/12/62 (later K Bristoe Station)

Company I *"Caldwell Guards*

1st Lt. Milton B. Blair 25 yr old enlisted Caldwell Co. 7/26/61 promoted 9/27/62 (later W-left ear Wilderness)
2nd Lt. James Greer 30 yr old enlisted Caldwell Co. 7/21/61 **W C 7/3**
3rd Lt. James Sudderth 22yr old enlisted Caldwell Co. 3/15/62 (later K Bristoe Station)
1st Sgt **Jacob Bush** 21 yr old enlisted Camp Vance 11/30/61 W-1862 **W 7/3 C 7/5** (later W Ream's Station)
Sgt. John Greer 29 yr old enlisted Caldwell Co. 7/26/61 **C 7/14**
Sgt. James Oxford 30 yr old enlisted Caldwell Co. 7/26/61 **C 7/14**
Private John Angelly 36 yr old enlisted Caldwell Co. 3/15/62 (later C Burgess Mill)
Private Thomas Barlow 21 yr old enlisted Caldwell Co. 3/15/62 (later W Bristoe Station)
Private Walter Barnett 40 yr old enlisted Caldwell Co. 3/15/62 (AWOL 8/1/63—returned W Spotsylvania)
Private L.B. Barnett 33 yr old enlisted Caldwell Co. 3/15/62 **K 7/3**
Private Milton Bush 22 yr old enlisted Caldwell Co. 3/15/62 **C 7/14**
Private Albert S. Caison 21 yr old enlisted Caldwell Co. 3/15/62 **C 7/3**
Private James Daniels 19 yr old enlisted Camp Holmes 1/12/63 (later C Bristoe Station)
Private William Deal 19 yr old enlisted Caldwell 7/26/61 (later W Bristoe Station)
Private James Downs 20 yr old enlisted Camp Wilkes 10/26/61 (later Corp W-right leg Cold Harbor)
Private John Friddle 35 yr old enlisted Northhampton Co. 1/10/63 **C 7/3**
Private Peyton Gibson 23 yr old enlisted Caldwell Co. 7/26/61 (later W Wilderness)
Private Goodwin Harris 40 yr old enlisted Camp Holmes 1/20/63 (later W-left thigh Bristoe Station)
Private Harvey Lafevers 27 yr old enlisted Caldwell Co.3/15/62 (later C Bristoe Station)
Private Ivan Laney 26 yr old enlisted Caldwell Co.3/15/62 (later C Bristoe Station)
Private Peter Laney 19 yr old enlisted Caldwell Co. 3/15/61 (later C Bristoe Station)
Private Thomas Matney 32 yr old minister enlisted Chatham Co (discharged 12/63)
Private Isaac Mayberry 24 yr old enlisted Caldwell Co. 7/26/61 **C 7/14**
Private Thomas Simmons 36 yr old enlisted Caldwell Co. 3/15/62 **W-left ankle C 7/14**
Private Kelly Small 21 yr old enlisted Caldwell Co 7/26/61 **C 7/14**

Private Urias Stallings 37 yr old enlisted Caldwell Co. 3/15/62 W Malvern Hill **W-left arm & eye 7/3**

Private George Summerow 23 yr old enlisted Caldwell Co 7/26/61 ***W-right knee 7/3***

Private Peter Summerow 20 yr old enlisted Caldwell Co. 3/15/62 ***W-right leg 7/3***

Private Miles Taylor 25 yr old enlisted Caldwell Co 7/26/61 **K 7/3**

Private Thomas Wilson 27 yr old enlisted 7/26/61 (later died disease 12/64)

Private William Wilson 20 yr old enlisted Caldwell Co. 3/15/62 W Malvern Hill slight **W 7/3**

Drummer William Loudermilk 23 yr old enlisted Caldwell Co 3/15/62 **C 7/5** serving a nurse

July 1 Casualties

Captain Nero G. Bradford 37 yr old enlisted Caldwell Co promoted 9/27/62 **W-left lung 7/1 C 7/5**

Sgt Jackson Henderson 32 yr old enlisted Caldwell 7/26/61 **W 7/1 C 7/5** "acted badly during battle (later detailed nurse by federals)

Sgt. John Houck 19 yr old enlisted Camp Vance 11/30/61 **W 7/1 C 7/4**

Corp. James Barnes 22 yr old enlisted Caldwell Co. 7/26/61 **W-right thigh 7/1** (later Sgt)

Corp. Robert Blair 36 yr old enlisted Camp Wilkes **W 7/1** (later W Bristoe Station)

Corp. Seth Dula 21 yr old enlisted Caldwell Co. 7/26/61 **W 7/1** (later K Bristoe Station)

Private Alfred Bradshaw 31 yr old enlisted Caldwell Co. 3/15/62 **W 7/1**

Private James Bradshaw 23 yr old enlisted Caldwell Co. 8/31/61 **W 7/1 C 7/4**

Private Alvin Brown 40 yr old enlisted Camp Holmes 1/12/63 (later AWOL 11/63—returned 1/64)

Private Thomas Chandler 18 yr old enlisted Camp Holmes 1/10/63 **W-left hand 7/1**

Private William Collins 19 yr old enlisted Caldwell Co. 3/15/62 **C Malvern Hill K 7/1**

Private Robert Cruise 46 yr old enlisted Caldwell Co. 3/15/62 **W 7/1** (died 7/31)

Private M.B. Dickson 35 yr old enlisted Camp Holmes 9/23/62 (later W 2/64)

Private William Earp enlisted Camp Holmes 9/23/62 **W-hand 7/1** (later guard duty)

Private Aaron Felts 23 yr old enlisted Caldwell Co. 7/26/61 **W 7/1** (later Corp C Wilderness)

Private John Ferguson 35 yr old enlisted Camp Holmes 1/10/63 (later died disease)

Private John Gibson 23 yr old enlisted Caldwell Co. 7/26/61 W Malvern Hill **W-right arm 7/1**

Private Murchison Gibson 31 yr old enlisted Caldwell Co. 3/15/62 **W-right foot 7/1**

Private William Green 23 yr old enlisted Caldwell Co. 3/15/62 **W 7/1 C 7/5** (later joined US Service)

Private Andrew Hall 20 yr old enlisted Caldwell Co 7/26/61 **W-left hand 7/1**

Private Tillman Hartley 23 yr old enlisted Caldwell 7/26/61 **W 7/1** (later W-left arm Ream's Station)

Private Jackson Henderson 32 yr old enlisted Caldwell Co. 7/26/61 **C 7/1** ("acted badly during battle")

Private Ed Hendren 25 yr old enlisted Camp Holmes 9/23/62 **C 7/1** (later C Burgess Mill)

Private Abraham Holden 24 yr old enlisted Hanover Junction 5/15/63 **W 7/1**

Private Henry Holden 22 yr old enlisted Caldwell Co.3/15/62 **W 7/1`**

Private Hezekiah Holder 30 yr old enlisted Caldwell Co. 7/26/61 **W 7/1**

Private J.C. Holder 22 yr old enlisted Camp Drury 7/8/62 **W 7/1**

Private William Hornby 25 yr old enlisted Camp French 9/23/62 (later K Wilderness)

Private Simon Johnson 22 yr old enlisted Camp Holmes 9/23/62 **W 7/1** (died Williamsport 7/20)

Private Walter "Wat" Jones transferred 2/23/63 from 12th NC brother of Major **W 7/1 C 7/5 died 8/63**

Private Thomas Justice 21 yr old enlisted Camp Vance 11/30/61 (later W 1/64)

Private James Laney 24 yr old enlisted Camp Drury 7/8/62 ***W 7/1*** *(later C Bristoe Station)*

Private Levi Laney 23 yr old enlisted Caldwell Co.3/15/62 ***K 7/1***

Private Levi Laxton 36 yr old enlisted Camp Holmes 1/12/63 **W-right thigh 7/1**

Private A.J. McGarie enlisted Camp Holmes 9/23/62 **K 7/1**

Private William McPherson 26 yr old enlisted Camp Holmes (later W Bristoe Station)

Private Clinton McRary 33 yr old enlisted Chatham Co. 7/26/61 (died disease 8/64)

Private Francis McRary 28 yr old enlisted Caldwell Co. 7/26/61 (later Corp & Sgt)

Private Hiram McRary 24 yr old 7/22/61 ***C 7/5*** *"acted badly during battle"*

Private John McRary 35 yr old enlisted Camp Holmes 1/12/63 (later died disease 4/64)

Private Benjamin Marley 36 yr old enlisted camp Holmes 9/23/62 **W-arm 7/1**

Private Allison Martin 33 yr old enlisted Chatham Co 10/21/61 **W-left leg 7/1**

Private John Matney 36 yr old enlisted Chatham Co.3/15/62 **K 7/1**

Private Thomas Pennel 26 yr old enlisted Caldwell Co. 3/15/62 **W 7/1 C Williamsport, Md 7/12**

Private W.M. Piercy 26 yr old enlisted Caldwell Co.3/15/62 **W-leg 7/1** (amp)

Private Murphy Pilkinton 31 yr old enlisted Orange Co CH, Va (later C Wilderness)

Private Fabius Prestwood 32 yr old enlisted Caldwell Co. 3/15/62 ***W 7/1 C 7/5***

Private Luther Prestwood 24 yr old enlisted Camp Vance 11/30/61 ***C 7/14***

Private William Reid 22 yr old enlisted Caldwell Co. 7/26/61

Private James Robinson 25 yr old enlisted Camp Drury 7/8/62 **W 7/1 C 7/4** (later c Spotsylvania)

Private Eli Setser 35 yr old enlisted camp French 9/23/62 **C 7/14**

Private William Siler 25 yr old enlisted Camp Holmes 9/23/62 **K 7/1**

Private James Simmons 22 yr old enlisted Camp Holmes 7/26/61 W Malvern Hill **W 7/1 C 7/5**

Private James M Simmons 32 yr old enlisted Caldwell Co. 3/15/62 **W-right thigh 7/1**

Private John Stallings 24 yr old enlisted Camp Wilkes 11/7/61 W Malvern Hill (later C Bristoe Station)

Private G.H. Sudderth 24 yr old enlisted Caldwell Co. 3/15/62 **K 7/1**

Private Calvin Summerow 18 yr old enlisted Caldwell Co 7/26/61 ***W-neck 7/1***

Private John Talbert 29 yr old enlisted Caldwell Co 7/26/61 W Malvern Hill **W-left hand 7/2**

Private John Teague 34 yr old enlisted Camp Wilkes 10/23/61

Private Julius Wakefield 30 yr old enlisted Caldwell Co. 3/15/62 **W 7/1**

Private Tilghman Watson 21 yr old enlisted Caldwell Co. 7/26/61 **W 7/1** (later C Bristoe Station)

Private Manly Watts 22 yr old enlisted Caldwell Co. **C 7/14**

Private Ambrose White 35 yr old enlisted Caldwell Co. ***C 7/14***

Private John White 21 yr old enlisted Caldwell Co 7/26/61 ***C 7/14*** (later W Petersburg)

Private Joseph Wilson 32 yr old enlisted Caldwell Co. 7/26/61 **K 7/1**

Company K *"Pee Dee Wild Cats"*

2nd Lt. Jesse Henry 34 yr old enlisted Anson Co 7/1/61 in command (later K Burgess Mill, Va)

1st Sgt. John Briley 24 yr old enlisted Anson Co 7/1/61 (later 1st Sgt-Private)

Sgt. William Smith 26 yr old enlisted Anson Co 7/1/61 color sergeant **W-head C 7/3 (died)**

Corp. Charles Braswell 22 yr old enlisted Anson Co 7/1/61 (later Sgt)

Private John Atkinson 23 yr old enlisted Anson Co 7/1/61 W Malvern Hill (later K Wilderness)

Private Riley Baker 16 yr old enlisted Anson Co 8/21/62 K Spotsylvania

Private Seaborn Benton 19 yr old enlisted Anson Co 7/17/62 **W-left leg C 7/3**

Private Thomas Bowman 18 yr old enlisted Anson Co 7/1/61 **C 7/14**

Private Tilman Briley 19 yr old enlisted Anson Co 9/19/62 **W-right thigh C 7/3** (died 9/4 buried Oakwod Cem Raleigh)

Private Jacob Burr 46 yr old enlisted Anson Co 10/17/62 **C 7/14**

Private Calvin Carpenter 24 yr old enlisted Anson Co 5/10/62 ***C 7/3***

Private Edmund Carpenter 32 yr old enlisted Anson Co 5/10/62 ***C 7/14***

Private Issac Carpenter 25 yr old enlisted Anson Co 7/1/61 ***WC 7/3*** *(died smallpox)*

Private William Dorsey 24 yr old enlisted Anson Co 7/1/61 (later Sgt)

Private John Eddings 23 yr old enlisted Anson Co 12/2/61 W Malvern Hill **W-left thigh 7/3**

Private A.B. Edwards 25 yr old enlisted Anson Co 5/10/62 ***WC 7/3*** *(died 8/1)*

Private John Edwards 20 yr old enlisted Anson Co 5/10/62 ***K 7/3***

Private Phillip Flake 19 yr old enlisted Anson Co 5/10/61 **K 7/3**

Private Elisha Gaddy 24 yr old enlisted Anson Co 12/2/61 **W-knee C 7/3**

Private Sherwood Gathings 20 yr old enlisted Anson Co 7/1/61 W-6/62 **C 7/3**

Private Thomas Green 23 yr old enlisted Anson Co 7/1/61 **K 7/3**

Private John Hyatt 18 yr old enlisted 5/1/63 **K 7/3**

Private Charles Jarman 23 yr old enlisted Anson Co 7/1/61 **W 7/3** (later W-Petersburg)

*Private **John Robert Jarman** 22 yr old enlisted Anson Co 7/1/61 (later W Bristoe Station—Corp)*
*Private Willis Jarman 36 yr old enlisted Anson Co 9/14/61 **W 7/3** (later W Wilderness)*
Private Moreland Johnson 24 yr old enlisted Anson Co 7/1/61 **W 7/3**
Private Stanmore Johnson 27 yr old enlisted Anson Co 5/10/61 **W 7/3**
Private Oliver Lahaise enlisted 9/17/61 W Barrington Ferry **C 7/14**
*Private Joseph Liles 19 yr old enlisted Anson Co 5/10/62 **K 7/3***
Private Jeremiah Mitchum 19 yr old enlisted Anson Co 5/10/62 **K 7/3**
Private Wilson Moore 28 yr old enlisted Anson Co 5/10/62 (died disease 8/2/63)
Private William Myers 20 yr old enlisted Anson Co 5/10/62 **W-leg 7/3**
Private William Sanders 19 yr old enlisted Anson Co 2/20/63 (later C Bristoe Station)
Private James Scarborough 28 yr old enlisted Anson Co 5/10/62 **K 7/3**
Private James Thomas 20 yr old enlisted Anson Co 5/10/62 **W 7/3 C 7/14**
Private Miles Teal 31 yr old enlisted Anson Co 5/10/62 **W-left elbow 7/3 C 7/5**
Private Calvin Thomas 28 yr old enlisted Anson Co 5/10/62 **C 7/3**
Private James Thomas 20 yr old enlisted Anson Co 5/10/62 **W 7/3 C 7/14**

July 1 Casualties

Captain J.C. McLaughlin 28 yr old enlisted Anson Co 7/1/61 **W-left hand (thumb amp.) 7/1**
1st Lt. Thomas Lilly 27 yr old enlisted Anson Co 7/1/61 **W-hip 7/1** (later W Five Forks)
3rd Lt. John Polk 23 yr old enlisted Anson Co 7/1/61 **W 7/1** (later Adjt. W Wilderness)
Sgt. William Broadway 23 yr old enlisted Anson Co 7/1/61 **W 7/1**
Sgt. David Dabbs 25 yr old enlisted Anson Co 7/1/61 **K 7/1**
Corp. Henry Crowson 19 yr old enlisted Anson Co 7/1/61 **WC 7/1**
Corp. William Dabbs 21 yr old enlisted Anson Co 9/17/61 W Malvern Hill
Corp. Joel Gaddy 23 yr old enlisted Anson Co 7/1/61 **W-right hand left shoulder 7/1** (later Sgt)
Private George Allen 25 yr old enlisted Anson Co 5/10/62 **W 7/1** (later Corp)
Private Robert Allen 28 yr old enlisted Anson Co 7/1/61 **W 7/1 C 7/5**
Private William Allen enlisted Anson Co 5/10/62 **W 7/1**
Private William Bowman 29 yr old enlisted Anson Co 5/10/62 **K 7/1**
Private William Boylin 18 yr old enlisted Anson Co 7/1/61 **K 7/1**
Private Daniel Braswell 23 yr old enlisted Anson Co 7/1/61 **W-left hand 7/1**
Private Thomas Brewer 26 yr old enlisted Anson Co 5/10/62 **W 7/1** (later C Wilderness)
Private John Broadway 24 yr old enlisted Anson Co 7/1/61 (later W Bristoe Station—died)
*Private James Carpenter 27 yr old enlisted Anson Co 5/10/62 **W 7/1***
Private Henry Clay Dumas 19 yr old enlisted Anson Co 12/2/61 **W 7/1** (later Corp / Sgt)
*Private Allen Edwards 24 yr old enlisted Anson Co 7/1/61 **W-left leg 7/1** (died 8/63)*
Private Francis Edwards 33 yr old enlisted Anson Co 5/10/62

Private John Edwards 34 yr old enlisted Anson Co 5/10/62 ***W-shoulder, back & side 7/1 C 7/5***

Private Elijah Flake enlisted in Anson Co. 2/1/63 after service with CS Navy (CSS Virginia) **W 7/3**

Private John Flake 19 yr old enlisted Anson Co 7/1/61 **K 7/1**

Private James Gadd 24 yr old enlisted Anson Co 7/1/61 **W-right arm 7/1**

Private Thomas C. Gathings 31 yr old enlisted Anson Co 5/10/62 **K 7/1**

Private William Gathings 35 yr old enlisted Anson Co 5/10/62

Private Sidney Griffin 23 yr old enlisted Anson Co 7/1/61 **K 7/1**

Private Thomas Gulledge 20 yr old enlisted Anson Co 5/10/62 W Barrington Ferry **W 7/1**

Private William Gulledge 21 yr old enlisted Anson Co 7/1/61 **W 7/1 C 7/5**

Private William Hall enlisted Craven Co 3/9/62 **W 7/1 C 7/5**

Private Robert Hanna 28 yr old enlisted Anson Co 7/1/61 **W-left leg 7/1**

Private Washington Harrington 23 yr old enlisted Anson Co 5/10/62 W Rawl's Mill, Va

Private James Henley 20 yr old enlisted Anson Co 12/2/61 W Malvern Hill **C 7/14**

Private Elijah Hildreth 27 yr old enlisted Anson Co 9/17/61 W Malvern Hill **W 7/1**

Private Robert Hildreth 17 yr old enlisted Anson Co 5/10/62

Private Louis Horn 30 yr old enlisted Anson Co 5/10/62 **W-hip 7/1** W-hand Petersburg

Private William Horn 29 yr old enlisted Anson Co 5/10/62 W Kings School House

Private James Howard 26 yr old enlisted Anson Co 7/1/61 **W-hip 7/1** (later W Petersburg)

Private Joseph Ingram enlisted Anson Co 5/1/61

Private William Ingram 29 yr old enlisted Anson Co 7/1/61 **W-leg 7/1 C 7/5** (later Corp)

Private ***Elijah Jarman*** *19 yr old enlisted Anson Co 7/1/61* ***W 7/1 C 7/14*** *(died 8/1)*

Private Thomas Jarman 27 yr old enlisted Anson Co 7/1/61 ***W 7/1***

Private Samuel Kendall 30 yr old enlisted Anson Co 7/1/61 **W 7/1 C 7/5**

Private William Laird 35 yr old enlisted Anson Co 5/10/62 **W-right leg 7/1 C 7/5**

Private Franklin Lee 25 yr old enlisted Anson Co 5/10/61

Private Henry Lee transferred 3/1/63 (later C Bristoe Station C Burgess Mill)

Private Joseph Lee 24 yr old enlisted Anson Co 7/1/61 **K 7/1**

Private Daniel Liles 24 yr old enlisted Anson Co 7/1/61 ***W 7/1***

Private Daniel McDiarmid enlisted 2/1/63 (died disease 4/18/64)

Private Martin McDiarmid 28 yr old enlisted 7/1/61 **W 7/1** (later W-leg Bristoe Station—died)

Private Terrell Phillips 29 yr old enlisted Anson Co 5/10/62 **C 7/14**

Private Washington Phillips 26 yr old enlisted Anson Co 5/10/62 **W 7/1**

Private John Pope 22 yr old enlisted Anson Co 7/1/61 **W-left thigh C 7/1**

Private John Poplin 32 yr old enlisted Anson Co 5/10/62 **W-left leg 7/1**

Private John Short 27 yr old enlisted Anson Co 7/1/61 W Malvern Hill W Rawls Mill ***W 7/1***

Private Samuel Short 22 yr old enlisted Anson Co 7/1/61 W Rawls Mill ***W 7/1***

Private William Short 19 yr old enlisted Anson Co 5/10/62 ***W 7/1***

Private William Smart 21 yr old enlisted Anson Co 7/1/61 (later C Bristoe Station)

Private Jesse Sullivan 25 yr old enlisted Anson Co 7/1/61 **W 7/1 C 7/5**

Private Albert Tyson 19 yr old enlisted Anson Co 5/10/62 **C 7/1**
Private John Tyson 20 yr old enlisted Anson Co 5/10/62 **W-leg 7/1**
Private James Wadsworth 21 yr old enlisted Anson Co 7/1/61 **W-back 7/1**
Private John Wiggins 20 yr old enlisted Anson Co 7/1/61 **K 7/1**
Private Rayford Willoughby 26 yr old enlisted Anson Co 7/1/61 W Malvern Hill (later C Bristoe Station)
Private John Woodburn 25 yr old enlisted Anson Co 7/1/62 **WC 7/1 7/5**

Captain James Adams Co D

1st Sgt Jacob Bush Co I

The 26th North Carolina Band

ELEVENTH NORTH CAROLINIA REGIMENT

Colonel Collett Leventhorpe

Major Egbert Ross

Field & Staff

Colonel Collett Leventhorpe took command 3/31/62 **W-left arm, hip 7/1 C 7/5 Greencastle, Pa**

Lieutenant Colonel William Martin 33 yr old Professor promoted 5/6/62 not at Gettysburg (sick—Fredericksburg) (later W, Jones Farm)

Major Egbert Ross 21 yr old enlisted Mecklenburg City appointed 5/6/62 **K 7/1**

Brevet Lt. Col 7/3 Captain William Grier appointed 3/10/62 (in command of regiment July 3)

Brevet Major 7/3 Captain Francis Bird (Co C) 33 yr old Bertie Co. Brown Univ & Wake Forest

Adjutant Henderson Lucas 22 yr old enlisted 9/30/61 appointed Adjt 7/11/62 **W 7/1 while carrying colors (three wounds) (died 7/25)**

Sergeant Major James McCorkle 22 yr old appointed 4/62 **C 7/3** (later 2nd Lt Co D)

Quarter Master John Tate appointed 4/22/62

Surgeon John Wilson 35 yr old enlisted Caswell Co. 3/25/62

Assistant. Surgeon James McCombs 25 yr old enlisted Mecklenburg Co 9/26/62 **C 7/5**

Assistant Surgeon Francis Gillam 23 yr old enlisted Bertie Co 1/23/62

Chaplin Aristides Smith appointed 11/17/62

Quarter Master Srgt James Sims **C 7/3**

Assistant Commissary Patrick Lowrie appointed 7/11/62

Commissary Sergeant. William Dickerson enlisted 4/29/62 appointed 8/9/62

Ordinance George Motz enlisted 11/3/62 appointed 11/3/62 (transferred to Co I 9/63)

Ord Sgt. George McDowell 33 yr old enlisted Chowan Co 2/15/62 **W-hip & foot 7/3** (later 1st Sgt)

Regimental Band

Senior Musician William Cline (Co I) 31 yr old enlisted Lincoln Co. 9/8/62 **C 7/5**
Musician Adlophus Coon (Co I) 20 yr old enlisted Lincoln Co. 3/14/62 promoed 9/62
Musician William Martin (Co I) enlisted 4/25/62 promoted to musician 9/62
Musician Charles Motz (Co I) 19 yr old enlisted Camp Mangum 5/3/62 promoted 9/62
Musician Monroe Seagle (Co I) 28 yr old enlisted Lincoln Co. 5/8/62 promoted 9/62

Company A *"The Charlotte Grays"*

Capt. William Hand 20 yr old Mecklenburg Co. enlisted 1/14/62 **C 7/3**
1st Lt. Charles Alexander appointed 2/1/62 absent from campiagn
2nd Lt. Robert Hand appointed 3/31/62 **W-back 7/3 C 7/5 (Greencastle, PA)**
3rd Lt. William Taylor 22 yr old enlisted 2/1/62 (later W Wilderness & Petersburg)
1st Sgt. Richard Alexander 22 yr old enlisted Mechlenburg Co. 2/1/62 **W-left shoulder 7/3**
Sgt. J. N. Ernheardt enlisted 2/1/62 **W-right side 7/3**
Sgt. John Elms enlisted 5/15/62 (later Lt.)
Cpl. J. Alexander 29 yr old enlisted Mechlenburg Co. 2/1/62
Corp. Emanuel Lewis 20 yr. old enlisted Mechlenburg Co. 2/1/62 (later W Wilderness/Sgt.)
Corp. Robert Gribble 23 yr. old enlisted Mechlenburg Co. 2/1/62 (later W-Petersburg/Sgt.)
Corp. Theo Rudock enlisted Mechlenburg Co. 2/1/62 **C 7/14** (later Sgt C Hatchers Run)
Pvt. M. Alexander 24 yr old enlisted Mechlenburg Co. 2/1/62 **W C 7/3**
Pvt. Milton Alexander 28 yr old enlisted Mechlenburg Co. 2/1/62 **C 7/3**
Pvt. Robert Alexander 19 yr old enlisted Mechlenburg Co. 2/1/62 **C 7/3**
Pvt. Cyrus Allen 20 yr old enlisted Mechlenburg Co. **C 7/3**
Pvt P. S. Auten 27 yr old enlisted Mechlenburg Co. 7/7/62 **W C 7/3 (died 8/1 Phila hospital buried PNC)**
Pvt. James Barnett 19 yr old enlisted Mechlenburg Co. 2/1/62
Pvt. J. H. Bigham 19 yr old enlisted Mechlenburg Co. 12/27/62
Pvt. John Bigham 20 yr old enlisted Mechlenburg Co. 2/1/62 **W-thigh & Right Buttock C 7/3**
Pvt. J.J. Blakely 19 yr old enlisted Mechlenburg Co. 3/1/63 **C 7/14**
Pvt. William Ernheardt 36 yr old enlisted Mechlenburg Co. 4/1/63 **C 7/3**
Pvt. J. W. Fisher 23 yr old enlisted 2/1/62 Mechlenburg Co.
Pvt. J. S. Garrison 18 yr old enlisted Mechlenburg Co. 12/29/62 **K 7/3**
Pvt. Frank Glenn 28 yr old enlisted Mechlenburg Co. 5/3/62
Pvt. William Goodrum 18 yr old enlisted Mechlenburg Co. 3/1/63 **W-7/3 C (died 7/18)**
Pvt. Walter Gray 21 yr. old enlisted Mechlenburg Co. 2/1/62
Pvt. N. O. Harris 24 yr. old Mechlenburg 5/3/62 **W-right shoulder (shell wound) 7/3**
Pvt. Milton Hill 32 yr. old enlisted Mechlenburg 7/7/62 **C 7/3**
Pvt. Monroe Hovis 24 yr. old enlisted Mechlenburg Co. 2/1/62 (later W Spotsylvania)

Pvt. Campbell King 26 yr. old Mechlenburg Co. 5/3/62 (later captured Bristoe Station)
Pvt. Thomas McConnel 19 yr. old enlisted Mechlenburg Co. 2/1/62
Pvt. Sidney McGinnis 27 yr. old enlisted Mechlenburg Co. 3/1/63 **WC 7/3**
Pvt. John McWhirter 21 yr. old enlisted Mechlenburg Co. 2/1/62 **K 7/3**
Pvt. H. Monteith 21 yr. old enlisted Mechlenburg Co. 2/1/62
Pvt. James Montgomery 27 yr old enlisted Mechlenburg Co. 2/1//62 **W C 7/3 (later Lt W-leg Reams Station—died)**
Pvt. A. Newell 20 yr. old enlisted Mechlenburg Co. 2/1/62 **W-left shoulder 7/3**
Pvt. J. Orman 18 yr old enlisted Mechlenburg Co. 2/1/62
Private R. L. Query 22 yr old enlisted Mechlenburg Co. 2/1/62
Private S.F. Query 22 yr old enlisted Mechlenburg Co. 2/1/62
Private Robert Simpson enlisted Mechlenburg Co. 2/1/62 **W 7/3 C 7/5**
Private John Smith 36 yr old enlisted Mechlenburg Co. 3/1/63 **W-head 7/3 died 7/15**
Private R.C. Taylor 20 yr old enlisted Mechlenburg Co. 2/1/62
Private Angus Wingate enlisted Mechlenburg Co. 2/1/62 **K 7/3**
Private Taylor Wright 18 yr old enlisted Mechlenburg Co. 3/1/63 **W-back 7/3 C 7/5**

July 1 Casualties

Sgt. William Brown enlisted 2/1/62 **W 7/1 C 7/5**
Sgt. Samuel McElroy enlisted 2/1/62 **W 7/1 C 7/5**
Sgt. Thomas Neily enlisted 2/1/62 **W 7/1** (later W Petersburg)
Corp. James Bigham 28 yr old enlisted Mechlenburg Co. 7/7/62 **W-arm 7/1**
Corp. William Icehower enlisted 2/1/62 **W 7/1 C 7/5**
Pvt. M.R. Alexander enlisted 2/1/62 **W-right shoulder 7/1**
Pvt. H. W. Allen 25 yr old enlisted Mechlenburg Co.7/3/62 **W-right arm 7/1 C 7/5**
Pvt. John Barnett 20 yr old enlisted Mechlenburg Co. 2/1/62 **W 7/1 (died 7/5)**
Pvt. John Cochrane 27 yr old enlisted Mechlenburg Co. 2/1/62 (later C Bristoe Station) (later Corp.) **W 7/1**
Pvt. J.J. Darnell 29 yr old enlisted Mechlenburg Co. 3/1/63 **W 7/1 C 7/5**
Pvt. Henry Duckworth 19 yr old enlisted Mechlenburg Co. 2/1/62 **W 7/1** (later Corp.)
Pvt. Daniel Dulin 22 yr old enlisted Mechlenburg Co. 4/20/62 **W-left hip 7/1 C 7/4**
Pvt. William Elliott 22 yr old enlisted Mechlenburg Co. 7/7/62 **K 7/1**
Pvt. J. H. Ernheardt 23 yr old enlisted Mechlenburg Co. 2/1/62 **K 7/1**
Pvt. Robert Ewing 21 yr old enlisted Mechlenburg Co. 2/1/62 **W 7/1 C 7/5**
Pvt. William Ewing 26 yr old enlisted Mechlenburg Co. 7/7/62 **W 7/1 C 7/5**
Pvt. James Galloway enlisted Mechlenburg Co. 2/1/62 **W-Breast 7/1/63 (died 7/21)**
Pvt. James Gibson enlisted Mechlenburg Co. 2/1/62 (later musician)
Pvt. David Glenn enlisted Mechlenburg Co. 2/1/62 **W-right arm 7/1**
Pvt. Joshua Glover 37 yr old enlisted Mechlenburg Co. 3/1/63 **W-left thigh 7/1 C 7/5**
Pvt. Robert Groves 23 yr. old enlisted Mechlenburg Co. 2/1/62 **W 7/1 C 7/14**
Pvt. Andrew Hand enlisted 2/1/62 **W 7/1 C 7/5**

Pvt. Isaac Henderson 21 yr. old enlisted Mechlenburg Co. 2/1/62
Pvt. Thomas Henderson 23 yr. old enlisted Mechlenburg Co. 2/1/62 **C 7/14**
Pvt. G. T. Herring enlisted 2/1/62 **W 7/1**
Pvt. F. Hobbs 18 yr. old enlisted Mechlenburg Co. 5/15/62 **W 7/1**
Pvt. David Hunter 21 yr old enlisted Mechlenburg Co. 2/1/62 **W 7/1 C 7/5**
Pvt. James Hutchison 25 yr. old enlisted Mechlenburg Co. 2/1/62 **W 7/1 (died 7/5)**
Pvt. David Jenkins 21 yr. old enlisted Mechlenburg Co. 2/1/62 **W-right thigh 7/1 C 7/5**
Pvt. Jacob Jenkins 23 yr. old enlisted Mechlenburg Co. 7/7/62 **W 7/1 C 7/14**
Pvt. Thomas Johnson enlisted 4/1/62 **W 7/1 C 7/5**
Pvt. John McConnel enlisted Mechlenburg Co. 2/1/62 **W 7/1 C 7/5 (died of wounds)**
Pvt. John H. McConnel 20 yr. old enlisted Mechlenburg Co. 2/1/62 **W 7/1**
Pvt. G. Neal 19 yr. old enlisted Mechlenburg Co. 2/1/62 **W-left shoulder 7/1 C 7/5**
Pvt. Robert McGinn 30 yr. old enlisted Mechlenburg Co. 5/1/6/62 **W 7/1 C 7/14**
Pvt. Isaac Norment enlisted 5/15/62 **W 7/1**
Private C. Paysour 33 yr old enlisted Mechlenburg Co. 3/1/63 **W 7/1 C 7/5**
Private Daniel Powell 28 yr old enlisted Mechlenburg Co. 4/20/62 **K 7/1**
Private Thomas Prim 18 yr old enlisted Mechlenburg Co. 3/1/63 **W 7/1 died**
Private Peyton Roberts 21 yr old enlisted Mechlenburg Co. 2/1/62 **W-right foot 7/1 C 7/5**
Private James Sims enlisted Mechlenburg Co. 2/1/62 **W 7/1 C 7/14** (later QM Sgt)
Private J.M. Stowe enlisted Mechlenburg Co. 2/1/62 **W-left thigh 7/1 C 7/5**
Private W. Wallace 20 yr old enlisted Mechlenburg Co. 2/1/62 **W 7/1 C 7/14**
Private William Wilson 20 yr old enlisted Mechlenburg Co. 4/1/63 **W 7/1 C 7/5** (later Hospital Steward)

Company B *"Burke County"*

Captain Mark Armfield appointed 12/3/61 **C 7/3**
1st Lt Thomas Parks appointed 2/15/62 **C 7/14** (later Capt)
2nd Lt Portland Warlick appointed 2/15/62 **W-left arm 7/3 (died 12/28/63)**
1st Sgt John Miller transferred from 1st NC—6 month)
Sgt John Michaux enlisted 12/20/61 **C 7/14** (later 1st Sgt)
Corp.H.H. Galloway enlisted 12/20/61 **C 7/14** (later Sgt)
Corp. R.J. Hennessa 21 yr old enlisted 12/20/61 **C 7/3** (later Sgt)
Corp. H.H. Parks enlisted Burke Co 4/29/62 **K 7/3**
Private James Andrews 18 yr old enlisted Wilkes Co 2/11/63 **W-left leg 7/3 C 7/14**
Private William Andrews 28 yr old enlisted Wilkes Co 2/1/62
Private Jacob Bowman 31 yr old enlisted Caldwell Co 2/1/62 **C 7/14**
Private A.C. Branch 21 yr old enlisted Burke Co 1/15/62 WC 7/3
Private Reuben Branch enlisted Burke Co 1/15/62
Private William Brewer 20 yr old enlisted McDowell Co. 2/9/63 **C 7/14**
Private Lambert Bristol 17 yr old enlisted Burke Co. (later discharged 4/1/64)

Private James Cannon 23 yr old enlisted Caldwell Co (later W Petersburg)

Private Nathan Carswell 28 yr old enlisted Burke Co 2/11/63 (deserted 8/5/63)

Private D.A. Causby 39 yr old enlisted Burke Co **C 7/14**

Private John Cook 21 yr old enlisted Burke Co. 2/1/62W 7/1 **C 7/3**

Private James Courtney 36 yr old enlisted Caldwell Co 2/1/62 **C 7/14**

Private J.W. Crawley 22 yr old enlisted Burke Co 1/15/62 **C 7/14** (later W Spotsylvania / Corp)

Private Eliphus Crouch 23 yr old enlisted Burke Co 1/15/62

Private B.L. Davis 18 yr old enlisted McDowell C 2/1/62 **C 7/14**

Private J.N. Duckworth enlisted 2/1/62 **WC 7/3**

Private William Duckworth 35 yr old enlisted Burke Co 12/15/62 **K 7/3**

Private Thomas Ferree 25 yr old enlisted Burke Co 2/1/62 (later Sgt / died illness 10/64)

Private William Fox 29 yr old enlisted Burke Co 2/1/62

Private Davis Griffin 31 yr old enlisted Burke Co 2/1/62 ***C 7/14***

Private James Griffin 29 yr old enlisted Burke Co 2/1/62 ***C 7/14*** *(joined US service)*

Private William Griffin 27 yr old enlisted Burke Co 2/1/62 (later C Hatcher's Run)

Private W.T. Harbinson 18 yr old enlisted Burke Co 2/1/62 (later W-right leg Cold Harbor)

Private L.B. Harris 18 yr old enlisted Burke Co 2/1/62 **C 7/14** (later W Burgess Mill, Va)

Private John Keller 18 yr old enlisted Caldwell Co 2/11/63 **WC 7/3**

Private J.N. Landis 35 yr old enlisted McDowell Co 2/1/62 (later W-both eyes Farmville, Va

Private Larkin Livingston 19 yr old enlisted Wilkes Co 2/1/62 (later C Bristoe Station / W—Jerusalem Plank)

Private James London enlisted 2/1/62 (later Sgt / W Burgess Mill, Va)

Private Joseph Moore 22 yr old enlisted Burke Co 2/1/62 (later transferred 41st NC)

Private P.W. Morgan 29 yr old enlisted Burke Co 2/1/62 ***C 7/14*** *(Took oath 8/63)*

Private J.P. Parks 19 yr old enlisted Burke Co 11/10/62 **C 7/14**

Private W.S. Patton 19 yr old enlisted Burke Co 2/1/62 (later C Bristoe Station)

Private Thomas Pearson 29 yr old enlisted Burke Co 2/1/62 (later W Petersburg)

Private C.S. Phillips 17 yr old enlisted Burke Co 2/1/62

Private E.W. Pucket 19 yr old enlisted Burke Co 2/1/62 **WC 7/3**

Private Harvey Shuffler 31 yr old enlisted Burke Co 2/1/62 (later W-foot & right leg Bristoe Station)

Private Sidney Shuffler 19 yr old enlisted Burke Co 2/1/62 **C 7/14**

Private William Shutter 28 yr old enlisted Burke Co 2/1/62 W White hall, Va **C 7/14**

Private J.V. Singleton 28 yr old enlisted Burke Co 2/1/62

Private M.D. Singleton 22 yr old enlisted Burke Co 2/1/62 (died 3/1/64)

Private S.S. Singleton 23 yr old enlisted Burke Co 2/1/62 **C 7/14**

Private Alva Smith 22 yr old enlisted Burke Co 2/1/62 **C 7/14**

Private George Stacey enlisted 2/1/62 **C 7/3**

Private Archibald Swink 27 yr old enlisted Burke Co 2/13/62

Private J.P. Teem 19 yr old enlisted Burke Co 4/1/62 **C 7/3**

Private S.D. Wakefield enlisted 2/1/62 **WC 7/3**

Private A.P. Warlick 20 yr old enlisted Burke Co 4/29/62 **W 7/3** (later Corp. W Petersburg)
Private R.G. Williams 23 yr old enlisted Burke Co 2/1/62 (later W Wilderness)
Musician George Keller enlisted Burke Co. 2/1/62 (later W Burgess Mill—died)

July 1 Casualties

3rd Lt Elisha Dorsey 27 yr old enlisted Burke Co. 2/15/62 **W-right leg 7/1 C 7/5** (later 1st Lt)
Sgt. John Duval enlisted 12/20/61 **W 7/1** C Hagerstown, Md. (died 8/63)
Sgt John Warlick enlisted Burke Co 5/15/62 **W 7/1 C 7/5** (later 2nd Lt))
Sgt. W.W. McGimsey 28 yr old enlisted Burke Co 12/20/61 **W 7/1**
Corp.R.W. Carlton enlisted 12/20/61 **W 7/1 C 7/5**
Private George Andrews 29 yr old enlisted Wilkes Co 2/1/62 **W-left leg 7/1 C 7/5**
Private P.B. Anthony 29 yr old enlisted Burke Co 2/1/62 **W 7/1 (died 7/18/63)**
Private M Branch 26 yr old enlisted Burke Co 2/1/62 ***W-left knee 7/1 C 7/5***
Private R.R.Carswell 30 yr old enlisted Burke Co. 2/11/63 ***W 7/1 C 7/5*** *(deserted 11/63)*
Private John Clarke 26 yr old enlisted Burke Co 1/15/62 **C 7/14**
Private B.B. Clarke 21 yr old enlisted Burke Co. 1/15/62 AWOL 8/63 to 10/63 returned AWOL 11/64
Private Samuel Day 39 yr old enlisted Caldwell Co 2/1/62 **W 7/1 C 7/5**
Private Thomas Dorsey enlisted Burke Co 1/15/62 **W 7/1 C 7/5** (later Corp)
Private John Fincannon 31 yr old enlisted Burke Co 2/1/62 **W 7/1**
Private W.T.Landis 25 yr old enlisted Burke Co 2/1/62 **W-left leg 7/1**
Private Jordan Livingston 22 yr old enlisted Wilkes Co 2/1/62 **W 7/1**
Private George Loudermilk 35 yr old enlisted Burke Co 2/1/62 (later W Spotsylvania)
Private Kinchen Mincey 30 yr old enlisted Burke Co 2/11/63 (deserted 9/63—returned)
Private Thomas Moore 22 yr old enlisted Burke Co 2/1/62 ***W 7/1 C 7/5*** *(later K New Market, Va)*
Private A.A. Morgan 26 yr old enlisted Burke Co 2/1/62 ***W-arm 7/1 (amputated) C 7/5***
Private A.H. Morrison 19 yr old enlisted Burke Co 2/1/62 W White Hall, Va **K 7/1**
Private Michael Pearson 46 yr old enlisted Burke Co 2/1/62 **W 7/1**
Private Alfred Perry 36 yr old enlisted Burke Co 2/1/62 **C 7/14**
Private Lucius Singleton 18 yr old enlisted Burke Co 2/1/62 **W-left arm 7/1** (later Corp)
Private Anderson Smith 26 yr old enlisted Burke Co 2/1/62 (AWOL 5/64) returned
Private Henry Smith 19 yr old enlisted Burke Co 2/1/62 **C 7/14** (later W-left eye Petersburg)
Private J.C. Smith 26 yr old enlisted Burke Co 2/1/62 **C 7/14**
Private William Smith 29 yr old enlisted Burke Co 2/1/62 **WC 7/1**
Private Elisha Walker 29 yr old enlisted Burke Co. 2/15/62 **W-shoulder & side 7/1** (later 3rd Lt)
Private J.B. Williams 21 yr old enlisted Burke Co 2/1/62 **W-left foot 7/1** (later C Hatchers Run)

Company C *"Bertie County"*

Captain Francis Bird 33 yr old Bertie Co. Brown Univ & Wake Forest appointed 1/22/62 (Promoted Major & Lt. Col. K Ream's Station)
2nd Lt Edward Outlaw appointed 1/22/62 (later Captain)
Sgt William Todd enlisted 1/23/62 **W 7/3** (later 1st Lt / W-right buttock Ream's Station)
Sgt Daniel Britton 19 yr old enlisted Bertie Co 1/23/62 (later Sgt)
Corp. Joseph Carter enlisted 1/23/62 (later Sgt / 1st Sgt K Reams's Station) **W 7/3**
Corp John Floyd 21 yr old enlisted Bertie Co 1/23/62 (later Sgt C Burges Mill, Va)
Private Armstead Bazemore 21 yr old enlisted Bertie Co 1/23/62 (later Sgt)
Private William Bazemore 26 yr old enlisted Bertie Co 1/23/62 W-left hand White Hall, Va
Private William Brogden 18 yr old enlisted Bertie Co 5/7/62 (later W Spotsylvania)
Private James Burden enlisted 22/15/62 (later Corp. W Cold Harbor)
Private Levin Butler enlisted 1/23/62 (later C Bristoe Station)
Private Thaddeus Butler transferred 1/62 (deserted 8/26/63)
Private Thomas Cale 19 yr old enlisted Bertie Co 1/23/62 (deserted 10/20/64)
Private George Casper 37 yr old enlisted Bertie Co 5/15/62 (deserted 10/24/64)
Private James Casper 22 yr old enlisted Bertie Co 1/23/62 ***C 7/14*** *(joined US Service)*
Private William Casper 27 yr old enlisted Bertie Co 1/23/62 (deserted 10/24/64)
Private Jonathan Corprew 21 yr old enlisted Bertie Co 1/23/62 W White Hall, Va **W 7/3**
Private Allen Davis 25 yr old enlisted Bertie Co 1/23/62 (later W-arm Spotsylvania)
Private Augustus Davis 23 yr old enlisted Bertie Co 1/23/62 **W 7/3**
Private Aaron Evans 20 yr old enlisted Bertie Co 1/23/62 (later C Bristoe Station)
Private James Floyd 19 yr old enlisted Bertie Co 1/23/62 **WC 7/3** (later Corp / Sgt)
Private John Gilliam enlisted 1/23/62 as 57 yr old substitute (discharged 4/9/64)
Private John Gregory 21 yr old enlisted Bertie Co 1/23/62 **C 7/3**
Private William Gregory 26 yr old enlisted Bertie Co 1/23/62 **W-foot shot off 7/3 C Williamsport (died)**
Private George Harrell enlisted 1/23/62 (later Corp.)
Private Thomas Holder 19 yr old enlisted Bertie Co 1/23/62 **WC 7/3 (died)**
Private Joseph Jackson 30 yr old enlisted Bertie Co 1/23/62 **C 7/14**
Private Joseph King 20 yr old enlisted New Hanover Co **C 7/3**
Private William Leggett 20 yr old enlisted Bertie Co 1/23/62
Private James Mitchell 18 yr old enlisted 4/22/62 (later C Bristoe Station /South Side RR)
Private Nathan Myers enlisted 4/22 /62 (later W-hand Spptsylvania)
Private Richard Owens enlisted Bertie Co 1/23/62 (later Corp / deserted 2/17/64)
Private James Rawls enlisted Bertie Co 1/23/62 (later C Bristoe Station / Corp.)
Private John Stone 17 yr old enlisted as substitute 5/17/62 (later C Bristoe Station—joined US service)
Private Elisha Todd 21 yr old enlisted Bertie Co 1/23/62 (later Chief Musician)
Private Lewis Todd 33 yr old enlisted Bertie Co 5/3/62 (later Corp / Sgt)
Private William Ward 22 yr old enlisted Bertie Co 1/23/62 (later Sgt)

Private James Williams 19 yr old enlisted Bertie Co 1/23/62 **WC 7/3 (died)**

Musician William Butler enlisted 1/23/62 (later Corp W Hatchers Run)

July 1 Casualties

1st Lt Thomas Cooper appointed 1/22/62 **K 7/1**
3rd Lt Edward Rhodes 21 yr old enlisted Bertie Co 1/22/62 **K 7/1**
1st Sgt Clingman Craige enlisted 1/23/62 **W 7/1 C Hagerstown 7/14** (later 2nd Lt—died in prison)
Sgt William Parker 43 yr old enlisted Bertie Co 1/23/62 **W 7/1** (died 7/20/63)
Sgt James Rayner enlisted Bertie Co 1/23/62 **W-left leg 7/1 C 7/5** (later ensign)
Corp. James Adams 21 yr old enlisted Bertie Co 1/23/62 **W-left hand 7/1**
Corp William Powell enlisted 1/23/62 **W 7/1 C 7/5** (later Sgt)
Private Jesse Byrum 27 yr old enlisted Bertie Co 1/23/62 ***C 7/14***
Private Reuben Byrum 23 yr old enlisted Bertie Co 1/23/62 ***C 7/14***
Private Benjamin Carter 23 yr old enlisted Bertie Co 5/7/62 **W 7/1 died 7/3**
Private Joseph Casper 21 yr old enlisted Bertie Co 1/23/62 ***W 7/1 (died 7/3)***
Private Asa Cooper enlisted Hanover Co 5/12/62
Private Jacob Freeman 34 yr old enlisted Bertie Co 1/23/62
Private William Mardre enlisted 7/7/62 **W 7/1** (later Ord Sgt)
Private Jeremiah Mitchell enlisted 1/23/62 **K 7/1**
Private John Parker 21 yr old enlisted Bertie Co 1/23/62 **W 7/1 C 7/14** (joined US service)
Private Thomas Parker enlisted Bertie Co 1/23/62 (later W-left hand Petersburg)
Private Joseph Pritchard 21 yr old enlisted Bertie Co 1/23/62 (later deserted 1/28/64)
Private Thomas Peele enlisted 4/22/62 **K 7/1**
Private James Pierce 23 yr old enlisted Bertie Co 1/23/62 **K 7/1**
Private Andrew Pritchard 20 yr old enlisted Bertie Co 1/23/62 **W-right leg, hip, arm 7/1**
Private Napolean Rice 19 yr old enlisted Bertie Co 1/23/62 **W 7/1** (died 7/17/63)
Private Henry Skiles enlisted 5/17/62 (later deserted 10/24/64)
Private Robert Skiles 33 yr old enlisted Bertie Co 1/23/62 **C 7/14**
Private David Stone 22 yr old enlisted Bertie Co 1/23/62 **K 7/1**

Company D *"Burke County"*

Captain Calvin Brown appointed 2/4/62 (resigned 1/7/64)
2nd Lt Louis Elias 18 yr old enlisted Burke Co 2/5/62 (later 1st Lt)
3rd Lt George Kincaid 24 enlisted Burke Co 2/15/62 **K 7/3**
1st Sgt O.J. Brittain enlisted Burke Co 2/8/62 **C 7/14**
Sgt. S.J. Black 41 yr old enlisted Burke Co. 2/22/62 **C 7/14**
Sgt. J.M. Clay 23 yr old enlisted Burke Co. 2/27/62 **W-eye C 7/3**

Sgt. John Lang 33 yr old enlisted Burke Co. 2/12/62 (later K Wilderness)
Sgt. William Womack 31 yr old enlisted Burke Co. 2/10/62 (later 1st Sgt)
Sgt. James Rozzell enlisted 5/9/62 (later K Wilderness)
Corp. Abraham Mace 19 yr old enlisted Burke Co. 2/28/62 **W 7/3 C 7/14** (later C Bristoe Station)
Corp. John Simpson enlisted 3/27/62 **C 7/3**
Private Lucius Baker 23 yr old enlisted Burke Co 3/1/62 (later W-hip Bristoe Station)
Private R.W. Bingham 26 yr old enlisted Burke Co 3/11/62 (later C Bristoe Station)
Private Samuel Brittain 22 yr old enlisted Burke Co 2/14/62
Private John Butler 18 yr old enlisted Burke Co. 2/15/62
Private William Butler 38 yr old enlisted Burke Co. 2/15/62 (later Corp / Sgt)
Private George Causby 19 yr old enlisted Burke Co. 2/24/62 W Fredericksburg ***C 7/5***
Private William Causby 19 yr old enlisted Burke Co. 3/12/62 ***W 7/3 C Greencastle, Pa 7/5***
Private Benjamin Clark 38 yr old enlisted Burke Co. 3/11/62 **C 7/3**
Private John Cook 23 yr old enlisted Burke Co. 2/15/62 **W-left cheek 7/3**
Private Alexander Giles 23 yr old enlisted Bernie Co. 5/1/62
Private S.L. Giles 38 yr old enlisted Burke Co. 2/22/62 **W-right leg 7/3**
Private W.W. Giles 29 yr old enlisted Burke Co. 5/1/62 **C 7/3**
Private P.W. Hennessee 25 yr old enlisted Burke Co. 2/4/62 **C 7/3**
Private John Hinson enlisted Burke Co **C 7/3** (later joined US Service)
Private Daniel Johnson 20 yr old enlisted Bertie Co. (later W-hand Cold Harbor)
Private J.W. Johnson 29 yr old enlisted Burke Co. 3/1/62 **C 7/14**
Private Robert Johnson 21 yr old enlisted Burke Co. 2/22/62 (later C Burgess Mill, Va)
Private W.W. Kincaid 33 yr old enlisted Burke Co. 2/12/62 (deserted 7/16/63—returned C Spotsylvania)
Private James McKesson enlisted 5/1/62 **WC 7/3**
Private E.A. Melton enlisted 2/10/62 **C 7/3** (later W Wilderness)
Private W.H. Melton 25 yr old enlisted Burke Co. 4/7/62 W White Hall, Va
Private Marshall Miller 29 yr old enlisted Burke Co. 2/12/62 **C 7/14** (later K Petersburg)
Private John Pearson enlisted 2/8/62 **W 7/1 W 7/3** (slight)
Private Moses Powell 19 yr old enlisted Burke Co. 2/21/62
Private William Powell 16 yr old enlisted Burke Co. 4/22/62 (later C Bristoe Station)
Private James Saulman 23 yr old enlisted Burke Co. 2/10/62
Private David Settlemire 39 yr old enlisted Burke Co. 2/28/62 **W-stomach 7/3**
Private E.M. Sudderth 38 yr old enlisted Burke Co. 3/4/62 **K 7/3**
Private Perry Summers 19 yr old enlisted Burke Co. 2/8/62 **W-breast 7/3** (later K Bristoe Station)
Private H.A. Tate enlisted 2/14/62 **W-right thigh C 7/3—died 8/25/63**
Private R.L. Todd 19 yr old enlisted Burke Co. 2/25/62 **WC 7/3 died 7/25/63**
Private E.H. Williams 27 yr old enlisted Burke Co. 2/8/62 ***W 7/1 C 7/5***
Private John Williams 29 yr old enlisted Burke Co. 3/18/62
Private Joseph Williams 26 yr old enlisted Burke Co. 3/12/62
Private Molton Williams 24 yr old enlisted Burke Co. 2/15/62 ***C 7/14***

July 1 Casualties

1st Lt W.J. Kincaid appointed 2/14/62 **W 7/1 C 7/5** (later Capt)
Corp. N.W. Jordan 26 yr old enlisted Burke Co. 2/14/62 (later Sgt) **W 7/1**
Corp. Moulton Winters enlisted 2/10/62 **K 7/1**
Private T.W. Benfield 26 yr old enlisted Burke Co 4/18/62 **W-thigh 7/1** (later W Petersburg) died
Private Thomas Chrisenberry 30 yr old enlisted Burke Co. 1/31/63 **K 7/1**
Private Michael Clark 30 yr old enlisted Burke Co. 3/17/62 **WC 7/1**
Private Hezehiah Fair 29 yr old enlisted Burke Co. 5/1/62 **C 7/14**
Private Adam Henson 23 yr old enlisted Burke Co. 2/18/62 (deserted 8/3/63—returned)
Private Abram Huffman 36 yr old enlisted Burke Co. 2/28/62 **C 7/14** (later K Jone's Farm, Va)
Private Rufus Hicks 29 yr old enlisted Burke Co. 9/14/62 (later C North Anna)
Private J.W. Kincaid 31 yr old enlisted Burke Co. 3/12/62 **K 7/1**
Private John Largent enlisted 5/1/62 **W 7/1 C 7/5** (later Corp)
Private Jackson Miller 23 yr old enlisted Burke Co. 2/12/62 **W-thigh 7/1 C 7/5**
Private Isaiah Mosteller 39 yr old enlisted Burke Co. 2/26/62 (later W Spotsylvania)
Private Samuel Poteet 25 yr old enlisted Burke Co. 2/22/62 **W 7/1**
Private John Poteet 38 yr old enlisted Burke Co. 2/12/62 **C 7/14**
Private John Saulman 19 yr old enlisted Burke Co. 2/12/62 **W-right ankle 7/1**
Private Charles Taylor 29 yr old enlisted Burke Co. 3/12/62 **W 7/1 C 7/14**
Private J.B. Wadkins 33 yr old enlisted Burke Co. 3/10/62 **W-left leg 7/1**
Private Lafayette Walls 34 yr old enlisted Burke Co. 3/8/62 W Fredericksburg **K 7/1**
Private B.R. Whisenhunt 31 yr old enlisted Burke Co. 2/22/62 **C 7/14**
Private J.A. Williams 36 yr old enlisted Burke Co. 2/13/62 (deserted 11/13/63—arrested—imprisoned)
*Private W.M. Williams 21 yr old enlisted Burke Co. 4/17/62 **W 7/1***
*Private William Williams 25 yr old enlisted Burke Co. 2/10/62 **W 7/1 C 7/5***
Private William Wood 19 yr old enlisted Burke Co. 3/1/62 **W 7/1 C 7/4**

Company E *"Mecklenburg & Iredell Counties"*

Captain William Kerr appointed 3/20/62 (later W-left leg Petersburg)
3rd Lt. William Turner 25 yr old enlisted Mecklenburg Co. 3/12/62 (later 1st Lt C Petersburg)
1st Sgt David McDonald enlisted 3/12/62 W 7/1 (later K Jone's Farm, Va)
Sgt. John Carmack 36 yr old enlisted Mecklenburg Co. 2/28/62
Sgt Robert Wilson 31 yr old enlisted Mecklenburg Co. 3/4/62 (later C Hatchers Run)
Corp. John McDonald enlisted 3/14/62 (later Sgt / 1st Sgt)
Private Enoch Abernathy 55 yr old enlisted Mecklenburg Co. 2/15/62 (discharged 11/10/64)

Private James Alexander 27 yr old enlisted Mecklenburg Co. 2/24/62 (later Sgt / 2nd Lt C Hatcher's Run)

Private Burton Bass 23 yr old enlisted Iredell Co. 2/26/62 C Hatchers Run

Private John Beaty 44 yr old enlisted Mecklenburg Co. 3/26/62 (later C Hatchers Run)

Private William Belk 20 yr old enlisted Mecklenburg Co. 3/2/62 (later C Bristoe Station)

Private William Dixon 44 yr old enlisted Mecklenburg Co. 3/6/63 **W 7/3** (died 9/1/63)

Private Samuel Eller 21 yr old enlisted Wake Co. (deserted 9/14/63)

Private John Finger 37 yr old enlisted Mecklenburg Co. 3/12/62 **W-neck 7/3** (later WC Bristoe Station)

Private Paul Grier enlisted 1862 Mecklenburg Co (later 2nd Lt K Bristoe Station)

Private John Hollingsworth 24 yr old enlisted Mecklenburg Co. 2/24/62 (later Corp)

Private James Jamison 26 yr old enlisted Mecklenburg Co. 3/7/63 (later Corp)

Private Jones Jamison 21 yr old enlisted Mecklenburg Co. 2/28/63 **C 7/14** (later C Hatchers Mill)

Private Thomas Jamison 35 yr old enlisted Mecklenburg Co. W White Hall **W 7/3**

Private Hugh McCorkle36 yr old enlisted Mecklenburg Co. 3/3/62 **C 7/14**

Private Cyrus McLure 29 yr old enlisted Mecklenburg Co. 3/12/62 **W-index finger 7/3 C 7/14**

Private James McQuay 36 yr old enlisted Mecklenburg Co. 4/30/62 **K 7/3**

Private John Mitschka 41 yr old enlisted Mecklenburg Co. 2/19/62 **C 7/3**

Private Francis Ostwalt 39 yr old enlisted Mecklenburg Co. 2/26/62 **C 7/3** (died smallpox 12/63)

Private George Pool 34 yr old enlisted Mecklenburg Co. 3/14/62 (later W-left hip Spotsylvania)

Private Alexander Stone 31 yr old enlisted Mecklenburg Co. 2/19/62 **C 7/3**

Private James Walker 34 yr old enlisted Mecklenburg Co. 5/9/62 (later Corp. C Hatchers Run)

Private John Walker 19 yr old enlisted Mecklenburg Co. 3/12/62

Private Edward Williamson 21 yr old enlisted Mecklenburg Co. 2/24/62 **C 7/3** (died 8/20)

July 1 Casualties

1st Lt. John Beatty Clanton 33 yr old enlisted Mecklenburg Co. 3/20/62 **WC 7/1** (died 8/1)

2nd Lt. William Rozzell enlisted 5/24/62 **W 7/1-C7/5 died 7/10**

Sgt. John Goodman 34 yr old enlisted Iredell Co. 2/26/62 **K 7/1**

Corp. William Cathey 27 yr old enlisted Mecklenburg Co. 3/12/62 **W-left arm 7/1 C 7/5 (amputated)**

Corp. William Hartgrove 33 yr old enlisted Mecklenburg Co. 3/10/62 W White Hall, Va **W-left thigh 7/1** (later Sgt)

Corp. Julius Puckett 29 yr old enlisted Mecklenburg Co. 3/12/62 **W-right leg 7/1** (later Sgt)

Private Samuel Auton 25 yr old enlisted Mecklenburg Co. 3/8/62
Private James Bass 29 yr old enlisted Iredell Co. 2/26/62 **W-left arm 7/1**
Private William Bird 26 yr old enlisted Mecklenburg Co. 3/8/62 W White hall, Va **W-right leg 7/1 C 7/4**
Private John Bradley 23 yr old enlisted Iredell Co. 2/26/62 **C 7/1**
Private John Brimer 27 yr old enlisted Mecklenburg Co. 4/7/62 **W-leg 7/1**
Private James Christy 26 yr old enlisted Iredell Co. 4/19/62 **W-right leg 7/1**
Private James Clark 39 yr old enlisted Mecklenburg Co. 4/1/63 **K 7/1**
Private Richard Hartgrove 24 yr old enlisted Mecklenburg Co. 2/27/62 W White Hall, NC **W 7/1**
Private David Hartline 28 yr old enlisted Iredell Co. 2/26/62 **W-right foot 7/1** (later Teamster)
Private Ezekiel Helms 29 yr old enlisted Mecklenburg Co. 3/12/62 **K 7/1**
Private James Hill 36 yr old enlisted Mecklenburg Co. 3/4/62 **W-hip 7/1 C 7/6** (later K Reams Station)
Private Lindsey Lewis 24 yr old enlisted Mecklenburg Co. **W-right foot 7/1**
Private William McLelland enlisted 5/5/62 **W 7/1 C 7/5**
Private William McQuay 21 yr old enlisted Mecklenburg Co. 3/10/62 **WC 7/1 (died 7/7)**
Private William Martin 20 yr old enlisted Mecklenburg Co. 3/5/62 **W 7/1**
Private William Murdock 28 yr old enlisted Mecklenburg Co. 4/19/62 **W-right foot 7/1**
Private ____________ (after Narron) 19 yr old enlisted Mecklenburg Co. 2/1/63 **W-left arm 7/1 C 7/5**
Private William Puckett 25 yr old enlisted Mecklenburg Co. 3/10/62 **W-left thigh 7/1**
Private William Richey 36 yr old enlisted Iredell Co. 4/19/63 **W 7/1 C 7/5 (died 7/9)**
Private William Rievs 27 yr old enlisted Mecklenburg Co. 3/12/62 **W 7/1**
Private David Smith 24 yr old enlisted Mecklenburg Co. 2/27/62
Private Levi Walker 33 yr old enlisted Mecklenburg Co. 3/8/62 **W 7/1 C 7/5** (later K Spotsylvania)
Private James Wingate 37 yr old enlisted Mecklenburg Co. 3/14/62 ***W 7/1 C 7/4***
Private Thomas Wingate 33 yr old enlisted Mecklenburg Co. 3/14/62 ***W 7/1*** *(later C Hatchers Run)*
Private Reuben Yaunts 29 yr old enlisted Mecklenburg Co. 2/14/62 **K 7/1**

Company F *"Chowan, Hertford & Perquimans Counties"*

Captain Edward Small appointed 2/15/62 **C 7/3**
1st Lt. Stephen Roberts 29 yr old appointed 2/15/62 **W-shoulder 7/3** (later W-left leg Wilderness)
Sgt.C.G. Davenport 32 yr old enlisted Chowan Co 2/15/62 (later 1st Sgt)

Sgt. Nathaniel Mardre enlistyed 2/15/62 **C 7/14** (later W Wilderness)
Sgt. Thomas Small 25 yr old enlisted Chowan Co 4/18/62 (later W Hatchers Run)
Sgt. Joseph Trotman 29 yr old enlisted Perquimans Co 2/15/62 **C 7/3** (later W Hatchers Run)
Corp. Robert Briscoe 43 yr old enlisted Hertford Co. 2/15/62 W-leg **C 7/3** (died Chester, Pa buried PNC)
Corp. James Creecy enlisted Perquimans Co **C 7/14**
Private Bryant Askew 19 yr old enlisted Hertford Co 2/15/62
Private Joshua Askew 24 yr old enlisted Hertford Co 2/15/62
Private T.C. Bateman 19 yr old enlisted Chowan Co 2/15/62 **C 7/14** (joined US Service)
Private A.J. Byrum 22 yr old enlisted Chowan Co 2/15/62 ***W-left leg*** *7/3 (amputated)*
Private Issac Byrum enlisted 2/15/62 ***W-left leg*** *7/3* ***C*** *7/5 (amputated)*
Private Henry Creecy 21 yr old enlisted Chowan Co 2/15/62 (later C Bristoe Station)
Private Louis Davidson 41 yr old enlisted Hertford Co 4/12/62 **WC 7/3 (died 7/27)**
Private Joseph Farmer 23 yr old enlisted Hertford Co 4/20/62 (later C Bristoe Station)
Private Henry Floyd 32 yr old enlisted Hertford Co 2/15/62 **C 7/3**
Private Thomas Harris 30 yr old enlisted Perquimans Co 4/28/62 **W-left side C 7/3** (later Corp)
Private Thomas Haskett 45 yr old enlisted Perquimans Co 2/15/62 **WC 7/3**
Private Hance Jordan 28 yr old enlisted Chowan Co 4/11/62 (later missing Wildernesss)
Private Caleb Lane 24 yr old enlisted Perquimans Co 4/28/62 ***K*** *7/3*
Private William Lane 23 yr old enlisted Perquimans Co 4/28/62 ***C*** *7/3*
Private George Lassiter 21 yr old enlisted Chowan Co 2/15/62
Private Joseph Long 21 yr old enlisted Perquimans Co 4/28/62 **W-left thigh & arm 7/3** (later Corp)
Private Calvin Mansfield 23 yr old enlisted Perquimans Co 4/28/62 **C 7/14**
Private James Miller 19 yr old enlisted Chowan Co 2/15/62 (later W-arm Wilderness)
Private Thomas Munds 21 yr old enlisted Chowan Co 2/15/62 (later W Bristoe Station)
Private Jacob Nowell 28 yr old enlisted Hertford Co 2/15/62 **C 7/28/63**
Private Job Pierce 24 yr old enlisted Hertford Co. 4/7/62 (later C Hatcher Run)
Private Timothy Perry 27 yr old enlisted Chowan Co 2/15/62
Private John Potter 28 yr old enlisted Perquimans Co 4/28/62 (later C Bristoe Station)
Private Samuel Potter 20 yr old enlisted Perquimans Co 2/15/62 (later C Bristoe Station)
Private William Saunders 19 yr old enlisted Hertford Co 2/15/62
Private Frederick Simpson 22 yr old enlisted Chowan Co 2/15/62
Private Charlton Smith 35 yr old enlisted Perquimans Co 4/28/62 ***K*** *7/3*
Private James Smith 22 yr old enlisted Perquimans Co 4/19/62
Private William Smith 27 yr old enlisted Perquimans Co 2/15/62 ***K*** *7/3*
Private David Stearns 20 yr old enlisted Chowan Co 2/15/62 (later C Bristoe Station)
Private James Stearns 35 yr old enlisted Chowan Co 2/15/62 (deserted 7/64)
Private S.S. Sutton 35 yr old enlisted Chowan Co 2/15/62 ***W-left arm*** *7/3* (later C Bristoe Station / W Burgess Mill))
Private Joseph Taylor 18 yr old enlisted Hereford Co **C 7/3** (later W Jone's Farm, Va)

Private Henry Thatch 25 yr old enlisted Perquimans Co 4/28/62 **K 7/3**
Private Anderson Ward 20 yr old enlisted Chowan Co
Private James White 21 yr old enlisted Perquimans Co 4/19/62 ***WC 7/3*** *(died 7/16)*
Private Issac White 20 yr old enlisted Perquimans Co 2/15/62 ***WC 7/3*** *(later Corp)*
Private James B White 33 yr old enlisted Hertford Co 4/19/62 **W-right arm 7/3**
Private Robert White Perquimans Co enlisted 2/15/62 ***C 7/14***
Private Joseph Wingate 21 old enlisted Perquimans Co 2/15/62

July 1 Casualties

2nd Lt. William Rea 21 yr old enlisted 2/15/62 **W-left hip & right foot 7/1** (later W-jaw Petersburg)
3rd Lt. Blake Hoskins appointed 4/7/62 **W 7/1 C 7/5 died 7/9**
Private Miles Askew 18 yr old enlisted Hertford Co 2/15/62 ***W-head 7/1 C 7/5*** (later W Ream's Station)
Private Richard Bailey 30 yr old enlisted Perquimans Co 4/28/62 (transferred CS Navy)
Private F.W. Bates 34 yr old enlisted Chowan Co 2/15/62 ***WC 7/1 C 7/5***
Private William Benbury 21 yr old enlisted Chowan Co 2/15/62 **W-arm 7/1** (later Sgt W Petersburg)
Private J.R. Conner 19 yr old enlisted Hertford Co 2/15/62 **W-thigh 7/1 C 7/5**
Private Adam Forehand 22 yr old enlisted Chowan Co 2/15/62 **W 7/1 C 7/14**
Private B.F. Goodwin 24 yr old enlisted Chowan Co 2/15/62 **W 7/1 C 7/14**
Private Stephen Garrett 40 yr old enlisted Chowan Co 2/15/62 (later C Bristoe Station)
Private N.C. Jordan 29 yr old enlisted Chowan Co 2/15/62 ***K 7/1***
Private Robert Jordan 22 yr old enlisted Perquimans Co 4/28/62 (later Corp) ***W 7/1***
Private John Long 29 yr old enlisted Perquimans Co 2/15/62 (later W-elbow Weldon RR)
Private Stephen Parrish enlisted 2/15/62 (later W Jone's Farm, Va)
Private William Parrish 22 yr old enlisted Chowan Co 2/15/62 ***W-left thigh 7/1***
Private John Proctor 19 yr old enlisted Perquimans Co 2/17/62 **WC 7/1** (died 8/63)
Private James Swain 48 yr old enlisted Perquimans Co 2/15/62 (later W-left ankle Bristoe Station)
Private George Whedbee 20 yr old enlisted Perquimans Co 2/15/62 **W 7/1 C 7/4**

Company G *"Orange & Chatham Counties"*

Captain John Freeland appointed 2/6/62
1st Sgt Jones Watson enlisted Orange Co 2/26/62 (later 3rd Lt)
Sgt. James Whitaker 25 yr old enlisted Orange Co 2/26/62 (later 2nd Lt C Hatcher's Run)
Sgt. William Whitted enlisted 2/26/62 **C 7/14** (later 3rd Lt)

Sgt. Henry McDade 25 yr old enlisted Orange Co 2/26/62 **C 7/14**
Corp. Wesley Harwood enlisted 2/26/62 (later Sgt)
Corp. David Norwood 21 yr old enlisted Orange Co 2/26/62 **C 7/3** (died 9/63)
Private Ruffin Allen 34 yr old enlisted Orange Co 2/1/63 (Later C Bristoe Station)
Private Wesley Andrews 30 yr old enlisted Orange Co 2/1/63 ***W C 7/3 (died 7/10)***
Private Robert Campbell 20 yr old enlisted Orange Co 2/26/62
Private John Cheek 31 yr old enlisted Orange Co 2/26/62 C 7/14
Private Nathaniel Cheek 27 yr old enlisted Orange Co 2/26/62 (later Corp & Sgt)
Private Virgil Cheek 19 yr old enlisted Orange Co 2/1/63 (later Sgt)
Private John Clements enlisted 2/26/62 **W-hip 7/3** (later Sgt)
Private William Clements 19 yr old enlisted Orange Co 2/26/62 (later W Cold Harbor)
Private Robert Daniel 25 yr old enlisted Orange Co 2/26/62 **C 7/14**
Private Henry Davis 19 yr old enlisted Orange Co 2/26/62 (later C Bristoe Station)
Private James Davis 19 yr old enlisted Orange Co 2/26/62 (later drummer)
Private Washington Fowler 30 yr old enlisted Orange Co 9/6/62
Private Esau Garratt 20 yr old enlisted Orange Co 2/26/62 **W-lung C 7/3 died 7/11 Williamsport**
Private John Hester 25 yr old enlisted Orange Co 2/26/62
Private Anderson Hunter 24 yr old enlisted Orange Co 2/1/63
Private William Huskey 25 yr old enlisted Orange Co 2/26/62 (deserted 10/64)
Private William Jolly 24 yr old enlisted Orange Co 2/26/62 **C 7/14**
Private Baxter King enlisted Orange Co 2/26/62 **W-hip 7/3**
Private Bellfield King 21 yr old enlisted Orange Co 2/26/62
Private Rufus King 21 yr old enlisted Orange Co 2/26/62 **C 7/14**
Private W.D. King enlisted Orange Co 2/26/62
Private John Mincy 21 yr old enlisted Orange Co 2/26/62 **W-left foot 7/3**
Private James Pendergrass 27 yr old enlisted Orange Co 2/26/62
Private James M Pendergrass 33 yr old enlisted Orange Co 8/29/62 (died 10/64 tyhoid)
Private John Pendergrass 30 yr old enlisted Orange Co 2/26/62 W 7/3 C 7/5
Private William H Pendergrass 21 yr old enlisted Orange Co 12/20/62
Private Edward Reeves 32 yr old enlisted Orange Co 2/26/62 **C 7/14**
Private Carney Smith 25 yr old enlisted Orange Co 2/26/62 (later Corp)
Private Houston Sparrow 23 yr old enlisted Orange Co 2/26/62
Private William Sparrow 21 yr old enlisted Orange Co 2/26/62 C 7/14
Private Thomas Strain 27 yr old enlisted Orange Co 3/1/63 **W-left shoulder 7/1** (later C Hatcher's Run)
Private William Suggs enlisted Orange Co 9/10/62 **C 7/3** (later Corp / Sgt)
Private William Thrift 23 yr old enlisted Orange Co 2/26/62 **W 7/3**
Private William Tilly enlisted Orange Co 2/26/62 (later Sgt W-right leg Mine Run)
Private George Walters 19 yr old enlisted Orange Co 4/25/63
Private Thomas Whitaker 19 yr old enlisted Orange Co 2/26/62 **C 7/14**

July 1 Casualties

1st Lt. John McDade appointed 2/6/62 **K 7/1**
2nd Lt. Nathaniel Tenney 27 yr old enlisted Orange Co 2/26/62 **K 7/1**
3rd Lt. James Williams enlisted 2/26/62 **K 7/1**
Sgt. Thomas Davis 25 yr old enlisted Orange Co 2/26/62 ***W-right ankle 7/1 C 7/5*** *(later 1st Sgt W Cold Harbor)*
Corp. William Ivey 24 yr old enlisted Orange Co 2/26/62 **W 7/1 C 7/5 (died 8/8)**
Corp. Jeter Snipes 20 yr old enlisted Orange Co 5/3/62 **W-left lung C 7/1** (died 7/19)
Private Thomas Bagley transferred 1/19/63 **C 7/14**
Private Philo Blackwood enlisted 2/26/62 **W 7/1**
Private A.J. Brockwell 37 yr old enlisted Orange Co 2/1/63
Private Washington Burgess 24 yr old enlisted Orange Co 2/26/62
Private Algernon Daniel 19 yr old enlisted Orange Co 2/26/62 **W-hips 7/1 C 7/5**
Private Benjamin Davis 50 yr old enlisted Orange Co 2/26/62 ***FATHER&SON***
Private Demarcus Davis 30 yr old enlisted Orange Co 2/26/62 (discharged 3/64 paralysis)
Private Fendall Davis 19 yr old enlisted Orange Co 5/3/62/62 ***W-right hip 7/1***
Private William Durham enlisted Orange Co 2/26/62 **W 7/1 (died 7/3)**
Private Cornelius Edwards 27 yr old enlisted Orange Co 2/26/62 **W 7/1** died Williamsport 7/6
Private William Flintoff 19 yr old enlisted Orange Co 2/26/62 **W-right side 7/1** (later W Petersburg)
Private Thadeus Lloyd 24 yr old enlisted Orange Co 2/26/62 ***W 7/1***
Private Henderson Marcom 36 yr old enlisted Orange Co 2/26/62 (deserted 10/10/63)
Private C.H. Pendergrass 19 yr old enlisted Orange Co 2/1/63 ***W-right shoulder 7/1*** (later C Hatcher's Run)
Private George Pendergrass 21 yr old enlisted Orange Co 2/26/62 (later C Bristoe Station)
Private George W Pendergrass 37 yr old enlisted Orange Co 5/9/62 (discharged 9/27/63 rheumatism)
Private William Pendergrass 27 yr old enlisted Orange Co 4/10/62 ***K 7/1***
Private Henry Petty 20 yr old enlisted Orange Co 2/26/62 (later C Bristoe Station)
Private Van Sparrow 29 yr old enlisted Orange Co 2/26/62 ***W 7/1*** *(C Bristoe Station)*
Private Bentley Suitt 23 yr old enlisted Orange Co 2/26/62 **W 7/1**
Private Jerry Tripp 21 yr old enlisted Orange Co 2/26/62 **W-breast &* left shoulder 7/1**
Private Lemuel Vann enlisted Orange Co 2/26/62 (deserted 7/21/63—returned)
Private Duncan Waddell 19 yr old enlisted Orange Co **W7/1 C 7/5 "gallant conduct 7/1"** (later 1st Lt)
Private Samuel Williams 19 yr old enlisted Orange Co 2/26/62 ***W 7/1***
Private Forrest Williams 23 yr old enlisted Orange Co 2/26/62
Private Norris Williams 21 yr old enlisted Orange Co 2/26/62

Company H *"Mecklenburg County"*

Captain William Grier appointed 3/10/62 (in command of regiment July 3)

Sgt. Stephen Blankenship 28 yr old enlisted Mecklenburg Co 5/1/62 (later 1st Sgt C Hatcher's Run)

Sgt. J.S. Caldwell 28 yr old enlisted Mecklenburg Co 3/14/62 **C 7/14**

Sgt. Robert Saville 25 yr old enlisted Mecklenburg Co 3/14/62 **W 7/3**

Corp. John Campbell 27 yr old enlisted Mecklenburg Co 5/1/62

Corp. John Smith 25 yr old enlisted Mecklenburg Co 3/12/62 (later Sgt)

Corp. Alex Thrower 19 yr old enlisted Mecklenburg Co 3/10/62 (later W Wilderness)

Private John Alexander 19 yr old enlisted Mecklenburg Co 3/24/63 (later FW Wilderness)

Private Stephen Blair 19 yr old enlisted Mecklenburg Co 3/14/62

Private James Brown 25 yr old enlisted Mecklenburg Co 3/14/62

Private Robert Burns 27 yr old enlisted Mecklenburg Co 3/14/62

Private James Carothers 34 yr old enlisted Mecklenburg Co 3/14/62 (later W Spotsylvania)

Private John Carothers 37 yr old enlisted Mecklenburg Co 3/14/63 (died disease 8/2/63)

Private James Cooper 33 yr old enlisted Mecklenburg Co 3/14/62 **C 7/14**

Private Elias Crowell enlisted 6/1/62 (later musician)

Private A.R. Hamel 34 yr old enlisted Mecklenburg Co 10/27/62 **WC 7/3 (died 8/28/63)**

Private Seth Hotchkiss 21 yr old enlisted Mecklenburg Co 3/14/62 **C 7/5**

Private Thomas Humphries 31 yr old enlisted Mecklenburg Co 5/1/62 (later Corp)

Private William Knox 23 yr old enlisted Mecklenburg Co 3/19/62 **C 7/14**

Private Robert Lowrie transferred 6/13/62 (later 1st Lt)

Private James McMillan 35 yr old enlisted Mecklenburg Co 3/14/62 (later Corp & Sgt FW Wilderness)

Private James McQuaige 31 yr old enlisted Mecklenburg Co 5/1/62 (later C Hatcher's Run)

Private James Madden 25 yr old enlisted Mecklenburg Co 3/15/62 (later died disease 1/64)

Private Wiley Mincy 21 yr old enlisted Mecklenburg Co 3/14/62 **C 7/14**

Private William Morrison transferred 11/1/62 **C 7/3** (later musician)

Private John Neely 21 yr old enlisted Mecklenburg Co 4/17/62 (later Corp & Sgt)

Private W.M. Reid 29 yr old enlisted Mecklenburg Co 5/1/62 (later Corp)

Private John Russell 23 yr old enlisted Mecklenburg Co 3/21/62 **C 7/3**

Private Alexander Sloop 48 yr old enlisted Mecklenburg Co 3/10/62 **C 7/5**

Private James Smith 28 yr old enlisted Mecklenburg Co 3/18/62 (later missing Bristoe Station W Wilderness)

Private Thomas Smith 20 yr old enlisted Mecklenburg Co 3/15/62 **C 7/14**

Private J.A. Snider 38 yr old enlisted Mecklenburg Co 1/21/63 **K 7/3**

Private C.B Watt transferred 4/13/63 (later Corp & Sgt)

Private William Wilkerson 20 yr old enlisted Mecklenburg Co 3/10/62 W-head Cold Harbor

Private R.J. Wingate 20 yr old enlisted Mecklenburg Co 3/10/62 (later W-thigh Wilderness)

July 1 Casualties

1st Lt. James Lowrie 25 yr old enlisted Mecklenburg Co 5/1/62 **K 7/1**

2nd Lt. John Knox 25 yr old enlisted Mecklenburg Co 3/14/62 **W-left wrist 7/1** (later K Wilderness)

3rd Lt. James Saville enlisted 3/14/62 W 7/1 (later W-left shoulder Jone's Farm / C Hatcher's Run)

1st Sgt Francis Harris 25 yr old enlisted Mecklenburg Co 3/14/62 **W-left arm 7/1 C 7/4**

Sgt. Patrick Clark 35 yr old enlisted Mecklenburg Co 3/14/62 W White Hall, Va **W 7/1**

Corp. Thomas Campbell 23 yr old enlisted Mecklenburg Co 3/14/62 **K 7/1**

Private Benjamin Coffey 20 yr old enlisted Mecklenburg Co 3/14/62 **W-left leg & right eye 7/1**

Private Peter Ingle 32 yr old enlisted Mecklenburg Co 3/14/62 **W 7/1** (later C Hatcher's Run)

Private Abel Key 36 yr old enlisted Mecklenburg Co 3/15/62 **W 7/1**

Private R.C. Porter 18 yr old enlisted Mecklenburg Co 3/2/63 **W-right thigh 7/1 C 7/5**

Company I *"Lincoln County"*

Captain Albert Haynes appointed 2/12/62 **W chest, shoulder & right fibula 7/3 C 7/5**

1st Lt. David Coon appointed 2/12/62 **W-right foot & both eyes W 7/3**

2nd Lt. Lemuel Hoyle appointed 3/12/62 **W 7/3**

3rd Lt.Oliver Ramseur appointed 3/12/62 **WC 7/3**

Sgt. Robert Bell 29 yr old enlisted Lincoln Co 3/17/62 **W 7/3** (later W Hatchers Run)

Sgt. William Jetton enlisted 3/11/62 **K 7/3**

Sgt. Walter Ramseur enlisted 3/21/62 (later W-back Bristoe Station—died)

Corp. Robert Cathey 26 yr old enlisted Lincoln Co. 3/21/62 **K 7/3**

Corp. Oliver Wells enlisted 3/9/62 **W 7/3**

Private William Abernathy enlisted Lincoln Co. 3/12/62 **W-mouth C 7/3**

Private Sidney Bolick 21 enlisted Lincoln Co. 3/17/62 **WC 7/3**

Private Joseph Boyles enlisted Lincoln Co. 7/15/62 **C 7/14 (later C Burgess Mill)**

Private Lorenzo Campbell 18 yr old enlisted Lincoln Co. 5/13/63 **C 7/21/63**

Private Michael Carpenter 19 yr old enlisted Lincoln Co. 3/15/62 (later W-leg Bristoe Station)

Private Sidney Cornwell 19 yr old enlisted Lincoln Co 3/13/62 **W 7/3** (later K Petersburg)

Private Fred Dellinger 19 yr old enlisted Lincoln Co. 3/15/62 ***W 7/3-C 7/14***

Private P. Dellinger 19 yr old enlisted Lincoln Co. 3/9/62 ***K 7/3***

Private Robert Finger 21 yr old enlisted Lincoln Co. **K 7/3**

Private Stanhope Glasscock 24 yr old enlisted Lincoln Co. 3/28/62 **WC 7/3** (died 7/19)

Private Adolphus Hafner 17 yr old enlisted Lincoln Co 3/15/62 ***K 7/3***

Private George Hafner enlisted Lincoln Co. 5/8/62 W Malvern Hill **W-left arm 7/3**

Private Hosea Hafner 17 yr old enlisted 3/15/62 **W 7/3**

Private Jacob Hafner 17 yr old enlisted Lincoln Co. 3/15/62 ***W-arm 7/3 (amp) C 7/4***

Private Christy Haun 19 yr old enlisted Lincoln Co. 3/13/62 **W 7/3**

Private Andrew Haynes 23 yr old enlisted Lincoln Co. 3/11/62 ***K 7/3***

Private John Haynes enlisted 4/24/62 ***C 7/3***

Private Daniel Hoover 18 yr old enlisted Lincoln Co. 5/8/62 **W 7/3**

Private Monroe Hovis enlisted Lincoln Co. 4/25/62 ***C 7/3***

Private Daniel Hubbard enlisted Lincoln Co. 3/23/63 (deserted 7/22/63—returned 11/63)

Private Jacob Huss 24 yr old enlisted Lincoln Co. 3/9/62 (later K Bristoe Station)

Private John Huss 21 yr old enlisted Lincoln Co. 3/9/62 **C 7/14**

Private Taylor Jetton 16 yr old enlisted Lincoln Co. 7/10/62 **C 7/14**

Private Leonidas Johnson 25 yr old enlisted Halifax Co. 1/2/63 **W-jaw 7/3**

Private Robert Johnson enlisted 3/3/62 **C 7/21/63**

Private John Kiser 31 yr old enlisted Lincoln Co. 3/15/62 (later W Bristoe Station—died)

Private Cameron Leonhardt enlisted 3/9/62 ***W-left shoulder C 7/3 (died 7/30)***

Private Jacob Leonhrdt enlisted 3/9/63 ***K 7/3***

Private Jacob Miller 28 yr old enlisted Lincoln Co.5/8/62 (later Sgt)

Private John Ramseur 24 yr old enlisted Lincoln Co. 3/21/62 (later Sgt)

Private Jacob Rhodes 29 yr old enlisted Lincoln Co. 5/8/62 (later Sgt)

Private Daniel Rincik 29 yr old enlisted Lincoln Co. 3/21/62 **C 7/14**

Private Anthony Shull 29 yr old enlisted Lincoln Co. 3/15/62 W White Hall, Va **C 7/14**

Private Daniel Stroup 20 yr old enlisted Lincoln Co. 3/15/62 **WC 7/3**

Private John Warlick 22 yr old enlisted Lincoln Co. 5/8/62 **W-right breast & left leg 7/3** (later W left arm Ream's Station)

Private Phillip Weaver enlisted Wayne Co. 12/20/62 (later W Bristoe Station & C Burgess Mill)

Private Perry Wood 21 yr old enlisted Lincoln Co. 3/17/62 **W-left hand 7/3** (later C Burgess Mill)

Private David Wyont enlisted Lincoln Co. 3/23/623 **W 7/3** (later C Burgess Mill)

Musician William Cline 31 yr old enlisted Lincoln Co 9/8/62 **C 7/5 caring for wounded**

Musician Adolhus Coon 20 yr old enlisted Lincoln Co 3/14/62 **C 7/5 caring for wounded**

Musician William Martin enlisted 4/25/62 (transferred regimental band 9/64)

Musician Charles Motz 19 yr old enlisted Camp Mangum 5/3/62 **C 7/5 caring for wounded**

Musician Monroe Seagle 28 yr old enlisted Lincoln Co. 5/8/62 (later regimental band)

July 1 Casualties

Corp. Laben Hovis yr old enlisted Lincoln Co. 3/14/62 **W-jaw 7/1 C 7/5**
Private James Abernathy 19 yr old enlisted Lincoln Co. 3/22/62 **W-left hand 7/1**
Private. Jacob Allran 35 yr old enlisted Lincoln Co 3/15/62 **W 7/1**
Private Absalom Avery 34 5/8/62 **W 7/1** (later C Burgess Mill)
Private Jacob Bisaner 19 yr old enlisted 3/11/62 **W-left side 7/1 C 7/5** (later Sgt)
Private Lafayette Blackburn 21 yr old enlisted Lincoln Co. 3/11/62 **W 7/1 C 7/5** (later W-left leg Jone's farm)
Private John Boyles enlisted Lincoln Co. 5/8/62 **WC 7/1 (died 8/10)**
Private David Carpenter enlisted Lincoln Co 3/26/62 **W 7/1 C 7/5**
Private Henry Carpenter enlisted 3/26/62 Lincoln Co. **WC 7/1 died 7/27**
Private Jacob Carpenter enlisted 3/13/62 Lincoln Co. **W 7/1 C 7/5 died 7/21**
Private William Carpenter 33 yr old enlisted Lincoln Co. 3/21/62 **W 7/1 C 7/5 (later C Burgess Mill)**
Private James Clark 32 yr old enlistyed Lincoln Co 3/21/62 **W 7/1 C 7/5 Chambersburg, Pa**
Private Absalom Cody 17 yr old enlisted Lincoln Co 3/23/63 **K 7/1**
Private Samuel Davis enlisted Lincoln Co. 3/23/62 **W 7/1**
Private Phillip Dellinger 23 yr old enlisted Lincoln Co. 3/11/62 W 7/1 C 7/5
Private David Glenn 18 yr old enlisted Lincoln Co. 3/13/62 **W 7/1** (later W Wilderness)
Private John Hafner 20 yr old enlisted Lincoln Co 3/15/62 K 7/1
Private David Hoover 21 yr old enlisted Lincoln Co. 3/15/62 W White Hall **K 7/1**
Private Henry Houser 23 yr old enlisted Lincoln Co. 3/17/62 **W 7/1 C 7/5**
Private David Hubbard enlisted 3/15/62 **W 7/1**
Private George Keever 19 yr old enlisted Lincoln Co. 3/15/62 **WC 7/1 (died 7/7)**
Private Hiram Kiser 27 yr old enlisted Lincoln Co. 3/21/62 **W-head 7/1**
Private Joseph Leonhardt 29 yr old enlisted 3/11/62 W 7/1 (later W Bristoe Station)
Private John Oats **W-head 7/1 C 7/5**
Private Albert Poole 21 yr old enlisted Lincoln Co. 3/12/62 **W 7/1** (later C Hanover Junction)
Private Nelson Ramsey 20 yr old enlisted Lincoln Co. 3/12/62 **K 7/1**
Private Robert Reinhardt enlisted Lincoln Co. 1/5/63 **W-left arm 7/1**
Private Joseph Richey 36 yr old enlisted Lincoln Co. 3/15/62 **W 7/1** (later K Wilderness)
Private Alfred Seagler 46 yr old enlisted Lincoln Co. 3/15/62 **K 7/1**
Private Elijah Sigmon enlisted Lincoln Co 3/26/63 **WC 7/1**
Private David Smith enlisted Lincoln Co. 3/26/63 **W 7/1-C 7/5**
Private Aaron Speagle enlisted Lincoln Co 4/8/63 **W 7/1**
Private Monroe Speagle 19 yr old enlisted Lincoln Co. 3/3/63 **K 7/1**
Private William Spreagle 19 yr old enlisted Lincoln Co. 3/21/62 **W-right shoulder 7/1**
Private Pinkney Strutt 20 yr old enlisted Lincoln Co. 3/15/62 **WC 7/1**
Private Aaron Tallant enlisted Lincoln Co 4/8/63 **W 7/1**
Private Adophs Wacaster enlisted 3/15/62 **WC 7/1** (later C Wilderness)

Company K *"Buncombe County"*

Captain James Young appointed 3/1/62 (later) W Ream's Station
1st Lt. John A. Burgin appointed 3/1/62 **K 7/3**
2nd Lt. John W. Burgin appointed 3/1/62 **K 7/3**
Sgt. John West 45 yr old enlisted Buncombe Co 3/1/62 (later 1st Sgt W Spotsylvania—died)
Corp. Jacob Bartlett enlisted 3/1/62 (later Sgt & 1st Sgt)
Corp. John Davidson 19 yr old enlisted Buncombe Co 3/1/62 (later Sgt C Bristoe Station)
Corp. William McKee enlisted Buncombe Co 3/1/62 (deserted 8/20 demoted returned C Burgess Mill)
Private Thomas Atkin 19 yr old enlisted Buncombe Co. 3/1/63 (later Corp & Sgt)
Private James Bartlett 39 yr old enlisted Buncombe Co. 4/27/63 **C 7/3**
Private John Bartlett 41 yr old enlisted Buncombe Co. 4/27/63
Private George Bell 19 yr old enlisted Buncombe Co. 3/1/63 (later W Spotsylvania)
Private George Bird 19 yr old enlisted Buncombe Co. 3/1/62 (later Corp W Wilderness)
Private Patrick Black 58 yr old enlisted Buncombe Co. 3/1/62 (discharged 10/64)
Private Thomas Brown 19 yr old enlisted Buncombe Co. 3/1/62 (later Corp)
Private Elisha Burns 21 yr old enlisted Buncombe Co 3/1/62 (deserted 8/20/63)
Private James Cordell enlisted Buncombe Co 4/27/63 **C 7/3**
Private Jasper Crook enlisted Buncombe Co 3/1/62 (later Corp)
Private Joseph Crow enlisted Buncombe Co 3/1/62 (later W Spotsylvania)
Private Levi Crow enlisted Buncombe Co 4/15/62
Private James Darnold enlisted New Hanover Co 8/19/62 **WC 7/1**
Private Joseph Glendown 20 yr old enlisted Buncombe Co 3/1/62 (later killed by accident)
Private Thomas Goodson enlisted Buncombe Co 3/1/62 **C 7/14**
Private John Hall 24 yr old enlisted Buncombe Co 3/1/62 **C 7/14**
Private Thomas Harris 27 yr old enlisted Buncombe Co 3/1/62 **C 7/3**
Privte Foster Justice 29 old enlisted Buncombe Co 4/15/62 (later C Bristoe Station)
Private James Kyles enlisted Buncombe Co 4/27/62 **C 7/14**
Private Charles Morris 36 yr old enlisted Buncombe Co 3/1/62 W-head&leftarm White Hall, Va **C 7/14**
Private Cornelius Morris 34 yr old enlisted Buncombe Co 3/1/62 W-White hall, Va **W-right elbow 7/14**
Private Monroe Morris 28 yr old enlisted Buncombe Co 10/27/62 **C 7/3**
Private Zebidee Morris 41 yr old enlisted Buncombe Co 4/27/62 (later W Bristoe Station)
Private George Patton 20 yr old enlisted Buncombe Co 3/1/62 (later W-left leg Wilderness)
Private James Patton 19 yr old enlisted Buncombe Co 3/1/62
Private William Poore 23 yr old enlisted Buncombe Co 3/1/62 **C 7/14**
Private James Powers 23 yr old enlisted Buncombe Co 3/1/62 **C 7/14**
Private Martin Roberts enlisted Buncombe Co 6/3/63 **C 7/14**
Private Richard Smith 26 yr old enlisted Buncombe Co 3/1/62 (deserted 6/30/64—returned)
Private William Smith enlisted Buncombe Co 3/1/62 (deserted 8/20/63 w Spotsylvania)

Private William Stroup 27 yr old enlisted Buncombe Co 3/1/62 **K 7/3**
Private John Trantham 19 yr old enlisted Buncombe Co 3/1/62 (later C Bristoe Station)
Private Joseph Trantham 21 yr old enlisted Buncombe Co 3/1/62 (later C Bristoe Station)
Private Jesse Watkins enlisted Buncombe Co 3/1/62 (deserted 8/20/63—returned C Spotsylvania)
Private Miniard Watkins enlisted Franklin, NC 10/27/62 **C 7/14**
Private Uriah Watkins enlisted Camp Davis 5/12/62 **C 7/14**
Private John West 19 yr old enlisted Buncombe Co 3/1/62 (later Corp)
Private George Wormley enlisted Buncombe Co 3/1/62 (later Corp)

Musician John Goodson 20 yr old enlisted Buncombe Co 3/1/62

July 1 Casualties

3rd Lt. Samuel Young 25 3/1/62 appointed 11/10/62 **WC 7/1 died 7/7**
1st Sgt James Triplett enlisted 5/1/62 **K 7/1**
Sgt. William Anderson enlisted 3/1/62 **K 7/1**
Sgt. John Patton enlisted Buncombe Co 3/1/62 **W 7/1 C 7/5** (later 2ndLt)
Sgt William West enlisted Buncombe Co 3/1/62 **W-head 7/1**
Corp. Lucius Gash 17 yr old enlisted Wake Co. 7/1/62 **W-foot 7/1/63** (later W Spotsylvania-died)
Private Jeremiah Ball 22 yr old enlisted Buncombe Co. 4/29/62 (deserted 11/63)
Private James Bell **WC 7/1** (died 7/10)
Private Thomas Burnett 18 yr old enlisted Buncombe Co 3/1/62 **W-left arm 7/1**
Private William Burnett 27 yr old enlisted Buncombe Co 3/1/62 (deserted 7/26/63)
Private John Burns 23 yr old enlisted Buncombe Co 3/1/62 W White Hall, Va **C 7/1**
Private John Cordell enlisted Buncombe Co 3/1/62 (deserted 8/20/63—returned)
Private Joseph Cordell enlisted Buncombe Co 3/1/62 (deserted 8/20/63—returned)
Private Joseph Creaseman enlisted Buncombe Co 4/27/63 ***K 7/1***
Private Abraham Creaseman Jr. enlisted Buncombe Co 4/15/62
Private William Creaseman enlisted Buncombe Co 3/1/62 (later deserted 6/30/64)
Private William L Creaseman enlisted *Buncombe Co* 3/1/62 (deserted 7/26/63)
Private Ezekiel Henderson 30 yr old enlisted Buncombe Co 3/1/62 **W 7/1 C 7/5** (later W-thigh Burgess Mill)
Private David Miller 24 yr old enlisted Buncombe Co 9/17/62 (deserted 8/20/63—returned)
Private Gabriel Miller 38 yr old enlisted Buncombe Co 4/27/62 (deserted 8/20/63—returned)
Private William Morrison 19 yr old enlisted Buncombe Co 3/1/62 **K 7/1**
Private Ferdinand Neighbour enlisted Buncombe Co 4/27/63 **SICK 7/3 C 7/5**
Private John Pittman 31 yr old enlisted Buncombe Co 3/1/62 **W-shoulder 7/1**
Private Alfred Smith enlisted 3/1/62 **W-neck & face 7/1 C 7/5**
Private John Suttles 23 yr old enlisted Buncombe Co 3/1/62 (deserted 8/20/63-returned)
Private John Wilson 44 yr old enlisted Buncombe Co 3/1/62 **W 7/1**
Private Marcus Young 18 yr old enlisted Buncombe Co 3/1/62 **W 7/1 C 7/5** (later W Wilderness)

Fourth Brigade Second Division Third Corps

Army of Northern Virginia
Commanded July 1 Brigadier General Joseph Davis
Commanded July 3 Brigadier General Joseph Davis

Assistant Adjutant General—Captain William T. Magruder 38 years old Upper Marlboro, Md—USMA—US Cavalry until 10/62 **K 7/3**

Assistant Adjutant & Inspector General—Captain Thomas C. Holiday 23 years old Aberdeen, Ms—UNC—W-Sharpsburg **W 7/3**

Aide-de-Camp—Lieutenant Henry Bacon Estes 24 years old Pulaski Tn—Lawyer

Aide-de-Camp—Cadet Joseph D. Reid 17 years old Sharon, Ms **K 7/1**

Volunteer Aide-de-Camp—Samuel M. Lowry 25 years old Crawfordsville, Ms **W 7/3**

Quarter Master—Major James S. Reid Canton, Ms—planter

Commissary of Substance—Major Samuel R. Harrison 44 years old New Orleans, La

Senior Brigade Surgeon Benjamin Ward—27 yrs old Tulane University / Atlanta Med College **left behind to care for wounded 7/4**

Brigade Clerk Walter Bennett (Co B 2nd MS)

Pioneer Corp Robert Cooper (Co. B 2nd MS)

Courier Private John Walker 26 yr old Tischomingo teacher enlisted 5/1/61 2nd MS

Wagonmaster Marcus McElhannon 27 yr old Tishomingo farmer enlisted 5/1/61 2nd MS

Brigade Scout William Nooner 23 yr old Tippah farmer enlisted 5/1/61 2nd MS

Scout William Nooner enlisted May 10, 1861 23 years old 2nd MS (W-Sharpsburg) **W 7/1**

Scout Alan Richie 27 years old painter enlisted 1861 2nd MS

FIFTY FIFTH NORTH CAROLINA REGIMENT

Captain James Whitehead Co E

Colonel John Connally

Captain Edward Satterfield Co H

Field & Staff

Colonel John Kerr Connally 24 yr old enlisted Yadkin Co. appointed Colonel 5/12/62 **W-left arm/right hip 7/1 C 7/5** (later W CH)

Lieutenant Colonel Maurice Thompson Smith 35 yr ld enlisted Granville NC appointed Lt Colonel 3/10/63 **K shot in side 7/1**

Major Alfred Horatio Belo 34 yr old journalist appointed 3/10/63 **W-left leg & lung by shell 7/1 evening (later Lt. Col / W-CH)**

Adjutant Henry Jordan appointed 11/18/62 **C 7/1**

Sergeant Major Jesse Allen Adams 21 yr old enlisted Wayne Co 5/30/62 appointed May-June 1863 **W-both thighs 7/1 C 7/5**

Surgeon Benjamin Green appointed 11/18/62 **C 7/5** with wounded

Assistant Surgeon Isaac G Cannady Granville Co doctor appointed 5/20/62

Assistant Surgeon W.T. Parker **C 7/5** with wounded

Hospital Steward A.J. Stone

Color Sergeant Marlin Galloway

Assistant Quartermaster William Webb appointed 4/30/63 (later QM Greensboro NC)

Quartermaster Sergeant Henry Furman appointed 10/7/62

Ordinance Sergeant J.W. Young appointed 11/19/62

Regimental Band

Musician Henry Adcock (Co K) 19 yr old enlisted Granville, NC

Musician Francis Bernard (Co E) 32 yr old enlisted Pitt Co. 7/8/62

Musician Jacob Ellington (Co E) 41 yr old enlisted Pitt Co 5/16/62

Musician William Horne (Co E) enlisted Pitt Co. 4/30/62

Drum Major / Chief Musician Charles Jacke (Co E)

Musician William Rowland (Co G) 25 year old enlisted Johnston Co. 5/1/62

Musician Burton Summerhill (Co E) 20 yr old enlisted Pitt Co. 4/2/62

Musician Henry Turnage (Co E) 20 yr old enlisted Pitt Co. 4/15/62

Musician Archibald Tyson (Co E) 23 yr old enlisted Lenoir Co. **C 7/5 (left behind as nurse)**

Company A *"Wilson County"*

Captain Albert Upchurch 27 yr old Wilson Co. merchant enlisted 5/30/62 **C 7/3**

1st Lt. Benjamin Briggs 26 yr old court clerk enlisted 6/2/62 **W 7/3** (later W Wilderness)

2nd Lt Thomas Bass 27 yr old Wilson Co farmer enlisted 4/19/62

3rd Lt Thomas Jefferson Hadley 23 yr old student enlisted 5/10/62 **W 7/14** (later W Wilderness)

Sgt. Lewellyn Jones 18 yr old enlisted in Wilson Co 5/7/62 (later W-knee North Anna)

Cpl. Joseph Marshbourn 23 yr old enlisted in Wilson Co 5/12/62 **WC 7/3**

Cpl. Haywood Scott 25 yr old enlisted in Wilson Co 4/19/62 K Wilderness ""gallantry"

Cpl. Sion Upchurch 29 yr old enlisted in Wilson Co 5/12/62 (later W-elbow Wilderness)

Private Richard Banks **C 7/14**

Private Caswell Barnes 41 yr old shoemaker enlisted Wilson Co.4/29/62 (later W-both legs Wilderness)

Private Enos Barnes 27 yr old enlisted Wilson Co.4/28/62 (later Corp)

Private William Barnes 38 yr old enlisted Wilson Co.2/14/63 **C 7/14**

Private Bryant Bass 50 yr old enlisted as substitute 1/26/63 (later W-groin Wilderness)

Private Larry Bass 17 yr old enlisted Wilson Co.1/26/63

Private James Bell 41 yr old enlisted Wilson Co.5/8/62 (later W Wilderness)

Private Amos Boyett 34 yr old enlisted Wilson Co.4/28/62 (later K Wilderness)

Private Enos Boyett 31 yr old enlisted Wilson Co.4/28/62 (later hospitalized 7/31/63)

Private Stephen Boyett 19 yr old enlisted Wilson Co.11/7/62 **W-back 7/3**

Private Daniel Campbell 28 yr old enlisted Wilson Co.5/2/62 (later W-shoulder Wilderness)

Private Henry R Davis 31 yr old enlisted Wilson Co.5/2/62 (later C Bristoe Station)

Private Leonard Dickinson 25 yr old enlisted Wilson Co.5/7/62 **WC 7/3**

Private Granberry Etheridge 24 yr old enlisted in Wilson Co 4/29/62 (later W-thigh Wilderness)

Private James Etheridge 27 yr old enlisted in Wilson Co 4/29/62

Private Justice Etheridge 20 yr old enlisted in Wilson Co 4/29/62 (later W-thigh Wilderness)

Private James Farrell 39 yr old enlisted in Wilson Co 12/19/62
Private Calvin Gardner 31 yr old enlisted in Wilson Co 4/26/62 (later W-shoulder Wilderness)
Private Jethro Harrison 35 yr old enlisted in Wilson Co 5/5/62
Private William Holland 19 yr old enlisted in Wilson Co 6/12/62 (later K Peeble's farm, Va)
Private Columbus Jones 24 yr old enlisted in Wilson Co 5/7/62
Private William Lamm 24 yr old enlisted in Wilson Co 5/5/62 **WC 7/14**
Private George Lane 21 yr old enlisted in Wilson Co 7/18/62
Private Henderson Love 26 yr old enlisted in Wilson Co 5/5/62 (later "gallantry at Globe Tavern")
Private James Mercer 23 yr old enlisted in Wilson Co 4/13/62 (later W-leg Petersburg)
Private John J Mercer 28 yr old enlisted in Wilson Co 7/2/62
Private John Moore 34 yr old enlisted in Wilson Co 4/29/62
Private Jacob Pearson 19 yr old enlisted in Wilson Co 4/29/62 (later musician)
Private Jackson Price 48 yr old enlisted in Wilson Co 12/15/62 **WC 7/14** Falling Waters
Private James Proctor 33 yr old bricklayer enlisted in Wilson Co 4/21/62 (later W-right shoulder Globe tavern)
Private Burkett Renfrow 22 yr old enlisted in Wilson Co 4/12/62 (died disease 11/64)
Private Elisha Scott 20 yr old enlisted in Wilson Co 4/29/62 (later W-shoulder Wilderness)
Private Alexander Smith 27 yr old enlisted in Wilson Co 4/19/62 (later W-shoulder Wilderness)
Private Willie Tomlinson 23 yr old enlisted in Wilson Co 5/5/62
Private Willis Watson 51 yr old enlisted in Wilson Co 7/28/62 (later W-ankle Wilderness)
Private Eli Williamson 18 yr old enlisted in Wilson Co 2/13/63 (later C Talley's Mill, Va)

Teamster James Stancill 24 yr old enlisted in Wilson Co 4/19/62 (detailed as wagon master & forager)
Teamster Eason Tomlinson 31 yr old enlisted in Wilson Co 5/2/62

July 1 Casualties

1st Sgt David Dew 30 yr old enlisted Wilson Co.5/14/62 **C 7/1**
Sgt. Augustus Barnes 28 yr old enlisted Wilson Co.4/29/62 **W-leg 7/1**
Sgt. John Hadley 19 yr old enlisted in Wilson Co 42/2/63 **WC 7/1**
Sgt. William Pearson 27 yr old enlisted in Wilson Co 4/29/62 **C 7/1**
Cpl. Henry Boswell 35 yr old enlisted Wilson Co.4/29/62 **W-left leg 7/1**
Cpl. Robert Pittman 23 yr old enlisted in Wilson Co 4/29/62 **C 7/1**
Private Duncan Adams 23 yr old enlisted Wilson Co.4/24/62 **W-head & both legs 7/1** (amp)
Private John Adams 25 yr old enlisted Wilson Co.4/24/62 **C 7/1** (later W Wilderness)
Private George Arquir 19 yr old enlisted Wilson Co.10/01/62 **C 7/1**

Private Issac Aycock 39 yr old enlisted Wayne Co 12/22/62 **W-head 7/1**
Private Jesse Aycock 38 yr old enlisted Wilson Co.12/19/62 **C 7/1**
Private Larry Barnes 25 yr old enlisted Wilson Co.4/28/62 **K 7/1**
Private Jesse Beaman 33 yr old carpenter enlisted Wilson Co.4/21/62 **C 7/1**
Private Jethro Boswell 24 yr old enlisted Wilson Co.4/29/62 **C 7/1**
Private Andrew Cook 31 yr old enlisted Wilson Co. 5/13/62 **C 7/1**
Private James Daniel enlisted Wilson Co 12/19/62 W-breast **C 7/1**
Private Henry Davis 38 yr old enlisted Wilson Co.12/19/62 **C 7/1**
Private Jonathan Davis 33 yr old enlisted Wilson Co.5/5/62 **C 7/1**
Private Edwin Etheridge 24 yr old enlisted Wilson Co.4/29/62 **W-groin 7/1**
Private Gabriel Farrell 35 yr old enlisted in Wilson Co 4/28/62 **W-right leg 7/1**
Private Granberry Farrell 19 yr old enlisted in Wilson Co 4/29/62 **W-leg 7/1** died 11/9
Private Nathaniel Hayes 33 yr old enlisted in Wilson Co. 5/13/62 **C 7/1**
Private John Hunt 23 yr old enlisted in Wilson Co 4/29/62 **W-neck C 7/1**
Private Henry Lucas 28 yr old enlisted in Wilson Co 4/12/62 **C 7/1**
Private Wright Pender 20 yr old enlisted in Wilson Co 5/5/62 **W-thigh 7/1** (later W Globe Tavern)
Private Calvin Raper 34 yr old enlisted in Wilson Co 5/2/62 **C 7/1**
Private Gordon Rountree 38 yr old enlisted in Wilson Co 2/12/63 **K 7/1**
Private Henry Scott 23 yr old enlisted in Wilson Co 4/29/62 **W-shoulder 7/1**
Private William Simpson 32 yr old enlisted in Wilson Co 5/12/62 **C 7/1**
Private Jacob Stancill 23 yr old enlisted in Wilson Co 5/2/62 **C 7/1**
Private Jesse Sullivan 20 yr old enlisted in Wilson Co 4/28/62 **C 7/1**
Private Josiah Thorn 24 yr old enlisted in Wilson Co 4/4/62 **W-right leg C 7/1**
Private Sanders Trevathan 32 yr old enlisted in Wilson Co 5/2/62 **W-groin 7/1**
Private Joseph Watson 35 yr old enlisted in Wilson Co 4/28/62 **WC 7/1**
Private Willie Williamson 33 yr old enlisted in Wilson Co 4/12/62 **W-breast 7/1**
Private Gray Woodward 35 yr old enlisted in Wilson Co 4/29/62 **K "opening minutes of battle" 7/1**

Company B "*Wilkes County*"

Captain George Gilreath 31 yr old enlisted Wilkes Co. 3/29/62 **K 7/3** commanding regiment
Captain John Peden transferred 11/25/62 promoted Captain 7/3 AM **W-head 7/3** (later W-hand Wilderness)
2nd Lt Hiram Greer 22 yr old enlisted Wilkes Co 5/19/62
3rd Lt Leander Gilbreath transferred 3/27/63 (later transferred to cavalry)
Sgt. Thomas Branch transferred 10/12/62
Sgt. Noah Gilreath 22 yr old enlisted Wilkes Co. 9/15/62 (later W thigh Wilderness)
Sgt. Ervin Higgins 29 yr old enlisted Wilkes Co 5/6/62 **W-head 7/3** (later W-right arm Wilderness)

Sgt. Elihu Lewis 26 yr old enlisted Wilkes Co 5/4/62 (later K Wilderness)
Corp. William Cockerham 28 yr old enlisted Wilkes Co 4/2/62 (later reduced in rank)
Cpl. James Sharp 32 yr old enlisted Wilkes Co 4/5/63 **C 7/14**
Private E. Anderson 30 yr old enlisted Wilkes Co 4/1/63 (later transferred CS Navy)
Private Jesse Anderson 39 yr old enlisted 4/14/62 (later K Glove Tavern)
Private Meredith Benge enlisted Wilkes Co K Wilderness
Private Samuel Benge 24 yr old enlisted 4/5/62 (later W-hand Wilderness "cited for gallantry")
Private Daniel Billings 25 yr old enlistyed Wilkes Co 3/12/63
Private John Bolin 34 yr old enlisted 4/5/63 **W-left hip C 7/3** (later W Globe Tavern)
Private John Brown 43 yr old enlisted 1862 **W-left hand 7/3**
Private Andrew Earp 35 yr old enlisted Wilkes Co 3/8/62 **C 7/14**
Private John Gregory 19 yr old enlisted Wilkes Co 3/18/62
Private Huander Higgins 23 yr old enlisted Wilkes Co 4/5/62 (later W-both thighs Wilderness)
Private William Love 24 yr old enlisted Wilkes Co 10/15/62
Private William McDonald Irish born enlisted Wilkes Co deserted 7/5 Cashtown, Pa
Private Winburn Minton enlisted Wilkes Co (later K Wilderness)
Private James Moore **C 7/14**
Private Riley Moore 21 yr old enlisted Wilkes Co 3/31/62 **C 7/14** (later joined US service)
Private James Pearson 24 yr old enlisted Wilkes Co 5/1/63 **C 7/3**
Private Israel Rash 22 yr old enlisted Wilkes Co 4/2/62 **W 7/3 C 7/5**
Private Leonidas St John 18 yr old substitute enlisted Wilkes Co 4/1/62 C Washington NC **K 7/14 Falling Waters**
Private Evan Shoemaker 35 yr old enlisted Wilkes Co 4/5/62 (later W Wilderness)
Private James A. Smith 23 yr old enlisted Wilkes Co 4/9/62 (later K 2/64)
Private Sidney Summerlin 33 yr old enlisted Wilkes Co 3/29/62

Teamster Henry Benge 29 yr old enlisted Wilkes Co 10/15/62

July 1 Casualties

Sgt. Edmund Greer 31 yr old enlisted Wilkes Co 3/22/62 **C 7/1**
Sgt Thomas Pearson 28 yr old enlisted Wilkes Co 4/24/62 **C 7/1**
Sgt Asa Rash 22 yr old enlisted Wilkes Co 10/15/62 **C 7/1**
Cpl. Thomas Bell 36 yr old enlisted Wilkes Co 3/8/62 **W-left arm & both thighs 7/1**
Private William Billings 18 yr old enlisted Wilkes Co 4/8/62 **W-left hip 7/1**
Private Willliam Bryant 29 yr old enlisted 10/23/62 **K 7/1**
Private Thomas Gregory 24 yr old enlisted Wilkes Co 3/19/62 **W-face 7/1**
Private Thomas Grutle 34 yr old enlisted Wilkes Co 5/5/62 **K 7/1**
Private John McNeill 29 yr old substitute enlisted Wilkes Co 10/10/62 **K 7/1**

Private David Marlow 19 yr old enlisted Wilkes Co 4/16/62 **K 7/1**
Private Elbert Marlow 25 yr old enlisted Wilkes Co 4/16/62 **W-hand 7/1** (later W Wilderness)
Private James Marlow 16 yr old enlisted Wilkes Co 4/25/63 **W-left arm C 7/1 (amp)**
Private Martin Marlow 18 yr old enlisted Wilkes Co 4/5/63 **W-arm 7/1**
Private Alfred Minton 35 yr old enlisted Wilkes Co 4/4/62 **W-arm & leg 7/1**
Private William pearson 34 yr old enlisted Wilkes Co 4/5/63 **K 7/1**
Private Franklin Privett 27 yr old enlisted Wilkes Co 4/2/62 **W-left knee C 7/1**
Private William Rose 18 yr old enlisted Wilkes Co 4/8/62 **W-left leg C 7/1**
Private David Sanders Irish born 21 yr old enlisted Wilkes Co 4/1/62 **C 7/1**
Private James Smith enlisted 10/4/62 as substitute **K 7/1**
Private William Wright 39 yr old enlisted Wilkes Co 10/9/62 **W-arm 7/1 (died 7/2)**

Company C *"Cleveland Grays"*

2nd Lt. Philip Elam 30 yr old Minster enlisted Cleveland Co. 3/29/62 **WC 7/3** (later W Globe Tavern)
3rd Lt. Thomas Falls 20 yr old clerk enlisted Cleveland Co. 3/29/62 **WC 7/3**
1st Sgt Aaron Beam 26 yr old transferred 3/29/62
Sgt. John Boggs 28 yr old enlisted Cleveland Co. 3/29/62 **W-both feet 7/3**
Sgt. Samuel Oates 32 yr old enlisted Cleveland Co. 3/29/62 **W-shoulder 7/3**
Sgt. Edward Lewis 34 yr old enlisted Cleveland Co. 3/29/62 (later WE-thigh Glove tavern)
Corp. Lewis McDonald 29 yr old enlisted Cleveland Co. 3/29/62
Private George Barrett 19 yr old enlisted 3/29/62 (later W-jaw Wilderness)
Private Joshua Beam 19 yr old enlisted Cleveland Co. 3/29/62 **W 7/3 C 7/5**
Private Rufus Beam 24 yr old enlisted Cleveland Co. 3/29/62 (later musician)
Private Jesse Blythe 26 yr old enlisted Cleveland Co. 11/4/62 **C 7/14**
Private William Bryant 21 yr old enlisted Cleveland Co. 10/28/62 (later W-hip Wilderness)
Private David Carpenter 33 yr old enlisted Cleveland Co. 3/29/62
Private John Carroll 19 yr old enlisted Cleveland Co. 3/29/62 **C 7/14**
Private Sylvester Cobb 18 yr old enlisted Cleveland Co. 3/29/62 (later K Wilderness)
Private David Elliot 19 yr old enlisted Cleveland Co. 3/29/62 **W-leg C 7/3**
Private Richard Eskridge enlisted Cleveland Co. 2/23/62 **W-right arm C 7/3**
Private A.N. Falls 19 yr old enlisted Cleveland Co. 11/15/62 **WC 7/3**
Private George Falls 19 yr old transferred 2/13/63 (later musician)
Private Aaron Froneberger 19 yr old enlisted Cleveland Co. 3/29/62 (later W-right forearm Wilderness)
Private Albert Gant 21 yr old enlisted Cleveland Co. 3/29/62 (later Sgt)
Private Simeon Gold 21 yr old enlisted Cleveland Co. 3/25/62 **K 7/3**
Private Farington Griffin 24 yr old enlisted Cleveland Co. 3/29/62 (hospitalized typhoid 8/31/63)

Private Eusibius Hendrick 20 yr old enlisted Cleveland Co. 3/29/62 **C 7/3**
Private Joseph Kistler 21 yr old enlisted Cleveland Co. 4/29/62 (hospitalized 8/3/63)
Private Jacob Lackey 36 yr old enlisted Cleveland Co. 3/29/62
Private J.L. Lattimer 19 yr old enlisted Cleveland Co. 3/18/63 **W-arm C 7/3**
Private William Lindsey 31 yr old enlisted Cleveland Co. 12/1/62
Private James Martin 21 yr old enlisted Cleveland Co. 3/29/62 **C 7/14** (later joined US Service)
Private Thomas Martin enlisted Cleveland Co. 3/29/62 **W-right arm 7/3** (later W-hip & right hand Wilderness)
Private Thomas Mitchum 33 yr old enlisted Cleveland Co.3/29/62 W-right arm Washington NC (later W-arm C Wilderness)
Private Abraham Mooney25 yr old enlisted Cleveland Co. 3/29/62
Private Jeremiah Morrison 18 yr old enlisted Cleveland Co. 6/7/62 **W-right leg 7/3**
Private James Moss 25 yr old enlisted Cleveland Co. 3/29/62 **W-left arm 7/3**
Private Thomas Sparrow enlisted Cleveland Co. 3/29/62 **C 7/5** as nurse for wounded
Private Hugh White 25 yr old enlisted Cleveland Co. 11/4/62
Private Michael White C Washington, NC **W 7/3 C 7/5**
Private William Williams 18 yr old enlisted Cleveland Co. 2/15/63 (hospitalized 5/64)
Private Moses Wilson 27 yr old enlisted Cleveland Co. 3/29/62 **C 7/14** Williamsport
Private Phillip Wilson 23 yr old enlisted Cleveland Co. 3/29/62 (later hospitalized 11/64)
Private Andersion Womack 20 yr old enlisted Cleveland Co. 3/29/62 (later W-arm Glove tavern)
Teamster Drury Goodson 19 yr old mechanic enlisted Cleveland Co. 3/29/62 (died typhoid 1/25/64)
Teamster Jacob Mooney 31 yr old enlisted Cleveland Co. 3/29/62 (later W-head Wilderness)
Teamster Newton Roach 21 yr old enlisted Cleveland Co. 3/29/62 **C 7/14**
Teamster S. Wilson 29 yr old enlisted Cleveland Co. 3/29/62

July 1 Casualties

Captain Edward Dixon 30 yr old enlisted Lincoln Co. 3/29/62 **WC 7/1**
1st Lt. George Bethel transferred 11/25/62 **C 7/1**
Sgt. William Brown 20 yr old enlisted Cleveland Co. 3/29/62 **WC 7/1**
Corp. John Eskridge enlisted Cleveland Co. 3/29/62 **C 7/1**
Corp. John Womack 23 yr old enlisted Cleveland Co. 3/29/62 **K 7/1**
Private James Brown 16 yr old enlisted Cleveland Co. 3/29/62 **W-left ankle 7/1 C 7/5**
Private Peter Carpenter 20 yr old enlisted Cleveland Co. 3/29/62 **C 7/1**
Private J.D. Costner 35 yr old enlisted Cleveland Co. 10/62 **C 7/1**

Private Joseph Crotts 26 yr old enlisted Cleveland Co. 3/29/62 **C 7/1**
Private George Crowder 19 yr old enlisted Cleveland Co. 3/29/62 **C 7/1**
Private John Crowder 21 yr old enlisted Cleveland Co. 3/29/62 **C 7/1**
Private George Davis 30 yr old enlisted Cleveland Co. 7/10/62 **W-left forearm C 7/1**
Private Crowell Digh 22 yr old enlisted Cleveland Co. 3/29/62 **C 7/1** died Point Lookout 10/63
Private Digh Crowel 21 yr old enlisted Cleveland Co. 3/29/62 **C 7/1**
Private John Gladden 27 yr old blacksmith enlisted Cleveland Co. 3/29/62 **K 7/1**
Private David Griffin 19 yr old enlisted Cleveland Co. 2/13/63 **W-shoulder C 7/1**
Private George Harden 19 yr old enlisted Cleveland Co. 5/6/62 **C 7/1** (later joined US Service)
Private Doctor Harmon 22 yr old enlisted Cleveland Co. 3/25/62 **C 7/1**
Private Jeremiah Heavener 19 yr old enlisted Cleveland Co. 5/15/62 **C 7/1**
Private J.D. Herner **C 7/1**
Private Levi Huffstetley 21 yr old enlisted Cleveland Co. 4/25/62 **W-leg 7/1 C 7/5**
Private J.M. Jones 26 yr old enlisted Cleveland Co. 5/15/62 **W-left arm 7/1**
Private Thomas Long 22 yr old enlisted Cleveland Co. 3/29/62 **C 7/1**
Private J.Z. Lowrence 18 yr old enlisted Cleveland Co. 2/13/63 **C 7/1** (later W—head Wilderness)
Private Reuben Martin 20 yr old enlisted Cleveland Co. 3/29/62 **C 7/1**
Private Neal Marion 20 yr old enlisted Cleveland Co. 7/10/62 **C 7/1**
Private J.F. Nowlin 44 yr old enlisted Cleveland Co. 6/1/62 **C 7/1**
Private James Oates 38 yr old enlisted Cleveland Co. 2/28/63 **W-shoulder 7/1** (later W Wilderness)
Private William Patterson 22 yr old enlisted Cleveland Co. 3/29/62 **W-shoulder 7/1** (later K Burgess Mill)
Private Henry Shitle 27 yr old enlisted Cleveland Co. 3/29/62 **C 7/1**
Private Monroe Simmons 18 yr old enlisted Cleveland Co. 3/29/62 **C 7/1**
Private Marcus Smith 17 yr old enlisted Cleveland Co. 3/29/62 **K 7/1**
Private James Spangler18 yr old enlisted Cleveland Co. 3/29/62 **C 7/1**
Private Crawford Spurlin 28 yr old tanner enlisted Cleveland Co. 3/29/62 **C 7/1**
Private William VanDyke 21 yr old enlisted Cleveland Co. 3/29/62 **C 7/1**
Private Franklin Warlick 19 yr old enlisted Cleveland Co. 2/13/63 **C 7/1** (later W-left ar Wilderness) amp.
Private Abram Weaver 21 yr old enlisted Cleveland Co. 3/29/62 **C 7/1** (later K Wilderness)
Private William Weaver **C 7/1**
Private Burrel White 21 yr old enlisted Cleveland Co. 3/29/62 **Missing 7/1 & 7/3**
Private Henry White 25 yr old enlisted Cleveland Co. 3/29/62 **W-left lung 7/1 died 8/8**
Private James White 19 yr old enlisted Cleveland Co. 3/29/62 **K 7/1**

Company D *"The Cleveland Farmers"*

1st Lt William Townes transferred 10/19/62 (commanded7/3 attack) (later W-breast Globe Tavern) died

1st Sgt. Romulus Randall 20 yr old enlisted Cleveland Co. 5/6/62 (later W-leg Wilderness)

Sgt B.H. Bridges 20 yr old enlisted Cleveland Co. 2/20/63 (later 1st Sgt)

Sgt. Burwell Blanton 27 yr old enlisted Cleveland Co. 5/12/62 (later K Wilderness)

Sgt. Thomas Green 31 yr old enlisted Cleveland Co. 5/6/62 C Washington, NC **C 7/14**

Corp. Benjamin Green 29 yr old enlisted Cleveland Co. 5/6/62 **C 7/5 with wounded (brother was surgeon**)

Corp. Charles Hamrick 29 yr old enlisted Cleveland Co. 5/6/62 (later W-arm Wilderness)

Corp. David Smith 31 yr old enlisted Cleveland Co. 3/26/62 (later W-hand Wilderness W-left knee Petersburg)

Private Peter Bean 28 yr old enlisted Cleveland Co. 5/12/62 **C 7/14**

Private Thomas Behcler 24 yr old enlisted Cleveland Co. 5/6/62 **C 7/14**

Private Jasper Blackwell 22 yr old enlisted Cleveland Co. 3/26/62 (hospitalized 8/3/63)

Private Andrew Bridges 19 yr old enlisted Cleveland Co. 5/6/62 (hospitalized 10/63 (later W-wrist Wilderness)

Private Isaac Bridges 29 yr old enlisted Cleveland Co. 3/26/62 (later W left Shoulder)

Private Marcus Carroll 30 yr old enlisted Cleveland Co. 3/26/62 (later W-hand WEilderness)

Private George Champion 24 yr old enlisted Cleveland Co. 5/29/62 **C 7/3** (later W Globe Tavern)

Private William Dickey 39 yr old substitute enlisted Cleveland Co. 3/26/62 (later K Wilderness)

Private M.L. Earls 23 yr old enlisted Cleveland Co 2/20/63 **W-hand 7/3**

Private William Gibson 38 yr old enlisted Cleveland Co. 2/20/63 (later K by sharpshooter Wilderness)

Private Drury Green 30 yr old enlisted Cleveland Co. 5/6/62

Private John Green 31 yr old enlisted Cleveland Co. 5/6/62 (later W-hand Wilderness)

Private John P. Green 29 yr old enlisted Cleveland Co. 5/12/62 (later W-left arm Wilderness)

Private Thomas Green Jr 26 yr old enlisted Cleveland Co. 5/6/62

Private Thomas Green Sr. 26 yr old enlisted Cleveland Co. 3/26/62

Private Aaron Hamrick 26 yr old enlisted Cleveland Co. 5/6/62 (later W—Glove Tavern)

Private Abram Hamrick 23 yr old enlisted Cleveland Co. 5/6/62 ***WC 7/3***

Private David Hamrick 34 yr old enlisted Cleveland Co. 5/6/62 ***W-left arm 7/3*** *(later W-left thigh Wilderness)*

Private David Hamrick Jr 20 yr old enlisted Cleveland Co. 2/20/63 ***K 7/3***

Private Elijah Hamrick 29 yr old enlisted Cleveland Co. 5/6/62 **W 7/3 C 7/5**

Private Gabriel Hamrick 23 yr old enlisted Cleveland Co. 5/6/62 (later W-left hip Petersburg)

Private Isaac Hamrick 24 yr old enlisted Cleveland Co. 5/6/62 ***C 7/14***

Private James Hamrick 29 yr old enlisted Cleveland Co. 5/26/62 ***K 7/3***

Private Oliver Hamrick enlisted 2/20/63 ***K 7/3***

Private William Harrill 35 yr old enlisted Cleveland Co. 2/20/63 hospitalized with rheumatism 7/16 (later W-head Wilderness)

Private William Hayes 20 yr old C 7/14 (later joined Us Service)

Private William Hendrick 29 yr old enlisted Cleveland Co. 5/26/62 (w-left leg Hatcher's Run—amp)

Private James Jenkins 25 yr old enlisted Cleveland Co. 5/6/62 (later W Burges Mill)

Private William Lovelace 29 yr old enlisted Cleveland Co. 5/6/62 **C 7/14**

Private Willis McKiney 27 yr old enlisted Cleveland Co. 5/6/62 ***K 7/14***

Private Berry McSwain enlisted Cleveland Co. 2/20/63 (later died disease 4/64)

Private Elijah McSwain 28 yr old enlisted Cleveland Co. 5/6/62

Private George McSwain 18 yr old enlisted Cleveland Co. 5/12/62 **W 7/3**

Private J.F. McSwain 21 yr old enlisted Cleveland Co. 2/20/63 ***W-left hand 7/3***

Private Oliver McSwain 19 yr old enlisted Cleveland Co. 5/12/62 ***C 7/14***

Private William Pruett 36 yr old enlisted Cleveland Co. 2/20/63 (hospitalized with ulcer of foot 7/16/63)

Private Wylie Pruett 30 yr old enlisted Cleveland Co. 5/13/62

Private James Ripley 38 yr old enlisted Cleveland Co. 2/20/62

Private Iredell Rollins 45 yr old enlisted Cleveland Co. 3/26/62

Private Jacob Runyan 27 yr old enlisted Cleveland Co. 3/26/62

Private Charles Smith 29 yr old enlisted Cleveland Co. 5/6/62

Private Hasiel Turner 21 yr old enlisted Cleveland Co. 5/6/62 (later hospitalized pneumonia 1/64)

Private Mastin Turner 20 yr old enlisted Cleveland Co. 5/6/62 (later Corp)

Teamster John Dellinger 35 yr old mechanic enlisted Cleveland Co. 5/12/62 (detailed as wheelwright)

Teamster Nero Hamrick 24 yr old enlisted Cleveland Co. 5/22/62 (later W Spotsylvania)

Teamster John Leinberger 28 yr old enlisted Cleveland Co. 5/12/62

Teamster Adolphus Runyan 33 yr old mechanic enlisted Cleveland Co. 3/26/62 (detailed as blacksmith)

Teamster John Sealy 37 yr old enlisted Cleveland Co. 3/26/62 **W-leg C 7/3 died**

Teamster Starling Weaver 25 yr old enlisted Cleveland Co. 3/26/62

Teamster John Weylie 30 yr old enlisted Cleveland Co. 3/26/62 (died typhoid fever 9/9/63)

Teamster Edward Yarboro 28 yr old enlisted Cleveland Co. 5/12/62 **W 7/3 C 7/7 Chambersburg** (later K Wilderness)

July 1 Casualties

Captain Silas Randall 33 yr old enlisted Cleveland Co. 3/29/62 **W-face C 7/1**

2nd Lt James Randall 27 yr old enlisted Cleveland Co 3/29/62 **W-face 7/1 C 7/5 Greencastle, Pa**

3rd Lt Joseph Cabaniss 24 yr old enlisted 3/26/62 **C 7/1**

Sgt. Lewis Smith 26 yr old enlisted Cleveland Co. 5/6/62 **W-hip & shoulder 7/1** (later W Wilderness)

Corp. David Dellinger 26 yr old enlisted Cleveland Co. 5/12/62 **C 7/1**

Corp. Joseph Green 29 yr old enlisted Cleveland Co. 5/6/62 **W-right hand 7/1**

Corp. James Runyan 26 yr old enlisted Cleveland Co. 5/6/62 **W-arm & side C 7/1 died 7/1**

Private Jacob Aderholt 33 yr old enlisted Cleveland Co. 3/26/62 **W-left leg C 7/1**

Private Charles Blanton 23 yr old enlisted Cleveland Co. 3/26/62 **W-right leg 7/1**

Private Hart Blanton 22 yr old enlisted Cleveland Co. 2/20/63 **C 7/1**

Private George Bowen 36 yr old enlisted Cleveland Co. 2/20/63 **C 7/1**

Private William Bryson 27 yr old enlisted 2/20/63 **C 7/1**

Private Richard Champion 20 yr old enlisted Cleveland Co. 5/6/62 **WC 7/1**

Private David Green 37 yr old enlisted Cleveland Co. 2/20/63 **W-abdomen C 7/1**

Private Reuben Green 22 yr old harness maker enlisted Cleveland Co. 5/6/62 **W-thigh C 7/1**

Private Zachariah Green 22 yr old enlisted Cleveland Co. 512/62 **W-hip 7/1**

Private Andrew Hamrick 30 yr old enlisted Cleveland Co. 5/12/62 ***W-foot 7/1***

Private Jerome Lankford 19 yr old enlisted Cleveland Co. 5/6/62 **C 7/1**

Private William Ledbetter 31 yr old enlisted Cleveland Co. 5/12/62 **K 7/1**

Private Samuel Ledford 35 yr old enlisted Cleveland Co. 5/6/62 **K 7/1**

Private Willis Lovelace 19 yr old enlisted Cleveland Co. 5/6/62 **C 7/1**

Private Doctor McSwain 19 yr old enlisted Cleveland Co. 5/6/62 **W-shoulder C 7/1**

Private Abraham Martin 21 yr old enlisted Cleveland Co. 2/20/63 **C 7/1**

Private George Mooney 19 yr old enlisted Cleveland Co. 3/26/62 **C 7/1**

Private Able Postin 36 yr old enlisted Cleveland Co. 2/20/63 **W-arm 7/1**

Private Miller Randall 32 yr old enlisted Cleveland Co. 3/6/62 **W-face 7/1** (later "gallantry" at Wilderness)

Private John Shitle 21 yr old enlisted Cleveland Co. 2/20/63 **W-side 7/1 C 7/5 Greencastle**

Private E.H. Wasson 20 yr old enlisted Cleveland Co. 2/20/63 **W-both thighs 7/1**

Private Lewis Weaver 22 yr old enlisted Cleveland Co. 3/26/62 **C 7/1** (later W-face Wilderness)

Company E *"Pitt County"*

Captain James S. Whitehead 26 yr old enlisted Pitt Co 4/1/62 **W-head & hand 7/3 C 7/5** Greencastle, Pa (later Major)

1st Lt James Hanraham 32 yr old enlisted Pitt Co. 4/1/62 **WC 7/14**
2nd Lt William Wilson 31 enlisted Pitt Co 4/30/62 **K 7/3**
3rd Lt Godfrey Taft 27 yr old enlisted Pitt Co. (hospitalized 11/63)
Sgt. John Hellen enlisted Pitt Co 4/2/62 (later W-left ankle Wilderness)
Sgt. J.Augustus. Whitley 21 yr old enlisted Pitt Co. 6/1/62 **K 7/3**
Corp. Elihu Braddy 25 yr old enlisted Pitt Co. 4/18/62 (later W-knee Wilderness)
Corp. Robert Ricks 27 yr old enlisted Pitt Co. 5/10/62 (later W-face & neck C Talley's Mill, Va)
Private Jesse Adams transferred 10/29/62
Private Henry Barnhill 28 yr old enlisted Pitt Co. 5/12/62 (later K Talley's Mill)
Private Francis Bernard 27 yr old enlisted Pitt Co 7/8/62 (later musician)
Private John Bernard 32 yr old enlisted 7/8/62 (later musician)
Private Joseph Braddy 35 yr old enlisted Pitt Co. 4/18/62 (later W-left arm Wilderness W Burgess Mill)
Private John Brown 23 yr old enlisted Pitt Co. 5/5/62 **W-left knee 7/3** (later W-left thigh Wildernes)
Private William Bullock transferred 4/6/62 (detached service)
Private John Cannon 22 yr old enlisted Pitt Co. 4/18/62 "captured 11 prisoners 7/1" **W-knee 7/3**
Private Alfred Carney enlisted 5/9/62 as substitute (later W-arm, Wilderness)
Private John Corbitt 25 yr old enlisted Pitt Co. 7/25/62 **W-arm 7/3**
Private Dennis Skelton 22 yr old turpentiner enlisted Pitt Co. 8/22/62
Private Simon Everett 21 yr old enlisted Pitt Co. 5/12/62 **K 7/3**
Private Kenneth Fleming 40 yr old enlisted Pitt Co. 7/8/62
Private John Gaskins 26 yr old enlisted Pitt Co. 4/30/62 (later W-left leg Wilderness)
Private Willie Gurganus 35 yr old enlisted Pitt Co. 4/23/62 (later K Glove Tavern "cited for gallantry")
Private James Horton 26 yr old mechanic enlisted Pitt Co. 4/30/62 **WC 7/3**
Private Richard Pollard 24 yr old enlisted Pitt Co. 4/17/62 (later W-neck Wilderness)
Private Charles Randolph 35 yr old enlisted Pitt Co. 4/28/62 (later W left side Wilderness)
Private Franklin Rogers enlisted Martin Co. 3/20/62
Private R.W. Smith 25 yr old enlisted Pitt Co. 7/8/62 (later detailed Pioneer Corps)
Private Allen Taft 33 yr old merchant enlisted Pitt Co. 7/8/62 (later musician)
Private William Taylor 20 yr old enlisted Pitt Co. 4/2/62 **W-abdomen C 7/3** (died)
Private Benjamin Teel 46 yr old enlisted Pitt Co. 4/28/62 (later W-left foot Wilderness)
Private James Teel 31 yr old enlisted Pitt Co. 4/14/62 **K 7/3**
Private Lemuel Tyson 18 yr old enlisted Pitt Co. 4/23/62 (later W-finger Globe Tavern)
Private Seth Tyson 21 yr old enlisted Pitt Co. 4/30/62 (later W-left hand Globe Tavern)
Private Lawrence White 29 yr old enlisted Pitt Co. 4/30/62 (later hospital guard)
Private Benjamin Whitehurst 27 yr old enlisted Pitt Co. 4/12/62

Chief Musician enlisted Pitt Co. 3/20/62 (appointed drum major 1862)

Musician William Horne 4/30/62 (detailed to regimental band)
Musician Jacob Ellington 41 yr old enlisted Pitt Co. 4/16/62
Musician Burton Summerell 20 yr old enlisted Pitt Co. 4/2/62 (detailed as musician)
Musician Henry Turnage 20 yr old enlisted Pitt Co. 4/15/62 (detailed to regimental band)
Musician Archibald Tyson 23 yr old enlisted Pitt Co. 9/9/62 **C 7/5** as nurse for wounded
Teamster John Worthington 27 yr old enlisted Pitt Co. 7/8/62

7/1 Casualties

Sgt. James B. Everett 23 yr old enlisted Martin Co 3/62 **C 7/1**
Sgt. Marlin Galloway enlisted Pitt Co. 4/30/62 W-head & arm Washington NC **W-leg C 7/1** (later 1st Lt)
Corp. James Cason 29 yr old enlisted Pitt Co. 5/1/62 **W-shoulder C 7/1** (later W-breast Wilderness)
Corp. James Fleming 28 yr old enlisted Pitt Co. 4/27/62 **C 7/1**
Corp. John Wilson enlisted 3/30/62 **C 7/1**
Private James Bullock 27 yr old enlisted Pitt Co. 4/14/62 **W-breast 7/1** (later W-thigh Wilderness)
Private James J. Bullock 27 yr old enlisted Pitt Co. 5/12/62 **W-right ankle 7/1**
Private McGilbra Cherry 24 yr old enlisted Pitt Co. 4/16/62 **W-right leg 7/1**
Private Joseph Dixon 25 yr old enlisted Pitt Co. 4/28/62 **W-arm 7/1**
Private William Bryan 33 yr old enlisted Pitt Co. 4/1/62 **W-left knee 7/1**
Private John Dudley 31 yr old enlisted Pitt Co. 7/8/62 **C 7/1 C 7/6 Greencastle**
Private William Dudley 31 yr old enlisted Pitt Co. 4/22/62 **W-breast C 7/1**
Private J.J. Edwards 20 yr old enlisted Pitt Co. 7/28/62 **W 7/1 C 7/6 Funkstown, Md** (Died 8/9 Williamsport)
Private James Edwards 19 yr old enlisted Pitt Co. 4/28/62 **W-neck 7/1**
Private William Edwards 20 yr old enlisted Pitt Co. 7/25/62 **C 7/1**
Private James L. Everett 23 yr old enlisted Pitt Co. 5/12/62 **K 7/1**
Private Wyatt Forbes 20 yr old enlisted Pitt Co. 5/5/62 **W-leg C 7/1** (amp) died 8/10 Chester hospital buried PNC
Private William Gardner 23 yr old enlisted Pitt Co. 4/23/62 **W-arm 7/1** (later W-thigh C Wilderness)
Private Henry Manning 20 yr old enlisted Pitt Co. 5/9/62 **W 7/1**
Private Jesse Manning 24 yr old enlisted Pitt Co. 4/7/62 **WC 7/1**
Private John Mills Jr. mason enlisted Pitt Co 3/20/62 **C 7/1**
Private John Mills Sr. 26 yr old enlisted Pitt Co. 7/25/62 **C 7/1**
Private Cicero Smith 26 yr old enlisted Pitt Co. 7/15/62 **W C 7/1** (later W-arm Wilderness
Private Joshua Tucker 18 yr old enlisted Pitt Co. 4/18/62 **WC 7/1** (later W-leg Globe Tavern)
Private McGilbra White 25 yr old enlisted Pitt Co. 5/12/62 **WC 7/1** (later W Tally's Mill, Va)

Private Jesse Woolard 24 yr old carpenter enlisted Pitt Co. 4/14/62 **W-left leg 7/1** (later Corp & Sgt)
Private Oscar Wooten 20 yr old enlisted Pitt Co. 4/30/62 **WC 7/1** (died 9/22)

Company F *"South Mountain Rangers"*

Captain Peter M. Mull absent W from head & lung at Washington, NC battle
1st Lt. Joseph Hoyle 25 yr old teacher enlisted Cleveland Co. 5/10/62 (hospitalized with fever 8/3/63)
2nd Lt. Peter P Mull 32 yr old tanner enlisted Burke Co 5/1/62 **W-right thigh C 7/3**
3rd Lt. Archibald Williams transferred 11/6/62 W-head 7/3 (later W-right hand Petersburg)
Sgt. Westley Williams enlisted Cleveland Co 5/31/62 "commended for leadership at Suffolk, Va"
Sgt. James Willis 34 yr old enlisted Cleveland Co. 4/24/62 (later W-side Globe Tavern)
Corp. Andrew Warlick 29 yr old enlisted Cleveland Co. 5/10/62 hospitalized 9/63 (later Sgt)
Private William Bigham 19 yr old enlisted Cleveland Co. 4/19/62 **W 7/3 C 7/4** (joined US service)
Private William Boyles 23 yr old enlisted Cleveland Co. 4/22/62 **W 7/3** (later K Petersburg)
Private Sidney Bradshaw 36 yr old enlisted Cleveland Co. 2/2/63 (died typhoid 8/22/63)
Private David Buff 23 yr old enlisted Cleveland Co. 2/10/63 (later W Wilderness)
Private Phillip Buff 19 yr old enlisted Cleveland Co. 2/10/63 (later W-right shoulder Wilderness)
Private Massenburg Burton 25 yr old enlisted Cleveland Co. 5/29/62 **WC 7/3**
Private Joseph Canipe 33 yr old enlisted Cleveland Co. 5/13/62 (later W-hip Wilderness)
Private Harrison Cook 18 yr old enlisted Cleveland Co. 2/25/63 **W-wrist 7/3**
Private Jesse Cook 31 yr old enlisted Cleveland Co. 4/19/62 (later K Tally's Mill, Va)
Private James Goodson 20 yr old enlisted Cleveland Co. 5/10/62 **W-hip C 7/3**
Private William Hicks 19 yr old enlisted Cleveland Co. 2/12/63
Private Eli Hoyle 57 yr old enlisted as substitute Cleveland Co. 4/19/62 (later W Bristoe Station discharged 3/64)
Private John Hudson 38 yr old enlisted Cleveland Co. 3/1/62
Private Allen Johnson 23 yr old enlisted Cleveland Co. 4/19/62 **W 7/3 C 7/5** (later joined US Service)
Private Ezra Mull 35 yr old enlisted Cleveland Co. 4/24/62 (detailed as recruiter 1864)
Private John Mull 33 yr old enlisted Cleveland Co. 5/3/62 (later C Wilderness)
Private Alfred Newton 27 yr old enlisted Cleveland Co. 4/24/62 **W 7/3**
Private Alfred Peeler 38 yr old enlisted Cleveland Co. 2/27/63
Private Joseph Prewit 30 yr old enlisted Cleveland Co. 2/12/63
Private Anderson Self 36 yr old enlisted Cleveland Co. 2/19/62 ***W-thigh 7/3***
Private Anderson Self 36 yr old enlisted Cleveland Co. 2/19/62 ***W-left thigh C 7/3*** *(later W-foot Wilderness)*

Private Robert Self 22 yr old enlisted Cleveland Co. 5/3/62
Private Rufus Self 19 yr old enlisted Cleveland Co. 10/7/62 **W-right hand 7/3**
Private Daniel Shuford 27 yr old enlisted Cleveland Co. 4/19/62 **C 7/14**
Private Peter Shuford 25 yr old enlisted Cleveland Co. 5/3/62 (later W-arm Wilderness W-forehead Globe Tavern)
Private James Stamley 44 yr old enlisted Cleveland Co. 4/22/62 **C 7/14**
Private Henry Willis transferred 2/17/63 (later W Petersburg)
Private Levi Wise 36 yr old enlisted Cleveland Co. 4/24/62 **K 7/14 Falling Waters**

Teamster Miles Goodson 17 yr old enlisted Cleveland Co. 4/19/62 (discharged 10/63)
Teamster Andrew McClurd 22 yr old enlisted Cleveland Co. 5/3/62 (later W-right leg Wilderness)
Teamster Wade McClurd 23 yr old enlisted Cleveland Co. 4/19/62 (detailed as blacksmith)
Ambulance Driver William Williams 29 yr old enlisted Cleveland Co. 5/10/62 (later W-shoulder Wilderness)

7/1 Casualties

1st Sgt John Cline 31 yr old enlisted Cleveland Co. 4/19/62 **C 7/1** (later W Spotsylvania)
Sgt. Issac Self 21 yr old enlisted Cleveland Co. 4/19/62 C 7/1
Corp. Albert Ivester 19 yr old enlisted Cleveland Co. 4/22/62 **C 7/1** (later Sgt)
Corp. Stepeh White 27 yr old enlisted Cleveland Co. 4/24/62 **C 7/1**
Private Peter Bivens 21 yr old enlisted Cleveland Co. 4/22/62 **C 7/1**
Private Williamson Brackett 19 yr old enlisted Cleveland Co. 4/19/62 **K 7/1**
Private Wesley Brendle 21 yr old enlisted Cleveland Co. 5/13/62 **C 7/1**
Private David Bumgarner 19 yr old enlisted Cleveland Co. 4/19/62 **C 7/1**
Private Daniel Canipe 28 yr old enlisted Cleveland Co. 5/13/62 **W-breast C 7/1**
Private John Canipe 28 yr old enlisted Cleveland Co. 4/19/62 **W-jaw 7/1**
Private Noah Canipe 19 yr old enlisted Cleveland Co. 5/13/62 **C 7/1**
Private Aaron Cook 19 yr old enlisted Cleveland Co. 5/3/62 **W-leg 7/1** (later detailed teamster)
Private William Craig 41 yr old enlisted Cleveland Co. 4/19/62 **C 7/1** (later W-face Petersburg)
Private William Elmore 27 yr old enlisted Cleveland Co. 4/19/62 **C 7/1** (later joined US service)
Private Joel Hoyle 23 yr old enlisted Cleveland Co. 4/19/62 detailed as Corp teamster—reduced to private **C 7/1**
Private Solomon Hoyle 25 yr old enlisted Cleveland Co. 5/10/62 **C 7/1**
Private Peter Lail 19 yr old enlisted Cleveland Co. 2/9/63 **C 7/1**
Private Jonathan McNeely 29 yr old substitute enlisted Cleveland Co. 5/3/62 **W-shoulder 7/1**
Private Samuel McNeily 41 yr old enlisted Cleveland Co. 4/19/62 **W-breast 7/1**

Private Eli Newton former 3rd Lt reenlisted 11/6/62 **W-arm 7/1**
Private Henry Norman 27 yr old enlisted Cleveland Co. 5/10/62 **W-groin & left arm 7/1** (later W Wilderness)
Private Robert Norman 31 yr old enlisted Cleveland Co. 5/13/62 **C 7/1**
Private William Seagle 19 yr old enlisted Cleveland Co. 4/22/62 **C 7/1**
Private William Self 22 yr old enlisted Cleveland Co. 4/24/62 **K 7/1**
Private John Smith 36 yr old enlisted Cleveland Co. 5/10/62 **W-hand 7/1**
Private John Swink 25 yr old enlisted Cleveland Co. 2/9/63 **C 7/1**
Private William Swink 22 yr old enlisted Cleveland Co. 2/9/63 **WC 7/1**
Private Robert Swofford 18 yr old enlisted Cleveland Co. 5/13/62 **K 7/1**
Private David Turner 35 yr old enlisted Cleveland Co. 2/23/63 **C 7/1**
Private Noah Warlick 23 yr old enlisted Cleveland Co. 5/10/62 **C 7/1**
Private Robert Willis 23 yr old enlisted Cleveland Co 4/19/62 ***C 7/1***
Private Samuel Willis 27 yr old enlisted Cleveland Co. 5/10/62 ***C 7/1***
Private Thomas Willis 21 yr old enlisted Cleveland Co. 5/10/62 ***K 7/1***

Company G *"North Carolina Rebels"*

1st Lt. Narcus Stevens 25 yr old enlisted Wayne Co. 5/1/62 (later K Burgess Mill, Va)
3rd Lt. Charles Jones enlisted 10/6/62 served as acting Adjt 8/63 (later 1st Lt)
Corp. James Best 19 yr old enlisted Wayne Co. 5/15/62 (later W-arm Wilderness)
Corp. Waitman Martin 24 yr old enlisted Wayne Co. 5/3/62 (hospitalized 9/2/63 typhoid fever)
Corp. Elezar Rich 33 yr old enlisted Wayne Co. 8/25/62 (later Sgt & 1st Sgt W-right arm Wilderness
Private William Fields 48 yr old enlisted Johnston Co. 5/14/62 **C 7/14**
Private William Grantham 21 yr old enlisted Wayne Co. 5/15/62 (later K Globe Tavern)
Private Stephen Morris 23 yr old enlisted Johnston Co. 5/3/62
Private John Powell 28 yr old enlisted Wayne Co. 2/28/63 (later K Glove Tavern—cited for "gallantry")
Private William Price 21 yr old enlisted Wayne Co. 5/1/62 C Washington NC
Private James Reeves 34 yr old enlisted Wayne Co. 2/28/63 **W 7/3 C 7/5** caring for wounded
Private Ryal Roberts 34 yr old enlisted Wake Co. 5/16/62 (died 11/7/63)
Private Henry Sasser 25 yr old enlisted Johnston Co 5/1/62 (sick 9/21/63)
Private Elisha Uzzell 29 yr old enlisted Wayne Co. 5/15/62 **W 7/3 died 7/21**

Teamster William Blackman 35 yr old enlisted Johnston Co. 5/1/62 (later W-left leg Wilderness)
Teamster Young Lee 24 yr old mechanic enlisted Johnston Co. 5/1/62 (later W-shoulder C Wilderness)

Teamster James Strickland 28 yr old mechanic enlisted Wayne Co. 5/6/62 (later court-martialed 12/63)
Teamster Pearsall 25 yr old enlisted Wayne Co. 5/3/62 Teamster 7&8/63 (later K Cold Harbor
Musician Eugene Geauffretean 25 yr old substitute enlisted Petersburg, Va (Chief Bugler)

July 1 Casualties

Captain Walter Whitted 28 yr old enlisted Wayne Co. 7/162 **W-face & left leg 7/1**
2nd Lt. Mordecal Lee 31 yr old enlisted Johnston Cop. 5/3/62 **K 7/1**
1st Sgt John Peacock 23 yr old enlisted Wayne Co. 5/3/62 **WC 7/1**
Sgt. Marshall Grantham enlisted Wayne Co. 5/10/62 **C 7/1**
Sgt.Adam Summerlin 23 yr old enlisted Wayne Co. 5/1/62 **W-left arm C 7/1 (amp)**
Corp. Lemuel Budd 28 yr old enlisted Wayne Co. 4/3/62 **C 7/1**
Corp. Bryant Ingram 24 yr old enlisted Johnston Co. 5/1/62 W-both thighs C Washington, NC **C 7/1**
Private Charles Benson 21 yr old enlisted Johnston Co. 5/15/62 **KW-arm & hip 7/1**
Private Fountain Bizzell 27 yr old enlisted Johnston Co. 5/15/62 **W 7/1**
Private John Brock 25 yr old enlisted Wayne Co. 5/1/62 **C 7/1**
Private John Chance 34 yr old enlisted Johnston Co. 4/3/62 **W-arm 7/1** (later W-left leg Wilderness)
Private John Cole 19 yr old enlisted Johnston Co. 12/15/62 ***W 7/1 C 7/5*** *(later C Wilderness)*
Private Thomas Cole 22 yr old enlisted Johnston Co. 4/3/62 **W-right lung & side C 7/1**
Private Calvin Dail 32 yr old enlisted Wayne Co. 2/28/63 **C 7/1**
Private William Darden 25 yr old enlisted Wayne Co. 5/15/62 **C 7/1**
Private John Faircloth 54 yr old enlisted Johnston Co 2/28/63 ***W-arm 7/1*** *(died 7/13)*
Private Stephen Faircloth 22 yr old enlisted Johnston Co. 5/18/62 ***W-hip 7/1*** *(later W-left hand Petersburg)*
Private William Faircloth 20 yr old enlisted Johnston Co. 5/8/62 ***W-head C 7/1***
Private Jesse Garris 9 yr old enlisted Wayne Co. 5/1/62 **W-thigh C 7/1** (later K Wilderness)
Private John Garris 33 yr old enlisted Wayne Co. 5/1/62 **C 7/1** (later W-chin Wilderness)
Private Hazy Goodson 27 yr old enlisted Wayne Co. 5/12/62 **C 7/1**
Private William Holloman 21 yr old enlisted Johnston Co. 5/1/62 **WC 7/1**
Private John Hood 19 yr old enlisted Wayne Co. 4/3/62 **C 7/1**
Private Abner Ingram 33 yr old enlisted Wayne Co. 4/9/62 **C 7/1**
Private John Ingram 29 yr old enlisted Johnston Co. 4/3/62 **C 7/1** (later C Wilderness)
Private Lovett Lee 26 yr old enlisted Johnston Co. 5/1/62 **C 7/14**
Private William lewis enlisted 7/62 **C 7/1**
Private Josiah McClenny 20 yr old enlisted 2/28/63 **K 7/1**
Private Lewis Martin 28 yr old enlisted Wayne Co. 5/3/62 **C 7/1**
Private Junius Outlaw 18 yr old enlisted Wayne Co. 5/1/62 **WC 7/1**

Private George Price 18 yr old enlisted Wayne Co. 4/3/62 C Washington, NC ***K 7/1***
Private Jesse Price 28 yr old enlisted Wayne Co. 4/3/62 ***C 7/1***
Private Levan Price 23 yr old enlisted Wayne Co. 5/10/62 ***W-foot 7/1*** *(later C Wilderness)*
Private W. Henry Price 26 yr old enlisted Wayne Co. 5/10/62 ***WC 7/1 died 7/28***
Private James Smith 26 yr old enlisted Wayne Co. 5/10/62 **C 7/1**
Private James Strickland 26 yr old enlisted Johnston Co. 5/1/62 ***C 7/1***
Private John Strickland 25 yr old enlisted Johnston Co. 5/1/62 ***C 7/1***
Private John Summerlin 43 yr old substitute enlisted Wayne Co. 5/1/62 **WC 7/1 died**
Private Josiah Thompson 28 yr old enlisted Wayne Co. 5/1/62 **C 7/1**
Private Major Williams 23 yr old enlisted Wayne Co. 5/6/62 **K 7/1**
Private John Woodall 21 yr old enlisted Wayne Co. 9/15/62 **W-left ankle 7/1** (later W-face Globe tavern)

Company H *"The Archer Boys*

Captain Edward Fletcher Satterfield appointed captain 3/10/63 **K 7/3**
3rd Lt William Holt former Sgt major promoted 5/8/63 W-left arm **C 7/3**
1st Sgt John Ellis transferred from 7th NC June 62 (later W Bristoe)
Sgt John Austin 32 yr old Burke Co farmer enlisted 4/3/62 **C 7/3**
Sgt Joseph Benfield 21 yr old Burke Co farmer enlisted 4/3/62 (later W Wilderness)
Sgt William Mullis 26 yr old Wilkes Co. farmer enlisted5/13/62
Sgt. Jesse Swinson 30 yr old Onslow Co. farmer enlisted 3/10/62 **C 7/14 Williamsport**
Cpl. John Grey enlisted 6/28/62 as substitute (deserted 10/63)
Cpl. William Hollar 25 yr old Alexander Co farmer enlisted 5/1/63 (discharged 7/20/63)
Cpl. Alexander Palmer enlisted at age 30 7/23/62 (later K Wilderness)
Private Michael Baker 31 yr old Wake Co farmer enlisted 10/11/62 (later WC Wilderness)
Private Abraham Bolick 26 yr old Alexander Co farmer enlisted 9/1/62
Private Alexander Bolick 40 yr old Alexander Co. farmer enlisted 4/3/62 (later W Wilderness)
Private John Davidson 29 yr old enlisted 12/1/62 **C 7/14**
Private Joseph Hayes 33 yr old enlisted 10/15/62 (later K-Wilderness)
Private Thomas Isenhower 25 yr old Caldwell Co farmer enlisted 4/3/62
Private Alfred Jolly 25 yr old Alexander Co.laborer enlisted 4/3/62 **W-left knee 7/3**
Private Daniel Kever 29 yr old Iredell Co farmer enlisted 1/22/62 **W-7/3** (later W-Wildernes/Globe Tavern)
Private Noah Logan 19 yr old Alexander Co farmer enlisted 7/23/62 (later W-Wilderness)
Private Andrew McGee 34 yr old Wilkes Co farmer enlisted 4/3/62 (later awarded at Wilderness)
Private Patrick McLain enlisted 1862 **C 7/14**
Private Washington Merritt enlisted at age 18 on 10/15/62 **K 7/14**

Private John Milstead 22 yr old Alexander C farmer enlisted 7/23/62 **W-knee 7/3**
Private McLane Padgett 34 yr old Onslow Co. cooper enlisted 3/29/62 **C 7/14**
Private Samuel Padgett 34 yr old Onslow Co. cooper enlisted 3/27/62 (later W-Wilderness)
Private Leander Price 23 yr old Burke Co farmer enlisted 4/3/62 (later W-Wilderness)
Private Curtis Simpson 18 yr old Craven Co. farmer enlisted 3/27/62 (later WC Sutherland Station)
Private James Starnes 19 yr old Caldwell Co. farmer enlisted 4/2/62 **W-back 7/3** (Later W-Wildernesss)
Private Wright Waller 27 yr old Onslow Co. farmer 4/24/62 (later teamster)
Private J.D. Williams 33 year old enlisted Onslow Co. 10/15/62 (saw Satterfield killed on slope)
Private Zachariah Winsett 28 yr old Jones Co. farmer enlisted 5/12/62 **W-right leg 7/3**

Teamster John Mullis 27 yr old Wilkes Co. farmer enlisted 4/5/62

July 1 Casualties

1st Lt. Nicholas Lillington Yadkin Co farmer appointed 1st Lt 3/10/63 W Sufflok, Va **W-thigh 7/1**
2nd Lt Benjamin Blount appointed 5/8/63 **C 7/1**
Sgt Michael Bebber 223 yr old Alexander Co farmer enlisted 4/10/62 **C 7/1**
Cpl. Abraham Autaway 27 yr old Onslow Co farm laborer enlisted 4/23/62 **W-face C 7/1**
Cpl.William Manning 19 yr old Duplin Co. farmer enlisted 4/7/62 **C 7/1**
Private John Baker 31 yr old Iredell Co farmer enlisted 4/3/62 **W 7/1**
Private Daniel Boan 36 yr old Duplin Co farmer enlisted 3/3/62 **C 7/1**
Private Solomon Dison 53 yr old Burke Co farmer enlisted 4/12/62 **W-arm C 7/1**
Private Lewis Gurganus 23 yr old Wake Co farmer enlisted 10/15/62 **C 7/1**
Private Amos Jones 33 yr old Duplin Co. farmer enlisted 5/12/62 **W-head C 7/1**
Private Alexander Matheson 21 yr old Alexander Co tobacconist enlisted 4/5/62 **C 7/1**
Private Eli Matheson 18 yr old Iredell Co farmer enlisted 4/3/62 **K 7/1**
Private Jerre Meadows 25 yr old Onslow Co. farmer enlisted 4/23/62 **C 7/1**
Private Philetus Moore 27 yr old Lincoln Co. farmer enlisted 4/3/62 **C 7/1**
Private Henry Otrich 21 yr old Iredell Co. farmer enlisted 4/3/62 **K 7/1**
Private Thomas Payne 18 yr old Alexander Co farmer enlisted 4/3/62 **C 7/1**
Private Benjamin Pearce 33 yr old Carteret Co farmer enlisted 3/23, 62 **C 7/1**
Private John Phipps 33 yr old Guilford Co mason enlisted 10/15/62 **C 7/1**
Private Michael Rawls 23 yr old Onslow Co laborer enlisted 10/15/62 **C 7/1**
Private Columbus Rector 26 yr old enlisted 10/15/62 **C 7/1**
Private Thomas Simpson 21 yr old Craven Co. farmer enlisted 3/27/62 **C 7/1**
Private Benjamin Sweet 20 yr old Iredell Co. laborer enlisted 4/19/62 as substitute **C 7/1**

Company I *"The Franklin Farmers"*

1st Lt. Charles Cooke 19 yr old Franklin Co student enlisted 5/12/62

1st Sgt Thomas Bragg 30 yr old Granville Co farmer enlisted 5/10/62 (later W Wilderness)

Sgt Shemuel Blackley 22 yr old Granville farmer enlisted 5/12/62 **W 7/3** (with negro servant)

Sgt Jesse Griffin 33 yr old Wake Co tenant farmer enlisted 5/10/62 **W 7/3** (later W Wilderness)

Cpl. Burgess Catlett Granville Co Catlett enlisted 10/10/62 **W-left arm C 7/14 hospitalized Williamsport**

Cpl. Leonidas Dent 26 yr old Granville Co mechanic enlisted 5/10/62 (later W Wilderness)

Private Atlas Allen 23 yr old Granville Co farmer (later Ambulance driver W Bristoe/Wilderness)

Private Benjamin Catlett 33 yr old Granville Co tobacconist enlisted 5/12/62 **C 7/3**

Private Sylvester Catlett 18 yr old Granville Co farmer enlisted 6/8/63 **W-right thigh C 7/3**

Private William Cleland 29 yr old Orange Co Texas farmer enlisted 1/163 as substitute (later musician)

Private Redin Davis 33 yr old Wilson Co farmer enlisted 10/25/62

Private George Evans 35 yr old **C 7/14**

Private Alsey Felce 41 yr old Franklin Co substitute 6/10/62 **K 7/3**

Private Howell Griffin34 yr old Franklin Co shoemaker enlisted 7/17/62

Private Richard Griffin 29 yr old Wake Co farmer enlisted 7/14/62 (later W Glove Tavern)

Private William Harp 24 yr old Granville farmer enlisted 2/16/63 (later W Wilderness)

Private William Holmes 18 yr old Franklin Co farmer enlisted 5/10/62

Private James Inscoe 18 yr old enlisted 2/9/63 **C 7/14**

Private Minton Jones 29 yr old Wake Co farmer enlisted 5/12/62

Private Richard Levister 37 yr old enlisted Franklin Co 2/11/63 (hospitalized 11/63)

Private Benjamin Mason 24 yr old enlisted Granville Co 5/10/62 **W-leg 7/14** (later W-arm Wilderness)

Private Nathan May 37 yr old enlisted Franklin Co 2/10/63 (hospitalized 11/63)

Private Thomas Neal 30 yr old mason enlisted Granville Co 10/17/62 **W 7/3 C 7/5**

Private Berry Pearce 33 yr old enlisted Franklin Co 2/11/63 (later "Gallantry at Wilderness")

Private Minton Perry 38 yr old mason enlisted Franklin Co 5/10/62 (later W-leg Wilderness)

Private Silas Stone 33 yr old enlisted Franklin Co 7/17/62 W Suffolk Va **W-both legs C 7/3 (amp)**

Private John Walker 21 yr old enlisted Pitt Co. 9/19/62 (later nurse)

Private Hinton Wiggins 34 yr old enlisted Franklin Co 7/17/62 (later AWOL)

Private Perry Wiggins 37 yr old enlisted Franklin Co 2/11/63 (later W-head Wilderness)

Private Henry Winston 29 yr old enlisted Franklin Co 5/10/62 (later W-leg Wilderness)
Private Peyton Winston 17 yr old enlisted Franklin Co 2/24/63 **C 7/14**
Private William Winston 31 yr old enlisted Franklin Co 5/10/62 (hospitalized 10/63) (later W Globe Tavern)

Teamster Sabret Card 32 yr old Franklin Co tenant farmer enlisted 5/10/62
Teamster Henry Standling 33 yr old enlisted Granville Co 7/14/62 **W-thigh C 7/3**

July 1 Casualties

Captain Wilson Williams 35 yr old Franklin Co. farmer enlisted 4/7/62 **C 7/1**
3rd Lt Burton Winston 26 yr old Franklin Co teacher enlisted 5/10/62 **W-side 7/1 C 7/5**
1st Sgt James Minga 28 yr old enlisted Granville Co 5/10/62 **C 7/1**
Sgt Alphonso Sherrod 31 yr old enlisted Granville Co 5/10/62 **C 7/1**
Cpl. Alfred Dent 35 yr old Franklin Co farmer enlisted 5/12/62 **W-left arm/right leg 7/1 (double amputee)**
Cpl. William Moore 29 yr old enlisted Franklin Co 5/10/62 **WC 7/1**
Private Calvin Bailey 20 yr old Granville Co farmer enlisted 5/13/62 **W-foot C7/1**
Private Lemuel Ball 38 yr old Granville Co farmer enlisted 2/9/62 **W-left arm 7/1**
Private James Bond 46 yr old Wake Co. farmer substituted 6/2/62 **W 7/1**
Private James Bowman 25 yr old enlisted 10/25/62 **C 7/1**
Private Joseph Bridges 19 yr old Franklin Co farmer enlisted 5/13/62 **C 7/1**
Private William Card 35 yr old Franklin Co farmer enlisted 5/10/62 **C 7/1**
Private George Catlett 30 yr old Granville Co farmer enlisted 5/12/62 **W 7/1**
Private George Cooley 40 yr old Wake Co farmer substituted 5/12/62 **C 7/1**
Private Allen Davis 34 yr old Granville Co farmer enlisted 10/2/62 **C 7/1**
Private William Dulin 29 yr old Burke Co farmer enlisted 10/20/62 **W-arm/left leg C 7/1**
Private John Ellington 28 yr old Chatham Co farmer enlisted 10/22/62 **W-arm 7/1**
Private William Fuller 31 yr old Franklin Co overseer enlisted5/1/62 **C 7/1**
Private Lemon Gay 30 yr old Franklin Co farmer enlisted 5/10/62 **C 7/1**
Private Sidney Gay transferred to 55th NC 11/17/62 **W 7/1**
Private William Green 18 yr old Franklin farmer enlisted 10/8/62 **W-left leg 7/1**
Private William Haley enlisted Granville Co 5/10/62 **C 7/1**
Private Levy Pearce 22 yr old enlisted Franklin Co 7/17/62 **C 7/1**
Private James Harris 20 yr old Franklin Co clerk enlisted 8/6/62 **C 7/1** (later Sgt)
Private William Harris 23 yr old enlisted 9/19/62 **W-face 7/1**
Private Henry Holden 19 yr old Franklin Co enlisted 2/9/63 **W-back C 7/1**
Private Miles Scarborough 30 yr old enlisted Wake Co. 7/17/62 **C 7/1**
Private Thomas Speed 18 yr old enlisted Franklin Co 5/10/62 **W-arm & right hip C 7/1** (later 1st St)
Private E.B. Williams 23 yr old enlisted Franklin Co 10/3/62 **W 7/1**
Private Green Williams 26 enlisted Burke Co. 10/25/62 **K 7/1**

Private Josiah Williams 21 yr old enlisted Franklin Co 4/13/62 **W-right arm, right hip & groin C 7/1**

Private Rufus Winston 36 yr old enlisted Franklin Co 2/9/63 **C 7/1**

Company K *"Granville County"*

Captain Robert Thomas 29 yr old enlisted Granville Co 5/1/62 **W-head 7/3** (later W-leg Burgess Mill, Va)

2nd Lt. William Webb transferred 5/6/62 **W-leg C 7/3**

Sgt. John Cannady transferred 8/1/62

Sgt. Jeremiah Currin 30 yr old enlisted Granville Co. 5/6/62 **W-head 7/3**

Sgt. Samuel Howard 30 yr old enlisted Granville Co. 5/6/62 (later W-right leg Wilderness)

Corp. John O'Bryant 26 yr old enlisted Granville Co. 5/6/62 K 7/3

Corp. Thomas Sanford 19 yr old enlisted Granville Co. 5/6/62 Corp.

Corp. Joseph Thomas 29 yr old enlisted Granville Co. 5/6/62

Corp William H. Veasey 35 yr old enlisted Granville Co. 5/6/62 **W-face & pelvis 7/14 Falling Waters C Williamsport Hospital**

Corp William Wilkerson 19 yr old enlisted Granville Co. 5/6/62

Private James Adcock 29 yr old enlisted Granville Co. 5/6/62 **W-hip & thigh C 7/3**

Private Joseph Allen 19 yr old enlisted Granville Co. 7/16/62 **W 7/3 W 7/10** Williamsport

Private Pomphret Blackwell 37 yr old enlisted Granville Co. **C 7/14**

Private William Blackwell 19 yr old enlisted Granville Co. 5/6/62 (later W-foot Wilderness)

Private Chesley Bowling 36 yr old enlisted Granville Co. 2/25/63 **C 7/14**

Private James Chandler 19 yr old enlisted Granville Co. 2/25/63 (later Corp)

Private John Cliborne 20 yr old enlisted Granville Co. 2/25/63 (died 1/14/64 typhoid fever)

Private Joseph Critcher 19 yr old enlisted Granville Co. 5/6/62 **W-both legs C 7/3** (later K Globe Tavern)

Private George Currin transferred 2/7/63 **K 7/3**

Private James C.Currin 27 yr old enlisted Granville Co. 5/6/62

Private Lotan Currin 37 yr old enlisted Granville Co. 2/10/63 (later W-right foot Wilderness)

Private Marcus Currin 19 yr old enlisted Granville Co. 5/6/62 (later W-leg Winderness)

Private Thomas Currin 24 yr old enlisted Granville Co. 5/6/62 **K 7/3**

Private John Daniel 19 yr old enlisted Granville Co. 5/6/62 **K 7/3**

Private Louis Daniel 20 yr old enlisted Granville Co. 3/1/63 **W-head, foot & shoulder 7/3**

Private Thomas Daniel 29 yr old enlisted Granville Co. 5/6/62 **W-head 7/3**

Private Zachariah Daniel 27 yr old enlisted Granville Co. 5/6/62 **WC 7/3**

Private John Dunn 36 yr old mason enlisted Granville Co. 5/6/62 (later detailed as mason)

Private Albert Eakes 23 yr old enlisted Granville Co. 5/6/62 **W-left elbow & left side 7/3**

Private Robert Eakes 26 yr old enlisted Granville Co. 5/6/62 (hospitalized 7/13/63)

Private John Elixson 21 yr old enlisted Granville Co. 5/6/62 (later sick with night blindness)

Private Robert Elixson 23 yr old enlisted Granville Co. 5/6/62 **W-hand 7/3**

Private Augustus Frazier 29 yr old enlisted Granville Co. 5/6/62 (later W-head Wilderness)

Private Rhodes Frazier 29 yr old enlisted Granville Co. 5/6/62 **WC 7/3**

Private George Hayes 37 yr old enlisted Granville Co. 2/10/63 (later W-arm Wilderness)

Private Marion Hester 23 yr old enlisted Granville Co. 5/6/62 **W-right knee C 7/3**

Private Amos Howard 18 yr old enlisted Granville Co. 6/15/62 (later K Wilderness)

Private Joseph Howard 19 yr old enlisted Granville Co. 5/6/62

Private Joseph T Howard 24 yr old enlisted Granville Co. 5/6/62 (later K Wilderness)

Private William Henry Howard 36 yr old enlisted Granville Co. 2/10/63 **W-left leg C 7/3** (amp) died 7/22

Private Edward Jones 31 yr old enlisted Granville Co. 5/6/62

Private Thomas Knott 37 yr old enlisted Granville Co. 2/10/63 (later W-neck & shoulder Wilderness)

Private William Knott 34 yr old enlisted Granville Co. 5/6/62 **W-abdomen C 7/3**

Private William Land 23 yr old enlisted Granville Co. 5/6/62 **K 7/3**

Private John Murray 27 yr old mechanic enlisted Granville Co. 5/6/62 (later W-left thigh Wilderness)

Private Samuel O'Bryant 23 yr old enlisted Granville Co. 3/1/62 ***K 7/3***

Private Drury Patterson 20 yr old enlisted Granville Co. 3/1/62 **W-right arm 7/3**

Private Stephen Puckett 18 yr old enlisted Granville Co. 5/6/62

Private William Puckett 20 yr old enlisted Granville Co. 5/6/62 **W-head & arm C 7/3** (died 7/23)

Private Nathaniel Riley 35 yr old enlisted Granville Co. 3/1/62 (later W Cold Harbor)

Private William Royster 35 yr old enlisted Granville Co. 3/1/62 (later Teamster)

Private Stephen Sanford 33 yr old enlisted Granville Co. 5/6/62 **C 7/5 as nurse for wounded** (later K Glove Tavern)

Private Charles Satterwhite 34 yr old enlisted Granville Co. 5/6/62

Private John Stovall 18 yr old enlisted Granville Co. 7/1/63 **W-thigh C 7/3** (later W-head Spotsylvania)

Private Benjamin Thorp18 yr old enlisted Granville Co. 6/1/63 **C 7/14**

Private Peterson Thorp transferred 8/4/62 (later Hospital Steward)

Private Bennett Veasey 19 yr old enlisted Petersburg, Va. 10/1/62 (later died typhoid 10/2/63)

Private George West 29 yr old enlisted Granville Co. 5/6/62 (later W-both legs Petersburg 10/1/64)

Private William West 31 yr old enlisted Granville Co. 5/6/62 **W-right ankle 7/3**

Private Joseph Wilkerson 35 yr old enlisted Granville Co. 5/6/62 (later "sick in camp" 7/31/63)

Private Peter Wilkerson 21 yr old enlisted Granville Co. 3/1/62

Private Robert Wilkerson 21 yr old enlisted Granville Co. 5/6/62 (hospitalized 11/63)

Private John Williams 28 yr old enlisted Granville Co. 5/6/62 (later K Hatcher's Run)
Private D.T. Wood 35 yr old enlisted Granville Co. 2/1/63 **C 7/5 (nurse for wounded)**
Private John Yancey 18 yr old enlisted Granville Co. 2/10/63 **W-side C 7/3**
Private Brantley York 23 yr old enlisted Granville Co. 3/1/62 (died typhoid 8/24/63)

Teamster Henry Adcock 19 yr old enlisted Granville Co. 3/1/62 (detailed as musician)
Teamster Richard Daniel 31 yr old enlisted Granville Co. 5/6/62
Teamster James Hobgood 28 yr old enlisted Granville Co. 5/6/62 C Washington NC
Teamster Robert Norwood 24 yr old enlisted Granville Co. 5/6/62 (later W-right thigh Wilderness)
Teamster Peter Phillips enlisted Granville Co 3/1/62 (later K Glove Tavern)
Teamster Sabret Card 32 yr old Franklin Co tenant farmer enlisted 5/10/62
Ambulance Driver John Currin 33 yr old enlisted Granville Co. 5/6/62

July 1 Casualties

1st Lt. Wilkins Stovall transferred 5/6/62 **W 7/1 C 7/14**
3rd Lt. Reuben Royster 32 yr old enlisted Granville Co 3/1/62 **W-hand 7/1**
Corp. Richard Russell 20 yr old enlisted Granville Co. 5/6/62 **W-thigh 7/1**
Private John Boyd 18 yr old enlisted Granville Co. 2/10/63 **C 7/1**
Private John H Boyd 36 yr old enlisted Granville Co. 2/10/63 **W-leg 7/1**
Private Edward Chalkley transferred 10/1/62 **W-right thigh 7/1**
Private James D. Currin 19 yr old enlisted Granville Co. 5/6/62 **K 7/1**
Private Hugh Currain enlisted Granville Co. 5/6/62 **W-foot 7/1 C** (died in Hagerstown Hospital 7/29)
Private Alex Greenway 37 yr old enlisted Granville Co. 4/1/63 **K 7/1**
Private Robert Harris 35 yr old enlisted Granville Co. 5/6/62 **W-leg 7/1 C 7/5 Chambersburg**
Private Elijah Frazier 26 yr old enlisted Granville Co. 5/6/62 **W-forearm C 7/1**
Private James Knott 30 yr old enlisted Granville Co. 5/6/62 **K 7/1**
Private William Phillips 21 yr old enlisted Granville Co. 3/1/62 **W-knee C 7/1** (later K Globe Tavern)
Private Robert Sanford 22 yr old enlisted Granville Co. 5/6/62 **W-right thigh C 7/1**
Private Samuel Slaughter 18 yr old enlisted Granville Co. 2/25/63 **W-head C 7/1**
Private William Vaugh 30 yr old enlisted Granville Co. 2/63 **W-thigh C 7/1**
Private Richard Wilkerson 26 yr old enlisted Granville Co. 5/6/62 **W-shoulder 7/1** (died 7/15)

SECOND MISSISSIPPI REGIMENT

Colonel John Stone

Private Elijah Mercer Co F

Field & Staff

Colonel John M Stone 33 yr old teacher & RR agent enlisted Tischomingo 5/1/61 W Sharpsburg **W 7/1 C 7/5 Greenscastle, Pa**

Lieutenant Colonel David Humphries Ripley businessman enlisted 4/30/61 as 2nd lt Co B then Major **K 7/3**

Major John Blair 28 yr old Tishomingo Lawyer enlisted 5/1/61 W 1st Manassas & Sharpsburg **C 7/1**

Adjutant Joseph Guyton 23 yr old Tippah druggist enlisted 5/1/61

Sergeant Major Walter Rutledge 22 yr old Tippah mail carrier enlisted 5/1/61

Surgeon H.H. Hubbard pre-war surgeon from Vicksburg appt. 4/27/61

Assistant Surgeon Joseph Holt pre-war surgeon enlisted 4/27/61

Assistant Surgeon James Hoyle 26 yr old Physician enlisted 4/29/61

Hospital Steward Newton Hunt (Co B)

Chaplin M.W. Frierson **C 7/5 Greencastle**

Assistant Commissary Sergeant Nathan Hay 23 yr old Tishomingo clerk enlisted 5/1/61

Ordinance Sergeant James Caraway (Co A) 23 yr old Tishomingo farmer enlisted 5/1/61

Quartermaster Malijak Suratt (Co A) 44 yr old Tishomingo farmer enlisted 5/1/61 **C 7/5 Greencastle**

Quartermaster Sergeant James Cayce 26 yr old Itawamba Co. farmer enlisted 8/7/61 C 7/5

Asst Quartermaster Lucas Byron (Co B)

Courier Private Miles Pegues 24 yr old Pontotoc teacher enlisted 5/1/61

Company A *"Tishomingo Rifleman"*

Captain Andrew Walker 22 yr old Tishomingo farmer enlisted 3/1/61 (later K Petersburg)
2nd Lt William Moody 21 yr old Tishomingo farmer enlisted 3/1/61 **WC 7/3 died 7/3**
Sgt George Turner Bynum 21 yr old Tishomingo clerk enlisted 3/1/61 **C 7/3**
Cpl. James Patrick 24 yr old Tischomingo farmer enlisted 5/1/61 **K 7/3**
Private John Adkins 21 yr old Jacinto farmer enlisted 3/1/61 **WC 7/3**
Private Toliver Atwood 19 yr old Itawamba farmer enlisted 3/1/61 **W right arm C 7/3**
Private James Brewer 21 yr old Alabama farmer enlisted 3/1/61 **C 7/3**
Private Charles Duncan 20 yr old Jacinto farmer enlisted 3/1/61 **C 7/14**
Private Robert Fowler 20 yr old Jacinto farmer enlisted 3/1/61 **W 7/3**
Private James Hancock 23 yr old farmer enlisted 7/10/61 W-hand Gaines Mill W-hip Sharpsburg (later W Wild)
Private Thomas J. McAnally 20 yr old Farmer enlisted Jacinto 3/1/61 **awarded Roll of Honor for action** (later K Wilderness)
Private John Parish 25 yr old Tischomingo farmer enlisted 5/1/61 **WC 7/3** W-2nd Manassas

Nurse John Lindsay (Co A)
Bugler Charles Williams (Co A)
Teamster William Carter 35 yr old Tishomingo farmer enlisted 3/1/61
Teamster Christopher Key 25 yr old Tischomingo farmer enlisted 5/1/61

July 1 Casualties

1st Lt George Ralston 29yr old Tishomingo farmer enlisted 3/1/61 **W 7/1 C 7/4** died 7/30
3rd Lt James McKay 35 yr old Jacinto farmer enlisted 3/1/61 **W 7/1**
1st Sgt William Frierson 22 yr old Tishomingo farmer enlisted 3/1/61 **W left leg 7/1 C 7/5 Greencastle, Pa**
Sgt A.H. Gelison **W 7/1 C 7/4**
Sgt James Harris 30 yr old Tishomingo farmer enlisted 3/1/61 (later K Tally's Mill) **C 7/1**
Sgt Robert Neeley 32 carpenter enlisted Winchester, Va 7/10/61 **W 7/1** (later Lt)
Sgt. George Bynum 23 yr old Tishomingo farmer enlisted 3/1/61
Private Oliver Adair 37 yr old Jacinto farmer enlisted 3/1/61 W 2nd Manassas **W 7/1**
Private Robert Adair 28 yr old Jacinto farmer enlisted 3/1/61 **W 7/1**
Private N.C. Beard 19 yr old Jacinto farmer enlisted 3/1/61 **W 7/1 C 7/5**
Private R.I. Beard 23 yr old Jacinto farmer enlisted 3/1/61 **WC 7/1**
Private David Beaty 24 yr old Jacinto farmer enlisted 3/1/61 **W-head C 7/1**
Private J.L. Beaty 21 yr old Jacinto farmer enlisted 3/1/61 **W 7/1 died**
Private Arthur Belcher 29 yr old Tishomingo farmer enlisted 3/1/61 **W 7/1 C 7/5**
Private James W Bonds Tischomingo farmer enlisted 3/1/61 K 7/1
Private Reuben Boone 20 yr old yr old Tishomingo farmer enlisted 3/1/61 **W 7/1**

Private John Burcham 24 yr old Jacinto farmer enlisted 3/1/61 **C 7/1**
Private Ralph Burns 26 yr old Jacinto farmer enlisted 3/1/61 **W 7/1**
Private Giles Burns 29 yr old Jacinto farmer enlisted 3/1/61 (later W-Wild) **C 7/1**
Private Thomas Butler 21 yr old Tishomingo farmer enlisted 3/1/61 **C 7/1**
Private Nathaniel Bynum 19 yr old Jacinto student enlisted 3/1/61 **C 7/1**
Private Andrew Dixon 27 yr old Tishomingo farmer enlisted 3/1/61 (later K-Wild) **C 7/1**
Private Micajah Faris **W 7/1 awarded Roll of Honor for action 7/1**
Private James Helton 20 yr old Farmer enlisted Jacinto 3/1/61 **C 7/1**
Private J.J. King **WC 7/1**
Private Francis Lee 27 yr old Farmer enlisted Jacinto 3/1/61 **W 7/1**
Private John Lindsey 26 yr old Farmer enlisted Jacinto 3/1/61 **C 7/1**
Private Samuel Lindsey 22 yr old Farmer enlisted Pontotoc 3/1/61 **W 7/1 C 7/5**
Private James Mayo 20 yr old Tishomingo farmer enlisted 5/1/61 **K 7/1**
Private William Miller Tishomigo farmer enlisted 3/1/61 **C 7/1**
Private Lewis Monroe 23 yr old Tishomingo farmer enlisted 5/1/61 **C 7/1**
Private **Color Bearer** William Murphy 22 yr old Tishomingo farmer enlisted 5/1/61 **C 7/1** (Captured at RR Cut by Corporal Frank Wallar 6th Wisconsin Infantry)
Private Samuel Neely 22 yr old Tischomingo farmer enlisted 7/10/61 W 1st & 2nd Manassas & Sharpsburg **W-thigh 7/1**
Private Thomas Parrish 26 yr old Tischomingo farmer enlisted 5/1/61 **C 7/1** W 2nd Manassas
Private A.M. Parrish **W 7/1 C 7/5** died 10/22/63 in prison
Private John Pitts 23 yr old Farmer enlisted Jacinto 3/1/61 **W 7/1 C 7/63 on furlough in MS**
Private S.N. Pitts Farmer enlisted Jacinto 3/1/61 **W 7/1 C 7/5**
Private James Reed 32 yr old Farmer enlisted Jacinto 3/1/61 **K 7/1**
Private Arthur Reynolds 20 yr old Tischomingo farmer enlisted 5/1/61 **W 7/1 C 7/5**
Private George Reynolds 19 yr old Tischomingo farmer enlisted 5/1/61 **C 7/1** (later Corporal)
Private Gilford Reynolds 28 yr old Farmer enlisted Jacinto 3/1/61 **W 7/1 C 7/5**
Private Arthur Robinson 21 yr old Tischomingo farmer enlisted 5/1/61 **W 7/1 C 7/5 died Ft Del** (buried at Finn's Point, NJ)
Private William Rollins 35 yr old Jacinto farmer enlisted 3/1/61 **W-left thigh 7/1 C 7/5**
Private James Sledge 27 yr old Tischomingo farmer enlisted 5/1/61 **C 7/1**
Private Balam Smith 29 yr old Tischomingo farmer enlisted 5/1/61 **W foot 7/1**
Private Lycurgus Tapcott 25 yr old Jacinto farmer enlisted 3/1/61 **W-left leg 7/1 C 7/5**
Private Arthur R Thompson Jacinto farmer enlisted 3/1/61 C 7/1
Private William Turner 25 yr old Tischomingo farmer enlisted 5/1/61 **W 7/1** W-Sharpsburg
Private Byron White 26 yr old Jacinto farmer enlisted 3/1/61 **W 7/1 C 7/5** (later W-Wild)

Company B *"O'Connor Rifles"*

Captain John Buchanan 43 yr old Tippah blacksmith enlisted 5/1/61 **W right leg 7/3 C 7/5 Greencastle Pa** (later Major)

2nd[t] Lt William Moody 26 yr old Tippah drugist enlisted 5/1/61 **W right leg C 7/3**

2nd Lt Hugh "Luke" Byrn 23 yr old Tippah clerk enlisted 5/1/61 **WC 7/3 with colors**

1st Sgt Augustus Vairin 43 Tippah watchmaker enlisted 5/1/61 **WC 7/3**

Corp. Stephen Braddock 23 yr old Tippah enlisted 5/1/61 **awarded Roll of Honor for action at Falling Waters** (later K Bristoe Stn)

Corp. Allen Talbott 22 yr old Tippah farmer enlisted 5/1/61 (later Brigade QM Sgt)

Corp. Pickney J. Ticer enlisted 8/23/61 W Seven Pines **awarded Roll of Honor for action 7/3 C 7/14**

Private Samuel Adams 27 yr old Tippah farmer enlisted 5/1/61 **C 7/3**

Private Rodolphus "Rose" Byrn enlisted 4/30/61 W-head 1st Manassas W 2nd Manassas

Private William Byrn enlisted at Ripley, MS 4/15/63

Private John Coltharp 37 yr old Ripley farmer enlisted 5/1/61 **C 7/3**

Private John Eubanks enlisted 3/1/62 in Verona, MS **C 7/3**

Private Joseph Glenn 20 yr old Tippah farmer enlisted 5/1/61 **C 7/14**

Private Virgil Grace 22 yr old Tippah farmer enlisted 5/1/61 **C 7/3**

Private Isaac N Gray 25 yr old Tippah farmer enlisted 5/1/61 (later W 8/28/64)

Private James Guyton 21 yr old Tippah farmer enlisted 5/1/61 **C 7/3**

Private Robert Henderson 26 yr old Tippah farmer enlisted 5/1/61 **W 7/3**

Private David J. Hill 35 yr old Tippah surveyor enlisted 5/1/61 **W-right leg C 7/3**

Private Samuel Lancaster 20 yr old Ripley farmer enlisted 3/3/62 (later W Wild)

Private John McCarver 23 yr old Ripley farmer enlisted 3/3/62 **C 7/3**

Private William McGowan 20 yr old Ripley farmer enlisted 3/8/62 **K 7/3**

Private Westley Monday 37 yr old Ripley farmer enlisted 3/3/62 **C 7/14**

Private John Nance 21 yr old Ripley farmer enlisted 3/3/62 **C 7/3**

Private William Neley 20 yr old enlisted Ripley, Ms 3/3/62 ambulance driver 1862 (later W Weldon RR)

Private Lazarus Pearce 36 yr old farmer enlisted 3 creek AK 3/1/62 **C 7/3**

Private Charles Taylor **WC 7/3** died US General Hospital Chester Pa 10/22

Private Zenas Vernor enlisted at Winchester Va 7/15/61 (later W-left leg Wilderness)

Private H.J. Whitehead **W-arm C 7/3**

Private Jasper Whitehead enlisted at Ripley, MS 9/18/61 W-**leg&thigh C 7/3**

Teamster William Jackson 25 yr old Tippah farmer enlisted 5/1/61

Ambulance Driver Alexander Neely 25 yr old Tippah farmer enlisted 5/1/61

July 1 Casualties

1st Lt John Lauderdale 30 yr old Tippah saddler enlisted 5/1/61 **K 7/1**
Sgt John Fryar 20 yr old Tippah student enlisted 5/1/61 **C 7/1**
Sgt Trussie McKay 23 yr old Tippah clerk enlisted 5/1/61 ROH Boonsboro W 2nd Manassas **K 7/1**
Sgt Luther Richie 23 yr old Tippah clerk enlisted 5/1/61 **C 7/1** (later W Cold Harbor)
3rd Sgt Harvey Smith 25 yr old Tippah farmer enlisted 5/1/61 **C 7/1**
5th Sgt Miles Bennett 23 yr old Tippah farmer enlisted 5/1/61 **W 7/1 awarded Roll of Honor for action 7/1**
Sgt Robert Young 20 yr old Ripley, Ms clerk enlisted 5/1/61 **W-arm 7/1**
Cpl Thomas Nance 26 yr old Tippah farmer enlisted 5/1/61 **W 7/1**
Cpl Daniel White 22 yr old Ripley, Ms farmer enlisted 9/18/61 **K 7/1**
Private Michael Blackwell 24 yr old Tippah farmer enlisted 5/1/61 **K 7/1**
Private William Thomas Blackwell Enlisted Ripley, MS 9/18/61 **K 7/1** (had brothers in 42nd MS)
Private Nathaniel Boyd 19 yr old Ripley farmer enlisted 3/19/62 **K 7/1**
Private Joseph Bratten 23 yr old Tippah farmer enlisted 5/1/61 **WC 7/1**
Private William McDuff Cochran 30 yr old Tippah farmer enlisted 5/1/61 **C 7/1** (later Cpl.)
Private William Cowen 19 yr old Ripley farmer enlisted 3/7/61 **C 7/1**
Private William Crase **C 7/1**
Private Benjamin Crum 24 yr old Ripley farmer enlisted 5/1/61 **W 7/1**
Private David Dacus 27 yr old Ripley farmer enlisted 3/11/62 **C 7/1**
Private Thomas Duncan 30 yr old Tippah farmer enlisted 5/1/61 **WC 7/1**
Private Granderson Fewel 23 yr old Tippah farmer enlisted 5/1/61 **C 7/1**
Private William Gray 22 yr old Ripley farmer enlisted 5/1/61 **CK 7/1**
Private Peter Hammerschmidt 19 yr old Tippah shoemaker enlisted 5/1/61 W Manassas W Gaines Mill **C 7/1**
Private Terrell Harris 27 yr old Tippah farmer enlisted 5/1/61 **WC 7/1 died Fort Delaware buried Finn's Point NJ**
Private George Holcombe 18 yr old Ripley student enlisted 5/1/61 **W 7/1** C on furlough
Private Charles Humphreys 22 yr old farmer enlisted Camp Fisher, Va 10/28/61 **C 7/1**
Private John Kelly 29 yr old Tippah farmer enlisted 5/1/61 **C 7/1**
Private Matthew Knox 21 yr old Tippah farmer enlisted 5/1/61 **W 7/1**
Private John Lancaster 24 yr old Ripley farmer enlisted 3/3/62 **W 7/1**
Private G.K. Lyons **WC 7/1**
Private W.M. Marton **C 7/1**
Private Green McCarley 24 yr old Tippah farmer enlisted 5/1/61 **WC 7/1**
Private Lewis McDonald 26 yr old Tippah farmer enlisted 5/1/61 **W 7/1**
Private Richmond Miller 30 yr old Ripley farmer enlisted 3/3/62 **W 7/1**
Private William Miller 34 yr old Jacinto farmer enlisted 3/1/62 **C 7/1**
Private Jacob Norton 23 yr old Tippah farmer enlisted 5/1/61 **C 7/1** (later W Bristoe & Wild)
Private William C. Norton 20 yr old Ripley farmer enlisted 3/3/62 **W leg 7/1 C 7/5**
Private John Ray 21 yr old Tippah farmer enlisted 5/1/61 **W-foot 7/1**

Private James Robertson 20 yr old Ripley farmer enlisted 3/3/62 **K 7/1**
Private Michael Saunders 27 yr old Tippah student enlisted 5/1/61 **C 7/1**
Private Thomas Saunders 23 yr old Ripley farmer enlisted 3/3/62 **K 7/1**
Private James Seargeant 35 yr old Ripley farmer enlisted 3/3/62 **W 7/1**
Private James Simpson 24 yr old Tippah student enlisted 5/1/61 **C 7/1**
Private George Sims 22 yr old Tippah laborer enlisted 5/1/61 **W-hipC 7/1**
Private Harvey Smith 25 yr old Tippah farmer enlisted 5/1/61 **C 7/1**
Private Milton Sweney enlisted at Ripley, MS 9/18/61 **W-leg C 7/1**
Private William Swinny 19 yr old Guntown, MS farmer **W-hip 7/1 C 7/5**
Private John Whitten 35 yr old Shannon MS farmer enlisted 3/21/61 **K 7/1**
Private Jesse Winburn 32 yr old Ripley farmer enlisted 3/3/62 **K 7/1**

Members of Company B, pictured with the Hatcher's Run colors (note that the battle honors have been inaccurately penciled in on the photo). The photo is believed to have been taken in Texas, possibly at the Dallas Reunion. From left to right, pictured are John H. Allen, William H. "Billy" Byrn, Isaac N. Gray, George P. Holcombe, Alexander Wolf, and Lucas H. Byrn. *(Photo courtesy of the Miss. Dept. of Archives and History)*

Company B 2nd Mississippi
"O'Connor Rifles"
Captain John Buchanan
Commanding

Company C *"Town Creek Rifleman"*

Captain John Storey 26 yr old Itawamba clerk enlisted 5/1/61 **K 7/3** W 2nd Manassas
1st Lt Romulus Sargent 24 yr old Itawamba farmer enlisted 5/1/61 **C/73**
1st Lt David Walker 29 yr old Itawamba clerk enlisted 5/1/61 **C 7/3**
2nd Lt William Bessonette 25 yr old Itawamba mason enlisted 5/1/61 **W 7/3**
1st Sgt Alfred Scales 22 yr old Itawamba clerk enlisted 5/1/61 **W 7/3**
Sgt—James Stovall 22 yr old Itawamba clerk enlisted 5/1/61 **W 7/3**
Sgt—William Davis 45 yr old Itawamba carpenter enlisted 5/1/61
Sgt—Ruffin A. Roberts 24 yr old Itawamba farmer enlisted 5/1/61 **K 7/3**
Corp—James Beachum 20 yr old Itawamba farmer enlisted 5/1/61 **C 7/3**
Corp—John Palmer 30 yr old Itawamba farmer enlisted 5/1/61 **C 7/3**
Private James Anderson 21 yr old Itawamba farmer enlisted 5/1/61 W Sharpsburg (later K Weldon RR)
Private William Bazemore 24 yr old Itawamba farmer enlisted 5/1/61 **K 7/3 awarded Roll of Honor for action**
Private William Crayton Verona, Ms farmer enlisted 10/1/61 (later W-Wild)
Private James Davis 30 yr old Itawamba farmer enlisted 5/1/61 **W 7/3**
Private Francis Devall 21 yr old Itawamba farmer enlisted 5/1/61 **W-left leg C 7/3**
Private John Eubanks Verona, Ms farmer enlisted 3/1/62 **C 7/3**
Private James Evans 23 yr old Itawamba farmer enlisted 5/1/61 **C 7/3**
Private Sylvester Harris 23 yr old Verona, Ms farmer enlisted 3/1/62 **C 7/3**
Private Thomas Harris Verona, Ms farmer enlisted 3/1/62 **C 7/14**
Private James Lamb Verona, Ms farmer enlisted 3/1/62 **K 7/3**
Private J.N. Lesley Verona, Ms farmer enlisted 3/1/62 **W-thigh C 7/3**
Private Thomas Mabry 26 yr old Itawamba farmer enlisted 5/1/61 **WC 7/14**
Private Osburn Marcy enlisted Verona, Ms 3/1/62 (later deserted 9/63)
Private John McDonald enlisted Verona, Ms 3/1/62 (later W Wilderness)
Private William Pettigrew enlisted Verona, Ms 3/1/62 W-Sharpsburg (later W-Wild & Ream's Station)
Private John Stevens enlisted Verona, Ms 3/1/62 W 2nd Manassas (later Corp)
Private Henry H. Storey 22 yr old Itawamba farmer enlisted 5/1/61 **Roll of Honor 7/1 K 7/3**
Private John Taylor enlisted Verona, Ms 3/1/62 W Sharpsburg (later W Wilderness)
Private Joseph Turner 21 yr old Itawamba farmer enlisted 5/1/61 **W-left thigh C 7/3**
Private Henderson Westmoreland 21 yr old Itawamba farmer enlisted 5/1/61 **W-right Foot C 7/3**

Teamster James Conner 23 yr old Itawamba farmer enlisted 5/1/61 (W-Wilderness)

7/1 Casualties

Sgt—John Beam Itawamba resident enlisted Richmond, MS 10/1/61 **W 7/1**
Sgt John Bell 33 yr old Itawamba farmer enlisted 5/1/61 **C 7/1**

Corp—Rubin Roberts 18 yr old Itawamba farmer enlisted 5/1/61 **C 7/1**
Private H.L. Beachum 24 yr old Itawamba farmer enlisted 5/1/61 **W-right leg 7/1**
Private John Bell Richmond, MS farmer enlisted 10/1/61 **W 7/1**
Private Joshua Birmingham Enterprise. Ms farmer enlisted 9/20/62 **C 7/1**
Private John Brazeal 21 yr old Itawamba farmer enlisted 5/1/61 **C 7/1**
Private John 21 yr old Itawamba farmer enlisted 5/1/61 **C 7/1**
Private Charles Clayton 29 yr old Itawamba farmer enlisted 5/1/61 **C 7/1**
Private Joshua Clayton 33 yr old Itawamba farmer enlisted 5/1/61 **C 7/1**
Private J.M. Compson **C 7/1**
Private Jesse Flinn **W 7/1**
Private John Flinn 22 yr old Itawamba farmer enlisted 5/1/61 **C 7/1**
Private Thomas Gray Verona, Ms farmer **W 7/1 C 7/5**
Private John W. Green Verona, Ms farmer enlisted 3/1/62 **K 7/1**
Private Dolphus Hughes Verona, Ms farmer enlisted 3/1/62 **W 7/1**
Private James Hughes 21 yr old Itawamba farmer enlisted 5/1/61 **C 7/1**
Private Chrstopher Kirksey Verona, Ms farmer enlisted 3/1/62 **W 7/1**
Private Wilson Lesley 26 yr old Verona, Ms farmer enlisted 3/1/62 **W 7/1**
Private John Looney enlisted Richmond, Ms **C 7/1**
Private J.T. Lyles 18 yr old Verona, Ms farmer enlisted 3/1/62 **W-left arm 7/1**
Private James Marshall 20 year old farmer enlisted Winchester.Va 6/28/61 **K 7/1**
Private George Martin enlisted Verona, Ms 3/1/62 **W 7/1**
Private Robert Marion 22 yr old Itawamba farmer enlisted 5/1/61 **C 7/1**
Private John Mayfield 27 yr old Itawamba farmer enlisted 5/1/61 **C 7/1** (later Sgt)
Private John McHenry 35 yr old Itawamba farmer enlisted 5/1/61 **C 7/1**
Private James Pettigrew enlisted Verona, Ms 3/1/62 **W 7/1**
Private Thomas Pettigrew enlisted Verona, Ms 3/1/62 **W 7/1**
Private John Sargent 30 yr old Itawamba farmer enlisted 5/1/61 **C 7/1**
Private J.F. Ray **W 7/1 C 7/5** Cashtown, Pa
Private Alfred Roberts 43 yr old Richmond, Ms blacksmith enlisted 3/15/62 **W 7/1**
Private Samuel Rollin Richmond, Ms farmer enlisted 10/1/61 **C 7/1**
Private Aaron Sargent Richmond, Ms farmer enlisted 10/1/61 **C 7/1**
Private Joseph Stockton enlisted Verona, Ms 3/1/62 **W 7/1**
Private John Sugar Verona farmer enlisted 3/1/61 **C 7/1**
Private John Tabler enlisted Verona, Ms 3/1/62 **C 7/1**
Private Thomas Traylor enlisted Verona, Ms 3/1/62 **W 7/1**
Private George Turner 24 yr old Itawamba farmer enlisted 5/1/61 **C 7/1** (later K Weldon RR)
Private Augustus Watson 21 yr old Itawamba farmer enlisted 5/1/61 **C 7/1**
Private R.A. West 35 yr old Verona, Ms farmer enlisted 3/1/62 **W 7/1**
Private Mayfield Wiygul enlisted Richmond, Ms 10/1/61 **C 7/1**
Private Leroy Wylie 21 yr old Itawamba farmer enlisted 5/1/61 **C 7/1**

Company D *"Joe Matthews Rifles"*

Captain Robert Brandon 24 yr old Tippah Co. farmer enlisted 5/1/61 **WC 7/3** died 7/15 Chester, Pa

1st Lt John Jasper Hicks 32 Tennessee born farmer enlisted Harper's ferry 5/15/61 W-Sharpsburg **W-back 7/3 while retreating**

2nd Lt Gideon Willis Iuka, Ms farmer enlisted 10/1/61 **WC 7/3**

1st Sgt Zachery Prescott 27 yr old Pine Grove, Ms farmer enlisted 4/27/61 W Gaines Mill, Sharpsburg, Wilderness **W 7/3**

Sgt Alfred Mooney 26 yr old Tippah Co. farmer enlisted 5/1/61 **W-left hand 7/3**

Cpl. William Cooper 20 yr old Tippah Co. farmer enlisted 5/1/61 W-1st Manassas (later W-Wilderness)

Cpl Joseph Jasper Cox 21 yr old Tippah Co. farmer enlisted 5/1/61 W-1st Manassas **K 7/3**

Private Henry Box 32 yr old Tippah Co farmer enlisted 5/1/61 **C 7/3**

Color Bearer Private Christopher Davis 23 yr old Tippah Co farmer enlisted 5/1/61 **Sick on 7/1 W-legs 7/3 died**

Private John Elliot 21 yr old Salem, Ms farmer enlisted 5/1/61 **W-left leg C 7/3**

Private William Jasper Gresham 19 yr old Ripley, Ms farmer enlisted 5/1/61

Private William Houston 20 yr old Tippah Co farmer enlisted 5/1/61 **K 7/3**

Private William T. Moore 24 yr old Tippah Co farmer enlisted 5/1/61 **W 7/3 awarded Roll of Honor for action**

Private Daniel Pogue 44 yr old Tippah Co farmer enlisted 5/1/61 W Sharpsburg (later W-Wilderness)

Private James Walker 24 yr old Tippah Co farmer enlisted 5/1/61 **C 7/14** Falling Waters

Teamster John Daniel 22 yr old Tippah Co farmer enlisted 5/1/61 W 1st Manassas

July 1 Casualties

Sgt Ezekiel Allen Tippah Co. mechanic enlisted 5/1/61 **C 7/1**

Cpl. James Walding 24 yr old Tippah Co. farmer enlisted 5/1/61 **W 7/1** (later W Wilderness)

Private Albury Bruton 21 yr old Tippah Co farmer enlisted 5/1/61 **C 7/1**

Private Gilbreath Cathy 22 yr old Tippah Co farmer enlisted 5/1/61 **C 7/1** W Gaines Mill

Private Joel Cherry 31 yr old Tippah Co farmer enlisted 5/1/61 **C 7/1**

Private Marion Cooper 20 yr old Tishomingo Co farmer enlisted 5/1/61 **W 7/1 C 7/5**

Private Jeremiah Fulton 29 yr old Tippah Co farmer enlisted 5/1/61 **W 7/1 awarded Roll of Honor for action**

Private Robert Grisham 20 yr old Tippah Co farmer enlisted 5/1/61 **W-left thigh 7/1**

Private Toleman Hammons 24 yr old Iuka farmer enlisted 5/1/61 **C 7/1** W 2nd Manassas & Sharpsburg

Private Joseph Houston Iuka, Ms farmer enlisted 5/1/61 **C 7/1**

Private John Johnson 27 yr old Tippah Co farmer enlisted 5/1/61 **W 7/1** W-Sharpsburg
Private Wilson Lesley 26 yr old Verona farmer enlisted 5/1/61 **W 7/1**
Private James Lewis 21 yr old Salem, Ms student enlisted 9/19/61 **WC 7/1** died David's island NY 7/20
Private Cornelius Robinson Iuka Farmer **C 7/1** died Fort Delaware buried Finn's Point, NJ
Private George Walker 22 yr old Ripley farmer enlisted 3/1/61 **K 7/1**
Private John Wilson 21 yr old Tippah Co farmer enlisted 5/1/61 **C 7/1**

Company E *"Calhoun Rifles"*

3rd Lt Benjamin Richardson 28 yr old Guntown farmer enlisted 8/7/61 **K 7/3**
Sgt William Keyes 23 yr old Itawamba Co. farmer enlisted 8/7/61 **W 7/3** (later W-Wilderness)
Sgt Rufus Jones 23 yr old Itawamba Co. farmer enlisted 8/7/61—*survived*
Private John Childers 18 yr old Itawamba Co. farmer enlisted 8/7/61 **C 7/3**
Private Robert Hughes 21 yr old Itawamba Co. farmer enlisted 8/7/61 **WC 7/3**
Private Wallace McFearson 21 yr old Saltillo, Ms farmer enlisted 5/1/61 **W 7/3**
Private William McGee 42 yr old Guntown farmer enlisted 5/1/61 **W 7/3**
Private Elijah Miller yr old Guntown farmer enlisted 5/1/61 **W 7/14**
Private Samuel "Berry" Scott 21 yr old Guntown farmer enlisted 5/1/61 *Survived*
Private Henry Stocks 20 yr old Baldwyn, Ms farmer enlisted 5/1/61 **W 7/3**

Teamster & Wheelwright James Watt 29 yr old Guntown farmer enlisted 5/1/61 (detached duty)
Blacksmith Francis Ford 33 yr old Guntown blacksmith enlisted 8/7/61 (detached brigade)
Pioneer Ephram McCully 23 yr old Saltillo, Ms farmer enlisted 5/1/61 (detached)

July 1 Casualties

1st Lt Peyton Bailey 23 yr old Itawamba Co. farmer enlisted 8/7/61 **C 7/1**
2nd Lt Robert Whitley 25 yr old Guntown farmer enlisted 5/1/61 **C 7/1**
W-1st Manassas W Gaines Mill
1st Sgt William McGee 42 yr old Itawamba Co. carpenter enlisted 8/7/61 **W 7/1** deserted 7/25
2nd Sgt Steven Smith 28 yr old Itawamba Co. farmer enlisted 8/7/61 **C 7/1** W-Sharpsburg
Sgt Edward Lesley 25 yr old Itawamba Co. farmer enlisted 5/1/61 **C 7/1**
Sgt James Stovall 22 yr old Itawamba Co. farmer enlisted 8/7/61 **W 7/1**
Cpl. James Knott 19 yr old Guntown farmer enlisted 8/7/61 **W 7/1**
Cpl. Ivy Woodward 23 yr old Itawamba Co. farmer enlisted 8/7/61 **C 7/1**
Cpl. Charles L. Humphries 23 yr old Itawamba Co. farmer enlisted 8/7/61 **W-right side & liver 7/1 left behind C 7/5 died awarded Roll of Honor for action**

Cpl. Samuel Hankins 18 yr old Guntown farmer enlisted 8/7/61 DIARY **W 7/1**
Private John Brawner 35 yr old Guntown farmer enlisted 8/7/61 **C 7/1**
Private Benjamin Bryant 27 yr old Guntown farmer enlisted 8/7/61 **W 7/1**
Private William Bryant 23 yr old Itawamba Co. farmer enlisted 8/7/61 **C 7/1**
Private William D. Bryson 24 yr old Itawamba Co. farmer enlisted 8/7/61 **C 7/1**
Private Pleasant Easley 23 yr old Guntown farmer enlisted 8/7/61 **C 7/1** died Fort Delaware buried Finn's Point, NJ
Private David Edge 28 yr old Guntown farmer enlisted 8/7/61 **C 7/1**
Private William Ellis 19 yr old Itawamba Co. farmer enlisted 8/7/61 **C 7/1**
Private Oliver Evans 19 yr old Itawamba Co. farmer enlisted 8/7/61 **W 7/1**
Private Newton Fisher 21 yr old Guntown farmer enlisted 8/7/61 **K 7/1**
Private Edward Flanagan 42 yr old Guntown farmer enlisted 8/7/61 **W 7/1**
Private John Flanagan 19 yr old Guntown farmer enlisted 8/7/61 **C 7/1**
Private Alexander Hartsfield 19 yr old Itawamba Co. farmer enlisted 8/7/61 **W 7/1**
Private James Hopkins 21 yr old Itawamba Co. farmer enlisted 8/7/61 **C 7/1**
Private Jasper Hopkins 23 yr old Itawamba Co. farmer enlisted 8/7/61 **W 7/1**
Private William Johnson 22 yr old Guntown farmer enlisted 8/7/61 **C 7/1** W-Sharpsburg
Private George Keeys 20 yr old Guntown farmer enlisted 8/7/61 **W-arm 7/1**
Private Stephen Kent 23 yr old Guntown farmer enlisted 8/7/61 (later W Bethesda Church) **C 7/1**
Private James Kyle 24 yr old Saltillo,Ms farmer enlisted 6/1/61 **C 7/1**
Private William Lassiter 21 yr old Guntown, Ms farmer enlisted 8/7/61 **C 7/1**
Private Doctor Franklin Leathers 31 yr old Saltillo farmer enlisted 3/1/62 **C 7/1**
Private Major McClain 24 yr old Guntown farmer enlisted 3/8/62 **C 7/1**
Private William McCombs 23 yr old Guntown farmer enlisted 5/1/62 **C 7/1**
Private James Daniel McCully 20 yr old Saltillo, Ms farmer enlisted 5/1/61 **C 7/1**
Private James McDonald 20 yr old Guntown farmer **C 7/1** W-Gaines Mill
Private George Monk Tupelo, Ms farmer reenlisted Guntown, Ms 2/22/62 (later K-Bristoe) **C 7/1**
Private John Newberry 22 yr old Saltillo, Ms farmer enlisted 5/1/61 (later W-Wilderness) **C 7/1**
Private Charles Nelson 23 yr old Guntown farmer enlisted 5/1/61 **W 7/1**
Private John Pryor 28 yr old Guntown farmer enlisted 5/1/61 **W 7/1**
Private Oliver T. Raines 20 yr old Guntown farmer enlisted 2/26/62 **C 7/1**
Private Condary Strickland 24 yr old Guntown farmer enlisted 2/20/62 **C 7/1**
Private William Swinny 19 yr old Baldwyn, Ms farmer enlisted 3/12/62 **W-hip C 7/1**
Private James Walker 21 yr old Marietta farmer enlisted 3/1/62 **C 7/1**
Private James Weems 19 yr old Guntown farmer enlisted 2/26/62 **C 7/1**
Private William Weems 23 yr old Guntown farmer enlisted 3/1/62 **W-left thigh 7/1 C left behind C 7/5**
Private J.J. Whitley Guntown farmer enlisted 5/1/61 **K 7/1**

Private Robert Whitley 25 yr old Guntown farmer enlisted 5/1/61 **C 7/1**
Private George Wilson 25 yr old Guntown farmer enlisted 5/1/61 **K 7/1**

Company F *"Magnolia Rifles"*

Captain Henry Powers 31 yr old lawyer enlisted Tippah 5/1/61 W Malvern Hill **W 7/3 C 7/5**

1st Lt James Saunders 25 yr old farmer enlisted Tippah 5/1/61 W Sharpsburg **W 7/3 C 7/5**

2nd Lt John Bearden 25 yr old carpenter enlisted Tupelo 5/1/61 W Gaines/Sharpsburg (resigned 11/63

3rd Lt. Thomas Storey 26 yr old Ripley farmer enlisted 3/3/62 **W 7/3** (later W Weldon RR)

Sgt John Lokey 32 yr old farmer enlisted Tippah 5/1/61 W Gaines Mill (Later W Wilderness)

Sgt Thomas Newton 36 yr old collector enlisted Tippah 5/1/61 W Gaines Mill (later W Wilderness)

Sgt Montgomery Selph 24 yr old farmer enlisted Tippah 5/1/61 W-1st Manassas

Private William Ayres 25 yr old Tupelo carpenter enlisted 4/30/61 W Gaine's Mill W 1st Manassas /(K CH)

Private Lewis Blythe 24 yr old farmer enlisted Tupelo 4/30/61 **awarded Roll of Honor for action 7/3**

Private James Burton 29 yr old farmer enlisted Ripley 3/3/62 **W-right thigh/left leg C 7/3**

Private Armistead Butler 21 yr old farmer enlisted Tippah 5/1/61 (later W-Wild)

Private Joseph C. Clark 23 yr old farmer enlisted Tippah 5/1/61 **W-right side&leg 7/14**

Private Daniel Cutberth 26 yr old farmer enlisted Ripley 3/1/62 (later K Wilderness)

Private Andrew Dixon 27 yr old farmer enlisted Tishomingo 5/1/61 (later K-Wilderness)

Private James Forsythe 24 yr old farmer enlisted Tippah 5/1/61 W Sharpsburg **K 7/3**

Private Samuel Frazier 28 yr old planter enlisted Tippah 5/1/61 **W 7/3**

Private Lawrence Gray 23 yr old Chesterville farmer enlisted 3/22/62 (later C Wilderness)

Private David Griffin 25 yr old farmer enlisted Ripley 3/1/62 **C 7/3**

Private Pickney Hardin 24 yr old planter enlisted Tippah 5/1/61 **C 7/14**

Private Albert Harris 22 yr old blacksmith enlisted Tippah 5/1/61 WC Sharpsburg **WC 7/3**

Private John Hedden 26 yr old planter enlisted Tippah 5/1/61 **C 7/14**

Private John King 22 yr old farmer enlisted Ripley 3/1/62 **W 7/3 C 7/5**

Private Elijah Messer / Mercer 22 yr old planter enlisted Tippah 5/1/61 **W-left arm & chest 7/3**

Private Mathew Patton enlisted at Ripley 9/30/61 **W 7/3**

Private Samuel Pennypacker 21 yr old farmer enlisted Tippah 5/1/61 (later W Bristoe)

Private Samuel Pickens 23 yr old Ripley farmer enlisted 3/1/62 **W-arm C 7/3**

Private William Stanfield 24 yr old farmer enlisted Tippah 5/1/61 **W 7/3**
Private Benjamin Tarver 23 yr old Ripley farmer enlisted 3/1/62 **W-left hand 7/3**

Teamster Jerome Patton 26 yr old planter enlisted Tippah 5/1/61
Pioneer Christopher Cutberth enlisted Ripley 9/30/61

July 1 Casualties

1st Sgt John McBride 21 yr old farmer enlisted Tippah 5/1/61 **C 7/1** died Fort Delaware buried Finn's Point NJ
Sgt Samuel Lidell 22 yr old farmer enlisted Tippah 5/1/61 W Malvern Hill **K 7/1**
Cpl. John Pitman 23 yr old planter enlisted Tippah 5/1/61 W SevenPines **W-left arm 7/1**
Cpl. Marion Messer 23 yr old planter enlisted Tippah 5/1/61 **C 7/1**
Cpl. James Norvell 28 yr old farmer enlisted Tippah 5/1/61 **C 7/1**
Cpl. John Smith 21 yr old farmer enlisted Tippah 5/1/61 **C 7/1**
Private John Booker 23 yr old farmer enlisted Tupelo 2/22/62 **W 7/1**
Private James Childers 21 yr old planter enlisted Tippah 5/1/61 **C 7/1**
Private James Clark enlisted at Ripley. Ms 3/4/61 **C 7/1**
Private Joseph Clark 21 yr old farmer enlisted Tippah 5/1/61 **C 7/1**
Private William Cox 20 yr old farmer enlisted Corinth 3/22/612 5/1/61 **C 7/1**
Private James Dalton 21 yr old planter enlisted Tippah 5/1/61 **W 7/1**
Private Henry Dawkins 26 yr old farmer enlisted Tippah 5/1/61 **W 7/1**
Private Greenlief Fortenbery 21 yr old farmer enlisted Ripley 3/3/62 **C 7/1**
Private William Gibson 23 yr old farmer enlisted Tippah 5/1/61 **W 7/1**
Private Robert Herring 23 yr old blacksmith enlisted Tippah 5/1/61 **C 7/1**
Private William Jones 23 yr old planter enlisted Tippah 5/1/61 **C 7/1** (later K Petersburg)
Private William Liles 20 yr old farmer enlisted Tippah 5/1/61 WC Sharpsburg **C 7/1**
Private Isaac Luna 23 yr old planter enlisted Tippah 5/1/61 **W 7/1 C 7/5**
Private James Luna 32 yr old planter enlisted Tippah 5/1/61 **K 7/1**
Private William Luna 34 yr old planter enlisted Tippah 5/1/61 W Manassas/Sharpsburg **W-arm 7/1 C 7/5** awarded Roll of Honor for action
Private John Martin 24 yr old planter enlisted Tippah 5/1/61 **C 7/1**
Private William Miller 23 yr old planter enlisted Tippah 5/1/61 **C 7/1**
Private Samuel Moore 24 yr old planter enlisted Tippah 5/1/61 **W 7/1**
Private James Raby 21 yr old Ripley farmer enlisted 3/1/62 **C 7/1** (later W Wilderness)
Private Cornelius Robinson 23 yr old farmer enlisted Tippah 5/1/61 **WC 7/1**
Private Michael Robinson 25 yr old farmer enlisted Tippah 5/1/61 **C 7/1**
Private Thomas Sauders 22 yr old Ripley farmer enlisted 3/3/62 W Sharpsburg **K 7/1**
Private George Smith 22 yr old farmer enlisted Tippah 5/1/61 **C 7/1**
Private Lemuel Smith 46 yr old Ripley farmer enlisted 3/3/61 **W 7/1**
Private James Stanley 20 yr old Tishomingo Co. laborer enlisted 5/1/61 W Malvern Hill **W 7/1**

Company G *"The Pontotoc Minutemen"*

1st Lt. John W. Dillard 25 yr old Pontotoc County businessman enlisted 5/1/61 **W 7/3 C 7/5**

2nd Lt James Combs 24 year old Alabama Farmer enlisted 5/1/61 **W 7/3** W 1st Manassas

Sgt Joel Donaldson 32 y old overseer W 2nd Manassas **W both legs C 7/3 awarded Roll of Honor for action 7/3**

1st Corp Thomas Cooper enlisted 04/30/61 sick 7/1 **fought 7/3** W Malvern Hill (later W Wild)

Corp George Easterwood 26 yr old Pontotoc planter enlisted 5/1/61 **W side 7/14 awarded Roll of Honor for action 7/14**

Private Levi Childers Tippah County farmer enlisted 7/15/62 as substitute (later W Wild)

Private William Combs 21 year old Alabama farmer enlisted 5/01/61 **C 7/14** (W Sharpsburg)

Private John T Dillard 20 yr old from Rock Ford enlisted 03/62

Private Esias Earle 27 yr old Redlands teacher enlisted 5/1/61 (later Corp)

Private William Handley 29 yr old Pontotioc farmer enlisted 5/1/61 **W 7/3** (later W Wild)

Private Thomas Miller 22 yr old farmer enlisted 8/15/61 **W 7/3**

Private Elijah Shelton 22 yr old Tennessee farmer enlisted 3/20/62 **Sick 7/1 fought 7/3** later W-thigh Wild

Nurse John Edington Okolona farmer enlisted 1862 **C 7/5 with wounded**

Teamster Thomas Lyons 24 yr old Pontotoc farmer enlisted 5/1/61

July 1 Casualties

Captain Thomas Crawford 29 yr old clerk enlisted 04/30/61 **fought 7/1 sick 7/3 C 7/14**

2nd Lt. John McCurley 26 yr old Pontotoc farmer enlisted 5/1/61 **W 7/1 C 7/5** Cashtown

1st Sgt John Wray old Pontotoc planter Private enlisted 5/1/61 **W 7/1 C 7/5 Cashtown**

2nd Sgt Frederick Daggett Pontotoc County farmer enlisted 5/01/61 **C 7/1 at RR Cut**

Sgt James Dilliard 23 yr old Pontotoc teacher enlisted 03/20/61 **W left leg 7/1 C 7/5**

Sgt William Nowlin 22 yr old **W 7/1**

Corp Robert McDole 21 yr old Pontotoc farmer enlisted 5/1/61 **W left thigh 7/1**

Private William Childers Tippah County farmer enlisted 3/20/ 62 **W 7/1**

Private John Donaldson 28 yr old farmer enlisted 9/16/61 **C 7/1**

Private Charles Earl 19 yr old Pontotoc County farmer enlisted 5/1/07 **C 7/1 at RR Cut**

Private Robert Eddington 33 yr old Pontotoc County farmer enlisted 5/1/61 **W right lung 7/1**

Private James Edwards 22 yr old Pontotoc county farmer enlisted 5/1/61 **W 7/1**

Private William Harrison 28 yr old Pontotoc stage driver enlisted 5/1/61 **W 7/1**

Private James Henry 28 yr old Pontotoc farmer enlisted 5/1/61 **W 7/1** W South Mtn

Private John Johnston 21 yr old Pontotoc farmer enlisted 9/18/61 **C 7/1 RR Cut**

Private Green Kidd 47 yr old Pontotoc farmer enlisted as substitute **K 7/1**
Private Samuel Lindsey 22 yr old Pontotoc planter enlisted 5/1/61 **W 7/1 C 7/5**
Private Patrick McNally 47 yr old Irish laborer enlisted 4/61 **W 7/1** (later W-Wild)
Private Houston Miller 21 yr old Pontotoc farmer enlisted 5/1/61 **K 7/1**
Private James Miller 28 yr old Pontotoc planter enlisted 5/1/61 **W 7/1 C 7/5**
Private Benjamin Rodgers 37 yr old Pontotoc farmer enlisted 3/20/62 **W 7/1 C 7/5**
Private Francis Smith 22 yr old SC Planter enlisted 5/1/61 **fought 7/1 sick 7/3**
Private William Wommack 24 yr old Ripley farmer enlisted 3/1/62 **C 7/1**

Company H *"Coonewah Rifles"*

1st Lt David Marlin 28 yr old Chesterville teacher enlisted 4/29/61 **K 7/3**
2nd Lt John C. Fears 25 yr old Chesterville farmer enlisted 4/29/61 W-Sharpsburg
Sgt Newton Clayton 27 yr old Pontotoc Co farmer enlisted 4/29/61 W Sharpsburg (later K Wilderness)
Cpl. William Moore 28 yr old Chesterville enlisted 2/24/62 **K 7/3**
Private Allen Bland 31 yr old Tupelo carpenter enlisted 4/30/61 C Seven Pines **WC 7/3**
Private William Bowen 35 yr old Richmond, Ms farmer enlisted 3/1/07 (later K Wilderness)
Private Philip Brandon 26 yr old Tupelo farmer enlisted 3/22/62 (later W Wilderness)
Private Samuel Brandon 28 yr old Tupelo farmer enlisted 8/10/61 (later W Wilderness)
Private Pleasant Clark 35 yr old Chesterville farmer enlisted 4/29/61 (later K Wilderness)
Private Levi Cochran 19 yr old Chesterville farmer enlisted 3/15/62 **WC 7/3**
Private William Cochran 20 yr old Chesterville farmer enlisted 4/29/61 W Sharpsburg (deserted 11/63)
Private William Coker 29 yr old Tupelo farmer enlisted 3/1/62 (later W Wilderness) died
Private Hampton Goza 23 yr old Chesterville farmer enlisted 2/24/62 (later W Wilderness K Weldon RR)
Private Lawrence Gray 23 yr old enlisted Corinth 3/22/62 (later C Wilderness)
Private John Harwell 20 yr old Tupelo clerk enlisted 4/29/61 (later W Wilderness / K Spotsylvania)
Private Samuel Kyle 20 yr old Saltillo farmer enlisted 5/1/61 W-2nd Manassas & Wilderness
Private Henry "Tobe" McPherson 21 yr old Chesterville farmer enlisted 4/29/61 W 2nd Manassas (later K Wilderness) **(Captured colors of 149th Pa by shooting Color Cpl Henry Spayd in the leg and seizing colors)**
Private James Nunnalee 18 yr old Tupelo student enlisted 3/17/62 **awarded Roll of Honor for action Falling Waters**
Private John Sanders 32 yr old Verona farmer enlisted 5/1/61 **W 7/14**
Private William Sullivan 23 yr old Tupelo farmer **WC 7/3**
Private William Thompson 29 yr old Tupelo teacher enlisted 4/29/61 W Sharpsburg **W 7/3**

Private Benton Weatherington 19 yr old Chesterville student W Sharpsburg (later W Wilderness)

Teamster Reuben Killian 25 yr old Alabama born farmer enlisted 4/29/61
Scout Emery Hooker 27 yr old Chesterville farmer enlisted 8/15/61—Scout for General Heth
Musician Benjamin Pierce

July 1 Casualties

Captain William Cunningham 33 yr old Pontontoe Co resident enlisted April 29, 61 **W-right arm and left hip 7/1**
3rd Lt Altas Roberts 21 yr old Chesterville farmer enlisted 4/29/61 W 2nd Manassas **K 7/1** (leading party to take 149th Pa colors)
1st Sgt Bruce Strain 22 yr old Chesterville farmer enlisted 4/29/61 **W-right thigh 7/1**
Sgt Henry Powell 22 yr old Chestervlle farmer enlisted 4/29/61 W 2nd Manassas **C 7/1**
Sgt Benjamin Rook 28 yr old Tupelo farmer enlisted 4/29/61 W-Sharpsburg **C 7/1**
Cpl. Edward Maxcy 21 yr old Chesterville farmer enlisted 4/29/61 **C 7/1**
Cpl. James Raines 19 yr old Tupelo farmer enlisted 4/29/61 **W-right foot C 7/1 awarded Roll of Honor for action 7/1**
Private William Ayers 25 yr old Tupelo carpenter enlisted 4/30/61 W 1st Manassas/ Gaines Mills **C 7/1** (later K CH)
Private J.H. Beam **W 7/1 sick C 7/5**
Private Richard Bennett 22 yr old Richmond, Ms farmer 3/23/62 W South Mtn **C 7/1**
Private James Bell 23 yr old Tupelo farmer enlisted 4/21/61 **W-right thigh 7/1 C 7/5**
Private James Bolen 23 yr old Chesterville Ms farmer enlisted 4/29/61 W Gaines Mill **C 7/1**
Private J.H. Bowen 24 yr old Chesterville, Ms farmer enlisted 3/15/62 **C 7/1**
Private Wilie Braden 20 yr old Tupelo farmer enlisted 4/29/61 **C 7/1**
Private James Brookshire 22 yr old Chesterville student enlisted 5/10/61 W-Sharpsburg **C 7/1**
Private James Charles enlisted 3/23/62 **W 7/1**
Private Stephen Cochran 21 yr old Chesterville farmer enlisted 4/29/61 **C 7/1** (later W Bethesda Church)
Private William Cox 19 yr old Corinth farmer enlisted 3/22/62 deserted 8/19/63
Private James Dale 19 yr old Chesterville farmer enlisted 3/1/62 **C 7/1**
Private John Duke 23 yr old Pontotoc Co, Ms farmer enlisted 4/29/61 **C 7/1** (later W Weldon RR)
Private Jeremiah Falkner 23 yr old Tupelo Merchant enlisted 8/10/61 **C 7/1** (later Killed Petersburg)
Private Andrew Fears 26 yr old Tupelo farmer enlisted 4/29/61 **W-right leg 7/1**
Private William D Freeman Tupelo farmer enlisted 3/10/62 **K 7/1**
Private Hezikiah Frost 21 yr old Tupelo farmer enlisted 4/29/61 W-2nd Manassas **K 7/1**

Private William Gill 24 yr old Chesterville farmer enlisted 3/15/62 **W 7/1**
Private James J. Green 23 yr old Chesterville farmer enlisted 3/10/62 **C 7/1**
Private John Helms 26 yr old Chesterville farmer enlisted 4/29/61 **W 7/1** (later W-Wilderness)
Private David Johnson 23 yr old Tupelo carpenter enlisted 4/29/61 **C 7/1**
Private James Kyle 24 yr old Saltillo farmer enlisted 6/1/61 **C 7/1**
Private William Lilly 23 yr old Chesterville farmer enlisted 4/29/61 WC 2nd Manassas **C 7/1**
Private John McGill 17 yr old Verona laborer enlisted 3/21/62 **C 7/1**
Private Thomas Logan 26 yr old Tupelo carpenter enlisted 4/29/61 W Sharpsburg **C 7/1**
Private Jacob Lowery 23 yr old Chesterville farmer enlisted 4/29/61 W Gaines Mill **W 7/1 C 7/5**
Private William Lummus 19 yr old Iuka farmer enlisted 3/1/62 **C 7/1**
Private William Mabry 31 yr old farmer enlisted 8/10/61 **W 7/1** (later W Wilderness & Weldon RR)
Private William McKinney 21 yr old Chesterville student enlisted 3/1/62 **C 7/1**
Private George Norwood 31 yr old Chesterville carpenter enlisted 4/29/61 **W 7/1 C 7/5** (later W CH)
Private Andrew Rea 27 yr old Verona mechanic enlisted 10/1/61 **W 7/1** (later W Weldon RR)
Private Thomas Rea 29 yr old Verona mechanic enlisted 10/1/61 **C 7/1**
Private Elvis Roberts 21 yr old Chesterville farmer enlisted 4/29/61 **W 7/1**
Private John Rucker 19 yr old Chestervlle farmer enlisted 3/1/62 **W 7/1 C 7/14**
Private William Smith 20 yr old Tupelo student enlisted 4/29/61 **K 7/1**
Private James Strain 20 yr old Chesterville cadet enlisted 3/15/62 (later Lt & Captain) **C 7/1**
Private James Wade 25 yr old Popular Springs, Ms farmer enlisted 4/29/61 **C 7/1** (later K Ft McRae)
Private John Ware 24 yr old Tupelo clerk enlisted 4/29/61 **W-leg 7/1**
Private George Weatherington 24 yr old Chesterville teacher W-2nd Manassas **K 7/1**
Private Moses Whitesides 19 yr old Chesterville farmer enlisted 3/15/62 **W 7/1** (K Bristoe)

Company I *"Cherry Creek Rifles"*

1st Lt Artaxeres Sory 29 yr old Pontotoc Co farmer enlisted 5/1/61 (later W Wilderness)
3rd Lt Joseph Owen 28 yr old Pontotoc Co farmer enlisted 5/1/61 (later K North Anna)
Sgt James B. Gambrell 21 yr old Pontotoc Co farmer enlisted 5/1/61 (later Lt) later a doctor
Cpl. John Mahon 24 yr old Pontotoc Co farmer enlisted 5/1/61 **W-right lung C 7/3**
Private Henry Andrews 28 yr old Pontotoc Co farmer enlisted 5/1/61 **K 7/14**
Private Martin Andrews 22 yr old Pontotoc Co farmer enlisted 5/1/61 (later W Wilderness)

Private Washington Ball Cherry Creek, Ms farmer enlisted 9/17/61 **C 7/14**
Private Willis Ball 26 yr old Pontotoc Co farmer enlisted 5/1/61 deserted 7/10
Private William Freeman 28 yr old Pontotoc Co farmer enlisted 5/1/61 **WC 7/3 died**
Private Willis Grant 22 yr old Pontotoc Co farmer enlisted 5/1/61 **W-thigh C 7/3**
Private Sargent Jones 28 yr old Jacinto, Ms farmer enlisted 5/1/61 **WC 7/3**
Private James Knight 22 yr old Pontotoc Co farmer enlisted 5/1/61 **C 7/3**
Private John Pitts 22 yr old Pontotoc Co farmer enlisted 5/1/61 **W 7/3 C 7/5**
Private George Shuttleworth 28 yr old Pontotoc Co farmer enlisted 5/1/61 **C 7/14**
Private George Simpson 19 yr old Chesterville, Ms farmer enlisted 3/1/62 **W-right leg C 7/3**
Private J.P. Ticer Pontotoc farmer enlisted 5/1/61 **C 7/14 awarded Roll of Honor for action 7/1**
Private Fleming Worthy 25 yr old Pontotoc Co farmer enlisted 5/1/61 **W-right shoulder C 7/3**
Private Monroe Yeager 20 yr old Pontotoc Co farmer enlisted 5/1/61 W-2nd Manassas **K 7/3 awarded Roll of Honor for action**
Pioneer John Freeman 20 yr old Pontotoc Co farmer enlisted 5/1/61 (later W-Wilderness)

July 1 Casualties

Captain Richard Leavell 24 yr old Pontotoc Co teacher enlisted 5/1/61 **C 7/1**
2nd Lt John Stevens 30 yr old Pontotoc Co farmer enlisted 5/1/61 **C 7/1**
1st Sgt George Young 22 yr old Pontotoc Co farmer enlisted 5/1/61 **W-chest 7/1**
Sgt Minett Smith 21 yr old Pontotoc Co farmer enlisted 5/1/61 W-Sharpsburg **C 7/1**
Sgt Martin Wells 25 yr old Pontotoc Co farmer enlisted 5/1/61 **C 7/1**
Cpl. James Wood 25 yr old Pontotoc Co farmer enlisted 5/1/61 **C 7/1**
Private John Adams 29 yr old Cherry Creek, Ms farmer enlisted 5/1/61 **K 7/1**
Private Weldon Armstrong Guntown, Ms farmer enlisted 5/1/61 **C 7/1**
Private Franklin Ball 21 yr old Pontotoc Co farmer enlisted 5/1/61 **K 7/1**
Private William M. Ball 28 yr old Pontotoc Co farmer enlisted 5/1/61 **C 7/1**
Private Thomas Billingsley 22 yr old Guntown, Ms farmer enlisted 5/1/61 **C 7/1** (later K Weldon RR)
Private Elijah Caldwell 23 yr old Pontotoc Co farmer enlisted 5/1/61 **C 7/1**
Private William Cobb 23 yr old Pontotoc Co farmer enlisted 5/1/61 **K 7/1 awarded Roll of Honor for action**
Private William Helms 24 yr old Pontotoc Co farmer enlisted 5/1/61 **C 7/1**
Private John Hill 21 yr old Pontotoc Co farmer enlisted 5/1/61 **W 7/1**
Private George Jones 19 yr old Chesterville, Ms farmer enlisted 5/1/61 **W-left leg C 7/1**
Private James McCarver 24 yr old Pontotoc Co farmer enlisted 5/1/61 W-Sharpsburg **C 7/1**
Private Amos McGregor 24 yr old Pontotoc Co farmer enlisted 5/1/61 **W 7/1**
Private Peyton McReynolds 23 yr old Pontotoc Co farmer enlisted 5/1/61 **W-Sharpsburg W-7/1**

Private Barney Moser Pontotoc farmer **C 7/1** died Fort Delaware buried Finn's Point NJ

Private Alexander Owens 25 yr old Pontotoc Co farmer enlisted 5/1/61 **C 7/1**

Private John Pitts Pontoc farmer enlisted 5/1/61 **C 7/1** died Fort Delaware buried Finn's Point NJ

Private Tuner Ray 33 yr old Pontotoc Co farmer enlisted 5/1/61 W-Sharpsburg **C 7/1**

Private Francis Rose 24 Guntown, Ms 24 farmer enlisted 9/10/61 **W-left thigh 7/1**

Private Newton Shirley 28 Guntown, Ms farmer enlisted 9/10/61 **K 7/1**

Private Ludy Wells 23 yr old Pontotoc Co farmer enlisted 5/1/61 W-Sharpsburg **WC 7/1 (died)**

Private Henry Wells 22 yr old Pontotoc Co farmer enlisted 5/1/61 **C 7/1**

Private Jesse Wells 26 yr old Pontotoc Co farmer enlisted 5/1/61 **W-left arm&leg 7/1**

Company K *"Iuka Rifles"*

Captain Henry Terry 26 yr old Iuka farmer enlisted 3/1/61 W 2nd Manassas (later K Wilderness)

1st Lt William Harvey 24 yr old farmer enlisted Tishomingo Co, Ms 5/1/61 (later captain)

2nd Lt Winchester Castleberry 25 yr old lumberman enlisted Tishomingo Co. 5/1/61 W 2nd Manassas (later K Petersburg)

3rd Lt Joseph Phillips 23 yr old Tishomingo Co, Ms clerk enlisted 5/1/61 **WC 7/3**

Sgt Joseph Moore 22 yr old farmer enlisted Tishomingo, Ms 5/1/61 **WC 7/14**

Sgt William Moore 28 yr old Tishomingo, Ms farmer enlisted 5/1/61 **W 7/3**

Cpl. John Moore 19 yr old farmer enlisted Iuka, Ms 4/1/62 (later K Spotsylvania)

Cpl. Albert Fetting 20 yr old Tishomingo, Ms Tinner enlisted 5/1/61 **C 7/14**

Private James Akers 18 yr old student enlisted Richmond, Va 7/1/62 **K 7/3 awarded Roll of Honor for action 9/62 & 7/3/63**

Private Aden Allen 36 yr old Iuka, Ms farmer enlisted 3/1/62 (later W Spotsylvania)

Private Absolom Bailey 22 yr old Tishomingo, Ms farmer enlisted 5/1/61

Private Joseph Barnett 19 yr old Iuka, Ms farmer enlisted 3/1/62 W Gaines Mill **C 7/14**

Private William Barnett 36 yr old Iuka, Ms farmer enlisted 3/1/62 **W 7/3 C 7/5**

Private James Curtis 22 yr old Iuka, Ms farmer enlisted 3/1/62 **W-right arm C 7/3**

Private William Davis 28 yr old Iuka, Ms enlisted 3/1/62 (later W Wilderness)

Private Rody Donohue **W 7/3 C 7/5** (Galvanized as Federal artilleryman)

Private James Eastman 19 yr old Iuka, Ms farmer enlisted 3/1/62 (Later K Spotsylvania)

Private George Hamilton 21 yr old Iuka, Ms farmer enlisted 3/1/62 W Seven Pines (later C Weldon RR)

Private Robert Harland 21 yr old Tishomingo, Ms farmer enlisted 5/1/61 (later W Spotsylvania)

Private Edward Hathaway 22 yr old Iuka farmer enlisted 3/1/62

Private Isaac Holt 37 yr ld Iuka, Ms farmer enlisted 3/1/62 (later W Bristoe Station)

Private John Horton 22 yr old Iuka, Ms farmer enlisted 5/1/61 (later W Spotsylvania)

Private Richard Lucas 19 yr old Iuka, Ms farmer enlisted 3/1/62 **C 7/3**

Private William T. Lummus 43 yr old Iuka farmer enlisted 3/1/62 C South Mtn (later K Wilderness)

Private Thomas Martin 20 yr old Tishomingo, ms laborer enlisted 5/1/61 (later K Wilderness)

Private Jesse Martindale 23 yr old Tishomingo, Ms laborer enlisted 5/1/61 **C South Mtn** (later W Wilderness)

Private Miles Martindale 25 yr old Tishomingo, Ms laborer enlisted 5/1/61 (later W Wilderness)

Private Andrew Owens 20 yr old Tishomnigo, Ms farmer enlisted 3/1/62 **C 7/14**

Private William Smith 19 yr old Iuka, Ms farmer enlisted 3/1/62

Private Francis Sutton 23 yr old Iuka, Ms enlisted 3/1/62 **WC 7/8 Williamsport (died 7/19)**

Private James Ward 30 yr old Tishomingo, Ms farmer enlisted 5/1/61 W Gaines Mill (later W Wilderness)

Private Lorenzo Whitaker 20 yr old Iuka farmer enlisted 3/1/62 **WC 7/2** (on skirmish line)

Teamster George Hubbard 30 yr old Tshomingo mechanic enlisted 5/1/61 (blacksmith) **deserted 7/25/63**

Nurse Anthony Cunningham 40 yr old enlisted Iuka, Ms 3/1/62

July 1 Casualties

Sgt James Graham enlisted Iuka, Ms 9/24/61 W Gaines Mill **C 7/1** (died in prison)

Sgt John McIntosh 21 yr old Tishomigo,Ms engineer enlisted 5/1/61 **W-left thigh C 7/1** (later W Wilderness)

Sgt William Houston 21 yr old enlisted Iuka, ms 3/1/62 W Gaines Mill **C 7/1**

Cpl. James Farmer 23 yr old farmer enlisted Iuka, Ms 3/1/62 **C 7/1**

Private William Atkins 25 yr old Iuka, Ms farmer enlisted 3/1/62 W Seven Pines **C 7/1**

Private William Brown 19 yr old Iuka, Ms farmer enlisted 3/1/62 **C 7/1**

Private George Charlton 22 yr old Iuka, Ms laborer enlisted 3/1/62 **W 7/1 C 7/5**

Private William Condrey 21 yr old Iuka farmer enlisted 9/24/61 **K 7/1 awarded Roll of Honor for action 7/1**

Private Samuel Dewoody 21 yr old Tishomingo, Ms Postmaster **C 7/1**

Private Albert Gibson 20 yr old Tishomingo, Ms farmer enlisted 5/1/61 **WC 7/1**

Private Edwin Hanners 23 yr old Tishomingo, Ms farmer enlisted 5/1/61 **W 7/1**

Private Ambrose Harland 30 yr old Iuka, Ms farmer enlisted 3/1/62 **C 7/1**

Private James Harland 22 yr old Tishomingo, Ms farmer enlisted 5/1/62 **C 7/1**

Private James Hubbard 20 yr ld Iuka farmer enlisted 3/1/62 **(deserted 7/1 C 7/5 served as nurse)**

Private James Hughes 27 yr old Iuka farmer enlisted 3/1/62 **W 7/1 RR Cut** (later W Wilderness)

Private Henry Inman 30 yr old Tishomingo, Ms merchant enlisted 5/1/61 W 1st Manassas **C 7/1**

Private John Jackson 22 yr old Tishomingo, Ms enlisted 5/1/61 **W 7/1**

Private William Lummus 19 yr old Iuka, Ms farmer enlisted 3/1/62 **C 7/1**

Private James McCoy 23 yr old Iuka, Ms farmer enlisted 3/1/62 **W 7/1 C 7/5**

Private Isaac McKeown 31 yr old Tishomingo, Ms carpenter enlisted 5/1/61 **W 7/1 C 7/5** (later K Wilderness)

Private Wallis Newton 21 yr old Iuka, Ms enlisted 3/1/62 **W 7/1** (later W Wilderness)

Private Augustus Riggs 34 yr old Tishomingo farmer enlisted 5/1/61 **W 7/1 C 7/5 (died)**

Private Henry Rowland 23 yr old Iuka, Ms farmer enlisted 3/1/62 **W-hip 7/1 C 7/5**

Private Richard Southall 23 yr old Iuka planter enlisted Winchester, Va 6/20/61 **W 7/1**

Private George Sutton 21 yr old Tishomingo, Ms farmer enlisted 5/1/61 **W 7/1**

Private Benjamin Trammell 26 yr old Iuka, Ms enlisted 3/1/62 **C 7/1** (later W Weldon RR)

Private James Wallis 26 yr old Iuka, Ms farmer enlisted 3/1/62 **C 7/1**

Private John Watts 24 yr old Tishomingo, Ms laborer enlisted 5/1/61 **W 7/1**

Company L *"Liberty Guards"*

Captain Robert Storey 39 yr old Riley, Ms farmer enlisted 3/3/62 Sick in Richmond (died 7/2)

1st Lt. Joshua Henson 30 yr old Ripley, Ms farmer enlisted 3/3/62 (later Capt)

2nd Lt. Thomas Storey 26 yr old Ripley, ms farmer enlisted 3/3/62 **W-calf 7/3**

3rd Lt. Ransom Jenkins 25 yr old Ripley, Ms farrier W-Wilderness K-Petersburg

Sgt Joseph Dalton 32 yr old Dumas farmer enlisted 3/3/62

Cpl. Micagah Clark 40 yr old Ripley, Ms farmer enlisted 3/3/62

Private Owen Carpenter 26 yr old Ripley, Ms farmer 3/3/62 **K 7/3 awarded Roll of Honor for action**

Private William Bounds Dumas, Ms farmer enlisted 3/13/63

Private James Burton 29 yr old enlisted Ripley, Ms 3/3/62 **W-right thigh & left leg C 7/3**

Private William Guy 23 yr old Dumas, Ms planter enlisted 5/1/61 **W 7/3** (later W-Wild)

Private John Hedden 25 yr old enlisted Tippah, Ms **C 7/14**

Private Richard Jeter 19 yr old Union Mills, ms farmer enlisted 3/3/62 (later K Wilderness)

Private Andrew Lee 20 yr old Ripley, ms farmer enlisted 3/3/62 (later W Weldon RR)

Private Moses Lewis 21 yr old Dumas, Ms farmer 3/3/62 **K 7/14**

Private John May 23 yr old farmer enlisted Ripley 3/1/62 W Sharpsburg (later W Wilderness)

Private John Mask 23 yr old Union Mills farmer enlisted 3/1/62 W-foot Sharpsburg (later W-Wild)

Private John Alexander McAllister 23 yr old Molina, Ms farmer enlisted 3/3/62 W Seven Pines (later W Weldon RR)

Private John Smith 19 yr old Ripley, Ms farmer enlisted 3/3/62

Private Lafayette Welty 20 yr old farmer enlisted Ripley, Ms 3/362 **W 7/3**
Private Robert Yancey 19 yr old Ripley farmer enlisted 3/3/62 (later W Petersburg)

July 1 Casualties

Sgt. Edwin Jordan 36 yr old New Albany, Ms farmer enlisted 3/3/62 **C 7/1**
Sgt Harvey Smith 24 yr old Ripley, Ms farmer enlisted 5/1/61 **C 7/1**
Cpl. Henry Coleman 30 yr old farmer enlisted 3/3/62 **K 7/1**
Cpl. James Murphy 37 yr old Baltimore, Md Seaman enlisted 7/13/62 W-Sharps **C 7/1**
Cpl. William Jenkins 23 yr old planter enlisted Tippah 5/1/61 **C 7/1**
Private James Bartlett 26 yr old Dumas, Ms farmer enlisted 3/3/62 **C 7/1 RR Cut**
Private Isaiah Beaseley 20 yr old Dumas farmer enlisted 3/3/62 **WC 7/1**
Private Surathia Bryan 30 yr old Ripley, Ms farmer **W 7/1**
Private James Commander 22 yr old Mooresville, Ms farmer enlisted 2/12/63 **C 7/1**
Private Jesse Dial 25 yr old Silver Springs, Ms farmer enlisted 3/3/62 **WC 7/1**
Private Samuel Green 35 yr old Dumas, Ms farmer enlisted 3/3/62 **W 7/1**
Private Charles Jordan 33 yr old Ripley, Ms farmer enlisted 3/3/62 **C 7/1**
Private Edwin Jordan 36 yr old New Albany, Ms farmer enlisted 3/3/62 **C 7/1**
Private John Murphy 31 yr old Arizabo, Ms laborer enlisted 3/3/62 **W-right shoulder 7/1**
Private James Riley 37 yr old enlisted 3/3/62 **K 7/1**
Private Thomas Robinson 19 yr old Dumas, ms farmer **W 7/1** (later K Weldon RR)
Private Edward Stricklin 31 yr old farmer enlisted Tippah 5/1/61 **W 7/1**
Private Wilson Swaine 25 yr ld Silver Springs, Ms farmer enlisted 3/3/62 **W 7/1**
Private Daniel White 23 yr old Ripley farmer enlisted 3/3/62 **K 7/1 awarded Roll of Honor for action**
Private Simon West 33 yr old Union Mills, Ms farmer enlisted 3/3/62 **W 7/1**

FORTY SECOND MISSISSIPPI REGIMENT

Captain Thomas Clark Co. F

Rev. Thomas Witherspoon

Private William Wooten

Field & Staff

Colonel Hugh Reed Miller 51 yr old former Pontotoc judge & legislator elected 5/14/62 **W-chest & knee C 7/3** died 7/19

Buried Old Fellows Rest Cemetery Aberdeen, MS

Lieutenant Colonel Hillary Moseley31 yr old physician enlisted Panola 3/27/62 **W-foot 7/1** (resigned 12/18/63)

Major William Feeney sadler who enlisted Grenada, Ms 5/14/62 **W 7/1-right breast** later Colonel (K-Wild)

Adjutant Oliver Carr 24 yr old Appointed 5/17/62 (later W-Wilderness)

Sergeant Major George Miller 21 yr old student enlisted Pontotoc, Ms appointed 7/9/62 **W-thigh 7/1** (father was Col.)

Surgeon Robert L. Taggart Oxford, MS physician appt asst surg. 5/17/62 Appt surgeon 12/62 (later hospital duty)

Assistant Surgeon Legrand James Wilson 27 yr old enlisted Grenada, Ms 5/14/62

Assistant Surgeon William McCreight 30 yr old enlisted Benela, Ms 5/13/62 **C 7/5** with wounded

Chaplin—Thomas Wright Witherspoon "took a gun and went into battle"—brought home Col Miller's body

Quartermaster—Lumsford Pitt Cooper enlisted into Co H Grenada, Ms 5/14/62 (later Brigade QM)

Quartermaster Sergeant Thomas Harris (Co. A) enlisted Grenada, Ms 5/14/62

Ordinance Sergeant Edwin Miller enlisted Grenada 5/14/62 **C 7/5 to be with father (Col. Miller)**

Commissary Sergeant John Stevens (later K-Bristoe Station)

Wagon Master—Quartermaster Steven Gunter (Co C) enlisted Grenada, Ms 5/14/62

Wagon Master—Richard Hall enlisted Grenada, Ms 5/14/62

Company A *"Carroll County Fencibles"*

Captain Andrew Nelson 32 yr old Carroll Co. judge enlisted Grenada, Ms 5/14/62 (later Lt. Col W Wilderness)

3rd Lt William West 35 yr old enlisted Grenada, Ms 5/14/62 Sick in Richmond fough tat falling Waters (later K-Wilderness)

Sgt. Rufus Holman 23 yr old enlisted Grenada 5/14/62 (later K Wilderness)

Sgt Frank Price 20 enlisted Grenada, Ms **C 7/14**

Sgt John Taliaferro 25 yr old enlisted Grenada, Ms 5/14/62 **K 7/3**

Cpl. Jesse Lott 30 yrs old enlisted Grenada 5/14/62 **W-left leg 7/1 C 7/3** (in attack)

Cpl. Joseph Timberlake 29 yr old enlisted Grenada, Ms **C 6/28/63 Greencastle, Pa**

Private Isaac Thomas Alderman enlisted Grenada, Ms 5/14/62 (later Corporal / K Hatcher's Run)

Private William Arnold enlisted Booneville, Ms 5/14/62 **W 7/16**

Private Joseph Bamburg enlisted Grenada, Ms 5/14/62

Private Isaac Brown enlisted Grenada, Ms 5/14/62 **W-head 7/3**

Private John Campbell enlisted Grenada, Ms 5/14/62 **C 7/3**

Private George Cheek enlisted Grenada, Ms 5/14/62 (later W-Wilderness / Weldon RR)

Private Riley Forbes enlisted Grenada, Ms 5/14/62 **C 7/3**

Private John Glenn enlisted Grenada, Ms 5/14/62 **C 7/3**

Private William Holland enlisted Grenada, Ms 5/14/62 **K 7/4**

Private William Holman enlisted Grenada, Ms 5/14/62 **C 7/14**

Private Joseph Howard enlisted Grenada, Ms 5/14/62 **W 7/3**

Private George Jones enlisted Grenada, Ms 5/14/62 **(under arrest 7/1) C 7/3**

Private Norwell McPherson 31 yr old enlisted Grenada, Ms 5/14/62 **K 7/3**

Private Richard Meux enlisted Grenada, Ms 5/14/62 **C 7/14**

Private John Rogers 18 yr old enlisted Grenada, Ms 5/14/62 **W 7/3** (later W-Wilderness)

Private Benjamin Shelton enlisted Grenada, Ms 5/14/62 **W-leg C 7/3**

Private William Sullivan enlisted Grenada, Ms 5/14/62 (later K-Wilderness)

Private Lee Taylor enlisted Grenada, Ms 5/14/62 (detached) (later K Weldon RR)

Private William Tindell enlisted Grenada, Ms 5/14/62 **C 7/3**

Private William Tyler 34 yr old enlisted Grenada, Ms 5/14/62 **WC 7/3**

Private James Whitley 22 yr old enlisted Grenada, Ms 5/14/62 **C 7/3**

Private William Wimberly enlisted Grenada, Ms 5/14/62 (later W-Wildwood)

Private Edward Wright 22 yr old enlisted Grenada, Ms 5/14/62 **C 7/3**

July 1 Casualties

1st Lt Thomas Pleasants enlisted Grenada 5/14/62 ***left sick in Fredericksburg sick 7/1-7/3*** **W-arm 7/14**

2nd Lt William Bamburg 31 yr old enlisted Grenada, Ms 5/14/62 **W 7/1** (later WC-Wilderness)

Sgt William Ingram 24 yr old enlisted Grenada 5/14/62 **W-left hand 7/1 C 7/5**

Private William Beck 29 yrs old enlisted Grenada, Ms 5/14/62 **K 7/1**

Private Hamilton Beck 22 yrs old enlisted Grenada, Ms 5/14/62 **(sick 7/3)**

Private Berry Blaylock enlisted Grenada 5/14/62 **C 7/14 (sick 7/3)**

Private William Cain enlisted Grenada, Ms 5/14/62 **W 7/1** (later W-Wilderness)

Private Richard Campbell enlisted Grenada, Ms 5/14/62 **W 7/1**

Private Nathan Carpenter enlisted Grenada, Ms 5/14/62 **W 7/1 (died 7/14)**

Private Hillard Cheek enlisted Grenada, Ms 5/14/62 **W-left breast C 7/1**

Private Callaway Collins enlisted Grenada, Ms 5/14/62 **W-breast 7/1**

Private William Collins enlisted Grenada, Ms 5/14/62 **W-left knee 7/1**

Private George Doss 28 yr old enlisted Grenada, Ms 5/14/62 **W 7/1**

Private Ira Eubanks enlisted Grenada, Ms 5/14/62 **W 7/1 C 7/5**

Private Sanders Ezell enlisted Grenada, Ms 5/14/62 **W 7/1**

Private Harvey Flanigan 27 yr old enlisted Grenada, Ms 5/14/62 **K 7/1**

Private William Forbes enlisted Grenada, Ms 5/14/62 **W 7/1**

Private Micajah Gant enlisted Grenada, Ms 5/14/62 **W 7/1**

Private Ezekiel Lancaster 26 yr old enlisted Carrolton, Ms **W-arm 7/1**

Private Osbourne Heath enlisted Grenada, Ms 5/14/62 **sick 7/1 7/3 at Falling Waters 7/14** (later K Wilderness)

Private James Howard enlisted Grenada, Ms 5/14/62 **K 7/1**

Private Stephen Lancaster 29 yr old Carrolton, Ms **sick 7/1 & 7/3 present 7/14**

Private James Loden enlisted Grenada, Ms 5/14/62 **sick 7/1 & 7/3 present 7/14**

Private Christopher Loving 19 yr old farmer **W-right arm& leg 7/1**

Private Turner Lumbley 30 yr old enlisted Grenada, Ms 5/14/62 **K 7/1**

Private Stephen Marshall 26 yr old farmer enlisted Grenada, Ms 5/14/62 **W 7/1**

Private Alexander McMillan farmer enlisted Grenada, Ms 5/14/62 **W 7/1**

Private John Minyard 22 yr old enlisted Grenada, Ms 5/14/62 **W-right side by shell fragment 7/1 C 7/5**

Private Reason Peters enlisted Grenada, Ms 5/14/62 **W-left leg 7/1 C 7/5**

Private Mathew Richmond enlisted Grenada, Ms 5/14/62 **sick 7/1-7/3 C 7/14**

Private William Rogers 26 yr old enlisted Grenada, Ms 5/14/62 **K 7/1**

Private Richard Taliaferro enlisted Grenada, Ms 5/14/62 **W-left knee 7/1**

Private Albert Terry enlisted Grenada, Ms 5/14/62 **Present 7/1 sick 7/3**

Private James William 38 yr old enlisted Grenada, Ms 5/14/62 **sick 7/1-7/3** (later W-Weldon RR)

Teamster William Lott enlisted Grenada, Ms 5/14/62 **W-left leg 7/1 C 7/5**

Company B *"Senatobia Invincibles"*

2nd Lt John Godfrey 36 yr old druggist enlisted Granada, Ms 5/14/62 **W 7/3** (later K Wilderness)

Sgt James McNeely 25 yrs old enlisted Grenada 5/14/62 **C 7/3**

Cpl. James Terry 28 yr old enlisted Grenada, ms 5/14/62 **W-leg C 7/3 (died)**

Private Lucius Britton enlisted Grenada, Ms 5/14/62 **W-thigh C 7/3**

Private Thomas Burns enlisted Grenada, Ms 5/14/62 **C 7/14** (sick 7/3)

Private Joseph Coppeye enlisted Grenada, Ms 5/14/62 **C 7/5**

Private Eli Deshazo enlisted Grenada, Ms 5/14/62 **W 7/3** (later W-Spotsylvania)

Private James Freeze enlisted Grenada, Ms 5/14/62 **W 7/3 C 7/5**

Private John Miller 18 yr old student enlisted Grenada, Ms 5/14/62 **WC 7/3** (Later Cpl)

Private William Mitchell 24 yr old farmer enlisted Grenada, Ms 5/14/62 (later K Bristoe)

Private James W Moore 26 yr old mechanic enlisted Grenada, Ms 5/14/62 (later teamster)

Private James Moore 22 yr old enlisted Grenada, Ms 5/14/62 sick in Fredericksburg **W-scalp 7/14**

Private Robert Phillips enlisted Grenada, Ms 5/14/62 **K 7/3**

Private David Roberts enlisted Grenada, Ms 5/14/62 **W 7/3**

Private James Scott enlisted Grenada, Ms 5/14/62 **WC 7/3**

Private William Terry 23 yr old enlisted Grenada, Ms 5/14/62 **C 7/14 detached with wagons**

Private William Veazey 17 yr old student enlisted Grenada, Ms 5/14/62 **W 7/3** (later Corp)

Private James Yarbough 24 yr old enlisted Grenada, Ms 5/14/62 (later K-Weldon RR)

Teamster John Singleton enlisted Grenada (later W Petersburg)

Musician William Quinn 24 yr old enlisted Grenada, Ms—Regimental bugler

Musician Lewis Robertson 30 yr old enlisted Grenada, Ms 5/14/62 **C 7/5** (Drummer)

7/1 Casualties

Captain Leander Woollard 28 yr old lawyer enlisted Grenada, Ms 5/14/62 **C 7/1**

3rd Lt Benjamin Wham 26 yr old enlisted Grenada, Ms 5/14/62 **W-thigh 7/1 C 7/5 died Baltimore**

Sgt Benjamin Hall 23 yr old enlisted Granada, Ms 5/14/62 **W 7/1**

Sgt John Wham 29 yr old enlisted Grenada, Ms 5/14/62 **MW 7/1 died 9/3/63**

Sgt Seth Wolllard 31 yr old enlisted Grenada, Ms 5/14/62 **W 7/1**

Cpl. Hampton Bradley 24 yr oldenlisted Grenada, Ms 5/14/62 **C 7/1**

Cpl. James Powell 24 yr old enlisted Grenada, Ms **WC 7/1**

Private Joseph Bachman enlisted 2/8/63 Carrolton, Ms **K 7/1**

Private James Blassingame enlisted Grenada, Ms 5/14/62 **K 7/1**

Private James Bradley 26 yr old enlisted Grenada, Ms 5/14/62 **W 7/1**

Private William Gabler enlisted Grenada, Ms 5/14/62 **W 7/1**

Private Marcus Campbell enlisted Grenada, Ms 5/14/62 **C 7/1**

Private William Chisholm enlisted Grenada, Ms 5/14/62 **C 7/1**
Private David Deshazo enlisted Grenada, Ms 5/14/62 **C 7/1**
Private John Deshazo enlisted Grenada, Ms 5/14/62 **C 7/1**
Private William Embry enlisted Grenada, Ms 5/14/62 **C 7/1**
Private William Fairless enlisted Grenada, Ms 5/14/62 **C 7/1**
Private James Green enlisted Grenada, Ms 5/14/62 **C 7/1**
Private Theodopolis Hall 19 yr old clerk enlisted Grenada, Ms 5/14/62 **C 7/1**
Private Monroe Harris enlisted Grenada, Ms 5/14/62 **C 7/1**
Private James Hunter enlisted Grenada, Ms 5/14/62 **WC 7/1**
Private Samuel Leonard enlisted Grenada, Ms 5/14/62 (present detached) (Later W-Wilderness)
Private James McIntosh 25 yrs old enlisted Grenada, Ms 5/14/62 **K 7/1 (carrying colors)**
Private Candor Miller enlisted Grenada, Ms 5/14/62 **W 7/1 C 7/5**
Private John T Miller 22 yr old student enlisted Grenada, Ms 5/14/62 **C 7/1**
Private Sylvanus Mitchell enlisted Grenada, Ms 5/14/62 **C 7/1**
Private Joseph Patton 34 yr old enlisted Grenada, Ms 5/14/62 **K 7/1**
Private William Patton enlisted Grenada, Ms 5/14/62 **W-foot 7/1 C 7/5**
Private Thomas Powell 21 yr old student enlisted Grenada, Ms 5/14/62 **C 7/1**
Private Abner Ridgeway enlisted Grenada, Ms 5/14/62 **WC 7/1**
Private Robert Robinson enlisted Grenada, Ms 5/14/62 **C 7/1**
Private Sanvel Rowell enlisted Grenada, Ms 5/14/62 **C 7/1**
Private John Saunders enlisted Grenada, Ms 5/14/62 **WC 7/1**
Private Eli Scott enlisted Grenada, Ms 5/14/62 **C 7/1**
Private John Scott enlisted Grenada, Ms 5/14/62 **W 7/1 C 7/5**
Private John A Scott enlisted Sardis, Ms **W 7/1**
Private Joseph Steele enlisted Grenada, Ms 5/14/62 **C 7/1**
Private William Swan enlisted Grenada, Ms 5/14/62 **K 7/1**
Private William Warren 31 yr old enlisted Grenada, Ms 5/14/62 **C 7/1** (Died Ft. Delaware)
Private William White 20 yr old enlisted Grenada, Ms 5/14/62 **W-arm 7/1**
Private John William 24 yr old enlisted Grenada, Ms 5/14/62 **K 7/1**

Private Rubin Loafman enlisted Grenada, Ms 5/14/62 (present detached)

Company C *"Nelm's Avengers"* aka *"Nelson's Avengers"*

Captain Wiley Smith 25 yr old physician enlisted Grenada, Ms—absent during campaign (later W-Wilderness)
1st Lt James Nail 28 yr old mechanic, enlisted Grenada, Ms in command **K 7/3**
3rd Lt John Wilburn 26 yr old enlisted Grenada, Ms 5/14/62 **W 7/3 died**

Sgt Richard Cobb 27 yr old enlisted Grenada, Ms 5/14/62
Sgt Americus Payne 27 yr old enlisted Grenada **W-left side 7/3 C 7/5**
Cpl. James Scott 23 yr old enlisted Grenada **C 7/3**
Cpl. Nathan Smith 25 yr old enlisted Grenada **W-lung & forearm C 7/3**
Private Samuel Anderson enlisted Grenada, Ms 5/14/62
Private Samuel Bailey enlisted Grenada, Ms 5/14/62 (later W-Petersburg)
Private Paul Boggan enlisted Grenada, Ms 5/14/62 **K 7/3**
Private Thomas Boyd enlisted Grenada, Ms 5/14/62 **C 7/3**
Private Sidney Castleberry enlisted Grenada, Ms 5/14/62 **W-arm 7/3**
Private Jacob Craft 32 yr old enlisted Grenada, Ms 5/14/62 **K 7/3**
Private Hiram Crumpler 34 yr old enlisted Grenada, Ms 5/14/62 **W-knee 7/3**
Private Ebenezer Davis 24 yr old enlisted Grenada, Ms 5/14/62 (later W-Wilderness)
Private Hezekial Davis 30 yr old enlisted Grenada, Ms 5/14/62 **C 7/3 died Ft Delaware / buried Finn's Point, NJ**
Private James Dye enlisted Grenada, Ms 5/14/62 W 7/1
Private Samuel Hall 23 yr old enlisted Grenada, Ms 5/14/62 **C 7/3**
Private Gabiel Ham 31 yr old enlisted Grenada, Ms 5/14/62
Private George Ham 21 yr old enlisted Grenada, Ms 5/14/62 **C 7/14**
Private Robert Holderly 21 yrs old enlisted Grenada, Ms 5/14/62 **W-right forearm 7/3**
Private James L Howard enlisted Grenada, Ms 5/14/62 **K 7/3**
Private James Humphries 21 yrs old enlisted Grenada, Ms 5/14/62 **K 7/3**
Private Samuel Hutchinson 27 yrs old enlisted Grenada, Ms 5/14/62 **W-left hand 7/3**
Private John Johnson student enlisted Grenada, Ms 5/14/62 **W 7/3**
Private Britton Jones enlisted Grenada, Ms 5/14/62 (later W Spotsylvania)
Private Stephen Jones 37 yr old enlisted Grenada, Ms 5/14/62 **W 7/3**
Private Christopher Manning enlisted Grenada, Ms 5/14/62 (present detached)
Private Thomas Marshall 23 yr old enlisted Grenada, Ms 5/14/62 **W 7/3 C 7/4**
Private James Phillips 24 yr old enlisted Grenada, Ms 5/14/62 **K 7/3**
Private Albert Pounders enlisted Grenada, Ms 5/14/62 **K 7/3**
Private John Pryor 20 yr old enlisted Grenada, Ms 5/14/62 **W-left knee C 7/3**
Private Pleasant Reed 26 yr old enlisted Grenada, Ms 5/14/62 **C 7/4**
Private Zalmon Reed enlisted Grenada, Ms 5/14/62 **K 7/3**
Private George Riggs enlisted Grenada, Ms 5/14/62 WC 7/3
Private William Rines 19 yr old enlisted Grenada, Ms 5/14/62 **C 7/3**
Private Alexander Stephens 19 yr old enlisted Grenada, Ms 5/14/62
Private Joseph Wheeler 19 yr old enlisted Grenada, Ms 5/14/62 **C 7/3**

Teamster Calvin Newberry enlisted Grenada, Ms 5/14/62 (later C Davis Farm)
Teamster James Norvis 35 yr old enlisted Grenada, Ms 5/14/62
Teamster Joseph Simmons 29 yr old enlisted Grenada, Ms 5/14/62
Private Josuha Teague 29 yr old enlisted Grenada, Ms 5/14/62 detailed to Ord train (Later W-Wilderness)

7/1 Casualties

2nd Lt Oliver Stevens 32 yr old enlisted Grenada, Ms **W-abdomen 7/1** (later W-Wilderness)
Sgt Robert Dennis 24 yr old enlisted Grenade, Ms 5/14/62 **K 7/1**
Sgt William Whitley 23 yr old enlisted Grenada, Ms 5/14/62 **K 7/1**
Cpl. Thomas Clifton 29 yr old enlisted Grenada, Ms 5/14/62 **C 7/1**
Cpl. Jordan Payne 20 yr old enlisted Grenada **C 7/1**
Private George Anderson enlisted Grenada, Ms 5/14/62 **W 7/1**
Private Felix Baker enlisted Grenada, Ms 5/14/62 **W-leg 7/1** (amputated-died 7/13)
Private John Black enlisted Grenada, Ms 5/14/62 **W 7/1**
Private William Danner 31 yr old enlisted Grenada, Ms 5/14/62 **C 7/1**
Private Robert Farley 30 yr old enlisted Grenada, Ms 5/14/62 **K 7/1**
Private James Gaddy enlisted Grenada, Ms 5/14/62 **W 7/1**
Private Stephen Ham 24 yr old enlisted Grenada, Ms 5/14/62 **K 7/1**
Private Stephen H ham 31 yr old enlisted Grenada, Ms 5/14/62 **W 7/1**
Private Thomas Ham 29 yr old yr old enlisted Grenada, Ms 5/14/62 **sick 7/1 7/3 present 7/14**
Private James Johnson enlisted Grenada, Ms 5/14/62 **absent sick 7/1 & 7/3 W 7/14**
Private Donald Jones enlisted Grenada, Ms 5/14/62 **sick 7/1 & 7/3 C 7/14**
Private John Jones enlisted Grenada, Ms 5/14/62 **sick 7/1 & 7/3 C 7/14**
Private Joseph Mason enlisted Grenada, Ms 5/14/62 **K 7/1**
Private Marion McCall enlisted Grenada, Ms 5/14/62 **sick 7/1 & 7/3**
Private John McNeal enlisted Grenada, Ms 5/14/62 **W-left side 7/3** (later W CH)
Private Moses McNeely enlisted Grenada, Ms 5/14/62 **W-nose by shell 7/1**
Private Charles Morgan enlisted Grenada, Ms 5/14/62 **W 7/1**

Company D *"Capt. Locke's Company"*

1st Lt Matthew Jones 35 yr old enlisted Grenada 5/14/62 (later W Bristoe Station)
3rd Lt Masselton Thompson 22 yr old enlisted Grenada, Ms 5/14/62 (later W-Bristoe Station)
1st Sgt William Smith 21 yr old enlisted Grenada, Ms CD 7/3 (died 12/63)
Sgt George Yocum 28 yr old enlisted Grenada, Ms 5/14/62
Cpl. Whitson Carter enlisted Grenada, Ms 5/14/62 **C 7/6 Williamsport** Paroled 7/6
Cpl. William Jackson enlisted Grenada 5/14/62 **C 7/14**
Private Monroe Blackwell enlisted Grenada, Ms 5/14/62
Private Robert Brown enlisted Grenada, Ms 5/14/62 **C 7/3**
Private Mitchel Marion Burford age 23 enlisted Grenada, Ms 5/14/62 **WC 7/3 died smallpox (Ft Delaware)buried Finn's Point,**
Private William Cannon enlisted Grenada, Ms 5/14/62 **C 7/3**
Private James Crawford 30 yr old enlisted Grenada, Ms 5/14/62

Private David Dean 31 yr old enlisted Grenada, Ms 5/14/62
Private Stephen Fielder student enlisted Grenada, Ms 5/14/62
Private Romulus Kersey 19 yr old student enlisted Grenada, Ms 5/14/62 **C 7/3** (escaped)
Private Frank King enlisted Grenada, Ms 5/14/62 **W 7/1 C 7/5**
Private Thomas Martin 20 yr old enlisted Grenada, Ms 5/14/62 "brave in battle" (later Sgt) later W-Wilderness
Private Joseph McClain 28 yr old mechanic enlisted Grenada, Ms 5/14/62 **WC 7/3 (died)**
Private John Miner 35 yr old enlisted Grenada, Ms 5/14/62
Private John Moore 20 yr old farmer enlisted Corinth, Ms (later W-Wilderness)
Private Albert Norfleet 17 yr old enlisted Grenada, Ms 5/14/62
Private Ben Rogers 28 yr old enlisted Grenada, Ms 5/14/62
Private John Sansom 39 yr old enlisted Grenada, Ms 5/14/62 **W-right arm C 7/3 (amp)**
Private Davidson Smith 31 yr old enlisted Grenada, Ms 5/14/62 **C 7/14**
Private Henderson Sowell 19 yr old enlisted Grenada, Ms 5/14/62 **W-face 7/3**
Private Willis Sulllivan 29 yr old enlisted Grenada, Ms 5/14/62 **W 7/3 C 7/5**
Private John Thompson 20 yr old enlisted Benola, Ms 5/14/62 **C 7/3**
Private Henry Wall 26 yr old enlisted Grenada, Ms 5/14/62 **C 7/14**
Private Flinn Wilson 22 yr old enlisted Grenada, Ms 5/14/62 **K 7/3**
Private Dan Yocum 21 yr old enlisted Grenada, Ms 5/14/62 (later K-Spotsylvania)

Teamster Thomas Williams 26 yr old enlisted Grenada, Ms 5/14/62 (later W-Wilderness)

July 1 Casualties

Captain Robert Locke 28 yr ld enlisted Grenada 5/14/62 **W-breast 7/1** (later Major)
2nd Lt George Houze 29 yr old Grenada, Ms 5/14/62 **K 7/1**
1st Sgt Joshua Martin Adkins 23 yr old merchant enlisted Grenada, Ms 5/14/62 **K 7/1**
Sgt Lafayette Morgan 34 yr old enlisted Grenada 5/14/62 **K 7/1**
Cpl. John Anderson 17 yr old enlisted Grenada, Ms 5/14/62 **W 7/1 C 7/6** (later Lt)
Cpl. William Caisson 34 yr old enlisted Grenada, Ms 5/14/62 **C 7/1**
Private John Bowden 31 yr old merchant enlisted Grenada, Ms 5/14/62 **C 7/14 (sick 7/3)**
Private John Boyd enlisted Grenada, Ms 5/14/62 **C 7/14 (sick 7/3)**
Private Robert Caisson 21 yr old enlisted Grenada, Ms 5/14/62 **C 7/1**
Private George Everson 19 yr old enlisted Grenada, Ms 5/14/62 **C 7/1**
Private James Farrow 19 yr old enlisted Grenada, Ms 5/14/62 **W 7/1**
Private Thomas Hancock 30 yr old enlisted Grenada, Ms 5/14/62 **W 7/1**
Private Ebenezer Ingram enlisted Grenada, Ms 5/14/62 **W 7/1 C 7/4**
Private Lovett Ingram enlisted Grenada, Ms 5/14/62 **W-thigh 7/1 C 7/5**
Private Lucius Johnson enlisted Grenada, Ms 5/14/62 **W-right leg 7/1**
Private William Kerr 25 yr old farmer enlisted Grenada, Ms 5/14/62 **W 7/1** (later Sgt)
Private William Kersey enlisted Grenada, Ms 5/14/62 **W 7/1**
Private William McCall enlisted Grenada, Ms 5/14/62 **W-right arm 7/1**

Private John McCurry enlisted Grenada, Ms 5/14/62 **W-back &abdomen 7/1 C 7/5**
Private Charles Ruby 28 yr old enlisted Grenada, Ms 5/14/62 **W-right leg 7/1 C 7/5**
Private Jacob Sansom 37 yr old enlisted Grenada, Ms 5/14/62 **W-left hand 7/1**
Private Perry Walker 25 yr old enlisted Grenada, Ms 5/14/62 **W 7/1 C 7/6 Williamsport died 7/19**
Private James Wall 23 yr old enlisted Grenada, Ms 5/14/62 **7/1 present 7/3 sick C 7/6 Williamsport**
Private R.M. White 18 yr old enlisted Grenada, Ms 5/14/62 **W 7/1**
Private Frank Wilson 19 yr old enlisted Grenada, Ms 5/14/62 **W-face 7/1**

Company E *"Davenport Rifles"*

Captain Henry Davenport 26 yr old enlisted Booneville, Ms 5/14/62 **K 7/3**
1st Lt Jordon Moores 43 yr old farmer enlisted Boonville, ms **K 7/3**
2nd Lt Henry Beardon 21 yr old enlisted Grenada, Ms 5/14/62 **C 7/3**
3rd Lt Lyman Mitchell 33 yr old enlisted Boonville, Ms **W-right hand 7/3**
First Sgt Lanceford Davis 27 yr old enlisted Booneville, Ms 5/14/62 **C 7/3**
Sgt. Franklin Smith 36 yr old enlisted Boonesville, Ms **W-right thigh 7/3**
Cpl. John Campbell enlisted Boonville, Ms 5/14/62 **C 7/14**
Cpl. Joseph Green enlisted Boonville, Ms 5/14/62 (later K-Wilderness)
Cpl. Daniel Wright 34 yr old Booneville, Ms enlisted 5/14/62 **W 7/3**
Private H.W. Adams enlisted Grenada, Ms 5/14/62 **C 7/6**
Private Columbus Akers enlisted Boonville, Ms 5/14/62 **K 7/3**
Private John Akers enlisted Boonville, Ms 5/14/62 **WC 7/3**
Private Henry Barlow Blackwell enlisted Boonville, Ms 5/14/62 **WC 7/3** (had brother in 2nd MS)
Private Joshua B. Blackwell enlisted Boonville, Ms 5/14/62 **W-left leg C 7/3** (had brother in 2nd MS)
Private William Burchum 19 yr old enlisted Boonville, Ms 5/14/62 **C 7/3**
Private James Couch enlisted Booneville, Ms 5/14/62
Private Lewis Evans enlisted Booneville, Ms 5/14/62 **C 7/3**
Private George Fagan enlisted Grenada, Ms 5/14/62 **C 7/3**
Private William Noah Fagan enlisted Grenada, Ms 5/14/62 **C 7/3**
Private Curtis Garner enlisted Booneville, Ms 5/14/62 **K 7/3**
Private Washington Green 29 yr old enlisted Booneville, Ms 5/14/62 **C 7/3**
Private David Jones enlisted Booneville, Ms 5/14/62
Private Robert Lard 23 yr old enlisted Tishimango, Ms **W-left thigh C 7/3**
Private Benjamin McBride enlisted Booneville, Ms 5/14/62 (later W-right thigh Spotsylvania)
Private Heziekiah Palmer enlisted Baldwyn, Ms 10/1/62 (later K Bristoe)
Private Thomas Palmer enlisted Boonville, Ms 5/14/62 **K 7/3**

Private William Palmer enlisted Booneville, Ms 5/14/62 **K 7/3**
Private George Plaxco enlisted Booneville, Ms 5/14/62
Private William Paxco enlisted Booneville, Ms 5/14/62
Private William Ragsdale enlisted Booneville, Ms 5/14/62 **C 7/14 (Died 9/28)**
Private Meredith Reynolds enlisted Booneville, Ms 5/14/62 **C 7/3**
Private William Searcy enlisted Booneville, Ms 5/14/62 **C 7/3**
Private Moses Smith enlisted Booneville, Ms 5/14/62 **K 7/3**
Private Charles Williams enlisted Booneville, Ms 5/14/62 **W-right elbow C 7/3**
Private Samuel Williams enlisted Booneville, Ms 5/14/62 **C 7/3**
Private William Yates enlisted Booneville, Ms 5/14/62 deserted 3/63/captured/returned **K 7/3**

July 1 Casualties

Sgt. William Lorick 27 yr old enlisted Boonville, Ms 5/14/62 **W-right foot 7/1**
Sgt Calvin McElroy 34 yrs old enlisted Boonville, Ms **W-leg 7/1**
Cpl. Rufus Lusk 27 yrs old enlisted Boonville, ms 5/14/62 **W-shoulder 7/1** (later K Petersburg)
Private William Carvan enlisted Booneville, Ms 5/14/62 **C 7/1**
Private Thomas Kinningham 24 yr old enlisted Booneville, Ms 5/14/62 **W-thigh 7/1**
Private James Rowell enlisted Booneville, Ms 5/14/62 **sick 7/1-7/3 K 7/14**
Private George Smith enlisted Booneville, Ms 5/14/62 **W 7/1**
Private John Smith enlisted Booneville, Ms 5/14/62 **sick 7/1-7/3**
Private Thomas Stevenson enlisted Booneville, Ms 5/14/62 **C 7/1**
Private John Yates enlisted Booneville, Ms 5/14/62 deserted 3/63/captured/returned **W-right thigh 7/1 C 7/5**

Company F *"Captain Clark's Company"*

1st Lt James Seals 24 yr old enlisted Oxford, Ms W-**thigh 7/3** (5 wounds) died 7/20
2nd Lt Nathan Coker 29 yr old enlisted Calhoun co. 4/29/62 **W 7/3** (later W-Bristoe)
3rd Lt Benjamin Grant merchant enlisted Sarepta, Ms 4/29/62 **W-thigh C 7/14**
Sgt Rowland Tankersley 29 yr old enlisted Sarepta, Ms 4/29/62 **C 7/3**
Cpl. Robert Brower 43 yr old mechanic enlisted Oxford, Ms 4/29/62 **W 7/3**
Private Mike Austin enlisted Oxford, Ms 4/29/62 (later W-leg Wild)
Private William Bachman enlisted Oxford, Ms 4/29/62 **C 7/3**
Private Hardy Berry enlisted Oxford, Ms 5/14/62
Private Larkin Bert enlisted Oxford, Ms 4/29/62
Private John Brown enlisted Calhoun Co. Ms 4/29/62 **C 7/3**
Private Robert Davis 23 yr old enlisted Oxford. Ms 4/29/62
Private John Flemens enlisted Sarepta, Ms 4/29/62 **C 7/4**

Private Joseph Goode 31 yr old mechanic enlisted Oxford, Ms 4/29/62 **WC 7/3**
Private John House 17 yr old Oxford, Ms enlisted 5/14/62
Private William Huckaby 19 yr old Oxford, Ms enlisted 4/29/62 **W-thigh C 7/3**
Private James Jenkins enlisted Sarepta, Ms 4/29/61 **W 7/3**
Private William Masey enlisted Oxford, Co, Ms 4/29/61 **WC 7/3**
Private Cealy McUlly farmer enlisted Sarepta, Ms
Private Jefferson Overby enlisted Oxford, Ms **W-groin 7/3**
Private Jefferson Prestage 24 yr old enlisted Oxford, Ms **W-knee C 7/3**
Private John Scott 20 yr old enlisted Oxford, Ms (later W-Bristoe Station)
Private Levi Shepard enlisted Sarepta, Ms **W-right thigh C 7/3**
Private Jeremiah Smith 20 yr old enlisted Oxford, Ms **C 7/3**
Private Joseph Tramel enlisted Oxford, Ms 5/14/62 **C 7/14**
Private William Trim enlisted Sarepta, Ms 4/29/62 **W-leg & shoulder 7/3**
Private Jacob Ward 26 yr old enlisted Oxford, Ms 5/14/62
Private James Webster 20 yr old enlisted Oxford, Ms 5/14/62 **W 7/3**
Private George W. Wilkins 19 yr old enlisted Oxford, Ms 5/14/62 **W-left thigh C 7/14**
Private John Wilkins 25 yr old enlisted Oxford, Ms 5/14/62 **W-leg C 7/3**
Private Samuel Wilkins 30 yr old enlisted Oxford, Ms 5/14/62 **W-right hand C 7/3**

Pioneer John Countess 39 yr old enlisted Calhoun Co. Ms 4/29/62
Private William Blaylock enlisted Oxford, Ms 4/29/62—guard on ordinance train
Teamster John Blout enlisted Calhoun Co. 4/29/62
Teamster Ranson Murphree enlisted Sarepta, Ms 4/29/62 (later W-Wildernesss)
Teamster Solomon Murphree 31 yr old enlisted Oxford, Ms 5/14/62
Teamster William Smallwood 19 yr old enlisted Oxford, Ms 5/14/62

July 1 Casualties

Captain Thomas Goode Clark 41 yr old enlisted Oxford, Ms **K 7/1 (with 2 sons)**
1st Sgt James Duncan 24 yr old teacher enlisted Calhoun Co. 4/29/62 **W 7/1**
Sgt Marcellus Church 24 yr old (half brother of Captain) enlisted Calhoun Co., Ms 4/29/62 **WC 7/3** died Pt Lookout
Sgt William Tatum 31 yr old enlisted Calhoun Co, Ms **W-right foot 7/1**
Private Lee Allen enlisted Oxford, Ms 4/29/62 **(sick 7/3)**
Private Abner Bagwell enlisted Calhoun, Ms 4/29/62 **(sick 7/3)**
Private Charles Bagwell enlisted Calhoun, Ms 4/29/62 **W 7/1 (died 7/18)**
Private Love Bagwell enlisted Calhoun, Ms 4/29/62 **W 7/1 C 7/4**
Private George Bratton enlisted Sarepta, Ms 4/29/62 **K 7/1**
Private Jesse Brown enlisted Calhoun Co. Ms 4/29/62 **WC 7/1**
Private Ensley Christman 19 yr old enlisted Oxford, Ms 4/29/62 **K 7/1**
Private Lawrence Christman 29 yr old enlisted Oxford, Ms 4/29/62 **W 7/1**
Private Samuel Christman 25 yr old enlisted Oxford, Ms 4/29/62 **W 7/1**

Private Albert H. Clark 19 yr old Oxford, Ms enlisted 4/29/62 **K 7/1 . . . sons**
Private Jonathan Clark 21 yr old Oxford, Ms enlisted 4/29/62 **K 7/1 . . . sons**
Private Ed Clemens 27 yr old enlisted Oxford, Ms 4/29/62 **W 7/1**
Private William Cotton 23 yr old enlisted Calhoun Co. Ms 4/29/62 **W 7/1**
Pioneer Henry Davis 25 yr old enlisted Oxford. Ms 4/29/62 **W-left leg 7/1 C 7/4**
Private Alexander Goad 29 yr old Blacksmith enlisted Sarepta, Ms 4/29/62 **W-right elbow 7/1**
Private Henry Jenkins enlisted Sarepta, Ms 4/29/61 **W 7/1 C 7/5**
Private William Johnson enlisted Sarepta, Ms 4/29/61 **W 7/1**
Private James Kinney enlisted Calhoun Co. **W 7/1 C 7/5 died of wounds**
Private Calvin Kirby **WC 7/1 (died of wounds)**
Private Milus Kirby 20 yr old enlisted Oxford, Ms 4/29/61 **WC 7/1**
Private William Murphree 22 yr old enlisted Oxford, Ms **W-right leg 7/1 C 7/4**
Private Alexander Palmer 34 yr old Sarepta, Ms enlisted 4/29/62 **W 7/1 C 7/7**
Private Dudley Patterson 22 yr old enlisted Oxford, Ms **W-right forearm 7/1**
Private John Patterson enlisted Oxford, Ms **K 7/1**
Private Moses Phillips enlisted Oxford, Ms 5/14/62 **W-left hip 7/1 C 7/4**
Private Reuben Pruett 18 yr old enlisted Oxford, Ms **W 7/1 C 7/5**
Private Elsiha Sharp enlisted Sare[pta, Ms 4/29/62 **W-left foot 7/1**
Private Sherwood Tankersly 32 yr old enlisted Oxford, Ms 5/14/62 **sick 7/1-7/3 C 7/14**
Private Jasper Vick 25 yr old enlisted Oxford, Ms 5/14/62 **7/1 present 7/3 sick**

Company G *"Gaston Rifles"*

1st Lt Thomas Smith 33 yr old Benola, Ms **W-thigh 7/3** (later W-Wilderness)
2nd Lt John Spencer 30 yr old enlisted Benela, Ms **K 7/3**
1st Sgt Cullen Lee enlisted Benela, Ms 5/15/62 **W-side 7/3** (later LT W Spotsylvania)
Cpl. William Killingsworth 33 yr old enlisted Benela, Ms 5/13/62 **C 7/3**
Cpl. Samuel Patterson 22 yr old enlisted Grenada, Ms
Private Thomas Anderson enlisted 8/30/62 Richmond, Va **WC 7/3** (died)
Private John Bryan enlisted Benela, Ms 5/13/62 **W 7/3**
Private James Burns enlisted Benela, Ms 5/13/62 **WC 7/3** (died 8/6 Chester hospital buried PNC))
Private Abraham Crutchfield enlisted Benela, Ms 5/13/62 **C 7/14**
Private Joseph Few 18 yr old enlisted Benela, Ms 5/13/62 **C 7/3**
Private Wiley Griffin 24 yr old enlisted Benela, Ms 5/13/62
Private Andrew Hamby 33 yr old enlisted Benela, Ms 5/13/62 **W 7/3 C 7/14**
Private John Hardin 20 yr old enlisted Benela, Ms 5/13/62
Private Edward Hardy 19 yr old enlisted Benela, Ms 5/13/62
Private Levi Harrelston enlisted Benela, Ms 5/13/62 **C 7/4**
Private William Hollingsworth enlisted Benela, Ms 5/13/62 **C 7/14**

Private David Lee enlisted Benela, Ms 5/13/62 **W-finger 7/3**

Private Darling Lowery enlisted Saltillo, ms 5/14/62 **C 7/3**

Private Jonathan May 21 yr old physician enlisted Benela, Ms 5/13/62

Private Levi T. McKee 23 yr old enlisted Benela, Ms Headquarters Guard **W/C 7/3 died Frederick, Md 8/13 buried Mt Olivet**

Private Bazzell Moore 30 yr old enlisted Benela, Ms 5/13/62 **C 7/14**

Private William Moore 29 yr old farmer enlisted Benela, Ms 5/13/62 (later W-right side Wilderness)

Private James Moreman 33 yr old enlisted Benela, Ms 5/13/62 **W-right arm C 7/3 (arm amputated)**

Private Thomas Murphree 28 yr old enlisted Benela, Ms 5/13/62 **W-shell right arm 7/3** (amp-died 7/20)

Private Aquiller Parker 22 yr old enlisted Grenada, Ms **C 7/3**

Private Elijah Parker 25 yr old enlisted Grenada, ms **K 7/3**

Private Issac Sims enlisted Benela, Ms 5/13/62 (later W-Weldon RR)

Private Alberry Stroup 20 yr old enlisted Benela, Ms 5/13/62 **W-left ankle 7/3**

Private Matthew Terry 33 yr old enlisted Benela, Ms 5/13/62 (later K Wilderness)

Private Pleasant Thompson 23 yr old enlisted Benela, Ms 5/13/62 **C 7/3**

Private Hardin Walker 24 yr old enlisted Benela, Ms 5/13/62 **W-shoulder C 7/3**

Private Frances Winter 25 yr old enlisted Benela, Ms 5/13/62 deserted 7/31/63

Private John Winter 29 yr old enlisted Benela, Ms 5/13/62 **left to care for wounded C 7/4**

Private Josiah Winter 20 yr old enlisted Benela, Ms 5/13/62 deserted 7/31/63

Private Lewis Winter 21 yr old enlisted Benela, Ms 5/13/62 deserted 7/31/63

Ambulance Driver Ephram Kea enlisted Benela, Ms 5/13/62 (later K-Wilderness)

Teamster James Barker enlisted 3/19/63 Benela, Ms

Teamster Mason Thurman enlisted Benela, Ms 5/13/62 (later W-Wilderness)

July 1 Casualties

Captain James Gaston 28 yr old enlisted Benela, Ms 5/14/62 **K 7/1**

Sgt Charles Bentley enlisted Benela, Ms 5/13/62 **(sick on 7/3)**

Sgt Joshua Hardy Benela, Ms 5/13/62 **WC 7/14 (sick left at Fredericksburg on march)**

Sgt Noah Shook 23 yr old enlisted Benela, Ms 5/13/62 **C 7/1**

Sgt James Vanlandingham 30 yr old Grenada, Ms **C 7/1**

Cpl. James Kea enlisted Benela, Ms 5/13/62 **C 7/1** (later W Turkey Run)

Private Nelson Alexander enlisted Benela, Ms 5/13/62 **W 7/1**

Private Nimrod Arnold enlisted Benela, Ms 5/13/62 **K 7/1**

Private J.D. Bowen enlisted Grenada, Ms 5/14/62 **W-right arm 7/1**

Private James Bulock enlisted Benela, Ms 5/13/62 **C 7/1**

Private Milton Burson 34 yr old enlisted Benela, Ms 5/13/62 **C 7/1**

Private John Chrosier 35 yr old enlisted Grenada, Ms 5/14/62 **W 7/1**

Private John Clark 22 yr old enlisted Grenada, Ms 5/14/62 **C 7/1**
Private Henry Clark enlisted Benela, Ms 5/13/62 **W 7/1**
Private Manning Crutchfield 31 yr old enlisted Benela, Ms 5/13/62 **W-left leg 7/1**
Private William Crutchfield 19 yr old enlisted Benela, Ms 5/13/62 **C 7/1**
Private Henry Dunkin 28 yr old enlisted Benela, Ms 5/13/62 **C 7/1**
Private John Dunkin enlisted Benela, Ms 5/13/62 **C 7/1**
Private John Easley enlisted Benela, Ms 5/13/62 **C 7/1**
Private William Embrey 30 yr old enlisted Benela, Ms 5/13/62 **C 7/1**
Private Andrew Few 30 yr old enlisted Benela, Ms 5/13/62 **W 7/1**
Private Hazekah Griffin 30 yr old enlisted Benela, Ms 5/13/62 **C 7/1**
Private Ira Griffin enlisted Benela, Ms 5/13/62 **C 7/1**
Private Riley Griffin enlisted Benela, Ms 5/13/62 **W 7/1 C 7/4**
Private Carroll Hardin 20 yr old enlisted Benela, Ms 5/13/62 **W 7/1** (later W-Wild)
Private Irodel Harrelson enlisted Benela, Ms 5/13/62 **W-ankle 7/1**
Private Abel Harris yr old Oxford, Ms enlisted 4/29/62 **C 7/1**
Private William W. Johnson enlisted Benela, Ms 5/13/62 **sick 7/1 & 7/3 WC 7/14**
Private Arthur Kea enlisted Benela, Ms 5/13/62 **C 7/1**
Private Gary Moore 31 yr old enlisted Benela, Ms 5/13/62 **sick 7/1 & 7/3 present 7/14** (later W-knee Wilderness)
James Moore 29 yr old enlisted Benela, Ms 5/14/62 **sick 7/1 & 7/3 present W 7/14** (later W-Wilderness)
Private John Monger 19 yr old enlisted Benela, Ms 5/14/62 **left sick at Fredericksburg C 7/14**
Private Daniel Munn 26 yr old enlisted Benela, Ms 5/13/62 **W-right thigh 7/1**
Private George Murff 32 yr old enlisted Benela, Ms 5/13/62 **sick 7/1-7/3 C 7/14**
Private James Pryor 26 yr old enlisted Benela, Ms **W-hand 7/1** (later W-Bristoe Station)
Private Solomon Shok 19 yr old enlisted Benela, Ms 5/13/62 **left sick Fredericksburg—C 7/14**
Private James Simms enlisted Benela, Ms 5/13/62 **left sick at Fredericksburg**
Private William Slaughter 33 yr old enlisted Benela, Ms 5/13/62 **C 7/1**
Private Edward Streeter 19 yr old enlisted Benela, Ms 5/13/62 **W-scalp 7/1** (later W Bristoe)
Private William Taylor 31 yr old enlisted Benela, Ms 5/13/62 **C 7/1**
Private Moses Vanlandingham 28 yr old enlisted Benela, Ms 5/13/62 **C 7/1**
Private Alonzo Weeks 25 yr old twin enlisted Benela, Ms 5/13/62 **C 7/1**
Private John Weeks 25 yr old twin enlisted Benela, Ms 5/13/62 **C 7/1**
Private Green Williard 24 yr old enlisted Benela, Ms 5/13/62 **C 7/1**

Company H *"Captain Powell's Company"*

1st Lt Frank Ingram enlisted Grenada 5/14/62—in command
2nd Lt John Milton enlisted Grenada 5/14/62 **W-left lung 7/3**

Sgt Calvin Hight 32 yr old enlisted Grenada 5/14/62 **W-left arm C 7/3**
Sgt Benjamin Murphree 19 yr old enlisted Grenada 5/14/62 **W 7/14** (later C-Wilderness)
Sgt Reuben Perry enlisted Grenada, Ms 5/14/62 **W 7/14**
Sgt Robert Taylor 30 yr old enlisted Grenada, Ms **C 7/3**
Cpl. William Taylor 32 yr old enlisted Grenada, Ms 5/14/62 **W-hand 7/3**
Cpl. John Weir 22 yr old enlisted Grenada, Ms 5/14/62 **K 7/3**
Cpl. John Womack 28 yr old enlisted Grenada, Ms 5/14/62 **C 7/3**
Pioneer John Abbott enlisted Grenada, Ms 5/14/62
Private John Brewer enlisted Grenada, Ms 5/14/62 **W-face 7/3**
Private Harvey Burgess 31 yr old enlisted Grenada, Ms 5/14/62 **C 7/3**
Private Adam Campbell 31 yr old enlisted Grenada, Ms 5/14/62 **C 7/3**
Private Alfred Charter 29 yr old enlisted Grenada, Ms 5/14/62 **W 7/3**
Private Chalmers Cofer 30 yr old enlisted Grenada, Ms 5/14/62 **C 7/3**
Private Hosea Countess 31 enlisted Grenada, Ms 5/14/62 **C 7/3**
Pioneer William Cowen 33 yr old enlisted Grenada, Ms 5/14/62
Private Henry Craven 22 yr old enlisted Grenada, Ms 5/14/62 **C 7/3**
Private George Denley 26 yr ld enlisted Grenada, Ms 5/14/62
Private George Earle enlisted Grenada, Ms 5/14/62 **W-cheek 7/3** (later W Bristoe)
Private James Eskew 24 yr old enlisted Grenada, Ms 5/14/62 **WC 7/3**
Private William Flanagin enlisted Grenada, Ms 5/14/62 **W-thigh C 7/3**
Private Andrew Goforth enlisted Grenada, Ms 5/14/62 **K 7/3**
Private Oliver hall 26 yr old enlisted Grenada, Ms 5/14/62 **C 7/3**
Private James Hanks 28 yr old enlisted Grenada, Ms 5/14/62
Private George Herron 25 yr old enlisted Grenada, Ms 5/14/62 **C 7/3**
Private James Heron 29 yr old enlisted Grenada, Ms 5/14/62 **C 7/3**
Private Samuel Herron 27 yr old enlisted Grenada, Ms 5/14/62 **C 7/3**
Private Thomas Johnson silversmith enlisted Grenada, Ms 5/14/62
Private James Jones enlisted Grenada, Ms 5/14/62 **C 7/3**
Private William Love 24 yr old enlisted Grenada, Ms 5/14/62 **W 7/3** (later K CH)
Private James R Mullins 28 yr old enlisted Grenada 5/14/62 **C 7/14**
Private James Rees enlisted Grenada 5/14/62 **K 7/3**
Private Marion Rees enlisted Grenada 5/14/62 **W-both thighs C 7/3**
Private Martin Rees enlisted Grenada 5/14/62 **C 7/14**
Private Matthew Rees 29 yr old enlisted Grenada 5/14/62 **W 7/3**
Private Charles Reynolds 25 yr old enlisted Grenada 5/14/62 **W 7/3**
Private John Rogers 25 yr old enlisted Grenada 5/14/62 **W-Right Hip C 7/3**
Private Daniel Sanderson 20 yr old enlisted Grenada 5/14/62 **W-left hip C 7/3** (amp-died)
Private Archibald Shaw 33 yr old enlisted Grenada 5/14/62 **C 7/3**
Private William Simpson 21 yr old enlisted Grenada 5/14/62 (later K-Bristoe Station)
Private Joshua Smith 31 yr old enlisted Grenada 5/14/62
Private William Springer 29 yr old enlisted Grenada 5/14/62 **W 7/3** (died 7/20)
Private William Vann 23 yr old enlisted Grenada, Ms 5/14/62 **C 7/3**

Private William Womack 20 yr old enlisted Grenada, Ms 5/14/62 **K 7/3**
Private Elisha Woodall 20 yr old enlisted Grenada, Ms 5/14/62 **C 7/6 Cashtown**
Private Francis Wright 31 yr old enlisted Grenada, Ms 5/14/62 **C 7/14**

Ambulance Corp Driver George Speir 31 yr old enlisted Grenada 5/14/62
Teamster William Hyde 25 yr old enlisted Grenada, Ms 5/14/62
Teamster James Mullins enlisted Grenada, Ms 5/14/62 **C 7/5**

July 1 Casualties

Captain John Powell 36 yr old sheriff enlisted Grenada 5/154/62 left at Front Royal sick—fought 7/14
Sgt Eli Spears 30 yr old enlisted Grenada **sick 7/1-7/3 C 7/14**
Cpl. Henry Cooper enlisted Grenada, Ms 5/14/62 **C 7/1** (later QM)
Private John English 24 yr old enlisted Grenada, Ms 5/14/62 **W 7/1 C 7/6**
Private John Eskew 27 yr old enlisted Grenada, Ms 5/14/62 **W 7/1**
Private John Flanagin 26 yr old enlisted Grenada, Ms 5/14/62 **W 7/1**
Private Burgess French 24 yr old enlisted Grenada, Ms 5/14/62 **W 7/1**
Private William Grizzard 27 yr old enlisted Grenada, Ms 5/14/62 **W-hand 7/1**
Private James Hendricks 25 yr old yr old enlisted Grenada, Ms 5/14/62 **(sick 7/1 & 7/3)**
Private Amos Langham 32 yr old enlisted Grenada, Ms 5/14/62 **W-right leg 7/1**
Private William Neely 32 yr old farmer enlisted Grenada 5/14/62 **sick 7/1-7/3 C 7/14**
Private Henry Sartin 28 yr old enlisted Grenada 5/14/62 **C 7/1**
Private Russell Sartin 34 yr old enlisted Grenada 5/14/62—**detached as ordinance guard**
Private James Schmitz 26 yr old enlisted Grenada 5/14/62 **W-right arm 7/1**
Private Jacob Smith 27 yr old enlisted Grenada 5/14/62 **sick 7/1-7/3** (later W-Weldon RR)
Private William Simmons 31 yr old enlisted Grenada 5/14/62 **K 7/1**
Private James Southern enlisted Grenada 5/14/62 **W 7/1**
Private Henry Speir 26 yr old enlisted Grenada 5/14/62 **K 7/1**
Private George Spradlyn 31 yr old enlisted Grenada 5/14/62 **W 7/1**
Private Stewart Taylor 23 yr old enlisted 4, Grenada Ms 5/14/62 **W-right leg 7/1**
Private James Thorpe 28 yr old enlisted Grenada, Ms 5/14/62 **W 7/1**
Private Christopher Vernon 34 yr old enlisted Grenada, Ms 5/14/62 **sick 7/1-7/3 C 7/5**

Company I *"Mississippi Reds"*

Captain Jefferson Meek 53 yrs old enlisted Panola, Ms 3/27/62 (on furlough during campaign)
1st Lt Robert Buchanan 24 yr old enlisted Grenada, Ms 5/14/62 (later Captain / W Wilderness)
Sgt John Bourland 23 yr old enlisted Sardis, Ms 2/29/62 **W-right arm C 7/3**

Sgt William Keel 20 yr old enlisted Sardis 4/21/62 **W-hip& abdomen 7/3 died**
Sgt James Meek 27 yrs old enlisted Sardis, Ms **WC 7/3**
Cpl. John Little 28 yr old enlisted Sardis, Ms 4/21/62 **W 7/3** (later Lt)
Private Calvin Billingley enlisted Grenada, Ms 5/14/62 **K 7/3**
Private George "Green" Cain 27 yr old enlisted Grenada 5/14/62 (later Sgt & Lt)
Private Marcellus Campbell 19 yr old enlisted Panola, Ms 3/27/62 **W 7/3** (later W Spotsylvania)
Private Henry Childress enlisted Sardis, Ms 6/1/62
Private Thomas Cloud 33 yr old enlisted Sardis, Ms 4/21/62 **WC 7/3**
Private James Cook 19 r old enlisted Panola, Ms 3/27/62 **WC 7/3**
Private William Evans 27 yr old enlisted Sardis, Ms 4/21/62 **W 7/3**
Private Robert Harlan 27 yr old enlisted Grenada 5/14/62 **W-head & hip 7/3**
Private William Harlan 30 yr old enlisted Grenada 5/14/62 **C 7/3**
Private James Harmon 22 yr old enlisted Grenada 5/14/62 **C 7/3**
Private Walter "Tince" Harmon 24 yr old enlisted Grenada 5/14/62
Private James Hudspeth 27 yr old enlisted Grenada, Ms 5/14/62 **C 7/3**
Private Thomas Johnson enlisted Sardis, Ms 4/21/61, **W-left thigh C 7/3**
Private William Josselyn enlisted Sardis, Ms 4/21/61, **K 7/3**
Private William Keating enlisted Sardis, Ms 4/21/61 **W-hip & abdomen C 7/3 (died)**
Private D.J. Kimes enlisted Sardis, Ms 4/21/61 **WC 7/3 died**
Private William Leaton 20 yr old enlisted Sardis, Ms 4/21/61 **K 7/3**
Private William Little enlisted Sardis, Ms 4/21/61 **K 7/3**
Private Martin Samuel enlisted Sardis, Ms 4/21/61—later Ambulance Corps
Private William McLeod enlisted Sardis, Ms 4/21/61 **W 7/3** (later W CH)
Private Andrew Parks enlisted Sardis, Ms 4/21/62 **W-knee 7/3**
Private Levi Rhodes enlisted Sardis, Ms 4/21/62 **W-left thigh C 7/3 (after war moved to Texas)**
Private Simon Rhodes enlisted Sardis, Ms 4/21/62
Private Joseph Rials enlisted Sardis, Ms 4/21/62 **W 7/3 C 7/7 Hagerstown, Md**
Private David Smith 25 enlisted Sardis, Ms 4/21/62 **WC 7/3**
Private Levi N. South 20 enlisted Sardis, Ms 4/21/62 **WC 7/3 (died Ft Delaware buried Finn's Point, NJ)**
Private Daniel Still 29 enlisted Panola, Ms 4/21/62
Private James Stogner 23 enlisted Grenada, Ms 4/21/62 **K 7/3**
Private John Watson 36 yr old enlisted Sardis, Ms 4/21/62
Private John Whitton 24 yr old enlisted Sardis, Ms 4/21/62

Teamster Lodd Allen enlisted Oxford, Ms 4/21/62
Ambulance Corps—William Carlton enlisted Panola, Ms 3/27/62

July 1 Casualties

2nd Lt William Waldron 34 yr old enlisted Grenada, Ms 5/14/62 **W 7/1 died 7/2**

3rd Lt. William Harmon 29 yr old enlisted Grenada 5/14/62 **WC 7/1 died in hospital**
Cpl. Rufus Cloud 33 yr old enlisted Sardis, Ms 4/21/62 **W-chest 7/1**
Cpl. Joseph Hoke 31 yr old Panola farmer enlisted 3/27/62 **W 7/1**
Cpl. Whitmel Roberts 31 yr old enlisted Grenada, Ms **W-knee 7/1 C 7/5** (died / buried Phila Nat cem)
Private V.A. Arnold enlisted Panola, Ms 3/2762 **(sick 7/3)**
Private Cornelius Cain 19 yr old enlisted Grenada 5/14/62 **W 7/1**
Private James Cain 24 yr old enlisted Grenada 5/14/62 **W 7/1**
Private James Alfred "Bud" Connor enlisted Sardis, Ms 4/21/62 **W-left hand 7/1** (middle finger amp)
Private Leonidas Campbell 20 yr old enlisted Sardis, Ms 4/21/62 **W 7/1**
Private William Fite 22 yr old enlisted Sardis, Ms 5/14/62 **W 7/1**
Private Robert Jackson enlisted Sardis, Ms 4/21/61, **K 7/1**
Private William Kennedy enlisted Sardis, Ms 4/21/61 **K 7/1**
Private Jordan Looney 23 yr old farmer enlisted Sardis, Ms 4/21/61 **K 7/1** buried Lee's Headquarters
Private Thomas Looney enlisted Sardis, Ms 4/21/61 **K 7/1**
Private William Robinson 24 yr old enlisted Sardis, Ms 4/21/62 **W-left thigh 7/1 C 7/4**
Private Joseph Rowland 29 yr old enlisted Panola, Ms 3/27/62 **sick 7/3**
Private William Simons 29 enlisted Sardis, Ms 4/21/62 **C 7/1**
Private William Wooten 31 yr old enlisted Sardis, Ms 4/21/62 **W-right hand 7/1**
Private Robert Workman 24 yr old enlisted Sardis, Ms 4/21/62 **W 7/1**
Sgt Henry King enlisted Sardis 4/21/62 (detached during battle)
Private Patrick Waits 27 yr old enlisted Sardis, Ms 4/21/62 **detached 7/1—7/3**

Company K *"Pontotoc Minutemen"*

Captain Goldsboro Mears 31 yrs old enlisted Grenada 5/14/62 **K 7/3**
2nd Lt Jones Donaldson 23 yr old student enlisted Grenada, Ms 5/14/62 (later Captain)
2nd Lt Granberry Strickland 32 yr old mechanic, enlisted Saltville, Ms **W 7/3**
3rd Lt Erving Mears 22 yrs old enlisted Saltillo, Ms (later W-Wilderness) (later Lt Col)
Sgt William Dixon 33 yr old enlisted Saltillo, Ms 5/14/62 (later K-Wilderness)
Sgt Wright Harris 29 yr old clerk enlisted Saltillo, Ms 5/14/62
Sgt Robert K. Houston 32 yr old enlisted Pontotoc, Ms 5/14/62
Sgt William Oswald 33 yr old enlisted Saltville, Ms 5/14/62 **K 7/3**
Cpl. James Strickland enlisted Saltville, Ms W 7/1 **C 7/5**
Private Robert Barkley enlisted Grenada, Ms 5/14/62 **K 7/14**
Private Samuel Cole enlisted Saltillo, Ms 5/14/62
Private G.W. Jennings enlisted Saltillo, Ms 5/14/62 **K 7/14**
Private Armstead Jones enlisted Saltillo, Ms 5/14/62 (later Cpl)
Private Patrick Keeff enlisted Saltillo, Ms 5/14/62

Private John Kidd enlisted Saltillo, Ms 5/14/62 (W Bristoe)
Private Curtis Kirby 25 yr old enlisted Saltillo, Ms **W-left hip 7/3 C 7/5**
Private James Lowery enlisted Saltillo, Ms 5/14/62 (later Sgt)
Private John Lynn enlisted Grenada 5/14/62 **W-fingers 7/3 C 7/5**
Private Jeremiah Phillips enlisted Saltillo, Ms 5/14/62 (later W Spots/ Weldon RR)
Private William Pitts enlisted Saltillo, Ms 5/14/62 **W-hip C 7/3**
Private Jesse Raper enlisted Saltillo, Ms 5/14/62 **C 7/14**
Private Thomas Waddle 27 yr old enlisted Saltillo, Ms 5/14/62
Private James Williams 25 enlisted Saltillo, Ms 5/14/62 (later K Bristol Station)

Teamster William Low enlisted Saltillo, Ms 5/14/62

July 1 Casualties

1st Lt Joseph Patterson 32 yr old enlisted Grenada left in Fredericksburg 6/14 ***Sick 7/1-7/3 W-arm 7/14***
Sgt John Crow enlisted Saltillo, Ms 5/14/62 **C 7/1**
Sgt William Yeargin enlisted Grenada, Ms 5/14/62 **fought 7/1 / deserted 7/2 / C 7/14**
Cpl. Tilman Howell enlisted Pontotoc, Ms 5/14/62 **C 7/1**
Cpl. John Malone 23 yrs old enlisted Saltillo, Ms 5/14/62 **W 7/1**
Cpl. Henderson Raper enlisted Saltville, Ms **C 7/1**
Private Wiley Ashley enlisted Pontotoc, Ms 5/14/62 **(absent 7/3) (later W-Bristoe)**
Private William Ashley enlisted Pontotoc, Ms 5/14/62 **(absent 7/3)**
Private George Cagle age 48 enlisted Grenada, Ms 5/14/62 **WC 7/1 exchanged died 12/24/63 Charlottesville hospital**
Private William Christopher enlisted Saltillo, Ms 5/14/62 **WC 7/1**
Private A.P. Cole enlisted Saltillo, Ms 5/14/62 **W 7/1 C 7/4**
Private Preston Crow enlisted Saltillo, Ms 5/14/62 **W 7/1**
Private Wiley Erwin enlisted Saltillo, Ms 5/14/62 **W 7/1 C 7/4**
Private James Johnson enlisted Saltillo, Ms 5/14/62 **W 7/1 C 7/5**
Private John Johnson farmer enlisted Saltillo, Ms 5/14/62 **C 7/1**
Private James Mahan 21 yr old enlisted Oxford, Ms **K 7/1**
Private William Pearson enlisted Saltillo, Ms 5/14/62 **W 7/1 C 7/5**
Private Ransom Rains enlisted Saltillo, Ms 5/14/62 **sick 7/1-7/3**
Private William Raper enlisted Saltillo, Ms 5/14/62 **W 7/1 (died 7/11)**
Private William Yeargen enlisted Saltillo, Ms 5/14/62 Sgt demoted after 1/63 AWOL **fought 7/1 deserted 7/3 C 7/14**

ELEVENTH MISSISSIPPI REGIMENT

Sgt. Eli Peel Co C

Corp. William Delbridge Co G

Field & Staff

Colonel Francis Marion Green 40 yr old lawyer in Oxford **W 7/3** (mortally wounded at Spotsylvania May 12th)

Lieutenant Colonel 38 yr old Alexander H. Franklin—promoted Lt. Colonel January 1863 absent

Major Reuben O Reynolds 31 yr old graduate of the University of Georgia and University of Virginia. Lawyer in Aberdeen enlisted 4/23/61 W Gaine's Mill **W 7/1 C 7/5 Greencastle, Pa** (later Col / W Petersburg)

Adjutant Thomas C. Holliday 22 yr old enlisted Aberdeen 2/20/61 W-Sharpsburg promoted to Brigade Staff

Sergeant Major Joseph J. Evans enlisted Aberdeen 4/27/61 **W 7/3** (later Adjt)

Ensign William O'Brien (Color Sergeant) enlisted Houston, Ms 4/25/61 **K 7/3 on advance**

Surgeon William Shields enlisted Harpers Ferry, Va 6/9/61 **C 7/14 Williamsport**

Assistant Surgeon Thomas Bennett enlisted Camp Fisher 2/7/62

Assistant Surgeon William Hopkins enlisted Macon, Ms 4/26/61

Quartermaster Silas Owen 24 yr old Oxford, Ms 5/13/61

Quartermaster Sgt Morris Houseman 24 yr old enlisted Houston, Ms 5/13/61 detailed 5/62 (later C-HR)

Quartermaster Clerk Thomas Chilton enlisted Camp Fisher 8/9/61 (later C Petersburg)

Ordinance Sgts Thomas Glenn enlisted Friars Point., Ms 5/13/61

James Morley enlisted Carrolton, Ms 5/13/61

QM Dept Saddler Private Asa Landon, G 28 yr old enlisted Houston, Ms 5/13/ 61

Company A *"The University Grays"*

Captain Simon Marsh enlisted Oxford, Ms 5/13/61 promoted Captain 9/62 resigned sick 6/63

Second Lieutenant John V. Moore 23 yr old yr old enlisted Oxford, Ms 5/13/61 **WC 7/3** (later Capt)

Third Lieutenant Frank O. Dailey—enlisted Oxford, Ms 5/13/61 **K 7/3**

2nd Sergeant Jeremiah Gage enlisted Oxford, Ms 5/13/61 **K artillery 7/3** (famous letter home)

Sergeant Thomas Heslep enlisted Oxford, Ms 5/13/61 W—Gaines Mill **K 7/3**

Sgt. Calvin Myers Harper's Ferry 6/8/61 W 1st Manassas W-shoulder/ Sharpsburg **W-both thighs C 7/3**

Private Andrew Jackson Baker enlisted Yalobusha, Ms 7/22/61 **WC 7/3** (never later a Lieutenant)

Private James E Ballard enlisted Camp Jones 9/18/61 **K 7/3**

Private Samuel M Brewer enlisted Oxford, Ms 4/26/61 **K 7/3** buried Hollywood Cemetery

Private Hugh Quinn Bridges enlisted Harpers Ferry 5/25/62 **W-leg 7/3** "dropped gun and retreated" (K Wilderness)

Private Richard C. Bridges enlisted Oxford, Ms 6/8/62 **W-shell fragment in leg below knee 7/3** (later W Wilderness)

Private William Cochran enlisted Oxford, Ms **K 7/3**

Private Needham J. Dabney enlisted Franklin, Va 3/20/63 **C 7/3**

Private James Dailey enlisted Oxford, Ms 5/13/61 served as liter bearer 7/3 **W 7/14**

Private W.F. DeGraffenreid enlisted Oxford, Ms **W 7/3** (later W at Weldon RR)

Private, William T. Estes enlisted Oxford, Ms 5/13/61 **WC 7/3 died 7/10**

Private R. W. Goodwin enlisted Fredericksburg, Va 3/62 **W-left leg C 7/3 died in hospital**

Private James W. Hale enlisted Oxford, Ms 5/13/61 W-Sharpsburg **WC 7/14**

Private Hall, William R. Hall enlisted 7/1/361 Winchester, Va **K 7/3**

Private Parmeneo Harding enlisted Oxford, Ms 5/13/61 **C 7/3**

Private Edward L. Harris—enlisted Marshall, Ms 7/13/62 **WC 7/3**

Private Almouth Heslep—enlisted Vicksburg 3/14/62 **W 7/3**

Private Rufus P. Heslep enlisted Winchester, Va 7/13/62 **W 7/3**

Private Charles A. Hicks enlisted Harper's ferry, va 6/8/61 **W-right arm C 7/3**

Private William J Hurt—.enlisted Crawfordville, Ms 4/26/61 **W right thigh 7/3** (later W Spotsylvania)

Private John H. Ivy—enlisted Springfield, Ms 4/1/61 **W 7/3**

Private Edmond G Jones 23 yr old enlisted 4/26/61 **W 7/3** (later K Wilderness)

Private James J. King enlisted 4/62 Ashland, Va **W 7/3 C 7/5 Cashtown**

Private Willis Monroe Lea enlisted camp Fisher 10/10/61 **W 7/3** (later K Weldon RR)

Private J. S. McKay enlisted Oxford, Ms 5/13/61 **WC 7/3**

Private Joseph L McKie enlisted Springdale. Ms 3/1/62 **W-right arm C 7/3**
Private Thomas Fondren McKie 18 yr old enlisted Springdale. Ms **K 7/3**
Private James R Montgomery 24 yr old enlisted Oxford, Ms 5/13/61 **C 7/3** (later K Spots)
Private Albert T Myers enlisted Winchester, Va 7/13/61 W Gaines Mill **W-both thighs 7/3**
Private Calvin Myers enlisted Oxford, Ms 5/13/61 **WC 7/3**
Private James Smith enlisted Winchester, Va 7/13/61 **W 7/3**
Private William Tabner enlisted Oxford 5/13/61 **WC 7/3**
Private James Taylor enlisted Oxford, Ms **C 7/14** (later Lieutenant—cavalry)
Private Joshua Taylor enlisted Oxford, Ms W-head Sharpsburg **C 7/14** (later C Petersburg)
Private George W.Wool enlisted Oxford, Ms **W-knee C 7/3**
Pioneer Peter J Saunders 24 yr old mechanic enlisted Oxford 5/13/61
Teamster R Estes enlisted Oxford, Ms W-Sharpsburg

July 1 Casualties

None

Company B *"Coahoma Invincibles"*

Captain William David Nunn 21 yr old enlisted Friars Point, Ms 2/16/61 **MW 7/3** died 7/13 (had watch of W.L. Magruder)
First Lieutenant George W. Morton enlisted Friars Point W-Sharpsburg **W-hand 7/3** (Later Captain)
2nd Lieutenant John L. Ashe enlisted Friars Point, Ms 4/27/61 (Later 1st Lieutenant 7/13) **C 7/14**
3rd Lt Henry McLeod 23 yr old doctor enlisted Friars Point 5/13/61 **W left leg 7/3**
1st Sgt John R. Garner,—enlisted Friars Point 5/13/61 **C 7/14** discharged disabled
Sgt John S. T Grubbs—26 yr old farmer enlisted Friars Point 3/1/62 **C 7/3**
Sergeant James Henderson enlisted Friars Point 5/13/61 **C 7/3**
Sgt Joseph G Richardson 24 yr old enlisted Friars Point, Ms 5/13/61 (later C Wilderness)
Sgt Benjamin A Sims 29 yr old enlisted Friars Point 5/13/61 **K 7/3**
Corp George Meneghan 24 yr old enlisted Friars Point 5/13/61
Corp. Frederick A. Ross,—captured at Petersburg 30 yr old enlisted Friars Point, Ms 5/13/61
Corporal Eldridge H. St. John 25 yr old enlisted Friars Point, Ms 5/13/61 **W-left arm C 7/14**
Private William Alley enlisted Lynchberg, Va 5/13/61
Private James Bartley enlisted Friars Point, Ms 5/13/61 **W 7/3**

Private Council Canfield sadler enlisted Friars Point, Ms 4/27/61 **W 7/14 C Williamsport Hospital**

Private Columbus Chambers enlisted Friars Point, Ms 4/27/61 (later W Wilderness)

Private Henry W. Chambers enlisted Friars Point, Ms 2/16/61 **C 7/5 Greencastle** (drowned trying to escape from prison)

Private Thomas J. Colburn enlisted Friars Point, Ms 3/1/62 (later WC Wilderness)

Private Robert Crenshaw enlisted Friars Point, Ms 5/13/61 **K 7/3**

Private Zederick Damrel enlisted Friars Point, Ms 4/27/61 **C 8/63** Northern Virginia

Private Marcellus C Garner,.—enlisted Friars Point, Ms 3/1/61 **W 7/3**

Private James Haines enlisted Friars Point 5/13/61 **WC 7/3** (later C Petersburg)

Private George W. Hurst—enlisted Friars Point 4/27/61 **W 7/3** (later deserted 8/63)

Private Nathaniel Kelly enlisted Friars Point 5/13/61 **C 7/5 Cashtown**

Private Louis A. Lawrence 35 yr old enlisted Friars Point, Ms 5/13/61 **K 7/3**

Private Archibald P. Mathews 22 yr old enlisted Friars Point 5/13/61 W-shoulder 7 Pines **K 7/14**

Private William M Maynard enlisted Friars Point 3/3/63 **K 7/3**

Private Charles E. Maynard enlisted Friars Point 3/1/62 **W 7/3**

Private Alkana McHenry 25 yr old carpenter enlisted Friars Point 5/13/61 **K 7/3**

Private J. F. McCloud enlisted Friars Point 3/1/63 **W 7/3** (later died of disease)

Private Henry C McMullin merchant enlisted Friars Point 5/13/61 **K 7/3**

Private John B Montroy 29 year old enlisted Friars Point 5/13/61 **W 7/3**

Private Thomas D. Musgraves 24 yr old enlisted Friars Point 5/13/61 **K 7/3**

Private William A. Pridgen 21 yr old enlisted Friars Point, Ms 2/16/61 (later C Wilderness)

Private Harrison P. Reid 24 yr old enlisted Friars Point, Ms 5/13/61 **C 7/5 Waterloo, Pa** (later W Cold Harbor)

Private Elisha N. Richardson enlisted 5/63 Richmond, Va **K 7/3**

Private Hopkins R Richardson 21 yr old enlisted Friars Point, Ms 5/13/61 **K 7/3**

Private Morgan M Richardson enlisted Friars Point, Ms.—**K 7/3**

Private John Sanguinette 24 yr old enlisted Friars Point, Ms 3/1/61 **C 7/14** (later C Petersburg)

Private William W. Ward merchant enlisted Friars Point, Ms **W 7/3** (later deserted)

Private Elijah Watson 32 yr old enlisted Friars Point (later W-right hand Spots / C Hatchers Run)

Private William Wright 45 yr old enlisted Friars Point 3/8/62 **K 7/14**

Private Martin Webb 22 yr old student enlisted Friars Point, Ms 4/27/61 **W 7/3 C 7/5**

Teamster John Dobson enlisted Friars Point, Ms 4/27/61

Musician William T. Wells merchant enlisted Friars Pont 4/27/61 deserted

July 1 Casualties

None

Company C *"The Prairie Rifles"*

Captain George W. Shannon 23 yr old enlisted Okolona, Ms 5/13/61 W Gaine's Mill **W 7/3** (later Major / Lt Col)

First Lieutenant William H. Peel 25 yr old enlisted Okolona, Ms **WC 7/3** (died in prison)

Second Lieutenant George Luster 26 yr old enlisted Okolona, Ms 5/13/61 promoted 2nd LT 4/62 **WC 7/3**

Third Lieutenant George F. Cole enlisted Okolona, Ms 4/25/61 **WC 7/3**

1St Sgt Eli H. Peel 22 yr old enlisted Okolona, Ms 5/13/61 W-Seven Pines **K 7/3 (Bryan Barn)**

Sgt Ashley Crumpton enlisted Okolona, Ms 4/30/61

Sgt. John Morris 25 yr old enlisted Oklona, Ms 5/13/61 **W-leg C 7/3**

Corporal George W Justice enlisted Okolona, Ms printer 4/25/61 **W 7/3**

Corporal Thomas J. Middlebrook 20 yr old Okolona, Ms **W 7/3**

Corporal William H Smith 20 yr old enlisted Okolona, Ms 4/25/61 **C 7/3**

Private Benjamin J. Abbot enlisted Okolona, Ms 4/25/61 **W 7/3**

Private William Cobb enlisted Okolona, Ms 4/26/61 **WC 7/3**

Private Larkin Cole enlisted Okolona, Ms 7/2/62 **W 7/3 C 7/5** (drowned while escaping)

Private Thophilus R. Davenport enlisted Okolona, Ms 3/2/61 **WC 7/3 died 7/10**

Private Thomas Hare, enlisted Okolona, Ms 4/25/61 (later W Bristoe Station)

Private George Kidd 26 yr old Okolona, Ms 4/25/61 W-arm 7 Pines **W-right thigh & hand C 7/3**

Private Abraham Klaus 25 yr old enlisted Okolona, Ms **W 7/3**

Private Green Kyle 23 yr old enlisted Okolona, Ms 4/25/61 **W 7/3**

Private James Kyle enlisted Camp Lidell 5/3/63 **K 7/3**

Private George M. Lusher, enlisted Okolona, Ms **WC 7/3**

Private David H. Meredith enlisted Okolona, Ms 5/13/61 (later captured at Culpeper August 1863)

Private Thomas F. Paramore 23 yr old enlisted Okolona, Ms 5/13/61 **C 7/14** (later deserted)

Private James M Parchman 20 yr old enlisted Okolona, Ms 5/13/61 **W 7/3**

Private James T. Ponder 27 yr old enlisted Okolona, Ms 5/13/61 W 7 Pines **W-left knee 7/3**

Private William A Robinson 22 yr old enlisted Okolona, Ms 5/13/61 **WC 7/3 died 7/10**

Private Robert D. Rodgers 26 yr old enlisted Okolona, Ms 5/13/61 (later W-CH)

Private Martin V. Smith 30 yr old enlisted Okolona, Ms 5/13/61 **C 7/2 Picket line** (later deserted)

Private George G. Temple 33 yr old enlisted Okolona, Ms 5/13/61 **K 7/3**

Private Franklin G. Thomas 25 yr old enlisted Okolona, Ms 5/13/61 **W 7/3** (later transferred to Cavalry)

July 1 Casualties

None

Company D *"Neshoba Rifles"*

Captain John R. Prince 26 yr old enlisted Philadelphia 4/24/61 promoted Captain January 1863 **W 7/14**
First Lieutenant Isaac M. Kelly—promoted 1st Lieutenant January 1863 dropped from roll 12/1864
Second Lieutenant William A. Whatley 20 yr old enlisted Philadelphia, Ms 4/24/61 (later W CH)
3rd Lt Henry Tyler Hester,—enlisted Neshoba 5/13/61 **W-left foot C 7/3**
1st Sgt James C. Wilson enlisted Pleasant Springs, Ms 7/8/61 (later W Weldon RR / C Hatchers Run)
Sgt John B Jones enlisted Pleasant Springs, Ms 7/8/61 **W 7/3**
Sgt. John C. William 23 yr old enlisted Neshoba, Ms 3/1/62
Sgt Joseph F Riley 24 yr old enlisted Philadelphia, Ms 5/13/61 **C 7/3**
Corporal Thomas M Cook enlisted Philadelphia, Ms 4/24/61 **C 7/14**—died in prison
Corporal Private James Bates enlisted Philadelphia, Ms 4/24/61
Corporal Thomas Cooper enlisted Philadelphia, Ms 4/24/61 **K 7/3**
Corporal Josiah Perry 21 yr old enlisted Neshoba, Ms 7/1/62
Corporal Joshua Threatt enlisted Philadelphia, Ms 4/24/61 **K 7/3**
Private William Adams enlisted Philadelphia, Ms 7/1/62 **C 7/3**
Private Samuel Y. Bardston enlisted Philadelphia, Ms 7/1/62 **K 7/3**
Private Daniel Bates enlisted Philadelphia, Ms 7/1/62 **W-shell to head 7/3**
Private Henry Bassett enlisted Philadelphia, Ms 3/1/62 W-Sharpsburg **WC 7/3**
Private G.Y. Boydston enlisted Philadelphia, Ms 7/1/62 **K 7/3**
Private Joseph T Brown enlisted Philadelphia, MS 7/1/61 **C 7/14**
Private William J. Brown enlisted Philadelphia, Ms 7/1/62 **K 7/14**
Private John Burmingham enlisted Philadelphia, Ms 3/1/62 **K 7/3**
Private Columbus Martin Cook enlisted Philadelphia, Ms 3/20/61 **K 7/3**
Private Jacob Harrison Cook enlisted Philadelphia, Ms 3/1/61 **WC 7/3**
Private James Michael Cook enlisted Philadelphia, Ms 3/1/61
Private John Henry Cook enlisted Philadelphia, Ms 3/1/61 **WC 7/3** (Later K Spotsylvania)
Private John W. Cook enlisted Philadelphia, Ms 3/20/61 (not a brother) **WC 7/3**
Private Thomas Melvin Cook enlisted Philadelphia, Ms 4/24/61 **C 7/14**—died in prison
Private William B. "Bill" Cook enlisted Philadelphia 4/24/61 (later C Hatcher's Run)
Private James Cooper enlisted Neshoba, Ms 5/13/61 **C 7/3** died in prison
Private David W. Copeland enlisted Neshoba, Ms 5/13/61 **W 7/3**
Private Solomon Edwards,—enlisted Philadelphia 3/20/61 **W 7/3 (later K Cold Harbor)**

Private Thomas J Evans,.—enlisted Philadelphia 4/24/61 **C 7/3** died of smallpox in prison

Private William H. Ferguson,—enlisted Philadelphia 4/24/61 **W 7/3** (later C Wilderness)

Private Jesse Gully enlisted Philadelphia, Ms 3/20/61 **W 7/3**

Private Peter Haney,—enlisted Philadelphia 4/24/761 **C 7/3**

Private Hiram Perry Harrison,—enlisted Camp Jones 9/8/61 **WC 7/3**

Private Wayne Harrison enlisted Camp Jones 9/8/61 **W 7/3**

Private Wiley P. Heflin 29 yr old farmer enlisted Neshoba 4/13/61 **W-left foot by shell fragment & left hip by minie' C 7/3**

Private James C Henderson,.—enlisted Camp Jones 9/8/61 **C 7/3**

Private Hampton J Herrington,. **WC 7/3**

Private James Hester enlisted Philadelphia, Ms 3/20/61 **W 7/3**

Private John T. Hunt enlisted Philadelphia, Ms 4/24/61 **W 7/3**

Private William D. Jones 22 yr old enlisted Philadelphia 5/13/61 **W 7/3** (later K Burgess Mill)

Private Nathaniel G Kelly 20 yr old enlisted Philadelphia 4/24/61 **C 7/5 Cashtown**

Private Andrew McDonald enlisted Philadelphia 3/1/62 **W-foot C 7/3**

Private Archibald McDonald enlisted Philadelphia, Ms 3/20/61 WC 7/3

Private Randall Mayo enlisted Philadelphia, Ms 3/1/62 **W-right arm 7/3** (later C Hatchers Run)

Private Henry A Morehead, 29 yr old enlisted Philadelphia Ms 4/24/61 **K 7/3**

Private George G. Morrell enlisted Pleasant Springs, Ms **C 7/3** (later K Wilderness)

Private James T. Petty enlisted Pleasant Springs, Ms **C 7/3**

Private David L Pigg enlisted Philadelphia, Ms 3/20/61 W 2nd Manassas **W-left foot C 7/3**

Private John L. Rawls enlisted Philadelphia, Ms 3/1/62 (later W Cold Harbor) **W 7/3**

Private T.J. Richardson enlisted Philadelphia, Ms 3/20/61 **K 7/3**

Private Miles M Rickard 22 yr old enlisted Neshoba, Ms 5/13/61 **K 7/3**

Private Charles Ridout enlisted Philadelphia 3/1/62 **W-leg C 7/3**

Private Eli Seale enlisted Philadelphia, Ms 4/24/61 **W-foot C 7/3**

Private John W Shepard,.—enlisted Philadelphia **K 7/3**

Private John A Stovall enlisted Philadelphia, Ms 3/20/62 **C 7/14** (later W Weldon RR)

Private Amos Thornell enlisted Philadelphia, Ms 3/20/61 **K 7/3**

Private Isaac C. Whitmire enlisted Philadelphia, Ms 3/1/62 (later W-Spots / C Hatchers Run

Private Hardy Williamson enlisted Philadelphia, Ms 3/1/62 **W-right leg C 7/3** died in prison

Private John M. Williamson 26 yr old enlisted Philadelphia, Ms 4/24/61 **C 7/3**

Wagon Master Richard H. Mardis enlisted Philadelphia, Ms 3/1/62 K 9/64

Teamster Cpl. Jesse S. Gully,—enlisted Philadelphia 4/24/61 no record after December 1864

Teamster Andrew J. McDonald enlisted Philadephia, Ms 3/1/62 C 7/5 with Train (later C Hatchers) Run

July 1 Casualties

None

Company E "P*rairie Guards*"

Captain Henry P. Halbert—enlisted Crawford, Ms 4/27/61 promoted Captain April 1862 **MW 7/3**

First Lieutenant William Henry Belton—enlisted Crawford, Ms 4/26/61 elected 1st Lieutenant April1862 **SW-face 7/3**

2nd Lt Thomas P. Mims enlisted Crawfordsville, Ms 5/13/61 **MW 7/3** died 7/13

3rd Lieutenant Goolsby,—enlisted Crawfordsville, Ms 4/26/61—scouted out attack route **K 7/3**

Sgt Thomas Carr enlisted Crawford, Ms 4/26/61 **K 7/3**

Sgt Alexander J. Halbert,—enlisted Crawfordsville, Ms 2/15/61 **WC 7/3**

Sgt William O Jones 28 yr old enlisted Crawfordsville, Ms 4/26/61 **W-face C 7/3**

Sgt. James D. Love enlisted Crawfordsville 5/13/61 **W-left leg C 7/3**

Corporal William A. Allen enlisted Crawford, Ms 4/30/61 **K 7/3**

Corporal John T Morgan 20 yr old enlisted Crawfordsville, Ms 5/13/61 **(ONLY SURVIVOR)**

Private John W. Ball enlisted Crawford, Ms 4/30/61 **K 7/3**

Private Hiliary B. Crouch enlisted Crawford, Ms 4/26/61 **W 7/3**

Private J.J. Day, enlisted Crawford, Ms 4/26/61 **C 7/3**

Private Jefferson L Edmonds,.—enlisted Crawfordsville, Ms 4/27/61 **WC 7/3**

Private George W Edwards,.—enlisted Crawfordsville, Ms 4/27/61 **WC 7/3**

Private Artemus J Erwin enlisted Crawfordsville **W 7/3**

Private Nathaniel H. Howard,—enlisted Crawfordsville, Ms 4/27/61 **W 7/3**

Private Leander Huckaby,—enlisted Crawfordsville, Ms 3/15/61 **W-thigh C 7/3 died**

Private Jones, John Thomas 24 yr old enlisted Crawfordville 2/15/61 **W 7/3 died 7/10**

Private Jehu Kirksey 20 yr old enlisted Crawfordsville 4/26/61 **W-right shoulder C 7/3** (later C Hatchers)

Private Liberty S Martin enlisted Columbus, Ms 8/1/62 **K 7/3**

Private John R. Mimms 23 yr old enlisted Crawfordsville, Ms 5/13/61 **MW 7/3 died 7/9** buried Conover farm

Private James Moorehead 22 yr old enlisted Crawfordsville, Ms 2/15/61 **WC 7/3 died**

Private Thomas B Moorhead enlisted Crawfordsville, Ms 2/15/61 **W 7/3**

Private William Nance 25 yr old enlisted Crawfordsville, Ms 4/25/61 (later K Wilderness)

Private Fletcher S Norwood enlisted Columbus, Ms 3/1/63 **K 7/3**

Private John Norwood enlisted Crawfordsville, Ms 2/15/61 WC 7/3

Private L. H. Petit—enlisted Crawfordsville 4/26/61 **C 7/3**

Private Montholon S Powell 21 yr old enlisted Crawforsville, Ms ***W-leg 7/3 C 7/4***

Private Thomas Powell 23 yr old enlisted Crawforsville, Ms ***W 7/3***

Private Walter Scales 17 yr old enlisted Crawford, Ms **W 7/3** (later C Hatchers Run)

Private John L. Sherman,—enlisted Crawford, Ms 5/8/62 **WC 7/3**

Private Charles D. Thompson enlisted Crawfordsville, Ms **C 7/14** (joined U.S. service in prison)

Private David S. Turner 18 yr old enlisted Crawfordsville, 1/25/63 **C 7/3**

Private John Turner 21 yr old enlisted Crawfordsville, Ms 4/26/61 **WC-chest & hands 7/3** (later K Wilderness)

Private Thomas A Walker enlisted Crawfordsville, Ms 4/26/61 **C 7/3**

Private John W. White 18 yr old enlisted Crawfordsville, Ms 4/10/61 **WC 7/3**

Private Charles Wilkins enlisted Crawfordsville enlisted Crawfordsville, Ms 4/25/61 (later W Spotsylvania)

Private David C. Wilkins enlisted Crawfordsville, Ms 4/26/61 ***K 7/3 in advance***

Private Henry M. Wilkins 27 yr old yr old enlisted Crawfordsville, Ms 2/15/61 ***K 7/3 in advance***

Private Thomas J Wilkins enlisted Crawfordsville, Ms 4/26/61 ***W-right thigh 7/3*** *(later W-left leg Weldon RR)*

Private Max M Williams 23 yr old enlisted Crawfordsville, Ms 2/15/61 **W 7/3**

Private John K Woods 31 yr old enlisted Crawfordsville, Ms 4/26/61 **W left buttock 7/3 C 7/4**

Private William G. Broadfoot enlisted Crawford, Ms 4/26/61 detailed for water 7/3 **C 7/14 died in prison**

Private Charles Cooper enlisted Crawford, Ms detailed for water 7/3 (later C Hatchers Run

Teamster Samuel J. Stephens, 28 yr old enlisted Crawford, Ms (later C Hatchers Run)

Nurse Joel Malone 21 yr old yr old enlisted Crawfordsville, Ms 5/13/61 **C 7/5**

July 1 Casualties

None

Company F *"Noxubee Rifles"*

Captain Thomas J. Stokes 25 yr old planter enlisted Macon, Ms 5/13/61 promoted to Captain 11/62 **WC 7/3**

First Lieutenant Charles O. Brooks enlisted Macon, Ms 4/26/61 W Sharpsburg promoted 1st LT November 1862 **C 7/3**

Second Lt. Daniel A. Featherstone—enlisted Macon, Ms 4/26/61 promoted 2nd Lieutenant 11/62 **K 7/3** (bombardment)

3rd Lt Newton L. Wood enlisted Macon, Ms 4/26/61 **C 7/3**

1st Sgt Francis A Moore 22 yr old enlisted Macon, Ms 5/13/61 **WC 7/14**

2nd Sgt Hiram Binion enlisted Noxuba, Ms 4/26/61 **W 7/14** (later C-Spotsylvania)

Sergeant Absolom Gavin enlisted Macon, Ms 5/13/61 **W 7/3**
Corp Dewitt Farmer enlisted Macon, Ms 4/26/61 **MW 7/3**
Corp. Rienzi Mahorner 22 yr old clerk enlisted Macon, Ms 5/13/61 **C 7/14** (later W Petersburg)
Corp. Alexander W Manees 27 yr old enlisted Macon, Ms 5/13/61 **W-right thigh 7/3** (later K Cold Harbor)
Private Samuel M. Bowen enlisted Macon, Ms 4/26/61 **WC 7/3**
Private John Dorrah enlisted Macon, Ms 4/26/61 **W 7/3**
Private Adoniram J Farmer,.—Macon student enlisted 4/26/61 **K 7/3**
Private Laban Freeman,—21 yr old enlisted Macon, Ms student 5/13/61 **WC 7/3**
Private Thomas Freeman enlisted Macan, Ms 4/26/61 **WC 7/3**
Private Gawin,. Absalom—enlisted Macon, Ms 4/26/61 W 2nd Manassas **C 7/3**
Private Augustus A. Greer,—Macon student enlisted 4/26/61 **K 7/3**
Private William F Hardy,. student enlisted Macon, Ms 5/13/61 **W-left arm 7/3 died 7/20**
Private Francis M. Hill, enlisted Macon, Ms 4/26/61 **C 7/3**
Private John J. Howell, enlisted Macon, Ms 4/16/61 **C 7/3** died in prison
Private Frank Howell student enlisted Macon, Ms 4/26/61 **W 7/3**
Private James T. L Jones 24 yr old enlisted Macon 4/26/61 wounded at 1st Manassas **WC 7/3**
Private Jones, John A 22 yr old enlisted Macon, Ms 4/26/61 (later C Hatchers Run) **W 7/3**
Private James W Hughes enlisted Macon, Ms **C 7/3**
Private Franklin J Lewis 26 yr old enlisted Macon student 5/13/61 **W-right thigh 7/3** (Later K-Petersburg)
Private Bernard Mahorner 21 yr old enlisted Macon, Ms 5/13/61 **W C 7/3 died 7/30**
Private Harris Mahorner 20 yr old enlisted Macon, Ms 5/13/61 **W-right leg grapeshot C 7/3 died 10/15**
Private Victor Mansion French born mechanic & substitute **C 7/14**
Private William "Neely" Nance enlisted Macon, Ms 5/13/61 **W 7/3**
Private William T. Parker 29 yr old enlisted Macon, Ms (later Asst Surgeon)
Private Joseph R. Pendleton enlisted Macon, Ms 4/26/61 **K 7/3**
Private Robert R Pierce enlisted Macon, Ms 5/13/61 **K 7/3**
Private Richard Pierce 23 yr old enlisted Macon, Ms 5/13/61 **K 7/3**
Private Asa B. Robinson 23 yr old enlisted Macon, Ms 5/13/61 **W 7/3 died**
Private Ira Russell enlisted Macon, Ms 5/13/61 **W 7/3**
Private Robert D Sanders enlisted Macon, Ms 4/26/61 **K 7/3**
Private Thomas J. Shaw 22 yr old student enlisted Macon 5/13/61 **WC 7/3** (later C Hatchers Run)
Private Henry Y Spoon,. 32 yr old enlisted Macon, Ms 5/13/61 (later W-ankle Bristoe Station)
Private Charles J. Stewart 23 yr old enlisted Oxford, Ms 5/13/61 **K 7/3**
Private Erasmus A Thomas enlisted Macon, Ms 2/24/61 **W-left hand C 7/3** (later W Cold Harbor)
Private Elbert Thompsopn enlisted Macon, Ms 5/13/61 **W 7/3**

Private John J Vincent enlisted Macon, Ms 11/1/62 **C 7/14 died in prison**
Private Richard White enlisted Macon, Ms 5/13/61 **W 7/3**
Private John C. Williams enlisted Macon, Ms 2/24/61 **C 7/14**
Private John Windham 18 yr old student enlisted Goldsboro, NC 1/1/63 **K 7/3**
Private Oliver H. P. Windham 29 yr old clerk enlisted Macon, Ms 4/26/61 **C 7/3**
Teamster Henry P. Burton enlisted Macon, Ms 4/26/61 (later K Cold Harbor)
Teamster Daniel Hill enlisted Macon, Ms 4/26/61
Teamster William Hill enlisted Macon, Ms 5/13/61
Blacksmith Richard C. White 28 yr old enlisted Yorktown, Va 5/5/62 no record after December 1864
Musician W. Massengale 22 yr old student enlisted Lynchburg, Va 5/13/61 (later K Hatcher Run)

July 1 Casualties

None

Company G *"Lamar Rifles"*

Captain William G. Nelms—27 yr old enlisted Oxford, Ms 5/13/61 W Sharpsburg **W-chest 7/3** (later W Weldon RR)
First Lieutenant Henry G. Fernandez enlisted Oxford, Ms 2/23/61 promoted 1st Lieutenant 9/ 1862 **W 7/3**
Second Lieutenant William A. Osborne 25 yr old enlisted Oxford, Ms 5/13/61 promoted 9/62 **K 7/3**
Third Lieutenant Robert W. Black enlisted Lafayette Co, Ms 4/26/61—detailed—promoted 2nd Lt July 1863 in command at war's end
Third Lieutenant Charles W. Orr 25 yr old enlisted Oxford, Ms 5/13/61 promoted 5/63 on furlough
1st Sgt James O Eades,.—enlisted Oxford, Ms 4/26/61 (later K Wilderness)
2nd Sergeant Joshua Harley enlisted Oxford, Ms 8/9/61 **W 7/14 C Williamsport 7/15**
Private John Robinson 22 yr old Oxford Student enlisted 8/4/61 Promoted Lt 7/4 (later C Hatcher's Run)
Corporal William Delbridge enlisted Oxford 2/23/61 (later W Petersburg)
Corporal James Howry enlisted Oxford 4/26/61 **W 7/3**
Corporal Robert H. Wyatt 23 yr old merchant enlisted Oxford, Ms 5/13/61 **WC 7/3** (later C Hatchers Run)
Private John R. Barry enlisted Caswell, Ms 4/26/61 **W-lower jaw C 7/3**
Private James W. Biggers enlisted Oxford, Ms 4/26/61 **C 7/14 died in prison**
Private Christopher Boyd enlisted Oxford, Ms 8/9/61 **C 7/3**

Private Theodore Burney enlisted Oxford 5/3/61 **K 7/14**

Private Christopher Christopher C. Boyd enlisted Oxford, Ms 8/9/61 **W 7/3** (later W Petersburg)

Private Parham M. Buford student enlisted College Hill, Ms 8/9/61 **W-leg C 7/3 amp**

Private John Coffey enlisted Oxford, Ms 8/9/61 **K 7/3**

Private Robert F Dickens enlisted Oxford, Ms 5/12/61 **WC 7/3**

Private James F. Dooley enlisted Camp Jones 8/9/62 **C 7/14**

Private Packolet Fernandez enlisted Oxford, Ms 4/26/61

Private James M Gilmer,.—enlisted Oxford, Ms 5/13/61 (later C Cold Harbor)

Private Robert J. Gilmer,—enlisted Oxford, Ms 4/26/61

Private Charles Harris,—23 yr old Student enlisted Oxford, Ms 5/13/61 **W-leg C 7/3 amp**

Private Franklin Hope enlisted Oxford, Ms 4/26/61 (later Cpl & LT)

Private Wesley A. Hyde,—enlisted Oxford, Ms 4/26/61 **K 7/3**

Private Dudley A. Isom,—22 yr old farmer enlisted Oxford, Ms 4/26/61 **K 7/3**

Private William H. Johnson enlisted Camp Jones 8/9/61 **C 7/3** (later W-Weldon RR)

Private Isaac W Listenbee 24 yr old enlisted Oxford **W-bowels 7/14 (died 8/63)**

Private John W. Morrow 21 yr old enlisted Oxford, Ms 4/26/61 **W 7/3** (later W-left hand Wilderness)

Private Patrick H. Neagle 24 yr old enlisted Oxford, Ms 5/13/61 (later W Wilderness)

Private Ira Baxter Orr 22 yr old enlisted Oxford, Ms 5/13/61 **W-left thigh C 7/3**

Private Armead Price 22 yr old Oxford student enlisted Oxford, Ms 8/4/61 W Sharpsburg

Private Huldric Price 24 yr old Oxford student enlisted Oxford, Ms 8/4/61

Private James Stowers 20 yr old student enlisted Oxford, Ms 5/13/61 **W 7/14**

Private Newton Wilkins 25 yr old clerk enlisted Oxford, Ms 4/26/61 **W-right shoulder 7/3** (later teamster)

Private Richard J. Wilson 25 yr old student enlisted Oxford, Ms 5/13/61 **slightly W 7/3** (later K Wilderness)

Private Thomas H Wilson 20 yr old clerk enlisted Oxford, Ms 4/26/61 **W-left ankle C 7/3**

Private William W Wyatt medical student enlisted Oxford, Ms 4/26/61 **W 7/3** (later W Wilderness /C Hatchers Run)

Teamster (Forage Train) Thomas K Turner enlisted Harper's Ferry 6/9/61 not in battle **C 7/5 died in prison**

Musician Edward J. Walton 24 yr old clerk enlisted Oxford, Ms 4/26/61

Private Thomas Chilton detached to Quarter Master

Private Thomas Franklin detached to Ambulance Corps

Teamster Private Wesley Hyde (detached)

July 1 Casualties

None

Absent July 3

Private Warren Boden enlisted Oxford, Ms 4/26/61 absent sick rejoined at Falling Waters

Private John F Brown student enlisted Lafayette, Ms 8/9/61 ***absent sick 7/1-7/3 returned WC 7/14***

Private Theodore Burney enlisted Oxford, Ms 3/28/62 (absent sick) rejoined ***K 7/14***

Private Gabriel N. Smither, enlisted Oxford 3/10/62 W Sharpsburg ***absent 7/1-7/3*** *with other regiment* ***returned for 7/14***

Private James Graham enlisted Oxford 3/28/61 ***absent 7/1-7/3 returned Falling Waters***

Company H *"Chickasaw Guards"* (Color Company)

Captain Jamison H. Moore—enlisted Houston, Ms 5/13/61 elected Captain April 1862 **K 7/3**

1st Lieutenant Thomas W. Hill—enlisted Houston, Ms 5/13/61 pro 1st Lieutenant July 1862 **K 7/3**

2nd Lt Robert A. McDowell 26 yr old clerk & bartender enlisted Houston, Ms 5/13/61 **WC 7/3**

Sgt Samuel Reid Carothers enlisted Houston, Ms 4/25/61 WC **7/3 died in prison**

Sgt. Robert N. Lyon 22 yr old enlisted Houston 4/25/61 **K 7/3**

Sgt E. C. Speares,—enlisted Houston, Ms 5/13/61 **C 7/14 Falling Waters**

Sgt Clay Turberville enlisted Aberdeen, Ms 5/13/61 **C 7/14** (later Sgt Major)

Sgt Warren D. Reid 22 yr old student enlisted Winchester, Va 6/24/61 **W C 7/3** (later W CH)

Corporal Francis P. Hamilton 21 yr old planter enlisted Houston, Ms 5/13/61 **W 7/3 died 7/5**

Corporal William Holland enlisted Houston, Ms 4/25/61 **W 7/3**

Corporal George T Shaw 20 yr old student enlisted Houston, Ms 3/19/61 **K 7/3**

Private William A. Barton enlisted Houston, Ms 4/25/61 **K 7/3**

Private Thomas J. Boatner enlisted Houston, Ms 4/25/61 **W-hip 7/3 (bombardment) C 7/5** Private

Thomas V. Gordon enlisted Houston, Ms 5/13/61 **C 7/3**

Private James M. Griffin enlisted Houston, Ms 3/18/62 **W-foot by shell fragment C 7/3**
Corporal Francis P. Hamilton enlisted Houston, Ms 5/13/61 **K 7/3**
Private John V. Harris enlisted Houston, Ms 4/25/61 **K 7/3**
Private Thomas J. Holladay 27 yr old farmer enlisted Houston, Ms 5/13/61 **C 7/3**
Private Kearney Guston enlisted Houston, Ms 3/18/61 (later W Cold Harbor)
Private W. Pendelton Knox 24 yr old enlisted Houston 3/18/62 **C 7/3**
Private George Lee, 22 yr old enlisted Houston, Ms student 5/13/61 **W-right leg C 7/3**
Private James Lyon, 21 yr old enlisted Houston 3/18/61 **W-left arm (amp) C 7/3**
Private John Marable, "Jolly John" 20 yr old enlisted Houston, Ms 5/13/61 W Malvern Hill **C 7/3**
Private Joseph Marable 23 yr old enlisted Houston, Ms 4/25/61 **C 7/3** (later 2nd Lt)
Private William H Marable 23 yr old enlisted Houston, Ms 5/13/61 **K 7/3**
Private Robert Bankhead Marion enlisted Houston, Ms 5/15/61 W Gaines Mill **W-left arm C 7/3**
Private, Robert K Marion 20 yr old enlisted Houston, Ms 5/13/61 W 1862 **C 7/3**
Private William Marion "Red Bristles" 27 yr old enlisted Corinth13/61 **C 7/3**
Private William P. Marion—18 yr old enlisted Houston, Ms 5/13/61 "picked up flag" **K 7/3**
Private George M Mathis enlisted Houston, Ms **C 7/14 Falling Waters**
Private William B. McDowell 21 yr old enlisted Houston, Ms 5/13/61 **W-right thigh 7/3 C 7/5**
Private Aberham McJunkin, "Leech" 20 yr old enlisted Houston, Ms 5/13/61 W Fredericksburg (later W CH))
Private William T Moore enlisted Gettysburg Pa 7/1/63 **W-right leg C 7/3**
Private Mordecai J. "Jack" Murphy 26 yr old clerk enlisted Houston, Ms **K 7/3**
Private Lemuel N Reid 29 yr old enlisted Houston, Ms 3/18/62 **W-left hip C 7/3** (later W Cold Harbor)
Private Samuel Reid 30 yr old enlisted Houston, Ms 5/13/61 **C 7/3**
Private Thomas Baskin "Back" Reid 27 yr old enlisted Houston, Ms 3/18/62 (later K Weldon Railroad) Private Abiah E Robinson enlisted Houston, Ms 5/13/61 **K 7/3**
Private Samuel Roberson enlisted Houston, Ms 4/25/61 **W 7/3**
Private David N Smith enlisted Houston, Ms 3/19/61 **W 7/3 Died 7/8**
Private Joseph M Smith 26 yr old enlisted Houston, Ms **W-mouth C 7/3** (later C Hatchers Run)
Private J. C. Wilkins enlisted Houston, Ms 5/13/61 **W-left side C 7/3**
Private Samuel L. Wilson 25 yr old planter enlisted Houston, Ms 5/13/61 **W-left thigh C 7/3**
Private Thomas Willson 29 yr old enlisted Houston, Ms 5/13/61 **W-left hand 7/3**
Private John Wright 21 yr old enlisted Houston, Ms 5/13/61 **W-left side 7/3 C 7/5**
Regt Blacksmith Private David G. Maloney 26 yr old enlisted Houston, Ms 5/13/61 (later deserted)

July 1 Casualties

None

Company I *"Van Dorn Reserves"*

Captain Stephen Cocke Moore 25 yr old enlisted Aberdeen, Ms 5/13/61 **W 7/3 C 7/6**
1st Lieutenant William Word enlisted Aberdeen 4/26/61 W-**left shoulder 7/3 C 7/5**
2nd Lieutenant William H. Clopton enlisted Aberdeen, Ms 2/20/61 **W-both thighs 7/3 during advance C 7/5**
3rd Lieutenant Walton P. Snowden 2 yr old enlisted Aberdeen, Ms 2/20/61 **W-left arm C 7/3**
Sgt William Elkin enlisted Aberdeen 4/27/61 **C 7/14** (later Brigade Commissary Sgt)
Sergeant William Gladney enlisted Aberdeen 4/26/61 **W 7/3**
Sgt Joseph B McAllister 25 yr old enlisted Houston, Ms 2/20/61 **W left foot C 7/3**
Sgt. William H Meek 22 yr old enlisted Aberdeen, Ms 5/13/61 **WC 7/3**
Sgt Richard C. Sarter 24 yr old enlisted Aberdeen, Ms **W-thigh 7/3 C 7/5**
Sgt. Eugene Turbeville enlisted Aberdeen, Ms 5/13/61 **C 7/14**
Sgt William Word 27 yr old enlisted Aberdeen, Ms 2/20/61 (later W-Bethesda Church / Capt)
Corporal. Lucien J Morgan 25 yr old enlisted Aberdeen, Ms 5/13/61 **K 7/3**
Corporal James D. Demoville, enlisted Aberdeen, Ms 4/27/61 **C 7/3**
Private William Awalt enlisted Camp Jones 11/1/61 **K 7/3**
Private Lucius G Beale enlisted Aberdeen, Ms 4/26/61 **WC 7/3**
Private Isaac G. Bell enlisted Aberdeen, Ms 4/26/61 **K 7/3**
Private James S. Boothe enlisted Aberdeen, Ms 4/26/61 **C 7/14 and died in prison**
Private Benjamin Bradford enlisted Aberdeen, Ms 2/20/61 **C 7/3**
Private Lucukkus Burnette enlisted Aberdeen, Ms 4/27/61 **K 7/3**
Private William H. Clopton enlisted Aberdeen, Ms 4/26/61 **WC 7/3**
Private James T. Conway enlisted Okolona, Ms 4/25/61 **WC 7/14 died**
Private Nathan Davison enlisted Aberdeen 4/26/61 **W 7/3**
Private Robert Doak enlisted Aberdeen, Ms 4/26/61 **C 7/5**
Private Robert Elder enlisted Aberdeen 4/26/61 **W 7/3**
Private James M.Gillespie—enlisted Aberdeen 4/26/61 **W-thigh 7/3** later captured at Hatchers Run
Private John Gilleylen enlisted Aberdeen 5/13/61 (later W CH)
Private Thomas A.Gilmer—enlisted Aberdeen 3/4/61 **K 7/3**
Private James B.Gladney—enlisted Aberdeen 4/25/61 **C 7/3** (later W Cold Harbor)
Private J. W. Hawkins enlisted Aberdeen 4/25/61 **C 7/3**
Private Joseph L King enlisted Aberdeen, Ms 8/1/61 **W-groin 7/3 C 7/5 Greencastle, Pa**
Private William H Lile 24 yr old enlisted Aberdeen, Ms 8/1/61 **W-knee 7/3 died 8/1**

Private Tranquillus "Tipp" C. Mann enlisted Camp Jones, Ms 9/61 **C 7/14** (later QM)
Private Norman T. McKay 24 yr old enlisted Houston, Ms 5/13/61 **W-left thigh C 7/3**
Private Norman T McNairy enlisted Aberdeen, Ms **WC 7/3**
Private William McNairy 32 yr old enlisted Aberdeen, Ms 5/13/61 **C 7/3**
Private David H Meredith 25 yr old enlisted Aberdeen, Ms 5/13/61 **C 7/14**
Private Lycurgus W. Morgan enlisted Aberdeen 4/26/61 **K 7/3**
Private John T Moore enlisted Aberdeen, Ms 5/13/61 (later QM)
Private Patrick J. Mulvihill enlisted Aberdeen, Ms 5/13/61 **W-wrist C 7/3**
Private William T Ourey enlisted Aberdeen, Ms 5/13/61 **W-penis 7/3** no record after December 1864
Private James F. Page 19 yr old enlisted Aberdeen, Ms 5/13/61 (later W-right shoulder Wilderness)
Private William Painter 26 yr old enlisted Aberdeen, Ms 5/13/61 deserted & **C 7/14**
Private L. Purnell enlisted Aberdeen, Ms 4/23/61 **WC 7/3**
Private Thomas C. Shell 26 yr old enlisted Aberdeen, Ms 4/13/61 **C 7/14 died in prison**
Private James D Schell enlisted Aberdeen, Ms 4/13/61 (later Hospital Steward)
Private John B Sims 32 yr old enlisted Aberdeen, Ms 5/13/61 **W-right arm C 7/3**
Private W. P. Snowden 22 yr ld enlisted Aberdeen 2/20/61 **W-left thigh 7/3**
Private Charles Strong enlisted Camp Jones 9/1/61 **K 7/3**
Private George W Wall 26 yr old enlisted Aberdeen, Ms 5/13/61 W**C 7/3**
Private Alexander S. Word Aberdeen, Ms 3/4/62 **W-right leg 7/3** captured in Mississippi died in prison
Private Beverly D Young. enlisted Aberdeen, Ms 4/27/61 **W 7/3 died 8/29/63** David's Island NY

July 1 Casualties

None

Company K *"Carroll Rifles"*

Captain James S. Standley—22 yr old enlisted Carrolton, Ms W-Seven Pines resigned disabled August 1863
Captain George Bird enlisted Carrolton, Ms 4/29/61 promoted 6/28 from 1st Lt. **K 7/3**
First Lieutenant John T. Stanford—promoted to 1st Lieutenant 6/63 W-right shoulder 7/3 C 7/5
Second Lieutenant Albert G. Drake student enlisted Carrolton., Ms 2/26/61 pro 2nd Lieutenant June 1863 **W 7/3** killed at Po River
1st Sgt Alexander L. Kimbrough 26 yr old enlisted Carrolton 4/27/61 **W 7/3** (later C Deep Bottom)
2nd Sergeant Samuel J. Harper,—enlisted Carrolton, Ms 5/15/61 W-right arm **C 7/3**

3rd Sgt John Kimbrough 23 yr old enlisted Carrolton, Ms 4/29/61
1st Corporal George Arnold enlisted Lynchberg, Va 4/29/61
Corporal Joseph W Liddell 20 yr old enlisted Carrolton, Ms 5/29/61 **K 7/3**
Corporal Thomas J. Roach 20 yr old enlisted Carrolton, Ms 5/13/61 **K 7/3**
Corporal John T Standley, enlisted Carrolton, Ms C 7/14 Falling Waters
Private J.E. Boatwright enlisted Grenada, Ms 4/14/62 **K 7/3**
Private Nathaniel Clarke enlisted Carrolton, Ms 4/29/61 **K 7/3**
Private James Cobb enlisted Carrolton, Ms 3/8/61 **K 7/3**
Private John M. Durham enlisted Carrolton, Ms 4/29/61 **K 7/3**
Private Thomas W. Freeman, **C 7/3** died in prison
Private Rhesa R. Hawkins,—enlisted Carrolton, Ms 3/8/61 **C 7/3**
Private Joseph Hughes enlisted Carrolton, Ms 4/29/61 **W 7/3**
Private John W Jennings 20 yr old enlisted Carrolton, Ms 4/29/61 **W 7/3** (later W Weldon RR)
Private John T. Johnson 20 yr old student Carrolton 3/8/62 **K 7/3**
Private James H Kimbrough enlisted Carrolton, Ms 3/8/62 **W 7/3** (later C Petersburg)
Private Thomas Kimbrough 20 yr old enlisted Carrolton, Ms **W 7/3** (later Sharpshooter)
Private Elisha Lac enlisted Carrolton, Ms **K 7/3**
Private DeWitt Lee 23 yr old enlisted Carrolton, Ms 5/13/61 **C 7/3**
Private Elisha Lee 28 yr old enlisted Carrolton, Ms 5/13/61 **K 7/3**
Private Duncan McRae 33 yr old enlisted Carlton, Ms 5/13/61 **C 7/3**
Private William Marshall enlisted Carrolton, Ms 4/29/61 **W 7/3**
Private Henry Moores 28 yr old enlisted Carrolton, Ms **C 7/3** (later W Cold Harbor)
Private Joseph B Nelson 35 yr old enlisted Carrolton, Ms 5/13/61 (later ambulance driver C HR)
Private George W Oury 20 yr old enlisted Carrolton, Ms 5/13/61 **C 7/3**
Private Thomas F. Oury enlisted Carrolton, Ms 5/13/61 **W-left leg 7/3** (later C Hatchers Run)
Private James Pearce 23 yr old enlisted Carrolton, Ms later C Wilderness, died in prison)
Private Daniel O. Ross 23 yr old enlisted Carrolton, Ms 5/13/61 **C 7/14 Falling Waters**
Private Henry C. Royall 20 yr old enlisted Carrolton, Ms 3/8/62 sick until 1st battle **K 7/3**
Private James W. Shackleford enlisted Carrolton, Ms 3/8/62 **W 7/14**
Private John Shackleford enlisted Camp Jones 8/21/61 **WC 7/3** (later W-left hand Cold Harbor)
Private John T Stanford enlisted Carrolton, Ms 5/13/61 **WC 7/3**
Private Marshall W. Stevens 25 yr old enlisted Carrolton, Ms 4/29/61 **WC 7/3** (later W Petersburg)
Private Cicero Thompson enlisted Carrolton 3/1/63 **W 7/3** (later C North Anna)
Private Alexander C. Turner 20 yr old enlisted Carrolton, Ms 5/13/61 (later sharpshooter)
Private Archibald J. Turner 21 yr old enlisted Carrolton, Ms 5/13/61 **C 7/3**
Private Green A Williams enlisted Carrolton, Ms 3/8/62 **W 7/3** (later K Petersburg)
Private Phillip Wacher born in Switzerland enlisted Carrolton, Ms 5/13/61 (later deserted 7/6/63)

Bugler G.D. Winston enlisted Lynchburg, Va 5/10/61 (later C Hatchers Run)
Musician Patrick Winston enlisted Okolona, ms 3/1/63 (later C Hatchers Run)
Musician William T. Bean—enlisted Lychburg, Va 4/29/61 (later C-Hatchers Run)
Musician Robert H Hicks,.—enlisted Carrolton, Ms 4/13/61

July 1 Casualties

None

Major General William Dorsey Pender
Commander Third Division
Third Corps
Army of Northern Virginia

Major General Isaac Trimble
Third Division
Third Corps
Army of Northern Virginia

Maj. Joseph A. Engelhard
Assistant Adjutant-General, Pender's Light Division.

Brigadier General James Lane
Commander Second Brigade
Third Division—Third Corps
Army of Northern Virginia

Brigadier General Alfred Scales
Commander Fourth Brigade
Third Division—Third Corps
Army of Northern Virginia

Third Division Third Corps

Army of Northern Virginia
Commanded 7/1 Major General William Dorsey Pender
Commanded 7/3 Major General Isaac Trimble

Assistant Adjutant General (Pender)—Major Joseph Engelhard (later W Ream's Station)

Assistant Adjutant General (Trimble)—Major William Carvel Hall **C 7/3**

Assistant Adjutant & Inspector General—Major Leonard Henderson Hunt 26 years old Granville, NC—druggist W-Gaines Mill

Aide-de-Camp—Captain Samuel A'Court Ashe 23 years old Wrigthsville Sound, NC USNA C 2nd Manassas

Aide—de-Camp—Lieutenant Samuel S Kirkland 32 years old—Wm & Mary—civil engineer

Aide-de-Camp—Lieutenant James Thomas Rosborough 22 years old Rideway SC—W-Malvern Hill & Sharpsburg

Volunteer Aide-de-Camp—Louis Gourdin Young 30 yr old Gramville S.C. **W-three wounds 7/1-7/3**

Aide-de-Camp (Trimble) Lieutenant Samuel Boyer Davis 19 years old nephew of Trimble Delaware **W-lung C 7/3**

Volunteer Aide-de-Camp (Trimble)—Charles Edward Grogan 22 years old Clark Co. Va—**W-twice 7/3 C 7/5**

Chief of Artillery (Trimble)—Major Lewis Terrell

Engineering Officer—Lieutenant Channing Moore Bolton 20 years old Richmond, Va—UVa

Ordinance Officer (Pender)—Captain Edward Willoughby Anderson 22 years old St. Augustine, Fl USMA

Ordinance Officer (Trimble)—Captain Lawrence Slaughter Marye 29 years old Fredericksburg, Va—UVa

Quarter Master (Pender)—Major Nathaniel Eldridge Scales 29 years old—UNC

Quarter Master (Trimble)—Major George Douglas Mercer 32 years old Anne Arundel, Md

Assistant Quarter Master—Captain Robert Marcus Oates 34 years old Cleveland Co. NC—grocer

Commissary of Substance—Major Daniel Tolson Carraway 30 years old

Maj. Daniel T. Carraway—Chief Surgeon

Second Brigade Third Division Third Corps

Army of Northern Virginia
Commanded July 1 Brigadier General James H. Lane
Commanded July 3 Brigadier General James H. Lane

Assistant Adjutant General—Captain George Johnston 23 years old Edenton, NC—UNC former Captain Co G 28th NC
C Hanover CH) appointed 1/19/63
Assistant Adjutant & Inspector General—Lieutenant Edward Alson Thorne Nicholson 20 years old UNC
Aide-de-Camp—Lieutenant Oscar Lane (brother) 28 years old (later K-Spotsylvania)
Ordinance Officer—Lieutenant James Augustus Washington Bryan 24 years old New Bern NC.—Princeton
Quarter Master—Major George Sidney Thompson 24 years old Chapel Hill, NC UNC
Commissary of Substance—Captain Thomas Hall McCoy 26 years old Clinton, NC former 2nd Lt Co C 7th NC appointed June 1863

THIRTY THIRD NORTH CAROLINA INFANTRY

Major Joseph Saunders

2nd Lt. Finley Jones

Field & Staff

Colonel Clark Moulton Avery 44 yr old appointed 1/17/62 C—New Bern W-Chancellorsville MW-Spotsylvania

Lt. Colonel Robert Cowen 23 yr old Iredel Co. promoted 8/5/62 W-right forearm Chancellorsville Absent W

Major Joseph H. Saunders 24 yr old Orange Co. planter appointed 5/13/63 **WC 7/3** (later Lt. Col)

Adjutant Spier Whitaker 22 yr old 2nd lt Co K 8/14/62 C New Bern appointed 1/3/63 C Fredreicksburg 5/3/63 (later sick 9/63)

Sergeant Major Lewis Lawrence 21 yr old enlisted Tarboro, NC 9/3/61 promoted 12/10/62 (later Lt Col.)

Assistantt Quartermaster John Sudderth appointed 4/30/63 (later Brigade QM)

Quartermaster Sergeant Francis Butler 28 yr old mechanic enlisted Forsythe Co 9/15/61

Ordinance Sergeant John Midyett enlisted 4/26/63 promoted May 1, 1863

Surgeon John Shaffner appointed 3/4/62 C Hanover CH (with wounded)

Assistant Surgeon Littlebury Rose appointed 3/62

Assistant Surgeon John Vigal appointed 5/28/62

Asst Surgeon John Tyler McLean appointed 6/11/63 **C 7/5 (with wounded)**

Chaplin Thomas Eatman appointed 2/12/63

Quartermaster Sergeant Francis Butner promoted 11/61

Assistant t Commissary of Substance Robert Hauser 30 yr old physician in Surray Co. enlisted 8/3/61

Commissary Sergeant Edward Burgess promoted 1/21/62
Ordinance Sergeants John Midyett detailed 5/1/63
John Gibson 38 yr old enlisted Cabarrus Co. appointed 2/13/62

Regimental Band

Chief Musician Edwin Dull promoted 2/1/62
Musician William Butner 27 yr old mechanic enlisted Forsyth Co 8/15/61 promoted 2/1/62
Musician Reuben Crator 23 yr old enlisted Forsyth Co. 3/15/62 promoted 5/62
Musician Lewis Hartman 21 yr old enlisted Forsyth Co. 7/1/8/61 promoted 2/1/62
Drummer Robert Jones 20 yr old enlisted Pitt Co 7/31/61 Musician in Co B until 9/63
Musician John Kimbrough 19 yr old enlisted Yadkin Co 3/15/62 promoted 5/1/62
Musician Oliver Lehman 19 yr old enlisted Forsyth Co. 7/1/61 promoted 2/15/63
Musician Gideon Miller (Co H) 118 yr old enlisted Forsyth Co. 7/15/62 promoted 7/62
Musician Virgil Miller 19 yr old enlisted Forsythe Co. 3/1/62promoted 3/62 (later deserted)
Musician Jesse Reynolds 17 yr old enlisted Cumberland Co. 8/29/61 (Co G) transferred 3/63
Musician Levin Stroupe 22 yr old teacher enlisted Forsyth Co. 7/22/61 promoted 2/1/62
Musician Robert Watson enlisted Hyde Co as Serg (Co F) C Fredericksburg appointed 5/64
Musician John Williard (Co I) 22 yr old enlisted Forsyth Co. 11/14/61 promoted 4/62
Musician William Williford (Co G) 16 yr ol;d enlisyed Cumberland Co. 2/11/62 promoted 2/62

Company A Iredell County

Captain Henry Baker 24 yr old enlisted Halifax Co. 4/25/62 promoted captain 5/13/63 **K 7/3**
1st Lt James Summers 34 yr old mechanic enlisted Iredell Co. C Chancellorsville
2nd Lt Thomas Cowan 20 yr old enlisted Iredell Co. W-thigh Ox Hill;, Va **K 7/3**
3rd Lt Martin Whalen transferred 2/1/62 (later C Fussell's Mill, Va)
1st Sgt Robert Shields21 yr old mechanic enlisted Iredell Co 6/25/61 C Fredericksburg **K 7/3**
Sgt. Gilbert Stamper 27 yr old enlisted Iredell Co 6/10/61 **C 7/3**
Sgt. Milus Hicks 22 yr old enlisted Iredell Co 3/1/62 WC Fredericksburg **C 7/3**
Sgt. John Powell 35 yr old enlisted Wake Co 7/1/62 (died smallpox 11/26/63)
Cpl. William Holland 31 yr old enlisted 3/6/62 (later AWOL 7/63 / returned / W Wilderness)
Cpl. Elias Jenkins 21 yr old enlisted 7/1/62
Cpl. David Troutman 27 yr old overseer enlisted Iredell Co 7/29/61 C Fredericksburg **C 7/5**

Cpl. Joseph Ward 26 yr old sailor enlisted Iredell Co 7/5/61 C Hanover CH

Priv. John Barbee 25 yr old enlisted Orange Co 11/24/61 C New Bern (later W Petersburg)

Priv. James Barrett 20 yr old enlisted Iredell Co.7/26/61 C Fredericksburg, Va

Priv. William Bowers 25 yr old enlisted Person Co.7/1/62 **WC 7/3 (died 7/10)**

Priv. Henry Campbell 27 yr old stonecutter enlisted Wake Co.11/8/62

Priv. Jones Cardon 22 yr old enlisted Cabarrus Co.3/29/62 C Fredericksburg (later W Petersburg 6/22/64)

Priv. Christopher Davis 27 yr old enlisted Orange Co 11/30/61 C Hanover CH

Priv. James Dearman 22 yr old enlisted Iredell Co.7/18/61 C Hanover CH **C 7/14**

Priv. Patrick Dolehite 20 yr old enlisted Orange Co 11/30/61 (later Corp W Wilderness)

Priv. Daniel Fink 29 yr old enlisted 2/26/62 C New Bern, NC C Fredericksburg (later W Wilderness)

Priv. Leander Guy 22 yr old painter enlisted in Iredell Co 11/4/61 **W 7/3 C 7/5**

Priv. W.M. Hallman 27 yr old enlisted Wake Co. enlisted 5/26/63 **K 7/2**

Priv. Jacob Halterman 22 yr old enlisted 6/12/61 C Fredericksburg (later W-Spotsylvania / Pioneer)

Priv. Daniel Heintzleman 31 yr old enlisted Cabarrus Co 3/29/62 **C 7/14** (later C Fussell Mills)

Priv. William Johnson 31 enlisted 7/1/62 C Fredericksburg (later W Wilderness)

Priv. William Jones enlisted Iredell Co. **C 7/5**

Priv. John Lazenby 20 yr old enlisted Iredell Co 7/25/61 C New Bern W Hanover CH (later Corp)

Priv. John Medlin 32 yr old enlisted Wake Co. 11/16/61 (later Corp) W 7/64

Priv. James Millsaps enlisted 3/26/63 (later Corp)

Priv. John Murph 28 yr old enlisted Cabarrus 12/26/61 C Hanover CH **C 7/14**

Priv. Alfred Ramseur enlisted in transfer 5/26/63 **K 7/3**

Priv. John Shinn 22 yr old enlisted Cabarrus 12/03/61 W Fredericksburg **W-right shoulder-arm 7/3 C 7/4**

Priv. William Shuford enlisted as transfer 5/16/62 (later Sgt)

Priv. Adolpus Stewart 23 yr old enlisted Iredell Co 2/26/62 C Fredericksburg **W-hand 7/3** (later W-right foot Jericho Mills)

Priv. John Scott 24 yr old enlisted wake Co 7/1/62 **K 7/3**

Priv. Edward Strickland 25 yr old enlisted Wake Co. 7/1/62 (later AWOL 7/63 returned 6/64)

Priv. Levi Tucker 24 yr old enlisted Wake Co. (later W-thumb,left arm and right shoulder Wilderness)

Priv. Gray Wasden 31 yr old enlisted Wake Co 7/1/62 C Fredericksburg W-left leg C Chancellorsville (Later K Petersburg)

Priv. Abel York 24 yr old enlisted Iredell Co 8/4/61 as drummer C New Bern W Ox Hill (later AWOL 8/63)

Priv. Isaiah York 23 yr old enlisted Iredell Co W-right foot Cedar Mtn (later Sgt)

July 1 Casualties

None

Company B *"Clark's Guard"*

1st Lt Ebenezer Price 20 yr old enlisted Edgecombe Co 9/20/61 W Cedar Mtn. **W-hip 7/14** (later Capt)

2nd Lt Peyton Anthony transferred 4/23/63 W Chancellorsville **W-ankle 7/3**

1st Sgt Burvin Stephenson 29 yr old carpenter enlisted Egdecombe Co 8/19/61 W Cedar Mtn. **C 7/3**

Sgt Major Lewis Lawrence 20 yr old enlisted Edgecombe Co. 9/3/61 (later 1st Lt)

Sgt William Calhoun 25 yr old enlisted Edgecombe Co. 5/1/62 **W-arm 7/3**

Sgt William Howard 19 yr old enlisted Edgecombe Co 5/1/62 **W 7/3 C 7/5**

Sgt Thomas Mayo 20 yr old enlisted Edgecombe Co 7/31/61 **W-hip 7/3** (later 1st Sgt W-left arm Reams Station)

Corp Jesse Braswell 28 yr old enlisted Lenoir Co. 3/21/62 ***W-shoulder** 7/3 (later Sgt)*

Corp William Godwin 20 yr old enlisted Edgecombe Co 8/29/61 **W-left thigh 7/3**

Corp John Purvis 21 yr old enlisted Edgecombe Co C Chancellorsville **W-left hip 7/3** (later Sgt)

Private William Andrews 22 yr old enlisted Edgecombe Co 7/31/61 **C 7/14**

Private Robert Armstrong 26 yr old enlisted Edgecombe Co 5/1/62 C Hanover CH C Chancellorsville **C 7/5**

Private Bullock Brsswell 19 yr old enlisted Edgecombe Co 5/1/62 C Chancellorsville **C 7/14**

Private David Braswell 29 yr old enlisted Edgecombe Co 5/1/62 (later W Jericho Mills, Va)

Private Joshua Braswell 25 yr old enlisted Edgecombe Co. 5/1/62 (later K Jones Farm, Va)

Private William Briley 26 yr old enlisted Pitt Co. 9/6/61 (later W-hip Jone's Farm, Va)

Private William Briley 23 yr old enlisted Edgecombe Co 8/26/61

Private Frestel Brown 18 yr old enlisted Edgecombe Co 7/31/61 (later Corp)

Private Edward Burk born in Ireland "gave up" at Gettysburg **C 7/3**

Private Daniel Calhoun 21 yr old enlisted Edgecombe Co.

Private Thomas Council 23 yr old enlisted "Jenkins" 9/7/61

Private John Crisp 26 yr old enlisted 8/13/61 **C 7/3**

Private Benjamin Davenport 20 yr old enlisted Edgecombe Co 7/31/61

Private James Denton 25 yr old enlisted Edgecombe Co 8/22/61 (w-right arm Petersburg picket)

Private Bethel Ford 39 yr old enlisted Pitt Co. C New Bern **C 7/14**

Private Burwell Gay 25 yr old enlisted Edgecombe Co 5/1/62 C Winchester, Va **C 7/3**

Private William Gay 20 yr old enlisted Edgecombe Co 7/15/61 **W-right arm (amp) 7/3 C 7/5**

Private James Graham 31 yr old enlisted Wake Co 7/1/62

Private Guilford Grimes 19 yr old enlisted Edgecombe Co 5/1/62 W Cedar Mtn

Private Nathan Grimes 21 yr old enlisted Edgecombe Co 7/31/61 (later Corp)

Private James Hagans 24 yr old enlisted Edgecombe Co 5/10/62 W Cedar Mtn **W-head & abdomen 7/3**

Private Warren Harrell 18 yr old enlisted Edgecombe Co 5/1/62 W Malvern Hill W Chancellorsville ***W-shoulder 7/3***

Private William Harrell 17 yr old enlisted Edgecombe Co 8/13/61 ***W 7/3***

Private William Hoard 34 yr old enlisted Edgecombe Co 9/10/61 **W-right shoulder 7/3 C 7/5**

Private William Hyatt enlisted Edgecombe Co 5/10/62 C Chancellorsville **WC 7/3 (died)**

Private Noah Jackson 22 yr old enlisted Wake Co. 7/1/62 (later AWOL 11/63—returned 1/64

Private James Johnson 19 yr old enlisted Edgecombe Co 5/1/62

Private Robert Jones 19 yr old enlisted Edgecombe Co 7/312/61 (later musician / Sgt Major)

Private Wilson Long 24 yr od enlisted Edgecombe Co 8/6/61 (later K Jericho Mills, Va)

Private Duncan McIntire 22 yr old enlisted wake Co 7/1/62 (AWOL 11/63—returned 1/64)

Private McGilvery Manning 20 yr old enlisted Edgecombe Co 7/31/61

Private Macon Morrison 25 yr old enlisted Wake Co. 7/1/62 (later W-head Reams's Station)

Private Joseph Peel 23 yr old enlisted Edgecombe Co. 8/13/61 W-right elbow Gaines Mill (later w-Gravel Hill,Va)

Private William Peel 21 yr old enlisted Edgecombe Co. (later Pioneer)

Private James Philpot 19 yr old enlisted 3/27/62 W-leg Ox Hill, Va (died at home 10/64)

Private John Raiford 22 yr old carpenter enlisted Edgecombe Co 9/20/61

Private Robert Randolph 27 yr old enlisted Edgecombe Co 8/20/61 C New Bern NC

Private John Ruffin 27 yr old enlisted Edgecombe 5/1/62 W Gaines Mill, Va

Private Timothy Sullivan Irish born enlisted Edgecombe Co **C 7/3**

Private William Tolston 24 yr old enlisted Edgecombe Co 5/1/62 **W-thigh 7/ 3 C 7/5**

Private William Vainwright 33 yr old enlisted Edgecombe Co 7/31/61 C Hanover CH **W-foot 7/3** (later K Jericho Mills, Va)

Private William Warbritton 20 yr old enlisted Edgecombe Co. 8/6/61 (later Corp K Wilderness)

Private James Williams 20 yr old enlisted Edgecombe Co. 8/11/61

July 1 Casualties

None

Company C *"Cabarrus Hornets"*

Captain David Corzine 37 yr old enlisted Cabarrus Co 9/20,61 W Chancellorsville **W-leg 7/3** (later K Gravel Hill, Va)

1st Lt. Willoughby Avery transferred 8/6/62 (later Captain)

2nd Lt. William Gibson 24 yr old enlisted Wake Co 10/24/62 **K 7/3**

1st Sgt Daniel Moore 24 yr old carpenter enisted Cabarrus Co. 9/7/61 C Fredericksburg (later 1st Lt)

Sgt. John Barnhardt 24 yr old enlisted Cararrus Co. 8/31/61 W 2nd Manassas (later W Spotsylvania)

Sgt James File 20 yr old enlisted Cabarrus Co 8/31/61 (later W Jerusalem Plank Rd)

Sgt Joseph Meisenheimer 25 yr old enlisted Cabarrus Co 8/31/61 **W 7/3** (later C Wilderness)

Sgt Valentine Plott 26 yr old enlisted Cabarrus Co 9/4/61 W-arm Fredericksburg **W 7/1 C 7/5**

Corp. John Goodman 21 yr old enlisted Cararrus Co 8/31/61 W-foot Malvern Hill W-left thigh 7/1 ***C 7/4***

Corp Daniel Sides 30 yr old enlited Cabarrus Co 8/31/61 C Sharpsburg (later W-right leg & arm Wilderness)

Private Jacob Barnhardt 24 yr old enlisted Cararrus Co. 8/31/61 ***C 7/5***

Private Rufus Barnhardt 26 yr old enlisted Cararrus Co. 8/31/61 C New Bern, NC C Hanover CH

Private Simon Barnhardt 30 yr old enlisted Cararrus Co. 8/31/61

Private Sandy Brantly 19 yr old enlisted Cararrus Co. 8/31/61 C New Bern, NC **W-left leg (amp) 7/3 C 7/5**

Private John Brown 29 yr old enlisted Cararrus Co.

Private Philip Carriker 26 yr old enlisted Cararrus Co. 11/9/61 W Fredericksburg (later Corp)

Private Franklin Cook 22 yr old blacksmith enlisted Cararrus Co 8/31/61 **C 7/4**

Private Henry Cope 22 yr old enlisted Cararrus Co 9/28/61

Private John Cornelius 23 yr old enlisted Cararrus Co 7/1/61

Private Presley Cornelius 25 yr old enlisted Cararrus Co 7/1/61 **W 7/3 (died)**

Private James C. Corzine served in 57th NC transferred 4/1//63

Private Frank Craig 18 yr old enlisted Rowan Co. (Later 2nd Lt)

Private Allen Craver 22 yr old enlisted Forsythe Co 7/1/62

Private Charles Daywalt 23 yr old enlisted Cararrus Co 8/31/61

Private Irdell Evans 21 yr old enlisted Forsythe Co 7/1/62 C Fredericksburg (AWOL 7/63 returned 9/63 C Spotsylvania)

Private Milton Fiddler 23 yr old enlisted Forsythe Co 7/1/62 (later C Wilderness)

Private Richard Gillespie 28 yr old enlisted Cabarrus Co 10/15/61 **W-side 7/3 C 7/5**

Private George Goodman 25 yr old enlisted Cabarrus Co 8/31/61 ***W-left thigh 7/1***

Private Jacob Goodman 21 yr old enlisted Cabarrus Co 8/31/61 ***C 7/5 (caring for brother)***

Private William Harris 40 yr old carpenter enlisted Cabarrus Co 8/31/61 **C 7/5**

Private Gaston Helsebeck 19 yr old enlisted Forsythe Co. 7/1/62 (AWOL 7-8/63 returned W-right leg Gravel Hill, Va)

Private Timothy Jenkins 25 yr old enlisted Cabarrus 2/21/62 (later C Wilderness)

Private William Jenkins 21 yr old enlisted Cabarrus 2/21/62 (later C Wilderness)

Private Parham Kirk 49 yr old blacksmith enlisted Wake Co **C 7/5**

Private William Lefler 21 yr old enlisted Cabarrus 2/27/62 **C 7/3**

Private Noah Lewis 31 yr old enlisted Forsythe Co. 7/1/62 C Fredericksburg **C 7/5**

Private David Livengood 23 yr old enlisted Cabarrus 2/26/62 (later W-right leg Spotsylvania)

Private William Louder 24 yr old enlisted Cabarrus Co 8/31/61 **C 7/5**

Private William McGraw 20 yr old enlisted Cabarrus Co 9/6/61

Private James Moore 21 yr old enlisted Cabarrus Co. C Peninsular Campaign

Private Jesse Moore 22 yr old enlisted Cabarrus Co 9/7/61 C Peninsular Campaign (later Corp K Wilderness)

Private Thomas Nading 29 yr old enlisted Forsythe Co 7/1/62 **C 7/5**

Private Charles Padget 26 yr old enlisted Forsythe Co 7/1/62 **C 7/14**

Private John Peninger 25 yr old enlisted Cabarrus Co 9/16/61 (later K Jericho Mills 5/23/64)

Private George Petrie 38 yr old enlisted Cabarrus Co 9/13/61 **W-arm 7/1 C 7/4**

Private Chalmers Plott 22 yr old enlisted Cabarrus Co. 8/31/62 W-foot&knee Cedar Mtn. (Later Corp)

Private Henry Rumage 30 yr old enlisted Cabarrus Co 8/31/61 (later W Spotsylvania)

Private Sanford Shelton 25 yr old enlisted Forsythe Co 7/1/62 **K 7/1**

Private Henry Clay Shive transferred 2/25/63 **C 7/14**

Private **Augustus Shore** 22 yr old enlisted Forsythe Co 7/1/62 **WC 7/14** (later W-Petersburg)

Private Naaman Shore 20 yr old enlisted Forsythe Co 7/1/62 (AWOL 11/63 returned)

Private David Sink 26 yr old enlisted Forsythe Co **C 7/14**

Private William Spainhour 21 yr ld enlisted Forsythe Co **C 7/14**

Private Allison Stough 41 yr old enlisted Cabarrus Co 9/28/61 **C 7/14**

Private William Stough 37 yr old enlisted Cabarrus Co 3/26/63 (later W-Jerusalem Plank)

Private Adam Tucker 26 yr old enlisted Cabarrus Co 2/2/62 **W-left eye both legs 7/3 C 7/4**

Private Charles Tucker 21 yr old enlisted Cabarrus Co 9/14/61 **WC groin 7/3** (later teamster)

Private Francis Walter 22 yr old blacksmith enlisted Cabarrus Co 9/13/61

July 1 Casualties

Private Amzi Petrie 37 yr old enlisted Cabarrus Co. **K 7/1**

Company D *"Wilkes Regulators"*

Captain Oliver Parks 26 yr old enlisted Wilkes Co 10/4/61 (dismissed 1/21/63) returned (Resigned 9/17/763) ** see record

1st Lt James Hunt 23 yr old enlisted Wilkes Co 10/4/61 W-chest CH (died 6/6/64)

2nd Lt Finley Jones 28 yr old enlisted Wilkes Co 10/4/61 W Chancellorsville **WC 7/3**

3rd Lt John Happoldt 22 yr old enlisted Burke Co 10/4/61

1st Sgt Shadrach Joins 20 yr old enlisted Wilkes Co 3/1/62 C Fredericksburg W-right arm **C 7/3**

Sgt. Eleazer Jennings 32 yr old enlisted Wilkes Co 10/4/61 ***W-face 7/3*** *(later W-thigh Wilderness)*

Sgt. James Lane 25 yr old enlisted Wilkes Co 10/4/61 deserted Mar-Apr 62 returned (later deserted Oct 64)

Sgt. Franklin Pardue 27 yr old enlisted Wilkes Co 10/4/61 ***K 7/3***

Cpl. Barton Durham 24 yr old enlisted Wilkes Co 10/4/61 C Fredericksburg **WC 7/3**

Cpl. William Pardue 21 yr old enlisted Wilkes Co 10/4/61 (later Sgt C-Petersburg)

Cpl. Benjamin Stiller 20 yr old enlisted Wilkes Co 10/4/61 C Fredericksburg **C 7/3**

Priv. Miles Blackburn 20 yr old enlisted Wilkes Co 3/22/62 C Gaines Mill (later AWOL)

Priv. Felix Brewer 21 yr old enlisted Wilkes Co 10/4/61 (deserted 8/63-10/63)

Priv. Joseph Brinegar 20 yr old enlisted Wilkes Co 10/4/61 (later Corp)

Priv. John Buttery 20 yr old enlisted Wilkes Co 10/4/61 deserted Jan-Feb 63 & April 64

Priv. Caleb Carter 22 yr old enlisted Wilkes Co 3/22/62 AWOL July-Oct 62 **WC 7/3** C Wilderness

Priv. Columbus Carter 19 yr old enlisted Wilkes Co 3/22/62 AWOL July-Oct 62 (later deserted)-returned C Spots

Priv. Jackson Grimes 24 yr old enlisted Wilkes Co 10/4/61 deserted 3/62 returned C Fredericksburg

Priv. Charles Hawkins 29 yr old enlisted Alleghany Co 10/4/61 **W 7/3 (died 7/14)**

Priv. Jesse Hawkins 25 yr old enlisted Sparks 3/22/62 AWOL Jan-Feb 63 returned (Deserted 8/63)

Priv. John Higgins 21 yr old enlisted Wilkes Co 10/4/61 C Fredericksburg

Priv. Lindsay Jennings 21 yr old enlisted Wilkes Co 10/4/61 (later Sgt)

Priv. George McCall 25 yr old enlisted Richmond Co 7/1/62 (AWOL Nov-Dec 63)

Priv. Charles McDaniel 52 yr old enlisted Wake Co 10/30/61 (discharged 2/64)

Priv. William McEntire enlisted in Rutherford C (later 3rd Lt W Spots)

Priv. James McLean 29 yr old enlisted Richmond Co 7/1/62 **WC 7/3**

Priv. Laughlin Oliver 24 yr old enlisted Richmond Co 7/1/62 **C 7/14**

Priv. Colbert Pardue 26 yr old enlisted Wilkes Co 10/4/61 (later W-right hip Wilderness)

Priv. John Pardue 24 yr old enlisted Wilkes Co 10/4/61 (later W Spotsylvania)

Priv. Augus Patterson 30 yr old enlisted Wilkes Co 7/1/62 W-left hand right arm Fred **W-right thigh 7/3**

Priv. Fletcher Peele 30 yr old enlisted Richmond Co 7/1/62 (later Corp.)

Priv. Jacob Perkins 23 yr old enlisted Richmond Co 7/1/62 (later W right leg Turkey Ridge, Va)

Priv. William Sanford 27 yr old enlisted Wilkes Co 10/4/61 C Gaines Mill (later K Gravel Hill, Va)

Priv. Samuel Stokes 20 yr old enlisted Wilkes Co 10/4/61 (deserted 8/9/63—returned C Spots)

Priv. Jacob Wagoner 31 yr old enlisted Lenoir Co 3/1/62 (deserted Sept-Oct 63—returned—C Spotsylvania

Private William Walker enlisted Orange Co. 7/8/62 (later C Wilderness)

Priv. William Wiles 19 yr old enlisted Wilkes Co 10/4/61 C Fredericksburg (later K Wilderness)

Musician Robert Watson enlisted Hyde Co as Sergeant C Fredericksburg Appointed 3/63 **C 7/3**

July 1 Casualties

None

Company E "*Gates County*"

Captain William Parker enlisted at age 41 Edgecombe Co. 10/2/61 W-head 2nd Manassas

2nd Lt. John "Jimmy" Caldwell 18 yr old enlisted Burke Co 5/3/63 **K 7/3**

2nd Lt John Cowper 21 yr old teacher enlisted Gates Co 10/5/61 **W-left lung C 7/3**

1st Sgt William Brinkley 31 yr old enlisted Gates Co 8/30/61

Sgt. William Duke enlisted Gates Co 2/20/62 **C 7/3**

Sgt. Robert Hinton transferred 7/14/62 (later W Jericho Mills)

Corp Alfred Eason transferred 7/14/62 **W-right foot 7/2 C 7/5**

Corp. Alfred Hayes 29 yr old mechanic enlisted Gates Co 10/22/61

Corp. Benjamin Smith 24 yr old enlisted Gates Co. 8/10/61 C new Bern NC (later W-neck Spotsylvania)

Private Micajah Anderson enlisted Edgecombe Co 7/1/62 (later K Wilderness)

Private Thomas Baucum 25 yr old enlisted Anson Co 7/1/62 (later C Wilderness)

Private John Benton enlisted Gates Co 2/15/62 (wounded several times during war)

Private David Boyet enlisted Gates Co 2/20/62 **C 7/3**
Private Burwell Branton 30 yr old enlisted gates Co 10/7/61 **W-hand C 7/3**
Private Moses Branton enlisted Gates Cop W Chancellorsville **C 7/3**
Private Reuben Brown 16 yr old enlisted Gates Co 10/20/61 (later deserted 12/63)
*Private William Corbett **20** yr old enlisted Gates Co 8/10/61 deserted 7/24/63 returned 4/64*
*Private Johnson Corbett **20** yr old enlisted Gates Co 8/21/61 deserted 7/24/63 returned 4/64*
Private Joseph Dildy 21 yr old enlisted Gates Co 4/26/62 AWOL 9/63
Private William Dildy transferred 7/14/62 (later C Wilderness)
Private Timothy Eason 23 yr old enlisted Gates Co 10/7/61 AWOL 9/63
Private Frank Eure enlisted 4/28/63 Deserted 7/24/63
Private George Eure 19 yr old enlisted Gates Co 8/3/61 W-left thigh Malvern Hill
Private James Eure enlisted Gates Co 2/20/62
Private Uriah Eure 31 yr old enlisted gates Co deserted 7/24/63
Private James Everett transferred 7/14/62 **K 7/3**
Private Calvin Gaither enlisted Edgecombe Co 7/1/62 **C 7/3**
Private Charles Griffin enlisted Anson Co 7/1/62 (later C Wilderness)
Private Henry Harrell enlisted Gates Co. 11/18/61 Deserted 7/24/63
*Private Joseph Harrell 19 yr old enlisted Gates Co. 1/1/62 C Glendale **C 7/14** (died Point Lookout 12/29/63)*
*Private Patrick Harrell enlisted gates Co 2/20/62 C Chancellorsville **C 7/14** (joined US Army 2/2/64)*
Private John Harrington enlisted Anson Co. 7/1/62 C Fredericksburg (later C Bristoe Station)
Private Anderson High enlisted Edgecombe Co 7/1/62 C Chancellorsville **W 7/3 C 7/5** (later K Jerusalem Plank Rd)
Private Alexander Holland 25 yr old enlisted Gates Co 8/1/61 C Hanover CH C Fredericksburg (later W Jericho Mills)
Private William Hughes enlisted Anson Co. 7/1/72 (AWOL after 11/63)
Private Warren Jones transferred 7/14/62 deserted 7/24/63
Private John Lannon 17 yr old enlisted Edgecombe Co 7/1/62 as substitute
Private Benjamin Mathias enlisted Gates Co. 1/25/62
Private Hardy O'Neal enlisted Edgecombe Co 7/1/62
Private L. Berry O'Neal enlisted Edgecombe Co. 7/1/62
Private Wiley Parker 17 yr old enlisted gates Co 2/11/62 (later Musician)
Private Jesse Porter 23 yr old enlisted Gates Co. C Wilderness)
Private James Smith **C 7/5/63** (died in prison)
Private Henry Traywick enlisted Anson Co. 7/1/62 C Chancellorsville **C 7/14**
Private Nathan Vick enlisted Edgecombe Co 7/1/62 W Chancellorsville **K 7/3**
Private William Weeks 29 yr old enlisted Edgecombe Co 7/1/62 (later C Spotsylvania)
Private William Wesley enlisted Edgecombe Co 7/1/62 **C 7/14**

Private N.W. Wick enlisted Edgecombe Co June 1863 **K 7/2**

Private John Wilson 26 yr old enlisted Gates Co 2/20/62 **C 7/14**

Private William Worsley enlisted Edgecombe Co 7/1/62 **C 7/14**

Private Frederick Wright 21 yr old enlisted gates co 8/10/61 W-left hip by shell Malvern Hill W-left hand Cedar Mtn W-left shoulder Sharpsburg

July 1 Casualties

None

Company F *"Dixie Invincibles"*

Captain James Weston 25 yr old Hyde Co Trinity College graduate enlisted 9/9/61 C New Bern, NC (later Maj W-leg Jericho Mills. Va.)

1st LT James Gibbs appointed 9/9/61 C-Fredericksburg **W 7/ 3** (later W left foot Jericho Mills, Va)

2nd LT Samuel Watson enlisted Hyde Co. Ms 9/9/61 **W/C 7/3**

3rd Lt Wilson Lucas 23 yr old Hyde Co enlisted 9/961

1st Sgt Joseph Swindell 21 yr old Hyde Co Farmer enlisted 9/9/61 W New Bern C Fred/Chan

Ord Sgt John Midyett detailed May 1, 1863

Sgt Joseph Gibbs 35 yr old enlisted Hyde Co. 9/9/61 C Fredericksburg **C 7/3**

Sgt Samuel Gibbs enlisted Hyde Co. 9/9/61 W-right side Malvern Hill / C Fredricksburg (later W North Anna)

Sgt Robert Watson enlisted Hyde Co. 9/9/61 C Fredericksburg **C 7/3**

Sgt William Farrow enlisted Hyde Co. 9/9/61 C New Bern (later Sgt)

Corp James Dailey enlisted Hyde Co. 9/9/61 **C 7/3** (later Sgt)

Corp Clement Daniels enlisted Hyde Co. 9/9/61 C Fredricksburg (later C Wilderness)

Corp Benjamin Neal enlisted in Hyde Co 9/9/61 C Malvern Hill C Fredericksburg (later C Wilderness)

Private **Martin Ball** enlisted Hyde Co. 9/9/61 C Hanover CH (later C Fussell's Mill, Va)

Private Richard Berry enlisted Hyde Co. 9/9/61 C Fredericksburg **W 7/1-3** (later W-right arm Petersburg)

Private Thomas Cates enlisted Orange Co 7/8/62 (later W Wilderness)

Private Sylvester Cutrell enlisted Hyde Co. 9/9/61

Private William Douglas enlisted Hyde Co. 9/9/61 (later W-leg Spotsylvania)

Private John Edwards enlisted Orange Co. 7/8/62 (later C Gravel Hill, Va)

Private John Emory enlisted Hyde Co. 9/9/61 **W 7/3**

Private William Ensley enlisted Hyde Co. 9/9/61

Private Henry Gibbs enlisted Hyde Co. 9/9/61 ***K 7/3***

Private Robert Gibbs enlisted Hyde Co. 9/9/61 W-neck C Sharpsburg (later WC Wilderness)

Private Thomas Gibbs enlisted Hyde Co. 9/9/61 (later W-m leg Farmville, Va)

Private Samuel Gill enlisted Organge co. 7/8/62 (later C Spotsylvania)

Private William Gray enlisted Hyde Co. 9/9/61 C Hanover CH / (laterW-left leg Jericho Mills, Va)

Private Samuel Hamilton enlisted Hyde Co. 9/9/61 C Fredericksburg (later W Wilderness)

Private Allison Harris 19 yr old enlisted Hyde Co. 9/9/61 (later drummer)

Private Robert Harris enlisted Hyde Co. 9/9/61 W Maryland 10/15/62

Private Thomas Hawkins enlisted Orange Co. 7/8/62 (later C Wilderness)

Private Robert Hinton enlisted Orange Co. 7/8/62

Private Henry Jennette 26 yr old enlisted Hyde Co. 9/9/61 W New Bern

Private Nathaniel King enlisted Orange Co. 7/8/62 (later W-left hip Jericho Mills, Va)

Private William Kirkland enlisted Orange Co. 7/8/62 **C 7/14**

Private Samuel Lloyd enlisted Orange Co 7/8/62 (later C Spotsylvania)

Private Charles Long enlisted Orange Co. 7/8/62 (later deserted 12/ 63—returned became a nurse)

Private Sidney Malone 25 yr old enlisted Orange Co. 7/8/62 (later W Wilderness)

Private B.F. Mayhew enlisted Hyde Co. 9/9/61 C New Bern / C Fredricksburg (later Corp)

Private Riley Midyett enlisted Hyde Co. 9/9/61 W-arm Fredricksburg (later W-arm Petersburg)

Private Issac Morris enlisted Orange Co. 7/8/62 C Chancellorsville **C 7/3**

Private Mathias O'Neal enlisted Hyde Co. 9/9/61 **W-face 7/3—bombardment**

Private Thomas Payne enlisted Hyde Co. 9/9/61 **C 7/14** (later Sgt)

Private Walter Riley enlisted Orange Co. 7/8/62

Private Reuben Rose enlisted Hyde Co. 9/9/61 C-Pennisula

Private Wallace Sadler enlisted Hyde Co. 9/9/61 deserted 1/63 "retaken"

Private Benjamin Sawyer enlisted Hyde Co 4/15/62 deserted 1/63 "retaken"

Private Henry Scott enlisted Orange Co. 7/8/62 W Fredericksburg (later K Wilderness)

Private Henry Selby enlisted Hyde Co. 9/9/61

Private William Selby enlisted yde Co 9/9/61 (deserted 8/63)

Private Christopher Spencer enlisted Hyde Co. 9/9/61 **W-left arm 7/2 skirmish line**

Private A.J. Stroud enlisted Orange Co. 7/8/62 (deserted 8/63)

Private Henry White enlisted Hyde Co 9/9/61

July 1 Casualties

None

Company G *"Cumberland Rangers"*

Captain William Callais appointed 2nd Lt 8/6/62 W Chancellorsville

1st Lt. Joseph Mills appointed 4/18/63 **W-right foot 7/3**

2nd Lt. John McDonald 27 yr old teacher enlisted Cumberland Co C New Bern NC

3rd Lt. John Wooten enlisted Cumberland Co 10/1/62

Sgt William Arnett 27 yr old enlisted Cumberland Co. 10/16/61 **W-right thigh 7/3 C 7/5**

Sgt Lewis Dixon 27 yr old mechanic enlisted Cumberland Co. C New Bern NC **C 7/3**

Corp. Benjamin Howell 30 yr old enlisted Hanover Co. 3/1/62 (AWOL 1/64 returned 11/64)

Corp. Emanuel Thompson 28 yr old enlisted Cumberland Co 3/1/62 W New Bern, NC

Private James Barnes 20 yr old enlisted Cumberland Co. 10/30/61 (later W Jones farm)

Private John Baxley 26 yr old enlisted Robeson Co. 11/2/61 **C 7/14**

Private Simeon Baxley 23 yr old enlisted Robeson Co. 11/2/61 C New Bern, NC (later C Wilderness)

Private Christian Bodenheimer 31 yr old enlisted Forsythe Co **K 7/1**

Private Evans Canady 22 yr old enlisted Cumberland Co 9/2/61 C New Bern, NC

Private Joshua Carman 32 r old enlisted Cumberland Co 11/6/61 (later AWOL 9-11/63 returned)

Private James Carter 24 yr old enlisted Cumberland Co 9/30/61

Private Edwin Cline 27 yr ld enlisted Forsythe Co 7/15/62 (later AWOL 9-11/63 returned)

Private Allen Davis 20 yr old enlisted Cumberland Co 3/1/62 W-shoulder New Bern NC **C 7/3**

Private Jonathan Deal 20 yr old enlisted Cumberland Co W-back New Bern NC

Private Francis Faircloth 26 yr old enlisted Cumberland Co. 9/3/61

Private Aaron Hair 22 yr old enlisted Cumberland Co 10/25/61 WC New Bern, NC (later W Jericho Mills)

Private Daniel Hair 24 yr old cooper enlisted in Cumberland Co.10/28/61 (later C Wilderness)

Private Nathan Hair 19 yr old enlisted Cumberland Co. 10/12/61 W-shoulder New Bern NC (later AWOL 8-11/63)

Private Edward Henning 31 yr old enlisted Forsythe Co. 7/15 (later AWOL 11/63 returned)

Private James Hudler 31 yr old enlisted Forsythe Co. **C 7/3**

Private George Hughes 28 yr old enlisted Cumberland Co. (later AWOL 8/63 returned 11/63 C Spotsylvania)

Private John Jones 38 yr old enlisted Forsythe Co. 7/1/562 **W 7/3** (later Corp)

Private John Long 2 yr old enlisted Forsythe Co. 7/15/62 (later C Wilderness)

Private John Martin 37 yr old enlisted Cumberland Co. C Cedar Mtn (later C Wilderness)

Private William Mitchell 24 yr old laborer enlisted Cumberland Co 11/4/61 C Hanover CH (later WC Spotsylvania)
Private James Powers 35 yr old enlisted Cumberland Co. 8/24/61 (later W-left hand Wilderness)
Private James Russell 19 yr old enlisted Cumberland Co. 3/1/62
Private Amos Singletary 21 yr old enlisted Bladen Co 10/28/62 (later C Spotsylvania)
Private Harrison Spaugh 30 yr old enlisted Forsythe Co 7/15/62 (Later AWOL 11/63-2/64)
Private William Strickland 18 yr old enlisted Cumberland Co 7/15/62 W-left foot Fredericksburg
Private Samuel Vest 35 yr old enlisted Forsythe Co 7/15/62 (later C Wilderness)

Musician William Williford 16 yr old enlisted Cumberland Co 2/11/62
Musician Jesse Reynolds 17 yr old enlisted Cumberland Co 8/29/61
Teamster William Powers 28 yr old enlisted Cumberland Co. 3/1/62

July 1 Casualties

None

Company H "*Hyde County*"

Captain Riddick Gatling appointed 8/9/62 **W 7/3** (later W Jerusalem Plank)
1st Lt George Sanderlin promoted 2/11/63 (later Capt)
Sgt. Nathan Topping enlisted Hyde Co 10/17/62 (later K Spotsylvania)
Corp. John Jarvis enlisted Hyde Co 10/17/61 C New Bern, NC (later Sgt)
Private Alexander Bailey enlisted Hyde Co 10/17/61 C New Bern NC W Fredericksburg (later C Gravel Hill, Va)
Private Simon Bailey enlisted Hyde Co 10/17/61 **C 7/5** (later joined US Service)
Private William Balance enlisted Hyde Co 10/17/61 C New Bern, NC W-right arm 7/3 (later Corp)
Private Elias Binkley enlisted Forsythe Co 7/1/62
Private Mathias Blake 35 yr old enlisted Hyde Co 10/17/61 C New Bern, NC W Chancellorsville **W-shoulder 7/3**
Private Zachariah Boomer enlisted 5/21/62 (later W-Left hand Wilderness)
Private Pinkney Buffkin enlisted Columbus Co 7/15/62 (later AWOL 11/1/63)
Private John Daniels enlisted 5/17/62 W-arm Fredericksburg later (AWOL 7/63-1/64 later Corp)
Private Syl Davis enlisted Forsythe Co 7/15/62 (later Hospital Steward)
Private Henry Gibbs enlisted Hyde Co 6/9/62 **C 7/5**
Private Amasa Miller enlisted Hyde Co 5/1/62

Private Francis Hauser enlisted Forsythe Co 7/15/62 **W 7/3 C 7/5**
Private Benson Herrington enlisted Hyde Co 10/17/62 C New Bern, NC (later W Gravel Hill, Va)
Private Nathaniel Jarvis enlisted Hyde Co 10/17/61 (later Sgt / W-right leg Spotsylvania)
Private Wiley Kiger enlisted Forsythe Co 7/1/62 (later AWOL 8/63—returned 11/63
Private John Kreeger enlisted Forsythe Co 7/15/62 (AWOL 11/63—returned 2/64)
Private Joseph Long enlisted Columbus Co. 7/15/62 (later C Spotsylvania)
Private Thomas Miller enlisted Forsythe Co 7/15/62 **C 7/14**
Private George Moore 27 yr old enlisted Forsythe Co 7/15/62 **W-left leg 7/3**
Private James Ryans enlisted Forsythe Co 7/1/62 (later deserted 9/63-10/63 K Wilderness)
Private Luther Sanderford enlisted Hertford Co 7/15/62 C Chancellorsville **C 7/14**
Private William Shoaf enlisted Forsythe Co. 7/15/62 **W-shoulder 7/3 C 7/5**
Private William Smith enlisted Columbus Co 7/15/62 (later AWOL 10/63-1/64 C Spotsylvania)
Private Lewis Swindall enlisted Hyde Co. 4/29/62 W-thigh Frayser's farm W-Petersburg / Sgt)
Private Nathaniel Swindall enlisted Hyde Co 10/17/61 **C 7/3**
Private Moses Teague 18 yr old enlisted Forsythe Co. 7/15/62 (AWOL 7/63 to 10/63 C Wilderness)
Private George Williams enlisted Forsythe Co. 10/17/61 **C 7/3**

Musician Gideon Miller 18 yr old enlisted Forsythe Co. 7/15/62

July 1 Casualties

None

Company I *"Confederate Stars"*

2nd Lt. Lafayette Goslin 21 yr old enlisted Forsythe Co. 7/1/61 (later W Gravel Hill, Va)
3rd Lt. Isaac Farrow appointed 12/25/62 (later transferred to Co H)
1st Sgt Jesse Marshall 23 yr old mechanic enlisted Forsythe Co. 7/1/61 (later W Wilderness)
Sgt Franklin Ketner 22 yr old enlisted Forsythe Co. 3/1/62 (later W-right leg Gravel Hill, Va)
Sgt John Long 20 yr old enlisted Forsythe Co. 9/12/61 C Fredericksburg
Corp William Glasscock 20 yr old enlisted Forsythe Co 8/5/61 C New Bern NC C Fredericksburg **C 7/5**
Corp Franklin Kiger 19 yr old enlisted Forsythe Co 8/10/61 C Fredericksburg **K 7/3**
Corp William Long 20 yr old enlisted Forsythe Co 7/8/62 **C 7/3**
Private Charles Anderson 23 yr old enlisted Forsythe Co 8/10/61 **C 7/12** (Funkstown, Md)
Private John Binkley 22 yr old enlisted Forsythe Co. 3/1/62 (later C Wilderness)
Private Henry Brinkley 23 yr old enlisted Forsythe Co. 3/1/62 **C 7/5** (later joined US Army)

Private Martin Brinkley 25 yr old enlisted Forsythe Co. 3/1/62 (AWOL 7/763-3/64)
Private William Brinkley 27 yr old enlisted Forsythe Co. 3/31/62 C Fredericksburg (AWOL 7/63-11/63)
Private David Collet 27 yr old enlisted Forsythe Co. 8/23/61
Private Banson Conrad 24 yr old enlisted Forsythe Co. 3/1/62 C Fredericksburg ***C 7/12*** *Funkstown, Pa deserted 2/19/65*
Private Carlos Conrad 21 yr old enlisted Forsythe Co. 3/1/62 (AWOL 7/63-9/63) deserted 2/19/65
Private Gideon Conrad 18 yr old enlisted Forsythe Co. 2/14/63 deserted 2/19/65
Private Wiley Conrad 22 yr old enlisted Forsythe Co 3/1/62 deserted 2/19/65
Private Allen Crater 25 yr old enlisted Forsythe Co. 7/8/62 **W 7/3 C 7/5**
Private William Faircloth 18 yr old enlisted Forsythe Co. 8/9/61 C Fredericksburg (later K Wilderness)
Private Romulus Flynt 22 yr old enlited Forsythe Co. 3/11/62 (later W Wilderness)
Private Joel Fulton 25 yr old enlisted Forsythe Co. 8/5/61 C Fredericksburg **K 7/3**
Private Andrew George 35 yr old enlisted Forsythe Co. 7/8/62 (AWOL 7/63 to 9/63)
Private William Griffin 19 hyr old enlisted Forsythe Co. 8/11/61 C 7/14 (later joined US Service)
Private Lewis Howerton 19 yr old enlisted Forsythe Co. 10/10/62 C Fredericksburg
Private Francis Ketner 20 yr old enlisted Forsythe Co 7/8/62 ***W-right leg C 7/3***
Private William Ketner 25 yr old enlisted Forsythe Co. 3/1/62 W 7/3 (later W Jerusalem Plank)
Private Edwin Kiger 33 yr old enlisted Forsythe Co. 7/8/62 (later W-left thigh Wilderness)
Private Samuel Kiger 21 yr old enlisted Forsythe Co. 8/3/61 **WC 7/3** W Spotsylvania
Private William Kiger 23 yr old enlisted Forsythe Co. 7/8/62 (AWOL 11/63 to 2/64)
Private Francis Lashmit 21 yr old enlisted Forsythe Co. 8/9/61 C New Bern, NC **K 7/3**
Private Jesse Ledford 19 yr old enlisted Forsythe Co. 3/1/62
Private Lewis Leinbach 23 yr old enlisted Forsythe Co. 12/17/61 W-thigh Fredericksburg (later C Jericho Mills, Va)
Private Adolphus Long 22 yr old enlisted Forsythe Co. C Fredericksburg C 7/14
Private Franklin McRary 22 yr old enlisted 7/8/62 (later C Wilderness)
Private Thomas Newsom 22 yr old enlisted Forsythe Co. C Fredericksburg
Private John Nicholson 26 yr old physician enlisted Forsythe Co. 9/15/61 (later Asst Surgeon)
Private Edward Pfaff 21 yr old enlisted Forsythe Co. 3/1/62 C Fredericksburg (later W Cold Harbor)
Private Eugene Rank 23 yr old enlisted Forsythe Co. **K 7/3**
Private Joseph Reich enlisted Forsythe Co 7/8/62 (later Corp W North Anna Sgt)
Private Charles Rothrock 35 yr old enlisted Forsythe Co.7/8/62 **W 7/14** (Later W-right leg Cold Harbor)
Private William Seat 21 yr old enlisted Forsythe Co. 3/1/62 W 2nd Manassas (later C Jerusalem Plank)
Private Joseph Seiwers 22 yr old enlisted Forsythe Co.7/8/62 **W 7/3 C 7/5** (later joined US Service)

Private Edward Shore 28 yr old enlisted Forsythe Co. 7/8/62 C Fredericksburg **C 7/3** (later W Spotsylvania)
Private John Shouse 21 yr old enlisted Forsythe Co. 3/1/62
Private John Shultz 29 yr old enlisted Forsythe Co. 3/20/62 C Fredericksburg (later C Jericho Mills, Va)
Private Samuel Shultz 18 yr old enlisted Forsythe Co. 2/14/63 **C 7/12 (Hagerstown, Pa)**
Private Milton Stewart 22 yr old enlisted Forsythe Co.8/5/61 C New Bern, NC C 7/12 (Funkstown. Pa)
Private Thomas Stewart 20 yr old enlisted Forsythe Co.12/10/62 C 7/12 (Funkstown, Pa)
Private Robert Tate 20 yr old enlisted Forsythe Co. 8/3/61 **K 7/3**
Private Columbus Thomas 27 yr old enlisted Forsythe Co. 7/8/62 (Later Sgt)
Private Alkana Wall 23 yr old enlisted Forsythe Co. 9/1/61 (later C Bristoe Station W-Richmond)
Private Kinison Wall 32 yr old enlisted Forsythe Co. 8/8/61 (Deserted 8/63 C Wilderness joined US Service)
Private John Westmoreland 27 yr old enlisted Forsythe Co.8/15/61 C Fredericksburg (later C Wilderness)
Private John Williams 32 yr old enlisted Forsythe Co.9/15/61 C Chancellorsville **W 7/3**
Private Tyree Williams 33 yr old enlisted Forsythe Co.3/1/62 W Shepardstown **W-left ankle C 7/3**
Private James Woodlieff 28 yr old enlisted Forsythe Co. 7/8/62 **K 7/3**

Musician Edgar Leinbeck 22 yr old enlisted Forsythe Co. 3/15/62 (later Corp)
Musician William T Ketner 22 yr old enlisted Forsyteh Co. 3/7/62 transferred to band

July 1 Casualties

none

Company K "*Greene County*"

Captain Henry Granger 23 yr old enlisted Greene Co. 1/23/62 (resigned 9/2/63)
1st Sgt James Dockery 19 yr old enlisted Richmond Co. 7/1/62 **C 7/12 Hagerstown, Md** (later C Gravel Hill, Va)
Sgt James Hughes 22 yr old enlisted Greene Co. 1/23/62 C Fredericksburg C 7/12 Hagerstown, Md
Sgt Henry Taylor 31 yr old Greene Co. 1/23/62
Corp James Bartlett 41 yr old enlisted Lenoir Co. 1/21/62 **W 7/3** (later Sgt W-Jerusalem Plank)
Corp John Hemby 17 yr old enlisted Greene Co 1/23/62
Corp Daniel Henderson 24 yr old enlisted Richmond Co.

Private William Adams 51 yr old enlisted Bernie Co. 7/1/62 as substitute
Private John Bailey 28 yr old enlisted Craven Co. 2/5/62 **C 7/5**
Private Hugh Barber 17 yr old enlisted Richmond Co. 5/8/62 (W Wilderness)
Private William Beaman 21 yr old enlisted Greene Co. 1/23/62 C New Bern
Private James Bunch 18 yr old enlisted Bernie Co. 7/1/62 (died 11/26/62)
Private Richard Capehart 20 yr old enlisted Bernie Co. 7/1/62
Private Pinkney Clark 36 yr old enlisted Greene Co. 1/23/62 **C 7/12 Hagerstown, Md**
Private Alfred Covington 19 yr old enlisted Richmond Co. 7/1/62 W Chancellorsville **C 7/12 Hagerstown**
Private Elisha Covington 20 yr old enlisted 7/1/62
Private Newsom Dail 33 yr old enlisted Greene Co. C Shepherdstown **K 7/3**
Private William Davis 18 yr old Bertie Co 7/1/62 (died 9/5/63)
Private Solomon Ford 28 yr old enlisted Richmond Co. 7/1/62 (later W-left knee Wilderness)
Private James Garris 19 yr old enlisted Greene Co. **C 7/5**
Private John Gay 20 yr old enlisted Greene Co. 1/23/62 W Richmond 6/62
Private W Gay 22 yr old enlisted Greene Co. 7/1/62 (later W Spotsylvania)
Private George Hinson 25 yr old enlisted Greene Co. 1/23/62
Private Jesse Hoggard 23 yr old enlisted Bernie Co. 7/1/62 (AWOL 9/63 to 1/64)
Private Jackson Howell 27 yr old enlisted Greene Co. 1/23/62 **K 7/3**
Private Jackson Meacham 32 yr old enlisted Richmond Co. 7/1/62 (later C Wilderness)
Private John Mizell 23 yr old enlisted Bernie Co. 7/1/62 (deserted 9/1/63)
Private James Rockwell Moore 24 yr old enlisted Burke County as Private (later 3rd Lt)
Private William Mooring 31 yr old enlisted Greene Co. 1/23/62 C Chancellorsville **W-left arm 7/3 C 7/5**
Private William Nicholson 21 yr old enlisted Richmond Co. 7/1/62 (later W Wilderness)
Private William Owens 19 yr old enlisted Greene Co.1/23/62
Private George Reddick 27 yr old enlisted Greene Co. 1/23/62 C Sharpsburg
Private John Rencher 25 yr old enlisted Chatham Co. as private (later 1st Lt)
Private John Sneed 17 yr old wagoner enlisted Richmond Co 7/1/62 **C 7/13 Hagerstown, Md**
Private Charles Vaughan 25 yr old enlisted Greene Co. 1/23/62 (AWOL 9/63 deserted)
Private John Webb 31 yr old enlisted Richmond, Co (deserted 6/64)
Private Alfred White 18 yr old enlisted Bertie Co. 7/1/62

July 1 Casualties

None

EIGHTEENTH NORTH CAROLINA REGIMENT

Colonel John Barry

Captain Van Richardson Co C

Field & Staff

Colonel John Decatur Barry 24 yr old Wilmington graduate of UNC W Fraysers farm promoted from Major May 27, 1863 (later W-right hand by sharpshooter 7/2/64)

Lt. Colonel John McGill 20 yr old Sampson City student promoted 5/3/63 W Frayer's farm **W 7/3** hospitalized Charlottesville 7/12/63

*Major Thomas Wooten 23 yr old Columbus Co. promoted 5/3/63 W Chancellorsville Absent W (*later commanded sharpshooters)

Adjutant Eugene Stuart Martin 22 yr old former Sgt Co I enlisted New Hanover Co. 8/17/61

Sergeant Major Franklin Mitchell 22 yr old clerk enlisted Wilmington NC 7/1/61 as Private appointed 9/30/62 (later C Spotsylvania)

Assistant Commissary of Subsistence Robert Tait previously served as Captain Co B (later resigned 7/18/63)

Surgeon Dr. Thomas Lane appointed 3/19/63

Assistant Surgeon Simpson Russ appointed 6/3/61

Assistant Surgeon Alexander Gordon appointed 3/31/63

Chaplin William Jordan appointed formally 8/19/63

Color Sergeant John Frink appointed 7/3 (later ensign C Spotsylvania)

Quartermaster Sergeant William Murray 26 yr old enlisted New Hanover Co. appointed 3/1/63 C near Greencastle 7/5/63

Commissary Sergeant Samuel Richardson promoted 4/24/62
Ordinance Sergeant Charles Flanner 21 yr old student enlisted New Hanover Co. 8/13/61 detailed 1/1/63 promoted 4/27/64

Company A *"The German Volunteers"*

- note—originally almost all German immigrants (April 1861) Most were relieved as foreign citizens in April 1862

Captain Benjamin Rinaldi appointed 5/27/62 W 2nd Manassas promoted 1/23/63
2nd Lt David Bullard 25 yr old enlisted New Hanover Co. appointed 1/23/63 (later C Spotsylvania)
Sgt Angus Bullard 23 yr old enlisted New Hanover Co. 6/15/61 **C Williamsport, Md 7/14/63 escaped**
Sgt White Smith 25 yr old enlisted New Hanover Co. 6/15/61 **C 7/3**
Sgt Marshall Tatum 21 yr old enlisted New Hanover Co. 6/15/61
Corporal Eli Rhyne 30 yr old enlisted New Hanover Co. 8/14/61 **W/ C 7/3**
Private Hugh Bandy 34 yr old enlisted Catawba Co. 8/14/62 (later C Fussell's Mill, Va)
Private John Barclay 32 yr old enlisted Iredell Co. 8/14/62 C Falling Waters. Md 7/14
Private Cephus Beattty 31 yr old enlisted Iredell Co. 8/14/62 (later C Spotsylvania)
Private James Chason transferred 3/1/63 W Chancellorsville **W/C 7/3**
Private Owen Davis 27 yr old enlisted 7/17/61 W Hanover CH (later K Wilderness)
Private Simon Deal 28 yr old enlisted Iredel Co. 8/14/62 **W 7/3**
Private William Deal 23 yr old enlisted Catawba Co. 8/14/62 **W 7/3**
Private Joseph Dellinger 34 yr old enlisted Catawba Co. 8/14/62 **W 7/3**
Private Thomas Faircloth 25 yr old enlisted Bladen Co. 7/23/62
Private Washington Hall 25 yr old enlisted Bladen Co. W-right thigh C Hanover CH W Sharpsburg **C Falling Waters, Md 7/14**
Private Joseph Hawn 26 yr old enlisted Catawba Co. 8/14/62 (later Corporal C Wilderness)
Private John Heffner 21 yr old enlisted Catawba Co. 8/14/62
Private Frederick Herman 21 yr old enlisted Catawba Co. 8/14/62 (later C Spotsylvania)
Private Miles Herman 35 yr old enlisted Catawba Co. 8/14/62 **K 7/3**
Private Jacob Hollar 30 yr old enlisted Catawba Co. 8/14/62 (later C Spotsylvania)
Private William Howard 24 yr old enlisted Catawba Co. 8/14/62 W-left thigh 7/1 (later Sgt)
Private Salathal Huffman 29 yr old enlisted Catawba Co. 8/14/62 (later W-head Wilderness)
Private Isaac Huntley 25 yr old enlisted Catawba Co. 8/14/62
Private John Johnson enlisted Catawba Co. 9/8/62
Private John Laughlin saddler born in Liverpool, England **C 7/3** (later joined US service)
Private Heartford Love 47 yr old enlisted Catawba Co. 9/8/62 (later C Wilderness)
Private Iredel Nickens 28 yr old enlisted New Hanover Co. C Chancellorsville C Front Royal, Va. 7/25/63

Private Frank Pope 19 yr old enlisted Catawba Co. 8/14/62 C Chancellorsville (later W Petersburg 6/22/64)

Private Henry Shook 29 yr old enlisted Catawba Co. 8/14/62 (later C Spotsylvania)

Private David Starns 25 yr old enlisted Catawba Co. 8/14/62 lost eye at Fredericksburg (later C Spotsylvania)

Private Osbourne Williams 36 yr old enlisted Catawba Co. 9/8/62

July 1 Casualties

None

Company B *"Bladen Light Infantry"*

Captain Marcus Buie 25 yr old appointed 5/3/63 (later W-right foot Ream's Station)

1st LT Thomas Wiggins 23 yr old enlisted Bladen Co. 5/3/61 promoted 1st LT 5/3/63

2nd LT Camden Lewis 21 yr old enlisted Bladen Co. 5/3/61 (later W=-arm Cold Harbor / K Fussell's Mill)

Sgt William Robeson transferred 2/1/63 (later 2nd & 1st Lt)

Sgt Philip Evers 31 yr old enlisted Bladen Co. 5/3/61 (later C Wilderness)

Sgt Dennis Storm 29 yr old enlisted Bladen Co. 5/3/61 W-left thigh / **C 7/3**

Sgt Calvin Ward 23 yr old enlisted Bladen Co. 5/3/61 **W 7/3** (later detailed as recruiter)

Corp Isaac Davis 20 yr old enlisted Camp Wyatt 9/27/61 (later transferred C.S. Navy)

Corp James Gause 28 yr old carpenter enlisted Bladen Co.5/3/61 (later W-leg Riddell's Shop, Va)

Corp Troy Russ 24 yr old carpenter enlisted Bladen Co.5/3/61 **W-7/3**

Corp Travis Singletary 28 yr old carpenter enlisted Bladen Co.5/3/61 **W/C 7/3** (later W-leg Gravel Hill, Va)

Private William Barlow 33 yr old enlisted Iredell Co. 8/20/62 (later C Spotsylvania)

Private Benjamin Carter 33 yr old enlisted wake Co. 9/10/62

Private Richard Cheshire 31 yr old carpenter enlisted Bladen Co.5/3/61 **C Falling Waters, Md 7/1/4**

Private Alfred Edwards 23 yr old carpenter enlisted Bladen Co.5/3/61

Private Haynes Edwards 32 yr old carpenter enlisted Bladen Co.5/3/61 C Hanover CH **W 7/3**

Private John Fields 25 yr old enlisted wake Co. 9/10/62 (later K Jone's Farm)

Private John Goodson 28 yr old enlisted Wake Co. **W-thigh C 7/3/63 died 7/14**

Private John Graves 31 yr old carpenter enlisted Bladen Co.5/3/61 (later transferred CS Navy)

Private Council Green 23 yr old carpenter enlisted Wake Co.5/3/61 (later deserted at Spotsylvania)

Private Eli Guffie 23 yr old carpenter enlisted Wake Co.5/3/61

Private Anderson Guyton 20 yr old carpenter enlisted Bladen Co.5/3/61
Private John Hagler 27 yr old enlisted Iredell Co. (later w-lung/ C Gravel Hill, Va
Private William Hagler 29 yr old enlisted Iredell Co 8/20/62 C-Chancellorsville later C Spotsylvania
Private Joseph Hester 29 yr old enlisted Bladen Co. 5/3/61
Private Snowden Hester 28 yr old enlisted Bladen Co.5/3/62 ***C 7/14***
Private Wright Hester 20 yr old carpenter enlisted Bladen Co.5/3/61 (later W-leg North Anna, Va)
Private George King 21 yr old enlisted Camp Wyatt 9/10/62 **W/C 7/3**
Private William Lovett 28 yr old enlisted Bladen Co.5/3/61 (later C Chester Gap,Va 7/21)
Private John Nance 27 yr old enlisted Bladen Co.5/3/61 W/C Hanover CH
Private David Pait 34 yr old enlisted Bladen Co.5/3/61 **W-left thigh 7/3 C 7/5**
Private Nelson Pate 23 yr old enlisted Bladen Co.5/3/61 W Antietam
Private James Rackley 28 yr old enlisted Bladen Co.5/3/61 **W-leg-hip 7/3**
Private John Rickman 26 yr old enlisted Wake Co 9/10/62 **C Funkstown, Md 7/11**
Private Love Simmons 29 yr old enlisted Iredell Co. 8/20/62 (later C Gravel Hill, Va)
Private David Singletary 19 yr old enlisted Bladen Co.5/3/61 (later C Petersburg)
Private Josuha Singletary 21 yr old enlisted Bladen Co.5/3/61
Private Snowden Singletary 24 yr old enlisted Bladen Co.5/3/61 (later W Spotsylvania) (later Corp)
Private William Starling 35 yr old enlisted Bladen Co.5/3/**61** **W right arm 7/3**
Private Bryant Thompson 29 yr old enlisted Fort Caswell 6/21/61

July 1 Casualties

None

Company C *"Columbus Guards No 3"*

Captain Van Richardson appointed 10/27/62 (later W Wilderness)
1st Lt Owen Smith 18 yr old enlisted Columbus Co. 4/24/61 (later W-right leg Petersburg)
2nd Lt Edward Fowler 23 yr old enlisted Columbus Co. 4/24/61 W-left shoulder Glendale (later W-thigh Petersburg)
Sgt Lamar Bryan 21 yr old enlisted Columbus Co 7/20/61 W Fredericksburg
Sgt Nathaniel Marlow 29 yr old painter enlisted 4/24/61 W Cedar Run **W-right arm 7/3/63**
Corp Jonathan Faulk 35 yr old enlisted Columbus Co. 4/24/61 (later C Gravel Hill, Va)
Private James Austin 20 yr old enlisted Camp Hill 9/5/62 (later W Cold Harbor)
Private James Baird 32 yr old enlisted Camp Hill 8/20/62 (later C Spotsylvania)
Private William Bell 22 enlisted Columbus Co. 4/24/61 **W/C 7/3**
Private William Benfield 35 yr old enlisted Camp Hill 8/20/62 (later C Spotsylvania)

Private Noah Bentley shoemaker who enlisted at Camp Hill 8/20/62 (later C Spotsylvania)

Private William Best 32 yr old enlisted Columbus Co. 4/24/61 C Hanover CH (later—eye shot out at Spotsylvania)

Private Alexander Bostin 35 yr old enlisted Camp Hill 9/6/62 (later W Cold Harbor / C Gravel Hill, Va)

Private Joshua Boswell 22 yr old enlisted gum swamp 7/4/61 **C 7/3/63**

Private Evander Canady 19 yr old enlisted Columbus Co. 4/24/61 (Later C Spotsylvania)

Private George Canady 26 yr old enlisted Columbus Co. 4/24/61

Private Silas Clover 28 yr old enlisted Camp Hill 8/20/62 **K 7/3**

Private Abraham Copening 20 yr old enlisted Camp Hill 8/27/62 (later C Spotsylvania)

Private James Craig 27 yr old enlisted Camp Hill 8/20/62 (later W-right arm Petersburg)

Private Daniel Crump 33 yr old enlisted Camp Hill 8/20/62 (later C Spotsylvania)

Private Daniel Green 28 yr old enlisted Columbus Co. 8/12/61 C Hanover CH / W-hip Fredericksburg (later deserted 8/20/63)

Private John Hartman 28 yr old enlisted Camp Hill 9/6/62 **C Williamsport, Md 7/7** (left behind)

Private George Howell 35 yr old enlisteed Camp Hill 9/5/62 (later C Spotsylvania)

Private Elijah Hudson 31 yr old enlisted Camp Hill 9/5/62 **C Hagerstown 7/12**

Private William Jackson 23 yr old enlisted Camp Hill; 9/6/62 (later deserted 8/1/63)

Private David Ketchey 28 yr old enlisted Camp Hill 9/6/62 (later C Spotsylvania)

Private DaVault Klutts 29 yr old enlisted Camp Hill 9/6/62

Private Adam Klutz 31 yr old enlisted Camp Hill 9/6/62 **C 7/12 Hagerstown, MD**

Private Crofford Landcaster 29 yr old teamster enlisted Columbus Co. 7/29/61 (later C Spotsylvania)

Private Elkana Lanier 30 yr old enlisted Camp Hill 9/6/62 (later deserted 8/26/63—shot 9/26/63

Private James Lee 24 yr old enlisted Camp Hill 9/5/62 C 7/3/63

Private William Lee 28 yr old enlisted Camp Hill 9/5/62 C Winchester 1862 / later deserted 8/26/63 . . . shot 9/26/63

Private John Long 22 yr old enlisted Columbus Co. 4/21/61 (later C Spotsylvania)

Private T.J. Martin 25 yr old enlisted Camp Hill 8/20/62 W Fredericksburg **K 7/3**

Private John Menius 29 yr old enlisted Camp Hill 9/6/62 (later C Spotsylvania)

Private David Mull 27 yr old enlisted Camp Hill 9/6/62 **W 7/3** deserted-returned

Private John Poovey 31 yr old enlisted Camp Hill 9/6/62 W-hand Fredericksburg (later C Spotsylvania)

Private George Sherrill 20 yr old enlisted Camp Hill 9/6/62 (later Musician)

Private John Sides 29 yr old enlisted Camp Hill 9/6/62 (later C Spotsylvania)

Private Owen Sowers 27 yr old enlisted Camp Hill 9/6/62 (later C Spotsylvania)

Private Asa Sowles 26 yr old enlisted Columbus Co. 4/24/61 (later C Spotsylvania)

Private Joseph Stevens 34 yr old enlisted Camp Stevesn SC 2/5/62 (later C Spotsylvania)

Private Josiah Thomas 31 yr old enlisted Columbus Co. 8/9/61 (later C Spotsylvania)

Private Edward Vause 24 yr old enlisted Columbus Co. 6/10/61 C Hanover CH W-left hand Fredericksburg **C 7/12** (later C Spotsylvania)
Private Martin Williams 20 yr old enlisted Columbus Co. W Cedar Mtn. (later Corp C Spotsylvania)
Private Doctor Willliamson 22 yr old enlisted Columbus Co. 4/24/61 W Hanover CH
Private Joseph Williamson 24 yr old enlisted Columbus Co. 4/24/61 (later C Spotsylvania)

July 1 Casualties

None

Company D *"The Robeson Rifle Guard"*

Captain Alexander Moore 21 yr old enlisted Robeson Co. 5/21/61 promoted 12/13/62
2nd Lt. Alfred Rowland 19 yr old enlisted Robeson Co. 5/1/61 (later C Spotsylvania)
3rd Lt. Aaron Inman 23 yr old enlisted Robeson Co. 5/18/61 **C 7/3**
1st Sgt Augustus Floyd 22 yr old enlisted Robeson Co. 7/21/61 **W 7/3**
Sgt. Ferdinand Odum 24 yr old enlisted Robeson Co 5/18/61 W Cedar Mtn. C Chancellorsville (later W-foot C Spotsylvania)
Sgt. Bright Watson 26 yr old enlisted Robeson Co. 7/15/61 W-arm 2nd Manassas **C 7/3**
Corporal James Hartman 20 yr old drummer enlisted Rutherford Co. 5/18/61 **WC 7/3**
Corp. Alexander McLellan 22 yr old enlisted Robeson Co. 5/18/61 (later reduced to Private C Spotsylvania)
Private William Allen 20 yr old enlisted Robeson Co. 6/27/61
Private William Andrews 22 yr old enlisted Robeson Co. 5/18/61 W Fredericksburg (later Corp C Spotsylvania)
Private Clark Barnes 28 yr old enlisted Robeson Co. 6/27/61 (later C Spotsylvania)
Private Robert Barnett 28 yr old enlisted Wilkes Co. 8/22/62 W Fredericksburg (died 8/23/63)
Private John Biggs 23 yr old enlisted Robeson Co. 7/24/61 W-elbow Malvern Hill (later W-bayonet-ankle Spotsylvania)
Private Francis Bryant 23 yr old enlisted Robeson Co. 8/5/61 (later C Spotsylvania)
Private Alfred Bullard 30 yr old enlisted Robeson Co. 5/18/61 (later W-shoulder, right leg Spotsylvania)
Private Augustus Clewis 27 yr old enlisted Robeson Co. 7/27/61 (later C Spotsylvania)
Private Zachariah Clewis 23 yr old enlisted Robeson Co. 5/18/61 W Hanover CH
Private Charles Davis 25 yr old enlisted Wilkes Co 8/22/62 (later C Wilderness)
Private George Dawkins 24 yr old enlisted Robeson Co. 5/18/61 **W 7/3**
Private Hinnant Edwards 23 yr old enlisted Robeson Co. 5/18/61 C Hanover CH **K 7/3**
Private Angus Harden 32 yr old enlisted Robeson Co. 7/24/61 (later C Spotsylvania)

Private Reuben Harmond 32 yr old enlisted Alexander Co. 9/5/62 WC Chancellorsville **W-side C 7/3**

Private Neill Hines 21 yr old enlisted Wilkes Co. 8/22/62 (later C Spotsylvania)

Private Alfred Ivey 25 yr old wagoner enlisted Robeson Co. 5/18/61 (later C Spotsylvania)

Private Jesse Joines 26 yr old enlisted Wilkes Co. 8/22/62 (later C Spotsylvania)

Private Richard Kellihan 22 yr old enlisted Robeson Co. 5/18/61 **C 7/14**

Private Columbus Kelly 26 yr old enlisted Wilkes Co. 9/5/62 deserted 7/5

Private Henry Lovett 25 yr old enlisted Robeson Co. 7/3/61 (later C Wilderness)

Private Forney Prevatt 22 yr old enlisted Robeson Co. 5/18/61 W Hanover CH (later C Wilderness)

Private Alfred Proffitt 22 yr old enlisted Wilkes Co 8/22/62 (later W Wilderness)

Private Andrew Profitt 29 yr old enlisted Wilkes Co 8/22/62 C Chancellorsville (later C Spotsylvania)

Private Ralph Regan 22 yr old enlisted Robeson Co. 5/18/61 W Hanover CH K 7/6 Hagerstown, Md

Private Stephen Thompson transferred from 12th NC 2/6/62 (reduced from Sgt)

Private McQueen Townsend 23 yr old enlisted Camp Watt 8/5/61 (later W Cold Harbor)

Private William Townsend 22 yr old enlisted Camp Wyatt 8/9/61

Private W.L. Tritt 31 yr old enlisted Alexander Co. 9/5/62 C Chancellorsville (later sick 8/63)

Private Joseph Waters 22 yr old enlisted Robeson Co. 5/18/61 **C 7/3**

Private Joseph Wright 26 yr old enlisted Wilkes Co. 9/5/62 **C 7/14** (later joined US Service)

July 1 Casualties

None

Company E *"The Moore's Creek Rifle Guards"*

Captain John Moore 33 yr old enlisted New Hanover Co 5/17/61 promoted 1/13/63 **C 7/14**

1st Lt. George Washington Corbett 26 yr old enlisted New Hanover Co 5/17/61 W Malvern Hill (later C Spotsylvania)

2nd Lt. Pearsall Colvin 27 yr old enlisted New Hanover Co 5/17/61 **W-left arm 7/3**

3rd Lt. Lewis Alderman 20 yr old enlisted New Hanover Co 5/17/61 appointed 1/13/63 (later K Petersburg)

Sgt. James Moore 27 yr old enlisted New Hanover Co 5/17/61 **WC 7/3**

Sgt. James Springfield 26 yr old enlisted New Hanover Co 5/17/61 C Hanover CH (later 2nd Lt)

Sgt. George Woodcock 26 yr old enlisted New Hanover Co 5/17/61 W-leg Cedar Mtn.) W Fredericksburg **W-shoulder C 7/3**

Corp. David Corbett 21 yr old enlisted New Hanover Co 5/17/61 W Hanover CH W-thigh 7/3

Corp. Gaston Costin 23 yr old enlisted New Hanover Co 5/17/61 W 7/3 (later W Wilderness—Sgt)

Private Columbus Barnhill 21 yr old enlisted New Hanover Co 5/17/61 W 2nd Manassas

Private William Barnhill 21 yr old enlisted New Hanover Co 5/17/61 (later C Spotsylvania)

Private Council Blake 21 yr old enlisted New Hanover Co 5/17/61 W 7/1 (died 7/27/63)

Private Edwin Blake 23 yr old teacher enlisted New Hanover Co 5/17/61

Private George Bonham 27 yr old enlisted New Hanover Co 5/17/61 (later transferred to cavalry)

Private Lafayette Briscoe 36 yr old enlisted Camp Hill 7/18/62 (later C Spotsylvania)

Private Richard Brown 20 yr old enlisted New Hanover Co 5/17/61 W Gaines Mill

Private Thomas Colvin 34 yr old clerk enlisted New Hanover Co 5/17/61 (later musician)

Private William Cook 24 yr old mechanic enlisted New Hanover Co 5/17/61 W Fredericksburg (later C Spotsylvania)

Private Henry Corbett 18 yr old enlisted New Hanover Co. 8/26/62

Private Stephen Costin 26 yr old enlisted New Hanover Co 5/17/61

Private William Covington 25 yr old enlisted camp Hill 7/18/62 **C 7/14** (later C Jerusalem Plank Rd)

Private William Davidson 23 yr old enlisted camp Hill 7/18/62 (later W Spotsylvania)

Private Zachariah Durham 17 yr old enlisted camp Hill 7/18/62 **C 7/12 Hagerstown**

Private Gideon Garris 20 yr old enlisted New Hanover Co 5/17/61 C Hanover CH **C 7/3**

Private Robert Henry 35 yr old enlisted New Hanover Co 5/17/61 as Sgt—reduced (later W-groin Wilderness—Corp)

Private George Keith 29 yr old mechanic enlisted New Hanover Co 5/17/61

Private Nathan Lewis 20 yr old enlisted New Hanover Co 5/17/61 (later C Spotsylvania)

Private Robert Lewis 21 yr old enlisted Camp Wyatt 8/15/61 **W 7/3** (later C Gravel Hill—Sgt)

Private Christopher McAuslan 20 yr old student enlisted New Hanover Co 5/17/61 (later W-leg Turkey Hill,Va)

Private Lewis Malpass 21 yr old enlisted New Hanover Co 5/17/61 C Hanover CH W Fredericksburg W-left arm & right hand **C 7/3**

Private David Mashburn 23 yr old student enlisted New Hanover Co 5/17/61 **C 7/3**

Private Nathaniel Miller 34 yr old enlisted New Hanover Co 7/18/61 (later C Spotsylvania)

Private Henry Moore 20 yr old enlisted 11/1/61 W-right leg Hanover CH

Private William Moore 22 yr old student enlisted New Hanover Co 5/17/61 W Ox Hill, Va (later W Fussell's Mill)

Private Haywood Peterson 20 yr old enlisted New Hanover Co 5/17/61 W Hanover CH (later Corp C Spotsylvania)

Private Jacob Pigford 19 yr old enlisted New Hanover Co 5/17/61 W Hanover Ch (later C Spotsylvania)

Private William Pigford 23 yr old enlisted New Hanover Co 5/17/61 (later W-left leg C Spotsylvania)

Private Charles Pridgen 30 yr old blacksmith enlisted Camp Wyatt 9/10/61 ***W 7/3*** *(later C Spotsylvania)*

Private Hinton Pridgen 23 yr old enlisted New Hanover Co 5/17/61 ***W-shoulder & leg C 7/3***

Private Richard Reeves 23 yr old turpentine maker enlisted New Hanover Co 5/17/61 W-leg Glendale **C 7/3**

Private Frederick Register 20 yr old enlisted New Hanover Co 6/13/61 W Glendale

Private Malery Smith 23 yr old enlisted Camp Hill 7/18/62 C 7/14 (later C Spotsylvania)

Private Edward Stanton 26 yr old born in Limerick Ireland enlisted New Hanover Co 5/17/61 **C 7/3**

Private Morris Taylor 20 enlisted new Hanover Co 2/6/62 **C 7/3**

Private Hampton Weaver 30 yr old enlisted Camp Hill 7/18/62 (later died of wounds 9/3/64)

Private John Weaver 25 yr old enlisted Camp Hill (later W-left arm Wilderness W-left hip Fussell's Mill)

Private William Weaver 33 yr old enlisted Camp Hill 7/18/62

Private John Wells 32 yr old enlisted camp Hill 7/18/62 **K 7/3**

Private James Wheeler 24 yr old enlisted New Hanover Co 5/17/61 W 2d Manassas (later W Fussell's Mill—died 8/29)

Private John Woodcock 23 yr old enlisted 5/17/61C Chancellorsville **W 7/3 C 7/5**

Drum Major Henry Woodcock 21 yr old enlisted New Hanover Co 5/17/61 promoted Drum Major 5/1/63

July 1 Casualties

None

Company F *"The Scotch Boys"*

Captain Alfred Moffit 24 yr old merchant enlisted Randolph Co. 6/1/61 promoted 11/28/62 **W-right thigh C 7/3**

1st Lt. Archibald McGregor 24 yr old enlisted Richmond Co. 6/1/61 **K 7/3**

2nd Lt. John Stewart 23 yr old enlisted Richmond Co 6/1/61 W Cedar Mtn **WC 7/3** (died 7/19/63)

3rd Lt. Franklin McIntosh 23 yr old enlisted Richmond Co. 6/1/61 W Chancellorsville (later C Spotsylvania)

Sgt. James Buchanan 26 yr old enlisted Richmond Co 6/1/61 (later 2nd Lt W Turkey Hill, Va)
Sgt. Neil Smith 25 yr old student enlisted Richmond Co 6/1/61 (later C Spotsylvania)
Corp. Edward McPherson 20 yr old enlisted Richmond Co 6/1/61 (later C Spotsylvania)
Corp. Daniel McKinnon 23 yr old enlisted Richmond Co 6/1/61 C Hanover CH C Chancellorsville (later Sgt W Gravel Hill, Va.)
Corp. Christopher Gibson 31 yr old enlisted Richmond Co 6/1/61 (later Sgt & 2nd Lt)
Private Neill Beasley 22 yr old enlisted Wake Co. 6/1/61 (later C Spotsylvania)
Private Neill Brown 22 yr old enlisted Richmond Co 6/1/61 W Hanover CH (later C Spotsylvania)
Private William Buchanan 21 yr old enlisted Richmond Co 6/1/61 W Hanover CH (later Sgt C Spotsylvania)
Private William Bullard 21 yr old enlisted Richmond Co 6/1/61 (later W Spotsylvania)
Private John Burge enlisted 8/20/62 (later C Spotsylvania)
Private James Calder 23 yr old enlisted Richmond Co 6/1/61 W Ox Hill, Va
Private Hugh Calhoun 23 yr old student enlisted Richmond Co 6/1/61 C Hanover CH (later C Spotsylvania)
Private Archibald Cameron 27 yr old enlisted Richmond Co 6/1/61 **C 7/3**
Private William Connelly 19 yr old enlisted Wayne Co. (later C Wilderness)
Private William Harris 27 yr old enlisted Iredell Co 8/20/62 W-left heel Fredericksburg (later W Spotsylvania)
Private Alexander Huckabee 28 yr old enlisted Richmond Co 6/1/61 W Hanover CH (later W-left hand Wilderness)
Private John Hughes 23 yr old enlisted Richmond Co 6/1/61 C Hanover CH
Private Albert Lovelace enlisted Iredell Co 8/20/62 **C 7/12 Hagerstown, Md** (later joined US Service)
Private John Lytch 24 yr old enlisted Richmond Co 6/1/61 (later died of disease 9/13/64)
Private Milton McEachin 19 yr old student enlisted Richmond Co 6/1/61 (later C Spotsylvania)
Private Martin McGregor enlisted Gordonsville, Va. 5/12/62 (later C Spotsylvania)
Private Archibald McKay 25 yr old mechanic enlisted Richmond Co 6/1/61 W Glendale (later C Spotsylvania)
Private John McKay enlisted Gordonsville, Va. 5/12/62 (later W Spotsylvania)
Private Malcolm McKay 25 yr old enlisted Richmond Co 8/1/61 (later C Spotsylvania)
Private Daniel McLean 21 yr old enlisted Richmond Co 6/1/61 (later C Spotsylvania)
Private Neil McNeill 20 yr old student enlisted Richmond Co 6/1/61 W-calf Fredericksburg **C 7/12 Hagerstown**
Private Neil McQueen 23 yr old teacher enlisted Richmond Co 6/1/61 **C 7/3**
Private John Martin 22 yr old enlisted Richmond Co 5/11/61 C Hanover CH W Fredericksburg (later C Spotsylvania)
Private L. Middleton enlistment at Richmond Co. (later C Spotsylvania)
Private William Murphy 23 yr old enlisted Richmond Co 6/1/61 C Hanover CH W-left hand Wilderness)

Private Elijah Norton enlisted Camp Wyatt 7/23/61 C Hanover Co K-Wilderness
Private John Norton 22 yr old enlisted Richmond Co 7/23/61 **W-arm 7/3**
Private Jesse Parsons enlisted Wake Co. 9/10/62 (later W-Wilderness)
Private Stephen Pate 24 yr old enlisted Richmond Co 6/1/61 (later C Spotsylvania)
Private John Patterson 21 yr old enlisted Richmond Co 6/1/61 (later Corp)
Private Amos Roper 24 yr old student enlisted Richmond Co 6/1/61 W Hanover CH (later Corp C Wilderness)
Private John Seals 20 yr old enlisted Richmond Co 6/1/61
Private James Smith 31 yr old enlisted Camp Stephens SC 11/17/62 (later C Spotsylvania)
Private Achilles Webb enlisted Iredell Co. 8/20/62 (later W-left hand Wilderness)
Private Mikaja Wilkerson 18 yr old enlisted as substitute 8/20/62 (later W Jone's farm)

July 1 Casualties

Private Henry Thrower 29 yr old enlisted Richmond Co 6/1/61 **W 7/1 C 7/5**
Private James Waters 19 yr old enlisted Iredell Co. 8/20/62 **W-arm 7/1** (later C Spotsylvania)

Company G

Captain John Poisson 31 yr old clerk enlisted New Hanover Co 4/15/61 promoted 11/12/62 W Fredericksburg
1st Lt. William Dixon 23 yr old enlisted New Hanover Co 7/16/61 **K 7/3**
2nd Lt. Thomas Shepard 21 yr old enlisted New Hanover Co 7/16/61 W-thigh Chancellorsville (dismissed 9/15/64)
Sgt. Shepard Averitt transferred 4/1/63 **W 7/3** C 7/5 (later C Spotsylvania)
Sgt. John Morrison 21 yr old teacher enlisted "Bolle's battery" 5/17/61 W Hanover CH W-Sharpsburg (later K Wilderness)
Sgt. James Poisson 20 yr old student enlisted New Hanover Co 8/15/61 (later discharged insane)
Corp. Richard Comron 30 yr old clerk enlisted New Hanover Co. (later CS Navy)
Corp. William Hall 24 yr old enlisted Brunswick Co 5/20/61 (later reduced to private)
Corp. Romanzo Reed 29 yr old printer enlisted New Hanover Co. 7/29/61 (later K Wilderness)
Private Jesse Adams enlisted in Iredell Co 9/6/62
Private Alexander Anderson 26 yr old enlisted New Hanover Co 5/24/61
Private Sherod Banther enlisted Iredell Co 8/14/62 (later K Spotsylvania)
Private Julius Bennett 20 yr old enlisted Camp Hyatt 8/26/61 (later died 8/5/64 disease)
Private William Blum enlisted as substitute Camp Gregg 1/1/63 (later K Jerusalem Plank Rd)
Private William Camp enlisted Iredell Co 8/14/62 **K 7/3**
Private William Canter enlisted Iredell Co 9/8/62 (later died typhoid 8/63)

Private Absalom Carlton enlisted Iredell Co 9/8/62 **C 7/3**
Private George Carlton enlisted Iredell Co 9/8/62 **missing 7/14** returned 9/63 (later C Spotsylvania)
Private James Dancey enlisted Iredell Co 9/8/62 (later Corp & Sgt)
Private John Dancey enlisted Ireell Co 9/8/62 (later C Spotsylvania)
Private W. Dancey enlisted Iredell Co 9/8/62 **C 7/14**
Private Samuel Dyer 21 yr old English born sailor enlisted New Hanover Co 10/31/61 C Hanover CH
Private William Dyer enlisted Iredell Co 8/14/62 **K 7/3**
Private Isaac Early enlisted Iredell Co 8/14/62 (AWOL 8/63)
Private William Flowers enlisted Iredell Co 8/14/62 **C 7/14**
Private Alfred Hamrick enlisted Iredell Co 8/14/62 W-right side Fredericksburg (later C Spotsylvania)
Private J.H. Hawkins enlisted Iredell Co 8/14/62 (AWOL 8/63)
Private William Hinchey enlisted Iredell Co 9/8/62 (later deserted 7/64)
Private J. Humphries enlisted Iredell Co 8/14/62 (later died 10/64 disease)
Private Thomas Humphries enlisted Iredell Co 8/14/62 (later died 10/64 disease)
Private John King 26 yr old enlisted New Hanover Co 7/29/61 (later Corp / chaplain 14th Tn)
Private Perry McGraw enlisted Iredell Co 8/14/62 (later transferred engineering troops)
Private David Matheny enlisted Iredell Co 8/14/62 (later W Wilderness)
Private George Matheny enlisted Iredell Co 8/14/62 (later Corp C Spotsylvania)
Private L.W. Russell enlisted Iredell Co 8/14/62 W Fredericksburg **W-ribs & right breast 7/3** (later C Spotsylvania)
Private Jackson Seavert enlisted Iredell Co 8/14/62
Private William Spears enlisted Iredell Co 8/14/62 (later C Gravel Hill, Va
Private Dugald Turner 22 yr old cooper enlisted New Hanover Co 8/15/61
Private John Whitted transferred 4/26/62 C Hanover CH W-2nd Manassas W-Fredericksburg (later 2nd Lt)

Musician Joseph Leslie 21 yr old shoemaker enlisted New Hanover Co 8/3/61 drummer from 6/1/62

July 1 Casualties

None

Company H *"Columbus Vigilants"*

Captain Francis Wooten transferred 4/24/62 (later C Spotsylvania)
1st Lt. Archibald McCollum 26 yr old carpenter enlisted Columbus Co. 4/23/61 (later W-right shoulder Spotsylvania)

3rd Lt. John Elkins 24 yr old merchant enlisted Columbus Co 6/15/61 (later C Spotsylvania (later 2nd Lt.)

Color Sgt. John Frink 20 yr old enlisted Columbus Co 4/23/61 C Chancellorsville (later C Spotsylvania)

Sgt. Henry Hall 20 yr old enlisted New Hanover Co 6/15/61 W Fredericksburg C Chancellorsville **W-leg 7/3 C** (amp) died 7/22/63

Sgt John McLeod 28 yr old enlisted New Hanover Co 4/23/61 (later 1st Sgt)

Corp. Dillion Baldwin 23 yr old enlisted Columbus Co 4/21/61

Corp. John Best 24 yr old enlisted Columbus Co 4/23/61 (later W-right thigh Wilderness—Sgt)

Corp. Alexander Lewis 21 yr old enlisted Camp Stephens, SC 1/1/62 C Chancellorsville (later Sgt W-right thigh Wilderness 2nd Lt)

Private Isham Baldwin 26 yr old enlisted Columbus Co 4/23/61 (later Sgt)

Private John Baldwin 26 yr old enlisted Columbus Co 4/23/61 W Fredericksburg **C 7/3**

Private Henry Barefoot 20 yr old enlisted Columbus Co 4/23/61 W-right shoulder Hanover CH **W-left leg C 7/3**

Private Alexander Brown 24 yr old enlisted Camp Stephens, SC 1/1/62 (later C Spotsylvania)

Private William Bullard 24 yr old enlisted New Hanover Co. 6/15/61 **C 7/3**

Private James Bullis enlisted Iredell Co 9/7/62 (later C Spotsylvania)

Private Wesley Bumgarner enlisted 9/7/62 (later C Spotsylvania)

Private John Chancey 28 yr old enlisted Columbus Co 4/23/61

Private Wiley Cornish 26 yr old carpenter enlisted Columbus Co 4/23/61 (later Hospital Steward)

Private Neill Downie 21 yr old distiller enlisted 4/23/61 (deserted 3/10/65)

Private Bryant Fisher 30 yr old enlisted Columbus Co 4/23/61 (later C Spotsylvania)

Private Joseph Fisher 29 yr old enlisted Columbus Co 4/23/61 C Hanover CH W Fredericksburg (later W-left hand Spotsylvania)

Private John Frink 20 yr old enlisted Columbus Co 6/15/61 (later transferred to Cavalry)

Private James Green enlisted 7/18/62 **W-left wrist, left arm & leg C 7/3**

Private Alfred Hall enlisted 7/18/62 **W-left shoulder 7/14**

Private William Harper 22 yr old enlisted Columbus Co 4/23/61 deserted 8/15/63—returned

Private Thomas Harris enlisted 7/18/62 **W-right shoulder C 7/3** died 8/16/63

Private James Hinson 23 yr old enlisted Columbus Co 4/23/61 (later Corp)

*Private Joshua Hinson 24 yr old enlisted Columbus Co 4/23/61 W-head 2nd Manassas W-thigh Fredericksburg **C 7/3***

Private John Jackson 30 yr old cooper enlisted Columbus Co 4/23/61 **W-left thigh 7/3 C 7/4**

Private William Joyner 31 yr old carpenter enlisted Columbus Co 4/23/61 W Fredericksburg (later W-Jerusalem plank—died)

Private Henry Long 25 yr old enlisted Columbus Co 4/23/61 **C 7/3** (later Corp)

Private Major McKeel 28 yr old mechanic enlisted Columbus Co 4/23/61 C Hanover CH **C 7/14** (later W—Ream's Station)
Private David Marshall enlisted 7/18/62 (AWOL 8/63)
Private James Mitchell enlisted 7/18/62 **K 7/3**
Private Ruffin Price 31 yr old enlisted Columbus Co 4/23/61 W Antietam
Private John Sutton 23 yr old enlisted camp Wyatt 8/31/61 (later W North Anna)
Private John Tedder 28 yr old enlisted New Hanover Co 6/15/61 C Hanover CH **C 7/3**
Private John Thompson enlisted 9/7/62 (later C Spotsylvania)
Private Kelly Wadkins 23 yr old enlisted Columbus Co 4/23/61 **W 7/3 C 7/14**
Private Richard Wootel 23 yr old enlisted Columbus Co 4/23/61 **K 7/3**

July 1 Casualties

None

Company I "*Wilmington Rifle Guards*"

Captain Thomas Lewis transferred 6/30/62 W-hip 2nd Manassas W Chancellorsville (later C Spotsylvania)
1st Sgt Benjamin White 22 yr old upholsterer enlisted New Hanover 7/24/61 (later 2nd Lt)
Sgt. Rufus Devane 21 yr old enlisted New Hanover Co. 7/3/61 (later 1st Sgt W-Spotsylvania)
Sgt. Shadrick Wells 24 yr old enlisted New Hanover Co. 7/1/61
Corp. James Brown 20 yr old mechanic enlisted New Hanover Co. (later Sgt W Jone's Farm)
Corp. Isiah **Carroll** 24 yr old enlisted New Hanover Co. (later Sgt W-thigh Spotsylvania)
Corp. Abraham Cook 24 yr old enlisted New Hanover Co. 7/6/61 (later Sgt)
Corp. Josiah Heath 21 yr old enlisted New Hanover Co. 7/6/61 W Glendale (later C Spotsylvania)
Corp. William Rogers 20 yr old enlisted New Hanover Co. 7/30/61 (later reduced to private)
Private John Arrowood 32 yr old enlisted Wake Co. 8/17/62 W Fredericksburg (later K Wilderness)
Private Samuel Ashe 22 yr old student enlisted Pender Co. 1/8/62 (later transferred to local defense)
Private J.E. Beggarly 26 yr old enlisted Wake Co. 9/10/62 **C 7/3**
Private Shadrach Bell 27 yr old enlisted Wake Co. 9/10/62 W-right lung Fredericksburg
Private Harmon Bland 23 yr old enlisted New Hanover Co. 7/1/61 **Deserted 7/2**—returned (later C Spotsylvania)
Private John Bland enlisted Fort Fisher 10/9/61 (later C Spotsylvania)

Private John Blanton 32 yr old enlisted New Hanover Co. **K 7/3**

Private Robert Burgess 28 yr old enlisted Wake Co. 9/10/62 W-hand & shoulder Fredericksburg

Private Thomas Casey enlisted Wake Co. 9/10/62 W-hand Fredericksburg **C 7/3**

Private John Cave 26 yr old enlisted Wake Co. 8/17/62 (later W-left leg Wilderness)

Private Benjamin Clark 27 yr old student enlisted Fort Caswell 5/1/61 W-right shoulder Cedar Mtn.

Private Daniel Fryar 30 yr old enlisted New Hanover Co. 7/1/61 **WC 7/3**

Private James Fryar 24 yr old enlisted New Hanover Co. 7/1/61

Private D.H. Gillespie 21 yr old enlisted New Hanover Co. 8/17/62 W Sharpsburg (died at home 12/21/63)

Private Henry Hall 24 yr old enlisted New Hanover Co. 7/1/61

Private Owen Hollingsworth 30 yr old enlisted New Hanover Co. (later CS Navy 1864)

Private William Hollingsworth 31 yr old enlisted New Hanover Co. 7/1/61 (later K Gravel Hill, Va.)

Private Hosea Horne 27 yr old enlisted Wake Co. 8/17/62 (later C Wilderness)

Private Davis Latta 23 yr old student enlisted Fort Caswell 7/3/61 W Fredericksburg

Private John Martin 20 yr old enlisted Wake Co. 8/17/62 (later deserted—return C Jericho Mills, Va)

Private J Massey enlisted Wake Co. 8/17/62 (died in camp 3/64)

Private James Melton 19 yr old enlisted Wake Co. 8/17/62 (later C Spotsylvania)

Private Henry Payne 27 yr old enlisted Wake Co. 8/17/62

Private James Pigford 24 yr old enlisted New Hanover Co. 7/1/61 W Glendale

Private Jesse Quinn 32 yr old enlisted New Hanover Co. 8/1/61 W Glendale **C 7/14**

Private Daniel Riggs 35 yr old enlisted Wake Co. 8/17/62 **C 7/3**

Private David Russell 19 yr old enlisted camp Stephens, SC 2/14/62

Private Miller Snow 26 yr old enlisted wake Co 8/17/62 **W-left arm, shoulder and thigh C 7/3**

Private Umberson Sothard 27 yr old enlisted wake Co 8/17/62 (died at home 11/64)

Private Mode Sprinkle 31 yr old enlisted Wake Co. 9/10/62 (later C Spotsylvania)

Private Daniel Wells 20 yr old enlisted New Hanover Co. 7/30/61 **C 7/3**

July 1 Casualties

None

Company K *"Bladen Guards"*

1st Lt. Alfred Tolar 21 yr old enlisted Bladen Co 4/26/61 **W-groin 7/3**

2nd Lt. Evander Robison 25 yr old enlisted Bladen Co 4/26/61

1st Sgt George Hall 26 yr old enlisted Bladen Co 4/26/61 (later transferred and reduced in rank 9/63)

Color Sgt. James Richardson 30 yr old mechanic enlisted Bladen Co 4/26/61 W Chancellorsville **K 7/3**

Sgt. Jesse Bloodworth 21 yr old merchant enlisted Bladen Co 4/26/61 (later 1st Sgt) (later W Jone's Farm)

Sgt. William King enlisted Bladen Co. 4/23/62 W Fredericksburg (later W Turkey Hill, Va)

Sgt. Archibald McNeill 20 yr old enlisted Bladen Co 5/11/61

Corp. James Cromartie 21 yr old enlisted New Hanover Co. 3/4/62 W-right side C Hanover CH

Corp. Alexander Patterson 31 yr old artist enlisted Bladen Co 4/26/61 (later Sgt. C Spotsylvania)

Private Alexander Franklin 32 yr old enlisted 9/7/62 (AWOL 11/64)

Private C.A. Blackwilder enlisted 7/18/62 **W-left arm 7/3**

Private Stephen Buie 29 yr old merchant enlisted Bladen Co 5/20/61 **C 7/12 Hagerstown**

Private John Burney 24 yr old enlisted Bladen Co 4/26/61 (later Corp & Sgt)

Private William Burney 21 yr old enlisted Bladen Co 4/26/61 **C 7/14**

Private John Cain enlisted Bladen Co 4/26/61 W Fredericksburg

Private Alexander Cambell 28 yr old enlisted Bladen Co 4/26/61 **W-heel C 7/3**

Private Calvin Davis 23 yr old enlisted Bladen Co 4/26/61 W Cedar Mtn. (later K Ream's Station)

Private Jonathan Dunham 31 yr old enlisted Fort Fisher 10/10/61 C Hanover CH **C 7/5** (hospital detail)

Private Daniel Ferguson 23 yr old enlisted New Hanover Co 8/1/61 C Hanover CH **W 7/3** (later C Spotsylvania)

Private John Gibson 35 yr old enlisted 7/18/62 (later W Turkey Hill)

Private Joseph Gillespie 24 yr old enlisted Bladen Co 4/26/61 **WC 7/3** (later C Wilderness)

Private William Ingram enlisted 9/7/62 **C 7/3**

Private Benjamin Lenair enlisted Bladen Co. 3/31/62

Private R.E.A. Lollar enlisted 9/7/62 C Chancellorsville **W-leg 7/3** (died 9/21/63)

Private Michael McConnis enlisted 9/7/62 **C 7/3**

Private Malcolm McDonald 22 yr old enlisted Bladen Co 5/1/61 (later C Gravel Hill, Va)

Private William McDuffie 22 yr old enlisted Bladen Co 4/30/61 C Hanover CH W-left leg Fredericksburg (later C Spotsylvania)

Private J.W. McKoy enlisted 7/18/62 **W-leg C 7/3**

Private Solomon McNorton 25 yr old enlisted New Hanover Co 6/1/61 (later W Jone's farm, Va.)

Private William Maultsby 23 yr old enlisted New Hanover Co. 6/16/61 C Hanover CH (later W Fussill's Mill)

Private George Meadows 27 yr old enlisted Bladen Co 4/26/61 W-left foot Sharpsburg (later W Wilderness)

Private William Melvin 38 yr old enlisted Bladen Co 4/26/61

Private Joseph Moore 22 yr old enlisted Bladen Co 9/7/61 (later C Wilderness)

Private James Mulford 27 yr old enlisted Bladen Co 7/17/61

Private Daniel Murphy 26 yr old mechanic enlisted Bladen Co 4/26/61

Private Abram Page 43 yr old enlisted New Hanover Co. 3/10/62 deserted 8/1/63—returned (later W Kelly's Ford

Private William Robeson 22 yr old enlisted Bladen Co 4/26/61 (later W-breast & arm Gravel Hill, Va.)

Private Nathan Sikes 22 yr old enlisted Bladen Co 4/26/61 (later W Wilderness W-left hand Jone's Farm))

Private John Singletary 20 yr old enlisted New Hanover Co. (later C Spotsylvania)

Private Murdock Smith 33 yr old enlisted Bladen Co 4/26/61 deserted 10/13/63

Private Daniel Sullivan 29 yr old enlisted Bladen Co 4/26/61 C Hanover CH (later deserted 12/7/64)

Private Daniel Sutton 22 yr old enlisted Bladen Co 5/1/61

July 1 Casualties

None

TWENTY EIGHTH NORTH CAROLINA REGIMENT

Captain James Linebarger *Private Alan Carpenter Co D*

Field & Staff

Colonel Samual D. Lowe Lincoln Co merchant promoted 11/1/62 C Hanover CH **W left thigh 7/3** (retired disabled)

Lt. Colonel William Asbury Speer 37 yr old Yadkin Co. promoted 3/12/63 C-Hanover CH W-Chancellorsville **W 7/3**

(later Col) (later K-head wound Ream's Station)

Major Samuel Stowe 41 yr old 6' 3" Gaston physician promoted 4/16/63 C-Hanover CH **W 7/3** (retired disabled)

Adjutant Romulus Folger 22 yr old enlisted Surry NC promoted 1/7/63

Sergeant Major William Rankin 38 yr old enlisted Wake Co. 4/7/63 previously Major of 37th NC promoted 4/29/63 **W 7/3**

Assistant Quartermaster Durant Parker appointed 5/2/63

Assistant Quartermaster George Thompson appointed 10/18/61

Assistant Commissary of Subsistence Nicholas Gibbon appointed 10/18/61

Surgeon Robert Gibbon appointed 9/25/61

Assistant Surgeon Lewis Mayo appointed 5/2/63

Hospital Steward Larkin Barker appointed 2/28/63

Chaplin Francis Milton Kennedy appointed 12/6/62

Quartermaster Sergeant Tullius Lowe promoted 5/ 63

Ordinance Sergeant Gabriel Johnston 21 yr old enlisted Orange Co 9/2/61

Commissary Sergeant William Mauney promoted 10/61
Ordinance Sergeant Gabriel Johnston appointed 12/9/61
Brigade Blacksmith Andrew Jackson Jenkins 28 yr old enlisted Gaston Co.,NC 7/30/61
Brigade Blacksmith Daniel Sifford 33 yr old enlisted Gaston Co, NC 4/8/62 C-Hanover CH C-Fredericksburg

Company A *"Surray Regulators"*

Captain Edward Lovell 21 yr old enlisted Surry County, NC 5/4/61 **W-right arm 7/3**
1st Lt. Elijah Thompson 28 yr old enlisted Surry County, NC 5/4/61 W 2nd Manassas **W-thigh 7/3 C 7/5**
2nd Lt. Matthew Norman 20 yr old enlisted Surry County, NC 5/4/61 (later C 9/63)
3rd Lt. F.M. Nixon 27 yr old enlisted Surry County, NC 5/4/61 W-Gaines Mill (later W CH) **slight wound 7/3**
1st Sgt. Watson Holyfield 22 yr old enlisted Surry Co., NC 5/4/61 W Gaines Mill **W 7/3** (later W Wilderness & Ream's Station)
Sgt.Jesse Cockerham 30 yr old enlisted Surry Co.NC 5/4/61 C Hanover CH **K 7/3 on advance**
Sgt. Charles Thompson 27 yr old enlisted Surry Co. NC 5/4/61 **slight W 7/3** (later died of disease)
Cpl. William Blackwood 18 yr old enlisted Surry Co., NC 3/18/62 W-Sharpsburg **W-back & left thigh C 7/3**
Cpl. Woodson Moody 23 yr old enlisted Surry Co., NC 5/4/61
Cpl. Harrison Patterson 21 yr old enlisted Surry Co., NC 3/18/62 C Hanover CH
(Later W-right leg Wilderness & left arm Spotsylvania & left leg Petersburg)
Cpl. Frost Snow 20 yr old enlisted Surry Co. NC 5/4/61 (later WC Spotsylvania)
Priv. Lemuel **Alberty** 20 yr old enlisted Surry Co. NC 3/18/62
Priv. Henry Anthony 21 yr old enlisted Surry Co., NC 5/4/61 (later W Spots)
Priv. James Asburn 19 yr old enlisted Surry Co., NC 3/18/62 (later W-Petersburg) *
Priv. John Benson 29 yr old enlisted Surry Co., NC 3/18/62 **W-left leg right side 7/3 C 7/5**
Priv. Julius Blackwood 17 yr old enlisted Surry Co., NC 3/18/62 W-mouth & hand 2nd Manassas **C 7/3**
Priv. Andrew Bobbitt 29 yr old enlisted Surry Co., NC 5/8/61 **W 7/3** (later W-Petersburg)
Priv. Arthur Bray 27 yr old enlisted Surry Co., NC 5/4/61 **WC 7/3**
Priv. Lee Burris 24 yr old enlisted Surry Co., NC 5/4/61 C-Hanover CH C-Wilderness
Priv. Wilson Center 26 yr old enlisted Surry Co., NC 3/18/62 **K 7/3**
Priv. Andrew Chandler 27 yr old enlisted Surry Co., NC 3/18/62 **K 7/3**
Priv. John Childress 21 yr old enlisted Surry Co., NC 5/10/62 **W 7/3** (later K-Wilderness)
Private William Cockerham enlisted Surry Co.NC 5/4/61 W Chancellorsville (later C Wilderness)
Priv. Isaac **Draughan** 22 yr old farmer enlisted Surry Co., NC 5/4/61

Priv. John **Draughan** 52 yr old blacksmith enlisted Surry Co., NC 5/4/61 (later K Wilderness)

Priv. William **Draughan** 25 yr old farmer enlisted Surray Co. 3/18,62

Priv. Solomon Gates 20 yr old enlisted Surry Co., NC 5/4/61 **WC 7/3**

Priv. George Hiatt 21 yr old farmer enlisted Surray Co, NC 3/18/62 C Hanover CH (later C Deep Bottom)

Priv. Jesse Holder 19 yr old farmer enlisted Surray Co, NC 3/18/62 (later Sgt)

Priv. William Marsh 21 yr old farmer enlisted Surray Co, NC 3/18/62 C Hanover CH **W-left Shoulder 7/3** (later C-Jericho Ford)

Priv. William H Marsh 18 yr old farmer enlisted Surray Co, NC 3/18/62 **W-hand 7/3**

Priv. John Phillips 18 yr old blacksmith enlisted Surray Co, NC 3/18/62 (later W-knees C-Spotsylvania)

Priv. John Reid 25 yr old farmer enlisted Surray Co, NC 3/18/62 C-Hanover CH (later C Spotsylvania CH)

Priv. Christopher Riggs 24 yr old enlisted Surry Co.NC 5/4/61 (later W-Spots promoted Sgt W-left arm Jone's Farm)

Priv. David Smith 21 yr old enlisted Surry Co. NC 5/4/61 W 2nd Manassas **K 7/3**

Priv. Thomas Sprinkle 27 yr old enlisted Surray Co, NC 3/18/62 **C 7/3**

Priv. Robert White 32 yr old enlisted Surray Co, NC 3/18/62 **W-right leg C 7/6**

Priv. William White 28 yr old enlisted Surry Co. NC 5/4/61 **W-abdomen C 7/3** (later W-Petersburg)

Priv. Ransom Wood 30 yr old enlisted Surray Co, NC 3/18/62 **W-right hand & right shoulder 7/3**

Priv Little York 15 yr old enlisted Surray Co, NC 3/12/62 **W-forehead C 7/3**

July 1 Casualties

Priv. John Hardy 20 yr old enlisted Surry Co., NC 5/4/61 W-Chancellorsville **W-left leg 7/1**

Company B "*The Gaston Invincibles*"

Captain Thomas Smith 31 yr old enlisted Gaston County, NC 7/30/61 **W-left high 7/3** (later K Reams's)

1st Lt. Robert Rhyne 22 yr old enlisted Gaston Co., NC 7/30/61 W-Chancellorsville (Later W-Ream's Station)

2nd Lt. Robert Ormand 29 enlisted at Camp Fisher 8/20/61 W-shoulder 2nd Manassas **W Falling Waters 7/14** (later W Spotsylvania)

3rd Lt. Hiram Costner 24 yr old enlisted Gaston Co., NC 7/30/61 C Hanover CH (later W Jericho Mills)

Sgt. John T.Carpenter 23 yr old enlisted Gaston Co., NC 7/30/61 C Hanover CH (later WC Petersburg)

Sgt. Hugh Torrence 23 yr old enlisted Gaston Co.,NC 7/30/61 W-Frayser's Farm **W-left eye 7/3** (later Hospital guard)

Sgt. John White 31 yr old enlisted Gaston Co.,NC 7/30/61 W-Gaines Mill **C 7/4**

Cpl. Foster Tilman 22 yr old enlisted Gaston Co.,NC 7/30/61 W-arm Cedar Mtn & W Chancellorsville WC 7/3

Cpl. George Hines 26 yr old enlisted Gaston Co.,NC 9/18/61 **W-head 7/3 C 7/5 (lost eye)** W-Spots

Cpl. John Hoffman 22 yr old enlisted Gaston Co.,NC 8/6/61 C-Hanover CH C-Fredericksburg (later W-right leg Wilderness)

Cpl. Christopher Neil 22 yr old enlisted Gaston Co.,NC 7/30/61 C Hanover CH C-Fredericksburg W-Chancellorsville **C-7/3**

Priv. S.M. Abernathy 20 yr old enlisted Gaston Co.NC 3/29/62 (later W-Right thigh Wilderness)

Priv. William Allison 23 yr old enlisted Gaston Co., NC 7/30/61 C Hanover CH

Priv. James Beaty 20 yr old enlisted Gaston Co., NC 7/30/61 C Fredericksburg

Priv. F.T. Carpenter 22 yr old enlisted Gaston Co., NC 7/30/61 W-Cedar Mtn C-Fredericksburg **WC 7/3 (died)**

Priv. John C. Carpenter 20 yr old enlisted Gaston Co., NC 7/30/61 C-Hanover CH C-Fredericksburg

Priv. Rufus Carson 20 yr old enlisted Bunker Hill, Va 10/5/62 W-Fredricksburg (later Cpl.)

Priv. John Clemmer 20 yr old enlisted Gaston Co.,NC 7/30/61 (later Sgt.)

Priv. Leander Clemmer 20 yr old enlisted Gaston Co., NC 7/30/61

Priv. James Cloninger 22 yr old enlisted New Hanover, NC 3/14/62 C-Hanover CHJ & Fredricksburg **W-right elbow C 7/3**

Priv. L.A. Cloninger 19 yr old enlisted Gaston Co., NC 3/29/62

Priv. John Costner 22 yr old enlisted Gaston Co.,NC 7/30/61 (Later W-Spotsylvania)

Priv. Jonas Costner 20 yr old enlisted Gaston Co.,NC 7/30/61 WC-Hanover CH

Priv. J.B. Crenshaw 20 yr old enlisted Gaston Co.,NC 7/30/61 **W-right thigh 7/1**

Priv. J.R. Dickson 20 yr old enlisted Gaston Co.,NC 7/30/61 C-Fredericksburg

Priv. Nathaniel Farrar 36 yr old enlisted Gaston Co.,NC 7/30/61

Priv. John Floyd 22 yr old enlisted Gaston Co.,NC 7/30/61 C-Hanover CH **W-right foot 7/3**

Priv. Lauson Ford 25 yr old enlisted Camp Fisher, NC 9/18/61 C Hanover CH

Priv. Andrew Friday 22 yr old enlisted Gaston Co.,NC 7/30/61 C Hanover CH C Fredericksburg (later W-Petersburg)

Priv. John Grice 27 yr old enlisted Gaston Co.,NC 7/30/61 C Hanover CH W Chancellorsville (later W-hip Spots)

Priv. James Groves 23 yr old enlisted Gaston Co.,NC 7/30/61 C-Hanover CH

Priv. Willis Hawkins 29 yr old enlisted Gaston Co.,NC 7/30/61 C-Fredericksburg **C 7/3**

Priv. Thomas Hoffman 21 yr old enlisted Gaston Co.,NC 7/30/61 C Fredericksburg K-Wilderness

Priv. Martin Hovis 23 yr old enlisted Gaston Co., NC 8/6/61 C-Fredericksburg

Priv. Rufus Jenkins 26 yr old enlisted Gaston Co.,NC 7/30/61 C-Fred **C 7/3**

Priv. Michael Kiser 20 yr old enlisted Gaston Co.,NC 7/30/61 C-Fredericksburg

Priv. William Lawing 33 yr old enlisted Gaston Co.,NC 7/30/**61** C-Fredericksburg **W-jaw C 7/3** (later W-Petersburg)

Priv. Franklin Leeper 33 yr old enlisted Gaston Co.,NC 7/30/61 C-Fredericksburg **W-forearm C 7/3** (later Corp)

Priv. John Lewis 19 yr old enlisted Gaston Co.,NC 3/29/62

Priv. W.F. Lewis 21 yr old enlisted Gaston Co.,NC 7/30/61 **W-leg C 7/3 (died)**

Priv. Davis Linebarger 32 yr old enlisted Gaston Co.,NC 7/30/61 C-Fredericksburg **W-right hand 7/1 (hand amputated)**

Priv. G.M. Logan 20 yr old enlisted Gaston Co.,NC 7/30/61 **WC 7/3**

Priv. Franklin McArver 22 yr old enlisted Gaston Co.,NC 7/30/61 C-Hanover CH

Priv. Isaac McIntosh 33 yr old enlisted Gaston Co.,NC 7/30/61 C-Fredericksburg **W-foot C 7/3**

Priv. William Miller 22 yr old enlisted Gaston Co.,NC 7/30/61 W-Gaines Mill

Priv. John Morrow 22 yr old enlisted Gaston Co.,NC 7/30/61 C-Fredericksburg W-Chancellorsville WC 7/3 (later C-Petersburg)

Priv. John Murphy 23 yr old enlisted Gaston Co.,NC 7/30/61

W-finger 2nd Manassas W-Chancellorsville **WC 7/3** (later W-left leg Petersburg)

Priv. John Murphy 20 yr old enlisted Gaston Co.,NC 7/30/61 W-Chancellorsville **W 7/3**

Priv. Peter Neil 24 yr old enlisted Gaston Co.,NC 7/30/61 **W-thigh C 7/3**

Priv. Abraham Nichols 20 yr old enlisted Gaston Co.,NC 7/30/61 C-Hanover CH C-Fredericksburg WC 7/3

Priv. Edward Pegram enlisted as 2nd Lt defeated enlisted 4/30/63 **W-face 7/3** (later wagonmaster)

Priv. John Ratchford 24 yr old enlisted Gaston Co, NC 3/17/62 W-left hip C Fredericksburg (later W-face Reams Station)

Priv. Alexander Rhyne 27 yr old enlisted Gaston Co.,NC 7/30/61 C Hanover CH **WC 7/3**

Priv. Alfred Rhyne 20 yr old enlisted Gaston Co.,NC 7/30/61 C-Sharpsburg

Priv. Thomas Sanders 20 yr old enlisted Gaston Co.,NC 7/30/61 C-Hanover CH

Priv. John Sarvis 19 yr old yr old enlisted Gaston Co.,NC 3/29/62 C Hanover CH **W-right eye 7/3** (later W-left thigh Ream's Station)

Priv. Isaac Shields 24 yr old enlisted Gaston Co.,NC 7/30/61 C Hanover CH **W-right leg C 7/3**

Priv. James Shields 18 yr old enlisted Gaston Co, NC 2/25/63 (later musician)

Priv. John Shrum 22 yr old enlisted Gaston Co.,NC 7/30/61

Priv. Lawson Smith 23 yr old enlisted Gaston Co.,NC 7/30/61 C-Spotsylvania

Priv. William Smith 20 yr old enlisted Gaston Co.,NC 7/30/61

Priv. Robert Stone 25 yr old enlisted Gaston Co.,NC 7/30/61 **C 7/14**

Priv. William Thomas 21 yr old enlisted Gaston Co.,NC 7/30/61 C-Hanover CH C-Fredericksburg
Priv. Francis Thompson C-Hanover CH **WC 7/3** (later clerk QM)
Priv. Jacob Thornburg 21 yr old enlisted Gaston Co, NC 3/29/62
Priv. William Whitesides 25 yr old enlisted Gaston Co.,NC 7/30/61
Priv. LeRoy Wilson 21 yr old enlisted Gaston Co.,NC 3/29/62 C-Fredericksburg **WC 7/14/63**
Priv. Wyley Wyatt 23 yr old enlisted Gaston Co.,NC 7/30/61 C-Hanover CH C Fredericksburg (later CSA Navy)

Drummer Ross Gaston 17 yr old enlisted Gaston Co.,NC 7/30/61
Teamster Alexander McCay 42 yr old enlisted Gaston Co.,NC 7/30/61

July 1 Casualties

Priv. William Carpenter 20 yr old enlisted Gaston Co., NC 7/30/61 C Hanover CH **W 7/1**

Company C *"South Fork Farmers"*

Captain James Linebarger 25 yr old enlisted 8/13/61 Catawba Co.NC W-Fredericksburg / Chancellorsville **W-groin 7/3**
1st Lt. Marcus Throneburg enlisted 8/13/61 Catawba Co. NC C Hanover CH (later W Ream's Station)
2nd Lt. Coleman Austin enlisted 8/13/61 Catawba Co. NC C Hanover CH **K 7/3**
1st Sgt. David Kincaid enlisted Camp Fisher 8/26/61 W Ox Hill W Chancellorsville **WC 7/1**
Sgt Mathias Throneberg 25 yr old enlisted 8/13/61 Catawba Co. NC W Gaines Mill
Sgt. John Williams enlisted 8/13/61 Catawba Co. NC (later 2nd Lt)
Sgt. James Grice enlisted Catawba Co. NC 8/13/61 C Hanover CH W Fredericksburg& Chancellorsville **W 7/3**
Sgt George Kayler enlisted Catwaba Co NC 8/13/61 **W 7/3 (died 7/19)**
Sgt Levi Linebarger 19 yr old enlisted Catawba, NC
Sgt Joshua Little 22 yr old enlisted Catawba Co. NC 8/13/61 W Ox Hill (later W-right leg C Gravel Hill, Va)
Cpl. Phanuel Herman 25 yr old enlisted Catawba Co. NC 8/13/61 C Hanover CH **WC 7/3 (later Sgt)**
Cpl. Maxwell Sigman enlisted Catawba Co, NC 8/13/61 C Hanover CH **W-left leg 7/3**
Priv. Allen Barger 23 yr old enlisted 3/15/62 Catawba Co. NC C Hanover CH
Priv. Marcus Barger 26 yr old enlisted 3/15/62 Catawba Co. NC C Hanover CH
Priv. Noah Barger 23 yr old enlisted 3/15/62 Catawba Co. NC
Priv. Aaron **Bolch** enlisted Catawba Co. NC 8/13/61 C Hanover CH **WC 7/3**

Priv. Abel **Bolch** enlisted 3/15/62 Catawba Co. NC W Gaines Mill *

Priv. Logan Bolch enlisted Catawba Co. NC 3/14/63 **WC 7/3 (died Phila hospital 9/30 buried PNC))**

Priv. Calvin Bowman 19 yr old enlisted Catawba Co. NC 3/15/62 (later C Spots) *

Priv. Allen Bumgarner enlisted Catawba Co. NC 8/13/61 C Hanover CH *

Priv. David Bumgarner enlisted Catawba Co. NC 8/13/61 C Hanover CH W Chanc *

Priv. Adophus Campbell Catawba Co NC 8/13/61 W-Chan **W-left shoulder C 7/3**

Priv. Alfred Cline 20 enlisted Catawba Co. NC 8/13/61

Priv. Ambrose Cline 24 yr old enlisted Catawba Co. NC 3/14/63 (late K-Richmond)

Priv. John Clippard 28 yr old enlisted 3/15/62 Catawba Co. NC (later W-jaw Wild)

Priv. Sidney Connell 23 yr old enlisted Catawba Co.NC 8/13/61 W-2nd Manassas **W 7/3**

Priv. Henry Conrad 18 yr old enlisted Catawba Co. NC 8/13/61 (later K-Gravel Hill)

Priv. Lawson Cook 33 yr old enlisted 3/15/62 Catawba Co. NC **W 7/3**

Priv. David Drum enlisted Catawba Co NC 8/13/61 W-2nd Manassas **W 7/3** (later W-Reams Station)

Priv. Adolphus Edwards enlisted Camp Fisher, NC 8/26/61 C Hanover CH (later W-Left leg Jericho Mills (amp)

Priv. Ephraim Fry 39 yr old enlisted Catawaba Co, NC 8/1/3/61 **W-forehead 7/3**

Priv. Jacob Fry enlisted Camp Fisher, NC 9/2/61 **C 7/3**

Priv. Phillip Goins 19 yr old enlisted Catawba Co. NC 8/13/61 C-Hanover CH W-Fredericksburg & Chancellorsville

Priv. James Goodson 19 yr old enlisted Catawba Co. NC 8/13/61 W-shoulder Frayser's farm (later W Spots) died

Priv. Watson Harwell enlisted Catawba Co. NC 3/14/63 **K 7/3**

Priv. Newton Haun enlisted Catawba Co, NC 3/15/62 **K 7/3**

Priv. David Hefner 35 yr old enlisted Catawba Co. NC 8/13/61 **W-4 times 7/3**

Priv. Levi Hefner 23 yr old enlisted Catawba Co. NC 8/13/61 W Ox Hill W Fredericksburg (later C Spotsylvania)

Priv. Serenus Hefner 22 yr old enlisted Catawba Co. NC 8/13/61 C Hanover CH (later W-left foot Jones Farm)

Priv. Wilson Hefner 18 yr old enlisted Catawba Co NC 3/15/62 C Hanover CH W Chancellorsville

Priv. Abel Herman enlisted Catawba Co. NC 8/13/61 W-Chan **C 7/14**

Priv Daniel Herman 26 yr old enlisted Catawba Co. NC 8/13/61 C-Hanover CH W-Chancellorsville (later Corp)

Priv. George Herman 24 yr old enlisted Catawba Co. NC 8/13/61 W-2nd Manassas (later Corp K—Spotsylvania)

Priv. Rufus Herman 19 yr old enlisted Catawba Co. NC 8/13/61 (later C Gravel Hill)

Priv. Lemuel Holler enlisted Catawba Co, NC 3/15/62 C Hanover CH **WC 7/3**

Priv. Jacob Houston 26 yr old enlisted Catawba Co NC 3/15/62 W-Shepardstown **W 7/3**

Priv. John Houston 20 yr old enlisted Catawba Co. NC 8/13/61 C Hanover CH

Priv. Daniel Huffman 20 yr old enlisted Catawba Co. NC 8/13/61 W-chest 2nd Manassas (later C Spotsylvania)

Priv. Jeremiah Huffman 28 yr old enlisted Catawba Co. NC 8/13/61 W-hip Gaine's Mill **left sick 7/3** (died typoid fever 10/20/63

Priv. Levi Huffman 24 yr old enlisted Catawba Co. NC 8/13/61 C Winchester, Va (later W Spotsylvania)

Priv. Joseph Killian 19 yr old enlisted Catawba Co, NC 3/15/62 C Hanover CH **W 7/3** (later K Ream's Station)

Priv. Cicero Lael 20 yr old enlisted Catawba Co NC 3/15/62 W Ox Hill (later WC Gravel Hill, Va)

Priv. Polycarp 18 yr old enlisted Catawba Co, NC 3/9/63 (later W-Spotsylvania)

Priv. Avery Linebarger 18 yr old enlisted Catawba Co NC 3/15/62 W-Sherpardstown (later C Deep Bottom)

Priv. Jacob Linebarger transferred from 13th NC 3/21/63 W-Chan **K 7/3**

Priv. Ephraim Link enlisted Catawba Co NC 3/15/62 C Hanover CH **K 7/3**

Priv. William Martin 27 yr old enlisted Catawba Co. NC 8/13/61 W-shell Frayser's farm **W-shell—left arm & shoulder 7/3**

Priv. David Miller enlisted Catawba Co, NC 3/14/63 (later W-Wilderness)

Priv. Hiram Miller enlisted Catawba Co NC 3/15/62 W-hand Frayser's farm W-Chancellorsville **WC 7/3**

Priv. Marcus Miller enlisted Catawba Co. NC 8/13/61 (later K-Spotsylvania)

Priv. William Miller enlisted Catawba Co. NC 8/13/61 **K-7/3**

Priv. Levi Poovey 18 yr old enlisted Catawba Co NC 1/27/63 **W-face & right arm 7/3**

Priv. David Poovey 23 yr old enlisted Catawba Co NC C Hanover CH W-Chancellorsville **K 7/3**

Priv. Henry Poovey enlisted Catawba Co, NC 3/14,63 **K 7/3**

Priv. Josiah Poovey 20 yr old enlisted Catawba Co, NC 3/15/62 **W 7/3**

Priv. Julius Poovey 18 yr old enlisted Catawba Co, NC 1/27/63 W-leg Chancellorsville (later W-head Wilderness)

Priv. Hiram Poovey 25 yr old enlisted Catawba Co, NC 3/15/62 (later W-Jone's Farm)

Priv. David Pryor enlisted Camp Fisher, NC 8/26/61 C Hanover CH **K 7/3**

Priv. Samuel Pryor enlisted Camp Fisher, NC 8/26/61 C Hanover CH **WC 7/3**

Priv. James Reynolds enlisted camp Fisher 9/2/61 C Hanover CH **K 7/3**

Priv. George Seaboch 35 yr old enlisted Camp Fisher 9/9/61 C Hanover CH

Priv. William Seaboch enlisted Camp Fisher 3/15/62 C Hanover CH (later K Jone's Farm)

Priv. Noah Simmons enlisted Catawba Co, NC 3/14/63 (later C-Wilderness) *

Priv. David Sipe enlisted Catawba Co, NC 8/13/61 **K 7/3**

Priv. Eli Spencer enlisted Catawba Co, NC 8/13/61 W Cedar Mtn

Priv. Pinkney Spencer enlisted Catawba Co, NC 8/13/61 W-hand-Gaines Mill

Priv. Heglar Summit 23 yr old enlisted Camp Fisher 9/2/61 (later C-Spotsylvania)

Priv. Aaron Townson 18 yr old enlisted Catawba Co, NC 3/15/62 C Hanover CH
Priv. Laban Turner 19 yr old Catawba Co, NC engineer enlisted 3/15/62
Priv. Noah Wagner 21 yr old enlisted Catawba Co. NC 3/15/62 C Hanover CH
Priv. Thomas Wagner 24 yr old enlisted Catawba Co, NC C Hanover CH (later W-Gravel Hill)
Priv. Robert White 24 yr old enlisted Gaston Co., NC 7/30/61 (later W Jericho Mills / 1st Lt)
Priv. Noah Yount enlisted Catawba Co, NC 3/14/63 W Chancellorsville (later Teamster) *

Teamster Joshua Carter 28 yr old enlisted Catawba Co. NC 8/13/61 W-Chancellorsville (later teamster)
Musician John Turbyville 23 yr old enlisted Catawba Co, NC 8/13/61 W-Mechanicsville
"Nurse" Priv. Elijah Killian Catawba blacksmith enlisted 8/13/61 **C 7/5 "nurse at hospital"**

July 1 Casualties

None

Company D "*Stanly Yankee Hunters*"

Captain John Randle 25 yr old Stanly County, NC enlisted 7/29/61 **W 7/3 (died)**
1st Lt. Edmund Moose 38 yr old enlisted Stanly Co, NC 7/29/61 **WC 7/3 (died)**
1st Sgt. Thomas Harris 31 yr old enlisted Stanly Co, NC 7/29/61
Sgt. Moses Eudy 27 yr old Stanly Co, NC 7/29/61 (later 2nd Lt / Capt W Spotsylvania)
Sgt. Howell Parker 20 yr old Stanly Co, NC 7/29/61 (later 1st Lt-W Hatchers Run)
Sgt. James Easley 21 yr old enlisted Stanly Co, NC 7/29/61 **K 7/3**
Sgt. Coleman Lefler 25 yr old enlisted Stanly Co, NC 7/29/61 C Hanover CH
Sgt Malachi Lowder 23 yr old enlisted Stanly Co, NC 7/29/61 **K 7/3**
Sgt Marvel Richie 18 yr old Stanly Co, NC 7/29/61 W-Richmond **W-left side 7/3**
Cpl. Jacob Lyerly 24 yr old enlisted Stanly Co, NC 7/29/61 (later died of Tyhoid)
Cpl. Roland Miller 26 yr old enlisted Stanly Co NC 3/15/62 (later W-North Anna)
Cpl. Daniel Plyler 22 yr old enlisted Stanly Co, NC 7/29/61 W Ox Hill
Priv. Ervin Almond 32 yr old enlisted Stanly Co, NC 7/29/61 C Hanover CH **C 7/3**
Priv. Henry Ary 21 yr old enlisted Stanly Co, NC 3/15/62 (later Deep Bottom)
Priv. Hiram Barbee 20 yr old enlisted Stanly Co, NC 3/15/62
Priv. Terrell Bolton 27 yr old enlisted Stanly Co, NC 7/29/61 (later W-leg C Wilderness)
Priv Adam Burleson—22 yr old enlisted Stanly Co, NC 7/29/61
Priv. John Burleson 24 yr old enlisted Stanly Co, NC 7/29/61 (later C Waterloo, Va)
Priv. Allen **Carpenter** 21 yr old enlisted Stanly Co, NC 7/29/61
Priv. Churchill **Carpenter** 19 yr old enlisted Stanly Co, NC 7/29/61 **K 7/3**

Priv. Uriah Crayton 24 yr old enlisted Stanly Co, NC 7/29/61 (later Corp)
Priv. John Crowell 20 yr old enlisted Stanly Co, NC C Hanover CH
Priv. William Crowell 24 yr old enlisted Stanly Co, NC 7/29/61
Priv. James Davis 20 yr old Stanly Co, NC 3/15/62 W Richmond W-right leg **C 7/3**
Priv. Charles Fisher 18 yr old enlisted Stanly Co, NC 3/15/62 (W-leg Petersburg)
Priv. Wilson Furr 29 yr old enlisted Stanly Co, NC 3/15/62 (later W-head Wildernesss)
Priv. John Hatley 31 yr old enlisted Stanly Co, NC 7/29/61 **K 7/3**
Priv. James Howell 21 Stanly Co, NC 3/1/62 W-Richmond (two fingers amp) **K 7/3**
Priv. Henry Honeycutt 26 yr old Stanly Co, NC 7/29/61 C Hanover CH W-head **C 7/3**
Priv. Monroe Lefler enlisted Camp Gregg, Va 3/26/63 (later K Wildernesss)
Priv. Jacob H Lyerly 19 yr old enlisted Stanly Co, NC (later Corp)
Priv. Benjamin Mauldin 24 yr old enlisted Stanly Co, NC 7/29/61 **W-head C 7/3**
Priv. Isaac Mault 18 yr old enlisted Camp Gregg, Va 4/27/63 (later K-Petersburg)
Priv. James Mault 23 yr old enlisted Stanly Co, NC 3/15/62 **W-left lung 7/3**
Priv. Arthur Miller 24 yr old blacksmith enlisted Stanly Co, NC 7/29/61 C Hanover CH C Chancellorsville **C 7/3**
Priv. Wilson Morris 25 yr ld enlisted Stanly Co, NC 3/15/62 **W-right foot C 7/3**
Priv. William Newby 33 yr old enlisted Stanly Co NC 3/15/62 (deserted 9/63—C Wild)
Priv. Nelson Pennington 22 yr old Stanly Co, NC 7/29/61 C Hanover CH W-left shoulder 7/3 (later hospital guard)
Priv. Benjamin Perry 20 yr old Stanly Co, NC 7/29/61 W 2nd Manassas **WC 7/3**
Priv. Henry Plyler 19 yr old enlisted Stanly Co, NC 3/15/62 (later W Petersburg)
Priv. Columbis Rowland 24 yr old enlisted Stanly Co NC 3/15/62 W Richmond
Priv. John Sell 27 yr old enlisted Stanly Co, NC 5/6/62 **K 7/3**
Priv. Samuel Sell 22 yr old enlisted Stanly Co, NC 3/15/62
Priv. *Alexander Sides Jr.* 22 yr old enlisted Stanly Co, NC 7/29/61
Priv. *Alexander Sides Sr.* 44 yr old enlisted Stanly Co, NC 7/29/61 **C 7/3**
Priv. Charles Sides 20 yr old Stanly Co, NC 3/15/62 C Fredericksburg **W-thigh C 7/3**
Priv. Joseph Sides 31 yr old enlisted Stanly Co, NC 7/29/61 **C 7/3**
Priv. William Sides 20 yr old enlisted Stanly Co, NC 7/29/61 C Fredericksburg (later deserted 9/63 returned C-Spotsylvania)
Priv. Doctor Smith 20 yr old enlisted Stanly Co, NC 7/29/61 **WC 7/3 (died)**
Priv. Josiah Smith 26 yr old enlisted Stanly Co, NC 7/29/61 (later C Spotsylvania)
Priv. Robert Stoker 41 yr old enlisted Stanly Co, NC 7/29/61 **W Fredericksburg C 7/4**
Priv. Francis Tally 23 yr old enlisted Stanly Co, NC 7/29/61 (later Sgt)
Priv. Harrison Tolbert 22 yr old Stanly Co, NC 7/29/61 C-Ox Hill (later C-Spots)
Priv. Ferdinand Turner 22 yr old enlisted Stanly Co, NC 7/29/61 C Hanover CH
Priv. James Turner 23 yr old enlisted Stanly Co, NC 3/15/62
Priv. James Whitaker 25 yr old Stanly Co, NC 7/29/61 W-Cedar Mtn **W-thigh C 7/3**
Priv William Yow 23 yr old enlisted Stanly Co, NC 7/29/61 (later W-thigh Spotsylvania)

July 1 Casualties

None

Company E *"Montgomery Grays"*

Captain Niven Clark 28 yr old enlisted Montgomery County, NC 8/1/61 W-Glendale (later K-Spots)
1st Lt. James Ewing 27 yr old enlisted Montgomery Co, NC 8/1/61 W-leg Fred
2nd Lt. Thomas Green 28 yr old Montgomery Co, NC 8/1/61 W-Richmond W-Reams
3rd Lt. Elias Hurley 29 yr old Montgomery Co, NC 8/1/61 **W 7/3** C-Wilderness
1st Sgt. Isaac Williams 26 yr old Montgomery Co, NC 8/1/61 C Hanover CH (later C Gravel Hill)
Sgt. Joshua Cranford 29 yr old Montgomery Co, NC enlisted 8/1/61 (later C Pickett's farm)
Sgt. John Fraser 21 yr old Montgomery Co, NC enlisted 8/1/61 (later K-Spotsylvania)
Sgt. Robert McKay 20 yr old Montgomery Co, NC enlisted 9/25/61
Cpl. William Chisholm joined company 3/62
Cpl. Calvin Smith 32 yr old Montgomery Co, NC enlisted 8/1/61 C Hanover CH (C Spots)
Cpl. Mathew Stutts 22 yr old Montgomery Co, NC enlisted 8/1/61
Priv. Dawson Allen 30 yr old Montgomery Co, NC enlisted 8/1/61 **WC 7/3**
Priv. James Ballard 28 yr old Montgomery Co, NC 8/1/61 C Hanover CH **W-ankle C 7/3**
Priv. Miles Ballard 23 yr old Montgomery Co, NC enlisted8/1/61 C Hanover CH
Priv. George Barringer 29 yr old Montgomery Co, NC enlisted8/1/61 (courier for Gen Lane)
Priv. Alexander Bass 42 yr old Montgomery Co, NC enlisted 8/1/61 **C 7/3**
Priv. Robert Bird 21 yr old Montgomery Co, NC 8/1/61 W Gaines Mill (later W-Spots)
Priv. Oliver Brewer 21 yr old Montgomery Co, NC enlisted 8/1/61 **WC 7/3**
Priv. Josiah Callais 24 yr old Montgomery Co, NC enlisted 8/1/61 **W 7/1 C 7/3 (died)**
Priv. David Chauncy 34 yr old Montgomery Co, NC enlisted 8/1/61 (deserted 8/63)
Priv. Nathaniel Cook 25 yr old Montgomery Co, NC enlisted 8/1/61 W-Richmond **W-left arm C 7/3**
Priv. William Gadd 37 yr old Montgomery Co, NC 8/1/61 **W 7/3** (later W-Petersburg)
Priv. William Green 22 yr old Montgomery Co, NC enlisted 8/1/61 C 2nd Manassas
Priv. B.L. Hall enlisted Camp Gregg, Va 2/1/63 (later K Wilderness)
Priv. John Haney 26 yr old Montgomery Co, NC enlisted 10/2/62 (later W-Petersburg)
Priv. James Harper 28 yr old Montgomery Co, NC enlisted 8/1/61 (later C-Spotsylvania)
Priv. John Hasten enlisted Wake Co, NC **W-thigh C 7/3 (died 7/7/63)**
Priv. Joel Henderson 20 yr old Montgomery Co, NC enlisted 8/1/61
Priv. George Hunsucker 29 yr old Montgomery Co, NC enlisted 3/4/62 **W 7/3**
Priv. James Lassiter 27 yr old Montgomery Co, NC enlisted 8/1/61
Priv. Josiah Lisk 21 yr old Montgomery Co, NC enlisted 3/20/62

Priv. William Lothrop 27 yr old Montgomery Co, NC enlisted 10/2/62 (later C Gravel Hill)
Priv. Jesse Luther 25 yr old Montgomery Co, NC enlisted 8/1/61 (later C Gravel Hill)
Priv. Howell McDonald 23 yr old Montgomery Co, NC enlisted 8/1/61
Priv. Evander McInnis 21 yr old Montgomery Co, NC enlisted 8/1/61 **WC 7/3 (died)**
Priv. George McRae 21 yr old Montgomery Co, NC enlisted 8/1/61 (later W-right arm Ream's)
Priv. James McRea Montgomery Co, NC enlisted 8/1/61 **W 7/3**
Priv. John Matheson 19 yr old Montgomery Co, NC enlisted 8/1/61 W-thigh Gaines Mill (later Corp)
Priv. George Morgan 20 yr old Montgomery Co, NC enlisted 3/3/63 (later C Spots)
Priv. Sampson Morris 34 yr old Montgomery Co, NC enlisted 8/1/61 **W 7/3** (later W-knee Jones farm)
Priv. Noah Nichols 20 yr old Montgomery Co, NC enlisted 8/1/61
Priv. John Parker 25 yr old Montgomery Co, NC enlisted 8/1/61 **K 7/3**
Priv. Thomas **Parsons** 23 yr old Montgomery Co, NC enlisted 8/1/61 (later deserted)
Priv. William Phillips 21 yr old Montgomery Co, NC enlisted 8/1/61 **K 7/3**
Priv. James Reden transferred 3/62 C Hanover CH **C 7/3**
Priv. John Sedberry 33 yr old Montgomery Co, NC enlisted 8/1/61 W-Frazier Farm **C 7/3**
Priv. Thomas Smith 35 yr old Montgomery Co, NC enlisted 8/1/61 (Later K Spots)
Priv. W.A. Smith 33 yr old enlisted New Hanover Co, 3/12/62 **WC 7/3 (died 7/11/63)**
Priv. John Stafford 23 yr old Montgomery Co, NC enlisted 3/20/62 **C 7/1**
Priv. James Wade 21 yr old Montgomery Co, NC enlisted 8/1/61 **W-arm C 7/3**
Priv. Solomon Waesner 25 yr old enlisted Montgomery 5/23/62 **W-right hip C 7/3**
Priv. David Waisner 24 yr old Montgomery Co, NC enlisted 3/20/62 C Hanover CH **C 7/3**

Musician William Lisk 31 yr old Montgomery Co, NC enlisted 8/1/61

July 1 Casualties

None

Company F "*The Yadkin Boys*"

Captain Thomas Apperson 25 yr old enlisted Yadkin County, NC 6/18/61 W-Hanover CH
1st Lt. John Truelove 31 yr old Yadkin County, NC 6/18/61 **W-neck 7/3** (later W-Petersburg)
2nd Lt. William Marler 24 yr old enlisted Yadkin County, NC 6/18/61 **C 7/3**
3rd Lt. James Starling 24 yr old enlisted Yadkin County, NC 6/18/61 W-Fredericksburg
1st Sgt. Peter Apperson 22 yr old Yadkin County, NC 6/18/61 W-Richmond **W-right shoulder C 7/3**

Sgt. John Brown 30 yr old enlisted Yadkin Co, NC 4/4/62 C Sharpsburg **C 7/3**
Sgt. Frederick Myers 23 yr old enlisted Yadkin County, NC 6/18/61 promoted 5/11/63
Sgt. Augustus Randleman 22 yr old enlisted Forsyth County, NC 6/18/61 **WC 7/3 (died)**
Cpl. Samuel Creson 25 yr old enlisted Yadkin County, NC 6/18/61 **W 7/3 (deserted 9/63)**
Cpl. **Issac Poindexter** 25 yr old enlisted Yadkin County, NC 6/18/61 (later Sgt C Wilderness)
Priv. Benjamin Adams 22 yr old Yadkin County, NC 6/18/61 **C 7/3** (later C Pickett's Farm)
Priv. John Apperson 18 yr old enlisted Yadkin Co, NC 2/1/63
Priv. George Blakely 24 yr old enlisted Yadkin County, NC 6/18/61 (later W Ream's Station)
Priv. Henry Bran 20 yr old enlisted Yadkin County, NC 6/18/61 (later Corp)
Priv. Azariah Brown 22 yr old enlisted Yadkin County, NC 3/25/62 **C 7/3**
Priv. James Brown 20 yr old enlisted Yadkin County, NC 6/18/61 (later Sgt)
Priv. Sidney **Choplin** 26 yr old enlisted Yadkin County, NC 6/18/61 **K 7/3**
Priv. James Conrad 18Yadkin Co, NC farmer **WC 7/3** (died 9/16)
Priv. John Donathan 18 yr old enlisted Yadkin Co, NC 4/1/62 (later W-Wilderness)
Priv. Alexander Fortner 23 yr old enlisted Yadkin County, NC 6/18/61 W-Ox Hill **K 7/3**
Priv. Martin Gough 19 yr old enlisted Yadkin County, NC 6/18/61 **W 7/3**
Priv. John Hicks 26 yr old enlisted 3/17/62 **W 7/3** (later W-right leg Wilderness)
Priv. Richard Hutchens 22 yr old enlisted Yadkin County, NC 6/18/61 W-Fred **C 7/3**
Priv. William Kelly 22 yr old enlisted Yadkin County, NC 6/18/61 **WC 7/3**
Priv. James Nicholson 29 yr old enlisted Yadkin County, NC 6/18/61 C Hanover CH
Priv. Henry Norman 19 yr old enlisted Yadkin Co, NC 2/18/63 (deserted 9/12/63)
Priv. Reason Pack 30 yr old enlisted Camp Fisher, NC **W-left thigh & left hand 7/3**
Priv. Clem Sprinkle 23 yr old enlisted Yadkin Co, NC 4/30/62
Priv. Carson Strickland 23 yr old enlisted Nash Co. 10/1/62 W-Fredericksburg (later W-Petersburg)
Priv. Stephen Strickland 23 yr old enlisted Yadkin Co, NC 10/1/62 **K 7/3**
Priv. James Tackett 22 yr old enlisted Yadkin Co, NC **WC 7/3**
Priv. John Tackett 22 yr old enlisted Yadkin County, NC 6/18/61 **C 7/3**
Priv Thomas Tackett 19 yr old enlisted Yadkin Co, NC (later W-Bethesda Church)
Priv. C.A. Tally 32 yr old enlisted Mecklenburg **K 7/3**
Priv. Thomas Wooten 21 yr old enlisted Yadkin County, NC 6/18/61 **W-left thigh C 7/3**
Priv. Andrew Yarbrough 21 yr old enlisted Yadkin County, NC 6/18/61 *

July 1 Casualties

None

Company G *"The Guards of Independence"*

Captain Elijah Morrow 30 yr old enlisted Orange Co,NC 9/2/61 W-Chan W-thigh **C 7/3 (died)**

1st Lt. George McCauley 31 yr old enlisted Orange Co,NC 9/2/61 (later Capt.)

2nd Lt. Henry Andrews 38 yr old Orange Co, NC 9/2/61 C Hanover CH (later C-Spots)

3rd Lt. Edwin Edwards 25 yr old enlisted Orange Co, NC 9/2/61 C Hanover CH (K Spots)

Sgt. Daniel Morrow 21 yr old Orange Co, NC Student C Hanover CH W-Chan

Sgt. Henry Edwards 20 yr old enlisted Orange Co, NC 6/1/62 W-Malvern Hill

Sgt. William Edwards 21 yr old enlisted Orange Co 9/2/61 3/5/62 C-Hanover CH / C-Fredericksburg / W-Chancellorsville

WC 7/3 (later K-Petersburg)

Sgt. Edward Martin 21 yr old enlisted Orange Co 3/5/62 C-Hanover CH

Sgt. Jesse Nevill 21 yr old enlisted Orange Co 9/2/61 C-Hanover CH C-Fredericksburg (later K-Wilderness)

Cpl. James Durham 21 yr old enlisted Orange Co, NC 9/2/61 C Fred W-Wild

Cpl. William Marcom enlisted Orange Co 9/2/61 C-Fredericksburg W-Chancellorsville (later C-Wilderness)

Cpl. Joseph Vickers 21 yr old enlisted Orange Co 9/2/61 C-Hanover CH (later C-Spots)

Priv. John Andrews 20 yr old enlisted Orange Co, NC bricklayer 9/2/61 W-Chancellorsville (deserted 12/3/63) (later C Spots)

Priv. James Brockwell 23 yr old enlisted Orange Co, NC farmer 9/2/61

Priv. John Brockwell 24 yr old enlisted Orange Co, NC 9/2/61

Priv. Joseph Brockwell 28 yr old enlisted Orange Co, NC 9/2/61

Priv. Dennis Cates 24 yr old enlisted Orange Co, NC 9/2/61 C Hanover CH C-Fred C—Spots

Priv. Enoch Cates 21 yr old enlisted Orange Co,NC 9/2/61 (later K-Wilderness)

Priv. Richard Cates 21 yr old Orange Co, NC 9/2/61 W-Gaines Mill **C-Falling Waters 7/14**

Priv. Jesse Cheek 19 yr old enlisted Orange Co, NC 9/2/61 **W 7/3 (died 7/16)**

Priv. William Cheek 20 yr old enlisted Orange Co, NC 9/2/61 C-Hanover CH C-Spots

Priv. William Cole 20 yr old enlisted Orange Co, NC 9/2/61

Priv. Dallas Crabtree 16 yr old enlisted 2/63 C Spotsylvania

Priv. William Crabtree 25 yr old enlisted Orange Co, NC 9/2/61 C-Hanover CH **K 7/3**

Priv. Addison Crawford 20 yr old enlisted Orange Co, NC 9/2/61 C Fred (later K-Wild)

Priv. Henry Crawford 20 yr old enlisted Orange Co, NC 9/2/61 C-Fred W-Chan C-Wild

Priv. Samuel Crawford 30 yr old enlisted Orange Co, NC 9/2/61 **W 7/3**

Priv. Lucien Daniel 22 yr old enlisted Orange Co, NC 9/2/61 (later K-Wilderness)

Priv. Joseph Durham 30 yr old Orange Co, NC C-Hanover **W left thigh right arm 7/3**

Priv. Robert Durham 21 yr old enlisted Orange Co, NC C Hanover CH (later Corp C-Spots)

Priv. William J. Durham 25 yr old enlisted Orange Co, NC (later W Fussell Mill)
Priv. William P. Durham 24 yr old enlisted Orange Co 9/2/61 (later C-Spots)
Priv. Samuel Edwards 22 yr old enlisted Orange Co 9/2/61 (later C-Spots)
Priv. James Johnson 22 yr old enlisted Orange Co 1/1/62
Priv. John Kennedy 22 yr old enlisted Orange Co 9/2/61
Priv. Bunk Lloyd 16 yr old enlisted Orange Co 1/63 (later C-Spots)
Priv. Henry Lloyd 19 yr old enlisted Orange Co 3/5/62 C-Fredericksburg (later C-Spots)
Priv. Lucian Lloyd 23 yr old enlisted Orange Co 9/2/61 C-Fredericksburg **WC 7/3** (died 7/10)
Priv. Issac Morris 25 yr old enlisted Orange Co 3/5/62 C-Hanover CH (later W-Kelly's Ford)
Priv. John Morris 20 yr old enlisted Orange Co 3/5/62 C-Hanover CH C-Fredericksburg W-Chancellorsville **K 7/3**
Priv. John Pendergrass 23 yr old enlisted Orange Co 9/2/61 C-Hanover CH
Priv. Nathaniel Pendergrass 23 yr old enlisted Orange Co 9/2/61 W-left hand Chancellorsville (later C-Spots)
Priv. Reuben Poe 27 yr old enlisted Orange Co 12/20/61 (later C-Spots)
Priv. Stephen Poe 21 yr old enlisted Orange Co 12/20/61 C-Fred
Priv. Pleasant Poindexter transferred 4/63 **W-back 7/3**
Priv. Roby Poindexter 28 yr old enlisted Orange Co 9/15/61
Priv. William Poindexter transferred 3/18/63 **WC 7/3 (died 7/5)**
Priv. John Roberson 21 yr old enlisted Orange Co12/20/61 C-Hanover CH (later K-Spots)
Priv. Alfred Robertson 23 yr old enlisted Orange Co 9/2/61
Priv. George Smith 23 yr old enlisted Orange Co 9/2/61 C-Hanover CH (later C-Wild)
Priv. James Smith 21 yr old enlisted Orange Co 9/2/61
Priv. Mitchell Smith 32 yr old enlisted Orange Co 9/2/61 C-Hanover CH **W-foot 7/3**
Priv Calvin Snipes 22 yr old enlisted Orange Co 9/2/61 (later C Hatcher's Run)
Priv. William Stanford 21 yr old enlisted Orange Co 9/2/61 WC Hanover CH
Priv. Robert Stephens 24 yr old enlisted Orange Co 9/2/61
Priv. George Straughan 32 yr old enlisted Orange Co 9/2/61 C-Fred W-Wild
Priv. Nathan Straughan 21 yr old enlisted Orange Co 9/2/61 C-Fred C-Chan **W 7/3**
Priv. Henry Sykes 22 yr old enlisted Orange Co 9/2/61 C-Fred **C 7/14**
Priv. Johnson Sykes 21 yr old enlisted Orange Co 9/2/61C-Hanover CH (later W-Peters)
Priv. Oregon Tenney 20 yr old enlisted Orange Co 12/20/61 W-Cedar Mtn
Priv. James Thompson 23 yr old enlisted Orange Co 9/2/61 (later W-Wild)
Priv. John Weaver 23 yr old enlisted Orange Co 9/2/61 (later C-Gravel Hill, Va)

1

July 1 Casualties

Priv. Thomas Howard 36 yr old enlisted Orange Co 9/2/61 **W-thigh 7/1 C 7/5**

Company H "*The Cleveland Regulators*"

Captain Gold Holland 43 yr old enlisted Cleveland Co, NC 3/17/62
1st Lt. Milton Lowe promoted 11/14/62 (Later C Gravel Hill, Va)
2nd Lt. David Smith 27 yr old mechanic enlisted Gaston Co. 7/30/61 Sgt Major then elected 4/6/63 resigned 9/28/64
3rd Lt. Stephen Simmons 20 yr old enlisted Cleveland Co 8/22/61 **K 7/3**
1st Sgt. Thomas Holland 20 yr old enlisted Cleveland Co 8/22/61 W—Mechanicville
Sgt. James Moore Green 20 yr old enlisted Cleveland Co 8/22/61 C Hanover CH
Sgt. Ransom Hawkins 25 yr old enlisted Cleveland Co 8/22/61
Sgt. Lewis Matheney 31 yr old enlisted Cleveland Co 8/22/61 (later K Wild)
Sgt James Rollins 29 yr old enlisted Cleveland Co 8/22/61 **W-left leg & right shoulder 7/3 C (died 7/22)**
Cpl. Perry Gold 22 yr old enlisted Cleveland Co 8/22/61
Cpl. Asa Hamrick 23 yr old enlisted Cleveland Co 8/22/61 C Hanover CH WC-Spots
Cpl. Orville Hardin 21 yr old enlisted Cleveland Co 8/22/61 K Spots CH
Cpl. James Holland 21 yr old enlisted Cleveland Co 8/22/61 **W 7/3** (later K-North Anna)
Cpl. Bery Hughes 22 yr old enlisted Cleveland Co 8/22/61 **C 7/3**
Cpl. Meredith Jolly 20 yr old enlisted Cleveland Co 8/22/61 **W 7/3** (later Sgt)
Priv. Crawford Barnett 22 yr old enlisted Cleveland Co 8/22/61
Priv. William Barnett 33 yr old enlisted Cleveland Co 8/22/61 **W-shoulder 7/3**
Priv. Samuel Bridges 20 yr old enlisted Cleveland Co 2/20/63 **W 7/1 C 7/5**
Priv. Elias Byars 32 yr old enlisted Cleveland Co 3/17/62 (later K-Spots CH)
Priv. David Champion 26 yr old enlisted Cleveland Co 8/22/61
Priv. James Champion 18 yr old enlisted Cleveland Co 3/17/62
Priv. Dilliard Dobbins 23 yr old enlisted Cleveland Co 8/22/61 W-Shepardtown
Priv. James Gillespie 24 yr old enlisted Cleveland Co 3/17/62 (later Corp)
Priv. John Gillespie 23 yr old enlisted Cleveland Co 3/17/62 W-Ox Hill, Va
Priv. George Green 20 yr old enlisted Cleveland Co 8/22/61 **K 7/3**
Priv. James Green 23 yr old enlisted Cleveland Co 8/22/61
Priv. John Green 19 yr old enlisted Cleveland Co 8/22/61 **W-leg 7/3**
Priv. Thomas Green transferred 4/2/63 (later 3rd Lt)
Priv. Phineas Holland 20 yr old enlisted Cleveland Co 8/22/61 C Jericho Mills, Va
Priv. James Hughes 20 yr old enlisted Cleveland Co 8/22/61 W-right hand Chanc C-Spots
Priv. William Jones 21 yr old enlisted Cleveland Co 3/17/62
Priv. John Lee 21 yr old enlisted Cleveland Co 3/17/62 **K 7/3**
Priv. Watson Lee 24 yr old enlisted Cleveland Co 3/17/62
Priv. William Lee 22 yr old enlisted Cleveland Co 3/17/62 (later W-abdomen Reams)
Priv. James Lovelace 19 yr old enlisted Cleveland Co 3/17/62 C Hanover CH
Priv. Tullius Lowe 19 yr old enlisted Lincoln Co (later QM Sgt)
Priv. Almerein McCraw 20 yr old enlisted Cleveland Co 8/22/61 (later K-Spots)
Priv. James McGinnis 18 yr old enlisted Cleveland Co 8/22/61 **WC 7/3 (died 7/14)**

Priv. Burrell McSwain 34 yr old enlisted Cleveland Co 3/17/62 W-Cedar Mtn **W 7/3**
Priv. John McWebb 22 yr old enlisted Cleveland Co 3/17/62
Priv. Weldon Martin 25 yr old enlisted Cleveland Co 3/17/62
Priv. James Pruett 25 yr old enlisted Cleveland Co 3/17/62
Priv. William Pruett 18 yr old enlisted Cleveland Co 3/17/62 **W-right leg 7/3**
Priv. Willis Webb 21 yr old enlisted Cleveland Co 3/17/62 (later W-left hand Wild)
Priv. James Wilson 23 yr old enlisted Cleveland Co 8/22/61 **W-face & neck 7/3**
Priv. Lewis Yarboro 24 yr old enlisted Cleveland Co 3/17/62 (later W-hand Wild)

July 1 Casualties

None

Company I "*The Yadkin Stars*"

Captain Simon Bohannon 28 yr old enlisted Yadkin Co, NC **W 7/3** (later C-Spots)
1st Lt. Jordan Snow 31 yr old enlisted Yadkin Co 8/13/61 **W-right thigh 7/3** (later C Pickett's Farm)
2nd Lt. Adam Whitman Stone 33 yr old enlisted Surry **W 7/3** (later W-chest Spotsylvania / later Captain)
1st Sgt Cleophus Hendricks 32 yr enlisted Yadkin Co 8/13/61 C Hanover CH **W-left leg C 7/3**
Sgt James Brindle 25 yr old enlisted Yadkin Co 8/13/61
Sgt Daniel Casey 22 yr old enlisted Yadkin Co 8/13/61 W 2nd Manassas C Chan **C 7/3**
Sgt. Greenberry Harding 20 yr old enlisted Yadkin Co 3/8/62 W Gaines Mill W Fred **W-3 times 7/3**
Sgt. Samuel Harding 25 yr old enlisted Yadkin Co 8/13/61 (later K-Ream's Station)
Sgt. John McBride 27 yr old enlisted Yadkin Co 8/13/61 C Hanover CH
Cpl. David Cockerham 32 yr old enlisted Yadkin Co 8/13/61 C New Bern
Cpl. Smith Dozier 21 yr old enlisted Yadkin Co 8/13/61 C Hanover CH
Cpl. Lewis Johnson 23 yr old enlisted Yadkin Co 8/13/61 C New Bern **W 7/3** (later W Spots)
Cpl. William Teach 19 yr old enlisted Yadkin Co 3/8/62
Priv. Pleasant Baity 19 yr old enlisted Yadkin Co 3/8/62 **W 7/3**
Priv. Nathan Benge 20 yr old enlisted Yadkin Co 8/13/61 (later C Spots)
Priv. William Buchannon 22 yr old enlisted Yadkin Co 8/13/61 C Hanover CH **K 7/3**
Priv. Henry Bundy 25 yr old enlisted Yadkin Co 8/13/61 C Hanover C **C 7/3**
Priv. William Carter transferred from Co. B 3/29/63 W Mechanicsville **W 7/3 C 7/4**
Priv. William Chappel enlisted Camp Holmes 11/14/62 (later C Pickett's farm, Va)
Priv. James Chappel 30 yr old enlisted Yadkin Co 8/13/61 (later W-thighs C Wild)
Priv. William Childress 21 yr old enlisted Yadkin Co 8/13/61 C Hanover CH **W 7/3**

Priv. Joshua Danner 20 yr old enlisted Yadkin Co 3/8/62 **W/3 (died 7/4)**
Priv. Nathan Dozier 20 yr old enlisted Yadkin Co 8/13/61 **W 7/3** (later W Jericho Mills)
Priv. Henry Eller 20 yr old enlisted Yadkin Co 8/13/61 C Hanover CH **C 7/3**
Priv. Iredell Evans 20 yr old enlisted Yadkin Co 8/13/61
Priv. Enoch Farris 20 yr old enlisted Yadkin Co 8/13/61 C Hanover CH (later K Wild)
Priv. W. Gross enlisted Yadkin Co 2/14/62
Priv. Daniel Hall 19 yr old enlisted Yadkin Co 3/8/62 **W 7/3 C 7/4**
Priv. Anderson Hayes 25 yr old enlisted Yadkin Co 8/13/61 C Han CH (later W-Spots)
Priv. Thomas Hayes 27 yr old enlisted Yadkin Co 8/13/61
Priv. Bloom Holcomb 18 yr old enlisted Yadkin Co 2/28/63 (later W-Gravel Hill) later Sgt
Priv. Daniel Holcomb 27 yr old enlisted Yadkin Co. 1st Lt. defeated for reelection (died smallpox12/63)
Priv. John Holcomb enlisted Yadkin as 3rd Lt defeated for reelection **W-thigh & hand 7/3 C 7/4**
Priv. Jones Holcomb 21 yr old enlisted Yadkin Co 8/13/61 **K 7/3 by shell on advance**
Priv. Isaac Hutchens 19 yr old enlisted Yadkin Co as substitute 3/8/62 **slight W 7/3**
Priv. Abner Joyce 21 yr old enlisted Yadkin Co 8/13/61 W-Chan **W 7/2**
Priv. Temple McKaughn 19 enlisted Yadkin Co 3/8/62 **W 7/3 (died)**
Priv. Jonas Macokey 19 yr old enlisted Yadkin Co 4/13/63 **K 7/3 by shell on advance**
Priv. Robert Mackie 24 yr old enlisted Caldwell Co. 8/28/62 (later W-right thigh C Spots)
Priv. Thomas Macy 21 yr old enlisted Yadkin Co 8/13/61 (later W Spots) **
Priv. William Macy 26 yr old enlisted Yadkin Co 11/12/61 C Hanover CH
Priv. John Martin 20 yr old enlisted Yadkin Co 8/13/61 C Hanover CH (later C Wild) *
Priv. John H. Martin enlisted Forsyth Co 10/20/62 (later C Fussell's Mill, Va) *
Priv. Elijah Petty 21 yr old enlisted Yadkin Co 8/13/61 (deserted 8/5/63)
Priv. **John Potts** 27 yr old enlisted Yadkin Co 3/8/62 (deserted 7/23/63)
Priv. James Reeves 20 yr old enlisted Yadkin Co 3/8/62
Priv. Evan Reece 20 yr old enlisted Yadkin Co 3/8/62 C Hanover CH **W 7/3**
Priv. George T. Reynolds 19 yr old enlisted Yadkin Co 3/8/62 C Hanover CH **K 7/3**
Priv. Lewis Shores 20 yr old enlisted Yadkin Co 8/13/61 W-Chancellorsville
Priv. John Smith 19 yr old enlisted Yadkin Co 1/6/62
Priv. Tapley Smith 23 yr old enlisted Yadkin Co 8/13/61 W 2nd Manassas W Cedar Mtn
Priv. Little Swaim 20 yr old enlisted Yadkin Co 8/13/61 W-2nd Manassas (later Corp)
Priv. Leander A. Todd 25 yr old enlisted Yadkin Co 3/8/62 (later 3rd Lt.)
Priv. Jacob Waggoner 21 yr old enlisted Yadkin Co 8/13/61 (later W-hip Wild)
Priv. Bartholomew Weatherman 22 yr old enlisted Yadkin Co 8/13/61 (later C Gravel Hill)
Priv. Henry Whitehead 24 yr old enlisted Yadkin Co 3/8/62 (later W Gravel Hill, Va)
Priv.James Wishon 21 yr old enlistedYadkin Co8/13/61 C New Bern (later K Jones farm)
Priv. Samuel Wishon 28 yr old enlisted Yadkin Co 3/8/62 C Hanover CH (deserted 7/15/63) returned (later WC Gravel Hill)

Musician Willie Royal 21 yr old enlisted Yadkin Co 8/13/61 C Hanover CH

July 1 Casualties

None

Company K "*The Stanley Guards*"

Captain John Moody 35 yr old enlisted 9/7/61 sick in Virginia

1st Lt. James Crowell 33 yr old enlisted Stanley Co, NC 9/7/61 W 2nd Manassas (later K Peter)

2nd Lt. Adam Stone 28 yr old enlisted in Stanley Co. **W 7/3** (later W Spots)

3rd Lt Isaac Biles 23 enlisted Stanley Co. 9/7/61 W Chancellorsville **W-right foot 7/3**

Sgt. Daniel Bost 30 yr old enlisted Lenoir Co 4/26/62 W Ox Hill (later 2nd Lt) K-9/5/64

Sgt. Crittenton Furr 23 yr old enlisted Stanly Co 9/7/61 W-Hanover CH (later C-Spots)

Sgt. Henry Page 21 yr old enlisted Stanly Co 9/7/61 W Hanover CH (later C Spots)

Sgt. Doctor Ross 27 yr old enlisted Stanly Co 9/7/61 C Hanover CH **W-right hip 7/3**

Sgt. William Ross 23 yr old enlisted Stanly Co 9/7/61 **W-right arm 7/3**

Cpl. William Biles 28 yr old enlisted Stanly Co 9/7/61 **W-head & side C 7/3**

Cpl. William Bost 20 yr old enlisted New Hanover Co 2/4/62

Cpl. Samuel Forrest 22 yr old enlisted Stanly Co 9/7/61 **W-right arm 7/1**

Cpl. Uriah Hathcock 21 yr old enlisted Stanley Co 3/15/62 W Cedar Mtn

Priv. Eben Burleyson 23 yr old enlisted Stanly Co 3/15/62

Priv. Adam Burris 18 yr old enlisted Stanly Co 9/7/61 W Chan **W-right thigh C 7/3**

Priv. Levi Burris 22 yr old enlisted Stanly Co 9/7/61 **W-left leg C 7/3**

Priv. Wiley Carkier 22 yr old enlisted Stanly Co 9/7/61

Priv. William Carkier 25 yr old enlisted Stanly Co 9/7/61 **W-right arm C 7/3**

Priv. John Coley 17 yr old enlisted 3/2/63 (later K-CH)

Priv. James Crowell 36 yr old enlisted Stanley Co 3/2/63 (later C-Spots)

Priv. William Crowell 36 yr old enlisted Stanley Co 3/2/63 ***W-right leg 7/3 C 7/5***

Priv. David Davis enlisted Stanley Co 9/7/61 W-left leg **C 7/3 (leg amputated)**

Priv. George Davis enlisted Stanley Co 9/7/61 (later C Spots)

Priv. David Eudy 24 yr old enlisted Stanly Co 9/7/61 **WC 7/3**

Priv. Leon Farmer 18 yr old enlisted Stanly Co 9/7/61 C Hanover CH

Priv. John Fesperman 37 yr old enlisted Stanly Co 9/7/61 (later W-left thigh CH)

Priv. Martin Harkey 25 yr old enlisted Stanly Co 3/15/62 W Hanover CH (later W 1864)

Priv. Solomon Harkey 35 yr old enlisted Stanly Co 3/15/62 ***C 7/3***

Priv. Edney Hathcock 19 yr old enlisted Stanly Co 9/7/61 (later C Wild)

Priv. Daniel Hatley 19 yr old enlisted Stanly Co 9/7/61 **W-thigh C 7/3 (Died 7/24)**

Priv. Joseph Hinson 35 yr old enlisted Stanly Co 9/7/61 **W 7/3**

Priv. William Hinson 30 yr old enlisted Stanly Co 3/10/62

Priv. Benjamin Holt 35 yr old enlisted Stanly Co 9/7/61 (later W Spots)

Priv. David Holt 27 yr old enlisted Stanly Co 9/7/61 **K 7/3**
Priv. John Howell 24 yr old enlisted Stanly Co 9/7/61 **W-pelvis C 7/3 (died 7/28)**
Priv. George Kirk 20 yr old enlisted Stanly Co 9/7/61 **K 7/3**
Priv. William Kirk 28 yr old enlisted Stanly Co 9/7/61 C Hanover CH **W-leg 7/3**
Priv. John McClarty 23 yr old enlisted Stanly Co 2/4/62
Priv. Steven McKinley 20 yr old enlisted New Hanover Co 9/7/61 2/4/62 C Hanover CH
Priv. Charles J. McSwain 39 yr old enlisted Stanly Co 9/7/61 (deserted 8/26/63) captured executed
Priv. Archibald Marberry 25 yr old enlisted Stanly Co 9/7/61 (later W Wild)
Priv. Elisha Milton 24 yr old enlisted Stanly Co wheelwright 9/7/61 **C 7/14**
Priv. George Milton 19 yr old enlisted Stanly Co 3/14/62 C Hanover CH W Fred
Priv. Daniel Moody 20 yr old enlisted New Hanover Co 2/4/62 **W-left hand C 7/3**
Priv. Daniel Moose 21 yr old enlisted Stanly Co 3/15/62
Priv. William Morton 22 yr old enlisted Stanly Co 3/10/62 C Hanover CH (later C Spots)
Priv. Simpson Nash 20 yr old enlisted Stanly Co 9/7/61 **WC 7/3**
Priv. John Nelson 32 yr old enlisted Stanly Co 9/27/62 **K 7/3**
Priv. David Rogers 27 yr old enlisted Stanly Co 9/7/61 **W 7/3** (later W-leg Spots)
Priv. George Ross 33 yr old enlisted Stanly Co 3/27/62 C Hanover CH **W-left hip C 7/3**
Priv. Gabriel Russell 19 yr old enlisted Stanly Co 3/18/62 **K 7/3**
Priv. Benjamin Smith 30 yr old enlisted Stanly Co 9/7/61 **W-both knees C 7/3**
Priv. David Smith 25 yr old enlisted Stanly Co 9/7/61
Priv. Edmund Smith 21 yr old enlisted Stanly Co 9/7/61 C Glendale (later C Spots)
Priv. Evan Smith 32 yr old enlisted Stanly Co 9/7/61 C Hanover CH (later C Spots)
Priv. Henry Swaringen 19 yr old enlisted New Hanover Co 9/7/61 C Fred **K 7/3**
Priv. Wilber von **Swaringen** 20 yr old enlisted New Hanover Co 2/4/62 W-neck **C 7/3** (later WC Wilderness)
Priv. Charles White 19 yr old enlisted New Hanover Co 2/4/62 (later Corp)

Musician William Coley 31 yr old enlisted Stanly Co 9/7/61
Musician George Hathcock 28 yr old enlisted Stanly Co 9/7/61 C Hanover CH
Musician Green Hathcock enlisted Stanly Co 3/15/62
Musician James Morton 33 yr old enlisted Stanly Co 9/7/61 (later W Petersburg)

July 1 Casualties

None

THIRTY SEVENTH NORTH CAROLINA REGIMENT

Lt Westley Battle—Co D

Lt. Iowa Royster—Co G

Field & Staff

Colonel William Barbour 29 yr old Rowen Co. elected 6/30/62 W-right arm Chancellorsville absent W

Lieutenant Colonel William Morris 36 yr old enlisted Gastion Co. W-ear Fredericksburg / W-r foot Chancellorsville **C 7/3**

Major Owen Brown 26 yr old enlisted Mecklenburg 9/16/61 appointed 5/29/63 **W 7/3 leg C** (amp) died—hosp 7/24/63 buried Hollywood Cemetery

Adjutant David Oates 18 yr old appointed Adjt. 12/1/62 (later W-neck /C Deep Bottom)

Sergeant Major William Wallace Glenn 26 yr old merchant enlisted Gaston, NC 11/20/61 W Chan. appointed 6/63 (later 2nd Lt)

Surgeon Dr George Trescott 31 yr old appointed 1/28/63

Asst Surgeon Daniel Graham transferred 6/11/63

Chaplin Albert Stough 36 yr old appointed 11/20/61 (resigned 9/63)

Quartermaster Sergeant John Alexander 31 yr old enlisted Mecklenburg 10/22/61 appointed 7/63

Assistant Commissary of Subsistance Miles Pegram (resigned 7/64)

Commissary Sergeant Charles Stowe transferred from 6th NC 6/62 appointed 1/63

Ordinance Sergeant James Abernathy 22 yr old enlisted Gaston Co 10/6/61 appointed 1/63

Drum Major John Carlton 27 yr old enlisted Watauga Co 9/14 appointed 3/1/62

Company A "*Ashe Beauregard Rifles*"

Captain William Alexander transferred 5/63 **C 7/3**

1st Lt Thomas Norwood 18 yr old enlisted Ashe Co. 7/62 **W-breast 7/3 C escaped 7/6**

2nd Lt Willis Whitaker transferred 3/9/63 **W-right arm 7/3 C (amp)**

Sgt William Miller 31 yr old enlisted Iredell Co 8/15/62 **C 7/3**

Sgt George Parsons 20 yr old enlisted Ashe Co 8/27/61 (later 1st Sgt)

Sgt Issac Sherwood (later W/C Spotsylvania)

Corp William Goss18 yr old enlisted Ashe Co 12/28/61 W 2nd Manassas "Badge of Distinction Chancellorsville **C 7/3 or 7/14**

Corp Robert Lane 19 yr old harness maker enlisted Ashe Co 8/27/61 C Hanover CH (later Sgt)

Corp Marshall May 26 yr old enlisted Iredell Co 8/15/62 **C 7/5**

Private Floyd Anderson 29 yr old enlisted Iredel Co. 8/15/62 former Sergt. **W-hand-arm-head 7/3**

Private James Baker 18 yr old enlisted Ashe Co 8/27/61 W 2nd Manassas W Chancellorsville **C 7/3**

Private Farrow Bare 21 yr old enlisted Ashe Co 8/15/62 **C 7/5**

Private Francis Capehart 26 yr old enlisted wake Co. 12/28/61 (later C Spotsylvania)

Private James Childers 49 yr old enlisted Camp Gregg, Va 2/24/63

Private Robert Comach enlistment date not reported (later C Spotsylvania)

Private Peyton Cox 23 yr old enlisted Ashe Co 8/27/61 as Corp. reduced in rank

Private William Davis 23 yr old enlisted Ashe Co 5/1/62 W Chancellorsville **C 7/3**

Private Jacob Eldrich 18 yr old enlisted Ashe Co 5/1/62 C Hanover CH **C 7/3 died**

Private Jackson Ham 23 yr old enlisted Gordonsville, Va 5/1/62 **K 7/3**

Private Rufus Holdaway 31 yr old enlisted Ashe Co 8/27/61 (later Corp & Sgt) **W 7/3**

Private Henry Hughes 18 yr old enlisted Ashe Co. 3/27/62 **WC 7/3 died**

Private Ambrose Liles 21 yr old enlisted Ashe Co 8/27/61

Private Edmond Marlow 23 yr old enlisted Ashe Co 8/27/61 **K 7/3**

Private George May 23 yr old enlisted Iredell Co 8/15/62 as Corp—reduced in rank **C 7/3**

Private Josiah Roten 21 yr old enlisted Irdell Co 8/15/62 **deserted after battle**

Private Richard Perry transferred 1/13/63 (later Sgt K Spotsylvania)

Private John Severt 20 yr old enlisted Ashe Co 8/27/61 **W-head 7/3**

Private James Testerman 25 yr old enlisted Gordonsville, Va 5/1/62 (later Corp)

Private Thomas Trivett 33 yr old enlisted 8/15/62 W-hand Fredericksburg (later Corp K Petersburg)

Private James Vannoy 23 yr old enlisted Ashe Co 8/27/61 W/C Chancellorsville (later W Bethesda Church & Sgt)

July 1 Casualties

None

Company B "*Watauga Marksmen*"

Captain Andrew Critcher absent from Chancellorsville wound

1st Lt. Joseph Todd transferred 5/15/62 W-arm Fredericksburg (later AWOL 10/63)

2nd Lt. Nathaniel Horton transferred 12/1/62 **W-left shoulder—lung C 7/3**

Corp. John Ball 28 yr old enlisted Watauga Co. 9/14/61

1st Sgt Joel Fairchild 28 yr old enlisted Watauga Co. 9/14/61 (Badge of Dist. Chancellorsville) 7/3

Sgt Jesse Story 30 yr old enlisted Watauga Co. 9/14/61 **W 7/3** died Lynchburg, Va 8/1/63

Private Abram Barlow 27 yr old enlisted 8/15/62 **W 7/3** C 7/5

Private John Bebber 27 yr old enlisted Iredell Co 8/15/62 **K 7/3**

Private William Beckham 25 yr old enlisted Iredell Co 8/15/62

Private Joseph Benfield 33 yr old enlisted Watauga Co 9/14/61 W Cedar Mtn deserted 7/22/63

Private Daniel Blevins 27 yr old enlisted Iredell 8/15/62 (later W-thigh Jericho Mills)

Private Felix Calhoun 31 yr old enlisted Iredell Co 8/15/62 **C 7/14**

Private David Campbell 18 yr old enlisted Watauga Co. 8/15/62 W Gaines Mill **C 7/3**-5

Private H.H. Campbell 27 yr old enlisted Iredell Co 8/15/62 later W-leg Spotsylvania—died

Private William Campbell 34 yr old enlisted Iredell Co 8/15/62 (later K Spotsylvania)

Private Cornelius Carlton transferred 2/28/63 **W 7/3** died

Private Lindsay Carlton 25 yr old enlisted Watauga Co. 9/14/61 **W 7/3** (later C Hanover CH)

Private William Cozzens 23 yr old enlisted Watauga Co. 9/14/61 (later C Petersburg)

Private William Danner 31 yr old enlisted Watauga Co. 9/14/61

Private Francis Gortney 27 yr old enlisted Iredell Co 8/15/62 (later W-knee Jericho Mills)

Private Solomon Green 20 yr old enlisted Watauga Co.9/14/61 C Hanover CH / W-left leg Fredericksburg (later K Spots)

Private Edmond Greer 22 yr old enlisted Watauga Co. 9/14/61 W Cedar Mtn **W-neck 7/3 C 7/5**

Private Alexander Hartley 26 yr old enlisted Watauga Co. 9/14/61 W-thigh 2nd Manassas **C 7/3**

Private Azor Hartley 25 yr old enlisted Watauga Co. 9/14/61 W 2nd Manassas (later W Spotsylvania)

Private Finley Hartley 21 yr old enlisted Watauga Co. 9/14/61 W Gaines Mill (discharged 3/64)

Private John Hayes 27 yr old enlisted Watauga Co. 3/15/62 later Sgt / C Spotsylvania

Private John Holdman 32 yr old cabinetmaker enlisted Watauga Co. 9/14/61 deserted 7/22/63

Private James Lowe transferred 10/30/62 W Chancellorsville **C 7/3-5**

Private William Lowe transferred 10/30/62 deserted 7/22/63 returned C Spotsylvania

Private Alfred Miller 29 yr old enlisted Iredell Co. 8/15/62 W-head Fredericksburg **K 7/3**
Private Jesse Miller 20 yr old enlisted Watauga Co. 9/14/61 W-thigh Fredericksburg (later AWOL 9/64)
Private William Nelson 21 yr old enlisted Watauga Co. 9/14/61 W-leg 2nd Manassas **C 7/3-5**
Private Larkin Oxendine 28 yr old enlisted Watauga Co. 9/14/61 (later C Ft Stedman)
Private Franklin Payne 22 yr old enlisted Watauga Co. 9/14/61 C 7/5 *
Private Anderson Stafford 30 yr old enlisted Iredell Co 8/15/62 (later W Ream's Statio)

July 1 Casualties

None

Company C "*Mecklenburg Wide Awakes*"

Captain Lawson Potts transferred 2/28/62 W-thigh 2nd Manassas / W-hip Ox Hill **W-leg 7/3** (later W-wrist Spotsylvania)
1st Lt. John Brown transferred 5/16/63 (later C Spotsylvania)
2nd Lt. William Doherty transferred 6/1/63 **K 7/3**
3rd Lt. Abraham Torrence 25 yr old enlisted Mecklenburg Co. 9/16/61 W-shoulder 2nd Manassas (later W-leg Ream's St.)
1st Sgt Barnabas Johnston later 3rd Lt K Spotsylvania
Sgt James Alexander 27 yr old enlisted Mecklenburg Co. 8/15/62 AWOL 7/15—returned later K Spotsylvania
Sgt Benjamin Brown 21 yr old enlisted Mecklenburg Co. 9/16/61 "Badge of Distinction" Chancellorsville (later 1st Sgt)
Corp. Marcus Dellinger 27 yr old enlisted gaston Co. 8/15/62 W-leg Fredericksburg
Private David Alexander 29 yr old enlisted Mecklenburg Co. 9/16/61 W 2nd Manassas (later Sgt / K North Anna)
Private Thomas L. Alexander 31 yr old enlisted Mecklenburg Co. 9/16/61
Private Thomas R. Alexander 23 yr old enlisted Mecklenburg Co. 9/16/61 W Chancellorsville **W-leg 7/3**
Recorded "Rebel yell" 1935
Private Thomas Armour 25 yr old enlisted Mecklenburg Co. 9/16/61 (AWOL Nov-Dec 1863—returned later W—North Anna)
Private John D. Barnette 32 yr old enlisted Mecklenburg Co. 9/16/61
Private John W Barnette 25 yr old enlisted Mecklenburg Co. 9/16/61
Private James Beard 21 yr old enlisted Mecklenburg Co. 3/1/62 (later Corp W North Anna)
Private Samuel Black 35 yr old enlisted Gaston Co. 8/15/62
Private James Boyles 27 yr old enlisted Mecklenburg Co. 9/16/61 (later AWOL 9/63-10/63 returned)

Private Joseph Benjamin Burleyson 22 yr old enlisted Mecklenburg Co. 9/16/61 W-hand Fredericksburg **WC 7/3**

Private William Caldwell 25 yr old enlisted Mecklenburg Co. 8/15/62 (AWOL 9-10/63 C Spotsylvania)

Private Jacob Carpenter 27 yr old enlisted Gaston Co. 8/15/62 (later W Spotsylvania—died)

Private John Carpenter 21 yr old enlisted Gaston Co. **W-hand & shoulder 7/3**

Private Samuel Christenburg 26 yr old enlisted Mecklenburg Co. 8/15/62 W-right arm 7/3 **C 7/5**

Private James Deaton 22 yr old enlisted Mecklenburg Co. 9/16/61 (later deerted 11/64)

Private John Deaton 19 yr old enlisted Mecklenberg Co. 5/24/62

Private John Goodrum 21 yr old enlisted Mecklenburg Co. 9/16/61 (later W-hand Wilderness)

Private William Harrison 20 yr old enlisted Mecklenburg Co. 9/16/61 (later Corp/Sgt)

Private Richard Holbrooks 22 yr old enlisted Mecklenburg Co. 9/16/61

Private John Houston 29 yr old enlisted Mecklenburg Co. 8/15/62 (later Corp C Ft Gregg)

Private Andrew Howie 33 yr old enlisted Mecklenburg Co. 8/15/62 W-shoulder 7/3

Private Samuel Hucks 23 yr old enlisted Mecklenburg Co. 9/16/61 C Hanover CH **W-shoulder 7/3**

Private James Hunter 23 yr old enlisted Mecklenburg Co. 9/16/61 **W-Abdomen 7/1 C 7/5** died Chester 7/23

Private John Jamison 29 yr old enlisted Mecklenburg Co. 8/15/62

Private Alexander Kelly 25 yr old enlisted Mecklenburg Co. 8/15/62 W-hip & leg 2nd Manassas

Private Thomas Kerns 32 yr old enlisted Mecklenburg Co. 9/16/61 (former 1st Lt of company—resigned 6/1/63—enlisted as Private)

Private Rufus Lentz 24 yr old enlisted Mecklenburg Co. 9/16/61 W-hip 2nd Manassas (later Sgt)

Private John Little 19 yr old enlisted Mecklenburg Co. 9/16/61

Private Columbus McCoy 30 yr old enlisted Mecklenburg Co. 8/15/62 (discharged 3/64 disease)

Private John McCoy 33 yr old enlisted Mecklenburg Co. 9/16/61 **K-7/3**

Private Robert Miller 28 yr old carpenter enlisted Mecklenburg Co. 5/24/62 **C 7/3**

Private John Pettus transferred 11/20/61 as 3rd Lt. W-head Fredericksburg Resigned—enlisted as Private

Private Milus Pippins 33 yr old enlisted Mecklenburg Co. 8/15/62 AWOL 11/63—returned C Spotsylvania

Private Elam Sample 19 yr old enlisted Mecklenburg Co. 8/15/62

Private Thomas Sloane 23 yr old enlisted Mecklenburg Co. 9/16/61

Private William Stearns 28 yr old enlisted Mecklenburg Co. 9/16/61

Private Cephus Stroup 30 yr old enlisted Mecklenburg Co. 8/15/62 C Fredericksburg

Private Hugh Torrence 26 yr old enlisted Mecklenburg Co. 9/16/61 W Gaine's Mill **C 7/3-5**

Private James Torrence enlisted Iredell Co 8/15/62 (later W-head Spotsylvania)

Private William Torrence 22 yr old enlisted Mecklenburg Co. 9/16/61 W-Shepardstown (later Corp W Spotsylvania)

Private James Wagstaff 24 yr old enlisted Mecklenburg Co. 8/15/62 (later W Petersburg)

Private Joseph Walker 31 yr old enlisted Mecklenburg Co. 8/15/62 C Fredericksburg **W-leg 7/3**

Private Joel White 22 yr old enlisted Mecklenburg Co. 9/16/61 (later W-leg Petersburg)

Private Thomas Worsham 33 yr old enlisted Mecklenburg Co. 9/16/61 K-7/3

Hospital Steward William Alexander 23 yr old enlisted 2/1/62 (detailed as Hosp steward)

July 1 Casualties

None

Company D "*North Carolina Defenders*"

Captain Jackson Bost 32 yr old physician enlisted Union Co. 9/18/61 C Hanover CH & WC Chancellorsville **W 7/3** (later Major)

3rd Lt Wesley Lewis Battle transferred 1/13/63 **W-left arm C 7/3** (amp.) died 8/22

1st Sgt George Baucom—Still in hospital with Chancellorsville wounds

Sgt Joseph Griffin 24 yr old enlisted Union Co. 9/16/61 W Glendale W Glendale (later 3rd Lt)

Sgt Ellis Griffin 27 yr old enlisted Union Co. 9/16/61 **K 7/3**

Sgt Thomas Horne 21 yr old enlisted Union Co. 9/16/61 C Hanover CH **W-knee 7/3 C 7/5**

Sgt Malachi Staton 28 yr old enlisted Union Co. 9/16/61 W Chancellorsville **W-shoulder C 7/3 died 8/16**

Corporal Thomas Trull 22 yr old enlisted Union Co. 9/16/61 W Glendale

Corporal George Walters 21 yr old enlisted Union Co. 9/16/61 (later Sgt W Petersburg)

Private John Austin 24 yr old enlisted Union Co. 9/16/61 W-leg Glendale / Badge of Dist Chanc **C 7/3**

Private Jonathan Austin 26 yr old enlisted Union Co. 1/9/62

Private Joseph Austin 19 yr old enlisted Union Co. 9/16/61 (later Corp / Sgt / Sgt Major)

Private Milton Austin 24 yr old enlisted Union Co. 1/9/62 later K Petersburg

Private Ellis Baucom 23 yr old enlisted Union Co. 9/16/61 W Cedar Mtn / W Chancellorsville. **W-head-leg 7/1 C 7/4**

Private James Baucom 24 yr old enlisted Union Co. 9/16/61 later W-left arm Petersburg
Private Henry Bennett 22 yr old enlisted Union Co. 9/16/61 W-hand 2nd Manassas / W Chancellorsville **C 7/5**
Private **Robert Bivens** 32 yr old enlisted Union Co. 9/16/61 **W-face & right leg 7/3**
Private Adam Black 24 yr old enlisted Union Co. 8/12/62 **C 7/3**
Private Ananias Broom 22 yr old enlisted Union Co. 9/16/61
Private Samuel Carelock 19 yr old enlisted Union Co. 9/16/61 C Sharpsburg / C Fredericksburg (later Corp)
Private Daniel Chambers 31 yr old enlisted Union Co. 9/16/61 (later W-thigh Cold Harbor)
Private Lawson Collins 21 yr old enlisted Union Co. 9/16/61 C Hanover CH (later C Wilderness)
Private Thomas Cuthbertson 23 yr old enlisted Union Co. 9/16/61 (later transferred to 53 NC)
Private Kenneth Dees 26 yr old teacher enlisted Union Co. 9/16/61 C Hanover CH (later Corp)
Private Hiram Eacher 28 yr old enlisted Iredell Co. 8/12/62 **W-hip/arm 7/3**
Private Miles Eacher 18 yr old enlisted Gaston Co 3/2/63 **W-right thigh C 7/3**
Private Thomas Eason 28 yr old enlisted Union Co. 9/16/61
Private David Gaddy 22 yr old enlisted Union Co. 9/16/61 **K 7/3**
Private Elijah Gaddy 19 yr old enlisted Gaston Co. 3/20/62 W Cedar Mtn. **W-shoulder 7/1 C 7/5**
Private James Gaddy 24 yr old enlisted Gaston Co. 8/8/62
Private John German 22 yr old enlisted Union Co. 9/16/61 **K 7/3**
Private Thomas Green 35 yr old enlisted Union Co. 8/8/62 **W 7/3 Died 11/19/63**
Private James Griffin 21 yr old enlisted Union Co. 9/16/61 deserted 1/61-returned **K 7/3**
Private William A.Griffin 24 yr old enlisted Union Co 9/16/61 **W 7/3** C 7/5
Private William T. Griffin 20 yr old enlisted Lenoir Co. 4/16/62 W Fredericksburg
Private William F Horne 19 yr old enlisted Lenoir Co. 4/16/62 W 2nd Manassas (later Corp)
Private John Huffstetler 19 yr old enlisted Iredell Co. 8/12/62 (later W-leg Spotsylvania)
Private Dennis Liles 26 yr old enlisted Union Co. 9/16/61 C Hanover CH **W-arm 7/3**
Private Ellis Little 26 yr old enlisted Union Co. 9/16/61 W-lung 7/3 C 7/5 died Gettysburg Hosp
Private Solomon Marsh 26 yr old enlisted Union Co. 9/16/61 **K 7/3**
Private Christopher Mauney 39 yr old enlisted Cleveland Co 3/17/63 **W-head 7/3**
Private Manassas Mauney 21 yr old enlisted Iredel Co 8/12/62 (later W Wilderness / C Gravel Hill)
Private Garrison Medlin 22 yr old enlisted Union Co. 3/5/62 C Fredericksburg (later C Spotsylvania)
Private David Neal 23 yr old enlisted Iredell Co 8/12/62
Private Green Neal 25 yr old enlisted Iredell Co. 8/12/62 **W-arm C 7/3** died
Private Elijah Parker 22 yr old enlisted Union Co. 9/16/61 W-leg 7/3 (later W-thigh North Anna)

Private John Parker 27 yr old enlisted Union Co. 9/16/61 C Harrison Landing (later W-head Jericho Mills)

Private Levi Parker 20 yr old enlisted Union Co. 9/16/61 W Glendale **W-arm/side 7/3**

Private Evan Phillips 18yr old enlisted Union Co. 3/23/63 (later W-thigh Spotsylvania—died)

Private Andrew Price 23 yr old enlisted Union Co. 9/16/61 C Fredericksburg (later W-left leg Wilderness)

Private Henry Rape 28 yr old enlisted Union Co. 9/16/61 W Gaine's Mill (later W-hand-shoulder Gravel Hill)

Private George Sellers 36 yr old enlisted Gaston Co. 3/2/63 AWOL 9/63 to 2/64 returned

Private William Sellers 40 yr old enlisted Gaston Co 3/2/63 **C 5/63**

Private Marcus Simpson 23 yr old enlisted Union Co. 9/16/61 **W-left thigh 7/3 C 7/5**

Private Moses Snider 22 yr old enlisted Union Co 8/8/62

Private David Thomas 19 yr old enlisted Union Co. 9/16/61 W-forehead Fredericksburg

Private Hampton Trull 20 yr old enlisted Union Co. 9/16/61 **C 7/5** later W-leg Gravel Hill, Va (amp) died

Private William Trull 30 yr old enlisted Union Co. 9/16/61 **C 3-5/63** (later C Fussell's Mill, Va

Private Emberry Walters 19 yr old enlisted Union Co 4/16/62 W 2nd—head Manassas

Private Bryant Williams 35 yr old enlisted Union Co. 9/16/61 W-thigh Glendale **C 7/3**

July 1 Casualties

None

Company E *"Watauga Minute Men"*

Captain William Nicholson 25 yr old previously Adjutant promoted 12/1/62 (later W North Anna / K Five Forks)

1st Lt Johiel Eggers 28 yr old enlisted Watauga Co 9/18/61 C Hanover CH (resigned health 1/65)

2nd Lt Edward Nicholson previously Sgt major 19th NC transferred 12/1/62 (later Adjut)

3rd Lt Octavius Wiggins trans from 41st NC 1/12/63 Wounded Chancellorsville absent wounded (later W-thigh North Anna River)

1st Sgt Jordan Phillips 22 yr old enlisted Watauga Co. 9/18/61 C Hanover CH

Sgt Jonathan Hartley 23 yr old enlisted Watauga Co 9/18/61 (later Lt / C Petersburg)

Sgt William Foster 21 yr old enlisted Lenoir Co. 4/12/62 (later reduced in rank 10/63 W Ream's Station)

Sgt Alfred Green 19 yr old enlisted Watauga Co. 9/18/61 C Hanover CH (later W-right arm Gravel Hill, Va)

Sgt James McLain 25 yr old enlisted Iredell Co. W-Chancellorsville **W-left arm / C 7/3**

Corp George Patrick 25 yr old enlisted Watauga Co. 9/18/61 C Hanover CH (later Sgt) **

Corp. Young Swift 29 yr old carpenter enlisted Watauga Co. 9/18/61 W gaine's Mill (later W-breast Spotsylvania)

Private James Adams 30 yr old enlisted Iredell Co 8/15/62

Private John Adams enlisted Iredell Co 8/15/62 (served through 10/64)

Private John Norman Adams 34 enlisted Iredell Co 8/15/62

Private Wellington Adams 34 enlisted Iredell Co 8/15/62 (later Corp / Sgt)

Private Andrew Baird 21 yr old enlisted Watauga Co. 9/18/61 deserted after battle 7/6

Private John Baird 20 yr old enlisted Lenoir Co 4/5/62 **K 7/3**

Private Henry Baker 22 enlisted Iredell Co 8/15/62 (later died Orange CH 12/15/63)

Private Henry S.Baker 24 enlisted Iredell Co 8/15/62 **W-foot / C 7/3 died 8/1/63 Phila hospital buried PNC)**

Private Lemon Beckham 20 enlisted Iredell Co 8/15/62 (later W Ream's Station)

Private James Blair 18 yr old enlisted Lenoir Co 4/5/62 sick 7-12/62 (later C Ft. Stedman)

Private William T Blair 20 yr old enlisted Watauga Co. 9/18/61 C Hanover CH **W 7/3**

Private Alexander Cable 21 yr old enlisted Watauga Co. 9/18/61 (later C Spotsylvania)

Private Cornelius Coffey 23 yr old enlisted Watauga Co. 9/18/61 W 2nd Manassas / Accidentally shot-right foot 7/16/63

Private James Coffey 23 yr old enlisted Watauga Co. 9/18/61 W 2nd Manassas

Private Joseph Coffey 24 yr old enlisted Watauga Co. 9/18/61 (detailed as musician)

Private Maxwell Coon 23 yr old enlisted Iredell Co. 8/12/63 **W-leg 7/3** (later C Fussell's Mill, Va)

Private David Dugger 23 yr old enlisted Watauga Co. 9/18/61 (later C Spotsylvania)

Private Brizilla Eggers 36 yr old enlisted Lenoir Co. 4/12/62 **W-arm 7/3** C Hanover (later Corp/ Sgt)

Private John Farthing 22 yr old enlisted Watauga Co. 9/18/61 **C 7/3-5** (later joined US Service)

Private Cicero Harmon 23 yr old enlisted Watauga Co. 9/18/61 AWOL 7-10/62 returned

Private Bartlett Hartley 22 yr old enlisted Watauga Co. 9/18/61 (later C Wilderness)

Private Michael Lamb enlisted date not reported (later C Bristoe Station)

Private George Lawrence 21 yr old enlisted Watauga Co. 9/18/61 AWOL 7-12/62 (later Corp / C Jericho Mills)

Private John Lusk 20 yr old enlisted Watauga Co 4/12/62 W-head(brusied by shell) Fredericksburg deserted 7/22/63 returned 10/8/63

Private John McLane 35 yr old enlisted Iredell Co. 8/15/62 AWOL 11/62 returned 1/63

Private John Mitchell 25 yr old enlisted Iredell Co.8/15/62 (later W-right shoulder Petersburg)

Private Amos Morrision 25 yr old enlisted Iredell Co. 8/15/62

Private George Munday 22 yr old enlisted Iredell Co. 8/15/62 **K 7/3 (lungs)**

Private William Munday 20 yr old enlisted Iredell Co 8/15/62

Private Jacob Orrant 19 yr old enlisted Camp Holmes 4/5/62 burnt 12/12/62 returned 1/63 (later W Fussell's Mill)

Private Lewis Orrant 19 yr old enlisted Watauga Co. deserted 8/62 returned 3/63 later deserted 7/64

Private Redmond Price enlisted Lenoir Co. 4/5/62 C Hanover CH (later W Spotsylvania)

Private Hugh Reece 25 yr old enlisted Lenoir Co. 4/5/62 C Hanover CH deserted 7/22

Private George Reece 24 yr old carpenter enlisted Watauga Co. 9/18/61 W-foot 2nd Manassas

Private Phillip Shull 21 yr old enlisted Watauga Co. 9/18/61

Private Simon Shull 23 yr old enlisted Watauga Co. 9/18/61 (later Sgt C Spotsylvania)

Private William Strickland 21 yr old enlisted Watauga Co. 9/18/61 **C 7/3** (later joined US service)

Private Sherman Swift 24 yr old enlisted Watauga Co. 9/18/61 deserted 2nd Manassas—returned (later Teamster)

Private Daniel Teague 18 yr old enlisted Camp Gregg, Va 5/10/63 **deserted sick 7/4 C**

Private Moses Teague 21 yr old enlisted Iredell Co 8/15/62 (later W-head Spotsylvania)

Private Harrison Teaser 21 yr old enlisted Watauga Co. 9/18/61 C Hanover CH **W-hip C 7/3**

Private James Webster 26 yr old enlisted Iredell Co 8/15/62 **W-both thighs C 7/3**

Musician Samuel Swift 32 yr old enlisted Watauga Co. 9/18/61

July 1 Casualties

None

Company F *"Western Carolina Stars"*

Captain John Petty 20 yr old enlisted Wilkes Co. W Chancellorsville **W 7/3** (later K Five Forks)

1st Lt. Felix Tankersley—absent wounded from Chancellorsville

2nd Lt. John Forrester 23 yr old enlisted Wilkes Co 9/24/61 W-knee Ox Hill C Fredericksburg **W-leg 7/3 C 7/4**

1st Sgt. Robert Staley 19 yr old enlisted Wilkes Co 9/24/61 W Ox Hill, Va (later ensign)

Sgt. Samuel Ferguson 22 yr old enlisted Wilkes Co 9/24/61 (later 1st Sgt)

Sgt. George Sale 24 yr old enlisted Wilkes Co 9/24/61 slightly wounded 1862 **C 7/3**

Sgt. Thomas Vannoy 21 yr old enlisted Wilkes Co 9/24/61 W-shoulder Fredericksburg

Corp. Robert Gibbs 29 yr old enlisted Wilkes Co 9/24/61 W Chancellorsville **C 7/3**

Corp. William McDaniel 23 yr old enlisted Wilkes Co 9/24/61 W Gaine's Mill **W 7/3 C 7/5** (later Sgt)

Corp. William Mastin 24 yr old enlisted Wilkes Co 9/24/61 W Chancellorsville **C 7/3** (later W Ream's Station)

Corp. George Pearson 28 yr old enlisted Wilkes Co 9/24/61 (later reduced in rank C Ft. Stedman)

Corp. Phillip Walsh 26 yr old enlisted Wilkes Co 9/24/61 W-finger Ox Hill, Va (later Sgt)

Private A.M. Anderson 29 yr old enlisted Wilkes Co 9/24/61 C Hanover CH C Fredericksbrg **W-left leg C 7/3**

Private Joshua Bowman 31 yr old enlisted Iredell Co 8/8/62 **W 7/3 C 7/5** (later W-left arm Petersburg 7/64 K "in breastworks 4/65)

Private Joseph Bumgarner 23 yr old enlisted Wilkes Co 9/24/61 C Hanover CH **C 7/4**

Private Benjamin Clary 21 yr old enlisted Wilkes Co.5/10/62 C Fredericksburg **W 7/3** (later Corp W-Ream's Station)

Private Simon Cline 31 yr old enlisted Iredell Co 8/8/62

Private Henry Crouse 22 yr old enlisted Wilkes Co 9/24/61 ***W-left arm C 7/3***

Private Shubel Crouse 20 yr old enlisted Wilkes Co 9/24/61 ***WC 7/3***

Private Rufus Cuiller 22 yr old enlisted Wilkes Co 9/24/61 **WC 7/3**

Private Nesbet Davis 20 yr old enlisted Wilkes Co 9/24/61 deserted 7/23/63—returned C Wilderness

Private Joseph Edwards 20 yr old enlisted Wilkes Co 5/10/62 (later teamster)

Private Alexander Fox 24 yr old enlisted Iredell Co 8/8/62 W Chancellorsville **C 7/3**

Private David Fox 26 yr old enlisted Iredell Co 8/8/62 W-foot 7/2 deserted 8/27/63

Private Edward Gaultney 24 yr old enlisted Wilkes Co 9/24/61 (hospitalized 11/63—died)

Private Noah Gilbreath 19 yr old enlisted Wilkes Co 9/24/61 W 2nd Manassas (later Corp W-Gravel Hill)

Private Simpson Hanner 21 yr old enlisted Wilkes Co 9/24/61 W-thigh C Hanover CH W-arm 2nd Manassas **C 7/3**

Private Samuel Hawkins 37 yr old enlisted Wilkes Co 9/24/61 (later W-right arm C Spotsylvania)

Private William Hefner 20 yr old enlisted Iredell 8/8/62

Private John Howell 19 yr old enlisted Wilkes Co 9/24/61 C Hanover CH deserted 7/23/63

Private Benjamin Kilby 23 yr old enlisted Wilkes Co 9/24/61 C Hanover CH deserted 7/23/63-returned W Bethesda Church

Private John Kilby 19 yr old enlisted Wilkes Co 9/24/61 deserted 7/23/63—returned (later Corp)

Private William Kilby 36 yr old enlisted Wilkes Co 9/24/61 W 2nd Manassas "Badge of Distinction Chancellorsville **W 7/3**

Private Jesse Luther 19 yr old enlisted Wilkes Co. (later C Darbytown)

Private James Lyon 36 r old enlisted Wilkes Co. 3/15/62 (later W Spotsylvania)

Private William McGee 36 yr old enlisted Wilkes Co 9/24/61 W-head C Fredericksburg (later 3rd Lt)

Private Willis Parks transferred 4/15/62 W-right thigh 2nd Manassas

Private Leonard Parlier 19 yr old enlisted Wilkes Co 9/24/61 W Fredericksburg **C 7/3**

Private John Parsons 28 yr old saddler enlisted Wilkes Co 9/24/61 "finger shot off" Fredericksburg **C 7/3**

Private William Perteete 24 yr old enlisted Wilkes Co 9/24/61 (later Corp)
Private Thomas Pollard 19 yr old enlisted Wilkes Co 9/24/61 W Hanover CH deserted 7/23/63—returned
Private Eli Roberts 25 yr old enlisted Wilkes Co 9/24/61
Private Langley Roberts 22 yr old enlisted Wilkes Co 9/24/61 **C 7/3**
Private Rufus Roberts 28 yr old enlisted Wilkes Co 9/24/61 (later C Spotsylvania)
Private John Rowe 26 yr old enlisted Wilkes Co 9/24/61 **C 7/3**
Private Daniel Spencer 25 yr old enlisted Wilkes Co 9/24/61 (later W-right shoulder North Anna)
Private Joel Thomas 25 yr old enlisted Wilkes Co 9/24/61 W Glendale
Private Elbert Wallace 18 yr old enlisted Wilkes Co 9/24/61 W Hanover CH deserted 7/20/63
Private Matthew Wallace 19 yr old enlisted Wilkes Co 9/24/61 deserted 7/20/63
Private Jesse Wyatt 24 yr old enlisted Wilkes Co 9/24/61 C Harrisons Landing, Va (later died 7/64 sickness)

July 1 Casualties

None

Company G *"Alexander Soldiers"*

This was the skirmish line 7/1

Captain Daniel Hudson 26 yr old enlisted Alexander Co. 10/9/61 (later W-head, right hand & right arm Spotsylvania)
1st Lt. James Pool 22 yr old enlisted Alexander Co. 10/9/61 W Cedar Mtn. W 2nd Manassas **WC 7/3**
3rd Lt. Iowa Michigan Royster transferred 6/5/63 **W 7/3 died 7/13**
1st Sgt. Lawson Robnett 20 yr old enlisted Alexander Co. 10/9/61 **WC 7/3 died 8/9**
Sgt. George Barnes 35 yr old enlisted Alexander Co. 10/9/61 W Chancellorsville **K 7/3**
Sgt. Noah Deal 32 yr old enlisted Iredell Co 8/8/62 (later C Deep Bottom)
Sgt. James Reed 27 yr old enlisted Iredell Co 8/8/62 **W 7/3 C7/5**
Sgt. Jesse Robnett 21 yr old enlisted Alexander Co. 10/9/61 W-both thighs C Hanover CH "Badge of Distinction" Chancellorsville **W-leg C 7/3 (amp) died 7/22**
Sgt John Russell 28 yr old enlisted 4/12/62 **W 7/3 C 7/5**
Corp. Smith Barnes 32 yr old enlisted Alexander Co. 10/9/61 **WC 7/3 died 7/20**
Corp. David Harmon 29 yr old enlisted Iredell Co W-head Fredericksburg (later 1st Sgt W Wilderness)
Corp Elcany Tritt 27 yr old enlisted Alexander Co. 10/9/61 W-arm, 2nd Manassas **WC 7/3** (later joined US Service)

Private William Austin 22 yr old enlisted Lenoir Co 4/8/62 W-shoulder Fredericksburg **C 7/3**

Private Tobias Barnes 20 yr old enlisted Alexander Co. 4/18/62 W-arm Fredericksburg (later Corp & Sgt)

Private William Brookshire 29 yr old enlisted Alexander Co. 10/9/61 (later died disease)

Private Lawson brown 19 yr old enlisted Lenoir Co 3/28/62 **C 7/3**

Private Noah Brown 17 yr ole enlisted Winchester, Va 9/28/62 W Chancellorsville (later W-1864)

Private Emmit Chapman 31 yr old enlisted Winchester, Va 9/26/62 (later C Ft. Stedman)

Private James Wiley Chapman 21 yr old enlisted Alexander Co. 10/9/61 (later Corp & Sgt W 7/64)

Private William Dison 33 yr old enlisted Lenoir Co. 4/8/62 W 7/1 C 7/5

Private Peter Echerd enlisted Iredell Co 8/8/62 (later Sgt C Ft. Stedman)

Private Miles Faulkner 40 yr old enlisted Alexander Co. 10/9/61 **C 7/3**

Private John Fortner 31 yr old enlisted Alexander Co. 10/9/61 **C 7/3**

Private George Hefner 27 yr old enlisted Iredell Co 8/8/62 W 7/62 W Chancellorsville (later Corp)

Private M.E. Hickman 19 yr ole enlisted Lenoir Co. 4/8/62 (died hospital disease 8/64)

Private Thomas Loudermilk 26 yr old enlisted Iredell Co 8/8/62 deserted 8/23—returned (later K Spotsylvania)

Private James Lawrence 35 yr old enlisted Iredell Co 8/8/62 **C 7/3**

Private Wesley Pearce 23 yr old enlisted Alexander Co. 10/9/61 (later died disease 8/11/63)

Private Jesse Pennell 30 yr old enlisted Guilford Co. 10/9/61 (later W-right elbow North Anna)

Private George Pool 25 yr old enlisted Alexander Co. 10/9/61 W-left thigh Gaines Mill

Private Samuel Pope 28 yr old enlisted Lenoir Co 4/30/62 W-back& thigh 2nd Manassas

Private William Smith 33 yr old enlisted Iredell Co 8/8/62 (later died of disease at home)

Private James Snow 41 yr old enlisted Alexander Co. 10/9/61 W-arm Fredericksburg

Private Benjamin Steele 25 yr old enlisted Iredell Co 8/8/62 W-left ankle **C 7/3**

Private Jonas Stine 27 yr old enlisted Iredell Co 8/8/62 (discharged with epilepsy 12/64)

Private James Summers 19 yr old student enlisted Iredell Co. 8/8/62 (discharged sick 4/64)

Private Van Diver Teague 44 yr old enlisted lenir Co 4/9/62 W-left elbow Hanover CH W Ox Hill

Private George Tritt 25 yr old enlisted Alexander Co. 10/9/61 (later Sgt)

Private William tritt enlisted Ireell Co 9/5/62 (later Corp C Deep Bottom, Va)

Private Thomas watts 25 yr old enlisted Alexander Co. 10/9/61 C Hagerstown, Md **W 7/3 C 7/5**

Private Merriman Webster 42 yr old enlisted Alexander Co. 10/9/61 AWOL 1/64—return (later C Fussell's Mill)

Private James Winkler 19 yr old enlisted Lenoir Co 4/30/62 **W 7/3 C 7/5**

Private Thomas Winkler 21 yr old enlisted Lenoir Co. C Hanover CH (later C North Anna)

July 1 Casualties

None

Company H *"Gaston Blues"*

Captain Henry Fite absent wounded from Chancellorsville

2nd Lt. George McKee 20 yr old enlisted 10/6/61 "Badge of Distinction" Chancellorsville (later 1st Lt)

1st Sgt. John Ormand enlisted 8/12/62 **W-arm 7/3** (later 3rd Lt.)

Sgt. James Polk 20 yr old enlisted Gaston Co.10/6/61 **W-breast 7/3** (later 1st Sgt)

Sgt. George Thomasson 28 yr old enlisted Gaston Co.10/6/61 **W-ankle 7/3 C 7/5**

Sgt. Robert Tucker 40 yr old millwright enlisted Gaston Co.10/6/61 C Hanover CH

Corp. Henry Elmore 20 yr old enlisted Gaston Co.10/6/61 (later Sgt)

Corp. Thomas Kendrick enlisted Iredell Co. 8/12/62 W Chancellorsville **W-leg C 7/3** (later Sgt)

Private Featherstone Armstrong 23 yr old enlisted Gaston Co.10/6/61 ***W-head &side 7/3***

Private James Armstrong enlisted Gaston Co. 3/2/63 ***W-leg 7/3***

Private John Armstrong 45 yr old enlisted Gaston Co.10/6/61 W Shepardstown (later Corp)

Private Whitten Armstrong enlisted Gaston Co.3/2/63 (served until 9/63)

Private Henry Beam enlisted Gaston Co 8/12/62 (later W-back & left shoulder Cold Harbor)

Private George Bell 28 yr old enlisted Gaston Co.10/6/61 WC Hanover CH (later Corp K Spotsylvania)

Private James Brimer 22 yr old enlisted Gaston Co.10/6/61 C Fredericksburg

Private Laben Canady 25 yr old enlisted Gaston Co.10/6/61 C Hanover CH (later C Spotsylvania)

Private Samuel Canley enlisted Gaston Co. 5/10/62 (later C Wilderness)

Private Lemuel Clemmer 26 yr old enlisted Gaston Co 8/12/62 W Fredericksburg

Private Lewis Clemmer 41 yr old enlisted Gaston Co.10/6/61 C Hanover CH (later W Jerusalem Plank)

Private Emanuel Cloninger 22 yr old enlisted Gaston Co.10/6/61 C Fredericksburg (later transferred CS Navy)

Private Porter Craig enlisted Iredell Co 8/12/62 **K 7/3**

Private John Craig enlisted Iredell Co. 8/12/62

Private Peter Dellinger enlisted Iredell Co. 8/12/62 **W 7/3 C 7/5**

Private William Dickson enlisted Iredell Co. 8/12/62 **W-arm 7/3**

Private Hugh Ewing 33 yr old enlisted Gaston Co.10/6/61 (discharged sick 2/64)

Private Thomas Furgusson enlistyed Iredell Co 8/12/62

Private Green Ford 20 yr old mechanic enlisted Gaston Co.10/6/61 deserted 7/63 (later captured & shot)

Private William Ford 20 yr old enlisted Gaston Co.10/6/61 (later W-neck Wilderness—Corp)
Private William Good 20 yr old enlisted Gaston Co.10/6/61 **W-left leg 7/3** (later Corp)
Private Samuel Hanna enlisted gaston Co 8/12/62 (later W Jone's farm)
Private Thomas Hanna enlisted Gaston Co 8/12/62
Private Jacob Hovis enlisted Gaston Co 8/12/62 W-head Fredericksburg **W-leg 7/3**
Private John Linebarger enlisted Gaston Co 5/11/62 (later W-breast Spotsylvania)
Private Jonas Linebarger 36 yr old enlisted Gaston Co.10/6/61 (detailed as teamster)
Private John Lynch 47 yr old enlisted Gaston Co.10/6/61 C Hanover CH (discharged overage 10/64)
Private George McAllister enlisted Gaston Co 3/2/63 (died typhoid 7/23/63)
Private John Moore enlisted Gaston Co. 8/12/62 (later W Jerusalem Plank)
Private Amos Morris 19 yr old enlisted Camp Holmes 4/4/62 (later WC Spotsylvania)
Private Levi Morrison enlisted Gaston Co. 5/10/62
Private Eli Paysour 20 yr old enlisted Gaston Co.10/6/61
Private William Ramsey enlisted Gaston Co 3/2/62
Private John Ratchford enlisted Gaston Co 8/12/62 **W-arm & right thigh 7/3 C 7/5**
Private John F Ratchford enlisted Gaston Co 8/12/62 (discharged disability 2/64)
Private Columbus Stroup 19 enlisted Iredell W-right hand Fredericksburg Co. 8/12/62
Private William Stroup enlisted Iredell Co 8/12/62 (later W-foot Spotsylvania)
Private John Thomasson 25 yr old enlisted Gaston Co.10/6/61 (later AWOL 3/64)
Private James Whitesides enlisted Iredell Co. 8/12/62 **W-foot 7/3 C 7/5**
Private John Whitesides enlisted Iredell 8/12/62 (later AWOL 1/64 returned 3/64)
Private Harvey Wright 22 yr old enlisted Gaston Co.10/6/61 C Fredericksburg **K 7/3**

Company I *"Mecklenburg Rifles"*

Captain William Stitt absent wounded—thigh at Chancellorsville
1st Lt. William Ellis transferred 8/1/62 (later Captain)
2nd Lt. Adam Yandle absent wounded-arm Chancellorsville
3rd Lt. John Elms transferred 5/1/63 **K 7/3**
1st Sgt. John Tally 47 yr old carpenter enlisted Mecklenburg 10/22/61 W-ear 2nd Manassas "badge of distinction" Chancellorsville (later K Spotsylvania)
Sgt. Thomas Brown 22 yr old enlisted Mecklenburg 10/22/61 (later 1st Sgt W Fussell's Mill)
Sgt. James Flow 43 yr old enlisted Mecklenburg 10/22/61 C Harrison's Landing
Sgt. Albert Montgomery 21 yr old enlisted Mecklenburg Co 1/11/62 W-leg **C 7/3**
Corp. Marshall McCoy 18 yr old enlisted Mecklenburg 1/11/61 **W 7/3** (later reduced to private)
Corp. John Nicholson transferred 1/1/62 W-neck Hanover CH (later W Jerusalem Plank)
Private James Alexander 20 yr old enlisted Mecklenburg Co. 11/15/61

Private John Alexander 31 yr old enlisted Mecklenburg 10/22/61 (later QM)
Private John Barnhill 22 yr old enlisted Mecklenburg 10/22/61
Private Samuel Blythe 28 yr old enlisted Mecklenburg 10/22/61 C Fredericksburg (later C Gravel Hill, Va)
Private James Brown 19 yr old enlisted Mecklenburg 5/21/62 **K 7/3**
Private Levi Carpenter 33 yr old enlisted Iredell Co. 8/15/62 (later C Gravel Hill, Va)
Private Marcus Carpenter 25 yr old enlisted Iredell Co. 8/145/62 (later C Spotsylvania)
Private James Clark 19 yr old enlisted Iredell Co. 8/15/62 W-neck Fredericksburg W Chancellorsville **C 7/7**
Private John Clark 35 yr old enlisted Iredell Co. 8/15/62 W-Fredericksburg
Private William Cross 36 yr old enlisted 3/11/62 W-Malvern Hill (later AWOL 1864)
Private John Edwards 28 yr old enlisted Mecklenburg 1/9/62 W Sharpsburg (later W-left hand Wilderness Corp)
Private Andrew Hargett 24 yr old enlisted Mecklenburg 12/1/61 (later Sgt)
Private John Hunsacker 19 yr old enlisted Mecklenburg 10/22/61 W Sharpsburg
Private George King 25 yr old enlisted Iredell Co. 8/15/62
Private George Kissiah 22 yr old enlisted Mecklenburg 10/22/61 W Glendale
Private Thomas Kissiah 24 yr old enlisted Mecklenburg 10/22/61
Private William Kissiah 27 yr old enlisted Mecklenburg 10/22/61 W Hanover CH W-groin 2nd Manassas
Private George Kistler 22 yr old enlisted Mecklenburg 10/22/61 W-shoulder Glendale **C 7/14**
Private Solomon Kizer 21 yr old enlisted Mecklenburg 8/15/62 W Chancellorsville WC 7/5
Private William Lawing 30 yr old enlisted Iredell Co 8/15/62 **W 7/3** K Petersburg "bomb shell"
Private James McCall 21 yr old enlisted Mecklenburg 11/20/61 C Fredericksburg (later Corp)
Private David McCord 32 yr old enlisted Iredell Co 8/15/62
Private Isaac McGee 27 yr old enlisted 8/15/62 C Spotsylvania
Private Dallas Maxwell 20 yr old enlisted Mecklenburg 10/22/61 W Chancellorsville W-right leg 7/3
Private Caleb Mooney 34 yr old enlisted Iredell Co. 8/15/62 W Chancellorsville **C 7/3**
Private Colman Mullis 46 yr old enlisted Mecklenburg Co. C Harrisons Landing (later died disease 7/64)
Private James Orr 28 yr old enlisted Mecklenburg Co 3/11/62 W-knee Glendale (later Corp)
Private Caleb Paysour 27 yr old enlisted Iredell Co. 8/15/62 C Fredericksburg (later C Wilderness)
Private Franklin Raffield 28 yr old enlisted Iredell Co. 8/15/62 (later W-left hand Jerusalem Plank)
Private Robert Sharpe 24 yr old enlisted Camp Mangum 12/24/61 WC Fredericksburg W-leg **C 7/3**

Private Jacob Shoe 22 yr old enlisted Mecklenburg 10/22/61 W-both arms C Hanover CH W Chancellorsville **WC 7/3**

Private Ira Simpson 24 yr old enlisted Mecklenburg 10/22/61 C 7/14 (later joined US Service)

Private Franklin Smith 26 yr old enlisted Mecklenburg Co. C Fredericksburg W-head 7/3

Private Andrew Spears 30 yr old enlisted Mecklenburg 10/22/61

Private James Taggart 21 yr old enlisted Mecklenburg 10/22/61 W Hanover CH **K 7/3**

Private Robert Todd 27 yr old enlisted Iredell Co. 8/15/62

Private Stephen Turner 25 yr old enlisted Mecklenburg 10/22/61 (later Corp)

Private William Woodall 25 yr old enlisted Mecklenburg Co 8/15/62 C 7/14

Teamster John Patterson 25 yr old enlisted Mecklenburg 10/22/61 W-left hand 10/22/61 C Winchester

July 1 Casualties

None

Company K *"Alleghany Tigers"*

Captain William Fetter 23 yr old enlisted Alleghany Co. 8/1/62 W-thigh 2nd Manassas (later Court-martialed 7/63)

1st Lt. Thomas Armstrong transferred 8/15/62 (later Captain w-chest Fussell Mill, Va)

2nd Lt. William Mickle transferred 5/3/63 **K 7/3**

Sgt. William Ross 20 yr old enlistyed Alleghany Co 9/15/61 W-face Fredericksburg (later 2nd Lt W-right hip Five Forks)

Sgt. Eli Blevins 29 yr old enlisted Idedell Co. 8/15/62 (later W Jericho Mills, Va)

Sgt. James Johnston 28 yr old enlisted Allegany Co. 9/15/62 W Hanover CH **W 7/3** (later 1st Sgt)

Sgt. Huston Waddell 25 yr old enlisted Allegany Co. 9/15/62 deserted 7/4

Corp. Wells Blevins 20 yr old enlisted Iredell Co 8/15/62 (later Sgt)

Corp.Calvin Caudill 23 yr old enlisted Idrell Co. C 7/5 (later Sgt)

Corp. George Duncan 22 yr old enlisted Alleghany Co 9/15/62 **C 7/3** (later C New Market, Va)

Corp. James Jones 22 yr old enlisted Lenoir Co 9/15/62 W-thigh New Bern W—Chancellorsville Co.

Corp. Levi Jones 20 yr old enlisted Allegany Co. 9/15/62 deserted 7/26/62—returned deserted 7/4/63-returned

Corp. William Sturgill 20 yr old enlisted Allegany Co. 9/15/61

Corp. Jesse Williams 21 yr old enlisted Allegany Co. 9/15/62

Private Marion Beamon enlisted 8/15/62 **W-left hand 7/3**

Private Alfred Blevins 30 yr old enlisted Iredell Co 8/15/62 ***W-right thigh*** *7/3 W-left hand Jericho Mills, Va—died*

Private Ephraim Blevins 19 yr old enlisted Iredell Co 8/15/62 ***C 7/3***

Private Francis Blevins 20 yr old enlisted Iredell Co. 20 yr old enlisted Iredell Co.8/15/62 W-foot Chancellorsville C 7/5

Private Isham Blevins 32 yr old enlisted Iredell Co 8/15/62 ***K 7/3***

Private Robert Blevins 33 yr old enlisted Iredell Co. 8/15/62 AWOL 9/63 (later C Wilderness)

Private Wesley Blevins 22 yr old enlisted Iredell Co. 8/15/62 **W 7/3**

Private William Caudill 39 yr old enlisted Alleghany Co. **W-left leg 7/3** (later C Wilderness)

Private Martin Cox 22 yr old enlisted Iredell Co. 8/15/62 (later Corp & Sgt)

Private Daniel Douglas 39 yr old enlisted Alleghany Co.

Private Jesse Duncan 20 yr old enlisted Allegany Co. 9/15/62 W Fredericksburg **C 7/3**

Private John Grubb 32 yr old enlisted Alleghany Co. C Hanover CH ***W 7/3 C 7/5***

Private Ira Halsey 20 yr old enlisted Allegany Co. 9/15/62 W Cedar Mtn. (later Corp & Sgt)

Private James Hensley 21 yr old enlisted Allegany Co. 9/15/62 W Fredericksburg **K 7/3**

Private Samuel Landreth 34 yr old enlisted Iredell Co. 8/15/62 C Fredericksburg **W 7/3** (later C Spotsylvania)

Private Jacob McGrady 29 yr old enlisted Iredell Co 8/15/62 W-side Fredericksburg **W-eye 7/3—died 7/14**

Private Obadiah Mendenhall 20 yr old enlisted Allegany Co. 9/15/62 **W7/3 C 7/5**

Private Franklin Parsons 26 yr old enlisted Allegany Co. 9/15/62 C Fredericksburg W Chancellorsville **C 7/3**

Private Zachariah Phillips 20 yr old enlisted Allegany Co. 9/15/62 W-neck Fredericksburg **W 7/3 C 7/5**

Private John Pugh 36 yr old enlisted Allegany Co. 9/15/62 W-left hip 7/3 C 7/5 (later W-right arm Spotsylvania)

Private William Saunders 30 yr old enlisted Iredell Co. 8/15/62 **W-back & right shoulder 7/3**

Private William Smithdeal 35 yr old enlisted Allegany Co. 9/15/62 **C 7/5**

Private Madison Stamper 25 yr old enlisted Allegany Co. 9/15/62 **W-left ankle C 7/3**

Private William Steadham 26 yr old enlisted Iredell Co 9/15/62 (later C Wilderness)

Private John Tilley 25 yr old enlisted Iredell Co. 8/15/62 W-head Fredericksburg **WC 7/3**

Private Henry Tredway 20 yr old enlisted Allegany Co. 9/15/61 W-face Fredericksburg **W 7/3 C 7/5**

Private Bower Walters 30 yr old enlisted Iredell Co. 8/15/62 AWOL 9/63 to 2/64

Private Andrew Weaver 20 yr old enlisted Iredell Co. 8/15/62

Private William Western enlisted Iredell Co. 8/15/62 (later hospitalized Richmond, Va 11/28/63)
Private Killis Williams 20 yr old enlisted Lenoir Co. **WC 7/3 died 8/19**
Private Thomas Wiggins (later 3rd Lt. W-right thigh Spotsylvania W-Jones Farm, Va)

July 1 Casualties

None

SEVENTH NORTH CAROLINA REGIMENT

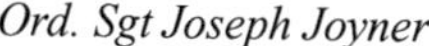

Ord. Sgt Joseph Joyner

Private Richard Fleming Co F

Field & Staff

Colonel Edward Haywood 32 yr old enlited Wake City promoted 6/27/62 W 2nd Manassas W Chancellorsville Absent W

Lt. Colonel William Lee Davidson 38 yr old Charlotte merchant promoted 5/3/63 W Chancellorsville Absent W

Major John McLeod Turner 23 yr old enlisted Rowen Co. Captain Co F until promoted **in command 7/3 W abdomen—C 7/3**

Adjutant John Williams Pearson appt Liberty Mills 6/22/63 mustered 7/8/63 (later W-knee & thigh—Spotsylvania)

Sergeant Major William Robinson 27 yr old enlisted Alexander Co. 7/29/61 C Hanover CH appointed 3/1/63

Quartermaster Sergeant Julius Boyd appointed 3/26/63 (later Brigade QM)

Assistant Quartermaster John Hughes 33 yr old enlisted Craven Co.

Surgeon Wesley Campbell 33 yr old enlistyed Iredell Co. 11/6/61

Assistant Surgeon Jesse Fraley appointed 2/17/63

Hospital Steward Edwin McAulay **C 7/5 with wounded**

Ordinance Sergeant **Joseph Joyner** enlisted 2/25/62 into Co C W—2nd Manassas appointed 11/10/62

Acting Ensign Samuel Van Pelt promoted from Co H 7/3/63

Brigade Butcher Private William Rowland Co B

Company A *"Iredell & Allegheny Counties"*

Captain John Knox 23 yr old student enlisted Mecklenburg Co. 5/16/61 W Fredericksburg (later C Wilderness)

1st Lt. Pinkney Carlton transferred 2/13/63 W Chancellorsville (later W-left Achilles tendon Cuilpepper, Va)

Sgt. Leander Connelly 21 yr old enlisted Mecklenburg 5/29/61 (later transferred)

Sgt. J.P. Marshall 26 yr old enlisted Mecklenburg Co.5/29/61 **K 7/3**

Sgt Joseph Millsaps 24 yr old enlisted Mecklenburg Co.5/29/61 **W (left ankle) 7/3 C 7/5** (later W Fussell's Mill)

Corp. Henry Alexander 24 yr old enlisted Lenoir Co 2/26/62 **K 7/3**

Corp. Robert Barnes Robert Barnes 24 yr old enlisted Mecklenburg Co. 6/1/61 (later Sgt)

Corp. William Millstead 23 yr old enlisted Mecklenburg Co.5/29/61 "Badge of Distinction Chancellorsville"

Corp. Abner Morrison 29 yr old enlisted Lenoir Co 2/26/62 W Chancellorsvile **C 7/3**

Corp. W.G. Morrison **C 7/3** (later sick with erysipelas—exchanged 3/17/64)

Private Benjamin Austin 20 yr old enlisted Mecklenburg Co. 5/29/61

Private William Baker 25 yr old enlisted Alamance Co. 8/17/61 **W (ankles) / C 7/3**

Private John Beard 23 yr old enlisted Iredell Co. 8/20/62 **C 7/3**

Private Jacob Benfield 50 yr old enlisted Mecklenbrg Co. 5/29/61 **W right thigh 7/3 / C Greencastle, Pa**

Private Hugh Bentley 26 yr old enlisted Mecklenburg Co. 5/29/62 **W left thigh 7/3 C 7/5**

Private Abner Brown 21 yr old enlisted Lenoir Co. 2/26/62 **W slightly 7/3** (later W Spotsylvania)

Private Bedford Brown 23 yr old enlisted Mecklenburg Co. 5/29/61 (later W-11/63)

Private George Brown 26 yr old enlisted Mecklenburg Co. 5/29/61 **W 7/3-C 7/5**

Private J.W. Broyhill 21 yr old enlisted Mecklenburg Co. 4/9/62 (later died disease 7/64)

Private William Caldwell 19 yr old enlisted Mecklenburg Co. 9/4/61 (later K Fussell's Mill)

Private Burrell Connolly 20 yr old enlisted Iredell Co 5/29/61

Private J.H. Connolly 25 yr old enlisted Iredell Co. 8/20/62 **W 7/3 C 7/5**

Private Silas Dagerheart 21 yr old enlisted Iredell Co 5/29/61 W 1862 (later W Wilderness)

Private David Dean (later joined US Service) deserted **C 7/5**

Private George Echard 20 yr old enlisted Mecklenburg Co 5/29/61 (later deserted 7/22/64)

Private James Eidson 28 yr old enlisted Iredell Co 2/26/62 (later K Wilderness)

Private John Fincannon 33 yr old enlisted Iredell Co 5/29/61 **K 7/3**

Private Josiah Gaultney 23 yr old enlisted Mecklenburg Co 5/29/61 C Hanover CH later **C 7/23**
Private Leander Guy 29 yr old enlisted Lenoir Co **K 7/3**
Private A.A. Howerton 23 yr old enlisted Camp Holmes 5/15/63 (served until 10/64)
Private John Isonhour 24 yr old enlisted Iredell Co. 8/20/62 **C 7/3**
Private Joseph Knox 21 yr old enlisted Camp Holmes 5/29/63 **K 7/3**
Private William May 22 yr old enlisted Mecklenburg Co.5/29/61 **W-elbow 7/3** (later QM department)
Private James Miller 22 yr old enlisted Mecklenburg Co.5/29/61 (later W Petersburg)
Private Thomas Miller 21 yr old enlisted Iredell Co. 8/8/62 (later discharged medical)
Private George Millsaps 17 yr old enlisted Iredell Co. (later W-left leg Well's Farm, Va)
Private Jeremiah Moore 27 yr old enlisted Mecklenburg Co.5/29/61 C Chancellorsville **W-leg C 7/3**
Private John Moore 25 yr old enlisted Mecklenburg Co.5/29/61 (later W 1/64)
Private Julius Moore 33 yr old enlisted Mecklenburg Co.5/29/61 C Winchester, Va **W 7/3**
Private Elam Morrison 34 yr old enlisted Lenoir Co. 2/26/62
Private R.A. Morrison 22 yr old enlisted Lenoir Co. 2/26/62 W 6/62 **W-left arm 7/3 (amp)**
Private William Oliphfant 21 yr old enlisted Alamance Co. 6/15/61 (present through 6/64)
Private M. Wilson Price enlisted 11/1/61 W Glendale (later Corp & Sgt)
Private James Robertson 21 yr old enlisted Mecklenburg Co 5/29/61 (later Corp)
Private William N. Sumers 23 yr old enlisted Lenoir Co. 2/26/62 ***W 7/3***
Private William R. Sumers 21 yr old enlisted Lenoir Co 2/26/62 ***K 7/3***
Private George Watts 27 yr old carpenter enlisted Mecklenburg Co.5/29/61 (later Corp)
Private William Watts 22 yr old enlisted Mecklenburg Co.5/29/61
Private T.M White 21 yr old enlisted Lenoir Co. 2/26/62

July 1 Casualties—1

Private Noah Baker 20 yr old enlisted Alamance Co 6/16/61 **W 7/1 C 7/5**

Company B "*Cabarrus County*"

Captain James Harris 23 yr old enlisted Cabarrus Co. 6/7/61
1st Lt. William Harris 21 yr old enlisted Cabarrus Co. 6/7/61
2nd Lt. Albert Bizzell transferred 3/14/63 (later W-right lung Jone's Farm, Va)
Sgt. W.G. Lawyer no record of enlistment W right thigh C 7/1-7/3
Sgt. William Sawyer 20 yr old enlisted Cabarrus Co. 6/10/61 "Badge of Distinction Chancellorsville" **W-right thigh C 7/3**
Sgt. Robert Shearer 32 yr old enlisted Cabarrus Co. 6/12/61 (discharged 2/64)

Corp. Francis Hartsell 23 yr old enlisted Cabarrus Co. 7/12/61 W Shepardstown, Va (later Sgt)

Corp Jackson Linker 24 yr old enlisted Cabarrus Co. 6/7/61 **W right leg 7/3 C 7/5**

Private Calvin Allman 21 yr old enlisted Cabarrus Co. 6/20/61

Private Green Allman 25 yr old enlisted Cabarrus Co. 6/23/61 (later W-right arm Petersburg)

Private Leonard Allman 30 yr old enlisted Cabarrus Co 3/1/62 **C 7/14**

Private Nathaniel Allman 24 yr old enlisted Cabarrus Co. 7/2/61 **W-leg 7/3**

Private John Barbra 23 yr old enlisted Cabarrus Co 3/8/62 **C 7/6** Williamsport

Private Julius Bost 19 yr old enlisted Cabarrus Co. 6/7/61 C Sharpsburg (later W Ream's Station)

Private Nelson Bost 31 yr old enlisted Cabarrus Co. 3/13/62 (later K Ream's Station)

Private M.A. Carriker enlisted Cabarrus Co **C 7/5**

Private Martin Carriker 21 yr old enlisted Cabarrus Co. 6/7/61 W-thigh 62 **C 7/3** (later K Spotsylvania)

Private W.M. Cleaner **C 7/3** no further records

Private Julius Cole 20 yr old enlisted Cabarrus Co. 8/17/61 (later deserted 11/7/64)

Private Levi Crimminger 36 yr old enlisted Cabarrus Co. 6/10/61 **WC 7/3** (later joined US Service)

Private Enoch Deaton 25 yr old enlisted Cabarrus Co. 3/11/62 (served through 10/64)

Private Allison Furr 25 yr old enlisted Cabarrus Co. 7/3/61 **C 7/3**

Private Israel Furr 27 yr old enlisted Cabarrus Co. 6/21/61 (later W-left hand Ream's Station)

Private Moses Furr 25 yr old enlisted Cabarrus Co. 6/27/61 (later W Ream's Station)

Private George Garman 19 yr old enlisted Cabarrus Co. 7/16/61 C Fredericksburg 5/63

Private David Herlocker 29 yr old enlisted Cabarrus Co. 6/15/61 C Hanover CH **W 7/3**

Private Edward Hill 21 yr old enlisted Cabarrus Co. 6/22/61

Private William Joyner 22 yr old enlisted Cabarrus Co. 2/1/62 **C 7/3** (later W 7/64)

Private William Linker 22 yr old enlisted Cabarrus Co. 3/6/62 W 7/62 (later discharged 12/63)

Private William Maxwell 20 yr old enlisted Cabarrus Co. 6/24/61 C Hanover CH **C 7/5** (later W-right leg Deep Bottom)

Private John Morton 42 yr old enlisted Cabarrus Co. 6/7/61 W Ox Hill, Va (later C Broad Creek)

Private Solomon Plumer 31 yr old enlisted Cabarrus Co. 6/7/61 **W right side C 7/3**

Private Ingram Reid 20 yr old enlisted Cabarrus Co. 6/26/61

Private David Shoe 36 yr old enlisted Cabarrus Co. 3/8/62 W Ox Hill, Va

Private Levi Shoe 20 yr old enlisted Cabarrus Co. 6/11/61 W-Fredericksburg (later K Spotsylvania)

Private Francis Smith 30 yr old enlisted Cabarrus Co. 5/13/62 (later Corp C Spotsylvania)

Private William Starns 23 yr old enlisted Cabarrus Co. 6/10/61

Private Jesse Still 28 yr old enlisted Cabarrus Co. 6/27/61 (later C Jericho Mills)

Private William Still 21 yr old enlisted Cabarrus Co. 6/29/61 **C 7/12 Hagerstown** (later W 8/64)

Private Franklin Turner 19 yr old enlisted Cabarrus Co. 6/11/61 (later W Ream's Station)

Private John Vanderburg 23 yr old enlisted Cabarrus Co. 6/20/61 (later W-hand Ream's Station)

Private John Vickers 29 yr old enlisted Cabarrus Co. 7/13/61 (later Corp)

Teamster John Boss on detail from 5/1/63 through 9/20/63

Private William Rowland 23 yr old enlisted Cabarrus Co. 6/25/61 (Brigade Butcher)

July 1 Casualties

None

Company C "*New Hanover County*"

1st Lt. Walter MacRae transferred 3/17/63 **W-left thigh 7/3** (later Captain)

2nd Lt. Richard Quince 25 yr old enlisted New Hanover Co 7/21/61 (later 1st Lt K Gravel Hill, Va)

2nd Lt. Pasqual Agostini 24 yr old merchant born Philadelphia Pa enlisted 7/26/61 **W-arm & left foot 7/3**

Sgt. John C Cameron 32 yr old enlisted New Hanover Co. 7/8/61 (served through 10/64)

Sgt. McKenzie Culbreth 24 yr old 7/15/61 W Sharpsburg **C 7/14** (later W-Petersburg)

Sgt. Lazarus Peavy 26 yr old enlisted New Hanover Co. 6/24/61 W-left arm Ox Hill 9/1/62 (later 1st Sgt)

Sgt Joseph Phipps 24 yr old enlisted New Hanover Co. 7/16/61 (later K Wilderness)

Corp. Calvin Smith 32 yr old enlisted Cumberland Co 7/8/61 (later Sgt W-left thigh Well's Farm)

Corp. Richard Smith 29 yr old enlisted 7/20/61 W-left leg Sharpsburg (served through 10/64)

Corp. Phillip Strickland 20 yr old enlisted New Hanover Co.7/16/61 "Badge of Distinction" Chancellorsville (later WC Gravel Hill)

Private Nathan Adams enlisted New Hanover Co 7/21/61 (later C Wilderness)

Private Wiley Atkinson enlisted Shephardsville 2/3/62 (later C Wilderness)

Private Handy Bass 25 yr old enlisted Shephardsville 12/21/61

Private Leonard Bass 28 yr old enlisted New Hanover Co.12/21/61 W Gaine's Mill (later K Wilderness)

Private Levi Bass 26 yr old enlisted New Hanover Co. 7/20 /61 (later W Spotsylvania)

Private William Blackman 26 yr old enlisted New Hanover Co. 3/13/62 deserted Sharpsburg **C 7/5**

Private William Blanchard **"gave up" 7/3** no further records

Private Kenyon Brock 27 yr old enlisted New Hanover Co. 7/13/61 (later W Gravel Hill)

Private Thomas Bullard 25 yr old enlisted New Hanover Co. 7/3/61 W Gaine's Mill (died 12/19/64)

Private Daniel Cameron enlisted 3/1/63 **C 7/3**

Private Thomas Cameron 26 yr old enlisted Harnett Co 6/29/61 W-hand 1/15/63 **C 7/3**

Private Alexander Carter 20 yr old cooper enlisted Cumberland Co 6/20/61 W Gaine's Mill (later Corp & Sgt)

Private Ollen Coates 28 yr old enlisted New Hanover Co. 7/20/61 (served through 10/64)

Private James Gainey 20 yr old enlisted New Hanover Co. 6/24/61 (later W-hand 5/5/64

Private Morris Gainey 30 yr old enlisted New Hanover Co. 6/10/61 (later W-left hand Wilderness)

Private Dillon Gaster 28 yr old enlisted New Hanover Co. 6/26/61 as Corp—reduced C 2nd Manassas

Private Riley Holder 20 yr old enlisted New Hanover Co. 7/8/61 W Gaine's Mill **W 7/3-C 7/5**

Private William Hudson 26 yr old enlisted New Hanover Co 7/20/61 (later Corp)

Private Retus Huffman 23 yr old enlisted Cumberland Co. 7/14/61 W-foot 2nd Manassas (later W—6/22/64)

Private M.F. Iddings 22 yr old enlisted wake Co. 5/15/63 (later W Ream's Station)

Private Fleet Johnson 31 yr old enlisted Cumberland Co. 6/18/61 W Fredericksburg (later Corp K Gravel Hill, Va)

Private John Mathews 42 yr old enlisted Cumberland Co. 6/26/61 C Hanover CH (later C Gravel Hill, Va)

Private James Morse 21 yr old enlisted Carteret Co. 1/25/62 (served through 10/64)

Private William Parker 31 yr old enlisted Wake Co. 8/20/62 (later detailed at Nitre Bureau)

Private John Patterson 31 yr old enlisted Wake Co. 8/20.62 (later W-left arm North Anna)

Private William Register 19 yr old substitute enlisted 3/4/62 (later C Wilderness)

Private John Shinn 23 yr old enlisted wake Co. 8/20/62 (died 4/18/64)

Private Daniel Strickland 40 yr old enlisted New Hanover Co. 7/16/61 W Ox Hill, Va (later C Fussell's Mill)

Private William Wilson 20 yr old enlisted New Hanover Co. 7/20 /61 **C 7/3**

Teamster Archibald Douglas 21 yr old enlisted Harnett Co 6/29/61

Teamster William McGarar 33 yr old well digger enlisted 6/24/61 W Gaine's Mill

July 1 Casualties

None

Company D *"Mecklenburg County" "auslanders"*

Captain Timothy Cahill 25 yr old enlisted Mecklenburg Co 6/24/61 **W right leg 7/3 C 7/5** (amp)

1st Lt Thomas Mulloy 22 yr old clerk enlisted Charleston, SC 8/3/61 (later W-right hip Spotsylvania)

2nd Lt Patrick Kirby 35 yr old bookkeeper enlisted Savannah, Ga 8/20/61 W Gaine's Mill

Corporal George Bennett Irish born 30 yr old enlisted Mecklenburg 7/25/61

Corporal Joseph Davidson 18 yr old enlisted Camp Gregg 3/1/63

Corporal Andrew Holshouser 31 yr old enlisted Iredell Co. 8/2/62 (served through 10/64)

Private Richard Anderson 25 yr old enlisted Camp Holmes 5/17/63 (later C Wilderness)

Sgt. Patrick Beglin Irish born 25 yr old enlisted Savannah **C during retreat** (later joined US Service)

Private George Bolton 25 yr old Philadelphia born harness maker enlisted Mecklenburg Co. 7/5/61 (later W Wilderness)

Private Patrick Brannon Irish born 22 yr old tinner enlisted Charleston, SC C Hanover CH **C 7/3**

Private Nathan Brennan enlisted Mecklenburg Co. **C 7/4**

Private John Brinkle 21 yr old enlisted Davidson Co. W-hands&face (later W Wilderness)

Private William Cashion 33 yr old enlisted Iredell Co. 8/2/62 (later W Wilderness)

Private James Clarke Irish born 26 yr old enlisted Charleston, SC 7/17/61 **C 7/3** (later joined US service)

Private Hiram Dobson 29 yr old enlisted Iredell Co. 8/8/62 (died disease 12/63)

Private John Eller 35 yr old enlisted Iredell Co. 8/18/62 (later W-left leg Wilderness)

Private Samuel Goodman 34 yr old enlisted Iredell Co. 8/18/62 (later C Wilderness)

Private Francis Horrace German born 22 yr old enlisted 7/12/61 W-head Fredericksburg **W C 7/3**

Private David Howell 21 yr old enlisted Mecklenburg 7/25/61 W Gaine's Mill (later W Spotsylvania)

Private James Howell 21 yr old enlisted Mecklenburg 6/29/61 W 6/62

Private John Howell 22 yr old enlisted Mecklenburg Co. (later W-Wilderness)

Private Alexander Kanapaux 20 yr old enlisted Charleston 7/17/61 C Hanover CH **K 7/3**

Private Lawrence Kelly Brooklyn born 20 yr old enlisted Savannah, Ga **W-right hand C 7/3**

Private William Kistler 27 yr old enlisted Iredell Co. 8/4/62 **K 7/3**

Private John Meredith 34 yr old enlisted Camp Holmes 5/9/63 (later C Wilderness)

Private E.A. Nantz 29 yr old enlisted Iredell Co. 8/2/62 (later W-right hand Wilderness)

Private William Varker 20 yr old miner enlisted Mecklenburg Co. 7/15/61 **W 7/3 C 7/5**

Private James Vincent English born 31 yr old miner enlisted Guilford Co (later C Wilderness)

July 1 Casualties

None

Company E "*Nash County*"

1st Lt Joshua Vick 20 yr old enlisted Nash Co. 5/25/61 C Winchester, Va **W left knee 7/3** (later Captain)

2nd Lt William Deans 24 yr old enlisted Wilson Co. 5/25/61 (later 1st Lt W Petersburg)

1st Sgt John Ballentine 28 yr old enlisted Wilson Co. 5/25/61 W Fredericksburg (later 2nd Lt W Wilderness)

Sgt. George Bains 22 yr old enlisted Alamance Co. 8/3/61 W 2nd Manassas (later 1st Sgt W Reams Station)

Sgt. Bennett Brantley 21 yr old enlisted Wilson Co. 5/25/61 (died 1/24/64 cause unknown)

Sgt John Winborn 24 yr old enlisted 6/1/62 (served through 10/64)

Corp Henderson Bains 23 yr old enlisted Wilson Co. 5/25/61 W Glendale C Chan **W-right hip 7/3 died**

Corp James Batchelor 26 yr old enlisted Wilson Co. 5/25/61 (later C Wilderness)

Private John Bottoms 26 yr old enlisted Wilson Co. 8/3/61 **deserted Hagerstown 7/6**

Private Micah Brantley 23 yr old enlisted Wilson Co. 5/25/61 W-thigh Gaine's Mill (present through 10/64)

Private James Brown **C 7/5** no further records

Private John Brown 29 yr old enlisted Northampton Co. 6/10/61 deserted Richmond 8/1463

Private Isaac Daniel 23 yr old enlisted Wilson Co. 5/25/61 W New Bern (later Corp & Sgt)

Private Dempsey Deans 27 yr old enlisted Wilson Co. 5/25/61 W—Glendale deserted—returned (C Wilderness)

Private Berry Earp 23 yr old enlisted Wilson Co. 5/27/61 (later W Wilderness)

Private Calvin Earp 22 yr old enlisted Wilson Co. 5/25/61 **W 7/3 died 7/15/63**

Private John Eatmon 21 yr old enlisted Gordonsville, Va 5/25/61 WGaines Mill (served through 11/64)

Private Wilson Eatmon 20 yr old enlisted Craven Co. 3/12/62 (later W Petersburg)
Private Elisha Eure 24 yr old enlisted Camp Advance WC-Malvern Hill/ "Badge of Distinction" Chancellorsville
Private George T.W. Finch 21 yr old enlisted Nash Co. 6/1/61 **W-left hip C 7/14** (later W Petersburg)
Private Adam Flowers 21yr old enlisted Alamance Co. W 2nd Manassas
Private Lane Hayman enlisted Wilson Co. (later 2nd Lt. K Wilderness)
Privae Neverson Hendrick 21 yr old enlisted Gordonsville, Va 5/24/62 W-Gaines Mill
Private Kinchen Liles 20 yr old enlisted 6/1/61 W-Glendale **C 7/3**
Private Wesley Liles 23 yr old enlisted Wilson Co. 5/25/61 W-knee Glendale W right thigh **C 7/3**
Private James Murray 47 W right thigh **C 7/3 W 7/3**
Private Joseph Murray 25 yr old enlisted Northampton Co. 6/10/61
Private Mark Page 23 yr old enlisted Wilson Co. 5/25/61 (late W Deep Bottom, Va)
Private Jesse Pope 39 yr old enlisted Wilson Co. **W 7/14—died**
Private Dolison Rice 22 yr old enlisted Wilson Co. 5/25/61 (later W-right knee Ream's Station)
Private William Saunders 22 yr old enlisted Wilson Co. 5/25/61
Private Mark Taylor 23 yr old enlisted Wilson Co. 5/25/61 (later K Spotsylvania)
Private Nathan Williams 41 yr old enlisted Craven Co. 3/12/62 W-2nd Manassas (later W Wilderness)
Private William Williams 21 yr old enlisted Lenoir Co (later Sgt)
Private Spencer Wood 25 yr old enlisted Wilson Co. 5/25/61 (dropped from rolls 12/31/63)

Teamster Griffin Lewis 21 yr old enlisted Northampton Co. 6/1/61
Teamster Hillsman Lewis 25 yr old enlisted Northampton Co. 6/1/61
Teamster Kinchen Lewis 23 yr old enlisted Northampton Co. 6/1/61

July 1 Casualties

None

Company F "*Rowan County*"

1st Lt Daniel Kinney 26 yr old enlisted Davidson Co. 6/29/61 promoted to Sgt 11/1/62 for "gallant conduct" **C 7/3**
Sgt Solomon Ayers 23 yr old enlisted Rowen Co. 6/21/61 promoted Sgt 2/1/63 for "gallantry" (later K Spotsylvania))
Sgt Calvin Reid 22 yr old enlisted Rowen Co. 6/15/61 **W left leg C 7/3** (amp) died 8/13/63

Corp Daniel Cauble 21 yr old enlisted Rowen Co. 6/13/61 W Gaine's Mill W-Cold Harbor—died

Private Howell Bassinger enlisted Iredell Co. 8/20/62 **W-foot C 7/3** (later W Spotsylvania)

Private Godfrey Bischerer 51 yr old enlisted Davidson Co. 2/22/62 C Hanover CH **C 7/5**

Private Joseph Blackburn 24 yr old enlisted Rowen Co. 6/15/61 W Ox Hill **W-right thigh 7/3 C Funkstown, Md 7/12**

Private John Blue enlisted Richmond Co. 8/6/6 (later 2nd Lt)

Private James Christenbury 20 yr old saddler enlisted Alamance Co. (later W Spotsylvania)

Private Joel Cranford 22 yr old enlisted Davidson Co. 3/2/62 (served through 10/64)

Private Wilburn Cranford 22 yr old enlisted Davidson Co. 6/30/61 **WC 7/3**

Private Silas Davis enlisted 5/1/63 **W-foot 7/3**

Private David DeBerry 19 yr old enlisted Rowen Co. 6/15/61 **C 7/3** (later joined US service)

Private Daniel Doby 37 yr old enlisted Davidson Co. 3/8/62 W Ox Hill, Va

Private Lorenzo Earnheardt 20 yr old enlisted Rowen Co. 6/13/61 **C 7/3**

Private D. Esterberry **C 7/3** "no further records"

Private **Richard Fleming** 22 yr old enlisted Iredell Co. 8/20/62 **W/C 7/3** (later W Wilderness)

Private William Fry 25 yr old enlisted Alamance Co. 6/15/61 W Fredericksburg (later Corp)

Private Robert Hall enlisted Davidson Co 3/1/62 W Ox Hill, Va. (present through 10/64)

Private George Hooks 27 yr old enlisted Rowen Co. 6/5/61 **W 7/3** (died of disease 5/64)

Private James C Johnson 23 yr old enlisted Rowen Co. 7/1/61 as Corp—reduced in rank **C 7/10**

Private James F Johnson 20 yr old enlisted Rowen Co.6/15/61 W Ox Hill, Va. **K 7/3**

Private John W Johnson 20 yr old bricklayer enlisted Rowen Co. 7/8/61 (later W Wilderness)

Private Gray Jordan 33 yr old enlisted Craven Co. **C 7/14**

Private Jeremiah Loftin 18 yr old enlisted Rowan Co 4/1/63 **W-thigh 7/3 C 7/5**

Private Giles Owens 24 yr old enlisted Rowen Co. 7/3/61 C Harrison's landing & Fredericksburg 5/3/63 **W-7/3**

Private David Phillips 19 yr old enlisted Rowen Co. 6/15/61 W Ox Hill, Va. **left as nurse C 7/7/63**

Private George Quillman 24 yr old enlisted Rowen Co. 6/27/61 **W-leg C 7/3**

Private John Pearson enlisted Rowen Co. (later 2nd Lt K Jone's Farm, Va.)

Private William Redwine 29 yr old enlisted Alamance 6/29/61 **W-right thigh & right foot 7/3**

Private William R Redwine 25 yr old enlisted Rowen Co. 7/1/61 (later C North Anna)
Private Jesse Reid enlisted Iredell Co. 8/20/62 (later promoted to Sgt 9/1/64)
Private George Richards 20 yr old enlisted Rowen Co. 6/27/61 (later K Wilderness)
Private Edward Ridenhour 24 yr old enlisted Rowen Co.6/15/61 **W-right arm 7/3**
Private Leonard Sills 26 yr old enlisted Davidson Co. 7/7/61 **W-right thigh C 7/3**
Private William Sills enlisted Davidson Co. W-jaw Fredericksburg (later Corporal)
Private John Surratt 31 yr old enlisted Davidson Co. 8/9/61 **W-right leg 7/3**
Private George Swink enlisted Rowan Co. 3/26/62 W-head C Sharpsburg deserted on retreat
Private William Turner 23 yr old enlisted Davidson Co. W-Glendale **W leg C 7/3**
Private Lewis Watkins 21 yr old enlisted Rowen Co. 6/4/61 W-hand Fredericksburg
Private John Wilkinson 32 yr old enlisted Rowen Co. 8/10/61 **C 7/3**
Private Edwin Williams 20 yr old enlisted Rowen Co. 6/15/61 "Badge of Distinction—Chancellorsville"
Private Eliphalet Worley 38 yr old blacksmith enlisted Davidson Co. C Fredericksburg **C 7/3**

Drummer John Rowe 20 yr old enlisted Rowen Co. 7/8/61
Musician William B Howard 36 yr old enlisted Chatham Co. 8/14/61 **K 7/3 during bombardment**
Ambulance Corps James Fry 26 yr old enlisted 3/11/62
Teamster Charles Kennerly 22 yr old enlisted Rowen Co. 6/15/61
Teamster James Knox 30 yr old enlisted Rowen Co. 6/15/61
Teamster Turner Pinkston 21 yr old enlisted Rowen Co. 6/21/61

July 1 Casualties

None

Company G "*The Wake Rangers*"

Captain Andrew Hill transferred 1/20/62 **W-ankle & right arm 7/3**
1nd Lt Simpson Weatherspoon transferred 6/17/61 W 2nd Manassas **C 7/3**
2nd Lt William Weatherspoon transferred 6/1/61
1st Sgt Fabius Haywood Jones 32 yr old enlisted Wake Co. 6/26/61 **WC 7/3 died**
Sgt William Herndon 22 yr old enlisted Wake Co. 6/26/61 W 6/62 (later wounded Cold harbor)
Sgt William Jenkins 34 yr old enlisted Wake Co. 6/26/61 **WC 7/63 died**
Sgt Paschal McGeehee 32 yr old enlisted Wake Co 7/8/61 W-Glendale C Fred **C 7/3**
Sgt William Henry McGhee 34 yr old enlisted Wake Co. 6/26/61 **C 7/3** (later 1st Sgt)
Corporal Mathews Edwards 23 21 yr old enlisted Wake Co. 7/3/61 (later Sgt K Spots)

Corporal Thomas Hopson 33 yr old enlisted Wake Co. 7/8/61 (later W—arm Wild)
Corporal Ira Smith 27 yr old enlisted Wake Co. 7/8/61 (Badge of Distinction at Chancellorsville) (later reduced)
Corporal James Sorrell 23 yr old enlisted Wake Co. 6/26/61 W Chancellorsville
Private John Barber **C 7/5** exchanged 5/3/64 retired to Invalid Corps
Private Richard Blackwelder 31 yr old enlisted Cararrus Co.
Private Thomas Bowden 21 yr old enlisted Wake Co. 6/26/61 (later W Richmond)
Private Benjamin Browning 22 21 yr old enlisted Wake Co. 6/26/61 (later W Fussell Mill)
Private Valentine Cook 29 yr old enlisted Cabarrus Co. (later W Petersburg)
Private Walter Crabtree 21 yr old enlisted Wake Co. 6/26/61 (later C Wilderness)
Private John Cress 21 yr old enlisted Cabarrus Co. (later C Wilderness)
Private Sidney Crocker 22 21 yr old enlisted Wake Co. 7/1/61 (transferred 8/63)
Private A. Daniel **C 7/5** exchanged 9/22/64
Private Willis Edwards 26 yr old enlisted Wake Co. 6/26/61 **left as nurse C 7/5** (later Corp)
Private Joseph Gilbert 25 yr old enlisted Wake Co. 6/26/61 (later Corp W-left arm Petersburg))
Private John Harward 21 yr old enlisted Wake Co. 3/26/62 **C 7/3**
Private Asel Hedgecock 30 yr old enlisted Montgomery Co. 5/17/63 **K 7/3**
Private Daniel Hedgecock 28 enlisted Montgomery Co 5/17/63 **W left leg 7/3**
Private Chesley Herndon 23 yr old enlisted Wake Co. 6/26/61 **C 7/3**
Private James Hicks 21 yr old enlisted Wake Co. 7/8/61 (later W Petersburg)
Private Rufus Hicks 25 yr old enlisted Wake Co. 7/8/61
Private D Hitchcock **C 7/3** paroled 8/1/63 no further records
Private William Howard 36 yr old enlisted Wake Co. 8/14/61 **K 7/3**
Private George King 24 yr old enlisted Wake Co 7/1/61 **K 7/3**
Private Solomon Ladd 22 yr old enlisted Wake Co. 7/8/61 **C 7/3**
Private Daniel Littles 25 yr old enlisted Cabarrus Co. (later W Spots Died 6/10/64)
Private William Lumley 29 yr old enlisted Wake Co. 7/8/61 (later C Deep Bottom)
Private E.A. McGee **C 7/3** no other records
Private Obediah McGhee 19 yr old enlisted Wake Co. 7/8/61 (later W Spots)
Private William Marshall 21 yr old enlisted Wake Co. 7/15/61 **WC 7/3**
Private William Medlin 20 yr old enlisted Wake Co. 7/28/61 (later W-head Jericho Mills, Va)
Private John Megehee 27 yr old enlisted Wake Co. 6/26/61 **W 7/3 C 7/5 (died 8/1)**
Private Wesley Mills 30 yr old enlisted Wake Co. 7/8/61 **W right thigh C 7/3** (later W Wilderness)
Private Wiley Pollard 22 yr old enlisted Wake Co. 6/26/61 C Sharpsburg **K 7/3**
Private Martin Propst 31 yr old enlisted Cabarrus 8/20/62 (later W-left thigh Wilderness)
Private Mathias Propst 29 yr old enlisted Cabaruus Co. **K 7/3**
Private Gaston Rigsbee 24 yr old enlisted Wake Co. 7/8/61 (later W Fussell's Mill)

Private Jacob Sattenfield 29 yr old enlisted Wake Co. 3/9/62 (later C Wilderness)
Private James Tilley 23 yr old enlisted Wake Co.7/8/61 W 2nd Manassas
Private Thomas Upchurch 23 yr old enlisted Wake Co. 7/8/61 **C 7/3**
Private Louis Weatherspoon 18 yr old enlisted Wake Co. 7/1/61 (later Sgt. W Spotsylvania)
Private Davis Welsh 27 yr old enlisted Montgomery Co 5/17/63 **W-left hand 7/3**
Private Merrit Yates 32 yr old mason enlisted Wake Co. 7/8/61 (later Corp / C Wilderness)

Teamster William Barbee 24 yr old enlisted wake Co. 6/21/61 W 6/62 W Fredericksburg
Teamster Willliam H Howard 24 yr old enlisted Wake Co. 6/26 /61
Teamster Richard Wamble 36 yr old enlisted Wake Co. 7/24/61

July 1 Casualties

None

Company H "*Cabarrus County*"

Captain James Harris 22 yr old enlisted Cabarrus Co. (later W-groin Jone's Farm promoted major)
1st Lt John Alexander 30 yr old enlisted Camp Mason (later W-right thigh Cold Harbor)
2nd Lt James Stafford 23 yr old enlisted Cabarrus Co. 7/20/61 (later W-left arm Spotsvania)
1st Sgt Thomas Erwin 36 yr old enlisted Cabarrus Co. 7/20/61 **K 7/3**
Sgt Shaw W White 22 yr old enlisted Cabarrus Co. (W Gaines Mill—W Petersburg)
Sgt William White 24 enlisted Cabarrus Co.7/20/61 (later K Jones Farm)
Corp Daniel Alexander 24 yr old enlisted Cabarrus Co. 7/20/61 (later promoted to 1st Sgt W-leg C Deep Bottom)
Corp Samuel Van Pelt transferred 7/62—acting Ensign at Pickett's Charge (later 1st Lt)
Corp David White 20 yr old enlisted Cabarrus Co. 7/20/61 **W 7/3-C 7/ 5** (later K Spotsylvania)
Private Adolphus Alexander 23 yr old enlisted Cabarrus Co. 7/29/61 **WC 7/3 died 9/7/63**
Private Dionysius Alexander 21 yr old enlisted Cabarrus Co. 7/29/61 **K 7/3**
Private Samuel Alexander 22 yr old enlisted Cabarrus Co. 7/20/61
Private Cyrus Archer 24 yr old enlisted Cabarrus Co. 7/20/61 (later W-leftarm Petersburg)
Private Felix Archibald 29 yr old enlisted Cabarrus Co. 3/12/62 (served through 10/64)
Private Asa Barnhardt 29 yr old enlisted Cabarrus Co. 7/20/61 (served through 10/64)
Private Loche Barnhardt 22 yr old enlisted Cabarrus Co. 7/20/61 W-Fredericksburg (later died of disease)
Private John Blackwelder 19 yr old enlisted Cabarrus Co. 7/25/61 **W 7/3 C 7/5**

Private Caleb Bost 20 yr old enlisted Cabarrus Co. 7/20/61 as butcher (later W Deep Bottom)

Private James Carter 33 yr old enlisted Cabarrus Co. 7/20/61 W-Fredericksburg **W-left leg 7/3 C 7/5**

Private Jeremiah Clouts 23 yr old enlisted Union Co. (served through 10/64)

Private Moses Dease 20 yr old enlisted 2/21/62 (served through 10/64)

Private John Dorton 23 yr old enlisted Cabarrus Co. 7/20/61

Private Miles Harris 27 yr old enlisted Cabarrus Co.7/20/61as Corporal—demoted (later W Spotsylvania)

Private Robert Holbrooks 34 yr old enlisted Cabarrus Co. 3/6/62 (served through 10/64)

Private William Hudson 18 yr old enlisted Cabarrus Co. 7/20/61 (later W-left thigh Gravel Hill)

Private Cicero McCarhern 20 yr old enlisted Cabarrus Co. 7/20/61 (later K Gravel Hill)

Private Daniel McEachearn 20yr old enlisted Cabarrus Co. 7/20/61 (W Gaines Mill)

Private James Martin 18 yr old enlisted Cabarrus Co. 7/20/61 (later C Deep Bottom)

Private Benjamin Moore 21 yr old enlisted Cabarrus Co.8/9/61 (later killed Gravel Hill)

Private Joseph Moore 22 yr old enlisted Lenoir Co. 4/26/62

Private Leroy Morrison 19 yr old enlisted Cabarrus Co. 12/11/61 (later W Petersburg)

Private Samuel Morrison 22 yr old enlisted Cabarrus Co. 8/5/61 W Glendale ***W 7/3*** *(later Corp)*

Private Andrew Myers 30 yr old enlisted Union Co. 2/22/62 **C 7/3**

Private William Nicholson 18 yr old enlisted Cabarrus Co. 2/24/62 W Gaines Mill (later C Wilderness)

Private Balis Parrish 20 yr old enlisted Cabarrus Co. 8/3/61 (later W Petersburg)

Private David Perviance 18 yr old enlisted Cabarrus Co. 2/18/62 **C 7/3—died**

Private Isaac Pharr 26 yr old enlisted Cabarrus Co. 7/20/61 W Gaines Mill (later Corp)

Private Samuel Phillips 24 yr old enlisted Cabarrus Co. 7/20/61 **C 7/12 Funkstown, Md**

Private Henry Polk 23 yr old enlisted Cabarrus Co.7/21/61

Private John Rodgers 31 yr old enlisted Union Co. **C 7/3**

Private James Spears 18 yr old enlisted Cabarrus Co. 9/6/61 as drummer—reduced 3/63 (later W Cold Harbor)

Private Charles Taylor 33 yr old enlisted Cabarrus Co. 3/1/62 C Fredericksburg (later W Jerusalem Plank)

Private Richard White 21 yr old enlisted Cabarrus Co. 7/20/61 (later K Spotsylvania)

Private David Winecoff 30 yr old enlisted Cabarrus Co 8/17/61 **C 7/3**

Private D.R. Winker **C 7/3** no further records

Private John York 19 yr old enlisted Cabarrus Co. 3/2/63

Teamster William Demarcus 22 yr old enlisted Cabarrus Co. 8/5/61 (also cook)

July 1 Casualties

None

Company I "*Iredell County*"

Captain James Mcauley wounded at Chancellorsville absent in hospital

Brevet 2nd Lt. DeWitt Smith 35 yr old teacher enlisted Iredell Co 7/22/61 **C 7/3**

1st Sgt George Morrow 23 yr old enlisted a Corporal Mecklenburg, NC 7/22/61 **W 7/3**

Sgt George Kistler 26 yr old enlisted Iredell Co 2/24/62

Corporal James Beaty 23 yr old enlisted Iredell Co 7/22/61 W Gaines Mill (later W Petersburg—died)

Corporal John Brown 25 yr old enlisted 7/22/61 **W left arm C 7/3**

Corporal William Cook 29 yr old enlisted 2/24/62 (later Sgt C Wilderness)

Corporal James Knox 20 yr old enlisted Iredell Co 7/22/61 W Gaines Mill

Private David Alley 22 yr old enlisted 7/22/61 W Ox Hill **W 7/3 C 7/5**

Private Robert Atwell 23 yr old enlisted Iredell Co. 2/24/62 (later W Ream's Station)

Private William Beam 18 yr old enlisted Iredell Co 2/26/62 (later W-left leg Cold Harbor)

Private Malvin Cavin 21 yr old enlisted Iredell Co 7/22/61 (serviced through 10/64)

Private Forrest Cornelius 31 yr old enlisted Iredell Co. **K 7/3**

Private William Deaton 23 yr old enlisted Iredell Co 7/22/61

Private James Freeman 18 yr old enlisted Iredell Co. W-right hand Gaines Mill

Private Asbury McDaniel 37 yr old enlisted Iredell Co. 2/24/62 **W left Ankle C 7/3** (later W Petersburg)

Private John McNeely 23 yr old enlisted Iredell 2/24/62 (later Sgt Major)

Private William McNeely 25 yr old enlisted Iredell Co 7/22/61 (later K Spotsylvania)

Private John Means 30 yr old enlisted Iredell Co 7/22/61 (later Corp)

Private Matthew Nesbit 21 yr old enlisted Iredell Co 7/22/61

Private Samuel Overcash 20 yr old enlisted Iredell Co 2/26/62 **K 7/3**

Private William Overcash 25 yr old enlisted Iredell Co 7/22/61 (present through 10/64)

Private Peter Parker 34 yr old enlisted Iredell Co. 2/26/62 **K 7/3**

Private Daniel Perry 24 yr old enlisted Iredell Co. 8/20/62 W-head Fredericksburg (later C Wilderness)

Private Lloyd Perry 29 yr old enlisted Iredell Co. C Sharpsburg (later W Wilderness)

Private Thomas Purdie 18 yr old enlisted Camp Graham 3/3/62 award badge of distinction Chancellorsville **W-right arm 7/3**

Private William Rose 37 yr old enlisted 7/22/61 **WC 7/3 died 7/20**

Private Robert Steel 29 yr old enlisted Iredell Co 7/22/61 **W-left leg C 7/3 (amp) died—8/27**

Private Joseph Templeton 25 yr old enlisted Iredell Co 6/27/61 W-right leg Gaines Mill

Private Joseph Templeton 21 yr old enlisted Iredell Co. W Hanover CH **C 7/3**

Private Julius Templeton 21yr old enlisted Iredell Co. 8/20/62 (served through 10/64)

Private David Williams 35 yr old enlisted Iredell Co 8/21/61 **C 7/3**

Private Francis Wilson 24 yr old enlisted Iredell Co 7/22/61 W Gaine's Mill **W-leg & right arm 7/3**

Private James Wilson 19 yr old mechanic enlisted Iredell Co 7/22/61 W Gaines Mill (later W Wells Farm, Va)

Private Benjamin Young 24 yr old enlisted Iredell Co. 8/20/62 (served through 10/64)

Pioneer William Mills 29 yr old enlisted Iredell Co. 2/26/62 C-Sharpsburg detailed to pioneer corps

Teamster Robert W McKay 23 yr old enlisted Iredell Co 7/22/61

Teamster Robert Brown 20 yr old enlisted Iredell Co 7/22/61 (later W-hand Wilderness)

Ambulance Driver James Creswell 25 yr old enlisted Iredell Co 7/22/61 W Gaine's Mill (detailed as driver)

July 1 Casualties

None

Company K "*Alexander County*"

Captain Nathan Pool 32 yr old enlisted Alexander Co. 5/16/61 W Fredericksburg (absent sick after 9/63)

1st Lt. Robert Teague 34 yr old enlisted Iredell Co. 6/18/61 W Gaine's Mill

2nd Lt Arthur Walker enlisted Alexander Co 7/11/61 W Malvern Hill "Badge of Distinction" Chancellorsville **W-gut & breast 7/3**

2nd Lt. William Haywood transferred 3/63 (later K Wilderness)

1st Sgt. Issac McCurdy 20 yr old enlisted Alexander Co. 7/11/61 Badge of Distinction-Chancellorsville (later K Spotsylvania)

Sgt. Orren Burgess 25 yr old enlisted Alexander Co. 7/11/61 (later 1st Sgt)

Sgt. McAmy Kirkpatrick 25 yr old enlisted Cabarrus Co. (later K Fussell Mill, Va)

Sgt. Daniel McIntosh 22 yr old enlisted Alexander Co. 7/11/61 **C 7/3**

Sgt. Francis Query 39 yr old enlisted Alexander Co. 7/4/61 W-Gaine's Mill (later K Spotsylvania)

Sgt. William Simmons 21 yr old enlisted Alexander Co 7/11/61 **K 7/3**

Corp. William Anderson 20 yr old enlisted Alamance 8/19/61 (later reduced in rank)

Corp. John Teague 31 yr old enlisted Alexander Co. 7/23/61 C Harrison Landing W Sharpsburg (later C Wilderness)

Private Leroy Alexander 21 yr old enlisted Iredell Co 8/12/62 **K 7/3**
Private Samuel Austin 24 yr old enlisted Alexander Co. 7/23/62 (later W Spotsylvania)
Private Timothy Brooks enlisted Camp Graham 12/21/61 W Gaine's Mill **C 7/3**
Private Alfred Bumgarner 39 yr old enlisted Alexander Co. 7/20/61 C Sharpsburg **W 7/3**
Private James Burgess 28 yr old enlisted Alexander Co. 7/11/61
Private Joseph A. Campbell 25 yr old enlisted 2/18/62 **WC 7/3 died Phila hospital buried PNC)**
Private Benjamin Childers 26 yr old enlisted Iredell Co. 8/16/62 (later W-hand Jones Farm)
Private Peter Childers 22 yr old enlisted Iredell Co 8/16/62 (later W Petersburg
Private Hosea Christopher 20 yr old enlisted Alexander Co. **C 7/3** (later W Well's Farm)
Private James Davis 16 yr old enlisted Iredell Co. 8/18/62 W Shepardstown, Va
Private William Deal 20 yr old enlisted Alexander Co. 8/11/61 **W 7/3**
Private William Elder 26 yr old enlisted Iredell Co. 8/9/62 (later C Wilderness)
Private George Hoke 31 yr old enlisted Iredell Co 2/19/62 W Fredericksburg) **WC 7/3**
Private Leroy Holsclaw 22 yr old enlisted Alexander Co. 7/23/61
Private John Howard 22 yr old enlisted wake Co 5/1/63 **C 7/3**
Private Washington Ingold 18 yr old enlisted Wake Co. 5/1/63 **C 7/3**
Private Hugh Lamberth 28 yr old enlisted Alexander Co. 7/29/61 **K 7/3**
Private Jesse Levi Laws 20 yr old enlisted Alexander Co. 7/25/61 (later arrested 8/64)
Private John McClelland 25 yr old enlisted Alexander Co. 3/29/62 W Malvern Hill (later W Wilderness)
Private George Patterson 26 yr old enlisted Iredell Co. 8/8/62 **W head-right cheek 7/3**
Private John Patterson 28 yr old enlisted Alexander Co. 2/26/62 (later Corp W-head/left arm right hand Wilderness))
Private William Patterson 28 yr old enlisted Alexander Co. 7/29/61 **WC 7/3**
Private Levi Phillips 25 yr old enlisted Alexander Co 2/26/62 **K 7/3**
Private Jesse Reid 21 yr old enlisted Alexander Co. 7/11/61 W Glendale
Private Lewis Smith 27 yr old enlisted Alexander Co. 7/11/61 **W 7/3**
Private Jeremiah Staley 28 yr old enlisted Wake Co. 5/1/63
Private Thomas Staley 21 yr old enlisted Wake Co. 5/1/63 **WC 7/3 died 7/22**
Private James Thompson 23 yr old enlisted Alexander Co. 7/11/61 **K 7/3**

Teamster Jacob McClelland 23 yr old enlisted Alexander Co. 7/11/61
Teamster Henry McLain 29 yr old enlisted Alexander Co. 7/11/61 (served through 10/64)

July 1 Casualties

None

Fourth Brigade Third Division Third Corps

Army of Northern Virginia
Commanded July 1 Brigadier General Alfred M. Scales
Commanded July 3 Colonel William J. Lowrance

Assistant Adjutant General Captain James Wilson Riddick 20 years old Nansemond Co, Va W Gaines Mill **W 7/1**

Acting Assistant Adjutant General—Lieutenant David Murdock McIntire 32 years old New Hanover, NC merchant

Assistant Adjutant & Inspector General—Captain Hugh L.Guerrant 28 year old merchant W-Chancellorsville (later W—Wilderness)

Aide-de-Camp—Captain John D Young promoted 7/1 from 34th NC

Aide-de-Camp—Lieutenant Alvis David Montgomery (Scale's brother in Law) 28 years old Caswell Co. NC

Commissary of Substance—Major Henry L. Biscoe 22 years old Lancaster Co. Va.

THIRTY EIGHTH NORTH CAROLINA REGIMENT

Lt. Ransom Middleton Co A

Private Marcus Bean Co I

Colonel William Hoke 26 yr old enlisted Lincoln Co. elected Colonel 1/17/62 W Mechanicsville **W-leg 7/1**

Lieutenant Colonel Ashford 26 yr old Sampson farmer appointed 1/14/63 W-leg 2nd Manassas **W 7/1** (later Colonel)

Major Murdock McRae McLauchlin 30 yr old teacher Cumberland Co. appointed 1/14/63 W-face Chancellorsville Absent W

Adjutant David McIntire 32 yr old merchant from Duplin Co. appointed 7/9/62 "Badge of Distinction" at Chancellorsville

Sergeant Major Agrippas Hardister 36 yr old enlisted Camp Mangum 12/31/61 promoted 4/24/63 (later W-hip North Anna)

Ordinance Sergeant Jason Andrews 22 yr old enlisted Randolph Co. promoted 12/17/62

Assistant Quartermaster William Edwards appointed 6/7/62

Assistant Commissary of Subsistance appointed 3/13/62

Surgeon Peter Young promoted 1/6/62

Assistant Surgeon James Darden appointed 2/14/63

Quartermaster Sergeant Daniel Hoke promoted 6/7/62

Hospital Steward Alfred Hambright promoted 1/3/63

Brigade Mail carrier Corporal John McGowen appointed 5/63

LT. G.F. Bason, Bde Ord Officer Ordinance Officer Lt. G.F. Bason

Company A *"Spartan Band"*

1st Lt. Alsa Brown 20 yr old enlisted Duplin Co "Badge of Distinction Chancellorsvile" **C 7/3**

3rd Lt. Henry C. Moore 27 yr old Duplin Co. 11/12/61 (Acting Adjutant) **C 7/3**

1st Sgt David Thompson enlisted Duplin County 10/1/61

Sgt William Hightower 23 yr old enlisted Duplin Co 10/1/61 **W 7/3 C 7/5** (later K Spotsylvania)

Sgt Leonidas Pearsall 20 yr old enlisted Duplin Co 10/1/61 **W 7/3** "left behind"(died 1/64)

Sgt John Pearsall 22 yr old enlisted Duplin Co 10/1/61 W 7/3

1st Sgt William Pearsall 27 yr old enlisted Duplin Co 10/1/61 promoted 3/15/63

Corp Thomas Armstrong 20 yr old enlisted Duplin Co 10/1/61 W-foot Cedar Mtn. (later Corp)

Corp Hosea Lanier 24 yr old enlisted Duplin Co 10/1/61 WC 7/3 (died 8/13)

Corp Lewis Thomas 24 yr old enlisted Duplin Co 10/1/61 **K 7/3**

Private William Barnett 20 yr old yr old enlisted Duplin Co 10/1/61 **W-arm 7/3 C 7/5 (amp)**

Private John Bishop 26 yr old enlisted Duplin Co 10/1/61 W Chancellorsville **W/C 7/3** (later W Wilderness)

Private William Boone 21 yr old enlisted Duplin Co 10/1/61

Private Nicholas Hall 26 yr old enlisted Duplin Co 10/1/61 W 2nd Manassas **W 7/3** (died 7/12)

Private Robert Houston 19 yr old enlisted Duplin Co 10/1/61

Private James Lanier 20 yr old enlisted Duplin Co 10/1/61 **W/ 7/3** (died Ft Delaware)

Private Jesse Nethercutt 28 yr old enlisted Duplin Co 10/1/61 "Badge of Distinction" Chancellorsville (later W Ream's Station)

Private Thomas Phillips 22 yr old enlisted Duplin Co 10/1/61 C Sharpsburg (later Corp & Sgt)

Private John Southerland 23 yr old enlisted Duplin Co 10/1/61

Private Daniel Thomas transferred 11/25/61 W-right arm Fredericksburg **W 7/1 "slight" & fought 7/3**

Private William Thigpen 33 yr old enlisted Duplin Co 10/1/61 C Sharpsburg **W-left thigh 7/3 C 7/5**

Teamster William Davis 20 yr old enlisted Duplin Co 10/1/61 (ambulance driver) (later W-right thigh Jerusalem Plank)

Brigade Mail Carrier Corp John McGowen

Musician George Miller 19 yr old enlisted Duplin Co 10/1/61 appointed 3/17/63

July 1 Casualties

2nd Lt. Ransom Middleton 32 yr old enlisted Duplin Co. 10/1/61 W-leg Chancellorsville **W-face, foot, right thigh 7/1**

Private John Frederick 20 yr old enlisted Duplin Co 10/1/61 W 2nd Manassas (later Corp)

Private Solomon Gore 27 yr old enlisted Duplin Co 10/1/61 W 2nd Manassas

Private Willis Grisham 20 yr old enlisted Duplin Co 10/1/61 W-abdomen Glendale **W 7/1**

Private Sylvanus Jones 29 yr old enlisted Duplin Co 10/1/61

Private Benjamin Marredy 26 yr old enlisted Duplin Co 10/1/61 C Sharpsburg (later K Jerusalem Plank)

Private Benjamin Pearsall transferred to regiment 3/13/63

Private John Pollack 28 yr old enlisted Duplin Co 10/1/61 (later AWOL 10/64)

Private Jesse Sandlin 22 yr old enlisted Duplin Co 10/1/61 W-Rappahannock (later W Wilderness)

Private Andrew Swinson 28 yr old enlisted Duplin Co 10/1/61 (discharged 2/64 "ulceration left leg) **W 7/1**

Private William Taylor 24 yr old enlisted Duplin Co 11/2/61

Private Merrill Wood 26 yr old enlisted Duplin Co 10/1/61

Company B *"Men of Yadkin"*

Capt. Augustin Blackburn (with slave "Alfred "teen" Blackburn) 28 yr old enlisted Yadkin Co 10/16/61 (later resigned 11/63)

1st Lt. Samuel Wilder 33 yr old cabinetmaker enlisted Yadkin Co 10/16/61 **K 7/3**

2nd Lt. Asa Lewis 21 yr old enlisted Yadkin Co 10/16/61 **C 7/14**

1st Sgt Hampton Brown 39 yr old enlisted Yadkin Co 4/19/62 W-thigh Mechanicsville W Fredericksburg **C 7/5 nurse for wounded**

Sgt John Grose 23 yr old enlisted Yadkin Co 10/16/61 (later C Wilderness)

Sgt John Martin 33 yr old enlisted Yadkin Co 10/16/61 **W 7/1 slight & fought 7/3** (later C Wilderness)

Cpl. Lewis Wooten 18 yr old enlisted Yadkin Co 4/19/62 W Mechanicsville W Fredericksburg

Private Stephen Adams 26 yr old enlisted Yadkin Co 4/24/62 **C 7/3**

Private James Angell 21 yr old enlisted Yadkin Co 10/16/61 (later Corp C Spotsylvania)

Private John Angell 53 yr old enlisted Yadkin Co 4/19/62 (later AWOL 9/64)

Private Thomas Dinkins 38 yr old enlisted Yadkin Co 4/19/62 "Badge of Distinction" Chancellorsville **C 7/3**

Private Horace Eddleman 26 yr old enlisted Yadkin Co 10/16/61 (later Sgt)
Private Nathan Grose 20 yr old enlisted Yadkin Co 10/16/61 ***C 7/3***
Private William Haynes 26 yr old enlisted Yadkin Co 10/16/61 (later C Wilderness)
Private Robert Joyce transferred 3/25/63 (later Sgt & 1st Sgt K Jerusalem Plank)
Private Andrew Joyner 21 yr old enlisted 2/15/63 Deserted 7/20/63

July 1 Casualties

Cpl. Thomas Martin 22 yr old enlisted Yadkin Co 9/1/62 **W 7/1** (Later C Wilderness)
Private Issac Atwood 19 yr old enlisted Yadkin Co 10/16/61 W-left arm Mechanicville
Private Henry Brown 20 yr old enlisted Yadkin Co 9/1/62 **W 7/1 C 7/12 Hagerstown**
Private Lewis Collins 21 yr old enlisted 10/16/61 **W 7/1 C 7/14**
Private David Collins 25 yr old enlisted Yadkin Co 10/16/61
Private Caleb Creedmore 28 yr old enlisted Yadkin Co 10/16/61 later AWOL 8/11/63—returned W-Spotsyvania
Private William Norman 22 yr old enlisted Yadkin Co 1/1/63 **K 7/1**
Private Daniel Pendry 20 yr old enlisted Yadkin Co 10/16/61 **W 7/1**
Private David Reniger 28 yr old enlisted Yadkin Co 2/3/63 (later C North Anna River)
Private Alexander Sprinkle 20 yr old enlisted Yadkin Co 4/19/62 (later musician)
Private Alfred Tate 19 yr old enlisted 2/19/63 (died disease 1/4/64)
Private James Veach 20 yr old enlisted Yadkin Co 10/16/61 (later musician)
Private Gary Warden transferred 1/31/62 deserted 7/21/63—returned

Company C "*Sampson Farmers*"

Capt. John Wilson 33 yr old enlisted Sampson Co 8/18/61 (later Major)
Sgt. Everett Bass 37 yr old enlisted Sampson Co 10/18/61 **C 7/14**
Sgt Randoln Jackson 29 yr old enlisted Sampson Co 10/18/61 (later W Jerusalem Plank)
Sgt William Royall 21 yr old enlisted Sampson Co 10/18/61 (later W Wilderness)
Cpl. Samson Warren 20 yr old enlisted Sampson Co 10/18/61
Private Joseph Buff 37 yr old enlisted Cleveland Co 2/27/63 **W 7/3 C 7/14 Williamsport**
Private Alexander House 19 yr old enlisted Sampson Co 10/18/61 **C 7/3**
Private T.C. Johnson 23 yr old enlisted Sampson Co 11/4/61 **C 7/3**

Private Benjamin Sutton 21 yr old enlisted Sampson Co 10/18/61 C Chancellorsville "Badge of Distinction"
Private Lawson Warlick 38 yr old enlisted 3/5/63 **W/C 7/3**
Private Jesse Willis 35 yr old enlisted Cleveland Co 2/28/63 **W 7/1 slight & fought 7/3**

Private Peter Willis 39 yr old enlisted Cleveland Co 2/28/63 **W 7/1 slight & fought 7/3**

Detached to Brigade Private Jesse Sanderson 26 yr old mechanic enlisted Sampson Co 10/18/61 W Mechanicsville

July 1 & 2 Casualties

1st Lt. Rufus Allen 34 yr old enlisted Sampson Co 10/18/61 **W 7/1** (died 8/20/63)
2nd Lt. Hosea Weeks 25 yr old enlisted Sampson Co 10/18/61 **W-scalp 7/1** (later K Spotsylvania)
3rd Lt. George Daughtry 21 yr old enlisted Sampson Co 10/18/61 W-foot Mechanicsville "gallantry at Chancellorsville" **K 7/1**
Cpl. John King 19 yr old enlisted Sampson Co 10/18/61 **W 7/1 C 7/5** died 7/19
Private Elijah Crow 36 yr old enlisted 2/27/63 **K 7/1**
Private William Glisson 20 yr old enlisted Sampson Co 10/18/61 **W 7/1**
Private David Glisson 23 yr old enlisted Sampson Co 10/18/61 W Fredericksburg
Private Robert Rathford transferred 3/5/63 **W 7/1**
Private William House 32 yr old enlisted Sampson Co 10/18/61 C Antietam **K 7/1**
Private M.S. King 37 yr old enlisted Camp Gregg 1/6/63 **K 7/1**
Private J.M. Martin 30 yr old enlisted Gaston Co. (later died disease 6/64)
Private William Pope 20 yr old enlisted Sampson Co 10/18/61 W-ankle Mechanicsville (later Musician)
Private Samuel Pursley transferred 3/5/63 **C 7/14**
Private Richard Smith 29 yr old enlisted Sampson Co 10/18/61
Private Thomas Smith 26 yr old enlisted Sampson Co 10/18/61 W-foot Mechanicsville (later detached)
Private Calvin Sutton 20 yr old enlisted Sampson Co 10/18/61 **K 7/2**

Company D *"Sampson Plowboys"*

1st Lt. John Robinson 24 yr old enlisted Sampson Co. 10/22/61 in command (later Captain)
Sgt John House 26 yr old enlisted Sampson Co. 2/4/62
Sgt Nathan King 25 yr old enlisted Sampson Co 10/22/61
Sgt Richard King 23 yr old enlisted Sampson Co 10/22/61 (later K Wilderness)
Cpl. Bryant Bell 21 yr old enlisted Sampson Co 10/22/61
Cpl. William Britt 23 yr old enlisted Sampson Co 10/22/61 (served until 10/64)
Cpl. George Carr 24 yr old enlisted Sampson Co 10/22/61 (later W Wilderness)
Private James King 21 yr old enlisted Sampson Co 10/22/61
Private Stephen Lucas 23 yr old enlisted Sampson Co 10/22/61 (later C Wilderness)

Private Ephraim Shipp 19 yr old substitute enlisted Sampson Co 10/22/61 (W left thigh Chancellorsville)

Private John Weeks 20 yr old enlisted Sampson Co 10/22/61 C Frederick, Md C 7/14 Williamsport, Md

July 1 Casualties

Captain Henry Darden enlisted Sampson Co. 10/22/61 **W-shoulder 7/1** (later W-Abdomen Ream's Station died 9/2/64)

3rd Lt. William Faison 24 yr old enlisted Sampson Co 10/22/61 **W-right leg 7/1**

1st Sgt David Thompson transferred 3/15/61 "Badge of Distinction" Chancellorsville **W-left shoulder W 7/1**

Sgt William King transferred to regiment 5/63 **C 7/14**

Sgt Nathan Lewis 19 yr old enlisted Sampson Co 10/22/61 **W 7/1 "left behind" C 7/5** (later W-left shoulder Jerusalem Plank)

Private Bermudus McClure 36 yr old enlisted Wake Co. 3/20/63 **W 7/1 "left behind" C 7/5**

Private Jesse Bowen 28 yr old enlisted Sampson Co 10/22/61 (died at home 9/9/63)

Private Alvin Odom 32 yr old enlisted Sampson Co 10/22/61 **W 7/1**

Private Edward Ramsour 25 yr old enlisted Camp Gregg 1/1/63

Private James Shipp 36 yr old enlisted Sampson Co 10/22/61

Private Robert Shipp 22 yr old enlisted Sampson Co 10/22/61 W-right shoulder Mechanicsville W—Fredericksburg **C 7/14**

Private John Stephens 22 yr old enlisted Sampson Co 10/22/61 **W-left arm 7/1**

Private William Stevens 21 yr old enlisted Sampson Co 10/22/61 **W-right leg 7/1**

Private Rufus Stroup 28 yr old enlisted Wake Co 3/20/63 **W 7/ 1 C 7/5**

Company E "*Richmond Boys*"

1st Lt. Olfred Dockery enlisted 4/18/62 (later W-right side Wilderness)

2nd Lt. William Covington 22 yr old enlisted Richmond Co.10/30/61 **C 7/3**

1st Sgt John Elliot 23 yr old enlisted Richmond Co 10/30/61 W Fredericksburg (later reduced in rank)

Sgt Jackson McRae 31 yr old enlisted Richmond Co 9/8/62 W Harper's ferry (later 1st Sgt)

Cpl. Kenneth Covington 20 yr old enlisted Richmond Co 10/30/61 **W-left thigh 7/3**

Cpl. William Harris 27 yr old enlisted Richmond Co 10/30/61 **C 7/ 3**

Cpl. Jesse Thrower 26 yr old enlisted Richmond Co 10/30/61 **C 7/14**

Private Elisha Batton 20 yr old planter enlisted Richmond Co 10/30/61 (later W Riddell's Shop)

Private Samuel Covington 21 yr old enlisted Richmond Co 10/30/61 **C 7/3**

Private Tristram Ford 20 yr old enlisted Richmond Co 10/30/61 **C 7/14**
Private James Gay 21 yr old planter enlisted Richmond Co 10/30/61 (later Corp)
Private James Hines 19 yr old enlisted Richmond Co 10/30/61 C Glendale (killed 1864)
Private Alexander McDuffie 22 yr old planter enlisted Richmond Co 10/30/61
Private Benjamin Smith 27 yr old blacksmith enlisted Richmond Co 10/30/61 (later W Ridell's Shop)
Private William Smith 23 yr old planter enlisted Richmond Co 10/30/61 **C 7/14**
Private Robert Wallace 22 yr old enlisted Richmond Co 2/7/63 (later AWOL 2/29/64)

Nurse Allen Crouch 24 yr old enlisted Richmond Co 10/30/61 W Glendale detailed 4/1/63
Private Alexander McIntyre 23 yr old enlisted Richmond Co 10/30/61 (detailed to pioneers)

July 1 Casualties

Private Benjamin Bolton 20 yr old enlisted Richmond Co.10/30/61 **W 7/1 C 7/14**
Private Bounds 26 yr old planter enlisted 10/31/61 **W 7/1 C 7/14**
Private Mason Garrett 22 yr old planter enlisted Richmond Co 10/30/61 (deserted 8/1/63)
Private Thomas McCaskill 30 yr old enlisted Richmond Co 10/30/61 (later K Wilderness)
Private William McCaskill 34 yr old enlisted Richmond Co 10/30/61 deserted 8/1/63
Private John Shepard 19 yr old enlisted Richmond Co 10/30/61 **K 7/1**
Private Harrison Shepard 22 yr old planter enlisted Richmond Co 10/30/61 **W 7/1 C 7/14**
Private William Shepard transferred 2/1/63 **W 7/1 C 7/14**
Private Noah Webb 22 yr old substitute enlisted Richmond Co 10/30/61 **W 7/1** (later C Mine Run)
Private William Webb 25 yr old enlisted Richmond Co 10/30/61 **"Missing" 7/16/63** (deserted 7/25/63)

Company F "*Catawba Wildcats*"

3rd Lt. Hiram Davis 31 yr old mechanic enlisted Catawba 10/31/61 (later court-martialed 4/9/64)
Sgt Alfred Hedrick 22 yr old enlisted Catawba 10/31/61
Sgt Nelson Sigman 20 yr old enlisted Catawba 10/31/61 W Mechanicsville (later W Jerusalem Plank)
Private Monroe Cloninger 22 yr old enlisted Catawba 10/31/61 (served to 10/64)
Private Adolphus Fox 24 yr old enlisted Catawba 10/31/61 (later C North Anna)
Private Elcanah Hunsucker 32 yr old enlisted Catawba 10/31/61
Private Miles Knup 38 yr old enlisted Catawba 10/31/61 deserted 8/15/63 (later K Spotsylvania)

Private Lawson Lael 21 yr old enlisted Catawba 10/31/61 W 2nd Manassas deserted 8/15/63
Private Daniel Null 29 yr old enlisted Catawba 10/31/61 (later C North Anna)
Private Augustus Parks 38 yr old enlisted Catawba 10/31/61 AWOL 8/1/63
Private Marcus Pope 21 yr old enlisted Catawba 10/31/61 (later C North Anna)
Private Alfred Setzer 25 yr old enlisted Catawba 10/31/61 C Chancellorsville (later W-left shoulder Jerusalem Plank)
Private Anson Sigman 36 yr old enlisted 3/16/63 deserted 9/63 (died 6/64 typhoid fever)
Private Davault Sigman 24 yr old enlisted camp Hill 8/14/62 (later W Wilderness)

Private Anderson Hetrick 27 yr old enlisted Catawba 10/31/61 (detailed as pioneer)

July 1 Casualties

2nd Lt. Alonzo Deal 22 yr old enlisted Catawba 10/31/61 W Mechanicsville **W-side 7/1** (later captain)
1st Sgt Marion Roseman 20 yr old enlisted Catawba 10/31/61 **W-right thigh 7/1 C 7/5**
Sgt Quinton Smith 19 yr old enlisted Catawba Co 10/31/61 W-Ox Hill **W 7/1**
Cpl. Jacob Lael 32 yr old enlisted Catawba 10/31/61 **K 7/1**
Cpl. Elcanah Hefner 37 yr old enlisted Catawba 10/31/61 deserted 7/29/63—returned C Wilderness
Private Gilbert Arwod 28 yr old enlisted Catawba 10/31/61 W-leg Mechanicsville W Chancellorsville **K 7/1**
Private George Baker 39 yr old enlisted Catawba 10/31/61 **W-right scapula 7/1** (later Corp C Wilderness)
Private Jacob Baker 31 yr old enlisted Catawba 10/31/61 **W 7/1 C 7/5**
Private Miles Bost 39 yr old enlisted Catawba Co. 10/31/61 **"Missing" 7/1** returned 9/63 (later W Spotsylvania)
Private Jefferson Cline enlisted Catawba Co. 3/16/763 AWOL 10/20/63
Private Sidney Crawford 24 yr old enlisted Catawba 10/31/61 **W 7/1 deserted returned 4/64**
Private Lenas Fullbright 37 yr old enlisted Catawba Co. **W 7/1 C 7/7 Williamsport**
Private Daniel Hefner 36 yr old enlisted Carawba Co. 3/16/63 **WC 7/1 C 7/5** died 8/18
Private John Hoke 39 yr old enlisted Catawba Co. 3/1/63 deserted 7/29/63—returned
Private Martin Hoke 32 yr old enlisted Catawba 10/31/61 deserted 7/29/63 (later C North Anna)
Private Miles Moser 21 yr old enlisted Catawba 10/31/61 W 2nd Manassas **K 7/1**
Private Elcanah Pope 36 yr old enlisted Catawba Co 3/16/63 ***W-leg & hand 7/1*** *(later W Spotsylvania)*
Private Miles Pope 27 yr old enlisted Catawba 10/31/61 **W-head "shell fragment" 7/1** (later C Spotsylvania)
Private Miles Logan Yount 38 yr old married with 4 children enlisted Catawba Co. 10/31/61 **K 7/1**

Company G *"Rocky Face Rangers"*

Capt. George Flowers 21 yr old teacher enlisted Alexander Co. 11/2/61 W-scalp Mechanicsville **W 7/3** (later Major & Lt. Col.))

1st Lt. Richard Sharp 23 yr old enlisted Alexander Co. 11/2/61 "awarded for gallantry at 2nd Manassas" (later Captain)

2nd Lt. Alfred Hines 21 yr old teacher enlisted Alexander Co. 11/2/61 (later 1st Lt)

3rd Lt. Thomas Murdah 21 yr old enlisted Alexander Co. 11/2/61 W Gaine's Mill

Sgt Samuel Adams 24 yr old enlisted Alexander Co 11/2/61 (later C North Anna River)

Sgt Wesley Matheson 20 yr old enlisted Iredell Co. 2/1/62 "Badge of Distinction" Chancellorsville (later Ensign)

Sgt Lewis Morrison34 yr old enlisted Alexander Co.11/2/61 (later W-right side face Jerusalem Pank)

Sgt William Norton 23 yr old enlisted Alexander Co.11/2/61 C 2nd Manassas (later K Wilderness)

Cpl. Albert Davis 21 yr old enlisted Alexander Co 11/2/61 C Boonsboro (later C Spotsylvania)

Private Samuel Ellis 20 yr old enlisted Alexander Co 3/7/63 (later Corp)

Private Samuel Hines 23 yr old enlisted Alexander Co 4/12/62 W Mechanicsville (later W Cold Harbor)

Private Erastus Kennedy 31 yr old mechanic enlisted Alexander Co 11/2/61 (later Corp)

Private Elisha Long 37 yr old enlisted Alexander Co 3/19/63 (served until 10/64)

Teamster John Patterson 25 yr old enlisted Alexander Co.11/2/61 **C 7/14** (later joined US Service)

Teamster Quintus Patterson 34 yr old enlisted Alexander Co 5/12/62

July 1 & 2 Casualties

1st Sgt Jonas Bradshaw 28 yr old enlisted Alexander Co 11/2/61 W 2nd Manassas **WC 7/1 "left behind" C 7/5**

Private Moses Austin 21 yr old enlisted Alexander Co 3/9/63 **W 7/1 C 7/5** (later W Spotsylvania)

Private Thomas Bruce 39 yr old enlisted Alexander Co. 7/21/62 (later W North Anna)

Private Milas Clary 21 yr old enlisted Alexander Co 11/2/61 W Mechanicville **W 7/1 C 7/5**

Private William Lackey 21 yr old enlisted Alexander Co.11/2/61 W Shepherdstown **K 7/1**

Private William Leroy Lackey 22 yr old enlisted Alexander Co.11/2/61 W Mechanicsville **W 7/1 (later Corp)**

Private James Allen Lackey **W 7/ 2 C 7/5 died 10/15**

Private James W. Lackey 23 yr old enlisted Alexander Co.11/2/61 W Mechanicsville C 2nd Manassas W Chancellorsville **W 7/2**

Private **Robert Lackey** 21 yr old enlisted Alexander Co.11/2/61 W Mechanicsville (later musician)

Private **Wesley Lackey** 30 yr old enlisted Alexander Co.11/2/61 deserted 8/13/63 (later W Jerusalem Plank)

Private **William Henry Lackey** 23 yr old enlisted Alexander Co.11/2/61 (later W Cold Harbor)

Private John Lackey 22 yr old enlisted Alexander Co.11/2/61 **W 7/1 C 7/5**

Private Thomas Sharpe 24 yr old enlisted Alexander Co.11/2/61 **W-both thighs 7/ 1 C 7/5**

Company H "*Uwharrie Boys*"

Capt. William Thornburg 26 yr old enlisted Randolph Co. 11/4/61 W Richmond **slight w-7/1 W-face 7/3**

1st Lt. Issac Kearns 29 yr old enlisted Randolph Co 11/4/61 **WC 7/3** died 7/24

2nd Lt. Alexander Murdock 26 yr old enlisted Randolph Co 11/4/61 **C 7/14**

Sgt O.C. Hamilton 24 yr old enlisted Randolph Co. 11/4/61 (transferred CS Navy 1864)

Sgt Henry Ingram 21 yr old enlisted Randolph Co. 11/4/61 W Fredericksburg

Sgt Thomas Russell 22 yr old enlisted Randolph Co. 11/4/61 W-left leg Mechanicsville **C 7/3**

Cpl. E.T. Kearns 28 yr old enlisted Randolph Co. 11/4/61 W Mechanicsville **K 7/3**

Private A.M. Bell 21 yr old enlisted Randolph Co 11/4/61 W-arm Mechanicsville (later Corp)

Private N.G. Campbell 18 yr old enlisted Randolph Co 11/4/61 **K 7/3**

Private Tyson Cranford 20 yr old enlisted Randolph Co 11/4/61 W Malvern Hill **K 7/3**

Private Julian Fletcher Hamilton 20 yr old enlisted Camp Hill Co. 3/5/63

Private C.H. Hancock 22 yr old enlisted Randolph Co. 11/4/61

Private Willis Hill 23 yr old enlisted Randolph Co. 11/4/61 **C 7/14**

Private B.H. Hopkins 23 yr old enlisted Randolph Co. 11/4/61 W Gaines Mill (later Sgt)

Private Martin Hopkins 23 yr old enlisted Randolph Co. 11/4/61

Private E.W. Ingram enlisted in Mississippi 3/27/63 (served through 10/64)

Private J.H. Lewis 20 yr old enlisted Randolph Co. 11/4/61 **C 7/14**

Private E.E. Luck 22 yr old enlisted Randolph Co. 11/4/61 W-thigh Mechanicsville (later Sgt)

Private N.C. Nance 24 yr old enlisted Randolph Co. 11/4/61 **K 7/3**

Private Harris Russell 25 yr old enlisted Randolph Co. 11/4/61 deserted 9/1/63 (later C Wilderness)

Private Harris Sanders 20 yr old enlisted Randolph Co. 11/4/61 (later W Fort Harrison 1864)

Private Jesse Scarlott 20 yr old enlisted Randolph Co. 11/4/61 W Mechanicsville **slight W 7/3**

Private Jesse Shaw 22 yr old enlisted Randolph Co. 11/4/61 **C 7/14**

Private J.M. Tomlinson 20 yr old enlisted Randolph Co. 11/4/61 **C 7/14**

Private Fenner Watkins 35 yr old enlisted Wake Co. 3/5/63 (died 1/64)

Private V.S. Wood 26 yr old enlisted Randolph Co. 11/4/61 (died 10/31/63 disease)

Teamster Z.A. Cranford 23 yr old enlisted Randolph Co 11/4/61

Teamster Jesse Lassiter 20 yr old enlisted Randolph Co. 11/4/61

July 1 Casualties

Cpl. D.P. Woodburn 26 yr old enlisted Randolph Co. 11/4/61 "Badge of Distinction Chancellorsville **K 7/1**

Private Calier Hamilton transferred 3/7/63 **K 7/1**

Private J.F. Hardister 23 yr old enlisted Randolph Co. 11/4/61 **W 7/1 C 7/5**

Private Lewis Harvell 22 yr old enlisted Randolph Co. 11/4/61 **WC 7/ 1 C 7/5**

Private James Harvell 35 yr old enlisted Randolph Co.11/4/61 deserted 9/1/63 returned W-back Wilderness)

Private David Hill 20 yr old enlisted Randolph Co. 11/4/61 **W-right thigh 7/1 C 7/5** (later joined US Service)

Private M.F. Hopkins enlisted camp Hill 3/18/63 **W-foot 7/1 C 7/5** (amp)

Private Stokes Hopkins 30 yr old enlisted Randolph Co. 11/4/61 W-Hanover CH

Private B.N. Kearns 38 yr old enlisted Randolph Co. 11/4/61 **W-face 7/1** (later W-lung Spotsylvania)

Private Thomas Kearns 20 yr old enlisted Randolph Co. 11/4/61 C 2nd Manassas **W-left leg 7/1 C 7/5**

Private Ezekiel Lassiter 29 yr old enlisted Randolph Co. 11/4/61 **K 7/1**

Private M.H. Lewis 39 yr old enlisted Randolph Co 3/23/63 **W-right arm & right thigh 7/1 C 7/5**

Private B.F. Luther 20 yr old enlisted Randolph Co. 11/4/61 **K 7/1**

Private A.H. Luther 20 yr old enlisted Randolph Co. 11/4/61 "left behind sick did not fight"

Private H.N. Tomlinson 21 yr old enlisted Randolph Co. 11/4/61 W Mechanicsville **W 7/1 C 7/5**

Desertion—Private Julian Fletcher Hamilton 20 yr old enlisted Camp Hill Co. 3/5/63 (Deserted June 1863)

"When he was just 18 his family pushed him into the Confederate army. One day he decided he couldn't stand it any longer, so he left. As he waded across a creek he was

captured by the Yankees . . . after (the war ended) he was ashamed to come home so he worked and made his living in the vineyards of a Catholic priest in Ohio" (North Carolina Division of Archives and History)

Private Benjanin Steed 26 yr old enlisted Camp Holmes 4/10/63 **C 7/5** Williamsport (not in battle)

Company I "*Cleveland Marksman*"

Capt. David Magness 28 yr old enlisted Cleveland Co 11/21/61 **C 7/3**

1st Lt. William Blanton previously Private in 56th NC elected 6/13/63

2nd Lt. Drury Suttle 26 yr old enlisted Cleveland Co 11/21/61 **C 7/3**

1st Sgt Harbert Fortenberry 29 yr old enlisted Cleveland Co 11/21/61 **W 7/3** (later W Wilderness)

Sgt William Hamrick 25 yr old enlisted Cleveland Co 11/21/61 W Gaine's Mill C Chancellorsville **C 7/3**

Sgt Doctor Panel 31 yr old enlisted Cleveland Co 11/21/61 W-Thigh Mechanicsville (reduced Corp 10/63)

Sgt John Waters 29 yr old enlisted Cleveland Co 11/21/61 (former Color Sgt)

Private **Marcus Beam** 6' 2" 28 yr old enlisted Cleveland Co 11/21/61 (later K Jerusalem Plank)

Private Thomas Costner 20 yr old enlisted Cleveland Co 11/21/61 W Cedar Run AWOL 12/63-returned

Private John Crowder 32 yr old enlisted Cleveland Co 11/21/61 (later Corp W Spotsylvania)

Private Pascal Crowder 33 yr old enlisted Cleveland Co 11/21/61 **WC 7/14**

Private J.M. Gardner 26 yr old enlisted Cleveland Co 11/21/61 (later K Spotsylvania)

Private Thomas Gardner 19 yr old enlisted Cleveland Co 11/21/61 W Sharpsburg **K 7/3**

Private William Gold 19 yr old enlisted Cleveland Co 5/9/62

Private Richard Hughes 19 yr old enlisted Cleveland Co 11/21/61 W Mechanicsville

Private Gabriel Kitchens 24 yr old enlisted Cleveland Co 11/21/61 W Gaine's Mill

Private Daniel Martin 20 yr old enlisted Cleveland Co 11/21/61 W Harper's ferry (nurse detail) **C 7/5**

Private Richard Philbeck 27 yr old enlisted Cleveland Co 11/21/61 **C 7/3**

Private C.B. Powell 18 yr old substitute enlisted Cleveland Co. W-leg Mechanicsville **W 7/3**

Private Jacob Williams 30 yr old enlisted Cleveland Co 11/21/61 W-leg Mechanicsville

Private Milton Williamson 28 yr old enlisted Cleveland Co 11/21/61

Teamster Hardin Tucker 19 yr old enlisted Fredericksburg 12/20/62

Teamster Asberry Wiggins 25 yr old enlisted Cleveland Co 11/21/61 W Gaine's Mill

July 1 Casualties

Cpl. William Covington 22 yr old enlisted Cleveland Co 11/21/61 AWOL 7/25/63 (later W Wilderness)

Cpl. Benjamin Durham 26 yr old enlisted Cleveland Co. (later reduced to private 12/63 W Riddell's Shop)

Cpl. Francis Hord 28 yr old enlisted Cleveland Co 11/21/61 (reduced to Private 11/25/63)

Private Francis Bridges 22 yr old enlisted Cleveland Co 11/21/61 **W 7/1** (later Sgt)

Private Richard S. Cogdell 22 yr old enlisted Cleveland Co 11/21/61 **K 7/1**

Private Elkanah Davis 36 yr old enlisted Cleveland 2/28/63

Private Howell Green 26 yr old enlisted Cleveland Co 11/21/61 W Mechanicsville

Private Pinkney Green 22 yr old enlisted Cleveland Co 11/21/61 W Mechanicsville **W 7/1 C 7/14**

Private Richard Grigg 38 yr old enlisted Cleveland Co 2/28/63 **C 7/14**

Private William Grigg 39 yr old enlisted Cleveland Co 2/28/63 **W-right foot 7/1 C 7/5**

Private Chapel Henrick 39 yr old enlisted Cleveland Co 2/28/63

Private Thomas Kearns **W 7/1 C 7/5**

Private William Pryor 27 yr old mechanic enlisted Cleveland Co 11/21/61 AWOL 8/22/63

Private Thomas Ramsey 33 yr old enlisted Cleveland Co. 11/21/61 "Badge of Distinction Chancellorsville" **K 7/1**

Private William Sansing 34 yr old enlisted Cleveland Co 11/21/61

Private L.P. Williams 39 yr old enlisted Cleveland Co 2/28/63 **W 7/ 1 C 7/5** (died 7/15)

Private George Wilson 26 yr old enlisted Cleveland Co 11/21/61 **K 7/1**

Private Drury Wright 26 yr old enlisted Cleveland Co 11/21/61 AWOL 9/1/64—returned

Company K "*Carolina Boys*"

Captain Daniel Monroe enlisted Cumberland Co. 1/27/62 (sick—died of disease 9/24/63)

2nd Lt. Hugh McDonald transferred 1/27/62 **C 7/14**

3rd Lt. John McArthur 22 yr old enlisted Cumberland Co. 11/9/61

Sgt Alexander Graham 29 yr old enlisted Cumberland Co. 11/9/61 W by shell Mechanicsville (later 1st Sgt)

Sgt Daniel K McDuffie 23 yr old enlisted Cumberland Co 2/15/62 **W 7/1 slight & fought 7/3**

Sgt Daniel McMillan 21 yr old enlisted Cumberland Co. 11/9/61 **C 7/14**

Cpl. Alexander Arnet 25 yr old enlisted Cumberland Co. 1/27/62 **W 7/1 slight & fought 7/3**

Cpl. Niven Culbreth 25 yr old enlisted Cumberland Co. 2/15/62 W Mechanicsville (later Sgt C Spotsylvania)

Cpl. James Geddie 25 yr old enlisted 2/15/62

Private Lauchlin Blue 25 yr old enlisted Cumberland Co 2/15/62 W Mechanicsville (later Corp)

Private Joseph Cain 18 yr old enlisted Cumberland Co. 3/1/63

Private Daniel Campbell 31 yr old enlisted Cumberland Co. 11/9/61 **C 7/14** (later Sgt)

Private John Culbreth 26 yr old enlisted Cumberland Co. 2/15/62 **W 7/3 C 7/5**

Private William Geddie 27 yr old enlisted Cumberland Co. 2/15/62 C Sharpsburg K Spotsylvania

Private Wiley Keen 32 yr old enlisted 3/19/62 **C 7/3**

Private J.A. McArthur 20 yr old enlisted Cumberland Co. W-slightly Mechanicsville **W-left leg C 7/3**

Private Daniel McLaurin 22 yr old enlisted Cumberland Co 2/15/62 W Mechanicsville

Private William McPhaul 21 yr old enlisted Cumberland Co. 11/9/61 "Badge of Distinction Chancellorsville" **W-face C 7/3**

Private Joseph Phillips 20 yr old enlisted Cumberland Co 2/15/62

Private David Ray 19 yr old enlisted Cumberland Co. 5/3/62 W Mechanicsville (later K Wilderness)

Private Neill Ray 27 yr old enlisted Cumberland Co. 11/9/61 (later W Jerusalem Plank)

July 1 Casualties

1st Lt. John Ray 35 yr old enlisted Cumberland Co. 11/9/61 W-mouth Mechanicsville **W-right ankle 7/1 C 7/5** (amp)

Sgt D.C. McCaskill 29 yr old enlisted Cumberland Co 2/15/62 **W 7/1**

Corp George McNeill 21 yr old enlisted Cumberland Co. 11/9/61 **K 7/1**

Private Duncan Black 19 yr old enlisted Cumberland Co. 11/9/61 **W-knee 7/1 "left behind" C 7/5**

Private Cornelius Haley 32 yr old enlisted Cumberland Co. 11/9/61 **W-left leg 7/1**

Private Richard Harrison 27 yr old enlisted Cumberland Co 2/15/62 **C 7/14**

Private Daniel McDuffie 28 yr old enlisted Cumberland Co 2/15/62 **K 7/1**

Private Archibald McDearmid 28 yr old enlisted Cumberland Co. 11/9/61 **C 7/14**

Private Dougald McDougald 28 yr old enlisted Cumberland Co. 11/9/61 **K 7/1**

Private John McGill 20 yr old enlisted Cumberland Co 2/15/62 **WC 7/1 "left behind" C 7/5**

Private Duncan Monroe 28 yr old enlisted Cumberland Co. 11/9/61 W-shell burn Sharpsburg **C 7/14**

Private Hugh Priest 19 yr old enlisted Cumberland Co 1/27/62 **C 7/14**

THIRTEENTH NORTH CAROLINA REGIMENT

Lt. James Williamson Co A

Private Caleb May

Field & Staff

Colonel Joseph Hyman 28 yr old enlisted 10/15/62 Edbecombe Co. promoted to Colonel 6/13/62 **W-right arch 7/1**

Lt. Colonel Henry Rogers 27 yr old teacher enlisted Casell City appointed 6/13/63 W Chancellorsville Absent W

Major Eilah Withers 26 yr old UNC graduate former Captain of Company A promoted 6/13/63 **W 7/1** (later Lt. Col)

Sergeant Major William Howard enlisted 4/29/61 Yanceyville appointed 4/30/63 (later transferred to State Troops)

Senior Captain Capt. Ludolphus Henderson 27 yr old dentist enlisted Caswell Co 4/29/61 In Command 7/3 **W 7/3**

Quartermaster Daniel Hill 21 yr old enlisted Caswell Co 4/24/61

Assistant Quartermaster Charles Hill appointed 9/20/61 (later Division Paymaster)

Assistant Commissary of Subsistance Eramus Scales appointed 11/14/61

Chaplin George T Williams transferred 4/28/63 (resigned 12/63)

Surgeon John McAden appointed 11/16/61 **C 7/5 (with wounded)**

Assistant Surgeon William Stephens appointed 2/14/63

Ordinance Sgt William Mebane 23 yr old enlisted Rockingham Co 5/3/61 promoted 6/15/62 (later Brigade Ordinance Officer)

Aide-de-camp for General Scales Alvis Montgomery age 25 enlisted Suffolk Va. **W/C 7/3**

Company A *"Yanceyville Grays"*

Capt. Ludolphus Henderson 27 yr old dentist enlisted Caswell Co 4/29/61 **W 7/3 advance** (later W Cold Harbor)

2nd Lt. David Lockett 22 yr old enlisted Caswell Co. elected 2nd Lt 5/11/63

Sgt. Allen Harralson 20 yr old clerk enlisted Caswell Co 4/29/61 (later W North Anna)

Private Franklin Dennis 29 yr old coach maker enlisted Caswell Co 4/29/61 **W slight 7/1 fought 7/3**

Private George Dickinson 20 yr old enlisted Camp Ruffin 7/27/61 (later Sgt Major)

Private Alexander Kimbrough 19 yr old enlisted Caswell Co 4/29/61 W-right hand Chancellorsville (later W Cold Harbor)

Private John Park 31 yr old enlisted Caswell Co 5/13/61 detailed as nurse for wounded **C 7/5**

Private John Reagan 23 yr old enlisted Caswell Co 4/29/61 W Fredericksburg **C 7/3**

Private William Roberts 23 yr old enlisted Caswell Co 4/29/61 detailed to care for wounded **C 7/5** (later Sgt)

Private Monroe Robertson 21 yr old enlisted Caswell Co 4/29/61 (later W North Anna)

Private Julius Thompson 23 yr old enlisted Caswell Co 4/29/61 **C 7/3**

Private John Duke 28 yr old wagoner enlisted Caswell Co 4/29/61 W Gaine's Mill (later W Spotsylvania)

7/1-7/2 Casualties

1st Lt. James Williamson 20 yr old enlisted Caswell Co 5/13/61 W Chancellorsville **W-thigh 7/1**

1st Sgt John Jones 24 yr old enlisted Caswell Co 9/3/61 **W 7/1** (later W-hand North Anna)

Corp. Henry Walters 26 yr old enlisted Caswell Co 4/29/61 W Sharpsburg **W 7/2 died 7/3**

Private William Ferrell 26 yr old enlisted Caswell Co 4/29/61 **C 7/5 as nurse** (later C Cold Harbor)

Private Joseph Gillespie 25 yr old enlisted Caswell Co 6/10/61 W-eye Williamsburg

Private Henry Howard 22 yr old enlisted Caswell Co 4/29/61 W Barnett's Ford **W 7/1** (later Color Sgt)

Private William Kennon 20 yr old enlisted Camp Ruffin 7/18/61 (later W North Anna)

Private David Long 27 yr old enlisted Camp Ruffin 7/10/61 W Gaine's Mill **sick did not fight C 7/5** (later K Ream's Station)

Private Joseph Moore 22 yr old enlisted Caswell Co 4/29/61 (later Corp K Spotsylvania)

Private John Robinson 23 yr old enlisted Caswell Co 4/29/61 **W 7/1 died 7/2**

Private Pleasant Scott enlisted Caswell Co 3/6/63 **W-right leg 7/1**

Private John Totten transferred 12/15/62 **W-leg 7/1 died 7/20**

Private Anglis Warren 20 yr old enlisted Caswell Co 3/6/63 **W 7/1**
Private William Womack 29 yr old enlisted Caswell Co 4/29/61 **C 7/15 Williamsport, Md**

Company B "*Raneleburg Rifleman*"

Capt. William Robinson 27 yr old doctor enlisted Mecklenburg 4/3/61 W Sharpsburg (later W Spotsylvania)
1st Lt. (Dr.) John McLean 28 yr old enlisted Mecklenburg Co 5/26/61
2nd Lt. Edward Smith 24 yr old enlisted Mecklenburg 4/3/61 **C 7/3**
3rd Lt. Henry "Harry" Walker 26 yr old enlisted Mecklenburg 5/20/61 **W-left leg 7/3 (amp) C 7/13** Hagerstown, Md
Sgt. John Todd 28 yr old enlisted Mecklenburg 4/3/61 (1st Sgt 7/3)
Sgt. William Whyte 21 yr old enlisted Mecklenburg 8/13/61 (later W-leg Wilderness)
Private Henry Cathey 32 yr old carpenter enlisted Mecklenburg 5/20/61 W-thigh Gaines Mill (later W North Anna)
Private Samuel Crowell 22 yr old enlisted Mecklenburg 5/20/61 (later C Hanover Junction)
Private Arthur Erwin 31 yr old enlisted Mecklenburg 6/12/61
Private John Groves 26 yr old enlisted Mecklenburg 4/3/61 **W-thigh 7/3 C 7/14**
Private Neely McGinn 22 yr old enlisted Mecklenburg 10/22/61
Private Randolph Nicholson 28 yr old enlisted Mecklenburg 4/3/61 **K 7/3**

Chief Musician 29 yr old enlisted Camp Ruffin 8/7/61 (later Drum major)
Musician Oswald Alexander 25 yr old enlisted Mecklenburg 7/17/61

7/1 Casualties

1st Sgt John Knox 33 yr old enlisted Mecklenburg 4/3/61 **K 7/1**
Corp. Robert Choate 25 yr old enlisted Mecklenburg 8/13/61 **W 7/1 C 7/5**
Private Hezekiah Alexander 23 yr old enlisted Mecklenburg 7/17/61 **K 7/1**
Private Alfred Brimer 26 yr old enlisted Mecklenburg 7/17/61 **K 7/1**
Private James Kimbrell 22 yr old enlisted Mecklenburg Co 4/3 /61 W South Mountain **K 7/1**
Private James Kirkpatrick 30 yr old enlisted Mecklenburg 7/17/61 W South Mountain **W 7/1 C 7/5**
Private William McGinn 32 yr old enlisted Mecklenburg 6/23/61 **W 7/1 C 7/5**
Private Stephen Marks 22 yr old enlisted Mecklenburg 4/3/61 W Sharpsburg **W-cheek & arm 7/1**
Private Henry Moser 25 yr old enlisted Mecklenburg 4/3/61 **K 7/1**
Private John Mulwee 23 yr old enlisted Mecklenburg 5/20/61 **W-shoulder 7/1**
Private James Neagle 19 yr old enlisted Mecklenburg 7/17/61 **W-right leg 7/1 C 7/5**

Private William Taylor 20 yr old enlisted Mecklenburg Co 7/17/61 W Williamsburg **W 7/1**
Private Levi "Jackson" Walker 21 yr old enlisted Mecklenburg 5/20/61 **W-left leg 7/1 (amp) C 7/5**
Private Henry Wolf 25 yr old enlisted Mecklenburg 7/17/61 W-bayonet Williamsburg **W 7/1 C 7/5**

Company C "*Milton Blues*"

Sgt. William Farley 23 yr old enlisted Caswell Co 4/24/61—in command **W 7/3 C 7/14**
Private Noah Alexander 38 yr old enlisted Gaston, Co. 3/5/63
Private William Allen 23 yr old enlisted Caswell Co 4/24/61
Private William Brandon 20 yr old enlisted Caswell Co 8/24/61 W-right hand Fredericksburg (later Corp)
Private Angus Burch 23 yr old enlisted Caswell Co 4/24/61 (later Corp)
Private Thomas Evans 23 yr old lawyer enlisted Caswell Co 4/24/61 drillmaster (later Captain 8/9/63)
Private James Hamlett 22 yr old enlisted Caswell Co 4/24/61
Private John Hendrick 26 yr old enlisted Caswell Co 4/24/61 W South Mountain (later Corp W Wilderness)
Private Samuel Johnson 29 yr old teacher enlisted Wake Co 9/27/62
Private John McCain 37 yr old enlisted Caswell Co 4/24/61 W Gaine's Mill (later Corp & Sgt)
Private James Phelps 23 yr old enlisted Caswell Co 4/24/61 W South Mountain (later W-hand Wilderness)
Private Watson Powell 22 yr old enlisted Caswell Co 4/24/61 W Malvern Hill **C 7/5**
Private John Brooks 19 yr old enlisted Caswell Co 4/24/61 detailed as courier

7/1 Casualties

Capt. William Rainey 24 yr old enlisted Caswell Co. 4/24/61 **W 7/1 C 7/5** (died 7/9/63)
1st Lt. William Brandon 24 yr old enlisted Caswell Co.4/24/61 **W 7/1 C 7/5** (died 7/9/63)
1st Sgt Henry Long 23 yr old trader enlisted Caswell Co 4/24/61 W South Mountain **W-hand 7/1**
Sgt. John Yarbrough 22 yr old mechanic enlisted Caswell Co 4/24/61 **W-right leg 7/1 C 7/5**
Corp. George W. Brandon 20 yr old enlisted Caswell Co 7/17/61 **W 7/1 C 7/5** (died 8/26/63 Phila hospital buried PNC))
Private John Allen 27 yr old enlisted Caswell Co 4/24/61 W Chancellorsville **W-left foot 7/1 C 7/5** (amp)

Private Adolphus Atkinson 19 yr old silversmith enlisted Caswell Co 4/24/61 **W 7/1 C 7/5**

Private William Bumganer 29 yr old enlisted Wake Co. 9/27/62

Private Samuel Covington 23 yr old enlisted Caswell Co 4/24/61 W Fredericksburg **W 7/1 C 7/5**

Private Henry Hamlett 29 yr old enlisted Caswell Co 4/24/61 W Gaine's Mill **K 7/1**

Private Lorenzo Kersey 22 yr old mechanic enlisted Caswell Co 4/24/61 **W 7/1 C 7/5 as nurse** (later W-right arm North Anna)

Private Eli Lefler 39 yr old enlisted Stanley Co. 2/28/63 **K 7/1**

Private Henry Powell 23 yr old enlisted Caswell Co 4/24/61 **W 7/1 C 7/5**

Private William Powell 21 yr old enlisted Caswell Co 4/24/61 W Malvern Hill **WC 7/1 C 7/5**

Private William Stone 38 yr old enlisted Rockingham Co 3/5/63 (later W Wilderness)

Company D "*Leasburg Grays*"

Capt. Thomas Stephens 24 yr old teacher enlisted Caswell Co. 5/1/61 (resigned 12/14/63)

1st Lt. William Woods 22 yr old student enlisted Caswell Co 5/1/61 **W 7/3 C 7/5** (later Captain)

Sgt. John Burton 25 yr old enlisted Caswell Co. 5/1/61 **C 7/14**

Sgt. John Harrison 30 yr old enlisted Caswell Co. 5/1/61 (later 1st Sgt C Mine Run)

Corp. Thomas Featherstone 26 yr old enlisted Caswell Co. 5/1/61 W-arm & leg Sharpsburg (later Sgt)

Private John Howard 21 yr old enlisted Caswell Co. 7/30/61 (later W-arm Wilderness)

Private Jerry Hughes enlisted as substitute Richmond, Va 8/3/62 **C 7/5 (detailed a nurse with wounded)**

Private Adolphus Parrott 22 yr old enlisted Caswell Co. 5/1/61 (later K North Anna)

Private John Whitlow 29 yr old enlisted Caswell Co 8/15/61 (later W-left arm Spotsylvania)

Private Robert Williams 24 yr old enlisted Caswell Co 7/30/61 W-arm & side Gaines Mill (later 2nd Lt)

Private John Woods 30 yr old enlisted Caswell Co. 5/1/61 (later W Well's Farm, Va)

Pioneer William Graham 26 yr old enlisted Caswell Co. 5/1/61

7/1 Casualties

2nd Lt. Thomas Chambers 24 yr old clerk enlisted Caswell Co. 5/1/61 **K 7/1**

Corp. Alexander Gordon 21 yr old enlisted Caswell Co. 7/1/61 W Gaine's Mill **K 7/1**

Corp. Bedford Stephens 21 yr old enlisted Caswell Co. 5/1/61 **W 7/1** (later K Spotsyvania)

Private William Bradford 21 yr old enlisted Caswell Co. 5/1/61 C Fredericksburg **W 7/1 C 7/5**

Private Dolphus Bradsher 31 yr old enlisted Caswell Co. 5/1/61

Private John Evans 21 yr old enlisted Caswell Co. 5/1/61 C Boonsboro WE Chancellorsville **K 7/1**

Private William Faucett 38 yr old enlisted Alamance Co. 3/13/63 **W 7/1 died 7/4**

Private John Hamilton 24 yr old enlisted Caswell Co. 5/1/61 W Malvern Hill (later W Cold Harbor)

Private Green Lea 20 yr old saddler enlisted Caswell Co. 5/1/61 **W 7/1**

Private Walker McFarland 21 yr old enlisted Caswell Co. 5/1/61 C Williamsburg **W 7/1 C 7/5** (died 7/10)

Private Anthony Norman 21 yr old enlisted Caswell Co. 8/15/61 W Gaine's Mill W Chancellorsville **K 7/1**

Private William Oakley 26 yr old enlisted Caswell Co. 5/1/61 **K 7/1**

Private John O'Brien 22 yr old clerk enlisted Caswell Co. 5/1/61 **W 7/1**

Private Squire Pruitt 30 yr old enlisted wake Co 9/27/62 (died 9/22 pneumonia)

Private William Scott 21 yr old enlisted Caswell Co. 7/30/61 W Gaine's Mill **W-right foot 7/1 C 7/5**

Private Andrew Stephens 32 yr old enlisted Caswell Co. 5/1/61 **K 7/1**

Private Clem Wagstaff 23 yr old enlisted Caswell Co. 7/30/61 **W 7/1 C 7/5** (later Corp)

Private Bartlett Warren 29 yr old enlisted Caswell Co. 5/1/61 W-left arm Malvern Hill **K 7/1**

Company E "*Alamance Regulators*"

2nd Lt. William Andrews 27 yr old enlisted Alamance Co 5/8/61 in command 7/3

3rd Lt. John Ireland 22 yr old enlisted Alamance Co 5/8/61 **W-right leg 7/3**

Corp. James Garrison 23 yr old blacksmith enlisted Alamance Co 5/8/61

Corp. Armistead Patterson 21 yr old enlisted Alamance Co 5/8/61

Private John R. Adams 23 yr old enlisted Alamance Co 5/8/61 W-right side C South Mountain (later Sgt)

Private Alfred Coble 21 yr old enlisted Bunker Hill, Va

Private Daniel Coble 23 yr old enlisted Bunker Hill, Va

Private R.B. Fooshee 20 yr old enlisted Camp Gregg 4/18/63 **W 7/3 C 7/5**

Private James Foster 28 yr old enlisted Alamance Co 5/8/61 (later W Wilderness)

Private George Holt enlisted Camp Gregg 4/18/63 **W 7/1 slight fought 7/3**

Private James Lackey 23 yr old enlisted Alamance Co 5/8/61 **W 7/1 slight fought 7/3** (later K Spotsylvania)

Private Matthew Patton 37 yr old enlisted camp Gregg, Va 4/18/63 **C 7/3**

Private Andrew Pyle 22 yr old enlisted Alamance Co 5/8/61

Private Andrew Rike 30 yr old enlisted camp Gregg 4/18/63 **W 7/1-7/3 W slightly**

Private James Rippey 21 yr old enlisted Alamance Co 5/8/61 **C 7/3**

Teamster John Murray 26 yr old enlisted Alamance Co 5/8/61

Musician Jacob Anthony 23 yr old enlisted Alamance Co 5/8/61 (later transferred to infantry 3/64 K Wilderness)

7/1 Casualties

Capt. Thomas Martin 22 yr old student enlisted Franklin Co. 5/8/61 **W-left hip 7/1** (later Major)

1st Lt. James Bason 27 yr old clerk enlisted Alamance Co 5/8/61 W Chancellorsville **W 7/1** (later Captain)

Color Sgt William F Faucette 30 yr old enlisted Alamance Co 5/8/61 **W-left arm 7/1 C 7/5**

Sgt. James Bradshaw 27 yr old enlisted Alamance Co 5/8/61 W Glendale **W 7/1 C 7/5** (died 8/9)

Sgt. James Dickey 21 yr old wagon maker enlisted Alamance Co 5/8/61 **W-right arm 7/1 C 7/5** (amp)

Corp. James Hicks 29 yr old enlisted Alamance Co 5/8/61 **K 7/1**

Private John J. Adams 23 yr old enlisted Alamance Co 5/8/61 **W-right thigh 7/1 C 7/5**

Private Alexander Andrews 26 yr old enlisted Alamance Co 5/8/61

Private Cadwalleder Andrews 20 yr old enlisted Alamance Co 5/8/61 **W 7/1** (later K Cold Harbor)

Private William Boggs 20 yr old enlisted Alamance Co 5/8/61 **W 7/1 C 7/5** (died 7/8)

Private Thomas Fonville 24 yr old saddler enlisted Alamance Co 5/8/61 C Sharpsburg **K 7/1**

Private Felty Gerringer 39 yr old enlisted Camp Gregg 3/13/63 **K 7/1**

Private Abel Horn 30 yr old enlisted Alamance Co 5/8/61

Private George Keck 26 yr old enlisted Alamance Co 5/8/61 **W-left arm 7/1**

Private **Caleb May** 28 yr old enlisted Alamance Co 5/8/61 **W 7/1 C 7/5**

Private William Murray 21 yr old enlisted Alamance Co 7/27/61 W Gaine's Mill **K 7/1**

Private William Thompson 20 yr old enlisted camp Gregg 4/18/63 **W-foot 7/1 C 7/5 (died 7/30)**

Company F "*Davie Greys*"

Corp. Matthew Ijams 21 yr old enlisted Davie Co. 8/6/61 in command 7/3 WC Williamsburg **C 7/14**

Corp. Grief Mason 23 yr old tobacconist enlisted Davie Co. 4/26/61 (later K Wilderness "carrying regimental colors)

Corp. Andrew Sain 23 yr old enlisted Davie Co. 8/6/61 (reduced to private 5/64)

Private John Briniger 21 yr old enlisted Davie Co. 8/6/61 (later died 11/4/63)
Private Thomas Butler 23 yr old teacher enlisted Davie Co. 4/26/61 W Chancellorsville **C 7/14**
Private Daniel Divire 29 yr old enlisted Davie Co. 4/6/61 (later Corp)
Private Matthew Fletcher 24 yr old enlisted Davie Co. 4/26/61
Private Arthur Hendren 25 yr old enlisted Davie Co. 4/26/61 C Sharpsburg (later 1st Sgt)
Private Randolph Pool 25 yr old enlisted Davie Co. 8/6/61 W-left knee Chancellorsville **C 7/14**
Private John Stonestreet 27 yr old enlisted Davie Co. 8/6/61 (later W Spotsylvania)
Private Pinkney Turner 29 yr old enlisted Davie Co. 8/6/61 **C 7/14**
Private Daniel Wallace 32 yr old tobacconist enlisted Davie Co. 4/26/61 **W 7/3** (died 7/7)

Musician Jasper Nail 21 yr old enlisted Davie Co. 4/26/61 W-left thigh Malvern Hill

7/1 Casualties

Capt. Franklin Williams 25 yr old teacher enlisted Davie Co. 4/26/61 W Fredericksburg **W-left leg 7/1 C 7/5**
2nd Lt. Nimrod Sain 34 yr old carpenter enlisted Davie Co 4/26/61 **W 7/1**
Sgt. John Nail 23 yr old enlisted Davie Co. 4/26/61 C Sharpsburg W Chancellorsville **W-right shoulder 7/1 C 7/5** (later Sgt)
Corp. William McGuire 20 yr old enlisted Davie Co. 4/26/61 W Chancellorsville **W 7/1** (later C Ream's Station)
Private Alfred Daywalt 22 yr old enlisted Davie Co. 8/6/61 **W-breast 7/1**
Private Henry Foster 31 yr old enlisted Davie Co 7/16/62
Private Jacob Foster 25 yr old enlisted Davie Co. 4/26/61 WC Fredericksburg
Private John Harris 24 yr old enlisted Davie Co. 4/26/61 W-left thigh **7/1 C 7/5**
Private George Hinkle 20 yr old enlisted Davie Co. 8/6/61 **W 7/1 C 7/4**
Private Robert Holt 24 yr old enlisted Davie Co. 4/26/61 **W-left foot 7/1 C 7/5**
Private Emanuel Leonard 30 yr old enlisted Davie Co. 4/26/61 **K 7/1**
Private James McDonald 21 yr old enlisted Davie Co. 8/6/61 W-3times Chancellorsville **K 7/1**
Private Urban May 21 yr old enlisted Davie Co. 8/4/61 **W 7/1 C 7/5** (later joined US Service)
Private William Penry 27 yr old enlisted Davie Co. 4/26/61 C Frederick, Md **K 7/1**
Private John Ridenhour 35 yr old enlisted Davie Co. 7/16/62 **W 7/1 C 7/5** (died 8/12)
Private Anderson Ridenhour 30 yr old enlisted Davie Co. 1/3/63 **W 7/1 C 7/5** (died 9/10)
Private John Sheets 23 yr old enlisted Davie Co. 8/6/61 **W 7/1 C 7/5**
Private John Tutterow 23 yr old enlisted Davie Co. 8/6/61 **W-left ankle 7/1** (later W-left lung Spotsylvania)

Private Thomas Vinagum 24 yr old enlisted Davie Co. 4/26/61—scout in several; battles **W 7/1** (died 8/28)

Private Jiles West 31 yr old enlisted Davie Co. 7/16/62 (furloughed sick 12/64)

Private Daniel Williams 22 yr old enlisted Davie Co. 4/26/61 **W 7/1 C 7/5** (later C Wilderness)

Company G *"Edgecombe Rifles"*

Sgt. Richard Stallings 27 yr old clerk enlisted Edgecombe Co 5/8/61 in command 7/3 **K 7/3**

Corp. Edmond Andrews 20 yr old enlisted Edgecombe Co 5/8/61 W Williamsburg (later Sgt)

Sgt. James Howard 20 yr old enlisted Edgecombe Co 5/8/61 **W 7/3** (later 1st Sgt W Jerusalem Plank)

Private Mark Atkinson 20 yr old enlisted Edgecombe Co 8/11/61 C Boonsboro **C 7/3**

Private Theodore Bell 26 yr old carpenter enlisted Edgecombe Co 5/8/61 W-arm C Boonsboro **W-right side 7/3**

Private George Burgess 20 yr old enlisted Edgecombe Co 5/8/61 (later W-right thigh Jerusalem Plank)

Private William Garrett 21 yr old enlisted Edgecombe Co 8/1/61 W Fredericksburg W-thigh Chancellorsville (later Corp)

Private Silas Gay 18 yr old enlisted Edgecombe Co 8/11/61 (later Corp)

Private Irvin Harris 24 yr old enlisted Edgecombe Co 5/8/61

Private Elisha Jones 24 yr old enlisted Edgecombe Co 5/8/61 **K 7/3**

Private James Lewis 23 yr old enlisted Edgecombe Co 8/10/61 C Williamsburg (later Corp W-arm Spotsylvania)

Private Silas Pippen 27 yr old enlisted Edgecombe Co 5/8/61 WC Williamsburg **C 7/14** (joined US Service)

Private John Ritter 25 yr old enlisted Edgecombe Co 5/8/61 **C 7/14**

Private John Savage 23 yr old enlisted Edgecombe Co 5/8/61 **C 7/3**

Private John Williams 24 yr old enlisted Edgecombe Co 5/8/61 WC Boonsboro (died 3/64)

Teamster Sherwood Harris 20 yr old teamster enlisted Edgecombe Co 5/8/61 (served to 4/64)

7/1 Casualties

2nd Lt. Rufus Atkinson 23 yr old teacher enlisted Edgecombe Co. 5/8/61 **W 7/1 C 7/30** Winchester, Va (died 8/2)

1st Sgt George Stancill 22 yr old enlisted Edgecombe Co.5/8/61 W Williamsburg **W 7/1-7/3 slight** (later 1st Lt)

Sgt. Joseph Keel 29 yr old enlisted Edgecombe Co 5/8/61 **W-left arm 7/1**

Corp. James Mayo 23 yr old enlisted Edgecombe Co 5/8/61 **W 7/1 C 7/5** (later Sgt served until 4/64

Private Lawrence Atkins 28 yr old carpenter enlisted Edgecombe Co 5/8/61 WC Williamsburg C Boonsboro W Chancellorsville **W 7/1**

Private Martin Barnhill 21 yr old enlisted Edgecombe Co 5/8/61 **W 7/1 C 7/5** (later Corp W Cold Harbor)

Private William Blout 19 yr old enlisted Edgecombe Co 5/8/61 C Chancellorsville **W 7/1 C 7/5** (died 8/13)

Private Thomas Cogins 23 yr old enlisted Edgecombe Co 5/8/61

Private John Elixon 20 yr old teamster enlisted Edgecombe Co 5/8/61 W Boonsboro **W 7/1 C 7/5**

Private Henry Lilly 26 yr old enlisted Edgecombe Co 5/8/61 **W-jaw 7/1** (later W Jerusalem Plank)

Private James Medford 23 yr old miller enlisted Edgecombe Co 5/8/61 C Boonsboro **W 7/1** (later W-left leg Cold Harbor)

Private Arthur Parker 22 yr old enlisted Edgecombe Co 5/8/61

Private Henry Parker 29 yr old enlisted Edgecombe Co 5/8/61 **W 7/1 C 7/5**

Private William Proctor 23 yr old blacksmith enlisted Edgecombe Co 5/8/61 W Williamsburg **W-left arm & knees 7/1 C 7/4**

Private John Rogers 19 yr old enlisted Edgecombe Co 8/13/61 W Chancellorsville **W-leg 7/1**

Private Robert Sherrod 30 yr old enlisted Edgecombe Co 5/8/61 W-left shoulder Gaine's Mill

Private John Summerlin 26 yr old enlisted Edgecombe Co 5/8/61 (served until 4/64)

Private John Whitehurst 26 yr old enlisted Edgecombe Co 5/8/61 C Sharpsburg **W-thigh 7/1 C 7/5** (later Corp)

Company H "*Rockingham Guards*"

Capt. Thomas Lawson 23 yr old enlisted Camp Ruffin, Va 9/11/61 (later died disease 2/24//64)

2nd Lt. Robert Moir W Chancellorsville **W 7/3 at start of advance** (later Captain)

3rd Lt. Nathaniel Smith 24 yr old student enlisted Northampton Co **C 7/14** (later 1st Lt)

Sgt. William Carter 22 yr old enlisted Rockingham Co 5/3/61 W Gaine's Mill (later K Fort Harrison)

Corp. Albert Combs 22 yr old enlisted Rockingham Co 5/3/61 (later W North Anna Sgt)

Corp. Milton Martin 25 yr old medical student enlisted Rockingham Co 5/3/61 (later Sgt C Wilderness)

Private John Cox 29 yr old enlisted Rockingham Co 5/3/61 (served until 10/64)

Private Smith Cox 27 yr old enlisted Cox Co. 9/27/62 (later W Spotsylvania—died)

Private Thomas Featherstone 22 yr old enlisted Rockingham Co 5/3/61 W-knee Fredericksburg (later K Cold Harbor)
Private Samuel Heggie 24 yr old enlisted Rockingham Co 5/3/61 (later Corp)
Private William Heggie 27 yr old enlisted Rockingham Co 5/3/61 (later Corp)
Private Peter Robertson 31 yr old enlisted Rockingham Co 5/3/61 **W-left arm 7/3 C 7/5**
Private Thomas Winston 20 yr old enlisted Rockingham Co 5/3/61 W-right toe Chancellorsville **C 7/3**

Musician James Easley 25 yr old enlisted Rockingham Co 5/3/61 (later W Spotsylvania)

7/1 Casualties

1st Lt. James Maclin Smith 25 yr old medical student enlisted Rockingham Co 5/3/61 **W-ankle 7/1 cited for meritorious conduct**
Sgt. James Ratliff 25 yr old enlisted Rockingham Co 5/3/61 W Mechanicsville **W 7/1 C 7/5**
Corp. John Robertson 20 yr old enlisted Rockingham Co 5/3/61 W-hip Gaine's Mill ***W-leg 7/1 C 7/5*** *(amp)*
Private Robert Covington 22 yr old enlisted Rockingham Co 5/3/61 C Winchester, Va **W-left thigh 7/1 C 7/5**
Private J.L. Hamington enlisted Rockingham, Co. C Spotsylvania
Private J.Z. Hathcock 21 yr old enlisted Stanly Co 2/28/63 C Fredericksburg **W 7/1 slight** (later C Wilderness)
Private Owen Joyce yr old enlisted Rockingham Co 5/3/61 **W 7/1**
Private Henry Melton 20 yr old enlisted Rockingham Co 2/28/63 **W 7/1 C 7/5**
Private Lawson Miles 38 yr old enlisted Rockingham Co 5/3/61 **C 7/14**
Private Henry Moir 20 yr old enlisted Rockingham Co 5/3/61 W Chancellorsville **W 7/1 C 7/5**
Private James Stephens 26 yr old enlisted Rockingham Co 5/3/61 **C 7/14**
Private James Vaugh 21 yr old enlisted Rockingham Co 5/3/61 W Gaine's Mill **K 7/1**
Private Thompson Walker 27 yr old enlisted Rockingham Co 5/3/61 (discharged "fractured thigh" 3/4/64)
Private Peter Walls 27 yr old enlisted Rockingham Co 9/27/62 W Fredericksburg (later AWOL 3/64)

Company I "*Rockingham Rangers*"

1st Lt. William Winchester 23 yr old clerk enlisted Rockingham Co 5/3/61 W Chancellorsville **W-right foot C 7/3**
2nd Lt. Abner Neal 24 yr old enlisted Rockingham Co 5/3/61C Sharpsburg (later 1st Lt) in command 7/3

3rd Lt. Rowland Williams 23 yr old enlisted Rockingham Co 5/3/61 W-finger Malvern Hill (later Captain)

Corp. Henry Sharp 21 yr old enlisted Rockingham Co 5/3/61 **C Williamsport, Md 7/14 (later Sgt)**

Private James Benton 29 yr old ditcher enlisted Rockingham Co 5/3/61 **W 7/1 slight & fought 7/3** (later Sgt)

Private Andrew Cobb 25 yr old enlisted Rockingham Co 5/3/61 W 2nd Manassas (later W Spotsylvania) died

Private Charles Ingram 22 yr old enlisted Caswell Co. 5/3/61

Private William Meador 24 yr old enlisted Rockingham Co 5/3/61 W Gaine's Mill C South Mountain

Private John Peay 23 yr old enlisted Rockingham Co 5/3/61 (AWOL 1/64)

Private Robert Stewart 21 yr old enlisted Rockingham Co 5/3/61 (later K Wilderness)

Private John Winchester transferred 3/4/63 (later W-left hand Wilderness)

July 1 Casualties

Sgt. Josephus Pratt 20 yr old enlisted Rockingham Co 5/3/61 **W-left thigh 7/1 C 7/5**

Private Henry Carter 22 yr old enlisted Rockingham Co 5/3/61 C Sharpsburg **W 7/1 C 7/5**

Private Lemuel Fry 24 yr old enlisted Rockingham Co 5/3/61 **W 7/1**

Private Lewis Gudenburg 38 yr old enlisted Richmond, Va 7/11/62 **W 7/1 C 7/5**

Private Thomas Haskell 48 yr old enlisted Stanly Co. 2/28/63 **W 7/1**

Private Craven Hosford 30 yr old enlisted Rockingham Co 2/28/63 (served until 10/64)

Private Joel Husdon 23 yr old enlisted Rockingham Co 5/3/61 **K 7/1**

Private Giles Jones 22 yr old cooper enlisted Rockingham Co 5/3/61 W as Color Sgt South Mountain **W-left leg 7/1 C 7/5**

Private David McCollum 25 yr old enlisted Rockingham Co 5/3/61 **C 7/14** (later W Jerusalem Plank)

Private James Rogers 27 yr old enlisted Rockingham Co 5/3/61 **W 7/1 C 7/5**

Private Alfred Stanly 27 yr old enlisted Rockingham Co 2/28/63 **(W-right eye 7/1**)

Private George Suits 22 yr old enlisted Rockingham Co 5/3/61

Private Thomas Webster 37 yr old enlisted Wake Co. 9/27/62 (later W Spotsylvania)

Private James Wray enlisted Rockingham Co 8/21/61 **K 7/1**

Company K "*Dixie Boys*"

Capt. Hugh Guerrant 28 yr old enlisted Rockingham Co 5/22/61 W Chancellorsville (later W-hand Wilderness)

2nd Lt. George Anderson 22 yr old plasterer enlisted Rockingham Co 5/22/61 **W 7/3** (later 1st Lt. & Adjutant)

1st Sgt Robert McCollum 30 yr old enlisted Rockingham Co 5/22/61 C Williamsburg (later 2nd lt.)

Sgt. James Jones 28 yr old enlisted Rockingham Co 5/22/61 C Sharpsburg (later 1st Sgt)

Corp. John Guerrant 21 yr old enlisted Rockingham Co 7/3/61 **W 7/3**

Corp. Robert Stanfield 22 yr old enlisted Rockingham Co 8/5/61 WC Williamsburg **C 7/3**

Corp. Jacob Trollinger 22 yr old clerk enlisted Rockingham Co 5/22/61 W-thigh Chancellorsville **W 7/3** (Later Sgt Major)

Private John Bateman 23 yr old enlisted Rockingham Co 5/22/61 W Williamsburg **C 7/3**

Private John Boyles 20 yr old enlisted Rockingham Co 5/22/61 C Williamsburg **C 7/3**

Private James Call 20 yr old enlisted wake Co. 9/27/62 (later C Wilderness)

Private James Warren 23 yr old enlisted Rockingham Co 5/22/61 "Only man in Co K unhurt at Gettysburg"

July 1 Casualties

1st Lt. William Nunally 28 yr old merchant enlisted Rockingham Co 5/22/61 **K 7/1**

3rd Lt. William Totten 25 yr old enlisted Rockingham Co 5/22/61 C Williamsburg **W-leg 7/1** (amp) died 7/10

Sgt. Robert Maxwell 23 yr old wheelwright enlisted Rockingham Co 5/22/61
WC Williamsburg W Fredericksburg W Chancellorsville

Private Thomas Loftis 20 yr old enlisted Rockingham Co 8/5/61 W-left breast Sharpsburg **W 7/1 slightly** (later W Wilderness)

Private Benjamin G Carter 33 yr old enlisted Rockingham Co 5/22/61 **W 7/1 C 7/5** (died 8/29 Phila hospital buried PNC))

Private Lewis Collins 25 yr old enlisted Rockingham Co 5/22/61 **W 7/1** (later teamster)

Private Julius Love 21 yr old blacksmith enlisted Rockingham Co 5/22/61 W-hand South Mountain **W-left elbow 7/1 C 7/5**

Private Calton Nunn 24 yr old enlisted Rockingham Co 8/5/61 **WC 7/1**

Private Richard Ramsey 22 yr old enlisted Rockingham Co 5/22/61 **K 7/1**

Private Roberson Sanders 22 yr old enlisted Rockingham Co 8/5/61 **W 7/1 C 7/5** (later W-left shoulder Spotsylvania)

Private Jesse Slade 39 yr old enlisted Rockingham Co 5/22/61 **K 7/1**

Private Pickney Summers 22 yr old enlisted Rockingham Co 5/22/61 **W 7/1**

Private William Summers 24 yr old enlisted Rockingham Co 5/22/61 C Williamsburg **W-right leg 7/1**

Private George Taylor 34 yr old enlisted Rockingham Co 8/5/61 W-left arm Williamsburg **C 7/14**

Private James Tulloch 29 yr old enlisted Rockingham Co 4/26/63 **W 7/1**

Private Isom Upton 29 yr old shoemaker enlisted Rockingham Co. 8/4/62 **K 7/1**
Private Alexander Walker 22 yr old enlisted Rockingham Co 5/22/61 **W 7/1 C 7/5**
Private James Walker 33 yr old enlisted Rockingham Co. 12/15/62 **K 7/1**
Private George Ware 33 yr old enlisted Rockingham Co 5/22/61 C Middletown, Md W-knee **W 7/1 C 7/5** (died7/12)
Private William Wright 22 yr old enlisted Rockingham Co 5/22/61 W Seven Pines **W 7/1**

Walker Brothers Pre War

Walker Brothers Post War

THIRTY FOURTH NORTH CAROLINA REGIMENT

Lt. Davis Harrill Co B

Private William Morris Co K

Colonel William Lowrance 27 yr old Davidson College graduate and teacher former Captain Co D enlisted Iredell Co. 9/9/61

Lt. Colonel George T. Gordon former British Army officer resided in Rockbridge Alum Springs, Va **W-left leg 7/3** (later W-right foot Bristoe Station)

Major George McIntosh Clark 24 yr old enlisted in Montgomery Co. former Captain Co K appointed 5/6/63 **K 7/1**

Major / Adjutant Francis Twitty 23 yr old enlisted Rutherford Co. former Captain Co C (acting Adjutant) appointed Major 7/1/63 **W-arm 7/3** died 9/10/64

Sgt Major George Atwell 20 yr old enlisted Rowan Co 9/9/61 promoted 3/1/63 (later 2nd Lt Co E)

Brigade QM John Clarke appointed 11/16/61
Surgeon John Miller transferred 5/17/62 (served until 10/64)
Assistant Surgeon John Richards appointed 6/15/63 (served until 10/63)
Chaplin Augustus Bennick appointed 2/12/63 (later resigned 12/19/63)
QM Sgt Willis Hargroves transferred 10/7/62
Commissary Sgt John McDowell Rutherford Co farmer appointed 6/63 (later Lt. Col.)
Ordinance Sgt Henry Rickert appointed 3/1/63

Company A "*Laurel Springs Guards*"

Captain Hiram Abernathy appointed 6/63 (later W Wilderness)
1st Sgt Hiram Stamper 37 yr old enlisted Ashe Co 8/10/61 (later C North Anna)
Sgt Levi Cox 37 yr old enlisted Ashe Co 8/10/61 (later C Brandy Station & C Fort Stedman)
Corp Hamilton Koonce 20 yr old enlisted Ashe Co 8/10/61 W-arm Ox Hill W Chancellorsville **W 7/3** (later Sgt)
Private William Liles 21 yr old enlisted Ashe Co 8/10/61 C Gaine's Mill (later Corp W Wilderness)
Private Jonathan Miller 34 yr old enlisted Ashe Co 8/10/61 W-thigh Shepherdstown (later deserted 4/10/64)
Private William Patrick 22 yr old enlisted Ashe Co 8/10/61 **W-right arm 7/3**
Private John Richardson 28 yr old enlisted Ashe Co 8/10/61 W-left shoulder Chancellorsville **W 7/3 C 7/5**
Private Joshua Richardson 21 yr old enlisted Ashe Co 8/10/61 (later Corp W-left arm Ream's Station)
Private James South 28 yr old enlisted Ashe Co 8/10/61 W 2nd Manassas **W-shell concussion 7/3** (later Corp)
Private Wiley Taylor 34 yr old enlisted Ashe Co 8/10/61 **C 7/3**

July 1 Casualties

1st Lt. Bartlett Martin W 7/1 35 yr old enlisted Ashe Co 8/10/61 **W 7/1 C 7/5**
2nd Lt. George Woody 35 yr old enlisted Ashe Co 8/10/61 **W-head 7/1** (later W-right foot Wildernesss)
Private Jacob Bare Jr. 21 yr old enlisted Ashe Co 8/10/61 deserted 8/27/63—returned
Private Jacob Bare Sr. 21 yr old enlisted Ashe Co 8/10/61 deserted 8/1/63 (later W Spotsylvania)
Private John Bare Jr. 23 yr old enlisted Ashe Co 8/10/61 W-right thigh C Chancellorsville AWOL 10/18/63
Private John Black 37 yr old enlisted Ashe Co 8/10/61 (later W Wilderness W-left leg Ream's Station)
Private Solomon Fisher 24 yr old enlisted Camp Vance 4/1/63 (later C Jericho Mills)
Private George Koonce 37 yr old enlisted Ashe Co 8/10/61 (later W Wilderness)
Private Calvin Osborn 29 yr old enlisted Ashe Co 8/10/61 **C 7/14**
Private Zadoc Osborne 36 yr old enlisted camp Gregg 3/29/63 (deserted 9/1/63)
Private Andrew Pennington 31 yr old enlisted Ashe Co 8/10/61 (deserted 8/27/63)
Private James Richardson 25 yr old enlisted Ashe Co 8/10/61 W-left thigh Gaines Mill
Private John Roope 27 yr old enlisted Ashe Co 8/10/61 (later AWOL 2/20/64)
Private Harvey Sheets 24 yr old enlisted Ashe Co 8/10/61 deserted 8/27/63—returned

Private Alexander Taylor 39 yr old enlisted Ashe Co 4/10/62 deserted 8/2/63—returned (later C North Anna)

Private Amos Viers 22 yr old enlisted Ashe Co 5/22/62 **W 7/1**

Private John Waggoner 29 yr old enlisted Ashe Co 8/10/61 as musician W Mechanicsville deserted 9/1/63

Private John Williams 24 yr old enlisted Ashe Co 8/10/61 **C 7/14**

Company B *"Sandy Run Yellow Jackets"*

Capt. Joseph Byers 31 yr old enlisted Cleveland Co 9/2/61 (dismissed 10/24/63 AWOL)

1st Lt. **David Harrill** 25 yr old enlisted Rutherford Co 9/2/61 C Chancellorsville

Sgt James Wilson 30 yr old enlisted Rutherford Co 9/2/61 W 2nd Manassas (later K Wilderness)

Sgt Sgt Doctor Hamrick 24 yr old enlisted Rutherford Co 9/2/61 (later 1st Sgt)

Private Washington Blankenship 34 yr old enlisted Camp Vance 6/8/63 (later C Cold Harbor)

Private William Brooks 24 yr old enlisted Rutherford Co 9/2/61 W Gaines Mill W Fredericksburg (later W Spotsylvania)

Private Abraham Davis 28 yr old enlisted Rutherford Co 9/2/61 W-arm Gaines Mill (later C North Anna)

Private John Davis 20 yr old enlisted Rutherford Co 9/2/61 W-left hand Fredericksburg AWOL 12/1/63

Private Ancil Dycus 23 yr old enlisted Rutherford Co 9/2/61 dismissed-reenlisted

Private William Philbeck 23 yr old enlisted Rutherford Co 9/2/61 (later W-eye Fort Stedman)

Private George Pinson 27 yr old enlisted Ceveland Co. 2/26/63 **C 7/14**

Private James Robbins 19 yr old enlisted Rutherford Co 9/2/61 (later died of disease 12/63)

Private Woody Wells 21 yr old enlisted Rutherford Co 9/2/61 (later W Jerusalem Plank)

Private Hiram White 20 yr old enlisted Rutherford Co 9/2/61 (later C Brandy Station)

Private Wallace Winn 37 yr old enlisted Cleveland Co 2/26/63 "Badge of Distinction" Chancellorsville

Private John Womack 19 yr old enlisted Rutherford Co 9/2/61 C Chancellorsville **C 7/14**

July 1 Casualties

Sgt Robert James 26 yr old enlisted Rutherford Co 9/2/61 **W-right ankle 7/1 C 7/5**

Private David Bowen 29 yr old enlisted Rutherford Co 9/2/61

Private David Bridges 22 yr old enlisted Rutherford Co 9/2/61 (died 6/14/64)

Private William Bridges 17 yr old enlisted Rutherford Co 9/2/61 (later C Petersburg)

Private Wilson Bridges 27 yr old enlisted Rutherford Co 10/19/61 (AWOL 10/23/63 W Riddell's Shop)
Private Whitson Davis 25 yr old enlisted Rutherford Co 9/2/61 **W 7/2**
Private Felix Dobbins 27 yr old enlisted Rutherford Co 9/2/61 (later W Williamsburg 64 C Fort Stedman)
Private Jesse Dobbins 22 yr old enlisted Rutherford Co 9/2/61 W 2nd Manassas (later K Wilderness)
Private Francis Green 26 yr old enlisted Rutherford Co 9/2/61 W Gaine's Mill **C 7/1**
Private Uel Green 29 yr old enlisted Cleveland Co 2/26/63 deserted 11/1/63
Private Jacob Holifield 18 yr old enlisted Rutherford Co 9/2/61 deserted 9/17/630
Private James McDaniel 33 yr old enlisted Rutherford Co 9/2/61 **C 7/1**

Company C *"Rutherford Rebels"*

Captain John Young enlisted Camp Gregg 3/6/63 promoted 7/1
2nd Lt. Lorenzo Wilkie 26 yr old enlisted Rutherford Co. 9/2/61
3rd Lt. William Wilkins transferred 4/15/63 appointed 7/1/63 **W-left hand & left thigh 7/3**
1st Sgt. Noah Whiteside 23 yr old enlisted Rutherford Co. 9/2/61 (later AWOL 1/64)
Sgt. James Henderson 24 yr old enlisted Rutherford Co. 9/2/61 W-right hip Fredericksburg (later W Jone's Farm)
Sgt. George Koonce 22 yr old enlisted Rutherford Co. 9/2/61 "Badge of Distinction" Chancellorsville **C 7/3**
Corp. Humphrey Lynch 26 yr old enlisted Rutherford Co. 9/2/61 (later W Petersburg 1864)
Corporal William Sorrell 31 yr old enlisted Rutherford Co. 9/2/61 C 8/1 Brandy Station
Private John Camp 25 yr old enlisted Rutherford Co. 9/2/61 **C 7/12/ Funkstown**
Private G.W. Coon W 7/2/62 near Richmond **W 7/3 C 7/5**
Private Calvin Crow 19 yr old enlisted Rutherford Co. 9/2/61 W Gaine's Mill (later Corp)
Private Andrew Flack 20 yr old enlisted Rutherford Co. 9/2/61 (later Corp & Sgt K Ream's Station)
Private Samuel Foster 30 yr old enlisted Rutherford Co. 9/2/61 **C 7/3**
Private John Freeman 25 yr old enlisted Rutherford Co. 9/2/61 **C 7/14**
Private Edward Goode 23 yr old enlisted Rutherford Co. 9/2/61
Private George Goode 22 yr old enlisted Rutherford Co. 9/2/61 W near Culpepper, Va 1863 (later Corp)
Private James Hudgins 20 yr old enlisted Rutherford Co. 9/2/61 C 8/1 Brandy Station
Private William Nailand 20 yr old enlisted Rutherford Co. 9/2/61 **C 7/14**
Private Drewry Nanney 19 yr old enlisted Rutherford Co. 9/2/61
Private James Scoggins 21 yr old enlisted Rutherford Co. 9/2/61
Private Esley Shitle 21 yr old enlisted Rutherford Co. 9/2/61 (later C North Anna)

Private Jeremiah Shitle 30 yr old enlisted Rutherford Co. 9/2/61 **C 7/14**
Private Jason Taylor enlisted Rutherford Co. 10/12/62 (later Corp)
Private John Wilson 20 yr old enlisted Rutherford Co. 9/2/61

Ambulance Driver William Conner 24 yr old enlisted Rutherford Co. 9/2/61 W-back Gaine's Mill

July 1 Casualties

Sgt. Robert Harrill 26 yr old miller enlisted Rutherford Co. 9/2/61 W Gaine's Mill (later W Jerusalem Plank)
Corp. Stephen Hensley 24 yr old enlisted Rutherford Co. 9/2/61 (later reduced in rank)
Private Thomas Carson 26 yr old enlisted Rutherford Co. 9/2/61 (later transferred Co I)
Private Alfred Cook 19 yr old enlisted Rutherford Co. 9/2/61 **W-jaw 7/1 C 7/5**
Private Elijah Daves 26 yr old enlisted Rutherford Co. 9/2/61 **W 7/1 K 7/6 Williamsport**
Private Alfred Foster 23 yr old enlisted Rutherford Co. 9/2/61 (later W Jone's Farm)
Private Henry Foster 25 yr old enlisted Rutherford Co. 9/2/61 (detailed as Pioneer)
Private Mills Higgins 28 yr old enlisted Rutherford Co. 9/2/61 **K 7/1**
Private Henry Keeter 19 yr old enlisted Rutherford Co. 9/2/61 **W-left leg 7/1 C 7/5**
Private John Ledbetter 29 yr old enlisted Rutherford Co. 9/2/61 **C 7/14**
Private Henry London 30 yr old enlisted Rutherford Co. 9/2/61 W Gaine's Mill
Private Ahijah Lynch 24 yr old enlisted Rutherford Co. 9/2/61 W Gaine's Mill W-hip Ox Hill **C 7/14**

Company D *"The Oakland Guards"*

Capt. Carmi McNeely 27 yr old enlisted Rowan Co 9/9/61 promoted 9/7/62 **C 7/14**
1st Lt. Monroe M. Gillon 22 yr old enlisted Rowan Co 9/9/61 (later W-shoulder Petersburg) **cited for meritorious conduct**
2nd Lt. Tilman Davis 35 yr old enlisted Rowan Co 9/9/61 (later arrested 1/64 to 2/64)
1st Sgt Joel Corriher 27 yr old enlisted Rowan Co 9/9/61 W Gaine's Mill (later W Ream's Station)
Sgt. John Ellis 22 yr old enlisted Rowan Co 9/9/61 (later W Jerusalem Plank)
Sgt. Samuel Torrence 30 yr old enlisted Rowan Co 9/9/61 (later W Culpepper 8/1/63)
Corp. Miles Freeze 27 yr old enlisted Rowan Co 9/9/61 (later W Petersburg)
Corp. Theodore Kistler 22 yr old enlisted Rowan Co 9/9/61 W 2nd Manassas (later Color Sgt W-abdomen Jericho Mills)
Corp. Reuben Overcash 21 yr old enlisted Rowan Co 9/9/61 W Gaine's Mill (later died of disease 3/64)
Private Joseph Douglas 22 yr old enlisted Rowan Co 9/9/61

Private Marshall Douglas enlisted Iredell Co 5/15/62 **W-left hand C 7/3**
Private Obediah Eller 23 yr old enlisted Rowan Co 9/9/61 "badge of gallantry" Chancellorsville (later promoted Color Sgt 9/1/63)
Private James Glover 19 yr old enlisted Rowan Co 9/9/61 **C 7/12 Hagerstown**
Private Robert Hart 22 yr old enlisted Rowan Co 9/9/61 (later W Spotsylvania)
Private Jacob Kurf 21 yr old enlisted Rowan Co 9/9/61 W Fredericksburg (later Corp)
Private Ibsom Miller 23 yr old enlisted Rowan Co 9/9/61 **K 7/3**
Private Hampton Overcash 23 yr old mechanic enlisted Rowan Co 9/9/61 (served through 10/64)
Private Henry Overcash 25 yr old enlisted Rowan Co 9/9/61 W Gaine's Mill AWOL 7/24—returned

Ambulance Driver John Woodside 20 yr old enlisted Rowan Co 9/9/61
Teamster Jacob Stirewalt 24 yr old enlisted Rowan Co 9/9/61

July 1 Casualties

Sgt. William Kirkpatrick 28 yr old enlisted Rowan Co 9/9/61 W Chancellorsville **W 7/1 C 7/14**
Corp. William Barnhart 31 yr old enlisted Rowan Co 9/9/61 **W 7/1 C 7/5 ***
Corp. George Overcash 20 yr old enlisted Rowan Co 9/9/61 **W 7/1**
Private Thomas Atkinson 23 yr old enlisted Rowan Co 9/9/61 as Sgt W Gaine's Mill (AWOL 9/63-11/63)
Private John Clotfelder 21 yr old enlisted Rowan Co 9/9/61 deserted 9/62 arrested on duty 3/63 (later K Ream's Station)
Private Green Eller 31 yr old miller enlisted Rowan Co 9/9/61 W Seven Pines (later W Spotsylvania)
Private John Hodgins 25 yr old enlisted Rowan Co 9/9/61 **W-left leg 7/1 C 7/5 (amp)**
Private James Lawrence 22 yr old enlisted Rowan Co 9/9/61
Private Eli McLaughlin 30 yr old enlisted Rowan Co 9/9/61 (detailed as clerk in QM office)
Private John McLaughlin 32 yr old enlisted Rowan Co 9/9/61
Private James McNeely 30 yr old enlisted Rowan Co 5/15/62 C 1862 (served until 12/64)
Private Stanhope Martin 20 yr old enlisted Rowan Co 9/9/61 W-left forearm Gaine's Mill
Private James Franklin Miller 27 yr old enlisted Rowan Co 9/9/61 (later AWOL 8/63 to 10/63 W Wilderness)

Company E *"Shady Grove Rangers"*

Capt. Micajah Davis 25 yr old enlisted Lincoln Co. 9/11/61 promoted 12/62 (resigned 10/63)

1st Lt. James Tiddy 23 yr old enlisted Lincoln Co. 12/1/62 Promoted 5/3/63 **W-right foot 7/3 (amp) C 7/5**

2nd Lt. Emmanuel Houser 22 yr old enlisted Lincoln Co 9/11/61 appointed 5/3/63 (later W-leg Wilderness)

1st Sgt David Taylor 27 yr old carpenter enlisted Lincoln Co 9/11/61 "Badge of distinction" Chancellorsville (later C Wilderness)

Sgt George Cauble 25 yr old enlisted Lincoln Co 9/11/61 W 2nd Manassas **W 7/3 C 7/5**

Sgt Marcus Holly 24 yr old enlisted Lincoln Co 9/11/61 **W 7/3 C 7/5**

Sgt Joseph Huss 21 yr old enlisted Lincoln Co 9/11/61 **K 7/3**

Sgt. John Yoder 21 yr old enlisted Lincoln Co 9/11/61 **W 7/3**

Corp. John Bess 20 yr old enlisted Lincoln Co 9/11/61 W Fredericksburg C Chancellorsville (later C Wilderness)

Corp. Wiley Childers 22 yr old carpenter enlisted Lincoln Co 9/11/61

Corp. Malachi Hovis 20 yr old enlisted Lincoln Co 9/11/61 **

Private Benjamin Carpenter 19 yr old enlisted Lincoln Co 5/11/62 (later W Reams Station Sgt)

Private Jacob Dellinger 22 yr old enlisted Camp Magnum 12/7/61

Private Abraham Eaker 32 yr old enlisted Lincoln Co 9/11/61 **C 7/14** (later joined US Service)

Private Daniel Eaker 24 yr old enlisted Lincoln Co 9/11/61 **C 7/14** (later joined US Service)

Private Jesse Eaker 21 yr old enlisted Lincoln Co 9/11/61 W Seven days W 2nd Manassas C Chancellorsville (later C Brandy Station)

Private Pickney Edmond 24 yr old enlisted Lincoln Co 9/11/61 W-Shoulder Gaines Mill

Private Able Hertzog 21 yr old enlisted Lincoln Co 9/11/61 WC Chancellorsville (later ensign)

Private Marcus Hevner 25 yr old enlisted Lincoln Co 9/11/61 W Gaine's Mill **C 7/3**

Private Daniel Holly 20 yr old enlisted Camp Gregg 3/8/63

Private Samuel Hoyle transferred 10/2/62 **W 7/3 C 7/5**

Private Pinkney Huss 18 yr old enlisted Camp Gregg 3/8/63 (later AWOL 1/64 to 4/64)

Private James Keever 27 yr old enlisted Lincoln Co 9/11/61 (later C Wilderness)

Private Emanuel Mooney 37 yr old enlisted Gaston Co. 3/5/63 W-"stabbed in abdomen" Chancellorsville (later W Spotsylvania)

Private Robert Price 29 yr old carriage maker enlisted Lincoln Co 9/11/61

Private Alexander Proctor 21 yr old enlisted Lincoln Co 12/9/61 (served through 11/64)

Private Berry Quenn 25 yr old enlisted Lincoln Co 9/11/61 (later K Wilderness)

Private David Reed 29 yr old enlisted Lincoln Co 2/2/62 W-ankle, arm & hip Gaine's Mill

Private Matthew Reynolds 20 yr old enlisted Lincoln Co 9/11/61 **W 7/3 C 7/5**

Private George Robinson 19 yr old tinner enlisted Camp Mangum 1/4/62 W 2nd Manassas W Fredericksburg

Private Jacob Sain 24 yr old enlisted Lincoln Co 9/11/61 **W 7/3 C 7/14**

Private Charles Shull 20 yr old enlisted Lincoln Co 9/11/61 W Gaine's Mill (later C Wilderness)
Private Philip Shull 20 yr old blacksmith enlisted Lincoln Co 9/11/61 W 2nd Manassas
Private Robert Taylor 23 yr old blacksmith enlisted Lincoln Co 9/11/61 C Chancellorsville **K 7/12**
Private Marcus Withers 23 23 yr old enlisted Lincoln Co 9/11/61 **C 7/3**

Teamster Jonas Hoyle 30 yr old enlisted Lincoln Co 9/11/61 W-side Fredericksburg (detailed as Teamster)
Teamster Joshua Queen 28 yr old enlisted Lincoln Co 9/11/61 W-finger Gaine's Mill (detailed as Teamster)

July 1 Casualties

Corp. George Fulbright 24 yr old enlisted Lincoln Co 9/11/61 W-left arm Ox Hill **W 7/1 C 7/5**
Corp. Devany Putham transferred 4/16/63
Private Jacob Friday 37 yr old enlisted Gaston Co 3/5/63 **W 7/1 C 7/5**
Private Noah Bess 18 yr old enlisted Camp Gregg 3/8/63 **W 7/1**
Private William Bess 23 yr old enlisted Lincoln Co 9/11/61 **W 7/1**
Private Frederick Carpenter 36 yr old enlisted Gaston Co 3/5/63 deserted 8/63—arrested
Private James Calvin 25 yr old stonemason enlisted Lincoln Co 9/11/61
Private Turner Cody 46 yr old enlisted Lincoln Co 9/11/61 (discharged 9/64 overage)
Private George Conner 27 yr old enlisted Lincoln Co 9/11/61 W Seven Days
Private Andrew Fulenwider transferred 6/8/63 **K 7/1**
Private Daniel Gilbert 29 yr old enlisted Lincoln Co 9/11/61 W Gaines Mill
Private Zimri Kiser 36 yr old enlisted Gaston Co 3/5/63
Private John Lemaster 20 yr old enlisted Lincoln Co 9/11/61 W-leg Gaines Mill W-left calf **7/1 C 7/5**
Private Andrew Metcalf 37 yr old enlisted Gaston Co. 3/5/63 **W 7/1** (later C North Anna)
Private Caleb Rhyne 38 yr old enlisted Gaston Co. 3/5/63 C Wilderness
Private Levi Wacaster 30 yr old enlisted Camp Mangum 12/7/61 **W 7/1 C 7/5**

Company F *"The Floyd Rifles"*

Capt. David Hoyle 33 yr old millwright enlisted Cleveland Co. 9/17/61 W Gaine's Mill (later resigned 11/64)

1st Lt. Jacob Hogue 38 yr old enlisted Cleveland Co. 9/17/61 **W 7/1 fought 7/3**

2nd Lt. Nathan McGinnis 30 yr old enlisted Cleveland Co. 9/17/61 (later Asst QM)

3rd Lt. Thomas **Lattimore** 19 yr old enlisted Cleveland Co. 10/5/61 (commander Co D early 1864)

1st Sgt. William White 25 yr old enlisted Cleveland Co. 9/17/61 W Chancellorsville **C 7/3**

Sgt William Goodson 27 yr old substitute enlisted Cleveland Co. 9/17/61 **W 7/3 slight**

Sgt. Maxwell Hoyle 22 yr old enlisted Cleveland Co. 9/17/61 (later AWOL 9/23/63—reduced in rank—W Petersburg)

Corp. Drury Price 24 yr old enlisted Cleveland Co. 9/17/61 W Mechanicsville

Corp. Lemuel Self 24 yr old enlisted Cleveland Co. 9/17/61 (later AWOL 9/23—reduced in rank—promoted Corp C North Anna

Corp. John Turner 31 yr old enlisted Cleveland Co. 9/17/61 (later W Petersburg—died)

Private James Blanton 23 yr old enlisted Cleveland Co. 9/17/61 W Gaine's Mill

Private William Gibbons 24 yr old enlisted Cleveland Co. 9/17/61 **C 7/3** (later K Wilderness)

Private Elphus Hamrick 27 yr old enlisted Cleveland Co. 9/17/61 (later C Ft Stedman)

Private Martin Hoyle 39 yr old enlisted Cleveland Co. 2/28/63 **C 7/14**

Private Abram Irvin 20 yr old enlisted Cleveland Co. 9/17/61 W Gaine's Mill **C 7/3**

Private James Lattimore 22 yr old enlisted Cleveland Co. 9/17/61 (later W Spotsylvania North Anna)

Private Jesse Lattimore 21 yr old enlisted Cleveland Co. 10/5/61

Private William Lee 22 yr old enlisted Cleveland Co. 9/17/61 **C 7/14** (under arrest 4/64) *

Private Presley Norman 24 yr old enlisted Cleveland Co. 9/17/61 W Gaine's Mill **C 7/14**

Private Miles Stroup enlisted Wayne Co 1/28/62 **C 7/5 left behind as nurse**

Private Simpson Warlick 32 yr old enlisted Cleveland Co. 4/15/63 AWOL 11/1/63

Private Emory Warren 29 yr old enlisted Orange County CH, Va 8/14/62 **C 7/14**

Private Adam Whisnant 27 yr old enlisted Cleveland Co. 9/17/61 **C 7/14**

Private Lawson Williams 19 yr old enlisted Cleveland Co. 2/28/63 **W 7/3 C 7/5**

Private Perry Wright 22 yr old enlisted Massaponax, Va 5/17/62 **C 7/14** (later W-left leg Petersburg)

Private William Wright 22 yr old enlisted Cleveland Co. 9/17/61 W-thigh Seven Pines

Drummer William Williams 20 yr old enlisted Cleveland Co. 9/17/61 (later infantry private)

Ambulance Driver Benjamin Ellis 26 yr old enlisted Cleveland Co. 10/10/61

Teamster Andrew Peeler 27 yr old enlisted Cleveland Co. 9/17/61

Private Andrew London 31 yr old enlisted Cleveland Co. 9/17/61 (detailed as blacksmith)

July 1 Casualties

Sgt Virgil Elliot 32 yr old enlisted Cleveland Co. 9/17/61 **W-right leg 7/1** (later C Ft. Stedman)

Sgt. Bedford Hendrick 28 yr old enlisted Cleveland Co. 9/17/61 W Chancellorsville **W 7/1 C 8/1 Brandy Station**

Private Jesse Carter 20 yr old enlisted Cleveland Co. 9/17/61 W 2nd Manassas **K 7/1**

Private Henry Clay 21 yr old enlisted Cleveland Co. 9/17/61 **W 7/1 C 7/5** died 8/17

Private John Eaker 22 yr old enlisted Cleveland Co. 10/10/61 **W 7/1 C 7/5**

Private John Crow 30 yr old enlisted Cleveland Co. 9/17/61 **C 7/14** (later under arrest 4/64) *

Private William Crowder 25 yr old enlisted Cleveland Co. 9/17/61 (later W Petersburg)

Private Jacob Earls 21 yr old enlisted Cleveland Co. 9/17/61 W-right arm Gaines Mills

Private John Gantt 19 yr old enlisted Cleveland Co. 9/17/61 **C 7/14** (later under arrest 4/64) *

Private William Gantt 23 enlisted Cleveland Co. 2/28/63 (later K Spotsylvania)

Private John Lutz 26 yr old tanner enlisted Cleveland Co. 9/17/61 **W 7/1 C 7/5**

Private John Newton 20 yr old enlisted Cleveland Co. 9/17/61 W-shell Gaine's Mill **W-left leg 7/1 C 7/5**

Private John Peeler transferred 2/8/63 **C 7/14** (later joined US service)

Private Moses Petty 24 yr old enlisted Cleveland Co. 9/17/61 W-Ox Hill, Va **W-left thigh 7/1 C 7/5**

Private Andrew Powell 23 yr old enlisted Cleveland Co. 9/17/61 **W 7/1 C 7/5**

Private Drury Turner 47 yr old enlisted Camp Greeg, Va 5/15/63

Private William Turner 24 yr old enlisted Cleveland Co. 9/17/61 W Chancellorsville **C 7/14**

Company G *"The Mecklenburg Boys"*

2nd Lt. James Todd 24 yr old enlisted Mecklenburg Co. 9/30/61 (later Captain)

1st Sgt Charles Todd 23 yr old enlisted Mecklenburg Co. 9/30/61 "Badge of Distinction Chancellorsville (later Sgt Major)

Sgt. Thomas Johnson 29 yr old enlisted Mecklenburg Co. 9/30/61 (later W Spotsylvania)

Sgt. William McCord 28 yr old enlisted Mecklenburg Co. 9/30/61 W 2nd Manassas (later 1st Sgt)

Sgt. Green Todd 27 yr old enlisted Mecklenburg Co. 9/30/61 (Later W-thigh leg & arm Wilderness)

Corp. John Lawing 22 yr old enlisted Mecklenburg Co. 9/30/61 (later AWOL 11/63—died of disease 9/64)

Corp. Charles Wriston 23 yr old enlisted Mecklenburg Co. 9/30/61 (later Sgt K Spotsylvania)

Private Joseph Carpenter 38 yr old enlisted 3/12/63 **K 7/3**

Private John Lawing 22 yr old enlisted Mecklenburg Co. 9/30/61 W Gaine's Mil **W 7/3** (later Corp)

Private Alexander McCall 23 yr old enlisted Mecklenburg Co. 9/30/61 C Gaine's Mill **C 7/14**

Private Thaddeus McGahey 23 yr old enlisted Mecklenburg Co. 1/4/62

Private George Parks 26 yr old enlisted Mecklenburg Co. 9/30/61 **C 7/3** (later C North Anna)

Private James Proctor 35 yr old enlisted Mecklenburg Co. 9/30/61 **C 7/14**

Private George Rosich 33 yr old enlisted Richmond, Va 5/30/62

Private James Sanford 20 yr old enlisted Mecklenburg Co. 9/30/61

Private John Sanford 21 yr old enlisted Mecklenburg Co. 9/30/61 **W slight 7/3**

Private John Todd 22 yr old enlisted Rappahannock, Va 5/12/62 **W 7/3 C 7/5**

July 1 Casualties

Capt. George Norment 29 yr old farmer enlisted Mecklenburg Co. 9/30/61 W Gaine's Mill **W-left hip 7/1** (later Lt. Col.)

1st Lt. Alexander Cathy 28 yr old enlisted Mecklenburg Co. 9/30/61 **W-leg 7/1 C 7/5** (amp)

3rd Lt. John Abernathy 21 yr old enlisted Mecklenburg Co. 9/30/61 **K 7/1**

Corp. John Cathey 21 yr old enlisted Mecklenburg Co. 9/30/61 W-fot Gaine's Mill **W-left shoulder 7/1 C 7/5**

Private Thomas Bennett 31 yr old enlisted Mecklenburg Co. 9/30/61 **(on detail after wounded 7/1)**

Private John Brotherton 38 yr old enlisted Lincoln Co. 3/12/63 **W 7/1** (later W-Jerusalem Plank Rd)

Private William Brotherton 39 yr old enlisted Lincoln Co.

Private Alexander Cathy 29 yr old enlisted Mecklenburg Co. 9/30/61 (later W Wilderness)

Private Almarine Clark 35 yr old enlisted Mecklenburg Co. 9/30/61 W-Richmond (served until 11/64)

Private John Clark 30 yr old enlisted Mecklenburg Co. 9/30/61 W-Richmond (later K Wilderness)

Private William Cox 28 yr old enlisted Mecklenburg Co. 9/30/61 W-hip & arm Gaine's Mill

Private Hugh Elliot 36 yr old enlisted Mecklenburg Co. 9/30/61 W 2nd Manassas (later died disease 2/64)

Private Scott Hutchinson 36 yr old enlisted Mecklenburg Co. 9/30/61 (later Corp)

Private Samuel Jarrett 38 yr old enlisted Lincoln Co 3/12/63 (Later K Spotsylvania)

Private John Hipp 37 yr old enlisted Mecklenburg 3/1/63 **W 7/1** (later W Spotsylvania)

Private James McCall 22 yr old enlisted Mecklenburg Co. 9/30/61 C Chancellorsville **W 7/1**

Company H *"The Rough and Readys"*

Captain John Roberts 31 yr old enlisted Cleveland Co. 10/1/61

1st Lt. Joseph Camp 23 yr old enlisted Cleveland Co. 10/1/61 **C 7/12** Funkstown, Md

2nd Lt.George Blanton 33 yr old blacksmith enlisted Cleveland Co. 10/1/61 C Winchester, Va (later W Spotsylvania)

3rd Lt. William Mittag 29 yr old enlisted Cleveland Co. 10/1/61 C Harrison's Landing

1st Sgt A.J. Webb 24 yr old enlisted Cleveland Co. 10/1/61 **K 7/3**

Sgt. James Wesson 20 yr old enlisted Cleveland Co. 10/1/61 C Savage Station (later 1st Sgt)

Sgt. Franklin Wilkins 30 yr old enlisted Cleveland Co. 10/1/61 as Sgt—reduced in rank—promoted Sgt

Corp. Romulus Hopper transferred 10/62 (later Sgt)

Corp. John Howell 21 yr old enlisted Cleveland Co. 10/1/61 (later Sgt)

Corp. Richard Morris transferred 7/62 **W 7/3**

Corp William Wesson 37 yr old enlisted Cleveland Co. 10/1/61 **C 7/14**

Private David Allen 35 yr old enlisted Cleveland Co. as Corp—reduced in rank (later W Spotsylvania)

Private Perry Allen 21 yr old enlisted Cleveland Co. 10/1/61 (later AWOL 11/63—returned C North Anna)

Private H.W. Barrett 24 yr old enlisted Cleveland Co. 10/1/61

Private William Brown 23 yr old enlisted Cleveland Co. 10/1/61 **C 7/14** (later joined US service)

Private Abner Camp 30 yr old enlisted Cleveland Co. 10/1/61 W-right leg Gaine's Mill deserted 8/18/63

Private J.A. Cobb 37 yr old enlisted Cleveland Co. 2/28/63 **C 7/14**

Private Timons Hughes 22 yr old enlisted Cleveland Co. 10/1/61 (later C Ft Stedman)

Private Alexander Shields 28 yr old carriage maker enlisted Cleveland Co. 10/1/61 (present through 2/64)

Private Robert Smith 30 yr old enlisted Cleveland Co. 10/1/61 **C 7/14**

Private H.M. Warren 22 yr old enlisted Wayne Co. 1/16/62

Private Joseph Weaver 18 yr old enlisted Cleveland Co. 2/26/63 **W 7/3** died 6/64

Private William Wilkins 26 yr old enlisted Cleveland Co. 10/1/61 W-left leg Gaine's Mill AWOL 12/63

Musician Champion Allen 27 yr old enlisted Cleveland Co. 10/1/61

Teamster James Scism 20 yr old enlisted Cleveland Co. 10/1/61 W Mechanicsville (detailed cattle driver & blacksmith)

July 1 Casualties

Private Laben Allen transferred 9/62 deserted 8/18/63

Private William Long 24 yr old enlisted Cleveland Co. 10/1/61 promoted Sgt—reduced private **C 7/14**

Private O.V. Mauney 29 yr old enlisted Cleveland Co. 10/1/61 W-left thigh Glendale **W 7/1**

Private D.W. Miller 37 yr old enlisted Cleveland Co. 2/28/63 **W 7/1 C 7/14**

Private William Moore 29 yr old enlisted Cleveland Co. 10/1/61 **K 7/1**

Private Ross Moore enlisted Cleveland Co 8/1/62 arrested 4/63 **deserted C 7/5 ***

Private James Overby 34 yr old enlisted Cleveland Co. 10/1/61 **C 7/14**

Private J.L. Putman 21 yr old enlisted Cleveland Co. 10/1/61 **W 7/1 C 7/14**

Private Perry Putham 39 yr old enlisted 2/28/63 **C 7/14**

Private E.H. Revel 21 yr old enlisted Cleveland Co. 10/1/61 W 9/62

Private Henry Revel 20 yr old enlisted Cleveland Co. 10/1/61 **C 7/14** (later joined US service)

Company I *"The Rutherford Band"*

2nd Lt. Thomas Phillips 19 yr old enlisted Rutherford Co. 10/6/61 W-right thigh 2nd Manassas

Sgt Leonard Fowler 32 yr old enlisted Rutherford Co. 10/6/61 W 2nd Manassas **W 7/3**

Sgt. Orson Mays 25 yr old enlisted Rutherford Co. 2/1/62 **C 7/3**

Corp. John Henson 20 yr old enlisted Rutherford Co. 10/6/61 (W Wilderness)

Corp. James Morrow 21 yr old enlisted Rutherford Co. 10/6/61 W-breast C Ox Hill W Chancellorsville **W 7/3 C 7/5**

Corp. James Wyatt 21 yr old enlisted Rutherford Co. 10/6/61 (present through 11/64)

Private William Blanton 21 yr old enlisted Rutherford Co. 10/6/61

Private James Brooks 39 yr old enlisted Person Co. 3/10/63 (later AWOL 1/64-returned)

Private William Fisher 41 yr old enlisted Lincoln Co. 3/12/63 **C 7/14**

Private Miles Flinn 39 yr old enlisted Rutherford Co. 10/6/61 W-left shoulder 2nd Manassas (later Sgt)

Private Daniel Fowler 27 yr old enlisted Rutherford Co. 10/6/61 as Corp—reduced in rank **C 7/3**

Private Thomas Hays 28 yr old enlisted Rutherford Co. 10/6/61 (later W Petersburg)

Private James Henderson 23 yr old enlisted Rutherford Co. 10/6/61 (later Corp)

Private Joseph Kennady 20 yr old enlisted Rutherford Co. 10/6/61 W-Malvern Hill **WC 7/3**

Private Little John Kennedy 20 yr old enlisted Rutherford Co. 10/6/61

Private Thomas Kennedy 32 yr old enlisted Rutherford Co. 10/6/61

Private Joseph Smith 25 yr old enlisted Rutherford Co. 10/6/61 as Sgt—reduced in rank later (transferred CS Navy)

Private James Steadman 20 yr old enlisted Rutherford Co. 10/6/61 W Gaine's Mill **W slight 7/3**

Private Marion Strickland 26 yr old enlisted Rutherford Co. 10/6/61 W Sharpsburg (later W Thigh Wilderness)
Private Thompson Wood 20 yr old enlisted Rutherford Co. 10/6/61 W Chancellorsville **W 7/3**

Teamster Hilman Phillips 29 yr old enlisted Rutherford Co. 10/6/61

July 1 Casualties

Capt. James Wood 31 yr old enlisted Rutherford Co. 10/6/61 **W-head & right arm 7/1**
1st Lt. Henry Jenkins 33 yr old enlisted Rutherford Co. 10/6/61 **W 7/1**
3rd Lt. George Job Huntley 22 yr old enlisted Rutherford Co. 10/6/61 **K 7/1**
1st Sgt. John Crawford 19 yr old enlisted Rutherford Co. 10/6/61 W Shepardstown **W 7/1 C 7/5**
Corp. Jackson Robbins 35 yr old enlisted Rutherford Co. 10/6/61 W Gaine's Mill **K 7/1**
Private James Griffin 33 yr old enlisted Rutherford Co. 10/6/61 **W 7/1 C 7/5** (later C North Anna)
Private John Hansel 37 yr old enlisted Gaston Co. 3/19/63 (later W Cold Harbor)
Private Nimrod Harris 22 yr old enlisted Rutherford Co. 10/6/61 (later died of disease 3/64)
Private Phillip Henson 19 yr old enlisted Rutherford Co. 10/6/61 **W 7/1 C 7/5**
Private Eli Jenkins 37 yr old enlisted Gaston Co. **W 7/1 C 7/5**
Private John Jenkins enlisted Rutherford Co. 6/28/63 **W 7/1 C 7/5** (later joined US Service)
Private William Smith 42 yr old enlisted Rutherford Co. 10/6/61 (later W-abdomen Wilderness)
Private John Steadman 17 yr old enlisted Rutherford Co. 10/6/61 W Shepardstown **W 7/1**
Private William Sutton 30 yr old enlisted Rutherford Co. 10/6/61 W 2nd Manassas
Private Hiram Tate 29 yr old enlisted Rutherford Co. 10/6/61 deserted 8/63
Private James Taylor 27 yr old enlisted Rutherford Co. 10/6/61 **K 7/1**
Private James Thompson 22 yr old enlisted Rutherford Co. 10/6/61 **W-arm & head 7/1**
Private Marcus Wood transferred 6/20/62 (later C North Anna)

Company K *"Montgomery Boys"*

1st Lt. Thomas Haltom 43 yr old merchant enlisted Montgomery Co. 9/9/61 W-leg Glendale (resigned 7/64)
3rd Lt. Burrel Cotton 26 yr old enlisted Montgomery Co. 9/9/61 W Glendale (later K Jerusalem Plank)

1st Sgt William Coogan 27 yr old enlisted Montgomery Co. 9/9/61 W-right leg Gaine's Mill

Sgt. George Coggin 28 yr old enlisted Montgomery Co. 9/9/61 **C 7/3**

Sgt. Wilson Kime 37 yr old enlisted Montgomery Co. 9/9/61

Sgt. Elijah Saunders 27 yr old enlisted Montgomery Co. 9/9/61 W-hip & arm Mechanicsville **W-right thigh 7/3**

Corp. Winbern Cranford 27 yr old millwright enlisted Montgomery Co. 9/9/61 (later C Jerusalem Plank)

Corp. James Elliot 28 yr old enlisted Montgomery Co. 9/9/61 **W 7/12 Hagerstown**—died 8/63

Corp. Elijah Reeves 22 yr old enlisted Montgomery Co. (later Sgt 7/4/63)

Private Hiram Brewer 22 yr old enlisted Montgomery Co. 9/9/61 deserted 8/14—returned

Private John Burroughs 22 yr old enlisted Montgomery Co. 9/9/61 W—Glendale deserted 8/14

Private Joel Cranford 24 yr old enlisted Montgomery Co. 9/9/61 (later W—arm Wilderness—amp)

Private William Dennis 24 yr old enlisted Montgomery Co. 9/9/61 W Gaine's Mill (later C Ft Stedman)

Private Gilbert Hamilton 24 yr old enlisted Montgomery Co. 9/9/61 (later Corp C North Anna)

Private Joseph Hogan 40 yr old enlisted Montgomery Co 9/8/61 "Badge of Distinction" Chancellorsville deserted 8/13/63—returned

Private James Hughes 35 yr old enlisted Montgomery Co. 9/9/61

Private Freeman Hurley 22 yr old enlisted Montgomery Co. 9/9/61 W-both thighs Gains Mill **C 7/3**

Private James McRae 32 yr old school teacher enlisted Camp Gregg 3/23/63 (later C Jerusalem Plank)

Private Anderson Morgan 40 yr old enlisted Montgomery Co. 3/5/63 **AWOL 7-10/63**

Private Joseph Morgan 23 yr old enlisted Montgomery Co. 9/9/61

Private Wililam **Morris** 22 yr old enlisted Montgomery Co. **C 7/14**

Private James Reeves 24 yr old enlisted Montgomery Co. 9/9/61 C Frederick, Md (later Corp 7/24/63)

Private David Richardson 19 yr old enlisted Montgomery Co. 9/9/61 (later K Petersburg)

Private Martin Rush 20 yr old enlisted Montgomery Co. 9/9/61 W Gaine's Mill (later W-foot Wilderness)

Private Eli Russell 27 yr old enlisted Montgomery Co. 3/5/63 **C 7/14**

Private Elijah Russell 25 yr old enlisted Montgomery Co. 12/25/61 W-right knee Gaine's Mill

Private Leonard Frank 38 yr old enlisted Montgomery Co. 3/5/63 (later C Ft. Stedman)

Private William Russell 37 yr old enlisted Montgomery Co. 3/5/63 (later AWOL 3-4/64 K-Petersburg

Private Elisha Saunders 27 yr old enlisted Montgomery Co. 3/5/63 **C 7/3**
Private James Sedberry 23 yr old enlisted Montgomery Co. 9/9/61 (later Corp W Cold Harbor—died)
Private Issac Smith 23 yr old enlisted Montgomery Co. 9/9/61 W Ox Hill, Va.
Private David Thompson 33 yr old enlisted Montgomery Co. 9/9/61 as Sgt—reduced in rank W Chancellorsville **C 7/14**

Teamster Pleasant Hurley 20 yr old enlisted Montgomery Co. 9/9/61

July 1 Casualties

2nd Lt. Nevin McLeod 27 yr old enlisted Montgomery Co. 9/9/61 **W-right leg 7/1** (later K North Anna)
1st Sgt Noramn McLeod 24 yr old enlisted Montgomery Co. 9/9/61 **K 7/1**
Corp. Allen McInnis 24 yr old enlisted Montgomery Co. 9/9/61 W-Gaines Mill **K 7/1**
Private Leonard Cranford 32 yr old enlisted Montgomery Co. 9/9/61 **W 7/1**
Private Titus Elliot 27 yr old enlisted Montgomery Co. 9/9/61 **K 7/1**
Private Thomas Elliot 27 yr old enlisted Montgomery Co. 9/9/61 (later C Jerusalem Plank)
Private Dewitt Hall 36 yr old enlisted Montgomery Co. 3/5/63
Private Littleton Hearn 38 yr old enlisted Montgomery Co. 3/5/63
Private John Hill enlisted Camp Holmes 5/23/63 (later K Wilderness)
Private Calvin Hogan 28 yr old enlisted Montgomery Co. 9/9/61 **K 7/1**
Private Jeremiah Moore 27 yr old enlisted Montgomery Co. 9/9/61 **W 7/1 C 7/5**
Private Joseph Ray transferred 5/63 **W-leg 7/1 C 7/5 (amp) died 7/31**
Private Elijah Reynolds 25 yr old enlisted Montgomery Co. 9/9/61 **W-right ankle 7/1 C 7/14**
Private James Talbert 37 yr old enlisted Montgomery Co. 3/5/63 (later W-left thigh Wilderness C Ft. Stedman)
Private Mark Talbert 22 yr old enlisted Montgomery Co. 9/9/61 (later C Ft. Stedman)
Private John Thomas 23 yr old enlisted Montgomery Co. 9/9/61 deserted 8/14 captured (shot for desertion)
Private George Walker 39 yr old enlisted Montgomery Co. 3/5/63 (later W-left thigh Ft. Stedman)
Private William Walker 37 yr old enlisted Montgomery Co. 3/5/63 (later AWOL 7-10/64)
Private Daniel Yarboro 37 yr old enlisted Montgomery Co. 3/5/63

TWENTY SECOND NORTH CAROLINA REGIMENT

Colonel Conner

Private James Powell Co G

Field & Staff

Colonel James Conner still absent wounded in the leg Mechanicsville (later resigned 8/13/63)

Lieutenant Colonel William Mitchell 35 yr old Alleghany Co. elected 5/3/63 . . . . in command

Major Lee Russell elected 5/3/63 27 yr old enlisted Montgomery Co. **C Falling Waters 7/14/63**

Adjutant John H Wilbourn previously Sgt Major appt 4/7/63 W Chancellorsville absent wounded

Sergeant Major John Brower appointed form Co I 7/62

Quartermaster Dickson Wilder appointed 7/12/62

Assistant Quartermaster Dickson Wilder 24 yr old enlisted Wake Co. 5/28/61 appointed 7/16/62

Commissary Sergeant Elisha Neal 34 yr old enlisted McDowell Co 3/1/62

Assistant Commissary Sergeant Henry Conner appointed 6/13/62 (later W-head Spots C-HR)

Surgeon Gervais Robinson appointed 12/24/62 **C 7/5** with wounded

Assistant Surgeon Benjamin Cheek—appointed 6/15/63 (later Surgeon 11/64)

Hospital Steward John Reid 24 yr old enlisted McDowell Co. 6/5/61 appointed 10/9/61

Chaplin F.H. Wood appointed 2/63 (served until 10/64)

Ensign (color Bearer) Jesse Pinkerton appointed 10/62

Quartermaster Sergeant Joseph Rush 22 yr old Randolph Co. enlisted 6/18/61appointed 10/10/62

Ordinance Sergeant George Russell 27 yr old Randolph Co. enlisted 6/18/61 appointed 8/4/62

Courier (for General William Pender) William Bailey 29 yr old enlisted McDowell Co. 6/5/61 C Seven Pines C Sharpsburg (later Sgt)

Company A *"Caldwell Rough & Ready Boys"*

Capt. William Clark transferred 5/10/62 W Malvern Hill W-hand Fredericksburg (later W-left heel Jerusalem Plank)

2nd Lt. Sion Oxford 27 yr old enlisted Caldwell Co 4/30/61 W Seven Pines (later ensign W Wilderness))

2nd Lt. William Dickson enlisted 8/8/61 **C 7/3**

3rd Lt. William Tuttle 21 yr old enlisted Caldwell Co 4/30/61

Sgt. A.B. Coffee 21 yr old enlisted Caldwell Co 4/30/61 (later W North Anna)

Corp. Lewis Dinkins 25 yr old enlisted Caldwell Co 4/30/61 **C 7/3**

Corp. A.C. McCrary 27 yr old enlisted Caldwell Co 3/19/62 W Sharpsburg (later Sgt)

Private H.A. Clark 20 yr old enlisted Caldwell Co 7/23/61 W 2nd Manassas **slight W 7/1 fought 7/3**

Private Rufus Deal 23 yr old enlisted Caldwell Co 4/30/61 C Seven Pines W-hand Fredericksburg (later K Cold Harbor)

Private Robert Diamond 19 yr old enlisted Caldwell Co 4/30/61 **W-right ankle 7/3 C 7/5**

Private Aurelius Dula 20 yr old enlisted Caldwell Co 4/30/61 W Gaine's Mill **W-right foot, right leg & left arm 7/3 during bombardment**

Private Thomas Field 20 yr old enlisted Caldwell Co 3/19/62 W 2nd Manassas **C 7/3**

Private Henry Fisher 20 yr old enlisted Caldwell Co 3/19/62 W-Glendale C Cold Harbor

Private Joseph Gaines 43 yr old enlisted Caldwell Co 3/19/62 **K 7/3**

Private Collet Greer 19 yr old enlisted Caldwell Co 4/30/61 W-hand Gaine's Mill W-right arm Fredericksburg W-left hand Wilderness

Private James Hamby 23 yr old enlisted Caldwell Co 4/30/61 **K 7/3**

Private John Justice transferred 2/18/63 **C 7/3**

Private E.P. Miller 21 yr old enlisted Caldwell Co 4/30/61 W Seven Pines **W 7/3 C 7/5**

Private Issac Palmer 19 yr old enlisted Caldwell Co 4/30/61 W-arm Fredericksburg W-groin Drewey's Bluff (later W Wilderness)

Private Benton Payne 22 yr old enlisted Caldwell Co 4/30/61 W Sharpsburg (later W Ream's Station Corp & Sgt)

Private S.B. Shell 22 yr old enlisted Caldwell Co 4/30/61 **C 7/14**

Private L.J. Sudderth 20 yr old enlisted Caldwell Co 3/19/62 W Sharpsburg W-hand Fredericksburg (later C Cold Harbor)
Private Randy Taylor 26 yr old enlisted Caldwell Co 3/19/62 C Chancellorsville **C 7/3**
Private John Wilson 20 yr old enlisted Caldwell Co 4/30/61 **C 7/3**

Teamster Stewart Hass 23 yr old enlisted Caldwell Co 4/30/61
Private Samuel Harper 19 yr old enlisted Caldwell Co 4/30/61 W Gaine's Mill (detailed surgeon's clerk)

July 1 Casualties

1st Lt. Joseph Clark 26 yr old enlisted Caldwell Co. **W-right arm 7/1 C 7/3**
Sgt. Pickens Barlow 25 yr old enlisted Caldwell Co 4/30/61 W-neck Fredericksburg **W 7/1**
Corp. Marcus Deal 25 yr old enlisted Caldwell Co 4/30/61 **W-right foot, right leg & right arm 7/1 C 7/5** (later W-thigh North Anna 1st Sgt)
Private W.A. Allen 23 yr old enlisted Caldwell Co 3/19/62 W-leg Fredericksburg
Private E.A. Banfield 22 yr old enlisted Caldwell Co 4/30/61 C Winchester, Va
Private W.P. Bryant 24 yr old enlisted Caldwell Co 4/30/61 (later WC Jericho Mills, Va)
Private D.P. Clark 19 yr old enlisted Caldwell Co 10/1/62 **W-thigh 7/1 C 7/5 (died 7/22 Chester Pa buried PNC)**
Private Henry Coffey 24 yr old enlisted Caldwell Co 4/30/61 W-arm Fredericksburg **C 7/14**
Private Larkin Coffey 23 yr old enlisted Caldwell Co 3/10/61 W 2nd Manassas (later C Jericho Mills)
Private John Coleman 24 yr old enlisted Caldwell Co 4/30/61 C 2nd Manassas W-hip Fredericksburg
Private **Michael Criger** 27 yr old enlisted Caldwell Co 4/30/61 (K Riddel's Shop 1864)
Private Mathew Helan 19 yr old enlisted Caldwell Co 3/19/62 W Seven Pines
Private Henry Keller 27 yr old enlisted Caldwell Co 3/19/62 W-right thigh Glendale (later C Jericho Mills)
Private Israel Keller 19 yr old enlisted Caldwell Co 3/19/62 W Shepherdstown
Private Thomas Knight 27 yr old enlisted Caldwell Co 12/12/61 W-leg Gaine's Mil!
Private Wade Lutz 19 yr old enlisted Caldwell Co 3/19/62 **W 7/1 C 7/5 died**
Private John McMillan 23 yr old enlisted Caldwell Co 4/30/61 W Seven Pines **K 7/1** at beginning of fight
Private George Sides 26 yr old enlisted Caldwell Co 4/30/61 W-arm Glendale W-hip Fredericksburg **C 7/14**
Private Marcus Sparks 23 yr old enlisted Caldwell Co 4/30/61 W-"bursting shell" Sharpsburg
Private Hosea Stallings 19 yr old enlisted Caldwell Co 3/19/62 W Sharpsburg
Private James Stallings 22 yr old enlisted Caldwell Co 4/30/61 W Seven Pines W-head 2nd Manassas W-leg Fredericksburg (later Sgt)

Private James Steel 19 yr old enlisted Caldwell Co 3/19/62 (later K Cold Harbor)
Private Alfred Story 23 yr old enlisted Caldwell Co 3/19/62 W-breast & arm Gaine's Mill **W 7/1 C 7/5**
Private Logan Teague enlisted Caldwell Co 2/14/62 (later C Five Forks, Va)
Private Nathan Teague22 yr old enlisted Caldwell Co 4/30/62 W-arm Malvern Hill (later C Turkey Hill, Va)
Private James Watts 22 yr old enlisted Burke Co. 8/9/61 W Sharpsburg
Private Joseph Williams 25 yr old enlisted Caldwell Co **K 7/1**

Company B *"McDowell Rifles"*

Capt. Joseph Conley transferred 5/20/63 **W 7/3 died 7/29 (Wagon w Dula)**
2nd Lt. George Gardin 20 yr old enlisted McDowell Co 5/8/61 C Seven Pines (later W-shoulder Wilderness)
Sgt Samuel Tate 23 yr old enlisted McDowell Co 5/8/61 W Seven Pines W-left shoulder 2nd Manassas (later 1st Lt)
Sgt. Walker James 20 yr old enlisted McDowell Co 8/10/61 **C 7/3**
Corp. Leander Chapman 23 yr old enlisted McDowell Co 5/8/61 C Chancellorsville (later W Jerusalem Plank)
Corp. George Lackey 23 yr old enlisted McDowell Co 5/8/61 **C 7/3**
Private George Conner 39 yr old enlisted McDowell Co 4/5/62 **W 7/3** (later K Spotsylvania)
Private Thomas Cuthbertson 19 yr old enlisted McDowell Co 5/8/61
Private Joseph Dickson 23 yr old enlisted McDowell Co 3/16/62 **W 7/3**
Private Alford Finley previously Captain WC Seven Pines W-face 2nd Manassas court-martialed 4/63 (later Sgt)
Private John Haney 47 yr old enlisted McDowell Co 4/15/62 **C 7/3**
Private Daniel Holland 23 yr old enlisted McDowell Co 4/15/62 **slightly W 7/1 fought 7/3**
Private Jacob Padgett 24 yr old enlisted McDowell Co 5/8/61 W Seven Pines **WC 7/3**
Private Jacob Washburn 19 yr old enlisted McDowell Co. 5/18/63 **K 7/3**

Musician Reuben James enlisted McDowell Co 5/8/61

18

July 1 Casualties—18 (7)

Sgt. William Garvin 22 yr old enlisted McDowell Co 5/8/61 **W 7/1 C 7/5**
Corp. B.F. Seagle 30 yr old enlisted McDowell Co 5/8/61 W-left shoulder Seven Pines deserted 7/17
Private Hampton Carven enlisted McDowell Co 3/19/62 (served until 10/64)

Private William Christy 25 yr old enlisted McDowell Co 3/21/62 **C 7/12** Hagerstown, Md
Private George Buchanan 19 yr old enlisted Mitchell Co. **W 7/1**
Private Hampton Cowen 26 yr old enlisted McDowell Co 4/15/62 WC Seven Pines deserted 7/63—returned
Private Martin Curtis 22 yr old enlisted McDowell Co 8/10/61 W-head Seven Pines **C 7/12 Funkstown, Md**
Private Alexander Glass 46 yr old enlisted McDowell Co 4/15/62 **C 7/14**
Private James Hensley 34 yr old enlisted McDowell Co 5/8/61 **W 7/1 C 7/5** (later C Wilderness)
Private J.L.Ingle 27 yr old enlisted McDowell Co 4/15/62 **K 7/1**
Private James Jaminson 25 yr old enlisted McDowell Co 4/15/62 **C 7/14** (joined US Service)
Private Hugh Laughrun 29 yr old enlisted McDowell Co 5/8/61 W-both hands 7/62 **K 7/1**
Private W.G. Poteet 28 yr old enlisted McDowell Co 4/15/62 **K 7/1**
Private Charles Pyatt 21 yr old enlisted McDowell Co 4/15/62 (later W-hand Spotsylvania)
Private E.P. Reid 26 yr old enlisted McDowell Co 4/15/62 W-head Gaines Mill C Chancellorsville (later Sgt)
Private William Walton 20 yr old enlisted McDowell Co 4/15/62 (later C Wilderness)
Private James Ward 35 yr old enlisted McDowell Co 10/10/62 (later W-leg Spotsylvania)
Private William Walker 29 yr old enlisted McDowell Co 4/15/62 **W 7/1 C 7/5**
Private William West 22 yr old enlisted McDowell Co 4/15/62 deserted 7/63 returned

Company E *"The Guilford Men"*

Capt. Martin Wolfe 33 yr old enlisted Guilford Co 5/23/61 W-leg 2nd Manassas **W-leg (cut tendon) 7/3** (resigned 8/26/63)
1st Lt. Robert Cole 26 yr old enlisted Guilford Co 11/14/61 W Chancellorsville (later Captain 9/15/63_
2nd Lt. Andrew Busick 24 yr old enlisted Guilford Co. 5/23/61 W Sharpsburg (later 1st Lt)
1st Sgt John Anderson 20 yr old enlisted Guilford Co. 5/23/61 (later reduced to private 5/64)
Sgt Alfred Gordon 24 yr old enlisted Guilford Co. 5/23/61 W 2nd Manassas (later provost guard)
Sgt. Thomas Hooper 27 yr old mechanic enlisted Guilford Co. 5/23/61 (later Sgt Major of regiment)
Sgt. Martin Wyrick 21 yr old enlisted Guilford Co. 5/23/61 W-foot Glendale **C 7/14** (later 1st Sgt)
Corp. Franklin Pegram 25 yr old enlisted Guilford Co. 7/5/62 W-left hand Chancellorsville (later Sgt W-thumb Ream's Station)

Private Alpheus Bagley 26 yr old enlisted Guilford Co. 2/22/62 C Chancellorsville (later W-thigh Ream's Station—amp—died)
Private Sidney Brown 26 yr old enlisted Guilford Co. 5/23/61 (later Corp)
Private Allen Davis 19 yr old enlisted 1862 (later C Brandy Station)
Private William Dean 23 yr old enlisted Guilford Co. 5/23/61 W Sharpsburg (later deserted 9/1/64)
Private William Grissom 23 yr old enlisted Guilford Co. 5/23/61
Private Elam Hunt 44 yr old enlisted Guilford Co. 2/22/62 C Sharpsburg **C 7/14**
Private William Irwin 27 yr old enlisted Guilford Co. 2/22/62 W Mechanicsville W Chancellorsville **W 7/3 C 7/7 Waynesboro**
Private Jesse Jester 20 yr old enlisted Guilford Co. 2/22/62 W-neck Glendale W-head & right shoulder Fredericksburg **C 7/5**
Private Harper Jones 24 yr old enlisted Guilford Co. 2/22/62 **C 7/14** (later W-arm Ream's Station
Private Jonathan Kellam 22 yr old enlisted Guilford Co. 5/23/61 **K 7/3**
Private John May 46 yr old enlisted Guilford Co. 2/22/62 ***K 7/3***
Private Maurice Oliver enlisted Guilfford Co. **C 7/3**
Private Nathaniel Oliver 18 yr old enlisted Guilford Co. 2/22/62 W-right shoulder Seven Pines (later W-accidentally 7/24/63)
Private Washington Orrell 24 yr old enlisted Guilford Co 5/23/61 (later 2nd Lt)
Private John Pegram 38 yr old enlisted Guilford Co. 2/22/62 (later W 1864) "cited for bravery at Gettysburg" (later W-left leg Ream's Station-amp)
Private Christopher Perkins 22 yr old enlisted Guilford Co. 2/22/62 **C 7/3**
Private Benjamin Roberts 25 yr old miner enlisted Guilford Co. 5/23/61 **W 7/3 C 7/5**
Private Pickney Smothers 23 yr old enlisted Guilford Co. 2/22/62 (discharged 2/1/64 disability)
Private John P. Stack 29 yr old enlisted Guilford Co. 2/22/62 W-both legs Seven Pines **W-right thigh C 7/3**
Private John W Stack 26 yr old enlisted Guilford Co. 2/22/62 W-leg Glendale **C 7/7 Waynesboro**
Private William Stack 33 yr old enlisted Guilford Co. 2/22/62 W Harper's Ferry **W 7/3**
Private John Thacker 25 yr old enlisted Guilford Co. 5/23/61 began as Commissary Sgt—reduced **C 7/3**
Private Alfred Wade 19 yr old enlisted Guilford Co. 2/22/62 W-"stunned y shell" Fredericksburg **C 7/3**
Private John Welch 22 yr old enlisted Guilford Co. 5/23/61 (later Corp)

Teamster John Clark 22 yr old enlisted Guilford Co. 5/23/61
Teamster Jesse Jackson 19 yr old enlisted Guilford Co. 2/22/62
Teamster Pleasant Pratt 23 yr old enlisted Guilford Co. 5/23/61 W Glendale W-head & hand Chancellorsville
Teamster George Smothers 27 yr old enlisted Guilford Co. 2/22/62

July 1 Casualties

Private James Bell 22 yr old enlisted Guilford Co. 5/23/61 (discharged 9/63—disabled)

Private John Bodenhammer enlisted Guilford Co. 5/23/61 (later C North Anna)

Private William Briggs 25 yr old enlisted Guilford Co. 5/23/61 W-eye 2nd Manassas

Private Peter Brown 29 yr old enlisted Guilford Co. 2/22/62

Private Durant Busick 20 yr old enlisted Guilford Co. 5/23/61 W-left knee Glendale **W-left leg 7/1 C 7/5** (amp)

Private Elisha Guyer 20 yr old enlisted Guilford Co. 5/22/62 **W 7/1** (later W Spotsylvania)

Private George Holt enlisted Guilford Co. 3/17/63 **W 7/1**

Private Nathaniel Kellam 24 yr old enlisted Guilford Co. 5/23/61 **W 7/1** (later C Wilderness)

Private James F. Loflin 20 yr old enlisted Guilford Co. 2/22/62 (later Corp)

Private James M. Loflin 23 yr old enlisted Guilford Co. 2/22/62 W-shoulder Manassas W Chancellorsville

Private Lazarus Loflin 26 yr old enlisted Guilford Co. 2/22/62 W Chancellorsville (later W Spotsylvania)

Private Richard Long 26 20 yr old enlisted Guilford Co. 2/22/62 W-arm & shoulder Fredericksburg

Private J.D. May 23 yr old enlisted 2/22/62 ***W 7/1 C 7/5 died 7/31***

Private Elcanah Merdiith 25 yr old enlisted Guilford Co. 2/22/62 **C 7/14**

Private W.S. Oliver 19 yr old enlisted Guilford Co. 2/22/62 **W 7/1** AWOL 7/24

Private Isiah Pegram 20 yr old enlisted Guilford Co. 5/23/61 **W-leg 7/1 C 7/5**

Private Samuel Pegram 25 yr old enlisted Guilford Co 3/17/63 W-back & left arm Chancellorsville **W-7/1**

Private William Rich 19 yr old enlisted Guilford Co. 5/23/61 **W-chest 7/1 C 7/6 Waynesboro**

Private Frederick Shaw 23 yr old enlisted Guilford Co. 2/22/62 W-shoulder 2nd Manassas **W-right shoulder 7/1** (later Sgt C Wilderness)

Private Harmon Wade 42 yr old enlisted Guilford Co. 2/22/62 W Mechanicsville **d eserted 7/2**

Private William Wall 20 yr old enlisted Guilford Co. 5/23/61 **K 7/1**

Private John Wood 18 yr old enlisted Guilford Co. 2/22/62 **C Hagerstown 7/6**

Company F *"Alleghany True Blues"*

2nd Lt. Shadrach Caudill 20 yr old enlisted Alleghany Co 5/27/61 C Glendale (later Captain 8/19/63)

1st Sgt Flemin Hampton 23 yr old enlisted Alleghany Co. 5/27/61 W-abdomen Gaine's Mill (later W Wilderness)

Sgt Berry Edwards 20 yr old enlisted Alleghany Co. 5/27/61 W 10/62 (later W Petersburg)
Sgt. Berry H Edwards 31 yr old enlisted Alleghany Co. 5/27/61 C Seven Pines W-left shoulder Fredericksburg (later 1st Sgt)
Sgt. Robert Gambill 29 yr old enlisted Alleghany Co. 5/27/61 W-left knee 2nd Manassas
Sgt Henry Waggoner 28 yr old enlisted Alleghany Co. 5/27/61 C Seven Pines
Corp. Charles Crouse 24 yr old enlisted Alleghany Co. 5/27/61 W Seven Pines **C 7/14**
Corp. Hiram S Edwards 24 yr old enlisted Alleghany Co. 5/27/61 as Sgt W-leg Gaines Mill reduced to private (later C Jericho Mills)
Corp. Calvin Toliver 31 yr old enlisted Alleghany Co. 5/27/61 W-Sharpsburg (later Sgt)
Private Jeremiah Caudill 22 yr old enlisted Alleghany Co. 5/27/61 W Glendale (later W Petersburg)
Private Nathaniel Reynolds 21 yr old enlisted Alleghany Co. 5/27/61 W-hand Seven Pines (later W-thigh Wilderness died)
Private Riley Sanders 24 yr old enlisted Alleghany Co. 5/27/61 (later W-left hand Jerusalem Plank)
Private Jonathan Sexton 20 yr old enlisted Alleghany Co. 5/27/61
Private Melvin Taliafero 27 yr old enlisted Alleghany Co. 5/27/61 (later Corp)

July 1-2 Casualties

Private Granville Billings 30 yr old enlisted Alleghany Co. 5/27/61 **W 7/1 C 7/14**
Private Francis "Frank" Bryan Cheek 23 year old enlisted Allegheny Co. (deserted 8/3/63)
Private Sowell Choat 22 yr old enlisted Alleghany Co. 5/27/61 **W 7/1 died 7/2**
Private John Collins 21 yr old enlisted Alleghany Co. 4/15/62 (later C Jericho Mills)
Private Levi Collins 18 yr old enlisted Alleghany Co. 4/15/62 (later W-head Wilderness C Cold Harbor)
Private William Cumby 37 yr old enlisted Alleghany Co. 4/15/62 (Later W Cold Harbor)
Private John Fender 21 yr old enlisted Alleghany Co. 5/27/61
Private Obediah Finney 30 yr old enlisted Alleghany Co. 3/15/62 W-left thigh Chancellorsville
Private John Mains 22 yr old enlisted Alleghany Co. 5/27/61 W Seven Pines **K 7/2**
Private Mathias Osborn 23 yr old enlisted Alleghany Co. 5/27/61 **W-left arm 7/1** (later Sgt) (later C North Anna)
Private George Richardson 20 yr old enlisted Alleghany Co. 5/27/61 **C 7/3**
Private William Whitaker 25 yr old enlisted Alleghany Co. 5/27/61 W-hip Mechanicsville W-thigh 2nd Manassas **C 7/14**
Private John Wiles 30 yr old enlisted Alleghany Co. 5/27/61 as Corp—reduced Private (later W-back Harper's Ferry)

Company G *"Caswell Rifles"*

Capt. George Graves 25 yr old Wake Forest graduate elected 5/1/62 W-Sharpsburg **W-arm 7/3 C 7/5**

Sgt. William Page 27 yr old enlisted Caswell Co 10/5/61 W Mechanicsville **W-hand 7/1 fought again W 7/3** (later Corp)

Sgt. James Powell 25 yr old enlisted Wake Co. 8/5/61 W-hand Shepherdstown

Sgt.Moses Sartin 25 yr old enlisted Wake Co. 5/28/61 W-side Fredericksburg **C 7/14** (later 1st Sgt)

Private Robert Bolton enlisted Caswell Co 2/1/62 W Sharpsburg **W 7/3** (later W Jerusalem Plank)

Private Lewis Brewer enlisted Forsythe Co 7/2/62 **W-right side C 7/3**

Private Starlin Brincefield 23 yr old enlisted Caswell Co 1/10/62

Private Alfonzo Burton 22 yr old enlisted Wake Co 5/28/61 (later W Jerusalem Plank Rd)

Private James Elliot 26 yr old enlisted Caswell Co 5/28/61 W Seven Pines (later Corp C Ream's Station)

Private George Hardy 32 yr old enlisted Wake Co. 7/12/61 **C 7/14**

Private John Jackson enlisted Stokes Co 2/12/63 (later C Mechanicsville 1864)

Private Richard Mitchell 23 yr old enlisted Caswell Co 5/28/61 (later C Turkey Hill, Va)

Private Washington Price 29 yr old enlisted Caswell Co 10/5/61 **C 7/14**

Private Turner Patterson 28 yr old enlisted Caswell Co 5/28/61 W-Sharpsburg (later C 1864)

Private William Patterson 33 yr old enlisted Caswell Co 7/12/61 **C 7/3**

Private Leander Perkins 22 yr old enlisted Wake Co. 5/28/61 W-right hip & breast Mechanicsville (later W-left side Jericho Mills)

Private **Charles Poteat** 29 yr old enlisted Wake Co. (present through 10/64)

Private Thompson Robertson 32 yr old enlisted Wake Co. 5/28/61 W Seven Pines W-hand Fredericksburg (later W-hand North Anna)

Private Joshua Rodgers 21 yr old enlisted Caswell Co. 5/28/61 W-foot Fredericksburg (later C Jericho Mills, Va)

Pioneer Stephen Sartin 21 yr old enlisted Wake Co. 5/28/61 W Glendale (later W-right hip Harper's Ferry)

Private Richard Simpson 22 yr old enlisted Wake Co. 5/28/61 W-hand Fredericksburg

Private Joseph Terry 20 yr old enlisted Stokes Co. 3/5/63

Private John Walker 26 yr old enlisted Guilford Co 3/2/63 **C 7/3**

July 1 Casualties

1st Lt. Peter Smith 24 yr old enlisted 5/28/61 W Sharpsburg **W-left hand 7/1**

1st Sgt R.T. Blackwell 30 yr old enlisted Wake Co 5/28/61 W-shoulder Fredericksburg **W-left side 7/1** "while carrying colors

Private I.E. Brown 18 yr old enlisted Wake Co. **K 7/1**

Private Nat Durham 35 yr old enlisted Caswell Co 3/6/63 (served through 10/64)
Private Richard Durham 22 yr old enlisted Wake Co 7/12/61 **W 7/1**
Private William Durham 24 yr old enlisted Wake Co 5/28/61 (later C Jericho Mills)
Private David Ingram enlisted Wake Co. **K 7/1**
Private Henry Lee 36 yr old enlisted Guilford Co 2/21/63 W Chancellorsville
Private Henry Lovelace enlisted Caswell Co 11/10/61 (later C Jericho Mills)
Private William Lovelace 25 yr old enlisted Wake Co. (later C Chickahominy River)
Private Levi Padget 35 yr old enlisted Forsythe Co 2/17/63 **W 7/1**
Private Romulus Rodgers 29 yr old enlisted Caswell Co. 5/28/61 (later Corp & Sgt)
Private George Strader 24 yr old enlisted Wake Co. 5/28/61 **C 7/14** (later joined US Service)
Private John Strader 29 yr old enlisted Wake Co. 5/28/61 (later W-back Spotsylvania)
Private Charles Thompson enlisted 11/61 (later hospitalized 8/64)
Private William Turner 36 yr old enlisted Caswell Co 3/5/63
Private Abner Walker 29 yr old enlisted Wake Co. 5/28/61 **W-right ankle 7/1**

Company H *"The Stokes Boys"*

brevet 1st Lt. John Martin 29 yr old enlisted Stokes Co. 6/1/61 (court—martialed 4/63) (later 1st Lt W-left side Wilderness)
2nd Lt. Calvin Graves 45 yr old enlisted Caswell Co 5/10/63
3rd Lt. Mason Mitchell 27 yr old enlisted Stokes Co. 6/1/61 W Seven Pines **slightly W 7/1 participated 7/3**
Sgt Cephus Joyce 20 yr old enlisted Stokes Co. 6/1/61 W-arm Fredericksburg (later C Jericho Mills)
Sgt Richard Martin 38 yr old enlisted Stokes Co. 6/1/61 W-left thigh Glendale W—face 2nd Manassas (later W 8/64)
Corp. John Corn 38 yr old enlisted Stokes Co 3/1/62 **C 7/14**
Private A.P. Alberty 39 yr old enlisted Stokes Co 3/10/62 **C 7/3**
Private Rolly Amos 24 yr old enlisted Stokes Co 3/1/62 (later W 2/64)
Private James Burge 25 yr old enlisted Stokes Co 3/1/62 W-Sharpsburg W Chancellorsville (later Corp)
Private N. Counterolt enlisted Stokes Co 1862 **C 7/5**
Private Samuel Claybrook 23 yr old enlisted Stoles Co. 6/1/61 **W-right leg C 7/3 (died Chester Pa 7/27 buried PNC)**
Private John Dunlap 23 yr old enlisted Stokes Co 3/1/62 (later W-hand Wilderness)
Private John Foddrill 29 yr old enlisted Stokes Co. 3/1/62 **W-elbow C 7/3**
Private Augustus Frazier 24 yr old cabinetmaker enlisted Stokes Co. 3/1/62 (later C Jericho Mills, Va)
Private Tison Frazier 20 yr old enlisted Stokes Co. 3/1/62 C Chancellorsville (later C Mechanicsville 6/64)

Private John Gatewood 22 yr old enlisted Stokes Co. 6/1/61 (later W Jerusalem Plank Rd)
Private Robert Griffin 22 yr old enlisted Stokes Co 3/1/62 (later C Mechanicsville 6/64)
Private William Hall 19 yr old enlisted Stokes Co 3/1/62 W Glendale C Chancellorsville **C 7/4**
Private Aaron Heath 24 yr old enlisted Stokes Co. 6/1/61 W "by a bomb" Seven Pines W Sharpsburg **C 7/3**
Private John Hopkins 21 yr old enlisted Stokes Co 3/1/62 **C 7/14** (later W Ox Hill, Va)
Private John Hunley 29 yr old enlisted Stokes Co. 6/1/61 (later C Wilderness)
Private W.A. Hutcherson 19 yr old enlisted Stokes Co 3/1/62 **K 7/3**
Private Livingston Joyce 18 yr old enlisted Stokes Co 3/1/63 **W C 7/3 died**
Private George Knight 18 yr old enlisted Stokes Co 3/1/63 **C 7/14**
Private Henry Lackey 25 yr old enlisted Stokes Co. 6/1/61 **C 7/3**
Private George Lawrence 28 yr old enlisted Stokes Co. 3/1/62 W Gaine's Mill W 2nd Manassas W-scalp Chancellorsville
Private Abner Manuel 21 yr old enlisted Stokes Co. 6/1/61 W-arm Glendale (later W-right leg Spotsylvania)
Private Andrew Martin 20 yr old enlisted Stokes Co. 6/1/61 **W-left hand 7/1 fought 7/3** (later W Wilderness)
Private William F Martin 19 yr old enlisted Stokes Co 3/1/62 (later W-hand Wilderness)
Private William Nicholson 24 yr old enlisted Stokes Co. 6/1/61 (later C Jericho Mills)
Private M.L. Smith 18 yr old enlisted 1/1/63 **C 7/14** (later served US service)
Private James Spencer 20 yr old enlisted Stokes Co. 6/1/61 **C 7/12 Hagerstown, Md** (later joined US Service)
Private William Spencer 18 yr old enlisted Stokes Co. 6/1/61 **C 7/14** (later joined US service)
Private Latney Stanley 28 yr old enlisted 3/1/63 (served to 10/64)
Private Andrew Steel 24 yr old enlisted Stokes Co 3/1/62 W Sharpsburg **C 7/14**
Private Burley Tilley 19 yr old enlisted Stokes Co. 3/1/62
Private Wesley Vernon enlisted Stokes Co **slightly W 7/3**
Private Samuel Ward 29 yr old enlisted Stokes Co. 3/1/62 (later Sgt)
Private William White 22 yr old enlisted Stokes Co. 3/1/62 **K 7/3**
Private Thomas Wilkins 29 yr old enlisted Stokes Co. 3/1/62 **C 7/3**
Private William Wilkins 21 yr old enlisted Stokes Co. 6/1/61 **W 7/3**
Private William Wilkins 26 yr old enlisted Stokes Co. 6/1/61
Private William Woods 24 yr old enlisted Stokes Co 3/1/62 W-face 2nd Manassas **W 7/3**
Private Alexander Young 19 yr old enlisted Stokes Co. 6/1/61 **C 7/14**

Teamster Pleasant Hutcherson 33 yr old enlisted Stokes Co (served until 10/64)
Teamster George Joyce 20 yr old enlisted Stokes Co. 6/1/61 (served until 10/64)

July 1 & 2 Casualties

Sgt William Cunningham 20 yr old enlisted Stokes Co as Corp (W Chancellorsville) **W 7/1 (wagon W Duba)**

Corp. Pleasant Padgett 22 yr old enlisted Stokes Co. 3/1/62 W Fredericksburg **W-chest 7/1 C 7/5**

Private Joshua Corn 20 yr old enlisted Stokes Co 3/1/62 W Sharpsburg **K 7-1**

Private William Duggins 29 yr old enlisted Stokes Co. 6/1/61 W-thigh Chancellorsville **W 7/1**

Private Franklin Kellam 36 yr old enlisted Stokes Co 3/1/62 W 2nd Manassas **K 7/1**

Private Raleigh Martin 20 yr old enlisted Stokes Co. 6/1/61 ***K 7/1***

Private William Martin 22 yr old enlisted Stokes Co 3/1/62 W-leg 2nd Manassas C Chancellorsville ***W-hip 7/1 C 7/5***

Private John Nelson 29 yr old enlisted Stokes Co. 3/1/62 **K 7/1**

Private Abram Nowlin 37 yr old enlistyed Stokes Co 3/1/62 **W 7/1 C 7/5** (later W Ream's Station)

Private Winston Powers 41 yr old enlisted 3/1/63

Private Austin Rhodes 27 yr old enlisted 3/1/62 W Glendale (later W Wilderness)

Private James Robertson 24 yr old enlisted Stokes Co. 6/1/61 **W-left arm 7/1 C 7/5** (later C Jericho Mills)

Private Columbus Sands 20 yr old enlisted Stokes Co. 6/1/61 as Corp—reduced to private W Mechanicsville (later C Jericho Mills)

Private William Shaffer 17 yr old enlisted Stokes Co. 3/1/62 deserted 7/8/63

Private William Sisk 18 yr old enlisted 3/1/63 **K 7/1**

Private William Smith 37 yr old enlisted 3/1/63 **K 7/1**

Private Reuben Vernon 30 yr old enlisted Stokes Co. 2/26/62 **W-left leg 7/2 C 7/5**

Private John Tilley enlisted Wake Co 6/1/61 W—knee Chancellorsville **K 7/1**

Private Hudson Williams 45 yr old enlisted Stokes Co. 3/1/62 W Mechanicsville **W-left thigh 7/1 C 7/5**

Private Thomas Yates 20 yr old enlisted Stokes Co. 6/1/61 **W-abdomen 7/1 C 7/5**

Company I "*Davis Guards*"

3rd Lt. Burwell Birkhead 24 yr old student enlisted Randolph Co 6/5/61 W Chancellorsville **slight W 7/1 fought 7/3** (later C North Anna)

1st Sgt Richard Winbourne 25 yr old enlisted Randolph Co 6/5/61 W Mechanicsville (later 2nd lt)

Sgt Augustus Kennett 24 yr old enlisted Randolph Co 6/5/61 (later transferred to CS Navy)

Sgt. Alpheus Lamb 23 yr old enlisted Randolph Co 6/5/61 W "on picket" Sharpsburg (later C Jericho Mills

Sgt. Henry Rush 22 yr old laborer enlisted Randolph Co 6/5/61 W Sharpsburg (later C Jericho Mills)

Sgt. Thomas Wood 23 yr old enlisted Randolph Co 6/5/61 (later C Jericho Mills 1st Sgt)

Corp. Robert Causey 22 yr old enlisted Randolph Co 11/14/61 W Chancellorsville (later C Jericho Mills)

Corp. Newton Lamb 21 yr old enlisted Randolph Co 6/5/61 ***C 7/14***

Corp. Watson Redding 25 yr old enlisted Randolph Co 3/1/62 W Sharpsburg W-both thighs 11/62 (later Sgt)

Corp. W.P. Wood 19 yr old enlisted Randolph Co 3/1/62 W-shoulder 2nd Manassas (later Sgt C Jericho Mills)

Private Parson Aldred 39 yr old enlisted Randolph Co 6/5/61 W Sharpsburg W-hip Fredericksburg **C 7/14**

Private John Alford 36 yr old cabinetmaker enlisted Randolph Co 6/5/61 (later C Wilderness)

Private Daniel Allred 24 yr old enlisted Randolph Co 6/5/61 (later W 8/63)

Private William Allred 25 yr old enlisted Randolph Co 6/5/61 W Glendale (later Sgt)

Private Henry Breedlove 21 yr old enlisted Randolph Co 11/14/61 ***K 7/3***

Private Lorenzo Breedlove 22 yr old enlisted Randolph Co 6/5/61 ***C 7/3*** *(later joined US Navy)*

Private William Breedlove 26 yr old enlisted Randolph Co 6/5/61 ***K 7/3***

Private Miles Cross 21 yr old enlisted Randolph Co 6/5/61 (later C Jericho Mills)

Private William Cross 25 yr old painter enlisted Randolph Co 3/4/62 (later C Jericho Mills)

Private David Faukner 25 yr old enlisted Randolph Co 6/5/61 W-right hip Seven Pines W-breast Fredericksburg

Private Silas Faukner 20 yr old enlisted Randolph Co 6/5/61 (later C Jericho Mills)

Private Elias Frazier 28 yr old enlisted Randolph Co 6/5/61 W 2nd Manassas **C 7/14**

Private W.S. Gardner 19 yr old enlisted Randolph Co 3/8/62 **K 7/3**

Private Robert Glenn 23 yr old enlisted Randolph Co 6/5/61 C Fredericksburg (later 2nd Lt C Jericho Mills, Va)

Private James Hanner 23 yr old enlisted Randolph Co 6/5/61 C Mechanicsville **C 7/14** Hagerstown, Md

Private Augustus Heath 20 yr old blacksmith enlisted Randolph Co 6/5/61 **C 7/3** (later joined US service)

Private Jonathan Heileg 23 yr old enlisted Randolph Co 6/5/61 W Seven Pines

Private Milton Jarrell 22 yr old enlisted Randolph Co 6/5/61 **C 7/3** (later joined US Service)

Private Zimri Jarrell enlisted Randolph Co 6/5/61 (later C Wilderness)

Private Eli Johnson 30 yr old enlisted Randolph Co 6/5/61 W-arm Fredericksburg **C 7/14**

Private Alpheus Julian 20 yr old enlisted Randolph Co 6/5/61 W Chancellorsville (later 1st Sgt)

Private Jesse King 21 yr old enlisted Randolph Co 6/5/61 (later AWOL 10/64)

Private Burgess Lamb 20 yr old enlisted Randolph Co 6/5/61 (later C Jericho Mills)

Private David Lamb 22 yr old mechanic enlisted Randolph Co 6/5/61 W-hip 10/62 ***C 7/3***

Private Dudley Lamb 24 yr old enlisted Randolph Co 6/5/61 W Mechanicsville (later W-neck Wilderness)

Private M. Lamb 26 yr old enlisted 3/1/62 (served until 3/64)

Private William Lamb 20 yr old enlisted Randolph Co 6/5/61

Private David Little enlisted Randolph Co 11/14/61

Private William McMasters 21 yr old enlisted Randolph Co 6/5/61 C Mechanicsville **C 7/14** (joined US Service)

Private Louis Morgan 19 yr old enlisted Randolph Co 6/5/61 **C 7/3** (later joined US Service)

Private Nathan Rich 22 yr old enlisted Randolph Co 3/1/62 **C 7/3** (later joined US Service)

Private William Rich 25 yr old enlisted Randolph Co 3/1/62 (AWOL 9/62) **C 7/3**

Private Franklin Robbins 24 yr old enlisted Randolph Co 6/5/61 C Fredericksburg **C 7/3**—deserter (later joined US Service)

Private Anderson Tucker 25 yr old enlisted Randolph Co 6/5/61 W Chancellorsville **C 7/14** Hagerstown, Md

Private William Walker 20 yr old enlisted Randolph Co 6/5/61 (later W Wilderness)

Private Albert Worth transferred 3/8/62 as Sgt—W Gaine's Mill—reduced in rank—(later transferred to local forces)

Teamster James Health 25 yr old enlisted Randolph Co 6/5/61

July 1 Casualties

Capt. Gaston Lamb 26 yr old enlisted Randolph Co 6/5/61 W-leg Mechanicsville **W-both thighs 7/1 (In Wagon w Dula)**

1st Lt. John Palmer 25 yr old enlisted Randolph Co 6/5/61 W Chancellorsville **K 7/1**

2nd Lt. Isaiah Robbins 25 yr old enlisted Randolph Co 6/5/61 W Chancellorsville **K 7/1**

Corp. W.S. Williams 20 yr old enlisted Randolph Co 3/1/62 (later K Ream's Station)

Private Sidney Alford 29 yr old enlisted Randolph Co 2/24/62 W Seven Pines (later W Ream's Station) **W 7/1**

Private David Allison enlisted Randolph Co 6/5/61 W-arm Mechanicsville **W 7/1** (later C Spotsylvania)

Private W.L. Boman 20 yr old enlisted Randolph Co 6/5/61 deserted 7/63

Private James Coletrane 27 yr old enlisted Randolph Co 6/5/61 **K 7/1**

Private Jackson Hicks 25 yr old enlisted Randolph Co 6/5/61 **W 7/1** (later W Ream's Station)

Private Enoch Latham 23 yr old enlisted Randolph Co 3/8/62 W Chancellorsville (later C Jericho Mills joined US service)

Private Henry Latham 22 yr old enlisted Randolph Co 6/5/61 **C 7/14**

Private Kelly Latham 21 yr old enlisted Randolph Co 3/8/62 C Seven Pines **C 7/14** Hagerstown. Md

Private Redell Robbins 26 yr old enlisted Randolph Co 3/1/62—deserter (later W-hand Spotsylvania)

Private Lemuel Robbins 25 yr old enlisted Randolph Co 3/1/62 W-Sharpsburg—deserted

Private Jonathan Rollins 25 yr old enlisted Randolph Co 3/1/62

Private James Smith 35 yr old enlisted Randolph Co 3/1/62 **K 7/1**

Company K *"McDowell Boys"*

2nd Lt. John Burgin 22 yr old enlisted McDowell Co. 6/5/61 commanding **WC 7/3**

1st Sgt John Crawford 22 yr old enlisted McDowell Co. 6/5/61 C Middletown, Md 9/13/63 **C 7/14**

Sgt John Curtis 22 yr old enlisted McDowell Co. 3/18/62 (later W-left foot Wilderness)

Corp. Joseph Bradley 19 yr old enlisted McDowell Co. 3/19/62 W 7/1 (later C Wilderness)

Corp. David Davis 19 yr old enlisted wake Co 7/24/62 **C 7/14** (later AWOL 1864)

Private Benjamin Allison 41 yr old enlisted McDowell Co. 3/18/62 C South Mtn. **C 7/3**

Corp. Jacob Allison 24 yr old enlisted McDowell Co. 6/5/61 W-hand & forehead 2nd Manassas

Private John Bailey 25 yr old enlisted McDowell Co. 1/4/62 (later 2nd Lt W-right shoulder Petersburg)

Sgt. Richard Bird 20 yr old enlisted McDowell Co. 7/24/61 W Seven Pines W-shoulder 2nd Manassas C 7/14

Private William Bradley 21 yr old enlisted McDowell Co. 3/19/62 (later W-groin Wilderness)

Private William M Brown 35 yr old enlisted McDowell Co. 3/15/62 (later Sgt)

Private Parker Cardwell transferred 3/12/62 W Chancellorsville (later W-arm & leg Wilderness)

Private Marion Duncan 22 yr old enlisted McDowell Co. 6/5/61 **C 7/3**

Private **John Greenlee** 20 yr old enlisted McDowell Co. 3/15/62 W Seven Pines C 7/12 Hagerstown, Md

Private James Hall 22 yr old enlisted McDowell Co. 6/5/61 (later died pneumonia 4/64)

Private James M Hall 23 yr old enlisted McDowell Co. 1/4/62 (later W Cold harbor)

Private Jonathan Hall 21 yr old enlisted McDowell Co. 5/18/62 (later C Jericho Mills)

Private John Harris 21 yr old enlisted McDowell Co. 6/5/61 **W 7/3 C 7/5** (later joined US Service)

Private Noah Hawkins 21 yr old enlisted McDowell Co. 6/5/61 W Malvern Hill **C 7/14**

Private Herbert Horton 28 yr old enlisted McDowell Co. 6/5/61 (later provost guard)

Private John Justice 22 yr old enlisted Wake Co. 6/5/61 C 7/12 Funkstown, Md

Private William Moody 21 yr old enlisted Wake Co. 6/5/61 (later C Jericho Mills)
Private J.B. Sauls 35 yr old enlisted Rockingham Co. 3/23/63 (later K Wilderness)
Private Ralph Wright 30 yr old enlisted Guilford Co 3/22/63 (later C Jericho Mills)

July 1 Casualties

Captain William Goodling 25 yr old enlisted McDowell Co. 6/5/61 promoted 12/1/62 **W-left arm 7/1** (amp) resigned 12/12/63
Corp. Elisha Ross 30 yr old enlisted McDowell Co. 6/5/61 **K 7/1**
Private Samuel Bradley 22 yr old enlisted McDowell Co. 6/5/61 **W 7/1** (later W-hand Wilderness)
Private George Curtis 23 yr ld enlisted Wake Co 7/24/61 C Seven Pines deserted 7/63-returned
Private James Gillespie 18 yr old enlisted McDowell Co 3/15/62 (later deserted 7/64)
Private Ephrain Gray 28 yr old enlisted Wake Co. 6/5/61 **K 7/1**
Private Zachariah Hawkins 24 yr old enlisted McDowell Co. 6/5/61 **W 7/1**
Private Edward A Haynes enlisted McDowell Co. 6/5/61 **W left arm 7/1** (later C Wilderness)
Private Edward L Haynes 21 yr old enlisted McDowell Co. 6/5/61 **W 7/1**
Private Hiram Joyce 40 yr old enlisted Wake Co 3/24/63 **W-left eye 7/1** (later W Wilderness)
Private Peter Justice 23 yr old enlisted McDowell Co. 6/5/61 **W-right arm 7/1** (later W-ankle Wilderness)
Private Richard McFarland 18 yr old enlisted Wake Co. 6/5/61 W-arm & leg Mechanicsville **W—right thigh 7/1 C 7/5**
Private Burton Mashburn 19 yr old enlisted Wake Co. 6/5/61 **W-left foot 7/1 C 7/5**
Private William ODear 20 yr old enlisted McDowell Co. 6/5/61 (later C Wilderness joined US service)
Private Albert Pleasant 36 yr old enlisted Caswell Co 5/22/63 deserted 7/29
Private B.W. Pleasants enlisted McDowell Co 1861 (later W 'bomb shell" Wilderness)
Private Joseph Quinn 25 yr old enlisted Wake Co. 6/5/61 **C 7/14** (later joined US Service)
Private Jasper Ross 20 yr old enlisted McDowell Co. 6/5/61 deserted 7/23

Company L *"The Uwharrie Grays"*

Captain Clarkson Horney 20 yr old Randolph Co enlisted 6/18/61 **W-ankle 7/3 (amp) died**
1st Lt. Yancey Johnson 22 yr old Randolph Co enlisted 6/18/61
Sgt Jacob Jones Randolph Co enlisted 6/18/61 W-Fredericksburg (later W-Wild)
Sgt Albert Lineberry 41 yr old Randolph Co enlisted 3/12/62 W-Chancelorsville

Sgt William Pike 20 yr old Randolph Co enlisted 3/12/62 as substitute
Cpl. Dennis Fox 26 yr old Randolph Co enlisted 6/18/61 W-Chan (later K Ream's)
Cpl. Hezekiah Perry 24 yr old Randolph Co enlisted 6/18/61 W-Fred **K 7/3**
Cpl. Allen Scott 28 yr old Randolph Co enlisted 10/1/61 (later W-Jones Farm)
Private Doctor Allred 20 yr old Randolph Co enlisted 6/18/61 (later C Wilderness)
Private Samuel Allred 24 yr old Randolph Co enlisted 6/18/61 deserted 8/1/63
Private Thomas Allred 21 yr old Randolph Co enlisted 3/19/62 **C 7/3**
Private Francis Birkhead 23 yr old Randolph Co enlisted 6/18/61 **W 7/3** (later 1st Sgt)
Private Lawrence Birkhead 21 yr old Randolph Co enlisted 6/18/61 **W 7/3 as colorbearer**
Private James Brown 21 yr old Randolph Co enlisted 3/18/62 (later W in foot)
Private Caswell Craven 19 yr old Randolph Co enlisted 6/18/61 W Seven Pines
Private Thomas Crisp Pitt Co farmer enlisted 6/18/61 (later C Wilderness)
Private William Curtis 19 yr old Chatham Co farmer enlisted 6/18/61 **W-arm 7/12**
Private David Ellison 23 yr old Randolph Co enlisted 6/18/61 **WC 7/3**
Private Daniel Hughes 29 yr old Randolph Co enlisted 6/18/62 (later W-Wilderness)
Private Arnold Hutton 22 yr old Randolph Co enlisted 6/18/61 W-Fred/Chan
Private Alsey Jackson 20 yr old Randolph Co enlisted 6/18/61 **W 7/1 C 7/5**
Private Jacob Kanoy 25 yr old blacksmith Randolph Co enlisted 6/18/61 (later C-Wild)
Private Inzar Latham 19yr old Randolph Co enlisted 3/15/63 (later W-Rapidan)
Private Josiah Luther Randolph Co enlisted 3/18/62 **C 7/14**
Private D. McMasters 20 yr old Randolph Co enlisted 6/18/61 W-Chan **W 7/3**
Private Samuel Marsh 21 yr old Randolph Co enlisted 6/18/61 (later C Jericho Mills)
Private William Marsh 24 yr old Randolph Co enlisted 3/12/62 **W-left arm 7/3**
Private Benjamin May 24 yr old Randolph Co substitute enlisted 3/18/62
Private Henry May 20 yr old Randolph Co enlisted 3/18.62 **C 7/14**
Private Alexander O'Brien 26 yr old Randolph Co enlisted 6/18/61 W-Mechanicville
Private John Reddick 28 yr old Randolph Co enlisted 6/18/61 (later W-Wilderness)
Private John Thornbrough 19 yr old Randolph Co enlisted 6/18/61 W-Seven Pines/ Chan
Private John Thrift 17 yr old Randolph Co enlisted 3/12/62 W-2nd Manassas/Chan
Private Alfred Walker 19 yr old Randolph Co enlisted 3/18/62 **C 7/14**
Private Minas Ward 21 yr old Randolph Co farmer enlisted 6/18/61 (later CM)
Private Calvin Welborn 26 yr old Randolph Co enlisted 6/18/61 (Later Lt)

Teamster John Gorley 21 yr old Randolph Co enlisted 6/18/61
Teamster Solomon York 26 yr old Randolph Co enlisted 6/18/61

July 1 Casualties

2nd Lt. Oliver Pike 24 yr old Randolph Co enlisted 6/18/61 **W-hand & leg 7/1** (**Wagon w Dula)**
Cpl. James Elder 20 yr old Randolph Co enlisted 6/18/61 W-Fredericksburg **W 7/1**

Cpl. Cyrus Nance 20 yr old Randolph Co enlisted 6/18/61 W-Chancellorsville **C 7/14**

Private Franklin Brady 27 yr old Randolph Co carpenter enlisted 6/18/61 **C 7/14**

Private A.J. Carter 19 yr old Randolph Co enlisted 3/18/62 **C 7/14**

Private Samuel Carter 25 yr old Randolph Co enlisted 6/18/61 (lost finger at Fredericksburg) (deserted 9/15/63—returned)

Private James Caveness 24 yr old Randolph Co. enlisted 3/18/62

Private John Caveness 36 yr old Randolph Co enlisted 6/18/61 **C 7/14**

Private Edward Hale 23 yr old Randolph Co enlisted 6/18/61 (later transferred to Artillery) **W 7/1**

Private Benjamin Lassiter 25 yr old Randolph Co enlisted 6/18/61 **W 7/1**

Private Henry Lassiter 23 yr old Randolph Co enlisted 6/18/61 W-2nd Manassas **W 7/1**

Private John O/Brien Randolph Co farmer **C 7/6**

Private Nelson Sumner 22 yr old Randolph Co enlisted 3/12/62

Private McKenzie Varner 27 yr old Randolph Co enlisted 3/18/62 **WC 7/2 died**

Private Zeno Ward 24 yr old Randolph Co farmer enlisted 6/18/61 W-Chancellorsville **W 7/1 C 7/5**

Private Benjamin Williams Randolph Co enlisted 6/18/61 W-Mechanicsville

Company M "*The Randolph Hornets*"

Capt. Columbus Siler 24 yr old enlisted Randolph Co. 6/10/61 W Glendale W Chancellorsville **W 7/3**

1st Lt. James Robbins 22 W Chancellorsville (later W-arm Wilderness & W Ream's Station)

2nd Lt. John Lawrence 22 yr old enlisted Randolph Co. W Seven Pines W Chancellorsville **WC 7/3**

Sgt. Thomas Hays 21 yr old enlisted Randolph Co. 6/10/61

Sgt.William Hays 27 yr old enlisted Randolph Co. 6/10/61 W-right arm Glendale

Sgt. William Pounds 20 yr old enlisted Randolph Co. 6/10/61 C Fredericksburg **C 7/14** (later joined US service)

Sgt William Willey 28 yr old enlisted Randolph Co. 6/10/61 W-Glendale (later reduced in rank detached Greensboro)

Corp. William Jones 23 yr old enlisted Randolph Co. 3/6/62 (later W-left hand Wilderness)

Private Simon Allen 19 yr old enlisted Randolph Co. 3/6/62 C 2nd Manassas C Cold Harbor (later joined US Service)

Private James Allred 18 yr old enlisted Randolph Co. 3/6/62 W head Fredericksburg W Chancellorsville (later C Cold Harbor)

Private Thomas Arnold 26 yr old enlisted Randolph Co. 6/10/61 W-thigh 2nd Manassas

Private John Coble 21 yr old enlisted Randolph Co. as Corporal reduced in rank 8/1/62

Private James Cox 22 yr old enlisted Randolph Co. 6/10/61 W-leg Mechanicsville
Private Thomas Cross 20 yr old enlisted Randolph Co. 6/10/61 (later W-head Wilderness)
Private Grandison Euliss 29 yr old enlisted Randolph Co. 2/25/62 (later C Jericho Mills)
Private Josiah Foster 30 yr old enlisted Randolph Co. 6/10/61 AWOL 7/62 to 9/62 **C 7/5 ***
Private Levi Foster 21 yr old enlisted Randolph Co. 6/10/61
Private Joel Kivett 22 yr old enlisted Randolph Co. 6/10/61 **C 7/3**
Private Talton Kivett 23 yr old enlisted Randolph Co. 6/10/61 AWOL 9/62 to 11/62 W Chancellorsville C Wilderness
Private Marshall Ranes 21 yr old enlisted Randolph Co. 6/10/61 W-foot 2nd Manassas **C 7/5** (later joined US Service)
Private Abner Steel enlisted Randolph Co. 6/10/61 W-leg & shoulder Seven Pines W-leg 2nd Manassas
Private Lyndon Trogden 24 yr old enlisted Randolph Co. 6/10/61 ***W-left foot 7/3 C 7/14***
Private Solomon Trogden 34 yr old enlisted Randolph Co. 6/10/61 W-face Mechanicsville (later teamster W Wilderness)
Private James Webster 21 yr old enlisted Randolph Co. 6/10/61 W-side C Fredericksburg
Private James Williams 37 yr old enlisted Randolph Co. 6/10/61 (later C Jericho Mills)
Private Joel Williams 25 yr old blacksmith enlisted Randolph Co. 3/6/62
Private Darius York 33 yr old enlisted Randolph Co. 6/10/61 W Seven Pines **C 7/14**

Wagon Master Riley Coble 20 myr old enlistyed Randolph Co **W 7/3** (later W—left hand 6/4/64)
Teamster Joseph Henson 25 yr old enlisted Randolph Co. 3/6/62 W Chancellorsville
Teamster James Scotton 20 yr old enlisted Randolph Co. 6/10/61
Teamster—Wheelwright Lorenzo Stout 31 yr old enlisted Randolph Co. 6/10/61
Teamster Andrew Turner 23 yr old enlisted Randolph Co. 6/10/61
Teamster Joseph York 21 yr old enlisted Randolph Co. 2/25/62
Teamster Solomon York 26 yr old enlisted Randolph Co. 6/10/61

July 1 Casualties

Sgt James Campbell 23 yr old blacksmith enlisted Randolph Co 3/6/62 **W 7/1 C 7/5**
Sgt. Stepehn Trogden 26 yr old enlisted Randolph Co. 6/10/61 C Fredericksburg **W-right thigh 7/1** (amp)
Corp. Wesley Siler 23 yr old enlisted Randolph Co. 6/10/61 **K 7/1**
Private Nathan Barker 29 yr old enlisted Randolph Co. 6/10/61 **W-big toe 7/1 C 7/5** (died 8/4 Phila hospital buried PNC))
Private John Burgess 21 yr old enlisted Randolph Co. 6/10/61 W Glendale W Sharpsburg **W-left thigh 7/1**
Private Christian Foust 31 yr old enlisted Randolph Co. 3/6/62 W-side Mechanicsville **C 7/12** Funkstown, Md

Private Peter Foust 22 yr old enlisted Randolph Co. 3/6/62 **C 7/14** (later joined US Service)

Private John Glasco 21 yr old enlisted Randolph Co. 3/6/62 deserted 3/64 (later joined US service)

Private Elias Hays 22 yr old enlisted Randolph Co. 6/10/61 C 6/62 **C 7/14**

Private James Hays 29 yr old enlisted Randolph Co. 3/6/62 **C 7/14**

Private John Jackson 38 enlisted Moore Co. 3/13/63 **K in Maryland 7/15**

Private Alfred Kivett 24 yr old enlisted Randolph Co. 6/10/61 **C 7/14** (later joined US Service)

Private Austin Lawrence 17 yr old enlisted Randolph Co. 3/6/62 W-side 2nd Manassas **C 7/1**

Private William Routh 28 yr old enlisted Randolph Co. 6/10/61

Private Madison Smith 23 yr old enlisted Randolph Co. 6/10/61 as Corp—reduced in rank deserted 11/63

Private Jeremiah Trogden 27 yr old enlisted Randolph Co. 6/10/61 ***W 7/1 C 7/5***

Private H.C. Trogden 30 yr old enlisted Randolph Co. 6/10/61 C Seven Pines (later AWOL)

Private Daniel Yergin 31 yr old enlisted Randolph Co. 6/10/61 W Chancellorsville **W 7/1 C 7/5**

SIXTEENTH NORTH CAROLINA REGIMENT

Corp. Marcus Deal Co A

Teamster David Brinkley Co C

Field & Staff

Colonel John S McElroy 28 yr old enlisted Yancey Co. elected Lt. Col. 4/26/62 promoted Col. 6/1/62 W Chancellorsville absent W

Lt. Colonel William Stowe 31 yr old Gaston Co. promoted 5/31/62 W-head & neck Chancellorsville absent W

Major Herbert Lee 32 Rutherford Co. promoted 5/31/62 W-left knee Fredericksburg absent W

Acting Colonel Calvin McCloud Captain of Company H enl Franklin Co. 5/14/61 as 1st Sgt W Mechanicville QM—commanding 7/3

Adjutant Solomon Hensley (acting commander) enl Burnesville 9/25/61 appointed 1/24/62 **W-thigh 7/1**

Sergeant Major—Harmon Sanders 30 yr old enlisted Franklin Co. 5/14/61 promoted 5/10/63 (later W-leg Petersburg)

Surgeon W.G. Stephens promoted from asst surgeon 2/16/63

Surgeon F.T. Fry appointed 3/16/63 W 7/1

Assistant Surgeon R.S. Baldwin appointed 7/19/62 (later Surgeon)

Assistant Surgeon Robert Murphy appointed 8/3/62

Quartermaster Sergeant Acais Francis formerly Co L promoted 9/62

Ordinance Sergeant Jesse Moore formerly Corp Co H appointed 11/5/62

Clerk Thomas Hayden 20 yr old enlisted Rutherford Co 5/9/61 (detailed as Division clerk)

Clerk Thomas Hayden 20 yr old enlisted Rutherford Co 5/9/61 (detailed as Division clerk)

Clerk P.D. Roberts 21 yr old enlisted Rutherford Co 5/9/61 (detailed as Brigade clerk 11/8/62)

Regimental Band

Musician Miles Becco (Co I) 24 yr old enlisted Henderson Co. 5/5/61
Musician Harrison Benson (Co I) 25 yr old enlisted Henderson Co. 5/5/61
Musician W.G. Brittain (Co K) 25 yr old enlisted Polk Co. 4/20/61
Musician James Cockram (Co I) 23 yr old enlisted Henderson Co. 7/1/61
Musician John Howard (Co E) 21 yr old enlisted Burke Co 7/14/62
Musician Joseph Johnson (Co I) 25 yr old enlisted Henderson Co. 7/1/61
Musician David Miller (Co. I) 22 yr old enlisted Rutherford Co. 5/9/61
Musician John Miller (Co I) 27 yr old enlisted Henderson Co 5/5/61
Drummer William Reese (Co I) 19 yr old enlisted Henderson Co. 5/5/61

Company B "*Madison County*"

Captain Solomon Carter Enlisted 4/29/61 elected Captain 4/26/62 W-Chancellorsville absent wounded

1st Lt Ira Proffit 29 yr old enlisted Madison Co. 4/29/61 promoted 5/3/63 **C 7/3**

2nd Lt John Rhea 31 yr old enlisted Madison Co. 4/29/61 promoted 12/20/62 (later arrested—court martialed)

1st Sgt Zachariah Peek 27 yr old enlisted Edray, Va. W-arm Chancellorsville

Sgt. Jacob Henderson 25 yr old enlisted Staunton, Va. **W 7/3** (later reduced to private 8/30/63)

Sgt. John Randall 22 yr old enlisted Madison Co. 4/29/61 (later 2nd Lt)

Private Elbridge Bartley 23 yr old enlisted Madison Co. 3/3/62

Private James Brooks 20 yr old enlisted Madison Co. 4/29/61 **W 7/3**

Private John Brown 21 yr old enlisted Staunton, Va 7/8/61 **WC 7/3**

Private Levi Callahan 24 yr old enlisted Madison Co 4/29/61 W Gaine's Mill **C 7/5** (on hospital duty)

Private Levi Hall 24 yr old enlisted Madison Co 4/29/61 C Fredericksburg

Private Joseph Hembree 24 yr old enlisted Madison Co 3/3/62 **C 7/3** (later joined US Service)

Private William Hensley enlisted Madison Co. 4/29/61 as fifer—reduced to Private **W 7/3**

Private Obediah Holcombe 22 yr old enlisted Staunton, Va. 7/8/61 **W 7/3**

Private Samuel Miliken 24 yr old enlisted Richmond Va. 6/23/62 **W 7/3**

Private John Proffitt 17 yr old enlisted Madison Co 3/3/62 **C 7/14**

Private Fincher Riley 28 yr old enlisted Madison Co 4/29/61 Badge of Distinction Chancellorsville **W 7/3 C 7/5**

Private William Stevens 24 yr old enlisted Madison Co 4/29/61 **C 7/3**

Private Thomas Stewman 20 yr old enlisted Staunton, Va. 4/29/61 (later C Mine Run)

Private John Sykes 20 yr old enlisted Orange Co. 1/27/63 **W 7/3** (later died disease 4/64)
Private Aaron Wardrope 23 yr old enlisted Madison Co. 4/29/61 **W-head 7/3**

Drummer John Calahan 31 yr old enlisted Madison Co 4/29/61 W Fredericksburg (later Sgt C Wilderness)

July 1 Casualties

Sgt. John Brown 53 yr old enlisted Madison Co 4/29/61 (later transferred to home guard 8/63)
Corp. William McElrath 25 yr old enlisted Madison Co 4/29/61 **W 7/1**
Private George Boone 25 yr old enlisted Madison Co 4/29/61
Private Mitchell Buckner 29 yr old enlisted Madison Co 4/29/61 **C 7/14**
Private William Clark 20 yr old enlisted Madison Co 4/21/61 **W 7/1** AWOL 11/63
Private Whitnel Dickerson enlisted Granville Co. 7/15/62
Private James Hembree transferred 4/62 **W-right leg 7/1 C 7/5**
Private Elisha Keith 22 yr old enlisted Madison Co 4/29/61 W-hand C Seven Pines **W 7/1**
Private Caleb Knott enlisted Granville Co. **W 7/1 C 7/14**
Private John Loudermilk enlisted Staunton Va. 7/8/61 (later C North Anna)
Private James McElrath 32 yr old enlisted Madison Co 4/29/61 (later K Spotsylvania) **W 7/1**
Private John Smart 24 yr old enlisted Madison Co 4/29/61 **C 7/14**
Private Henry Stout 28 yr old enlisted Wake Co. 9/10/62 (later C North Anna)
Private John Thomas 25 yr old enlisted Madison Co 4/29/61 C Fredericksburg ***C 7/14*** *(later C North Anna)*
Private William Thomas 25 yr old enlisted Madison Co 4/29/61 C Fredericksburg (later C North Anna)
Private Richard Woodson 28 yr old enlisted Madison Co 4/29/61 (later W-leg Mine Run C Hatcher's Run)

Company C "*Black Mountain Boys*"

Capt Nelson Wilson 26 yr old enlisted Yancey Co. appointed 10/16/62 (later C North Anna)
1st Lt William Jasper Edney 27 yr old enlisted Yancey Co. 5/1/61 W-Seven Pines C Fredericksburg (resigned 10/64)
2nd Lt William Byrd 26 yr old enlisted Yancey Co. 5/1/61 **C 7/3** (later C Hatcher's Run)
1st Sgt Hiram Hensley 26 yr old enlisted Yancey Co. 5/1/61 (reduced to Sgt 6/64 W-head C North Anna)

1st Sgt William McCleland 21 yr old enlisted Yancey Co. 5/1/61 C Fredericksburg **WC 7/14**

Sgt. Alfred Buchanan 21 yr old enlisted Yancey Co. 5/1/61 W Gaines Mill (later K North Anna)

Corp. Thomas Baker 29 yr old enlisted Yancey Co. 5/1/61 (Reduced to Private 10/64)

Corp. Henry Wiggins 36 yr old enlisted Yancey Co. 5/1/61 "badge of distinction at Chancellorsville" deserted "on picket" 8/2/63

Private Daniel Abernathy 28 yr old enlisted Raleigh 9/26/62 (later C Hatcher's Run)

Private John Collis 26 yr old enlisted Yancey Co. 5/1/61 W-left arm Glendale (later C Hatcher's Run)

Private Alexander Fortner 24 yr old enlisted Yancey Co. 5/1/61 (later W Wilderness)

Private Wilson Hensley 25 yr old enlisted Yancey Co. 5/1/61 **C 7/14** (later Sgt)

Private John Honeycutt 23 yr old teacher enlisted Yancey Co. 5/1/61 **W 7/3** deserted 8/1/63

Private Oliver McCourry 22 yr old enlisted Yancey Co. 3/25/62 (later C North Anna)

Private William Riley Robinson 32 yr old enlisted Yancey Co 5/1/61 **W 7/3**

Private Jesse Young 21 yr old enlisted Yancey Co. 5/1/61 W Mechanicsville (thumb amp.) **C 7/14 Falling Waters**

Drummer Samuel Robinson 32 yr old enlisted Yancey Co. 9/25/61

Teamster David Brinkley 33 yr old enlisted Yancey Co. 5/1/61 (on detail)

July 1 Casualties

Corp. Alexander McAlister 25 yr old enlisted Yancey Co. 5/1/61 **W 7/1** missing at Falling Waters **7/14**

Corp. Logan Thomason 21 yr old enlisted Yancey Co. 5/1/61 W Seven Pines **W-left leg 7/1 C 7/5**

Private David Crites 28 yr old enlisted Yancey Co. 9/25/61 **W-right arm 7/1 C 7/5 (amp)**

Private John Deyton 19 yr old enlisted Yancey Co. 3/31/62 **C 7/14**

Private William Fox 30 yr old enlisted Yancey Co. 5/1/61 (later W Wilderness)

Private David Hager 21 yr old enlisted Wake Co 9/26/62 **W-right foot 7/1 C 7/5** (later W Wilderness)

Private James Hall 33 yr old enlisted Yancey Co. 5/1/61 W Seven Pines C Fredericksburg

Private Joseph Hall 25 yr old enlisted Yancey Co. 5/1/61 (later Corp C Hatcher's Run)

Private Pinkney McCourry 18 yr old enlisted Yancey Co. 3/21/62 (later Corp. C Hatcher's Run)

Private Malcolm McCurry 22 yr old enlisted 3/15/62 W Seven Pines deserted 8/2/63

Private Samuel Price 24 yr old enlisted Yancey Co. 5/1/61 (later W-left thigh Ream's Station)

Private Elisha Randolph 26 yr old enlisted Yancey Co. (later W-Wrist Spotsylvania)

Private David Robinson 26 yr old enlisted Yancey Co 9/25/61 (later Sgt C Hatcher's Run) **W 7/1**

Private Ephraim Shepherd 25 yr old enlisted Yancey Co. 5/1/61 deserted 9/63
Private Valentine Tipton 33 yr old enlisted Yancey Co. 5/1/61 (later W North Anna)
Private John Turbyfield 25 yr old enlisted Yancey Co. 5/1/61 W-leg Gaines Mill (later C Hatcher's Run)
Private John Wheeler 19 yr old enlisted Yancey Co. 5/1/61 deserted 8/2/63

Company D *"Rutherford County"*

Capt Adolphus McKinney 24 yr old promoted 6/1/62 **C 7/3**
1st Lt King 20 yr old enlisted Rutherford Co 5/1/61 appointed 9/1/62 **W 7/3 (died 7/28/63)**
2nd Lt Wells 27 yr old enlisted Rutherford Co. 5/1/61
1st Sgt Raymond Owens 23 yr old enlisted Rutherford Co 5/27/61 W Mechanicsville **W 7/3** (later 2nd Lt)
Sgt. James Bostick 23 yr old enlisted Rutherford Co 5/1/61 (later W-knee Petersburg-died)
Sgt. William Goode 22 yr old enlisted Rutherford Co 5/1/61 W-arm Mechanicville (later 1st Sgt W-Wilderness)
Corp. Peter Mintz 32 yr old enlisted Rutherford Co 5/18/61 C Seven Pines **K 7/3**
Corp. James Suttle 24 yr old enlisted Rutherford Co 5/1/61 (later C Hatcher's Run)
Private Kenneth Blanton 20 yr old enlisted Rutherford Co 5/1/61 W Seven Pines Badge of Distinction Chancellorsville (later C Hatcher's Run)
Private Robert Gatlin 30 yr old enlisted wake Co. 3/5/63 **C 7/3**
Private Lorraine Griffin 25 yr old enlisted Rutherford Co 5/1/61 (later Sgt)
Private Pinkney Martin 20 yr old enlisted Rutherford Co 5/1/61 W-head Seven Pines
Private Albert Padgett 21 yr old enlisted Rutherford Co 5/3/61 (later W Riddell's Shop)
Private Marcus Padgett transferred 5/30/62 (later C Mine Run & Hatcher's Run)
Private Drury Scruggs 23 yr old enlisted Rutherford Co 5/6/61 **K 7/3**
Private Aaron **Wall** 24 yr old enlisted Rutherford Co 6/3/61 **W "shell shock" 7/3**

Teamster James Aters 20 yr old enlisted Rutherford Co 5/1/61

July 1 Casualties

3rd Lt Thorn 25 yr old enlisted Rutherford Co 5/1/61 **W 7/1 C 7/5** (died 7/30/63)
Corp. Samuel Harrill 27 yr old enlisted Rutherford Co 5/1/61 (later reduced to Private)
Corp. John Sutton 26 yr old enlisted Rutherford Co 5/29/61 (reduce to Private 8/13/63)
Private Amos Bailey 25 yr old enlisted Rutherford Co 5/18/61 deserted 8/2/63—returned
Private J.C. Bailey 29 yr old enlisted Rutherford Co 5/18/61 deserted 8/2/63
Private Lorenzo Baily 23 yr old enlisted Rutherford Co 5/1/61 deserted 8/2/63 (returned K Spotsylvania)

Private Riley Baily W at Seven Pines (later died prior to 1/11/65)
Private James Clark 31 yr old enlisted Wake Co. 9/27/62 (later deserted 10/4/63)
Private Aaron Compton 22 yr old enlisted Wake Co. 9/27/62 (later C South Anna)
Private William Cooper 22 yr old enlisted Rutherford Co 5/3/61 W Seven Pines
Private Newton Cooper 28 yr old enlisted Rutherford Co 3/18/62
Private Reuben Cooper 20 yr old enlisted Rutherford Co 5/1/61 W 2nd Manassas (later Corp) **W 7/1**
Private George Harris 28 yr old enlisted Rutherford Co 5/23/61 **W 7/1 C 7/5 as hospital nurse**
Private Lawson Haney 28 yr old enlisted Rutherford Co 5/1/61 **C 7/14**
Private William Hawkins 30 yr old enlisted Rutherford Co 5/1/61 (later W Riddell's Shop, Va.)
Private Craven Jenkins 26 yr old enlisted Rutherford Co 5/10/61 **C 7/14**
Private Charles McPeters 22 yr old enlisted Yancey Co. 5/1/61 (later Corp & Sgt) **W 7/1**
Private James Quakenbush 29 yr old enlisted Wake Co. 3/5/63 (later C Hatcher's Run)
Private Luther Robertson 29 yr old enlisted Rutherford Co 5/1/61 (died at home 6/2/64)
Private David Parker 29 yr old enlisted Wake Co. 9/27/62 **W-elbow 7/1 C 7/14**
Private Guilford Young 19 yr old enlisted Rutherford Co 6/27/61 (discharged 10/1/63)

Company E *"The Burke Tigers"*

Capt Able S Cloud 22 yr old enlisted Burke Co. 5/10/61 promoted 5/31/62 **C 7/3** (later Lt. Col)
1st Lt Kaylor 28 yr old enlisted Burke Co. 5/10/61 **W-forearm 7/3**
2nd Lt John Sides 22 yr old enlisted Burke Co. 5/10/61 W-right leg 2nd Manassas
3rd Lt Henry Branch 25 yr old enlisted Burke Co. 5/10/61 **C 7/14**
1st Sgt James Henson 23 yr old enlisted Burke Co. 5/10/61 (later C Hatcher's Run)
Sgt. Sampson Cannon 26 yr old enlisted Burke Co. 5/10/61 W Fredericksburg deserted 7/25/63
Corp. William Dale 21 yr old enlisted Burke Co. 9/1/62 (later C Hatcher's Run)
Private David Branch 24 yr old enlisted Burke Co. 5/10/61 **C 7/14** (later C Hatcher's Run)
Private Thomas Causby 21 yr old enlisted Burke Co. 5/10/61
Private Lawrence Cook 34 yr old enlisted Burke Co. 5/10/61 Badge of Distinction Chancellorsville **C 7/3**
Private William Cook 27 yr old enlisted Wake Co 9/23/62
Private Calvin Copeland 25 yr old enlisted Burke Co. 5/10/61 **W 7/3**
Private Lawson Corpening 20 yr old enlisted Burke Co. 5/10/61
Private Joseph Dale 21 yr old enlisted Burke Co. 5/10/61 **W 7/3**
Private Thomas Garrison 23 yr old enlisted Burke Co. 5/10/61 (later C Riddell's Shop)
Private John Hines 25 yr old enlisted Burke Co. 5/10/61 W Fredericksburg (later Sgt C Wilderness)

Private Henry Lail 26 yr old enlisted wake Co. 9/23/62 (later W Wilderness)
Private John Lane 23 yr old enlisted Burke Co. 5/10/61 W-head Mechanicsville **W 7/3**
Private Francis Pearson 27 yr old enlisted Burke Co. 5/10/61 W 2nd Manassas **W 7/3**
Private Thomas Wishon transferred from Co B 4/26/62 **C 7/3**
Private Peter Young enlisted Burke Co 5/10/61 **WC 7/3 died 7/8**

Teamster William Causey 24 yr old enlisted Burke Co. 5/10/61

July 1 Casualties

Private James Beach 25 yr old enlisted Burke Co. 5/10/61 W Sharpsburg (later teamster)
Private Eli Burns 21 yr old enlisted Burke Co. 5/10/61 **C 7/14** (later K Petersburg)
Private Alexander Chapman 31 yr old enlisted Wake Co 9/23/62 W Fredericksburg (AWOL 12/18/63)
Private Nathaniel Chapman 23 yr old enlisted Burke Co. 5/10/61 (later C Wilderness)
Private Joel Cloud 33 yr old enlisted Wake Co. 9/23/62 (later Corp C Hatcher's Run)
Private Joseph Denton 22 yr old enlisted Wake Co. 9/23/62 (later C North Anna)
Private John Duckworth 34 yr old enlisted Burke Co. 5/10/61 deserted 7/25/63—returned 11/63
Private Harvey Fisher enlisted camp Vance 2/28/63
Private John Giles 25 yr old enlisted Burke Co. 5/10/61 **W 7/1**
Private Henry Goins 20 yr old enlisted Burke Co. 5/10/61 **W-left arm & right elbow 7/1 C 7/5 (amp)**
Private Alexander Hoffman 26 yr old enlisted Wake Co. 9/23/62
Private Azer Hoffman 20 yr old enlisted Wake Co. 9/23/62 (later C Hatcher's Run)
Private John Howard 21 yr old enlisted Richmond, Va. 7/14/62 (later musician)
Private Amos Huffman 22 yr old enlisted wake Co. 9/23/62 (later C Hatcher's Run)
Private William Huffman 25 yr old enlisted Burke Co. 5/10/61 deserted 7/20/63-returned 10/63
Private Samuel Lane 33 yr old enlisted Burke Co. 5/10/61 (later C Hatcher's Run)
Private Jackson Lawman 26 yr old enlisted Burke Co. 5/10/61 W Ox Ford (later W Hatcher's Run)
Private Pinkney Martin enlisted Cam Gregg 1/16/63 deserted 7/25/63—returned (later C Liddell's Shop)
Private James Murphey 32 yr old enlisted Burke Co. 5/10/61 (transferred to CS Navy 4/64)
Private John Propst 20 yr old enlisted Burke Co. 5/10/61 (later C Hatcher's Run)
Private Ransom Smith 24 yr old enlisted Burke Co. 5/10/61 ***C 7/5*** *nursing wounded (later joined US Service)*
Private Harvey Smith 26 yr old enlisted Burke Co. 5/10/61 ***W-right leg 7/1 C 7/5***
Private Joseph Van Horn 26 yr old enlisted Burke Co. 5/10/61 **C 7/14**

Company F *Buncombe County*

1st Lt. Milton Blackwell 25 yr old enlisted Buncombe Co. 5/7/61 appointed 3/62 (later Court-martialed 9/63 reduced to Private)

2nd Lt William Boyd appointed 7/30/62 sick during this period

3rd Lt. Dowe Alexander 26 yr old enlisted Buncombe Co. 5/7/61 W-shoulder 2nd Manassas (died 2/64 disease)

Sgt. Fidelia Dover 28 yr old enlisted Buncombe Co. 5/7/61 W Mechanicsville (later 1st Sgt—reduced to Private)

Corp. Benjamin Capps 24 yr old enlisted Buncombe Co. 5/7/61 W-foot Mechanicsville (later deserted 2/64)

Corp. Abijah Meadows 22 yr old enlisted Buncombe Co. 5/7/61 W Mechanicville Badge of distinction Chancellorsville (later Sgt)

Private William Dover 20 yr old enlisted Buncombe Co. 5/7/61 (later Corp. 3/64—reduced 7/64—deserted)

Private John Edwards 20 yr old enlisted Buncombe Co. 5/7/61 (joined Co. 1/63)

Private John Green 33 yr old enlisted Buncombe Co. 5/7/61 W Fredericksburg **C 7/3**

Private George Harper 19 yr old enlisted wake Co. 9/30/62 (later C Hatcher's Run)

Private William Harper 23 yr old enlisted Wake Co. 9/30/62 (later W Wilderness)

Private James Hawkins 25 yr old enlisted Buncombe Co. 5/7/61 **C 7/3** (later C Hatcher's Run)

Private John Hunter 32 yr old enlisted Buncombe Co. 5/7/61 **C 7/3**

Private Charles Luther 21 yr old enlisted Buncombe Co. 5/7/61 (later W Liddell's Shop)

Private William Rollins 21 yr old enlisted Buncombe Co. 5/7/61 W 2nd Manassas (later Corp W Riddell's Shop)

Private Jesse Stroup 23 yr old enlisted Buncombe Co. 5/7/61 W Chancellorsville **K 7/3**

Private Mias Wilson 20 yr old enlisted Buncombe Co. 5/7/61 missing Gettysburg **Hid at local family farm**

Private Hodge Young 25 yr old enlisted Buncombe Co. 5/7/61 W Glendale **C 7/3**

Fifer J.N. Snelson 21 yr old enlisted Buncombe Co. 5/7/61 W Mechanicsville deserted 10/16/63

7/1 & 7/2 Casualties (Skirmish duty)

Sgt. Joseph Reynolds 25 yr old enlisted Buncombe Co. 5/7/61 W Fredericksburg W Chancellorsville **W 7/1**

Private Benjamin Cole 24 yr old enlisted Buncombe Co. 5/7/61 (later W-knee Hatcher's Run)

Private Joseph Dover 24 yr old enlisted Buncombe Co. 5/7/61 (later K North Anna) **W 7/1**

Private James Hampton 23 yr old enlisted Buncombe Co. 5/7/61 **K 7/2**

Private Alfred Haney 24 yr old enlisted Buncombe Co. 5/7/61 **W 7/2**

Private James Ingle 23 yr old enlisted Buncombe Co. 5/7/61 W Mechanicsville (later 1st Sgt & 1st Lt) **W 7/1**
Private John Jones 23 yr old enlisted Buncombe Co. 5/7/61 AWOL 7/11/63—returned
Private Dallas James 18 yr old enlisted Buncombe Co. 7/8/61 W Mechanicsville
Private Alexander Jimison 21 yr old enlisted Buncombe Co. 5/7/61 W Mechanicsville (later W-Petersburg)
Private Montraville Jones 34 yr old enlisted Buncombe Co. 5/7/61 **C 7/14**
Private Martin King 21 yr old enlisted Buncombe Co. 5/7/61
Private John Ledford 22 yr old enlisted Buncombe Co. 7/8/61 W-leg Mechanicsville AWOL 7/11/63—returned
Private Benjamin Lewis 24 yr old enlisted Buncombe Co. 5/7/61 W Seven Pines **deserted 7/4 Chambersburg, Pa**
Private Gustus Mears 24 yr old enlisted Buncombe Co. 5/7/61 **W 7/1 C 7/14**
Private William Roper 24 yr old enlisted Buncombe Co. 5/7/61 W Mechanicsville
Private James Snelson 20 yr old enlisted Buncombe Co. 7/8/61 W Mechanicsville **W 7/2**
Private William Stroup 21 yr old enlisted Buncombe Co. 5/7/61

Company G *"Rutherford County Men"*

1st Lt John McEntire 26 yr old enlisted Rutherford Co 5/9/61 W-Seven Pines **C 7/3**
Sgt. Joseph Alexander 23 yr old enlisted Rutherford Co 5/9/61 W Seven Pines W Sharpsburg (later 3rd Lt)
Corp. John Davis enlisted Rutherford Co. 3/13/62 **C 7/3**
Corp. Thomas Houser 26 yr old enlisted Rutherford Co 5/9/61 W-thigh & arm Seven Pines
Private R.M. Barbee 24 yr old enlisted enlisted Chatham Co. 3/18/63
Private Benton Bradley 24 yr old enlisted Rutherford Co 5/9/61 (later C Wilderness)
Private Robert Callahan 20 yr old enlisted Rutherford Co 5/13/61 W Mechanicsville
Private John Crain 38 yr old enlisted Chatham Co. 3/18/63 **K 7/3**
Private James Davis 26 yr old enlisted Rutherford Co 5/9/61 (later W-hand Jone's farm)
Private John Eaves 29 yr old enlisted Rutherford Co 5/9/61 (later transferred to Signal Corps)
Private W.W. Gunter 39 yr old enlisted Chatham Co. 3/18/63 **W-left arm C 7/3**
Private Benjamin Hicks 23 yr old enlisted Rutherford Co 5/9/61 (later discharged 2/7/64)
Private Israel Higgins 20 yr old enlisted Rutherford Co 5/9/61 W Shepherdstown (later W Wilderness)
Private Joseph Holland 27 yr old enlisted Chatham Co. 3/18/63 **W 7/3 C 7/5**
Private James Hoyle 21 yr old enlisted Rutherford Co 5/9/61 W-leg Seven Pines **W-7/3 C 7/5**
Private Thomas Huntsinger 25 yr old enlisted Rutherford Co. (later W Wilderness)

Private James Ketter 24 yr old enlisted Rutherford Co. 5/9/61 W-hand Mechanicsville **W 7/3 C 7/5 as nurse**

Private Elijah Turner 20 yr old enlisted Rutherford Co 5/9/61 W-arm Seven Pines **C 7/14**

Private James Turner 19 yr old enlisted Rutherford Co 3/13/62

Private James Twitty 22 yr old enlisted Rutherford Co 5/9/61

Private David Wicker 38 yr old enlisted 3/18/63 **WC 7/3**

Private John Williams transferred 5/63 **C 7/3**

Ambulance Driver Joseph Cole 33 yr old enlisted Rutherford Co 3/18/61

Teamster W.A. Mitchell 21 yr old enlisted Rutherford Co 5/9/61

July 1 Casualties

2nd Lt George Mills 33 yr old salesman enlisted Rutherford Co. 5/9/61 **W 7/1 shell**

3rd Lt John Ford 30 yr old enlisted Rutherford Co 5/9/61 Color Sgt 1862 W Fredericksburg **K 7/1**

Corp. Amassa Williams 28 yr old enlisted Rutherford Co 5/9/61 **W-left thigh 7/1 C 7/14** (later 1st Sgt)

Private Gaither Arrowood 21 yr old enlisted 5/9/61 **W-left foot 7/2**

Private John Bradley 28 yr old enlisted Rutherford Co 5/9/61 W-hip Seven Pines **W-both legs 7/1 C 7/5** (amp)

Private Pinkney Carpenter 21 yr old enlisted Rutherford Co 5/9/61 **W 7/2 Arm (amp) C 7/5**

Private James Carrier 22 yr old enlisted Rutherford Co 5/9/61 (later served in signal corps)

Private James Carson 21 yr old enlisted Rutherford Co 5/9/61 **C 7/14**

Private James Church 27 yr old enlisted Rutherford Co 5/9/61 **C 7/14**

Private Daniel Coleman 32 yr old enlisted Rutherford Co 5/9/61

Private Daniel Dallas 36 yr old enlisted Robeson Co 3/363

Private Alfred Davis 20 yr old enlisted Rutherford Co 5/9/61 (died of disease 8/11/63)

Private J.G. Freeman 28 yr old enlisted Rutherford Co 3/13/62 **W-left hand 7/1**

Private Marcus Good 26 yr old enlisted Rutherford Co. 5/9/61 W-neck Mechanicsville **W-chest 7/1 C 7/5**

Private Hawkins Johnson 24 yr old enlisted Rutherford Co 3/13/62 **W 7/1**

Private Samuel Ledbetter 25 yr old enlisted Rutherford Co 5/9/61 **C 7/14**

Private John Logan 28 yr old enlisted Rutherford Co 5/9/61 W Valley River, Va

Private Benjamin Long 21 yr old enlisted Rutherford Co 5/9/61 W-forearm Gaine's Mill

Private Reuben Simon 27 yr old enlisted Wake Co. 2/25/63 (AWOL 12/63-10/64)

Private Alfred Smith enlisted Rutherford Co 3/13/62 W Mechanicsville **W-left hand 7/1**

Private Arch Spratt 24 yr old enlisted Rutherford Co 5/9/61 **W 7/1**

Private John Steadman 24 yr old enlisted Rutherford Co. 5/9/61 **W-right leg 7/1 C 7/5**

Private I.S. Upchurch 38 yr old enlisted Chatham Co. 3/18/63

Private J.D. Weaver enlisted 1861 reported for duty 7/63 deserted 7/17/63
Private Samuel Williams 21 yr old enlisted Rutherford Co 5/9/61 **W-face 7/1 C 7/5**
Private Samuel Willis 37 yr old enlisted 3/3/63 **W 7/1 C 7/5**

Company H *"Macon County"*

Captain Calvin McLoud 23 yr old (acting Colonel 8/63) promoted 7/14/63
2nd Lt Lee Allman appointed 5/3/63 (later resigned 12/16/63)
3rd Lt Bell 25 yr old saddler enlisted Macon County 5/14/61 W-head Seven Pines W 2nd Manassas **W-right arm 7/3**
Sgt. Moses Brooks 28 yr old mechanic enlisted Macon Co. 5/14/61 W Mechanicsville **W-thigh 7/3** died 7/18
Corp. David Robinson 21 yr old enlisted Macon Co 5/14/61 (later Sgt)
Corp. Thomas Stanfield 24 yr old enlisted Macon Co 5/14/61 C Chancellorsville **C 7/14** Falling Waters (joined US Service)
Private John Amick enlisted Wake Co. 3/2/63 **C 7/3** (died 7/23)
Private Rufus Cunningham 22 yr old enlisted Macon Co 5/14/61 **C 7/3**
Private Lorenzo Drake 30 yr old enlisted Macon Co 5/14/61 W Chancellorsville **W 7/3** (later detailed as teamster)
Private Joseph Huggins 38 yr old enlisted 3/31/63 **C 7/3**
Private Alfred Layton enlisted Wake Co. 5/19/63 **C 7/3**
Private Isaac Layton enlisted Wake Co. 5/9/63 **C 7/3**
Private Henry Lineberry enlisted Wake Co. 5/2/63 **C 7/3**
Private Robert London 49 yr old substitute enlisted Macon Co 3/21/63 **C 7/14** (later joined US Service)
Private Andrew Love 38 yr old enlisted 3/21/63 **W 7/3 C 7/5 as nurse**
Private George Oliver 37 yr old enlisted Macon Co. 3/21/63 **C 7/3**
Private John Oliver 23 yr old enlisted Macon Co 6/20/61 W-right shoulder Chancellorsville **C 7/14**
Private Madison Oliver19 yr old enlisted Macon Co 6/20/61
Private W.L. Westall 27 yr old enlisted Macon Co 5/14/61 W Mechanicsville 6/26/62 W-shoulder Chancellorsville (later K Cold Harbor)

Private Phillip Roberts 24 yr old enlisted Macon Co 5/14/61 (detailed as teamster)

July 1 Casualties

1st Sgt. George Angel 23 yr old enlisted Macon Co 5/14/61 W Mechanicsville **W 7/1**
Private William Allison 37 yr old enlisted Macon Co. 3/21/63 **W-left leg 7/1 C 7/5**
Private Thomas Angel 24 yr old enlisted Macon Co 5/14/61 W Mechanicville (died disease 9/63)

Private John Blain 24 yr old enlisted Macon Co 6/20/61 **C 7/14**
Private Robert Brooks 26 yr old enlisted Macon Co 5/14/61 (later W Ream's Station)
Private Alfred Brown 28 yr old enlisted Macon Co 5/14/61 (later C Hatcher's Run)
Private William Cline 20 yr old enlisted Macon Co 5/14/61 **W-jaw 7/1 C 7/5**
Private William Cunningham enlisted Macon Co 3/31/63 (AWOL 7/30/63)
Private James Donaldson 25 yr old enlisted Macon Co 5/14/61
Private James Gray 27 yr old enlisted Macon Co 5/14/61
Private Eli Henson 28 yr old enlisted Macon Co 5/14/61
Private Wiley Jones enlisted Camp Vance (served til 10/63)
Private Joab Moore 19 yr old enlisted Macon Co 5/14/61 **W 7/1** (later 1st Sgt)
Private Ephraim Parish 28 yr old enlisted Macon Co 5/14/61
Private G.W. Parrish 20 yr old enlisted Macon Co. 5/14/61 **W-both legs 7/1**
Private William Parrish 29 yr ld enlisted Macon Co. 6/20/61 **W 7/1**
Private James Raby 24 yr old enlisted Macon Co 3/8/62 deserted 12/6/63
Private Lewis Sorrells 24 yr old enlisted Macon Co 5/14/61
Private William Sorrells 20 yr old enlisted Macon Co 5/14/61 W-left arm Fredericksburg
Private William Winstead 22 yr old enlisted Macon Co 5/14/61 **W-right leg 7/1 C 7/5 (amp)**

Company I *"Henderson County"*

Sgt. Alfred Gash 20 yr old enlisted Henderson Co 7/1/61 commanded company (reduced in rank 8/63)
Sgt. James Whitaker 23 yr old enlisted Henderson Co. 5/5/61 W Mechanicsville (later K North Anna)
Corp. Hyman Rucker 25 yr old enlisted Henderson Co. 5/5/61 (later Sgt)
Private Richard Brannon 21 yr old enlisted Henderson Co 5/5/61 W 2nd Manassas **W 7/3 C Williamsport, Md 7/10/63**
Private James Bryson 25 yr old enlisted 5/5/61 W Seven Pines **slight W 7/1 fought 7/3**
Private Jonas Cannon 36 yr old enlisted Caldwell Co. 3/5/63 W-accidentally **C 7/3**
Private Thomas Dauson 22 yr old enlisted Henderson 5/5/61 **slight W 7/1 fought 7/3**
Private Ebenezer Girvin transferred 3/10/63 **slight W 7/1 fought 7/3**
Private George Jones 23 yr old enlisted Henderson Co 7/1/61 (later died disease 8/9/64)
Private James Jones 20 yr old enlisted Henderson Co 5/5/61 (later W North Anna)
Private John Lowrey 22 yr old enlisted Henderson Co 5/5/61 W Seven Pines W Fredericksburg
Private William Posey 23 yr old enlisted Henderson Co. 5/5/61 (later C Wilderness)
Private Adolphus Tounsend 20 yr old enlisted Henderson Co. 5/5/61 W-right thigh Gaines Mill

Musician George Barnette 21 yr old enlisted Henderson Co. 7/1/61

Musician Harrison Benson 26 yr old enlisted Henderson Co 5/5/61 W Mechanicsville W Ox Hill

Musician James Cockram 24 yr old enlisted 7/1/61 W Seven Pines

Musician Enoch Hollingsworth 36 yr old shoemaker enlisted Henderson Co. 3/3/62 W Seven Pines

Musician Joseph Johnson 26 yr old enlisted Henderson Co 7/1/61 W-neck Shepherdstown

Private Wilson Justin 23 yr old enlisted Henderson Co 5/5/61 C Sharpsburg (later Musician)

Private Harrison Loflin 25 yr old mechanic enlisted Henderson Co 5/5/61 (later Corp C Wilderness)

Musician John Martin 28 yr old enlisted Henderson Co. 5/5/61 W neck Mechanicsville

Musician John Miller 28 yr old enlisted Henderson Co. 5/5/61

Private Wesley Middleton 19 yr old enlisted Henderson Co. 3/15/61 W Mechanicsville (detailed as nurse)

July 1 Casualties

1st Lt John Mills 21 yr old enlisted Henderson Co 5/5/61 **W-right leg 7/1**

1st Sgt Joseph Gash 22 yr old enlisted Henderson 7/1/61 **W-left leg 7/1**

Corp. Payton Dewberry 24 yr old enlisted Henderson Co 5/5/61 (reduced in rank 8/63)

Private John T. Bowman 22 yr old enlisted Henderson C 7/1/61 **W-left leg 7/1 C Williamsport Md 7/10/63 died Harrisburg**

Private Mack Bowman 26 yr old enlisted Henderson Co 5/5/61 (served until 11/64)

Private J.E. Cox 31 yr old enlisted 3/18/62 W Seven Pines (later K Riddel's Shop)

Private Leonard Crabtree 38 yr old enlisted Orange Co. 1/27/63 **K-"leg shot off" 7/1**

Private William Dearman 25 yr old enlisted Henderson Co 5/5/61 **W-right thigh 7/1 C 7/5** died 10/13

Private John Dewberry 21 yr old enlisted Henderson Co. 7/1/61 W-hand Fredericksburg

Private John Erwin 25 yr old enlisted Henderson Co. 5/5/61 **W Seven Pines W 7/1**

Private Ephraim Ferree 33 yr old enlisted Henderson Co 5/5/61 (later transferred to Co. E)

Private James Lewis 24 yr old enlisted Henderson Co 5/5/61 **K 7/1**

Private Richard Liverett 22 yr old enlisted Henderson Co. 5/5/61 **C 7/1**

Private King McCarson 22 yr old enlisted Henderson Co. 3/10/62 W-left arm & thigh Fredericksburg (deserted 8/63—returned)

Private Elisha Nelson 22 yr old enlisted Henderson Co. 5/5/61 W-Fredericksburg (d eserted 8/1/63)

Private John Williams 23 yr old enlisted Henderson Co. 5/5/61 C 2nd Manassas (later AWOL 3/1/64—returned)

Company K "*Polk County*"

Captain John Camp 28 yr old enlisted Polk County 5/20/61 (later court—martial and dismissed)
2nd Lt Whitefield Morgan 28 yr old enlisted Polk Co. 4/20/61 **K 7/3**
1st Sgt. Otis Nelson 23 yr old enlisted Polk Co. 4/20/61 (later 2nd Lt C North Anna)
Corp. Charles Sims 22 yr old enlisted Polk Co. 4/20/61 (later detailed as Musician)
Private Thomas Alwine 23 yr old enlisted Polk Co. 4/20/61 (later W Wilderness)
Private John Ellison 27 yr old enlisted Polk Co. 4/20/61 (later Corp & Sgt)
Private George Feagans 21 yr old enlisted Polk Co. 4/20/61 (later C North Anna)
Private David Foster 22 yr old enlisted Polk Co. 4/20/61 (later Corp C North Anna)
Private James Giles 21 yr old enlisted Polk Co. 4/20/61 (later Corp & Sgt C North Anna)
Private Jacob Keever 20 yr old enlisted Polk Co. 4/20/61 (served until 11/64)
Private George Painter 21 yr old enlisted Polk Co. 4/20/61 **W 7/3 died 12/5/63**
Private Elias Taber 25 yr old enlisted Polk Co. 4/20/61 (later W Wilderness)
Private John Williams 27 yr old enlisted Polk Co 4/20/61 **W 7/2 by piece of shell fought on 7/3**

Musician Joseph Johnson enlisted Polk Co W Shepherdstown

July 1 Casualties

Sgt. James Copeland W Glendale **W 7/1 C 7/14** (later C North Anna)
Sgt. James Wilson 24 yr old enlisted Polk Co. 4/20/61 W-arm Fredericksburg **W 7/1 C 7/5**
Corp. Spencer Cantrell 25 yr old enlisted Polk Co. 4/20/61 W Gaines Mill **W 7/1 C 7/14**
Corp. Robert Dalton 24 yr old enlisted Polk Co. 4/20/61 W-mouth Seven Pines **K 7/1**
Corp. Watson Edwards 25 yr old enlisted Polk Co. 4/20/61 W 2nd Manassas **W-foot 7/1 C 7/5**
Private William Ballard 23 yr old enlisted Wake Co 9/25/62 C Chancellorsville **C 7/14**
Private David Childers 33 yr old enlisted Polk Co. 4/20/61 Deserted 8/2/63
Private John Cowart 25 yr old enlisted Polk Co. 4/20/61 W Gaine's Mill **W 7/1 C 7/14**
Private Murray Dunahoo 23 yr old enlisted Polk Co. 4/20/61 **W 7/1 C 7/14**
Private William Colbert 20 yr old enlisted Polk Co. 4/20/61 W-neck Seven Pines W Chancellorsville **K 7/1**
Private Charles Green 23 yr old enlisted Polk Co. 4/20/61 (AWOL 10/63—returned)
Private Columbus Lankford 25 yr old enlisted Polk Co. 4/20/61 **W 7/1 C 7/5**
Private John McDowell 21 yr old enlisted Polk Co. 4/20/61 Deserted 8/2/63
Private James Morrow 22 yr old enlisted Polk Co. 4/20/61 Deserted 8/8/62 arrested (later C North Anna)
Private Bartlett Nixon 30 yr old enlisted Wake Co. Deserted 7/23/63—returned
Private Ransom Thompson 30 yr old enlisted Polk Co. 4/20/61
Private Elijah Warren enlisted Camp Vance 6/1/63

Brigadier General John Daniel Imboden
Independent Cavalry Command
Army of Northern Virginia

Photo Credits

Private Issac Caldwell—"From the Charles M Woodruff Sr. Memorial Collection"
QM Sgt Francis Turner—"From the Charles M Woodruff Sr. Memorial Collection"
Corporal James Averiit—Courtesy Averitt Family
Private Evan Ballard—Tennessee Archives and History
Lt. Furgis Harris Co H—Courtesy of Susan Daniel Harris—great great grandniece"
Harris group Photo—"Tennessee Archives & History"
Co B 2nd Mississippi—Courtesy Mississippi Dept. of Archives and History
Private Drury Wall Co D—Courtesy Marcus Flynt—descendant
Lt. Romulus Cox Co K—Courtesy Ted Meredith Boca Raton, Fl / North Carolina Troops
Private Elijah Joyner Co A—Courtesy Mrs. Karen Griffin—descendant
Private James Yates Co H—North Carolina Troops
Colonel Henry Burgwyn—Library of Congress
Lt. Colonel John Lane—UNC Department of Archives & History
Major John Jones—Courtesy Society for the Historical Preservation of the 26th Regiment
Captain James Adams Co D—Courtesy Richard Holleman—descendant
Colonel Collett Leventhorpe—Library of Congress
Major Egbert Ross—Courtesy Douglas Moore
Captain James Whitehead Co E—North Carolina State Archives, Raleigh
Colonel John Connally—Library of Congress
Captain Edward Satterfield Co H—Satterfield & Merrit Papers, UNC—Chapel Hill
Colonel John Stone—Library of Congress
Private Elijah Mercer Co F—Courtesy of Joycie Mercer-Allen & Sharon Mercer-Holbert & Joseph Mercer
Captain Thomas Clark Co. F—Courtesy of Charlie W. Clark—descendant
Rev. Thomas Witherspoon—Courtesy The Historical Center of the Presbyterian Church in America
Private William Wooten Co I—Courtesy of Chris Marks—descendant
Sgt. Eli Peel Co C—Courtesy of David Pell—descendant
Corp. William Delbridge Co G—University of Mississippi Archives
Major Joseph Saunders—Library of Congress

2nd Lt. Finley Jones—North Carolina Troops
Colonel John Barry—Library of Congress
Captain Van Richardson Co C—North Carolina Museum of History
Captain James Linebarger—North Carolina Troops
Private Alan Carpenter Co D—Mrs. Lorene Carpenter Curlee—descendant
Lt Westley Battle—Co D courtesy North Carolina State Archives
Lt. Iowa Royster—Co G courtesy North Carolina State Archives
Ord. Sgt Joseph Joyner—Courtesy Clarence Hollowell Jr.
Private Richard Fleming Co F—Courtesy Mrs. Lynn Fleming Simpson
Lt. Ransom Middleton Co A—Us Army War College, Carlisle, Pa
Private Marcus Bean Co I—Courtesy Miss Mary Gordon Elliot—descendant
Lt. James Williamson Co A—Courtesy Alamance Historical Society
Private Caleb May Co A—Courtesy Walter Brown Jr.
Walker Brothers Pre War—Courtesy of the North Carolina Office of Archives and History, Raleigh, North Carolina
Walker Brothers Post War—Courtesy of the North Carolina Office of Archives and History, Raleigh, North Carolina
Lt. Davis Harrill Co B Courtesy Mrs. Sara Blanton Johnston
Private William Morris Co K—Courtesy Martha Lunsford
Colonel Conner—Library of Congress
Private James Powell Co G—Courtesy James Powell—descendant
Corp. Marcus Deal Co A—US Army War College Carlisle, Pa
Teamster David Brinkley Co C—Courtesy Paul Kardulis